Handbook of
Clinical
Psychoneuroendocrinology

Edited by

CHARLES B. NEMEROFF
Duke University Medical Center

PETER T. LOOSEN
Veterans Administration Medical Center, Nashville

THE GUILFORD PRESS
New York   London

To
Arthur J. Prange, Jr., MD.,
who taught both of us.
And to our families:
Melissa, Matthew, and Amanda
Laura, Max, and Alexander

© 1987 The Guilford Press
Distributed by John Wiley & Sons Ltd.
in UK, Europe, Middle East, Africa

Last digit is print number: 9 8 7 6 5 4 3 2 1

Printed in the United States of America

Library of Congress Cataloging-in-Publication Data

Handbook of clinical psychoneuroendocrinology.

  Includes bibliographies and index.
  1. Mental illness—Endocrine aspects.   2. Endocrine
glands—Diseases—Psychological aspects.
  3. Psychoneuroendocrinology.   I. Nemeroff, Charles B.
II. Loosen, Peter T.   [DNLM: 1. Behavior—drug
effects.   2. Endocrine Diseases—complications.
3. Mental Disorders—etiology.   4. Neuroendocrinology.
5. Psychophysiology.   WM   100 H23365]
RC455.4.E54H36   1987   616.89′071   86-31837
ISBN 0 471 91768 0

British Library Cataloguing in Publication Data Available

CONTRIBUTORS

Huda Akil, Ph.D Mental Health Research Institute, Medical Center, The University of Michigan, Ann Arbor, Michigan 48109

Gregory M. Asnis, M.D. Affective Disorders Program, Albert Einstein College of Medicine/Montefiore Medical Center, Bronx, New York 10467

Peter C. Avgerinos, M.D. Section on Clinical Neuroendocrinology, National Institute of Mental Health, Bethesda, Maryland 20892

Mark S. Bauer, M.D. Department of Psychiatry, Hospital of the University of Pennsylvania, Philadelphia, Pennsylvania 19104

Joseph R. Calabrese, M.D. Department of Psychiatry, The Cleveland Clinic, Cleveland, Ohio 44106

Magda Campbell, M.D. Department of Psychiatry, New York University Medical Center, New York, New York 10016

George P. Chrousos, M.D. Developmental Endocrinology Branch, National Institute of Child Health and Human Development, Bethesda, Maryland 20892

David L. Copolov, M.D. Mental Health Research Institute, Melbourne, Australia

Stephen I. Deutsch, M.D., Ph.D. Department of Psychiatry, New York University Medical Center, New York, New York 10016

Marian Droba, M.D. Department of Psychiatry, Hospital of the University of Pennsylvania, Philadelphia, Pennsylvania 19104

Hinderk M. Emrich, M.D. Max Planck Institute for Psychiatry, Munich, Federal Republic of Germany

Dwight L. Evans, M.D. Division of Health Affairs, School of Medicine, Department of Psychiatry, University of North Carolina, Chapel Hill, North Carolina 27514

Max Fink, M.D. Department of Psychiatry and Behavioral Science, Health Sciences Center, State University of New York at Stony Brook, Stony Brook, New York 11794-2990

Paul E. Garfinkel, M.D. Department of Psychiatry, University of Toronto, Toronto, Ontario, Canada M5G 2C4

Judith S. Gavaler, Ph.D. Department of Medicine, School of Medicine, University of Pittsburgh, Pittsburgh, Pennsylvania 15261

Philip W. Gold, M.D. Section on Clinical Neuroendocrinology, National Institute of Mental Health, Bethesda, Maryland 20892

Robert N. Golden, M.D. Division of Health Affairs, School of Medicine, Department of Psychiatry, University of North Carolina, Chapel Hill, North Carolina 27514

Susanna Goldstein, M.D. Cornell University Medical Center, Payne Whitney Clinic, New York, New York 10021

Wayne H. Green, M.D. Department of Psychiatry, New York University Medical Center, New York, New York 10016

Gary A. Gudelsky, M.D. Department of Psychiatry, School of Medicine, Case Western Reserve University, Cleveland, Ohio 44106

Uriel Halbreich, M.D. Department of Psychiatry, School of Medicine, State University of New York at Buffalo, Buffalo, New York 14215-3098

Roger F. Haskett, M.D. Department of Psychiatry, University of Michigan, Ann Arbor, Michigan 48109-0118

Lewis L. Judd, M.D. Department of Psychiatry, University of California, San Diego, La Jolla, California 91093

Konstantine Kalogeras, M.D. Section on Clinical Neuroendocrinology, National Institute of Mental Health, Bethesda, Maryland 20892

Sidney H. Kennedy, M.D. Department of Psychiatry, Toronto General Hospital, Toronto, Ontario, Canada M5G 2C4

Mitchel A. Kling, M.D. Section on Clinical Neuroendocrinology, National Institute of Mental Health, Bethesda, Maryland 20892

James Koenig, M.D. Department of Psychiatry, School of Medicine, Case Western Reserve University, Cleveland, Ohio 44106

Dean D. Krahn, M.D. Department of Psychiatry, University of Michigan Medical Center, Ann Arbor, Michigan 48109

Carmen Z. Lemus, M.D. Research Department, Hillside Hospital, Long Island Jewish Medical Center, Glen Oaks, New York 11004

Peter T. Loosen, M.D. Veterans Administration Medical Center, Nashville, Tennessee 37203

D. Lynn Loriaux, M.D., Ph.D. National Institute of Child Health and Human Development, Bethesda, Maryland 20892

Herbert Y. Meltzer, M.D. Department of Psychiatry, School of Medicine, Case Western Reserve University, Cleveland, Ohio 44106

Margaret L. Moline, Ph.D. Institute of Chronobiology, New York Hospital/Cornell Medical Center, Westchester Division, White Plains, New York 10605

John E. Morley, M.D. Veterans Administration Medical Center, Sepulveda, California 91343

Charles B. Nemeroff, M.D., Ph.D. Departments of Psychiatry, Pharmacology, and the Center for Aging and Human Development, Duke University Medical Center, Durham, North Carolina 27710

Seymour Reichlin, M.D., Ph.D. Endocrinology Division, Department of Medicine, Tufts University School of Medicine, Boston, Massachusetts 02111

June Machover Reinisch, Ph.D. The Kinsey Institute for Research in Sex, Gender, and Reproduction, Indiana University, Bloomington, Indiana 47405

Victor I. Reus, M.D. Langley Porter Neuropsychiatric Institute, School of Medicine, University of California, San Francisco, San Francisco, California 94143

S. Craig Risch, M.D. Department of Psychiatry, University of California, San Diego, La Jolla, California 92093

Robert T. Rubin, M.D., Ph.D. Division of Biological Psychiatry, Department of Psychiatry, Harbor UCLA Medical Center, Torrance, California 90509

Stephanie A. Sanders, Ph.D. The Kinsey Institute for Research in Sex, Gender, and Reproduction, Indiana University, Bloomington, Indiana 47405

Claudia Schmauss, Ph.D. Section of Molecular Neurobiology, School of Medicine, Yale University, New Haven, Connecticut 06510

Michael H. Sheard, M.D. The Connecticut Mental Health Center, New Haven, Connecticut 06508

Mark A. Smith, M.D. Department of Psychiatry, Pharmacology, and the Center for Aging and Human Development, Duke University Medical Center, Durham, North Carolina 27710

H. M. van Praag, Ph.D. Department of Psychiatry, Albert Einstein College of Medicine, Bronx, New York 10461

David H. Van Thiel, M.D. Department of Medicine, School of Medicine, University of Pittsburgh, Pittsburgh, Pennsylvania 15261

Daniel R. Wagner, M.D. Institute of Chronobiology, New York Hospital/Cornell Medical Center, Westchester Division, White Plains, New York 10605

Stanley J. Watson, M.D., Ph.D. Mental Health Research Institute, Medical Center, The University of Michigan, Ann Arbor, Michigan 48109

Peter C. Whybrow, M.D. Department of Psychiatry, Hospital of the University of Pennsylvania, Philadelphia, Pennsylvania 19104

Elizabeth Young, Ph.D. Mental Health Research Institute, Medical Center, The University of Michigan, Ann Arbor, Michigan 48109

CONTENTS

FOREWORD

This monograph provides a comprehensive and interpretive view of the relationship between the central nervous system and the endocrine systems (the major homeostatic regulatory systems) with a consideration of the relevance of these relationships to the understanding of the psychiatric aspects of endocrine disease, and the endocrine implications of psychiatric disorder.

Several millennia separate the first neuroendocrine observations from the beginning of understanding of the nature of hormones and of endocrine glands. For example, seasonal breeding of animals is environmentally regulated, and castration leads to striking changes in the behavior of domestic animals such as bulls, boars, and roosters. These phenomena were exploited by the early pastoralists. The effects of castration on personality and sexual function were known to antiquity and are recorded in the Bible and other ancient writings, but it was not until 1849 that the internal secretions of the testicles were demonstrated by transplantation experiments (Berthold), not until the 1920s that modern views of the pituitary as "the master gland" began to emerge, and not until the 1940s that the concept of hypothalamic–pituitary control was seriously entertained. Acceptance of the role of brain peptides in pituitary control did not come until the structure of thyrotropin-releasing hormone (TRH) was elucidated in 1969; and the current widespread interest in neuropeptides in neurobiology did not begin to emerge until the discoveries of the structures of substance P, somatostatin, and the endogenous opioids which made possible the application of modern methods to the study of the substances.

Psychoneuroendocrinology, which deals specifically with the interactions between hormones and the nervous system, is now a major focus of research. These studies can be considered at many levels of abstraction from reductionist to symbolic. Virtually every hormone exerts effects on nerve cells through specific receptors, and emotional states can influence most endocrine functions. Because both the pituitary and behavior are influenced by central bioaminergic, peptidergic, and cholinergic neuronal functions, the endocrine disturbances that occur in the major psychiatric disorders such as depression and schizophrenia have been considered by many workers as potential "windows to the brain," useful in inferring the nature of underlying disturbance in central neurotransmitter function. The field of psychiatry has been indelibly marked by the concept of the stress reaction of Selye, taken from the pituitary–adrenal system as a heuristic model of adaptive and coping responses. In fact the adrenocorticotropic hormone (ACTH) response has been used in some studies to define the term "stress." In several psychiatric diseases such as anorexia nervosa and maternal deprivation syndrome, extreme alterations in endocrine function are encountered which can dominate the clinical picture.

In certain psychiatric diseases, endocrine abnormalities, though rather subtle, and not well explained pathophysiologically have become important as disease trait or state markers. For example, the abnormal suppression of cortisol by dexamethasone and the blunted thyroid stimulating hormone (TSH) response to TRH in depression have been used in diagnosis, in genetic studies, and for prognosis, although the basis of the response is not known, and not necessarily related etiologically to the underlying disorder.

Psychoneuroendocrine concepts and insights have thus proven to be important to behaviorists and psychiatrists. In addition, changes induced by hormones have revealed the inherent plasticity of the brain. During development, hormones can exert an effect on the process of differentiation of structure and function. In rats, for example, gonadal hormones are essential in organizing functional pathways that define maleness and femaleness and actually change neuronal morphology. Gonadal hormones can modify already established patterns by their activating functions, such as the effect of testosterone on sex drive.

The editors of this volume have assembled a number of distinguished psychoneuroendocrinologists to summarize the state of current knowledge in these various areas, and to provide conceptual models of interpretation. Many of the chapters include outlines of future work to be done and of problems to be solved. They have produced a valuable guide to the field.

Seymour Reichlin, MD, PhD
Tufts–New England Medical Center

PART I

INTRODUCTION

1 ENDOCRINOLOGY FOR THE PSYCHIATRIST

JOHN E. MORLEY

Sepulveda VA Medical Center

DEAN D. KRAHN

University of Michigan Medical Center

INTRODUCTION

That hormones affect behavior has been recognized since antiquity. Nearly 2,000 years ago, Areteus the Cappadocian documented some of these effects as follows:

For it is the semen, when possessed of vitality, which makes us to be men, not well braced in limbs, hairy, well voiced, spirited, strong to think and to act, as the characteristics of men prove. For when the semen is not possessed of its vitality, persons become shrivelled, have a sharp tone of voice, lose their hair and their beard, and become effeminate, as the characteristics of eunuchs prove.

The first experiments in psychoendocrinology were undertaken by Leonardo da Vinci who again stressed the relation of male hormones to emotion and libido:

Testicles witness of caution. These contain in themselves ardour, that is they are augmenters of the animosity and ferocity of the animals; and experience shows us this clearly in the castrated animals, of which one sees the bull, the boar, the ram and the cock, very fierce animals, which after having been deprived of these testicles remain very cowardly; so one sees a ram drive before it a herd of whethers, and a cock put to flight a number of capons; and I have seen the same thing happen with a hen and also with oxen.

By 1922 the hypothesized role of endocrinopathies in the regulation of behavior was delineated as follows by B. R. Tucker writing in the *American Journal of Psychiatry*:

It has been observed that a large number of delinquent girls have hypothyroidism. Hyperpituitary cases are frequently called incorrigible, opinionated and hypersexual, while the hypo cases may be lazy, truant and ungrateful and deficient in integrity. Hyperadrenal cases may be cowardly and easily led to fear. Hypergonads show sexual irregularity and go to extremes in dress and action, and hypogonad cases may be perverts, asocial, cunning, cruel or cringing.

In fact, it has only been in the last decade that psychoneuroendocrinology has truly come of age, and such rampant speculations have been replaced with a more refined scientific knowledge. Much evidence is now available showing that hormones modulate behavior and that, in turn, behavior can alter hormonal secretion. Thus, in the 1980s we have at last come within striking distance of proving that Harvey Cushing was at least partly correct when, in 1913, he wrote in what was then the *American Journal of Insanity*, "It is quite probable that the psychopathology of everyday life hinges upon the effect of the ductless glands' discharge upon the nervous system."

The evolution of multicellular organisms from primitive, unicellular ancestors was only possible with the coincident development of control systems that allowed the many parts of an organism to work together

3

for a common goal. For example, while a group of unicellular organisms that each sensed a lack of nutrients could each begin to feed, the cells of a multicellular organism could not take such unilateral action. Rather, systems for coordinating adaptation to environmental and metabolic challenges such as food deprivation were developed so that each cell could participate in differentiated roles in the collective act of meeting needs such as obtaining food. Endocrinological, neurological, and psychological mechanisms play closely allied roles in this coordination process. While the study of these three mechanisms has usually been carried on by separate medical disciplines, the coordination of behavior and metabolism cannot be understood without integration of knowledge lying in the premises of neurology, psychology, and endocrinology. This chapter is aimed at providing a basis for the endocrinological contribution to this integrative effort.

PRINCIPLES OF ENDOCRINOLOGY

The endocrine system (like the neurological system) depends fundamentally on the ability of cells to communicate by sending and receiving chemical messages. In the endocrine system the chemical messengers are known as hormones. While hormones were classically defined as blood-borne messengers, recently this definition has been amended to include messengers present in other extracellular fluids as well. Therefore, the difference between hormones and neurotransmitters is blurring, but remains primarily that neurotransmitters traverse only the distance across one synaptic cleft while hormones may influence cells several feet away. This distance difference makes for some of the differences between neurological and endocrinological control systems. While the neurological systems of cell-to-cell communication might be compared to the relatively private and direct interaction of a pair of telephones, the endocrine system uses a system like radio in which radiowaves (like hormones) are sent from a central station (like a gland) and received by radios tuned to an appropriate frequency (like cells with appropriate receptors for the hormone). These differences make the endocrine system more suited to directing re-

sponses requiring the actions of many cells or organs while the nervous system is capable of more subtle responses.

Hormones have three basic chemical structures, namely, peptide, steroid, or tyrosine derivatives. The tyrosine derivatives include two classes of hormones: the biogenic amines such as epinephrine, and the thyroid hormones. In general, the molecular mechanisms of action of the biogenic amines closely resemble those of the peptide hormones, whereas thyroid hormone acts similarly to the steroid hormones.

Hormone Receptors

As was noted, chemically mediated communication requires the recognition and interpretation as well as the sending of chemical messengers. All hormones produce their effects by binding to a receptor. This binding sets into motion a chain of events leading to changes in cell function. The receptors have sites in their configuration which specifically accommodate and bind only one hormone. If a cell does not have a population of receptors with the appropriate binding site, then that cell cannot respond to that particular hormone. However, a cell may have receptor populations specific for several hormones.

The receptors may reside either on the cell membrane (as do receptors for biogenic amines and peptides) or on the chromatin within the nucleus of the cell (steroid and thryoid hormones). While the recognition sites on receptors are unique, the overall structure and function of membrane receptors have several characteristics in common. These receptors consist of a hydrophilic hormone binding region exposed on the external cell surface, a hydrophobic region anchoring the receptor within the lipid bilayer of the cell membrane, and an activity site which can interact with membrane proteins or interior cell constituents. While the membrane receptors are anchored in the plane of the cell membrane, within this plane the receptors are mobile. They are also constantly turning over; the half-life of the insulin receptor is about 7 hours. After hormones bind to receptors and produce their effects on cell function (by a mechanism to be discussed later), they cluster in the cell membrane, are internalized by endocytosis, and are either recycled or degraded. A high rate of receptor binding as would occur during periods of increased hormone concentration in the extracellular fluid bathing the cell membrane would then lead to a higher rate of receptor degradation, gradually leading to a lower number of receptors and decreased responsiveness of that cell to that hormone (down-regulation).

We have so far followed the chemical messenger from its secretion to recognition by a receptor. If, however, that recognition was not translated into changed cellular function, this process would be as ineffectual as a radio that, after recognizing waves of a given frequency, failed to translate that signal into verbal output. The translation process for those peptide and biogenic amines that bind to membrane receptors depends on second messengers. The change in a receptor configuration induced by binding the appropriate hormone causes a change in a coupling unit allowing the binding of GTP. The binding of GTP to the coupling unit in turn activates adenyl cyclase which converts ATP to cAMP. cAMP interacts with the regulatory subunit of a protein kinase which catalyzes the phosphorylation (and change in activity) of another enzyme. This, then, fulfills the efferent leg of the endocrine system. A hormonal signal has been sent, recognized, and translated into altered cellular function.

Other mechanisms also exist to bridge the gap between the binding of hormone by receptor and alteration of cellular function. They include a proposed mechanism by which the hormone–receptor complex causes an activation of enzymes which methylate phospholipids in the cell membrane, leading to altered membrane fluidity activating enzymes and changing calcium permeability. A third means by which hormones interacting with membrane receptors can alter cell function is by changing calmodulin activity and thereby changing calcium uptake.

Steroid and thyroid hormones function via intracellular receptors which, like membrane receptors, are specific for one hormone. Because these hormones are hydrophobic, they can passively diffuse across the lipid membrane. Once a steroid hormone binds to a receptor in the cytosol, an activated hormone–receptor complex migrates to the nucleus and binds to the chromatin. There the complex stimulates the rate of transcription of specific mRNAs which eventuates in new enzymes being produced and the cell function being changed. Thryoid hormones also achieve their effects at the nuclear level, but do not first bind to receptors in the cytosol.

Hypothalamic–Pituitary–Endorgan Axis

Hormonal actions on cells represent the effector arm of the endocrine system. But, in a control system, the regulatory arm of this system is vital. There are several mechanisms by which the endocrine system is regulated. One major site for control and coordination with the other behavioral–metabolic adaptation systems is the hypothalamus. The hypothalamus sits atop the hierarchically structured endocrine system (Figure 1.1). It integrates information from widespread neurological sources regarding external environment and internal milieu. It then secretes an appropriate group of chemical messengers known as releasing factors into the portal capillary system. These releasing factors act via receptors on the anterior pituitary to elicit (or sometimes inhibit) the secretion of tropic hormones. These hormones effect, by the same mechanisms described earlier, the secretion of hormones from target organs or glands such as the thyroid, adrenal, or gonads (Table 1.1).

While the hypothalamus obtains much information regarding the effects of its function from its widespread nervous system inputs, its most direct feedback is via the process of feedback inhibition. Each level in the hierarchy of the endocrine system has receptors that respond to the hormones secreted by all levels distal to them in the cascade leading to hormone secretion. Usually the binding of hormone to such receptors causes a decrease in the secretion of the hormones upstream, although there are exceptions to this pattern of feedback inhibition.

Beside feedback inhibition and the integration via the hypothalamus with the nervous system, down-regulation of receptors also serves to keep hormonal actions in check.

Thus, there are many steps between the hypothalamic control center and the production of the appropriate effect at the target tissue. Abnormalities of any of these steps can result in either excessive functioning

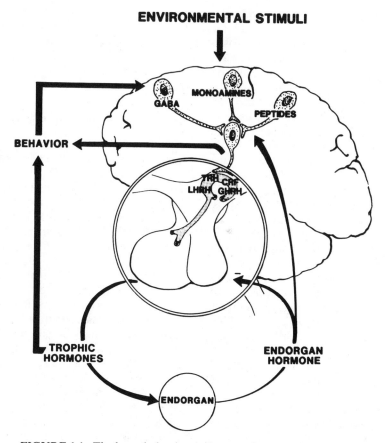

FIGURE 1.1. The hypothalamic–pituitary–endorgan axis. This figure
diagrammatically illustrates that the interplay of neurotransmitters in
the hypothalamus, often activated by environmental and/or behavioral
stimuli, leads to the release of releasing factors from the median eminence. These releasing factors then release trophic hormones from the
pituitary. The trophic hormones then produce the release of the endorgan hormones which then feed back both at the pituitary and the
hypothalamic level to modulate release of the releasing factors. In turn,
the interplay of the neurotransmitters, releasing factors, trophic, and
endorgan hormones all lead to modification of behavior. GABA, γ-
aminobutyric acid; TRH, thyrotropin-releasing hormone; CRF, corticotropin-releasing factor; LHRH, luteinizing hormone-releasing
hormone; GHRH, growth hormone-releasing hormone.

(e.g., hyperthyroidism) or deficient functioning (e.g., hypothyroidism). If this dysfunction occurs at the target organ (gland) level,
it is termed *primary* disorder (e.g., primary
hypothyroidism). The term *secondary* disorder (e.g., secondary hyperthyroidism) is used
to denote pituitary level dysfunction. Sometimes the term *tertiary* disorder is used to denote hypothalamic dysfunction as an etiology
for an endocrinopathy. More unusual are

syndromes in which the target tissue is insen-
sitive to the endorgan hormone due to abnormal hormone, abnormal receptor, or a
postreceptor defect (e.g., insulin resistance
syndrome). Examples of three types of hor-
mone-insufficiency syndromes are given in
Figure 1.2. Examples of the hormone excess
syndromes are given in Figure 1.3.

Because hormones affect many tissues, an
abnormal amount of hormone produces a

TABLE 1.1. Hypothalamic Hormones and the Pituitary and Endorgan Hormones Regulated by Them

Hypothalamic hormone		Pituitary hormone		Endorgan		Endorgan hormone or response
A. Releasing						
Thyrotropin-releasing hormone	→	Thyrotropin	→	Thyroid	→	Thyroxine Triiodothyronine
		Prolactin	→	Prepared breast	→	Lactation
Gonadotropin-releasing hormone	→	Luteinizing hormone	→	Ovarian follicle Testis	→	Progesterone Testosterone
	→	Follicle-stimulating hormone	→	Ovarian follicle	→	Estrogens
				Testis	→	Spermatogenesis
Growth hormone-releasing hormone	→	Growth hormone	→	Liver	→	Somatomedin
Corticotropin-releasing hormone	→	ACTH	→	Adrenal cortex	→	Cortisol
	→	β-Lipotropin	→	?		
	→	γ-MSH	→	?		
B. Inhibitory						
Somatostatin	→	Growth hormone	→	Liver	→	Somatomedin
	→	Thyrotropin	→	Thyroid	→	Thyroxine, triiodothyronine
Dopamine (prolactin inhibitory factor)	→	Prolactin	→	Prepared breast	→	Lactation
	→	Thyrotropin	→	Thyroid	→	Thyroxine, triiodothyronine

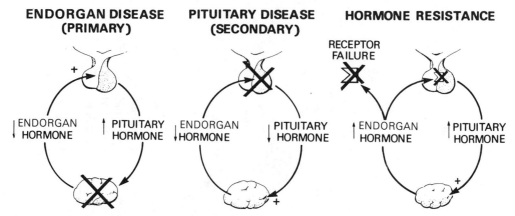

FIGURE 1.2. Examples of the three types of hormone insufficiency syndromes (hypo-endocrine disease).

plethora of nonspecific symptoms. Due to this nonspecificity, the clinician's task is to develop an index of suspicion that a patient has a given endocrine disorder. In endocrinology, biochemical tests are the gold standard and the proper interpretation of these tests supersedes clinical judgment in making diagnoses. If the subset of symptoms presented by the patient is sufficiently suggestive, biochemical tests should be carried out to determine the diagnosis.

The first task is to verify that the suspected excess or deficiency of the hormone does exist. While this is most often done by direct measurement of the hormone in question, the endocrinologist can also detect more subtle abnormalities by taking advantage of the endocrine system's own attempts at regulatory response. For example, in a patient suspected of hypothyroidism, routine measures of thyroid hormone levels may be within normal limits. However, the level of thryoid stimulating hormones (TSH, the tropic hormone secreted by the pituitary) may be high in the case of a primary thyroid deficit. Thus, a high TSH not only identifies a patient as suffering from a disease threatening to produce formal chemical hypothyroidism, but also localizes the dysfuntion to the thyroid gland.

The preliminary screening test(s) should identify whether the patient has *hyper* or *hypo* disease. Further workup should then address

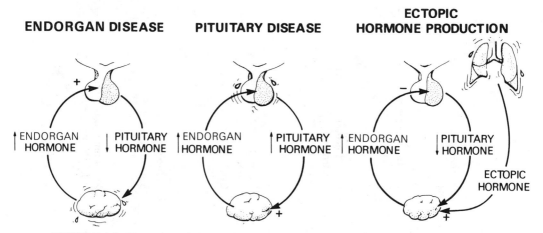

FIGURE 1.3. Examples of the hormone excess syndromes (hyper-endocrine diseases).

TABLE 1.2. Comparison of the Basic Causes of Hyper- and Hypo-Endocrine Disease

Hyper disease	Hypo disease
1. Hyperplasia	1. Congenital
A. Excess tropic hormone	A. Aplasia
B. Abnormal stimulant	B. Enzyme defect
2. Primary tumors	2. Acquired
A. Benign (adenoma)	A. Infection
B. Malignant (cancer)	B. Granulomatous
3. Ectopic production	C. Autoimmune
4. Irritation/inflammation	D. Vascular
5. Exogenous hormone excess	E. Trauma
	F. Tumor
	i. Benign
	ii. Malignant—primary
	—secondary
	G. Iatrogenic
	i. Drugs
	ii. Surgery
	iii. Irradiation
	H. Idiopathic

the following points:

1. Is the biochemical anomaly clinically significant?
2. Is the disease involving the endorgan (primary disease) or the pituitary (secondary disease)? (Points 1 and 2 are further elaborated on in the next section.)
3. What is the etiology? The basic causes of hyper and hypo disease are outlined in Table 1.2.

TABLE 1.3. Management Choices in Hyper- and Hypo-Endocrine Disease

Hyper disease	Hypo disease
1. Surgery	1. Replacement
2. Radiation—external	2. Rx treatable causes
—internal	
3. Drugs	
4. Observation	

4. Are there associated diseases? (See Polyglandular Diseases.)
5. What is the appropriate management (Table 1.3)?

Diagnostic Tests

In endocrinology the majority of circulating hormone levels are measured by *radioimmunoassays*. Radioimmunoassays depend on the concept that radioactively labeled and unlabeled hormones will compete for specific binding sites on antibodies to the hormone. A standard curve can be constructed using known concentrations of unlabeled hormone, and the results obtained with unknown serum samples can then be compared to the standard curve. Before the advent of radioimmunoassays, most hormones were assayed by *bioassays* which utilized the fact that human hormones often produce similar effects in animals. Bioassays are still utilized occasionally when the clinical situation suggests an altered hormone effect, but radioimmunoassays show normal values. This is because some circulating hormones may be altered so that they no longer exert their effect, but are still recognized by the antibody to the hormone or, alternatively, an ectopic hormone is being produced which cross-reacts with another hormone's receptor, but not with the antibody to the hormone. In general, radioimmunoassays have much greater sensitivity and precision than bioassays, though recently some bioassays have been developed that perform as well or better than the radioimmunoassay. Because of the problem that circulating levels of the hormone do not always reflect the activity level of the hormone, *radioreceptor assays* have been developed. These utilize the normal receptor for the hormone in place of an antibody and otherwise utilize the same displacement principles as radioimmunoassays. In general, they display less precision than radioimmunoassays.

Steroid and thyroid hormones (and very occasionally peptide hormones) circulate bound to carrier proteins with only a small proportion being free, **yet it is the free hormone that is available to tissues**, therefore it is important to take into account abnormalities in circulating binding proteins. This can be done by utilizing indirect measurements of done by utilizing indirect measurements of the binding capacity of the binding protein; for example, thryoid hormone is bound to thyroid binding globulin (TBG)—a variety

of *in vitro* tests are available to indirectly measure TBG. If the total thyroid hormone (T4 or T3) is multiplied by this correction factor, an *index* of the free hormone level can be obtained; if the index is normal, this usually correlates with normal levels of free hormone. In certain instances, more sophisticated (and invariably more expensive) tests are necessary to measure the true free hormone level, for example, utilization of equilibrium dialysis. Because steroid hormones are only loosely bound to circulating proteins and these proteins pass poorly into the saliva whereas the hormones pass freely, estimations of free hormone levels are now being made by measuring salivary hormone levels. Unfortunately, this approach does not work for thyroid hormones which are more tightly bound to serum proteins and accumulate bound to prealbumin in the saliva.

Another problem in determining the circulating hormone levels revolves around the fact that many hormones demonstrate marked circadian rhythms (Figure 1.4). In addition, some hormones alter their levels following a meal. For these reasons, most hormone levels should be measured at a fixed time preferably in fasting subjects. In addition, some hormones, for example, testosterone and luteinizing hormone, are secreted in rapid oscillations, necessitating the measurement of multiple samples or the pooling of a number of samples. Because a single

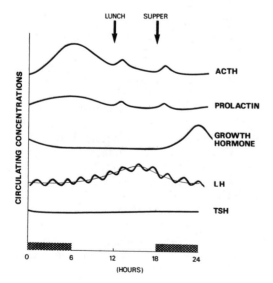

FIGURE 1.4. Diagrammatic demonstration of the various rhythms of pituitary hormones. Note particularly the circadian rhythms, the oscillating ryhthms (LH), and the effect of feeding (ACTH and prolactin).

TABLE 1.4. Multiple Endocrine Neoplasia Syndromes (Hypercluster)

Type I (triple P)	Type II (PAT)
Parathyroid hyperplasia	Parathyroid hyperplasia
Pituitary adenomas, e.g., prolactinoma	Adrenal, e.g., pheochromocytoma
Pancreas, e.g., insulinoma	Thyroid, e.g., medullary carcinoma
(Carcinoid)	

sample or even a few samples fail to give an indication of the 24-hour secretion of the hormone, it is sometimes necessary to collect a 24-hour urine sample and measure the hormone or its metabolites in the urine. Finally, it needs to be remembered that normal ranges are generated as a convenience and always represent an approximation. Some "normals" will lie outside the normal range and some abnormals within the normal range. Because of this overlap, it is often necessary to utilize dynamic testing to confirm the diagnosis. Generally, if the patient has hypo-endocrine disease, the appropriate dynamic test involves stimulating the hormone whereas where hyper disease is suspected, an attempt to suppress the hormone is in order.

Polyglandular Disease

Endocrine disease often tends to cluster such that if a patient has one disease there is an increased likelihood that the patient will develop another endocrine disease or that endocrine disease will be present in other family members. Hyper-endocrine diseases tend to cluster together, as do hypo-endocrine diseases. The hyper disease clusters are called the multiple endocrine neoplasia (MEN) syndromes (Table 1.4) and the hypo cluster, the polyglandular insufficiency syndromes (Table 1.5). Hyperthyroidism violates the rule in that it clusters with the hypo disorders. This is most probably because the natural history of the majority of cases of hyperthyroidism is that after 5–20 years they evolve into hypothyroidism. This clustering makes it extremely important to screen patients carefully on follow-up visits for the development of associated diseases. The etiology of the polyglandular insufficiency syndromes involves an autoimmune mechanism. The recent suggestion that depression is related to immune dysfunction raises the

TABLE 1.5. Polyglandular Insufficiency Syndromes (Hypocluster)

Aspect	Type I	Type II
Age	Children	Adults
Genetic linkage	—	HLAB8-DW3
Diseases	Addison's (adrenal)	Addison's (adrenal)
	Thyroid	Thyroid
	Diabetes	Diabetes
	Pernicious anemia	Pernicious anemia
	Hypoparathyroid	Coeliac disease
	Hypogonadism	Myasthenia gravis
	Moniliasis (hypo T cell)	Vitiligo
	Chronic aggressive hepatitis	
	Vitiligo	

possibility that it may be associated at a higher than expected rate with the polyglandular insufficiency syndrome.

SPECIFIC ENDOCRINE DISORDERS AND THEIR DIAGNOSIS

Pituitary Disorders

Pituitary tumors (adenomas) can either produce symptoms by producing an excess of a pituitary hormone (especially prolactin, growth hormone, or ACTH) or by destruction of pituitary tissue leading to pituitary hormone deficiency (hypopituitarism) or by invasion of surrounding tissues, for example, optic chiasm or hypothalamus. Involvement of the optic chiasm eventually leads to a bitemporal hemianopsia (i.e., inability to see to either side). However, early symptoms of tumor impinging on the optic chiasm may often lead to the patient being referred to the psychiatrist. A classic early complaint is that the patient sees images floating apart or that one half of the face is higher than the other

half (the Picasso effect or the hemifield slide phenomenon). These symptoms tend to occur when the patient is tired or anxious and are due to an inability to fuse the images from both eyes because of the lack of the nasal fields (Figure 1.5). Patients who complain of such visual disturbances should have formal visual testing to rule out early bitemporal hemianopsia. Involvement of the hypothalamus leads to the classical hypothalamic symptoms, including appetite disturbances, diabetes insipidus, excessive thirst, memory disturbances, sleep disturbances (both narcolepsy and insomnia), and disturbances of temperature regulation and abnormal sweating. The overlapping of these symptoms with those found in psychiatric disorders has led to frequent speculation regarding hypothalamic involvement in psychiatric syndromes.

Prolactin is a 198 amino acid polypeptide secreted from the lactotrophs of the anterior pituitary. The major known function of prolactin is the development of breast tissue in preparation for milk production and the maintenance of lactation during the postpartum period. Prolactin is the only anterior

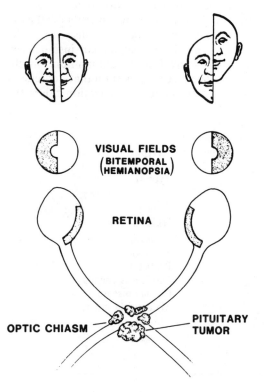

VISUAL FIELDS (BITEMPORAL HEMIANOPSIA)

RETINA

OPTIC CHIASM

PITUITARY TUMOR

FIGURE 1.5. Illustration of the classical visual field defect of pituitary tumors (the Picasso effect, hemifield slide phenomenon), that is, bitemporal hemianopsia, and the fact that this can lead to failure of fusion of visual images.

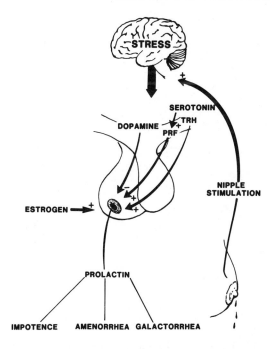

FIGURE 1.6. Regulation of prolactin secretion from the anterior pituitary. PRF, Prolactin-releasing factor; TRH, thyrotropin-releasing hormone.

pituitary hormone which is predominantly under control of an inhibitory factor, namely, dopamine (Figure 1.6). Excess production of prolactin leads to amenorrhea and galactorrhea in the female and impotence, gynecomastia, and galactorrhea in the male. Prolactinomas are the commonest type of pituitary tumors, accounting for 60% of primary pituitary tumors. The diagnosis of a prolactinoma is made by demonstration of an elevated prolactin level and the demonstration of a pituitary tumor on CT scan. Multiple dynamic pharmacological tests for the differentiation of a prolactinoma from other causes of elevated prolactin have been proposed, but lack the sensitivity or specificity to be generally useful. Other causes of chronically elevated prolactin levels include hypothalamic tumors, for example, craniopharyngioma, pituitary stalk lesions, hypothyroidism, chronic renal failure, severe liver disease, chronic irritation of the chest wall following chest wall surgery or chronic nipple stimulation, and opiates and dopaminergic antagonists, for example, phenothiazines, butyrophenones, and metoclopramide. This has led to the proposal that monitoring prolactin levels could be used in

patients on antidopaminergic drugs to follow treatment compliance.

Growth hormone (GH) is a 191 amino acid polypeptide hormone produced by the somatotrophs of the anterior pituitary. Most of the effects of GH are produced by the GH-stimulated release of somatomedins (insulin growth factor, IGF) from the liver. The release of GH from the pituitary is under the dual control of two hypothalamic factors including a GH-releasing factor, a 40–44 amino acid peptide that stimulates GH release, and somatostatin, a 14 amino acid inhibitory substance (Figure 1.7). In addition, circulating somatomedins both directly inhibit GH release at the level of the anterior pituitary and stimulate the release of hypothalamic somatostatin. Excess GH secretion leads to acromegaly in adults and gigantism in children before the closing of epiphyses. Diagnosis of GH excess is made by demonstrating that levels of circulating somatomedin are elevated and that GH levels fail to suppress below 5μg/ml from 1 to 2 hours after 100 g of glucose. Besides pituitary tumors, pathological causes of GH excess include protein malnutrition, including anorexia nervosa, chronic renal failure, and ectopic production

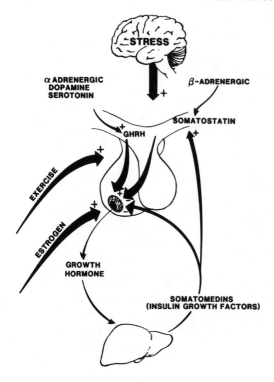

FIGURE 1.7. Regulations of growth hormone secretion from the anterior pituitary.

of GH releasing hormone from lung and pancreatic tumors.

Arginine vasopressin (AVP; antidiuretic hormone) is synthesized in the supraoptic and paraventricular nuclei of the hypothalamus where it is packaged into neurosecretory granules together with its carrier protein, neurophysin. These neurosecretory granules are then transported along the axons to the posterior pituitary. The major function of AVP is to prevent diuresis by increasing water permeability of the collecting duct epithelium in the kidney.

Diabetes insipidus (lack of secretion or effect of AVP) is of importance to the psychiatrist in the differential diagnosis of psychogenic polydipsia (potomania). Both groups of patients present with polyuria and polydipsia. They can both be differentiated from the other forms of polyuria by the fact that both diabetes insipidus and psychogenic polydipsia are characterized by a dilute urine (specific gravity < 1.005 and osmolality < 200 mOsm/kg), whereas in other forms of polyuria (e.g., diabetes mellitus) the osmolality of the urine tends to be closer to that

of the plasma. Diabetes insipidus leads to a more concentrated plasma osmolality, whereas in psychogenic polydipsia the plasma osmolality tends to be dilute. The differential diagnosis of diabetes insipidus and psychogenic polydipsia is given in Table 1.6. Thioridazine (Mellaril) can result in a syndrome indistinguishable from psychogenic polydipsia while another psychiatric drug, lithium can block the effect of AVP at the level of the kidney, producing a syndrome similar to diabetes insipidus.

An excess of vasopressin production (syndrome of inappropriate secretion of antidiuretic hormone—SIADH) leads to water retention, hyponatremia, and often mental disturbances. Common causes of SIADH include tumors, tuberculosis, central nervous system (CNS) trauma and infections, and a variety of drugs including carbamazepine and phenothiazines. The diagnosis is established in patients without other endocrine disease who have low plasma osmolality and sodium and inappropriately elevated urine osmolality and sodium.

TABLE 1.6. Differential Diagnosis of Diabetes Insipidus and Psychogenic Polydipsia

Symptom	Diabetes insipidus	Psychogenic polydipsia
Polydipsia	+ +	+ +
Polyuria	+ +	+ +
Plasma osmolality	↑	↓
Urine osmolality	↓	↓
Effect of water deprivation on urine osmolality	None	↑
Effect of hypertonic saline infusion on urine osmolality	None	↑
Urine osmolality response to vasopressin	↑	↑
Plasma vasopressin	↓	↓

Thyroid Disorders

The thyroid gland synthesizes, stores, and releases thyroxine (T4), and triiodothyronine (T3). The predominant form of thryoid hormone released from the thyroid gland is T4, with the majority of the T3 being formed in the periphery by enzymatic deiodination of T4. These hormones have widespread effects on many tissues, increasing oxygen consumption as well as increasing carbohydrate absorption, regulating growth and maturation, especially of the nervous system (hypothyroidism in infants results in cretinism), and decreasing cholesterol levels. The release of thyroid hormones from the thyroid is under control of thyrotropin (TSH) released from the anterior pituitary (Figure 1.8). The release of TSH is, in turn, under the regulation of thyrotropin-releasing hormone (TRH) as well as a number of hypothalamic inhibitory factors.

Hypothyroidism (myxedema) is a clinical syndrome resulting from deficiency of thyroid hormones and is characterized by a general slowing of metabolism. Hypothyroidism can be due to failure of the thyroid gland itself (primary hypothyroidism) due to failure of the pituitary to produce TSH (secondary hypothyroidism) or rarely due to hypothalamic dysfunction (tertiary hypothyroidism—lack of TRH). A small group of patients develop the signs of hypothyroidism in the presence of elevated circulating thryoid hormones. They appear to have peripheral resistance to the action of thyroid hormone (Refetoff syndrome). A comparison of the features of hypo- and hyperthyroidism is given in Table 1.7. Diagnosis of hypothyroidism is made by the demonstration of an elevated TSH in the presence of a low free T4 index (FT4I). Note that T3 may actually be normal in patients with hypothyroidism. A number of illnesses including major psychiatric disorders can on rare occasions result in a low free T4 index (euthyroid sick syndrome), but in all these cases the TSH is within the normal range.

Hyperthyroidism results from an excess of circulating thyroid hormones. The clinical features are given in Table 1.7. The diagnosis rests in the first instance on the demonstration of an elevated FT4I. However, there is a small subgroup of thyrotoxic patients who have a normal FT4I, but a greatly elevated T3 level (T3 toxicosis). There are a number of causes of an elevated T4, as listed below:

1. Hyperthyroidism
2. Acute illness with liver dysfunction
3. Endorgan resistance to thyroid hormones (Refetoff syndrome)
4. Abnormal T4 binding albumin
5. Factitious thyrotoxicosis
6. Propranolol
7. Psychiatric illness

Some of these do not result in hyperthyroidism, including acute psychiatric illness.

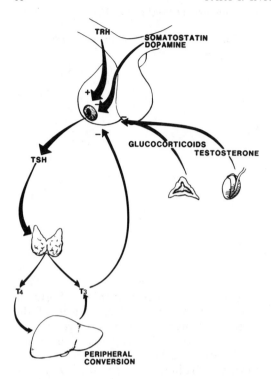

FIGURE 1.8. Regulation of the·hypothalamic–pituitary–thyroid axis.

TABLE 1.7. Clinical Manifestations of Hyper- and Hypothyroidism

Area	Hyperthyroidism	Hypothyroidism
Nutritional	Weight loss, increased appetite	Weight gain
Skin	Heat intolerance, sweating, onycholysis, finger tremor	Cold intolerance, pale, dry
Cardiovascular	Tachycardia, high output failure, atrial arrythmias	Bradycardia, pericardial effusion
Gastrointestinal	Diarrhea	Constipation
Muscular	Proximal myopathy	Weakness
Neurological	Hyperactive reflexes phase	Delayed relaxation
Eyes	Lid lag	Periorbital swelling
Psychological	Hyperactive, irritable emotional lability	Lethargy, depression
Gonads	Impotence, amenorrhea, infertility	Impotence, menorrhagia/amenorrhea, infertility
Hematological	Anemia	Anemia

For this reason, it is recommended that screening psychiatric patients for hyperthyroidism be delayed until 2 weeks after hospital admission unless there are clinically compelling reasons to begin the investigation earlier. Also, a urinary drug screen for amphetamine and phencyclidine should be carried out on all psychiatric patients who are having thyroid function testing as these drugs can elevate thyroid functions. In patients with elevated T4 levels, a TSH rise following the administration of TRH rules out true hyperthyroidism. Unfortunately, a flat TSH response does not necessarily confirm the presence of hyperthyroidism as there are a number of other causes of failure of TSH to respond to TRH, including aging in males and acute or chronic physical illness and depressive disorders in males and females.

Graves' disease is a specific form of hyperthyroidism due to antibodies to the TSH receptor stimulating the thryoid gland to produce hyperthyroidism. Patients with Graves' disease, besides having thyrotoxicosis and goiter, may also have ophthalmopathy (exophathalmus), pretibial myxedema (deposition of mucopoly saccharides in the pretibial area), and thyroid acropachy (subperiorteal inflammation in the fingers, giving the impression of clubbing). Definitive diagnosis of Graves' disease can be made by the demonstration of the presence of circulating thyroid stimulating immunoglobulin.

A subset of older patients with thyrotoxicosis present with a very atypical picture, with apathy and depression representing the major symptoms rather than the hyperkinetic anxious type of individual who is characteristic of the younger hyperthyroid (Figure 1.9). This presentation is called apathetic thyrotoxicosis and is characterized by fatigue, weight loss, proximal myopathy, and cardiovascular abnormalities (heart block, atrial fibrillation, and/or cardiac failure). The classical eye signs of hyperthyroidism are often lacking and the patient may not have a goiter.

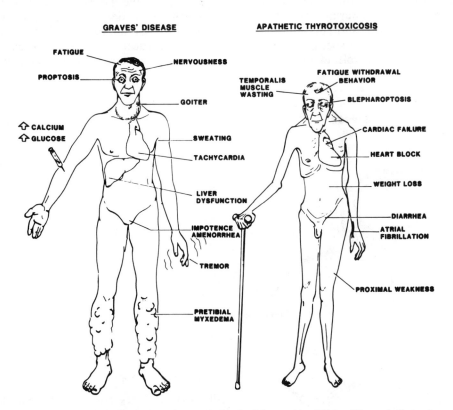

FIGURE 1.9. Comparison between classical hyperthyroidism (Graves' disease) and apathetic thyrotoxicosis.

Of particular note for the psychiatrist is the need to avoid tricyclic antidepressants in hyperthyroid patients. In hyperthyroidism, there is increased toxicity of these agents, probably due to the increased sensitivity to catecholamines that exists in these patients.

Recently, it has been recognized that the development of thyroiditis may be extremely common in the general population. The subacute form of thyroiditis is due to a viral infection, classically presents with a painful thyroid gland, and may be associated with the development of transient hyper- or hypothyroidism. In some cases, there is not pain in the thyroid gland and this is then called painless thyroiditis.

Adrenal Disorders

The adrenal gland consist of two organs: the medulla, which is essentially a sympathetic ganglion that secretes catecholamines, and the cortex, which synthesizes and releases gluco- and mineralocorticoids. While the norepinephrine, epinephrine, and dopamine secreted by the medulla during times of stress are part of the flight or fight response to emergencies seen in most species, the glucocorticoids also play a role in resistance to stress. The role of glucocorticoid increase in response to stress is not understood, but apparently is vital for survival. However, stress has been defined by endocrine researchers as that stimulus that increases ACTH and cortisol levels. The release of ACTH is under the control of the recently identified corticotropin-releasing factor (CRF) (Figure 1.10). CRF may well represent Hans Selye's mystical stress-releasing factor as central administration also leads to catecholamine release. It is important to realize that many events thought to be psychologically stressful have not been demonstrated to be stressors as defined by ACTH/cortisol response. Other functions of cortisol, the primary human glucocorticoid, include maintenance of vascular reactivity to catecholamines, increasing protein catabolism, hepatic glycogenesis and gluconeogenesis, exertion of an antiinsulin effect peripherally, and modulation of peripheral blood cell counts. The primary mineralocorticoid in humans, aldosterone, acts to increase reabsorption of Na^+ from urine, sweat, saliva, and gastric juice in response to hemorrhage, anxiety, surgery, high potassium or low sodium levels, and other stimuli.

Adrenocortical insufficiency is characterized by weakness, fatigue, weight loss,

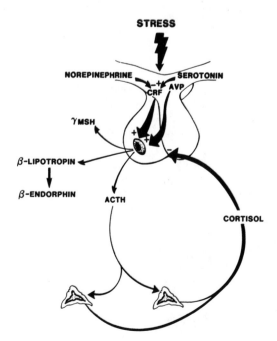

FIGURE 1.10. Regulation of the hypothalamic–pituitary–adrenal axis. CRF, Corticotropin–releasing factor; AVP, arginine vasopressin.

anorexia, hyperpigmentation, postural hypotension, gastrointestinal disturbances (especially nausea and vomiting), salt craving, and hypoglycemia. About 80% is due to autoimmune disease (Addison's disease) and 15% to tuberculosis. Rare causes include adrenal hemorrhage, fungal disease, sarcoidosis, amyloidosis, and metastates from a variety of cancers. Adrenal cortical insufficiency can also occur after disease of the pituitary and is commonly seen after withdrawal of corticosteroid medication that is too rapid to allow the pituitary to recover from suppression of function induced by exogenous steroids. One needs to be particularly aware that prolonged administration of steroid creams to the skin can result in absorption of the corticosteroid with suppression of ACTH and adrenocortical insufficiency. Diagnosis of adrenal insufficiency is made by stimulating the adrenal administration of 0.25 mg of a synthetic human α_{1-24}-ACTH (cosyntropin) intramuscularly or intravenously and measuring a plasma cortisol 30–60 minutes later. If the plasma cortisol level in response to cosyntropin is greater than 20 μg/dl, primary adrenocortical insufficiency is ruled out. Most cases of secondary adrenocortical insufficiency and adrenocortical insufficiency secondary to prolonged exogenous steroids will also fail to respond to this bolus of cosyntropin. Measurement of a plasma ACTH will then distinguish primary (very high ACTH) from the other causes of adrenocortical insufficiency (low or normal ACTH). Psychotropics need to be avoided in patients with Addison's disease because of their tendency to exacerbate the hypotensive episodes.

Cushing's syndrome (Figure 1.11) is characterized by truncal and facial ("moon facies") obesity, hypertension, proximal

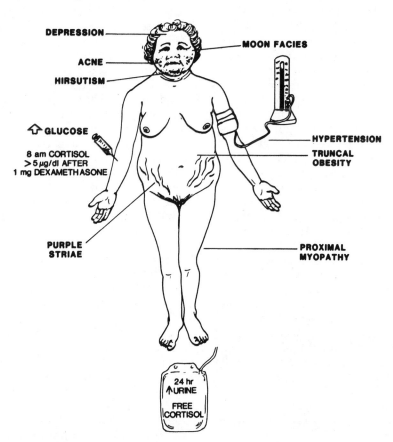

FIGURE 1.11. Classical features of Cushing's syndrome.

myopathy, purple striae, acne, mental disturbances, and easy bruisability. By far the commonest cause of Cushing's syndrome is
iatrogenic. Of the other causes, about two-
thirds is due to either pituitary tumors producing ACTH or excess production of CRF
by the hypothalamus (i.e., Cushing's disease), 15% is due to ectopic ACTH production by tumors, and another 15% is due to
adrenal adenomas or carcinomas. The diagnosis, when suspected, is screened for by
demonstrating failure of the plasma cortisol
to be reduced below 5 μg/dl at 8 A.M. after
administration of 1 mg of dexamethasone at
11 P.M. the previous night and/or the presence
of an elevated urinary free cortisol, particularly when the value is related to the creatinine excreted in the urine. However, there
are a number of false-positive responses, especially in hospitalized (25%) and obese
(15%) patients (Table 1.8). Failure of sup-
pressionafter 8 A.M. should be ignored as this
greatly increases the false-positive rate. Thus,
a positive overnight dexamethasone suppression test is followed by the 2-day low-dose
dexamethasone test. In this test, 0.5 mg of
dexamethasone is given hourly for 2 days.
Urine collections (for 24 hours) for either urinary free cortisol or 17-hydroxycortico-
steroids are made before and on the second
day of the test. Normal subjects should
demonstrate at least a halving of their baseline values when expressed per gram of urine
creatinine, and the final values should be well
within the normal range. False-positive responses are much less common with this test.
About 5% of Cushing's syndrome patients
may have a normal response to this test. This
is particularly true of some patients who develop cyclical Cushing's disease. For this reason, if the clinical index of suspicion is high,
this test should be repeated on at least three
occasions if a normal response is obtained.
Patients with abnormal responses should be
referred to an endocrinologist for the differentiation of Cushing's disease from primary
adrenal hyperfunction or ectopic ACTH production. With the recent availability of CRF
for clinical testing, it was hoped that the diagnosis of Cushing's disease would be sim-
plified. However, early testing has suggested
poor specificity for the ACTH/cortisol response to CRF in this regard.

The group of autosomal recessive enzyme

TABLE 1.8. False-Positive Responses to Dexamethasone Suppression[a]

1. Depression*
2. Alcohol*
3. Illness*
4. High estrogen states
5. Uremia*
6. Obesity
7. Inducers of hepatic microsomal enzymes
     Phenytoin*
     Barbiturates*

---

[a] The asterisk (*) denotes false-positives to the 2-day
low-dose dexamethasone test as well as to the overnight
1-mg dexamethasone test.

defects in the synthesis of cortisol, producing
the syndromes of congenital adrenal hyperplasia, are of importance to the psychiatrist
because they can result in patients having ambiguous genitalia or external genitalia opposed to that predicted by their genetic sex.
Thus, genetic females with 21α-hydroxylase
or 11β-hydroxylase deficiency will have varying degrees of labioscrotal fusion and clitoral
enlargement. Genetic males with 17α-hydrox-
ylase and 3β-hydroxysteroid dehydrogenase
deficiencies will have either female or ambiguous external genitalia. Other nonadrenal
causes of male pseudohermaphroditism include inborn errors of testosterone biosynthesis, endorgan insensitivity to androgens
(testicular feminization), and maternal ingestion of estrogens and progestins. It is essential
from the psychological point of view that the
sex of rearing of the patient is assigned as soon
as possible after birth and subsequently rein-
forced by appropriate surgical, hormonal,
and psychological management.

Phaeochromocytoma

Phaeochromocytoma is a tumor of the
adrenal medulla or sympathetic ganglia that
produces catecholamines. The syndrome produced by phaeochromocytomas has been
characterized as the panic syndrome (Figure
1.12). Patients present with hypertension,
tachycardia, hyperventilation, tremor, anxiety, weakness, weight loss, flushing, excessive
sweating, headaches, and postural hypoten-

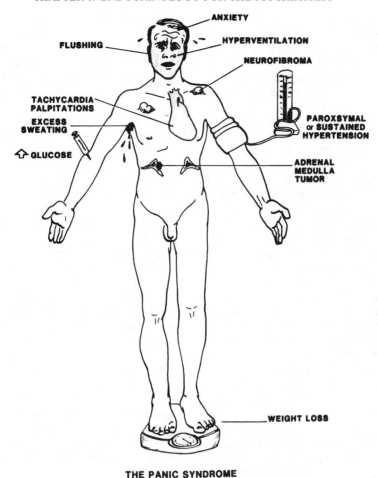

THE PANIC SYNDROME

FIGURE 1.12. Classical features of a phaeochromocytoma.

sion. A small percentage of patients with phaechromocytoma have neurofibromas on their skin. When the diagnosis of phaeochromocytoma is suspected three 24-hour urine specimens for metanephrines, vanillymandelic acid, or normetanephrine are collected. Elevated levels of catecholamines or their metabolites make the diagnosis of phaeochromocytoma extremely likely. Measurement of plasma catcholamines has proved to be less useful than the 24-hour urine values. Recently, the response of plasma catecholamines to clonidine has proved to be an effective diagnostic test for phaeochrocytoma.

Pancreatic Disorders—Hypoglycemia

While the steroid and thyroid hormones affect brain tissue function by directly bind-ing to brain tissue receptors, insulin and glucagon change CNS function by modulating the level of blood glucose, the primary foodstuff of neurons. Insulin, synthesized and secreted by the β cells of the pancreatic islets of Langerhans, acts on the insulin receptors (found on nearly every cell in the body) to increase glucose uptake, thus lowering the blood glucose level. It also stimulates the incorporation of amino acids into proteins. Glucagon, synthesized and secreted by the islet A cells, counters insulin's hypoglycemic actions primarily by its stimulation of hepatic glycogenolysis and gluconeogenesis. Other hormones that respond to hypoglycemia (antiinsulin hormones) include GH and cortisol.

The brain, under normal feeding circumstances, is an obligate glucose consumer, using 115 g of glucose per day. Because of this circumstance, the body has powerful homeostatic mechanisms which respond to any significant decrease in blood glucose. These include most prominently the secretion of epinephrine which stimulates glucagon secretion and hence, glycogenolysis, the activation of the sympathetic nervous system, the secretion of cortisol which increases gluconeogenesis, and the secretion of GH which increases blood glucose by decreasing glucose usage by peripheral tissue. The activation of the sympathetic nervous system and the increase of epinephrine secretion along with the effects of glucose deficiency on cerebral neurons combine to account for the symptoms of hypoglycemia. In general, acute hypoglycemia results in symptoms due to both increased autonomic nervous system activity and depressed CNS function, while chronic hypoglycemia evokes less autonomic arousal.

The symptoms of hyperepinephrinemia and autonomic arousal include weakness, tingling of the extremities, and periodically, sweating, palpitations, anxiety, and tremulousness. Cerebral glucopenia is reflected by headache, faintness, and mental confusion. However, in the chronically hypoglycemic, autonomic symptoms are often absent and the cerebral glucopenia can be reflected in more subtle symptoms such as personality changes, depression, and schizophrenia-like symptoms. Acute hypoglycemia, if untreated, can progress to loss of consciouness, coma, and death.

Diagnosis of organic mental disorders secondary to acute hypoglycemia depends on the measurement of low plasma glucose (usually less than 40 mg/100 ml) *and* the reversal of the symptoms with the administration of intravenous glucose. However, chronic hypoglycemia is often intermittent and nocturnal and is not always present at the time when symptoms are present. Where the diagnosis is suspected (and the patient is not receiving insulin) the patient may need to be hospitalized and fasted for 72 hours and then exercised, following which the diagnosis can be made by measuring insulin and glucose levels.

The most common cause of hypoglycemia is excessive insulin dosage in diabetic patients. Insulin-secreting β cell tumors of the pancreas, adrenal, thyroid, or pituitary in-

sufficiency, liver damage, alcoholism, and hereditary carbohydrate metabolism disorders can also cause this syndrome. Functional or reactive hypoglycemia may also occur, usually 2–4 hours after meals when blood sugar drops to low levels and symptoms of hyperepinephrinemia ensue. While this disorder, thought secondary to poor matching of insulin and subsequent anti-insulin hormonal responses, clearly occurs in situations such as "dumping" syndrome after gastrectomy, the diagnosis of reactive hypoglycemia has been invoked to explain all types of behavioral abnormalities, especially anxiety and antisocial disorders. The chief problem with this diagnosis is that it has often been invoked without validation of the following strict criteria: (1) Hypoglycemia after a carbohydrate meal must be documented; (2) symptoms must occur simultaneously with the hypoglycemia; (3) the symptoms must be relieved promptly by eating; (4) the pattern of hypoglycemic symptoms 2–4 hours after meals and the relief of symptoms by eating is a regular one. Furthermore, the diagnosis has not been sufficiently differentiated from the one-third of normal subjects who have plasma glucose $< 60 \mu g/$ 100 ml after meals. It would seem that in most patients who develop major mental symptoms associated with "reactive" hypoglycemia, the symptomology depends mainly on an excessive psychological response to a physical situation that represents a variant of normality. Treatment of reactive hypoglycemia, therefore, involves psychological counseling as well as the institution of six small meals a day, in an attempt to limit the degree of glucose excursion compared to that seen after two or three large meals. The use of fructose as a sweetener and high-fiber foods to slow gastric emptying and reduce the glycemic response may also prove useful.

While treatment of acute hypoglycemia is obviously providing glucose either orally or intravenously, depending on the severity of the hypoglycemia, more specific therapy for the disorders underlying this syndrome is beyond the scope of this chapter. Chronic hypoglycemia can lead to brain damage if the problem has been of sufficient duration and severity. Therefore, these symptoms may not reverse with the resolution of the metabolic imbalance.

Pancreatic Disorders—Diabetes Mellitus

Hyperglycemia is most frequently due to poorly controlled diabetes mellitus, but can also be due to Cushing's syndrome, hyperthyroidism, or phaechromocytoma. Diabetes mellitus is a syndrome including both metabolic and vascular components. We will focus on the organic mental disorders due to hypoinsulinemia and consequent hyperglycemia. If the impairment of glucose metabolism is only mild to moderate, the patient may complain of fatigue. With worsening glucose tolerance and glucose levels exceeding the usual threshold, polyuria, polydipsia, blurry vision, and polyphagia ensue while fatigue worsens. At this point, fatigue, malaise, and associated appetite changes could be confused with depression or hypochondriasis. The appearance of ketone bodies due to excessive lipolysis can lead to anorexia, and progression to ketoacidosis is accompanied by abdominal pain, nausea, vomiting, shortness of breath, and stupor proceeding to coma. Impotence is occasionally the first sign of diabetes vascular complications, and diabetes should be ruled out before psychological explanations are invoked. Like hypoglycemia, recurrent and chronic hyperglycemia can result in organic mental disorders that may mimic depression or schizophrenia and may be irreversible.

Besides direct effects of hormones and nutrients on brain cell function, there are other more subtle psychological effects on the patient. While the level of glucose has prominent effects on mental functions, there are many effects of diabetes mellitus on psychological mechanisms of patients not directly explained by glucose levels.

As discussed, neurological, endocrinological, and psychological mechanisms are inextricably intertwined in the process of behavior control. Rarely are people with normal endocrine systems aware of the automatic, unconscious endocrine contributions to their behavior. However, diabetic patients and others with endocrinopathies become acutely aware of the anxiety, irritability, mood changes, and other symptoms experienced during abnormal metabolic fluctuations. This awareness of endocrine status leads both patients and families to continually question the validity of any psychological reaction. An outburst of anger in response to a perceived injustice is met with the frustrating reply, "your blood sugar must be low." Certainly this type of interaction can have serious repercussions for identity formation as well as successful conflict resolution within families. Other psychosocial burdens for the diabetic patient include (1) the need to cope with an illness that may range from having undetectable to life-threatening symptoms, (2) the necessity of adhering to a strict regimen, and (3) the belief that failure to adhere to this regimen makes one responsible for one's long-term disabilities or death. More recently, the introduction of insulin pumps (human machine dependency syndrome) and the use of pancreatic and renal transplantation have added further psychological problems to deal with for the diabetic family and physician.

Of all chronically ill patients, diabetics have been shown to complain more often of painful symptoms. This is particularly prominent in the case of the painful diabetic neuropathy. It has now been shown that hyperglycemia and/or rapid excursions in blood glucose heighten the perception of pain and that diabetic patients, even in the face of a peripheral neuropathy, have a decreased pain tolerance.

Parathyroid Disorders

Calcium is vital to proper neuronal membrane function. The calcium level in blood is controlled by the interplay of parathyroid hormone (PTH), vitamin D, and calcitonin.

The parathyroid glands secrete PTH, which is responsible for the maintenance of serum calcium levels by increasing resorption of calcium from bone and decreasing renal excretion of calcium. Thus, disorders of the parathyroid glands are manifested by alterations in circulating calcium levels. As calcium is essential for neuronal function, these disorders are often associated with neurological and psychiatric manifestations.

Hypoparathyroidism is characterized clinically by signs and symptoms of neuromuscular hyperactivity and biochemically by low calcium elevated phosphorus, and low PTH.

Hypoparathyroidism is due either to surgical removal of the parathyroids, prolonged periods of hypomagnesemia (such as may occur in alcoholics), or is idiopathic. The neuromuscular symptoms include paresthesical tetany, hyperventilation, convulsions, and expyramidal (Parkinsonian-like) neurological syndromes. In patients with latent tetany, inflating a sphygmomanometer cuff results in carpal spasm (Trousseau's sign) and tapping the facial nerve anterior to the earlobe causes twitching of the facial muscles on the stimulated side (Chovstek's sign). Pseudohypoparathyroidism is a rare familial disorder characterized by tissue resistance to PTH. Besides developing hypocalcemia, these patients also often are mentally retarded and have a variety of congenital growth and skeletal developmental defects. Hypoparathyroidism also makes patients more susceptible to extrapyramidal side effects of neuroleptics and more likely to experience symptomatic hyperventilation.

Hyperparathyroidism is due to excessive production of PTH by either parathyroid gland hyperplasia or a parathyroid adenoma. Biochemically, this disorder is characterized by hypercalcemia, a low serum phosphate, and an inappropriately high PTH level. Clinically, these patients are often asymptomatic or complain of nonspecific symptoms such as weakness, easy fatigability, depressive symptoms, or loss of memory for recent events. In more severe cases they develop renal stones, bony disease (osteitis fibrosa cystica), and gastrointestinal complaints ("stones, bones, and moans"). The differential diagnosis of the causes of hypercalcemia is listed in Table 1.9. From the psychiatric point of view, it should be particularly noted that lithium can produce hypercalcemia.

Hypogonadism

Estrogens and androgens, like thyroid and steroid hormones, bind directly to brain cells. Deficiencies in estrogen levels and their regulation in females have been thought to underlie several poorly defined mental syndromes including menopausal distress, premenstrual

TABLE 1.9. Causes of Hypercalcemia

Etiology	Diagnostic test
1. Hyperparathyroidism	PTH, PO_4
2. Multiple myeloma	Serum protein electrophoresis
3. Ectopic malignant syndromes	
A. Ectopic PTH	PTH
B. Production of osteoclastic activating factor	Malignancy workup
C. Prostaglandins	Urinary prostaglandins
4. Granulomatous diseases	
A. Sarcoid	Muscle biopsy
B. Tuberculosis	Mantoux
5. Endocrine disease	
A. Hyperthyroid	Thyroxine
B. Addison's disease	Cosyntropin test
6. Prolonged immobilization	History
7. Drugs	History
A. Thiazides	
B. Vitamin D	
C. Vitamin A	
D. Lithium	
8. Benign familial hypocalciuric hypercalcemia	Low urine calcium

tension, postpartum blues, and psychogenic amenorrhea. As yet no good evidence exists relating hormonal changes to the psychiatric syndromes in any of these conditions (although certain physical symptoms such as hot flushes do seem related). It is important for the psychiatrist to remember that although psychological disturbances lead to amenorrhea, equally there are a variety of organic medical and endocrine disorders that can present with amenorrhea, for example, hypothalamic and pituitary tumors, thyroid disease, chronic illness, and hemochromatosis, and these need to be excluded. Also the menstrual cycles appear to require a certain critical amount of body fat which appears to account for the amenorrhea that has been reported in ballet dancers, serious joggers, and anorectic patients.

Hypoandrogenemia may reflect impaired testicular or pituitary functioning. As testosterone and luteinizing hormone (LH, the pituitary hormone controlling secretion of testosterone from the Leydig cells) are both secreted in episodic bursts 2–4 hours apart, it is essential that either more than one sample is obtained or that three specimens of blood each 30 minutes apart are pooled before being sent to the laboratory to give an idea of the integrated hormonal values (this is the most cost-effective method). An isolated testosterone without an LH level obtained at the same time is of little value, as it is the combination of both hormones that is used to make the diagnosis. Thus, if the patient has primary hypogonadism (testicular disease), the diagnosis is made by a low serum testosterone in the presence of a high LH, whereas in the case of secondary hypogonadism (pituitary or hypothalamic disease), the patient has a low testosterone, often in the presence of an inappropriately low normal (rather than overtly low) LH level. Many authors have suggested that Klinefelter syndrome (primary hypogonadism associated with an XXY karyotype) results in a psychiatric disorder, but the symptoms described are so variable as to make this syndrome nonspecific if, indeed, it exists.

Impotence

Impotence (failure to obtain an erection adequate for intercourse) can be psychogenic or organic in nature. In many cases both organic and psychogenic causes are involved. However, in the older male (over 40), it appears that the primary cause is organic in the overwhelming majority of patients.

The major organic cause of impotence is vascular disease. The penile artery is of similar size to that of the coronary arteries and is just as prone to develop atherosclerosis. Yet the older patient presenting to the physician with chest pain is immediately evaluated for angina, whereas the same patient presenting with impotence ("penile angina") is often referred directly for sex therapy without first having his vascular status checked by Doppler studies or penile plethysmography.

The second major cause of impotence is iatrogenic. Of the top 200 prescription drugs in America, 16 cause impotence. These include thiazide diuretics, antihypertensive medications, phenothiazines, butyrophenones, amphetamines, spironolactone, barbiturates, tricyclic antidepressants, monoamine oxidase inhibitors, cimetidine, and opiates.

Endocrine causes of impotence include primary hypogonadism (low testosterone and elevated LH), secondary hypogonadism (low testosterone and normal or low LH), elevated prolactin, and hypo- and hyperthyroidism. It has recently been reported that patients with temporal lobe epilepsy can have hypothalamic hypogonadism due to suppression or release of gonadotropin-releasing hormone.

Other causes of impotence include peripheral and autonomic neuropathies, diabetes mellitus, multiple sclerosis, cerebrovascular accidents involving the limbic system, spinal cord lesions, urological surgical procedures, and Peyronie's disease (fibrous bands in the penis).

ENDOCRINE CONDITIONS AS A CAUSE OF ORGANIC MENTAL DISORDERS

Central to modern efforts to understand behavior is the idea that psychological events are reflections of physiological events in the brain. Therefore, disorders that alter brain physiology may change behavior. Many, perhaps most, endocrine disorders alter brain function, and if this alteration is sufficiently severe, an organic mental disorder secondary to the endocrinopathy may be diagnosed.

Endocrine disorders may alter brain function in several ways. First, the hypothalamus and pituitary may develop tumors or infiltrations of sufficient size that brain function may be disrupted. Second, the brain is apparently a target tissue for a variety of hormones, as these hormones bind specifically to receptors on brain cells (e.g., cortisol binding is greatest in the hippocampus, with smaller amounts in the limbic system and cortex) and, presumably, alter brain cell function. Third, the endocrine system has wide-ranging effects, on peripheral metabolism which affect the brain's supply of nutrients necessary to neuronal function (e.g., insulin/glucagon affect glucose availability, parathyroid hormone alters calcium availability).

These three mechanisms tend to affect the function of nervous tissue in a relatively global manner. Therefore, the disorders in mental functioning they produce are quite nonspecific. Diagnosis of mental dysfunction as an organic mental disorder (OMD) due to endocrinopathy is not reliable without confirmatory laboratory results. There are no pathognomonic signs or symptoms for OMD due to a given endocrine disorder. However, there are mental symptoms that are more frequent in some endocrine disorders than others, and their presence may encourage the clinician to seek screening laboratory tests for certain hormonal disorders. An extensive baseline hormonal screen in the typical patient with a psychological com-

TABLE 1.10. Mental and Physical Signs and Symptoms of Major Endocrinopathies

Endocrinopathy	Symptoms of organic mental disorder	Physical signs and symptoms
Hyperthyroidism	Anxiety, distractibility, emotional lability which may progress to psychosis; small percentage, usually elderly, are apathetic and depressed; insomnia	Heat intolerance, appetite increase with weight loss, palpitation, warm skin, change in bowel and menstrual patterns, goiter, hyperactive reflexes, tachyarrhythmias, proximal weakness
Hypothyroidism	Fatigue, lethargy, decreased initiative, cognitive slowing, increased response latency, and slowed speech, depression, occasional psychosis (myxedema madness)	Cold intolerance, mild weight gain despite decreased appetite, constipation, menstrual irregularity, skin dryness, delayed tendon reflexes
Hypercortisolemia (Cushing's syndrome)	Exogenous steroids: Euphoria > depression, memory deficits, pressure of speech, irritability, psychosis Endogenous steroids: Depression > euphoria, especially in Cushing's disease, memory deficits, suicidal ideation	Weakness, muscle wasting, hypertension, increased appetite, truncal and facial obesity, abdominal striae, hyperglycemia
Hypocortisolemia (Addison's syndrome)	Fatigue, apathy, cognitive deficits, depressed mood in Addisonian crisis, psychosis, coma, stupor	Weakness, hypotension, anorexia, skin pigmentation, abdominal symptoms, weight loss
Hypoestrogenemia (in females)	Anxiety, tension, emotional lability, irritability, depression, changes in libido (all of these are hypothesized, not proven to be related to hypoestrogenemia	Hot flushes, atrophy of skin and mucosa, headaches, myalgias, painful intercourse

TABLE 1.10. (*Continued*)

Endocrinopathy	Symptoms of organic mental disorder	Physical signs and symptoms
Hypoandrogenemia	Decreased libido, fatigue	Impotence
Hyperinsulinemia (recurrent hypoglycemia	Acute: Anxiety, panic mental confusion Chronic: Personality changes, depression, or schizophrenic-like symptoms, dementia	Acute: Weakness, tingling periorally and of extremities, sweating, palpitation, tremulousness Chronic: Minimal physical symptoms
Hypoinsulinemia (diabetes mellitus)	Fatigue, lethargy, cognitive impairment, stupor, coma	Fatigue, polyuria, polydipsia, polyphagia, impotence, blurry vision
Hyperparathyroidism	Can range from asymptomatic to extremely dysfunctional; fatigue, depression, dementia	Polyuria, renal colic, epigastric distress, hyporeflexia, bone pain
Hypoparathyroidism	Irritability, nervousness, fatigue, confusion	Hyperreflexia, paresthesias periorally, muscle cramps, convulsions, acute dystonia with phenothiazines
Hyperaldosteronism	May present with nervousness, irritability, depression, weakness, or as acute organic syndrome with lethargy, stupor, coma, and impaired cognition	Weakness, paresthesias, multiple aches and pains, anorexia, hypokalemia
Hypopituitarism	Apathy, indifference, fatigue, depression, loss of libido, cognitive deficits	Loss of pigment, loss of body hair, loss of menstrual periods, loss of weight (differentiate from anorexia nervosa by AN patients having pubic hair and losing more weight)
Hyperprolactinemia (prolactinoma)	Decreased libido, depression	Impotence, amenorrhea galactorrhea, visual disturbances
Aromegaly	Narcolepsy, decreased libido	Large extremities, excessive sweating, proximal weakness, visual disturbances

plaint is not indicated at this time unless the clinician's index of suspicion is raised by specific physical or historical findings. Routine screening of the thyroid axis may be appropriate in psychiatric patients, however, as these diseases are of sufficient frequency as to make the cost–benefit analysis more favorable.

As was mentioned, specific endocrinopathies have profiles of mental symptoms that regularly accompany them. Table 1.10 delineates the common mental syndromes which have been described as accompanying specific endocrine disorders.

ENDOCRINE EFFECTS OF PSYCHIATRIC DISEASE

In addition to the plethora of effects of endocrine disorders on the psyche, it is now quite clear that the psyche is equally capable of modulating the secretion of hormones.

The effects of psychiatric disease on hormones are hypothetically mediated via alterations in neurotransmitter interactions at the level of the hypothalamus, leading to altered release into the portal system of the hypothalamic-releasing and -inhibiting hormones, although there is also some evidence for peripheral changes in hormonal secretion and metabolism. These changes will be fully discussed in the remainder of this volume and as such are only briefly alluded to here.

The most dramatic documented effect of psychiatric disease on the endocrine system is the increased activity of the hypothalamic–pituitary–adrenal axis in endogenous depression, which has led to the use of the dexamethasone suppression test as an extremely useful research tool in the diagnosis of this disorder. Unfortunately, this test has not proved to have the sensitivity or specificity necessary to be useful as a diagnostic tool in individual patients. Similarly, the failure of TSH to rise in response to TRH in depressed patients represents another example of a useful biological marker for psychiatric research. The presence of elevated thyroid hormone levels in acute psychiatric admissions (stress hyperthyroninemia) represents another example of psychiatric disease altering endocrine status. From the endocrinological point of view these abnormal test results need to be seen as false-positive results interfering with the diagnosis of endocrine disorders. From the psychiatric point of view these test results often represent a quandary (especially when they are extremely abnormal), as the psychiatrist then has to decide whether these results are due to the underlying mental disease or whether the mental disease is due to an endocrine disorder which requries further workup. Thus, careful clinical assessment of the patient and endocrinological consultation when in doubt are of paramount importance in patients with abnormal psychoneuroendocrine test results.

Another area where psychiatric disease can impinge upon endocrine disease is that where a stressful situation leads to precipitation of a full-blown systemic disease. Much evidence now exists favoring the ability of the CNS to modulate the immune system, possibly secondary to altered hormone release (see below). As a number of endocrine diseases are thought to be secondary to autoimmune processes, this alteration in immune function could theoretically allow the expression of an underlying autoimmune disease. Much anecdotal and some experimental evidence exists supporting the idea that this process may actually occur, especially in the case of hyperthyroidism.

There exists one major pitfall in research attributing onset of an endocrine disease to a stressful event. This problem has been characterized as the *dating phenomenon*. The classical example of this phenomenon is in the first case of Graves' disease (hyperthyroidism) which, in fact, was described by Caleb Hillier Parry. The patient was a young lady in her 20s who developed the classical signs and symptoms of hyperthyroidism following falling out of a wheelchair while being pushed down a hill. The stress of falling out of the wheelchair was identified as the etiological factor precipitating the hyperthyroidism. However, it is clear that most normal 20-year-olds are not pushed around in wheelchairs (she had no broken bones), and since proximal myopathy and weakness are major signs and symptoms of hyperthyroidism, it is probable that her hyperthyroidism predated her fall. This tendency to date the onset of physical signs and symptoms to a specific event is prevalent and makes research into the role of stress as a precipitant of disease extremely complex.

ENDOCRINE EFFECTS OF PSYCHIATRIC DRUGS

One of the clinical areas most directly applicable in endocrinology for the psychiatrist is the effect of psychiatric drugs on endocrine function.

The most commonly observed endocrine abnormality during psychiatric therapy is hyperprolactinemia. Both classes of the major antipsychotic drugs (i.e., phenothiazines and butyrophenones) elevate prolactin levels. They produce this effect by inhibiting dopamine action. Prolactin release from the anterior pituitary is under tonic inhibition by dopamine. The increase in prolactin is so characteristic of antipsychotic drugs that it has been used as a laboratory screening test for drugs with antipsychotic activity. In addition, during therapy, decrease in psychotic behavior is reported to be inversely correlated with increase in prolactin levels.

Clinical manifestations of hyperprolactinemia are amenorrhea, breast engorgement, and galactorrhea in the female and impotence, gynecomastia, and, rarely, galactorrhea in the male. In addition, in tissue cultures approximately one-third of breast tumors have been shown to be prolactin dependent, and in animal experiments high doses of phenothiazines increase the incidence of mammary tumors. The relevance of this increased tumor incidence to human populations is unknown. Whether the false-positive urinary, but not serum, pregnancy test that has been reported to occur with neuroleptics is related to the increased prolactin is not known.

Recently, a number of studies have suggested that prolonged elevations of prolactin may lead to an accelerated loss of bone mass (osteoporosis). Thus, investigations to determine benefits from calcium supplementation in female patients on chronic neuroleptic therapy are in order. Estrogen supplementation should be considered in perimenopausal women to forestall changes in bone mass as well as the increase in mortality due to cardiovascular disease characteristic of post-menopausal females. Measurement of 1,25-dihydroxyvitamin D (the active metabolite of vitamin D) should be considered, and if the value is at the lower range of normal or below, vitamin D supplementation should be undertaken.

A number of psychiatric drugs alter vasopressin (antidiuretic hormone) release and/or action and as such can result in abnormalities in water metabolism. Diphenylhydantoin inhibits the release of vasopressin and as such can lead to central diabetes insipidus. Lithium greatly reduces the sensitivity of the renal tubule to vasopressin by inhibiting the vasopressin-sensitive renal medullary adenylate cyclase. This results in a form of nephrogenic diabetes insipidus. As previously discussed, diabetes insipidus presents with polyuria and polydipsia and an increase in serum sodium levels and serum osmolality. Drug-induced diabetes insipidus needs to be distinguished from the polydipsia produced by Mellaril, which directly affects the thirst center, producing polydipsia. These patients tend to have hyponatremia rather than hypernatremia.

Inappropriate secretion of antidiuretic hormone resulting in hyponatremia can be produced by carbamazepine, monoamine oxidase inhibitors such as isocarboxazid, and tranylcypromine opiates and barbiturates. In general, the SIADH produced by these drugs responds to mild water deprivation. However, in some cases discontinuation of the drug is warranted.

A variety of psychiatric drugs alters thyroid function and thyroid function tests. The classical effect is the hypothyroidism produced by lithium. Amphetamine, Ritalin, and phencyclidine have been shown to produce an increase in thyroid hormones, most probably by activating the hypothalamic-pituitary–thyroid axis. Diphenylhydantoin can decrease both total and free thyroid hormone values by competing for binding sites on thyroid transport proteins, by inducing alterations in the enzymes responsible for metabolizing T4, and by producing a form of hypothalamic hypothyroidism. Barbiturates can produce a similar lowering in T4 levels by inducing T4 metabolizing enzymes, and diazepam lowers T4 levels by competing for binding sites on the transport proteins.

In patients with diabetes mellitus the effect of electroconvulsive therapy (ECT) needs to be kept in mind. ECT leads to an increase in a variety of stress hormones (e.g., GH and cortisol) that antagonize the effects of insulin. This can lead to the development of hyperosmolar diabetic coma over a course of therapy in a patient who already has borderline diabetes. Thus, a fasting and 2-hour postprandial serum glucose or an HbA_1C (glycosylated hemoglobin) should be checked before commencing therapy. If the HbA_1C or the fasting glucose (> 120 mg/dl) or the postprandial (> 140 mg/dl) is elevated, the serum glucose should be followed at weekly intervals during ECT. Any patient in whom polyuria and polydipsia develops during ECT should also have blood glucose checked. Patients who already have a diagnosis of diabetes mellitus should be carefully monitored during ECT, ideally by fingerstick blood glucose monitoring four times a day. They are likely to develop poor control during ECT insulin dosage as adjusted to maintain adequate blood glucose levels. Lithium has insulin-like actions and thus care should be taken of not precipitating hypoglycemic reactions when placing a diabetic on lithium. Again, careful monitoring of blood glucose is the key to successful management.

Chronic administration of methadone and other opiates leads to a number of hormonal changes. The most marked of these are hyperprolactinemia and a decrease in testosterone and LH, all of which play a role in the hypogonadism seen in these patients. In addition, 24-hour urinary free cortisol levels may be low and the patients may respond poorly to cosyntropin.

Nonpsychotropic Drug Effects

Certain endocrine tests can only be correctly interpreted if the physician is aware of the effects of frequently prescribed drugs. The average patient in a geriatric nursing facility receives six different drugs. This makes it incumbent upon the physician to be acutely aware of the possibility of drug–drug interaction and the effects of drugs on laboratory tests in the aged.

Salicylates, for example, are extremely common over-the-counter drugs used by the aged which can potentiate the action of the hypoglycemic agents and increase the incidence of gastrointestinal ulceration when used in combination with steroids. In addition, salicylates can falsely alter a number of laboratory results, for example, giving false-positive urinary glucose and low serum T4 levels. Many drugs can increase serum glucose levels or potentiate hypoglycemia, and their actions need to be taken into account in the diagnosis and treatment of diabetes in the elderly.

Finally, the elderly often take nutritional supplements and home remedies that can alter endocrine function or laboratory test results; for example, megadoses of vitamin C can alter urinary glucose level, megadoses of vitamin A can produce hypercalcemia, and ginseng tea can produce hypertension. Few patients mention vitamins or health foods when asked whether they are taking any drugs.

NEUROPEPTIDES

What Are They and Where Are They?

The dawning of the age of neuropeptides came with the isolation of the first of the hypothalamic-releasing factors, TRH, by Guillemin and Schally in the late 1960s. This was rapidly followed by the isolation of the gonadotropin-releasing factor (LHRH), the growth hormone inhibitory factor (somatostatin), and more recently by the corticotropin-releasing factor (amurine—from the Greek, "to ward off") and GH-releasing hormone (somatocrinin). Traditionally, these substances have been termed factors until fully isolated and characterized, after which they are referred to as hormones.

These hypothalamic hormones were originally thought to be only chemical messengers passing down the portal vessels to produce release of anterior pituitary hormones. Because of this classical theory, the study of these neuropeptides fell previously into the province of endocrinology, while the classical neurotransmitters were studied by others. However, it soon became obvious that TRH was not only present in the hypothalamus and pituitary, but also widely distributed throughout the CNS. TRH had a variety of effects on the CNS which led it to be characterized as an ergotropic (arousal producing) substance. These effects (and those of other neuropeptides) were achieved by TRH being emitted by one cell and affecting a receptor on a nearby cell. Thus, neuropeptides have much in common with other neurotransmitters, and many of the subsequent observations regarding neuropeptides may be equally applicable to monamine and amino acid transmitters. Further surprises came with the discovery that a TRH-like substance was distributed throughout the gastrointestinal tract, with high concentrations in the pancreas. Thus, TRH joined somatostatin as a peptide which appeared to belong both to the brain and the gastrointestinal tract. The recent demonstration of TRH in the reproductive tract and of a TRH-like material in the plant material alfalfa served only further to underline the ubiquitous distribution of neuropeptides.

With the demonstration that classical hypothalamic hormones occur in the gut, it came as no surprise that classical gut hormones are also present in the brain. In 1975, the gallbladder-contracting hormone, cholecystokinin, was demonstrated to be present in the brain. Recent studies have demonstrated that cholecystokinin produces a variety of effects on the CNS and on anterior pituitary hormone release. In general, chole-cystokinin appears to be a CNS depressant which in many instances antagonizes the stimulating effects of TRH. A number of other gut peptides, including vasoactive intestinal peptide and bombesin-like peptide, have also been found to be present in the brain. Other peptides such as the enkephalins, substance P, and neurotensin were demonstrated to occur in both the gut and the brain. In addition, pituitary peptides such as ACTH have been found to be present in the CNS. Many of the neuropeptides occur in the retina, especially in the ganglia responsible for integrating light impulses and, as such, appear to have an important potential role in vision. The easy accessibility of the retina makes this an area in which rapid advances in the knowledge of the relationship of neuropeptides to disease processes can be expected. A partial list of neuropeptides is presented in Table 1.11.

Besides being present in classical neurons, neuropeptides have been shown to be present in nonneuronal cells, although some of these have been demonstrated to have elongated processes extending from the cell bodies that are reminiscent of classical neurons. One such system is the somatostatin-containing cells in the gastric mucosa which have processes extending onto gastrin cells some distance away. Cells that modulate the function of other cells in this way or by elaborating neuropeptides to act on cells in juxtaposition to themselves have been termed "paracrine" (or cybernin) cells and act as a local regulatory system (Figure 1.13). Recent studies have suggested that neuropeptides may also feed directly back on the cells from which they are released (autocrine system). Such self-regulatory functions are common to other examples of chemical transmission.

As has been alluded to, neuropeptides appear to be ubiquitously distributed in nature. Le Roith and his colleagues have shown that insulin (which also occurs in the brain), somatostatin, ACTH, and β-endorphin are present in unicellular organisms. In addition, an LHRH-like substance has been found in oats, TRH in alfalfa, and opiate-like peptides—the exorphins—in casein and gluten. The possible significance of these food peptides (formones) as regulators of gastrointestinal or other functions has yet to be

TABLE 1.11. The Neuropeptides

A. Classical hypothalamic hormones
   1. Thyrotropin-releasing hormone (TRH)
   2. Gonadotropin-releasing hormone (GnRH)
   3. Somatostatin
   4. Corticotropin-releasing hormone (amunine)
   5. Growth hormone-releasing hormone (somatocrinin)
   6. Vasopressin
   7. Oxytocin

B. Classical gut hormones
   1. Cholecystokinin (CCK)
   2. Vasoactive intestinal peptide (VIP)
   3. Secretin-like peptide
   4. Bombesin-like peptide

C. Pituitary peptides
   1. ACTH
   2. β-Endorphin
   3. TSH
   4. γ-MSH

D. Others
   1. Enkephalins
   2. Dynorphin
   3. α-Neoendorphin
   4. Substance P
   5. Neurotensin
   6. Angiotensin
   7. Carnosine
   8. Calcitonin-like peptide
   9. Calcitonin gene-related peptide
   10. Neuropeptide Y

explored. However, the saying "You are what you eat" may turn out to be more true than any of us imagined.

Why Neuropeptides?

Not only has there been a proliferation of neuropeptides, but with the advent of each new neuropeptide, it has been discovered that each has multiple effects. Table 1.12 lists the multiple effects ascribed to the endogenous opioids as an illustration of this problem. While this proliferation of effects is almost overwhelming, the production of a series of closely related effects by a neuropeptide would make excellent teleological sense; for example, TRH produces central effects leading to general arousal as well as releasing

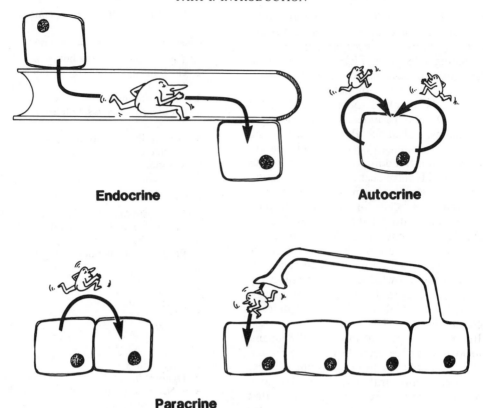

Endocrine

Autocrine

Paracrine

FIGURE 1.13. Examples by which neuropeptides (and other neurotransmitters) can reach their target organ.

TSH to activate release of thyroid hormone to allow mobilization of energy. In addition, if two neuropeptides are released simultaneously, both of which produce one similar set of effects and one opposite set of effects, this would allow synergistic reinforcement of the one group while allowing cancellation of the other group of effects; for example, both TRH and cholecystokinin suppress appetite, but TRH increases temperature and cholecystokinin produces hypothermia. Such packaging of information would allow the organism more flexibility in responding to a spectrum of stressors.

Another criticism of neuropeptide investigations is that these multiple effects have often been found after injection of the substance in question in amounts larger than those previously measured. However, high dosages may be necessary to achieve the concentrations possible at the postsynaptic receptor where these substances act.

The simplest example of the advantages of one peptide modulating more than one behavior is seen in the *Pleurobranchea*. This mollusk is a voracious and cannabalistic carnivore that devours anything up to one-third of its size which comes in its vicinity. This habit of eating everything would have rapidly led to extinction of this species, as every time it laid eggs they would have been eaten. Nature therefore gave this shellfish an interesting hormone called the egg-laying hormone. About 15 minutes after injecting the *Pleurobranchea* with egg-laying hormone, it stops eating and shortly after lays its eggs. The dual function of the egg-laying hormone in producing satiety as well as egg laying nicely demonstrates the advantages of a single substance regulating two closely related functions. However, such a simple correspondence between the presence of a single hormone and the performance of a discrete set of behaviors has not been as clearly elucidated in the human.

TABLE 1.12. Some of the Postulated Effects of Endogenous Opiates

1. Analgesia

2. Cataplexy/epilepsy

3. Memory: Facilitates passive avoidance and inhibits extinction
   of active avoidance

4. Hypo/hyperthermia

5. Sexual behavior: Decrease copulatory behavior

6. Blood pressure regulation: Hypotension, ? role in endotoxic shock

7. Decrease gastric acid release

8. Hormonal effects: ↓ ACTH and cortisol

   ↓ Luteinizing hormone

   ↑ Growth hormone

   ↑ Prolactin

9. Variable effects on carbohydrate metabolism; possibly plays a role in chlorpropamide–alcohol-induced flushing

10. Appetite regulation: Increased feeding

Another curious example of a peptide modulating behavior is found in the analysis of frog skin. Frog skin is an abundant source of a variety of neuropeptides, but their functional significance was initially unclear. Bombesin, one of the peptides present in frog skin, does seem to have an adaptive function. As bombesin has particularly potent effects on the gastrointestinal tract, the predator who eats such a frog will self-administer a large dose of bombesin-creating gastrointestinal distress. This paring of the consumption of the frog with sickness leads to a conditioned taste aversion in the predator and the protection of other frogs. The behavioral significance of peptides may only become apparent by considering the significance of the behavior for the species instead of the individual (human behavior has rarely been analyzed at this level by psychiatric researchers).

It is becoming apparent that it is perhaps more profitable to think of neuropeptides as acting as neuromodulators (as in the case for a number of other neurotransmitters). We have classically thought of neuronal activation as being an "all or none" phenomenon. It appears that one of the roles of neuropeptides is to modify the all or none response, allowing recruitment of some neurons while inhibiting others.

To understand the need for neuromodulation, it is necessary to appreciate the "1% advantage." Physicians and scientists are used to thinking of meaningful changes as being fairly large. Normal ranges are set with a large margin for error. The 1% advantage is the antithesis of this approach and is perhaps best understood by examining the progressive lowering of the world record for the 1-mile run in the past 100 years. On the average, it has taken 6–7 years for every 1% reduction in the record for the mile. The tremendous effort by many athletes that goes into producing this 1% advantage attests to the importance of small improvements. It seems likely that before we fully understand the role of neuropeptides as neuromodulators, we will have to readjust our thinking to take into account the importance of small day-to-day changes in behavior and in our general feeling of well-being. The investigation of these changes awaits the development of appropriate, reliable measurement devices for such small behavioral differences.

Another function of neuropeptides appears to be to switch off release of monoamines and other neuropeptides. It is now well recognized that neuropeptides can occur in the same neuron as monamines and other neuropeptides. In the posterior pituitary, vasopressin and enkephalin occur in the same neurons and are released in equal quanta. While the vasopressin is being released into the bloodstream, the enkephalin feeds back on the neuron from which it is released to inhibit further vasopressin release.

An important point concerning neuropeptides (as well as other neurotransmitters) is that they tend to alter in concert rather than in isolation. In a series of experiments in which we morphine addicted and withdrew rats, we found that the concentrations of a variety of neuropeptides in different areas of the brain were altered. This suggests that administration of a single neuropeptide may produce effects which are due either directly to the peptide itself or are secondary to alterations it produces in the release and/or synthesis of a number of other neuropeptides and neurotransmitters.

Neuropeptides act by binding to membrane receptors. Recent studies have suggested that the nutrient milieu may profoundly alter the membrane receptor characteristics. Thus, animals with elevated glucose levels have been shown to have a markedly decreased sensitivity to opiates and a supersensitivity to the opiate antagonist, naloxone. This appears to be due to a direct effect of glucose producing an alteration in the opiate receptor. A number of effects of alcohol appear to be similar to that of the endogenous opioids, leading to the suggestion that alcohol produces some of its effects by activation of the endogenous opiates. Alcohol has been shown to produce major alterations in opiate agonist and antagonist binding, possibly secondary to its effects on membrane fluidity. Finally, zinc has been reported to alter opiate receptors. These findings suggest that the nutritional milieu bathing the cells may play an important role in the expression of neuropeptide effects.

At present, the exact role or roles of the neuropeptides cannot be delineated with any degree of certainty. Whatever final roles are assigned to the neuropeptides, at present the most useful approach remains an open-minded one in which we neither dogmatically accept nor reject any claims made for these whimsical peptides.

Of Peptides and Pathology

Our knowledge of the pathophysiological processes in which neuropeptides are involved is rudimentary. The peptide system in which the best evidence for a role in pathology has been demonstrated is the edogenous opioid system. Endogenous opioid peptides have been shown to play a role in analgesia. Congenital indifference to pain has been shown to be associated with high levels of endogenous opioids. Endogenous opioid excess has been associated with a syndrome of cutaneous flushing and cyclical psychosis. Leigh syndrome (subacute necrotizing encephalomyelopathy), a recessive degeneratve neurological disorder, also has been associated with opioid excess. In addition, a variety of studies in animals have clearly established a role for endogenous opioid peptides in the pathogenesis of circulatory collapse (shock)

in animals. These studies have been extended to show that the opiate antagonist, naloxone, increases blood pressure in patients with septic shock.

A number of studies in animals and humans have suggested a role for neuropeptides in memory. ACTH and related peptides enhance motivational and attentional processes, whereas vasopressin facilitates consolidation and retrieval of memory processes. A number of animal studies have suggested a role for a variety of neuropeptides, in the consolidation and retrieval of memory. Recently, one of these neuropeptides, AVP, has been demonstrated to slightly improve memory in elderly subjects and patients with senile dementia, Korsakoff syndrome, and posttraumatic dementia. Levels of a number of neuropeptides have been shown to be abnormal in a variety of neurological disorders, including Huntington's chorea, Parkinson's disease, multiple sclerosis, and Shy–Drager syndrome. Bombesin-like activity has been shown to be decreased in the cerebrospinal fluid of schizophrenics.

Peptides have been shown to be abnormal in some peripheral disease states. The classical example is increased levels of vasoactive intestinal peptide (VIP) in watery diarrhea hypokalemia and achlorhydria (WDHA) syndrome. In addition, VIP content of nerves is increased in Crohn's inflammatory bowel disease, possibly consistent with the diarrhea seen in this condition. Finally, numerous neuropeptides, including bombesin, neurotensin, and substance P, have been shown to be produced ectopically by a variety of tumors.

Psychoneuroimmunology

There is a growing body of evidence showing that the CNS (and emotions) can modulate the immune system. It appears that these effects depend on an intact pituitary. Recently, γ-endorphin has been shown to be a potent enhancer of natural killer cell activity (cells which are important in the regulations of cancer immunosurveillance). Corticosteroids are well recognized to be immunosuppressive. The increased incidence of autoimmune disease in females has been shown in animal experiments to be linked to gonadal hormone production. Thymosin, a thymic hormone, has been shown to be elevated in patients at risk for acquired immune deficiency syndrome (AIDS). The next decade promises to see exciting advances in our knowledge of the role of neuropeptides and hormones as modulators of the immune system.

THE AGING ENDOCRINE SYSTEM

Along with other physicians, the psychiatrist needs to have a heightened awareness of endocrine changes that occur with aging. This is particularly important at the moment, since over 10% of the population is 65 or older and

it is predicted that this figure will double during the next 50 years. An awareness of the interactive effects of physiological changes that occur with aging together with intercurrent pathological processes is essential if the psychiatrist is going to be able to adequately apply the principles of psychoendocrinology delineated in this volume to the aged population. In addition, psychoneuroendocrinological research needs to be extended to define whether the effects of psychiatric disease on hormones remain the same in the elderly.

First, diseases and disabilities are more likely to develop in the old old (>75 years) than in the young old (60–75 years). With age, the loss of functional reserve in many

TABLE 1.13. Hormonal Changes Commonly Seen in the Aged

Hormone	Status
Sex	
Male	
Testosterone	Normal or decreased
Gonadotropins	Increased, normal, or decreased
Estradiol	Increased
Sex hormone-binding globulin	Increased
Female	
Estrogens	Decreased
Luteinizing hormone	Increased
Follicle-stimulating hormone (FSH)	Increased
Thyroid	
Thyroxine (T4)	Normal or decreased[a]
Triiodothyronine (T3)	Normal or decreased[a]
Thyroid-stimulating hormone (TSH, thyrotropin)	Normal or decreased
Thyroxine-binding globulin (TBG)	Increased
Adrenal	
Cortisol	Normal[b]
Androgens	Decreased
Calcium metabolism related	
Parathormone (PTH)	
Intact hormone	Decreased
C-terminal fragment	Increased
Calcitonin	Decreased
25-OHD$_3$ and 1,25-(OH)$_2$D$_3$[c]	Decreased
Posterior pituitary	
Arginine vasopressin	Increased

[a] Decrease often associated with or due to concomitant illness (euthyroid sick syndrome).

[b] Cortisol secretion and disposal rates and tissue responsiveness are decreased. Sensitivity to action of parathormone is decreased. Sensitivty to AVP at renal tubule is decreased.

[c] 25-OHD$_3$, 25-hydroxyvitamin D$_3$; 1,25-(OH)$_2$D$_3$, 1,25-dihydroxyvitamin D$_3$.

organs tends to lead to deficiency diseases (e.g., hypothyroidism, diabetes mellitus, hypogonadism). This, coupled with decreasing immune competence related to aging and the autoimmune basis of many endocrine disorders, leads to an increasing prevalence of hypoendocrine disease with increasing age and a tendency for more than one endocrine disease to occur in the same person (polyglandular failure syndromes). Further, decreased functional reserve with aging leads to poorer responses to releasing hormones (e.g., blunted TSH response to TRH and a blunted growth hormone response to GHRH).

Second, older persons tend to have multiple diseases that affect the clinical and laboratory manifestations of endocrine disease and often complicate management. This proclivity for multiple diseases, together with the tendency toward atypical (e.g., apathetic thyrotoxicosis) and nonspecific presentations (e.g., weight loss, fatigue, dementia), leads older persons to delay seeing a physician and often causes the physician to miss the diagnosis.

Third, most normal laboratory values have been developed from tests on young, healthy people, and abnormal results may merely reflect the aging process. Hormonal changes commonly seen in the aged are listed in Table 1.13. A psychiatric example of the problems of not taking the hormonal changes with aging into account comes from studies suggesting that melatonin/cortisol ratio may be abnormal in depression. Secretion of melatonin, which is produced by the pineal gland, is markedly decreased with aging, giving a simple explanation for the discrepant results in the literature where age-matched controls have not been employed. Finally, ectopic hormone production from neoplasms can mimic classical endocrine diseases.

Endocrine diseases tend to be easily treatable, and correction of impaired endocrine function often leads to dramatic improvements in the quality of life. In the elderly, atypical and/or nonspecific presentations tend to be the rule rather than the exception. Of the 15%–25% of causes of dementia that are reversible, a large proportion is due to metabolic diseases such as thyroid dysfunction, hyperparathyroidism, pituitary insufficiency, and pernicious anemia. For these reasons, clinicians need a heightened awareness of the possibility of an endocrine disorder in their elderly patients.

FURTHER READING

Principles of Endocrinology

Federman, D. D. (1981). General principles of endocrinology. In R. H. Williams (Ed.), *Textbook of endocrinology* (6th ed., pp. 1–4). Philadelphia: Saunders Co.

Hershman, J. M. (1977). *Endocrine pathophysiology: A patient oriented approach.* Philadelphia: Lea & Febiger.

Trence, D. L., Morley, J. E., Handwerger, B. S. (1984). Polyglandular autoimmune syndromes. *American Journal of Medicine 77,* 107–116.

Williams, J. A. (1983). Mechanisms in hormone secretion, action, and response. In F. S. Greenspan & P. H. Forsham (Eds.), *Basic and clinical endocrinology* (pp. 1–17). Los Altos, CA: Lange Medical Publications.

Specific Endocrine Disorders

Blum, M. (1972). Myxedema coma. *American Journal of the Medical Sciences, 264,* 432.

Broadus, A. E., & Rasmussen, H. (1981). Clinical evaluation of parathyroid function. *American Journal of Medicine, 70,* 475–478.

Davidson, M. B. (1981). *Diabetes mellitus: Diagnosis and treatment* (Vols. 1 & 2). New York: Wiley.

Davis, P. J., & Davis, F. B. (1974). Hyperthyroidism in patients over the age of 60 years. *Medicine (Baltimore), 53,* 161.

Findling, J. W., & Tyrell, J. B. (1983). Anterior pituitary and somatomedins. I. Anterior pituitary. In F. S. Greenspan & P. H. Forsham (Eds.), *Basic and clinical endocrinology* (pp. 38–88). Los Altos, CA: Lange Medical Publications.

Frantz, A. G. (1978), Prolactin. *New England Journal Medicine, 298,* 201.

Gold, E. M. (1979). The Cushing syndromes: Changing views of diagnosis and treatment. *Annals of Internal Medicine, 90,* 829.

Hershman, J. M. (1980). *Management of endocrine disorders.* Philadelphia: Lea & Febiger.

Modlin, I. M., Farndon, J. R., Shepherd, A., Johnston, I. D. A., Kennedy, T. L., Montgometry, D. A. D., & Welbourn, R. B. (1979). Phaeochromocytomas in 72 patients: Clinical and diagnostic features, treatment and long-term results. *British Journal of Surgery, 66,* 456–465.

Morley, J. E. (1981). Neuroendocrine control of thyrotropin secretion. *Endocrine Reviews, 2,* 396–436.

Morley, J. E., Slag, M. F., Elson, M. K., & Shafer, R. B. (1983). The interpretation of thyroid function tests in hospitalized patients. *JAMA, Journal of the American Medical Association, 249,* 2377–2379.

Odell, W. D., & Swerdloff, R. S. (1978). Abnormalities of gonadal function in men. *Clinical Endocrinology, (New York), 8,* 149.

Robertson, G. L. (1979). The pathophysiology of ADH secretion. In G. Toles (Ed.), *Clinical neuroendocrinology: A pathophysiological approach* (pp. 247–260). New York: Raven Press.

Slag, M. F., Morley, J. E., Elson, M. K., Trence, D. L., Nelson, C. J., Nelson, A. E., Kinlaw, W. B., Beyer, H. S., Nuttall, F. Q., & Safer, R. B. (1983). Impotence in medical clinic outpatients. *JAMA, Journal of the American Medical Association, 249,* 1736–1740.

Tolis, G. (1980). Prolactin: Physiology and pathology. *Hospital Practice, 15,* 85.

Volpe, R. (1978). Thyrotoxicosis. *Clinics in Endocrinology and Metabolism, 7,* 1–243.

Young, C. W., & Karom, J. H. (1983). Hypoglycemic disorders. In F. S. Greenspan & P. H. Forsham (Eds.), *Basic and clinical endocrinology* (pp. 546–556). Los Altos, CA: Lange Medical Publications.

Endocrine Conditions as a Cause of Organic Mental Disorders

Jacobson, A. M., & Hauser, S. T. (1983). Behavioral and psychological aspects of diabetes. In M. Ellenberg & H. Rifkin (Eds.), *Diabetes mellitus—Theory and practice* (pp. 1037–1053). New Hyde Park, NY: Medical Exam. Publishing Co.

Marks, V., & Rose, F. C. (1965). *Hypoglycemia.* London: Oxford University Press.

Popkin, M. K., & Mackenzie, T. B. (1980). Psychiatric presentations of endocrine dysfunction. In R. C. W. Hall (Ed.), *Psychiatric presentations of medical illnesses—Somatopsychic disorders* (pp. 139–156). New York: Spectrum Publications.

Whybrow, P. C., & Hurwitz, T. (1976). Psychological distrubances assoicated with endocrine deisease and hormone therapy. In E. J. Sacher, (Ed.), *Hormones, behavior and psychotherapy* (pp. 125–144). New York: Raven Press.

Wilkinson, D. G. (1981). Psychiatric aspects of diabetes mellitus. *British Journal of Psychiatry, 138,* 1–9.

Endocrine Effects of Psychiatric Disease

Prange, A. J. (Ed.). (1974). *The thyroid axis, drugs, and behavior.* New York: Raven Press.

Rose, R. M., & Sachar, E. (1981). Psychoendocrinology. In R. H. Williams (Ed.), *Textbook of endocrinology* (6th ed., pp. 645–670). Philadelphia: Saunders.

Sachar, E. J., & Baron, M. (1979). The biology of affective disorders. *Annual Review of Neuroscience, 2,* 505.

Endocrine Effects of Psychiatric Drugs

Meltzer, H. Y., & Goode, D. J. Effects of psychotropic drugs on endocrine function. In M. A. Lipton, A. DiMarcio (Eds.), *Psychopharmacology: A generation of progress.* New York: Raven Press.

Morley, J. E., Shafer, R. B., Elson, M. K., Slag, M. F., Raleigh, M. J., Brammer, G. L., Yuwiler, A., & Hershman, J. M. (1980). Amphetamine-induced hyperthyroidism. *Annals of Internal Medicine, 93,* 707–709.

Reisberg, B., & Gershon, S. (1979). Side-effects associated with lithium therapy. *Archives of General Psychiatry, 36,* 879.

Wurtman, R. J., & Fernstrom, J. D. (1976). Neuroendocrine effects of psychotropic drugs. In E. J. Sacher (Ed.), *Hormones, behavior and psychopathology* (pp. 145–152). New York: Raven Press.

Neuropeptides

Ferrier, I. N., Roberts, G. W., Crow, T. J., Johnstone, E. C., Owens, D. G. C., Lee, Y. C., O'Shaughnessy, D., Adrian, T. E., Polak, J. M., & Bloom, S. R. (1983). Reduced cholecystokinin-like and somatostatin-like immunoreactivity in limbic lobe is associated with negative symptoms in schizophrenia. *Life Sciences, 33,* 475–482.

Gerner, R. H., & Yamada, T. (1982). Altered neuropeptide concentrations in cerebrospinal fluid of psychiatric patients. *Brain Research, 238,* 298–302.

Krieger, D. T. (1983). Brain peptides: What, where and why? *Science, 222,* 975–985.

Krieger, D. T., & Martin, J. B. (1981). Brain peptides. *New England Journal of Medicine, 304,* 876–885.

Morley, J. E. (1982). Food peptides: Are they a new class of hormones? *JAMA, Journal of the American Medical Association, 247,* 2379–2380.

Morley, J. E. (1983). Neuroendocrine effects of endogenous opioid peptides in human subjects: A review. *Psychoneuroendocrinology, 8,* 361–379.

Reichlin, S. (1981). Neuroendocrinology. In R. H. Williams (Ed.), *Textbook of endocrinology* (6th ed., pp. 589–645). Philadelphia: Saunders.

Scanlon, M. F. (1983). Neuroendocrinology. *Clinics in Endocrinology and Metabolism, 12,* 467–858.

The Aging Endocrine System

Morley, J. E. (1983). The aging endocrine system. *Postgraduate Medicine, 73,* 107–120.

PART II

NEUROPSYCHIATRIC DISTURBANCE IN ENDOCRINE DISEASE

2 DISORDERS OF THE THYROID AND PARATHYROID

MARK S. BAUER
MARIAN DROBA
PETER C. WHYBROW
University of Pennsylvania School of Medicine

Despite their common location in the neck, the thyroid and parathyroid glands are distinct in embryology and function. This was not recognized until the turn of the century when the relationship between parathyroidectomy and tetany, the precise embryology, and the association of the gland to bone disease were all described. From the standpoint of the endocrinology of behavior, however, there is some interesting overlap; for example, the production of calcitonin by the C cells of the thyroid gland together with parathormone have a profound effect on mineral metabolism. Hence, in some cases of medullary carcinoma of the thyroid gland excessive amounts of thyrocalcitonin are produced, at times in association with pheochromocytomas, leading to disturbed mental states.

To preserve clarity in this review, therefore, the two systems are treated separately, with the effects of calcitonin discussed with the parathyroid system.

NEUROPSYCHIATRIC CHANGES ASSOCIATED WITH THYROID DYSFUNCTION

Introduction

Adequate thyroid function has long been recognized as necessary for normal mental life. However, the past 25 years have seen a burgeoning of interest in and knowledge of the role of thyroid metabolism in psychiatric disorders. Several developments have been important in elucidating these brain–thyroid relationships, including sensitive radioimmunoassay techniques for measuring thyroid hormones, methods for assessing central nervous system (CNS) receptor changes (Weiss, Heydorn, & Frazer, 1983), the localization of thyroid hormones (Dratman, Crutchfield, Gordon, & Jennings, 1983) and thyroid-related peptides (Witten & deWied, 1980) in the CNS, the use of thyroid hormones in the treatment of affective disorders (Prange, Wilson, Rabon, & Lipton, 1969; Stancer & Persad, 1982), and the discovery of abnormal thyroid-stimulating hormone (TSH) responses to thyrotropin-releasing hormone (TRH) in various psychiatric disturbances, particularly the affective disorders (Loosen & Prange, 1982).

The intimate relationship of thyroid function to psychiatric homeostasis was noted in the earliest descriptions of thyroid dysfunction. In the early nineteenth century psychiatric symptoms were described in close association with gross alterations in the thyroid economy. Caleb Parry (1825), in his description of what was later to become known as Graves' disease, referred to "palpitations of the heart and various nervous affectations" (p. 478). Robert Graves described a 3-month prodrome of "some symptoms which were supposed to be hysterical" in a woman who later developed tachycardia, weakness, exopthalmos, and thyromegaly (Graves, 1940). Similarly, the majority of 109 hypothyroid persons reported upon by the Clinical Society of London (1888) were found to have psychiatric symptoms, including depression, irritability, delusions, and delirium.

Hypothyroidism

Clinical Features

Hypothyroidism is associated with a spectrum of neuropsychiatric findings, from subtle cognitive, motoric, and affective symptoms and signs, to various major affective disorders, psychosis, and delirium.

Such persons complain of decreased ability to concentrate, subjective slowing of thought processes, and decreased short- and sometimes long-term memory. Gull (1873), in his initial description of hypothyroidism, "a Cretinoid State supervening in adult life," noted: "The mind, which had previously been active and inquisitive, assumed a gentle, placid indifference . . . but the intellect was unimpaired."

Fifteen years later, the Committee Report to the Clinical Society of London (1888) found a "slowness of apprehension, thought and action" in all but 3 of over 100 cases, and noted also, unlike Gull, that "dementia" was found in a significant number.

Motor functions and deep tendon reflexes are also slowed, sometimes being detectable on clinical exam. Measured by kinemometer, the ankle reflex time is usually in excess of the normal 200–280 msec (Abraham, Atkinson, & Roscoe, 1966). There may be a paucity of speech and perseveration, with anergy, fatigue, and hypersomnia dominating the clinical complaints. A variety of neurological and neuromuscular abnormalities may also be found, as reviewed elsewhere (Swanson, Kelly, & McConahey, 1981).

Affective changes can include dysphoria, hopelessness, crying spells, anhedonia, and even suicidal ideation. These symptoms may be mild, but sometimes present the clinical picture of a major depression. Depressive symptoms, however, need not predominate. Irritability, anxiety, insomnia, and depersonalization may all be significantly present.

Thyroid hypofunction can be associated with less common affective disorders as well.

Clinical and subclinical hypothyroidism are often found in a rapid-cycling form of bipolar (Cowdry, Wehr, Zis, & Goodwin, 1983) or unipolar (Oppenheimer, 1982; Siris, Chertoff, & Perel, 1979) affective illness; these persons experience a minimum of four affective episodes per year (Dunner, 1979; Roy-Byrne, Joffe, Udhe, & Post, 1984) and may cycle continuously. Such persons may have had previously diagnosed hypothyroidism (Cowdry et al., 1983), may have developed thyroid dysfunction while taking lithium carbonate for their preexisting affective disorder (Cho, Bone, Dunner, Colt, & Fieve, 1979), or may begin to cycle rapidly while taking antidepressants and then be discovered to have a subtle thyroid dysfunction (Extein, Pottash, & Gold, 1982).

The definition of subclinical hypothyroidism deserves special mention here. Wenzel, Meinhold, Raffenberg, Adlkoffer, and Schleusener (1974) described three grades of hypofunction based on biochemical parameters (Table 2.1). Grade I, defined by low serum free thyroxine index (FTI), includes persons with multiple myxedematous findings, including weight gain, dry skin, hoarseness, constipation, cold intolerance, and fatigue. Grade II persons, defined by normal FTI but elevated serum TSH level, show no more than one symptom or sign of hypothyroidism. Grade III persons, who have normal basal TSH levels but an exaggerated TSH response to TRH infusion, are euthyroid by clinical examination, although in the original study behavioral issues were not precisely discussed. Cooper, Halpern, Wood, Levin, and Ridgway (1984) recently assessed the efficacy of treating persons with subclinical hypothyroidism (Grade II) with thyroxine. They found that subtle systemic symptoms such as fatigue, constipation, and temperature intolerance tended to resolve when serum TSH levels returned to the normal range. Unfortunately again, no mention was made of cognitive or affective symptoms.

Although such endocrinological literature reveals little if any physical morbidity with subclinical hypothyroidism, psychiatric investigators have become increasingly aware of the association between Grade II and III hypothyroidism and pathological behavior, particularly severe mood disorder. In addition to a 92% incidence of elevated TSH

TABLE 2.1 Grades of Hypothyroidism[a]

Grade	FTI	Basal THS	ΔTSH[b]	Clinical findings
I	↓	↑	↑	Multiple signs and symptoms
II	Normal	↑	↑	At least one sign or symptom
III	Normal	Normal	↑	Asymptomatic

[a]After Wenzel, Meinhold, Raffenberg, Adlkoffer, and Schleusener (1974).

[b]After administration of 500 μg TRH.

levels in rapid-cycling bipolar persons (Cowdry *et al.*, 1983), Gold, Pottash, and Extein (1981) have reported Grade II or III hypothyroidism in 20 of 250 consecutive persons with major depression admitted to their inpatient unit. Therefore these grades of hypothyroidism may not be "subclinical" at all when the full spectrum of hypothyroid symptomatology, including its neuropsychiatric manifestations, is considered. In reviewing the entity of subclinical hypothyroidism, it is of interest to recall the reposts of Brockman and Whitman (1952) and Nordgren and von Scheele (1976). The former described six persons who developed psychosis after thyroidectomy despite normal peripheral thyroid function; they ascribed the syndrome to some aspect of the operation itself. At that time the TSH assay had not yet been developed, but it is conceivable that these persons may have had Grade II or III hypothyroidism. Nordgren and von Scheele described a patient with "myxedema madness without myxedema," who in present-day nosology would have been diagnosed as having Grade III hypothyroidism.

Hypothyroidism may also present as a gross alteration of mental status, such as with a nonspecific psychosis or delirium. The psychosis of myxedema may occur within the context of depressive symptomatology or may present a picture that more closely resembles a schizophreniform psychosis (Asher, 1949; Karnosh & Stout, 1934; Treadway, Prange, Doehne, Edens, & Whybrow, 1967), with paranoia, insomnia, agitation, and auditory hallucinations.

Delirium may supervene, with or without psychosis, leading to coma and death (Jellinek, 1962); seizures may also occur (Levin & Daughaday, 1955). Asher's classic study (1949) on "myxoedematous madness"

details 14 cases which illustrate the variety of psychotic and delirious symptoms that can develop during hypothyroidism.

Objective Assessment of Neuropsychological and Neuropsychiatric Findings

Instruments for measuring neuropsychiatric dysfunction confirm the clinical impression that Grade I hypothyroidism is associated with impairment of such cognitive functions as memory and mathematical and problem-solving ability. For example, Whybrow, Prange, and Treadway (1969) reported that hypothyroid persons have significantly impaired performance on the Porteus Maze and Trailmaking tests, reflecting problem-solving and abstraction ability, respectively; they also found significant conceptual disorganization as rated on global clinician rating scales such as the Brief Psychiatric Rating Scale (BPRS).

Crown (1949) compared four hypothyroid persons' scores on nonverbal and vocabulary intelligence tests before and after treatment. Each person's pretreatment scores yielded a "deterioration index," comparing abstraction ability with recall of vocabulary. The indices were subnormal initially and rose beyond a practice effect after 3 months of replacement therapy.

Reitan (1953) compared 15 hypothyroid persons to age- and sex-matched controls diagnosed as "neurotic" or "brain damaged." The control groups were heterogeneous, with the former made up predominantly of depressed persons and the later, including persons with various focal and generalized types of neurological dysfunction, from postoperative brain tumor residua to epilepsy. The neurotic depressed group was chosen as a control because they were thought to show no impairment of intellectual function; this assumption is open to question in view of what is now known about cognitive dysfunction in depressive illness (Weingarten & Silberman, 1984). Scores on the subtests of the Rorschach intelligence test most clearly differentiated the neurotic from the brain-damaged group, with the hypothyroid group falling in between. Reitan found no specific pattern of impairment, despite a longer response time in the hypothyroid group, but suggested that "there is a generalized suppression of intellectual functions in myxedema which would become significant statistically if the groups were larger" (p. 444).

Objective testing also corroborates the clinical impression that a panoply of psychiatric symptoms can accompany hypothyroidism and that although depressive symptoms may predominate, there is neither characteristic type nor degree of dysfunction. The Minnesota Multiphasic Personality Inventory (MMPI) given to hypothyroid persons shows high scores on the depressive scale, along with smaller peaks in the "psychotic triad" of schizophrenia, psychasthenia, and paranoia; the mean scores on almost all scales are higher than hyperthyroid persons' scores (Whybrow et al., 1969). Similarly, clinician rating on the BPRS shows higher total scores for hypothyroid persons when compared to a hyperthyroid group, with significantly higher scores in motor retardation and depressive mood (Figure 2.1).

Jain (1972) studied 30 hypothyroid persons, comparing scores on the Hamilton Depression and Anxiety Scales and the Beck Depression Inventory to the severity of hypothyroidism as measured by radioactive iodine uptake by the thyroid gland at 4 hours. He divided the patients into mild, moderate, and severe groups on this basis; unfortunately, no other parameters of thyroid function are reported. He found 13 patients to be "clinically depressed," with Beck and Hamilton Depression mean scores and Hamilton Anxiety scores highest for the moderately hypothyroid group (Table 2.2). Interestingly, the severely hypothyroid group scored lowest on all measures. Two persons had experienced hallucinations and two had "paranoid ideas," although one with each of these symptoms (unclear if the same person) had a preexisting diagnosis of schizophrenia; the other had "severe" hypothyroidism. Of the 30 persons,

8 were judged "psychiatrically normal," and 6 of these were in the "mild" hypothyroid group. Analysis of family psychiatric histories showed a trend which failed to reach significance for the 13 depressed hypothyroid persons to have more first-degree relatives treated for depression.

Finally, electroencephalographic (EEG) changes in hypothyroidism support the claim that CNS derangement is an integral part of the clinical picture. A diffuse slowing, an EEG pattern consistent with metabolic dysfunction, is found (Nieman, 1959); claims for a tracing pathognomonic of hypothyroidism (Browning, Atkins, & Weiner, 1954) await confirmation.

Incidence of Neuropsychiatric Dysfunction in Hypothyroidism

The incidence of cognitive and affective symptoms in the hypothyroid population is difficult to estimate. As improvements in diagnostic tests increase the incidence of hypothyroidism by identifying those with more subtle dysfunction and a wider array of presenting compliants, more refined neuropsychiatric instruments and a changing nosology alter the frequency and classification of findings. Nonetheless, certain statements can be made.

In the classic study of untreated myxedema in 1888, the Clinical Society of London found delusions and hallucinations in almost half of the 109 cases surveyed. They found intellectual "slowness" in all but 3 cases, and decreased memory, particularly short-term, in 46 of 71. Hun and Prudden (1888), in a contemporaneous American study, found a similar prevalence of intellectual deficits and psychosis.

There are scant data in the modern literature with which to estimate the incidence of mental changes in hypothyroidism. Over the past 40 years, there have been only three studies of unselected hypothyroid persons reporting the presence or absence of cognitive or psychiatric changes in each individual (Table 2.3).

Jain's study (1972) provides a group of 30 consecutive hypothyroid persons. Of 30, 22 persons showed some sort of psychopathology; he further suggested that "there appears to be no relationship between the severity of

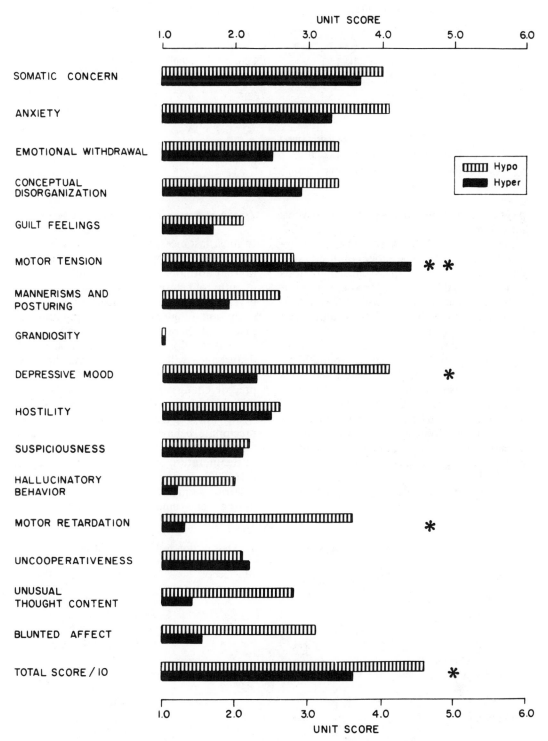

FIGURE 2.1. Hypo- and hyperthyroidism may produce various neuropsychiatric symptoms, as reflected in Brief Psychiatric Rating Scale scores.

TABLE 2.2. Quantitative Ratings of Affective Symptoms in Hypothyroidism[a]

Severity	n	[132]I uptake	HAM-D[b]	BDI[c]	HAM-A[d]
Mild	11	10–15.1	8.90	10.09	6.81
Moderate	11	5–10.1	12.36	17.81	8.45
Severe	8	< 5.1	6.25	9.37	4.00

[a]After Jain (1972).
[b]Hamilton Depression Rating Scale (mean).
[c]Beck Depression Inventory (mean).
[d]Hamilton Anxiety Rating Scale (mean).

physical symptoms and severity of psychiatric symptoms" (p. 128). Whybrow et al. (1969) found each of seven consecutive hypothyroid persons to be either confused (six), depressed (five, one with psychosis), anxious (one), or irritable (one); no patient was without some symptom. Crown (1949) found cognitive deficits in each of 24 unselected hypothyroid persons.

It therefore seems that some degree of neuropsychiatric dysfunction can be found in almost all persons who are diagnosed with hypothyroidism on clinical grounds; furthermore, Jain's data suggest that the degree of such behavioral dysfunction may not correlate with the physical manifestations of the disease. Although this latter finding requires confirmation, it is consistent with the finding of Gold et al. (1981) of significant affective illness in the subclinically hypothyroid population.

Treatment Response and Behavioral Change

In most instances, the behavioral syndromes associated with hypothyroidism remit with thyroid hormone replacement and the return of euthyroid status. When there is associated psychosis, however, exacerbation of the symptomatology may occur during initial replacement therapy. With therapeutic persistence at low doses, such increased behavioral disturbance will rapidly decrease, however, and a return of normal mental status may precede changes in the peripheral indices of thyroid function (Threadway et al., 1967).

Thyroid replacement therapy may also precipitate behavioral change in apparently "uncomplicated" hypothyroidism. A review of the literature by Josephson and MacKenzie (1980) revealed 18 cases of significant psychiatric sequelae, predominantly mania, during replacement therapy for hypothy-

TABLE 2.3. Incidence of Neuropsychiatric Dysfunction in Hypothyroidism

Study	n	Incidence[a]	Findings
Clinical Society of London (1888)	109	50%	Delusions, hallucinations
		46/71	Decreased memory
		98%	Mental "slowness"
Crown (1949)	4	4	Cognitive, IQ deficits
Whybrow, Coppen, Prange, Noguera, and Bailey (1972)	7	6	Subjective confusion
		7	Affective symptoms
		1	Psychosis
Jain (1972)	30	13	Depression
		10	Anxiety
		8	Confusion
		2	Delusions, hallucinations

[a]Total number of persons with findings unless otherwise noted.

roidism. However, all but one of these cases had had some psychiatric symptomatology documented prior to the initiation of replacement therapy; thus, it seems justified to proceed carefully when correcting hypothyroid status in persons who have experienced any behavioral dysfunction.

Do all people recover from their cognitive and emotional symptoms when their hypothyroidism is corrected? Numerous case reports summarized by Jain (1972) suggest that they do. A retrospective review by Tonks (1964) and the classic study by Asher (1949) suggest that where the neuropsychiatric disturbance is servere, there is a less rosy picture. Tonks reviewed the charts of 18 psychiatric inpatients who were found to be clinically hypothyroid; their psychiatric symptoms included depression, "atypical psychosis," a "schizophrenic-type psychosis," and delirium. Only eight of these responded to replacement therapy in addition to their primary psychiatric treatment. Age, sex, the presence of other physical illnesses, number of prior episodes of mental illness, and presence of clinical signs of hypothyroidism could not distinguish responders from nonresponders, although the total number studied was small. Those whose episode during which hypothyroidism was diagnosed was longer than 2 years tended to be nonresponders.

Asher's 14 patients were almost all severely myxedematous; all were psychotic or delirious. Two died shortly after admission, three did not improve over 3–12 weeks of treatment, and the remaining nine returned to their baseline level of function.

There have been three prospective studies of recovery in unselected groups of hypothyroid persons (Table 2.4). Crown's four patients (1949) all showed significant improvement on cognitive testing, as described above. Schon, Sutherland, and Rawson (1961) evaluated 24 patients "with no gross emotional disturbance" with the Wechsler vocabulary, digit span, and block design subtests, the Thurston Temperament Scale, and an unstructured clinical interview. All cognitive tests were significantly improved after 5 months of treatment, although interestingly the time to complete the tasks was unchanged. There was no statistical difference between the pre- and posttreatment temperament scales, but the interviewer's impression was that each subject had substantially improved in mood, organization of thought, and sense of general well-being.

Whybrow et al. (1969) were able to retest four of their seven hypothyroid persons after return to euthyroid status. Three persons, including one with psychosis, showed substantial reduction in psychiatric symptomatology as measured by the BPRS and the Clyde Mood Scale; one person remained mildly depressed and conceptually disorganized. In distinction to the dramatic subjective and objective improvement in these psychiatric measures, formal cognitive testing on the Porteus Maze and Trailmaking test did not consistently improve.

Selection bias may account for the differences between the results of the prospective studies and the results reported by Tonks and by Asher who investigated severely psychiatrically ill persons. It does seem justified to conclude that the majority of persons with hypothyroid-induced cognitive, affective, and psychotic findings can return to normalcy even, as Asher pointed out, when those

TABLE 2.4. Recovery from Neuropsychiatric Dysfunction in Hypothyroidism

Study	n	Outcome
Crown (1949)	4	Each improved cognitive functioning
Schon, Sutherland, and Rawson (1961)	24	Group mean improved on cognitive tests at 5 months
Whybrow, Prange, and Treadway (1969)	4	Three with improvement on BPRS and Clyde Mood Scale; one with resolution of psychosis; none with substantial change on cognitive testing

symptoms have existed for years. However, response is not uniform, and nonresponse may be due to other concurrent neuropsychiatric illness or to duration or severity of myxedema.

One final treatment response issue is that of defining an adequate replacement regimen. Regarding the time course of replacement therapy, it is clear from the endocrinological literature that up to 3 months may be necessary for reequilibration of the thyroid axis after perturbation (Krugman et al., 1975; Matte et al., 1981); it is to be expected, therefore, that while initial response may be dramatic, a complete reversal of neuropsychiatric symptoms may take 6–12 weeks.

Guidelines are less well established for defining the specific dose of replacement hormone required. For example, subclinical hypothyroidism is clearly associated with some affective syndromes and yet, it is not clearly established whether correcting the thyroid deficit alone will reverse the symptoms in all cases. However, there is anecdotal evidence in persons with rapid-cycling bipolar illness that treatment with thyroxine is effective in some patients (Stancer & Persad, 1982), but it is not clear whether those who respond are the ones who have subclinical thyroid dysfunction. Furthermore, our own experience suggests that those who do respond seem to require hypermetabolic doses of thyroxine.

Similarly, it is not clear whether the two standard deviation norm established in the "normal" population for peripheral indices such as the FTI is indeed normal, that is, sufficient to assure one that thyroid dysfunction does not contribute to neuropsychiatric symptoms. For example, Prange et al. (1969) found that in a series of treatment-resistant depressed women, there was a high frequency of serum thyroxine levels near the lower limit of normal; these women responded only after T3 was added to their antidepressant regimen.

Hence, operationally, when confronted with a depressed person who has normal peripheral thyroid function and an elevated serum TSH level or who has thyroid indices near the lower end of the normal range, the question of whether to "correct" thyroid status, or what "correction" of thyroid status is, is as yet unanswered.

Adjuvant psychotropic medication may be necessary in some persons either because the symptoms do not fully remit with normalization of thyroid status or because the exigencies of the clinical situation so dictate. However, certain caveats worthy of note have accumulated in the literature regarding such treatment of hypothyroid individuals with psychotropic medications.

Lithium carbonate can, of course, cause hypothyroidism (Jefferson & Griest, 1983), sometimes irreversibly (Perrild, Madson, & Hansen, 1978), and this must be considered when using this medication in those with a history of thyroid dysfunction. Carbamazepine, although associated with the lowering of serum levels of T4 and T3, has not been found to cause hypothyroidism (Strandjord, Aanderud, & Myking, 1980).

The antipsychotic agents have been the subject of a few case reports of untoward effects in hypothyroidism. For instance, chlorpromazine was associated with hypothermia and coma in one hypothyroid person (Schader, Belfer, & DiMascio, 1970). Gomez and Scott (1980) further suggested that hypothyroidism can predispose to neuroleptic-induced cardiac dysrhythmias, although in that case a diminutive woman received some 270 mg of haloperidol, 400 mg of thioridazine, and 40 mg of trifluoperizine in the 4 days prior to her cardiac arrest. The use of sedative–hypnotics of the benzodiazepine and barbiturate classes has not been associated with untoward effects, although there is some evidence that hypothyroidism may slow drug metabolism by liver microsomal enzyme (R. Kato, Takanaka, Takahashi, & Oneda, 1969).

Antidepressant therapy may not be efficacious until thyroid status is corrected, as may be expected on theoretical grounds (Whybrow & Prange, 1981). As noted, rapid-cycling affective illness in clinical or subclinical hypothyroidism may be induced by tricyclic (Extein et al., 1982) or occasionally monoamine oxidase inhibitor (Mattson & Seltzer, 1981) antidepressants, although there are little data suggestive of increased toxicity otherwise in using these drugs in hypothyroid persons.

Hyperthyroidism

Clinical Features

As in hypothyroidism, motoric, cognitive, and affective symptoms can all be prominent features of the hyperthyroid syndrome; gross mental status changes, including psychosis and delirium, can also occur. The earliest descriptions of hyperthyroidism frequently cited prominent motor findings such as restlessness, tremulousness, and a general increase in motor activity. Cognitive symptoms including difficulty with concentration, flightiness, and depersonalization may also accompany hyperthyroidism, as can decreased memory and attention.

Insomnia is frequently present, but energy levels are usually decreased, a distinction from mania where increased energy, irritability, and decreased sleep are prominent features. Speech can be rapid, however, with thought processes tangential and even somewhat disjointed. Irritability, chronic or episodic anxiety (often associated with cardiac findings such as atrial dysrhythmias or mitral valve prolapse), and affective lability are often present. In sum, the behavioral state in hypothyroidism is best characterized as that of tense dysphoria. Some of these hyperthyroid symptoms have been reported in normal volunteers given T4 or T3 (Bierwaltes & Ruff, 1958).

Although frank melancholia is uncommon in hyperthyroidism, the symptoms of dysphoria, anxiety, irritability, insomnia, anergy, weight loss, and cognitive dysfunction can resemble symptoms of a major depression. This is particularly so in the syndrome of apathetic hyperthyroidism, which may be clinically indistinguishable from major depression (Lakey, 1931). This syndrome occurs primarily in the elderly and often in the absence of tachycardia, goiter, and exophthalmos (Peake, 1981). In such patients, lethargy, withdrawal, depressive affect typical of a melancholic depression, and cognitive deficits resembling pseudodementia can make the differential diagnosis very difficult.

True mania and hypomania have been occasionally reported in uncomplicated hyperthyroidism (Villani & Wertzel, 1979). Typically, however, persons who develop manic symptoms during an episode of hyperthyroidism (Checkley, 1978; Corn & Checkley, 1983; Hasan & Mooney, 1981) or hyperthyroxinemia (Reus, Gold, & Post, 1979) have an underlying unipolar or bipolar affective disorder or develop such later when clinically euthyroid.

Thyroid hyperfunction may also lead to a nonspecific psychosis or delirium, either stuporous or agitated; convulsions can also occur. Such gross mental status changes associated with hyperthyroidism in general can accompany the rare but often lethal complication of thyroid storm (Greer & Parsons, 1968; Ingbar, 1966).

Objective Assessment of Neuropsychiatric Symptoms

As with hypothyroidism, objective neuropsychiatric assessment confirms the clinical impression of at least subtle cognitive dysfunction often in combination with affective symptoms.

Robbins and Vinson (1960) compared ten thyrotoxic persons to matched mormal controls, persons with a variety of psychiatric diagnoses (with somatization, obsessive–compulsive, or psychotic features), and persons with structurally or metabolically based organic brain syndromes. Using three standardized measures to assess neurotic traits and cognitive deficits, they found thyrotoxic individuals to most closely resemble those with organic brain syndromes, leading them to conclude that "thyrotoxicosis is a metabolic disease manifested by impaired psychobiologic integration" (p. 128).

Wilson, Johnson, and Smith (1962) found that although subjective depression was reported by a majority of hyperthyroid patients, their Clyde Mood Scale scores did not differ from normals; however, ratings for anxiety and cognitive disorganization corroborated the patients' subjective complaints.

Artunkal and Togrol (1964) found cognitive and affective deficits in a carefully studied group of Turkish women. Visual reaction time, visual–motor coordination, and mirror drawing were slowed, less accurate, and worsened more quickly with fatigue; auditory reaction times were intact. Rorschach testing revealed responses most closely resembling those of organically impaired individuals. Finally, MMPI scores for depression, paranoia, and schizophrenia were significantly higher than those of matched normals.

Greer, Ramsey, and Bagley (1973) found hyperthyroid persons' anxiety levels, as measured by a standardized questionnaire, similar to outpatients with "neurotic anxiety states." Galvanic skin response measurements were also similar in the two groups, but the physiological measures did not correlate with the subjective reports in either group.

Whybrow *et al.* (1969) studied ten thyrotoxic persons in addition to the seven hypothyroid persons described above. Porteus Maze and Trailmaking results were again significantly abnormal, though less so than those of the hypothyroid individuals. BPRS scores were abnormal, although with a somewhat different profile than the hypothyroid group (Figure 2.1). MMPI and Clyde Mood Scale confirmed the abnormal global scale scores, with relatively higher scores for hysteria and agitation and lower depressive scores than the hypothyroid group.

MacCrimmon, Wallace, Goldberg, and Streiner (1979) compared 19 thyrotoxic women with matched controls using Spitzer and Endicott's Psychiatric Status Schedule (PSS), the MMPI, and five cognitive tests. PSS results revealed higher depression–anxiety scores and more symptoms in general, but the symptoms did not appear to be consistent with established patterns associated with particular psychiatric illnesses. The MMPI profile more consistently differentiated thyrotoxic individuals, with higher scores in somatic distress, depression, anxiety, and subjective loss of control. Performance on cognitive tests showed similar group means but more variability in the hyperthyroid group than in the controls on Spokes, Competing Voices Messages, Stroop Color-Word, finger-tapping, and paired-associative learning tests; higher serum thyroxine levels were correlated with poorer performance on concentration and memory tasks, but not with those relying on motor speed or coordination.

Gross brain function in thyrotoxic individuals has been studied by EEG recordings since the late 1930s; characteristically increased α rhythms and paroxysmal slow features have been found. The most recent studies include those by Wilson and Johnson (1964) and Olsen *et al.* (1972). Wilson and Johnson found abnormal slow activity, including increased α activity and augmented response to photic stimulation. These abnormalities were least prominent in postmenopausal females, leading them to hypothesize that gonadal steroids might somehow increase brain sensitivity to thyroid hormones. They also evaluated 11 young normal subjects given 300 μg/day of T3 for 3 days; there were no wave changes, but they again found increased response to photic stimulation. Olsen's group found slow paroxysmal and fast abnormalities which were correlated with the severity of hyperthyroidism in what was considered a characteristic pattern, but, as in hypothyroidism, the EEG tracings have not proved pathognomonic.

Personality, Traumata, and Thyrotoxicosis

Thyrotoxicosis, unlike hypothyroidism, has been the subject of intense psychosomatic debate. Since Parry's first description (1825) in which thyrotoxicosis closely followed a young girl's frightening ride in a runaway wheelchair, hyperthyroidism has been examined in relation to psychosocial stressors and the individual's experience of such stressors. Investigations have addressed three interrelated questions: Does a particular personality or set of psychodynamic patterns predispose a person to hyperthyroidism? Can environmental stressors precipitate the disease in vulnerable persons? Can stressors cause relapses in hyperthyroid persons?

In contrast, hypothyroidism, since its initial description by Gull as acquired cretinism (1873), has been viewed as a deficiency state which merits primarily a description of symptoms and an elucidation of physiological mechanisms rather than an investigation of psychosocial precipitants. Hence, Eayrs (1960), in reviewing brain–thyroid relationships, remarked: "The effects of thyroid hyperfunction may be regarded as secondary functional signs insofar as they represent an exaggeration of existing personality characteristics, whereas those of hypothyroidism are due to mental disorders primarily attributable to the endocrine dysfunction" (p. 122).

As Gregory (1956) succinctly put it: " . . . hypothyroidism is usually recognized as somatopsychic in its etiology and manifestations. Hyperthyroidism, on the other hand, is commonly considered as a psychosomatic disorder, with emotional factors playing a prominent role in its etiology."

Conrad (1934), Lidz (1949), and Ham, Alexander, and Carmichael (1951), for example, proposed that a particular constellation of personality traits and intrapsychic conflict predispose one to thyrotoxicosis. These hypotheses emphasized two main themes. First, vulnerable persons, usually women, had significant unmet dependency needs; they evidenced a premorbid pattern either of overt dependency or of pseudomaturity, functioning in a seemingly independent manner, but compensating for their unmet needs with various defense mechanisms; such individuals are prone to thyrotoxicosis due to external circumstances (Bennett & Cambor, 1961). Second, such persons find it difficult to express hostility, coping by means of repression and denial. These hypotheses were supported by numerous case studies, with material gathered through semistructured interview, extended psychotherapy experience, or psychoanalysis.

The hypotheses further hold that traumatic experiences, which can be acute single episodes but are more often chronic dysfunctional interpersonal relationships (Lidz, 1949), for the prethyrotoxic individual lead to the dissolution of previously stable defenses and the precipitation of thyroid overactivity.

The methodological difficulties in validating such hypotheses, even with appropriate control groups, are legion. They are well outlined by Hermann and Quarton (1965) who separated the hypotheses of Ham and Alexander into two groups, those open to objective examination and those where the inference of the investigator was dominant. Studying the former set, they compared consecutive hyperthyroid, hypothyroid, and euthyroid persons evaluated at a thyroid clinic and found no group differences in demographics, personality, or family structure except that hyperthyroid persons tended to have larger numbers of children. Paykel similarly found no differences in the personality structure between thyrotoxic and control groups (Paykel, 1966). Gibson (1962) reviewed the literature which addressed the specific question of whether environmental stressors precede thyrotoxic episodes; he found no convincing relationship.

An approach that has been more successful in testing the putative relationship between psychosocial factors and thyroid function has been the study of iodine kinetics in the thyroid. Dongier, Wittkower, Stephens-Newsham, and Hoffman (1956) studied serum protein-bound iodine (PBI) levels and the gland half-life of ^{131}I in 25 volunteers and 27 anxious persons, including 5 with a past history of hyperthyroidism and 5 with a family history of hyperthyroidism. While they found no correlation between degree of anxiety and speed of radioactive iodine metabolism, they did find faster metabolism in those with a personal or familial hyperthyroid history, as well as in those with the personality styles and intrapsychic conflicts hypothesized. They found no change in PBI levels during stressful interviews, however, although such alterations have been documented in response to similar interviews by Flagg, Clemans, and Michael (1965) who found marked PBI changes in persons with thyroid disease.

Wallenstein, Holzman, Voth, and Uhr (1965) found that persons with thyroid "hot spots," areas of accelerated ^{131}I uptake, commonly had personality patterns reflecting unmet dependency needs and pseudomaturity. This personality pattern predicted the presence of hot spots in persons referred for thyroid evaluation, but not in normal controls or psychiatric patients. Although Voth, Holzman, Katz, and Wallenstein's 12-year follow-up study (1970) could not document that persons with hot spots later became thyrotoxic, there was some evidence that these thyroid abnormalities did wax and wane with life stressors. There is some data as well from a series of 20 patients (Ferguson-Rayport, 1956) and from a few case reports (Alexander, Hardin, & Shimminis, 1968; Cushman, 1967) that exacerbations of existing hyperthyroidism may follow life stressors.

Finally, Reusch, Christiansen, Patterson, Dewees, and Jacobson (1947) investigated 42 postthyroidectomy patients and found delayed or incomplete recovery in those with abnormal MMPI scores on the psychasthenia and psychopathic scores. Although they suggest that personality patterns contributed to delayed recovery, the majority of these patients had systemic signs and symptoms of either hyper- or hypothyroidism; this suggests that the psychological abnormalities may have been secondary to continued disruption of thyroid function rather than the cause of continued abnormal thyroid parameters.

In summary, the literature does not support a role for personality in predisposing a person to hyperthyroidism; indeed, the heuristic value of the concept of "organ specificity" has been questioned in psychosomatic circles in general (Mason, 1970; Weiner, 1977). However, there is some evidence that the clinical course of established hyperthyroidism may by affected by psychosocial factors and that such factors may alter the activity of thyroid hot spots in a temporary and largely subclinical manner.

Incidence of Neuropsychiatric Dysfunction

Studies estimating the incidence of cognitive and emotional dysfunction in hyperthyroidism are subject to the same caveats as in hypothyroidism. The investigations of unselected patients with hyperthyroidism, from which incidence figures can be estimated, are summarized in Table 2.5.

Certain trends emerge. First, some neuropsychiatric symptoms are ubiquitous in hyperthyroid persons; second, subjective or objective cognitive deficits are particularly common. Finally, psychosis does occur, although the two older studies by Lindz and Whitehorn and by Burstein which produced high-incidence figures deserve further comment.

Lidz and Whitehorn (1949) quotes a 20% incidence of at least "moderate" psychosis in his hyperthyroid sample; however, all were outpatients, and it is unclear what criteria were used to define psychosis beyond the inability to cooperate with treatment.

Burstein (1961) reviewed all admissions to the psychiatric unit of a county general hospital over 3 years. Of 8,000 cases, 54 had evidence of thyrotoxicosis, and 10 of these thyrotoxic persons were psychotic. However, it is unstated whether all of Burstein's thyrotoxic patients actually had signs or symptoms

TABLE 2.5. Incidence of Neuropsychiatric Dysfunction in Hyperthyroidism

Study	n	Incidence[a]	Dysfunction
Lidz (1949)	?	20%	Psychosis
Mandelbroth and Wittkomer (1955)	25	65%	"Neurotic"
Kleinschmidt and Waxenberg (1956)	17	2	Psychosis
Burstein (1961)	54	10	Psychosis
Wilson, Johnson, and Smith (1962)	26	14	Cognitive deficit
		15	Depression
		2	Elation
Hermann and Quarton (1965)	24	1	Psychosis
Whybrow, Prange, and Treadway (1969)	10	10	Fatigue and/or irritability
		2	Depression
		4	Subjective confusion
MacCrimmon, Wallace, Goldberg, and Streiner (1979)		2	Paranoia
Wallace, MacCrimmon, and Goldberg (1980)	19	18	Fatigue
		> 50%	Nervousness, irritability
Rockey and Griep (1980)	14	10	Fatigue
		11	Nervousness
		9	Social difficulties (irritability or withdrawal)
		1	Major depression

[a]Total number of persons with findings unless otherwise noted.

of clinical thyrotoxicosis or simply chemical evidence of thyroid hyperfunction (e.g., increased PBI). The definition of thyrotoxicosis is crucial in evaluating such studies, as it is now known that psychiatric distress sufficient to merit hospitalization can be associated with increased serum thyroxine levels in persons without progressive thyroid disease (Cohen & Swigar, 1979).

Treatment Response and Behavioral Change

The role of psychotropic medications in the treatment of hyperthyroidism raises several clinical issues. There is both experimental (Coville & Telford, 1970a) and clinical (Prange, 1970) evidence that increasing levels of thyroid hormones potentiate catecholamines, perhaps by increasing β-adrenergic sensitivity. This may be one of the mechanisms which underlies the T3 potentiation of tricyclic antidepressants (Prange et al., 1969). Elevated thyroid function may also increase the toxicity of medications which affect catecholamines. Tricyclic antidepressants have been found to worsen cardiac dysrhythmias and tachycardia in thyrotoxic persons, either through adrenergic or anticholinergic mechanisms (Blackwell & Schmidt, 1984). Although little has been written on the effects of monoamine oxidase inhibitors (MAOIs) in hyperthyroidism, hyperthyroxinemia in laboratory animals has been shown to increase the acute toxicity of these drugs (Carrier & Buday, 1961).

The ability of lithium to alter thyroid function both peripherally (Jefferson & Greist, 1983) and centrally (Bagchi, Brown, & Mack, 1982) has been well surveyed elsewhere and is beyond the scope of this review. However, the use of lithium in hyperthyroid persons deserves brief comment. Although lithium now has little place as a suppressant of thyroid metabolism, its ability to decrease thyroxine synthesis and release must be kept in mind when simultaneous treatment of hyperthyroidism and an affective disorder requiring lithium are undertaken. Frank hypothyroidism can occur in some individuals, and conversely abrupt discontinuation of lithium can induce hyperthyroxinemia and may precipitate mania (Reus et al., 1979).

Although benzodiazepines seem to have no effect on thyroid function directly (Barnes, Greenberg, Owings, & Blizzard, 1972), changes in the activity of hepatic microsomal enzyme activity with altered thyroid status (R. Kato et al., 1969) theoretically may dictate dosage adjustment when using drugs metabolized through that pathway.

Neuroleptics have been the subject of a number of case reports of increased toxicity in hyperthyroid persons. Such persons may be at risk for severe and even lethal dystonic reactions (Witschy & Redmond, 1981). There is also one case report of thyroid storm induced by haloperidol in a 13-year-old girl (M. Weiner, 1979). The anticholinergic effects of neuroleptics also necessitate careful monitoring for tachycardia and cardiac dysrhythmias in hyperthyroid persons.

The degree to which the neuropsychiatric findings in hyperthyroidism remit with restoration of a normal thyroid economy has been addressed by numerous investigators; six studies have used an unselected series of hyperthyroid individuals (Table 2.6).

Kleinschmidt found 8 of 17 persons with various nonpsychotic and psychotic symptoms to be improved with the reestablishment of normal thyroid status (Kleinschmidt & Waxenberg, 1956). Robbins and Vinson's 10 hyperthyroid persons, who initially resembled organically impaired persons on test of neuroticism and cognition, normalized with treatment (Robbins & Vinson, 1960).

Artunkal and Togrol's 20 women (1964) had improved MMPI profiles (51), while Whybrow et al. (1969) found improvement in magnitude of MMPI scores without change in pattern. Whybrow also found significant decreases in the BPRS and Clyde Mood Scale scores, while scores on the Porteus Maze and Trailmaking test normalized.

Wallace and colleagues (MacCrimmon et al., 1979; Wallace et al., 1980) found their 19 patients to have normal posttreatment cognitive testing and MMPI profiles, with the former normalizing at 3 weeks, but the latter only after 6–12 months of treatment. Finally, Rockey and Griep (1980) used the Sickness Impact Profile, a symptom rating scale which estimates disruption of normal life-style and function, to evaluate 14 hyperthyroid women before and after treatment. They found significantly reduced posttreatment scores in all but one woman who had concurrent symptoms of a major depression.

TABLE 2.6. Recovery from Neuropsychiatric Dysfunction in Hypothyroidism

Study		Outcome
Kleinschmidt and Waxenberg (1956)	17	Eight with decreased affective and psychotic symptoms
Robbins and Vinson (1960)	10	Group mean on cognitive and neuroticism tests normalized
Artunkal and Togrol (1964)	20	Little change
Whybrow, Prange, and Treadway (1969)	10	Group means on cognitive and psychopathology assessment normalized
MacCrimmon, Wallace, Goldberg, and Streiner (1979); Wallace, MacCrimmon, and Goldberg (1980)	19	Group means on cognitive testing normalized earlier than MMPI profile
Rockey and Griep (1980)	14	Sickness impact profile decreased in all but one who had a major depression

It therefore seems that the neuropsychiatric symptoms of hyperthyroidism are by and large reversible. There is little evidence to support the presence of a pathological personality pattern associated specifically with hyperthyroidism. Rather, it seems that scores on various personality tests, pathological in the throes of the thyrotoxic episode, return to baseline with resolution of the episode. This does not disprove the hypothesis that there is an underlying set of personality or intrapsychic factors which predispose to hyperthyroidism; however, it does imply that any psychopathology described during the episode, whether based on clinical interview or anamnestic data, is to a significant degree secondary to the metabolic derangement.

Pathophysiology: Possible Mechanisms

As yet we understand no single mechanism or unifying concept that can explain the many neuropsychiatric symptoms that are associated with an altered thyroid economy. The manifestations of both hypo- and hyperthyroidism are protean, from mild cognitive deficits and dysphoria to psychosis and delirium. In addition, thyroid hormones have a multitude of effects on the central and peripheral nervous systems. Many of those systems that are linked to thyroid function have themselves been implicated in the pathogenesis of mental disorders. The known effects of

thyroid action that may be relevant to psychopathoogy are summarized in Table 2.7.

In addition to the evidence gathered from the study of the close association of changes in the thyroid economy with affective symptoms, much has been learned from the study and treatment of affective disorders with thyroid hormones.

Thyroid status may predict the effectiveness of traditional antidepressant therapy. Positive response to imipramine (IMI) is correlated with increased tissue thyroid activity, measured by ankle reflex time and serum cholesterol levels (Whybrow, Coppen, Prange, Noguera, & Bailey, 1972). In addition, normalization of TSH response to TRH stimulation after successful treatment of depression is correlated with good prognosis, while continued blunting of the TSH response is predictive of relapse (Kirkegaard, Norlem, Lauridsen, Bjorum, & Christiansen, 1975).

Persons with a rapid-cycling form of bipolar affective disorder often have clinical or laboratory evidence of hypothyroidism (Cho et al., 1979; Cowdry et al., 1983; Dunner, 1979; Extein et al., 1982; Oppenheim, 1982; Roy-Byrne et al., 1984; Siris et al., 1979). Many of these persons respond to replacement or hypermetabolic doses of thyroxine (Extein et al., 1982; Stancer & Persad, 1982). In the 1920s, R. R. Gjessing (L. Gjessing, 1974) treated a group of persons who had a pattern of periodic psychoses with desiccated thyroid in hypermetabolic doses (sufficient to raise their pulse to 120 and induce protein catabolism) and their symptoms resolved. The basic means, however, by which altering thyroid status abolishes such cyclic psychiatric symptoms is as yet poorly understood.

The use of thyroid hormones as adjuvant treatment in depression has also provided some clues. With the possible exception of TRH given intravenously, the thyroid hormones and thyroid-related peptides have no antidepressant effects when given alone (Prange, Loosen, Wilson, & Lipton, 1980). However, T3 can potentiate the effects of tricyclic antidepressants, either hastening clinical recovery (Prange et al., 1969) or inducing remission in otherwise refractory depression (Earle, 1970). There is some evidence that TSH has a similar effect (Prange, Wilson, Knox, McClane, & Lipton, 1970).

It has been suggested that the explanation of adjuvant thyroid effects lies in the close linkage of thyroid and adrenergic function (Whybrow & Prange, 1981). There is general agreement from studies of heart and adipose tissue, as well as some data from CNS studies, that increasing thyroid activity increases β-adrenergic activity and decreases α_1-adrenergic activity, while decreasing thyroid activity leads to the reverse (Table 2.8), although there appears to be some organ specificity to these effects (Scarpace & Abrass, 1981; Williams, Guthrow, & Lefkowitz, 1979). Those studies that demonstrate an effect consistently show that alterations in at least β-adrenergic activity seem to be due to a change in receptor number rather than affinity.

Studies of norepinephrine (NE) synthesis and effects have yielded complementary results. For example, hypothyroid rats increase their NE synthesis (Lipton, Prange, & Dairman, 1968), while rats given exogenous thyroxine decrease their NE synthesis (Prange, Meek, & Lipton, 1970). When dopamine β-hydroxylase activity is assayed, parallel changes are seen in both animals and man (Stolk & Whybrow, 1976). In human adipose tissue, NE responsiveness significantly correlates with thyroid status (Arner, Wennlund, & Ostman, 1981).

These findings have led to the hypothesis that a β-adrenergic predominance occurs

with thyroid adjuvant treatment which aids in inducing a remission of depressive symptoms via increased or maintained cAMP production. However, this postulated mechanism of thyroid hormone effect is not easily reconciled with the current catecholamine hypothesis of depression, which states that recovery from depression is correlated with a decrease in β-receptor activity (Stone, 1983; Sulzer, 1978; Vetulani, Stawarz, Dingell, & Sulzer, 1976).

Furthermore, attempts to document thyroid hormone potentiation of tricyclic antidepressant effects in laboratory animals have yielded conflicting results. Schildkraut, Winokur, Draskoczy, and Hensle (1971) found that acute IMI treatment decreased NE turnover without changing brain NE content, while 10-day treatment yielded little change in NE turnover while decreasing brain NE content. When T4 was added to IMI for 10 days, NE metabolism increased as compared to IMI treatment alone, and the authors speculated that there may be a ralationship between increased NE turnover and the onset of clinical antidepressant effects.

However, Frazer et al. (174) found that 5 days of IMI treatment inhibited NE-stimulated cAMP production, an index of β-adrenergic receptor activity. When T3 was added, the IMI effect was mitigated, although T3 alone had no effect. More recently, Schmidt and Schultz (1985) found a decrease in β-adrenoceptor density and cAMP production after 7 days of treatment with T3 or T4 alone. Furthermore, when T4 was added to low-dose IMI treatment over 9 days, the cAMP response to NE was diminished in an additive fashion; there was no further effect when T4 was added to high-dose IMI treatment.

In summary, although adjuvant thyroxine treatment potentiated the IMI effect on NE metabolism in Schildkraut's system, T3 compromised the effect of IMI on cAMP production in Frazer's study. Schmidt and Schultz found no effect of adding T4 to a high dose of IMI, while the addition of T4 to a low dose of IMI could duplicate the effect of the higher dose. In addition, these authors found an actual decrease of cAMP generation with T3 and T4 alone. It is unclear at present whether the variability of these results is due to methodological (e.g., dosage of length of IMI

TABLE 2.7. Systems Relevant to Neuropsychiatric Function Altered by Thyroid Function Changes—Selected References

System	Animal studies	Human studies
	NEUROCHEMICAL EFFECTS	
Adrenergic function	See Table 2.8; also reviewed in Nilsson and Karlberg (1983)	
Calcium	Coville and Telford (1969)	
Catechol degradation	Singhal and Rastogi (1978)	
Cholinergic function	Coville and Telford (1970a)	
Cyclic AMP	Brodie, Davies, Hymie, Krishna, and Weiss (1976)	
Cyclic GMP	Tse, Wrenn, and Kuo (1980)	
Dopamine	Crocker and Overstreet (1984)	
Histamine	Coville and Telford (1970a)	
Serotonin	Coville and Telford (1970a)	
	NEUROENDOCRINE EFFECTS	
Growth hormone		Dunleavy, Oswald, Brown, and Strong (1974) Brown, Seggle, and Chambers (1975)
Prolactin		Bowers, Friosen, and Wang (1971)
TSH		Loosen and Prange (1982)
CNS thyroid hormones		Dratman, Crutchfield, Gordon, and Jennings (1983)
	SENSITIVITY TO CNS ACTIVE DRUGS	
Via central mechanisms	Coville and Telford (1970b)	
Via peripheral mechanisms	R. Kato, Takanaka, Takahashi, and Oneda (1969)	

NEUROPHYSIOLOGIC MEASURES

Sleep architecture	Kales et al. (1967) Dunleavy, Oswald, Brown, and Strong (1974) Jones et al. (1975)
Electroencephalogram	Browning, Atkins, and Weiner (1954) Nieman (1959) Wilson and Johnson (1964) Olsen et al. (1972)
Evoked potential	Kopell, Wittner, Lunde, Warrick, and Edwards (1970)
Seizure threshold	Shutov and Prostakova (1970)
Sato, Koramoto, and Wada (1984)	
Cerebral blood flow	Scheinberg, Stead, Brannor, and Warren (1950)

BIOLOGICAL RHYTHMS

Thyroid function affects rhythms	Richter, Jones, and Biswanger (1959) Hertz (1965)
Rhythms affect thyroid function	Konno (1979)

IMMUNE FUNCTION

Telford (1969)	Konno and Mosikawa (1982) Tatar, Starar, and Vegas (1983) Caroff and Winokur (1983)

TABLE 2.8. Effect of Thyroid Function on Adrenergic Receptor Activity

Thyroid function and receptor activity	Animal studies	Human studies
Increased thyroid and increased β receptor	Kunos, Vermes-Kunos, and Nickerson (1974) Kunos (1977) Williams, Lefkowitz, Watanabe, Hathoway, and Besch (1977) Tse, Wrenn, and Kuo (1980) Scarpace and Abrass (1981)	Grossman, Rubin, and Johnson (1971) Ginsberg, Clutter, Shah, and Cryer (1981)
Increased thyroid and decreased α receptor	Kunos et al. (1974) Kunos (1977)	Guttler, Shaw, and Otis
Decreased thyroid and decreased β receptor	Kunos et al. (1974) Fregly, Nelson, and Resch (1975) Kunos (1977) Gross, Brodde, and Schumann (1980)[a] Marwaha and Prasad (1981)[a]	
Decreased thyroid and increased α receptor	Rosenqvist and Borens (1972) Kunos et al. (1974) Kunos (1977)	Harlan, Laslo, and Bogderoff (1963) Grill and Rosenqvist (1973) Guttler et al. (1975)

[a]Denotes central nervous system study; otherwise peripheral organ system.

58

treatment, choice and dosage of thyroid hormone, age of animal, output variable measured) or other factors.

Although it is clear that central thyroid hormones affect many of the adrenergic parameters which are altered during depression and its treatment, the mechanisms by which those alterations occur are not known. Such mechanisms may be very complex. For example, Dratman and Crutchfield (1978) have shown that synaptosomes generate T3 from injected T4 and that T3 levels are higher there than in cytosol. The function of such locally generated T3 in unknown; it may be stored and released into the synaptic cleft, taken by retrograde transport into the presynaptic nucleus, or may function in other ways.

The control of the 5′-deiodinase which converts T4 to T3 is undoubtedly important to the control of CNS thyroid activity. There is evidence that CNS T3 levels are autoregulated in at least some species (Dratman et al., 1983), and it is conceivable that CNS deiodinase activity may play a role in this autoregulation. Further evidence indicates that it is T3 which is locally generated by pituitary 5′-deiodinase that determines TSH production, and that this pituitary deiodinase is regulated independently from its peripheral counterparts (Larsen, Silva, & Kaplan, 1981).

The T3 control of TSH synthesis may be only one example of the more general phenomenon of T3 control of CNS peptide synthesis. It appears that T3 generated in the pituitary controls TSH synthesis by a mechanism which involves the occupancy of nuclear receptor sites (Silva & Larsen, 1978). These sites are also found in the cortex, hypothalamus, telencephalon, and cerebellum of the rat (Schwartz & Openheimer, 1978) as well as peripherally in the liver and kidney. Further investigation will determine whether nuclear receptor-mediated control of peptide synthesis is relevant to control of the synthesis of larger proteins as well, such as the 5′-deiodinases, adrenergic receptors, and regulatory proteins.

The central adrenergic changes induced by altering thyroid function have been the most extensively studied CNS thyroid effects, but it is not clear whether these are its only or even most important CNS effects. It is also not certain to what extent data from peripheral investigations can be generalized to central thyroid function. Furthermore, within the CNS the regulatory processes by which the thyroid hormones, particularly T3, exert their effects are not known: deiodinase activity, nuclear binding, and ultimately peptide and protein synthesis may all be involved (Figure 2.2). What is clear, however, is that without optimal thyroid function, neuropsychiatric and particularly affective symptoms often do emerge and thus, despite our lack of understanding of fundamental mechanisms, the evaluation of thyroid status is of vital concern to the clinician of behavior.

Summary and Conclusion: A Possible Homeostatic Role for Thyroid Function?

Since Claude Bernard introduced the concept of le milieu intereur, biological scientists have been increasingly interested in the means by which the organism maintains its functions in the face of internal or external perturbations. Whether the thyroid system dose indeed play such a role in behavior or whether thyroid alterations are epiphenomena or secondary effects is very difficult to sort out. Nevertheless, there are certain indications that the thyroid system does play a homeostatic role in preventing neuropsychiatric symptoms.

First and foremost, it is clear normal thyroid function is necessary for normal mental function; deviations either toward hyper- or hypofunction disrupt affective and cognitive processes whether these deviations occur de novo or are iatrogenically induced. Furthermore, certain thyroid parameters (e.g., TSH response to TRH, ankle reflex time) are of prognostic significance in the treatment of affective symptoms, implying that certain thyroid states may aid and others may hinder the reestablishment of normal mental functioning.

Additional evidence for a homeostatic role comes from the adjuvant treatment data. Exogenously administered thyroid hormone hastens the response to antidepressants and can achieve remission in otherwise refractory cases.

That thyroid altérations cause adrenergic changes, and vice versa, has been well documented. If it is true, as the hypotheses hold, that catecholamines are involved in the

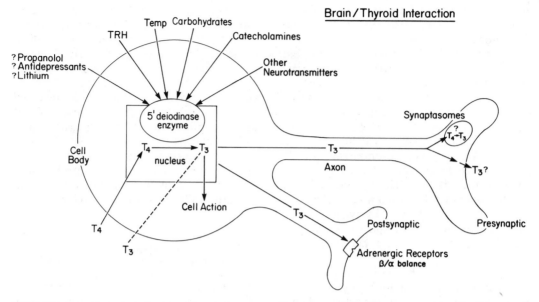

FIGURE 2.2. Alterations in thyroid function may affect numerous regulatory processes in the central nervous system.

pathogenesis of affective disorders and that central thyroid function affects central adrenergic function, then a homeostatic role in maintaining normal mental functioning is indeed possible for the thyroid system.

Regardless of such uncertainties about the teleological role of thyroid function, a number of conclusions can be drawn from the current data:

1. Neuropsychiatric symptoms can be caused by thyroid changes and typically remit when thyroid status is normalized.
2. Clinical and subclinical thyroid dysfunction are associated with certain types of major affective disorders; the mechanism responsible for this association is not completely understood.
3. Given certain neuropsychiatric syndromes (e.g., major depression), alterations in thyroid status, either exogenous or endogenous, may assist or impede the restoration of normal mental function.
4. It is unclear whether thyroid function plays a similar adaptive role in stressor-induced states.
5. Although it is probable that several stressor-induced neuropsychiatric states can induce alterations in thyroid parameters, it

is unclear whether gross thyroid disease can be precipitated by such states.

NEUROPSYCHIATRIC CHANGES ASSOCIATED WITH PARATHYROID DISORDERS

Introduction

Hypoparathyroidism is an endocrine disorder characterized biochemically by hypocalcemia, hyperphosphatemia, and low serum parathyroid hormone (PTH). Primary hypoparathyroidism may be idiopathic, or more commonly may result from excision of the parathyroids or damage to their blood supply during neck surgery. Secondary hypoparathyroidism results from severe hypomagnesemia which interferes with PTH secretion (Chase & Slatapolsky, 1974). Pseudohypoparathyroidism is an X-linked dominant hereditary disorder with variable penetrance characterized phenotypically by short stature, round face, short neck, metacarpal brachydactyly, cataracts, thick stocky body build, and increased or decreased bone density on X-ray. Biochemically there is endorgan resistance to PTH or ineffective circulating PTH. PTH levels are increased with concomitant hyperplasia of the parathyroid glands. Despite high levels of PTH, patients are hypocalcemic. Relatives of patients with pseudohypoparathyroidism who share the bony abnormalities and developmental defects but are spared the symptoms and biochemical evidence of hypoparathyroidism have so-called pseudopseudohypoparathyroidism.

Hypoparathyroidism leads to signs and symptoms associated with hypocalcemia. The medical aspects are summarized in Table 2.9. Neurological manifestations of decreased ionized calcium are secondary to increased neuromuscular excitability. Patients may exhibit the signs of Trousseau or Chvostek, parasthesias, or tetany with muscle cramps and onvulsions (Fonesca & Calverley, 1967). Increased sensitivity to dystonic reactions to phenothiazines has been reported (Schaff & Payne, 1966). Intracranial calcifications, particularly in the basal ganglia, may lead to Parkinsonism (P. Levin, Kunin, Peardon-Donaghy, Hamilton, & Maurer, 1961). Patients with idiopathic and pseudohypoparathyroidism, due to their usually longer course, are more likely to have evidence of ectopic calcification than patients with surgical hypoparathyroidism when onset is more rapid.

Assessment of Neuropsychiatric Findings

The neuropsychiatric manifestations of hypoparathyroidism were comprehensively reviewed by Denko and Kaebling (1962). They reviewed 378 case reports between 1907 and 1960. Reports were included which contained a description of the patient's intellectual or emotional features. Cases with a history of psychiatric illness prior to the onset of hypoparathyroidism were excluded. Their findings were arranged by subtypes of hypoparathyroidism, as summarized in Table 2.10. The psychiatric manifestations may be classified in three groups: (1) psychosis, often presenting similarly to a toxic delirium in which delusions and hallucinations develop; (2) disturbed cognition with intellectual impairment or features of organic brain syndrome; and (3) "unclassifiable" psychiatric diseases that today would include personality disorders, affective disorders such as major depression and dysthymia, and the anxiety disorders.

The investigators thus concluded that idiopathic hypoparathyroidism produced a wide

TABLE 2.9. Medical Aspects of Hypoparathyroidism[a]

Aspect	Pseudo	Idiopathic	Postsurgical
Increased neuromuscular excitability	+	+	+
Cataracts	+	+	+
Basal ganglia calcification	+	+	+
Prolonged Q-T interval on EKG	+	+	+
Papilledema	+	+	+
Dental defects	+	+	+
Alopecia	−	+	−
Vitiligo	−	+	−
Moniliasis	−	+	−
Hypothyroidism	+	+	+
Hypoadrenalism	−	+	−
Primary hypoganadism	+	+	−
Albright's hereditary osteodystrophy (brachydactyly, short, obese, round face)	+	−	−
Subcutaneous calcification (and bone formation)	+	−	−

[a]After Aurbach, Marx, and Spiegel (1985).

TABLE 2.10. Mental Changes in Hypoparathyroidism[a]

Type	Number of cases	Psychosis	Disturbed cognition	Unclassifiable psychiatric diseases
Idiopathic	178	9	93	57
Surgical	111	20	54	35
Pseudo	68	0	51	10
Pseudopseudo	21	0	11	3
Total cases	378			

[a]After Denko and Kaelbling (1962).

spectrum of psychiatric symptoms, including affective symptoms, personality changes, delirium, and frank psychosis. Surgical hypoparathyroidism produced a like array of psychiatric findings, with cognitive disturbances predominating. Pseudohypoparathyroidism and pseudopseudohypoparathyroidism patients and primarily intellectual impairment. Mental status changes in all groups were reversed or improved with treatment, except in pseudopseudohypoparathyroidism where there is no known effective treatment.

Most investigators have ascribed the mental status changes in hypoparathyroidism to alterations in calcium homeostasis rather than to the direct effects of parathyroid hormone per se. To test this assumption, Fourman, Rawnsley, Davis, Jones, and Morgan (1967) compared the effect of calcium and an inert substance, kaolin, on the mental status of 7 controls and 17 postthyroidectomy patients who had partial parathyroid insufficiency, defined as a plasma calcium at the lower limit of normal, which fell to lower values under calcium deprivation. Treatment efficacy was assessed by a mood questionnaire. Prior to treatment, eight patients were "anxious and tense" with moderate depression, five were anxious without depression, and four patients complained of chronic fatigue. The investigators reported a significant increase in symptoms after 2 months in those treated with kaolin compared to calcium treatment for 2 months. There was no change in mood ratings for the control group with either treatment. Mood improvement in the patient group was correlated with calcium treatment, but not with serum calcium levels. The authors concluded that subtle mental status changes were increased in mild

parathyroid insufficiency when exogenous calcium was deprived.

Possible Mechanisms

Sudden changes in serum calcium have been implicated as responsible in postparathyroidectomy psychosis (Mikkelson & Reider, 1979). There are no specific identifying features in this psychosis, which may resemble other postoperative psychoses. Calcium changes in brain could disturb neurotransmitter metabolism, as calcium has been shown to play a role in the activation of brain enzymes such as tryptophan hydroxylase (Knapp, Mandell, & Bullard, 1975) and tryosine hydroxylases (Morgenroth, Boadle-Biber, & Roth, 1975). The rate of change in calcium concentration—the more rapid change in ionic concentration, the more deleterious—may also affect neurotransmitter metabolism and general ionic shifts across the neuronal membrane. Prolonged exposure to an abnormal concentration of ions may lead to compensatory changes in receptor and transmitter release such that when a further abrupt shift in calcium concentration occurs, normal adaptive mechanisms are inadequate.

Hyperparathyroidism

Clinical Features

Primary hyperparathyroidism is a chronic disorder characterized by hypersecretion of parathyroid hormone (PTH), constant or intermittent hypercalcemia, hypophosphatemia, and hypercalciuria. About 80% of cases of primary hyperparathyroidism are secondary to a single parathyroid adenoma, the remainder due to chief cell hyperplasia and, rarely, parathyroid carcinoma. Lithium may also cause hyperparathyroidism, probably through an intracellular mechanism that decreases the ability of parathyroid cells to sense serum calcium levels accurately, thus interfering with feedback regulation of PTH secretion (Franks, Dubovsky, Lifshitz, Coen, Subryan, & Walker, 1982; Shen & Sherrard, 1982).

The prevalence of primary hyperparathyroidism has been estimated as 1:1000. It is uncommon in persons less than 40 years old, but the incidence increases sharply in patients 60 years of age and older (Heath, Hodgson, & Kennedy, 1980). The behavioral symptoms of hyperparathyroidism are secondary to hypercalcemia and may appear in the absence of recognized medical symptoms of hyperparathyroidism such as renal dysfunction, urolithiasis, bone disease, peptic ulcer disease, and pancreatitis. The differential diagnosis of primary hyperparathyroidism includes nonparathyroid causes of hypercalcemia (Potts, 1977), for example, malignancy, demineralization of bone, nephrolithiasis, and hypophosphatemia.

Assessment of Neuropsychiatric Findings

The neuropsychiatric manifestations of hyperparathyroidism and hypercalcemia have been reviewed recently by Alarcon and Franceschini (1984) (Table 2.11). Their extensive review was inspired by the study of a patient who presented with a mixture of paranoid symptoms like those seen in paranoid schizophrenia and a shallow, smiling, slightly euphoric affect without clouding of consciousness or any other organic feature. They found surprisingly few cases resembling theirs in the literature from 1940 to 1975. Once they documented the presence of a parathyroid adenoma as the cause of hypercalcemia in their patient, they retrospectively called her psychiatric condition a mixed organic disorder (delusional and affective). They concluded from their literature review that affective symptoms, primarily depression, are the most common psychopathological features of hyperparathyroidism, with the second largest group of manifestations encompassed by the label organic brain syndrome showing varying degrees of cognitive impairment. These authors contend that the described reports of paranoid psychosis are better labeled organic brain syndrome of a

TABLE 2.11. Patient Series Reporting Psychiatric Symptoms in Hyperparathyroidism[a]

Report	Number of patients	General "neuropsychiatric" symptoms, $n(\%)$	Dominant psychiatric symptoms
Eitinger (1942)	50	7(14)	
St. Goar (1957)	45	7(16)	
Hellstrom and Ivermark (1962)	138	11(8)	
Karpati and Frame (1964)	33	14(42)	4(12)
Henson (1966)	35	6(17)	3(8.5)
Cope (1966)	343	14(4)	3(1)
Anderson (1968)	36	7(23)	3(10)
Petersen (1968)	60	34(57)	5(9)
Flanagan (1970)	32	—	8(25)
Hecht et al. (1975)	73	7(10)	—
Gatewood (1975)	5	3(60)	2(40)
Totals	844	110	28

[a]From Alarcon and Franceschini (1984).

delirious type, as the "paranoid psychosis" usually occurred with clouded consciousness, psychomotor agitation, and altered cognition. The severity of psychiatric symptoms was correlated with the level of serum calcium in some series (Peterson, 1968), but there were many exceptions, including the patient described by Alarcon and Franceschini whose psychiatric symptoms were florid despite only a moderate elevation of serum calcium.

Specific neuropsychiatric symptoms may be a function of the time course of the illness. Sometimes it is only after a prolonged period of subclinical hypercalcemia that psychiatric manifestations emerge; patients may have subtle personality or mood disturbances for years before more clear manifestations of hyperparathyroidism appear. In another series, acute organic psychosis was said to have a "violent onset" (Peterson, 1968).

With appropriate management and definitive treatment of the underlying hyperparathyroidism, neuropsychiatric manifestations of the illness are reversible. Borer and Bhanot (1985) offer suggestions for the psychiatric consultant in managing these patients, including the use of antidepressants and low-dosage neuroleptics for depressive and psychotic or delirious features pending the definitive treatment of the hyperparathyroidism and hypercalcemia.

Possible Mechanisms

The cause of the clinical psychiatric changes seen in hyperparathyroidism has been attributed to the general dampening effect of hypercalcemia on neurological function (G. Kato & Somjen, 1969; Kelly, Krnjevic, & Somjen, 1969). This may adequately account for the lethargy and muscle weakness attributed to the effects of hypercalcemia on the myoneural junction, but is probably too simplistic an explanation of the diverse changes in CNS function reported here. A positive correlation between symptom severity in patients with major depressive disorders and cerebrospinal fluid (CSF) calcium concentrations has been found (Jimerson et al., 1979). Some cycling bipolar patients have higher CSF calcium during periods of mania than depression (Jimerson et al., 1979). Besides a "general dampening effect" on neu-

ronal function, Dubovsky and Franks (1983) have stressed the role of intracellular calcium in the synthesis and release of those neurotransmitters thought to be important in affective disorders. They have extended their theoretical findings to the successful use of verapamil, a calcium channel blocker, in the treatment of mania (Dubovsky, Franks, & Lifshitz, 1982).

Mention should also be made of the contribution of magnesium deficiency to the neuropsychiatric symptoms in hyperparathyroidism. This occurs secondary to the mobilization of magnesium in addition to calcium from bones and its subsequent urinary excretion (Potts & Roberts, 1958). Isolated hypomagnesemia is often associated with organic mental symptoms. In addition, 50% of patients with hypomagnesemia report auditory or visual hallucinations (Hall & Joffe, 1973). There are some reports of improved mental status in hyperparathyroid patients after the administration of magnesium, but it has not been demonstrated that this response is specific (Gatewood, Organ & Mead, 1975).

Calcitonin-Related Disorders

Calcitonin is a peptide hormone secreted by the parafollicular cells (C cells) of the thyroid. Its primary physiological effect is to decrease plasma calcium and phosphorus by inhibiting osteoclastic activity.

As mentioned in the introduction, medullary carcinoma, composing 5–10% of all thyroid tumors, involves neoplasia of the parafollicular cells. It is the first disease state in which an abnormality of calcitonin secretion has been described. The tumor occurs with a familial incidence in about 20% of the causes and is often associated with multiple endocrine adenomatosis syndrome, type II. Hypocalcemia is not found in the majority of patients, nor are definite skeletal abnormalities reported (Potts, 1977) despite overproduction of calcitonin by the tumor.

Recently, a substantial literature has begun to accumulate suggesting that the brain is another major site of calcitonin action (Freed, Bing, Andersen, & Wyatt, 1984). Calcitonin has been shown to have tranquilizing or depressant effects in patients with psychotic agitation or mania (Carman & Wyatt, 1979) and to act as an anorectic agent in rats

(Freed *et al.*, 1984). Further research is needed to elucidate the specific mechanisms underlying these effects.

Conclusions

The neuropsychiatric changes in parathyroid disease are profound and may affect all aspects of mental function. They are not easily predicted by the serum levels of calcium, although most patients' symptoms improve with treatment of the underlying parathyroid disorder and the concomitantly disturbed calcium metabolism. Nonetheless, appropriate serum electrolyte screening including serum calcium is warranted in the differential diagnosis of nonspecific psychiatric syndromes in patients whose affective symptoms or other vague subjective behavioral dysfunction have been refractory to standard treatment.

References

Abraham, A., Atkinson, M., & Roscoe, B. (1966). Value of ankle jerk timing in the assessment of thyroid function. *British Medical Journal, 1*, 830–833.

Alarcon, R. D., & Franceschini, J. A. (1984). Hyperparathyroidism and paranoid psychosis. Case report and review of the literature. *British Journal of Psychiatry, 145*, 477–486.

Alexander, W., Hardin, R., & Shimminis, J. (1968). Emotions and nonspecific infection as possible etiologic factors in Graves' disease. *Lancet, 2*, 196–198.

Anderson, J. (1968). The psychiatric aspects of disturbed calcium metabolism. *Proceedings of the Royal Society of Medicine, 61*, 1123–1124.

Arner, P., Wennlund, A., & Ostman, J. (1981). Thyroid hormone regulation of rat heart, lymphocyte, and lung β-adrenergic receptors. *Endocrinology (Baltimore), 108*, 1007–1011.

Artunkal, B., & Togrol, B. (1964). Psychological studies in hyperthyroidism. In M. Cameron & M. O'Connor (Eds.), *Brain thyroid relationships*. Boston: Little, Brown.

Asher, R. (1949). Myxoedematous madness. *British Medical Journal, 22*, 555–562.

Aurbach, G. P., Marx, S. J., & Spiegel, A. M. (1985). Parathyroid hormone and the calciferols. In J. D. Wilson & D. W. Foster (Eds.), *Textbook of endocrinology*. Philadelphia: Saunders.

Bagchi, N., Brown T., & Mack, R. (1982). Effect of chronic lithium treatment on hypothalamic–pituitary regulation of thyroid function. *Hormone and Metabolic Research, 14*, 92–93.

Barnes, V., Greenberg, A., Owings, J., & Blizzard, R. (1972). The effect of chlordiazepoxide on thyroid function and thyrotoxicosis. *Johns Hopkins Medical Journal, 131*, 298–300.

Bennett, A., & Cambor, C. (1961). Clinical study of hyperthyroidism: Comparison of male and female characteristics. *Archives of General Psychiatry, 4*, 160–165.

Beierwaltes, W., & Ruff, G. (1958). Thyroxin and triiodothyroxine in excessive dosage to euthyroid humans. *Archives of Internal Medicine, 101*, 569–576.

Blackwell, B., & Schmidt, G. (1984). Drug interactions in psychopharmacology. *Psychiatric Clinics of North America, 7*, 625–636.

Borer, M. S., & Bhanot, U. K. (1985). Hyperparathyroidism: Neuropsychiatric manifestations. *Psychosomatics, 26*, 597–601.

Bowers, C., Friosen, H., & Wang, P. H. (1971). Prolactin and thyrotropin release in may by synthetic pyroglutamyl-histadyl-prolinamide. *Biochemical and Biophysical Research Communications, 45*, 1033–1041.

Brockman, D., & Whitman, R. (1952). Postthyroidectomy psychoses. *Journal of Nervous and Mental Disease, 16*, 340–345.

Brodie, B., Davies, J., Hymie, S., Krishna, G., & Weiss, B. (1976). Interrelationships of catecholamine and other endocrine systems. *Pharmacological Reviews, 13*, 273–289.

Brown, G., Seggle, J., & Chambers, Psychoendocrinology and growth hormone: A review. *Psychoneuroendocrinology, 3*, 131–153.

Browning, T., Atkins, R., & Weiner, H. (1954). Cerebral metabolic disturbances in hypothyroidism: Clinical and encephalographic studies in the psychoses of myxedema and hypothyroidism. *AMA Archives of Internal Medicine, 93*, 938–942.

Burstein, B. (1961). Psychoses associated with thyrotoxicosis. *Archives of General Psychiatry, 4*, 267–273.

Carman, J. S., & Wyatt, R. J. (1979). Use of calcitonin in psychotic agitation or mania. *Archives of General Psychiatry, 36*, 72–75.

Caroff, S., & Winokur, A. (1984). Hormonal response to thyrotropin-releasing hormone following rest-activity reversal in normal man. *Biological Psychiatry, 19*, 1015–1025.

Carrier, R., & Buday, P. (1961). Augmentation of toxicity of microamine oxidase inhibitors by thyroid feeding. *Nature (London), 191*, 1107.

Chase, L. R., & Slatapolsky, E. (1974). Secretion and metabolic efficacy of parathyroid hormone in patients with severe hypomagnesemia. *Journal of Clinical Endocrinology and Metabolism, 38*, 363–371.

Checkley, S. (1978). Thyrotoxicosis and the course of manic–depressive illness. *British Journal of Psychiatry, 133*, 219–223.

Cho, J., Bone, S., Dunner, D., Colt, E., & Fieve, R. (1979). The effect of lithium on thyroid function in patients with primary affective disorder. *American Journal of Psychiatry, 136*, 115–116.

Clinical Society of London. (1888). Report on myxedema. *Transactions of the Clinical Society of London, 21* (Suppl.), 18.

Cohen, K., & Swigar, M. (1979). Thyroid function screening in psychiatric patients. *JAMA, Journal of the American Medical Association, 242*, 254–257.

Conrad, A. (1934). The psychiatric study of hyperthyroid patients. *Journal of Nervous and Mental Disease, 79*, 505–556.

Cooper, D., Halpern, R., Wood, L., Levin, A., & Ridgway, E. (1984). L-Thyroxine therapy in subclinical hypothyroidism. *Annals of Internal Medicine, 101*, 18–24.

Cope, D. (1960). Hyperparathyroidism: diagnosis and management. *American Journal of Surgery, 99*, 394–403.

Corn, T., & Checkley, S. (1983). A case of recurrent mania with recurrent hyperthyroidism. *British Journal of Psychiatry, 143*, 74–76.

Coville, P., & Telford, J. (1969). Changes in drug sensibility in hyperthyroidism. *British Journal of Pharmacology, 36*, 189–190.

Coville, P., & Telford, J. (1970a). Influence of thyroid hormones on the sensitivity of cardiac and smooth muscle to biogenic amines and other drugs. *British Journal of Pharmacology, 39*, 49–68.

Coville, P., & Telford, J. (1970b). The effect of thyroid hormones of the action of some centrally active drugs. *British Journal of Pharmacology, 40*, 747–760.

Cowdry, R., Wehr, T., Zis, A., & Goodwin, F. (1983). Thyroid abnormalities associated with rapid-cycling bipolar illness. *Archives of General Psychiatry, 46*, 414–420.

Crocker, A., & Overstreet, D. (1984). Modification of the behavioral effects of haloperidol and of dopamine receptor regulation by altered thyroid status. *Psychopharmacology, 82*, 102–106.

Crown, S. (1949). Notes on an experimental study of intellectual deterioration. *British Medical Journal, 2*, 684–686.

Cushman, P. (1967). Recurrent hyperthyroidism after normal response to triiodethyronine (letter). *JAMA, Journal of the American Medical Association, 199*, 588.

Denko, J. D., & Kaebling, R. (1962). The psychiatric aspects of hypoparathyroidism. *Acta Psychiatrica Scandinavica, Supplementum, 164*, 5–38.

Dongier, M., Wittkower, E., Stephens-Newshan, L., & Hoffman, M. (1956). Psychophysiological studies in thyroid function. *Psychosomatic Medicine, 4*, 310–323.

Dratman, M., & Crutchfield, F. (1978). Synaptosomal ^{125}I triiodothyroxine after intravenous ^{125}I thyroxine. *American Journal of Physiology, 235*, 638–647.

Dratman, M., Crutchfield, F., Gordon, J., & Jennings, A. (1983). Iodothyronine homeostasis in rat brain during hypo- and hyperthyroidism. *American Journal of Physiology, 245*, E185–E192.

Dubovsky, S. L., & Franks, R. D. (1983). Intracellular calcium ions in affective disorders, a review and a hypothesis. *Biological Psychiatry, 18*, 781–797.

Dubovsky, S. L., Franks, R. D., & Lifshitz, M. L. (1982). Effectiveness or verapamil in the treatment of a manic patient. *American Journal of Psychiatry, 139*, 502–504.

Dunleavy, D., Oswald, I., Brown, P., & Strong, J. (1974). Hyperthyroidism, sleep, and growth hormone. *Clinical Neurophysiology, 36*, 259–263.

Dunner, D. (1979). Rapid-cycling bipolar manic–depressive illness. *Psychiatric Clinics of North America, 2*, 461–467.

Earle, B. (1970). Thyroid hormone and tricyclic antidepressants in treatment-resistant depression. *American Journal of Psychiatry, 126*, 1667–1669.

Eayrs, J. (1960). The influence of the thyroid on the central nervous system. *British Medical Bulletin, 16*, 122–127.

Eittinger, L. (1942). Hyperparathyroidism with mental changes. *Nordvick Medicine, 14*, 1581–1585.

Extein, I., Pottash, A., & Gold, M. (1982). Does subclinical hypothyroidism predispose to tricyclic-induced rapid mood cycles? *Journal of Clinical Psychiatry, 43*, 290–291.

Ferguson-Rayport, S. (1956). The relation of emotional factors to recurrence of thyrotoxicosis. *Canadian Medical Association Journal, 75*, 993–999.

Flagg, G., Clemens, T., & Michael, E. (1965). A psychobiological investigation of hyperparathyroidism. *Psychosomatic Medicine, 27*, 497–504.

Flanagan, T. A., Goodwin, D. W., & Anderson, P. (1970). Psychiatric illness in a large family with familial hyperparathyroidism. *British Journal of Psychiatry, 117*, 693–698.

Fonesca, O. A., & Calverley, J. R. (1967). Neurological manifestations of hypoparathyroidism. *Archives of Internal Medicine, 120*, 202–206.

Fourman, D., Rawnsley, K., Davis, R. H., Jones, K. H., & Morgan, D. B. (1967). Effect of calcium on mental symptoms in partial parathyroid insufficiency. *Lancet, 2*, 914–915.

Franks, R. D., Dubovsky, S. L., Lifshitz, M., Coen, P., Subryan, V., & Walker, S. H. (1982). Long-term lithium carbonate therapy causes hyperparathyroidism. *Archives of General Psychiatry, 39*, 1074–1077.

Frazer, A., Pandy, G., Mendels, J., Neely, S., Kane, M., & Hess, M. (1974). The effect of triiodothyronine in combination with imipramine on cyclic AMP production in slices of rat cerebral cortex. *Neuropharmacology, 13*, 1131–1140.

Freed, W. J., Bing, L. A., Andersen, A. E., & Wyatt, R. J. (1984). Calcitonin as an anorectic agent. In N. S. Shah & A. G. Donald (Eds.), *Psychoneuroendocrine dysfunction* (pp. 83–109). New York: Plenum Press.

Fregly, M., Nelson, E., & Resch, G. (1975). Reduced β-adrenergic responsiveness in hypothyroid rats. *American Journal of Physiology, 229*, 916–924.

Gatewood, J. W., Organ, C. H., Jr., & Mead, B. T. (1975). Mental changes associated with hyperparathyroidism. *American Journal of Psychiatry, 132*, 129–132.

Gibson, J. (1962). Emotions and the thyroid gland: A critical appraisal. *Journal of Psychosomatic Research, 6*, 93–97.

Ginsberg, A. W., Clutter, W., Shah, S., & Cryer, P. (1981). Triiodothyronine-induced thyrotoxicosis increases mononuclear leukocyte β-adrenergic receptor density in man. *Journal of Clinical Investigation, 67*, 1785–1791.

Gjessing, L. (1974). A review of periodic catatonia. *Biological Psychiatry, 8*, 23–45.

Gold, M., Pottash, A., & Extein, I. (1981) Hypothyroidism and depression: Evidence from complete thyroid evaluation. *JAMA, Journal of the American Medical Association, 245*, 1919–1921.

Gomez, J., & Scott, G. (1980). Hypothyroidism, psychotropic drugs, and cardiotoxicity. *British Journal of Psychiatry, 134*, 89–91.

Graves, R. (1940). Clinical lectures. *Medical Classics, 5*, 35.

Greer, S., & Parsons, V. (1968). Schizophrenia-like psychosis in thyrotoxic crisis. *British Journal of Psychiatry, 114*, 1357–1359.

Greer, S., Ramsey, I., & Bagley, C. (1973). Neurotic and thyrotoxic anxiety: Clinical, psychological, and physiologic measurements. *British Journal of Psychiatry*, *122*, 549–554.

Gregory, I. (1956). Mental disorders associated with thyroid dysfunction. *Canadian Medical Association Journal*, *75*, 489–492.

Grill, V., & Rosenqvist, U. (1973). Inhibition of the neuroadrenergic-induced adenyl cyclase stimulation by augmented α-adrenergic response in subcutaneous adipose tissue from hypothyroid subjects. *Acta Psychiatrica Scandinavica*, *194*, 129–133.

Gross, G., Brodde, O., & Schumann, H. (1980). Decreased number of β-adrenoceptors in the cerebral cortex of hypothyroid rats. *European Journal of Pharmacology*, *61*, 191–197.

Grossman, W., Rubin, N., & Johnson, L. (1971). Effects of β blockade on peripheral manifestations of thyrotoxicosis. *Annals of Internal Medicine*, *74*, 875–881.

Gull, W. (1873). On a cretinoid state supervening in adult life. *Transactions of the Clinical Society of (London)*, *7*, 180–185.

Guttler, R., Shaw, J., & Otis, C. (1975). Epinephrine-induced alterations in urinary cyclic AMP in hyper- and hypothyroidism. *Journal of Clinical Endocrinology and Metabolism*, *41*, 707–711.

Hall, C. W., & Joffe, J. R. (1973). Hypomagnesemia: Physical and psychiatric symptoms. *JAMA, Journal of the American Medical Association*, *224*, 1749–1751.

Ham, G., Alexander, F., & Carmichael, H. (1951). A psychosomatic theory of thyrotoxicosis. *Psychosomatic Medicine*, *13*, 19–35.

Harlan, W., Laslo, I., & Bogderoff, (1963). Alterations to free fatty acid metabolism in endocrine disorders. I. The effect of thyroid hormone. *Journal of Clinical Endocrinology and Metabolism*, *23*, 33–40.

Hasan, M., & Mooney, R. (1981). Mania and thyrotoxicosis. *Journal of Family Practice*, *13*, 113–117.

Heath, H., Hodgson, S. F., & Kennedy, M. A. (1980). Primary hyperparathyroidism. Incidence, morbidity and potential economic impact in a community. *New England Journal of Medicine*, *302*, 189–193.

Hecht, A., Gershberg, H., & St. Paul, H. (1975). Primary hyperparathyroidism: Laboratory and clinical data in 73 cases. *JAMA, Journal of the American Medical Association*, *233*, 519–526.

Hellstrom, J., & Ivermark, B. I. (1962). Primary hyperparathyroidism. *Acta Chirurgica Scandinavica*, Suppl. 294, 5–113.

Henson, R. A. (1966). The neurological aspects of hypercalcemia: With special reference to primary hyperparathyroidism. *Journal of the Royal College of Physicians, London*, *1*, 41–50.

Hermann, H., & Quarton, (1965). Psychological changes and psychogenesis in thyroid hormone disorders. *Journal of Clinical Endocrinology and Metabolism*, *25*, 527–538.

Hertz, M. (1965). On rhythmic phenomena in thyroidectomized patients. *Acta Psychiatrica Scandanavica*, Supplementum, *180*, 449–456.

Hun, H., & Prudden, T. (1888). Myxoedema. *American Journal of the Medical Sciences*, *96*, 140–146.

Ingbar, S. (1966). Thyrotoxic storm. *New England Journal of Medicine*, *274*, 1251–1254.

Jain, V. (1972). A psychiatric study of hypothyroidism. *Psychiatrica Clinica*, *5*, 121–130.

Jefferson, J., & Greist, J. (1983). *Lithium encyclopedia for clinical practice*. Washington, DC: APA Press.

Jellinek, E. (1962). Fits, faints, coma, and dementia in myxedema. *Lancet*, *2*, 1010–1011.

Jimerson, D. C., Post, R. M., Carman, J. S., van Kammen, D. P., Wood, J. H., Bunney, W. E. Jr., & Goodwin, F. K. (1979). CSF calcium, clinical correlates in affective illness and schizophrenia. *Biological Psychiatry*, *14*, 37–51.

Johns, M., Masterson, J., Paddle-Ledinek, J., Patel, Y., Winikoff, D., & Malinee, M. (1975). Variations in thyroid function and sleep in healthy young men. *Clinical Science and Molecular Medicine*, *49*, 629–632.

Josephson, A., & MacKenzie, T. (1980) Thyroid-induced mania in hypothyroid patients. *British Journal of Psychiatry*, *137*, 222–228.

Kales, A., Heuser, G., Jacobson, A., Kales, J., Hanley, J., Zweizig, L., & Paulson, M. (1967). All night sleep studies in hypothyroid patients before and after treatment. *Journal of Clinical Endocrinology and Metabolism*, *27*, 1593–1599.

Karnosh, L., & Stout, R. (1934). Psychoses of myxedema. *American Journal of Psychiatry*, *91*, 1263–1265.

Karpati, G., & Frame, B. (1964). Neuropsychiatric disorders in primary hyperparathyroidism: Clinical analysis with review of the literature. *Archives of Neurology*, *10*, 387–397.

Kato, G., & Somjen, G. G. (1969). Effects of microiontophoretic administration of magnesium and calcium on neurons in the central nervous system of cats. *Journal of Neurobiology*, *2*, 181–195.

Kato, R., Takanaka, A., Takahashi, A., & Oneda, K. (1969). Species differences in the alterations of drug metabolizing activity of liver microsomes by thyroxine therapy. *Japanese Journal of Pharmacology*, *19*, 5–18.

Kelly, J. S., Krnjevic, K., & Somjen, G. (1969). Divalent cations and electrical properties of cortical cells. *Journal of Neurobiology*, *2*, 197–208.

Kirkegaard, C., Norlem, Lauridsen, Bjorum, N., & Christians, A. (1975). Protirelin stimulation test and thyroid function during the treatment of depression. *Archives of General Psychiatry*, *32*, 1115–1118.

Kleinschmidt, H., & Waxenberg, S. (1956). Psychophysiology and psychiatric management of thyrotoxicosis: A two-year follow-up study. *Journal of the Mount Sinai Hospital (New York)*, *23*, 131–153.

Knapp, S., Mandell, A., & Bullard, W. (1975). Calcium activation of brain tryptophan hydroxylase. *Life Sciences*, *16*, 1583–1594.

Konno, N. (1979). Comparison between the thyrotropin response to thyrotropin-releasing hormone in summer and that in winter in normal subjects. *Endocrinologia Japonica*, *25*, 635–638.

Konno, N., & Mosikawa, L. (1982). Seasonal variation of serum thyrotropin concentration and thyrotropin response to thyrotropin-releasing hormones in patients with primary hypothyroidism on constant replacement dosage of thyroxine. *Journal of Clinical Endocrinology and Metabolism*, *54*, 1118–1124.

Kopell, B., Wittner, W., Lunde, D., Warrick, G., & Edwards, D. (1970). Influence of triiodothyronine on selective attention in mood as measured by the visual averaged evoked potential. *Psychosomatic Medicine*, *32*, 495–502.

Krugman, L., Hershman, J., Chopra, I., Levine, G., Perkary, E., Geffner, D., & Teco, G. (1975). Patterns of recovery of the hypothalamic-pituitary-thyroid axis in patients taken off chronic thyroxine therapy. *Journal of Clinical Endocrinology and Metabolism*, *41*, 70–80.

Kunos, G. (1977). Thyroid hormone-dependent interconversion of myocardial α and β adrenoreceptors in the rat. *British Journal of Pharmacology*, *59*, 177–190.

Kunos, G., Vermes-Kunos, I., & Nickerson, M. (1974). Effects of thyroid state on adrenoreceptor properties. *Nature (London)*, *250*, 779–781.

Lakey, F. (1931). Apathetic hyperthyroidism. *Annals of Surgery*, *93*, 1026–1031.

Larsen, P., Silva, J., & Kaplan, M. (1981). Relationships between circulating and intracellular thyroid hormone: Physiologic and clinical implications. *Endocrine Reviews*, *2*, 87–102.

Levin, M., & Daughaday, W. (1955). Fatal coma due to myxedema. *American Journal of Medicine*, *18*, 1017–1019.

Levin, P., Kunin, A. S., Peardon-Donaghy, R. M., Hamilton, W. H., & Maurer, J. J. (1961). Intracranial calcifications and hypoparathyroidism. *Neurology*, *2*, 1076–1080.

Lidz, T. (1949). Emotional factors in the etiology of hyperthyroidism. *Psychosomatic Medicine*, *11*, 2–8.

Lidz, T., & Whitehorn, J. (1949). Psychiatric problems in a thyroid clinic. *JAMA, Journal of the American Medical Association*, *139*, 698–701.

Lipton, M., Prange, A., & Dairman, W. (1968). Increased rate of norepinephrine biosynthesis in hypothroid rats. *Federation Proceedings, Federation of American Societies for Experimental Biology*, *22*, 399–400.

Loosen, P., & Prange, A. (1982). Serum thyrotropin response to thyrotropin-releasing hormone in psychiatric patients. *American Journal of Psychiatry*, *139*, 405–416.

MacCrimmon, D., Wallace, J., Goldberg, W., & Streiner, D. (1979). Emotional disturbance and cognitive deficits in hyperthyroidism. *Psychosomatic Medicine*, *41*, 31–40.

Mandelbrote, B., & Wittkomer, E. (1955). Emotional factors in Graves' disease. *Psychosomatic Medicine*, *17*, 109–123.

Marwaha, J., & Prasad, K. (1981). Hypothyroidism elicits electrophysiological neuroadrenergic subsensitivity in the rat cerebellum. *Science*, *214*, 675–677.

Mason, J. (1970). Strategy in psychosomatic research. *Psychosomatic Medicine*, *32*, 427–438.

Matte, R., St. Marie, L., Comtois, R., D'Amour, P., LaCroix, A., Chartrand, R., Poisson, R., & Stonesky, C. (1981). The pituitary–thyroid axis after hemithyroidectomy in euthyroid man. *Journal of Clinical Endocrinology and Metabolism*, *53*, 377–380.

Mattson, A., & Seltzer, R. (1981). MAOI-induced rapid-cycling affective disorder in an adolescent. *American Journal of Psychiatry*, *138*, 677–679.

Mikkelson, E. J., & Reider, A. A. (1979). Postparathyroidectomy psychosis: Clinical and research implications. *Journal of Clinical Psychiatry*, *40*, 352–357.

Morgenroth, V., Boadle-Biber, M., & Roth, R. (1975). Activation of tyrosine hydroxylase from central noradrenergic neurons by calcium. *Molecular Pharmacology*, *11*, 427–435.

Nieman, E. (1959). The electroencephalogram in myxedema coma: Clinical and electroencephalographic study of three cases. *British Medical Journal*, *1*, 1204–1206.

Nilsson, O., & Karlberg, B. (1983). Thyroid hormone and the adrenergic nervous system. *Acta Psychiatrica Scandinavica Supplementum*, *672*, 27–32.

Nordgren, L., & von Scheele, C. (1976). Myxedematous madness without myxedema. *Acta Psychiatrica Scandinavica*, *199*, 233–236.

Olsen, P., Starer, M., Siersback-Nielsen, K., Hanson, J., Schioler, M., & Kirstensen, M. (1972). Electroencephalographic findings in hyperthyroidism. *Electroencephalography and Clinical Neurophysiology*, *32*, 171–177.

Oppenheimer, G. (1982). Drug-induced rapid-cycling: Possible outcomes and management. *American Journal of Psychiatry*, *137*, 939–941.

Parry, C. (1825). *Collected works* Vol. I. London.

Paykel, E. (1966). Abnormal personality and thyrotoxicosis. *Journal of Psychosomatic Research*, *10*, 143–152.

Peake, R. (1981). Recurrent apathetic hyperthyroidism. *Archives of Internal Medicine*, *141*, 258–262.

Perrild, H., Madson, S., & Hansen, J. (1978). Irreversible myxedema after lithium carbonate. *British Medical Journal*, *1*, 1108–1109.

Petersen, P. (1968). Psychiatric disorders in primary hyperparathyroidism. *Journal of Clinical Endocrinology and Metabolism*, *28*, 1491–1497.

Potts, J. T. (1977). Disorders of parathyroid glands. In T. W. Thorn, R. D. Adams, & E. Braunwald (Eds.), *Harrison's principles of internal medicine*. New York: McGraw-Hill.

Potts, J. T., & Roberts, B. (1958). Clinical significance of magnesium deficiency and its relation to parathyroid disease. *American Journal of the Medical Sciences*. *235*, 206–219.

Prange, A., Loosen, P., Wilson, I., & Lipton, M. (1980). The therapeutic use of hormones of the thyroid axis in depression. In R. Post & J. Ballenger (Eds.), *The neurobiology of mood disorders*. Baltimore: Williams & Wilkins.

Prange, A., Meeks, J., & Lipton, M. (1970). Catecholamines: Diminished rate of norepinephrine biosynthesis in rat brain and heart after thyroxine pretreatment. *Life Sciences*, *9*, 401–406.

Prange, A., Wilson, I., Knox, A., McClane, T., & Lipton, M. (1970). Enhancement of imipramine by thyroid-stimulating hormone: Clinical and theoretical implications. *American Journal of Psychiatry*, *127*, 191–199.

Prange, A., Wilson, I., Rabon, A., & Lipton, M. (1969). Enhancement of imipramine antidepressant activity by thyroid hormone. *American Journal of Psychiatry*, *126*, 457–460.

Reitan, R. (1953). Intellectual functions in myxedema. *AMA Archives of Neurology and Psychiatry*, *69*, 436–448.

Reus, V., Gold, P., & Post, R. (1979). Lithium-induced thyrotoxicosis. *American Journal of Psychiatry*, *136*, 724–725.

Reusch, J., Christiansen, C., Patterson, L., Dewees, S., & Jacobson, A. (1947). Psychological invalidism in thyroidectomized patients. *Psychosomatic Medicine*, *9*, 77–89.

Richter, C., Jones, G., & Biswanger, L. (1959). Periodic phenomena and the thyroid. *AMA Archives of Neurology and Psychiatry*, *81*, 233–255.

Robbins, L., & Vinson, D. (1960). Objective psychological assessment of the thyrotoxic patient and response to treatment. *Journal of Clinical Endocrinology and Metabolism*, *20*, 120–129.

Rockey, P., & Griep, R. (1980). Behavioral dysfunction in hyperthyroidism: Improvement with treatment. *Archives of Internal Medicine*, *140*, 1194–1197.

Rosenqvist, U., & Borens, L. (1972). Enhancement of the α-adrenergic response in aorta from hypothyroid rabbits. *Life Sciences*, *2*, 595–604.

Roy-Byrne, P., Joffe, R., Uhde, E., & Post, R. (1984). Approaches to the evaluation and treatment of rapid-cycling affective illness. *British Journal of Psychiatry*, *145*, 543–550.

Sato, M., Koramoto, K., & Wada, J. (1984). Antiepileptic effects of thyrotropin-releasing hormone and its new derivation, DN-1417, examined in feline amygdaloid kindling preparation. *Epilepsia (New York)*, *25*, 537–544.

Scarpace, P., & Abrass, I. (1981). Thyroid hormone regulations of rat heart, lymphocyte, and lung β-adrenergic receptors. *Endocrinology (Baltimore)*, *108*, 1007–1011.

Schader, R., Belfer, M., & DiMascio, A. (1970). Thyroid function. In R. Schader & A. DiMascio (Eds.), *Psychotropic drug side effects*. Baltimore: Williams & Wilkins.

Schaff, M., & Payne, C. A. (1966). Dystonic reaction to prochlorperazine in hypoparathyroidism. *New England Journal of Medicine*, *275*, 991–994.

Scheinberg, D., Stead, E., Brannon, E., & Warren, J. (1950). Correlative observations on cerebral metabolism and cardiac output in myxedema. *Journal of Clinical Investigation*, *29*, 1139–1150.

Schildkraut, J., Winokur, A., Draskoczy, P., & Hensle, J. (1971). Changes in norepinephrine turnover in rat brain during chronic administration of imipramine: A possible explanation for the delay in onset of clinical antidepressant effects. *American Journal of Psychiatry*, *127*, 72–79.

Schmidt, B., & Schultz, J. (1985). Chronic thyroxine treatment of rats down-regulates the noradrenergic cyclic AMP generating system in cerebral cortex. *Journal of Pharmacology and Experimental Therapeutics*, *233*, 466–472.

Schon, M., Sutherland, A., & Rawson, R. (1961). Hormones and neuroses—the psychological effects of thyroid deficiency. *Proceedings of the Third World Congress of Psychiatry* (Vol. 2, pp. 835–839). Montreal: McGill University Press.

Schwartz, H., & Openheimer, J. (1978). Nuclear triiodothyronine receptor sites in brain: Probable identity with hepatic receptors and regional distribution. *Endocrinology (Baltimore)*, *103*, 267–273.

Shen, F., & Sherrard, D. J. (1982). Lithium-induced hyperparathyroidism: An alteration of the "set-point." *Annals of Internal Medicine*, *96*, 63–65.

Shutov, A., & Prostakova, T. (1970). Clinical features of temporal lobe epilepsy and the functional state of the thyroid [Abstract]. *Zhurnal Nevropatologii Psikhiatrii imeni S.S. Korsakova*, *92*, 459–502.

Silva, J., & Larsen, P. (1978). Contributions of plasma triiodothyronine and local thyroxine monodeiodination to triiodothyronine to nuclear receptor saturation in pituitary, liver, and kidney of hypothyroid rats. *Journal of Clinical Investigation*, *61*, 1247–1259.

Singhal, R., & Rastogi, R. (1978). Neurotransmitter mechanisms during mental illness induced by alterations in thyroid function. *Advances in Pharmacology and Chemotherapy*, *15*, 203–262.

Siris, S., Chertoff, H., & Perel, J. (1979). Rapid-cycling affective disorder during imipramine treatment: A case report, *American Journal of Psychiatry*, *136*, 341–342.

Stancer, H., & Persad, E. (1982). Treatment of intractable rapid-cycling manic–depressive disorder with levothyroxine. *Archives of General Psychiatry*, *37*, 311–312.

Strandjord, R., Aanderud, S., & Myking, O. (1980). Serum levels of thyroid hormones in patients treated with carbamazepine. In R. Conger, F. Angeleri, & J. Perry (Eds.), *Advances in epileptology—Twelfth Epilepsy International Symposium* (pp. 439–443). New York: Raven Press.

St. Goar, W. T. (1957). Gastrointestinal symptoms as a clue to the diagnosis of hyperparathyroidism: A review of 45 cases. *Annals of Internal Medicine*, *XX*, 102–108.

Stolk, J., & Whybrow, P. (1976). Clinical and experimental interrelationships between sympathetic nervous activity and pituitary–thyroid function. In *Cellular and Molecular Bases of Neuroendocrine Processes, Symposium of the International Society of Psychoneuroendocrinology*. Budapest, Hungary: Academy of Sciences Press.

Stone, E. (1983). Problems with the current catecholamine hypotheses of antidepressant agents: Speculations leading to a new hypothesis. *Behavioral and Brain Sciences*, *6*, 535–577.

Sulzer, F. (1978). Functional aspects of the norepinephrine-coupled adenylate cyclase system in the limbic forebrain and its modification by drugs that precipitate or alleviate depression: Molecular approaches to an understanding of affective disorders. *Psychopharmakologie*, *11*, 113–152.

Swanson, J., Kelly, J., & McConahey, W. (1981). Neurologic aspects of thyroid dysfunction. *Mayo Clinic Proceedings*, *56*, 504–512.

Tatar, P., Starar, V., & Vegas, M. (1983). Different response of TSH to TRH in the morning and evening. *Hormone and Metabolic Research*, *15*, 461.

Taylor, J. (1975). Depression in thyrotoxicosis. *American Journal of Psychiatry*, *132*, 552–554.

Telford, J. (1969). Hormonal influences on mediators of allergic reactions. *International Archives of Allergy and Applied Immunology*, *36*, 29–30.

Tonks, C. (1964). Mental illness in hypothyroid patients. *International Journal of Psychiatry*, *110*, 706–710.

Treadway, C., Prange, A., Doehne, E., Edens, C., &

Whybrow, P. (1967). Myxedema psychosis: Clinical and biochemical changes during recovery. *Journal of Psychiatric Research, 5,* 289–296.

Tse, J., Wrenn, R., & Kuo, J. (1980). Thyrotoxicosis-induced changes in characteristics and activities of β-adrenergic receptors and adenosine 3′,5′-monophosphate and quanosine 3′,5′-monophosphate systems in heart may be related to reputed catecholamine supersensitivity in hyperthyroidism. *Endocrinology (Baltimore), 107,* 6–16.

Vetulani, J., Stawarz, R., Dingell, J., & Sulzer, F. (1976). A possible common mechanism of action of antidepressant treatments. *Naunyn-Schmiedeberg's Archives of Pharmacology, 273,* 109–114.

Villani, S., & Wertzel, W. (1979). Secondary mania [Letter]. *Archives of General Psychiatry, 36,* 1031.

Voth, H., Holzman, P., Katz, J., & Wallenstein, R. (1970). Thyroid "hot spots": Their relationship to life stress. *Psychosomatic Medicine, 32,* 561–568.

Wallace, J., MacCrimmon, D., & Goldberg, W. (1980). Acute hyperthyroidism: Cognitive and emotional correlates. *Journal of Abnormal Psychology, 89,* 519–527.

Wallenstein, R., Holzman, P., Voth, H., & Uhr, N. (1965). Thyroid "hot spots": A psychophysiological study. *Psychosomatic Medicine, 6,* 508–523.

Weiner, H. (1977). Psychobiological contributions to human disease. In H. Weiner (Ed.), *Psychobiology and human disease.* Amsterdam: Elsevier Press.

Weiner, M. (1979). Haloperidol, hyperthyroidism, and sudden death. *American Journal of Psychiatry, 136,* 717–718.

Weingarten, H., & Silberman, E. (1984). Cognitive changes in depression. In R. Post & J. Ballenger (Eds.), *Neurobiology of mood disorders.* Baltimore: Williams & Wilkins.

Weiss, B., Heydor, W., & Frazer, A. (1983). Modulation of β-adrenergic receptor–adenylate cyclase system following acute and repeated treatment with antidepressants. In E. Costa & G. Racogni (Eds.), *Typical and atypical antidepressants: Molecular mechanisms.* New York: Raven Press.

Wenzel, K., Meinhold, H., Raffenberg, M., Adlkoffer, F., & Schleusener, H. (1974). Classification of hypothyroidism in evaluating patients after radioactive therapy by serum cholesterol, T3 uptake, total T4, FT4-index, total T3, basal TSH, and TRH test. *European Journal of Clinical Investigation, 4,* 141–148.

Whybrow, P., Coppen, A., Prange, A., Noguera, R., & Bailey, J. (1972). Thyroid function and the response to liothyronine in depression. *Archives of General Psychiatry, 26,* 242–245.

Whybrow, P., & Prange, A. (1981). A hypothesis of thyroid–catecholamine–receptor interaction: Its relevance to affective illness. *Archives of General Psychiatry, 38,* 106–113.

Whybrow, P., Prange, A., & Treadway, C. (1969). Mental changes accompanying thyroid gland dysfunction. *Archives of General Psychiatry, 20,* 48–62.

Williams, L., Guthrow, C., & Lefkowitz, R. (1979). β-Adrenergic receptors of human lymphocytes are unaltered in hyperthyroidism. *Journal of Clinical Endocrinology and Metabolism, 48,* 503–505.

Williams, L., Lefkowitz, R., Watanabe, A., Hathoway, D., & Besch, R. (1977). Thyroid hormone regulation of β-adrenergic receptor number. *Journal of Biological Chemistry, 253,* 2787–2789.

Wilson, W., & Johnson, J. (1964). Thyroid hormone and brain function. I and II. *Electroencephalography and Clinical Neurophysiology, 16,* 321–331.

Wilson, W., Johnson, J., & Smith, R. (1962). Affective changes in thyrotoxicosis and experimental hypermetabolism. *Recent Advances in Biological Psychiatry, 4,* 234–242.

Witten, A., & deWied, D. (1980). Hypothalamic polypeptides and behavior. In P. Morgane & J. Panksepp (Eds.), *Handbook of the hypothalamus.* New York: Marcel Dekker.

Witschy, J., & Redmond, F. (1981). Extrapyramidal reaction to fluphenazine potentiated by thyrotoxicosis. *American Journal of Psychiatry, 138,* 246–249.

3 DISORDERS OF THE ADRENAL CORTEX AND GONADS

VICTOR I. REUS

University of California, San Francisco School of Medicine

INTRODUCTION

Disorders of adrenal and gonadal function represent some of the earliest examples of medical interest in the relationship between behavioral and hormonal function. Speculations that certain behavioral changes derived from pathological changes in gonadal anatomy can be found in the Egyptian papyri. Similar observations have continued to appear the the medical literature until the present day. Although definitive systematic investigations are rare and most current textbooks of endocrinology ignore such symptomatology entirely, a report by the superintendent of the New York State Lunatic Asylum in the year 1852 attributed one-quarter of 366 cases of insanity to causes directly connected with the reproductive system (Storer, 1871). Similarly, Bucknill and Tuke noted in 1858 in the foremost textbook of the time that "the reproductive organs are frequently the seat of disease, or abnormal function. Among male idiots and imbeciles, instances of deficit and excessive development of these organs are common; and the female population of every large asylum contains several instances of that masculine development of frame and constitution which indicates an abnormal formation of the sexual organ" (Bucknill & Tuke, 1858, p. 436). Disorders of the adrenal cortex were not specifically identified until more recent times, but behavioral signs and symptoms have been recognized as prominent and integral aspects of these disorders since the original reports. Cushing himself, in an early report (Cushing, 1913), noted that primary secretory disturbances were frequently associated with behavioral change, as did Addison in his original description in 1855 of the disease which now bears his name (Addison, 1855/1968). Medical interest in the effects of endocrinological disturbances on human behavior peaked in the 1920s and 1930s with the publication of a number of enthusiastic monographs (Berman, 1922; Fay, 1922).

Despite recent technological advances in assay techniques and the delineation of specific endocrinological pathology in primary psychiatric conditions which have led to a resurgence of interest in this literature, much of the actual data available are anecdotal and unquantified. Why behavioral symptomatology is either ignored or considered nonspecific in otherwise exhaustive and refined explorations of primary endocrine disorders is unclear. It should not be too controversial, however, to suggest that a closer inspection of behavioral changes in such disorders may aid in an understanding of the basic mechanisms of behavioral change in primary psychiatric disorders and, ultimately, of the regulation of normal behavioral function as well.

DISORDERS OF GONADAL FUNCTION

The Testes

Male Hypogonadism

Male hypogonadism has been classified according to etiology, hormone level, or anatomic pathology. The behavioral consequences of alteration in gonadal function depend largely on the stage in development in which the alteration occurs, the degree and pattern of change in gonadal hormone level, and the psychosocial response to such alterations. With the onset of puberty in the male, the secretion of testosterone increases almost 20-fold. Although there is some evidence that increases in these hormones are associated with increased aggressiveness and impulsive behavior in normal individuals, the most clear associations between androgen level and behavior have been reported in individuals suffering from decreased gonadal function. Such individuals show a significant decrement in sexual libido and aggressiveness. These effects are usually more evident if the reduction in hormone levels occurs before puberty, as acknowledged by a writer in 1640 who, in referring to the castration of prepubertal boys in order to preserve their high-pitched voices, noted that "they are all (considered) cowards, devoid of genius for literature, or any solid study. . ." (quoted in Heriot, 1975). That decrease in libido was not an invariable characteristic of castration can be noted in descriptions of the lives of some of the most famous castrati who were noted to have been involved in, if anything, greater than normal sexual activity.

The behavioral effects of hypogonadism have been most prominently studied in Klinefelter syndrome, a genetic disorder in which individuals have at least one extra X chromosome (47, XXY) (Ratcliffe, Bancroft, Axworthy, & McLaren, 1982). In addition to the prominent physical changes of increased height, decreased facial hair, small testes, and absent sperm production, a number of such individuals also suffer from mental retardation or a behavioral syndrome which includes features of passivity, mental dullness, and decreased libido. Laignel-Lavastine (1919), in a definitive monograph outlining the most common behavioral changes associated with

disorders of "internal secretions," observed that "testicular insufficiency" was associated with "loss of desire, impotency, senility . . . and asthenia" (p. 18). He also noted a "persistence of youth, and no arterial hypertension, activity, moral or physical energy" (p. 18). As was noted in the case of castration, however, certain individuals may present with none of these signs or symptons.

Specific behavioral effects are also noted with the onset of androgen therapy. These may include, besides increased libido and aggression, insomnia, irritability, and pressured thought. If replacement therapy is not initiated until adulthood, restoration of sexual libido and sexual maturity is seldom complete.

Testosterone and Aggression

The relationship between behavioral function and testosterone level in pathological gonadal disorders has also been examined in studies of the 47, XYY karyotype. Several early studies purported an increased incidence of aggressive behavior in individuals carrying this genetic profile and suggested that such behavior might be mediated by increased testosterone secretion (Money et al., 1975). Unfortunately, most current evidence, although not definitive, would suggest no clear relationship. Operational difficulties in the characterization of aggressive behavior and inclusion of many patients with mental retardation have confounded the interpretation of several salient studies.

Despite these factors, some investigations have shown beneficial behavioral effects associated with antiandrogen therapy, most commonly medroxyprogesterone acetate or cyproterone (R. T. Rubin, Reinisch, & Haskett, 1981). The effect on decreasing sexual paraphilias was most evident, with the effect on aggression and antisocial behavior less clear. In addition to papers describing XYY males as impulsive and prone to sociopathy, associations with schizophrenia have been reported (Haberman, Hollingsworth, Falek, & Michael, 1975). There is no evidence that this association is anything other than fortuitous, however. Several complete reviews of this conflictual literature have recently appeared for the reader wishing a more detailed summary (R. Rubin, 1982).

One of the most common causes of hypogonadism in adult life is testicular cancer. There is some evidence that men with testicular cancer of the germ cell type experience significant psychic disturbance *before* the onset of cancer. In a careful controlled study, Gorzynski, Lebovits, Holland, and Vugrin (1981) found a significantly higher rate of psychiatric disturbance in a testicular cancer group than a control group of males with acute leukemia. This was most evident in areas of somatic concern, level of general functioning, impulse control, and reality testing. Schizophenia was diagnosed in seven individuals, four of whom had associated cryptorchidism. In addition, a high incidence of opiate drug abuse was found among the testicular cancer group. Although this study did not address issues of etiology, the authors speculated that these behavioral findings may be examples of secondary effects of pituitary gonadal dysregulation on endogenous opiates and dopamine.

Androgen Insensitivity Syndrome (Testicular Feminization)

In this syndrome, particularly in its more incomplete presentation, a genetic and gonadal male who has the capacity to synthesize testosterone will fail to become masculinized. This appears to be a genetically transmitted defect in which the sensitivity of the target organ to testosterone is blocked. Because in the complete form of the disorder the external genitalia may be identical to that of a normal female, testicular feminization syndrome has attracted the attention of investigators who wished to distinguish the contributions of psychological mechanisms and hormonal agents to normal feminine sexual behavior. In an early paper, Money, Ehrhardt, and Masica (1968) found such individuals to be exclusively feminine in their gender role. Such individuals tended to play with dolls in childhood and expressed a desire for historically female occupations in adulthood. Generally normal sexual libido and response as well as maternal behavior have also been reported (Vague, 1983).

The hormonal findings associated with testicular feminization syndrome are somewhat variable. Androgen levels may be normal or elevated while serum estradiol levels are usually normal. Some specific changes have been noted in association with increased estrogen levels in male adulthood. In one particularly provocative but unreplicated study, Dawson (1966) found that certain males manifested gynecomastia as a result of liver damage secondary to kwashiorkor protein deficiency disease. In addition to an acquired testicular atrophy, these feminized males also exhibited significant change in sex-associated cognitive functions; that is, the usual male ratio of higher spatial to lower verbal skills had been reversed.

Homosexuality

Several early studies suggested alterations in absolute androgen level or in ratio of androsterone to other steroids in homosexual males. Most investigations since, however, have failed to reproduce these findings, although there are reports that unbound levels of testosterone as well as response to estrogens may be altered in some individuals. It has also been suggested that findings of decreased testosterone concentration in association with elevated luteinizing hormone in some homosexual men may represent a down-regulation of testicular receptors (Gladue, Green, & Hellman, 1984). The absence of independent validation of these findings makes their interpretation difficult at this time.

Disorders of Ovarian Function

Ovarian dysfunction may take many forms and no satisfactory classification of etiology currently exists. In general, observations of behavioral change in these disorders have been anecdotal and have focused principally on the psychological response to the absent or increased development of secondary sexual characteristics. In this regard, an early report (Laignel-Lavastine, 1919) notes that precocious puberty and "hyperovaria" were associated with "uneasiness, causing movement and action, nervous debility, tendency to loquacity, and erotic crises" (p. 18). Similarly, primary or secondary ovarian failure and subsequent delay of secondary sexual characteristics have been found to be associated with psychological trauma during adolescence and productive of anxiety and social withdrawal. One disorder that has received more specific attention is that of polycystic ovary disease. Several reports have noted that this diagnosis may be associated with complaints of depression, decreased libido, agitation, and irritability (Orenstein & Raskind, 1983). A number of such women have also been found to suffer from complex partial seizures, leading to a hypothesis of an extra-hypothalamic pathogenesis (Herzog, Seibel, Schomer, Vaitukaitis, & Geschwind, 1984).

Another estrogen deficiency state that appears to be associated with behavioral change is Turner's Syndrome (XO). Although such individuals are not genetically female and lack ovaries, they develop normal female external genitalia because of a lack of exposure to androgen prenatally. In addition to a characteristic physical appearance involving short stature and webbing of the neck, Turner's Syndrome patients appear to have a characteristic personality pattern as well, being described as "generally open, friendly, warm-hearted, and lacking in aggressiveness and sex drive" (Brown, 1975, p. 78). When a group of patients with Turner's Syndrome was compared to controls by Ehrhardt, Greenberg, and Money (1970), the patients were noted to be more passive during fights in childhood and more likely to withdraw from a fight than to defend themselves. Similarly, they showed a greater interest in doll play than in more characteristic male-oriented activities. These findings have been interpreted as showing that a feminine gender identity can develop in the absence of prenatal gonadal hormones or a second X chromosome (Al-Issa, 1982).

In general, libido in both males and females appears to be controlled more by androgen levels than by ovarian steroids. Estrogen is clearly necessary for the maturation and maintenance of female secondary sexual characteristics and, when administered to males in the course of cancer chemotherapy, results in behavioral effects similar to those observed in castration. How these effects are mediated is as yet unclear. Estrogens and progestins have many complex independent and interactive effects on nerve cells (Pfaff & McEwen, 1983) and have been localized to a variety of specific sites in brain, including the medial preoptic area, midline hypothalamus, and such limbic structures

as the medial amygdala and lateral septum. In addition to modulation of different parameters of sexual motivation and action, ovarian hormones have significant regulatory effects on most of the major neurotransmitter systems (McEwen, 1981). The combined use of autoradiography and fluorescence histochemistry has revealed that sex steroid target sites can be identified in the nuclei of many catecholamine cell bodies and catecholamine nerve terminals localized to specific steroid hormone target neurons (Heritage, Stumpf, Madhabananda, & Grant, 1980). Physiological alteration in estrogen level may also be associated with functional change in the number of serotonergic, noradrenergic, and dopaminergic receptors in brain (Biegon, Reches, Snyder, & McEwen, 1983; Euvrard, Oberlander, & Boissier, 1980). Even in the absence of specific behavioral studies, these data suggest that disorders of ovarian function affecting steroid production and release would have pronounced effects on neurochemical and behavioral activity (Salmon & Geist, 1943; Sopchak & Sutherland, 1960; Waxenburg, Finkbeiner, Drellich, & Sutherland, 1960).

DISORDERS OF THE ADRENAL CORTEX

Addison's Disease

Thomas Addison made the observation in 1855 that hypofunction of the adrenal cortex could result in "mind wandering," "delirium," "indisposition to mental exertion," and "languor" (Addison, 1855/1968). Some years later the esteemed German psychiatrist Griesinger (1882) noted that "in Addison's Disease there is generally great depression of sentiment . . ." (p. 138). It is interesting that despite their physiological differences, the psychiatric picture of Addison's disease is often much like that of Cushing's syndrome. The most salient symptoms include depression, apathy, fatigue, anhedonia, poverty of thought, negativism, and social withdrawal (Brown, 1975; Whitlock, 1982). In acute stages of the disease, an organic psychosis can occur, complete with cognitive impairment, delirium, and in extreme cases, stupor or coma. As concluded by Engel and

Margolin (1941), the frequency of these symptoms in this syndrome is high, with apathy and negativism appearing in 80% of the cases and depression and irritability in approximately one-half of all patients studied. Classic paranoid and catatonic states and bipolar affective disorders have been seen in as many as 10% of the patient population and, like the more usual physiological symptoms, have responded dramatically to glucocorticoid treatment (Cleghorn & Pattee, 1953). Correction of the electrolyte imbalance commonly seen in this disorder does not in itself result in improvement in behavioral symptomatology. Resolution of behavioral pathology by glucocorticoid replacement is seldom complete, however, since exogenous replacement can never match the fine-tuned circadian and stress-responsive release characteristic of the histologically normal gland. These observations would indicate that a chronological review of the medical history of one of the most well-known sufferers from Addison's disease, former President John F. Kennedy, might be of interest.

Psychiatric symptoms may sometimes present as primary features. In one recent particularly well-described case, a patient with Addison's disease was initially diagnosed as suffering from bereavement and conversion disorder (Demilio, Dackis, Gold, & Ehrenkranz, 1984). This individual complained of weakness and shortness of breath during exertion and reported a 3-week history of "empty" mood, anhedonia, crying, decreased concentration, impaired sleep, nausea, and appetite and weight loss. Depression per se does not appear to be characteristic of adolescents with juvenile Addison's disease (Money & Jobaris, 1977), but it should be noted that the assessment of the patients in this study was retrospective, occurring after a course of treatment ranging from 1 to 23 years. Apathy, less school achievement, and reduced play participation were, however, prominent in the history of these individuals, paralleling earlier observations in adults (Michael & Gibbons, 1963).

In addition to these more gross descriptions of behavior, changes in sensory function and sleep regulation have been reported. Henkin and colleagues, in a series of papers (Henkin, 1975; Henkin & Bartter, 1966; Henkin & Daly, 1968), demonstrated that in the absence of glucocorticoids sensory detection acuity for several sensory modalities was enhanced, while sensory "integration" was depressed. Correction of this deficiency was associated with a return of sensory detection and integration to normal levels. Individuals with Cushing's syndrome were found to have both depressed acuity and impaired sensory integration. Direct investigation of the visual-evoked response in Addison's patients revealed that when steroid levels were low, the potentials were of small amplitude and short latency. Increasing steroid level in normal subjects prolonged latency of visual-evoked response while administration of glucocorticoids increased and corticotropin decreased it in a patient population (Buchsbaum & Henkin, 1975; Koppell et al., 1970). Patients with Addison's disease were also found to have a relative decrease in δ sleep (stages 3 and 4) and δ percentage, both of which rose following withdrawal of hormonal replacement therapy (Gillin, Jacobs, Snyder, & Henkin, 1974a). Delta sleep also appeared to increase after the direct administration of ACTH to patients with adrenal cortical insufficiency, in the absence of any other effects on rapid eye movement sleep or total sleep (Gillin, Jacobs, Schneider, & Henkin, 1974b).

The actual mechanisms involved in these alterations of behavioral response remain obscure. It is still not clear, for example, whether such changes as have been described should be attributed to the adrenocortical deficiency itself or to the markedly increased levels of corticotropin (ACTH) and corticotropin-releasing factor (CRF) that arise in the disorder as the result of loss of feedback inhibition. Evidence for specific effects of ACTH and, more recently, CRF on attentional and affective processes and social behavior would appear to indicate that earlier conclusions regarding the primacy of the influence of glucocorticoids themselves might be premature (Beckwith & Sandman, 1982; Kalin, Shelton, Kraemer, & McKinney, 1983; Britton, Koob, Rivier, & Vale, 1982).

Cushing's Syndrome

The term Cushing's syndrome is applied to a family of disorders differing in etiology, with the same primary endocrine abnormality, an excessive production of cortisol and, sometimes, adrenal androgens (Krieger, 1983). Although adrenal tumors were originally thought to be the most common cause of the syndrome, current data would indicate that in most cases of the syndrome the causal agent is a pituitary tumor, usually a small, benign, basophil adenoma which rarely increases in size sufficient to increase intracranial pressure. The term Cushing's syndrome has also been applied to syndromes of secondary hypercortisolism such as may occur with ACTH-secreting bronchial malignancies. In an unknown percentage of cases the primary pathological locus is neither at the adrenal nor pituitary, but at a hypothalamic or limbic site. The hypercortisolism that appears in such cases of "diencephalic" Cushing's disease is theoretically secondary to an excessive production of CRF, and a consequent increased secretion of ACTH and cortisol. Although the term Cushing's disease is most accurately applied to those disorders in which the hypercortisolism is secondary to intracranial pathology, most investigations of behavioral change in these disorders historically made no distinction between the terms. Accordingly, for the sake of consistency this review will use the more general term Cushing's syndrome, including individuals with hypothesized Cushing's disease as well.

Physical Features

Twenty years before his classic monograph, "The Basophil Adenomas of the Pituitary Body and Their Clinical Manifestations," Harvey Cushing described a patient who exhibited central obesity, increased body hair, amenorrhea, muscle weakness, abdominal striae, and a round dusky face. Other features now recognized in classic presentations include supraclavicular fat distribution, hypertension, glycosuria, osteoporosis, and impotence and testicular atrophy in the male. Though such textbook examples would seldom pose a diagnostic problem for the nonspecialist, it has become clear that these signs are neither invariably found nor specific to individuals who meet laboratory criteria for Cushing's syndrome (Reus, 1984; Reus & Berlant, 1986). Several objective surveys have found that fewer than half the cases diagnosed according to laboratory standards present with classical features, while the signs themselves occur in high prevalence in the general population (Aron, Tyrrell, Fitzgerald, Findling, & Forsham, 1981; Ross & Linch, 1982).

Behavioral Symptoms

Regardless of the specific etiology, patients with Cushing's syndrome frequently report or show signs of a change in mental status. Thus far, there is no agreement that hypercortisolemic states are associated with a specific behavioral profile, but changes in affect and cognition are most frequently reported. In presenting his original series, Cushing noted that one of his patients was "without energy, easily fatigued, unable to concentrate his mind on his work, and fits of unnatural irritability alternated with periods of depression" (Cushing, 1932, p. 177). Since that time, most investigators have found evidence for psychiatric disturbance in more than 50% of cases studied (Carroll, 1977; Spillane, 1951; Whybrow & Hurwitz, 1976). As in Trethowan and Cobb's (1952) original series of 25 patients, depression emerges as the most common type of mental alteration, with psychosis also occurring in 10–15% of cases (Hurxthal & O'Sullivan, 1959; Starr, 1952).

Suicidal ideation or action may accompany the depressed mood in approximately 10% of patients and sleep disturbance is common (Krieger & Glick, 1974). The character of the mood disorder may vary from that of a chronic depression to that of a more cyclic alteration, with associated features of irritability, sleeplessness, disturbed concentration and memory, anxiety, and motoric overactivity. In a consecutive unselected series of 29 patients collected by Cohen (1980), 86% of the patients demonstrated symptoms of tearfulness, irritability, somatic preoccupation, sleeplessness, and depersonalization. Interestingly, there was a family history of depression or suicide in half the cases and, in 20%, a major emotional disturbance preceded the onset of somatic symptomatology. These behavioral findings were essentially confirmed by a prospective study conducted by Kelly, Checkley, and Bender (1980). A follow-up study of this same group demonstrated a significant decrease in symptoms of depression in association with reduction of urinary-free cortisol values after 3 and 12 months of treatment (Kelly, Checkley, Bender, & Mashiter, 1983).

Some patients diagnosed as having Cushing's syndrome present with a lifelong history of bipolar affective disorder antedating as well as associated with the characteristic somatic changes associated with the disorder. Reed, Watkins, and Dobson (1983) presented one such case in which a pituitary tumor was uncovered and where surgical removal led to the resolution of the psychiatric symptomatology. Another patient with diagnosed intermittent or "transient" Cushing's syndrome was described by Bochner, Burke, Lloyd, and Nurnberg (1979). This individual had five episodes of severe suicidal depression, each associated with recurrence of the signs and symptoms of Cushing's syndrome. The behavioral symptomatology remitted following bilateral adrenalectomy. Similar presenting histories and resolutions have been reported by Smith, Kohler, Helminiak, and Carroll (1982), Pasqualini and Gurevicj (1956), and Zondek and Leszynsky (1956).

In some cases, the behavioral change may be the most prominent presenting feature of the syndrome. Though such signs and symptoms may be merely harbingers of somatic changes to come, in some cases, particularly those individuals with episodic rather than constant hypercortisolemia, the cushingoid pathology may be mild, evanescent, and nonprogressive. In a particularly intriguing case report by Saad et al. (1984), a 37-year-old woman presented with acute psychosis and cognitive impairment, but no cushingoid feature other than mild generalized obesity. She showed both transient hypersecretion of cortisol and a paradoxical response to dexamethasone. Removal of a Crooke's cell adenoma resulted in resolution of her manic symptomatology, which included agitation, insomnia, visual hallucinations, religious delusions, and compulsive behaviors.

In an effort to objectify the neuropsychological deficit frequently occurring in Cushing's syndrome, Whelan, Schteingart, Starkman, and Smith (1980) administered a general neuropsychological test battery to a series of 35 patients. One-third of the group had moderate to severe impairment in language and nonlanguage tests of higher cortical and sensory and motor system function. Ten patients had more mild altrations, while 13 patients showed no deviations from normal performance. The deficits were most marked in spatial and visual ideational assessments and were particularly evident in the Picture Arrangement subtest of the Weschler and the Symbol Digit subtest (Starkman & Schteingart, 1981). This same series of patients was found in a later paper (Starkman, Schteingart, & Schork, 1981) to exhibit parallel alterations in mood and physiological function (i.e., decreased libido and sleep disturbance) consistent with the changes described by previous investigators. Interestingly, a statistically significant relationship was reported between an overall index of behavioral impairment and plasma ACTH level. Patients with primary adrenal adenomas, having high cortisol but low ACTH levels, did not appear to experience severe affective symptoms or the same degree of cognitive impairment.

Other more rare examples of behavioral disorders have also been linked to Cushing's syndrome in the medical literature. In one case report, a female patient developed pituitary-based Cushing's syndrome following a number of years in which she experienced the classic somatic and psychological symptoms of anorexia nervosa (Kontula, Mustajoki, Paetau, & Pelkonen, 1984). This pathological association may be simply coincidental, but many of the changes in hypothalamic–pituitary–adrenal function evident in anorexia nervosa bear striking similarity to changes occurring in Cushing's syndrome. Since systematic investigation of the prevalence of pituitary adenoma in anorexia nervosa is lacking, it is unknown to what extent this hypothesized etiology may occur in other individuals presenting with the syndrome.

Etiological Considerations

As noted by Pepper and Krieger (1984), the high incidence of mood and cognitive changes in Cushing's syndrome has led to questions as to whether these behavioral signs and symptoms represent the secondary effects of alteration in central neurotransmitter function in parallel with the endocrine disturbance or whether, conversely, the behavioral alterations are reflective of an antecedent alteration in central nervous system function *induced* by the primary endocrine disorder. It has also been suggested that in some cases the ACTH and cortisol hypersecretion are triggered in some fashion by a primary emotional stress, perhaps in genetically vulnerable individuals or, alternatively, that the behavioral changes occur only in individuals who have some underlying psychological vulnerability to the stresses attendant to the disease process. This latter hypothesis, although of historical interest, is not supported by current data.

The best evidence that behavioral changes in Cushing's syndrome are directly related to alteration of ACTH or cortisol level comes from observations of similar behavioral phenomena resulting in individuals who, for one reason or another, have changes in the levels of these hormones from exogenous sources. The relative contribution of ACTH versus cortisol to the induction of behavioral change remains controversial and obscure. Carroll (1977) found a considerably greater rate of depression in patients with Cushing's disease than individuals with Cushing's syndrome, a finding supported by some investigators (Cohen, 1980; Gifford & Gunderson, 1970; Taft, Martin, & Melick, 1970), but not others (Jeffcoate, Silverstone, Edwards, & Besser, 1979). Metyrapone, which dramatically increases ACTH, has been used therapeutically for mental symptoms secondary to Cushing's syndrome (Kramlinger, Peterson, Watson, & Leonard, 1985). One illness model that would be particularly useful for examining the specific contribution of corticotropin to the alteration in mental state is Nelson's syndrome in which high circulating levels of corticotropin develop following bilateral adrenalectomy for Cushing's disease. Specific behavioral assessments of patients with Nelson's syndrome are rare, although Kelly, Checkley, and Bender (1980) noted that none of their four patients met criteria for Major Depression.

Early reports of the therapeutic usage of corticotropin and cortisone noted a frequent occurrence of minor emotional changes such as euphoria and irritability, but also, more selectively, the development of psychotic conditions in certain patients, usually characterized by a paranoid/depressive presentation, but sometimes as mania or stupor (Glaser, 1953; Rome & Braceland, 1952). There did not seem to be any differences between the responses to cortisone and to ACTH or any relation to the pathological condition for which these treatments were administered. A review of the available clinical literature would suggest that the behavioral effects can be predicted to a degree by the dosage of medication administered and the length of time it is given. Acute treatment is more classically associated with a marked feeling of well-being, hyperactivity, increased appetite, insomnia, and mild anxiety or irritability. As a result, some individuals develop a marked dependency on glucocorticoids and self-administer these drugs in an abusive fashion (Dixon & Christy, 1980; Flavin, Frederickson, Richardson, & Merritt, 1983; Gifford, Murawski, Kline, & Sachar, 1977). Generally, patients on an equivalent daily dose of 40 mg of prednisone or more appear to be at greatest risk for the development of steroid psychosis, the onset usually occurring within several days from the start of treatment (R. C. W. Hall, Popkin, Stickney, & Gardner, 1979). In rare circumstances, however, very low doses of steroid (i.e., 7.5 mg of prednisolone) have resulted in psychotic experiences in a much shorter period of time (Greeves, 1984). In the large majority of cases, the behavioral pathology abates quickly in response to decreased corticosteroid administration. Again, exceptions have been reported, such as a case in which steroid administration precipitated bipolar illness which persisted despite discontinuation of the medication (Pies, 1981).

More recent studies have attempted to quantify the character of the behavioral pathology more specifically and the various risk factors involved (Lewis & Smith, 1983; Ling, Perry, & Tsuang, 1981; von Zerssen, 1974). There is no characteristic pathognomonic presentation, although emotional lability, "sensory flooding," intermittent memory impairment, and mutism stand out as rather unique qualities to the traditional symptom structure of the affective disturbances usually recorded (R. C. W. Hall *et al.*,

1979). The acute development of obsessive–compulsive behavior may be yet another unique sign of steroid-induced behavioral change (Bick, 1983) in light of animal studies in which the administration of steroids centrally results in marked stereotypical behaviors.

A continuing theme linking the behavioral changes associated with Cushing's syndrome and those induced by exogenous steroids is the similarity of the symptoms delineated to those of primary bipolar affective disorder (Becker, Gold, & Chrousos, 1983). This is best illustrated with patients who receive alternate day corticosteroid therapy and who can develop a syndrome of rapid mood cycling akin to that observed in bipolar patients (Sharfstein, Sack, & Fauci, 1982). The available data regarding efficacy of treatment of steroid psychosis are supportive as well in that tricyclics appear to exacerbate the syndrome (R. C. W. Hall, Popkin, & Kirkpatrick, 1978) while lithium is prophylactic (Falk, Mahnke, & Poskanzer, 1979; Goggans, Weisberg, & Koran, 1983).

Possible Mechanisms of Action

Given that exogenous or endogenous alteration of adrenocortical function will result in frequent and to some extent characteristic changes in behavioral expression, how are such effects mediated? Unfortunately, the complexity of the manner in which glucocorticoids interact with the central nervous system function prohibits a definitive response to this question, and it is likely that genetic, state-dependent, and pharmacodynamic factors are important variables in assessing the organismic response to an alteration in this system at any particular point. Glucocorticoids are phylogenetically old substances, the specific receptor sites for these hormones being found in every tissue in the body. Glucocorticoids may have both immediate and more prolonged effects, acting genomically on cell nuclei where they appear to be involved in the synthesis of messenger RNA and affect the modulation of gene expression through the recognition of specific DNA sequences (Firestone, Payvar, & Yamamoto, 1982; Karin *et al.*, 1984; Pfahl, McGinnis, & Hendricks, 1983). Some of the enzymes regulated are involved directly in the synthesis of

major neurotransmitters. Those areas of brain, such as the hippocampus, septum, and hypothalamus, which have the highest affinity for glucocorticoids are ideally situated for the regulation of neurotransmitter systems affecting attention, perception, and mood (E. D. Hall, 1982). Electrophysiologically, glucocorticoids have important effects on the modulation of unit cell activities in these sites. Biochemically, both glucocorticoids and ACTH directly affect catecholamine, indolamine, and GABAergic synthesis, release, and receptor sensitivity (Schubert, La Corbiere, Klier, & Steinbach, 1980; Versteeg, 1980). Glucocorticoids, for example, decrease norepinephrine turnover (Iuvone, Morasco, & Dunn, 1977), increase tyrosine hydroxylase activity (Sze & Hedrick, 1983), regulate the sensitivity of noradrenaline receptor-coupled adenylate cyclase (Mobley & Sulser, 1980), promote a high-affinity state of β-adrenergic receptors (Davies & Lefkowitz, 1981), induce tryptophan oxygenase (Altar, Bennett, Wallace, & Yuwoler, 1983), modify serotonin uptake (Lee & Chan, 1984), increase serotonergic monosynaptic reflex activation (E. D. Hall, 1980), increase plasma-free dopamine (Rothchild *et al.*, 1984), modify the activity of dopamine receptors (E. D. Hall & Tyler, 1983), affect phospholipid metabolism (Farese, 1984), and decrease GABA receptor binding (Kendall, McEwen, & Enna, 1982). Corticotropin has been found to have somewhat parallel regulatory effects (Dunn & Gispen, 1977; Dunn & Schotman, 1981; Enna & Duman, 1983; Gothert, 1981; Olpe & Jones, 1982). Interactions of both ACTH and cortisol with other neuropeptide systems such as the opiomelanotropinergic system may also be relevant to an understanding of a mental state (O'Donohue & Dorsa, 1982). Alternatively, of course, the neurorendocrine and behavioral changes may simply be secondary effects of a primary neurotransmitter alteration. Sachar (1975) suggested, for example, that the hypercortisolemia and depressive symptomatology seen in some psychiatric patients might be the result of a central norepinephrine deficiency state. More recent evidence would indicate that serotonergic (Lewis & Sherman, 1984), dopaminergic (Snider & Kuchel, 1983), cholinergic, and GABAergic (Jones *et al.*, 1984) systems are also important in the regulation of adreno-cortical function and should not be excluded prematurely.

In a few cases, structural changes induced by glucocorticoids may be responsible for the mental changes noted. A number of patients with Cushing's syndrome exhibit cerebral atrophy on CT scan (Heinz, Martinez, & Haenggeli, 1977), and animal studies indicate that alteration of adrenal hormone level significantly affects gross and microscopic brain structure (DeKosky, Scheff, & Cotman, 1984; Devenport & Devenport, 1982). An association between cortisol hypersecretion and increased ventricular size on CT scan has also been reported in depressed patients (Kellner, Rubinow, Gold, & Post, 1983).

Adrenocortical Virilizing Syndrome

In certain individuals, the adrenal cortex hypersecretes androgens in association with, or independently from adrenocorticoids. In the few patients studied from a behavioral standpoint, there is no definitive evidence that the disorders were associated with alteration in sexual habit or choice (in the male) (Money & Lewis, 1982). In the female, the behavioral effects rest on relatively indirect studies relying on evaluation of exogenous androgenic treatment. Research in this area is confounded by the small number of subjects available, marked variance in the age of onset and symptomatic effect, and an anecdotal case history approach to behavioral evaluation.

References

Addison, T. (1968). *A collection of the publisher's writings of the late Thomas Addison, M.D, physician to Guys Hospital*. London: New Sydenham Society. (Original work published 1855.)

Al-Issa, I. (1982). Gender, hormones, and psychopathology In I. Al-Issa (Ed.), *Gender and psychopathology* (pp. 279–304). New York: Academic Press.

Altar, C. A., Bennett, B. L., Wallace, R., & Yuwoler, A. (1983). Glucocorticoid induction of tryptophan oxygenase: Attenuation by intragastrically administered carbohydrates and metabolites. *Biochemical Pharmacology, 32*, 979–984.

Aron, D. C., Tyrrell, J. B., Fitzgerald, P. A., Findling, J. W., & Forsham, P. H. (1981). Cushing's syndrome: Problems in diagnosis. *Medicine (Baltimore), 60*, 25–35.

Bancroft, J., Axworthy, O., & Ratcliffe, S. (1982). The personality and psycho-sexual development of boys with 47XXY chromosome constitution. *J. Child Psychology & Psychiatry, 23*(2), 169–180.

Becker, L., Gold, P., & Chrousos, G. (1983). Analogies between Cushing's disease and depression: A case report. *General Hospital Psychiatry, 5*, 89–91.

Beckwith, B. E., & Sandman, C. A. (1982). Central nervous system and peripheral effects of ACTH, MSH, and related neuropeptides. *Peptides (New York), 3*, 411–420.

Berman, L. (1922). *The glands regulating personality*. New York: Macmillan.

Bick, P. A. (1983). Obsessive–compulsive behavior associated with dexamethasone treatment. *Journal of Nervous and Mental Disease, 171*, 253–254.

Biegon, A., Reches, A., Snyder, L., and McEwen, B. S. (1983). Serotonergic and noradrenergic receptors in the rat brain: Modulation by chronic exposure to ovarian hormones. *Life Sciences, 32*, 2015–2021.

Bochner, F., Burke, C. J., Lloyd, H. M., & Nurnberg, B. J. (1979). Intermittent Cushing's disease. *American Journal of Medicine, 67*, 507–509.

Britton, D. R., Koob, G. F., Rivier, J., & Vale, W. (1982). Intraventricular corticotropin-releasing factor enhances behavioral effects of novelty. *Life Sciences, 31*, 363–367.

Brown, G. M. (1975). Psychiatric and neurologic aspects of endocrine disease. *Hospital Practice, 10*, 71–79.

Buchsbaum, M. S., & Henkin, R. I. (1975). Effects of carbohydrate-active steroids and ACTH on visually evoked responses in patients with adrenal cortical insufficiency. *Neuroendocrinology, 19*, 314–322.

Bucknill, J., & Tuke, D. (1858), *A manual of psychological medicine*. Philadelphia: Blanchard & Lea.

Carroll, B. J. (1977). Psychiatric disorders and steroids. In E. Usdin, D. A. Hamburg, & J. D. Barchas (Eds.), *Neuroregulators and psychiatric disorders* (pp. 276–283). New York: Oxford University Press.

Cleghorn, R. A., & Pattee, C. L. (1953). Psychological changes in three cases of Addison's disease during treatment with cortisone. *Journal of Clinical Endocrinology and Metabolism, 14*, 344–352.

Cohen, S. I. (1980). Cushing's syndrome: A psychiatric study of 29 patients. *British Journal of Psychiatry, 136*, 120–124.

Cushing, H. (1913). Psychic disturbances associated with disorders of the ductless glands. *American Journal of Insanity, 69*, 965–990.

Cushing. H. (1932). The basophil adenomas of the pituitary body and their clinical manifestations (pituitary basophilism). *Bulletin of the Johns Hopkins Hospital, 50*, 137–195.

Davies, A. O., & Lefkowitz, R. J. (1981). Agonist-promoted high-affinity state of the β-adrenergic receptor in human neutrophils: Modulation by corticosteroids. *Journal of Clinical Endocrinology and Metabolism, 53*, 703–708.

Dawson, J. (1966). Kwashiorkor gynecomastia and feminization process. *Journal of Tropical Medicine, 69*, 175–179.

DeKosky, S. T., Scheff, S. W., & Cotman, C. W. (1984). Elevated corticosterone levels: A possible cause of reduced axon sprouting in aged animals. *Neuroendocrinology, 38*, 33–38.

DeMilio, L., Dackis, C. A., Gold, M. S., & Ehrenkranz, J. R. L. (1984). Addison's disease initially diagnosed as bereavement and conversion disorder. *American Journal of Psychiatry*, *141*, 1647–1648.

Devenport, L. D., & Devenport, J. A. (1982). The effects of adrenal hormones on brain and body size. *Physiological Psychology*, *10*, 339–404.

Dixon, R. B., & Christy, N. P. (1980). On the various forms of corticosteroid withdrawal syndrome. *American Journal of Medicine*, *68*, 224–229.

Dunn, A. J., & Gispen, W. H. (1977). How ACTH acts on the brain. *Behavioral Reviews*, *1*, 15–23

Dunn, A. J., & Schotman, P. (1981). Effects of ACTH and related peptides on cerebral RNA and protein synthesis. *Pharmacology & Therapeutics*, *12*, 353–372.

Ehrhardt, A., Greenberg, N., & Money, J. (1970). Female gender identity and absence of fetal gonadal hormones: Turner's syndrome. *Johns Hopkins Medical Journal*, *126*, 237–248.

Engel, G., & Margolin, S. (1941). Neuropsychiatric disturbances in Addison's disease and the role of impaired carbohydrate metabolsim in production of abnormal cerebral function. *Archives of Neurology and Psychiatry*, *45*, 881–884.

Enna, S. J., & Duman, R. S. (1983). Beta-adrenergic receptor regulation and antidepressants: The influence of adrenocorticotropin. *Journal of Neural Transmission*, *57*, 297–307.

Euvard, C., Oberlander, C., & Boissier, J. R. (1980). Estrogens and the extrapyramidal system. In E. Usdin, T. L. Sourkes, & M. B. H. Youdim (Eds.), *Enzymes and neurotransmitters in mental disease*. New York: Wiley.

Falk, W. E., Mahnke, M. W., & Poskanzer, D. C. (1979). Lithium prophylaxis of corticotropin-induced psychosis. *New England Journal of Medicine*, *299*, 1011–1012.

Farese, R. V (1984). Phospholipids as intermediates in hormone action. *Molecular and Cellular Endocrinology*, *35*, 1–14.

Fay, D. (1922). *A psychoanalytic study of psychoses with endocrinoses* (Monograph Series No. 33). Washington, DC: Nervous and Mental Disease Publishing Company.

Firestone, G. L, Payvar, F., & Yamamoto, K. R. (1982). Glucocorticoid regulation of protein processing and compartmentalization. *Nature (London)*, *300*, 221–224.

Flavin, D. K., Frederickson, P. A., Richardson, J. W., & Merritt, T. C. (1983). Corticosteroid abuse—An unusual manifestation of drug dependence. *Proceedings of the Mayo Clinic*, *58*, 764–766.

Gifford, S., & Gunderson, J. G. (1970). Cushing's disease as a psychosomatic disorder. *Medicine (Baltimore)*, *49*, 397–409.

Gifford S., Murawski, B. J., Kline, N. S., & Sachar, E. J. (1977). An unusual adverse reaction to self-medication with prednisone: An irrational crime during a fugue state. *International Journal of Psychiatry in Medicine*, *7*, 97–122.

Gillin, J. C., Jacobs, L. S., Snyder, F., & Henkin, R. I. (1974a). Effects of ACTH on the sleep of normal subjects and patients with Addison's disease. *Neuroendocrinology*, *15*, 21–31.

Gillin, J. C., Jacobs, L. S., Snyder, F. & Henkin, R. I. (1974b). Effects of decreased adrenal corticosteroids: Changes in sleep in normal subjects and patients with adrenal cortical insufficiency. *Electroencephalography and Clinical Neurophysiology*, *36*, 283–289.

Gladue, B. A., Green, R., & Hellman, R. E. (1984). Neuroendocrine response to estrogen and sexual orientation. *Science*, *225*, 1496–1500.

Glaser, G. H. (1953). Psychotic reactions induced by corticotropin (ACTH) and cortisone. *Psychosomatic Medicine*, *4*, 280–291.

Goggans, F. C., Weisberg, L. J., & Koran, L. M. (1983). Lithium prophylaxis of prednisone psychosis: A case report. *Journal of Clinical Psychiatry*, *44*, 111–112.

Gorzynski, G., Lebovits, A., Holland, J., & Vugrin, D. (1981). A comparative study of psychosexual adjustment in men with testicular cancer and acute leukemia. *Cancer Detection and Prevention*, *4*, 173–179.

Gothert, M. (1981). ACTH$_{1-24}$ increases stimulation-evoked noradrenaline release from sympathetic nerves by acting on presynaptic ACTH receptors. *European Journal of Pharmacology*, *76*, 295–296.

Greeves, J. (1984, May 19). Rapid onset psychosis with very low dosage of prednisone. *Lancet*, *1*, 1119–1120.

Griesinger, W. (1882). *Mental pathology and therapeutics*. New York: William Wood & Company.

Haberman, M., Hollingsworth, F., Falek, A., & Michael, R. P. (1975). Gender identity confusion, schizophrenia and a 47 XXY karyotype: A case report. *Psychoendocrinology*, *1*, 207–209.

Hall, E. D. (1980). Glucocorticoid effects on serotonergic and noradrenergic facilitation of spinal monosynaptic transmission. *Psychiatry Research*, *2*, 241–250.

Hall, E. D. (1982). Glucocorticoid effects on central nervous excitability and synaptic transmission. *International Review of Neurobiology*, *23*, 165–195.

Hall, E. D., & Tyler, C .V., Jr. (1983). Glucocorticoid modification of spinal dopamine receptor activation by apomorphine. *Brain Research*, *267*, 380–383.

Hall, R. C. W., Popkin, M. K., & Kirkpatrick, B. (1978). Tricyclic exacerbation of steroid psychosis. *Journal of Nervous and Mental Disease*, *166*, 738–742.

Hall, R. C. W., Popkin, M. K., Stickney, S. K., & Gardner, E. R. (1979). Presentation of the steroid psychoses. *Journal of Nervous and Mental Disease*, *167*, 229–236.

Heinz, E. R., Martinez, J., & Haenggeli, A. (1977). Reversibility of cerebral atroply in anorexia nervosa and Cushing's syndrome. *Journal of Computer Assisted Tomography*, *1*, 415–418.

Henkin, R. I. (1975). Effects of ACTH, adrenocorticosteroids and thyroid hormone on sensory function. In W. E. Strumpf & L. D. Grant (Eds.), *Anatomical neuroendocrinology* (pp. 298–316). New York: S. Karger.

Henkin, R. I., & Bartter, F. C. (1966). Studies on olfactory thresholds in normal man and in patients with adrenal cortical insufficiency: The role of adrenal coritcal steroids and of serum sodium concentration. *Journal of Clinical Investigation*, *45*, 1631–1639.

Henkin, R. I., & Daly. R. L. (1968). Auditory detection and perception in normal man and in patients with adrenal cortical insufficiency: Effect of adrenal cortical steroids. *Journal of Clinical Investigation*, *47*, 1269–1280.

Heriot, A. (1975). *The castrati in opera*. New York: Da Capo Press, Inc.

Heritage, A. S, Stumpt, W. E., Madhabanada, S., & Grant, L. D. (1980). Brain stem catecholamine neurons are target sites for sex steroid hormones. *Science, 207*, 1377–1379.

Herzog, A. G., Seibel, M. M., Schomer, D., Vaitukaitis, J., & Geschwind, N. (1984). Temporal lobe epilepsy: An extrahypothalamic pathogenesis for polycystic ovarian syndrome? *Neurology, 34*, 1389–1393.

Hurxthal, L., & O'Sullivan, S. (1959), Cushing's syndrome: Clinical differential diagnosis and complications. *Annals of Internal Medicine, 51*, 1–16.

Iuvone, P. M., Morasco, J., & Dunn, A. J. (1977). Effects of corticosterone on the synthesis of [^{3}H]catecholamines in the brains of CD-1 mice. *Brain Research, 120*, 571–576.

Jeffcoate, W., Silverstone, J., Edwards, C., & Besser, G. (1979). Psychiatric manifestations of Cushing's syndrome: Response to lowering of plasma cortisol. *Quarterly Journal of Medicine, 48*, 465–472.

Jones, M. T., Gillham, B., Altaher, A. R. H., Nicholson, S. A., Campbell, E. A., Watts, S. M., & Thody, A. (1984). Clinical and experimental studies on the role of GABA in the regulation of ACTH secretion: A review. *Psychoneuroendocrinology, 9*, 107–123.

Kalin, N. H., Shelton, S. E., Kraemer, G. W., & McKinney, W. T. (1983). Associated endocrine, physiological and behavioral changes in Rhesus monkeys after intravenous corticotropin-releasing factor administration. *Peptides (New York), 4*, 211–215.

Karin, M., Haslinger, A., Holtgreve, H., Richards, R. I., Krauter, P., Westphal, H. M., & Beato, M. (1984). Characterization of DNA sequences through which cadmium and glucocorticoid hormones induce human metallothionein-IIW$_A$ gene. *Nature (London), 308*, 513–519.

Kellner, C., Rubinow, D., Gold, P., & Post, R. (1983). Relationship of cortisol hypersecretion brain CT scan alterations in depressed patients. *Psychiatry Research, 8*, 191–197.

Kelly, W. F., Checkley, S. A., & Bender, D. A. (1980). Cushing's syndrome, tryptophan and depression. *British Journal of Psychiatry, 136*, 125–132.

Kelly, W. F., Checkley, S. A., Bender, D. A., & Mashiter, K. (1983). Cushing's syndrome and depression—A prospective study of 26 patients. *British Journal of Psychiatry, 142*, 16–19.

Kendall, D. A., McEwen, B .S., & Enna, S. J. (1982). The influence of ACTH and corticosterone of [^{3}H]GABA receptor binding in rat brain. *Brain Research, 236*, 365–374.

Kontula, K., Mustajoki, P., Paetau, A., & Pelkonen, R. (1984). Development of Cushing's disease in a patient with anorexia nervosa. *Journal of Endocrinological Investigation, 7*, 35–40.

Koppell, B. S., Wittner, W. K., Lunde, D., Warrick, G., & Edwards, D. (1970). Cortisol effects on averaged evoked potential, alpha-rhythm, time estimation, and two-flash fusion threshold. *Psychosomatic Medicine, 32*, 39–49.

Kramlinger, K. G., Peterson, G. C., Watson, P. K., & Leonard, L. L. (1985). Tyrapone for depression and delirium secondary to Cushing's syndrome. *Psychosomatics, 26*, 67–71.

Krieger, D. T. (1983). Physiopathology of Cushing's disease. *Endocrine Reviews, 4*, 22–43.

Krieger, D. T., & Glick, S. M. (1974). Sleep EEG stages and plasma growth hormone concentration in states of endogenous and exogenous hypercortisolemia or ACTH elevation. *Journal of Clinical Endocrinology and Metabolism, 39*, 986–1000.

Laignel-Lavastine, M. (1919). *The internal secretions and the nervous system* (Monograph Series No. 30). Washington, DC: Nervous and Mental Disease Publishing Company.

Lee, P. H. K., & Chan, M. (1984). Effects of adrenalectomy and adrenal steroids on the uptake of serotonin in rat platelets. *Clinical and Experimental Pharmacology and Physiology, 11*, 53–59.

Lewis, D. A., & Sherman, B. M. (1984). Serotonergic stimulation of adrenocorticotropin secretion in man. *Journal of Clinical Endocrinology and Metabolism, 58*, 458–462.

Lewis, D. A., & Smith, R. E. (1983). Steroid-induced psychiatric syndromes: A report of 14 cases and a review of the literature. *Journal of Affective Disorders, 5*, 319–332.

Ling, M. H. M., Perry, P. J., & Tsuang, M. T. (1981). Side effects of corticosteroid therapy. *Archives of General Psychiatry, 38*, 471–477.

McEwen, B. S. (1981). Neural gonadal steroid actions. *Science, 20*, 1303–1311.

Michael, R., & Gibbons, J. (1963). Interrelationships between the endocrine system and neuropsychiatry. *International Review of Neurobiology, 5*, 243–302.

Mobley, P. L., & Sulser, F. (1980). Adrenal corticoids regulate sensitivity of noradrenaline receptor-coupled adenylate cyclase in brain. *Nature (London), 286*, 608–609.

Money, J., Ehrhardt, A. A., & Masica, D. N. (1968). Fetal feminization induced by androgen insensitivity in the testicular feminization syndrome: Effects on marriage and maternalism. *Johns Hopkins Medical Journal, 123*, 105–114.

Money, J., & Jobaris, R. (1977). Juvenile Addison's disease: Follow-up behavioral studies in seven cases. *Psychoneuroendocrinology, 2*, 147–157.

Money, J., & Lewis, V. (1982). Homosexual/heterosexual status in boys at puberty: Idiopathic adolescent gynecomastia and congenital virilizing adrenocorticism compared. *Psychoneuroendocrinology, 7*, 339–346.

Money, J., Wiedeking, C., Walker, P., Migeon, C., Meyer, W., & Borgaonkar, D. (1975). 47,XYY and 46,XY males with antisocial and/or sex-offending behavior: Antiandrogen therapy plus counseling. *Psychoneuroendocrinology, 1*, 165–178.

O'Donohue, T. L., & Dorsa, D. (1982). The opiomelanotropinergic neuronal and endocrine systems. *Peptides (New York) 3*, 353–395.

Olpe, H. R., & Jones, R. S. G. (1982). Excitatory effects of ACTH on noradrenergic neurons of the locus coeruleus in the rat. *Brain Research, 251*, 177–179.

Orenstein, J., & Raskind, M. A. (1983). Polycystic ovary disease in two patients with Briquet's disorder. *American Journal of Psychiatry, 140*, 1202–1204.

Pasqualini, R. Q., & Gurevicj, N. (1956). Spontaneous remission in a case of Cushing's syndrome. *Journal of Clinical Endocrinology and Metabolism, 16*, 406–411.

Pepper, G. M., & Krieger, D. T. (1984). Hypothalamic–pituitary–adrenal abnormalities in depression: Their possible relation to central mechanisms regulating ACTH release. In R. Post & J. Ballenger (Eds.), *Neurobiology of mood disorders*. Baltimore, MD: Williams & Wilkins.

Pfaff, D. W., & McEwen, B. S. (1983). Actions of estrogens and progestins on nerve cells. *Science, 219*, 808–814.

Pfahl, M., McGinnis, D., & Hendricks, M. (1983). Correlation of glucocorticoid receptor binding sites on MMTV proviral DNA wit hormone-inducible transcription. *Science, 222*, 1341–1343.

Pies, R. (1981). Persistent bipolar illness after steroid administration. *Archives of Internal Medicine, 141*, 1087.

Ratcliffe, S. G., Bancroft, J., Axworthy, D., & McLaren, W. (1982). Klinefelter's syndrome in adolescence. *Archives of Disease in Childhood, 57*, 6–12.

Reed, K., Watkins, M., & Dobson, H. (1983). Mania in Cushing's syndrome: Case report. *Journal of Clinical Psychiatry, 44*, 460–462.

Reus, V. I. (1984). Diagnosis and treatment in endocrinology and psychiatry: From Cushing's syndrome to disorders of mood. In C. Van Dyke, L. Temoshok, & L. S. Zegans (Eds.), *Emotions in health and illness* (pp. 23–34). New York: Grune & Stratton, 1986.

Reus, V. I., & Berlant, J. L. (1986). Behavioral disturbances associated with disorders of the hypothalamic–pituitary–adrenal system. In I. Extein (Ed.), *Medical mimics of psychiatric disorders*. Washington, DC: APA Press.

Rome, H. P., & Braceland, F. J. (1952). The psychological response to ACTH, cortisone, hydrocortisone and related steroid substances. *American Journal of Psychiatry, 108*, 641–651.

Ross, E. J., & Linch, D. C. (1982, September 18). Cushing's syndrome—killing disease: Discriminatory value of signs and symptoms aiding early diagnosis. *Lancet, 2*, 646–649.

Rothschild, A. J., Langlais, P. J., Schatzberg, A. F., Walsh, F. X., Cole, J. O., & Bird, E. D. (1984). Dexamethasone increases plasma-free dopamine in man. *Journal of Psychiatric Research, 18*, 217–223.

Rubin, R. (1982). Testosterone and aggression in men. In P. Beumont & G. Burrows (Eds.), *Handbook of psychiatry and endocrinology* (pp. 355–356). New York: American Elsevier.

Rubin, R. T., Reinisch, J. M., & Haskett, R. F. (1981). Postnatal gonadal steroid effects on human hebavior. *Science, 221*, 1318–1324.

Saad, M. F., Adams, F., Mackay, B., Ordonez, N.G., Leavens, M. E., & Samaan, N. A. (1984). Occult Cushing's disease presenting with acute psychosis. *American Journal of Medicine, 76*, 759–766.

Sachar, E. (1975). Neuroendocrine abnormalities in depressive illness. In E. Sachar (Ed.), *Topics in psychoendocrinology*. New York: Grune & Stratton.

Salmon, U. J., & Geist, S. H. (1943). Effects of androgens upon libido in women. *Journal of Clinical Endrocrinology, 3*, 235–238.

Schubert, D., LaCorbiere, M., Klier, F. G., & Steinbach, J. H. (1980). The modulation of neurotransmitter synthesis by steroid hormones and insulin. *Brain Research, 190*, 67–79.

Sharfstein, S. S., Sack, D. S., & Fauci, A. S. (1982). Relationship between alternate-day corticosteroid therapy and behavioral abnormalities. *JAMA, Journal of the American Medical Association, 248*, 2987–2989.

Smith, D. J., Kohler, P. C, Helminiak, R., & Carroll, J. (1982). Intermittent Cushing's syndrome with an empty sella turcica. *Archives of Internal Medicine, 142*, 2185–2187.

Snider, S. R., & Kuchel, O. (1983). Dopamine: An important neurohormone of the sympathoadrenal system. Significance of increased peripheral dopamine release for the human stress response and hypertension. *Endocrine Reviews, 4*, 291–309.

Sopchak, A. L., & Sutherland, A. M. (1960). Psychological impact of cancer and its treatment. VII. Exogenous hormones and their relation to lifelong adaptation in women with metastatic cancer of the breast. *Cancer (Philadelphia), 13*, 528–531.

Spillane, J. D. (1951). Nervous and mental disorders in Cushing's syndrome. *Brain, 74*, 72–95.

Starkman, M. N, & Schteingart, D. E. (1981). Neuropsychiatric manifestations of patients with Cushing's syndrome; relationship to cortisol and adrenocorticotropic hormone levels. *Archives of Internal Medicine, 141*, 215–219.

Starkman, M. N., Schteingart, D. E., & Schork, M. A. (1981). Depressed mood and other psychiatric manifestations of Cushing's syndrome: Relationship to hormone levels. *Psychosomatic Medicine, 43*, 3–18.

Starr, A. (1952). Personality changes in Cushing's syndrome. *Journal of Clinical Endocrinology and Metabolism, 12*, 502–505.

Storer, H. (1871), *Reflex insanity in women*. New York. Lee & Shepard.

Sze, P. Y., & Hedrick, B. J. (1983). Effects of dexamethasone and other glucocorticoid steroids on tyrosine hydroxylase activity in the superior cervical ganglion. *Brain Research, 265*, 81–86.

Taft, P., Martin, F., & Melick, R. (1970). Cushing's syndrome—A review of the response to treatment in 42 patients. *Australasian Annals of Medicine, 19*, 295–303.

Trethowan, W. H., & Cobb, S. (1952). Neuropsychiatric aspects of Cushing's syndrome. *Archives of Neurology and Psychiatry, 67*, 283–309.

Vague, J. (1983). Testicular feminization syndrome. *Hormone Research, 18*, 62–68.

Versteeg, D. H. G. (1980). Interaction of peptides related to ACTH, MSH, β-LPH with neurotransmitters in the brain. *Pharmacology & Therapeutics, 11*, 535–557.

von Zerssen, D. (1974). Mood and behavioral changes under corticosteroid therapy. In T. M. Itil, G. Laudahn, & W. M. Herrmann (Eds.), *Psychotropic action of hormones*. New York: Spectrum Publications.

Waxenburg, S. E., Finkbeiner, J. A., Drellich, M. G., & Sutherland, A. M. (1960). The role of hormones in human behavior. II. Changes in sexual behavior in relation to vaginal smears of breast cancer patients after oophorectomy and adrenalectomy. *Psychosomatic Medicine, 22*, 435–442.

Whelan, T., Schteingart, D., Starkman, M., & Smith, A. (1980). Neuropsychological deficits in Cushing's syndrome. *J. Nervous & Mental Disease, 168*, 753–757.

Whitlock, F. A. (1982). *Symptomatic affective disorders: A study of depression and mania associated with physical disease and medication.* New York: Academic Press.

Whybrow, P. C., & Hurwitz, T. (1976). Psychological disturbances associated with endocrine disease and hormone therapy. In E. J. Sachar (Ed.), *Hormones, behavior, and psychopathology* (pp. 125–143). New York: Raven Press.

Zondek, H., & Leszynsky, H. E. (1956). Transient Cushing's syndrome. *British Medical Journal, 16*, 197–200.

4 PHYSIOLOGICAL, DIAGNOSTIC, AND PATHOPHYSIOLOGICAL IMPLICATIONS OF CORTICOTROPIN-RELEASING HORMONE

PHILIP W. GOLD

MITCHEL A. KLING

JOSEPH R. CALABRESE

KONSTANTINE KALOGERAS

PETER C. AVGERINOS

D. LYNN LORIAUX

GEORGE P. CHROUSOS

National Institute of Mental Health

INTRODUCTION

We now appreciate that the brain is the most prolific of all endocrine organs, producing scores of neurohormones within and beyond the boundaries of the endocrine hypothalamus. The idea that the brain functions as a gland, however, is not new. Indeed, the evolution of thought leading to the identification of corticotropin-releasing hormone (CRH) began around 400 B.C. (Iason, 1946; Zuingenus, 1669). At this time, Hippocrates, in his work entitled *De glandulus*, stated explicitly, "The flesh of the glands is different from the rest of the body, being spongy and full of veins; they are found in the moist part of the body where they become humid . . . and the brain is a gland as well as the mammae."

Following this farsighted postulate of Hippocrates, elucidation of the brain's endocrine functions proceeded at an extraordinarily slow pace. For instance, 500 years passed before one of the principal target tissues of the neurohormones was inadvertently identified by Galen, which he mistook for a mucous (pituita) secretion of the brain (Medvei, 1984). Then 1,600 more years passed un-

til the hypothalamic–pituitary system of portal vessels was described (Lieutaud, 1742), and another 200 more years elapsed until its functional significance was understood. It was then, in 1948, that Harris advanced the hypothesis that the hypothalamus produced humoral factors which traversed they hypophyseal portal system to regulate the secretion of anterior pituitary hormones into the systemic circulation (Harris, 1948).

By 1955, stimulated by Harris's postulate, the major groundwork for the identification of CRH was laid when Saffran, Schally, and Bentey (1955) showed that hypothalamic fragments possessed remarkable corticotropin (ACTH) -releasing properties when incubated with pituicytes *in vitro*. Within 15 years, Vale, Spiess, Rivier, and Rivier (1981) announced the sequence of a 41 amino acid peptide isolated from ovine hypothalami, which showed greater *in vivo* and *in vitro* corticotropin-releasing potency than any previously identified synthetic or endogenous peptide (Vale *et al.*, 1981). Shortly thereafter, Schally *et al.* (1981) described the sequence of porcine CRH, and J. Rivier, Spiess, and Vale

(1983) that of rat CRH (rCRH). Finally, Numa's group sequenced the genes of both ovine CRH (oCRH) and human CRH (hCRH) and deduced the amino acid sequence of the corresponding peptides (Furatani *et al.*, 1983; Shibahara *et al.*, 1983). Surprisingly, both the rCRH and the hCRH appeared to be chemically identical. Moreover, oCRH and hCRH are also structurally similar, each containing 41 amino acids and showing 83% homology (Figure 4.1).

The sequencing and subsequent synthesis of CRH has greatly enhanced the capacity for clinical neuroendocrinologists to explore the hypothalamic–pituitary components of Cushing's disease and adrenal insufficiency. CRH is also of importance to clinical psychoneuroendocrinologists, since its discovery occurred in the context of two other discoveries which have heightened their interest in the hypothalamic–pituitary–adrenal (HPA) axis and its regulation. First, many patients with depression (Carroll, Curtis, & Mendels, 1976; Sachar, Hellman, Fukushima, & Gallagher, 1970), anorexia nervosa (Gerner & Gwirtsman, 1981), alcoholism (Stokes, 1973), and obsessive–compulsive neurosis (Insel, Kalin, Guttmacher, Cohen, & Murphy, 1982) manifest a hyperactive pituitary–adrenal axis. In fact, the hypercortisolism seen in depressive illness and alcoholism can be so severe that it

is difficult to distinguish them from Cushing's disease; hence, each of these psychiatric entities has been referred to colloquially by some endocrinologists as a pseudo-Cushing's state. Second, it has been shown that ACTH is secreted synchronously with β-endorphin, one of the principal endogenous opioid peptides (Guillemin *et al.*, 1977), and that both hormones are contained within the sequence of a common precursor molecule, proopiomelanocortin (POMC) (Mains, Eipper, & Ling, 1977). CRF is the principal central signal for the cleavage of pituitary POMC into biologically active peptides.

CRH is also of interest to psychiatrists and neurobiologists for reasons other than its putative role in regulating the pituitary-adrenal axis. Hence, CRH is synthesized not only by the hypothalamus for transport by hypophyseal portal blood, but like other hypothalamic hormones such as TRH and somatostatin, is distributed and/or synthesized beyond the boundaries of the hypothalamus in many brain regions (Bloom, Battenberg, Rivier, & Vale, 1982; De Souza *et al.*, 1984; Olschowka, O'Donohue, Mueller, & Jacobowitz, 1982) and, like these peptides, seems to play a role in coordinating complex behavioral and/or physiological processes. Specifically, it has been shown that there are extensive hypothalamic aggregations of CRH cell bodies and terminal fields in the limbic system, cortex, and in close association with the central autonomic system and the locus ceruleus (Bloom *et al.*, 1982; De Souza *et al*, 1984; Olschowka *et al.*, 1982). This distribution of CRH within and beyond the hypothalamus provides an anatomical context for the observation that CRH can simultaneously activate and coordinate metabolic (Brown *et al.*, 1982), circulatory (Brown *et al.*, 1982), and behavioral responses that are adaptive in stressful situations (Britton, Koob, & Rivier, 1982; Sirinathsinghji, Rees, Rivier, & Vale, 1983; Sutton, Koob, Le Moal, Rivier, & Vale, 1982). Hence, in the rat, intracerebroventricular (ICV) administration of CRH leads not only to activation of the HPA axis, but also to activation of the sympathetic nervous system (Brown *et al.*, 1982) and to several behavioral changes characteristic of the stress response, including decreased feeding (Britton *et al.*, 1982) and sexual behavior (Sirinathsinghji *et al.*, 1983), assumption of a

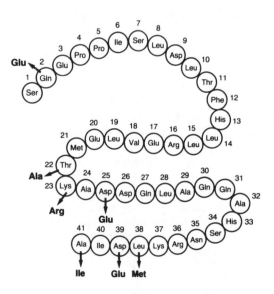

FIGURE 4.1.

freeze posture in a foreign environment (Sutton *et al.*, 1982), and increased exploration in familiar surroundings (Sutton *et al.*, 1982). In addition, in collaboration with Weiss and Post, our group has shown that CRH given ICV to the rat causes a marked increase in hostility and induces limbic seizures which show cross-sensitization with electrically kindled seizures (Weiss, Post, Gold, Chrousos, & Pert, in press).

Given CRH's significant role in HPA regulation and its intriguing effects on central nervous system (CNS) function, we embarked on a series of clinical studies with CRH both in normal volunteers and in psychiatric patients with major psychiatric disorders whose illnesses are at times characterized by hypercortisolism (e.g., primary affective disorder, anorexia nervosa, panic anxiety disorder, and schizophrenia). In addition, we studied patients with endocrine disturbances characterized by abnormal HPA function, including subjects with Cushing's disease, ectopic ACTH secretion, primary and secondary adrenal insufficiency, and Nelson's syndrome. In volunteers, we hoped to examine the physiological relevance of CRH to pituitary–adrenal function in man as well as to explore the differential biological effects and pharmacokinetics of oCRH and hCRH under varying conditions. In our patient populations, we asked the following questions:

1. Can CRH help determine whether the hypocortisolism in depression reflects an alteration in the set point for feedback inhibition of cortisol on ACTH secretion at the pituitary locus versus the possibility of an alteration in the secretion of endogenous CRH?
2. Can CRH help in the differential diagnosis of the various hypercortisolemic psychiatric syndromes?
3. Can CRH help determine whether depression and Cushing's disease lie on a common pathophysiological continuum or represent distinct abnormalities of the HPA axis?
4. Can CRH help establish the differential diagnosis of disturbances in HPA function which can be difficult to distinguish from one another, such as depression from Cushing's disease, ectopic ACTH production from Cushing's disease, or hypothalamic from pituitary–adrenal insufficiency?
5. Is CRH of possible relevance to the overall symptom complex of major psychiatric illnesses such as depression and anorexia nervosa?

RELEVANCE OF CRH TO PITUITARY–ADRENAL REGULATION IN MAN

Even before the sequencing of CRH, this peptide was postulated to play a major role in the regulation of pituitary–adrenal function. This role ascribed to CRH is schematically illustrated in Figure 4.2, which depicts the classic formulation of HPA regulation that has held sway for at least the past two decades. According to this formulation, CRH is secreted in seven to ten discrete episodes per day (during unstressed conditions), which in turn produce a similar number of ACTH and cortisol secretory episodes. The majority of these pulses occur in the early morning hours. Since cortisol has a longer half-life than ACTH (and presumably CRH), the frequent cortisol pulses occurring in the early morning produce a situation in which a new cortisol secretory episode may be initiated before the last episode is terminated, producing a rise in cortisol with each successive ACTH pulse. Hence, with an increasing frequency of CRH and ACTH pulses, there emerges an increase in the level or amplitude of plasma cortisol

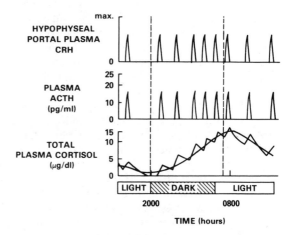

FIGURE 4.2.

secretion which we recognize as the early morning plasma cortisol surge. This phenomenon of the early morning rise in the amplitude of cortisol secretion is an example in which frequency modulation (i.e., timing of CRH, ACTH, and cortisol pulses) is translated into amplitude modulation (i.e., amplitude of cortisol secretion).

Over the years (and particularly since the sequencing of CRH), this classic formulation has been modified by additional information. For instance, it has been known for some time that vasopressin is capable of stimulating the pituitary corticotroph cell, and it has even been postulated to be the major hypothalamic CRH peptide. It is now known that arginine vasopressin (AVP) itself is not as potent as hCRH 1–41 in stimulating ACTH secretion, but the AVP markedly potentiates CRH's corticotropin-releasing properties (Gillies, Lingo, & Lowry, 1982). Moreover, other substances such as the catecholamines also potentiate CRH-induced ACTH secretion (Vale *et al.*, 1983). In light of these data and because of a paucity of clinical studies with hCRH, one of the first studies our group undertook with this peptide was to explore its possible relevance to the physiological regulation of the pituitary–adrenal axis in humans. To address this question, we first studied normal controls to compare naturalistically occurring ACTH pulses to those induced by hCRH administration. Figure 4.3 shows that a comparison of spontaneous endogenous ACTH and cortisol surges (isolated during normative circadian studies) is identical to those induced by an intravenous bolus of 1 µg/kg of hCRH (Avgerinos *et al.*, in press-a). This finding, that hCRH-induced plasma ACTH and cortisol pulses mimicked the spontaneously occurring secretory episodes of these hormones, provided the first compelling evidence that CRH may be of physiological relevance to the pituitary–adrenal axis in humans.

The finding that hCRH produces ACTH pulses which closely resemble endogenous ACTH secretory episodes led to an additional experiment designed to further explore the relationship between pulsatile CRH secretion and the pattern of ACTH and cortisol secretion in the basal state. In this study by Avgerinos *et al.*, we asked the following question: Could hCRH, given in pulses that simulate the hypothetical pattern shown in Figure

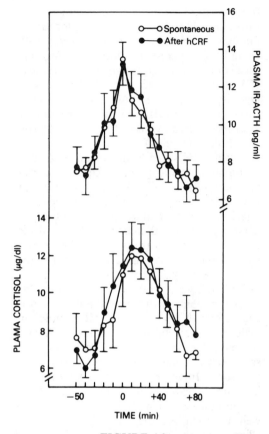

FIGURE 4.3.

4.2, restore the function of the pituitary–adrenal axis shown in patients with CRH deficiency [i.e., secondary adrenal insufficiency due to corticotropin-sparing (superpituitary) lesions] (Avgerinos *et al.*, in press-b)? The patients included in this study had secondary adrenal insufficiency determined by a standard 48-hour ACTH stimulation test. Thus, during a standard 3-hour evening oCRH test (see below), the plasma cortisol response of these patients was diminished while the plasma ACTH response was normal or exaggerated and showed a delayed pattern, suggestive of a hypothalamic lesion. Human CRH was given as a 1 µg/kg bolus eight times during the 24-hour period. The timing of each pulse of hCRH was chosen to correspond to the expected times of ACTH pulsation under naturalistic conditions. Hence, the majority of the pulses were given in the early morning hours to correspond with the A.M. cortisol surge. To a degree which was unexpected, such a paradigm of hCRH pulsatile administration reproduced the normal amplitude and circadian variation of cortisol secretion in patients with hypothalamic-CRH deficiency (Figure 4.4). Moreover, the administration of eight pulses of synthetic hCRH, as described above, normalized 24-hour urinary 17-hydroxysteroid and urinary free cortisol secretion in these patients (Avgerinos et al., in press-b). Parenthetically, we have previously noted that a continuous infusion of oCRH in normal volunteers for 24 hours produces a pattern of cortisol secretion which includes preservation of a circadian rhythm (Figure 4.5), though the amplitude is blunted compared to the naturalistic rhythm of that induced by the hCRH pulses (Schulte et al., 1985). Thus, al-

though basal circadian cortisol secretion may be dependent on endogenous CRH secretion, this circadian pattern of pituitary–adrenal function may also involve a component of a circadian rhythm in the responsiveness to CRH itself (Schulte et al., 1985). This is further suggested by our pulsatile hCRH administration data in patients with hypothalamic CRH deficiency (in which the responses to the early morning pulses are greater than the responses to the daytime pulses) (Avgerinos et al., in press-b) and by our own delineation of the naturalistic pattern of circadian ACTH secretion in normal volunteers. This latter study showed that the early morning cortisol surge is associated with an increase in both the pulse frequency and amplitude of ACTH secretion (T. H. Schuermeyer et al., unpublished observations).

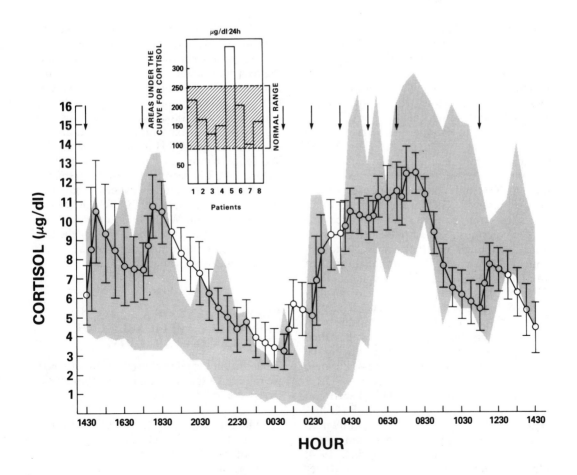

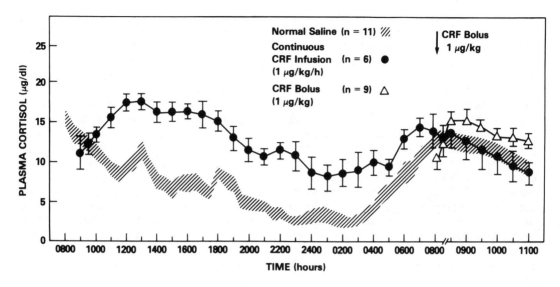

FIGURE 4.5.

In addition to studies of the relevance of CRH to basal and circadian ACTH and cortisol secretion, we have attempted to assess the relationship of CRH to pituitary–adrenal function during stress. To accomplish this task, we have attempted to see whether the ACTH responses to frequent pulses of hCRH given at 30- to 90-minute intervals from 6 P.M. to 8 P.M. would produce an ACTH secretory pattern resembling that seen during the standard insulin tolerance test. We noted that ACTH and cortisol responses to repeated pulses of hCRH were much less than those seen during the insulin tolerance test (P. C. Avgerinos et al., unpublished observations). Although neutralization of endogenous CRH in rats by administration of anti-CRH antibodies abolishes more than 75% of the ACTH responses to insulin-induced hypoglycemic stress (C. Rivier & Vale, 1983), our data are compatible with previous suggestions that factors other then CRH play an important role in producing the ACTH responses seen during stress. Putative factors which may underlie these extra-CRH influences on stress-induced ACTH secretion include the catecholamines and AVP (Gillies et al., 1982), both of which are known to increase during hypoglycemia and other forms of stress (Axelrod & Reisine, 1984; Plotsky, Rubin, & Vale, 1985; C. Rivier

& Vale, 1983). In support of the possible role of vasopressin are our recent data obtained in normal volunteers which show that osmotic-induced vasopressin secretion markedly potentiates CRH-induced ACTH secretion (Rittmaster et al., unpublished observations), compatible with other studies showing synergism between exogenous vasopressin administration and CRH in human volunteers. We doubt that oxytocin participates in CRH-induced ACTH secretion, despite a suggestion from in vitro studies, where it has been shown to have synergy with CRH in causing ACTH secretion. We have observed no synergy of oxytocin with hCRH in eliciting ACTH secretion in man (L. Nieman et al., unpublished observations).

DEVELOPMENT OF A CLINICALLY APPLICABLE CRH STIMULATION PARADIGM

To ascertain the clinical application of CRH, we initiated a series of studies in volunteers to assess the following questions:

1. Which peptide (oCRH or hCRH) might be best to use in acute challenges of the pituitary–adrenal axis?
2. What dose should be administered in

these studies and for how long should hormonal responses be sampled?

3. What time of day would be best suited for the performance of dynamic stimulation of the human pituitary–adrenal axis?

To assess these questions, we conducted pharmacokinetic and dose–response studies with both oCRH and hCRH. Some of these studies were performed at different times of day to correspond to periods when the HPA axis is normally quiescent or most active.

The first dose–response study with oCRH in primates was performed by our group in cynamolgus macaques (Schulte, Chrousos, Oldfield et al., 1982). Corresponding studies in humans yielding similar results were performed by Grossman et al. (1982) and Orth et al. (1983). These studies show that the lowest maximal stimulatory dose for cortisol secretion was 1 μg/kg (Figure 4.6); moreover,

this dose produced clear-cut plasma cortisol and ACTH secretion in all volunteers and experimental animals without detectable adverse effects. Of particular interest was the fact that the ACTH and cortisol responses to oCRH were prolonged, remaining clearly elevated at the end of the 3-hour sampling period (Schulte, Chrousos, Oldfield et al., 1982).

In our similar dose–response studies with hCRH in nonhuman primates (Schuermeyer et al., 1985) and man (Schuermeyer et al., 1984), Schuermeyer et al. noted a dose-dependent increase of plasma ACTH and cortisol concentrations with greater doses of hCRH (Figures 4.6 and 4.7). Peak plasma ACTH and cortisol responses to hCRH were significantly lower than those achieved by oCRH (Schuermeyer et al., 1984, 1985). Moreover, the ACTH and cortisol responses to hCRH were of much shorter duration than

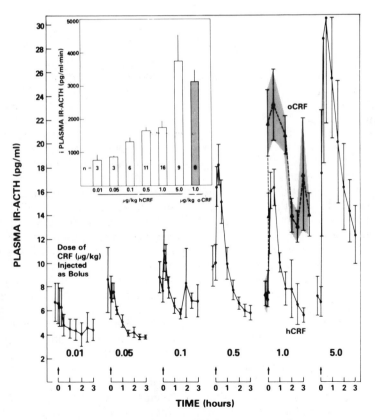

FIGURE 4.6.

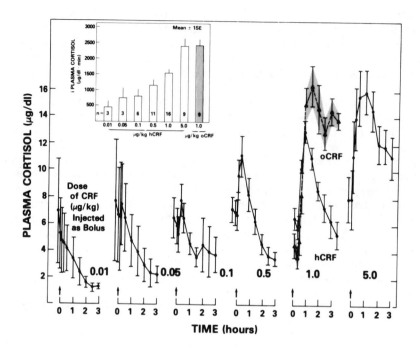

FIGURE 4.7.

those with oCRH. Accordingly, comparisons of the integrated secretory responses of both ACTH and cortisol following hCRH administration indicate that oCRH is at least five times more potent than hCRH (Schuermeyer et al., 1984, 1985). This difference is mainly due to the longer-lasting effect of oCRH upon ACTH and cortisol secretion.

These longer-lasting effects of oCRH on ACTH and cortisol secretion can be presumably accounted for on the basis of the differential pharmacokinetic properties of oCRH (Schulte, Chrousos, Gold et al., 1982) and hCRH (Schuermeyer et al., 1984, 1985) in human plasma. Hence, in our study directly comparing the metabolic clearance rate of these two peptides in human volunteers, Schuermeyer et al. (1984, 1985) noted that hCRH is cleared from plasma much more rapidly than oCRH (Figure 4.8). On the basis of the relatively slower clearance and more prolonged biological effects of oCRH, we elected to use this peptide for characterizing the functional integrity of the pituitary corticotroph in our clinical populations. We reasoned that the extra information provided

by a pulse of oCRH might provide the kind of additional information that could be helpful in exploring the pathophysiology of HPA activity in different patient subgroups. Moreover, we felt that this additional information could also be helpful in determining subtle differences in responses between patient subgroups and hence more helpful in establishing differential diagnoses between clinical entities. On the other hand, as illustrated by the studies in patients with hypothalamic CRH deficiency (Argerinos et al., in press-b), the much more rapidly cleared hCRH seems far more suitable than oCRH for studies of pulsatile ACTH secretion.

An additional factor of relevance to the establishment of a clinically applicable CRH stimulation test is the determination of an optimal time of day for administration of the peptide to patient populations. To explore this question, we administered a 1 μg/kg bolus of oCRH at 9 A.M., near the time of day when the axis is most active, and at 8 P.M., when the axis is normally dormant. It was found that owing to the lower baseline cortisol levels seen in the evening, the net inte-

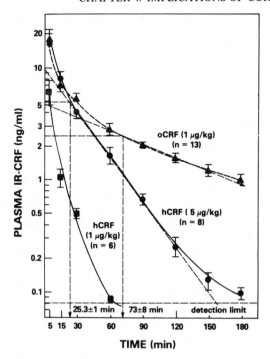

FIGURE 4.8.

grated cortisol responses to oCRH are greater at this time (Schulte *et al.*, in press). Hence, we decided that our CRH stimulation test would consist of the 1 μg/kg bolus of oCRH given at the 8 P.M. time.

CLINICAL STUDIES WITH oCRH IN PATIENTS WITH MAJOR PSYCHIATRIC DISORDERS

The first major finding utilizing CRH in psychiatry was made by our group when we noted that 12 of our drug-free depressed patients showed a significantly blunted response to oCRH (Gold *et al.*, 1984). We have continued to see this pattern in a larger series of depressed patients (see Figure 4.9) and most recently have replicated our finding in a large series of 32 patients (Gold *et al.*, in press-b). This finding has been further reproduced by Holsboer, Genken, Stalla, and Muller (1984) in 12 subjects using hCRH rather than oCRH. In light of the fact that hCRH is so much weaker a stimulus to ACTH secretion

than oCRH (Schuermeyer *et al.*, 1984, 1985), this finding of Holsboer is somewhat surprising. Indeed, we have been unable to replicate the finding of blunted ACTH responses to hCRH in a group of 15 depressed patients despite the fact that these same patients showed a markedly attenuated ACTH response to oCRH (J. R. Calabrese & P. W. Gold, unpublished observations). In light of these data, we recommend the use of oCRH rather than hCRH for diagnostic testing in psychiatry.

The finding of an attenuated response to oCRH in depression suggested that the pituitary corticotroph cell in depressed patients was appropriately restrained by the negative feedback effects of elevated cortisol levels (Gold & Chrousos, in press; Gold *et al.*, 1984, in press-b). This hypothesis was supported by the finding of a significant negative correlation between basal cortisol levels and the ACTH response to CRH in depression (Gold & Chrousos, in press; Gold *et al.*, 1984, in press-b).

In light of the apparently normal corticotroph cell function in depressed patients, we first advanced the hypothesis that hypercortisolism in depression represents a defect at or above the hypothalamus which results in the hypersecretion of endogenous CRH. To test this hypothesis, we attempted to replicate in normal controls a situation in which the pituitary corticotroph cell is exposed to excessive CRH. In order to accomplish this, we administered a continuous infusion of oCRH for 24 hours and evaluated the ACTH and cortisol responses (Schulte *et al.*, 1985). As noted earlier, Figure 4.5 shows the cortisol responses to this continuous infusion of oCRH. Of interest is the fact that the circadian rhythm of cortisol is preserved despite the continuous administration of oCRH, suggestion that the pituitary corticotroph cell shows a diurnal sensitivity to exogenous CRH. This is of interest in light of the fact that the circadian rhythm of cortisol is also generally preserved in depression (Halbreich, Asnis, Slindledecker, Zurnoff, & Nathan, 1985). Of additional interest is the fact that the mean amplitude of cortisol secretion during continuous CRH infusion is elevated about 40–50%, and that the urinary free cortisol secretion during CRH infusion averaged 150–200 μg/day (Schulte *et al.*, 1985). Hence,

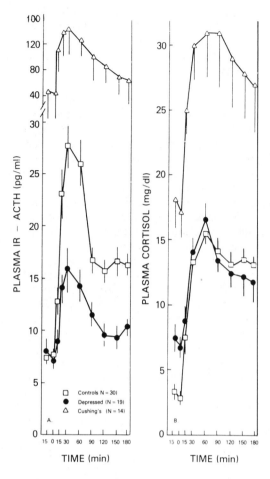

FIGURE 4.9.

the amplitude of plasma cortisol during the 24-hour period and the magnitude of urinary free cortisol hypersecretion are very similar during conditions of continuous administration of oCRH to controls and in the endogenously depressed state. We concluded, therefore, that a continuous CRH infusion to normal volunteers reproduces the pattern and magnitude of hypercortisolism, typically associated with depression. Additional data compatible with the idea that CRH is hypersecreted in depressed patients derive from the data of Nemeroff et al. (1984) who showed that the level of cerebrospinal fluid (CSF) CRH is elevated in depression. Although we could not demonstrate a significant elevation of CSF

CRH in depressed patients (A. Roy & P. W. Gold, unpublished observations), these subjects did manifest a significant positive correlation between postdexamethasone cortisol levels in depressed patients and the CSF level of CRH (Roy et al., in press-a). Moreover, we noted that CSF CRH is significantly higher in depressed patients who are dexamethasone nonsuppressors than in dexamethasone suppressors.

Inspection of our ACTH and cortisol responses to CRH in depression revealed other salient features of HPA dysfunction in depressed patients. For instance, we noted that depressed patients showed a robust total and free cortisol response despite the very small ACTH released during CRH stimulation (Gold & Chrousos, in press; Gold et al., 1984, in press-b). In fact, the free cortisol response to CRH was even greater in depressed patients than in controls (Gold et al., in press-b). We surmise from these data that the adrenal cortex in depression has grown hyperresponsive to ACTH (Gold & Chrousos, in press; Gold et al., 1984 in press-b), compatible with the well-described phenomenon of progressive functional and anatomical hypertrophy of the adrenal cortex seen during either experimentally induced stress (Selye, 1936) or during the course of chronic and repeated hyperstimulation of the adrenal cortex by ACTH in man (Renold, Jenkins, & Thorn, 1952). This suggestion of adrenal hyperresponsiveness to ACTH in depression is compatible with the data of Amsterdam, Winokur, Abelman, Lucki, and Rickels (1983) which showed that chronically depressed patients manifest greater cortisol responses to a bolus of exogenous ACTH than normal subjects.

Although our depressed patients were hypercortisolemic, it is noteworthy that basal ACTH levels remained in the normal range (Gold & Chrousos, in press; Gold et al., 1984, in press-b). This "normal" plasma ACTH level in depression most likely reflects a normal corticotroph cell caught in the balance between forces (i.e., negative feedback exerted by a hyperactive adrenal cortex from below and a predominating excess of CRH drive from above). Hence, the corticotroph cell, though restrained by the negative feedback to secrete at a rate that produces ACTH levels in the normal range, is nevertheless sufficiently driven by CRH topromote excessive cortisol secretion by hyperplastic adrenals. Presumably, depressed patients would have shown elevated levels of ACTH in the beginning of their depressive illness. a schematic diagram of these proposed relationships is shown in the first three panels in Figure 4.10 (Gold *et al.*, in press-b).

We have also explored the pathophysiology of hypercortisolism and other major psychiatric disorders, including anorexia nervosa. We note that underweight patients with anorexia nervosa show hypercortisolism even more severe than that seen in depressed patients. However, like the depressed patients, these underweight anorexics manifest a markedly attenuated ACTH response to exogenous CRH (Gold *et al.*, in press-a). This finding strongly suggests that like the depressed patients, the pituitary corticotroph cell in anorexia nervosa is appropriately restrained by the negative feedback effects of hypercortisolism and also suggests that anorexics, like depressed patients, show a defect in the secretion of CRH. In support of this hypothesis is our finding that underweight patients with anorexia nervosa show significantly higher CSF CRH levels than controls (W. Kaye & P. W. Gold, unpublished observations). When these underweight anorexic subjects were restudied after

their weight had stabilized at 100% of normal body weight, their basal hypercortisolism had resolved, suggesting normalization of the central defect which resulted in the hypersection of endogenous CRH (Grossman *et al.*, 1982). Moreover, the level of CRH in the CSF also returned to normal at this time (W. Kaye & P. W. Gold, unpublished observations). However, despite normalization of the apparent central defect in CRH secretion which had produced their hypercortisolism, these normal weight anorexics continued to show a markedly attenuated ACTH response to CRH (Gold *et al.*, in press-a). Although we cannot definitively account for this finding, it may represent the persistence of a functionally hypertrophied adrenal cortex into this phase of short-term recovery. On the other hand, normal weight bulimic subjects studied for 10 days after a voluntary absence from binging and vomiting and a group of anorexia nervosa subjects who had maintained normal body weight for at least 6 months showed normal basal ACTH and cortisol values and their responses to exogenous CRH (Gold *et al.*, in press-a). From these studies, we conclude that the basic pathophysiology of hypercortisolism in anorexia nervosa is similar to that seen in the depressed phase of primary affective disorder and that subtle defects in HPA function

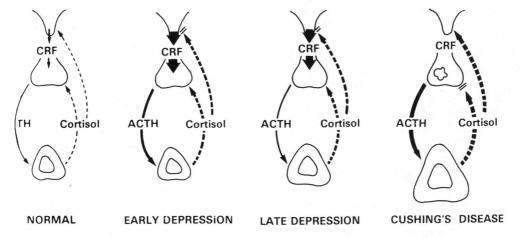

NORMAL   EARLY DEPRESSION   LATE DEPRESSION   CUSHING'S DISEASE

FIGURE 4.10.

persist in patients with anorexia nervosa despite the return to eucortisolism after the short-term correction of weight loss.

The apparently similar pathophysiology of hypercortisolism in depression and anorexia nervosa supports the notion that these two disorders lie on a pathophysiological continuum. Clinical data also support this idea. For instance, both patients with depression and anorexia nervosa manifest not only hypercortisolism, but also hypothalamic hypogonadism and anorexia nervosa. Moreover, many anorexia nervosa patients are depressed and show strong family histories for depression (Cantwell et al., 1977). Parenthetically, we observed a significant positive correlation between depression ratings and CSF CRH levels in anorexic patients (W. Kaye & P. W. Gold, unpublished observations), suggesting that CRH may be an important link between primary affective disorder and anorexia nervosa. Parenthetically, we have also noted attenuated ACTH responses to CRH in hypercortisolemic patients with anxiety disorder (Roy-Byrne et al., in press), suggesting that these patients show a similar pathophysiology of HPA functioning to that seen in subjects with depression and anorexia nervosa.

In contrast to the three hypercortisolemic psychiatric subgroups who showed the blunted ACTH responses to CRH, a group of severely psychotic schizophrenic patients showed normal basal cortisol values and normal ACTH responses to exogenous CRH (Roy et al., in press-b). These data are compatible with the previously published data of Nemeroff et al. (1984) showing normal CSF CRH in schizophrenia. Moreover, these data are compatible with previous studies which show that a smaller percentage of patients with schizophrenia than those with affective disturbance or other hypercortisolemic psychiatric disorders manifest overt basal hypercortisolism or fail to suppress their cortisol levels after dexamethasone. Parenthetically, when eight of these drug-free schizophrenic patients were studied after treatment with fluphenazine, the ACTH and cortisol response to CRH was similar to those seen during the drug-free state. In light of this eucortisolism and the normal ACTH responses to CRH in these psychotic schizophrenic patients, it is intriguing

to speculate that perhaps there is some defect in the transmission of the actual experience of distress and danger these subjects clearly feel to the hypothalamic neurons that translate this experience of distress and danger into activation of the CRH neuron. Additional work on exploring the perturbability of the CRH neuron in schizophrenic subjects following other stresses would seem warranted to further test this hypothesis.

Whether CRH plays a role in any human disease apart from the rare cases of Addison's disease secondary to CRH deficiency remains to be established. However, we have previously noted that its possible involvement in depression is intriguing in light of the following four sets of findings taken from the disciplines of developmental psychology, clinical psychiatry, and neurophysiology (Gold et al., 1984):

1. Laboratory animals subjected to maternal deprivation during the neonatal period show significant hyperactivity of the HPA axis during stress throughout adult life (Thomas, Levine, & Arnold, 1968). Hence, such animals presumably show a permanent change in the responsivity of their CRH neuron.

2. Individuals who are depression prone are thought to show greater than usual incidence of early noxious stress or maternal deprivation. Clinical experience shows that such a history seems to produce a tendency to repetitively relive the intense anxiety and dysphoria associated with this early deprivation throughout adult life whenever a significant frustration or important loss occurs. Thus, such individuals also seem prone to a hyperresponsivity of their CRH neutron intermittently throughout life.

3. CRH given ICV to primate animals not only stimulates the HPA axis (Rock et al., 1984), but also activates the locus ceruleus (Valentino, Foote, & Aston-Jones, 1983), produces decreased eating (Britton et al., 1982) and sexual behavior (Sirinathsinghji et al., 1983), and causes significant changes in activity (Sutton et al., 1982).

4. CRH has been eported to induce limbic seizures which cross-sensitize with electri-

cally kindled seizures (Weiss *et al.*, in press).

These findings, taken together, suggest that a CRH model of depression could help integrate dynamic formulations which take into account early losses and subsequent internal and external stress as factors that can predispose to or precipitate major depression, and the observations that depressed subjects often show hypercortisolism, significant anxiety, anorexia, diminished libido, hypo- or hyperactivity, and respond at times to limbic anticonvulsants. A schematic representation of this model is shown in Figure 4.11. That changes in CRH may be related to depressive symtomatology is also supported by empirical observations that depression is perhaps the only major symptom represented in a substantial number of patients, with each of the various psychiatric disorders characterized during their course by sustained or episodic hypercortisolism.

CRH STIMULATION TEST: IMPLICATIONS FOR THE DIAGNOSIS AND PATHOPHYSIOLOGY OF HYPERCORTISOLISM IN DEPRESSION AND CUSHING'S DISEASE

The hypercortisolism of depression can be of sufficient magnitude that it has been termed a pseudo-Cushing's state. Conversely, patients with Cushing's disease often show signs of clinical depression. Although there has been controversy over the years concerning the etiology of the hypercortisolism associated with affective illness and Cushing's disease, the overlap in the clinical and biochemical manifestations of these illnesses has prompted some to suggest that they share common pathophysiological features. Of clinical significance is the fact that patients with primary depression who may be hirsute or obese and who manifest high plasma and urinary free cortisol levels can be impossible to distinguish from patients with mild or early Cushing's disease. Indeed, depression can often be the first manifestation of Cushing's disease preceding the physical stigmata such as the buffalo hump or purple striae by months or even years.

Data from our group and others show that despite profound basal hypercortisolism, patients with Cushing's disease show a marked hyperresponsiveness of the pituitary corticotroph cell to exogenous CRH (Chrousos *et al.*, in press; Gold *et al.*, in press-b; Lytras *et al.*, 1984; Muller, Stalla, B. Werder, 1983; Nakahara *et al.*, 1983; Orth, 1984; Orth *et al.*, 1982; Pieters *et al.*, 1983) (Figure 4.9). Thus, in contrast to patients with depression who show a pituitary corticotroph cell normally responsive to the negative feedback effects of

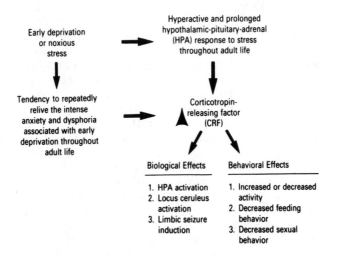

FIGURE 4.11.

glucocorticoids, patients with Cushing's disease manifest a pituitary corticotroph cell which is grossly unresponsive to cortisol negative feedback effects. Our data also suggest that the differences in pituitary corticotroph cell function between depressed and Cushing's disease patients seem accompanied by differences in hypothalamic CRH neuron function. Specifically, we have shown that many of our patients with Cushing's disease whom we studied 1 week after selective transsphenoidal adenectomy (at a time when basal ACTH and cortisol were uniformly undetectable) showed normal or nearly normal plasma ACTH responses to exogenous CRH (E. H. Oldfield et al., unpublished observations). We surmise that the adrenal insufficiency in each of these postoperative patients reflects hypofunction of corticotropin-releasing factor neurons which had been physiologically suppressed by exposure to the negative feedback of their long-standing hypercortisolism. This formulation is supported by our recent finding that compared to depressed patients and controls, CSF CRH is significantly lower in Cushing's disease patients (M. Kling & P. W. Gold, unpublished observations). A schematic diagram of the proposed differences in pituitary and hypothalamic function between patients with depression and Cushing's disease is shown in Figure 4.10.

The differential pathophysiology of hypercortisolism which we propose for Cushing's disease and depression is manifested by the fact that responses to CRH in these disorders are in the opposite direction (e.g., an exaggerated ACTH response in Cushing's disease and a blunted one in depression) (Figure 4.9). In all other diagnostic tests that have been utilized to differentiate depression from Cushing's disease, such as the dexamethasone suppression test and serial urinary free cortisol determinations, responses and/or levels in depression and Cushing's disease were in the same direction. Thus, the CRH stimulation is in a unique position to assist in the differential diagnosis between depression and early Cushing's disease. Indeed, our data do indeed show that the CRH stimulation test is helpful in the differential diagnosis of these disorders, with only a small percentage of depressed patients showing ACTH responses to CRH in the Cushing's disease range, and vice versa (Gold et al., in press-b).

DIFFERENTIAL DIAGNOSIS OF CUSHING'S DISEASE FROM OTHER CAUSES OF CUSHING'S SYNDROME

Cushing's syndrome, as a spontaneous pathophysiological entity, can be divided into three types (for a review, see Gold, 1979) (Valentino et al., 1983): Cushing's syndrome due to pituitary hypersecretion of ACTH (Cushing's disease, as discussed previously), hypercortisolism secondary to ectopic secretion of ACTH, and the autonomous secretion of cortisol by an adrenal adenoma or carcinoma. Thus, Cushing's syndrome can be divided into ACTH-dependent (the pituitary and ectopic ACTH secretion syndromes) and ACTH-independent (the cortisol-producing adrenal neoplasms) subsets. The differential diagnosis between the two types of ACTH-dependent Cushing's syndrome is often difficult. In contrast, adrenal tumors are usually diagnosed radiologically or by ultrasound. The most sensitive procedure for this diagnosis is high-resolution computerized axial tomography of the adrenal glands.

We and others have shown that the CRH stimulation test appears to differentiate between Cushing's disease and the ectopic ACTH syndrome (Chrousos et al., 1984, in press; Lytras et al., 1984; Muller et al., 1983; Pieters et al., 1983). Thus, whereas almost all patients with Cushing's disease show exaggerated or robust ACTH responses to CRH, patients with the ectopic ACTH syndrome generally fail to respond to CRH. Nine such patients were examined by us (Chrousos et al., 1984, in press) and four by other groups (Lytras et al., 1984; Muller et al., 1983; Pieters et al., 1983). Only one patient with ectopic ACTH secretion demonstrated responsiveness to CRH (Muller et al., 1983). This response was not found in repetition of the test, suggesting that randomly occurring secretory episodes of ACTH may provide a spurious diagnosis during a CRH test. Since medical or surgical correction of the hypercortisolism in these patients is followed by a rapid return (within 3 days) of pituitary–adrenal axis responsiveness to CRH, hypercortisolism in these patients is followed by a rapid return (within 3 days) of pituitary–adrenal axis responsiveness to CRH, hypercortisolism during testing is a prerequisite for assessing the response to CRH in these conditions.

Patients with ACTH-independent Cushing's syndrome had undetectable levels of plasma ACTH throughout the test and their plasma cortisol concentrations remained unaltered, like the patients with ectopic ACTH secretion. Medical or surgical correction of the hypercortisolism was followed quickly by normalization of the CRH response (Chrousos *et al.*, 1984, in press).

We have concluded that CRH testing assists in the differential diagnosis between Cushing's disease, the ectopic ACTH syndrome, and adrenal causes of Cushing's syndrome. The available data, cited above, indicate about 2 out of 44 (4.5%) false negatives and 1 out of 13 (7.6%) false positives in differentiating pituitary from ectopic causes of Cushing's syndrome.

CRH STIMULATION TEST IN NELSON'S SYNDROME

About 15% of patients who are treated for Cushing's disease show a marked increase in basal ACTH concentrations and hyperpigmentation associated with the pituitary tumor (Nelson's syndrome) (Nelson *et al.*, 1958). We and others have shown that the microadenomas caused in Cushing's disease respond to CRH. Whether the tumors associated with Nelson's syndrome respond in a similar manner is unknown. We examined the plasma ACTH response to CRH in patients with Nelson's syndrome. All patients had tumors visible by a CT scan associated with elevated basal ACTH values which showed marked rises after CRH. Thus, the ACTH-secreting adenomas in Nelson's syndrome, similar to the adenomas of Cushing's disease, respond to exogenous CRH.

It would represent an important advance in the treatment of Nelson's syndrome if the continuous infusion of CRH would "desensitize" the secretion of ACTH by these tumors. The phenomenon of pituitary desensitization was first described by Knobil

(1980), who observed that the pituitary secretion of luteinizing hormone and follicle-stimulating hormone can be interrupted by the frequent or continuous infusion of LHRH. This has been found to have extensive clinical application in treatment of idiopathic precocious puberty, palliative therapy for prostatic carcinoma, and other conditions where suppression of the hypothalamic–pituitary–gonadal axis is required, such as endometriosis. To examine the possibility of pituitary desensitization with CRH, we measured plasma ACTH concentrations in three patients who received continuous, maximal stimulatory infusions of oCRH for 24 hours. ACTH concentrations increased over the entire course of CRH administration and no evidence of desensitization was seen in any of these patients (Oldfield *et al.*, unpublished observations). We can conclude from this that CRH stimulates ACTH secretion in Nelson's syndrome. The tumors in this syndrome may be under the trophic influence of the hypothalamus, since the CRH neuron should be recovered from the suppressed state in these patients. The ACTH response in Nelson's syndrome compared to that observed in Cushing's disease is probably related to the larger tumor size and the lack of hypercortisolism in these subjects. Continuous infusions of CRH for 24 hours failed to desensitize the pituitary secretion of ACTH in patients with Nelson's syndrome. The stimulation of ACTH released in these tumors by CRH implies the presence of CRH receptors or CRH antagonists and therefore might prove useful in the management of these patients who frequently cannot be cured by current techniques.

CRH STIMULATION TEST IN THE DIFFERENTIAL DIAGNOSIS OF ADRENAL INSUFFICIENCY

Adrenal insufficiency is divided pathophysiologically into two types: primary, when the adrenals are primarily responsible, and secondary, when either the pituitary gland or the hypothalamus fails. We administered CRH to patients with adrenal insufficiency to determine whether the CRH stimulation test would be useful in the differential diagnosis of this condition (Schulte *et al.*, 1984).

Twenty-three patients with primary and secondary adrenal insufficiency were studied. All but one were on replacement glucocorticoid therapy, which was discontinued from 12 to 60 hours before testing.

Patients with primary adrenal failure had high basal plasma ACTH levels and low basal cortisol values. Cortisol levels were low or undetectable throughout the test. Plasma ACTH values were markedly stimulated by CRH (Figure 4.12). Similarly, patients with secondary adrenal insufficiency also had low or undetectable basal levels of cortisol, and cortisol responses to CRH were generally absent or minimal. However, in contrast to the

group with primary adrenal insufficiency, though plasma ACTH concentrations were also low in these subjects, the plasma ACTH responses were variable (Figure 4.12). Some patients had no ACTH responses to a CRH bolus, in contrast to the majority of patients who showed an early ACTH response similar to normal subjects. The response of these latter subjects, however, did not plateau, but continued to increase during the test. The difference ACTH response pattern in patients with secondary adrenal insufficiency cannot be accounted for by different clearance rates of CRH. All patients had immunoreactive CRH disappearance curves

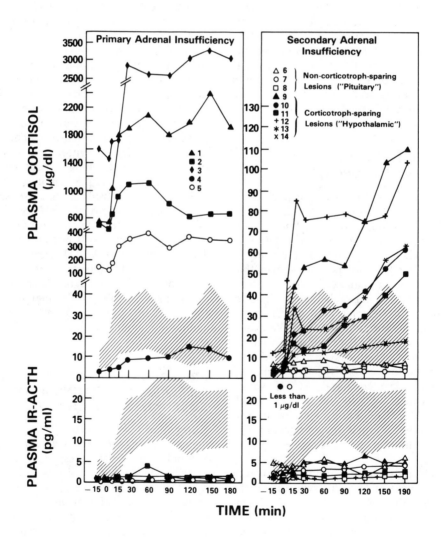

FIGURE 4.12.

from plasma, which were similar to normal controls. We postulate that the patients who showed no ACTH response to CRH represent corticotroph cell failure (pituitary adrenal insufficiency); on the other hand, the patients who responded to CRH have endogenous CRH insufficiency (hypothalamic adrenal insufficiency). We conclude from these data that, in contrast to the experience with other hypothalamic-releasing factors such as with LHRH and TRH, CRH may differentiate pituitary from hypothalamic causes of secondary adrenal insufficiency without a need for priming by multiple CRH injections.

Two patients with the rare syndrome of acquired idiopathic isolated ACTH deficiency had adrenal insufficiency, with adrenocorticol responses to a 48-hour ACTH stimulation test characteristic of the secondary form. These subjects also failed to respond to insulin-induced hypoglycemia and to vasopressin. These patients had undetectable plasma ACTH and cortisol response to a bolus of CRH. Thus, they appeared to have pituitary rather than hypothalamic adrenal insufficiency.

Patients with corticotroph-sparing secondary adrenal insufficiency present a rare opportunity to define the regulatory mechanism of the HPA axis. It is these subjects in whom, after priming with ACTH, we replicated the physiological CRH secretion by administering eight pulses of hCRH spaced strategically over the 24-hour period to mark the temporal sequence of expected ACTH pulsatile episodes.

SUMMARY AND CONCLUSIONS

CRH is a 41 amino acid peptide first isolated from ovine and subsequently from porcine, rat, and human hypothalami. We have conducted a series of clinical studies with oCRH and hCRH in volunteers and patients with various disorders of HPA function. In volunteers, we demonstrated that hCRH administration produced ACTH and cortisol responses which closely mimic naturalistically occurring secretory episodes. These data as well as our demonstration that pulsatile hCRH can reestablish normal ACTH and cortisol secretion in patients with hypo-

thalamic CRH deficiency strongly argue that CRH is of physiological relevance to the human pituitary–adrenal axis. However, since the ACTH response to an insulin tolerance test is greater than the maximal ACTH response to CRH, other factors such as vasopressin may be relevant to stress-induced ACTH secretion in man.

Following the demonstration that CRH seems to be of physiological relevance to human subjects, we developed a CRH stimulation test based on pharmacokinetic and dose–response studies with oCRH and hCRH. Based on these data, which revealed that oCRH functions as a long-acting analogue of hCRH and the demonstration that hormonal responses to CRH are greatest in the evening, patient groups with abnormalities of the HPA axis were tested with intravenous oCRH with a dose of 1 μg/kg given at 8 P.M.

This CRH stimulation test has proved helpful in clarifying the pathophysiology of hypercortisolism in a variety of psychiatric disorders characterized by this endocrine abnormality. Thus, blunted ACTH responses in hypercortisolemic patients with depression, anorexia nervosa, and panic anxiety disorder indicate normality of the pituitary corticotroph in these patient subgroups. These data, along with the finding that a continuous infusion of CRH to normal volunteers reproduces the pattern and magnitude of hypercortisolism in depression and anorexia nervosa, suggest that the hypercortisolism in these disorders represents a defect at or above the hypothalamus, resulting in the hypersecretion of CRH. This hypothesis is particularly intriguing in light of the demonstration that CRH administration to experimental animals produces many of the physiological and behavioral responses classically associated with depression and anorexia nervosa, including hypercortisolism, hypothalamic hypogonadism, and decreases in libido and appetite.

The CRH stimulation test has also helped to resolve one of the oldest endocrinological dilemmas, namely, whether the hypercortisolism of depression and Cushing's disease share a common or dissimilar pathophysiological basis. As noted, our data indicate a hypothalamic locus for depression and a pituitary locus for Cushing's disease.

Moreover, the CRH stimulation test has also proved helpful in the often difficult differential diagnosis between depression and early Cushing's disease. Hence, the wide divergence of ACTH responses to CRH in depression and Cushing's disease constitutes the basis for distinguishing most cases of Cushing's disease from depression.

The CRH test has also proved helpful in the differential diagnosis of Cushing's syndrome. Hence, in contrast to patients with Cushing's disease, patients with ectopic ACTH secretion show no response of either ACTH or cortisol to CRH, whereas patients with the hypercortisolism of adrenal origin have low or undetectable plasma ACTH, high plasma cortisol, and no response to CRH. Patients with primary adrenal insufficiency had increased plasma ACTH and diminished cortisol responses to CRH.

Patients with secondary adrenal insufficiency also had diminished plasma cortisol responses to CRH, but either diminished or normal to augmented and prolonged ACTH responses. Thus, these patients could be classified as having corticotroph-nonsparing and corticotroph-sparing lesions. We believe that the former represent pituitary and the latter hypothalamic adrenal insufficiency.

We conclude that CRH is an important modulator of the human pituitary–adrenal axis which has helped to elucidate the pathophysiology of abnormalities in HPA function in patients with depression, anorexia nervosa, panic anxiety disorder, Cushing's disease, and secondary adrenal insufficiency. Moreover, CRH has proved helpful in the differential diagnosis of pseudo-Cushing's from Cushing's disease, Cushing's disease from ectopic ACTH secretion, and pituitary from hypothalamic–adrenal insufficiency. Although no therapeutic applications of CRH have yet been implemented, administration of CRH by implantable infusion pumps should constitute a more physiological treatment of hypothalamic–CRH deficiency than glucocorticoid replacement. Moreover, we speculate that it is possible that centrally active CRH antagonists may be helpful in the treatment of pseudo-Cushing's states, and the peripherally active CRH antagonists may prove capable of managing the complications of Nelson's syndrome.

References

Amsterdam, J. D., Winokur, A., Abelman, E., Lucki, I., & Rickels, K. (1983). Cosyntropin (ACTH 1–24) test in depressed patients and healthy subjects. *American Journal of Psychiatry, 140*, 907–909.

Avgerinos, P. C., Schuermeyer, T. H., Gold, P. W., Nieman, L., Udelsman, R., Loriaux, D. L., & Chrousos, G. P. (in press-a). Synthetic human CRH as a probe of pulsatile ACTH and cortisol secretion. In *Hormones and pulsatility* (W. Crowley, ed.). New York: Plenum Press.

Avgerinos, P. C., Schuermeyer, T. H., Gold, P. W., Tomai, T. P., Loriaux, D. L., Sherins, R. J., Cutler, G. P., Jr., & Chrousos, G. P. (in press-b). Pulsatile administration of human corticotropin-releasing factor (hCRF) in patients with secondary adrenal insufficiency in restoration of normal cortisol secretory pattern. *Journal of Clinical Endocrinology and Metabolism*.

Axelrod, J., & Reisine, T. D. (1984). Stress hormones: Their interaction and regulation. *Science, 224*, 452–459.

Bloom, F. E., Battenberg, E. L. F., Rivier, J., & Vale, W. (1982). Corticotropin-releasing factor (CRF): Immunoreactive neurons and fiber in rat hypothalamus. *Regulatory Peptides, 4*, 43–48.

Britton, D. R., Koob, G. F., & Rivier, J. (1982). Intraventricular corticotropin-releasing factor enhances behavioral effects of novelty. *Life Sciences, 31*, 363–367.

Brown, M. R., Fisher, L. A., Spiess, J., Rivier, C., Rivier, J., & Vale, W. (1982). Corticotropin-releasing factor: Actions on the sympathetic nervous system and metabolism. *Endocrinology (Baltimore), 111*, 928–931.

Cantwell, D. P., Sturzenberger, S., Burnough, J. *et al.* (1977). Anorexia nervosa. An affective disorder? *Archives of General Psychiatry, 34*, 1087–1094.

Carroll, B. J., Curtis, G. C., & Mendels, J. (1976). Neuroendocrine regulation in depression. I. Limbic system–adrenocortical dysfunction. *Archives of General Psychiatry, 33*, 1039–1044.

Chrousos, G. P., Oldfield, E. H., Nieman, L., Nisula, B., Cutler, G. B., Jr., Schulte, H. M., Gold, P. W., & Loriaux, D. L. (in press). The corticotropin-releasing factor test in Cushing's syndrome [Letter]. *New England Journal of Medicine*.

Chrousos, G. P., Schulte, H. M., Oldfield, E. H., Gold, P. W., Cutler, G. B., Jr., & Loriaux, D. L. (1984). The corticotropin-releasing factor stimulation test: An aid in the differential diagnosis of patients with Cushing's syndrome. *New England Journal of Medicine, 310*, 622–627.

De Souza, E. B., Perrin, H. M., Insel, T., Rivier, J., Vale, W. W., & Kuhar, M. J. (1984). Corticotropin-releasing factor receptors in rat forebrain: Autoradiographic identification. *Science, 224*, 1449–1450.

Furatani, Y., Morimoto, Y., Shubahara, S., Noda, M., Takahashi, H., Hirose, T., Asai, M., Inayama, S., Hayashida, H., Miyata, T., & Numa, S. (1983). Cloning and sequence analysis of cDNA for ovine corticotropin-releasing factor precursor. *Nature (London), 301*, 537–540.

Gerner, G. H., & Gwirtsman, H. E. (1981). Abnormalities of dexamethasone suppression test and urinary MHPG on anorexia nervosa. *American Journal of Psychiatry*, 138, 650–653.

Gillies, G. E., Lingo, E. A., & Lowry, P. J. (1982). Corticotropin-releasing activity of the new CRF is potentiated several times by vasopressin. *Nature (London)*, 299, 355–357.

Gold, P. W., & Chrousos, G. P. (in press). Clinical studies with corticotropin-releasing factor: Implications for the diagnosis and pathophysiology of depression, Cushing's disease, and adrenal insufficiency. *Psychoneuroendocrinology*.

Gold, P. W., Chrousos, G. P., Kellner, C. H., Post, R. M., Roy, A., Avgerinos, P., Schulte, H. M., Oldfield, E. H., & Loriaux, D. L. (1984). Psychiatric implications of basic and clinical studies with corticotropin-releasing factor. *American Journal of Psychiatry*, 141, 619–627.

Gold, P. W., Gwirtsman, H., Avgerinos, P. C., Nieman, L., Jimerson, D., Kaye, W., Loriaux, D. L., & Chrousos, G. P. (in press). Abnormal hypothalamic–pituitary–adrenal function in anorexia nervosa: Pathophysiological mechanisms in underweight and weight-recovered patients. *New England Journal of Medicine*.

Gold, P. W., Loriaux, D. L., Roy, A., Kellner, C. H., Post, R. M., Kling, M., Calabrese, J. R., Oldfield, E. H., Pickar, D., Avgerinos, P. C., Paul, S. M., Cutler, G. B., Jr., & Chrousos, G. P. (in press-b). The CRH stimulation test: Implications for the diagnosis and pathophysiology of hypercortisolism in depression and Cushing's disease. *New England Journal of Medicine*.

Grossman, A., Perry, L., Schally, A. V., Rees, L. H., Tomlin, D., Coy, D., Comary-Schull, A. M., & Besser, G. M. (1982). The new hypothalamic hormone corticotropin-releasing factor specifically stimulates the release of adrenocorticotropic hormone and cortisol in man. *Lancet*, 8278, 921–922.

Guilemin, R., Vargo, T., Rossier, J., Minick, S., Ling, N., Rivier, C., Vale, W., & Bloom, F. (1977). β-Endorphin and adrenocorticotropin are secreted concomitantly by the pituitary gland. *Science*, 197, 1367–1368.

Halbreich, V., Asnis, G. M., Slindledecker, R., Zumoff, B., & Nathan, R. S. (1985). Cortisol secretion in endogenous depression II time-related functions. *Archives of General Psychiatry*, 42, 909–915.

Harris, G. W. (1948). Neural control of the pituitary gland. *Physiological Reviews*, 28, 134–179.

Holsboer, F., Genken, H., Stalla, G. K., & Muller, G. H. (1984). Blunted ACTH responses to human CRH in depression [Letter]. *New England Journal of Medicine*, 311, 1127.

Iason, A. H. *The thyroid gland in medical history.* New York: Froben Press.

Insel, T. R., Kalin, W. H., Guttmacher, L. B., Cohen, R. M., & Murphy, D. L. (1982). The dexamethasone suppresssion test in obsessive–compulsive disorder. *Psychiatry Research*, 6, 153–160.

Knobil, E. (1980). The neuroendocrine control of the menstrual cycle. *Reviews of Physical Hormone and Research*, 36, 53–88.

Lieutaud, J. (1742). *Essais anatomiques, contenant l'histoire exact de toutes les parties qui composent le corps de l'homme, avec la manière de Disséquer.* Paris: Huart.

Lytras, N., Grossman, A., Tomlin, P. S., Wass, J. A. H., Coy, D. H. Schally, A. V., Rees, L. H., & Besser, G. M. (1984). Corticotropin-releasing factor responses in normal subjects and patients with disorders of the hypothalamus and pituitary. *Clinical Endocrinology (Oxford)*, 20, 71–84.

Mains, R., Eipper, E., & Ling, N. (1977). Common precursor to corticotropin and endorphins. *Proceedings of the National Academy of Sciences of the U.S.A.*, 74, 3014–3018.

Medvei, V. C. (1984). *A history of endocrinology.* Boston: MTP Press.

Muller, O. A., Stalla, G. K., & Werder, K. (1983). Corticotropin-releasing factor: A new tool for the differential diagnosis of Cushing's syndrome. *Journal of Clinical Endocrinology and Metabolism*, 56, 227–229.

Nakahara, M., Shibasaki, T., Shizume, K., Kiyosawa, Y., Odagiri, E., Toshihiro, S., Yamaguchi, H., Tsushima, T., Demura, H., Maeda, T., Wakabayashi, I., & Ling, N. (1983). Corticotropin-releasing factor test in normal subjects and patients with hypothalamic–pituitary–adrenal disorders. *Journal of Clinical Endocrinology and Metabolism*, 57, 963–968.

Nelson, D. H., Meakin, J. W., Denby, J. B., Matson, D. D., Emerson, K., & Thorn, G. W. (1958). ACTH-producing tumor of the pituitary gland. *New England Journal of Medicine*, 259, 161–164.

Nemeroff, C. B., Widerlov, E., Bissette, G., Wallens, H., Karllson, I., Eklund, K., Kilts, G., & Loosen, P. (1984). Elevated immunoreactive corticotropin-releasing hormone in depressed patients. *Science*, 224, 1342–1344.

Olschowka, J. A., O'Donohue, T. L., Mueller, G. P., & Jocobwitz, D. M. (1982). The distribution of corticotropin-releasing factor-like immunoreactive neurons in rat brain. *Peptides (New York)*, 3, 995–1015.

Orth, D. N. (1984). The old and the new in Cushing's syndrome [Editorial]. *New England Journal of Medicine*, 310, 649–651.

Orth, D. N., Debold, C. R., Decherney, G. S., Jackson, R. V., Alexander, A. N., Rivier, J., Rivier, C., Spiess, J. & Vale, W. (1982). Pituitary microadenomas causing Cushing's disease respond to corticotropin-releasing factor. *Journal of Clinical Endocrinology and Metabolism*, 55, 1017–1019.

Orth, D. N., Jackson, R. V., DeCherney, G. S., Debold, C. R., Alexander, A. N., Island, D. P., Rivier, J., Rivier, G., Spiess, J., & Vale, W. (1983). Effect of synthetic ovine corticotropin-releasing factor: Dose–response of plasma adrenocorticotropin and cortisol. *Journal of Clinical Investigation*, 71, 587–595.

Pieters, G. F. F. M., Hermus, A. R. M. M., Smals, A. G. H., Bartelink, A. K. M., Benraad, T. H. J., & Kloppenborg, P. W. G. (1983). Responsiveness of the hypophyseal adrenocortical axis to corticotropinreleasing factor in pituitary-dependent Cushing's disease. *Journal of Clinical Endocrinology and Metabolism*, 57, 513–515.

Plotsky, P. M., Rubin, T. O., & Vale, W. (1985). Hypophysiotropic regulation of adrenocorticotropin secretion in response to insulin-induced hypoglycemia. *Endocrinology (Baltimore)*, *117*, 323–329.

Post, R. M. (1982). Use of the anticonvulsant carbamazepine in primary and secondary affective illness: Clinical and theoretical implications. *Psychological Medicine*, *12*, 70–104.

Renold, A. E., Jenkins, D., & Thorn, G. W. (1952). The use of intravenous ACTH. A study in quantitative adrenocortical stimulation. *Journal of Clinical Endocrinology and Metabolism*, *12*, 763–797.

Rivier, C., & Vale, W. (1983). Modulation of stress-induced ACTH release by corticotropin-releasing factor, catecholamines, and vasopressin. *Nature (London)*, *303*, 325–327.

Rivier, J., Spiess, J., & Vale, W. (1983). Characterization of rat hypothalamic corticotropin-releasing factor. *Proceedings of the National Academy of Sciences of the U.S.A.*, *80*, 4851–4855.

Rock, J. P., Oldfield, E. H., Schulte, H. M., Chrousos, G. P., Gold, P. W., Cutler, G. B., Jr., Kornblith, P. L., & Loriaux, D. L. (184). Corticotropin-releasing factor administered into vertricular CSF stimulates pituitary ACTH release. *Brain Research*, *323*, 365–368.

Roy, A., Pickar, D., Chrousos, G. P., Doran, A., Paul, S. M., Loriaux, D. L., & Gold, P. W. (in press-a). Postdexamethasone cortisol levels in depression correlate positively with immunoreactive CSF CRH. *American Journal of Psychiatry*.

Roy, A., Pickar, D., Doran, A., Paul, S. M., Chrousos, G. P., & Gold, P. W. (in press-b). Normal ACTH and cortisol responses to CRH in schizophrenia. *American Journal of Psychiatry*.

Roy-Byrne, P. P., Uhde, T., Post, R. M., Gallucci, W. T., Chrousos, G. P., & Gold, P. W. (in press). Blunted ACTH response to ovine CRH in panic–anxiety disorder. *American Journal of Psychiatry*.

Sachar, E. J., Hellman, L., Fukushima, D. K., & Gallagher, T. F. (1970). Cortisol production in depressive illness: A clinical and biochemical classification. *Archives of General Psychiatry*, *23*, 289–298.

Saffran, M., Schally, A. V., & Bentey, B. G. (1955). Stimulation of the release of corticotropin from the adenohypophysis by a neurohypophyseal factor. *Endocrinology (Baltimore)*, *57*, 439–444.

Schally, A. V., Chang, R. C., Arimura, A., Redding, T. W., Fishback, J. B., & Vigh, S. (1981). High molecular weight peptide with corticotropin-releasing factor activity from porcine hypothalami. *Proceedings of the National Academy of Sciences of the U.S.A.*, *78*, 5197–5201.

Schuermeyer, T. H., Avgerinos, P. C., Gold, P. W., Tomai, T. P., Gallucci, W. T., Cutler, G. B., Jr., Loriaux, D. L., & Chrousos, G. P. (1984). Human corticotropin-releasing factor: Dose–response and time course of ACTH and cortisol secretion in man. *Journal of Clinical Endocrinology and Metabolism*, *59*, 1103–1108.

Schuermeyer, T. H., Gold, P. W., Gallucci, W. T., Tomai, T. P., Cutler, G. B., Jr., Loriaux, D. L., & Chrousos, G. P. (1985). Effect and pharmacokinetic properties of the rat/human corticotropin-releasing factor (r/h CRF) in rhesus monkeys. *Endocrinology (Baltimore)*, *117*, 300–306.

Schulte, H. M., Chrousos, G. P., Avgerinos, P. C., Gold, P. W., Oldfield, E. H., Cutler, G. B., & Loriaux, D. L. (1984). The corticotropin-releasing factor stimulation test: A possible aid in the diagnosis of adrenal insufficiency. *Journal of Clinical Endocrinology and Metabolism*, *58*, 1064–1067.

Schulte, H. M., Chrousos, G., Gold, P. W., Booth, J. P., Oldfield, T. H., Cutler, G. B., Jr., & Loriaux, D. L. (1985). Continuous infusion of CRF in normal volunteers. Physiological and pathophysiological implications. *Journal of Clinical Investigation*, *75*, 1781–1785.

Schulte, H. M., Chrousos, G. P., Gold, P. W., Oldfield, E. H., Phillips, J. M., Munson, P. J., Cutler, G. B., Jr., & Loriaux, D. L. (1982). Metabolic clearance rate and plasma half-life of radioiodinated ovine corticotropin-releasing factor in a primate. *Journal of Clinical Endocrinology and Metabolism*, *55*, 1023–1027.

Schulte, H. M., Chrousos, G. P., Oldfield, E. H., Gold, P. W., Cutler, G. B., Jr., & Loriaux, D. L. (1982). The effects of corticotropin-releasing factor on the anterior pituitary function of stalk-sectioned cynomolgus macaques: Dose–response of cortisol secretion. *Journal of Clinical Endocrinology and Metabolism*, *55*, 810–812.

Schulte, H. M., Chrousos, G. P., Oldfield, E. H., Gold, P. W., Cutler, G. B., Jr., & Loriaux, D. L. (in press). Corticotropin-releasing factor administration in normal men: Pituitary and adrenal responses in the morning and evening. *Hormone and Metabolic Research*.

Selye, H. (1936). Stress syndrome. A syndrome produced by diverse noxious agents. *Nature (London)*, *138*, 32.

Shibahara, S., Morimoto, Y., Furatani, Y., Notake, M., Takahashi, H., Shimizu, S., Horikawa, S., & Numa, S. (1983). Isolation and sequence analysis of the human corticotropin-releasing factor precursor gene. *EMBO Journal*, *2*, 775–779.

Sirinathsinghji, D. J. S., Rees, L. H., Rivier, J., & Vale, W. (1983). Corticotropin-releasing factor is a potent inhibitor of sexual receptivity in the female rat. *Nature (London)*, *305*, 232–235.

Stokes, P. E. (1973). Adrenocortical activation in alcoholics during chronic drinking. *Annals of the New York Academy of Sciences*, *215*, 77–81.

Sutton, R. E., Koob, G. F., Le Moal, M., Rivier, J., & Vale, W. (1982). Corticotropin-releasing factor produces behavioral activation in rats. *Nature (London)*, *297*, 331–333.

Thomas, E. B., Levine, E. S., & Arnold, W. J. (1968). Effects of maternal deprivation and incubation rearing upon adrenocortical activity in the adult rat. *Developmental Psychobiology*, *1*, 21–23.

Vale, W., Spiess, J., Rivier, C., & Rivier, J. (1981). Characterization of a 41-residue ovine hypothalamic peptide that stimulates secretion of corticotropin and β-endorphin. *Science*, *213*, 1394–1397.

Vale, W., Vaughn, J., Smith, M., Yamamoto, G., Rivier, J., & Rivier, C. (1983). Effects of synthetic ovine corticotropin-releasing factor, glucocorticoids, catecholamines, neurohypophyseal peptides, and other substances on cultured corticotropic cells. *Endocrinology (Baltimore)*, *113*, 1121–1131.

Valentino, R., Foote, S. L., & Aston-Jones, G. (1983). Corticotropin-releasing factor activates noradrenergic neurons of the locus coeruleus. *Brain Research*, *220*, 363–367.

Weiss, S. R. B., Post, R. M., Gold, P. W., Chrousos, G. P., & Pert, A. (in press). Behavioral activation and amygdala seizures following central CRH administration. *Brain Research*.

Zuingenus, T. (1669). *Commentaru Hippocrates, Basilae: Episcoporium Opera* (pp. 324–385).

PART III

ENDOCRINE DISTURBANCES IN PSYCHIATRIC DISORDERS

5 PSYCHOSOCIAL DWARFISM, INFANTILE AUTISM, AND ATTENTION DEFICIT DISORDER

WAYNE H. GREEN
STEPHEN I. DEUTSCH
MAGDA CAMPBELL
New York University Medical Center

INTRODUCTION

Psychosocial dwarfism (PSD), infantile autism (IA), and attention deficit disorder (ADD) are psychiatric disorders of childhood which may manifest abnormal endocrine findings.

In PSD, the child, although perhaps biologically vulnerable, typically has normal endocrine functioning once removed from the stressful environment. The abnormalities are felt to be related to psychosocial stresses—specifically a malignant caretaker/child relationship. These stresses appear to yield the endocrine abnormalities and the resultant growth retardation through their influence on the cerebral cortex and its relays to the hypothalamus. With removal of the stresses, but without medical or hormonal treatment, abnormal endocrine findings usually normalize over a period of from a few days to 2 years.

Infantile autism is a pervasive developmental disorder characterized by distortions in the development of various behaviors, including language and social relations. The accumulated evidence implicates central nervous system (CNS) dysfunction as causative in the etiology of IA. Various neurotransmitter and endocrine abnormalities have been reported in subgroups of IA, but none of the abnormalities has been found to be specific for this syndrome. The precise re-lationship between IA and the biological abnormalities is unclear. However, one major treatment strategy in IA is to use psychopharmacological agents in an attempt to normalize these findings and ameliorate the autistic symptomatology.

In ADD, the endocrine disturbances which have been of most concern to date are those subsequent to psychopharmacological treatment of the disorder, in particular their effects on growth. Endocrinological abnormalities are not usually a part of the clinical picture in untreated ADD children.

In this chapter, we shall review these three disorders, emphasizing the endocrinological aspects and their clinical relevance.

PSYCHOSOCIAL DWARFISM

Classical PSD was first described in a relatively homogenous group of 13 children by Powell and his colleagues in their classic papers, "Emotional deprivation and growth retardation simulating idiopathic hypopituitarism" (Powell, Brasel, & Blizzard, 1967; Powell, Brasel, Raiti, & Blizzard, 1967). These children were differentiated from those with idiopathic hypopituitarism by markedly disturbed home environments and by physical, endocrinological, and behavioral abnormalities which rapidly and significantly normalized following hospitalization. This normalization occurred without any specific medical, hormonal, or psychiatric treatment, although removal of a child from the nuclear family is one of the most powerful psychiatric interventions. The authors hypothesized psychic factors or the emotional disturbance in these children may have decreased "pituitary tropic hormone via the central nervous system" (Powell, Brasel, Raiti, & Blizzard, 1967, p. 1282) and noted that growth increased remarkably when the child was removed from the emotionally disturbed environment and that growth markedly and abruptly decreased upon discharge home. Only 1 of the 13 children was felt to be malnourished, and the authors felt the rapidity of change in growth rates precluded malabsorption or malnutrition as causative.

A recent critical review of classical PSD concluded the preponderance of evidence strongly supports the existence of such children and proposed specific diagnostic criteria for classical psychosocial dwarfism, given in Table 5.1 (Green, Campbell, & David, 1984).

Endocrinological Findings

Although endocrine abnormalities are characteristically found in PSD, they are heterogeneous (for critical review, see Campbell, Green, Caplan, & David, 1982). To date the only consistently abnormal endocrine finding has been somatomedin levels in the hypopituitary range, but this was in a total of only 9 PSDs aged 2 years or older. The endocrine deviations normalize following re-

---

TABLE 5.1. Diagnostic Criteria for Classical Psychosocial Dwarfism

I. Age of onset: Usually between 2 and 3 years

II. Physical manifestations: Severe linear growth retardation after a period of normal growth (height usually markedly < third percentile); children typically are *not* malnourished, delayed bone age usually present, decreased head circumference is sometimes found; dental eruption is typically normal

III. Endocrine manifestations: Majority have initial decreased fasting GH, decreased GH release following provocative stimuli, and when reported, abnormally low somatomedin levels; some have abnormal pituitary–adrenal axis findings

IV. Behavioral manifestations: The child exhibits some of the following:
    A. Bizarre behavior involving abnormal acquisition and intake of food and liquids, for example, polyphagia, polydispia, gorging, vomiting, eating garbage and pets' food, drinking toilet water
    B. Sleep disorders, some have nocturnal roaming
    C. Irritability, temper tantrums
    D. Apathy, withdrawal
    E. Poor peer relations, elective mutism
    F. Pain agnosia, self-injury, accident proneness
    G. Developmental lags, for example, psychomotor retardation, delayed language, IQs in the borderline or retarded ranges

V. Psychosocial environment: A severely disturbed mother(ing figure)/child relationship is present; child abuse is also present in some cases; mothers are heterogeneous in their psychopathology

VI. Disqualifiers: Not secondary to another physical or psychiatric disorder, for example, idiopathic hypopituitarism, infantile autism, mental retardation or primary malnutrition

VII. Confirmation of diagnosis: Growth and normalization of endocrine abnormalities begin rapidly following removal of the child to a new environment (which may include hospitalization) and without medical, hormonal, or psychiatric treatment

moval from the inimical environment with no specific medical, hormonal, or psychiatric treatment. This normalization may occur within days or take as long as 2 years, depending upon the specific endocrine disturbance and the methodology used to measure endocrine function. None of the abnormal endocrine findings correlates directly with either growth failure or catch-up growth. Thus, the etiology of growth failure in PSD is still unknown.

Growth Hormone

Growth hormone (GH) abnormalities are the most typical and best studied endocrine dysfunction in PSD. Psychosocial environment, sleep, nutrition, and pharmacological agents all influence GH production.

GH secretion by the anterior pituitary is regulated primarily by the median eminence (ME) of the hypothalamus which, in turn, is significantly influenced by other areas of the brain, including centers important in emotional expression such as the amygdala, the septal region, the hippocampus, and the midbrain (Brown, Seggie, Chambers, & Ettigi, 1978).

The predominant influence of the hypothalamus on pituitary GH secretion is stimulatory. This has been shown in patients following transection of the pituitary stalk and the very low GH levels which followed (Glick, Roth, Yalow, & Berson, 1965). The GH response to either insulin-induced hypoglycemia or arginine is blocked following pituitary stalk section (Antony et al., 1969; Lister, Underwood, Marshall, Friesen, & Van Wyk, 1974). This strongly suggests these stimuli act above this point, most likely in the hypothalamus. At least two hypothalamic factors influence GH secretion. GH release-inhibiting hormone (GIH), also known as somatostatin, has been identified in the ME of the hypothalamus (Pelletier, Labrie, Arimura, & Scally, 1974).

Although GH-releasing factor (GRF) from the human hypothalamus has not yet been isolated and synthesized, bioactive factors that are extremely similar or identical both immunologically and physiochemically have been isolated from human pancreatic islet tumors (Bloch et al., 1983; Böhlen et al., 1983; Guillemin et al., 1983). These factors are known as human pancreatic GRFs (hp-GRFs). The amino acid sequences of these hpGRF factors have been determined and at least one, hpGRF-44, has been synthesized and been found to be both a specific and a potent releaser of GH in clinical trials, including some in children with growth disturbances (Takano et al., 1984). Lal and Martin (1980) note that α-adrenergic, dopaminergic and serotonergic mechanisms stimulate GH secretion and a β-adrenergic mechanism inhibits GH secretion.

Sleep is the most important physiological regulator of GH, and the release of GH in children occurs primarily during slow wave sleep (SWS), especially Stage IV sleep (Honda et al., 1969; Takahashi, Kipnis, & Daughaday, 1968). GH release appears to be inhibited during periods of wakefulness and paradoxical (REM) sleep (Takahashi et al., 1968).

Although malnutrition is not typical of PSD, it clearly overlaps clinically in some cases. Acute starvation in rats both depletes GRF in hypothalami (Meites & Fiel, 1965) as well as pituitary GH content (Friedman & Reichlin, 1965). Decreased GH production has been reported in severely undernourished children (Mönckeberg, Donoso, Oxman, Pak, & Meneghello, 1963); however, GH levels are typically normal or elevated in infants or very young children with maternal deprivation (reactive attachment disorder of infancy) which has a severe malnutrition component (Krieger & Mellinger, 1971). Likewise, elevated GH levels have been reported with severe chronic protein–calorie malnutrition (Kwashiorkor) (Pimstone, Becker, & Hansen, 1973) and in about 50% of patients with anorexia nervosa (Vigersky & Loriaux, 1977).

GH Findings in PSD

GH findings are summarized in Table 5.2. Determinations of fasting GH levels immediately upon or soon after admission to hospital and before increased growth rates occurred were abnormally low in 20 out of 21 (95%) PSDs. Serum GH levels following provocative stimulation (nearly always insulin-induced hypoglycemia) at or soon after hospitalization and before increased growth rates were abnormally low in slightly over one-half of the PSDs tested (49 of 87; 56%).

TABLE 5.2. Growth Hormone Studies in Psychosocial Dwarfism

Authors	n	Chronological age (years)	Diagnosis	Early fasting GH (before growth)	GH after insulin stimulation (before growth)	GH after stimulation (after growth)
Frasier, Hilburn, and Matthews (1967)	1	$4\frac{11}{12}$	Dwarfism associated with environmental deprivation	Low	Normal	—
Powell, Brasel, Raiti, and Blizzard (1967)	15	3.3–11.5	Emotional deprivation and growth retardation	—	6/10 low, 4/10 normal	7/7 normal
Kaplan, Abrams, Bell, Conte, and Grumbach (1968)	9	$3\frac{1}{12}$–10	Psychosocial dwarfism	9/9 low	7/9 normal, 2/9 low	Only 1 of the 2 children with low values was retested; now normal
Krieger and Mellinger (1971)	7	$3\frac{5}{12}$–$10\frac{2}{12}$	Psychosocial dwarfism	6/7 low, 1/7 normal	5/7 low, 2/7 normal	5/6 normal, 1/6 low
Imura, Yoshimi, and Ikekubo (1971)	1	16	Deprivation dwarfism	—	Low	Normal
Frasier and Rallison (1972)	1	$5\frac{5}{12}$ (follow-up at $6\frac{2}{12}$, $10\frac{7}{12}$)	Deprivation dwarfism	—	Low (at $5\frac{5}{12}$ and $6\frac{2}{12}$)	Normal (age $10\frac{7}{12}$)

Reference	n	Age	Diagnosis			Majority normal (number not specified)
Brasel (1973)[a]	22	$1\frac{9}{12}-15\frac{3}{12}$	Psychosocial dwarfism	—	8/15 low, 7/15 normal	—
Lacey, Hewison, and Parkin (1973)	2	11 ± 0.4	Psychosocial short stature	—	2/2 low	—
Powell, Hopwood, and Barratt (1973)	1	5.7	Emotional deprivation and short stature	—	Low (plus arginine)	Normal (plus arginine)
Rayner and Rudd (1973)	3	$9\frac{2}{12}-10\frac{4}{12}$	Emotional deprivation	3/3 low	2/2 low, 1 normal on day 5	3/3 normal
Van Den Brande et al. (1975)	2	8	Emotional deprivation and short stature	—	1/2 low, 1/2 normal	2/2 normal
D'Ercole, Underwood, and Van Wyk (1977)	6	$4\frac{1}{2}-13$	Psychosocial dwarfism	—	5/6 low, 1/6 normal	—
Saenger et al. (1977)	1	$6\frac{10}{12}$	Psychosocial dwarfism	Low	Borderline low	Normal
Hopwood and Becker (1979)	35	2.0-14.0	Psychosocial dwarfism	—	14/28 "blunted"	—

[a] Includes patients from Powell, Brasel, and Blizzard (1967) and Powell, Brasel, Raiti, and Blizzard (1967).

Interestingly, 3 PSDs who had random GH levels determined on the day after admission when they were neither fasting nor resting had normal GH values (8.8, 19.5, and 38.0 ng/ml) (Krieger & Mellinger, 1971). Two of these were not tested with provocative stimuli because of poor physical condition secondary to malnutrition (weights 66% and 68% of normal mean for height) and the third for technical reasons. Later, GH values in these 3 patients after both fasting and insulin stimulation were abnormally low. Thus, although these provocations did not cause normal GH release by the pituitary, at other times normal serum levels existed. After growth rates had increased, 22 of 23 (96%) PSDs had normal GH responses to insulin-induced hypoglycemia.

Levels of GH are very responsive to the psychosocial environment. Typically values normalize and growth begins within a few days following removal from the inimical environment. Thus, GH function tests must be done rapidly following admission to hospital or the abnormality may be missed. Likewise, in children who return to the unfavorable environment, there is usually prompt recurrence of growth failure and abnormal GH levels (Powell, Brasel, Raiti, & Blizzard, 1967). The remarkable rapidity of these changes is strong evidence that malnutrition or malabsorption is not of primary importance, as growth failure and resumption would be expected to be more gradual if that were the case.

Imura, Yoshimi, and Ikekubo (1971) and Parra (1973) administered propranolol and methoxamine to PSDs. These drugs caused significant increases in GH output, suggesting to the authors that the low GH production by the pituitary is functional, not organic, and that pituitary GH reserve may be normal.

It must be noted that there are no absolute correlations between GH levels and growth in PSDs. Normal GH levels have appeared in some PSDs during periods of growth failure, and growth rate has increased while abnormally low GH levels remain. The exact relationship between GH function and growth rate in PSD must yet be determined.

Somatomedin

The somatomedins (SMs) are the effector hormones of GH which stimulates their production, primarily by the liver. While there is some evidence that GH can act directly on tissue (Isaksson, Jansson, & Gause, 1982), growth velocity usually correlates better with SM levels than with GH levels (Laron, 1983). Deficiency of GH either alone or with deficiency of other tropic hormones always shows very low SM values (LaCauza et al., 1983).

SMs in PSD

Four PSDs did not respond adequately when administered exogenous GH in their home environment (Frasier & Rallison, 1972; Tanner, Whitehouse, Hughes, & Vince, 1971). Because of this, Tanner (1973) speculated that decreased growth might be secondary to defective action or production of SM.

Van Den Brande and co-workers (1975) reported on SM activity in 2 PSDs aged 8 years. On admission, the male weighed 82% of the median for his height and had a subnormal response of GH to arginine infusion. The female weighed 109% of the median for her height and had a normal response of GH to arginine infusion. Both children, however, had SM activity levels in the hypopituitary range. Both children were growing at catch-up rates and had normal GH values 1 month after hospitalization, but SM activity was still below normal. In both, maximal plasma GH and plasma SM increased with time. The authors noted that one child's having normal GH level and a low SM activity suggested that growth failure was secondary to deficient SM levels. They felt the unexpectedly low SM activity levels in both children during catch-up growth implied that tissues had become hypersensitized to SM secondary to the low SM activity levels prior to hospitalization.

D'Ercole, Underwood, and Van Wyk (1977) determined SM-C levels in 6 PSDs (4 males, 2 females) ages $4\frac{1}{2}$–13 years. Five had both subnormal serum SM concentrations and a below normal GH response to a provocative test. All 6 children responded to hospitalization with marked personality improvements, catch-up growth rates, and normalization of pituitary GH responses. Serum SM returned to normal in 5. In the sixth, however, despite a marked acceleration of linear growth over a 4-month period, SM remained unchanged after the third week. While SM levels may have subsequently risen, this child's older brother's SM levels nearly doubled during the same 3-week period.

Saenger and colleagues (1977) reported a male PSD with SM activity in the hypopituitary range on admission to hospital; GH was low after fasting and borderline low after insulin stimulation. Both GH and SM normalized with onset of catch-up growth. Later, however, during his nurse's vacation growth rate abruptly decreased. SM level remained normal during this period while GH level again fell to a subnormal value.

The subnormal SM levels are the only consistently abnormal endocrine finding to date in PSD, but this is in a total of only 9 children in three studies. Again as with GH, catch-up growth appears to have occurred with a subnormal SM value and slow growth occurred with normal SM activity levels.

Somatostatin

Although somatostatin (SS) or GH release-inhibiting hormone (GH-RIH) has been isolated and synthesized (Mortimer, 1977) and it inhibits the sleep-related peak in physiological human GH release (Parker et al., 1974), its role in PSD is at present unknown. Because considerable evidence suggests that aberrant GH function is secondary to factors controlling its release by the pituitary rather than an absolute deficiency of GH, SS could prove to be of etiological significance.

Thryoid

Thyroid dysfunction is not typically associated with PSD; the large majority of cases have normal thyroxine (T4) levels (Campbell, Green et al., 1982). If present, abnormalities tend to be subnormal. Occasionally low initial protein-bound iodine (PBI) has been reported. In only one study (Krieger & Good, 1970) were markedly low initial T4 values reported. Krieger and Good (1970) found T4 values were less than 3 sigmas below the normal mean in 3 out of 4 PSDs. The most malnourished child whose weight was only 57% of the normal mean for her height had an unusually low basal metabolic rate (BMR) as well. The other 3 PSDs had elevated BMRs per weight predicted from

height and were not hypothyroid. The authors felt the low T4 values reflected a decrease in thyroxine binding proteins secondary to malnutrition. This was supported by follow-up of the hypometabolic child. She was retested at age 4, 1 year following her discharge home. She had acquired the bizarre eating habits typical of PSD and was no longer emaciated for her height; however, linear growth arrest had recurred. At this time, T4, ^{131}I uptake, and BMR for age were within normal limits. Thus, once the severe malnutrition was eliminated and while the full clinical picture of PSD was still present, thyroid functions were normal.

Pituitary–Adrenocortical Axis Function

There are few studies on adrenal functioning, and these have varied regarding the specific metabolites measured and methodology, making conclusions in this area difficult (for a critical review, see Campbell, Green et al., 1982).

The major studies are those of Powell, Brasel, Raiti, and Blizzard (1967), Krieger and Good (1970), and Krieger and Mellinger (1971). Both groups used metyrapone to evaluate the pituitary's capacity to secrete ACTH. Powell et al., using 17-hydroxycorticosteroids (17-OHCS) to evaluate adrenal cortisol secretion, found 9 of 13 to have low baseline values and 12 of 13 to have low values following metyrapone. When retested during catch-up growth, only 2 of 10 had recovered normal responses. In a follow-up of these patients, Brasel (1973) found some children required up to 2 years for normalization of the ACTH response to metyrapone.

Powell, Brasel, Raiti, and Blizzard (1967) found 6 of 7 PSDs had normal responses of adrenal function following exogenous ACTH administration, suggesting that decreased cortisol secretion after metyrapone was secondary to decreased ACTH production or release by the pituitary.

Krieger and Mellinger (1971), however, found the rise in 17-ketogenic steroids following metyrapone was normal in 5 of 6 PSDs. The authors accounted for the discrepancy with Powell's data by differences in metyrapone administration. Powell, Brasel, Raiti, and Blizzard gave 300 mg/100 lb body weight every 4 hours for 24 hours whereas they (Krieger & Mellinger, 1971) gave 300 mg/m² (surface area) every 4 hours for 48 hours.

Krieger and Good (1970) found all 4 PSDs whom they tested with exogenous ACTH had responses in the normal range. Moreover, they determined cortisol secretion rates in these 4 PSDs. On admission, 2 were elevated, 1 was normal, and 1 was low; by 4–5 weeks after admission, all were normal. It was suggested the elevated cortisol secretion rates were secondary to emotional stress. Plasma cortisol concentrations at time of admission, however, were normal in all 4 PSDs.

Based on these studies, it appears that ACTH release or production by the pituitary may be mildly to moderately compromised in some PSDs. The adrenal cortex appears to respond adequately in the presence of ACTH.

Sleep Studies in PSD

Since sleeping disturbance sometimes accompanied by night roaming has been anecdotally reported in many cases of PSD and sleep is the physiological regulator of GH release par excellence in prepubertal children (Finkelstein, Roffwarg, Boyar, Kream, & Hellman, 1972), the reports in this area are of particular interest.

Wise, Burnet, Geary, and Berriman (1975) have pointed out that provocative tests may successfully promote normal GH release while GH release may be deficient under normal physiological conditions such as sleep. The serotonin receptor blocker, methysergide, diminishes insulin-induced GH release while it enhances sleep-related GH secretion, suggesting different mechanisms of control of GH secretion.

Wolff and Money (1973) reported, in a partly retrospective study, 27 PSDs ages 1 year, 10 months to 16 years, 2 months who showed a significant correlation between good sleep and growth rate. During periods of poor sleep, growth of the PSDs averaged 0.34 cm/month versus 1.04 cm/month during periods of good sleep ($p < .001$). GH levels in these children were subnormal during periods of poor growth and normalized during the catch-up growth period. Sleep EEGs and concomitant GH assays were not performed.

Powell, Hopwood, and Barratt (1973) performed the first study which looked at the relationship between sleep pattern and GH release. They employed both sleep EEG and an indwelling catheter to monitor GH secretion in a female PSD age 9.3 years. There was no evidence of sleep disturbance during hospitalization. Total Stage III and Stage IV sleep was 41.5% of total on night 6 and the much larger portion of slow wave sleep (SWS) was Stage IV. Although SWS was normal, no significant GH secretion occurred during the fifth and sixth nights of hospitalization (4.4 and 5.6 ng/ml, respectively). On the 40th night, sleep was again normal and total Stages III and IV sleep was 49%. There was a marked output of GH (> 30 ng/ml) coincident with the onset of the first period of SWS. On day 1 of admission, arginine–insulin infusion resulted in a serum GH level of 9.6 ng/ml; on day 40 this rose to > 30 ng/ml. Powell et al. (1973) noted that their results did not support the hypothesis that an abnormal sleep pattern (or decreased amount of SWS) was responsible for the decreased GH output in this child.

Howse et al. (1977) compared nocturnal secretion of GH in 3 children (a male age 4.0 years and 2 females ages 4.5 and 13.0 years) with psychosocial GH deficiency with 14 normal children (ages 6.5–15.0 years, 13 males and 1 female) of short stature. GH levels were monitored via a continuous blood sampling technique over a 5-hour sleep period (22:30–03:30) and were correlated with sleep EEGs. An insulin stimulation test was then performed at 06:00 and peak GH value noted. These tests were performed on the first evening of hospitalization for the psychosocial GH deficiency children and on the third evening of hospitalization for the controls; since GH secretion can normalize very rapidly following removal from the home in PSDs, this minimized the likelihood of its occurring. The psychosocial GH deficiency children spent 97 ± 42 minutes in Stages III–IV sleep; this was longer than the time 87 ± 37.8 minutes normal short children spent in Stages III–IV sleep, but the difference was not significant ($p > .5$). The nocturnal GH sleep profile for the psychosocial GH deficiency group over the 5-hour period showed GH release to be of a shorter duration and lesser amount, particularly during the earlier episodes of Stages III–IV sleep, with the peak levels occurring during the later episodes of Stages III–IV sleep. All the psychosocial GH deficiency children showed lower peak GH values, lower 5-hour mean GH levels, and subnormal (< 20 mU/liter) GH responses to insulin-induced hypoglycemia when compared to the group of normal short children.

These authors suggested the delayed but definite GH response in the psychosocial GH deficiency group suggests "either a delay or a reduction in sleep mediated release of GH releasing factor (GHRF), or alternatively, reduced pituitary responsiveness to GHRF priming action, in association with a low pituitary secretion potential" (p. 356).

Guilhaume, Benoit, Gourmelen, and Richardet (1982) reported on the relationship between sleep Stage IV deficit and reversible human growth hormone (HGH) deficiency in PSD. Four children (3 males, 1 female) ages 12–36 months who exhibited the main characteristics of PSD were studied with polygraphic sleep recordings. Initial recordings were taken within the first 3 nights in 3 cases and on the ninth night in the fourth case. The second sleep recordings were performed after 21–105 days in the new environment and during catch-up growth. Ten healthy children of similar ages were used as controls.

Total sleep period was significantly lower ($p < .05$) in PSDs (439.5 min) than in controls (513.8 min). There was increased Stage I sleep ($p < .01$) and a tendency to increased intervening wakefulness in PSDs. Stage III sleep was normal in PSDs. However, in 3 of them Stage IV sleep was totally absent and in the fourth, it was markedly less than controls. Because of this, SWS (Stage III + Stage IV) in PSDs was less than in controls (11.9% vs. 29%). In addition, PSDs had fewer SWS episodes than controls (2.8 ± 0.7 vs. 4.0 ± 0.4), they were of shorter duration (13.0 ± 4.8 vs. 31.1 ± 4.5 min), and all controls had at least one SWS episode of 26 minutes or more, while only one PSD had episodes this long. Paradoxical sleep (or REM sleep) showed a tendency to be of shorter duration in the PSDs. The sleep efficiency index was significantly decreased ($p < .001$) in the PSDs. In only one PSD, however, were there long periods of wakefulness.

At follow-up sleep recording, marked improvements in sleep were noted. Stage IV sleep was present in all 4 PSDs and no longer significantly different from controls, although 3 of the 4 still had values below controls. The sleep efficiency index and paradoxical sleep also had improved significantly. Although total sleep period increased and Stage I sleep decreased (i.e., normalized) in 3 of the 4 PSDs, both parameters remained significantly different from controls ($p < .05$). In the same study, low plasma GH levels following ornithine stimulation were observed during the first 2 days of hospitalization in 2 subjects (9 and 10 ng/ml; normal value 11 ng/ml) during the catch-up growth both had normal tests (38 and 30 ng/ml). The same test in a third subject was normal on the ninth day after hospitalization (20 ng/ml).

The simultaneous improvements in sleep and growth suggested to the authors that the reduced GH and resultant growth failure may be caused by the lack of Stage IV sleep, the decreased length of SWS episodes, or both. These findings were consistent with the authors' speculation but, unfortunately, GH levels were not monitored during sleep.

Thus, as was the case with endocrine abnormalities, the studies of the relationship between duration and stage of sleep and GH secretion in PSD are also discrepant. While GH output correlated especially well with Stage IV sleep in one study, in another, subnormal GH output occurred with normal SWS. This may be additional evidence that the normal physiological apparatus for secreting GH may be operational, but can be overridden, possibly by CNS mechanisms.

Etiology

All workers in the field of PSD have been struck with the rapidity with which GH dysfunction normalizes and the rapidity with which physical growth begins upon removal of the PSD from the inimical environment. This rapidity precludes malnutrition and/or malabsorption as a primary cause.

It has been speculated that the cause of PSD is secondary to the psychosocial environment's influence on the child. Specifically, the cerebral cortex through its relays to the hypothalamus leads to intermittent and reversible inhibition of hypothalamic releasing factors, causing hormonal abnormalities and growth failure (Green *et al.*, 1984). The exact mechanisms of this are still unclear. It seems however, that two distinct factors may be psychologically important. One is the removal of a stress (the malignant caretaker/child relationship). The other appears to be the development of a mutual strong, emotionally positive relationship between the child and the new caretaker (Green *et al.*, 1984). Table 5.3 summarizes the relationships among psychosocial environment, growth rate, and hormonal levels in a PSD meticulously studied over a 10-month period by Saenger and his colleagues (1977).

It can be seen that slow growth—but decidedly more rapid than in the unfavorable environment—can occur with either or both GH and SM activity at subnormal levels. During catch-up growth, however, normal levels of both GH and SM appear to be necessary. These hormonal changes rapidly reflected environmental changes and especially the absence or presence of the special nurse once a strong positive attachment to her had been made. Caloric intake was measured and did not account for these differences. Additional data supporting the relationship between psychosocial environment and growth failure include growth lines at the ends of the long bones on X ray (Hernandez, Poznanski, Hopwood, & Kelch, 1978) and laboratory abnormalities (serum turbidity and serum triglycerides), which appeared to relate to separation and contact with parents (Hopwood & Becker, 1979; Hopwood, Becker, Hengstenberg, & Drash, 1977). These have been reviewed in detail elsewhere and a hypothetical model was proposed to clarify the relationships among environments, hormonal levels, and growth (Green *et al.*, 1984).

Animal Models

Although animal studies will not be reviewed here, an exception is made in the case of the recent work of Schanberg, Evoniuk, and Kuhn (1984) which provides a fascinating animal model in which findings are strikingly parallel to those in PSD. They found that restricting preweanling rat pups from active tactile interaction with their mother by sepa-

TABLE 5.3. Relationships among Environments, Growth Rates, Growth Hormone Levels, and Somatomedin Activity in a 7-Year-Old Male with Psychosocial Dwarfism[a]

Environment	Type of growth	GH level	SM activity
Home (prehospital)	Extremely slow	Not determined	Not determined
Hospital soon after admission	Slow	Low	Low
Hospital and relationship with special nurse	Catch-up	Normal	Normal
Hospital special nurse on vacation	Slow	Low	Normal
Hospital and special nurse returned	Catch-up	Normal	Normal
Home (posthospital)	Slow	Normal	Low
Hospital and reunited with special nurse	Catch-up	Not determined	Normal

[a] Based on data from Saenger *et al.* (1977) and P. Saenger (personal communication, 1982).

ration or anesthetizing the mother produced specific abnormalities in at least three biochemical processes involved in growth. There was an immediate and significant decrease in tissue ornithine decarboxylase (ODC) in all tissues studied, including brain; a selective decrease in GH levels while other hormones, including corticosterone, which usually alter during stress did not change; and decreased peripheral sensitivity to GH. Tactile stimulation by the mother rat restored these parameters to normal, but interactions with litter mates did not. However, when the experimenters tactilely stimulated the pups by stroking them heavily to approximate maternal grooming, ODC activity normalized.

Activity of ODC is an accurate and sensitive measure of cell growth and development, and GH is intimately involved in its regulation. When exogenous GH was given to deprived rat pups, however, tissue ODC was unresponsive and did not normalize. This selective loss of tissue sensitivity to GH is strikingly similar to the increased peripheral resistance to exogenous GH found in some PSDs. Likewise, the GH deficiency occurs in the presence of normal nutrition and is the primary hormonal abnormality (decreased SM activity levels in PSD being secondary to decreased circulating GH). While one obviously cannot generalize from the rat pups to the young human child, the marked similarities of physiological responses to abnormal mothering gives additional support for the psychosocial environment's ability to rapidly cause GH dysfunction and growth retardation in the presence of normal nutritional state in PSD.

Treatment

There is virtually unanimous agreement that the treatment of choice for PSD is removing the child from the inimical environment. Indeed, this is how PSD was identified serendipitously as a diagnostic entity. Treatment may initially include hospitalization, but later, placement with relatives, foster care, adoption, or a group home may be necessary. Return home results in rapid recurrence of growth failure in an alarming number of children and most then require rehospitalization or placement.

Although there is normalization of the endocrine findings as reviewed above, upon placement in a favorable environment, intellectual and behavioral symptoms do not always improve to a similar degree. Follow-up studies and outcome of these parameters have been reviewed elsewhere (Campbell, Green et al., 1982; Green, 1986).

If the child must return home or be treated in the home, intensive interventions with parents and close monitoring of the child are essential. The basic thrusts must be to alter and improve the caretaker–child relationship, enhance parental functioning and parenting abilities, and decrease stresses in the home (Green, 1985).

A few strategies employing pharmaceutical agents may eventually prove useful, particularly if the child must be treated in an unfavorable environment. It has been noted above that exogenous GH produces very disappointing results when administered in the growth-retarding environment.

Wolff and Money (1973) reported a PSD with insomnia whose growth failure occurred in a foster home. Both sleep pattern and growth rate improved when removed to other domiciles, but recurred when she returned to her foster family. Because replacement was not immediately possible, she was treated with a soporific (Seconal, 3/4 gr (50 mg) at bedtime for 5 months). Sleep improved markedly and the growth rate increased by 55.8% over the 11-month period prior to treatment (0.43 cm/month vs. 0.67 cm/month). Although this single case cannot rule out changes in intrafamilial or the child's psychodynamics, hypnotics may be a useful treatment for sleep disturbance in some cases which must remain temporarily or longer in the inimical environment.

The specific hypnotic and the dosage must be chosen carefully. Barbiturates usually considerably shorten Stages III and IV sleep (Harvey, 1980). Thiopental, however, has been reported to increase Stage IV sleep and to increase nocturnal peaks of GH (Harvey, 1980). Feinberg (1969) noted that in some adult psychiatric patients, secobarbital in low doses (200 mg) moderately increased Stage IV sleep, while higher doses (400–500 mg) significantly decreased Stage IV sleep. Since the benzodiazepines decreased the amount of Stage IV sleep in virtually all sleep studies reported (Greenblatt & Shader, 1974), their use in PSD would theoretically be contraindicated.

β-Adrenergic blocking agents which increase GH secretion can be of potential therapeutic value. Imura et al. (1971) and Parra (1973) have administered propranolol to a total of 6 PSDs with initially favorable results. Similarly, α-adrenergic stimulating agents enhanced GH release; methoxamine, when administered to a single PSD, caused a significant rise in plasma GH (Imura et al., 1971).

The role of neurotransmitters in causing GH abnormalities has not been determined. Selective stimulation of noradrenergic and dopaminergic receptors known to enhance GH secretion would be of possible therapeutic importance. Thus, clonidine, which selectively stimulates noradrenalin receptors, and L-dopa, a dopamine agonist are known to increase GH secretion, but have not yet been reported in PSD (Lal, Tolis, Martin, Brown & Guyda, 1975; Meltzer, Busch, & Fang, 1981). Methysergide, a serotonin receptor blocker, has been shown to enhance sleep-related GH secretion, although it does not appear to have been used in PSDs as yet (Mendelson et al., 1975).

In conclusion, PSD is a most challenging clinical disorder whose study presents a unique opportunity for further clarification of the relationship between psyche and soma and the intricate interrelationships among CNS, neurotransmitters, the endocrine system, and the psychosocial environment.

INFANTILE AUTISM

The syndrome of infantile autism (IA) was first described by Kanner in 1943. Following this, children with IA were usually labeled childhood schizophrenics or a variant thereof. Only in 1980, with DSM-III, did the official psychiatric nomenclature recognize IA as a behavioral syndrome. Despite its recognition, there is little information regarding its etiology and underlying neurochemical or neuroendocrine abnormalities.

Early Studies Involving
Multiple Hormones

In an attempt to identify endocrine "cofactors" in the development of a heterogeneous group of childhood psychiatric disorders, a variety of endocrine measures was examined in 2 girls and 1 boy (ages 6–13 years) with the diagnosis of "early primary psychosis" (Brambilla, Viani, & Rossotti, 1969). These children had an onset of illness in the first or second year and showed many of the symptoms incorporated into the DSM-III (American Psychiatric Association, 1980) criteria for IA, full syndrome present. In addition to an autistic manner of relating, the symptoms included deviant speech development and stereotypies. One of these children had evidence of gross organic pathology, including EEG and pneumoencephalographic abnormalities, and the other 2 were characterized as "physically underdeveloped." One of the underdeveloped children, a 13-year-old boy, presented evidence of delayed puberty. The major findings were reduced urinary 17-ketosteroid secretion in 2 patients, deficient endogenous ACTH secretion in all 3 patients, and basal thyroid functions (PBI) at the lower limits of normal in 2 patients (Brambilla et al., 1969). Although this pilot screening of abnormal endocrine functions suffered from major methodological flaws, including a small and heterogeneous sample, and the absence of current technology for hormone measurement (e.g., radioimmunoassay), it did support the existence of biological abnormalities in at least some autistic children.

In view of the frequently seen insistence upon the maintenance of "sameness" in autistic children, these children have been viewed as less capable of adapting to a variety of stressors (for discussion, see Maher, Harper, Macleay, & King, 1975). Although basal hormonal secretion could be normal in many autistic children, their inability to respond to stress would be expected to be associated with a failure or dysregulation of the activation of neuroendocrine responses. Therefore, basal levels of cortisol, GH, and glucose in blood and changes in these measures following the stress of insulin-induced hypoglycemia were examined in 11 autistic children (Maher et al., 1975). The 11 autistic children (9 males and 2 females; ages 4–13 years) were assessed independently by two psychiatrists and fulfilled criteria of Rutter et al. (1969). The neuroendocrine data of the autistic children were compared with a matched sample, including IQ, of mentally retarded patients.

Hypoglycemia was induced by the bolus injection of insulin (0.15 units/kg) between the hours of 9:30 A.M. and 1:00 P.M. Glucose, cortisol, and GH levels were measured at regular intervals for a period of 3 hours post-insulin infusion. A potential source of variance includes this large time period (i.e., $3\frac{1}{2}$ hours) within which individual subjects received insulin. Thus, detection of differences could be influenced by normal diurnal patterns of hormone secretion. Also, subjects received premedication for sedation and individual subjects differed in the amount and type of premedication received. The effect of this pretreatment on the various measures is unknown. The authors stated, however, that the autistic and subnormal children were treated identically in terms of premedication. Cortisol was measured by a competitive protein-binding assay, and a radioimmunoassay method was used to measure GH. Data were analyzed using a 2-way repeated measures analysis of variance.

Basal levels of glucose, cortisol, and GH were within normal limits for both groups and could not be used to distinguish the autistic and intellectually subnormal samples from each other (Maher et al., 1975). Both groups showed about a 50% reduction of blood glucose values between 15 and 30 minutes after insulin administration. The comparison group of subnormal children showed a significantly faster recovery of baseline blood glucose levels than the autistic group ($p < .05$). These results were in marked contrast to the results of the cortisol response to insulin-induced hypoglycemia. The postinsulin cortisol levels of the autistic children were elevated and failed to return to the baseline values up to 3 hours after insulin infusion ($p < .05$). These data suggest a complex metabolic disruption in at least some autistic children, as glucose mobilization is the usual response to cortisol elevation. No difference in the GH response to insulin-induced hypoglycemia could be detected between the two groups. This failure to detect a difference in GH secretion could have been due to the small sample sizes ($n = 11$ for both groups) and the large interindividual variablity of this measure. Also, the failure could reflect the high incidence of hyperserotonemia reported

in autistic and mentally retarded samples (Campbell, Friedman, DeVito, Greenspan, & Collins, 1974; Campbell et al., 1975; Ritvo et al., 1970; Young, Kavanagh, Anderson, Shaywitz, & Cohen, 1982). Serotonin is a neurotransmitter involved in the regulation of GH secretion (Willoughby, Menadue, & Jervois, 1982). In view of serotonin abnormalities in autism and mental retardation, the inclusion of a mentally retarded comparison group as the only comparison group was a major limitation of this study. However, the data do support an abnormality or alteration of endocrine responses to a specific stressor in some autistic patients (Maher et al., 1975). The normal basal cortisol secretion in the autistic subjects in the study by Maher et al. (1975) is at variance with the earlier report of a deficiency of endogenous ACTH secretion in the 3 patients of Brambilla et al. (1969).

Hypothalamic–Pituitary–Adrenal Axis

The circadian rhythm of adrenal corticosteroid secretion and elevation of specific steroids in plasma in response to specific stressors, for example, intravenous pyrogen, are dependent upon the intactness of the CNS (for discussion, see Yamazaki, Saito, Okada, Fujieda, & Yamashita, 1975). Circadian rhythmicity of adrenal corticosteroid secretion occurs later in development than the steroid response to intravenous pyrogen, but is usually established by at least age 4 years. A failure to develop the normal secretory pattern could reflect a disruption in the maturation of the cerebro-hypothalamic–pituitary axis (Yamazaki et al., 1975). The circadian rhythm of plasma 11-hydroxycorticosteroid (11-OHCS) secretion and plasma 11-OHCS response to an intravenous injection of a standard pyrogen were examined in 7 children (5 males and 2 females; ages 6–10 years) with "early infantile autism" (Yamazaki et al., 1975). A review of the clinical descriptions of these 7 patients suggests that at least 5 of them would fulfill DSM-III (American Psychiatric Association, 1980) criteria for IA. To assess circadian rhythmicity, blood was sampled at 6-hour intervals over the course of 24 hours. The reactivity to a fixed dose of standard pyrogen, based on weight, was determined by measuring plasma

11-OHCS concentration on baseline, between 8:00 and 9:00 A.M., and 2, 4, and 6 hours after injection. The concentration of 11-OHCS in plasma was determined using a specific fluorometric method. The circadian rhythms of plasma 11-OHCS levels showed irregular patterns in 5 of the 7 patients. Although most of the children failed to show a normal secretory pattern, 4 of the 6 children for whom data were presented showed sufficient reactivity to intravenous pyrogen (Yamazaki *et al.*, 1975). These data are consistent with clinical observations that autistic patients often fail to develop normal rhythmic patterns, for example, sleep and wakefulness. A general disruption in the development of normal biological rhythms may exist in autistic patients. Moreover, the data demonstrate the heterogeneity of the disorder; that is, although autistic patients may fail to mount a normal response to one type of stressor, for example, insulin-induced hypoglycemia, they may respond with sufficient reactivity to a different stressor, for example, intravenous pyrogen.

Hypothalamic–Pituitary–Thyroid Axis

The pituitary thyrotropin (TSH) response over a 2-hour period to an intravenous infusion of 400 μg of thyrotropin-releasing hormone (TRH) was examined in 10 autistic children (7 boys and 3 girls, ages 2.5–7.6 years) in order to obtain additional data on hypothalamic–pituitary function in this population (Campbell, Hollander *et al.*, 1978). The 10 preschool-age patients met the diagnostic criteria for IA of Creak (1964), Kanner (1943), and Rutter (1966), as determined by three child psychiatrists. Prior to their TRH infusions, 5 of the children had never received psychotropic medication and all children were medication-free for at least 3 months. None of the children had evidence of systemic disease, although 1 child was biochemically hyperthyroid at the time of study. Inspection of available clinical and laboratory data suggested the presence of subtle hypothalamic dysfunction and/or neurochemical abnormality in 9 of the children. Seven of the children showed evidence of growth disturbance (i.e., height percentile ≤ 10 and/or retarded bone age $> 2SD$) and 5 had elevated serotonin levels in blood (above 300 ng/ml).

In addition, many of the patients had pre- and perinatal histories suggestive of possible CNS insult. The results of the TRH infusions were heterogeneous and compatible with the occurrence of hypothalamic–pituitary dysfunction in most patients. Several patients showed a delay in the kinetics of their TSH responses to TRH. Two patients showed hyperresponsiveness and one showed attenuation of their TSH responses. Similarly, the triiodothyronine (T3) responses showed marked individual variability, with blunted or delayed (abnormal kinetics) responses observed. In addition to supporting a high basal rate of occurrence of hypothalamic–pituitary dysfunction among autistic patients, the heterogeneous nature of the TSH and T3 responses supports the existence of subgroups within samples identified according to similar descriptive diagnostic criteria. In this regard, the short-term behavioral responses to the TRH infusions were of interest. Some patients showed a reduction of activity level, whereas others showed a more responsive affect, increased spontaneous speech, and improved attention.

Although subtle abnormalities in the pituitary TSH response to TRH stimulation seem to exist in some autistic patients (Campbell, Hollander *et al.*, 1978), alterations of basal thyroid functions [i.e., thyroxine (T4), T3, and TSH] have not been consistently demonstrated (Abbassi, Linscheid, & Coleman, 1978; Cohen, Young, Lowe, & Harcherik, 1980; Khan, 1970; for discussion, see Campbell, Green *et al.*, 1982). The salutary effects of T3 reported in a few autistic patients (Campbell, Small *et al.*, 1978; Campbell *et al.*, 1973; Sherwin, Flach, & Stokes, 1958) prompted studies of basal thyroid functions in this disorder (Abbassi *et al.*, 1978; Campbell, Hollander, Ferris, & Greene, 1978; Cohen *et al.*, 1980). The clinical observations suggested either a state of T3 deficiency, impairment in the peripheral monodeiodination of T4 to T3, insensitivity to physiological levels of T3, or an unidentified central action of T3 in some autistic patients (Abbassi *et al.*, 1978). Thyroid functions were measured in 13 autistic patients (ages 7–21 years) and found to be within normal limits (Abbassi *et al.*, 1978). A limitation of this study was the wide age range of the sample and lack of information regarding ages at which diagnoses were determined. Of these 13 patients, 2 with retarded bone ages were selected for clinical trials of T3. In these two patients, clinical evidence of hyperthyroidism emerged when T3 levels exceeded 200 ng/dl and treatment was terminated (Abbassi et al., 1978). Thus, in these 2 patients, there was no suggestion of peripheral insensitivity to the metabolic effects of T3.

In another study, T4 levels were measured in 58 patients (53 males and 5 females; mean age 12.5 ± 5.1 years) who fulfilled DSM-III (1980) criteria for IA (Cohen et al., 1980). A subset of 20 of these children was randomly selected for measurement of T3 and TSH. No parameter of thyroid function could be used to distinguish the autistic sample from a control sample of 75 normal children (Cohen et al., 1980). These data are consistent with T3's having an undefined central therapeutic effect in those patients who benefited from its administration. Also, although basal abnormalities of thyroid indices may not be detected, the inability of at least some autistic patients to respond normally to TRH stimulation suggests a functional impairment in thyroid regulation (Campbell, Hollander et al., 1978).

The importance of obtaining repeated measures of basal thyroid function is emphasized by clinical observations of wide fluctuations in thyroxine and thyroxine-binding capacity in IA (Campbell, Green et al., 1982; Cohen, Shaywitz, Johnson, & Bowers, 1974). For example, in a study examining neurotransmitter metabolites in the CSF of 9 autistic and 11 "atypical" children, 3 of the autistic children (2 boys and 1 girl; ages 6.9–9.9 years) showed low serum thyroxine values on the initial determination (Cohen et al., 1974). However, on repeated investigation of their thyroid status, 2 of these children had high normal T4 levels and the third child was above the normal range. In this study, significant negative correlations between thyroxine, thyroxine-binding capacity, and the acidic central metabolites of dopamine and serotonin were shown (Cohen et al., 1974). Although the exact relationship of atypical to autistic children in this study is not known, these data suggest that fluctuations in thyroid status may reflect alterations in the central activity of dopamine and serotonin in autistic children. The atypical children were described as having pervasive developmental disabilities from the first years of life. Also, wide fluctuation in thyroid func-

tion is additional evidence of impairment in regulation of the hypothalamic–pituitary–thyroid axis in some autistic children.

In contrast to the above studies which found no or only the rare occurrence of abnormalities of basal thyroid functions, in a letter, Khan (1970) reported a very high incidence of abnormal thyroid function in 62 autistic children. Although information regarding characteristics of his sample (e.g., ages, sex composition, IQ) and procedures were omitted, the 62 children were diagnosed according to the nine points outlined by Creak (1964). Forty-five of the children (72.6%) were hypothyroid and an additional two were hyperthyroid, as determined by T3 uptake. These data are intriguing and consistent with hypothesized hypothalamic–pituitary dysfunction in subgroups of autistic patients. However, the failure to report detailed selection criteria and methodology severely limits the interpretation of these results.

In a study examining a large number of variables related to the physical growth and development of 101 young autistic children (Campbell et al., 1980), thyroid studies were performed within the first 2 weeks of admission in a subsample of 64 children. In contrast to many other studies of thyroid functions in autism, repeated measures were obtained in all children. On admission, the mean age of the larger sample was 3.97 ± 1.01 years (age range 2.0–7.0 years) and the children fulfilled diagnostic criteria of Kanner (1943), Creak (1964), Rutter (1978), and the American Psychiatric Association (1980), as determined by three child psychiatrists independently. Although all children were clinically euthyroid, biochemical evidence of hyperthyroidism was present in a higher than expected frequency. On more than one occasion, T4 levels exceeded the normal range in 22 (34%) of the 64 children. T3 levels were determined in 31 children and shown to be elevated in about half of them. Of the 31 children, 14 had T3 levels above 172 ng/dl: 56% had T3 values greater than 1 SD and 30% had T3 values greater than 2 SD above the mean of a normal age-matched sample. The potential relevance of these elevated thyroid functions to disturbances of central neural development was studied in 42 of the children who, in addition to measurement of T4 levels, were examined for minor congenital anomalies (Campbell et *al.*, 1980). In these 42 children, there was a positive correlation between weighted anomaly scores and T4 levels ($r = .46$; $p < .01$). The presence of minor congenital anomalies may reflect disturbances in the development of the nervous system during the first 3 months of gestation (Campbell, Geller, Small, Petti, & Ferris, 1978; Quinn & Rapoport, 1974). These peripheral measurements of thyroid status are consistent with the existence of subtle hypothalamic–pituitary dysfunction in subgroups of clinically euthyroid autistic patients. That disturbances in the regulation of the hypothalamic–pituitary–thyroid axis, as opposed to basal abnormalities, may be present in autism was also suggested by the salutary effects of T3 in 4 of 30 carefully diagnosed children (23 boys and 7 girls; ages 2.25–7.17 years) (Campbell, Small, Hollander *et al.*, 1978). In this study, no measure of baseline thyroid status was associated with any behavioral response despite elevations of T3 levels in 13 patients. Positive responses were associated with low IQ scores and reduction of serum T4 levels. In addition to the occurrence of subtle perturbations of the hypothalamic–pituitary–thyroid axis, these results are consistent with an undefined central effect of exogenous T3 in some autistic children.

Hypothalamic–Pituitary Studies Involving Growth Hormone

Data pertaining to the physical growth and development of 101 hospitalized autistic patients (ages 2–7 years), each of whom fulfilled several sets of diagnostic criteria as assessed by three child psychiatrists independently, showed that, as a group, the patients were shorter, abnormally distributed in terms of height percentiles with an overrepresentation in the lower third of percentiles for height, and had radiographic evidence of a greater than expected frequency of retarded bone age (Campbell *et al.*, 1980). As these measures were obtained within the first 2 weeks of admission, they could not be ascribed to the effects of institutionalization. The authors viewed these data as consistent with hypothalamic–pituitary dysfunction in a large number of these patients.

A major etiological role for dopamine has been implicated in the production of autistic symptomatology in a series of systematic pharmacological investigations (Anderson *et al.*, 1984; Campbell, Anderson *et al.*, 1978, 1982; Campbell *et al.*, 1972, 1976). In general, these studies have shown that specific symptoms (e.g., abnormal object relationships, affective lability, hyperactivity, stereotypies, and withdrawal) are exacerbated or attenuated by highly selective dopamine agonists and antagonists, respectively. In addition, higher levels of homovanillic acid (HVA), the principal central dopamine metabolite, have been detected in a subgroup of severely impaired autistic patients with increased locomotor activity and stereotypies (Cohen, Caparulo, Shaywitz, & Bowers, 1977). An elevation of this metabolite in spinal fluid is consistent with increased central turnover and release of dopamine in at least some autistic patients.

In order to examine a possible relationship between hypothalamic dysfunction and dopaminergic abnormalities in IA, the plasma GH response to oral L-dihydroxyphenylalanine (L-dopa) was examined in 22 autistic children (Deutsch, Campbell, Sachar, Green, & David, 1985). L-Dopa acts as a dopamine agonist after its transport into brain, selective concentration in dopaminergic terminals, decarboxylation, and release. Dopamine agonists are potent inducers of pituitary GH release. Dopamine receptors in the hypothalamus are probably the major locus mediating regulation of this agonist-induced GH secretion. Thus, a neuroendocrine strategy has been adopted to explore the sensitivity of hypothalamic dopamine receptors, as reflected in an elevation of plasma GH concentrations from baseline subsequent to provocative challenges with dopamine agonists (for discussion, see Meltzer *et al.*, 1981). Of course, the possibility of noradrenergic influences must be considered with the use of L-dopa as the sole provocative stimulus.

The 22 autistic children (ages 2.6–7.2 years) fulfilled DSM-III (American Psychiatric Association, 1980) criteria for IA as determined independently by at least two board-certified child psychiatrists, and were a subset of a larger sample participating in a study of the effects of haloperidol, behavior therapy, and their interaction on behavioral symptoms and language acquisition (Campbell, Anderson *et al.*, 1978). The L-dopa provocative tests were conducted as described by Weldon et al. (1973) and plasma GH determined by homologous radioimmunoassay. The oral dose of L-dopa was 250 mg in children under 70 lb and 500 mg for heavier children (Weldon et al., 1973). An indwelling butterfly was used to obtain serial heparinized blood samples. Samples were obtained at baseline (i.e., 20 and 10 minutes prior to and immediately upon L-dopa ingestion) and at regular 15-minute intervals for 135 minutes after L-dopa administration. A failure to mount a GH response greater than 6 ng/ml was considered to be an abnormal response to L-dopa provocation. In addition, the results were compared with a "control" series of published raw data on 42 children who received L-dopa provocative tests (Weldon et al., 1973). The majority of the control children were referred for evaluation of short stature and determined to have a nonendocrine cause for this complaint. The results showed that about 30% of this descriptively homogeneous sample of autistic children had blunted (≤ 6 ng/ml) plasma GH responses to L-dopa provocation (Deutsch et al., 1985). In fact, if 6 of the 22 autistic children with zero-time GH levels above 3 ng/ml are eliminated from the sample, then 6 out of the remaining 16 patients (38%) showed peak GH values below 5 ng/ml. The autistic sample showed blunted GH responses over the entire 135 minutes after L-dopa administration and differences between the autistic and control samples were significant at 90 ($p = .004$) and 120 ($p = .011$) minutes post L-dopa administration. These data imply the existence of a subsensitivity of hypothalamic dopamine receptors and impaired regulation of GH secretion in a subgroup of autistic patients. GH responses to L-dopa provocation were repeated in 8 patients after a 5-week period of treatment with optimal daily doses (0.5–4.0 mg/day) of haloperidol (Campbell, Anderson et al., 1978). These children were rechallenged with L-dopa in order to determine if short-term treatment with a highly selective antagonist had obvious adverse effects on the regulation of GH secretion. Although conclusions must be viewed as tentative due to the small sample size and large pre- and posttreatment within-group variance, short-term haloperidol treatment did

not result in a significant alteration of the GH response to oral L-dopa. The absence of any inferred alteration of hypothalamic dopamine receptor sensitivity after 5 weeks of optimal daily dose haloperidol treatment is consistent with the failure to detect a reduction of therapeutic efficacy (tolerance) with prolonged administration (Campbell, Perry et al., 1983). However, neuroleptic-induced abnormal movements were observed in about 20% of a sample of autistic children followed prospectively on these doses (Campbell, Grega, Green, & Bennett, 1983; Campbell, Perry et al., 1983). The various observations suggest that discrete neuroanatomic regions (i.e., tuberoinfundibular, nigrostriatal, mesolimbic, and mesocortical) may differ in ability to regulate dopamine receptor sensitivity. The neuroendocrine strategy may prove useful in the discrimination of these differences.

The blunted GH responses to L-dopa provocation observed in about 30% of a sample of 22 autistic children (Deutsch et al., 1985) prompted further investigation to see if this reflected a general hypothalamic–pituitary dysfunction, unrelated to a specific neurotransmitter, or a specific dopaminergic abnormality. Also, the authors wondered if plasma GH responses of autistic children varied according to the nature of the specific stressor. Therefore, a pilot study was conducted in which plasma GH responses to insulin-induced hypoglycemia were measured in 8 autistic children (Deutsch et al., 1986). All children had been free of psychoactive medication for at least 4 weeks prior to their enrollment in the study. During the final 2 weeks of the active 4-week medication period, the children were maintained on their optimal daily dose (range 0.5–3.0 mg/day) of haloperidol. Insulin-induced hypoglycemia was chosen as the provocative stimulus because it is known to stimulate GH secretion and is widely used in the evaluation of hypopituitary conditions (Kaplan, Abrams, Bell, Conte, & Grumbach, 1968; Puig-Antich et al., 1981). The 8 autistic children (6 boys and 2 girls; age range 3.5–5.33 years) fulfilled DSM-III (American Psychiatric Association, 1980) criteria for IA, as determined independently by three research child psychiatrists. They were a subsample of 40 preschool-age autistic children who participated in a larger study examining the effects of haloperidol on behavioral symptoms and discrimination learning (Anderson et al., 1984; Campbell, Anderson et al., 1982). After an overnight fast, baseline determinations of glucose and GH levels were made at 20 minutes, 10 minutes, and immediately prior to insulin infusion. An intravenous bolus of crystalline insulin (0.05 U/kg) was rapidly administered and blood glucose and plasma GH responses determined at 15-minute intervals over the course of a 135-minute period. Of the 8 children, 6 received insulin infusions both during the placebo wash-out period prior to beginning haloperidol and after 4 weeks of receiving daily doses of haloperidol (Campbell, Anderson et al., 1982). In 2 children, growth hormone responses to insulin-induced hypoglycemia were measured on only one occasion: either during the placebo wash-out period or after receiving medication for 4 weeks.

The results showed that with this dose of insulin, about a 50% reduction of blood glucose levels was achieved in most patients (Deutsch et al., 1986). In this sample, short-term administration of optimal daily doses of haloperidol did not interfere with the pituitary's ability to secrete GH in response to insulin-induced hypoglycemia. Therefore, in consideration of the raw data, medication condition was disregarded. On repeated testing, no patient showed evidence of a blunted response (less than 7 ng/ml). In fact, visual inspection of the data revealed that on at least one occasion, half of the sample showed a persistent elevation of GH levels with a failure to return to baseline values over the course of the 135-minute period postinsulin infusion. Furthermore, if a zero-time GH level of less than or equal to 3.0 ng/ml and about a 50% reduction of baseline glucose levels were adopted as criteria for inclusion in the study, then 4 out of 6 children displayed evidence of persistently elevated GH values, with a failure to return to baseline on at least one occasion. These results contrasted with the GH responses to insulin infusion in a comparison group of 7 children (ages 6–12 years) with nondepressed neurotic disorder presented by Puig-Antich et al. (1981). In these 7 "control" children, GH levels returned to baseline at about 90 min-

utes postinsulin infusion. The results were viewed as consistent with the occurrence of subtle hypothalamic–pituitary dysfunction in at least a few autistic patients. These data also emphasized the complexity of pituitary GH regulation in IA; that is, autistic patients may show blunted GH responses to L-dopa and prolonged reponses to insulin-induced hypoglycemia. It is likely that the prolonged GH response to insulin infusion observed in some autistic patients reflects an abnormality in a neurotransmitter system other than dopamine. Evidence for impaired serotonin regulation in subgroups of autistic patients has been reported (for review, see Young et al., 1982). This evidence includes hyperserotonemia in blood, abnormal handling of serotonin by platelets, and lowered levels of 5-hydroxyindoleacetic acid, the principal serotonin metabolite, in CSF of autistic patients. Unfortunately, other than to suggest the possible existence of a neurotransmitter abnormality in addition to dopamine, prolonged GH responses to insulin-induced hypoglycemia do not help to delineate a subgroup of autistic patients with a specific neurotransmitter abnormality.

Other Hormonal Data (Follicle-Stimulating Hormone and Luteinizing Hormone)

In addition to the results reviewed above, there are isolated endocrine data consistent with the occurrence of hypothalamic–pituitary dysfunction in at least some autistic patients. Of the 10 patients, 3 (1 boy and 2 girls; ages 4.0–7.6 years) who received TRH infusions (Campbell, Hollander et al., 1978) showed elevated levels of follicle-stimulating hormone (FSH). In these 3 patients, FSH values ranged from 5.5 to 7.5 IU/ml, whereas normal values for prepubertal children are less than 5 IU/ml. In another study (Campbell et al., 1976), two groups of 3 patients out of a sample of 12 patients (ages 3.0–6.9 years) showed deviations of luteinizing hormone and FSH levels.

In summary, the collective results of the available neuroendocrine studies in IA support the occurrence of hypothalamic–pituitary dysfunction in subgroups of patients. Thus, there is the possibility that the neuroendocrine approach may be useful in the delineation of subgroups among autistic patients who fulfill similar descriptive criteria. The identification of neurotransmitter abnormalities would assist in the development of more rational and specific pharmacological interventions. To date, with the possible exception of identifying a subgroup of patients with dopaminergic abnormalities (Deutsch et al., 1985), the measurement of peripheral hormones has not led to the identification of subgroups with specific neurotransmitter abnormalities (for discussion, see Campbell, Green et al., 1982).

ATTENTION DEFICIT DISORDER

Pituitary hormones, particularly GH and PRL, have been measured in response to provocative challenges and during sleep in hyperactive children to assess treatment effects of stimulant medications on the regulation of hormone secretion and neurotransmitter receptor sensitivity (Aarskog, Fevang, Klove, Stoa, & Thorsen, 1977; Greenhill et al., 1981; Greenhill, Puig-Antich, Sassin, & Sachar, 1977; Gualtieri et al., 1981; Hunt, Cohen, Shaywitz, & Shaywitz, 1982; Puig-Antich, Greenhill, Sassin, & Sachar, 1978; Schultz, Hayford, Wolraich, Hintz, & Thompson, 1982; Shaywitz et al., 1982; Stahl, Orr, & Griffiths, 1979). In large part, these studies were prompted by reports of growth retardation in hyperactive children following treatment with stimulants (Mattes & Gittelman, 1983; Roche, Lipman, Overall, & Hung, 1979; Safer & Allen, 1973) and the possibility that an effect on inhibition of height velocity could be mediated by a disruption in the regulation of GH secretion. Moreover, a relationship between administration of stimulant medications and emergence of tics in a subgroup of hyperactive patients has been proposed (Lowe, Cohen, Detlor, Kremenitzer, & Shaywitz, 1982) and, if true, would be consistent with effects of stimulants on the sensitivity of central catecholamine receptors.

Application of the neuroendocrine strategy to hyperactive children can be used to address a number of significant questions. First, the ability of stimulant medications to influence secretion of specific hormones (e.g., GH and prolactin) may reflect their relative pharmacological activities as indirect-acting dopamine agonists. The correlation of stimulant dose and/or serum levels at specific times postadministration with ability to influence hormonal concentrations could, perhaps, reveal important relationships between stimulant blood levels and their peaks and central effects. Second, the detection of differences in the sensitivities of hyperactive samples and comparison groups in their hormonal responses to challenge with stimulants could indicate an alteration of the sensitivity of dopamine receptors in hyperactive patients. The salutary effect of stimulants in hyperactive children, as well as neurochemical and animal data, has led to a proposal of the existence of a hypodopaminergic state in at least a subgroup of hyperactive patients (for review, see Hunt et al., 1982). In this regard, the few reports of salutary clinical effects of L-dopa in some hyperactive children and adults are consistent with hypothesized dopaminergic underactivity (Jackson & Pelton, 1978; Langer, Rapoport, Brown, Ebert, & Bunney, 1982; Reimherr, Wood, & Wender, 1980). If a chronic state of diminished dopaminergic transmission were to exist in some hyperactive patients, then postsynaptic dopaminergic receptor supersensitivity and altered neuroendocrine responses to challenge with stimulants would be predicted. Exaggerated responses would occur if receptors are supersensitive and the presynaptic elements are intact or diminished responses could occur due to a selective degeneration of presynaptic dopaminergic elements. In subjects with degeneration of presynaptic elements, exaggerated neuroendocrine responses would be expected upon challenge with a direct agonist. Finally, the neuroendocrine strategy can be used to detect age- associated alterations in the regulation of hormone secretion and dopamine receptor sensitivity.

In this critical and selective review, we shall focus on several representative neuroendocrine studies in hyperactive children which examine these issues.

The abilities of single oral doses of dextroamphetamine (15 mg) and methylphenidate (20 mg) to provoke plasma GH responses in a group of 20 hyperactive children (ages 6–13 years; 17 boys and 3 girls) were evaluated and compared to the action of L-dopa, a known oral stimulus for GH secretion used in the evaluation of hypopituitarism (Aarskog et al., 1977). In this series, provocative challenges with dextroamphetamine and methylphenidate were shown to be as potent as L-dopa in stimulating the secretion of GH. These stimuli resulted in at least 80% of the children responding with a plasma GH concentration greater than 5 ng/ml by 60–90 minutes following ingestion. Thus, acute challenges with either of these stimulants are capable of influencing the hypothalamic–pituitary axis and its regulation of GH secretion. The normal GH responses to L-dopa argue against any intrinsic abnormalities of GH regulation in this sample (Weldon et al., 1973). Seven of these children were rechallenged with L-dopa and dextroamphetamine after receiving methylphenidate (dose range 5–35 mg/day), as therapy for hyperactivity, for periods of 6–8 months. Although the sample size was small, chronic methylphenidate treatment was associated with higher basal GH levels, as well as alterations and heterogeneity in the GH responses to challenge with dextroamphetamine. In response to dextroamphetamine, 4 of the chronically treated children with basal GH values greater than 5 ng/ml showed a paradoxical decline of GH levels in the initial 30-minute period following dextroamphetamine. Of these 4 children, 2 failed to mount a GH response greater than 5 ng/ml to dextroamphetamine challenge over the course of a 3-hour period. The elevation of basal GH levels in some children following chronic methylphenidate treatment (i.e., at least 5 out of 7 children had values greater than 5 ng/ml on baseline) is contrary to the expected result occurring secondary to receptor subsensitization due to chronic treatment with an indirect-acting agonist. At least 3 of the 4 chronically treated children with elevated basal GH levels and paradoxical decline of GH in the initial 30 minutes following dextroamphetamine displayed basal GH values below 5 ng/ml prior to treatment with methylphenidate. Thus, although sample size was small and conclusions must be viewed as tentative, in this study chronic treatment with a stimulant appeared to disrupt hypothalamic–pituitary regulation of GH secretion in some hyperactive children. That the mechanism was not simply due to an effect on receptor sensitivity was suggested by the fact that the pattern of response to challenge with L-dopa in these 7 chronically treated children

appeared normal (Aarskog et al., 1977). The absence of detailed criteria for inclusion, other than simply the presence of "hyperactivity," is an unfortunate limitation of this study. The observed heterogeneity of GH responses to challenge with dextroamphetamine in the 7 chronically treated children could be explained, in part, by the absence of uniform selection criteria. Also, the fact that only 7 of the original 20 children were selected for long-term methylphenidate treatment could indicate something unique about this subsample. These issues make comparisons of these data to other studies problematic.

In a careful prospective study, growth, sleep EEG patterns, and neuroendocrine measures were examined in 13 hyperactive boys (aged 6–9.5 years) treated with d-amphetamine (10–30 mg/day; mean dose 0.84 mg/kg/day) for periods of at least 1 year and up to 21 months (Greenhill, Puig-Antich, Chambers et al., 1981; Greenhill, Puig-Antich, Sassin, & Sachar, 1977; Puig-Antich et al., 1978). Prior to their enrollment in this prospective study, these boys participated in a 2-week clinical trial and were shown to be reponsive to this stimulant, as reflected in at least a 25% reduction of the total Abbreviated Conners Parent–Teacher Questionnaire score. The selection criteria were defined carefully and included many "associated features" of the DSM-III (American Psychiatric Association, 1980) criteria for attention deficit disorder with hyperactivity (ADDH). In addition to hyperactivity, impulsivity, aggressiveness, and short attention span, the children had at least two of the following: history of speech delay, reading disability, neurological soft signs, and scatter on the WISC-R (Wechsler Intelligence Scale for Children—Revised). Children with a history of seizures or a grossly abnormal EEG were excluded from participation.

In this study, 12 months of continuous d-amphetamine treatment resulted in 16 percentile ($p < .001$) and 10 percentile ($p < .025$) reductions in weight and height, respectively (Greenhill et al., 1981). These reductions in weight and height percentiles were associated with significant reductions of mean weight and height velocities from their expected values ($p < .001$ and $p < .005$, respectively). A linear dose-dependent relationship appeared to exist between the loss of expected percentile height after 1 year and daily dosage of d-amphetamine (Puig-Antich et al., 1978). The authors' initial hypothesis was that the growth retardation observed with d-amphetamine was due to a disruption in the regulation of GH secretion (Greenhill, Puig-Antich, Chambers et al., 1981; Greenhill, Puig-Antich, Sassin, & Sachar, 1977; Puig-Antich et al., 1978). In order to test this hypothesis, they measured nocturnal secretion of growth hormone, especially during periods of SWS and the first 3 hours of sleep, and secretion in response to insulin-induced hypoglycemia. Physiologically, most GH is secreted during sleep in association with periods of SWS (Puig-Antich et al., 1978; Takahashi et al., 1968). Thus, the measurement of nocturnal GH secretion and its association with SWS can be used as a reflection of intact GH regulation. Similarly, the rate of GH secretion increases in response to insulin-induced hypoglycemia, and a failure to do so can indicate a disruption in the normal regulation of secretion (Kaplan et al., 1968). Contrary to the expected result, 6 months of continuous treatment with d-amphetamine, in dosages which positively influenced behavioral symptoms, did not alter any of the measures of GH regulation. GH secretion throughout the total sleep period and during the first 3 hours, secretory peaks in association with SWS, and secretion in response to insulin-induced hypoglycemia were unaffected by chronic d-amphetamine treatment. The failure to observe any desynchronization between SWS and GH secretion was explained, in part, by the lack of effect of chronic d-amphetamine treatment on critical sleep variables or patterns. Noradrenergic mechanisms have been implicated in the plasma GH response to insulin-induced hypoglycemia, as this response can be inhibited by an α-adrenergic antagonist, phentolamine (Martin, 1976; Puig-Antich et al., 1978). The failure to demonstrate, albeit indirectly, evidence of a possible alteration of adrenergic receptor sensitivity was consistent with the absence, or limited degree, of tolerance to the behavioral effects of d-amphetamine in this study. The development of tolerance to the behavioral effects and blunting in response to insulin-induced hypoglycemia would have been evidence consistent with receptor desensitization. Although no significant effects of 6

months of continuous d-amphetamine treatment on GH secretion were observed in this sample, a significant reduction of mean sleep-related (MSR) prolactin concentration was an unexpected finding (Greenhill, Puig-Antich, Chambers, et al., 1981; Greenhill, Puig-Antich, Sassin, & Sachar, 1977; Puig-Antich et al., 1978). In their preliminary report involving 7 patients (Puig-Antich et al., 1978), this reduction of MSR prolactin secretion was observed as early as 1 month after the beginning of treatment. Moreover, there was a significant correlation between the reduction of MSR prolactin secretion and inhibition of height velocity ($r = .57$, $p < .05$). An increased dopaminergic tone due to chronic d-amphetamine administration was proposed to account for the reduction of prolactin secretion. Although the half-life of d-amphetamine is about 4 hours and, in this study, the last dose was administered about 8 hours prior to the onset of sleep, significant nocturnal levels of this stimulant were detected (Puig-Antich et al., 1978). Thus, a sustained hyperdopaminergic tone could be maintained during sleep. As no tolerance to the suppression of prolactin secretion was observed, these data argue against a down-regulation of dopamine receptors in the pituitary and the utilization of this neuroendocrine measure to reflect alterations of dopamine receptor sensitivity in response to chronic d-amphetamine administration. However, these data do raise important issues regarding the role of prolactin in the regulation of growth.

In order to examine possible relationships between hyperactivity, sleep, and GH regulation, the secretory pattern of GH during sleep was evaluated in 5 hyperactive boys (ages $6\frac{3}{12}$–$12\frac{5}{12}$ years) with short stature (height percentile ≤ 10) (Stahl et al., 1979). These subjects were selected for study because it was hoped that they would have an increased likelihood of showing an abnormality of GH regulation. At the time of the study, 3 subjects had not received any stimulant medications for about 2 years, 1 had been off medication for 2 weeks, and only 1 subject was receiving methylphenidate (30 mg/day). All of these children showed peak nocturnal GH concentrations above (greater than 7 ng/ml) the values seen in children with isolated GH deficiency. Moreover, the results showed no abnormality in sleep architecture, as measured electroencephalo-graphically. The authors concluded that in these 5 hyperactive children, short stature could not be explained on the basis of abnormalities of sleep-related GH secretion. However, despite the absence of complete data sets during the period of 10 P.M. to 12 A.M., there is the suggestion of blunted GH responses during, or a dissociation of GH responses with, SWS in two cases. Neither of these two cases had received stimulant medications for periods of about 2 years prior to study. Unfortunately, the authors do not address either the absence of reasonably complete data sets between 10 P.M. and 12 A.M. in 4 of the 5 hyperactive patients and the possibility of blunting or dissociation in secretion of GH during SWS. Although the approach to detecting altered regulation of GH secretion is sound, there are several serious problems with this study. First, the selection of these children with short stature as the only subgroup of hyperactive children to be examined would confuse the interpretation of any positive findings. For example, an abnormality could be related to a primary disturbance of growth rather than indicate brain stem or hypothalamic–pituitary dysfunction in hyperactivity. Second, the data are graphed from 10 P.M. onward and there is no indication of the time of sleep onset for any of the children. Finally, although hyperactivity and short stature were listed as selection criteria, additional criteria for inclusion as well as diagnostic and demographic information were omitted from this report. Despite the many limitations of the study, the methodological approach is endorsed because a correlation of the secretory pattern of pituitary hormone secretion with brain electrical activity during sleep should yield valuable information regarding the functional state of the CNS.

Gualtieri et al. (1981) examined the GH and prolactin responses of 27 hyperactive children, 8 "hyperactive" adults, and 8 normal adults to challenges with single doses of methylphenidate (0.3 mg/kg and 0.6 mg/kg) in an acute placebo-controlled, double-blind crossover study. The hyperactive children (mean age less than 10 years) were medication-free at the time of the study, had IQ scores greater than 70, and fulfilled DSM-III (American Psychiatric Association, 1980) criteria for attention deficit disorder with hy-peractivity (ADDH). The hyperactive adults (mean age greater than 25 years) were referred with histories of childhood hyperkinesis and fulfilled DSM-III (American Psychiatric Association, 1980) criteria for ADDH, Residual Type. They continued to display many prominent symptoms including problems with restlessness, impulsivity, short attention span, and affective lability. In addition, impaired vocational performance, chronic interpersonal difficulties, and occasional drug or alcohol abuse were reported by some patients. The normal adults were university or hospital staff volunteers. All adult subjects were male and there was about 4:1 preponderance of male children. Subjects were fasted from 12 A.M. and the study began at 9 A.M. with the administration of a single oral dose of methylphenidate or placebo. One hour after the administration of the study medication, a blood sample was obtained for the determination of methylphenidate, GH, and prolactin levels. The study was double-blind and included a crossover after a period of 5 days during which the patient groups received drug or placebo followed by a 68-hour wash-out period. The normal adults did not receive drug or placebo during the 1 week between their crossover. The order of drug or placebo administration was randomized.

There were several significant findings and conclusions as well as hypotheses drawn from the above acute dose study (Gualtieri et al., 1981). Serum methylphenidate levels at 1 hour did not differ significantly between the three groups and, in the hyperactive children, levels correlated with oral dose on a milligram per kilogram basis ($r = .52$; $p < .05$). Thus, there are no apparent age-related differences in methylphenidate absorption. In the comparison of mean hormone levels between hyperactive and normal adults following placebo or stimulant challenge, there were no significant differences in the GH and prolactin concentration in either condition. Despite large interindividual variability, both adult groups showed an increase in GH and decrease in prolactin concentrations in response to methylphenidate. When the data from the adult groups were combined, these alterations in GH and prolactin concentrations correlated significantly ($r = .53$ and $-.49$, respectively) with serum levels of methylphenidate ($p < .01$). These data imply that acute changes (e.g., within 1 hour) in neuroendocrine measures may be a useful guide to the detection and selection of centrally effective doses. In view of the relatively short half-life of methylphenidate, acute changes of GH and prolactin concentrations occurring 1 hour after a single oral dose, corresponding to the approximate time of peak blood levels, may be most relevant to a study of the central action of methylphenidate (for discussion, see Gualtieri et al., 1981). In a related study, peak levels of methylphenidate were shown to occur at about 1 hour after oral administration (Gualtieri et al., 1982). These data are consistent with an absence of any difference in the sensitivity of dopamine receptors between adult patients with ADDH, Residual Type, and normal adults. However, this conclusion must be viewed as tentative and cannot be generalized to samples of hyperactive children. Although the authors reported their selection criteria for hyperactive adult patients carefully, the retrospective assignment of childhood diagnoses is a task of uncertain reliability. Thus, despite descriptive similarities, the adult hyperactive sample may, in fact, be diagnostically heterogeneous. Also, the sizes of the adult patient and normal samples ($n = 8$ for both) were small. A failure to detect any difference in dopamine receptor sensitivity between hyperactives and normals could be due to either of these factors alone or in combination. Finally, as determined by these authors and to be reviewed below, there is also the possibility of age-related differences in the sensitivities of dopamine receptors between children and adults. In the hyperactive children, there was a significant positive correlation between the serum level of methylphenidate and the concentration of GH 1 hour after drug administration ($r = .43$; $p < .01$). A surprising finding, however, was a greater sensitivity of the adult subjects to methylphenidate-induced prolactin suppression than the hyperactive children. The hyperactive children required a higher dose of methylphenidate on a milligram per kilogram basis to reduce their prolactin levels below those observed following placebo. Moreover, in the hyperactive children, there was no significant relationship between serum levels of methylphenidate and prolactin 1 hour after drug administration. The increased sensitivity

to prolactin suppression in adults may be clinically relevant as these subjects (adults only) experienced severe toxicity (including hallucinations) at the higher methylphenidate dose (0.6 mg/kg). Thus, in adults, a relationship between prolactin suppression and CNS toxicity in response to challenge with methylphenidate may exist. The increased prolactin suppression and CNS toxicity of adults to methylphenidate challenge could be due to maturational changes in the regulation of dopamine receptor sensitivity. In any event, the authors showed that changes in GH and prolactin concentrations are useful correlates of serum methylphenidate levels in terms of indicating centrally effective doses (Gualtieri et al., 1981). In addition, although many more questions were raised than answered, this study is a model of the application of the neuroendocrine strategy to ADDH.

The relationships between methylphenidate dosage, peak serum levels, and effects on levels of GH and prolactin, as well as on behavior, were examined further in studies involving "drug-naive" hyperactive boys and children receiving either low- or high-dose methylphenidate therapy (Shaywitz et al., 1982). All of the children in the acute study, involving 14 drug-naive boys (ages 7–12.4 years; mean age 10.4 years), and chronic study, involving 26 children (ages 4.75–16.25 years; mean age 11.2 years), were of normal intelligence and satisfied DSM-III (American Psychiatric Association, 1980) criteria for attention deficit disorder with hyperactivity (ADDH). In the acute study, children were admitted at 7:30 A.M. at which time an indwelling intravenous line was inserted. Methylphenidate, either a low dose (mean = 0.34 mg/kg) or a high dose (mean = 0.65 mg/kg), was administered orally at 9 A.M. and, thereafter, blood was sampled at regular intervals for determination of methylphenidate, GH, prolactin, and glucose concentrations. In the chronic study, children received "spot" sampling of blood at $1\frac{1}{2}$ or 2 hours after administration of their usual morning dose. In addition to measures of drug levels in blood, in the chronic study, behavioral effects were assessed, both prior to and after 1 month of treatment, in 21 children using the Conners Abbreviated Parent–Teacher Rating Scale (CAPTRS).

Pharmacokinetic data obtained during

the acute study showed that peak methylphenidate serum levels occurred at about 2.5 hours postadministration, with a relatively constant half-life of about 2.5 hours. Methylphenidate levels approximating at least 80% of peak values were observed between 1.5 and 3 hours after drug administration. The serum methylphenidate levels obtained after 2 hours in the chronic study approximated the values obtained at the same time in the acute study and suggest that chronic administration does not influence drug absorption or metabolism. A significant elevation of GH and reduction of prolactin levels were observed after methylphenidate administration. The alterations in levels of these hormones corresponded to the serum levels of methylphenidate. For example, in 11 drug-naive children receiving 0.34 mg/kg of methylphenidate, peak drug levels of about 8.5 ng/ml were sustained between 1.5 and 3 hours after administration. The GH peak occurred at about 2 hours and prolactin nadir at about 1.5 hours after administration. The return of these hormonal levels toward baseline values followed the time course of methylphenidate elimination. The reduction of prolactin levels is most consistent with a central agonist effect of methylphenidate on dopamine receptors. That these effects were due to stimulation of dopamine receptors and independent of a more general effect on metabolism was suggested by the absence of any change in glucose concentrations over the 3 hours post drug administration. No changes in hormone levels were observed in 4 of the hyperactive children challenged with placebo on a separate occasion. However, the observed reduction of prolactin with low-dose (0.34 mg/kg) methylphenidate in this study conflicts with the earlier observations of Gualtieri et al. (1981). In the chronic study, a relationship between peak serum levels of methylphenidate and behavioral improvement, as reflected in a reduction of scores on the CAPTRS, was found. In fact, the 3 children who failed to respond behaviorally had peak serum levels below 7 ng/ml at 2 hours postadministration. Thus, a failure to absorb methylphenidate adequately, as reflected in suboptimal serum levels or little or no effect on hormonal levels, could account for an absence of therapeutic effects in some patients. Also, the ability to influence hormonal levels acutely could predict therapeutic response. Despite the discrepant observations regarding prolactin suppression, in general, the results of this study (Shaywitz et al., 1982) agree with those of Gualtieri et al. (1981). Unfortunately, hormonal data were not presented in the chronic study and therefore no information regarding the effect of chronic methylphenidate administration on hypothalamic–pituitary function could be inferred.

The influence of chronic methylphenidate administration on the hypothalamic–pituitary axis of hyperactive children was further explored using a continuous blood withdrawal procedure in a sample of 9 ambulatory patients (Schultz et al., 1982). The patients were studied while receiving chronic medication and after a period of drug withdrawal. With this procedure, data regarding diurnal patterns of GH and prolactin secretion and integrated (over 24 hours) concentrations of these hormones were obtained. In addition, GH responses, after an overnight fast, to provocative and sequential challenges with arginine and insulin-induced hypoglycemia were measured. Fasting levels of SM-C were measured as well. Hormonal responses of the children were compared on and off medication and to available data on normal control subjects. The hyperactive children were referred for neuroendocrine evaluation with histories of childhood hyperkinesis and positive response to methylphenidate; the authors acknowledged potential differences in the diagnostic criteria of the referring clinicians. The mean age of the 9 children was 11.1 ± 1.7 years and the sample included 7 boys and 2 girls. Seven of the children were first studied while receiving chronic treatment with methylphenidate. Thus, it is possible that this prior long-term treatment with methylphenidate for periods ranging from 3 months to 4 years resulted in long-lasting changes in the hypothalamic–pituitary axis and/or sensitivity of dopamine receptors. Methylphenidate dosages ranged between 20 and 120 mg/day (mean = 1.1 ± 1.1 mg/kg/day) and, for purposes of some analyses, the children were stratified according to whether their dose was above (high dose) or below (low dose) 0.90 mg/kg/day. Blood was continuously sampled (4 ml/hour) over a 24-hour period and collected as 1-hour aliquots.

Children were permitted their usual diets and levels of activity.

The results of this investigation were unexpected and, with the possible exception of integrated prolactin concentrations, which were greater than values for normal children, irrespective of medication condition, do not support either basal abnormalities or any disruption of hypothalamic–pituitary function due to chronic methylphenidate therapy in hyperactive children (Schultz *et al.*, 1982) . In fact, the suggestion of elevated mean 24-hour prolactin concentrations in medicated hyperactive patients was contrary to the prediction based upon the known pharmacology of methylphenidate and earlier published reports (Greenhill, Puig-Antich, Chambers *et al.*, 1981; Greenhill, Puig-Antich, Sassin, & Sachar, 1977; Puig-Antich *et al.*, 1978). However, the published values for comparison of integrated prolactin concentrations determined in normal 7- to 15-year-old boys may be less than optimal, as they were obtained via an intermittent blood sampling procedure (for discussion, see Schultz *et al.*, 1982). The diurnal pattern of prolactin secretion and the integrated prolactin concentration in these patients were not affected by chronic treatment with methylphenidate. The normal diurnal pattern of GH secretion with peaks occurring during sleep, between about 10 P.M. and 2 A.M., was observed. There was no effect of medication on this secretory pattern. Integrated concentrations of GH did not differ significantly between patients on and off medication and between patients and published values for normal 7- to 16-year-old control subjects. Stratification of patients according to methylphenidate dose failed to reveal any significant effects. Similarly, the GH responses to provocative challenge with insulin-induced hypoglycemia in patients, irrespective of drug condition, did not differ from normal subjects. In contrast to the results with insulin-induced hypoglycemia, acute administration (morning dose) of methylphenidate appeared to augment the GH response to arginine. The interpretation of this finding is unclear, but does suggest a possible unique interaction of arginine with acute methylphenidate administration. There were no differences in fasting levels of SM-C between patients on and off medication and normal control subjects. In an effort to reconcile their failure to observe a methylphenidate-induced disruption of hypothalamic–pituitary function with reports of stimulant suppression of growth velocity, the authors raised the interesting possibility of methylphenidate-induced endorgan resistance to hormonal influences (Schultz *et al.*, 1982). In their discussion, they cited data suggesting that stimulants may interfere with cartilage metabolism. This suggestion is interesting and should be pursued. Clearly, these results were obtained in a small, heterogeneous sample of hyperactive patients and must await replication before it can be concluded that methylphenidate exerts little effect on the hypothalamic–pituitary axis. As mentioned, the results are contrary to any predictions based on the pharmacology of this stimulant and previous studies.

In a prospective study, effects of 6 months of continuous methylphenidate administration on the sleep-related patterns of GH and prolactin secretion and mean sleep-related hormonal concentrations were examined in 8 hyperactive boys (Greenhill *et al.*, 1984). The design of this study was similar to a previous prospective study, reviewed earlier, examining effects of chronic *d*-amphetamine administration in 13 hyperactive boys (Greenhill, Puig-Antich, Chambers *et al.*, 1981; Greenhill, Puig-Antich, Sassin, & Sachar, 1977; Puig-Antich *et al.*, 1978). In this study, 8 previously unmedicated boys (ages 6–10 years; mean age 8.5 ± 0.4 years) of normal intelligence were enrolled who fulfilled DSM-III (American Psychiatric Association, 1980) criteria for attention deficit disorder with hyperactivity and showed pervasive evidence of the disorder both at home and in school. Prior to their enrollment in the prospective study, they had to show behavioral evidence of methylphenidate responsiveness during a 2-week medication trial. The methylphenidate dosage ranged between 10 and 60 mg/day (mean dosage 1.3 mg/kg/ day), given in two divided doses, and was adjusted monthly according to symptom severity, as assessed by the Abbreviated Conners Rating Scale. Hormone analyses were performed on blood sampled at 20-minute intervals during the sleep period until awakening the following day. In addition, polysomnography was performed during the sleep period. Mean sleep-related hormone

TABLE 5.4. Major Neuroendocrine Studies of Attention Deficit Disorder with Hyperactivity

Authors	Subjects and diagnosis	Stimulant, duration of administration	Neuroendocrine procedures	Conclusions	Comments
Aarskog, Fevang, Klove, Stoa, and Thorsen (1977)	$n = 20$; ages 6 to 13 years; 17 males and 3 females; hyperactivity	Acute challenges: d-AMPHET. (15 mg), MPH (20 mg)	GH response to provocative challenge	Acute challenges stimulated GH secretion	GH response could reflect central activity of indirect DA agonists
		Chronic therapy: MPH ($n = 7$); 6 to 8 months		Heterogeneity and altered patterns of GH response to d-AMPHET. with chronic MPH therapy	Possible long-term effect of MPH on hypothalamic–pituitary function
Greenhill, Puig-Antich, Chambers et al. (1981); Greenhill, Puig-Antich, Sassin, and Sachar (1977); Puig-Antich, Greenhill, Sassin, and Sachar (1978)	$n = 13$; ages 6–9.5 years; males; ADDH with "associated" features	Chronic d-AMPHET. (10–30 mg; mean 0.84 mg/kg/day); 6 months	Nocturnal secretion of GH and PRL	No effect of chronic d-AMPHET. on measures of GH secretion	Data suggest no long-term effect of chronic d-AMPHET. on hypothalamic–pituitary function
			GH response to insulin-induced hypoglycemia	Chronic d-AMPHET. reduced MSR–PRL concentration	Possible role of reduced MSR–PRL concentration in growth suppression

Study	Subjects	Design	Measure	Results	Comments
Stahl, Orr, and Griffiths (1979)	$n = 5$; ages $6\frac{3}{12}$ to $12\frac{5}{12}$ years; males; hyperactivity and short stature (height percentile ≤ 10)	Four subjects off stimulant medication for 2 weeks to 2 years; 1 subject receiving MPH (30 mg/day) for unspecified duration	Nocturnal pattern of GH secretion	All subjects showed peak nocturnal GH levels above 7 ng/ml	Incomplete data sets and failure to include hyperactive subjects of normal stature limit conclusions; methodological approach, i.e., correlation with sleep EEG, is useful
Gualtieri et al. (1981)	A. Children $n = 27$; mean age ≤ 10 years; 22 males and 5 females; ADDH B. Hyperactive adults $n = 8$; mean age 27.9; males; ADD, Residual Type C. Normal adults $n = 8$; mean age 29.6; males	Acute challenges with placebo and single doses of MPH (0.3 and 0.6 mg/kg)	GH and PRL responses 1 hour after acute challenge	No differences between hyperactive and normal adults; in adults, increases of GH and decreases of PRL correlated with serum MPH levels; in hyperactive children, positive correlation between serum MPH level and GH concentration	Placebo-controlled, double-blind, crossover study; hormonal responses could reflect centrally effective doses; maturational changes in DA receptor sensitivity were suggested
Shaywitz et al. (1982)	A. Acute study "drug-naive" $n = 14$; ages 7–12.4 years; males; ADDH	Acute challenges; MPH (0.34 mg/kg or 0.65 mg/kg)	GH and PRL responses to provocative challenge	GH elevation and PRL reduction occurred upon acute challenge with MPH; hormonal alterations corresponded to serum MPH levels	Hormonal responses could reflect centrally effective doses

135

TABLE 5.4. (*Continued*)

Authors	Subjects and diagnosis	Stimulant, duration of administration	Neuroendocrine procedures	Conclusions	Comments
	B. Chronic study $n = 26$; ages 4.75–16.25 years; sex composition not specified; ADDH	Chronic therapy: MPH (0.34 mg/kg or 0.68 mg/kg); duration not specified			
Schultz, Hayford, Wolraich, Hintz, and Thompson (1982)	$n = 9$; ages $8\frac{2}{12}$ to $12\frac{11}{12}$ years; 7 males and 2 females; childhood hyperkinesis and positive MPH response	MPH (20–120 mg/day; mean 1.1 ± 1.1 mg/kg day); 3 months to 4 years	Continuous blood withdrawal procedure to measure (a) diurnal patterns of GH and PRL secretion, and (b) integrated (mean 24-hour) GH and PRL concentrations; GH response to arginine and insulin-induced hypoglycemia; fasting levels of somatomedin	No significant effect of chronic MPH administration on a variety of neuroendocrine measures; greater integrated PRL concentration in these patients	Results were contrary to predictions based on pharmacology of MPH; sample was small and diagnostically heterogeneous
Greenhill et al. (1984)	$n = 8$; ages 6–10 years; males; ADDH	MPH (10–60 mg/day; mean 1.3 mg/kg/day); 6 months	Measurement of sleep-related patterns of GH and PRL secretion and MSR hormonal concentrations	Modest elevation of MSR–GH concentration, no effect on MSR–PRL concentration	Suggests differences in the pharmacology of *d*-AMPHET. and MPH

Note. ADDH, Attention deficit disorder with hyperactivity; GH, growth hormone; PRL, prolactin; MPH, methylphenidate; *d*-AMPHET., *d*-amphetamine; MSR, Mean sleep-related.

CHAPTER 5. PSD, INFANTILE AUTISM, AND ATTENTION DEFICIT DISORDER

levels were correlated with measures of height and weight velocities and percentiles.

At baseline, sleep architecture of the hyperactive children did not reveal any evidence of major abnormalities. Continuous methylphenidate treatment showed only minimal effects on the EEG patterns of sleep; these included increases of stage shifts, REM activity and fragmentation, as well as the number of REM periods. Chronic methylphenidate administration did not influence the amount of time spent in SWS or the mean percentages of sleep stages (Greenhill et al., 1984).

In contrast to the study of Schultz et al. (1982) in which no effects of chronic methylphenidate administration on the secretory pattern and integrated 24-hour concentration of GH were observed, in this study, effects on the sleep-related pattern of GH secretion and mean sleep-related GH concentration were detected (Greenhill et al., 1984). There was a nonsignificant elevation (34%) of mean sleep-related GH concentration after 6 months of continuous treatment with methylphenidate. When the sleep night was divided into discrete time periods, statistical analyses showed that during drug treatment there was a significantly greater mean GH concentration in the period between the time of the first sample, that is, about 10 minutes prior to sleep onset, and 120 minutes after the first sample was obtained ($p < .05$). Thus, these data are consistent with methylphenidate's exerting its greatest effect during the onset of SWS. Moreover, two of the samples, which were obtained at 220 and 240 minutes after the first sample, showed significant methylphenidate-induced increases of GH concentrations ($p < .01$ and $p < .05$, respectively). In contrast to their findings with continuous d-amphetamine administration (Greenhill, Puig-Antich, Chambers et al., 1981; Greenhill, Puig-Antich, Sassin, & Sachar, 1977; Puig-Antich et al., 1978), the authors did not detect any suppression of nocturnal prolactin secretion with chronic methylphenidate administration (Greenhill et al., 1984). Moreover, no relationships between mean sleep-related hormonal concentrations and measures of growth velocity or percentile were detected when children were treated continuously for 6 months with methylphenidate. Although both methylphenidate and d-amphetamine are indirect-

acting dopamine agonists, methylphenidate appears to lack effect or have little effect, in comparison to d-amphetamine, on linear growth (for discussion, see Greenhill et al. 1984). In contrast to these data, Mattes and Gittelman (1983) rated significant decreases in height percentiles in a sample of 86 hyperactive children after 2, 3, and 4 years of treatment with the same drug; these were not apparent after 1 year; significant losses in weight percentiles paralleled these changes. The absence of an adverse effect of chronic methylphenidate administration on height velocity and percentile in the study by Greenhill et al. (1984) could be explained by the modest elevation in mean sleep-related GH concentration. Also, the lack of effect on skeletal growth could reflect differences in the pharmacology of the two drugs; that is, d-amphetamine may release dopamine from a more labile, reserpine-resistant pool of storage granules (Braestrup, 1977). Although the suggestion of mild tolerance to the behavioral effects of methylphenidate existed, as reflected in a minimal increase of dose on a milligram per kilogram basis at 6 months and 1 year after the start of the study, there was little or no neuroendocrine evidence consistent with dopamine receptor desensitization.

The results of the major neuroendocrine studies in the area of attention deficit disorder with hyperactivity are summarized in Table 5.4. The absence of any consistent neuroendocrine finding suggests that the diagnostic category, attention deficit disorder with hyperactivity, is an etiologically heterogeneous group of disorders.

CONCLUSION

Although considerable data concerning the psychoneuroendocrinology of PSD, IA, and attention deficit disorder have been accumulated, no pathognomonic findings have been reported. In fact, with the possible exception of PSD, no consistent abnormality has been found and some seemingly discrepant results have occurred among the various studies. Much further work remains to clarify how these psychoneuroendocrinological findings relate to these particular diagnostic entities and whether their variability represents diagnostic heterogeneity, etiological subgroups, circadian variations and sampling problems, individual differences, or different points in the clinical course. Even now, however, we can use our knowledge in selecting more rational treatment approaches and in monitoring clinical progress.

Acknowledgment

This work was supported in part by Public Health Service Grants MH-04665 and MH-32212 and by a grant from Stallone Fund for Autism Research (Dr. Campbell).

References

Aarskog, D., Fevang, F. O., Klove, H., Stoa, K. F., & Thorsen, T. (1977). The effect of the stimulant drugs, dextroamphetamine and methylphenidate, on secretion of growth hormone in hyperactive children. *Journal of Pediatrics, 90*, 136–139.

Abbassi, V., Linscheid, T., & Coleman, M. (1978). Triiodothyronine (T3) concentration and therapy in autistic children. *Journal of Autism and Childhood Schizophrenia, 8*, 383–387.

American Psychiatric Association. (1980). *Diagnostic and statistical manual of mental disorders* (3rd ed.). Washington, DC: Author.

Anderson, L. T., Campbell, M., Grega, D. M., Perry, R., Small, A. M., & Green, W. H. (1984). Haloperidol in the treatment of infantile autism: Effects on learning and behavioral symptoms. *American Journal of Psychiatry, 141*, 1195–1202.

Antony, G. J., Van Wyk, J. J., French, F. S., Weaver, R. P., Dugger, G. S., Timmons, R. L., & Newsome, J. F. (1969). Influence of pituitary stalk section on growth hormone, insulin, and TSH secretion in women with metastatic breast cancer. *Journal of Clinical Endocrinology and Metabolism, 29*, 1238–1250.

Bloch, B., Brazeau, P., Ling, N., Böhlen, F., Esch, F., Wehrenberg, W. B., Benoit, R., Bloom, F., & Guillemin, R. (1983). Immunohistochemical detection of growth hormone-releasing factor in brain. *Nature (London), 301*, 607–608.

Böhlen, P., Brazeau, P., Bloch, B., Ling, N., Gaillard, R., & Guillemin, R. (1983). Human hypothalamic growth hormone-releasing factor (GRF): Evidence for two forms identical to tumor derived GRF-44-NH$_2$ and GRF-40. *Biochemical and Biophysical Research Communications, 114*, 930–936.

Braestrup, C. (1977). Biochemical differentiation of amphetamine vs. methylphenidate and nomifensine in rats. *Journal of Pharmacy and Pharmacology, 29*, 463–470.

Brambilla, F., Viani, F., & Rossotti, V. (1969). Endocrine aspects of child psychoses. *Diseases of the Nervous System, 30*, 627–632.

Brasel, J. A. (1973). Review of findings in patients with emotional deprivation. In L. I. Gardner & P. Amacher (Eds.), *Endocrine aspect of malnutrition: Marasmus, kwashiorkor and psychosocial deprivation*, (pp. 115–127). Santa Ynez, CA: Kroc Foundation.

Brown, G. M., Seggie, J. A., Chambers, J. W., & Ettigi, P. G. (1978). Psychoendocrinology and growth hormone: A review. *Psychoneuroendocrinology, 3*, 131–153.

Campbell, M., Anderson, L. T., Meier, M., Cohen, I. L., Small, A. M., Samit, C., & Sachar, E. J. (1978). A comparison of haloperidol and behavior therapy and their interaction in autistic children. *Journal of the American Academy of Child Psychiatry, 17*, 640–655.

Campbell, M., Anderson, L. T., Small, A. M., Perry, R., Green, W. H., & Caplan, R. (1982). The effects of haloperidol on learning and behavior in autistic children. *Journal of Autism and Developmental Disorders, 12*, 167–175.

Campbell, M., Fish, B., David, R., Shapiro, T., Collins, P., & Koh, C. (1972). Response to triiodothyronine and dextroamphetamine. A study of preschool schizophrenic children. *Journal of Autism and Childhood Schizophrenia, 2*, 343–358.

Campbell, M., Fish, B., David, R., Shapiro, T., Collins, P., & Koh, C. (1973). Liothyronine treatment in psychotic and nonpsychotic children under 6 years. *Archives of General Psychiatry, 29*, 602–608.

Campbell, M., Friedman, E., DeVito, E., Greenspan, L., & Collins, P.J. (1974). Blood serotonin in psychotic and brain-damaged children. *Journal of Autism and Childhood Schizophrenia, 4*, 33–41.

Campbell, M., Friedman, E., Green, W. H., Collins, P. J., Small, A. M., & Breuer, H. (1975). Blood serotonin in schizophrenic children. A preliminary study. *International Pharmacopsychiatry, 10*, 213–221.

Campbell, M., Geller, B., Small, A.M., Petti, T.A., & Ferris, S. (1978). Minor congenital anomalies in young psychotic children. *American Journal of Psychiatry, 135*, 573–575.

Campbell, M., Green, W. H., Caplan, R., & David, R. (1982). Psychiatry and endocrinology in children: Early infantile autism and psychosocial dwarfism. In P. J. V. Beumont & G. D. Burrows (Eds.), *Handbook of psychiatry and endocrinology* (pp. 15–62). Amsterdam: Elsevier Biomedical Press.

Campbell, M., Grega, D. M., Green, W. H., & Bennett, W. G. (1983). Neuroleptic-induced dyskinesias in children. *Clinical Neuropharmacology, 6*, 207–222.

Campbell, M., Hollander, C. S., Ferris, S., & Greene, L. W. (1978). Response to thyrotropin-releasing hormone stimulation in young psychotic children: A pilot study. *Psychoneuroendocrinology, 3*, 195–201.

Campbell, M., Perry, R., Bennett, W. G., Small, A. M., Green, W. H., Grega, D., Schwartz, V., & Anderson, L. (1983). Long-term therapeutic efficacy and drug-related abnormal movements: A prospective study of haloperidol in autistic children. *Psychopharmacology Bulletin, 19*(1), 80–83.

Campbell, M., Petti, T. A., Green, W. H., Cohen, I. L., Genieser, N. B., & David, R. (1980). Some physical parameters of young autistic children. *Journal of the American Academy of Child Psychiatry, 19*, 193–212.

Campbell, M., Small, A. M., Collins, P. J., Friedman, E., David, R., & Genieser, N. B. (1976). Levodopa and levoamphetamine: A crossover study in schizophrenic children. *Current Therapeutic Research, 18*, 70–86.

Campbell, M., Small, A. M., Hollander, C. S., Korein, J., Cohen, I. L., Kalmijn, M., & Ferris, S. (1978). A controlled crossover study of triiodothyronine in autistic children. *Journal of Autism and Childhood Schizophrenia, 8,* 371–381.

Cohen, D. J., Caparulo, B. K., Shaywitz, B. A., & Bowers, M. B., Jr. (1977). Dopamine and serotonin metabolism in neuropsychiatrically disturbed children: CSF homovanillic acid and 5-hydroxyindoleacetic acid. *Archives of General Psychiatry, 34* 545–550.

Cohen, D. J., Shaywitz, B. A., Johnson, W. T., & Bowers, M., Jr. (1974). Biogenic amines in autistic and atypical children. Cerebrospinal fluid measures of homovanillic acid and 5-hydroxyindoleacetic acid. *Archives of General Psychiatry, 31,* 845–853.

Cohen, D. J., Young, J. G., Lowe, T. L., & Harcherik, D. (1980). Thyroid hormone in autistic children. *Journal of Autism and Developmental Disorders, 10,* 445–450.

Creak, M. (1964). Schizophrenic syndrome in childhood. Further progress report of a working party (April 1964). *Developmental Medicine and Child Neurology, 6,* 530–535.

D'Ercole, A. J., Underwood, L. E., & Van Wyk, J. J. (1977). Serum somatomedin-C in hypopituitarism and in other disorders of growth. *Journal of Pediatrics, 90,* 375–381.

Deutsch, S. I., Campbell, M., Perry, R., Green, W. H., Poland, R. E., & Rubin, R. T. (1986). Plasma growth hormone response to insulin-induced hypoglycemia in infantile autism: A pilot study. *Journal of Autism and Developmental Disorders, 16,* 59–68.

Deutsch, S. I., Campbell, M., Sachar, E. J., Green, W. H., & David, R. (1985). Plasma growth hormone response to oral L-dopa in infantile autism. *Journal of Autism and Developmental Disorders, 15,* 205–212.

Feinberg, I. (1969). Drugs and sleep: Discussion 4. In A. Kales (Ed.), *Sleep: Physiology and pathology* (pp. 344–351). Philadelphia: Lippincott.

Finkelstein, J. W., Roffwarg, H. P., Boyar, R. M., Kream, J., & Hellman, L. (1972). Age-related change in the twenty four-hour spontaneous secretion of growth hormone. *Journal of Clinical Endocrinology and Metabolism, 35,* 665–670.

Frasier, S. D., Hilburn, J. M., & Matthews, N. L. (1967). The serum growth hormone response to hypoglycemia in dwarfism. *Journal of Pediatrics, 71,* 625–638.

Frasier, S. D., & Rallison, M. L. (1972). Growth retardation and emotional deprivation: Relative resistance to treatment with human growth hormone. *Journal of Pediatrics, 80,* 603–609.

Friedman, R. C., & Reichlin, S. (1965). Growth hormone content of the pituitary gland of starved rats. *Endocrinology (Baltimore), 76,* 787–788.

Glick, S. M., Roth, J., Yalow, R. S., & Berson, S. A. (1965). The regulation of growth hormone secretion, *Recent Progress in Hormone Research, 21,* 241–283.

Green, W. H. (1985). Attachment disorders of infancy and early childhood. In H. I. Kaplan & B. J. Sadock (Eds.), *Comprehensive textbook of psychiatry/IV* (4th ed., pp. 1722–1731). Baltimore: Williams & Wilkins.

Green, W. H. (1986). Psychosocial dwarfism: Psychological and etiological considerations. In B. J. Lahey & A. E. Kazdin (Eds.), *Advances in Clinical Child Psychology* (Vol. 9, pp. 245–278). New York: Plenum Press.

Green, W. H., Campbell, M., & David, R. (1984). Psychosocial dwarfism: A critical review of the evidence. *Journal of the American Academy of Child Psychiatry, 23,* 39–48.

Greenblatt, D. J., & Shader, R. I. (1974). *Benzodiazepines in clinical practice* (p. 191). New York: Raven Press.

Greenhill, L. L., Puig-Antich, J., Chambers, W., Rubinstein, B., Halpern, F., & Sachar, E. J. (1981). Growth hormone, prolactin, and growth responses in hyperkinetic males treated with *d*-amphetamine. *Journal of the American Academy of Child Psychiatry, 20,* 84–103.

Greenhill, L. L., Puig-Antich, J., Novacenko, H., Solomon, M., Anghern, C., Florea, J., Goetz, R., Fiscina, B., & Sachar, E. J. (1984). Prolactin, growth hormone, and growth responses in boys with attention deficit disorder and hyperactivity treated with methylphenidate. *Journal of the American Academy of Child Psychiatry, 23,* 58–67.

Greenhill, L. L., Puig-Antich, J., Sassin, J., & Sachar, E. J. (1977). Hormone and growth responses in hyperkinetic children on stimulant medication. *Psychopharmacology Bulletin, 13,* 33–36.

Gualtieri, C. T., Kanoy, R., Hawk, B., Koriath, U., Schroeder, S., Youngblood, W., Breese, G. R., & Prange, A. J., Jr. (1981). Growth hormone and prolactin secretion in adults and hyperactive children: Relation to methylphenidate serum levels. *Psychoneuroendocrinology, 6,* 331–339.

Gualtieri, C. T., Wafgin, W., Kanoy, R., Patrick, K., Shen, D., Youngblood, W., Mueller, R., & Breese, G. (1982). Clinical studies of methylphenidate serum levels in children and adults. *Journal of the American Academy of Child Psychiatry, 21,* 19–26.

Guilhaume, A., Benoit, O., Gourmelen, M., & Richardet, J. M. (1982). Relationship between sleep stage IV deficit and reversible HGH deficiency in psychosocial dwarfism. *Pediatric Research, 16,* 299–303.

Guillemin, R., Brazeau, P., Böhlen, P., Esch, F., Ling, N., & Wehrenberg, W. B. (1982). Growth hormone-releasing factor from a human pancreatic tumor that caused acromegaly. *Science, 218,* 585–587.

Harvey, S. C. (1980). Hypnotics and sedatives. In A. G. Gilman, L. S. Goodman, and A. Gilman (Eds.), *The pharmacological basis of therapeutics* (6th ed., pp. 339–375). New York: Macmillan.

Hernandez, R. J., Poznanski, A. K., Hopwood, N. J., & Kelch, R. P. (1978). Incidence of growth lines in psychosocial dwarfs and idiopathic hypopituitarism. *American Journal of Roentgenology, 131,* 477–479.

Honda, Y., Takahashi, K., Takahashi, S., Azumi, K., Irie, M., Sakuma, M., Tsushima, T., & Shizume, K. (1969). Growth hormone secretion during nocturnal sleep in normal subjects. *Journal of Clinical Endocrinology and Metabolism, 29,* 20–29.

Hopwood, N. J., & Becker, D. J. (1979). Psychosocial dwarfism: Detection, evaluation and management. In A. W. Franklin (Ed.), *Child abuse and neglect* (Vol. 3, pp. 439–447). Oxford: Pergamon Press.

Hopwood, N. J., Becker, D. J., Hengstenberg, F. H., & Drash, A. L. (1977). Lipid changes associated with psychosocial dwarfism [Abstract] *Pediatric Research, 11*, 516.

Howse, P. M., Rayner, P. H. W., Williams, J. M., Rudd, B. T., Betrande, P. V., Thompson, C. R. S., & Jones, L. A. (1977). Nyctohemeral secretion of growth hormone in normal children of short stature and in children with hypopituitarism and intrauterine growth retardation. *Clinical Endocrinology (Oxford), 6*, 347–359.

Hunt, R. D., Cohen, D. J., Shaywitz, S. E., & Shaywitz, B. A. (1982). Strategies for study of the neurochemistry of attention deficit disorder in children. *Schizophrenia Bulletin, 8*, 236–252.

Imura, H., Yoshimi, T., & Ikekubo, K. (1971). Growth hormone secretion in a patient with deprivation dwarfism. *Endocrinologica Japonica, 18*, 301–304.

Isaksson, O. G. P., Jansson, J.-O., & Gause, I. A. M. (1982). Growth hormone stimulates longitudinal bone growth directly. *Science, 216*, 1237–1239.

Jackson, R. T., & Pelton, E. W. (1978). L-Dopa treatment of children with hyperactive behavior [Abstract]. *Neurology, 28*, 331.

Kanner, L. (1943). Autistic disturbances of affective contact. *Nervous Child, 2*, 217–250.

Kaplan, S. L., Abrams, C. A. L., Bell, J. J., Conte, F. A., & Grumbach, M. M. (1968). Growth and growth hormone. I. Changes in serum level of growth hormone following hypoglycemia in 134 children with growth retardation. *Pediatric Research, 2*, 43–63.

Khan, A. A. (1970). Thyroid dysfunction [Letter]. *British Medical Journal, 4*, 495.

Krieger, I., & Good, M. H. (1970). Adrenocortical and thyroid function in the deprivation syndrome. *American Journal of Diseases of Childhood, 120*, 95–102.

Krieger, I., & Mellinger, R. C. (1971). Pituitary function in the deprivation syndrome. *Journal of Pediatrics, 79*, 216–225.

LaCauza, C., Salti, R., Galluzzi, F., Seminara, S., Generoso, M., Nania, C., Becherucci, P., Chiccoli, A., & Merello, G. (1983). Clinical remarks on somatomedin activity. In G. Chiumello & M. Sperling (Eds.), *Recent progress in pediatric endocrinology* (pp. 85–105). New York: Raven Press.

Lacey, K. A., Hewison, A., & Parkin, J. M. (1973). Exercise as a screening test for growth hormone deficiency in children. *Archives of Diseases of Childhood, 48*, 508–512.

Lal, S., & Martin, J. B. (1980). Neuroanatomy and neuropharmacological regulation of neuroendocrine function. In H. M. Van Praag, M. H. Lader, O. J. Rafaelsen, & E. J. Sachar (Eds.), *Handbook of biological psychiatry: Part III. Brain mechanisms and abnormal behavior-genetics and neuroendocrinology* (pp. 101–167). New York: Marcel Dekker.

Lal, S., Tolis, G., Martin, J., Brown, G., & Guyda, H. (1975). Effect of clonidine on growth hormone, prolactin, LH, FSH, and TSH in the serum of normal men. *Journal of Clinical Endocrinology and Metabolism, 41*, 827–832.

Langer, D. H., Rapoport, J. L., Brown, G. L., Ebert, M. H., & Bunney, W. E., Jr. (1982). Behavioral effects of carbidopa/levodopa in hyperactive boys. *Journal of the American Academy of Child Psychiatry, 21*, 10–18.

Laron, Z. (1983). Somatomedin, insulin, growth hormone, and growth. In G. Chiumello & M. Sperling (Eds.), *Recent progress in pediatric endocrinology* (pp. 67–80). New York: Raven Press.

Lister, R.-C., Underwood, L. E., Marshall, R. N., Friesen, H. G., & Van Wyk, J. J. (1974). Evidence for a direct effect of TRH on prolactin release in humans. *Journal of Clinical Endocrinology and Metabolism, 39*, 1148–1150.

Lowe, T. L., Cohen, D. J., Detlor, J., Kremenitzer, M. W., & Shaywitz, B. A. (1982). Stimulant medications precipitate Tourette's syndrome. *Journal of the American Medical Association, 247*(12), 1729–1731.

Maher, K. R., Harper, J. F., Macleay, A., & King, M. G. (1975). Peculiarities in the endocrine response to insulin stress in early infantile autism. *Journal of Nervous and Mental Disease, 161*, 180–184.

Martin, J. B. (1976). Brain regulation of growth hormone secretion. In L. Martini, & W. F. Ganong, (Eds.), *Frontiers in neuroendocrinology* (Vol. 4, pp. 129–168). New York: Raven Press.

Mattes, J., & Gittelman, R. (1983). Growth of hyperactive children on maintenance methylphenidate. *Archives of General Psychiatry, 40*, 317–321.

Meites, J., & Fiel, N. J. (1965). Effect of starvation on hypothalamic content of "somatotropin releasing factor" and pituitary growth hormone content. *Endocrinology (Baltimore), 77*, 455–460.

Meltzer, H. Y., Busch, D., & Fang, V. S. (1981). Hormones, dopamine receptors, and schizophrenia. *Psychoneuroendocrinology, 6*, 17–36.

Mendelson, W. B., Jacobs, L. S., Reichman, J. D., Othmer, E., Cryer, P. E., Trivedi, B., & Daughaday, W. H. (1975). Methysergide: Suppression of sleep-related prolactin secretion and enhancement of sleep-related growth hormone secretion. *Journal of Clinical Investigation, 56*, 690–697.

Mönkeberg, F., Donoso, G., Oxman, S., Pak, N., & Meneghello, J. (1963). Human growth hormone in infant malnutrition. *Pediatrics, 31*, 58–64.

Mortimer, C. H. (1977). Growth hormone release-inhibiting hormone (GH-RIH, somatostatin). In L. Martini & G. M. Besser (Eds.), *Clinical neuroendocrinology* (pp. 279–294). New York: Academic Press.

Parker, D. C., Rossman, L. G., Siler, T. M., Rivier, J. Yen, S. S. C., & Guillemin, R. (1974). Inhibition of the sleep-related peak in physiologic human growth hormone release by somatostatin. *Journal of Clinical Endocrinology and Metabolism, 38*, 496–499.

Parra, A. (1973). Discussion in I. Krieger, Endocrines and nutrition in psychosocial deprivation in the U.S.A.: Comparison with growth failure due to malnutrition on an organic basis. In L. I. Gardner & P. Amacher (Eds.), *Endocrine aspects of malnutrition, kwashiorkor and psychosocial deprivation* (p. 155). Santa Ynez, CA: Kroc Foundation.

Pelletier, G., Labrie, F., Arimura, A., & Schally, A. V. (1974). Electron microscopic immunohistochemical localization of growth hormone–release–inhibiting hormone (somatostatin) in the rat median eminence. *American Journal of Anatomy, 140*, 445–450.

Pimstone, B. L., Becker, D. J., & Hansen, J. D. L. (1973). Human growth hormone and sulphation factor in protein–calorie malnutrition. In L. J. Gardner & P. Amacher (Eds.), *Endocrine aspects of malnutrition: Marasmus, kwashiorkor and psychosocial deprivation* (pp. 73–90). Santa Ynez, CA: Kroc Foundation.

Powell, G. F., Brasel, J. A., & Blizzard, R. M. (1967). Emotional deprivation and growth retardation stimulating idiopathic hypopituitarism. I. Clinical evaluation of the syndrome. *New England Journal of Medicine, 276,* 1271–1278.

Powell, G. F., Brasel, J. A., Raiti, S., & Blizzard, R. M. (1967). Emotional deprivation and growth retardation simulating idiopathic hypopituitarism. II. Endocrinologic evaluation of the syndrome. *New England Journal of Medicine, 276,* 1279–1283.

Powell, G. F., Hopwood, N. J., & Barratt, E. S. (1973). Growth hormone studies before and during catch-up growth in a child with emotional deprivation and short stature. *Journal of Clinical Endocrinology and Metabolism, 37,* 674–679.

Puig-Antich, J., Greenhill, L. L., Sassin, J., & Sachar, E. J. (1978). Growth hormone, prolactin and cortisol responses and growth patterns in hyperkinetic children treated with dextro-amphetamine. *Journal of the American Academy of Child Psychiatry, 17,* 457–475.

Puig-Antich, J., Tabrizi, M. A., Davies, M., Goetz, R., Chambers, W. J., Halpern, F., & Sachar, E. J. (1981). Prepubertal endogenous major depressives hyposecrete growth hormone in response to insulin- induced hypoglycemia. *Biological Psychiatry, 16,* 801–818.

Quinn, P. O., & Rapoport, J. L. (1974). Minor physical anomalies and neurological status in hyperactive boys. *Pediatrics, 53,* 742–747.

Rayner, P. H. W., & Rudd, B. T. (1973). Emotional deprivation in three siblings associated with functional pituitary growth hormone deficiency. *Australian Paediatric Journal, 9,* 79–84.

Reimherr, F. W., Wood, D. R., & Wender, P. H. (1980). An open clinical trial of L-dopa and carbidopa in adults with minimal brain dysfunction. *American Journal of Psychiatry, 137,* 73–75.

Ritvo, E., Yuwiler, A., Geller, E., Ornitz, E. M., Saeger, K., & Plotkin, S. (1970). Increased blood serotonin and platelets in early infantile autism. *Archives of General Psychiatry, 23,* 566–572.

Roche, A. F., Lipman, R. A., Overall, J. E., & Hung W. E. (1979). The effects of stimulant medication on the growth of hyperkinetic children. *Pediatrics, 63,* 847–850.

Rutter, M. (1966). Behavioural and cognitive characteristics of a series of psychotic children. In J. K. Wing (Ed.), *Early childhood autism* (pp. 51–81). Oxford: Pergamon Press.

Rutter, M. (1978). Diagnosis and definition. In M. Rutter & E. Schopler (Eds.), *Autism: A reappraisal of concepts and treatment* (pp. 1–25). New York: Plenum Press.

Rutter, M., Lebovici, S., Eisenberg, L., Sneznevzskij, A. B., Sadoun, R., Brooke, E., & Tsung-yi Lin. (1969). A triaxial classification of mental disorders in childhood. *Journal of Child Psychology and Psychiatry, 10,* 41–61.

Saenger, P., Levine, L. S., Wiedemann, E., Schwartz, E., Korth-Schutz, S., Pariera, J., Heinig, B., & New, M.I. (1977). Somatomedin and growth hormone in psychosocial dwarfism. *Pädiatrie und Pädologie, 5,* (Suppl.), 1–12.

Safer, D. & Allen, R. (1973). Factors influencing the suppressant effects of two stimulant drugs on the growth of hyperactive children. *Pediatrics, 51,* 660–667.

Schanberg, S. M., Evoniuk, G., & Kuhn, C. M. (1984). Tactile and nutritional aspects of maternal care: Specific regulators of neuroendocrine function and cellular development. *Proceedings of the Society for Experimental Biology and Medicine, 175,* 135–146.

Schultz, F. R., Hayford, J. T., Wolraich, M. L., Hintz, R. L., & Thompson, R. G. (1982). Methylphenidate treatment of hyperactive children: Effects on the hypothalamic–pituitary–somatomedin axis. *Pediatrics, 70,* 987–992.

Shaywitz, S. E., Hunt, R. D., Jatlow, P., Cohen, D. J., Young, J. G., Pierce, R. N., Anderson, G. M., & Shaywitz, B. A. (1982). Psychopharmacology of attention deficit disorder: Pharmacokinetic, neuroendocrine, and behavioral measures following acute and chronic treatment with methylphenidate. *Pediatrics, 69,* 688–694.

Sherwin, A. C., Flach, F. F., & Stokes, P. E. (1958). Treatment of psychoses in early childhood with triiodothyronine. *American Journal of Psychiatry, 115,* 166–167.

Stahl, M. L., Orr, W. C., & Griffiths, W. J. (1979). Nocturnal levels of growth hormone in hyperctive children of small stature. *Journal of Clinical Psychiatry, 40,* 225–227.

Takahashi, Y., Kipnis, D. M., & Daughaday, W. H. (1968). Growth hormone secretion during sleep. *Journal of Clinical Investigation, 47,* 2079–2090.

Takano, K., Hizuka, N., Shizume, K., Asakawa, K., Miyakawa, M., Hirose, N., Shibasaki, T., & Ling, N. C. (1984). Plasma growth hormone (GH) response to GH-releasing factor in normal children with short stature and patients with pituitary dwarfism. *Journal of Clinical Endocrinology and Metabolism, 58,* 236–241.

Tanner, J. M. (1973). Letter to the Editor. Resistance to exogenous human growth hormone in psychosocial short stature (emotion deprivation). *Journal of Pediatrics, 82,* 171–172.

Tanner, J. M., Whitehouse, R. H. Hughes, P. C. R., & Vince, F. P. (1971). Effect of human growth hormone treatment for 1 to 7 years on growth of 100 children, with growth hormone deficiency, low birth weight, inherited smallness, Turner's syndrome, and other complaints. *Archives of Diseases of Childhood, 46,* 745–782.

Van Den Brande, J. L., Van Buul, S., Heinrich, U., Van Roon, F., Zurcher, T., & Van Steirtegem, A. C. (1975). Further observations on plasma somatomedin activity in children. *Advances in Metabolic Disorders, 8,* 171–181.

Vigersky, R. A., & Loriaux, D. L. (1977). Anorexia nervosa as a model of hypothalamic dysfunction. In R. A. Vigersky (Ed.), *Anorexia nervosa* (pp. 109–122). New York: Raven Press.

Weldon, V. V., Gupta, S. K., Haymond, M. W., Pagliara, A. S., Jacobs, L. S., & Daughaday, W. H. (1973). The use of L-dopa in the diagnosis of hyposomatotropism in children. *Journal of Clinical Endocrinology and Metabolism, 36,* 42–46.

Willoughby, J. O., Menadue, M., & Jervois, P. (1982). Function of serotonin in physiologic secretion of growth hormone and prolactin: Action of 5,7-dihydroxytryptamine, fenfluramine and *p*-chlorophenylalanine. *Brain Research, 249,* 291–298.

Wise, P. H., Burnet, R. B., Geary, T. D., & Berriman, H. (1975). Selective impairment of growth hormone response to physiological stimuli. *Archives of Diseases in Childhood, 50,* 210–214.

Wolff, G., & Money, J. (1973). Relationship between sleep and growth in patients with reversible somatotropin deficiency (psychosocial dwarfism). *Psychological Medicine, 3,* 18–27.

Yamazaki, K., Saito, Y., Okada, F., Fujieda, T., & Yamashita, I. (1975). An application of neuroendocrinological studies in autistic children and Heller's syndrome. *Journal of Autism and Childhood Schizophrenia, 5,* 323–332.

Young, J. G., Kavanagh, M. E., Anderson, G. M., Shaywitz, B. A., & Cohen, D. J. (1982). Clinical neurochemistry of autism and associated disorders. *Journal of Autism and Developmental Disorders, 12,* 147–165.

6 DISORDERS OF EATING

SIDNEY H. KENNEDY

Toronto General Hospital

PAUL E. GARFINKEL

University of Toronto

NEUROENDOCRINE FUNCTION IN ANOREXIA NERVOSA AND BULIMIA

Introduction

Richard Morton is credited with the first medical description of anorexia nervosa in 1689. Almost 2 centuries later, William Gull (1874/1964) coined the term "anorexia nervosa" and Lasegue (1873/1964) independently described "anoréxie hystérique." Since then, various disciplines within medicine and psychiatry, including endocrinology, psychoanalysis, behavior therapy and family therapy, have established further research directions and added to our understanding of the disorder.

Today, anorexia nervosa (AN) and bulimia share equal prominence as the two most prevalent disorders of eating. To make a diagnosis of AN the latest revision of the Diagnostic and Statistical Manual of Mental Disorders (DSM-III-R, American Psychiatric Association, August 1986) requires weight loss of 15% or more below expected body weight for age and height; an intense fear of becoming obese even when underweight; a disturbance in the way one's body weight size or shape is experienced and in females an absence of at least three consecutive menstrual cycles which otherwise would be expected to occur.

Bruch (1970) has provided the most detailed descriptions of the psychological disturbances in AN. She has delineated three major areas of psychological disturbance. These relate to (1) the distortion of body image; (2) faulty perception of inner sensations including such visceral sensations as hunger and satiety, but extending to affective states; and (3) a pervasive sense of personal ineffectiveness. According to Bruch, AN represents the individual's attempt to obtain a sense of mastery or personal control, given these deficits in personal functioning and self-esteem. Cognitive distortions also contribute, in particular a dichotomous style of reasoning which relates to all areas of functioning and limits the individual's ability to accept "workable compromises" in life, whether it involves dieting, school, work performance, or relationships (Garfinkel & Garner, 1982).

Bulimia nervosa (BN), as defined by DSM-III-R (American Psychiatric Association, August 1986) is characterized by recurrent episodes of binge-eating (rapid consumption of a large amount of food within a relatively short period of time, usually less than 2 hours). During the eating binges there is a feeling of lack of control over the eating behavior, and the individual regularly engages in either self-induced vomiting, use of laxatives, strict dieting, fasting, or vigorous exercise in order to prevent weight gain. A minimum average of two binge-eating episodes per week for at least 3 months and a persistent overconcern with body weight and shape are also required.

The term bulimia has been used as a symptom, as a subtype of AN, and as a distinct syndrome. As a symptom, bulimia has been known to occur in various illnesses for at least 100 years (see Casper, 1983). However, recent interest in bulimia derives from its relationship to AN and from the fact that an increasing proportion of patients with AN present with bulimia (Garner, Garfinkel, & O'Shaughnessy, 1985). At least half of all anorexics also display bulimia today, whereas only 10–25% did 15 years ago (Bruch, 1973). Bulimic anorexics have been shown to differ from typical dietary restricting patients on a variety of parameters, including their familial weight histories, degree of impulse control, complications and outcome (Garfinkel & Garner, 1982), cognitive impulsivity (Toner, Garfinkel, & Garner, 1987), and concomitant personality disorder (Piran, Lerner, Kennedy, Garfinkel, & Brouilette, submitted for publication).

More recently, the study of bulimic anorexics has led to an awareness of a group of people with bulimia who present with many of the features of AN, but who never meet diagnostic criteria because of insufficient weight loss. A variety of terms have been used to describe this group of people, including "the dietary chaos syndrome" (Palmer, 1979), "bulimarexia" (Boskind-Lodahl, 1976), and "bulimia nervosa" (Russell, 1979). Various other classification systems have been proposed for bulimics; however, a recent study has found that bulimics with various weight histories are very similar on a battery of psychological and behavior indices (Garner, Olmsted, & Garfinkel, 1985). At present, it is not known why some bulimics lose large amounts of weight and others are unable to.

Prevalence studies indicate that the disorders have increased in the 1970s, particularly in women. For example, using data from case registries, Jones, Fox, Babigian, and Hutton (1980) reported a dramatic increase in AN in white females (15–24 years) from 0.55 per 100,000 per year between 1960 and 1969 to 3.26 per 100,000 between 1970 and 1976. Similarly, Willi and Grossman (1983) reported a dramatic increase in the number of treated cases of AN in Switzerland over three time periods: the incidence was 0.38 per 100,000 from 1956 to 1958, 0.55 per 100,000 from 1963 to 1965, and 1.12 per 100,000 from 1973 to 1975.

Other studies of untreated cases in the 1970s have shown AN to be very common; various estimates of 0.4–1.0% have been given (A. M. Crisp, Palmer, & Kalucy, 1976; Nylander, 1971; Szmukler, 1983). Recent estimates of bulimia have shown it to be even more common; about 2–4% of college females meet criteria for bulimia as a syndrome (Cooper & Fairburn, 1983; Strangler & Printz, 1980). It has been estimated that about 95% of anorexics are female and, while bulimia is also much more common in women, it also may occur in men (Gwirtsman, Roy-Byrne, Lerner, & Yager, 1984).

The origins of these disorders are thought to be multidetermined and relate to risk factors within the individual, the family, and the culture (Garfinkel & Garner, 1982). Psychological theories have emphasized the role of difficulties in achieving separation and autonomy, because of specific deficit states in the individual (Bruch, 1973) or because of particular family constellations (Minuchin, Rosman, & Baker, 1978). Disturbances in the regulation of self-esteem (Garfinkel & Garner, 1982) and in cognition (Garner & Bemis, 1982) have also been suggested to be risk factors. Premorbid obesity may represent a risk factor, particularly in those individuals who subsequently develop bulimia (Garfinkel, Moldofsky, & Garner, 1980). Recent evidence suggests that diabetes mellitus may also increase the risk for developing an eating disorder (Rodin, Daneman, Johnson, Kenshale, & Garfinkel, 1985).

The cultural pursuit of an ideal body shape has been emphasized and certain career groups in which thinness is "desirable" such as models and ballet students have been shown to have a higher incidence of AN (Garner & Garfinkel, 1980). Some investigators have emphasized changing cultural pressures on women, in particular having to perform and achieve in order to please others (Bruch, 1973). Selvini Palazzoli (1974) has emphasized the role conflict for women between the active pursuit of a career and the previously expected passive role in relationships.

There has also been a growing interest in

the relationship between affective disturbance and eating disorder. Evidence for a relationship between the two comes from (1) the high frequency of depressive symptoms in patients with eating disorders (see Garfinkel & Garner, 1982), (2) depressive syndromes in eating disorders over time (e.g., see Cantwell, Sturzenberger, Burroughs, Salkin, & Green, 1977), (3) family history data (Hudson *et al.*, 1983; Pyle, Mitchell, & Eckert, 1981; Strober, Salkin, Burroughs, & Morrell, 1982; Winokur, March, & Mendels, 1980), including recent evidence of a genetic link (Biederman, Rivinus *et al.*, 1984), and (4) shared biological markers (Walsh *et al.*, 1978). The latter relates to the fact that both groups of disorders are felt to have a hypothalamic disturbance and many neuroendocrine tests done in anorexic and bulimic patients have also been done in depressed patients. However, common findings do not necessarily imply common etiology.

Typical of recent findings relating affective and eating disorders is a study recently completed by our group (Piran, Kennedy, Garfinkel, & Owens, 1985). We found that 38% of patients with bulimic and restrictive AN fulfilled DSM-III criteria for major depressive disorder. As well, 61% of the bulimics had a positive family history of affective disorder while only 23% of restricters had such a family history. Of the parents in the combined group, 27% met criteria for alcoholism. With regard to the presence of a depressive syndrome on long-term follow-up, we have recently studied a large group of patients who were initially seen between 1970 and 1978; about 60% have met DSM-III criteria for affective disorder using a structured interview (Toner, Garfinkel, & Garner, 1986).

The self-perpetuating nature of starvation has previously been understated (Garfinkel & Kaplan, 1985). Many of the symptoms formerly attributed to AN and bulimia have been described in normal males who voluntarily remained on a semistarvation diet for 6 months. These included excessive preoccupation with food and bizarre eating behavior, cognitive changes including decreased concentration and increased apathy as well as depressed mood, and sleep disturbances (Keys, Brozek, Henschel, Mickelsen, & Taylor, 1950). Other prominent signs of starva-

tion, beside the weight loss and loss of body fat, include amenorrhea, hypotension, bradycardia, reduced core temperature, loss of scalp hair, and the development of lanugo. Starvation-related symptoms may play an important role in AN in that they are part of the reason the syndrome can become autonomous; when dieting anorexics experience these starvation-induced changes in their thinking and feeling, they perceive them to be a threat to their sense of personal control and worth, to which they respond by increasing the diet (Garfinkel & Garner, 1982).

A number of features of AN have prompted investigators over the years to propose a primary endocrine disturbance. These include the prominence of particular physical signs such as amenorrhea, hypothermia, hypotension, and lanugo. The facts that amenorrhea may precede any significant weight loss and that menses do not automatically resume with weight restoration have been used to substantiate a primary hypothalamic dysfunction. For example, amenorrhea has been reported to precede weight loss in up to 25% of cases (Russell, 1970; Warren & Vande Wiele, 1973). It is not clear from these series to what extent psychological stress, changes in diet, and errors in retrospective recall could have contributed to such findings.

Evidence linking anatomic lesions to disturbances of eating is sparse. In an intriguing case report, Weller and Weller (1981) described a 13-year-old girl with classical AN and a fatal brain tumor in the left hypothalamic region. However, when this subject was reviewed by Garfinkel and Garner (1982), they concluded that the number of cases in which AN coincided with a demonstrable hypothalamic or other brain tumor could be explained on the basis of chance alone. The role of the endocrine changes in AN and bulimia remains unclear. Which represent the consequences of weight loss, alterations in diet, vomiting, excessive exercising, or nonspecific emotional stress, and which relate to the basic process of the disorders? While some of these issues have been clarified in the past 10 years, others remain obscure, and a further area of new and at present speculative research has attempted to relate neuroendocrine changes to neurotransmitter mechanisms. Beumont and Russell (1982) concluded that the functional changes arising out of hypothalamic mechanisms are best considered as adaptive to behavioral and weight changes rather than as pathological.

Hypothalamic–Pituitary–Ovarian Axis

Menstrual Dysfunction and the Hypothalamus

Menstrual disturbances are prevalent in both AN and bulimia (Pyle *et al.*, 1981) and are associated with low and noncyclic levels of ovarian sex hormones. Low estrogen levels are thought to account for vaginal atrophy and dyspareunia and may also play a role in the amenorrhea (Parvizi & Ellendorff, 1975). Cystic ovaries may be a further complication (Treasure, Gordon, Wheeler, & Russell, 1985).

Plasma levels of estrogen and progesterone are known to be reduced (Russell, Loraine, Bell, & Harkness, 1965) in AN, and although levels rise with weight gain, relative estrogen deficiency and amenorrhea may persist (Wakeling, DeSouza, & Beardwood, 1977; Wakeling *et al.*, 1979).

Young (1975) has argued that the disturbances in food intake, appetite, sleep, hormone levels, and thermoregulation seen in AN are similar to the physiological effects of estrogen. He has postulated a primary hypothalamic hypersensitivity to estrogen or a failure of maturation in the hypothalamus at puberty in AN, with consequent decreased plasma levels. In support of the effect of estrogen on appetite, Dalvit (1981) proposed that women consume more food in the 10 days after ovulation than during the 10 days before when estrogen levels are higher.

Frisch and McArthur (1974) have found that onset and maintenance of regular menstrual function in women depended on the maintenance of a minimum weight for height, apparently representing a critical level of fat storage. Being too fat or too thin can be associated with amenorrhea. Resumption of menses after weight gain has also been associated with this factor, although at a somewhat higher weight than is necessary for menarche (Frisch, 1977). Weight may not be the only critical factor determining menstruation; studies of female athletes have shown that amenorrhea may also relate to the extent of exercise or the degree of stress the individual

is under as well as to body weight and body fat (Dale, Gerlach, & White, 1979; Feicht, Johnson, Martin, Sparks, & Wagner, 1978).

Patients with AN usually resume menses when their weights are restored. This can be true for patients who have been amenorrheic for many years. Estimates from large studies have found that between 50 and 75% of anorexics resumed normal menses (see Garfinkel & Garner, 1982). Two recent follow-up studies have documented the relationship between return of menses and weight. Morgan and Russell (1975) found that 50% of their patients had normal menses at 4- to 8-year follow-up; regular menses with only one exception were confined to those women whose weight had returned to normal. Hsu, Crisp, and Harding (1979) followed up 102 patients, of whom 28 had persistent amenorrhea. Of the latter, only 11 were at a normal body weight.

Menstrual disturbances are also common in bulimia (Pyle *et al.*, 1981), although amenorrhea is reported less often and for a shorter duration than in AN (Beumont, George, Pimstone, & Vinik, 1976). In a large case review of 499 bulimic subjects by Fairburn and Cooper (1982), almost half reported irregular menstruation, suggesting that abnormal eating habits may disrupt the menses, irrespective of weight.

Gonadotropins in AN

Despite disagreement over its origins, there is general agreement that hypothalamic hypogonadism is responsible for the menstrual disturbances in AN (Brown, 1983). Decreasing levels of luteinizing hormone (LH) parallel weight loss (Beumont, George, Pimstone, & Vinik, 1976; Hurd, Palumbo, & Gharid, 1977) and normalize with weight restoration (Brown, Garfinkel, Jeuniewic, Moldofsky, & Stancer, 1977; Sherman & Halmi, 1977). The same is true for follicle-stimulating hormone (FSH) (Sherman & Halmi, 1977; Beumont, George, Pimstone, & Vinik, 1976), although Beumont, Abraham, Argall, and Turtle (1978) failed to replicate the relationship between FSH and body weight.

Likewise, in emaciated patients, the circadian rhythm of LH secretion is either absent (as is normally the case in prepubertal girls) or shows a decrease during waking hours and an increase during sleep (similar to mid-pubertal girls) (Boyar & Katz, 1977; Boyar *et al.*, 1974). This abnormality of circadian hormone secretion is likely related to dietary intake and weight; studies of food restriction in normal women can replicate this pattern of LH secretion (Pirke, Fichter, Lund, & Doerr, 1979). Weight restoration produces a hormonal sequence which recapitulates puberty (Donovan, VanderWerfften, & Bosch, 1965), although resumption of cyclical LH secretion and menstruation does not always return with normal weight (Beumont, George, Pimstone, Vinik, 1976; Katz, Boyar, Roffwarg, Hellman, & Weiner, 1978).

The LH response to luteinizing-releasing hormone (LRH) is most dramatically reduced at 15% or more below ideal weight (Warren, 1977; Warren *et al.*, 1975). Beumont and associates (1978) also noted that bromocriptine did not increase the LH response in patients with normal prolactin levels and concluded that the amenorrhea of AN is probably not related to changes in prolactin secretion. The time delay in plasma LH and FSH response to a bolus injection of LRH (Vigersky, Andersen, Thompson, & Loviaux, 1977) appears to be a function of weight loss as it occurs in other patients with secondary amenorrhea and weight loss who do not have AN.

The peak LH response to clomiphene is also weight related, only releasing LH in those who have gained weight (Brown *et al.*, 1977). Claims in support of clomiphene use as a treatment for amenorrhea in AN (Parsons, Szmukler, & Brown, 1983), particularly in older patients, refer to impairment of calcium metabolism (Crilly, Francis, & Nordin, 1981) and the risk of osteoporosis. Recent studies by Rigotti, Brotman, and Herzog (1985) document a risk of osteoporosis secondary to chronic illness though the mechanism for its development remains unclear. Since this may not be due to trypoestrogenism alone, it is premature to recommend replacement therapy.

In a study of 12 male anorexics, A. H. Crisp, Hsu, and Chen (1982) reported findings similar to those in women: initially low levels of plasma testosterone increased with weight gain; LH levels were reduced and correlated with low body weight in contrast to FSH levels which did not; LH responses to LRH were varied but appeared normal at higher weights, while the FSH response to LRH was retained, even at very low weights. At the present time, little is known about gonadal hormones in bulimia.

Hypothalamic–Pituitary–Adrenal Axis

Direct measurement of ACTH in peripheral blood has not yet become a routine measure. Most studies have concentrated instead on its target hormone cortisol and the effect on cortisol of standardized "challenges" such as the dexamethasone suppression test (DST). When only urinary metabolites of cortisol (17-hydroxycorticosteroids and 17-ketosteriods) could be measured, their low levels in patients with AN (Bliss & Migeon, 1957; Emanuel, 1956; Garfinkel, Brown, Stancer, & Moldofsky, 1975) appeared to be evidence in support of an adrenal insufficiency. Subsequent studies of plasma cortisol, however, have generally shown an elevated morning level (Alvarez *et al.*, 1972; Brown *et al.*, 1977; Hurd *et al.*, 1977; Landon, Greenwood, Stamp, & Wynn, 1966), although one study did report normal levels (Vigersky, Loriaux, Andersen, & Lipsett, 1976). In addition, urinary free cortisol is elevated (Boyar *et al.*, 1977; Walsh *et al.*, 1978). This means that the hypothalamic–pituitary–adrenal (HPA) axis is intact and, if anything, overactive. Weiner and Katz (1983) have suggested two possible reasons for this apparent paradox where elevated cortisol production and decreased levels of cortisol metabolites coexist. First, there is evidence that cortisol metabolism is delayed (Boyar *et al.*, 1977; Doerr, Fichter, Pirke, & Lund, 1980) and this appears related to a physiological adaptation to starvation whereby T3 levels are reduced and elevated "reverse T3" can be detected (Leslie, Isaacs, Gomez, Raggatt, & Bayliss, 1978). At this time, T4 and thyroid stimulating hormone (TSH) levels are not altered (Croxson & Ibbertson, 1977) and treatment with T3 or T4 should be avoided. The second reason stems from the finding that, relative to body weight, there is an excess production of cortisol in emaciated patients with AN (Boyar *et al.*, 1977), which normalizes with slight weight gain (Walsh *et al.*, 1981).

The cortisol response to a standard dose of dexamethasone is abnormal in about 90% of emaciated patients with AN (Halmi, 1984) and is normal in about 90% of weight-restored AN patients. While there has been some lack of uniformity of dexamethasone dosage and of sampling times which makes comparison between studies difficult, Doerr and associates (1980) showed a convincing relationship between cortisol nonsuppression and weight change. Initially, 15 out of 16 female patients with AN showed nonsuppression or early escape, while only 3 remained abnormal after a 10% increase in body weight. Gerner and Gwirtsman (1981) also evaluated DST response in 22 emaciated AN patients. All but the 1 male patient had an abnormal result. More recently, our group (Kennedy, Piran, Stoke, Garfinkel, Wilkes, & Stern, 1984) assessed the effect of weight gain on DST and depression ratings (based on the Beck Depression Inventory and the Hamilton Depression Rating Scale). When 9 anorexic patients with DST nonsuppression were retested after they regained weight, 7 had converted to suppress cortisol normally without change in depression.

The HPA axis also appears to be overactive in bulimic subjects. Approximately 50% had a positive DST in a study reported by Hudson et al. (1983). These individuals weighed not less than 80% of ideal body weight at the time of testing. Using similar criteria, however, Musisi and Garfinkel (1985) found only 20% of bulimics to be nonsuppressors. Gwirtsman et al. (1984) noted a positive DST in 2 out of 3 male bulimics who were within 15% of ideal body weight at evaluation and had concurrent affective disorder diagnoses.

At this time, the meaning of cortisol nonsuppression in response to dexamethasone is unclear. Carroll et al. (1981) have claimed a high specifity for "melancholia" within an affective disorder population, while others have noted equally high rates of abnormality in mania (Graham et al., 1982), dementia (Spar & Gerner, 1982), alcoholism (Newsom & Murray, 1983), and eating disorders (Kennedy et al., 1984). Nonspecific effects such as weight loss have also been suggested as possible explanations (Berger, Pirke, Doerr, Krieg, & Von Zersen, 1983) and certainly in a group of emaciated anorexics, this is a major factor. Fichter, Pirke, and Holsober (1986) have also reported rapid reversal of DST (in both directions) following changes in caloric intake. However, not all abnormal DSTs normalize with weight restoration. This has led to speculation that eating disorders, especially bulimia, may represent a variant of affective disorder (Hudson et al., 1983).

Hypothalamic–Pituitary–Thyroid Axis

As has already been stated, the most significant changes in thyroid hormones appear to represent an adaptive function during relative starvation. Thyroxine (T4) levels in AN have been found to be within the normal range (Brown et al., 1977; Lundberg, Walinder, Werner, & Wide, 1972; Moshang et al., 1975). However, Wakeling et al. (1979) found that the levels were lower than in matched controls and did not rise after 4–6 weeks of weight gain. A correlation between the resting T4 and serum cortisol levels has been found (Brown et al., 1977), while serum triiodothyronine (T3) levels are reduced (Burman et al., 1977; Croxson & Ibbertson, 1977; Hurd et al., 1977; Miyai, Yamaruoto, Azukizawa, Ishibashi, & Kumahara, 1975; Moshang et al., 1975). This reduction is associated with an increase in the inactive reverse form of T3 (Burman et al., 1977) and occurs in other conditions associated with starvation (Vagenakis, 1977), including obese individuals who fast (Vagenakis et al., 1975). As TSH levels remain normal (Beumont, George, Pimstone, & Vinik, 1976; Brown, Garfinkel, Jeuniewic, Moldofsky, & Stancer, 1977), it can be concluded that abnormalities in the thyroid axis are not a result of endorgan failure.

The TSH response to thyrotropin-releasing hormone (TRH) has been studied in patients with AN, bulimia, and depression. Gwirtsman, Roy–Byrne, Yager, and Gerner (1983) reviewed 12 reports on 116 AN patients and found 12% had a blunted TSH response to TRH. In contrast, the same author found 8 out of 10 bulimic patients, not meeting criteria for AN at the time, had a blunted TSH response.

In their study of 6 female bulimic patients, Mitchell and Bantle (1983) noted normal T3 and T4 values in all but 1 individual, who had mild hypothyroid values. Following TRH administration, a different individual failed to show the normal TSH elevation demonstrated by the other 5. Similarly, only 1 of the 3 male bulimics reported on by Gwirtsman *et al.* (1984) showed a "blunted" TSH response to TRH.

Growth Hormone

There are a number of abnormal growth hormone (GH) responses, which may be influenced by the decreased estrogen levels found in AN (Wakeling *et al.*, 1979; Wakeling, Marshall, Beardwood, DeSouza, & Russell, 1976). Increased resting GH levels occur in some patients with AN (Brown *et al.*, 1977; Frankel & Jenkins, 1975; Garfinkel *et al.*, 1975; Hurd *et al.*, 1977) and also occur in marasmus (Pimstone, Becker, & Hausen, 1973). In the latter, these elevated basal levels of GH correlate with the degree of hypoalbuminemia and protein malnutrition (S. R. Smith, Bledsoe, & Chhetri, 1975). It is increased calorie intake rather than weight gain which promotes restoration of normal GH levels (Garfinkel *et al.*, 1975). The GH response to TRH is elevated in AN (Lundberg *et al.*, 1972; Maeda *et al.*, 1976) and bulimia (Gwirtsman *et al.*, 1983) as well as depression (Maeda *et al.*, 1976).

Insulin-induced hypoglycemia results in a diminished GH response in patients with AN (Brauman and Grégoire, 1975; Devlin, 1975) and in depressed patients (Carroll, 1978). There have been reports of both a normal GH response to oral glucose (Garfinkel *et al.*, 1975) and a paradoxical rise in GH (Alvarez *et al.*, 1972; Casper, Davis, & Pandey, 1977); the latter is reversed by improved nutrition (Casper *et al.*, 1977) and is reduced by the dopamine (DA) agonist bromocriptine (Harrower *et al.*, 1977).

Patients with AN have also been challenged with other dopaminergic agents such as L-dopa and apomorphine. The GH response to L-dopa is flattened and has been found not to normalize after weight gain (Sherman & Halmi, 1977), while the reduced apomorphine response normalizes with weight gain (Casper *et al.*, 1977).

Mitchell and Bantle (1983) reported significant abnormalities in GH regulation in 6 bulimic women. Four demonstrated an abnormal increase in GH following oral glucose. Normal subjects usually do not demonstrate a change in GH concentration following TRH administration (Irie & Tsushima, 1972), and they show a GH suppression response following oral glucose.

At normal weight a larger group of bulimics have been found to have normal responses to intravenuous cloindine (Kaplan, Garfinkel, Warsh, Brown, 1986).

Prolactin

Dopamine also appears to be the hypothalamic factor which inhibits prolcatin (PRL). If AN represented a primary failure of the hypothalamic pituitary axis, then elevated levels of PRL would be expected. Knowing also that secondary amenorrhea is frequently due to hyperprolactinemia (Bohnet, Dahlen, Wuttke, & Schneider, 1976; Franks *et al.*, 1975), this may appear reasonable. However, a number of studies have reported normal levels of daytime resting PRL (Beumont, George, Pimstone, & Vinik, 1976; Mecklenberg, Loriaux, Thompson, Andersen, & Lipsett, 1974; Wakeling *et al.*, 1979), and Darby, Brown, and Garfinkel (1983) found generally low levels of PRL, with no nocturnal rise in 5 low-weight patients. This is in contrast to the normal adult pattern of PRL elevation which occurs shortly after the onset of sleep (Wetterberg *et al.*, 1976). The blunted nighttime levels in emaciated anorexics are likely of dietary origin; there is evidence that alterations in diet in normal individuals may result in reduced nocturnal PRL secretion (Hill & Wynder, 1976). Hafner, Crisp, and McNeilly (1976) reported a normal PRL response to the DA receptor blocker chlorpromazine (CPZ) in AN, while Owen, Halmi, Lasley, and Stokes (1983) found a reduced PRL response, citing this as evidence in support of impaired DA regulation of PRL.

In six bulimic women, elevated basal PRL levels were found. These appeared to correlate with irregular menses (Mitchell & Bantle, 1983).

Melatonin

Secretion of melatonin from the pineal gland is also known to have a circadian rhythm with elevated nighttime levels (Vaughan *et al.*, 1976). Functionally, it has been implicated in the timing of the onset of puberty

(Waldhauser *et al.*, 1984). Since melatonin production is mainly under noradrenergic control, and anorexics appear to have reduced peripheral noradrenergic activity (Gerner & Gwirtsman, 1981; Biederman, Herzog, Rivinus, Ferber, Harper, Orsulak, Harmatz, & Schildkraut, 1984), low levels of melatonin would be predicted in anorexia nervosa. However, there are conflicting reports of elevated, decreased and normal levels in anorexics (Brown, Kirwan, Garfinkel, & Moldofsky, 1979; Birau, Alexander, Bertholdt, & Meyer, 1984; Dalery, Claustrat, Brun, & de Villard, 1985). Preliminary studies of melatonin in low and normal weight bulimia have found normal values (Kennedy, Costa, Parienti, & Brown, 1987).

Carbohydrate Metabolism

Low fasting blood glucose has been reported in many patients with AN, but symptomatic hypoglycemia rarely occurs (A. H. Crisp, Ellis, & Lowy, 1967; Mecklenberg *et al.*, 1974). Insulin secretion is abnormal in response to intravenous glucose, as is the response to oral glucose tolerance testing (A. H. Crisp *et al.*, 1967; Silverman, 1977). The peripheral effects of insulin have been reported to be both increased (Mecklenberg *et al.*, 1974) and decreased (A. H. Crisp *et al.*, 1967; Kanis *et al.*, 1974). Mecklenberg *et al.* (1974) documented persistent hypoglycemia after intravenous insulin injection in some patients. Consistent with these observations, Wachslicht-Rodbard, Gross, Rodbard, Ebert, and Roth (1979) showed increased insulin binding to circulating red blood cells and monocytes due to an increased receptor number. Recently, Zuniga-Guajardo, Garfinkel, and Zinman (in press) studied insulin metabolism in AN patients using a glucose clamp technique. They found marked changes in insulin metabolism as characterized by decreased basal insulin levels, increased sensitivity as assessed by glucose metabolism, and increased insulin clearance. They found these changes reversed when patients gained weight and speculated on their adaptive value in preventing severe hypoglycemia in starvation.

Gut–Brain Axis

Until recently, neuroendocrinology had focused on the various hypothalamic axes.

Within the past decade, a series of peptides initially found in secretory elements of the gastrointestinal tract, including cholecystokinin (CCK) and vasoactive intestinal polypeptide (VIP), have been shown to have both endocrine and neurotransmitter function. They are important in the regulation of carbohydrate metabolism, gastric acid secretion, pancreatic exocrine function, and gallbladder function as well as gastrointestinal motility and blood flow (Garfinkel & Coscina, 1982). CCK appears to be found in largest concentration in the central nervous system (CNS) and is most closely implicated in satiety regulation and pancreatic growth (McLaughlin, Baile, & Peikin, 1983). Animal studies support its role in inducing short-term satiety (G. P. Smith & Gibbs, 1976), although reports on humans remain conflicting (Greenway & Bray, 1977; Sturdevant & Goetz, 1976). In a review of the neuroendocrine control of appetite, Morley (1980) has suggested that CCK may mediate serotonin (5-HT)-induced satiety.

The relationship between CCK and other gut hormones, such as somatostatin and VIP, and human eating behavior remains to be clarified. This may further add to our understanding of AN and bulimia.

Arginine Vasopressin

Also of interest in patients with AN is the abnormal secretion of antidiuretic hormone arginine vasopressin (AVP). This neurohypophysial hormone is also secreted into the cerebrospinal fluid (CSF) (Luerrson & Robertson, 1980) and may mediate human cognitive and behavioral changes (Weingartner, Gold, & Ballenger, 1981). Patients with AN show a defect in urinary dilution and concentration (Mecklenberg *et al.*, 1974; Russell & Bruce, 1966; Vigersky *et al.*, 1976). More recently, Gold, Kaye, Robertson, and Ebert (1983) reported erratic vasopressin secretion before and immediately after weight restoration in 4 patients with AN. However, in 5 of 7 other patients studied at least 6 months after weight recovery, the results were normal. Since it is known that individuals who are grossly overweight also have instability in their AVP responses to osmotic stimuli which are corrected by weight reduction (Drenick, Carlson, Robertson, & Hershman, 1977), it is possible that abnormalities of eating and food intake may be linked to water balance.

NEUROENDOCRINE DISTURBANCES IN RELATION TO NEUROTRANSMITTERS

An extensive animal literature links brain monoamine systems to the regulation of appetite and eating behavior (Leibowitz, 1980). Similarly, the neurotransmitters are very important in regulating the release or inhibition of release of the various hormones. In general, there are concerns about extrapolating evidence from animal studies to clinical populations, particularly here, where evidence suggests that AN patients do not, in fact, lose their appetite 'until they are severely emaciated (Garfinkel, 1974) and where the desire for slimness can be linked to cognitive changes and defects in self-esteem. Nevertheless, underweight patients with AN do show evidence of decreased monoamine excretion.

Several studies have attempted to separate those abnormalities which appear to be associated with the state of low weight from those which remain after weight restoration.

The three major neurotransmitter substances most under investigation are noradrenaline (NA) and its major metabolite 3-methoxy-4-hydroxphenylglycol (MHPG), serotonin (5-HT) and its main metabolite 5-hydroxyindoleacetic acid (5-HIAA), and dopamine (DA) and its metabolite homovanillic acid (HVA).

Reduced urinary MHPG values have been reported in AN. Halmi, Dekirmenjian, Davis, Casper, and Goldberg (1978) reported significantly lower MHPG levels in acutely ill AN patients than in control subjects. The levels increased with weight gain and were significantly correlated with a decrease in depressive symptomatology. Based on previous associations between reduced urinary MHPG excretion and endogenous depression, Schildkraut (1973) and Halmi *et al.* (1978) suggested there was a relationship between MHPG levels and the symptoms of depression in AN patients. Two other studies (Abraham, Beumont, & Cobbin, 1981; Gerner & Gwirtsman, 1981) also found reduced MHPG excretion in emaciated AN patients, which was not related to measures of depression. However, Biederman, Herzog *et al.* (1984) have recently reported on lower levels of urinary MHPG among anorexic patients with concomitant major depression when compared to nondepressed anorexic patients and controls. In addition, weight restoration did not significantly alter the findings in both anorexic groups. Gross, Lake, Ebert, Ziegler, and Kopin (1979) and Darby, Van Loon, Garfinkel, Brown, and Kirwan (1979) additionally reported reduced plasma NA levels. Urinary MHPG appears to be influenced by such factors as diet and exercise and to be most closely related to levels of body fat (Johnson, Lieter, Burrow, Garfinkel, & Anderson, 1984)

Kaye, Ebert, Raleigh, and Lake (1984) measured CSF concentrations of NA, the DA metabolite HVA and the 5-HT metabolite 5-HIAA in patients with AN while underweight and after correction of weight loss. They reported significant decreases in HVA and 5-HIAA metabolites in the CSF at low weight, with normal values shortly after weight recovery. CSF concentrations of NA, however, were lower in the weight-recovered group than in either nonanorexic controls or in underweight anorexics. Could this represent a "masking effect" by starvation of a more specific trait abnormality within the noradrenergic system, similar to that proposed in the etiology of depression?

Studies in psychopharmacology link eating patterns to four monoaminergic systems. Within the medial hypothalamus the noradrenergic system is believed to be involved in appetite stimulation. Leibowitz (1983) has provided evidence from a number of studies linking hyperphagia in animals to an increase in medical hypothalamic NA functions. Schlemmer, Casper, Elder, and Davis (1981) reported that clonidine, an α-noradrenergic agonist, caused hyperphagia and weight gain in monkeys, and they speculated that it could have a role in the treatment of AN. Casper, Schlemmer, Gibbons, and Javaid (1984) have recently presented results on 4 patients who were treated with both clonidine and placebo; no differences in rate of weight gain were observed.

The β-adrenergic system may also be implicated in inhibiting eating behavior by releasing and inhibiting the reuptake of catecholamines as in the case of amphetamines (Checkley & Crammer, 1977). Interestingly,

Ong, Checkley, and Russell (1983) reported temporary elimination of bulimic behavior in 8 patients receiving intravenous methylamphetamine under double-blind conditions.

The serotonin (5-HT) system has been linked to control mechanisms involving appetite, mood, and sleep. It is likely that food consumption affects the synthesis of brain 5-HT (Wurtman & Wurtman, 1979), with the dietary predursor L-tryptophan playing a particularly important regulatory role here (Biggio, Fadda, Fanni, Tagliamonte, & Gessa, 1974). Of particular interest in understanding patients with AN, bulimia, and obesity is the suggestion made by Wurtman and Wurtman (1979) that the conversion of tryptophan to 5-HT is influenced by the proportion of carbohydrate in the diet; the synthesis of 5-HT in turn affects the proportion of carbohydrate an individual subsequently chooses to eat.

In a controlled study of anorexic patients Johnston, Leiter, Burrow, Garfinkel, and Anderson (1984) showed both a reduced fasting plasma tryptophan level and a reduced ratio of tryptophan to large neutral amino acids, suggesting a decrease in tryptophan availability and ultimately a reduction of central 5-HT activity.

Differences between restricter and bulimic subgroups of anorexic patients were reported by Kaye, Ebert, Gwirtsman, and Weiss (1984) using the probenicid blocking technique to measure the 5-HT metabolite 5HIAA in CSF. Weight recovered bulimic patients continued to show significantly reduced 5HIAA levels compared to weight recovered restricting anorexics or controls.

Tricyclic antidepressants improve appetite and restore weight in the course of successful treatment of depression. Amitriptyline has been reported to be a particular culprit in producing further undesirable weight gain during maintenance treatment. Paykel, Mueller, and De La Vergne (1973) reported carbohydrate craving as a particular problem. At the neurotransmitter level it has been shown to reduce presynaptic reuptake of 5-HT, leading to feedback inhibition and decreased 5-HT synthesis. Clinically there would be concerns about promoting increased carbohydrate craving in a bulimic population. Nevertheless, in a recent study Mitchell and Groat (1984) found amitrip-

tyline to be of clinical benefit without any increase in carbohydrate craving in a bulimic population.

A number of clinical studies have also reported a reduction in binge-eating behavior among bulimic patients treated with monoamine oxidase inhibitor (MAOI) therapy (Kennedy, Piran, & Garfinkel, 1985; Walsh, Stewart, Roose, Gladis, & Glassman, 1984). This may relate to the elevation of brain levels of 5-HT and NA reported with MAOI therapy (Murphy, Garrick, Aulakh, & Cohen, 1984).

Further understanding of the role of 5-HT in mediating hunger and satiety comes from clinical studies involving cyproheptadine, a 5-HT antagonist, and fenfluramine, a 5-HT agonist. Cypropheptadine has been reported to increase feeding and cause weight gain (Ghosh & Parvathy, 1973). While weight gain has been marginally better in anorexic patients treated with cyproheptadine in a controlled trial (Goldberg, Halmi, Casper, Eckert, & Davis, 1979), its value in treating patients with AN appears limited.

Fenfluramine is an anorexic agent which, in contrast to the other amphetamine congeners, exerts its effect through depletion of the 5-HT system (Blundell & Leshem, 1974). Stunkard (1982) has proposed that this anorectic effect may represent a lowering of a body weight "set point" and only secondarily a suppression of appetite. Since premorbid obesity is particularly common in bulimia (Garfinkel & Garner, 1982) and has been linked to an attempt to reduce the set point weight (Herman & Polivy, 1975; Wardle, 1980), further research into the 5-HT system in bulimia may prove fruitful. Fluoxetine is another potent and highly selective inhibitor of 5-HT uptake, that appears to have antidepressant and anorectic (Ferguson, 1985) properties. Results of a current multicenter double-blind placebo controlled trial of fluoxetine in bulimia will be of particular interest.

The DA system also plays an important role in linking neurotransmitter and neuroendocrine function. Barry and Klawans (1976) proposed that there is an increased synthesis of DA in AN, secondary to a defect in the negative-feedback control. As stated earlier, high basal levels of GH have been reported in AN. Since DA has been shown to regulate

GH production, defects in GH responses and elevated resting GH levels in AN appear to support this hypothesis. In a clinical test of this hypothesis, Vandereycken and Pierloot (1983) administered the DA blocker pimozide to patients with AN. However, they noted only a modest improvement in the rate of weight again.

In contrast, Mawson (1974) proposed a DA depletion hypothesis for AN and recommended treatment with L-dopa, a DA agonist which reduces PRL secretion, while Harrower et al. (1977) treated 8 AN patients with the DA agonist bromocriptine and observed only minimal effect on weight gain. Darby et al. (1979) added further support in reporting reduced levels of DA and NA, which were weight related. If DA is, in fact, an inhibitor of PRL release, then this DA depletion theory would predict elevated PRL levels in AN. This is rarely seen (Darby et al., 1983). Owen et al. (1983) proposed that PRL levels are not elevated because of the inhibitory effect of increased cortisol secretion on PRL. In order to assess the dopaminergic effect on PRL secretion in AN, they measured the PRL response to CPZ, a neuroleptic known to act as a DA blocker. Out of 9 AN patients, 6 at normal weight had either no or a minimal PRL response to CPZ. In addition, there was no relation between fasting morning cortisol levels and the PRL response to CPZ. The authors concluded in support of a deficiency or impairment at the DA postsynaptic receptor sites.

ROLE OF THE OPIATE SYSTEM

Evidence that endogenous opiate peptides (endorphins) are involved in eating behavior is derived mainly from animal studies (Baile, Della-Fera, McLaughlin, & Keim, 1980; Margules, Moisset, & Lewis, 1978). In humans, weight loss is common when people are administered opiate antagonists chronically. Opioid agonists appear to stimulate eating, while antagonists diminish eating. Kaye, Pickar, Naber, and Ebert (1982) reported a correlation between decreased CSF levels of "total opioid activity" and decreased weight in AN. Plasma β-endorphin activity has also been found to be reduced in normal weight bulimics (Waller et al., 1986). Moore,

Mills, and Forster (1981) have proposed that the endorphin antagonist naloxone may have an antilipolytic effect in man and hence could have a role in the treatment of AN. They reported significantly more weight gain in 12 anorexic patients during naloxone infusion compared to the period following drug withdrawal. This seems contradictory to the findings of reduced food intake following opiate antagonist infusion in both rats and humans (Margules, 1979), but may relate to a compensatory increase in opioid production at low weights in an effort to decrease metabolic rate (Kaye, Pickar, Ebert, & Naber, 1983). Alternatively, Gillman and Lichtigfeld (1981) suggested that naloxone may exert its effect through inhibiting vomiting and hence promote weight gain. How endorphin production relates to stress is not known, although recent work by Leibowitz and her colleagues (Leibowitz, 1980; Leibowitz & Hor, 1982) has shown a link between eating behavior in rats and β-endorphin release under noradrenergic control. In this way, increased β-endorphin release could promote the release of ACTH and hence activate the HPA system.

CONCLUSION

While much has been learned about anorexia nervosa and bulimia nervosa in the past 15 years, there is a great deal that is not yet understood and this is apparent from the current nonspecific approaches to treatment and from data on outcome. The mortality remains at about 8% 5 to 8 years after treatment (Garfinkel & Garner, 1982). However, long-term outcome indicates a much higher mortality—approaching 18% (Theander, 1985). Suicide among the chronically ill was particularly common in the Theander study. When patients recover, about 65% do so within 6 years of onset, but recoveries after even 12 years occur. About 35% continue with serious morbidity.

Acknowledgments

We gratefully acknowledge the support of the Canadian Psychiatric Research Foundation (Dr. Kennedy) and the Ontario Mental Health Foundation (Dr. Garfinkel). Technical assistance was provided by Sheila Walton, Brenda Lediett, Shirley Kartuz, and Celine Brouillette.

References

Abraham, S. F., Beumont, P. J. V., & Cobbin, D. M. (1981). Catecholamine metabolism and body weight in anorexia nervosa. *British Journal of Psychiatry*, *138*, 244–247.

Alvarez, L. C., Dinas, C. O., Castro, A., Rossman, L. G., Vanderlaan, E. F., & Vanderlaan, W. P. (1972). Growth hormone in malnutrition. *Journal of Clinical Endocrinology and Metabolism*, *34*, 400–409.

American Psychiatric Association. (1980). *Diagnostic and statistical manual of mental disorders* (3rd ed.). Washington, DC. Author.

Baile, C. A., Della-Fera, M. A., McLaughlin, C. L., & Keim, D. A. (1980). Opiate antagonist and agonist and feeding in sleep. *Federation Proceedings, Federation of American Societies for Experimental Biology*, *39*, 782.

Barry, V. C., & Klawans, H. L. (1976). On the role of dopamine in the pathophysiology of anorexia nervosa. *Journal of Neural Transmission*, *38*, 107–122.

Berger, M., Pirke, K. M., Doerr, R., Krieg, C., & von Zersen, D. (1983). Influence of weight loss on the dexamethasone suppression test. *Archives of General Psychiatry*, *40*, 585–586.

Beumont, P. J. V., Abraham, S. F, Argall, W. J., & Turtle, J. R. (1978). Plasma gonadotrophins and LHRH infusions in anorexia nervosa. *Australian and New Zealand Journal of Medicine*, *8*, 509–514.

Beumont, P. J. V., George, G. C. W., Pimstone, B. L., & Vinik, A. I. (1976). Body weight and the pituitary response to hypothalamic releasing hormones in patients with anorexia nervosa. *Journal of Clinical Endocrinology and Metabolism*, *43*, 487–496.

Beumont, P. J. V., George, G. C. W., & Swat, D. E. (1976). "Dieters" and "vomiters and purgers" in anorexia nervosa. *Psychological Medicine*, *6*, 617–622.

Beumont, P. J. V., & Russell, J. (1982). Anorexia nervosa. In P. J. V. Beumont & G. D. Burrows (Eds.), *Handbook of psychiatry and endocrinology* (pp. 63–96). New York: Elsevier Biomedical Press.

Biederman, J., Herzog, D. B., Rivinus, T. M., Ferber, R. A., Harper, G. P., Orsulak, P. J., Harmatz, J. S., & Schildkraut, J. J. (1984). Urinary MHPG in anorexia nervosa patients with and without a concomitant major depressive disorder. *Journal of Psychiatric Research*, *18*, 149–160.

Biederman, J., Rivinus, T. M., Herzog, D. B., Harmatz, J. S., Shanley, K., & Yunis, E. J. (1984). High frequency of HLA-Bw 16 in patients with anorexia nervosa. *American Journal of Psychiatry*, *141*, 1109–1110.

Biggio, G., Fadda, F., Fanni, P., Tagliamonte, A., & Gessa. G. L. (1974). Rapid depletion of serum tryptophan, brain tryptophan, serotonin, and 5-hydroxyindoleacetic aid by a tryptophan-free diet. *Life Sciences*, *14*, 1321–1329.

Birau, N., Alexander, D., Bertholdt, S., Meyer, C. (1984). Low nocturnal melatonin serum concentration in anorexia nervosa—further evidence for body weight influence. *IRCS Medical Sciences*, *12*, 477.

Bliss, E. L., & Migeon, C. J. (1957). Endocrinology of anorexia nervosa. *Journal of Clinical Endocrinology and Metabolism*, *17*, 766–776.

Blundell, J. E., & Leshem, M. B. (1974). Central action of anorexia agents. Effects of amphetamine and feufluramine in rats with hypothalamic lesions. *European Journal of Pharmacology*, *28*, 81–88.

Bohnet, H. G., Dahlen, H. G., Wuttke, W., & Schneider, H. P. G. (1976). Hyperprolactinemic anovulatory syndrome. *Journal of Clinical Endocrinology and Metabolism*, *42*, 132–143.

Boskind-Lodahl, M. (1976). Cinderella's stepsisters: A feminist perspective on anorexia nervosa and bulimia. *Journal of Women in Culture and Society*, *2*, 342–356.

Boyar, R. M., Hellman, L. D., Roffwarg, H., Katz, J., Zumoff, B., O'Connor, J., Bradlow, H. L., & Fukushima, D. K. (1977). Cortisol secretion and metabolism in anorexia nervosa. *New England Journal of Medicine*, *296*, 190–193.

Boyar, R. M., & Katz, J. (1977). 24-hour gonadotrophin secretory patterns in anorexia nervosa. In R. A. Vigersky (Ed.), *Anorexia nervosa* (pp. 177–187). New York: Raven Press.

Boyar, R. M., Katz, J., Finkelstein, J. W., Kapen, S., Weiner, H., Weitzman, E. D., & Hellman, L. (1974). Anorexia nervosa: Immaturity of the 24-hour luteinizing hormone secretory pattern. *New England Journal of Medicine*, *291*, 861–865.

Brauman, H., & Grégoire, F. (1975). The growth hormone response to insulin-induced hypoglycemia in anorexia nervosa and control underweight or normal subjects. *European Journal of Clinical Investigation*, *5*, 389–295.

Brown, G. M. (1983). Endocrine alterations in anorexia nervosa. In P. L. Darby, P. E. Garfinkel, D. M. Garner, & D. V. Coscina (Eds.), *Anorexia nervosa: Recent developments in research* (pp. 231–247). New York: Alan R. Liss.

Brown, G. M., Garfinkel, P. E., Jeuniewic, N., Moldofsky, H., & Stancer, H. C. (1977). Endocrine profiles in anorexia nervosa. In R. A. Vigersky (Ed.), *Anorexia nervosa* (pp. 123–135). New York: Raven Press.

Brown, G. M., Kirwan, P., Garfinkel, P., & Moldofsky, H. (1979, June). *Overnight patterning of prolactin and melatonin in anorexia nervosa* [Abstract]. Paper presented at the Second International Symposium on Clinical Psycho-neuro-endocrinology in Reproduction, Venice.

Bruch, H. (1970). Instinct and interpersonal experience. *Comprehensive Psychiatry*, *11*, 495–506.

Bruch, H. (1973). *Eating disorders*. New York: Basic Books.

Burman, K. D., Vigersky, R. A., Loriaux, D. L., Strum, D., Djuh, Y. Y., Wright, F. D., Wartofsky, L. (1977). Investigations concerning thyroxine deiodinative pathways in patients with anorexia nervosa. In Vigersky, R. A. (Ed.), *Anorexia nervosa* (pp. 255–261). New York: Raven Press.

Cantwell, D. P., Sturzenberger, S., Burroughs, J., Salkin, B., Green, J. K. (1977). Anorexia nervosa: An affective disorder? *Archives of General Psychiatry*, *34*, 1087–1093.

Carroll, B. J. (1978). Neuroendocrine function in psychiatric disorders. In M. A. Lipton, A. DiMascio, & K. F. Killam (Eds.), *Psychopharmacology: A generation of progress* (pp. 487–497). New York: Raven Press.

Carroll, B. J., Feinberg, M., Greden, J. F., Tarika, J., Albala, A. A., Haskett, R. F., James, N. McI., Kronfol, Z., Lohr, N., Steiner, M., de Vigne, J. P., & Young, E. (1981). A specific laboratory test for the diagnosis of melancholia. *Archives of General Psychiatry, 38*, 15–22.

Casper, R. C. (1983). On the emergence of bulimia as a syndrome. *International Journal of Eating Disorders, 21*, 3–16

Casper, R. C., Davis, J. M., & Pandey, C. N. (1977). The effect of the nutritional status and weight changes on hypothalamic function tests in anorexia nervosa. In R. Vigersky (Ed.), *Anorexia nervosa* (pp. 137–147). New York: Raven Press.

Casper, R. C., Schlemmer, R. F., Gibbons, R., & Javaid, J. (1984, September). *Effects of oral clonidine on weight and other measures in acute anorexia nervosa* [Abstract]. Paper presented at the International Conference on Anorexia Nervosa and Related Disorders, Swansea.

Checkley, S. A., & Crammer, J. L. (1977). Hormone responses to methylamphetamine in depression. A new approach to the noradrenaline depletion hypothesis. *British Journal of Psychiatry, 131*, 582–586.

Cooper, P. J., & Fairburn, C. G. (1983). Binge eating and self-induced vomiting in the community. A preliminary study. *British Journal of Psychiatry, 142*, 139–144.

Crilly, R. G., Francis, R. M., & Nordin, B. E. C. (1981). Steroid hormones, aging and bone. *Clinics in Endocrinology and Metabolism, 10*, 115–139.

Crisp, A. H., Ellis, J., & Lowy, C. (1967). Insulin response to a rapid intravenous injection of dextrose in patients with anorexia nervosa and obesity. *Postgraduate Medical Journal, 43*, 97–102.

Crisp, A. H., Hsu, L. K. G., & Chen, C. N. (1982). Reproductive hormone profiles in male anorexia nervosa before, during and after weight restoration of body weight to normal. A study of 12 patients. *International Journal of Eating Disorders, 1*, 3–9.

Crisp, A. H., Palmer, R. L., & Kalucy, R. S. (1976). How common is anorexia nervosa? *British Journal of Psychiatry, 128*, 549–554.

Croxson, M. S., & Ibbertson, H. K. (1977). Low serum triiodothyronine (T3) and hypothyroidism in anorexia nervosa. *Journal of Clinical Endocrinology and Metabolism, 44*, 167–174.

Dale, E., Gerlach, D. H., & White, A. L. (1979). Menstrual dysfunction in distance runners. *Obstetrics and Gynecology (New York), 54*, 47–53.

Dalery, J., Claustrat, B., Brun, J., & de Villard, R. (1985). Plasma melatonin and cortisol levels in 8 patients with anorexia nervosa. *Neuroeudocrinology letters, 7*, 159–164.

Dalvit, S. P. (1981). The effect of the menstrual cycle on patterns of food intake. *American Journal of Clinical Nutrition, 34*, 1811–1815.

Darby, P. L., Brown, G. M., & Garfinkel, P. E. (1983). Circadian patterning of protection in anorexia nervosa. In P. L. Darby, P. E. Garfinkel, D. M. Garner, & D. V. Coscina (Eds.), *Anorexia nervosa: Recent developments in research* (pp. 65–82). New York: Alan R. Liss.

Darby, P. L., Van Loon, G., Garfinkel, P. E., Brown, G., & Kirwan, P. (1979). LH growth hormone, prolactin and catecholamine responses to LHRH and bromocriptine in anorexia nervosa [Abstract]. *Psychosomatic Medicine, 41*, 585.

Devlin, J. G. (1975). Obesity and anorexia nervosa, a study of growth hormone release. *Irish Medical Journal, 68*, 227–231.

Doerr, P., Fichter, M., Pirke, K. M., & Lund, R. (1980). Relations between weight gain and hypothalmic pituitary adrenal function in patients with anorexia nervosa. *Journal of Steroid Biochemistry, 13*, 529–537.

Donovan, B. T., & Van Der Werfften Bosch, J. J. (1965). Physiology of puberty. *Monographs of the physiological society*. London: Edward Arnold.

Drenick, E. J., Carlson, H. E., Robertson, G. L., & Hershman, J. M. (1977). The role of vasopressin and prolactin in abnormal salt and water metabolism of obese patients before and after fasting and during refeeding. *Metabolism, Clinical and Experimental, 26*, 309–317.

Emanuel, R. W. (1956). Endocrine activity in anorexia nervosa. *Journal of Clinical Endocrinology and Metabolism, 16*, 801–816.

Fairburn, C. G., & Cooper, P. J. (1982). Self-induced vomiting and bulimia nervosa: An undetected problem. *British Medical Journal, 284*, 1153–1155.

Feicht, C. B., Johnson, T. S., Martin, B. J., Sparks, K. E., & Wagner, W. W., Jr. (1978). Secondary amenorrhea in athletes [Letter]. *Lancet, 2*, 1145–1146.

Fichter, M. M., Pirke, K.-M., & Holsober, F. (1986). Experimental study in healthy, starved subjects. *Psychiatry Research, 27*, 61–72.

Frankel, R. J., & Jenkins, J. S. (1975). Hypothalamic-pituitary function in anorexia nervosa. *Acta Endocrinologicle (Copenhagen), 78*, 209–221.

Franks, S., Murray, M. A. F., Jequier, A. M., Steele, S. J., Nabarro, J. D. M., Jacobs, H. S. (1975). Incidence and significance of hyperprolactinemia in women with amenorrhea. *Journal of Clinical Endocrinology, 4*, 597–607.

Frisch, R. E. (1977). Food intake, fatness, and reproductive ability. In R. A. Vigersky (Ed.), *Anorexia nervosa* (pp. 149–161). New York: Raven Press.

Frisch, R. E., & McArthur, J. W. (1974). Menstrual cycles: Fatness as a determinant of minimum weight for height necessary for their maintenance and onset. *Science, 185*, 949–951.

Garfinkel, P. E. (1974). Perception of hunger and satiety in anorexia nervosa. *Psychological Medicine, 4*, 309–315.

Garfinkel, P. E., Brown, G. M., Stancer, H. C., & Moldofsky, H. (1975). Hypothalamic pituitary function in anorexia nervosa. *Archives of General Psychiatry, 32*, 739–744.

Garfinkel, P. E., & Coscina, D. V. (1982). The physiology and psychology of hunger and satiety. In M. Zales (Ed.), *Eating, sleeping, and sexuality* (pp. 5–42). New York: Brunner/Mazel.

Garfinkel, P. E., & Garner, D. M. (1982). *Anorexia nervosa: A multidimensional perspective*. New York: Brunner/Mazel.

Garfinkel, P. E., & Kaplan, A. S. (1985). Starvation-based perpetuating mechanisms in anorexia nervosa and bulimia. *International Journal of Eating Disorders, 4*, 651–665.

Garfinkel, P. E., Moldofsky, H., & Garner, D. (1980). The heterogenity of anorexia nervosa. *Archives of General Psychiatry, 37*, 1036–1040.

Garner, D. M., & Bemis, K. (1982). A cognitive-behavioral approach to anorexia nervosa. *Cognitive Therapy and Research, 6,* 1–27.

Garner, D. M., & Garfinkel, P. E. (1980). Sociocultural factors in the development of anorexia nervosa. *Psychological Medicine, 10,* 647–656.

Garner, D. M., Garfinkel, P. E., & O'Shaughnessy, M. (1985). Validity of the distinction between bulimia with and without anorexia nervosa. *American Journal of Psychiatry, 142,* 581–587.

Garner, D. M., Olmsted, M. P., & Garfinkel, P. E. (1985). Similarities among bulimic groups selected by weight and weight history. *Journal of Psychiatric Research, 19,* 129–139.

Gerner, R. H., & Gwirtsman, H. E. (1981). Abnormalities of dexamethasone suppression test and urinary MHPG in anorexia nervosa. *American Journal of Psychiatry, 138,* 650–653.

Ghosh, M. N., & Parvathy, S. (1973). The effect of cyproheptadine on water and food intake and on body weight in the fasted adult and weanling rat. *British Journal of Pharmacology, 48,* 328–329.

Gillman, M. A., & Lichtigfeld, F. J. (1981). Naloxone in anorexia nervosa—the role of the opiate system. *Journal of the Royal Society of Medicine, 74,* 631–632.

Gold, P. W., Kaye, W., Robertson, G. L., & Ebert, M. (1983). Abnormalities in plasma and cerebrospinal fluid arginine vasopressin in patients with anorexia nervosa. *New England Journal of Medicine, 308*(19), 1117–1123.

Goldberg, S. C., Halmi, K. A., Casper, R., Eckert, E. D., & Davis, J. M. (1979). Cyproheptadine in anorexia nervosa. *British Journal of Psychiatry, 134,* 67–70.

Graham, P. M., Booth, J., Boranga, E., Galhenage, S., Myers, C. M., Teok, C. L., & Cox, I. S. (1982). The dexamethasone suppression test in mania. *Journal of Affective Disorders, 4,* 210–211.

Greenway, F. L., & Bray, G. A. (1977). Cholecystokinin and satiety. *Life Sciences, 21,* 769.

Gross, H. A., Lake, C. R., Ebert, M. H., Ziegler, M. G., & Kopin, I. J. (1979). Catecholamine metabolism in primary anorexia nervosa. *Journal of Clinical Endocrinology and Metabolism, 49,* 805–809.

Gull, W. W. (1874). Anorexia nervosa. *Transactions of the Clinical Society of London, 7,* 22–28. [Reprinted in Evolution of psychosomatic concepts. In M. Herman & R. M. Kaufman (Eds.), *Anorexia nervosa: A paradigm.* New York: International Universities Press, 1964.]

Gwirtsman, H. E., Roy-Byrne, P., Lerner, L., & Yager, J. (1984). Bulimia in men: Report of three cases with neuroendocrine findings. *Journal of Clinical Psychiatry, 45,* 78–81.

Gwirtsman, H. E., Roy-Byrne, P., Yager, J., & Gerner, R. H. (1983). Neuroendocrine abnormalities in bulimia. *American Journal of Psychiatry, 140,* 559–563.

Hafner, R. J., Crisp, A. H., & McNeilly, A. S. (1976). Prolactin and gonadotrophin activity in females treated for anorexia nervosa. *Postgraduate Medicine, 52,* 76–79.

Halmi, K. A. (1984, April). *Controversies on the significance of depression in anorexia nervosa and bulima.* Paper presented at the First International Conference on Eating Disorders, New York.

Halmi, K. A., Dekirmenjian, H., Davis, J. M., Casper, R., & Goldberg, S. (1978). Catecholamine metabolism in anorexia nervosa. *Archives of General Psychiatry, 35,* 458–460.

Harrower, A. D. B., Yap, P. L., Nairn, I. M., Walton, H. J., Strong, J. A., & Craig, A. (1977). Growth hormone, insulin, and prolactin secretion in anorexia nervosa and obesity during bromocriptine treatment. *British Medical Journal, 2,* 156–159.

Herman, C. P., & Polivy, J. (1975). Anxiety, restraint and eating behavior. *Journal of Abnormal Psychology, 84,* 666–672.

Hill, P., & Wynder, F. (1976). Diet and prolactin release. *Lancet, 2,* 806–807.

Hsu, L. K. G., Crisp, A. H., & Harding, B. (1979). Outcome of anorexia nervosa. *Lancet, 1,* 61–65.

Hudson, J. I., Pope, H. G., Jr., Jonas, J. M., Laffer, P. S., Hudson, M. S., & Melby, J. C. (1983). Hypothalamic–pituitary–adrenal axis hyperactivity in bulimia. *Psychiatry Research, 8,* 111–117.

Hurd, H. P., Palumbo, P. J., & Gharid, H. (1977). Hypothalamic–endocrine dysfunction in anorexia nervosa. *Mayo Clinic Proceedings, 52,* 711–716.

Irie, M., & Tsushima, T. (1972). Increase of serum growth hormone concentration following TRH injection in patients with acromegaly or gigantism. *Journal of Clinical Endocrinology and Metabolism, 35,* 97–100.

Johnson, J., Lieter, L., Burrow, G., Garfinkel, P., & Anderson, H. (1984). Excretion of urinary catecholamines in anorexia nervosa: Effects of body composition and energy intake. *American Journal of Clinical Nutrition, 40,* 1001–1006.

Jones, D. J., Fox, M. M., Babigian, H. M., & Hutton, H. E. (1980). Epidemiology of anorexia nervosa in Monroe County, New York, 1960–1976. *Psychosomatic Medicine, 42,* 551–558.

Kanis, J. A., Brown, P., Fitzpatrick, K., Hibbert, D. J., Horn, D. B., Nairn, I. M., Shirling, D., Strong, J. A., & Walton, H. J. (1974). Anorexia nervosa: A clincal, psychiatric and laboratory study. I Clinical and laboratory investigation. *Irish Journal of Medicine, 43,* 321–338.

Kaplan, A. S., Garfinkel, P. E., Warsh, J. J., & Brown, G. (1986). Neuroendocrine responses in bulimia. *Advances in Biosciences, 60,* 241–245.

Katz, J. L., Boyar, R., Roffwarg, H., Hellman, L., & Weiner, H. (1978). Weight and circadian luteinizing hormone secretory pattern in anorexia nervosa. *Psychosomatic Medicine, 40,* 549–567.

Kaye, W. H., Ebert, M. H., Gwirtsman, H. E., & Weiss, S. R. (1984). Differences in brain serotonergic metabolism between nonbulimic and bulimic patients with anorexia nervosa. *American Journal of Psychiatry, 141,* 1598–1601.

Kaye, W. H., Ebert, M. H., Raleigh, M., & Lake, R. (1984). Abnormalities in CNS monoamine metabolism in anorexia nervosa. *Archives of General Psychiatry, 41,* 350–355.

Kaye, W. H., Pickar, D., Ebert, M. H., & Naber, D. (1983). The opioid system in anorexia nervosa [Reply]. *American Journal of Psychiatry, 140,* 371–372.

Kaye, W. H., Pickar, D., Naber, D., & Ebert, M. H. (1982). Cerebral spinal fluid opioid activity in anorexia nervosa. *American Journal of Psychiatry, 139,* 643–645.

Kennedy, S., Costa, D., Parienti, V., & Brown, G. M. (1987). Is melatonin a neuroendocrine marker in bulimia? In H. G. Pope & J. Hudson (Eds.), *Psychobiology of bulimia*. Washington, DC: American Psychiatric Association.

Kennedy, S., Piran, N., & Garfinkel, P. E. (1985). Monoamine oxidase inhibitor therapy for anorexia nervosa and bulimia. A preliminary trial of isocarboxazid. *Journal of Clinical Psychopharmacology, 5*, 279–285.

Kennedy, S., Piran, N., Stokl, S., Garfinkel, P. E., Wilkes, B., & Stern, D. (1984, October). *The effect of weight change on the dexamethasone suppression test*. Paper presented at the Canadian Psychiatric Association, Banff.

Keys, A., Brozek, J., Henschel, A., Mickelsen, D., & Taylor, H. L. (1950). *The biology of human starvation*. Minneapolis: University of Minnesota Press.

Landon, J., Greenwood, F. C., Stamp, T. C. B., & Wynn, V. (1966). The plasma sugar, free fatty acid, cortisol and growth hormone response to insulin, and the comparison of this procedure with other tests of pituitary and adrenal function II in patients with hypothalamic or pituitary dysfunction of anorexia nervosa. *Journal of Clinical Investigation, 45*, 437–449.

Lasegue, C. (1873). De L'anorexie hystérique. *Archives Generales de Medecine*. [Reprinted in Evolution of psychosomatic concepts. In R. M. Kaufman & M. Heiman (Eds.), Evolution of psychosomatic concepts. *Anorexia nervosa: A paradigm*, (pp. 141–155). New York: International Universities Press, 1964.]

Leibowitz, S. F. (1980). Neurochemical systems for the hypothalamus. Control of feeding and drinking behavior and water–electrolyte excretion. In P. J. Morgane & J. Panksepp (Eds.), *Handbook of the hypothalamus: Vol. 3, Part A. Behavioral studies of the hypothalamus* (pp. 299–437). New York: Marcel Dekker.

Leibowitz, S. F. (1983). Hypothalamic catcholamine systems controlling eating behavior. A potential model for anorexia nervosa. In P. L. Darby, P. E. Garfinkel, D. M. Garner, D. V. Coscina (Eds.), *Anorexia nervosa: Recent developments in research* (pp. 221–229). New York: Alan R. Liss.

Leibowitz, S. F., & Hor, L. (1982). Endorphinergic and α-noradrenergic systems in the paraventricular nucleus. Effects on eating behavior. *Peptides (New York), 3*, 421–428.

Leslie, R. D. G., Isaacs, A. J., Gomez, J., Raggatt, P. R., & Bayliss, R. (1978). Hypothalamo-pituitary–thyroid function in anorexia nervosa. Influence of weight gain. *British Medical Journal, 2*, 526–528.

Luerrson, T. B., & Robertson, G. L. (1980). Cerebrospinal fluid vasopressin and vasotocin in health and disease. In J. R. Wood (Ed.), *The neurobiology of cerebrospinal fluid* (pp. 613–623). New York: Plenum Press.

Lundberg, P. O., Walinder, J., Werner, I., & Wide, L. (1972). Effects of thyrotropin-releasing hormone on plasma levels of TSH, FSH, LH, and GH in anorexia nervosa. *European Journal of Clinical Investigations, 2*, 150–153.

Maeda, K., Kato, Y, Yamaguchi, N., Chiliara, K., Ohga, S., Iwasaki, Y., Yoshimoto, Y., Morider, K., Kuromaru, S., & Imura, H. (1976). Growth hormone release following thyrotropin releasing hormone injection into patients with anorexia nervosa. *Acta Endocrinologica (Copenhagen), 81*, 1–8.

Margules, D. L. (1979). β-Endorphin and endoloxone: Hormones of the autonomic nervous system for the conservation or expenditure of bodily resources and energy in anticipation of famine or feast. *Neuroscience and Biobehavioral Reviews, 3*, 155–162.

Margules, D. L., Moisset, B., & Lewis, M. J. (1978). β-Endorphin is associated with overeating in genetically obese mice (ob/ob) and rats (fa/fa). *Science, 202*, 988–991.

Mawson, A. R. (1974). Anorexia nervosa and the regulation of intake: A review. *Psychological Medicine, 4*, 289–308.

McLaughlin, C. L., Baile, C. A., & Peikin, S. R. (1983). Hyperphagia during lactation: Satiety response to CCK and growth of the pancreas. *American Journal of Physiology, 244*, E61–E65.

Mecklenberg, R. S., Loriaux, D. L., Thompson, R. H., Andersen, A. E., & Lipsett, M. B. (1974). Hypothalamic dysfunction in patients with anorexia nervosa. *Medicine (Baltimore), 53*, 147–159.

Minuchin, S., Rosman, B. L., & Baker, L. (1978). *Psychosomatic families: Anorexia nervosa in context*. Cambridge, MA: Harvard University Press.

Mitchell, J. E., & Bantle, J. P. (1983). Metabolic and endocrine investigations in women of normal weight with the bulimia syndrome. *Biological Psychiatry, 18*, 355–365.

Mitchell, J. E., & Groat, R. (1984). A placebo-controlled double-blind trial of amitriptyline in bulimia. *Journal of Clinical Psychopharmacology, 4*, 186–193.

Miyai, K. Yamaruoto, T. Azukizawa, M. Ishibashi, K., Kumahara, Y. (1975). Serum thyroid hormones and thyrotropin in anorexia nervosa. *Journal of Clinical Endocrinology and Metabolism, 40*, 334–338.

Moore, R., Mills, I. H., & Forster, A. (1981). Naloxone in the treatment of anorexia nervosa: Effect on weight gain and lipolysis. *Journal of the Royal Society of Medicine, 74*, 129–131.

Morgan, H. G., & Russell, G. F. M. (1975). Value of family background and clinical feautres as predictors of long-term outcome in anorexia nervosa: Four-year follow-up study of 41 patients. *Psychological Medicine, 5*, 355–371.

Morley, J. E. (1980). The neuroendocrine control of appetite. *Life Sciences, 27*, 355.

Moshang, T., Jr., Parks, J. S., Baker, L., Vaidya, V., Utiger, R. D., Bougiovanni, A. M., & Synder, P. J. (1975). Low serum triiodothyronine in patients with anorexia nervosa. *Journal of Clinical Endocrinology and Metabolism, 40*, 470–473.

Murphy, D. L., Garrick, N. A., Aulakh, C. S., & Cohen, R. M. (1984). New contributions from basic science to understanding the effects of monoamine oxidase inhibiting antidepressants. *Journal of Clinical Psychiatry, 45*, 37–43.

Musisi, S., & Garfinkel, P. E. (1985). Comparative dexamethasone suppression test measurements in bulimia, depression, and normal controls. *Canadian Journal of Psychiatry, 30*, 190–194.

Newsom, G., & Murray, N. (1983). Reversal of dexamethasone suppression test nonsuppression in alcohol abusers. *American Journal of Psychiatry, 14,* 353–354.

Nylander, I. (1971). The feeling of being fat and dieting in a school population. An epidemiologic interview investigation. *Acta Sociomedica Scandinavica, 3,* 17–26.

Ong, Y. L., Checkley, S. A., & Russell, G. F. M. (1983). Suppression of bulimic symptoms with methyl amphetamine. *British Journal of Psychiatry, 143,* 288–293.

Owen, W. P., Halmi, K. A., Lasley, E., & Stokes, P. (1983). Dopamine regulation in anorexia nervosa. *Psychopharmacology Bulletin, 19,* 578–581.

Palmer, R. L. (1979). The dietary chaos syndrome: A useful new term? *British Journal of Medical Psychology, 52,* 187–190.

Parsons, V., Szmukler, G., & Brown, S. J. (1983). Fracturing osteoporosis in young women with anorexia nervosa. *Calcified Tissue International, 35* (Suppl.), A72.

Parvizi, N., & Ellendorff, F. (1975). 2-Hydroxyoestradiol-17β as a possible link in steroid brain interaction. *Nature (London), 256,* 59–60.

Paykel, E. S., Mueller, P. S., & De La Vergne, P. (1973). Amitriptyline, weight gain and carbohydrate craving: A side effect. *British Journal of Psychiatry, 123,* 501–507.

Pimstone, B. L., Becker, D. J., & Hausen, J. D. L. (1973). Human growth hormone in protein calorie malnutrition. In A. Pecile & E. E. Muller (Eds.), *Growth and growth hormone* (pp. 389–401). Amsterdam: Excerpta Medica.

Piran, N., Kennedy, S., Garfinkel, P. E., & Owens, M. (1985). Affective disturbance in eating disorders. *Journal of Nervous and Mental Disease, 173,* 395–400.

Piran, N., Lerner, P., Kennedy, S., Garfinkel, P., & Brouillette, C. (1984). Personality organization in bulimic and restrictive anorexia nervosa patients. (Submitted for publication.)

Pirke, K. M., Fichter, M. M., Lund, R., & Doerr, P. L. (1979). 24-hour sleep–wake pattern of plasma LH in patients with anorexia nervosa. *Acta Endocrinologica (Copenhagen), 92,* 193–204.

Pyle, R. L., Mitchell, J. E., & Eckert, E. D. (1981). Bulimia: A report of 34 cases. *Journal of Clinical Psychiatry, 42,* 60–64.

Rigotti, N. A., Nussbaum, S. R., Herzog, D. B., Neer, R. M. (1984). Osteoporosis in women with anorexia nervosa. *New England Journal of Medicine, 311,* 1601–1606.

Rodin, G. M., Daneman, D., Johnson, L. E., Kenshole, A., & Garfinkel, P. (1985). Anorexia nervosa and bulimia in female adolescents with insulin-dependent diabetes mellitus: A systematic study. *Journal of Psychiatric Research, 19,* 381–384.

Russell, G. F. M. (1970). Anorexia nervosa: Its identity as an illness and its treatment. In J. H. Price (Ed.), *Modern trends in psychological medicine* (Vol. 2, pp. 131–164). London: Butterworth.

Russell, G. F. M. (1979). Bulimia nervosa: An ominous variant of anorexia nervosa. *Psychological Medicine, 9,* 429–448.

Russell, G. F. M., & Bruce, J. T. (1966). Impaired water diuresis in patients with anorexia nervosa. *American Journal of Medicine, 40,* 38–48.

Russell, G. F. M., Loraine, J. A., Bell, E. T., & Harkness, R. A. (1965). Gonadotrophin and estrogen excretion in patients with anorexia nervosa. *Journal of Psychosomatic Research, 9,* 79–85.

Schildkraut, J. J. (1973). Norepinephrine metabolites as biochemical criteria for classifying depressive disorders and predicting responses to treatment, preliminary findings. *American Journal of Psychiatry, 130,* 695–699.

Schlemmer, R. S, Casper, R., Elder, J. K., & Davis, J. M. (1981). Hyperphagia and weight gain in monkeys treated with clonidine. In H. Lal & S. Fielding (Eds.), *Psychopharmacology of clonidine* (pp. 197–210). New York: Alan R. Liss.

Selvini Palazzoli, M. P. (1974). *Self-starvation.* London: Chaucer Publishing Co.

Sherman, B. M., & Halmi, K. A. (1977). Effect of nutritional rehabilitation on hypothalamic–pituitary function in anorexia nervosa. In R. Vigersky (Ed.), *Anorexia nervosa* (pp. 211–223). New York: Raven Press.

Silverman, J. A. (1977). Anorexia nervosa: Clinical and metabolic observations in a successful treatment plan. In R. A. Vigersky (Ed.), *Anorexia nervosa* (pp. 331–339). New York: Raven Press.

Smith, G. P., & Gibbs, J. (1976). Cholecystokinin and satiety: Theoretic and therapeutic implications in hunger. In D. Noviu, W. Wyrwicka, & G. A. Bray (Eds.), *Hunger: Basic mechanisms and clinical implications* (pp. 349–355). New York: Raven Press.

Smith, S. R., Bledsoe, T., & Chhetri, M. K. (1975). Cortisol metabolism and the pituitary–adrenal axis in adults with protein–calorie malnutrition. *Journal of Clinical Endocrinology and Metabolism, 42,* 197–200.

Spar, J. E., & Gerner, R. (1982). Does the dexamethasone suppression test distinguish dementia from depression? *American Journal of Psychiatry, 139,* 238–240.

Strangler, R. S., & Printz, A. M. (1980). DSM-III psychiatric diagnosis in a university population. *American Journal of Psychiatry, 137,* 937–940.

Strober, M., Salkin, B., Burroughs, J., & Morrell, W. (1982). Validity of the bulimia restricter distinction in anorexia nervosa: Parental personality characteristics and family psychiatric morbidity. *Journal of Nervous and Mental Disease, 170,* 345–351.

Stunkard, A. J. (1982). Anorectic agents lower a body weight set point. *Life Sciences, 30,* 2043–2055.

Sturdevant, R. A. L., & Goetz, H. (1976). Cholecystokinin both stimulates and inhibits human food intake. *Nature (London), 261,* 713–715.

Szmukler, G. (1983). Weight and food preoccupation in a population of English school girls. In G. J. Bargman (Ed.), *Understanding anorexia nervosa and bulimia* (pp. 21–27). Columbus, OH: Ross Laboratories.

Toner, B. D., Garfinkel, P. E., & Garner, D. M. (1986). Long-term follow-up of bulimic and dietary-restricting anorexics. *Psychosomatic Medicine, 48,* 520–529.

Toner, B. D., Garfinkel, P. E., & Garner, D. M. (1987). Cognitive style in bulimic and dietary-restricting anorexia nervosa. *American Journal of Psychiatry, 144,* 510–512.

Treasure, J., Gordon, P., Wheeler, M., Russell, G. F. M. (1985, September). Weight restoration and ovarian morphology as revealed by ultrasounds. Paper presented at International Symposium on Disorders of Eating Behaviour. Pavia Italy.

Vagenakis, A. G. (1977). Thyroid hormone in prolonged experimental starvation in man. In R. Vigersky (Ed.), *Anorexia nervosa* (pp. 243–252). New York: Raven Press.

Vagenakis, A. G., Burger, A., Portnay, G. I., Rudolph, M., O'Brian, J. I., Azizi, R., Arky, R., Nicod, P., Ingbar, S. H., & Braverman, L. E. (1975). Diversion of peripheral thyroxine metabolism from activating to inactivating pathways during complete feeding. *Journal of Clinical Endocrinology and Metabolism, 41,* 191–194.

Vandereycken, W., & Pierloot, R. (1983). Combining drugs and behavior therapy in anorexia nervosa: A double-blind placebo/pimozide study. In P. L. Darby, P. E. Garfinkel, D. M. Garner, & D. V. Coscina (Eds.), *Anorexia nervosa: Recent developments in research* (pp. 365–375). New York: Alan R. Liss.

Vaughan, G. M., Pelham, R. W., Pang, S. F., Loughlin, L. L., Wilson, K. M., Sandok, K. L. Vaughan, M. K., Koslow, S. H., & Reiter, R. J. (1976). Nocturnal elevation of plasma melatonin and urinary 5-hydroxyindoleacetic acid in young men. Attempts at modification by brief changes in environmental lighting and sleep and by autonomic drugs. *Journal of Clinical Endocrinology and Metabolism, 42,* 752–764.

Vigersky, R. A., Andersen, A. I., Thompson, R. H., & Loviaux, D. L. (1977). Hypothalamic dysfunction in secondary amenorrhea associated with simple weight loss. *New England Journal of Medicine, 297,* 1141–1145.

Vigersky, R. A., Loriaux, D. L., Andersen, A. E., & Lipsett, M. B. (1976). Anorexia nervosa behavioral and hypothalamic aspects. *Clinics in Endocrinology and Metabolism, 5,* 517–535.

Wachslicht-Rodbard, H., Gross, H. A., Rodbard, D., Ebert, M. H., & Roth, J. (1979). Increased insulin binding to erythrocytes in anorexia nervosa. Restoration to normal with refeeding. *New England Journal of Medicine, 300,* 882–887.

Wakeling, A., DeSouza, V., & Beardwood, C. J. (1977). Effects of administered estrogen on luteinizing hormone release in subjects with anorexia nervosa in acute and recovery stages. In R. A. Vigersky (Ed.), *Anorexia nervosa.* New York: Raven Press.

Wakeling, A., DeSouza, V. A., Gore, M. B. R., Sabur, M., Kingstone, D., & Boss, A. M. B. (1979). Amenorrhea, body weight and serum hormone concentration with particular reference to prolactin and thyroid hormones in anorexia nervosa. *Psychological Medicine, 9,* 265–272.

Wakeling, A., Marshall, C. J., Beardwood, C. J., DeSouza, V. F. A., & Russell, G. F. M. (1976). The effects of clomiphene citrate on the hypothalamic-pituitary-gonadal axis in anorexia nervosa. *Psychological Medicine, 6,* 371–380.

Waldhauser, F., Wieszenbacher, G., Zeithuber, U., Waldhauser, M., Frisch, H., & Wurtman, J. (1984). Fall in nocturnal serum melatonin levels during prepuberty and pubescence. *Lancet, 1,* 362–365.

Waller, D. A., Kiser, R. S., Hardy, B. W., Fuchs, I., Feigenbaum, L. P., & Uany, R. (1986). Eating behavior and plasma beta-endorphin in bulimia. *American Journal of Clinical Nutrition, 44,* 20–23.

Walsh, B. T., Katz, J. L., Levin, J., Kream, J., Fukushima, D. K., Hellman, L., Weiner, H., & Zumoff, B. (1978). Adrenal activity in anorexia nervosa. *Psychosomatic Medicine, 40,* 499–506.

Walsh, B. T., Katz, J. L, Levin, J., Kream, J., Fukushima, D. K., Weiner, H., & Zumoff, B. (1981). The production rate of cortisol declines during recovery from anorexia nervosa. *Journal of Clinical Endocrinology and Metabolism, 53,* 203–205.

Walsh, B. T., Stewart, J. W., Roose, S. P., Gladis, M., & Glassman, A. H. (1984). Treatment of bulimia with phenelzine. A double-blind placebo-controlled study. *Archives General of Psychiatry, 41,* 1105–1109.

Wardle, J. (1980). Dietary restraint and binge eating. *Behavioral Analysis and Modification, 4,* 201–209.

Warren, M. P. (1977). Weight loss and responsiveness to LH-RH. In R. A. Vigersky (Ed.), *Anorexia nervosa* (pp. 189–198). New York: Raven Press.

Warren, M. P., Jewelewicz, R., Dyrenfurth, I., Ans, R., Khalaf, S., & Vande Wiele, R. L. (1975). The significance of weight loss in the evaluation of pituitary response to LH-RH in women with secondary amenorrhea. *Journal of Clinical Endocrinology and Metabolism, 40,* 601–611.

Warren, M. P., & Vande Wiele, R. L. (1973). Clinical and metabolic features of anorexia nervosa. *American Journal of Obstetrics and Gynecology, 117,* 435–449.

Weiner, H., & Katz, J. L. (1983). The hypothalamic-pituitary-adrenal axis in anorexia nervosa: A reassessment. In P. L. Darby. P. E. Garfinkel, D. M. Garner, & D. Coscina (Eds.), *Anorexia nervosa: Recent developments in research* (pp. 249–270). New York: Alan R. Liss.

Weingartner, H., Gold, P., & Ballenger, J. C. (1981). Effects of vasopressin on human memory functions. *Science, 211,* 601–603.

Weller, R. A., & Weller, E. B. (1981). Anorexia nervosa in a patient with an infiltrating tumor of the hypothalamus. *American Journal of Psychiatry, 139,* 824–825.

Wetterberg, L., Arendt, J., Paunier, L., Sizouenko, P. C., Van Douselaar, W., & Heydon, T. (1976). Human serum melatonin changes during the menstrual cycle. *Journal of Clinical Endocrinology and Metabolism, 42,* 185–188.

Willi, J., & Grossman, S. (1983). Epidemiology of anorexia nervosa in defined region of Switzerland. *American Journal of Psychiatry, 140,* 564–567.

Winokur, A., March, V., & Mendels, J. (1980). Primary affective disorder in relatives of patients with anorexia nervosa. *American Journal of Psychiatry, 137,* 695–698.

Wurtman, J. J., & Wurtman, R. J. (1979). Drugs that enhance central serotoninergic transmission diminish effective carbohydrate consumption by rats. *Life Sciences, 24,* 895–904.

Young, J. K. (1975). A possible neuroendocrine basis of two clinical syndromes: Anorexia nervosa and the Kleine-Levin syndrome. *Physiological Psychology, 3,* 322–330.

Zuniga-Guajardo, S., Garfinkel, P. E., & Zinman, B. (1986). Changes in insulin sensitivity and clearance in anorexia nervosa. *Metabolism: Clinical and Experimental, 35,* 1096–1100.

7 ENDOCRINE DISTURBANCES IN AFFECTIVE DISORDERS AND SCHIZOPHRENIA

DAVID L. COPOLOV

Mental Health Research Institute, Melbourne, Australia

ROBERT T. RUBIN

Harbor UCLA Medical Center

INTRODUCTION

The major neurotransmitter hypotheses of the main functional psychiatric illnesses—the affective disorders and schizophrenia—originated post hoc as the result of observations of the neurobiological effects of potent psychotropic drugs. To such work is owed the continuing currency of the hypotheses. Measurements of neurotransmitters in the periphery have been made in an attempt to investigate the validity of various neurotransmitter dysfunction theories of the major psychiatric illnesses. These studies have been thwarted by the fact that there is a substantial peripheral contribution to the amount of neurotransmitters circulating in the plasma (Esler, 1984).

Endocrine investigations of psychiatric patients constitute a second line of research into the existence of neurotransmitter abnormalities. The advantages of such studies include the facts that the relationships between hypothalamic and pituitary function have been considerably clarified and that the sources of plasma hormones are usually discrete and identifiable. Nevertheless, it is difficult to hypothesize any particular set of changes in pituitary function as the result of a specific neurotransmitter abnormality, because each hormone is controlled by a complex set of neurotransmitters (Frohman & Berelowitz, 1984), and there is no firm reason to believe

that neurotransmitter function in the hypothalamus necessarily reflects neurotransmitter function elsewhere in the brain. However, while psychoendocrine strategies have met with limited success as methods by which neurotransmitter theories of mental illness can be tested, they have added valuable information to our understanding of one important limb of biological function in psychiatric patients.

It is best to consider the psychoendocrinology of major functional psychiatric disorders to be at a descriptive rather than a theoretical stage at present. Challenge tests with neurotransmitter agonists and antagonists and with synthetic hormones have revealed many provocative findings. Such work ideally should have been carried out on the foundation of studies which have reported "naturalistic" observations of endocrine function in psychiatric patients throughout the 24-hour period. This foundation is only partially laid because of the difficulty in obtaining drug-free patients and because of the time and effort required to perform multiple-sample circadian studies. However, such studies are of great importance to the understanding of pituitary function because disturbances of circadian function are prominent in psychiatric disorders and because hormonal secretory patterns may reveal information about the function of discrete brain regions, such as the suprachiasmatic nucleus, in these patients (Menaker, Takahashi, & Eskin, 1978). Also, circadian rhythm analyses of hormone secretion provide a more reliable index of the state of an endocrine system than single measures. As pointed out by Rusak (1984), single samples taken at a given clock time may in fact be taken at a different physiological time if there is phase advance or delay in the circadian rhythm of particular hormones. Studies that extrapolate from single-value increases or decreases to heightened or lowered activity of a particular endocrine axis therefore should be questioned, because the actual phenomenon being reflected may be that of a phase shift.

The following account primarily describes endocrine function in patients with affective disorder and schizophrenia as ascertained by studies which, on the whole, did not use pharmacological challenge. However, passing reference will be made to those provocative tests, such as the gonadotropin-releasing hormone (GnRH) stimulation test, which are not specifically covered in other chapters in this volume. Also, the major findings which relate to the postulated roles of opioid peptides in psychotic illness will not be reviewed here, as they are covered in other chapters in this volume.

DEPRESSION

Introduction

Many hormones have been proposed as successors to black bile as the humoral agent responsible for melancholia. Although, on the whole, evidence has not supported an etiological role for hormones in depression, the disorder has been shown to be associated with more endocrine changes than other major psychiatric illnesses. The circadian rhythm disturbances of hormone secretion represent only a small segment of the many chronobiological changes seen in this disorder. Such changes often include significant diurnal variation in clinical symptoms, decreased rapid eye movement (REM) sleep latency and total amount of REM sleep, increased REM density, forward shift (phase advance) of minimum body temperature, and periodicity to the onset and offset of the illness in certain patients (von Zerssen, 1983).

In order to critically analyze studies which claim specificity for certain chronoendocrinological changes in depressive disorders, one must be attuned to the nature of the problems faced by psychiatric nosologists. Depression tends to grade into normalcy, whereas, for example, schizophrenia separates from normalcy rather well. Thus, there is a need to reach consensus about the clinical definition of the more severe depressions in order to circumvent the potential problem of falsely low sensitivity of endocrine changes associated with broad definitions of depression. Sadly, however, no consensus has been found; indeed, the diagnosis of endogenous-pattern depression can vary from 24% to 72% of a given population of depressed patients, depending on the diagnostic scheme used (Davidson, Turnbull, Strickland, & Belyea, 1984).

Many studies from the mid-1970s to the early 1980s utilized the Research Diagnostic Criteria (RDC) (Spitzer, Endicott, & Robins, 1978) to diagnose endogenous depression. The RDC define endogenous-pattern depression more permissively than does DSM-III melancholia (Davidson et al., 1984). Although both the RDC and the DSM-III criteria for depression subtypes are based on empirical findings, they have no firm, independent validating criteria. For example, it has been noted that the RDC endogenous category includes patients who, on other clinical grounds, are not considered to have endogenous-pattern depression (Feinberg, Carroll, Steiner, & Commorato, 1979). In the absence of external validation for any one of the many definitions of endogenous-pattern depression, it is best to use several competing definitions to maximize the chance of relating biological changes to the endogenous symptom pattern with maximum sensitivity and specificity (Kendell, 1982). Most of the studies discussed herein used definitions of depression and of endogenous-pattern depression based on one system only. Therefore, the frequency of the endocrine abnormalities reported in such studies must be considered approximate.

Hypothalamic–Pituitary–Adrenal (HPA) Axis

This axis has been the most extensively studied of all endocrine systems in relation to affective illness. The specificity, stability, and implications of abnormalities of the HPA axis in depression have been the subject of great contention (Berger, Pirke, Doerr, Krieg, & von Zerssen, 1984; Carroll et al., 1981; Stokes et al., 1984). Less contentious is the fact the HPA hyperactivity occurs quite commonly in patients with affective disorder. Many issues relating to this will be discussed in this volume in the chapters on the cortisol system and the dexamethasone suppression test. Here, we will limit discussion to (1) the consideration of circadian patterns of HPA hormone secretion and their relation to sleep, and (2) proposed analogies between depression and Cushing's disease.

A number of studies have demonstrated increased adrenocortical activity in depressed patients throughout the 24-hour period (e.g., Carroll, Curtis, & Mendels, 1976; Rubin & Poland, 1982; Sachar, Hellman et al., 1973). There is no firm consensus on either the time of maximum differences or whether there is an attenuation of the amplitude of circadian cortisol rhythm in depressed patients. There is reasonable consensus among a number of studies that there is a phase advance of the circadian cortisol rhythm in depressive illness. Wehr, Gillin, and Goodwin (1983) fitted cosine functions to the cortisol data in five studies in which cortisol rhythms had been estimated in depressed patients and compared to those found in either normal controls or in patients with other psychiatric conditions (Conroy, Hughes, & Mills, 1968; Fullerton, Wenzel, Lohrenz, & Fahs, 1968; Knapp, Keane, & Wright, 1967; Sachar, Hellman et al., 1973; Yamaguchi, Maeda, & Kuromaru, 1978). In four of the five studies, the acrophase (or time of the fitted maximum) of the cortisol rhythm in depressed patients was 1–4 hours earlier than in the control groups. Other rhythms which have been shown to be phase advanced in affective disorder include body temperature (Cahn, Folk, & Huston, 1968; Wehr, Muscettola, & Goodwin, 1980), the circadian rhythm of REM activity (Papousek, 1975), and the urinary excretion of 3-methoxy-4-hydroxyphenylglycol (MHPG), a metabolite which partly reflects noradrenergic activity in the central nervous system (CNS) (Wehr et al., 1980).

The relationship between REM sleep rhythms and cortisol secretory rhythms also has been examined. Asnis et al. (1983) showed that in 17 unipolar and 8 bipolar depressed patients there was a shortened REM latency in patients with cortisol hypersecretion, defined by a mean plasma cortisol between 1300 and 1600 hours greater than the 94th percentile for a normal population (Asnis et al., 1982). REM latencies of 20 minutes or less occurred with particular specificity in those with cortisol hypersecretion thus defined. In a more detailed study, Jarrett, Coble, and Kupfer (1983) examined the relationship between sleep electroencephalographic (EEG) parameters and nocturnal cortisol secretion in 9 patients with moderately severe depression, 6 asymptomatic patients with a past history of such a disorder, and in 14 age- and sex-matched controls. The major finding was a significant reduction (51 minutes, $p < .02$) in the mean time from the onset of sleep to the early morning increase in plasma cortisol secretion in both the symptomatic and the recovered depressives compared to the controls. The patient groups showed no difference in the relationship between cortisol secretion and the offset of REM sleep periods. Jarrett et al. pointed to evidence which indicates that under normal conditions cortisol secretion in inhibited for 2–3 hours by the onset of sleep (Weitzman, Czeisler, & Moore-Ede, 1979). Their findings therefore indicate that the suppressive effect of sleep onset on cortisol secretion is reduced in depression, and that this permits the circadian cortisol secretory rhythm to move closer to the commencement of sleep, as does the onset of REM cycling. Jarrett et al. suggest that the relationship between sleep onset and the circadian cortisol rhythm may serve as a trait market for depressive illness.

Circadian rhythm abnormalities such as these may reflect neurophysiological processes which are either critical or peripheral to the initiation and maintenance of depressive illnesses (Wehr et al., 1983; also see Chapter 9, this volume). Evidence supporting an important role for such changes is the findings that some drugs used in the treatment of depression, including imipramine, lithium, and the monoamine oxidase inhibitor clorgyline, can induce a slowing of circadian rhythms (Wirz-Justice & Wehr, 1983), and that phase advance of the sleep–wake cycle in depressed patients may have antidepressant properties (Wehr, Wirz-Justice, Goodwin, Duncan, & Gillin, 1979).

The occurrence of dexamethasone non-suppressibility of cortisol secretion in depression, plus abnormalities of both mean daily cortisol concentrations and the circadian cortisol rhythm, have raised a question regarding the relationship of depression to Cushing's disease. Carroll and Mendels (1976) postulated that similar brain dysfunctions might underlie both melancholia and Cushing's disease on the reciprocal basis of HPA axis abnormalities in depression and the high prevalence of depressive and dysphoric changes in patients with Cushing's disease (S. Cohen, 1980). The etiology of Cushing's disease—the specific designation for cases of Cushing's syndrome in which there is inappropriately high secretion of ACTH by the pituitary—is an elusive as the etiology of affective disorder. A number of investigators have suggested neurotransmitter abnormalities in the hypothalamus, especially involving dysfunction of the serotonergic system (Krieger, Amorosa, & Linick, 1975). This amine system also has been implicated in the pathogenesis of depression (Maas, 1975). Such reasoning has led investigators to question why there is a notable absence of even mild physical stigmata of Cushing's disease in patients with severe depressive illness. A number of explanations have been forwarded to account for this finding, including postulated glucocorticoid receptor defects, the milder severity of HPA dysregulation in depression, and the fact that the cyclic nature of affective disorder results in intermittent rather than continuous tissue exposure to increased cortisol (Reus, 1984). Before the status of this question is raised to that of a dilemma, it must be noted that the analogy between Cushing's disease and depressive illness requires critical attention in a number of areas. For example, there is only limited evidence to show that depression is found more commonly in Cushing's disease than in other types of Cushing's syndrome (Cohen, 1980; Hurxthal & O'Sullivan, 1959; Jeffcoate, Silverstone, Edwards, & Besser, 1979; Starkman, Schteingart, & Schork, 1981; Trethowan & Cobb, 1952). Such studies report clinically significant affective disorder occurring in patients with, for example, adrenal adenomas. The implication is that depression may occur secondary to adrenocortical hyperfunction of any

cause rather than being specific to pituitary-dependent Cushing's disease. Furthermore, although two serotonin antagonists, cyproheptadine and methysergide, have been used effectively in the treatment of some patients with Cushing's disease (Krieger et al., 1975), they do not have proven efficacy in the treatment of depression. In fact, the postulated abnormality of serotonin neurotransmission in depression is that of deficiency rather than excess. Finally, a number of studies suggest that "disinhibition" of the HPA axis, as reflected by the dexamethasone suppression test (DST) nonsuppression (Stokes et al., 1984; von Zerssen, & Doerr, 1980), may be related to general factors occurring in a number of psychiatric illnesses rather than being specific to and reflecting a distinct functional lesion in endogenous depression.

Hypothalamic–Pituitary–Thyroid (HPT) Axis

According to many studies, depression is associated with both hyper- and hypofunction of the HPT axis in a sizable proportion of patients. Decreased thyroid function in depression has been suggested by Rybakowski and Sowinski (1973), Rinieris, Christodoulou, Souvatzoglou, Koutras, and Stefanis (1978a, 1978b), M. S. Gold, Pottash, and Extein (1981), and M. S. Gold, Pottash, Müller, and Extein (1981). Rinieris et al. demonstrated that, although circulating T4 and FT4 concentrations were lower than in control subjects, they were within normal limits. They also showed that the decrements were found in patients with psychotic but not neurotic depression. Belmaker, Kon, Ebstein, and Dasberg (1980), as well, demonstrated that plasma T4 concentrations were lower in depressed patients with psychotic symptomatology than in those who were neurotically depressed. They demonstrated an inverse relationship between free thyroxine index (FTI) values and Hamilton Depression Rating Scale scores. Of the depressed patients studied by Rybakowski and Sowinski (1973) 20% had low T4 and FT4 values; in contrast, only 1 of their 15 manic patients showed subnormal T4 and FT4 values. A larger number of patients were studied by M. S. Gold, Pottash, and Extein (1981) and M. S. Gold, Pottash, Müller, and Extein (1981), and, although it was stated that they were referred to a research facility with complaints of depression and anergia, specific psychiatric diagnoses were not included. M. S. Gold, Pottash, Müller, and Extein (1981) first reported subclinical mild or overt hypothyroidism in 9 out of 100 patients and in a later study (M. S. Gold, Pottash, & Extein, 1981) reported 20 out of 250 patients with evidence of the same abnormalities. A further study by M. S. Gold, Pottash, and Extein (1982) indicated that 60% of psychiatric patients found to be "biochemically hypothyroid" had positive thyroid microsomal antibodies, with titers > 1:10, suggesting that these patients suffered from autoimmune thyroiditis. The majority of these investigators' "hypothyroid" patients were designated so on the basis of an exaggerated response of thyroid-stimulating hormone (TSH) to thyrotropin-releasing hormone (TRH) administration. However, in the absence of symptoms and traditional biochemical indices of hypothyroidism, one can argue against such a diagnosis (see later). Nevertheless, the presence of some unequivocally hypothyroid patients highlights the fact that a number of patients presenting to psychiatrists with depressive symptomatology in fact may be suffering from an organic affective disorder. Thus, in certain cases, it may be difficult to distinguish a depressed patient with a neuroendocrine disturbance from a patient with the psychiatric manifestations of a mild neuroendocrine disease (Reus, 1984).

The validity of such conjectures must await further studies which examine the "boundary" problem, that is, the difficulty in separating patients with mild disorder from the normal population. There is much controversy regarding this problem, both in endocrinology and psychiatry. Thus, the definition of subclinical hypothyroidism proposed by Wenzel, Meinhold, Raffenberg, Adlkofer, and Schleusener (1974), which is based on an exaggerated TSH response to TRH in the absence of other thyroid function abnormalities and which has been used extensively by M. S. Gold, Pottash, and Extein (1981) has not been established, on the basis of prospective studies, to be a valid criterion for thyroid hypofunction. For example, Kutty, Bryant, and Farid (1978) reported that patients with such a biochemical profile,

unlike patients with the more generally accepted biochemical indices of hypothyroidism, are normocholesterolemic.

A number of investigators (Cho, Bone, Dunner, Colt, & Fieve, 1979; Cowdry, Wehr, Zis, & Goodwin, 1983; O'Shanick & Ellinwood, 1982) have presented evidence for a differential effect of lithium on the thyroid function of rapidly cycling versus nonrapidly cycling patients with bipolar affective disorder. The studies demonstrated that the prevalence of clinical hypothyroidism and elevated TSH levels was significantly higher in the rapidly cycling patients. Cho et al. (1979) reported that the prevalence of hypothyroidism increased from 0 to 31% in 16 rapidly cycling women after treatment with lithium, whereas the comparable change in 99 nonrapidly cycling women was from 4% to 6%. In the study by Cowdry et al. (1983), 51% of rapidly cycling patients on lithium were found to be hypothyroid, in contrast to no hypothyroidism in the nonrapidly cycling patients who were also taking lithium. Of the rapidly cycling group, 92% demonstrated elevated serum TSH concentrations in comparison to 32% of the nonrapidly cycling group. These findings are analogous to reports which describe patients who develop abnormalities of glucose tolerance following the administration of glucocorticoids. The long-term tendency for such patients to become spontaneously diabetic is unknown (Porte & Halter, 1981). Similarly, no evidence is yet at hand to suggest that patients with affective disorder in whom lithium-induced hypothyroidism occurs would have a higher incidence of spontaneous hypothyroidism than the general population. Nevertheless, if "latent" or covert hypothyroidism is associated with rapid cycling, such findings could be related to animal studies (Richter, 1965) and clinical studies (Herz, 1964) which demonstrated that partial thyroidectomy induced cyclic changes in locomotor activity and affect. If changes in the HPT axis contribute to the phenomenon of rapid cycling, then this might account for the efficacy of thyroid hormone treatment for patients with periodic catatonia (Gjessing, 1976) and rapidly cycling manic–depressive illness (Stancer & Persad, 1982).

As already mentioned, elevations in thyroid function test values also have been noted in depressed patients. There is less convincing evidence that such changes, when present, have anything to do with the pathogenesis of the affective state. Rather, it appears that such changes are epiphenomena related to the acute phase of the illness. The changes appear to be very similar to those found in hyperthyroxinemic patients with nonthyroidal medical illnesses—the so-called euthyroid sick syndrome. Spratt *et al.* (1982), based on thyroid function tests in the first 24 hours postadmission, found that 34% of a population of 119 patients with unipolar and bipolar depression had serum T4 concentrations greater than the upper limit for their normal reference range (10.9 μg/dl). Of the depressed patients, 21% had an increased FTI. In the total population of 645 psychiatric patients, 33% had elevated serum thyroxine and 18% had an elevated FTI. A similar study was performed by K. L. Cohen and Swigar (1979) on 480 newly admitted psychiatric patients. Specific diagnoses were not listed in this study. Increases in thyroid indices were noted, but these occurred less frequently than in the study by Spratt *et al.* (1982). In Cohen and Swigar's patients, T4 was increased above the normal range in 13%, and in 9% the FTI was greater than normal. In both studies, follow-up was associated with substantial decreases in thyroid function test values. In Cohen and Swigar's study, 27 out of the 31 patients who had shown abnormally high estimated free thyroxine levels on admission reverted to normal spontaneously, usually within a 2-week period. Similar normalizations occurred in the patients in the study by Spratt *et al.*; of 9 patients with depression and elevated T4, 8 showed normal T4 values on follow-up, mean serum T4 having dropped from 13.9 to 9.0 μg/dl.

The mechanism for such transient changes in thyroid function tests has not been fully ascertained. In the hyperthyroxinemia of the euthyroid sick syndrome, the changes have been attributed either to changes in T4 binding globulin (TBG) and prealbumin (Lutz, Gregerman, Spaulding, Hornick, & Dawkins, 1972) or to decreased conversion of T4 to triiodothyronine (T3) (Braverman & Vagenakis, 1979). The latter interpretation is supported by reports of decreased T3 and elevated metabolically inactive reverse T3 in

such patients. In the psychiatric population studied by K. L. Cohen and Swigar (1979), increases in the estimated free T4 level in 48% of the cases were due solely to decreased protein binding capacity. Decreased conversion of T4 to T3 may have contributed to the hyperthyroxinemia noted in other patients. This explanation gains some support from the findings of Spratt *et al.* (1982), who showed that less than 10% of patients with an increased FTI had an increased T3 concentration. However, no reverse T3 measurements on larger groups of hyperthyroxinemic psychiatric patients have been performed (Caplan, Pagliara, Wickus, & Goodlund, 1983).

Two considerations arise from these findings. First, thyroid function test results in newly admitted psychiatric patients, including those with depression, should be interpreted cautiously in view of the relatively common ocurrence of transiently abnormal test results in such patients. Second, transient hyperthyroxinemia may be important insofar as it contributes to a blunted TSH response to TRH (Ingbar & Woeber, 1981). However, some studies cast doubt on this as an important mechanism in psychiatric patients; for example, Takahashi, Kondo, Yoshimura, and Ochi (1974) found low basal thyroid function test values in those patients demonstrating a blunted TSH response to TRH.

Findings relevant to baseline functioning of the hypothalamic and pituitary components of the HPT axis are less common than those related to the thyroid. Kirkegaard, Faber, Hummer, and Rogowski (1979) reported that cerebrospinal fluid (CSF) TRH may be elevated in depression. If this finding is confirmed, it would suggest a mechanism (down-regulation of TRH receptors on pituitary thyrotrophs) which could account for blunting of the TSH response to TRH. However, the failure of CSF TRH levels to decline in treated patients after both clinical improvement and normalization of the TSH response to TRH argues against this explanation.

Two groups have studied the circadian patterns of TSH secretion in depressed patients. Both groups (Goldstein, Van Cauter, Linkowski, Vanhaelst, & Mendlewicz, 1980; Weeke & Weeke, 1978, 1980) demonstrated a reduction or absence of the normal nocturnal increase in serum TSH. The earlier study of Weeke and Weeke (1978) showed a correlation between the magnitude of the TSH blunting and the severity of the depression. Their later study (1980) suggested that the blunting was the result of a specific effect on nocturnal TSH secretion rather than being due to a phase shift of the TSH circadian rhythm. Goldstein *et al.* (1980) reported that the absence of a nocturnal rise in TSH was restricted to patients with unipolar depression.

In summary, apart from transient changes in thyroid activity in acutely disturbed psychiatric patients or findings which only equivocally indicate thyroid dysfunction (elevated baseline TSH), the vast majority of patients with depression have normal thyroid function (Grégoire, Brauman, de Buck, & Corvilain, 1977; Hatotani, Nomura, Yamaguchi, & Kitayama, 1977; Leichter, Kirstein, & Martin, 1977).

Hypothalamic–Pituitary–Gonadal (HPG) Axis

A number of findings suggest that abnormalities of the HPG axis may occur in some depressed patients. Differences in the function of this axis between the sexes have been nominated (Prange, Wilson, Bresse, & Lipton, 1976) as a factor which contributes to the almost universal finding of a higher prevalence of depressive disorder in women than in men (Silverman, 1968).

Impaired libido is often present in depression. Gonadal steroids have major effects on brain morphology and function and on sexual differentiation and behavior (W. A. Brown, 1980; Gorski, 1979; Rubin, Reinisch, & Haskett, 1981; Schiavi & White, 1976; vom Saal, 1979). In view of these effects, it is reasonable to hypothesize that reduced HPG activity might contribute to decreased sexual function in some depressed individuals.

Changes due to HPG dysfunction may not be limited to sexual symptoms in view of the wide range of effects of gonadal steroids on nonsexual behaviors (Kuhn & Schanberg, 1984) and neurochemistry. For example, estrogens affect two neurotransmitter systems which have been implicated in the etilogy of depression. There is indirect evidence that es-

trogens decrease the availability to the brain of tryptophan, the precursor to serotonin (Adams *et al.*, 1973; Green & Curzon, 1970; Greengard, 1971), a neurotransmitter which has been implicated in depression (van Praag, 1981; Wynn, Adams, Folkard, & Seed, 1975). Monoamine oxidase activity also is influenced by estrogens (Baron, Levitt, & Perlman, 1980; Klaiber, Broverman, Vogel, & Kobayashi, 1979; Luine & McEwen, 1977).

There is a dearth of studies which have systematically examined the HPG axis in depression. This deficiency is heightened by the fact that only one or two of the extant studies have examined more than one level within the HPG axis.

Studies on the secretory patterns of the gonadotropins, luteinizing hormone (LH) and follicle-stimulating hormone (FSH), have included only small numbers of patients and have reached inconsistent conclusions. Plasma LH was measured serially every 15 minutes for 4 hours by Benkert (1975) in 12 males with affective disorder. Abnormal LH concentrations were found in only 1 of the 7 patients with unipolar depression. In this patient and in 1 of the 5 bipolar manic patients, abnormally high spiking levels of LH were noted. In both patients, LH levels returned to normal after recovery from the affective illness. This study contained a paucity of clinical data and no demographic or treatment data. Ettigi, Brown, and Seggie (1979), in substantial agreement with Benkert, found that the mean baseline plasma LH level in depressed patients (5 men with primary depression and 4 with secondary depression) was not statistically different from 6 normal, age-matched male control subjects. Amsterdam, Winokur, Caroff, and Snyder (1981) also found no mean differences in either basal LH or FSH levels (based on single blood samples) among 12 unipolar and 11 bipolar depressed men and 18 male control subjects, as well as no mean LH or FSH differences among 19 unipolar and 7 bipolar premenopausal depressed women and 19 premenopausal controls.

In contrast, other studies suggest that LH secretion may be impaired in some depressed men and women. Altman, Sachar, Gruen, Halpern, and Eto (1975) measured morning plasma LH concentrations every 15 minutes over a 2-hour period in postmenopausal women with depression and in normal age-matched postmenopausal controls. In the former group, the mean plasma LH concentration was approximately 30% less than that of the matched control group, a statistically significant difference. In agreement with Altman *et al.* and in contrast to their findings in premenopausal depressives (Amsterdam *et al.*, 1981), Amsterdam, Winokur, Lucki, and Snyder (1983) reported a mean basal LH concentration for postmenopausal depressed women about one-third lower than that for normal postmenopausal controls (both means based on single blood samples from the subjects). A preliminary study by Rubin, Poland *et al.* (1981) demonstrated, by means of one-half hourly plasma sampling during the day (0730–1500 hours) and during sleep (2300–0700 hours), that there was a 15–30% reduction in both LH and FSH in 9 primary endogenously depressed men in comparison to 6 age- and race-matched normal male control subjects. Because of the small sample size, this difference was statistically nonsignificant. Therefore, there is tentative evidence that mild to moderate impairments of gonadotropin secretion may occur in depression. Such suggestions need to be studied further with larger numbers of patients and also a sampling framework which takes into account the prominent and random secretory bursts of LH and FSH (Goldzieher, Dozier, Smith, & Steinberger, 1976; Santen & Bardin, 1973).

A few studies have addressed the question of the pituitary gonadotrophic response to GnRH administration in depressed patients. Ettigi *et al.* (1979) and Rubin, Poland *et al.* (1981) studied male subjects and used the same dose of GnRH (100 μg). Both studies suggested that the LH response to GnRH is normal in patients with primary depressive illness. Rubin, Poland, *et al.* demonstrated that the FSH response to GnRH was reduced by approximately half in depressed patients compared to controls; FSH was not measured by Ettigi *et al.* These latter researchers demonstrated that the LH response to GnRH was approximately doubled in patients with depression secondary to other psychiatric conditions; such patients were not studied by Rubin, Poland *et al.* In contrast to these studies, Amsterdam *et al.* (1981, 1983)

reported LH and FSH responses to GnRH in their depressed men and pre- and postmenopausal depressed women that were not significantly different from the responses in their control subjects.

Reports of gonadal steroid concentrations in depressed patients are comparably sparse, and the findings from such reports should be considered tentative. Three studies have dealt with the concentration of testosterone in depressed patients. Sachar, Halpern, Rosenfeld, and Hellman (1973) reported on single time point, morning plasma testosterone concentrations in 15 severely depressed men during illness and shortly after recovery. A control group was not used in this study, but the values both during the dpressive phase and after recovery were within normal limits for the investigators' laboratory. In contrast, Vogel, Klaiber, and Broverman (1978) found that both total and free mean plasma testosterone concentrations (based on single samples) were approximately 30% lower in 27 men with primary unipolar depression compared to 13 age-matched control men.

The direction of change in plasma testosterone was similar in the previously mentioned study of Rubin, Poland *et al.* (1981). In addition to measurement of gonadotropins, diurnal and nocturnal changes in plasma testosterone were measured over a $15\frac{1}{2}$-hour period, in contrast to the single time-point sampling used by Vogel *et al.* and Sachar *et al.* In the study by Rubin, Poland *et al.*, the mean plasma testosterone concentration was 20% lower in the male patients than in the male controls; again, this was not statistically significant. The small sample size highlights the preliminary nature of these data and indicates the need for larger replication studies.

Only one study, by Vogel *et al.* (1978), examined mean plasma testosterone concentrations in female depressed patients. The weekly mean plasma testosterone value was 90–100% higher in 22 primary, unipolar, premenopausal depressives compared to 10 normal, aged-matched, premenopausal controls. Decreased testosterone binding to plasma protein also was noted in the depressed women, which contributed to the fact that the patients had a mean free testosterone concentration approximately 300% higher than that of the control subjects.

Plasma estradiol has been reported to be significantly increased in both male and female depressives. In their study on men, Vogel *et al.* (1978) showed that 15 depressives had a mean plasma estradiol level 50% higher than that in 12 control subjects. Vogel *et al.* also reported that the weekly mean plasma estradiol concentration in 22 premenopausal depressives was 60–80% of that found in 10 normal age-matched premenopausal controls. All subjects were studied across one full menstrual cycle.

In summary, the few published studies suggest that there may be reduced circulating levels of gonadotropins and testosterone in depressed men. Depressed women also may have decreased circulating gonadotropins, but in contrast to men, they may have increased gonadal steroid levels. These findings are not robust and are in need of replication. Even if subsequent studies confirm that HPG abnormalities exist in depression, it is not clear how such changes relate to the primary symptoms of the disorder in view of the fact that treatment of depression with gonadal steroids has not been a notably successful undertaking (Prange *et al.*, 1976).

Melatonin

The first studies on plasma melatonin in depression appeared 20 years after Lerner, Case, and Heinzelman (1959) first isolated the substance from the bovine pineal gland. The delay in studying the hormone was occasioned by technical problems with early assay systems. Only since the mid-1970s have reliable and sensitive assays been available (Arendt, Paunier, & Sizonenko, 1975; Arendt, Wetterberg, Heyden, Sizonenko, & Paunier, 1977; Rollag & Niswender, 1976).

There are three reasons why the examination of melatonin secretory rhythms is of interest to researchers studying depressive illness. First, melatonin has a prominent circadian rhythm which may be affected by many of the chronobiological abnormalities seen in depression (see Chapter 9, this volume). Melatonin concentrations are low during the day, but rise 10- to 50-fold during the night (Arendt *et al.*, 1975; Pelham, Vaughan, Sandock, & Vaughan, 1973). Second, there is evidence, especially in experimental animals,

that melatonin secretion is controlled by β-adrenergic activity (Hansen, Heyden, & Sundberg, 1977; G. M. Vaughan *et al.*, 1979); thus, melatonin secretion may be useful in testing noradrenergic deficit theories of depression. Finally, melatonin appears to have an important inhibitory influence on both the pituitary gland and the adrenal cortex. Pinealectomy results in increased enzyme activity in the rat pituitary gland (Urry & Ellis, 1975) and leads to melatonin-reversible adrenal hypertrophy (M. K. Vaughan, Reiter, & Benson, 1972). It therefore is possible that abnormalities of melatonin secretion may contribute to the frequency reported HPA dysfunction in depression.

The earliest study on melatonin secretory patterns in depression examined urinary melatonin in 6 patients with severe primary depression and 8 healthy control subjects (Jimerson, Lynch, Post, Wurtman, & Bunney, 1977). No significant differences in the urinary secretion of melatonin were noted, either under basal conditions or after sleep deprivation. This study involved bioassay and sampling every 8 hours. In contrast, plasma studies using frequent sampling and sensitive radioimmunoassays have suggested that significant abnormalities of nocturnal melatonin secretion are present in depressed subjects. Mendlewicz, Branchey *et al.* (1980) and Branchey, Weinberg, Branchey, Linkowski, and Mendlewicz (1982) reported that normal nocturnal melatonin increases were absent in 3 out of 4 depressed women. In a larger study involving control subjects, the mean nocturnal melatonin concentration in depressed patients ($n = 11$) was less than half that in control subjects (32.7 pg/ml versus 73.8 pg/ml) ($p < .01$) (Claustrat, Chazot, Brun, Jordan, & Sassolas, 1984). Although of considerable interest, these findings still must be considered preliminary in view of the study designs: The investigations of Mendlewicz *et al.* and Branchey *et al.* did not contain control subjects, and the subjects used as controls in the study by Claustrat *et al.* were not age and sex matched.

The changes in melatonin secretion, if confirmed, might reflect altered neurotransmitter function of either the serotonergic or the noradrenergic systems. Systemic tryptophan (Preslock, 1984), and perhaps serotonin (Ducis & Distefano, 1980), may act as precursors to melatonin. It thus is possible that a deficiency of tryptophan may lead to both decreased melatonin production and decreased brain serotonin. Low melatonin secretion also may reflect decreased β-adrenergic input to the pineal. Such hypotheses need to be made cautiously, because in man only those studies using β-antagonists are congruent with the animal studies which clearly suggest a functional role for the β-adrenoreceptors on pinealocytes; β-adrenergic agonists do not increase melatonin secretion in humans (D. C. Moore, Paunier, & Sizonenko, 1979).

Changes in melatonin secretion also may be secondary to changes in sleep patterns and other body rhythms. However, this hypothesis is difficult to reconcile with other studies which have investigated the relationship between melatonin secretion and both physical and sleep physiology parameters. Because depressed patients spend less time asleep (von Zerssen, 1983), it might be expected that they may be exposed to more melatonin-suppressing light. But, although low-intensity light has an inhibitory effect on the synthesis of melatonin in experimental animals (Klein, Buda, Kapoor, & Krishna, 1978; Taylor & Wilson, 1970; Wurtmann, Axelrod, & Phillips, 1963), only light intensities approximately five times those used in home or industrial situations can suppress the nocturnal secretion of melatonin in normal human subjects (Åkerstedt, Froberg, Friberg, & Wetterberg, 1979; Jimerson et al., 1977; Lewy, Wehr, Goodwin, Newsome, & Markey, 1980). Furthermore, in one study, normal spontaneous waking episodes during the night were shown to be associated with melatonin secretory episodes (Birkeland, 1982). Thus, on this basis, the increased intermittent and terminal wakening seen in depression (Wehr et al., 1983) might be expected to be associated with higher melatonin concentrations.

Several investigators have explored the relationship between melatonin secretion and the HPA axis. Wetterberg et al. (1981) measured serum cortisol and melatonin concentrations in 12 patients with major depression before and after a dexamethasone suppression test. They noted an inverse relationship between the degree of cortisol escape from dexamethasone suppression and the nocturnal concentration of serum melatonin. These findings were confirmed in subsequent studies of 32 patients with acute depression (Wetterberg, 1983). Adding weight to previous evidence that low nocturnal melatonin may be a trait marker for depression is the fact that 26 of the 32 depressed patients, when studied in remission, did not have a higher mean nocturnal melatonin concentration than during their illness episode. In addition, subjects with a greater family history of depressive illness had a lower mean nocturnal melatonin concentration (Wetterberg, Beck-Friis, Kjellman, & Ljunggren, 1984). In another report from these investigators (Beck-Friis et al., 1985), the relationship between lower melatonin concentrations and abnormal dexamethasone suppression tests in depressed patients was confirmed, but it should be noted that those depressed patients with normal cortisol suppression in response to 1 mg of dexamethasone ($n = 15$) had cortisol secretory rhythms which were almost identical to those of age- and sex-matched control subjects. This suggests that low nocturnal melatonin secretion may be associated more with HPA dysfunction than with affective disorder specifically. Adding weight to this suggested lack of diagnostic specificity, Ferrier, Johnstone, and Crow (1982) demonstrated a low melatonin/cortisol ratio in chronic schizophrenic patients compared to controls. This ratio had been suggested by Wetterberg, Beck-Friis, Aperia, and Petterson (1979) as a possible marker of affective disorder; Wetterberg et al. (1981) suggested that the pineal might secrete a corticotropin releasing factor (CRF)-inhibiting factor. They postulated that low melatonin secretion might be a marker for reduced CRF-inhibiting factor production, which thus might account for the HPA disinhibition seen in some depressives. This hypothesis does not account for the fact that in many studies, cortisol nonsuppression following dexamethasone is a transient, state-dependent phenomenon, whereas low melatonin secretion appears not to be.

Prolactin

Three sets of findings predict that prolactin secretion may be altered in depression. First, prolactin has a sleep-dependent rhythm, with blood levels beginning to increase shortly after sleep onset and reaching maximum values in the last hour or two of sleep (Rubin & Poland, 1982); thus, the circadian rhythm of prolactin may be expected to be abnormal in view of the sleep disturbance commonly seen in this disorder (Kupfer, 1977). Second, depression is a distressing disorder, often associated with considerable anxiety (A. J. Lewis, 1966); increased plasma prolactin therefore might be found in patients with this condition in view of the stress responsiveness of this hormone (Rose, 1980). Third, drug and somatic treatments which either cause or alleviate depressive symptomatology can markedly affect plasma prolactin concentrations. Tricyclic antidepressants and, more consistently, electroconvulsive therapy, have been shown to increase plasma prolactin (O'Dea, Gould, Hallberg, & Welland, 1978; Ohman, Wallinder, Balldin, Wallin, & Abrahamson, 1976; Turkington, 1972). However, the newer nontricyclic antidepressant nomifensin, a drug which inhibits both dopamine and norepinephrine reuptake, lowers plasma prolactin levels (Genazzani et al., 1980). In addition, two antihypertensive agents which induce depression quite commonly, reserpine and α-methyl-dopa, cause pronounced elevation in plasma prolactin concentrations, similar to the tricyclic antidepressants (Turkington, 1972). These effects do not permit a simple hypothesis regarding prolactin secretion in unmedicated depressed patients.

At least eight studies have included data on basal plasma prolactin concentrations in depressed patients during the day (usually the morning). The lack of consistency in findings relates to variables such as patient selection and differences in sampling times. Some studies indicate little or no change in prolactin concentrations of depressed patients as a group (Ehrensing et al., 1974; Garfinkel, Brown, Warsh, & Stancer, 1979; P. W. Gold, Goodwin, Wehr, Rebar, & Sack, 1976; Gregoire et al., 1977; Nielsen, 1980). Other studies report increases in prolactin concentrations (Horrobin, Mtabaji, Karmali, Manku, & Nasar, 1976; Maeda et al., 1975; Sachar, Frantz, Altman, & Sassin, 1973). Still others report decreases (Asnis, Nathan, Halbreich, Halpern, & Sachar, 1980; Mendlewicz, Linkowski, & Brauman, 1980).

Few studies have examined circadian patterns of prolactin secretion in depressed patients. Halbreich, Grunhaus, and Ben-David (1979) measured half-hourly serum prolactin

concentrations in 7 patients with endogenous depression and 5 normal controls over a 24-hour period. They reported that the sleep-related release of prolactin was essentially normal. Preliminary data from R. T. Rubin, R. E. Poland, and I. M. Lesser (unpublished observations) suggest that nocturnal sleep-related prolactin secretion may be decreased in depressed patients compared to matched normal controls. Such a finding, if confirmed, might relate to disruption of sleep architecture rather than to primary abnormalities of prolactin release. Blunting of nocturnal prolactin release also has been noted in 8 patients with bipolar depression, but not in two groups of comparison patients: 10 patients with unipolar depression and 10 control subjects (Mendlewicz, van Cauter, Linkowski, L'Hermite, & Robyn, 1980). These investigators reported that the mean 24-hour prolactin concentration was highest in the unipolar depressives, intermediate in the control subjects, and lowest in the bipolar patients. In view of the fact that plasma prolactin concentrations tend to be lower in males than in females, the comparison between the patient groups, which were mostly women, and the normal controls, who were all men, must be questioned. However, the differences between bipolar and unipolar depressed patients stand, and they may be of eventual diagnostic significance.

Growth Hormone

In view of the disturbed sleep architecture of patients with depression and the close association between specific sleep phases and growth hormone secretion, it is surprising to find so little work on the circadian rhythm of growth hormone in depressed patients. Schilkrut et al. (1975) showed that in a group of 6 endogenously depressed patients, there was diminished nocturnal growth hormone release. In normal subjects, the greatest surge in growth hormone secretion occurs approximately 1 hour after the onset of sleep, usually coinciding with the onset of sleep Stages III and IV (slow wave sleep—SWS). Smaller secretory peaks may occur later during the night, and surges also occur during waking hours, usually 3–4 hours after meals (Frohman & Berelowitz, 1984). The patients in the study of Schilkrut et al. (1975) demonstrated a shortened total sleep period, prolonged sleep latency, increased wake time, and reduced amounts of both SWS and REM sleep. These findings are characteristic of depressed patients and suggest that the growth hormone abnormalities were secondary to disrupted sleep architecture rather than being primary abormalities. An earlier study, which made a similar observation about decreased sleep-related release of growth hormone (Sachar, Frantz et al., 1973), was, after a subsequent study using age-matched controls, considered to be related more to the age of the subjects than to their affective status (Carroll & Mendels, 1976).

Growth hormone peaks decrease in number and magnitude after adolescence (Finkelstein, Roffwarg, Boyar, Kream, & Hellman, 1972). In addition to age, other factors must be taken into account when examining the validity of changes in the circadian secretion of growth hormone. These include food intake (Fineberg, Horand, & Merimee, 1972; Knopf et al., 1965; Roth, Glick, Yalow, & Berson, 1963), exercise status (Buckler, 1972), and ovarian function (Frohman & Berelowitz, 1984). Studies examining growth hormone secretion thus need to be more rigorous than many other hormone studies. In the face of such demands, there still is a very good case for greater interest to be shown in growth hormone. Not only is growth hormone secretion linked to a nonhormonal biological event (SWS), but also, substantial knowledge has accumulated about the areas of the brain involved in growth hormone sercretion (G. M. Brown, Seggie, Chambers, & Ettigi, 1978). Such facts led an international study group (Checkley & Rush, 1983) to recommend that the study of growth hormone release during SWS might provide a more definitive "functional neuroanatomy" of depressive disorders.

Glucose Metabolism

In 1935, Menninger suggested that there might be an association between diabetes and emotional stress. In addition, a number of studies have suggested that there might be a specific relationship between affective disorder and disturbed glucose metabolism. In the absence of prospective stuides using well-defined criteria for both patient selection and the diagnosis of diabetes mellitus, such a conclusion must remain tentative. Van der Velde

and Gordon (1969) reported that 16 of 32 manic–depressive patients who were older than 40 had abnormal oral glucose tolerance tests. This study included neither patient selection criteria nor a control group. The investigators suggested that this 50% prevalence of abnormal response was significantly greater than the predicted prevalence of diabetes in this age group, even accounting for underestimation of the latter in large-scale population surveys. However, the appropriate comparison was not the prevalence of diabetes in the community, but the prevalence of an abnormal response to oral glucose loading as defined by the investigators. A later study by Lilliker (1980), based on a retrospective analysis of hospital records, found a 10% prevalence of diabetes mellitus in an inpatient population of 203 manic–depressives. This was five times the prevalence expected from a normative nationwide survey. In an effort to determine whether these findings were specific to affective disorder, an analysis of the prevalence of diabetic diets in different diagnostic groups was carried out. This revealed that the prevalence of diabetes, using this unorthodox criterion, was several times higher in the manic–depressive patients than in patients from six other diagnostic groups. These findings are interesting, but the strength of the conclusions depends upon the validity of the illness criteria and of the diabetes prevalence estimates of the National Health Survey for 1960–1962, which were used as the basis for the nomative data.

Several case reports have indicated that a striking improvement in glucose tolerance may occur in depressed, diabetic patients after electroconvulsive therapy (ECT) (Crammer & Gillies, 1981; Fakhri, Fadhli, & El Rawi, 1980; Thomas, Goldney, & Phillips, 1983). Although these findings are provocative, they do not rule out the possibility that the higher insulin dosages required at the outset of treatment were due to metabolic derangements resulting from diabetes treatment nonadherence due to the depressive illness, and that the improvements reported after ECT were no greater than might be expected as the result of adequate medical management. Alternatively, the normalization might have been due to a decrease in the rate of secretion of hormones which counteract the effects of insulin, such as cortisol, growth hormone, and epinephrine (Kronfol,

Greden, & Carroll, 1981). Such hypotheses, of course, remain speculative.

MANIA

Introduction

The neuroendocrine investigation of manic states has received much less attention than similar investigations of patients with depressive disorders. The relative rarity of manic patients must contribute to this circumstance. Leonhard (1959) first suggested that patients with affective disorder should be divided into unipolar and bipolar categories, depending upon the occurrence of mania. The proportion of bipolar to unipolar patients is approximately 20% (Bratfos & Haug, 1968; Perris, 1966), and the proportion of manic episodes to all affective episodes ranges from 8% to 17% (Parker & Neilson, 1976; Winokur, Clayton, & Reich, 1969). It is likely that the paucity of studies also stems from the fact that it is difficult to maintain manic patients in a drug-free state while metabolic studies are being undertaken. An additional problem, a nosological one, arises in relation to patients manifesting manic symptoms. It is likely that a number of patients reported in the psychoendocrine literature as schizophrenic, especially those in earlier reports from the United States, were in fact manic. This occurred because many investigators of the Bleulerian tradition gave pathognomonic significance to certain psychotic symptoms, whether or not they occurred in the setting of prominent affective change (Bleuler, 1950). For example, it has been noted that if the presence of Schneiderian first-rank symptoms is considered sufficient for the diagnosis of schizophrenia, then a substantial number of manic patients will be misclassified (Brockington, Wainwright, & Kendell, 1980; W. T. Carpenter, Strauss, & Muleh, 1973).

An overview of the literature on the neuroendocrinology of mania suggests that the hormonal effects of the antimanic agent lithium acted as a stimulus for some studies, and that there is a relatively greater interest in the physiology of electrolytes, including their hormonal control, in this condition in comparison to depression.

Hypothalamic–Pituitary–Adrenal, Thyroid, and Gonadal Axes; Prolactin and Growth Hormone

Most studies which have used frequent blood sampling have demonstrated that there is a significant increase in cortisol secretion in mania. High cortisol concentrations at midnight have been reported in manic patients by Platman and Fieve (1968) and W. C. Carpenter and Bunney (1971), a time when cortisol concentration should be suppressed. Platman and Fieve's patients' mean midnight plasma cortisol concentration dropped to near normal levels once the patients had made a clinical recovery. A study by Akesode, Hendler, and Kowarski (1976) is worthy of comment, even though only 3 patients were included. These investigators used a portable, constant blood-withdrawal system to study the 24-hour fluctuations in cortisol secretion. Their 3 manic patients had a high 24-hour mean plasma cortisol concentration and failed to demonstrate normal circadian rhythmicity in cortisol secretion.

A number of findings implicate possible thyroid dysfunction in manic states. Syndromes similar to and either indistinguishable (Villani & Weitzel, 1979) or distinguishable (Krauthammer & Klerman, 1979) from mania on psychopathological grounds have been reported to occur secondary to thyrotoxicosis. It has been claimed that the antimanic effect of lithium may be related to its ability to interfere with thyroid function (Temple, Berman, Carlson, Robbins, & Wolff, 1972; Whybrow, 1972). An etiological hypothesis arising from such propositions and findings might involve hyperfunction of the hypothalamic–pituitary–thyroid axis in mania, but this has not been found to be the case. Basal TSH concentrations (Kirkegaard, Bjørum, Cohn, & Lauridsen, 1978; Takahashi, Kondo, Yoshimura, & Ochi, 1975) and FTI values (Kirkegaard et al., 1978; Rinieris et al., 1978a) have been reported as normal in manic patients. The only abnormality reported in this axis in mania has been that of lowered T3 and free T3 index (Kirkegaard et al., 1978); these changes were attributed to a change in the balance of monodeiodination of T4 in favor of reverse T3 rather than T3. However, the findings of Kirkegaard et al. were not confirmed by Bech, Kirkegaard, Bock, Johanesson, and Rafaelson (1978).

Few studies have been performed on patterns of gonadotropin secretion in mania. Benkert (1975) reported abnormally high, spiking plasma LH concentrations in 1 of 5 manic patients. Whalley et al. (1985) studied 7 manic, 3 schizoaffective manic, 13 schizophrenic, and 13 control subjects, all drug-free young men, by multiple blood sampling. Compared to the schizophrenic and control men, the manic and schizoaffective manic subjects as a group had a significantly higher mean plasma LH concentration than the schizophrenics and control subjects, but mean FSH and testosterone concentrations were similar for the three groups. This finding of an isolated increase in LH, but not in FSH or testosterone, in manic men needs to be replicated, and its physiological significance remains to be determined.

Although the plasma concentrations of prolactin in unmedicated patients with mania fall within the normal range, Cookson, Silverstone, and Rees (1982) reported that the clinical response of manic patients to antipsychotic medication follows a course which more closely reflects the prolactin response to such drugs than is seen in schizophrenic patients treated with similar drugs. For example, Cotes, Crow, Johnstone, Bartlett, and Bourne (1978), studying acute schizophrenic patients, reported a delay of at least 2 weeks between increases in prolactin concentration and drug-related clinical improvements after treatment with flupenthixol. A similar dissociation between prolactin concentrations and clinical improvement in schizophrenics was noted by Mielke, Gallant, and Kessler (1977) and Kolakowska et al. (1979). In the studies by Cookson et al. and Cotes et al., the prolactin response to antipsychotic medication in both manics and schizophrenics was brisk; the main difference was in the slower rate of clinical response to antipsychotic medication in the schizophrenics. It is not clear whether this difference reflected a prompt but nonspecific tranquilizing effect in manic patients versus a slower but more specific effect on psychotic symptomatology in the schizophrenic patients (Shopsin & Gershon, 1975).

Two reports on growth hormone secretion in mania suggest that abnormalities of this hormone are not a feature of the disorder (Cookson et al., 1982; Janowsky, Judd, Huey, Rottman, & Parker, 1979).

Salt and Aldosterone

A steady stream of research into sodium metabolism in mania occurred as the result of the report of Coppen, Shaw, Malleson, and Costain (1966) which presented the finding that in mania, "residual sodium," a measure of intracellular sodium, was substantially increased. Because this study has had a considerable influence on subsequent research, it is important to consider in some detail the methodology used by Coppen et al., an isotope dilution technique, to estimate residual sodium. The method involves administration of a sodium radioisotope, for example, $^{24}Na^+$, followed by an estimate of radioisotope excretion over 24 hours, as well as determinations of the serum concentrations of both labeled and unlabeled sodium. In addition, an estimate of extracellular fluid volume is required. The need for caution when considering residual sodium as an indication of intracellular sodium is well summarized by Durell, Baer, and Green (1971), including the fact that residual sodium calculations are influenced by the portion of bone sodium which equilibrates with the isotope and the fact that extracellular fluid volume is difficult to compute reliably (Gamble, Robertson, Hannigan, Foster, & Farr, 1953). In the study by Coppen et al. (1966), 13 patients were investigated during a manic episode. The mean values of residual sodium averaged more than 420 mEq greater than would be predicted for each patient on the basis of total body weight.

To put this result in context, the total intracellular sodium content in normal man is 100–150 mEq (Levinksy, 1980), and the increase in residual sodium in manic patients was approximately twice as great as that seen in a previously reported depressed population (Coppen & Shaw, 1963). After recovery, residual sodium values returned to values which were close to predicted. In the manic phase, 4 of the patients had very high values. These findings led Durell et al. (1971) to consider the possibility of a systematic error in residual sodium estimation, because the strikingly high values were found in this cluster of

4 patients who were apparently studied sequentially. Finally, all patients studied were on medication, including antipsychotic agents; the influence of such medication on the findings is not clear. A subsequent study by Baer *et al.* (1970), which included findings from 4 manic patients prior to lithium treatment, showed that residual sodium, corrected for total body weight, was similar in manic and depressed patients.

Changes in Na^+, K^+-ATPase have been suggested as an explanation for the possible increases in intracellular sodium in mania and depression. Na^+, K^+-ATPase is the membrane system responsible for pumping sodium out of cells—the "sodium pump." Reduced activity of this enzyme might lead to reduced sodium efflux and increased intracellular sodium. Studies on erythrocyte membrane preparations from patients both in the manic phase and after mood normalization suggest that Na^+, K^+-ATPase increases with the onset of euthymia (Naylor *et al.*, 1976, 1980). Furthermore, lithium produces an *in vivo* increase in erythrocyte Na^+, K^+-ATPase activity in manic–depressives, but not in normal subjects (Naylor, Dick, Dick, & Moody, 1974; Naylor *et al.*, 1977), and a high erythrocyte Na^+, K^+-ATPase activity in patients with affective disorder is associated with a good prognosis over the subsequent year (Glen, 1978; B. B. Johnstone, Naylor, Dick, Hopwood, & Dick, 1980). Other defects in the sodium pump in patients with manic illness are suggested by the finding that lymphocytes from recently recovered manic–depressive patients have a reduced *in vitro* ability to produce new sodium pump sites in response to increased cell sodium, in comparison to lymphocytes from age- and sex-matched controls (Naylor & Smith, 1981b). These erythrocyte studies suggested that Na^+, K^+-ATPase is altered in manic–depressive illness and that this alteration is unrelated to genomic influences, because it occurs in formed, nonnucleated cells. This led this group of researchers to investigate plasma factors which might influence Na^+, K^+-ATPase. Vanadium was a target for such research. It is an essential trace element, which in physiological concentrations (Allaway, Kubota, Losee, & Roth, 1968) is a powerful inhibitor of Na^+, K^+-ATPase (Cantley *et al.*, 1977; Wallick, Lane, &

Schwarts, 1979). Dick, Naylor, and Dick (1982) reported that plasma vanadium was present in significantly greater concentration in a small number of manic patients ($n = 6$) than in controls. Three patients were studied after recovery from the manic phase, and their plasma vanadium levels had not returned to control values. Naylor and Smith (1981a) also administered a vanadium-depleted diet and a vanadium chelator (ethylene–diaminetetraacetic acid, EDTA) to manic and depressed patients in a double-blind crossover study. Preliminary results indicated that the treatment was more effective than a control diet. Similarly, positive effects were found in a parallel double-blind study using high-dose ascorbic acid, a vitamin which is an effective treatment for vanadium poisoning. These studies were based on small numbers of subjects and brief treatments (5 and 2 days, respectively), so the results are very preliminary and in need of replication with greater patient numbers.

Studies on the role of sodium in manic–depressive disorder led to the investigation of aldosterone in such patients because it is the most potent hormonal regulator of electrolyte excretion. Aldosterone, like cortisol, is an adrenocortical hormone, but its concentration in blood is approximately 0.1% that of cortisol. Aldosterone increases sodium and chloride reabsorption from the renal tubule and increases the secretion of both hydrogen ion and potassium into the tubule. A number of studies suggest that aldosterone secretion is increased in mania. Hendler (1975) compared single-sample, morning plasma aldosterone concentrations in 7 untreated manic patients to those in 18 control subjects and 5 untreated schizoaffective patients studied in an "excited" phase. Aldosterone concentrations in the normal controls and the schizoaffective patients were similar, while aldosterone concentrations in the manic patients were significantly higher than those in both these groups. Treatment of the manic patients for 14 days with lithium carbonate resulted in both a significant decrease in plasma aldosterone concentrations and a marked clinical improvement. Monitoring for 24 hours of plasma aldosterone concentrations was performed in 3 manic patients (Akesode *et al.*, 1976); the mean integrated concentration of aldosterone was found to be higher than the range found in healthy subjects in an earlier study.

Comparisons of aldosterone in the manic and depressive phases of affective disorder have not provided convincing evidence that changes in aldosterone are specific to the manic phase. Jenner *et al.* (1967) reported that urinary aldosterone secretion was greater during the depressive phase of rapidly cycling manic–depressive patients. On the other hand, Murphy, Goodwin, and Bunney (1969) reported higher urinary aldosterone secretion in untreated manics than in untreated depressives. This difference lost significance, however, when corrected for body weight. Allsopp, Levell, Stitch, and Hullin (1972) demonstrated in 2 patients that aldosterone production rates decreased during the transition from mania to depression at a time when urinary sodium excretion exceeded dietary intake. In view of the fact that aldosterone usually increases in response to a decrease in total body sodium, the investigators suggested that manic–depressive disorder was associated with a disturbance in the regulatory mechanism for aldosterone production. A subsequent study by Hullin, Jerram, Lee, Levell, and Tyrer (1977) purported to show that one such abnormality was the presence in manic–depressive patients of a high recumbent plasma renin activity in relation to aldosterone production levels. Such conclusions were based on a small number of patients and did not include appropriate statistical tests of significance. Both this study and the one by Allsopp *et al.* at least took into account factors which might lead to artifactual changes in renin and aldosterone, including salt intake and posture.

Spironolactone, an aldosterone antagonist, has been used as a prophylactic agent in manic–depressive illness, as a consequence of some of the findings reported above. When given to 6 manic–depressive patients, only 1 patient relapsed in a 12-month follow-up period (Hendler, 1978). It was suggested by Hendler that lithium and spironolactone might affect similar neurobiological systems and that spironolactone might be a suitable alternative prophylactic medication to lithium for patients with affective disorder, especailly those patients who suffer side effects from the latter drug.

Calcium

A number of early studies suggested that low calcium concentrations may play a role in mania. Perfusion of low calcium solutions into patients resulted in "maniacal attacks" (Weston & Howard, 1922). Later work in experimental animals suggested that lowering cerebrospinal fluid calcium concentrations produced behavioral arousal (Pappenheimer, Heisey, Jordan, & Downer, 1962), while increasing calcium concentrations had a sedative effect (Feldberg & Sherwood, 1957). In fact, no studies have demonstrated lower than normal serum or CSF calcium in manic patients compared to control subjects, although in patients with affective disorder CSF calcium levels have been reported significantly lower during the manic phase than during the depressed phase (Jimerson *et al.*, 1979).

Another set of findings indicates that there might be an alteration in calcium effects in the opposite direction (an increase) in mania. Lithium has similar properties to calcium-blocking agents (Dubovsky, Franks, Lifschitz, & Coen, 1982). Furthermore, and in contrast to the changes described in CSF calcium, a small but significant increase has been reported in plasma calcium concentration in patients who switch into a manic phase (Carman, Post, Runkle, Bunney, & Wyatt, 1979). A sedative effect in agitated patients has been claimed for the calcium-lowering peptide, calcitonin (Carman & Wyatt, 1979b). The calcium channel blocker, verapamil, also has been proposed as an effective drug in the treatment of mania (Dubovsky *et al.*, 1982). Conversely, the oral administration of dihydrotachysterol, a synthetic vitamin D analogue, was reported to be associated with increased agitation in 8 psychotic patients (Carman & Wyatt, 1979a).

There has been little work on the function of calcium transport across membranes in mania. Meltzer and Kassir (1983) reported that erythrocyte membranes taken from manic–depressive outpatients showed selective abnormalities of calmodulin-activated Ca^+-ATPase. Manic–depressive patients ($n = 27$) showed a greater increase in activity than controls when a lithium-containing medium was used in the assay. No differences in activity were noted when a lithium-free medium was used.

SCHIZOPHRENIA

Introduction

Recent studies on the endocrinology of schizophrenia must give little posthumous comfort to the many psychiatrists who warmly embraced endocrine theories of this disorder during the early part of the twentieth century. Discussion of postulated links between hormones and schizophrenia was raised by Kraepelin (1910). Early reviews summarize clinical and autopsy findings relevant to this question (e.g., McCartney, 1929), and there are anecdotal reports of the therapeutic efficacy of glandular extracts in the treatment of schizophrenia (Hoskins, 1929). In an era which lacked sensitive and reliable hormone assay technology, Reiss (1958) drew together the disparate findings then at hand about the endocrinology of schizophrenia and formulated many questions and research strategies, a number of which have been taken up by contemporary researchers. Much of this recent research has been kindled by an interest in investigating the dopamine excess theory of schizophrenia, at present the most compelling neurotransmitter hypothesis of the disorder (see discussion later).

In addition to such postulated neurotransmitter abnormalities, data converging from a number of disciplines suggest that structural changes occur in the brains of a number of schizophrenics, especially those suffering from the "defect" state (Henn & Nasrallah, 1982). Patchy, primarily diencephalic, periventricular, fibrillary gliosis has been described in chronic schizophrenics (Stevens, 1982), commonly in the hypothalamus. Furthermore, third ventricular dilation has been described in schizophrenia (Pandurangi et al., 1984). Such changes might be associated with functional hypothalamic disturbance, as reflected by alterations in pituitary hormone secretion.

The fact that no neuroendocrine markers for schizophrenia have been described (Meltzer, 1984) may be because hypothala-

mic–pituitary function indeed is normal in the disorder or because the results have been confounded by the presence of biological heterogeneity among the study populations. Key investigators (e.g., Bleuler, 1950; Kety, 1959) have suggested that schizophrenia is a group of disorders rather than a single disease entity. Thus, psychiatric investigators face a major challenge in the quest to define subgroups of patients who might be expected to share neurobiological commonalities, especially in view of the fact that the validity of traditional clinical categories of schizophrenia (e.g., paranoid, catatonic, hebephrenic, and simple subtypes) has been brought into question (W. T. Carpenter, Bartko, Carpenter, & Strauss, 1976). For neurobiologists, a more promising approach to the problem of categorization within schizophrenia may be the Type I/Type II scheme proposed by Crow (1980). The Type I syndrome, characterized by a relatively acute course, positive symptoms including hallucinations, delusions, and thought disorder, and a good response to neuroleptics, is in contrast to the Type II syndrome in which patients have negative symptoms such as flattening of affect, respond poorly to neuroleptics, and are more likely to show intellectual impairment and structural brain abnormalities on computerized axial tomographic (CT) scan. Validating studies of Crow's hypothesis will be of great importance.

Prolactin

Dopamine is the most important neurotransmitter involved in the control of prolactin release from the pituitary. Anterior pituitary cells possess specific, high-affinity dopamine binding sites (G. M. Brown, Seeman, & Lee, 1976; Caron et al., 1978). By occupying these receptors, dopamine inhibits prolactin release. This has been shown to occur in vivo (Besses, Burrow, Spaulding, & Donabedian, 1975), in vitro (MacLeod & Lehmeyer, 1974), and also after the infusion of dopamine into hypophysial portal blood vessels (Takahara, Arimura, & Schally, 1974). Ben-Jonathan, Oliver, Weiner, Mical, and Porter (1977) showed that dopamine is present in portal blood at concentrations high enough to inhibit prolactin release *in vivo* (Gibbs & Neill, 1978). This suggests that dopamine's effect on prolactin is physiological rather than pharmacological.

The inhibitory dopaminergic influence on prolactin secretion provided the rationale for a large number of studies on prolactin concentrations in medicated and unmedicated schizophrenic patients (Rubin & Hays, 1980). Such studies have been used to test the dopamine excess hypothesis of the disorder. Measurements of basal prolactin concentrations in schizophrenic subjects have failed to reveal any significant abnormality (Brambilla, Guastalla *et al.*, 1976; Ettigi, Nair, Lal, Cervantes, & Guyda, 1976; Gruen *et al.*, 1978; Langer, Sachar, & Gruen, 1978; Meltzer & Fang, 1976; Meltzer, Sachar, & Frantz, 1974; Rotrosen *et al.*, 1979; Rotrosen, Angrist, & Panguin, 1978). These studies are subject to the caution that, in many, the patients were not drug-free for an adequate period in view of the fact that the metabolites of antipsychotic agents (especially chlorpromazine) may be detected weeks (Sved, Perales, & Palaic, 1971) or even months (Caffey, Forrest, Frank, & Klett, 1963) after drug administration. Many studies, on the other hand, describe drug-free patients who only have been free of medication for a minimum of 1 or 2 weeks (Ettigi *et al.*, 1976; Kleinman *et al.*, 1982; Meltzer, 1984). Residual effects of antipsychotic agents theoretically could be responsible for the increased prolactin concentrations in these "basal" studies, thereby masking the low prolactin concentrations one would expect to find if schizophrenic-related dopaminergic overactivity were present. However, it is possible to overestimate the likely effect of residual antipsychotic drug influences on prolactin, since tolerance within the tuberoinfundibular dopamine system may occur in patients on antipsychotic medication. Davis, Vogel, Gibbons, Pavkovic, and Zhang (1984) review reported studies involving 291 patients on long-term antipsychotic medication; approximately 50% had prolactin concentrations within the normal range. Most importantly, there is no consistent evidence from studies on patients who have been

drug-free for a number of months that their prolactin concentrations are below the normal range.

A number of variables have been shown to affect basal prolactin concentration in schizophrenic patients. Meltzer *et al.* (1974) and Ferrier, Johnstone, and Crow (1984) reported that basal prolactin concentrations were lower in chronic schizophrenic patients compared to patients with acute schizophrenia. Ferrier *et al.* (1984) suggested that this may be an age-related effect, but the literature on age effects on prolactin does not provide strong support for this interpretation. For example, Yamaji, Shimamoto, Ishibashi, Kosaka, and Orimo (1976) did not demonstrate any significant effect of aging on prolactin, whereas Vekemans and Robyn (1975) reported that there was a significant age-related fall in prolactin in women, in contrast to a slight age-related increase in prolactin concentrations in men. In the study by Ferrier *et al.* (1984), there was a negative correlation between prolactin concentration and age in the total group, including control subjects. In addition, the chronic schizophrenic patients were older than the acute schizophrenics. However, it is not clear how much of the negative correlation in the total patient group was due to low prolactin concentrations in the older chronic schizophrenics, in which case it would be difficult to resolve the age versus disease process explanation for the prolactin differences.

Several investigators have suggested that in both acute and chronic schizophrenics an inverse relationship exists between positive symptoms (hallucinations, delusions, and formal thought disorder) and basal prolactin concentrations (Ferrier *et al.*, 1984; E. C. Johnstone, Crow, & Mashiter, 1977). Kleinman *et al.* (1982) also found an inverse relationship between plasma prolactin and positive symptomatology, but only an a subgroup of patients—those with normal cerebral ventricular size as determined by CT scans. This study by Kleinman *et al.* is important because it suggests that within the chronic schizophrenic population there may be at least two groups of patients: those with normal ventricular size in whom dopaminergic activity influences psychotic phenomenology, and those with large ventricular size in whom dopaminergic activity may be less salient. This proposition is in part supported by the findings of Weinberger *et al.* (1980), who showed that dopamine-blocking antipsychotic drugs had less effect on patients with cerebral ventricular enlargement. Such findings provide indirect support for Crow's (1980) Type I/Type II hypothesis.

The facts that most studies of basal prolactin have failed to support the dopamine excess theory of schizophrenia and that prolactin concentrations are normal in patients with Parkinson's disease (Hornykiewicz, 1984), a disorder in which well-defined brain dopamine deficits have been documented, have led to a thorough appraisal of the relationship between the dopamine system controlling prolactin secretion and other brain dopamine systems. Seven distinct dopamine systems have been characterized in the CNS (Lindvall, 1979), three of which are relevant to schizophrenia. The cell bodies of the tuberoinfundibular system are located in the arcuate nucleus, and their axons terminate in the median eminence of the hypothalamus. This system influences prolactin secretion. Neurons in the mesolimbic–cortical dopamine system are situated in the ventromedial tegmental area and project to limbic and cortical areas. This system is hypothesized to be the main dysfunctional system in schizophrenia. The third system, the nigrostriatal dopamine system, contains cell bodies in the substantia nigra which project to the putamen and caudate.

Dopamine involved in the control of prolactin secretion is released from the axons of tuberoinfundibular neurons into the hypophysial portal blood vessels. This bloodborne neurotransmission stands in contrast to the direct interneuronal communication in other dopamine systems. Given the anatomy of this system, it might be expected that dopamine feedback control and reuptake might be of less importance in the function of tuberoinfundibular system axons than in the function of axons of the other dopamine systems. In fact, tuberoinfundibular dopaminergic neurons appear to lack both dopamine autoreceptors and high-affinity reuptake mechanisms (K. E. Moore & Demarest, 1980; K. E Moore, Demarest, Johnston, & Alper, 1980), features which are present in a number of other dopamine systems in the brain (K. E. Moore & Wuerthelel, 1979). Instead, the feedback system on tuberoinfundibular neurons seems to be mediated by prolactin, but the cells respond only after some hours (K. E. Moore, Demarest, & Johnston, 1980). Dopamine receptors on the lactotrophs also have properties which seem to be different from those in other brain dopamine systems. Some studies suggest that the receptors on lactotrophs are not linked to adenylate cyclase (Kebabian & Calne, 1979) and are therefore similar to D_2 receptors. Other studies indicate that the receptors are linked to adenylate cyclase, but unlike D_1 receptors (which stimulate the enzyme), dopamine receptors on lactotrophs are reported to inhibit the enzyme (Giannattasio, Elisabetta de Ferrari, & Spada, 1981). These particular and distinguishing characteristics of both tuberoinfundibular dopamine neurons and dopamine receptors on anterior pituitary cells suggest that much caution is required when extrapolating findings from human studies on prolactin secretion to help elucidate the functioning of brain dopamine systems which are thought to be involved with emotion and perception. Brain dopamine systems are not identical to each other, and the tuberoinfundibular system possesses unique features, as previously noted. Bacopoulos, Spokes, Bird, and Roth (1979), based on homovanillic acid concentrations in postmortem brain areas of patients who had been on chronic neuroleptic treatment, showed that tolerance to antipsychotic drugs did not develop in the mesocortical system; in contrast, the findings suggested that tolerance did occur in the mesolimbic and nigrostriatal systems. The tolerance in the latter system is reminiscent of the tolerance within the tuberoinfundibular system, as reflected by the normal prolactin concentrations in approximately 50% of patients on chronic neuroleptic treatment mentioned previously (Davies *et al.*, 1984). Dopamine autoreceptors appear to be absent not only on tuberoinfundibular neurons, but also on the neurons of the mesocortical system (Bannon, Michaud, & Roth, 1981), which contrasts with the probable presence of such autoreceptors in the nigrostriatal and mesolimbic systems (Bannon & Roth, 1983).

In view of the fact that prolactin secretion

is influenced by sleep (Rubin & Poland, 1982), it is surprising to note the absence of circadian rhythm studies of prolactin secretion in unmedicated schizophrenic patients.

Hypothalamic–Pituitary–Gonadal Axis

Abnormalities of gonadal function in schizophrenia have been postulated for more than 60 years (N. D. C. Lewis & Davies, 1921, 1922; Mott, 1922). Fertility among schizophrenics is lower than in comparison groups, including those with other psychiatric illnesses, a finding which is still apparent when the lower marriage rate for schizophrenics is taken into account (Kendell, 1983; MacSorley, 1964; Ødegaard, 1960). Several earlier studies also described schizophrenic patients with either physical or psychological signs of gonadal hypoactivity or incomplete sexual maturation (e.g., Bullmore, Reiss, & Smith, 1958; Hoskins, 1943). Both male and female schizophrenic patients have been reported to have more feminine physiques than patients in comparison groups (Rey & Coppen, 1959). The results of Rey and Coppen's study, which used Tanner's index as the dependent variable, could not be accounted for by sex chromosome abnormalities, and it therefore was postulated that the abnormal physique might be caused by a hormonal dysfunction during development.

No coherent picture emerges from a review of the literature on gonadal steroid measurements in schizophrenia. In fact, most of the early studies measured urinary 17-ketosteroids, which are derived mainly from weakly androgenic adrenocortical steroids (Cryer, 1979). A number of studies have reported normal sex steroid concentrations in schizophrenic patients (e.g., Arato, Erdos, & Polgar, 1979; Brooksbank et al., 1970). The most striking data are those of Brambilla and Penati (1978), who reported markedly reduced serum testosterone levels in more than 90% of a group of 29 chronic schizophrenic patients. This finding apparently has not yet been confirmed by other investigators.

The weak adrenal androgen, dehydroepiandrosterone (DHEA), is the primary precursor of urinary 17-ketosteroids. Tourney

and Hatfield (1972, 1973) suggested that the mean concentration of DHEA was lower in chronic schizophrenic outpatients than in acute schizophrenics and normal controls. In a more detailed, subsequent study (Erb et al., 1981), the diurnal rhythm of plasma DHEA was characterized in 10 chronic schizophrenic outpatients and 10 age-, sex-, height-, and weight-matched control subjects. The study demonstrated that 0800 hour values of DHEA in the schizophrenic patients were higher than those in the controls, whereas the 1600 hour values were lower. Using a linear programming technique, Erb et al. were able to discriminate with 100% accuracy between schizophrenics and controls on the basis of their diurnal DHEA rhythms. They also reported that there was a greater desynchronization between DHEA and cortisol secretion in the schizophrenics. Replication of this discrimination between groups needs to be attempted on an independent sample of patients.

Studies on the gonadotropins, LH and FSH, in plasma are less contradictory than other HPG studies in schizophrenia, perhaps because fewer studies have been published and relatively standard assay methodologies have been used. Significantly lower concentrations of plasma gonadotropins have been reported by Brambilla, Rovere, Guastalla, Guerrini, and Riggi (1976), and Brambilla et al. (1977) in drug-free chronic male schizophrenic patients compared to control subjects. Reductions in these hormones in chronic schizophrenics also were noted by Ferrier, Johnstone, Crow, and Rincon-Rodriguez (1983); there also was a reduction in the fluctuation of LH concentrations in serial plasma samples. In another group of unmedicated male chronic schizophrenics, E. C. Johnstone et al. (1977) reported low plasma LH values. In their study, however, mean plasma FSH concentrations were either at the upper end of the normal range or above it. Perhaps there is a difference in the physiology of the HPG axis in chronic and acute schizophrenics; a study by Siris et al. (1980) reported normal LH values in male patients with acute schizophrenia.

Three studies have been published on the response of gonadotropins to GnRH in schizophrenia. Each yielded a different result. Brambilla, Rovere et al. (1976) described increased LH and FSH responses to GnRH administration. A normal LH response to GnRH was reported by Naber, Ackenheil, Laakman, Fischer, and von Werder (1980), while a reduced FSH response to GnRH in male schizophrenics was reported by Ferrier *et al.* (1983). The latter investigators considered that the differences in response may have been due to varying drug-free intervals prior to GnRH administration. Hypotheses regarding the pathophysiology of HPG axis abnormalities in schizophrenia must await consolidation of reseach in this area because, at present, nonconsistent changes are apparent. In addition, the HPG axis in female schizophrenics remains largely unexplored due to the difficulties of controlling for variables such as menstrual phase and menopausal status.

Fluid Balance and Antidiuretic Hormone (ADH)

No systematic studies of ADH have been performed in schizophrenic patients. However, there is reason to suggest that such studies might be valuable because of an association between psychogenic polydipsia and psychoses, especially schizophrenia. It is not so much that this association exists, but that in some schizophrenic patients with psychogenic polydipsia there seems to be a defect in water handling, as reflected by an apparently frequent occurrence of water intoxication.

The occurrence of psychogenic polydipsia in patients with major psychiatric disorder has been noted for many years (e.g., Barlow & de Wardener, 1959; Robertson, 1980; Sleeper & Jellinek, 1936). Blum, Tempsey, and Lynch (1983) found a 17.5% prevalence of psychogenic polydipsia in 241 hospitalized psychiatric patients. The most frequent diagnosis found among the patients was schizophrenia. Deleterious biochemical consequences of large, even huge, fluid intake are usually prevented by a powerful homeostatic mechanism involving the osmoreceptor-regulated decrease of plasma ADH, which allows a rapid increase in free-water excretion under such circumstances. Under controlled conditions, healthy volunteers can drink 10 liters of water daily without an effect on serum osmolality (Habener, Dashe, & Solomon, 1964). Barlow and de Wardener (1959) studied patients with psychogenic polydipsia who consumed up to 20 liters per day. These patients did not manifest signs of hyponatremia or low serum osmolality unless they were given exogenous ADH. It therefore is intriguing to note that although patients with psychogenic polydipsia have a variety of psychiatric diagnoses, when water intoxication is described secondary to psychogenic polydipsia, the patient usually has been diagnosed as psychotic. Raskind (1974) reported that in the published literature, 11 out of 12 cases of water intoxication in compulsive water drinkers were psychotic. Smith and Clark (1980) noted that of 27 psychiatrically ill patients with water intoxication secondary to compulsive water drinking, 21 were schizophrenic. Inappropriate ADH secretion has been postulated as the mechanism for water intoxication in such patients. Becaue most of the patients were medicated, it was not clear whether the abnormality was related to the medication or to the underlying psychosis; many psychotropic agents are considered capable of inducing inappropriate ADH secretion (Moses & Miller, 1974). Of the antipsychotic agents, thiothixene has been best characterized as a stimulus of ADH secretion (Ajlouni, Kern, & Tures, 1974). In other cases, the concomitant use of thiazide diuretics has been implicated in the development of water intoxication (Beresford, 1970; Kennedy & Earley, 1970). Water intoxication also has been attributed to heavy cigarette smoking on the basis of nictone-stimulated ADH release (Blum *et al.*, 1983; Chin, Cooper, Crapo, & Abruch, 1976). In some studies (e.g., Rendell, McGrane, & Cuesta, 1978), the patients were drug free at the time of the development of symptoms.

Studies such as these raise clinician awareness about the occurrence of psychogenic polydipsia in patients with schizophrenia, especially those who have been hospitalized. Awareness also is needed of the symptoms of water intoxication, a syndrome which can and does lead to death (Raskind, 1974; Rendell *et al.*, 1978). The morbidity associated with water intoxication includes confusion, weakness, weight gain, convulsions, and eventually coma (Wynn & Rob, 1954). Water intoxication should be included in the list of differential diagnoses in the psychiatric patient with convulsions.

Although inappropriate ADH secretion has been postulated as the cause of water intoxication in compulsive water drinkers, there are very few reports of plasma ADH concentrations in these individuals. Hariprasad, Eisinger, Padmanambhan, and Nadler (1978) suggested, on the basis of a study of 6 psychiatric patients, that the underlying pathology is that of a "reset osmostat." Their patients, although unable to dilute their urine when plasma osmolality was low, were able to achieve maximal dilution once plasma osmolality was lowered further by sustained self-induced water loading. Thus, rather than normally decreasing plasma ADH concentrations once plasma osmolality falls below 275–285 mOsm/kg (Robertson, Shelton, & Athar, 1976), the osmostat has been reset to start decreasing ADH concentrations only after plasma osmolality has become significantly lower. Robertson (1980) proposed an alternative hypothesis to account for the findings of Hariprasad *et al.* by suggesting that in some patients with compulsive water drinking, there may be a relative increase in renal tubular sensitivity to the low levels of plasma ADH which are normally found in conditions of water loading.

The neurobiology of ADH osmostat resetting is unclear. ADH-producing magnocellular neurons are not directly responsive to osmotic stimuli (Hayward & Vincent, 1970). Osmoreceptor cells have been identified in the paraventricular and supraoptic nuclei and also in other areas of the anterior hypothalamus (Peck & Blass, 1975; Vincent, Aranaud, & Bioulac, 1972). The neurophysiology of the osmoreceptor set point has been a matter of some controversy. It is not clear, for example, whether there is a linear or exponential relationship between plasma osmolality and plasma ADH concentrations (Rodbard & Munson, 1978; Valiquette, 1980). It is uncertain whether, in normal humans, there is a random or specific distribution of osmoreceptor cells with particular osmotic thresholds and whether, in the case of patients who are liable to develop water intoxication, there is a change in the nature of this distribution.

Many studies have attempted to identify the neurotransmitters involved in the communication between the osmoreceptors and the magnocellular neurons. Acetylcholine (Dreifuss & Kelly, 1970; Sladek & Knigge, 1977) and angiotensin II (Sladek & Joynt, 1978) appear to be involved. Of heuristic interest with respect to water intoxication in schizophrenic patients, dopamine also has been implicated in osmoreceptor–magnocellular neuron communication in experimental animals (Bridges, Hillhouse, & Jones, 1976; Milton & Paterson, 1973; Ungerstedt, 1971). If dopamine is involved in ADH release, then the syndrome of water intoxication in some schizophrenic patients might be an indication of increased dopaminergic neurotransmission. Dopaminergic influence may not be that important in man, however; dopamine blockade in normal human subjects does not result in changes in plasma ADH (Kendler, Weitzman, & Rubin, 1978). This finding highlights the difficulty of assuming that studies in experimental animals are applicable to human physiology.

Much additional work needs to be undertaken before definitive statements can be made about ADH and osmoreceptor function in schizophrenia. The majority of schizophrenic patients have not exposed themselves to abnormal fluid loads, and it therefore has not been determined whether there is a general predisposition for the water homeostasis of schizophrenics to become compromised after fluid loading. To test this, larger numbers of schizophrenic and control subjects would need to be given high fluid loads under experimental conditions. Such studies, especially if undertaken in conjunction with the measurement of plasma ADH, might add an important dimension to our understanding of the neuroendocrinology of schizophrenia.

Growth Hormone

Growth hormone concentrations are of interest to the psychoneuroendocrinology of schizophrenia because growth hormone is secreted under the influence of dopamine, which stimulates its release. However, dopamine has less primacy in the control of growth hormone than it does in the control of prolactin. Other neurotransmitter influences on growth hormone release include the stimulatory effects of serotonin and α-adrenergic neurons and the inhibitory effect of β-adrenergic neurons (G. M. Brown et al., 1978). There is considerable agreement that basal growth hormone secretion is similar in schizophrenic and control subjects (Beg, Varma, & Dash, 1979; Brambilla, Guerrini et al., 1975; Janowsky et al., 1978; Nathan et al., 1981; Rotrosen, Angrist, Gershon, Sachar, & Halpern, 1976). Many types of pharmacological challenge have been used to test growth hormone secretion in schizophrenics. Results from these findings are discussed in Chapter 16, this volume.

Glucose Metabolism

The heyday of research into glucose metabolism in schizophrenia in the 1940s and 1950s coincided with the popularity of insulin coma therapy in psychiatry. Schizophrenia was more readily diagnosed in this era, and it is likely that many of the patients in fact had affective illnesses. Even if these qualifiers are disregarded, no consistent conclusions emerge from the early studies. Thus, hyper-, hypo-, and normoglycemia have been reported in schizophrenia (Brambilla, Guastalla et al., 1975; Freeman, 1946; Freeman & Elmadjian, 1950; Henneman, Altschule, & Goncz, 1954). Glucose tolerance tests have suggested both prediabetes and, in contrast, increased tolerance (Braceland, Meduna, & Vaichulis, 1945; Henneman et al., 1954; Meduna, Gerty, & Urse, 1942; Nadeau & Rouleau, 1953). Other findings have included a decreased rate of utilization of glucose (Dobrzanski & Kaczanowski, 1976) and hypoinsulinemia, the latter being diagnosed indirectly on the basis of tolbutamide test results (Kallio & Saarimaa, 1967). A high prevalence of diabetes mellitus has been described in long-stay mental hospital patients (Clayer & Dumbrill, 1967; Waitzkin, 1966a, 1966b), a population which would be expected to contain a significiant proportion of schizophrenic individuals. However, Lilliker (1980) found that the prevalence of diabetes in schizophrenic inpatients was not significantly greater than would be expected from national norms. In the face of such contradictory findings, one enduring theme seems worthy of further attention, relating to the postulated hyperglycemic effect of phenothiazines. Several studies have reported that these antipsychotic agents adversely affect glucose metabolism and are associated in a number of patients with the onset of clinical and biochemical diabetes (Arneson, 1964; Charatan & Bartlett, 1955; Hiles, 1956; Thonnard-Neumann, 1968). Schwarz and Munoz (1968) also described 5 patients who developed diabetes after commencing phenothiazines, but noted that these drugs did not affect diabetic control in 22 previously diagnosed diabetics. It is not known how much phenothiazine-associated weight gain (Amdisen, 1964) contributes to glucose dysregulation in such patients.

Calcium

Changes in circulating calcium concentrations and in the hormonal control of its metabolism have been investigated only to a limited extent in schizophrenia. This area has been of interest because of the significant role calcium has in the control of neuronal function (e.g., Killey, Kinjevic, & Somjen, 1969; Morgenroth, Boadte-Biber, & Roth, 1975). The effect of the phenothiazine trifluoperazine of calmodulin has aroused interest in the possibility that the antipsychotic effect of phenothiazines may be mediated by changes in calcium and that there may be an underlying calcium disturbance in schizophrenia. Calmodulin is a calcium-binding protein which is present in all nucleated cells. It plays an important role in the phosphorylation of various proteins in nerve cells and may be involved in the control of the synthesis and release of neurotransmitters (DeLorenzo, Freedman, Yohe, & Maurer, 1979). Calmodulin is inactivated by trifluoperazine, which binds avidly to it (Levin & Weiss, 1977). Studies to date have not convincingly demonstrated differences in plasma calcium concentrations in neuroleptic-free schizophrenic patients; however, such studies cast little light on calmodulin's intracellular calcium-binding properties in such patients because intracellular calcium concentrations are some 10,000 times lower than concentrations outside the cell. Although calcium concentrations are not lower, on the whole, in schizophrenic patients compared to normal values (Alexander, van Kammen, & Bunney, 1978; Gour & Chaudhry, 1957; Pandey, Devpura, Bedi, & Babel, 1973), there is some preliminary evidence that catatonic symptomatology is associated with increased serum calcium (Alexander *et al.*, 1978; Athanassenas *et al.*, 1983). These latter reports also indicated that serum calcium decreased significantly during treatment with antipsychotic agents.

CONCLUDING COMMENTS

Psychoneuroendocrinology, in both its clinical and research aspects, has undergone an important evolution in the past 50 years. Commencing with anecdotal clinical reports of associations between various endocrinopathies and altered behavioral states, psychoneuroendocrinology has developed into an important interdisciplinary inquiry into the influence of the brain on endocrine function and, conversely, the influence of hormones on the brain. The refinement in our understanding of the relationship between mental disturbances and endocrine changes has paralleled advancements in both clinical psychiatry and clinical endocrinology. The formulation of operational criteria for psychiatric diagnosis, the development of sensitive and specific assay techniques for the measurement of low concentrations of many hormones, and the availability of synthetic hypothalamic and pituitary peptide hormones for use in neuroendocrine challenge tests have contributed to a substantial and impressive expertise in neuroendocrine physiology, based on both preclinical and clinical research.

The promise of applying objective, biologically based measures, such as alterations in hormones, to the diagnostic process in psychiatry has inspired much of the work covered in this review. However, rather than neuroendocrine testing being an established laboratory diagnostic aid, its clinical utility remains controversial and in need of further definition (Rubin, 1985). Many of the conflicting data presented in this review can be understood on the basis of methodological difficulties in some of the studies, including insufficient sampling schedules for hormone measurement, small numbers of subjects,

lack of matched comparison groups, and inappropriate statistical analyses. Nevertheless, important consistencies in the data have emerged, such as increased HPA activity in endogenous depression, elevated circulating prolactin in patients treated with neuroleptic drugs, and water intoxication in psychotic patients with psychogenic polydipsia. The ultimate clinical application of these psychoneuroendocrine findings will be established only by the conduct of many more studies which are methodologically rigorously controlled.

To reiterate and summarize, clear changes in endocrine function occur in depression, and suggestive changes occur in mania and schizophrenia as well. These changes encompass multiple endocrine axes, and the pattern of endocrine disturbance can vary from patient to patient. The CNS control of the pituitary and other endocrine glands is complex, and a number of CNS neurotransmitters are involved. As disturbances in several of these neurotransmitters have been implicated in the pathogenesis of affective disorders and schizophrenia, the study of endocrine changes in these psychiatric disorders is of considerable heuristic value. Many of the data gathered in psychoneuroendocrine research investigations to date are conflicting, but several areas of consensus have emerged. The applicability of these consensus findings to clinical diagnosis and treatment of affective disorders and schizophrenia remains an urgent task for future research.

Acknowledgments

The authors gratefully thank Jay Jethwa for help in compilation of the bibliography and Mieke van Weel, Patricia Lynch, and Debra Hanaya for their secretarial assistance.

References

Adams, P. W., Wynn, V., Rose, D. P., Seed, M., Folkard, J., & Strong, R. (1973). Effects of pyridoxine hydrochloride (vitamin B_6) upon depression associated with oral contraception. *Lancet*, *1*, 899–904.

Ajlouni, K., Kern, W. W., & Tures, J. F. (1974). Thiothixene-induced hyponatremia. *Archives of Internal Medicine*, *134*, 1103–1105.

Åkerstedt, T., Froberg, J. E., Friberg, Y., & Wetterberg, L. (1979). Melatonin excretion, body temperature and subjective arousal during 64 hours of sleep deprivation. *Psychoneuroendocrinology*, *4*, 219–225.

Akesode, A., Hendler, N., & Kowarski, A. A. (1976). A 24-hour monitoring of the integrated plasma concentration of aldosterone and cortisol in manic patients. *Psychoneuroendocrinology*, *1*, 419–426.

Alexander, P. E., van Kammen, D. P., & Bunney, W. E., Jr. (1978). Serum calcium and magnesium in schizophrenia: Relationship to clinical phenomena and neuroleptic treatment. *British Journal of Psychiatry*, *133*, 143–149.

Allaway, W. H., Kubota, J., Losee, F., & Roth, M. (1968). Selenium, molybdenum and vanadium in human blood. *Archives of Environmental Health*, *16*, 342–348.

Allsopp, M. N. E., Levell, M. J., Stitch, S. R., & Hullin, R. P. (1972). Aldosterone production rates in manic–depressive psychosis. *British Journal of Psychiatry*, *120*, 399–404.

Altman, N., Sachar, E. J., Gruen, P. H., Halpern, F. S., & Eto, S. (1975). Reduced plasma LH concentrations in postmenopausal depressed women. *Psychosomatic Medicine*, *37*, 274–276.

Amdisen, A. (1964). Drug-produced obesity: Experiences with chlorpromazine, perphenazine and clophenthixol. *Danish Medical Bulletin*, *11*, 182–189.

Amsterdam, J. D., Winokur, A., Caroff, S., & Snyder, P. (1981). Gonadotropin release after administration of GnRH in depressed patients and healthy volunteers. *Journal of Affective Disorders*, *3*, 367–380.

Amsterdam, J. D., Winokur, A., Lucki, I., & Snyder, P. (1983). Neuroendocrine regulation in depressed postmenopausal women and healthy subjects. *Acta Psychiatrica Scandinavica*, *67*, 43–49.

Arato, H., Erdos, A., & Polgar, M. (1979). Endocrinological changes in patients with sexual dysfunction under long-term neuroleptic treatment. *Pharmakopsychiatrie Neuropsychopharmakologie*, *12*, 426–431.

Arendt, J., Paunier, L., & Sizonenko, P. C. (1975). Melatonin radioimmunoassay. *Journal of Clinical Endocrinology and Metabolism*, *40*, 347–350.

Arendt, J., Wetterberg, L., Heyden, T., Sizonenko, P. C., & Paunier, L. (1977). Radioimmunoassay of melatonin: Human serum and cerebrospinal fluid. *Hormone Research*, *8*, 65–75.

Arneson, G. A. (1964). Phenothiazine derivates and glucose metabolism. *Journal of Neuropsychiatry*, *5*, 181–185.

Asnis, G. M., Halbreich, U., Sachar, E. J., Nathan, R. S., Davies, M., Novacenko, H., Ostrow, L. C., Endicott, J., & Puig-Antich, J. (1982). Relationship of dexamethasone (2 mg) and plasma cortisol hypersecretion in depressive illness: Clinical and neuroendocrine parameters. *Psychopharmacology Bulletin*, *18*(4), 122–126.

Asnis, G. M., Halbreich, U., Sachar, E. J., Nathan, R. S. Ostrow, L. C., Novacenko, H., Davies, M., Endicott, J., & Puig-Antich, J. (1983). Plasma cortisol secretion and REM period latency in adult endogenous depression. *American Journal of Psychiatry*, *140*(6), 750–753.

Asnis, G. M., Nathan, R. S., Halbreich, U., Halpern, F. S., & Sachar, E. J. (1980). Prolactin changes in major depressive disorders. *American Journal of Psychiatry*, *137*, 1117–1118.

Athanassenas, G., Papadopoulos, E., Kourkoubas, A.,

Tsitouridis, S., Gabriel, J., Hoidas, S., & Srangos, E. (1983). Serum calcium and magnesium level in chronic schizophrenics. *Journal of Clinical Psychopharmacology*, *3*, 212–216.

Bacopoulos, N. C., Spokes, E. G., Bird, E. D., & Roth, R. H. (1979). Antipsychotic drug action in schizophrenic patients: Effect on cortical dopamine metabolism after long-term treatment. *Science*, *205*, 1405–1407.

Baer, L., Durell, J., Bunney, W. E., Murphy, D., Levy, B. S., Greenspan, K., & Cardon, P. V. (1970). Sodium balance and distribution in lithium carbonate therapy. *Archives of General Psychiatry*, *22*, 40–44.

Bannon, M. J., Michaud, R. L., & Roth, R. H. (1981). Mesocortical dopamine neurones: Lack of autoreceptors modulating dopamine synthesis. *Molecular Pharmacology*, *19*, 270–275.

Bannon, M. J., & Roth, R. H. (1983). Pharmacology of mesocortical dopamine neurones. *Pharmacological Reviews*, *35*, 53–68.

Barlow, E. D., & de Wardener, H. E. (1959). Compulsive water drinking. *Quarterly Journal of Medicine*, *28*, 235–258.

Baron, M., Levitt, M., & Perlman, R. (1980). Human platelet monoamine oxidase and the menstrual cycle. *Psychiatry Research*, *3*, 323–327.

Bech, P., Kirkegaard, C., Bock, E., Johanesson, M., & Rafaelson, O. J. (1978). Hormones, electrolytes and cerebrospinal fluid proteins in manic–melancholic patients. *Neuropsychobiology*, *4*, 99–112.

Beck-Friis, J., Ljunggen, J. G., Thoren, M., von Rosen, D., Kjellman, B. F., & Wetterberg, L. (1985). Melatonin, cortisol and ACTH in patients with major depressive disorder and healthy humans with special reference to the outcome of the dexamethasone suppression test. *Psychoneuroendocrinology*, *10*, 173–186.

Beg, A. A., Varma, V. K., & Dash, R. J. (1979). Effect of chlorpromazine on human growth hormone. *American Journal of Psychiatry*, *136*, 914–917.

Belmaker, R. H., Kon, M., Ebstein, R. P., & Dasberg, H. (1980). Partial inhibition by lithium of the epinephrine-stimulated rise in plasma cyclic GMP in humans. *Biological Psychiatry*, *15*, 3–8.

Ben-Jonathan, N., Oliver, C., Weiner, M. J., Mical, R. S., & Porter, J. C. (1977). Dopamine in hypophysial portal plasma of the rat during the estrus cycle and throughout pregnancy, *Endocrinology* (*Baltimore*), *100*, 452–458.

Benkert, O. (1975). Studies in pituitary hormones and releasing hormones in depression and sexual impotence. *Progress in Brain Research*, *42*, 25–36.

Beresford, H. R. (1970). Polydipsia, hydrochlorothiazide and water intoxication. *JAMA, Journal of the American Medical Association*, *214*, 879–883.

Berger, M., Pirke, K.-M., Doerr, P., Krieg, J.-C., & von Zerssen, D. (1984). The limited utility of the dexamethasone suppression test for the diagnostic process in psychiatry. *British Journal of Psychiatry*, *145*, 372–382.

Besses, G. S., Burrow, G. N., Spaulding, S. W., & Donabedian, R. K. (1975). Dopamine infusion acutely inhibits the TSH and prolactin response to TRH. *Journal of Clinical Endocrinology and Metabolism*, *41*, 985–988.

Birkeland, A. J. (1982). Plasma melatonin levels and nocturnal transitions between sleep and wakefulness. *Neuroendocrinology, 34,* 126–131.

Bleuler, E. (1950). *Dementia praecox or the group of schizophrenias* (J. Zinkin, Trans.). New York: International Universities Press.

Blum, A., Tempsey, F. W., & Lynch, W. J. (1983). Somatic findings in patients with psychogenic polydipsia. *Journal of Clinical Psychiatry, 44,* 55–56.

Braceland, C., Meduna, M. D., & Vaichulis, J. A. (1945). Delayed action of insulin in schizophrenia. *American Journal of Psychiatry, 102,* 108–110.

Brambilla, F., Guastalla, A., Guerrini, A., Riggi, F., Rovere, C., Zanoboni, A., & Zanoboni-Muciaccia, W. (1975). Glucose–insulin metabolism in chronic schizophrenia. *Progress in Brain Research, 42,* 373–374.

Brambilla, F., Guastalla, A., Guerrini, A., Rovere, C., Legnani, P., Sarno, M., & Riggi, F. (1976). PRL secretion in chronic schizophrenia. *Acta Psychiatrica Scandinavica, 54,* 275–286.

Brambilla, F., Guerrini, A., Rovere, C., Guastalla, A., Riggi, F., & Recchia, M. (1975). Growth hormone secretion in chronic schizophrenia. *Neuropsychobiology, 1,* 267–276.

Brambilla, F., & Penati, G. (1978). Schizophrenia: Endocrinological review. In F. Brambilla, P. K. Bridges, E. Endroczi, & G. Henser (Eds.), *Perspectives in endocrine psychobiology* (pp. 309–422). London: Wiley.

Brambilla, F., Rovere, C., Guastalla, A., Guerrini, A., & Riggi, F. (1976). Gonadotropin response to synthetic gonadotropin hormone-releasing hormone (GnRH) in chronic schizophrenia. *Acta Psychiatrica Scandinavica, 54,* 131–145.

Brambilla, R., Rovere, C., Guastalla, A., Guerrini, A., Riggi, F., & Burbati, G. (1988). Effects of clomiphene citrate administration on the hypothalamic–pituitary gonadal axis of male chronic schizophrenics. *Acta Psychiatrica Scandinavica, 56,* 399–406.

Branchey, L., Weinberg, U., Branchey, M., Linkowski, P., & Mendlewicz, J. (1982). Simultaneous study of 24-hour patterns of melatonin and cortisol secretion in depressed patients. *Neuropyschobiology, 8,* 225–232.

Bratfos, O., & Haug, J. O. (1968). The course of manic-depressive psychosis: A follow-up investigation of 215 patients. *Acta Psychiatrica Scandinavica, 44,* 89–112.

Braverman, L. E., & Vagenakis, A. G. (1979). The thyroid. *Clinical Endocrinology and Metabolism, 8,* 621–639.

Bridges, T. E., Hillhouse, E. W., & Jones, M. T. (1976). The effect of dopamine on neurohypophysial hormone release *in vivo* and from the rat neural lobe and hypothalamus *in vitro*. *Journal of Physiology (London), 260,* 647–666.

Brockington, I. F., Wainwright, S., & Kendell, R. E. (1980). Manic patients with schizophrenic or paranoid symptoms. *Psychological Medicine, 10,* 73–83.

Brooksbank, B. W. L., MacSweeny, D. A., Johnson, A. L., Cunningham, A. E., Wilson, D. A., & Coppen, A. (1970). Androgen excretion and physique in schizophrenia. *British Journal of Psychiatry, 117,* 413–420.

Brown, G. M., Seeman, P., & Lee, T. (1976). Dopamine/neuroleptic receptors in the basal hypothalamus and pituitary. *Endocrinology (Baltimore), 99,* 1407–1410.

Brown, G. M., Seggie, J. A., Chambers, J. W., & Ettigi, P. G. (1978). Psychoendocrinology and growth hormone: A review. *Psychoneuroendocrinology, 3,* 131–153.

Brown, W. A. (1980). Testosterone and human behavior. *International Journal of Mental Health, 9*(3–4), 45.

Buckler, J. M. H. (1972). Exercise as a screening test for growth hormone release. *Acta Endocrinologica (Copenhagen), 69,* 219–229.

Bullmore, G. H. L., Reiss, M., & Smith, D. W. (1958). Endocrine investigations in a juvenile psychiatric unit. In M. Reiss (Ed.), *Psychoneuroendocrinology* (pp. 63–75). New York: Grune & Stratton.

Caffey, E. M., Jr., Forrest, I. S., Frank, T. V., & Klett, C. J. (1963). Phenothiazine excretion in chronic schizophrenics. *American Journal of Psychiatry, 120,* 578–582.

Cahn, H. A., Folk, G. E., & Huston, P. E. (1968). Age comparison of human day–night physiological differences. *Aerospace Medicine, 39,* 608–610.

Cantley, L. C., Josephson, L., Warner, R., Yanagisawa, M., Lechene, C., & Guidotti, G. (1977). Vanadate is a potent Na$^+$, K$^+$-ATPase inhibitor found in ATP derived from muscle. *Journal of Biological Chemistry, 252,* 7421–7423.

Caplan, R. H., Pagliara, A. S., Wickus, G., & Goodlund, L. S. (1983). Elevation of free thyroxine index in psychiatric patients. *Journal of Psychiatric Research, 17,* 267–274.

Carman, J. S., Post, R. M., Runkle, D. C., Bunney, W. E., & Wyatt, R. J. (1979). Increased serum calcium and phosphorus with the "switch" into mania or excited psychotic states. *British Journal of Psychiatry, 135,* 55–61.

Carman, J. S., & Wyatt, R. J. (1979a). Calcium: Pacesetting the periodic psychoses. *American Journal of Psychiatry, 136,* 1035–1039.

Carman, J. S., & Wyatt, R. J. (1979b). Use of calcitonin in psychotic agitation or mania. *Archives of General Psychiatry, 136,* 72–75.

Caron, M. G., Beaulieu, M., Raymond, V., Gagne, B., Drouin, J., Lefkowitz, R. J., & Labrie, F. (1978). Dopaminergic receptors in the anterior pituitary gland. *Journal of Biological Chemistry, 253,* 2244–2253.

Carpenter, W. C., & Bunney, W. E. (1971). Diurnal rhythm of cortisol in mania. *Archives of General Psychiatry, 25,* 270–273.

Carpenter, W. T., Jr., Bartko, J. J., Carpenter, C. L., & Strauss, J. S. (1976). Another view of schizophrenia subtypes. *Archives of General Psychiatry, 33,* 508–516.

Carpenter, W. T., Jr., Strauss, J. S., Muleh, S. (1973). Are there pathognomonic symptoms in schizophrenia? An empiric investigation of Schneider's first-rank symptoms. *Archives of General Psychiatry, 28,* 847–852.

Carroll, B. J., Curtis, G. C., & Mendels, J. (1976). Neuroendocrine regulation in depression. I. Limbic system–adrenocortical dysfunction. *Archives of General Psychiatry, 33,* 1039–1044.

Carroll, B. J., Feinberg, M., Greden, J. F., Tarika, J., Albala, A. A., Haskett, R. F., James, N. McI., Kronfol, Z., Lohr, N., Steiner, M., de Vigne, J. P., & Young, E. (1981). A specific laboratory test for the diagnosis of melancholia. *Archives of General Psychiatry*, *38*, 15–22.

Carroll, B. J., & Mendels, J. (1976). Neuroendocrine regulation in affective disorders. In E. J. Sachar (Ed.), *Hormones, behaviour and psychopathology* (pp. 193–224). New York: Raven Press.

Charatan, F. B. E., & Bartlett, N. G. (1955). The effect of chlorpromazine (Largactil) on glucose tolerance. *Journal of Mental Science*, *101*, 351–353.

Checkley, S. A., & Rush, A. J. (1983). Functional indices of biological disturbance: Group report. In J. Angst (Ed.), *The origins of depression: Current concepts and approaches* (pp. 425–445). New York: Springer-Verlag.

Chin, W. W., Cooper, D. S., Crapo, L., & Abruch, J. (1976). Water intoxication caused by smoking in a compulsive water drinker. *Clinical Research*, *24*, 625A.

Cho, J. T., Bone, S., Dunner, D. L., Colt, E., & Fieve, R. R. (1979). The effect of lithium treatment on thyroid function in patients with primary affective disorder. *American Journal of Psychiatry*, *136*, 115–116.

Claustrat, B., Chazot, G., Brun, J., Jordan, D., & Sassolas, G. (1984). A chronobiological study of melatonin and cortisol secretion in depressed subjects: Plasma melatonin—a biochemical marker in major depression. *Biological Psychiatry*, *19*, 1215–1227.

Clayer, J. R., & Dumbrill, N. N. (1967). Diabetes mellitus and mental illness. *Medical Journal of Australia*, *1*, 901–904.

Cohen, K. L., & Swigar, M. E. (1979). Thyroid function screening in psychiatric patients. *JAMA, Journal of the American Medical Association*, *242*, 254–257.

Cohen, S. (1980). Cushing's syndrome: A psychiatric study of 29 patients. *British Journal of Psychiatry*, *136*, 120–124.

Conroy, R. T. W. L., Hughes, B. D., Mills. J. N. (1968). Circadian rhythm of plasma 11-hydroxycorticosteroid in psychiatric disorders. *British Medical Journal*, *3*, 405–407.

Cookson, J. C., Silverstone, T., & Rees, L. (1982). Plasma prolactin and growth hormone levels in manic patients treated with pimozide. *British Journal of Psychiatry*, *140*, 274–279.

Coppen, A., & Shaw, D. M. (1963). Mineral metabolism in melancholia. *British Medical Journal*, *2*, 1439–1444.

Coppen, A., Shaw, D. M., Malleson, A., & Costain, R. (1966). Mineral metabolism in mania. *British Medical Journal*, *1*, 71–75.

Cotes, P. M., Crow, T. J., Johnstone, E. C., Bartlett, W., & Bourne, R. C. (1978). Neuroendocrine changes in acute schizophrenia as a function of clinical state and neuroleptic medication. *Psychological Medicine*, *8*, 657–665.

Cowdry, R. W., Wehr, T. A., Zis, A. P., & Goodwin, F. K. (1983). Thyroid abnormalities associated with rapid-cycling bipolar illness. *Archives of General Psychiatry*, *40*, 414–420.

Crammer, J., & Gillies, C. (1981). Psychiatric aspects of diabetes mellitus: Diabetes and depression. *British Journal of Psychiatry*, *139*, 171–172.

Crow, T. J. (1980). Molecular pathology of schizophrenia: More than one disease process? *British Medical Journal*, *280*, 66–68.

Cryer, P. E. (1979). *Diagnostic endocrinology*. London: Oxford University Press.

Davidson, J., Turnbull, C., Strickland, R., & Belyea, M. (1984). Comparative diagnostic criteria for melancholia and endogenous depression. *Archives of General Psychiatry*, *41*, 506–511.

Davis, J. M., Vogel, C., Gibbons, R., Pavkovic, I., & Zhang, M. (1984). Pharmacoendocrinology of schizophrenia. In G. M. Brown, S. H. Koslow, & S. Reichlin (Eds.), *Neuroendocrinology and psychiatric disorders* (pp. 29–53). New York: Raven Press.

DeLorenzo, R. J., Freedman, S. D., Yohe, W. B., & Maurer, S. C. (1979). Stimulation of Ca^{2+}-dependent neurotransmitter release and presynaptic nerve terminal protein phosphorylation by calmodulin and calmodulin-like protein isolated from synaptic vesicles. *Proceedings of the National Academy of Sciences of the U.S.A.*, *76*, 1838–1842.

Dick, D. A. T., Naylor, G. J., & Dick, E. G. (1982). Plasma vanadium concentration in manic–depressive illness. *Psychological Medicine*, *12*, 533–537.

Dobrzanski, T., & Kaczanowski, F. (1976). Studies in the blood insulin level in patients with schizophrenic depression. *Polish Medical Journal*, *6*, 247.

Dreifuss, J. J., & Kelly, J. S. (1970). Excitation of identified supraoptic neurones by iontophoretic application of acetylcholine. *Journal of Physiology (London)*, *210*, 170P–172P.

Dubovsky, S. L., Franks, R. D., Lifschitz, M., & Coen, P. (1982). Effectiveness of verapamil in the treatment of a manic patient. *American Journal of Psychiatry*, *139*, 502–503.

Ducis, I., & Distefano, V. (1980). Evidence for a serotonin uptake system in isolated bovine pinealocyte suspensions. *Molecular Pharmacology*, *18*, 438–446.

Durell, J., Baer, L., & Green, R. (1971). Electrolytes and psychoses. In H. E. Himwich (Ed.), *Biochemistry, schizophrenias and affective illnesses* (pp. 283–307). Baltimore: Williams & Wilkins.

Ehrensing, R. H., Kastin, A. J., Schalch, D. S., Friesen, H. G., Vargas, J. R., & Schally, A. V. (1974). Affective state and thyrotropin and prolactin responses after repeated injections of thyrotropin-releasing hormone in depressed patients. *American Journal of Psychiatry*, *131*, 714–718.

Erb, J. L., Kadane, J. B., Tourney, G., Mickelsen, R., Trader, D., Szabo, R., & Davis, V. (1981). Discrimination between schizophrenic and control subjects by means of plasma dehydroepiandrosterone measurements. *Journal of Clinical Endocrinology and Metabolism*, *52*, 181–186.

Esler, M. (1984). How can we measure sympathetic nervous system "tone" in patients? *Australian and New Zealand Journal of Medicine*, *14*, 4–5.

Ettigi, P. G., Brown, G. M., & Seggie, J. A. (1979). TSH and LH responses in subtypes of depression. *Psychosomatic Medicine*, *41*, 203–208.

Ettigi, P. G., Nair, N. P. V., Lal, S., Cervantes, P., & Guyda, H. (1976). Effect of apomorphine on growth hormone and prolactin secretion in schizophrenic patients, with or without oral dyskinesia, withdrawn from chronic neuroleptic therapy. *Journal of Neurology, Neurosurgery and Psychiatry, 39*, 870–876.

Fakhri, O., Fadhli, A. A., & El Rawi, R. M. (1980). Effect of electroconvulsive therapy on diabetes mellitus. *Lancet, 2*, 775–777.

Feinberg, M., Carroll, B. J., Steiner, M., & Commorato, A. J. (1979). Misdiagnosis of endogenous depression with research diagnostic criteria. *Lancet, 1*, 267.

Feldberg, W., & Sherwood, S. L. (1957). Effects of calcium and potassium injected into the cerebral ventricles of the cat. *Journal of Physiology (London), 139*, 408–416.

Ferrier, I. N., Johnstone, E. C., & Crow, T. J. (1982). Melatonin/cortisol ratio in psychiatric illness. *Lancet, 1*, 1070.

Ferrier, I. N., Johnstone, E. C., & Crow, T. J. (1984). Hormonal effects of apomorphine in schizophrenia. *British Journal of Psychiatry, 144*, 349–357.

Ferrier, I. N., Johnstone, E. C., Crow, T. J., & Rincon-Rodriguez, I. (1983). Anterior pituitary hormone secretion in chronic schizophrenics. *Archives of General Psychiatry, 40*, 755–761.

Fineberg, E. S., Horand, A. A., & Merimee, T. J. (1972). Free fatty acid concentrations and growth hormone secretion in man. *Metabolism, Clinical and Experimental, 21*, 491–498.

Finkelstein, J. W., Roffwarg, H. P., Boyar, R. M., Kream, J., & Hellman, L. (1972). Age-related change in the 24-hour spontaneous secretion of growth hormone. *Journal of Clinical Endocrinology and Metabolism, 35*, 665–670.

Freeman, H. (1946). Resistance to insulin in mentally disturbed soldiers. *Archives of Neurology and Psychiatry, 56*, 74–78.

Freeman, H., & Elmadjian, F. (1950). Carbohydrate and lymphoid studies in schizophrenia. *American Journal of Psychiatry, 106*, 660–667.

Frohman, L. A., & Berelowitz, M. (1984). The physiological and pharmacological control of anterior pituitary hormone secretion. In C. B. Nemeroff & A. J. Dunn (Eds.), *Peptides, hormones and behaviour* (pp. 119–172). New York: Spectrum Publications.

Fullerton, D. T., Wenzel, F. J., Lohrenz, F. N., & Fahs, H. (1968). Circadian rhythm of adrenal cortical activity in depression. II. A comparison of types in depression. *Archives of General Psychiatry, 19*, 682–688.

Gamble, J. L., Jr., Robertson, J. S., Hannigan, C. A., Foster, C. G., & Farr, L. E. (1953). Chloride, bromide, sodium and sucrose spaces in man. *Journal of Clinical Investigation, 32*, 483–489.

Garfinkel, P. E., Brown, G. M., Warsh, J. J., & Stancer, H. C. (1979). Neuroendocrine responses to carbidopa in primary affective disorders. *Psychoneuroendocrinology, 4*, 13–20.

Genazzani, A. R., Camanni, F., Massara, F., Picciolini, E., Cocchi, D., Belforte, L., & Müller, E. (1980). A new pharmacological approach to the diagnosis of hyperporlactinemic states: The nomifensine test. *Acta Endocronologia (Copenhagen), 93*, 139–148.

Giannattasio, G., Elisabetta de Ferrari, M., & Spada, A. (1981). Dopamine-induced adenylate cyclase in female rat adenohypophysis. *Life Sciences, 28*, 1605–1612.

Gibbs, D. M., & Neill, J. D. (1978). Dopamine levels in hypophysial stalk blood in the rat are sufficient to inhibit prolactin secretion *in vivo. Endocrinology (Baltimore), 102*, 1895–1900.

Gjessing, R. R (1976). Synchronous-syntonic type A cases. In L. Gjessing & F. A. Jenner (Eds.), *Contributions to the somatology of periodic catatonia* (pp. 11–39). Oxford: Pergamon Press.

Glen, A. I. M. (1978). Lithium regulation of membrane ATPases. In F. N. Johnson & S. Johnson (Eds.), *Lithium in medical practice* (pp. 183–192). Lancaster, England: MTP Press.

Gold, M. S., Pottash, A. L. C., & Extein, I. (1981). Hypothyroidism and depression. *JAMA, Journal of the American Medical Association, 245*, 1919–1922.

Gold, M. S., Pottash, A. L. C., & Extein, I. (1982). Symptomless autoimmune thyroiditis in depression. *Psychiatry Research, 6*, 261–269.

Gold, M. S., Pottash, A. C., Müller, E. A., & Extein, I. (1981). Grades of thyroid failure in 100 depressed and anergic psychiatric inpatients. *American Journal of Psychiatry, 138*, 253–255.

Gold, P. W., Goodwin, F. K., Wehr, T., Rebar, R., Sack, R. (1976). Growth hormone and prolactin response to levodopa in affective illness. *Lancet, 2*, 1308–1309.

Goldstein, J., Van Cauter, E., Linkowski, P., Vanhaelst, L., & Mendlewicz, J. (1980). Thyrotropin nyctohemeral pattern in primary depression: Difference between unipolar and bipolar women. *Life Sciences, 27*, 1695–1703.

Goldzieher, J. W., Dozier, T. S., Smith, K. D., & Steinberger, E. (1976). Improving the diagnostic reliability of rapidly fluctuating plasma hormone levels by optimized multisampling techniques. *Journal of Clinical Endocrinology and Metabolism, 43*, 824–830.

Gorski, R. A. (1979). Nature of hormone action in the brain. In T. H. Hamilton, J. H. Clark, & W. A. Sadler (Eds.), *Ontogeny of receptors and reproduction hormone action* (pp. 37–392). New York: Raven Press.

Gour, K. N., & Chaudhry, H. M. (1957). Study of calcium metabolism in electric convulsive therapy (ECT) in certain mental diseases. *Journal of Mental Science, 193*, 275–285.

Green, A. R., & Curzon, G. (1970). The effect of tryptophan metabolites on brain 5-hydroxytryptamine metabolism. *Biochemical Pharmacology, 19*, 2061–2068.

Greengard, O. (1971). Relationship between urinary excretion of kynurenine and liver tryptophan oxygenase activity. *American Journal of Clinical Nutrition, 24*, 709–711.

Grégoire, F., Brauman, H., de Buck, R., & Corvilain, J. (1977). Hormone release in depressed patients before and after recovery,. *Psychoneuroendocrinology, 2*, 303–312.

Gruen, P. H., Sachar, E. J., Langer, G., Altman, N., Leifer, M., Frantz, A., & Halpern, F. S. (1978). Prolactin responses to neuroleptics in normal and schizophrenic subjects. *Archives of General Psychiatry, 35*, 108–116.

Habener, J. F., Dashe, A. M., & Solomon, D. H. (1964). Response of subjects to prolonged high fluid intake. *Journal of Applied Physiology, 19*, 134–136.

Halbreich, U., Grunhaus, L., & Ben-David, M. (1979). Twenty-four-hour rhythm of prolactin in depressive patients. *Archives of General Psychiatry, 36*, 1183–1186.

Hansen, T., Heyden, T., & Sundberg, L. (1977). Effect of propranolol on serum melatonin. *Lancet, 2*, 309–310.

Hariprasad, M. K., Eisinger, R. P., Padmanambhan, C. S., & Nadler, I. M. (1978). Reset osmostat associated with hyponatremia and dementia in psychotic patients. *Kidney International, 14*, 653.

Hatotani, N., Nomura, J., Yamaguchi, T., & Kitayama, I. (1977). Clinical and experimental studies on the pathogenesis of depression. *Psychoneuroendocrinology, 2*, 115–130.

Hayward, J. N., & Vincent, J. D. (1970). Osmosensitive single neurones in the hypothalamus of unanaesthetized monkeys. *Journal of Physiology (London), 210*, 947–972.

Hendler, N. H. (1975). Lithium responsiveness hyperaldosteronism in manic patients. *Journal of Nervous and Mental Disease, 161*, 49–54.

Hendler, N. H. (1978). Spironolactone prophylaxis in manic–depressive disease. *Journal of Nervous and Mental Disease, 166*, 517–520.

Henn, F. A., & Nasrallah, H. A. (Eds.). (1982). *Schizophrenia as a brain disease.* New York: Oxford University Press.

Henneman, D. H., Altschule, M. D., & Goncz, R. M. (1954). Carbohydrate metabolism in brain disease. II. Glucose metabolism in schizophrenic, manic–depressive and involutional psychoses. *Archives of Internal Medicine, 94*, 402–416.

Herz, M. (1964). On rhythmic phenomena in thyroidectomized patients. *Acta Psychiatrica Scandinavica, 40*(Suppl. 180), 449–456.

Hiles, B. W. (1956). Hyperglycemia and glycosuria following chlorpromazine therapy. *JAMA, Journal of the American Medical Association, 162*, 1651.

Hornykiewicz, O. (1984). Discussion: Schizophrenia. In G. M. Brown, S. H. Koslow, & S. Reichlin (Eds.), *Neuroendocrinology and psychiatric disorder* (pp. 85–87). New York: Raven Press.

Horrobin, D. F., Mtabaji, J. P., Karmali, R. A., Manku, M. S., & Nasar, B. A. (1976). Prolactin and mental illness. *Postgraduate Medical Journal, 52*(Suppl. 3), 79–85.

Hoskins, R. G. (1929). Endocrine factors in dementia praecox. *New England Journal of Medicine, 200*, 361–369.

Hoskins, R. G. (1943). Psychosexuality in schizophrenia—some endocrine consideration. *Psychosomatic Medicine, 5*, 3–9.

Hullin, R. P., Jerram, T. C., Lee, M. R., Levell, M. J., & Tyrer, S. P. (1977). Renin and aldosterone relationships in manic–depressive psychosis. *British Journal of Psychiatry, 131*, 575–581.

Hurxthal, L. M., & O'Sullivan, J. B. (1959). Cushing's syndrome: Clinical differential diagnosis and complications. *Annals of Internal Medicine, 51*, 1–16.

Ingbar S. H., & Woeber, K. A. (1981). The thyroid gland. In R. H. Williams (Ed.), *Textbook of endocrinology* (6th ed., pp. 117–248). Philadelphia: Saunders.

Janowsky, D. S., Judd, L., Huey, L., Rottman, N., & Parker, D. (1979). Naloxone effects on serum growth hormone and prolactin in man. *Psychopharmacology, 65*, 95–97.

Janowsky, D. S., Leichner, P., Parker, D., Judd, L. L., Huey, L., & Clopton, P. (1978). The effect of methylphenidate on serum growth hormone. *Archives of General Psychiatry, 35*, 1384–1389.

Jarrett, D. B., Coble, P. A., & Kupfer, D. J. (1983). Reduced cortisol latency in depressive illness. *Archives of General Psychiatry, 40*, 506–511.

Jeffcoate, W. J., Silverstone, J. T., Edwards, C. R. W., & Besser, G. M. (1979). Psychiatric manifestations of Cushing's syndrome: Response to lowering of plasma cortisol. *Quarterly Journal of Medicine, 48*, 465–472.

Jenner, F. A., Gjessing, L. R., Cox, J. R., Davis-Jones, A., Hullin, R. P., & Harma, S. M. (1967). A manic–depressive psychotic with a persistent 48-hour cycle. *British Journal of Psychiatry, 113*, 895–910.

Jimerson, D. C., Lynch, H. L., Post, R. M., Wurtman, R. J., & Bunney, W. E. (1977). Urinary melatonin rhythms during sleep deprivation in depressed patients and normals. *Life Sciences, 20*, 1501–1508.

Jimerson, D. C., Post, R. M., Carman, J. S., van Kammen, D. P., Wood, J. H., Goodwin, F. K., & Bunney, W. E., Jr. (1979). CSF calcium: Clinical correlates in the affective illnesses and schizophrenia. *Biological Psychiatry, 14*, 37–51.

Johnstone, B. B., Naylor, G. J., Dick, E. G., Hopwood, S. E., & Dick, D. A. T. (1980). Prediction of clinical course of bipolar manic–depressive illness treated with lithium. *Psychological Medicine, 10*, 329–334.

Johnstone, E. C., Crow, T. J., & Mashiter, K. (1977). Anterior pituitary hormone secretion in chronic schizophrenia—an approach to neurohumoral mechanisms. *Psychological Medicine, 7*, 223–228.

Kallio, I. V. I., & Saarimaa, H. A. (1967). Changes in blood lipids, postprandial lipemia and intravenous tolbutamide test response after insulin-shock treatment. *American Journal of the Medical Sciences, 254*, 619–622.

Kebabian, J. W., & Calne, D. B. (1979). Multiple receptors for dopamine. *Nature (London), 277*, 93–96.

Kendell, R. E. (1982). The choice of diagnostic criteria for biological research. *Archives of General Psychiatry, 39*, 1334–1339.

Kendell, R. E. (1983). Schizophrenia. In R. E. Kendell & A. K. Zealley (Eds.), *Companion to psychiatric studies* (3rd ed., pp. 275–296). Edinburgh: Churchill-Livingstone.

Kendler, K. S., Weitzman, R. E., & Rubin, R. T. (1978). Lack of arginine vasopressin response to central dopamine blockade in normal adults. *Journal of Clinical Endocrinology and Metabolism, 47*, 204–297.

Kennedy, R. M., & Earley, L. E. (1970). Profound hyponatremia resulting from a thiazide-induced decrease in urinary diluting capacity patient with primary polydipsia. *New England Journal of Medicine, 282*, 1185–1186.

Kety, S. S. (1959). Biochemical theories of schizophrenia. Part I. *Science, 129*, 1528–1532.

Killey, J. S., Kinjevic, K., & Somjen, G. (1969). Divalent cations and electrical properties of cortical cells. *Journal of Neurobiology, 2*, 197–201.

Kirkegaard, C., Bjørum, N., Cohn, D., & Lauridsen, U. B. (1978). Thyrotropin-releasing hormone (TRH) stimulation test in manic–depressive illness. *Archives of General Psychiatry*, 35, 1017–1021.

Kirkegaard, C., Faber, J., Hummer, L., & Rogowski, P. (1979). Increased levels of TRH in cerebrospinal fluid from patients with endogenous depression. *Psychoneuroendocrinology*, 4, 227–235.

Klaiber, E. L., Broverman, D. M., Vogel, W., & Kobayashi, Y. (1979). Estrogen therapy for severe persistent depressions in women. *Archives of General Psychiatry*, 36, 550–554.

Klein, D. C., Buda, M. J., Kapoor, C. L., & Krishna, G. (1978). Pineal serotonin *N*-acetyltransferase activity: Abrupt decrease in adenosine 3',5'-monophosphate may be signal for "turnoff." *Science*, 199, 309–311.

Kleinman, J. E., Weinberger, D. R., Rogol, A. D., Bigelow, L. B., Klein, S. T., Gillin, J. C., & Wyatt, R. J. (1982). Plasma prolactin concentration and psychopathology in chronic schizophrenia. *Archives of General Psychiatry*, 39, 655–657.

Knapp, M. W., Keane, P. M., & Wright, J. G. (1967). Circadian rhythm of plasma 11-hydroxycorticosteroids in depressive illness, congestive heart failure and Cushing's syndrome. *British Medical Journal*, 2, 27–30.

Knopf, R. F., Conn, J. W., Fajans, S. S., Floyd, J. C., & Guntsche, E. M., & Rull, J. A. (1965). Plasma growth hormone response to intravenous administration of amino acids. *Journal of Clinical Endocrinology and Metabolism*, 25, 1140–1144.

Kolakowska, T., Orr, M., Gelder, M., Heggie, M., Wiles, M., & Franklin, M. (1979). Clinical significance of plasma drug and prolactin levels during acute chlorpromazine treatment: A replication study. *British Journal of Psychiatry*, 135, 352–359.

Kraepelin, E. (1910). *Geschlachtliche Verirrungen und Volksvermehrungpsychiatrie*. Leipzig: Barth.

Krauthammer, C., & Klerman, G. (1979). Mania secondary to thyroid disease. *Lancet*, 1, 827–828.

Krieger, D. J., Amorosa, L., & Linick, F. (1975). Cyproheptadine-induced remission in Cushing's disease. *New England Journal of Medicine*, 293, 53–56.

Kronfol, Z., Greden, J., & Carroll, B. (1981). Psychiatric aspects of diabetes mellitus: Diabetes and depression. *British Journal of Psychiatry*, 139, 172–173.

Kuhn, C., & Schanberg, S. (1984). Hormones and brain development. In C. B. Nemeroff & A. J. Dunn (Eds.), *Peptides, hormones and behavior* (pp. 775–819). New York: Spectrum Publications.

Kupfer, D. J. (1977). EEG sleep correlates of depression in man. In I. Hanin & E. Usdin (Eds.), *Animal models in psychiatry and neurology* (pp. 181–188). Oxford: Pergamon Press.

Kutty, K. M., Bryant, D. G., & Farid, N. R. (1978). Serum lipids in hypothyroidism—a reevaluation. *Journal of Clinical Endocrinology and Metabolism*, 46, 55–60.

Langer, G., Sachar, E. J., & Gruen, P. H. (1978). Prolactin response to neuroleptic drugs in normal and schizophrenic subjects. *Psychopharmacology Bulletin*, 14, 8–9.

Leichter, S. B., Kirstein, L., & Martin, N. D. (1977). Thyroid function and growth hormone secretion in amitriptyline-treated depression. *American Journal of Psychiatry*, 134, 1270–1272.

Leonhard, K. (1959). *Aufteilung der Endogenen Psychosen*. Berlin: Akademie-Verlag.

Lerner, A. B., Case, J. D., & Henizelman, R. V. (1959), Structure of melatonin, *Journal of the American Chemical Society*, 81, 6084.

Levin, R. M., & Weiss, B. (1977). Binding of trifluoperazine to the calcium-dependent activator of cyclic nucleotide phosphodiesterase. *Molecular Pharmacology*, 13, 609–697.

Levinsky, N. G. (1980). Fluids and electrolytes. In K. J. Isslbacker, R. D. Adams, E. Braunwald, R. G. Petersdorf, & J. D. Wilson (Eds.), *Harrison's principles of internal medicine* (pp. 434–444). New York: McGraw-Hill.

Lewis, A. J. (1966). Affective disorder. In B. R. Scott (Ed.), *Price's textbook of the practice of medicine* (pp. 1177–1185). London: Oxford University Press.

Lewis, N. D. C., & Davies, G. R. (1921). A correlative study of endocrine imbalance and mental disease. *Journal of Nervous and Mental Disease*, 54, 385–405, 493–512.

Lewis, N. D. C., & Davies, G. R. (1922). *Journal of Nervous and Mental Disease*, 55, 13–32.

Lewy, A. J., Wehr, T. A., Goodwin, F. K., Newsome, D. A., & Markey, S. P. (1980). Light suppresses melatonin secretion in humans. *Science*, 210, 1267–1269.

Lilliker, S. L. (1980). Prevalence of diabetes in manic–depressive population. *Comprehensive Psychiatry*, 21, 270–275.

Lindvall, O. (1979). Dopamine pathways in the rat brain. In A. S. Horn, J. Korf, & B. H. C. Westsrink (Eds.), *The neurobiology of dopamine*. New York: Academic Press.

Luine, V. N., & McEwen, B. S. (1977). Effect of estradiol on turnover of type A monoamine oxidase in brain. *Journal of Neurochemistry*, 28, 1221–1227.

Lutz, J. H., Gregerman, R. I., Spaulding, S. W., Hornick, R. B., & Dawkins, A. T., Jr. (1972). Thyroxine binding proteins, free thyroxine and thyroxine turnover interrelationships during acute infectious illness in man. *Journal of Clinical Endocrinology and Metabolism*, 35, 230–249.

MacLeod, R. M., & Lehymeyer, J. D. (1974). Studies on the mechanism of the dopamine-mediated inhibition of prolactin secretion. *Endocrinology (Baltimore)*, 94, 1077–1085.

MacSorley, K. (1964). An investigation into the fertility rates of mentally ill patients. *Annals of Human Genetics*, 27, 247–256.

Maas, J. W. (1975). Biogenic amines and pharmacological separation of two types of depression. *Archives of General Psychiatry,, 32*, 1357–1361.

Maeda, K., Kato, Y., Ongo, S., Chihara, K., Yoshimoto, Y., Yamaguchi, N., Kuromaru, S., & Imura, H. (1975). Growth hormone and prolactin release after injection of thyrotropin-releasing hormone in patients with depression. *Journal of Clinical Endocrinology and Metabolism*, 40, 501–503.

McCartney, J. L. (1929). Dementia praecox as an endocrinopathy, with clinical and autopsy reports. *Endocrinology (Baltimore)*, 13, 73–87.

Meduna, S. L., Gerty, F. G., & Urse, V. G. (1942). Biochemical disturbances in mental disorders. I. Anti-insulin effect of blood in cases of schizophrenia. *Archives of Neurology and Psychiatry*, 47, 38–52.

Meltzer, H. Y. (1984). Neuroendocrine abnormalities in schizophrenia: Prolactin, growth hormone and gonadotrophins. In G. M. Brown (Ed.), *Neuroendocrinology and psychiatric disorder* (pp. 1–28). New York: Raven Press.

Meltzer H. Y., & Fang, Y. (1976). The effects of neuroleptics on serum prolactin in schizophrenic patients. *Archives of General Psychiatry, 33,* 279–286.

Meltzer, H. Y., & Kassir, S. (1983). Abnormal calmodulin-activated Ca^+-ATPase in manic–depressive subjects. *Journal of Psychiatric Research, 17,* 29–35.

Meltzer, H. Y., Sachar, E. J., & Frantz, A. G. (1974). Serum prolactin levels in unmedicated schizophrenic patients. *Archives of General Psychiatry, 31,* 564–569.

Menaker, M., Takahashi, J. S., & Eskin, A. (1978). The physiology of circadian pacemakers. *Annual Review of Physiology, 40,* 501–526.

Mendlewicz, J., Branchey, L., Weinberg, U., Branchey, M., Linkowski, P., & Weitzman, E. D. (1980). The 24-hour pattern of plasma melatonin in depressed patients before and after treatment. *Communications in Pyschopharmacology, 4,* 49–55.

Mendlewicz, J., Linkowski, P., & Brauman, H. (1980). Reduced prolactin release after thyrotropin-releasing hormone in manic depression. *New England Journal of Medicine, 302,* 1091–1092.

Mendlewicz, J., van Cauter, E., Linkowski, P., L'Hermite, M., & Robyn, C. (1980). The 24-hour profile of prolactin in depression. *Life Sciences, 27,* 2015–2024.

Menninger, W. C. (1935). Psychological factors in the etiology of diabetes. *Journal of Nervous and Mental Disease, 81,* 1–13.

Mielke, D. H., Gallant, D. M., & Kessler, C. (1977). An evaluation of a unique antipsychotic agent, sulpiride: Effects on serum prolactin and growth hormone. *American Journal of Psychiatry, 134,* 1370–1375.

Milton, A. S., & Paterson, A. T. (1973). Intracranial injections of 6-hydroxydopamine (6-OH-DA) in cats: Effects of the release of the release of antidiuretic hormone. *Brain Research, 61,* 423–427.

Moore, D. C., Paunier, L., & Sizonenko, P. C. (1979). Effect of adrenergic stimulation and blockade on melatonin secretion in the human. *Progress in Brain Research, 52,* 517–521.

Moore, K. E., & Demarest, K. T. (1980). Effects of baclofen on different dopaminergic neuronal systems. *Brain Research Bulletin, 5*(Suppl. 2), 531–536.

Moore, K. E., Demarest, K. T., & Johnston, C. A. (1980). Influence of prolactin on dopaminergic neuronal systems in the hypothalamus. *Federation Proceedings, Federation of American Societies for Experimental Biology, 39,* 2912–2916.

Moore, K. E., Demarest, K. T., Johnston, C. A., & Alper, R. H. (1980). Pharmacological and endocrinological manipulation of tuberoinfundibular and tuberohypophyseal dopaminergic neurons. In E. E. Müller (Ed.), *Neuroactive drugs in endocrinology* (pp. 109–121). Amsterdam: Elsevier/North-Holland.

Moore, K. E., & Wuerthele, S. M. (1979). Regulation of nigrostriatal and tuberoinfundibular–hypophyseal dopaminergic neurons. *Progress in Neurobiology, 13,* 325–359.

Morgenroth, V. H., Boadte-Biber, M. C., & Roth, R. (1975). Activation of tyrosine hydroxylase from central noradrenergic neurons by calcium. *Molecular Pharmacology, 11,* 427–435.

Moses, A., & Miller, M. (1974). Drug-induced dilutional hyponatremia. *New England Journal of Medicine, 291,* 1234–1239.

Mott, F. W. (1922). The reproductive organs in relation to mental disorder. *British Journal of Medicine, 1,* 463–467.

Murphy, D. L., Goodwin, F. K., & Bunney, W. E. (1969). Aldosterone and sodium response to lithium administration in man. *Lancet, 2,* 458–461.

Naber, D., Ackenheil, G., Laakman, G., Fischer, H., & von Werder, K. (1980). Basal and stimulated levels of prolactin, TSH and LH in serum of chronic schizophrenic patients, long-term treated with neuroleptics. *Pharmakopsychiatrie/Neuro-Psychopharmakologie, 13,* 325–330.

Nadeau, G., & Rouleau, Y. (1953). Insulin tolerance in schizophrenia. *Journal of Clinical and Experimental Psychopathology, 14,* 69–77.

Nathan, R. S., Sachar, E. J., Ostrow, L., Asnis, G. M., Halbreich, U., & Halpern, F. S. (1981). Failure of dopaminergic blockade to effect prolactin, growth hormone and cortisol responses to insulin-induced hypoglycemia in schizophrenics. *Journal of Clinical Endocrinology and Metabolsim, 52,* 807–809.

Naylor, G. J., Dick, D. A. T., Dick, E. G., & Moody, J. P. (1974). Lithium therapy and erythrocyte membrane cation carrier. *Psychopharmacologia, 37,* 81–86.

Naylor, G. J., Dick, D. A. T., Dick, E. G., Worrall, E. P., Peck, M., Dick, P., & Boardman, L. J. (1976). Erythrocyte membrane cation carrier in mania. *Psychological Medicine, 6,* 659–663.

Naylor, G. J., Dick, E. G., Smith, A. H. W., Dick, D. A. T., McHarg, A. M., & Chambers, C. A. (1980). Changes in erythrocyte membrane cation carrier with age in women. *Gerontology, 26,* 327–329.

Naylor, G. J., & Smith, A. H. W. (1981a). Vanadium: A possible etiological factor in manic–depressive illness. *Psychological Medicine, 11,* 249–256.

Naylor, G. J., & Smith, A. H. W. (1981b). Defective genetic control of sodium-pump density in manic–depressive psychosis. *Psychological Medicine, 11,* 257–263.

Naylor, G. J., Smith, A., Boardman, L. J., Dick, D. A. T., Dick, E. G., & Dick, P. (1977). Lithium and erthyroctye membrane cation carrier studies in normal and manic–depressive subjects. *Psychological Medicine, 7,* 229–233.

Nielsen, J. L. (1980). Plasma prolactin during treatment with nortriptyline. *Neuropsychobiology, 6,* 52–55.

O'Dea, J. P. R., Gould, D., Hallberg, M. A., & Welland, R. G. (1978). Prolactin changes during electroconvulsive therapy. *American Journal of Psychiatry, 135,* 609–611.

Ødegaard, Ø. (1960). Marriage rate and fertility in psychotic patients before hospital admission and after discharge. *International Journal of Social Psychiatry, 6,* 25–33.

Ohman, R., Wallinder, J., Balldin, J., Wallin, L., & Abrahamson, L. (1976). Prolactin response to electroconvulsive therapy. *Lancet, 2,* 936–937.

O'Shanick, G. J., & Ellinwood, E. H. (1982). Persistent elevation of thyroid-stimulating hormone in women with bipolar affective disorder. *American Journal of Psychiatry, 139*, 513–514.

Pandey, S. K., Devpura, J. C., Bedi, H. K., & Babel, C. S. (1973). An estimation of magnesium and calcium in serum and CSF in schizophrenia. *Journal of the Association of Physicians of India, 21*, 203–205.

Pandurangi, A., Dewan, M., Lee, S. H., Ramachandren, T., Levy, B. F., Boucher, M., Yozawitz, A., & Major, L. (1984). The ventricular system in chronic schizophrenic patients—a controlled computer tomography study. *Britith Journal of Psychiatry, 144*, 172–176.

Papousek, M. (1975). Chronobiologische Aspekte der Zyklothymie. *Fortschritte der Neurologie, Psychiatrie und ihrer Grenzgebiete, 43*, 381–440.

Pappenheimer, J. R., Heisey, S. R., Jordan, E. G., & Downer, J. C. (1962). Perfusion of the cerebral ventricular system in unanesthetized goats. *American Journal of Physiology, 203*, 763–774.

Parker, G., & Neilson, M. (1976). Mental disorder and season of birth—a southern hemisphere study. *British Journal of Psychiatry, 129*, 355–361.

Peck, J. W., & Blass, E. M. (1975). Localization of thirst and antidiuretic osmosreceptors by intracranial injections in rats. *American Journal of Physiology, 228*, 1501–1509.

Pelham, R. W., Vaughan, G. M., Sandock, K. L., & Vaughan, M. K. (1973). Twenty-four-hour cycle of a melatonin-like substance in the plasma of human males. *Journal of Clinical Endocrinology and Metabolism, 37*, 341–344.

Perris, C. (1966). A study of bipolar (manic–depressive) and unipolar depressive psychoses. *Acta Psychiatrica Scandinavica, Supplementum, 194*, 1–189.

Platman, S. R., & Fieve, R. R. (1968). Lithium carbonate and plasma cortisol response in the affective disorders. *Archives of General Psychiatry, 18*, 591–594.

Porte, D. J., & Halter, J. B. (1981). The endocrine pancreas and diabetes mellitus. In R. H. Williams (Ed.), *Textbook of endocrinology* (6th ed., pp. 716–843). Philadelphia: Saunders.

Prange, A. J., Wilson, I. C., Bresse, G. R., & Lipton, M. A. (1976). Hormonal alteration of imipramine response: A review. In E. J. Sachar (Ed.), *Hormones, behaviour and psychopathology* (pp. 41–67). New York: Raven Press.

Preslock, J. P. (1984). The pineal gland: Basic implications and clinical correlations. *Endocrine Reviews, 5*, 282–308.

Raskind, M. (1974). Psychosis, polydipsia and water intoxication. *Archives of General Psychiatry, 30*, 112–114.

Reiss, M. (Ed.). (1958). *Psychoendocrinology*. New York: Grune & Stratton.

Rendell, M., McGrane, D., & Cuesta, M. (1978). Fatal compulsive water drinking. *JAMA, Journal of the American Medical Association, 240*, 2557–2559.

Reus, V.I. (1984). Diagnosis and treatment in endocrinology and psychiatry: From Cushing's syndrome to disorder to mood. In C. van Dyke, L. Temoshok, & L. S. Zegans (Eds.), *Emotions in health and illness: Applications to clinical practice* (pp. 23–34). New York: Grune & Stratton.

Rey, J. H., & Coppen, A. J. (1959). Distribution of androgyny in mental patients. *British Medical Journal, 2*, 1445–1447.

Richter, C. P. (1965). *Biological clocks in medicine and psychiatry* (pp. 21–48). Springfield, IL: Charles C. Thomas.

Rinieris, P. M., Christodoulou, G. N., Souvatzoglou, A., Koutras, D. A., & Stefanis, C. N. (1978a). Free thyroxine index in mania and depression. *Comprehensive Psychiatry, 19*, 561–564.

Rinieris, P. M., Christodoulou, G. N., Souvatzoglou, A., Koutras, D. A., & Stefanis, C. N. (1978b). Free thyroxine index in psychotic and neurotic depression. *Acta Psychiatrica Scandinavica, 58*, 56–60.

Robertson, G. L. (1980). Psychogenic polydipsia and inappropriate antidiuresis. *Archives of Internal Medicine, 140*, 1574–1575.

Robertson, G. L., Shelton, R. L., & Athar, S. (1976). The osmoregulation of vasopressin. *Kidney International, 10*, 25–37.

Rodbard, D., & Munson, R. J. (1978). Is there an osmotic threshold for vasopressin release? *American Journal of Physiology, 234*, 340–342.

Rollag, M. D., & Niswender, G. D. (1976). Radioimmunoassay of serum concentrations of melatonin in sheep exposed to different lighting regimens. *Endocrinology (Baltimore), 98*, 482–489.

Rose, R. M. (1980). Endocrine responses to stressful psychological events. *Psychiatric Clinics of North America, 3*, 251–275.

Roth, J., Glick, S. M., Yalow, R. S., Berson, S. A. (1963). Hypoglycemia: A potent stimulus to the secretion of growth hormone. *Science, 140*, 987–988.

Rotrosen, J., Angrist, B. M., Gershon, S., Panguin, J., Branchey, L., Oleshanky, M., Halpern, F., & Sachar, E. J. (1979). Neuroendocrine effects of apomorphine characterization of response patterns and application to schizophrenia research. *British Journal of Psychiatry, 135*, 444–456.

Rotrosen, J., Angrist, B., Gershon, S., Sachar, E. J., & Halpern, F. S. (1976). Dopamine receptor alteration in schizophrenia: Neuroendocrine evidence. *Psychopharmacology, 51*, 1–7.

Rotrosen, J., Angrist, B., & Panguin, J. (1978). Neuroendocrine studies with dopamine agonists in schizophrenia. *Psychopharmacology Bulletin, 14*(1), 14–17.

Rubin, R. T. (1985). Editorial: The prospects for clinical psychoneuroendocrinology: Has the curtain been drawn across the neuroendocrine window? *Psychological Medicine, 15*, 451–454.

Rubin, R. T., & Hays, S. E. (1980). The prolactin secretory response to neuroleptic drugs: Mechanisms, applications, and limitations. *Psychoneuroendocrinology, 5*, 121–137.

Rubin, R. T., & Poland, R. E. (1982). The chronoendocrinology of endogenous depression. In E. E. Müller & R. M. MacLeod (Eds.), *Neuroendocrine perspectives* (Vol. 1, pp. 305–337). Amsterdam: Elsevier Biomedical Press.

Rubin, R. T., Poland, R. E., Tower, B. B., Hart, P. A., Blodgett, A. L. N., & Forster, B. (1981). Hypothalamo–pituitary–gonadal function in primary endogenously depressed men: Preliminary findings. In K. Fuxe, J.-A. Gustafsson, & L. Wetterberg

(Eds.), *Steroid hormone regulation of the brain* (pp. 387–396). Oxford: Pergamon Press.

Rubin, R. T., Reinisch, J. R., & Haskett, R. F. (1981). Postnatal gonadal steroid effects on human sexually dimorphic behavior: A paradigm of hormone–environmental interaction. *Science, 211,* 1318–1324.

Rusak, B. (1984). Assessment and significance of rhythm disruptions in affective illness. In G. M. Brown, S. H. Koslow, & S. Reichlin (Eds.), *Neuroendocrine and psychiatric disorder* (pp. 267–279). New York: Raven Press.

Rybakowski, J., & Sowinski, J. (1973). Free thyroxine index and absolute free-thyroxine in affective disorders. *Lancet, 1,* 889.

Sachar, E. J., Frantz, A. B., Altman, N., & Sassin, J. (1973). Growth hormone and prolactin in unipolar and bipolar depressed patients: Responses to hypoglycemia and L-dopa. *American Journal of Psychiatry, 130,* 1362–1367.

Sachar, E. J., Halpern, F., Rosenfeld, R. S., Gallagher, T. F., & Hellman, L. (1973). Plasma and urinary testosterone levels in depressed men. *Archives of General Psychiatry, 28,* 15–18.

Sachar, E. J., Hellman, L., Roffwarg, H. P., Halpern, F. S., Fukushima, D. K., & Gallagher, R. F. (1973). Disrupted 24-hour patterns of cortisol secretion in psychotic depression. *Archives of General Psychiatry, 28,* 19–24.

Santen, R. J., & Bardin, C. W. (1973). Episodic luteinizing hormone secretion in man: Pulse analysis, clinical interpretation, physiological mechanisms. *Journal of Clinical Investigation, 52,* 2617–2628.

Schiavi, R. C., & White, D. (1976). Androgens and male sexual function: A review of human studies. *Journal of Sex and Marital Therapy, 2,* 214.

Schilkrut, R., Chandra, O., Osswald, M., Rüther, E., Baarfüsser, B., & Mattussek, N. (1975). Growth hormone during sleep and with thermal stimulation in depressed patients. *Neuropsychobiology, 1,* 70–79.

Schwarz, L., & Munoz, R. (1968). Blood sugar levels in patients treated with chlorpromazine, *American Journal of Psychiatry, 125,* 253–255.

Shopsin, B., & Gershon, S. (1975). Psychoactive drugs in mania. *Archives of General Psychiatry, 32,* 34–42.

Silverman, C. (1968). *The epidemiology of depression.* Baltimore: Johns Hopkins Press.

Siris, S. G., Siris, E. S., van Kammen, D. P., Docherty, J. P., Alexander, P. E., & Bunney, W. E. (1980). Effects of dopamine blockade on gonadotropins and testosterone in men. *American Journal of Psychiatry, 137,* 211–214.

Sladek, C. D., & Joynt, R. J. (1978). Cholinergic involvement in the osmotic control of vasopressin release by the organ-cultured rat hypothalamo–hypophyseal system. *Neurology, 28,* 366.

Sladek, C. D., & Knigge, K. M. (1977). Cholinergic stimulation of vasopressin release from the rat hypothalamo–neurohypophysial system in organ culture. *Endocrinology (Baltimore), 101,* 1834–1838.

Sleeper, F. H., & Jellinek, E. M. (1936). A comparative physiologic, psychotic and psychiatric study of polyuric and nonpolyuric schizophrenic patients. *Journal of Nervous and Mental Disease, 83,* 557–563.

Smith, W. O., & Clark, M. L. (1980). Self-induced water intoxication in schizophrenic patients. *American Journal of Psychiatry, 137,* 1055–1060.

Spitzer R. L., Endicott, J., & Robins, E. (1978). Research diagnostic criteria: Rationale and reliability. *Archives of General Psychiatry, 35,* 773–782.

Spratt, D. I., Pont, A., Miller, M. B., McDougall, I. R., Bayer, M. F., & McLaughlin, W. T. (1982). Hyperthyroxinemia in patients with acute psychiatric disorders. *American Journal of Medicine, 73,* 41–48.

Stancer, H. C., & Persad, E. (1982). Treatment of intractable rapid-cycling manic–depressive disorder with levothyroxine. *Archives of General Psychiatry, 39,* 311–312.

Starkman, M. N., Schteingart, D. E., & Schork, M. A. (1981). Depressed mood and other psychiatric manifestations of Cushing's syndrome: Relationship to hormone levels. *Psychosomatic Medicine, 43,* 3–18.

Stevens, J. (1982). Neuropathology of schizophrenia. *Archives of General Psychiatry, 39,* 1131–1139.

Stokes, P. E., Stoll, P. M., Koslow, S. H., Mass, J. W., Davis, J. M., Swann, A. C., & Robins, E. (1984). Pretreatment DST and hypothalamic–pituitary–adrenocortical function in depressed patients and comparison groups. *Archives of General Psychiatry, 41,* 257–267.

Sved, S., Perales, A., & Palaic, D. (1971). Chlorpromazine metabolism in chronic schizophrenics. *British Journal of Psychiatry, 119,* 589–596.

Takahara, J., Arimura, A., & Schally, A. V. (1974). Suppression of prolactin release by a purified porcine PIF preparation and catecholamines infused into rat hypophysial portal vessels. *Endocrinology (Baltimore), 95,* 462–465.

Takahashi, S., Kondo, H., Yoshimura, M., & Ochi, Y. (1974). Thyrotropin response to TRH in depressive illness: Relation to clinical subtypes and prolonged duration of depressive episode. *Folia Psychiatrica Neurologica Japonica, 28,* 355–365.

Takahashi, S., Kondo, H., Yoshimura, M., & Ochi, Y. (1975). Thyroid function levels and thyrotropin response to TRH administration in manic patients receiving lithium carbonate. *Folia Psychiatrica Neurologica Japonica, 29,* 231–237.

Taylor, A. N., & Wilson, R. W. (1970). Electrophysiological evidence for the action of light in the pineal gland in the rat. *Experientia, 26,* 267–269.

Temple, R., Berman, M., Carlson, H. E., Robbins, J., & Wolff, J. (1972). The use of lithium in Graves' disease. *Mayo Clinic Proceedings, 47,* 872–878.

Thomas, A., Goldney, R., & Phillips, P. (1983). Depression, electroconvulsive therapy and diabetes mellitus. *Australian and New Zealand Journal of Psychiatry, 17,* 289–291.

Thonnard-Neumann, E. (1968). Phenothiazines and diabetes in hospitalized women. *American Journal of Psychiatry, 124,* 978–982.

Tourney, G. L., & Hatfield, H. L. M. (1972). Plasma androgen in male schizophrenics. *Archives of General Psychiatry, 27,* 753–755.

Tourney, G. L., & Hatfield, H. L. M. (1973). Androgen metabolism in schizophrenics, homosexuals and normal controls. *Biological Psychiatry, 6,* 23–36.

Trethowan, W. H., & Cobb, S. (1952). Neuropsychiatric aspects of Cushing's syndrome. *Archives of Neurology and Psychiatry, 67,* 283–309.

Turkington, R. W. (1972). Prolactin secretion in patients treated with various drugs. *Archives of Internal Medicine, 130,* 349–354.

Ungerstedt, V. (1971). Adipsia and aphagia after 6-hydroxydopamine-induced degeneration of the nigrostriatal dopamine system. *Acta Physiologica Scandinavica, 367*(Suppl.), 95–122.

Urry, R. L., & Ellis, L. C. (1975). Monoamine oxidase activity of the hypothalamus and pituitary: Alterations after pinealectomy, changes in photoperiod, or additions of melatonin *in vitro. Experientia, 31,* 891–892.

Valiquette, G. (1980). Posterior pituitary hormones and neurophysins. In M. Motta (Ed.), *The endocrine function of the brain* (pp. 385–417). New York: Raven Press.

Van Der Velde, C. D., & Gordon, M. W. (1969). Manic–depressive illness, diabetes mellitus and lithium carbonate. *Archives of General Psychiatry, 21,* 478–485.

van Praag, H. M. (1981). Management of depression with serotonin precursors. *Biological Psychiatry, 16,* 291–310.

Vaughan, G. M., McDonald, S. D., Jordan, R. M., Allen, J. P., Bell, R., & Stevens, E. A. (1979). Melatonin, pituitary function and stress in humans. *Psychoneuroendocrinology, 4,* 351–362.

Vaughan, M. K., Reiter, R. J., & Benson, B. (1972). Effect of melatonin and other pineal indoles on adrenal enlargement produced in male and female mice by pinealectomy, unilateral adrenalectomy, castration, and cold stress. *Neuroendocrinology, 10,* 139–154.

Vekemans, M., & Robyn, C. (1975). Influence of age on serum prolactin levels in women and men. *British Medical Journal, 4,* 738–739.

Villani, S., & Weitzel, W. D. (1979). Secondary mania. *Archives of General Psychiatry, 36,* 1031.

Vincent, J. D., Aranaud, E., & Bioulac, B. (1972). Activity of osmosensitive single cells in the hypothalamus of the behaving monkey during drinking. *Brain Research, 44,* 371–384.

Vogel, W., Klaiber, E. L., & Broverman, D. M. (1978). Roles of the gonadal steroid hormones in psychiatric depression in men and women. *Progress in Neuropsychopharmacology, 2,* 487–503.

vom Saal, F. S. (1979). Prenatal exposure to androgen influences morphology and aggressive behavior of male and female mice. *Hormones and Behavior, 12,* 1–11.

von Zerssen, D., & Doerr, P. (1980). The role of the hypothalamo–pituitary–adrenocortical system in psychiatric disorders. *Advances in Biological Psychiatry, 5,* 85–106.

von Zerssen, D. (1983). Chronobiology of depression. In J. Angst (Ed.), *The origins of depression: Current concepts and approaches* (pp. 253–271). Berlin: Springer-Verlag.

Waitzkin, L. (1966a). A survey for unknown diabetics in a mental hospital. 1. Men under age 50. *Diabetes, 15,* 97–104.

Waitzkin, L. (1966b). A survey for unknown diabetics in a mental hospital. 2. men from age 50. *Diabetes, 15,* 164–172.

Wallick, E. T., Lane, L. K., & Schwartz, A. (1979). Regulation by vanadate of ouabain binding to Na$^+$,

K$^+$-ATPase. *Journal of Biological Chemistry, 254,* 8107–8109.

Weeke, A., & Weeke, J. (1978). Disturbed circadian variation of serum thyrotropin in patients with endogenous depression. *Acta Psychiatrica Scandinavica, 57,* 281–289.

Weeke, A., & Weeke, J. (1980). The 24-hour pattern of serum TSH in patients with endogenous depression. *Acta Psychiatrica Scandinavica, 62,* 69–74.

Wehr, T. A., Gillin, J. C., & Goodwin, F. K. (1983). Sleep and circadian rhythm in depression. In M. Chase & E. D. Weitzman (Eds.), *Sleep disorders: Basic and clinical research* (pp. 195–224). New York: Spectrum Publications.

Wehr, T. A., Muscettola, G., & Goodwin, F. K. (1980). Urinary 3-methoxy-4-hydroxphenylglycol circadian rhythm: Early timing (phase advance) in manic–depressives compared with normal subjects. *Archives of General Psychiatry, 37,* 257–263.

Wehr, T. A., Wirz-Justice, A., Goodwin, F. K., Duncan, W., & Gillin, J. C. (1979). Phase advance of the sleep–wake cycle as an antidepressant. *Science, 206,* 710–713.

Weinberger, D. R., Bigelow, L. B., Kleinman, J. E., Klein, S. T., Rosenblatt, J. E., & Wyatt, R. J. (1980). Cerebral ventricular enlargement in chronic schizophrenia is associated with poor response to treatment. *Archives of General Psychiatry, 37,* 11–14.

Weitzman, E. D., Czeisler, C. A., & Moore-Ede, M. C. (1979). Sleep–wake, endocrine, and temperature rhythms in man during temporal isolation. *Advances in Sleep Research, 7,* 77–93.

Wenzel, K. W., Meinhold, H., Raffenberg, M., Adlkofer, F., & Schleusener, H. (1974). Classification of hypothyroidism in evaluating patients after radioiodine therapy by serum cholesterol, T3-uptake, total T4, FT4-index, total T3, basal TSH and TRH test. *European Journal of Clinical Investigation, 4,* 141–148.

Weston, P. G., & Howard, M. Q. (1922). The determination of sodium, potassium, calcium and magnesium in the blood and spinal fluid of patients suffering from manic–depressive insanity. *Archives of Neurology and Psychiatry, 8,* 179–183.

Wetterberg, L. (1983). The relationship between the pineal gland and the pituitary–adrenal axis in health, endocrine, and psychiatric conditions. *Psychoneuroendocrinology, 8,* 75–89.

Wetterberg, L., Aperia, B., Beck-Friis, J., Kjellman, B. F., Ljunggren, J.-G., Petterson, U., Sjolin, A., Tham, A., & Unden, F. (1981). Pineal–hypothalamic–pituitary function in patients with depressive illness. In K. Fuxe, J.-A. Gustaffson, & L. Wetterberg (Eds.), *Steroid hormone regulation of the brain* (pp. 397–403). Oxford: Pergamon Press.

Wetterberg. L., Beck-Friis, J., Aperia, B., & Petterson, U. (1979). Melatonin/cortisol ratio in depression. *Lancet, 2,* 1361.

Wetterberg, L., Beck-Friis, J., Kjellman, B. F., & Ljunggren, J.-G. (1984). Circadian rhythms in melatonin and cortisol secretion in depression. In E. Usdin, M. Asberg, L. Bertilsson, & F. Sjöqvist (Eds.), *Frontiers in biochemical and pharmacological research* (pp. 197–205). New York: Raven Press.

Whalley, L. J., Christie, J. E., Bennie, J., Dick, H., Blackburn, I. M., Blackwood, D., Sanchez Watts, G., & Fink, G. (1985). Selective increase in plasma luteinizing hormone concentrations in drug-free young men with mania. *British Medical Journal, 290,* 99–102.

Whybrow, P. C. (1972). Synergistic action between iodine and lithium. *JAMA, Journal of the American Medical Association, 221,* 506.

Winodur, G. W., Clayton, P. J., & Reich, T. (1969). *Manic–depressive illness.* St. Louis, MO: C. V. Mosby.

Wirz-Justice, A., & Wehr, A. (1983). Neuropsychopharmacology and biological rhythms. *Advances in Biological Psychiatry, 11,* 20–34.

Wurtman, R. J., Axelrod, J., & Philips, L. S. (1963). Melatonin synthesis in the pineal gland: Control by light. *Science, 142,* 1071–1073.

Wynn, V., Adams, P. W., Folkard, J., & Seed, M. (1975). Tryptophan, depression and steroidal contraception. *Journal of Steroid Biochemistry, 6,* 965–970.

Wynn, V., & Rob, C. G. (1954). Water intoxication: Differential diagnosis of hypotonic syndromes. *Lancet, 1,* 587–594.

Yamaguchi, N., Maeda, K., & Kuromaru, S. (1978). The effect of sleep deprivation on the circadian rhythm of plasma cortisol levels in depressive patients. *Folia Psychiatrica Neurologica Japonica, 32,* 479–487.

Yamaji, T., Shimamoto, K., Ishibashi, M., Kosada, K., & Orimo, H. (1976). Effect of age and sex on circulating and pituitary prolactin levels in humans. *Acta Endocrinologica (Copenhagen), 83,* 711–719.

8 ENDOCRINE CONSEQUENCES OF ALCOHOL ABUSE

JUDITH S. GAVALER
DAVID H. VAN THIEL

University of Pittsburgh School of Medicine

INTRODUCTION

Hypoandrogenization is commonly seen in chronic alcoholic men: 70–90% of such men experience reduced libido and/or impotence (Lloyd & Williams, 1948; Van Thiel & Lester, 1976). Reproductive as well as Leydig cell failure is common also in such men, with 70–80% of them demonstrating both gross testicular atrophy and infertility after years of preceding alcohol abuse (Lloyd & Williams, 1948; Van Thiel, 1983). Histological studies of the testicular tissue obtained from chronic alcoholic men usually demonstrate seminiferous tubular atrophy with loss of mature germ cells. Many of the residual, less mature germ cells have an abnormal morphology (Van Thiel, 1983).

Evidence for hyperestrogenization is also present in such men, but occurs less often. Thus, a female escutcheon and palmar erythema are seen in 50%, spider angiomata in 40%, and gynecomastia in 20% of chronic alcoholic men. These "estrogenic" signs of chronic alcoholism, unlike the transient impotence experienced with an acute alcoholic bout, persist in the absence of intoxication and are due in large measure to alcohol-induced permanent injury.

Until recently, liver disease was considered to be of primary importance in the pathogenesis of these evidences of sexual dysfunction in alcoholic men (Van Thiel, 1983). However, during the past 15 years, this concept has been challenged severely and a diametrically opposite point of view has gained currency. This change in thinking has occurred as a result of the demonstration that sexual dysfunction can occur in alcoholic men with a wide spectrum of morphological alcohol-associated hepatic injuries, varying from essentially normal liver to that of severe alcoholic hepatitis and/or cirrhosis. Moreover, testosterone concentrations can be shown to fall in normal male volunteers within hours of their ingesting sufficient amounts of alcohol to produce a hangover (Gordon, Altman, Southren, Rubin, & Lieber, 1976; Van Thiel, 1983). In addition, many of the features of the syndrome of alcohol-induced sexual dysfunction can be produced in experimental animals and appear in such animals at a time when hepatic biochemical function and morphological appearance are altered only minimally (Gavaler, Van Thiel, & Lester, 1980; Van Thiel, Gavaler, Cobb, Sherins, & Lester, 1979; Van Thiel, Gavaler, Lester, & Goodman, 1975; Van Thiel, Lester, & Vaitukaitis, 1978). Thus, the concept that the sexual changes observed in chronic alcoholic men are the result of alcohol abuse per se rather than the indirect consequence of alcohol-induced liver disease has gained considerable credence.

THE ALCOHOLIC MALE

A dose-dependent decline in plasma testosterone has been reported in mice receiving graded amounts of alcohol over a 5-day period. Alcohol-induced chronic testicular injury characterized by atrophy, loss of germ cells, and reduced testosterone levels has been reported in alcohol-fed rats after only 6 weeks of alcohol administration. Both adult and weanling rats fed a diet in which ethanol accounts for 36% of their caloric intake, but which contains sufficient vitamins, trace minerals, and proteins for normal growth and development, become hypogonadal (Gavaler et al., 1980; Van Thiel, Gavaler, Lester, & Goodman, 1975). The hypogonadism seen in these animals was characterized by atrophy of androgen-dependent target organs and testes and destruction of the germinal epithelium.

The most direct evidence that alcohol and possibly acetaldehyde may disturb testicular function has been developed in studies utilizing the isolated perfused rat testes and isolated rat Leydig cells maintained in tissue culture (Cobb, Ennis, Van Thiel, Gavaler, & Lester, 1978, 1980). In the perfusion studies, testes were perfused with a defined tissue culture medium which contained chorionic gonadotropin. When alcohol or acetaldehyde was added to the perfusion medium at concentrations comparable to those found in the blood of chronic alcoholic and acutely intoxicated individuals, testosterone production and secretion were markedly reduced. In the cell culture studies, ethanol levels equal to one-quarter of the legal limit of intoxication in most states inhibited testosterone synthesis and secretion by the cultured cells by greater than 40%. Larger doses of ethanol produced even greater effects.

Specific mechanisms by which alcohol adversely affects testicular function are being unraveled slowly. Alcohol may interfere with testicular vitamin A activation which is essential for normal spermatogenesis (Van Thiel, Gavaler, & Lester, 1974). In addition, alcohol metabolism may shift the testicular balance between NAD and NADH as it does in the liver, thereby secondarily inhibiting testosterone biosynthesis (Chiao, Johnston, Gavaler, & Van Thiel, 1981; Gordon, Vittek, & Southren, 1980; Johnston, Chiao, Gavaler, & Van Thiel, 1981). Similarly, acetaldehyde, either produced directly in the testes as a result of testicular metabolism of ethanol or entering the testes from the plasma as a result

of ethanol metabolism by the liver, may have a deleterious effect upon testicular mitochondria, organelles which are critical for steroidogenesis. Thus, it has been reported that the conversion of cholesterol to pregnenolone, a reaction that occurs in mitochondria, is inhibited as a result of exposure of mitochondria to either ethanol or acetaldehyde. In addition, several groups have demonstrated reduced activity of several microsomal enzymes which are important for testosteronogenesis, particularly 17α-hydroxylase, 3β-hydroxysteroid dehydrogenase/isomerase, and desmolase (Chiao et al., 1981; Gordon et al., 1980; Johnston et al., 1981). Not only is testicular testosterone production inhibited as a result of alcohol exposure, but recent studies have demonstrated that ethanol interferes with luteinizing hormone (LH) binding to testicular tissue and that chronic alcohol exposure is associated with a hypothalamic–pituitary defect in gonadotropin secretion (Van Thiel, 1983; Van Thiel, Lester, & Vaitukaitus, 1978). Thus, alcoholic individuals not only have inappropriately low plasma gonadotropin concentrations for the degree of their gonadal failure, but also demonstrate inadequate responses to exogenous stimuli which normally provoke gonadotropin release such as clomiphene and luteinizing hormone-releasing factor (LHRH). Similarly, inadequate gonadotropin responses can be demonstrated in chronic alcohol-fed rats and in normal rats following alcohol administration. The foregoing suggests that chronic alcohol ingestion induces gonadal injury through its direct effects on the gonad as well as through indirect effects exerted at the level of the hypothalamus and pituitary.

In addition to being hypogonadal, chronic alcoholic men are often grossly feminized (Van Thiel, 1983). Thus, palmar erythema, spider angiomata, a female escutcheon, and gynecomastia are common physical findings in such men. Biochemical evidence of "hyperestrogenization" is documented by increases in estrogen-responsive proteins, such as sex steroid-binding globulin and estrogen-responsive neurophysin (Lloyd & Williams 1948; Van Thiel, 1983; Van Thiel & Lester, 1976). It is probable also that the increase in prolactin levels seen in alcoholics with cirrhosis is related to increased estrogen levels or estrogen responsiveness (Van Thiel, Gavaler, Lester, Loriaux, & Braunstein, 1975). Moreover, because testicular atrophy can be produced by estrogen administration, the testicular damage in alcoholic men with cirrhosis can, at least in part, be ascribed to a hyperestrogenemic state. However, when plasma estradiol levels are actually measured in chronic alcoholic men, they are found to be either normal or only slightly increased. In contrast, plasma estrone levels are increased moderately (Van Thiel, Gavaler, Lester, Loriaux, & Braunstein, 1975).

This finding of normal to near normal estrogen levels in the presence of androgen deficiency is paradoxical in that estrogens can only be produced by conversion from preformed androgens. Thus, the mechanism of normal or moderately increased plasma estrogen levels in the presence of markedly reduced plasma androgen levels requires explanation. Preliminary results would suggest that the hyperestrogenemic state is a result of both the direct effects of alcohol and the indirect effects of alcohol mediated through the development of liver disease. Unlike what was initially expected, the metabolic clearance rate for estradiol in men with Laennec's cirrhosis is normal, not reduced (Olivo, Gordon, Rafii, & Southren, 1975).

Moreover, evidence has accumulated to suggest that the adrenal overproduction of weak androgens and estrogen precursors regularly occurs in chronic alcoholic men (Frajria & Angeli, 1977; Smals, Njo, Knoben, Ruland, & Kloppenborg, 1977). Furthermore, signs and symptoms of adrenocorticoid hyperresponsiveness resembling Cushing's syndrome have been described in such men. Thus, these patients not infrequently develop loss of peripheral muscle mass, truncal obesity, hypertension, facial erythema, increased plasma cortisol and androstenedione levels, loss of the normal diurnal variation of plasma cortisol, and failure to show dexamethasone suppression. The mechanism responsible for this overproduction of adrenocortical precursors of estrone is as yet uncertain. Recent studies would suggest, however, that ethanol and acetaldehyde directly stimulate the adrenal cortex by activating adenyl cyclase (Cobb et al., 1980). Thus, in an isolated perfused rat adrenal sys-

tem, concentrations of ethanol and acetaldehyde observed in the plasma of intoxicated males have been shown to increase corticosterone secretion. Moreover, in clinical studies, weakly androgenic steroids, such as androstenedione and dehydroepiandrosterone sulfate, have been shown to undergo aromatization to estrogens in various tissues, including skin, fat, muscle, bone, and brain. Such peripheral aromatization has been shown to be enhanced in men with Laennec's cirrhosis (Gordon, Olivo, Rafii, & Southren, 1975; Southren, Gordon, Olivo, Rafii, & Rosenthal, 1973). In addition, aromatase activity in the liver and presumably other tissues is enhanced in experimental animlas as a result of ethanol administration (Gordon et al., 1980). Thus, a normal metabolic clearance rate and an increased production rate of androstenedione and estrone account for the observed increases in plasma concentrations of these two steroids seen in alcoholic individuals (Gordon et al., 1976, 1980; Southren et al., 1973).

Compounding this overproduction of adrenal androgens which can be converted to estrogens, portosystemic shunting, which occurs as a consequence of alcoholic liver disease, has been shown to allow steroidal estrogen precursors such as androstenedione and dehydroepiandrosterone, secreted into the systemic circulation, to escape the confines of the enterohepatic circulation (Van Thiel et al., 1980). As a result, these steroids are converted to estrogens at peripheral sites where aromatase activity is increased. The slight increase in plasma estrogen levels observed in alcoholics therefore reflects the levels that reflux back into the plasma from these peripheral sites after aromatization has occurred.

Compounding the effect of this increased peripheral aromatization of androgens to estrogens is the observation that cytosolic estrogen receptor activity is enhanced in the liver and testes of chronic alcohol-fed animals and presumably also in man (Eagon, Porter, & Van Thiel, 1980). Normal male rat liver contains one-third the amount of cytoplasmic estrogen receptor present in normal female liver (Eagon, Fisher et al., 1980). After castration of the male, cytoplasmic estrogen receptor activity increases toward female values (Eagon, Porter & Van Thiel, 1980).

Treatment of the castrated rat with dihydrotestosterone (DHT) prevents the castration-induced change towards the female pattern. Moreover, chronic alcohol feeding of otherwise normal male rats is associated with a decline in the hepatic cytosolic content of a male-specific estrogen-binding protein and an increase in the classic estrogen receptor, in effect converting the male alcohol-fed rat liver to that of a female in terms of its cytosolic estrogen-binding characteristics. In the testes, chronic ethanol feeding reduces androgen levels and androgen receptor activity and enhances estrogen receptor activity. Exogenous androgen therapy reverses the defects in androgen levels and receptors, but not the estrogenic events. Such increased estrogen receptor activity and reduced levels of the nonreceptor male-specific estrogen-binding protein in the liver allows the male liver obtained from alcohol-fed animals to hyperrespond to the normal or only moderately increased plasma estrogen levels present.

THE ALCOHOLIC FEMALE

In contrast to the male, the alcoholic female is not superfeminized, but instead shows severe gonadal failure manifested as oligo-amenorrhea, loss of secondary sex characteristics (such as breast and pelvic fat accumulation), and infertility (Tables 8.1–8.3). Histologic studies of the ovaries obtained at autopsy from chronic alcoholic women who have died of cirrhosis while still in their reproductive years (20–40 years of age) have shown a paucity of developing follicles and few of no corpora lutea, documenting reproductive failure (Jung & Russfield, 1972). Moreover, these findings have been reproduced in an animal model (Van Thiel & Gavaler, 1982). Endocrine failure of the ovary of alcoholic women is manifested by reduced plasma levels of estradiol and progesterone, loss of secondary sex characteristics, and ovulatory failure (Van Thiel, & Gavaler, 1982).

The data that address the effects of alcohol exposure on reproductive function in female animals can be divided into those concerned with the estrus cycle (Table 8.1), those addressing the issue of ovulatory failure (Table 8.2), and, finally, those examining fertility (Table 8.3).

Since 1958, nine separate studies by seven different investigative groups have examined the effect of alcohol exposure in mice, rats, rabbits, and monkeys upon the estrus cycle of animals (Table 8.1). In general, as the alcohol

TABLE 8.1. Effects of Alcohol on the Estrus Cycle of Female Animals

Author (Year)	Species	Findings
Cranston (1958)	Mouse	Increased number of noncycling animals and increased number of abnormal cycling animals
Aron et al. (1965)	Rabbit	Increased number of abnormal cycles
Kieffer and Ketchel (1970)	Rat	Abnormal vaginal cytology
Van Thiel, Gavaler, and Lester (1978)	Rat	Increased number of noncycling animals and animals showing an absence of estrogen effect
Gavaler, Van Thiel, and Lester (1980)	Rat	Absence of any estrogen effect
Eskay, Ryback, Goldman, and Majchrowicz (1981)	Rat	Reduced number of cycling animals and increased number of animals having abnormal cycles
Bo, Krueger, Rudeen, and Symmes (1982)	Rat	Absence of estrus cycles
Mello, Bree, Mendelson, and Ellingboe (1983)	Monkey	Absence of cycles (amenorrhea)

TABLE 8.2. Effects of Alcohol on Ovulatory Function

Author (Year)	Species	Dose of ethanol	Finding
Chaudhury and Matthews (1966)	Rabbit	5 ml/kg	No progeny if mated at time of expected ovulation
Kieffer and Ketchel (1970)	Rat	7.9 g/kg	Absence of tubal ova 1 and 2 days following alcohol
Van Thiel, Gavaler, & Lester (1978)	Rat	5% diet	Absence of corpora hemorrhagicum and corpora lutea
Blake (1978)	Rat	0.6 ml/kg	Inhibits LH midcycle surge
Gavaler, Van Thiel, and Lester (1980)	Rat	5% diet	Absence of corpora hemorrahagicum and corpora lutea
Bo, Krueger, Rudeen, and Symmes (1982)	Rat	5% diet	Absence of corpora lutea
Mello, Bree, Mendelson and Ellingboe (1983)	Monkey	2.9 g/kg	Atrophic sexual organs and absence of corpora lutea
Gavaler (1983)	Rat	5% diet	Dose-dependent atrophy of sexual organs and reduced levels of estradiol and progesterone

exposure either increases in dose or is prolonged over time, the number of female animals demonstrating a total loss of estrus cyclicity or a disruption of the existing cycles (usually with irregular prolongations of their cycle) increases. Similarly, in rabbits, mice, rats, and monkeys, an increased incidence of ovulatory failure documented by a failure to conceive, absence of expected ova in the fallopian tubes following the time of expected ovulation, absence of ovarian corpus hemorrhagicum and corpora lutea, a loss of the midcycle ovulatory gonadotropin surge, and a failure of plasma estradiol and progesterone levels to increase in the latter half of the cycle have been seen following ethanol exposure to female animals (Table 8.2). Not

unexpectedly, as a result of this increased prevalence of ovulatory failure with increasing alcohol exposure, the fertility of alcohol-exposed female animals is affected adversely (Table 8.3).

In contrast to the considerable amount of data available concerning the adverse effects of ethanol exposure upon endocrine and reproductive function in female animals, little data exist in which human subjects have been studied (Table 8.4).

Moreover, in contrast to the generally negative acute studies performed in human female subjects, chronic ethanol abuse by human females has been shown to disturb hypothalamic–pituitary–gonadal function by most authors who have studied the problem

TABLE 8.3. Effects of Ethanol Exposure on Female Fertility

Author (Year)	Dose of ethanol	Species	Finding
Cranston (1958)	10–20%	Mouse	Number of anovulatory (infertile) animals increases
Chaudhury and Matthews (1966)	5 ml/kg	Rabbit	Markedly reduced fertility
Merari, Ginton, Heifez, and Lev-Ran (1973)	1 mg/kg	Rat	Abnormal lordosis/mating behavior

TABLE 8.4. Acute Effects of Alcohol in Human Female Subjects

Author (Year)	Findings
Positive studies	
H. Valimaki, Harkonen, and Ylikahri (1983)	Increased sex steroid levels and reduced gonadotropin levels
Negative studies	
McNamee, Grant, Ratcliffe, and Oliver (1979)	No consistent effect on hormone levels studied in the early follicular period
Mendelson et al. (1983); Mendelson, Mello, and Ellingboe (1981)	No effect on sex steroids studied in the midfollicular period
Mendelson, Mello, Ellingboe and Bavli (1985)	No effect upon postmenopausal LH levels

(Table 8.5). As can be seen from the data in Table 8.5, in general, chronic alcohol use by women leads to early menopause, lower postmenopausal gonadotropin levels, and increased plasma levels of the classic female sex hormones despite the presence of amenorrhea.

The biochemical mechanisms for such endocrine failure are probably the same as those occurring within the testes of the male, as the pathways for steroidogenesis are the same in the gonads of the two sexes and an alcohol dehydrogenase has been reported to be present within the ovary as well as the testes.

The fetal alcohol syndrome does exist. Thus, alcohol abuse, which is quite common, does not invariably produce sterility, at least in females. This of course does not mean that alcohol abuse by females does not lead to infertility. In fact, considerable data exist to suggest precisely the converse, that is, that excessive alcohol consumption does indeed reduce female fertility and, in some cases, leads to overt sterility or early menopause. In general, however, chronic alcohol exposure in female animals or women leads to relative infertility rather than sterility, which is manifested as increased difficulty in becoming

TABLE 8.5. Chronic Effects of Alcohol Abuse in Human Female Subjects

Author (Year)	Findings
Moskovic (1975) ($n = 321$)	61% experience menstrual problems; 9% experience early menopause
Ryback (1977) ($n = 2$)	Amenorrhea dissipates with alcohol abstinence
Hugues, Perret, Adessi, Coste, and Modigliani (1978) ($n = 11$)	Early menopause and arithmetically reduced FSH levels
Jones-Saumty, Fabian, and Parsons (1981) ($n = 100$)	Early onset of menopause and increased frequency of other menstrual problems
James et al. (1983) ($n = 2$)	Alcoholic postmenopausal women have increased levels estrone, estradiol, and androstenedione
Valimaki et al. (1984) ($n = 9$)	Amenorrheic alcoholic women have increased levels of estrone, estradiol, and reduced levels of gonadotropins

pregnant. Moreover, despite the considerable data available concerning the fetal dysmorphogenic consequences of maternal alcohol abuse, little if anything is known about the effect of such maternal alcohol exposure upon placental (fetal) endocrine function, despite the fact that considerable data exist to suggest that placental structure and some transport functions are disturbed as a consequence of maternal alcohol exposure. Moreover, data have recently become available to suggest that the progeny of animals exposed to alcohol *in utero* and during the early neonatal period are not neuroendocrinologically normal as adults. Such male progeny can be shown to have reduced testes size, reduced plasma testosterone levels, and reduced sexual motivation and performance as compared to that of control animals not exposed to alcohol *in utero*. Similarly, data exist to suggest that when one used tests of behavior reflecting differences in sexual orientation, the adult female progeny of these same alcohol-exposed pregnant animals are less feminized than are control animals not exposed to alcohol *in utero* and in the early neonatal period.

HYPOTHALAMIC–PITUITARY INJURY

In addition to demonstrating evidence of primary gonadal failure, chronic alcoholics, whether male or female, demonstrate evidence for a central hypothalamic–pituitary defect in gonadotropin secretion. Thus, in both sexes, despite severe gonadal injury, follicle-stimulating hormone (FSH) levels, although increased, are well below levels expected for the degree of reproductive failure present. Further, in both sexes, despite the marked reduction in sex steroid levels, LH concentrations range from normal to only moderately increased.

EFFECTS OF ETHANOL ON THE HYPOTHALAMIC– PITUITARY–ADRENAL AXIS

The earliest animal studies examining the effect of alcohol on this endocrine axis were based upon indirect evidence of adrenal activation and suggested but did not prove that

ethanol altered adrenal cortical function. Hion-Jon (1928) was the first to demonstrate histologic changes in rabbit adrenal gland after acute and chronic alcohol administration. Subsequently, others have demonstrated that alcohol administration either by gavage or interperitoneal injection altered adrenocortical activity as determined by reductions in adrenal ascorbic acid and cholesterol content (Smith, 1951). Moreover, such studies demonstrated that these changes can be prevented by prior hypophysectomy (Ellis, 1966). This latter observation suggests that the primary effect of ethanol on the hypothalamic–pituitary–adrenal axis is at the level of the hypothalamus and pituitary rather than at the level of the adrenal gland. Additional evidence for a primary hypothalamic–pituitary effect of ethanol is the observation that pretreatment with dexamethasone blocks the expected adrenal response to ethanol administration. Moreover, it could be shown that alcohol administration results in an acute decrement in pituitary ACTH content.

Ellis (1966) was the first to measure corticosterone levels in response to ethanol treatment. Using dogs and rats, he was able to demonstrate increases in corticosterone levels and no change in the metabolic clearance rate of corticosterone following ethanol administration (Ellis, 1966). Alcohol, when given chronically to mice, has been shown to disturb the normal diurnal variation in plasma corticosterone levels (Kakihana, Butte, Hathaway, & Noble, 1971; Kakihana & Moore, 1976). Similarly, in normal human subjects, ethanol at intoxicating doses produces an immediate increase in plasma cortisol (Fazekas, 1966; Jenkins & Connolly, 1968; Linkola, Fyhrquist, & Ylikahri, 1977; Mendelson, Ogata, & Mello, 1971; Merry & Marks, 1972). Moreover, the cortisol response appears to parallel the blood ethanol level (Jenkins & Connolly, 1968; Suzuki, Hayashi, Hirose, Ikeda, & Tamura, 1972; Torro, Kolodny, Jacobs, & Masters, 1973). This response is probably due to a hypothalamic stress reaction and pituitary release of ACTH. Such stress responses can be blocked in experimental animals by prior pituitary stalk transection, morphine administration, or dexamethasone. In contrast, ethanol intoxication and withdrawal have been shown to be associated with an enhanced adrenergic activity in the brain, a factor known to inhibit hypothalamic release of corticotropin-releasing factor, and thereby impair the normal ACTH stress response (Bjorkquist, 1975; Littleton, 1978; Tabakoff & Hoffman, 1980).

Because acute exposure to ethanol causes an increase in plasma cortisol levels in normal persons, the effect of sustained ethanol levels on adrenal function is of interest. Plasma cortisol levels remain elevated in mice chronically fed alcohol, and the presence of ethanol disturbs the normal diurnal variation of corticosterone levels in such animals (Kakihana & Moore, 1976). Studies using human subjects given ethanol for 4–29 days similarly have demonstrated persistent elevations of plasma cortisol in response to alcohol administration. Moreover, pseudo-Cushing's syndrome has been recognized recently in chronic alcoholic individuals (Smals & Klopopenborg, 1977; Smals et al., 1977). Patients manifesting this syndrome have many of the classic features of true Cushing's syndrome and exhibit increased plasma cortisol levels and abnormal responses to dexamethasone. Despite such evidence for direct ethanol-induced adrenocortical hypersecretion, most investigators have found no pathological changes at autopsy in the adrenal glands of patients dying of Laennec's cirrhosis.

In the 1960s, Peterson reported decreased urinary excretion of glucocorticoids in cirrhotic individuals (Peterson, 1960). Zumoff, Bradlow, Gallagher, and Hellman (1967) subsequently demonstrated that there was a distinctly abnormal pattern of urinary cortisol metabolites in cirrhotic patients with a decreased glucuronidate fraction (34% vs. 54% for normals) as well as a marked increase in the fraction excreted as cortolones. Moreover, recent studies by Gordon et al. (1980) have demonstrated that the A-ring reductase activity of the liver is reduced in cirrhotic individuals. Despite these various findings, the plasma levels of cortisol observed in cirrhosis generally have been reported to be normal. However, the normal diurnal pattern of glucocorticoid plasma levels is frequently absent in such patients. In addition, the metabolic clearance rate of cortisol is decreased in cirrhosis while the volume of distribution for cortisol is increased slightly, suggesting that the production rate of cortisol is reduced somewhat (Peterson, 1960).

The urine of patients with Laennec's cirrhosis, especially those with edema, contains increased amounts of aldosterone. Consistently, an increased secretion rate and increased plasma levels of aldosterone are reported in such individuals. It is well known that chronic liver disease is associated with a significant decrease in hepatic blood flow. As a result, the metabolic clearance rate of aldosterone is reduced and the half-life of the hormone is prolonged. It should be noted, however, that the resultant elevated plasma levels of aldosterone in cirrhotic individuals reflect not only a decreased metabolic clearance, but also an increased secretion rate occurring, at least in part, to an increased level of activity of the renin–angiotensin system.

The state of the hypothalamic–pituitary–adrenal axis during alcohol withdrawal has been studied extensively. Cessation of chronic alcohol administration to mice is followed by an abstinence syndrome characterized by hyperactivity, seizures, and increased plasma corticosterone levels. Chronic alcoholics also experience hypercortisolism during ethanol withdrawal. Interestingly, the pituitary response of ACTH in individuals experiencing alcohol withdrawal frequently is abnormal. In contrast to the apparent lack of ACTH reserve seen with withdrawal, adrenal reserve of cortisol, when stimulated by exogenous ACTH, is normal. Alcoholics who abstain from drinking often show persistent abnormalities of the hypothalamic–pituitary–adrenal axis when tested during abstinence (Mendelson, Ogata, & Mello, 1971; Mendelson & Stein, 1966; Stokes, 1973).

In addition to altering adrenocortical function, alcohol also enhances the adrenomedullary secretion of catecholamines and induces an increase in adrenal medullary content of phenylethanolamine N-methyltransferase activity (Pohorecky, Jaffe, & Berkeley, 1974). Studies in rats have suggested that acetaldehyde is principally responsible for the occurrence of these changes in catecholamine secretion and synthesis in response to alcohol administration (Pohorecky et al., 1974).

EFFECTS OF ALCOHOL ON THE HYPOTHALAMIC–PITUITARY–THYROIDAL AXIS

The most consistent effect of alcohol on the function of the thyroid is moderately decreased serum thyroxine (T4) levels and markedly decreased serum triiodiothyronine (T3) levels (Israel, Videla, MacDonald, & Bernstein, 1973; Israel, Walfish, Orrego, Blake, & Kalant, 1979; Orrego, Kalant, & Israel, 1979). It appears that the low T3 levels seen in alcoholics and normals after acute alcohol administration reflect primarily hepatic injury and reduced hepatic deiodination of T4 to T3, as T4 and TSH levels are only moderately reduced or are normal (Green et al., 1977; Israel, Videla, MacDonald, & Bernstein, 1973; Orrego, Kalant, & Israel, 1979). Despite the considerable data suggesting that alcohol adversely affects the hypothalamic–pituitary–thyroidal axis indirectly through hepatic injury, some data exist to show that ethanol also increases the uptake of iodine by the thyroid. Moreover, Wright, Merry, Fry, and Marks (1975) and Van Thiel, Smith, Wight, and Abuid (1979) have reported a diminished TSH response to thyrotropin-releasing factor (TSH) in chronic alcoholics.

Recent studies indicate that the administration of TRH to alcohol-naive male rats may antagonize the acute hypnotic and hypothermic effects of ethanol. In addition, recent studies have suggested that alterations in thyroid hormone metabolism may play a role in the clinical management of alcoholic hepatitis. It has been reported that propylthiouracil reverses the adverse effects of alcohol on the liver (Bernstein, Videla, & Israel, 1975; Israel, Walfish, & Orrego, 1979; Orrego, Kalant, & Israel, 1979). Moreover, the therapeutic value of propylthiouracil was found to be greatest in those patients with the most severe liver disease. However, others have not be able to substantiate the beneficial effects of propylthiouracil in the treatment of alcoholic hepatitis.

EFFECTS OF ALCOHOL ON GROWTH HORMONE AND PROLACTIN

Considerable evidence has accrued to suggest that ethanol ingestion blocks stimulated growth hormone release both in normal individuals and chronic alcoholics. Based on histologic examinations of laboratory animals, early studies suggested that alcohol feeding produced degenerative changes in the pituitary. More recently, the acute administration of large amounts of ethanol to laboratory rats has been shown to abolish spontaneous growth hormone secretion. In contrast, chronic alcoholics with cirrhosis have elevated basal levels of growth hormone and frequently show abnormal growth hormone responses to stimuli such as TRH (Van Thiel, Gavaler, Wight, Smith, & Abuid, 1979). Torro and co-workers (1973) have reported no effect of a single dose of ethanol on prolactin levels. Similarly, Earll, Gaunt, Earll, and Diuh (1976) have found no change in prolactin levels following ethanol ingestion. In contrast, Loosen and Prange (1977) reported reduced basal prolactin levels and minimally impaired prolactin responses to TRH during alcohol withdrawal by alcohol abusers.

It is of some interest that Jung and Russfield (1972) have reported an increased prevalence of prolactin-secreting cells in the pituitaries examined at autopsy of male and female patients who died of alcoholic liver disease. Consistent with such a finding, Ylikahri, Huttunen, and Harkonen (1976) noted increased prolactin responses to TRH in alcoholics, a finding which has been confirmed by Van Thiel, Smith, Wight, and Abuid (1979). Van Thiel and his co-workers (1979) have reported that individuals with cirrhosis have elevated basal prolactin levels and reduced prolactin responses to TRH; in contrast, individuals with fatty liver demonstrate reduced basal prolactin levels and exaggerated prolactin responses to TRH.

EFFECTS OF ALCOHOL ON VASOPRESSIN AND OXYTOCIN

Acute alcohol administration to man and animals produces an immediate diuresis which seems to occur as a result of inhibition of vasopressin secretion (Kleeman, 1973). Thus, several groups have reported reduced vasopressin levels in normal volunteers and animals after acute ethanol administration (Heiderman et al., 1978; Linkola, Fyhrquist,

& Forsander, 1977; Linkola, Ylikahri, Fyhrquist, & Wallenius, 1978). Little or no tolerance to the antidiuretic effects of ethyl alcohol or its inhibition of vasopressin secretion has been observed in chronic alcoholics (Marquis, Marchetti, Burlet, & Bowlange, 1975; Sereny, Rapport, & Hudson, 1966). The site of alcohol suppression of vasopressin release appears to be at the level of the hypothalamus. Thus, stimuli applied directly to the superoptic nucleus can override the diuretic effects of alcohol. Moreover, alcohol inhibits the electrically evoked discharges of the superoptic nucleus and prevents the degranulation produced by large doses of sodium chloride (Raiba, 1960). More recently, Marquis and co-workers (1975) in rats, and Linkola and co-workers (1977) in human subjects were able to demonstrate, using radioimmunoassay, transient suppression of antidiuretic hormone during the phase of increasing blood levels of alcohol followed by a decrease in vasopressin levels during the period of maximal alcohol levels.

On the basis of bioassay data, ethanol appears to inhibit the release of oxytocin (Wagner & Fuchs, 1968). No data, however, are available as yet on the actual blood levels of oxytocin during ethanol administration and withdrawal.

EFFECTS OF ALCOHOL ON CALCIUM METABOLISM

A dose-related acute sustained hypocalcemic effect of alcohol which is unrelated to the alterations produced in serum phosphate has been reported recently in both dogs and rats (Peng, Cooper, & Munson, 1972). Parathormone administration does not reverse this hypocalcemic effect (Peng & Gitelman, 1974). Tracer studies utilizing radioactive calcium have suggested that the fall in calcium is related to a shift of the ion out of the serum which is unrelated to any change in pH, magnesium, or binding protein levels (Peng *et al.*, 1972). Studies in normal volunteers and in alcoholic subjects have suggested that alcohol produces an increased urinary secretion of both calcium and magnesium (Jones, Shane, Jacob, & Flink, 1969; Kalbfleish, Lindenman, Ginn, & Smith, 1963). Both *in vitro*

and *in vivo*, ethanol has been shown to reduce duodenal transport of calcium (Krawitt, 1975).

The defect in calcium homeostasis found in chronic alcoholics with hypocalcemia, however, is most likely due to an ethanol-induced depression in serum magnesium levels (Estep, Shaw, & Watlington, 1969). Magnesium is well known to be important in the regulation of parathormone secretion and in the mediation of the hormone's peripheral action (Rasmussen, 1974). It must be said, however, that both malabsorption of calcium as well as a primary dietary deficiency of vitamin D probably are responsible, at least in part, for the hypocalcemia seen in individuals with advanced alcoholic cirrhosis. Finally, Williams, Bowser, and Hargis (1981) have reported recently that the oral administration of alcohol to normal volunteers results in an increased calcitonin level which may play a role, at least in part, in the pathogenesis of the hypocalcemia seen with alcohol use.

It is of some interest that a decreased density of tibial bone has been reported in rats fed ethanol chronically when compared to pair-fed control animals (Saville & Lieber, 1965). In this regard, it is important to note that alcoholic patients have a decreased bone mass and that they have an increased incidence of fractures (Nilsson, 1970). Finally, hypophosphatemia, which is seen commonly in alcoholics, may contribute, at least in part, to the pathogenesis of metabolic bone disease seen in such individuals (Knochel, 1977).

EFFECTS OF ALCOHOL ON THE ENDOCRINE PANCREAS

Singh and Patel (1976) and Shah, Wongsurawat, and Aran (1977) have reported that alcohol administration increases insulin secretion in response to orally or parenterally administered glucose loads. It has further been observed that alcohol pretreatment augments insulin release in normal volunteers to an administered glucose load (Metz, Berger, & Mako, 1969). Similar studies and results have been reported using normal volunteers and diabetics. Interestingly, alcohol pretreatment also increases insulin response to other secretagogues such as tolbutamide.

In contrast to these acute effects of alcohol

on the endocrine pancreas, glucose intolerance is common in individuals with established alcoholic liver disease, particularly those with portal hypertension. Both insulin and glucagon levels are increased, with glucagon levels being increased to a greater extent than are insulin levels. It is thought that glucose intolerance in such individuals is due primarily to hyperglucagonemia. It is important to remember, however, that abnormal glucose tolerance can occur in chronic alcoholic individuals as a result of chronic pancreatitis as well as advanced liver disease.

In patients with well-compensated cirrhosis, the levels of branched chain amino acids in muscles and plasma are depressed and plasma clearance of branched chain amino acids is increased. Sherwin, Joshi, and Hender (1974) observed that the degree of depression of branched chain amino acids present in the plasma of such patients might be related, at least in part, to the degree of portal systemic shunting observed in these patients. As noted earlier, portosystemic shunting is accompanied by hyperglucagonemia and hyperinsulinemia. Sherwin et al. postulate that the hyperinsulinemia in such patients explains the depression of plasma branched chain amino acids and the increased catabolism of these amino acids in peripheral tissues, especially in skeletal muscle. In contrast, Soeters and Fischer (1982) propose that the role of hyperglucagonemia in this regard might be more important than is hyperinsulinemia and that it contributes pathogenetically to branched chain amino acid uptake by fat rather than by muscle.

The consequences of portosystemic shunting on plasma insulin levels as well as branched chain amino acids have been studied also by Iwaski, Sato, and Ohkubo (1980). They noted that the ratio of insulin C peptide to insulin was significantly decreased in patients with cirrhosis compared to controls, but not in patients with idiopathic portal hypertension. Similarly, when compared to controls, plasma immunoreactive insulin was significantly increased in patients with cirrhosis, but not in those with idiopathic portal hypertension, suggesting that a decreased degradation of insulin occurs in patients with cirrhosis.

Finally, the syndrome of fasting alcoholic hypoglycemia is known to develop within 6–36 hours after ingestion of alcohol by individuals who are previously malnourished or fasting. No age group appears to be exempt from this alcohol-induced reaction, but children seem to be particularly susceptible to its occurrence. The most important clues to the correct diagnosis of such cases are an accurate history of ethanol use, blood alcohol level, blood glucose levels, and a fasting insulin determination made on blood collected at the time of the hypoglycemic episode. Freinkel, Singer, and Arky (1963), Field, Willaims, and Mortimore (1963), and Marks and Medd (1964) have reported that alcohol is capable of producing severe and conceivably fatal hypoglycemia. In addition to children, individuals who utilize sulfonylurea drugs as well as athletes are at particular risk for the development of severe hypoglycemia following the combination of alcohol ingestion, fasting, or strenuous exercise.

As is obvious from the preceding, ethanol and possible acetaldehyde, the first metabolic product of ethanol metabolism, have numerous effects upon the endocrine system. For some organs they act to enhance function, but for most, they inhibit function. Moreover, although much is known about these effects, much more yet remains to be learned.

Acknowledgments

This work was supported in part by grants from the NIAAA AA04425, AA06772, and AA0660 and NIAMDD RO1 AM32556 and the Gastroenterology Medical Research Foundation of Southwestern Pennsylvania.

References

Aron, E., Flanzy, M., Combescot, C., Puisais, J., Demaret, J., Reynouard-Brault, F., & Igbert, C. (1965). L'alcool, est-il dans le vin l'élément qui perturbe, chez la ratte, le cycle vaginal? *Bulletin de l'Academie Nationale de Medecine (Paris)*, 149, 112–120.

Bernstein, J., Videla, L., & Israel, Y. (1975). Hormonal influences in the development of the hypermetabolic state of the liver produced by chronic administration of ethanol. *Journal of Pharamacology and Experimental Therapy*, 192, 583–591.

Bjorkquist, S. E. (1975). Clonidine in alcohol withdrawal. *Acta Psychiatrica Scandinavica*, 52, 256–263.

Blake, C. A. (1978). Paradoxical effects of drugs acting on the central nervous system on the preovulatory release of pituitary luteinizing hormone in proestrous rats. *Journal of Endocrinology*, 79, 319–326.

Bo, W. J., Krueger, W. A., Rudeen, P. K., & Symmes, S. K. (1982). Ethanol-induced alterations in the morphology and function of the rat ovary. *Anatomical Record, 202,* 255–260.

Chaudhury, R. R., & Matthews, M. (1966). Effects of alcohol on the fertility of female rabbits. *Journal of Endocrinology, 34,* 275–276.

Chiao, Y.-B., Johnston, A. B., Gavaler, J. S., & Van Thiel, D. H. (1981). Effect of chronic ethanol feeding on testicular content of enzymes required for testosteronogenesis. *Alcoholism: Clinical and Experimental Research, 5,* 230–235.

Cobb, C. F., Ennis, M. F., Van Thiel, D. H., Gavaler, J. S., & Lester, R. (1978). Acetaldehyde and ethanol are direct testicular toxins. *Surgical Forum, 29,* 641–644.

Cobb, C. F., Ennis, M. F., Van Thiel, D. H., Gavaler, J. S., & Lester, R. (1980). Isolated testes perfusion: A method using a cell- and protein-free perfusate useful for the evaluation of a potential drug and/or metabolic injury. *Metabolism, Clinical and Experimental, 29,* 71–79.

Cranston, E. M. (1958). Effect of tranquilizers and other agents on sexual cycle of mice. *Proceedings of the Society for Experimental and Biological Medicine, 98,* 320–322.

Eagon, P. K., Fisher, S. E., Imhoff, A. F., Porter, L. E., Stewart, R. R., Van Thiel, D. H., & Lester, R. (1980). Estrogen binding proteins of male rat liver: Influences of hormonal changes. *Archives of Biochemistry and Biophysics, 201,* 486–499.

Eagon, P. K., Porter, L. E., & Van Thiel, D. H. (1980). Effect of hormonal alterations of levels of a hepatic estrogen binding protein. *Alcoholism: Clinical and Experimental Research, 4,* 213A.

Earll, J. M., Gaunt, K., Earll, L. A., & Diuh, Y. Y. (1976). Effect of ethyl alcohol on urine calcium and prolactin in man. *Aviation, Space and Environmental Medicine, 47,* 808–812.

Ellis, F. W. (1966). Effect of ethanol on plasma corticosterone levels. *Journal of Pharmacology and Experimental Therapy, 153,* 121–128.

Eskay, R. L., Ryback, R. S., Goldman, M., & Majchrowicz, E. (1981). Effect of chronic ethanol administration on plasma levels of LH and the estrous cycle in the female rat. *Alcoholism: Clinical and Experimental Research, 5,* 204–206.

Estep, H., Shaw, W. A., and Watlington, C. (1969). Hypocalcemia due to hypomagnesemia and reversible parathyroid hormone unresponsiveness. *Journal of Clinical Endocrinology and Metabolism, 29,* 842–848.

Fazekas, J. G. (1966). Hydrocortisone content of human blood and alcohol content of blood and urine after wine consumption. *Quarterly Journal of Studies on Alcohol, 27,* 439–446.

Field, J. B., Williams, H. E., & Mortimore, G. E. (1963). Studies on the mechanism of ethanol-induced hypoglycemia. *Journal of Clinical Investigation, 42,* 497–503.

Frajria, R., & Angeli, A. (1977). Alcohol-induced pseudo-Cushing's syndrome. *Lancet, 1,* 1050–1051.

Freinkel, N., Singer, D. L., & Arky, R. A. (1963). Alcohol hypoglycemia. I. *Journal of Clinical Investigation, 42,* 1112–1133.

Gavaler, J. S. (1983). Sex-related differences in ethanol-induced hypogonadism and sex steroid-responsive tissue atrophy: Analysis of the weanling ethanol-fed rat model using epidemiologic methods. In T. J. Cicero (Ed.), *Ethanol tolerance and dependence: Endocrinologic aspects* (Alcohol and Health Monograph Series No. 13). Washington, DC: National Institute on Alcohol Abuse and Alcoholism.

Gavaler, J. S., Van Thiel, D. H., & Lester, R. (1980). Ethanol: A gonadal toxin in the mature rat of both sexes. *Alcoholism: Clinical and Experimental Research, 4,* 271–276.

Gordon, G. G., Altman, L., Southren, A. L., Rubin, E., & Lieber, C. S. (1976). The effect of alcohol administration on sex hormone metabolism in normal men. *New England Journal of Medicine, 295,* 793–797.

Gordon, G. G., Olivo, J., Rafii, F., & Southren, A. L. (1975). Conversion of androgens to estrogens in cirrhosis of the liver. *Journal of Clinical Endocrinology and Metabolism, 40,* 1018–1026.

Gordon, G. G., Vittek, J., & Southren, A. L. (1980). Effects of chronic alcohol ingestion on the biosynthesis of steroids in rat testicular homogenate *in vitro*. *Endocrinology (Baltimore), 106,* 1880–1885.

Green, J. G., Snitcher, E. J., Mowat, N. A., Elkins, R. P., Rees, L. H., & Dawson, A. M. (1977). Thyroid function and thyroid regulation in euthyroid men with chronic liver disease. *Clinical Endocrinology (Oxford), 7,* 453–461.

Heiderman, J., Vestal, R., Rowe, J., Tobin, J., Andres, R., & Robertson, G. (1978). The response of arginine vasopressin to intravenous ethanol and hypertoxic saline in man. *Journal of Gerontology, 33,* 39–47.

Hion-Jon, V. (1928). The influence of alcohol on the endocrine glands. *Folia Neuropathologica Estoniana, 3,* 288–301.

Hughes, N. D., Perret, G., Adessi, G., Coste, T., & Modigliani, E. (1978). Effects of chronic alcoholism on the pituitary–gonadal function of women during menopausal transition and in the postmenopausal period. *Biomedicine, 29,* 279–283.

Israel, Y., Videla, L., MacDonald, A., & Bernstein, J. (1973). Metabolic alterations produced in the liver by chronic ethanol administration. Comparison between effects produced by ethanol and by thyroid hormones. *Biochemical Journal, 134,* 523–529.

Israel, Y., Walfish, P. G., & Orrego, H. (1979). Thyroid hormones in alcoholic liver disease. Effect of treatment with 6-*N*-propylthiouracil. *Gastroenterology, 76,* 116–122.

Iwaski, Y., Sato, H., & Ohkubo, A. (1980). Effect of spontaneous portal systemic shunting on plasma insulin and amino acid concentrations. *Gastroenterology, 78,* 677–683.

James, V. H. T., Green, J. R. B., Walker, J. G., Goodall, A., Short, F., Jones, D. L., Noel, C. T., & Reed, M. J. (1983). The endocrine status of postmenopausal cirrhotic women. In M. Langer, L. Chiandussi, I. J. Chopra, & L. Martini (Eds.), *The endocrines and the liver* (Sorono, Foundation Symposium No. 51). New York: Academic Press.

Jenkins, J. S., & Connolly, J. (1968). Adrenocortical response to ethanol in man. *British Medical Journal, 2,* 804–806.

Johnston, E. E., Chiao, Y.-B., Gavaler, J. S., & Van Thiel, D. H. (1981). Inhibition of testosterone synthesis by ethanol and acetaldehyde. *Biochemical Pharmacology, 30,* 1827–1831.

Jones, J. E., Shane, R. R., Jacob, W. H., & Flink, E. B. (1969). Magnesium balance studies in chronic alcoholism. *Annals of the New York Academy of Sciences, 162,* 934–939.

Jones-Saumty, D. J., Fabian, M. S., & Parsons, O. A. (1981). Medical status and cognitive functioning in alcoholic women. *Alcoholism: Clinical and Experimental Research, 5,* 372–377.

Jung, Y., & Russfield, A. B. (1972). Prolactin cells in the hypophysis of cirrhotic patients. *Archives of Pathology, 94,* 265–270.

Kakihana, R., Butte, J. C., Hathaway, A., & Noble, E. P. (1971). Adrenocortical response to ethanol in mice: Modification by chronic ethanol consumption. *Acta Endocrinologica (Copenhagen), 67,* 753–764.

Kakihana, R., & Moore, J. A. (1976). Circadian rhythm of corticosterone in mice: The effect of chronic consumption of alcohol. *Psychopharmacology (Berlin), 46,* 301–305.

Kalbfleisch, J. M., Lindenman, R. D., Ginn, H. E., & Smith, N. O. (1963). Effects of ethanol administration of urinary excretion of magnesium and other electrolytes in alcoholic and normal subjects. *Journal of Clinical Investigation, 42,* 1471–1475.

Kieffer, J. D., & Ketchel, M. (1970). Blockade of ovulation in the rat by ethanol. *Acta Endocrinologica (Copenhagen), 65,* 117–124.

Kleeman, C. R. (1973). Water metabolism. In H. Maxwell & C. R. Kleeman (Eds.), *Clinical disorders of fluid and electrolyte metabolism.* New York: McGraw-Hill.

Knochel, J. P. (1977). The pathophysiology and clinical characteristics of severe hypophosphatemia. *Archives of Internal Medicine, 137,* 203–220.

Krawitt, E. L. (1975). Effect of ethanol ingestion of duodenal calcium transport. *Journal of Laboratory and Clinical Medicine, 85,* 665–671.

Linkola, J., Fyhrquist, F., & Forsander, O. (1977). Effects of ethanol in urinary arginine vasopressin excretion in two rat strains selected for their different ethanol preferences. *Acta Physiologica Scandinavica, 101,* 126–128.

Linkola, J., Ylikahri, R., Fyhrquist, F., & Wallenius, M. (1978). Plasma vasopressin in ethanol intoxication and hangover. *Acta Physiologica Scandinavica, 104,* 180–187.

Littleton, J. (1978). Alcohol and neurotransmitters. *Clinics in Endocrinology and Metabolism, 7,* 369–384.

Lloyd, C. W., & Williams, R. H. (1948). Endocrine changes associated with Laennec's cirrhosis of the liver. *American Journal of Medicine, 4,* 315–330.

Loosen, P. T., & Prange, A. J. (1975). Alcohol and anterior pituitary hormone secretion. *Lancet, 2,* 985.

Marks, V., & Medd, W. E. (1964). Alcohol-induced hypoglycemia. *British Journal of Psychiatry, 110,* 228–232.

Marquis, C., Marchetti, J., Burlet, C., & Bowlange, M. (1975). Secretion urinaire et hormone antidiuretique chez der rats soumis a une administraiton répétée of ethanol. *Comptes Rendus des Seances de la Societe de Biologie et de ses Filiales, 54,* 555–562.

McNamee, B., Grant, J., Ratcliffe, J., Ratcliffe, W., &

Oliver, J. (1979). Lack of effect of alcohol on pituitary–gonadal hormones in women. *British Journal of Addiction, 74,* 316–317.

Mello, N. K., Bree, M. P., Mendelson, J. H., & Ellingboe, J. (1983). Alcohol self-administration disrupts reproductive function in female Macaque monkeys. *Science, 211,* 677–679.

Mendelson, J. H., Mello, N. K., Bavli, S., Ellingboe, J., Bree, M., Harvey, K., King, N., & Seghal, R. (1983). Alcohol effects on female reproductive hormones. In T. J. Cicero (Ed.), *Ethanol tolerance and dependence: Endocrinologic aspects* (Research Monograph No. 13, Washington, DC: National Institute on Alcohol Abuse and Alcoholism. DHHS Publ. No. (ADM) 83–1285).

Mendelson, J. H., Mello, N. K., & Ellingboe, J. (1981). Acute alcohol intake and pituitary gonadal hormones in normal human females. *Journal of Pharmacology and Experimental Therapy, 218,* 23–26.

Mendelson, J. H., Mello, N. K., Ellingboe, J., & Bavli, S. (1985). Alcohol effects of plasma luteinizing hormone levels in postmenopausal women. *Pharmacology, Biochemistry and Behavior, 22,* 233–236.

Mendelson, J. H., Ogata, M., & Mello, N. K. (1971). Adrenal function and alcoholism. *Psychosomatic Medicine, 33,* 145–157.

Mendelson, J. H., & Stein, S. (1966). Serum cortisol levels in alcoholic and nonalcoholic subjects after experientially induced alcohol intoxication. *Psychosomatic Medicine, 28,* 616–621.

Merari, A., Ginton, A., Heifez, T., & Lev-Ran, T. (1973). Effects of alcohol on the mating behavior of the female rat. *Quarterly Journal of Studies on Alcohol, 34,* 1095–1098.

Merry, J., & Marks, V. (1972). The effect of alcohol barbiturate and diazepan on hypothalamic pituitary adrenal function in chronic alcoholics. *Lancet, 2,* 990–991.

Metz, R., Berger, S., & Mako, M. (1969). Potentiation of the plasma insulin response to glucose by prior administration of alcohol. *Diabetes, 18,* 517–522.

Moskovic, S. (1975). Effect of chronic alcohol intoxication on ovarian dysfunction. *Stiar, 20,* 2–5.

Nillson, B. E. (1970). Conditions contributing to fracture of the femoral neck. *Acta Chirurgica Scandinavica, 136,* 383–384.

Olivo, J., Gordon, G. G., Rafii, F., & Southren, A. L. (1975). Estrogen metabolism in hyperthyroidism and in cirrhosis of the liver. *Steroids, 26,* 47–56.

Orrego, H., Kalant, H., & Israel, Y. (1979). Effect of short-term therapy with propylthiouracil in patients with alcoholic liver disease. *Gastroenterology, 76,* 105–110.

Peng, T. C., Cooper, C. W., & Munson, P. L. (1972). The hypocalcemia effect of alcohol in rats and dogs. *Endocrinology (Baltimore), 91,* 586–591.

Peng, T. C., & Gitelman, H. J. L. (1974). Ethanol-induced hypermagnesemia and inhibition of the serum calcium-raising effect of parathyroid hormone in rats. *Endocrinology (Baltimore), 94,* 608–612.

Peterson, R. E. (1960). Adrenocortical steroid metabolism and adrenal cortical function in liver disease. *Journal of Clinical Investigation, 39,* 320–331.

Pohorecky, L. A., Jaffe, L. S., & Berkeley, H. A. (1974). Effects of ethanol on the adrenal medulla of the rat. *Pharmacology, 12,* 340–346.

Raiba, N. (1960). Effect of ethanol on cytological changes induced by salt load in nucleus supraopticus of rat. *Proceedings of the Society for Experimental Biology and Medicine, 103,* 387–391.

Rasmussen, H. (1974). Parathyroid hormone, calcetonin, and the calciferals. In R. E. Williams (Ed.), *Textbook of endocrinology* (5th ed.). Philadephia: Saunders.

Ryback, R. S. (1977). Chronic alcohol consumption and menstruation. *JAMA, Journal of the American Medical Association, 238,* 2143.

Saville, P. D., & Lieber, C. S. (1965). Effect of alcohol on growth bone density and muscle magnesium in the rat. *Journal of Nutrition, 87,* 477–484.

Sereny, G., Rapport, A., & Hudson, H. (1966). The effect of alcohol withdrawal on electrolyte and acid–base balance. *Metabolism, Clinical and Experimental, 15,* 896–899.

Shah, J. H., Wongsurawat, N., & Aran, P. O. (1977). Effect of ethanol on stimulus-induced insulin secretion and glucose tolerance. A study of mechanisms. *Diabetes, 26,* 271–277.

Sherwin, R., Joshi, P., & Hendler, R. (1974). Hyperglucagonemia in Laennec's cirrhosis. *New England Journal of Medicine, 290,* 239–242.

Singh, S. P., & Patel, D. G. (1976). Effects of ethanol on carbohydrate metabolism. I. Influence on oral glucose tolerance test. *Metabolism, Clinical and Experimental, 25,* 239–242.

Smals, A. G., & Kloppenborg, P. W. (1977). Alcohol-induced Cushingoid syndrome. *Lancet, 1,* 1369.

Smals, A. G., Njo, K. T., Knoben, J. M., Ruland, C. M., & Kloppenborg, P. W. (1977). Alcohol-induced Cushingoid syndrome. *Journal of the Royal College of Physicians of London, 12,* 36–41.

Smith, J. J. (1951). The effect of alcohol on the adrenal ascorbic acid and cholesterol content of the rat. *Journal of Clinical Endocrinology, 11,* 792–795.

Soeters, P. B., & Fischer, J. E. (1982). Insulin, glucagon, amino imbalance, and hepatic encephalopathy. *Lancet, 2,* 880–882.

Southren, A. L., Gordon, G. G., Olivo, J., Rafii, F., & Rosenthal, W. S. (1973). Androgen metabolism in cirrhosis of the liver. *Metabolism, Clinical and Experimental, 22,* 695–702.

Stokes, P. E. (1973). Adrenocortical activity in alcoholics during chronic drinking. *Annals of the New York Academy of Science, 215,* 77–82.

Suzuki, T., Hayashi, R., Hirose, T., Ikeda, H., & Tamura, K. (1972). Adrenal 17-hydroxysteroid secretion in the dog in response to ethanol. *Acta Endocrinologica (Copenhagen), 70,* 736–740.

Tabakoff, B., & Hoffman, P. L. (1980). Alcohol and neurotransmitters. In H. Rigter & J. Crabbe (Eds.), *Alcohol tolerance and dependence.* Amsterdam: Elsevier/North-Holland Biomedical Press.

Torro, G., Kolodny, R. C., Jacobs, L. S., & Masters, W. H. (1973), Failure of alcohol to alter pituitary and target organ hormone levels. *Clinical Research, 21,* 505.

Valimaki, M., Harkonen, M., & Ylikahri, R. (1983). Acute effects of alcohol on female sex hormones. *Alcoholism: Clinical and Experimental Research, 7,* 289–293.

Valimaki, M., Penkonen, R., Salaspuro, M., Harkonen, M., Hirvonon, E., & Ylikahri, R. (1984). Sex hormones in amenorrheic women with alcoholic liver disease. *Journal of Clinical Endocrinology and Metabolism, 59,* 133–138.

Van Thiel, D. H. (1983). Ethanol: Its adverse effects upon the hypothalamic–pituitary–gonadal axis. *Journal of Laboratory and Clinical Medicine, 101,* 21–33.

Van Thiel, D. H., & Gavaler, J. S. (1982). The adverse effects of ethanol upon hypothalamic–pituitary–gonadal function in males and females compared and contrasted. *Alcoholism: Clinical and Experimental Research, 6,* 179–185.

Van Thiel, D. H., Gavaler, J. S., Cobb, C. F., Sherins, R. J., & Lester, R. (1979). Alcohol-induced testicular atrophy in the adult male rat. *Endocrinology (Baltimore), 105,* 888–895.

Van Thiel, D. H., Gavaler, J. S., & Lester, R. (1974). Ethanol inhibition of vitamin A metabolism in the testes: Possible mechanism for sterility in alcoholics. *Science, 186,* 941–942.

Van Thiel, D. H., Gavaler, J. S., & Lester, R. (1978). Alcohol-induced ovarian failure in the rat. *Journal of Clinical Investigation, 61,* 624–632.

Van Thiel, D. H., Gavaler, J. S., Lester, R., & Goodman, M. D. (1975). Alcohol-induced testicular atrophy: An experimental model for hypogonadism occurring in chronic alcoholic men. *Gastroenterology, 69,* 326–332.

Van Thiel, D. H., Gavaler, J. S., Lester, R., Loriaux, D. L., & Braunstein, G. D. (1975). Plasma estrone, prolactin, neurophysin, and sex steroid binding globulin in chronic alcoholic men. *Metabolism, Clinical and Experimental, 24,* 1015–1019.

Van Thiel, D. H., Gavaler, J. S., Slone, F. L., Cobb, C. F., Smith, W. I., Jr., Bron, K. M., & Lester, R. (1980). Is feminization in alcoholic men due in part to portal hypertension? A rat model. *Gastroenterology, 78,* 81–91.

Van Thiel, D. H., & Lester, R. (1976). Alcoholism: Its effect on hypothalamic–pituitary–gonadal function. *Gastroenterology, 71,* 318–327.

Van Thiel, D. H., Lester, R., & Vaitukaitis, J. (1978). Evidence for a defect in pituitary secretion of luteinizing hormone in chronic alcoholic men. *Journal of Clinical Endocrinology and Metabolism, 47,* 499–507.

Van Thiel, D. H., Smith, W. I., Jr., Wight, C., & Abuid, J. (1979). Elevated basal and abnormal thyrotropin-releasing hormone-induced thyroid-stimulating hormone secretion in chronic alcoholic men with liver disease. *Alcoholism: Clinical and Experimental Research, 3,* 302–308.

Wagner, G., & Fuchs, A. R. (1968). Effects of ethanol on uterine activity during suckling in postpartum women. *Acta Endocrinologica (Copenhagen), 58,* 133–141.

Williams, G. A., Bowser, E. N., & Hargis, G. K. (1981). Effect of ethanol on parathyroid hormone and calcitonin secretion in man. *Proceedings of the Society for Experimental Biology and Medicine, 159,* 187–191.

Wright, J., Merry, J., Fry, D., & Marks, V. (1975). Pituitary function in chronic alcoholism. *Advances in Experimental Medicine and Biology, 59,* 253–255.

Ylikahri, R. H., Huttunen, M. O., & Harkonen, M. (1976). Effect of alcohol on anterior pituitary secretion of trophic hormones. *Lancet, 1,* 1351.

Zumoff, G., Bradlow, H. G., Gallagher, T. F., & Hellman, L. (1967). Cortisol metabolism in cirrhosis. *Journal of Clinical Investigation, 46,* 1735–1741.

9 NEUROENDOCRINE AND OTHER BIOLOGICAL RHYTHMS IN PSYCHIATRIC ILLNESS

MARGARET L. MOLINE

DANIEL R. WAGNER

New York Hospital/Cornell Medical Center

INTRODUCTION TO CIRCADIAN RHYTHMS

Rhythmicity is a fundamental property of life on earth. All organisms, from single cells to complex multicellular plants and animals, have physiological rhythms. Many of these rhythms undergo repetitive cycles of approximately 24 hours and are therefore called circadian (circa = about; dies = day). Variables such as core temperature, subjective alertness, urine volume, and most hormones show distinctive circadian rhythms. Biological rhythms less than 24 hours (ultradian) [e.g., secretory episodes of luteinizing hormone and rapid eye movement (REM) sleep cycles], greater than 24 hours (infradian) (e.g., menstrual cycles), and yearly (circannual) (e.g., antler growth and seasonal reproduction) are also present in many species.

Chronobiologists use several terms to define the characteristics of a rhythm. "Phase" refers to a specific point within a cycle [e.g., acrophase (highest point) or nadir (lowest point)]. "Period" refers to the length of time between successive appearances of any given phase reference point (e.g., from one acrophase to the next). "Amplitude" refers to the range of values through which a rhythm varies.

An internal physiological timing system (or biological "clock") enables an organism to maintain synchronized temporal relationships to the environment and to react to and anticipate both short- and long-term environmental changes. For example, human core temperature is low during sleep and rises before waketime, possibly a mechanism to conserve metabolic energy. Long-term time measurement is evident in those mammalian species whose reproductive behavior is limited to a particular time of year. In this way, young are born at seasons advantageous for survival. Organisms obtain and use environmental time information, usually from the light–dark cycle, to set (entrain) their internal clocks to a precise 24-hour day. Via this mechanism, consistent internal temporal relationships (phases) among biological rhythms are maintained. Longer rhythms, such as reproductive cycles, are often multiples of circadian days.

Isolation of an organism from entraining environmental time cues permits the internal timing system to express its endogenous or inherent period(s), a process termed free-running. Usually the period of a rhythm lengthens. This indicates that the underlying clock is slower than 24 hours. In humans, the free-running period of most rhythms is about 25 hours (Weitzman, Moline, Czeisler, & Zimmerman, 1982).

Free-running can be either synchronized or desynchronized. In synchronized free-running, rhythms have the same free-running periods, but their relative phases to each other are often different from the entrained condition. For example, when entrained to 24-hour days, low temperature occurs during sleep. During free-running in temporal isolation, a different phase relationship between low temperature and sleep may develop quickly at the beginning of free-running, but is then maintained. Both rhythms free-run at the same period, but low temperature now occurs earlier or later relative to sleep when compared to entrainment. During desynchronized free-running, rhythms have different periods so that the phase relationships change in each circadian cycle. Phase relationships during entrainment and free-running have import in certain psychiatric disorders, as will be described later.

The region of the central nervous system (CNS) most clearly associated with biological rhythms is the hypothalamus. It now seems clear that one biological clock or "oscillator" is probably located in the hypothalamic nuclei (SCN) in mammals (Kawamura & Ibuka, 1978; Menaker, Takahashi, & Eskin, 1978; Moore, 1979). Even without afferent and efferent neuronal connections, the neurons of the SCN demonstrate a circadian variation of intrinsic firing activity. Information about the light–dark cycle is thought to reach the SCN via the retinohypothalamic tract which terminates in the SCN in all mammals studied thus far, including subhuman primates (Moore, 1979).

Several groups have proposed that there must be at least two endogenous clocks in the mammalian CNS in order to explain the phenomenon of desynchronized free-running (Kronauer, Czeisler, Pilato, Moore-Ede, & Weitzman, 1982) and the fact that some rhythms are not abolished by SCN lesions (Albers, Lydic, Gander, & Moore-Ede, 1984). The first such clock, a "deep" or "stable" oscillator, is thought to be responsible for timing temperature, cortisol, and REM sleep rhythms (Weitzman, Czeisler, Zimmerman, & Ronda, 1980). The second, more labile oscillator is thought to time the sleep–wake cycle. Other brain loci, especially the limbic and reticular nuclei, locus coeruleus, raphe system, and gigantocellular tegmental field cells (FTG cells) in the brain stem are important regulators of rhythmic functions such as sleep. However, no clear evidence exists that any of these is the second clock.

Circadian rhythms are important to psy-chiatry, and specifically to psychoneuroendocrinology, in several ways. First, all of the hypothalamic, pituitary, and peripheral hormones that are of interest to biological psychiatrists have distinct ultradian or circadian rhythms of secretion. It is crucial to recognize and control for hormonal rhythms in the design of provocative tests. Second, the natural history of major affective disorders includes both long-term cycling and profound circadian changes in hormones, mood, sleep, and other variables during the depressed phase. Third, psychotropic drugs, specifically antidepressants, have been shown to modify circadian rhythms. Certain affective disorders have been successfully treated by chronobiological techniques. Finally, perturbations of the circadian system that occur during travel across time zones and in shift workers are frequently associated with symptoms of dysphoria.

CIRCADIAN RHYTHMS IN HORMONES

The circadian secretion of several hormones is altered during psychiatric illness. This section covers the normal rhythmic secretion of pituitary and pineal hormones and the modification of these rhythms in psychiatric disease. The reader is also advised to consult Chapter 1 for additional information on endocrine disorders.

Adrenocorticotropic Hormone and Cortisol

Adrenocorticotropic hormone (ACTH) and cortisol are secreted in tandem, cortisol following ACTH. Cortisol is normally secreted in 8–15 discrete episodes during each 24-hour period in response to several short bursts of ACTH secretion (Gallagher et al., 1973). Peak cortisol values occur in the morning as a result of a series of secretory bursts of ACTH of increasing frequency and amplitude. These begin in the latter half of sleep and continue for 2–3 hours after awakening. At that point, a progressive decline in frequency and amplitude of ACTH secretory episodes ensues. The lowest values of cortisol are reached in the 4–6 hours preceding the onset of sleep. In addition, the initial hours of sleep appear to cause a decrease in cortisol concentrations directly (Weitzman, Zimmerman, Czeisler, & Ronda, 1983).

The circadian pattern of cortisol is only loosely coupled to the sleep–wake cycle and is unlike that of growth hormone and prolactin in this respect. In humans, neither total deprivation of sleep (Halberg et al., 1961; Poland, Rubin, Clark, & Gouin, 1972), constant light (Krieger, Kreuzer, & Rizzo, 1969), constant dark (Orth, Island, & Liddle, 1969), blindness (Weitzman et al., 1971), seasons (Weitzman et al., 1975), nor prolonged coma (Okuyama, Endo, Ohara, Takase, & Itahara, 1977) has a major effect on the basic circadian pattern of secretion of ACTH or cortisol.

Disorders of adrenal cortical function such as Cushing's disease are associated with abnormally increased cortisol secretion (see Chapter 1). However, patients may retain circadian rhythms of secretion that have elevated means (Glass, Zavadil, Halberg, Cornelissen, & Schaaf, 1984). The suggestion of a psychoendocrine connection between Cushing's disease and psychiatric disorders is based on the observation that patients with Cushing's disease often manifest serious mood disorders, especially depression (Brown, 1975). Patients with Addison's disease have abnormal ACTH and cortisol rhythms and often are depressed as well.

The secretory pattern of cortisol in patients with endogenous depression differs from normal in several respects. First, cortisol is secreted more frequently during a 24-hour period in depression (Carpenter & Gruen, 1982; Carroll, Curtis, & Mendels, 1976a, 1976b; Gruen, 1978; Sachar, 1975; Sachar, Hellman, Fukushima, & Gallagher, 1970; Sachar et al., 1973). Second, many depressives become "cortisol hypersecretors" as a result of the increase in secretory bursts (Fullerton, Wenzel, Lohrenz, & Fahs, 1968a; Halbreich, Sachar, Asnis, Nathan, & Halpern, 1981). Third, the increased secretion occurs predominantly during the late evening and early morning, resulting in a secretory curve that is flatter than normal, that is, has a lower amplitude (Sachar, 1975). Fourth, the nadir of the secretory pattern occurs earlier (is *phase advanced*) in depression relative to normal (Fullerton et al., 1986a).[1]

[1]This point will be described more fully later.

These four characteristics of cortisol secretion in depression usually revert to normal after clinical remission (Sachar, 1975).

The abnormal rhythm of cortisol secretion in depression may depend on the type of depression. Fullerton, Wenzel, Lohrenz, and Fahs (1968b) found significant differences between patients with endogenous and reactive depression, with higher mean morning plasma cortisol concentrations found in the group with endogenous depression.

Many other studies of cortisol rhythms in psychiatric disorders have focused on the response of the hypothalamic–pituitary–adrenal axis to provocative tests, particularly the dexamethasone suppression test (DST). The results of these studies can be found in other chapters of this volume. The relationship of cortisol and melatonin rhythms is discussed in the later section on melatonin.

Growth Hormone

Human growth hormone (GH) is one of a few hormones in which a major component of the daily secretory rhythm is normally determined by another rhythm, in this case, the sleep–wake cycle. There are typically one or two major secretory episodes of GH during sleep and two to four smaller episodes during waking hours. In men, the largest episode of the 24-hour day normally occurs 30–45 minutes following sleep onset and in association with slow wave sleep. Sleep architecture also appears to be an important factor in GH release (Moline, Monk, Wagner, Pollak, Kream, Fookson, Weitzman, & Czeisler, 1986). The sleep dependence of GH release was demonstrated when sleep episodes were delayed since the typical nocturnal rise in GH was also delayed (Sassin et al., 1969). Women may have additional major secretory episodes during waking hours; with GH showing a less robust relationship to sleep than in men (Moline, Wagner, Pollak, & Kream, 1986). GH is secreted at other times of the day in both sexes, often 4–5 hours after meals (D. C. Parker, Rossman, Kripke, Gibson, & Wilson, 1979). In addition, a 6-hour ultradian pattern of GH secretion has been described during wakefulness even in the fasting state and is independent of oral or intravenous administration of glucose (D. C. Parker et al., 1979).

In acromegaly, a pituitary adenoma continuously hypersecretes GH. GH is elevated throughout the entire day in all patients, and there is a loss of the clear association between maximal GH and sleep in most patients (Carlson, Gillin, Gordon, & Snyder, 1972; Mims & Bethune, 1974; Sassin, Hellman, & Weitzman, 1974).

GH secretion is also altered in psychiatric disorders. Most neuroendocrine studies to date have focused on the short-term effects of provocative tests using releasing hormones and neuropharmacological agents on diurnal (waking) secretion of GH. The relationship between circadian and sleep-related secretion of GH and the wide range of psychiatric disease has also been studied on a lesser scale.

Mendlewicz et al. (1985) reported that men with endogenous depression (both uni- and bipolar) secreted more GH during the 24-hour day. The differences between patients and controls were evident only in the daytime secretion; no differences were found in the amount of sleep-related GH release. Similar increases in diurnal secretion in unipolar depressed women have been observed in our laboratory (Moline, Pollak, & Wagner in preparation-a).

This finding may explain the blunted GH response to provocative testing found in some depressed patients. Either short-term feedback inhibition or pituitary depletion from an undetected burst of GH secretion, occurring prior to a provocative test session, could account for lack of GH responsiveness to pharmacological stimulation.

A decrease in both slow wave sleep and GH has been reported in young schizophrenic patients (Vigneri, Pezzino, Squatrito, Callandra, & Maricchiolo, 1974) and in children with psychosocial dwarfism (Wolff & Money, 1973).

Gonadotropins

The majority of luteinizing hormone (LH) secretion occurs in the form of pulsatile bursts lasting from 5 to 40 minutes (Baker et al., 1975; Rebar & Yen, 1979) in response to similar pulses of gonadotropin-releasing hor-

mone (GnRH) from the hypothalamus (Baker et al., 1975; Carmel, Araki, & Ferin, 1976). Following episodes of secretion of LH, plasma concentrations decrease at different rates, suggesting that there is an underlying low-amplitude pulsatile secretion (Reame, Sauder, Kelch, & Marshall, 1984; Ross et al., 1984; Yen, Vanderberg, Tsai, & Parker, 1974). Follicle-stimulating hormone (FSH) is also released episodically, but shows much less fluctuation due to both a longer half-life (Yen, Llerena, Pearson, & Littel, 1970) and less sensitivity to GnRH (Besser et al., 1972; Newton & Collins, 1972).

Studies of LH rhythms in mature women have revealed differences in the period and amplitude of secretion, depending on the phase of the menstrual cycle. During the follicular phase of the cycle, low-amplitude LH pulses are released with an ultradian period of approximately 90 minutes (Rebar & Yen, 1979; Yen et al., 1974). In addition, LH values decrease during the first 4 hours of sleep during the early follicular phase (Kapen, Boyar, Hellman, & Weitzman, 1976), suggesting an influence of sleep on LH secretion during this phase of the cycle (Rebar & Yen, 1979; Yen et al., 1974). At midcycle, an LH surge occurs superimposed on progressively elevated basal values (Kapen, Boyar, Hellman, & Weitzman, 1970). This surge usually begins in the latter half of a sleep episode (Kapen et al., 1970; Kapen, Boyar, Perlow, Hellman, & Weitzman, 1973; Kapen et al., 1976), but not in relation to any specific sleep stage. In the mid and late luteal phases, the ultradian period of LH release increases to 180–240 minutes. These differences in ultradian hormone release during the menstrual cycle may be due to alterations in gonadal steroid concentrations and/or in hypothalamic sensitivity to the steroids. FSH secretion displays an increased frequency only during the early follicular phase and at the midcycle surge (Rebar & Yen, 1979).

Adult men and prepubertal children of both sexes do not demonstrate the infradian variations in gonadotropin secretion described above in mature women, nor is there a relationship between LH secretion and sleep in adult men and prepubertal children (Boyar, Perlow et al., 1972; Penny, Olambiwonnu, & Frasier, 1977). Puberty, however, is characterized by a relationship between

LH and sleep rhythms. Puberty begins with an increase in mean plasma and urinary LH and FSH during sleep compared to the waking state (Kulin, Moore, & Santner, 1976; Lee, Plotnick, Steele, Thompson, & Blizzard, 1976). This is due to an increase in the amplitude of gonadotropin secretory episodes during sleep (Boyar, Finkelstein, & Roffwarg, 1972). Sleep-related increases of gonadal hormone secretion also occur. As puberty progresses in males, daytime gonadotropin and testosterone values progressively increase until both the waking and sleeping mean concentrations are the same. At sexual maturity in males, sleep–wake differences in LH have disappeared (Baker et al., 1975). The hypothalamic–pituitary–gonadal system then functions in the low-amplitude, ultradian pattern seen before puberty, but with higher mean hormonal concentrations.

As puberty proceeds in females, gonadotropin pulses increase in amplitude. As in males, these pulses initially occur only during sleep, but later progress into the waking hours. However, the hypothalamic–pituitary axis becomes differentially sensitive to the feedback effects of estrogen and progesterone in females, leading to menstrual cycling.

As menopause approaches, menstrual cycles increase in length for 40–50 cycles and then cease altogether (Vollman, 1974). Marked increases in FSH concentrations occur throughout the premenopausal cycles (Vollman, 1974). Secretion of LH increases in amplitude, with an ultradian period of about 120 minutes. A circannual rhythm in LH secretion has recently been reported in elderly women (and men), with a seasonal peak in spring (Touitou, Lagoguey, Bogdan, Reinberg, & Beck, 1983).

Several clinical conditions have been found to affect the rhythms of the hypothalamic–pituitary–gonadal axis, but not to alter the sequence of maturation of gonadotropin rhythms. Patients with gonadal dysgenesis have the same pattern of sleep-related increases in LH secretion at the time of puberty as normal individuals, with increases in daytime concentrations of LH through the pubertal years and loss of circadian sleep–wake differences in adulthood (Boyar, Finkelstein, & Roffwarg, 1973). Thus, the initial pubertal changes in gonadotropin secretory patterns appear to be gonad independent. Idiopathic precocious puberty is also associated with sleep-related increases in LH release (Rebar & Yen, 1979). In most instances, sexual precocity appears to be due to an abnormally early activation of the CNS sleep-related gonadotropic "program" for puberty.

The best studied psychiatric disorder associated with changes in the pattern of gonadotropin secretion is anorexia nervosa (see Chapter 6). The 24-hour pattern of LH secretion in this disorder reverts to either an early or a midpubertal pattern characterized by augmented release of LH during sleep and lower values during the waking day (Boyar, Katz, & Finkelstein, 1974). These patterns are seen when patients are "actively" anorexic (and amenorrheic) and have been found to return to the mature, adult pattern after symptomatic improvement, including weight gain.

Gonadotropin secretion may also be altered in affective illness. In unipolar depressed, postmenopausal women, mean plasma LH concentrations have been reported to be lower than age-matched controls (Altman, Sachar, Gruen, Halpern, & Eto, 1975).

Prolactin

Prolactin is normally secreted episodically throughout the day. However, a clear circadian rhythm is present that is associated with the sleep–wake cycle. Augmented secretion characteristically begins within 60 minutes after sleep onset. Prolactin continues to increase in concentration through the night, peaking at the end of the sleep period. The concentration falls rapidly upon awakening and continues to decrease until a nadir is reached in the late morning. Prolactin then rises steadily during the remainder of the day (Sassin, Frantz, Weitzman, & Kapen, 1972). Daytime naps are also associated with sharp elevations of prolactin (D. C. Parker, Rossman, & VanderLaan, 1973). That sleep rather than time of day determines the nocturnal increase in prolactin secretion was suggested by the finding that delays of sleep also delay the rise in prolactin (Sassin, Frantz, Kapen, & Weitzman, 1973). However, following a phase shift of the light–dark cycle, a peak of prolactin secretion was measurable at the original preshift phase (Desir et al., 1982).

These data suggest that the circadian rhythm of prolactin is not solely dependent on sleep. The sleep-related rises of prolactin secretion vary with sleep stages, with nadirs in REM sleep and maxima in non-REM sleep (D. C. Parker, Rossman, & VanderLaan, 1974). However, unlike GH, the prolactin pattern as described is not altered by slow wave sleep deprivation (Beck & Marquetand, 1976).

Prolactin concentrations vary across the menstrual cycle. At the time of the midcycle LH and FSH surges, prolactin also increases. Daytime values are higher in the luteal than in the follicular phase (Vekemans, Delvoye, L'Hermite, & Robyn, 1977).

Prolactin rhythms are modified in affective disorders. In depression, elevations in daytime secretion have been reported (Halbreich, Grunhaus, & Menashe, 1979; Mendlewicz, van Cauter, Linkowski, L'Hermite, & Robyn, 1980), and significant increases occur several hours before sleep (Halbreich et al., 1979). In bipolar patients, nocturnal prolactin secretion was abnormal in a majority of patients (Linkowski et al., 1983; Mendlewicz et al., 1980), with surges that occurred later in sleep or not at all instead of at sleep onset. These studies suggest that prolactin rhythms in patients with affective disorders are less associated with sleep than in normal individuals.

Thyroid-Stimulating Hormone (TSH)

The circadian rhythm of TSH secretion and the role of sleep in this rhythm had been the subject of some controversy. Two groups reported that peak TSH secretion usually occurred well after sleep onset (Patel, Alford, & Burger, 1972; Vanhaelst, van Cauter, Degaule, & Golstein, 1972). Neither of these early studies recorded sleep polygraphically, however. Later studies reported that TSH values rose for 2–4 hours prior to sleep (Chihara, Kato, Maeda, Ohgo, & Imura, 1976; Lucke, Hehrmann, & von Mayersbach, 1977; J. Weeke, 1973). In a more definitive study with sleep recordings and frequent sampling, greater mean TSH secretion was found to occur during the night compared to daytime, and maximum daily TSH secretion occurred prior to or just after sleep onset (Azuzikawa,

Pekary, Hershman, & Parker, 1976; D. C. Parker, Pekary, & Hershman, 1976). Sleep may have an inhibitory "masking" influence on TSH secretion since (1) peak values are prolonged if sleep onset is delayed, (2) peak values are diminished if sleep onset occurs earlier than usual, and (3) sharp drops in TSH concentration occur soon after onset of sleep, whether under normal or reversed sleep conditions (D. C. Parker et al., 1976).

The circadian rhythm of TSH in endogenous depression has been examined by several groups. In a 24-hour study, A. Weeke and Weeke (1980) did not find differences in TSH rhythms between severely depressed patients and normal subjects. However, in female unipolar depressed patients, Golstein, van Cauter, Linkowski, Vanhaelst, and Mendelwicz (1980) reported that 24-hour mean TSH secretion was lower than in controls and that phase relationships to sleep were abnormal. Bipolar patients did not show these changes. In a study of depressed older (65–80 years old) subjects, Kijne et al. (1982) did not observe differences in the diurnal variation of serum TSH before and after recovery. Since no control subjects were included in the latter study, it is unclear whether TSH rhythms are abnormal in depression or whether the discrepancy is the result of age or other factors (Mendlewicz, 1982).

Melatonin

Melatonin is a biologically active indole produced by the pineal gland. The circadian rhythm of melatonin is still being characterized in humans. In other mammals studied to date, the rhythm is clearly entrained to the light–dark cycle, with elevated plasma concentrations occurring during darkness, and low to absent values occurring in the presence of light (Tamarkin, Repert, & Klein, 1979). The rhythm is not passively dependent on light cycles, however, since neither constant dark nor blinding totally abolishes the rhythm in rats (Deguchi, 1978). Blind humans also retain melatonin rhythms. However, unusual phase relationships to other circadian rhythms occur in many blind individuals. Lewy (1983) reported that some blind people displayed melatonin rhythms that were phase advanced with respect to the light–dark cycle, while others were phase delayed. The melatonin rhythm of another blind subject free-ran even though his rest–activity cycles were entrained to 24 hours. These findings suggest that the light–dark cycle plays a major, but not exclusive role in regulating melatonin secretion in mammals.

In sighted humans, normal environmental lighting conditions (dim) probably have a less important influence on melatonin secretion than in other mammals. Neither sleeping in lighted conditions (Wetterberg, 1978) nor sleep deprivation during the night (with exposure to lights; Jamerson, Lynch, Post, Wurtman, & Bunney, 1977) abolished the nocturnal rise of melatonin in human subjects. However, extending darkness for an additional 4 hours in human subjects prolonged high plasma melatonin concentrations (Wetterberg, 1978). Significant amounts of immunoreactive melatonin have also been measured in human plasma during lighted conditions (Vaugh et al., 1978; Weinberg, D'Eletto, Weitzman, Erlich, & Hollander, 1979). These results may be explained by the finding that exposure to 2,500 lux is required to suppress nocturnal secretion to low, but detectable levels in normal humans (Lewy, Wehr, Goodwin, Newsome, & Markey, 1980). This light intensity is the equivalent of indirect daylight in the spring. Indeed, in a recent paper by Lewy, Sack, and Singer (1985), bright light either at "dawn" or "dusk" in the laboratory was shown to shift the onset of melatonin secretion based on a hypothetical phase response curve to light. Since such bright light is required to suppress or to shift melatonin concentrations, it is possible that humans living in ordinary habitats may not receive that level of light stimulation for more than a fraction of their waking hours (Okudaira, Kripke, & Webster, 1983), leading to measurable concentrations of the hormone throughout the day,

Manic–depressive patients may be more sensitive to light. Light intensities too low to suppress melatonin levels in controls were effective in this regard in depressed patients (Lewy, Wehr, Goodwin, Newsome, & Rosenthal, 1981). A further study compared 11 euthymic manic–depressives with normal controls and found that melatonin was suppressed more in the recovered patients (Lewy, Nurnberger, Wehr, Pack, Becker, Powell, & Newsome, 1985). These studies suggest that supersensitivity to light, like short REM sleep latency (see later) may be trait characteristics of affective disorders.

Melatonin reportedly has an annual rhythm of secretion in addition to its circadian rhythm. Arendt, Wirz-Justice, and Bradtke (1977) obtained monthly morning blood samples from normal subjects and found the highest values in January and July and the lowest in April and October. It is unclear whether these data indicate a change in the amount or timing of secretion, since only a single time point was sampled. The finding of a trough in April is intriguing, since spring is a time of increased incidence of hospital admission for depression (see later) and since melatonin concentrations are lower in depressed patients (see later). There may also be an annual rhythm in the ability of light to suppress melatonin levels, since subjects suppressed more in winter than in summer (Lewy, Wehr et al., 1982).

Differences in melatonin rhythms have been described in major affective disorders. Beck-Friis, von Rosen, Kjellman, Ljunggren, and Wetterberg (1984) found that peak melatonin concentrations during the night were lower in acutely depressed patients than in both normal subjects and unipolar and bipolar patients in remission. Mendlewicz et al. (1979) found lower nocturnal secretion and a smaller day–night difference in depressed patients than in controls. This finding did not reverse after treatment, even in patients who clinically improved, raising the possibility that it represents a trait marker for depression.

Patients with acute major depression and abnormal DST had lower nocturnal melatonin than similarly depressed patients with normal DST (Wetterberg, Beck-Friis, Kjellman, & Ljunggren, 1984). Wetterberg (1983) suggests a link between the pineal melatonin and the ACTH–cortisol systems, since (1) patients with Cushing's disease or pituitary adenomas have abnormal melatonin rhythms, and (2) large cortisol to melatonin ratios correlate positively with more severe depressive symptoms (Wetterberg, Beck-Friis, Aperia, & Peterson, 1979).

Melatonin may also affect depression. When melatonin was administered orally to depressed patients, an exacerbation of dysphoric mood occurred in every patient (Carmen, Post, Buswell, & Goodwin, 1976). Patients given melatonin also slept less, in contrast to reports based on normal subjects where melatonin induced euphoria, sedation, and sleep (Watson & Madden, 1977). Rosenthal, Sack, James et al. (1984) administered melatonin to patients with seasonal affective disorder (SAD) and found an increase in sadness, sleep disturbances, appetite, and weight, which are all symptoms of SAD. These studies suggest that melatonin may be involved in mediating some of the mood and behavioral changes in affective disorders, even though plasma concentrations of melatonin are lower in depression.

RHYTHMIC ASPECTS OF AFFECTIVE DISORDERS

Many of the clinical characteristics of affective disorders are rhythmic. These factors may be classified either as long term (infradian) or as circadian influences. This section will describe these rhythmic components, the integration of many facets of affective illness into the phase advance theory of depression, and experimental treatments for depression based on the theory.

Long-Term Rhythmic Influences

Cyclicity of Affective Disorders

Bipolar affective disorder is rhythmic, with a variable periodic time course between manic and depressive episodes. Some patients have episodes separated by years, while in the opposite extreme, some patients have 48-hour cycles of mania and depression. Indeed, case reports of precisely timed manic–depressive psychosis (Dirlich et al., 1981; Jenner, Goodwin, Sheridan, Tauber, & Lobban, 1968; Welsh, Nino-Murcia, Gander, Keenan, & Dement, 1986) stimulated much interest in chronobiological aspects of affective disorders.

Three rapidly cycling (48-hour) manic–depressives have been studied under conditions of temporal isolation. In the first study (Jenner et al., 1968), the patient was exposed to 22-hour days, during which the period of his affective cycle shortened to 44 hours, two

times the period of the entraining day. Another patient was allowed to free-run in the absence of time cues (Dirlich et al., 1981). His affective cycle remained approximately 48 hours, which was two times the period of his circadian temperature cycle. Both studies suggest a role of the circadian timing system in rapidly cycling bipolar disorders. In the third study (Welsh et al., 1986), regularly alternating short and long sleep periods coincided with mood changes. Treatment with lithium attenuated the mood cycles and shortened the period of the sleep–wake cycle.

Seasonality of Affective Illness

A seasonal or circannual influence on the occurrence of affective illness has been reported by many groups. Eastwood and Stiasny (1978) and Zung and Green (1974) studied the admission patterns of endogenously depressed patients in the Western Hemisphere and found significant increases in admissions in spring. Frangos et al. (1980) studied the onset of depressive episodes in Greece and reported an increase in May through August. That this pattern is related to season and not dependent on the actual month was demonstrated by a study of depressed patients in the Southern Hemisphere. G. Parker and Walter (1982) found more hospital admissions for depression in the month before spring (August), 6 months out of phase with the other studies.

Hospital admissions for mania also show seasonal trends. Studies in the United Kingdom (Jauhar & Weller, 1982; Meyers & Davies, 1978; Symonds & Williams, 1976; Walter, 1977), Greece (Frangos et al., 1980), and Hungary (Rihmer, 1980) showed similar spring and autumn peaks in onset of illness and hospital admission for mania, respectively. In Indiana, however, more admissions for mania occurred in winter and spring (Milstein, Small, Shelbourne, & Small, 1976). Thus, there is agreement among locations regarding increases in mania admissions in spring. The age groups, population size, or sex of patients included in each study may have led to the discrepancies among studies for the other times of year.

A subgroup of bipolar patients exhibits marked seasonality in the onset of yearly recurring depressions (Jefferson, 1986; Rosenthal, Lewy, Wehr, Kern, & Goodwin, 1983; Rosenthal, Sack, Gillin *et al.*, 1984; Rosenthal, Sack, James *et al.*, 1984). Seasonal affective disorder (SAD) is characterized by annual depression that begins in fall and winter and remits by spring and summer. The clinical syndrome differs from that of typical endogenous depression in that appetite and weight generally increase; there is an increase in sleep duration; and DST is generally normal (James, Wehr, Sack, Parry, Rogers, & Rosenthal, 1986; Rosenthal, Sack, James *et al.*, 1984). Symptoms may also be mild. The disorder is more common in women (4 : 1) and has been reported in prepubertal children as well as adults (Rosenthal, Carpenter, James, Parry, Rogers, & Wehr, 1986).

Since the photoperiod (duration of light per day) is shortening at the time that the seasonal depressions characteristically begin, attempts have been made to reverse the depression through the use of light. These will be described later. This syndrome may reflect an underlying circannual rhythm in affect. One patient, studied over many years, had a phase shift in his annual pattern as a result of a depressive episode that lasted 1 year (Rosenthal *et al.*, 1983). Thus, the manic phase occurred 6 months late. Over the next several years, the onset of his annual depression moved closer to winter. This pattern of gradual phase readjustment is analogous to circadian rhythms that resynchronize to their original phases over the course of several days following phase shifts.

Changes in Circadian Rhythms

The circadian physiology of patients with affective disorders differs from normal in several aspects besides in the endocrine rhythms previously described. Other changes in the circadian system will be described below.

Changes in Sleep Parameters

The sleep of psychiatric patients has been extensively studied over the past 20 years, with the majority of recent interest and findings focused on affective disorders. Earlier studies concentrated on sleep in schizophrenia (Caldwell & Domino, 1967; Feinberg, Braun, Koresko, & Gottlieb, 1969; Feinberg,

Koresko, & Gottlieb, 1965; Feinberg, Koresko, Gottlieb, & Wander, 1964; Stern, Fram, Wyatt, Grinspoon, & Tursky, 1969), alcoholism (Zarcone, 1978), and the effects of psychotropic drugs on sleep (Williams & Karacan, 1976). Since chronobiological abnormalities have not been suggested (nor looked for very vigorously) in schizophrenia or alcoholism, the following discussion is limited to the rhythmic aspects of normal sleep, how these are abnormal in affective disorders, and the effects of antidepressants on sleep and circadian rhythms. How sleep research fits into current chronobiological theory concerning circadian rhythm abnormalities in depression is also outlined. The tantalizing prospect that manipulating the sleep–wake cycle (without drugs) may be an effective treatment of depression is also discussed later.

It is well known that sleep consists of two distinct states: REM and non-REM (Aserinsky & Kleitman, 1953). Non-REM sleep is further subdivided into Stages I–IV, based on the electroencephalograph (EEG) characteristics of a given polygraphic epoch (Rechtshaffen & Kales, 1968). A full discussion of the differences among the various sleep stages is not germane here. Suffice it to say that non-REM sleep stages are periods of considerable physiological stability at a lower level compared to wakefulness (Orem, 1984). During REM sleep, cardiopulmonary functions are highly variable, oxygen consumption is comparable to wakefulness, penile erections occur in men, and most dreaming occurs. Although tone in skeletal muscles is reduced in non-REM sleep, it is absent during REM sleep (Orem, 1984). During normal sleep, these two states alternate about every 90 minutes. The night begins with a period of non-REM sleep and usually ends with a final awakening from REM sleep. However, the organization of normal sleep is more complex than a simple 90-minute alternation through four or five cycles per night. First, most of the 20–25% of the total sleep time spent in Stages III and IV (also called slow wave or "delta" sleep because 0.5–3 Hz activity predominates on the EEG) occurs during the first two non-REM–REM cycles of the night. Second, each successive REM period tends to be longer than the previous one, at least through the first four cycles. Thus, much of the 20–25%

of total sleep time spent in REM occurs during the last half of a normal night.

The sleep stages and temporal order of sleep are often disrupted in psychiatric patients. Increased awakenings and stage changes, but reduced slow wave sleep, are common in many psychiatric conditions. However, similar changes occur to a greater or lesser extent with normal aging (Weitzman *et al.*, 1982), in chronic insomnia (Gillin, Duncan, Pettigrew, Frankel, & Snyder, 1979), in degenerative brain diseases (Loewenstein *et al.*, 1982; Prinz *et al.*, 1982; Wagner, 1984), and in clearly organic sleep disorders such as the obstructive sleep apnea syndrome (Guilleminault, van den Hoed, & Mitler, 1978; Weitzman, Kahn, & Pollak, 1980). In patients with major depression, fairly specific abnormalities of REM sleep occur in addition to the changes listed above. These specific differences are (1) reduced latency to the first REM period, (2) lengthening of the first REM period such that REM becomes more evenly distributed across the night, and (3) an increase in the REM density (number of eye movements per minute) during the first REM period (Coble, Kupfer, Spiker, Neil, & McPartland, 1979; Kupfer, 1976, 1983; Kupfer, Foster, Coble, McPartland, & Ulrich, 1978; Kupfer, Shaw, Ulrich, Coble, & Spiker, 1982; Kupfer *et al.*, 1983; Mendlewicz, Kerkhofs, Hoffman, & Linkowski, 1984; Svendsen & Christensen, 1981).

Vogel, Vogel, McAbee, and Thurmond (1980) postulated that the abnormal temporal distribution of REM sleep in endogenous depression was due to "weakened" generator and inhibitor functions of brain stem REM sleep structures. They also pointed out that the REM sleep of depressives across the whole night is quite similar to that of normals in the last part of the night. The first REM period of depressives tends to be long, with a high density of eye movements; subsequent REM periods are of equal or lesser duration, while the density of eye movements increases further. The fourth REM period in normals tends to be the longest and contains a larger number of eye movements than the first three. The fifth, sixth, or, in very extended sleep, seventh REM periods in normals are progressively shorter than the fourth, yet eye movement density increases. In other words, what would be a normal REM pattern for the end of a sleep period is shifted into the early part of sleep in endogenous depression.

Shortened REM latency is the polygraphic hallmark of narcolepsy (Dement, 1976) and also occurs transiently during withdrawal from REM-suppressant drugs such as amphetamines, barbiturates, tricyclics, and MAOIs (Oswald, 1970). Nevertheless, narcolepsy and drug withdrawal are readily distinguishable from depression clinically. The REM latency in such patients is generally extremely short (< 10 minutes), a finding commonly referred to as SOREM (sleep-onset REM). Although SOREMs are observed in about 20% of sleep onsets in major depression (Coble, Kupfer, & Shaw, 1981), the REM latency in depression is more characteristically between 40 and 60 minutes, that is, between normal (70–110 minutes) and narcoleptic or acute drug withdrawal states.

Until very recently, the above abnormalities of REM sleep were regarded as very sensitive and fairly specific "biological markers" of the primary group of major depressive disorders (Kupfer, 1976, 1983) as defined by Research Diagnostic Criteria (Spitzer, Endicott, & Robins, 1977). However, similar findings in dysthymic characterological depression (Akiskal *et al.*, 1980), mildly to moderately depressed obsessive–compulsive disorder patients (Insel *et al.*, 1982), anorexia nervosa with depression (Neal *et al.*, 1980), and in both primary and secondary depressed outpatients (Rush, Giles, Roffwarg, & Parker, 1982) raised questions about the specificity of REM sleep abnormalities for the primary–secondary dichotomy. Recently, when depressed inpatients were matched for age and severity of depression, the REM sleep abnormalities were present in both primary and secondary depressed inpatients (Thase, Kupfer, & Spiker, 1984). Diagnostic specificity may be improved, however, by using the shortest REM latency from at least 3 consecutive nights of sleep recording (Ansseau, Kupter, & Reynolds, 1985)

Across all studies, however, the endogenous subtype of depression, as defined by Research Diagnostic Criteria (Spitzer *et al.*, 1977), is distinguishable from the nonendogenous subgroup using REM sleep measures. Primary major depressives are a more homogeneous group than the secondary subgroup. Such patients also tend to have more numerous and severe endogenous (vegetative, biological) symptoms. It has also been suggested that the lack of a short REM latency may predict lack of response to somatic therapy in atypical depressions (Svendsen & Christensen, 1981). There are indications that normalization of REM timing of the first 2 nights of tricyclic drug therapy predicts clinical improvement of the depressive episode with continued therapy (Kupfer et al., 1981).

REM sleep abnormalities may persist for at least 6 months following clinical remission (Rush, Ermen, Giles, Schlesser, Carpenter, Vasavada, & Roffwarg, 1986). Whether shortened REM latency is a trait of endogenous depression, a slowly normalizing feature or a hallmark of relapse is as yet undetermined.

The association of specific REM sleep abnormalities with the endogenous symptoms of major depression is one part of the body of evidence that circadian rhythm abnormalities are involved in the pathophysiology, if not the pathogenesis, of endogenous depression. As pointed out previously, our current understanding of the human circadian system includes the postulated presence of at least two endogenous clocks (oscillators), each of which primarily governs the timing of a variety of functions. Under ordinary 24-hour days, the two clocks are synchronized to each other and the external world by the regular input of daily time cues from the environment. In this way, phase relationships among the various rhythms are maintained in a stable, normal pattern. Evidence from free-running studies of normal individuals strongly suggests that the endogenous rhythms of core temperature, cortisol, and REM sleep are governed by the more stable of the two oscillators (see Introduction). In turn, the REM sleep abnormalities observed in endogenous depression may be understandable in terms of an abnormality in the phase relationship between the stable oscillator driving REM sleep and the more labile oscillator that governs the sleep–wake cycle. The following section reviews the background for this hypothesis.

A number of characteristic sleep disturbances occur when sleep is experimentally shifted (delayed) by 8–12 hours (Hume, 1980; Weitzman & Kripke, 1981; Weitzman, Kripke, Goldmacher, McGregor, & Nogeire, 1970), a situation analogous to the phenomenon of jet lag (Aschoff, Hoffman, Pohl, & Wever, 1975; Klein & Wegmann, 1974). Subjects (and travelers) have difficulty maintaining sleep, particularly in the second half of the new night after such phase shifts. In addition, the latency to the first REM period shortens and the amount of REM in the first half of the sleep period increases. These phenomena may persist for as long as 2 or 3 weeks following the phase shift.

The effects of phase shifts of the sleep–wake cycle on the timing of REM sleep were the first suggestion that there also might be a circadian rhythm of REM sleep propensity. Further evidence for such a rhythm came from studies of subjects placed on 90- or 180-minute "days." In these studies, subjects were permitted to sleep for 30 of every 90 minutes for 5–6 days (Carskadon & Dement, 1975, 1980) or 60 of every 180 minutes for 10 days (Weitzman et al., 1974). Despite mild to moderate sleep deprivation as a result of the ultradian schedules, subjects in these studies had most (70%) of their sleep between 3 A.M. and 2 P.M. and little sleep between 6 P.M. and 1 A.M., supporting the existence of a circadian phase of sleepiness. Importantly, slow wave sleep occurred in a fairly even distribution across 24 hours, but almost all of the REM sleep occurred during the sleep obtained between 7 A.M. and 2 P.M. In addition, SOREM periods were frequently present only during these same hours, and no REM sleep occurred between 9 P.M. and 1 A.M. Thus, studies of human sleep on an ultradian sleep–wake schedule further suggested the probability of a circadian rhythm of REM sleep. Different temporal distributions of slow wave and REM sleep also implies that these two physiologically different sleep states might be governed by two different endogenous oscillators.

Finally, studies of human subjects living in temporal isolation clearly demonstrate that there is a circadian rhythm of REM sleep propensity and, of greater significance, that this rhythm is synchronized to the rhythm of core body temperature (Czeisler, Zimmerman, Ronda, Moore-Ede, & Weitzman, 1980). In these studies, the majority of REM sleep occurred in conjunction with the rising phase of temperature, similar to what occurs in the last half of a normal, entrained sleep period. However, in the free-running condition, temperature reaches its nadir early in the sleep period or even before sleep onset. Latency to REM sleep shortens (including the occurrence of SOREMs), and the first REM period lengthens. Both phenomena are similar to the REM sleep timing abnormalities in endogenous depression. However, the free-running condition is not perfectly analogous to depression, since the REM density does not increase in the first REM period (Zimmerman, Czeisler, Laxminarayan, Knauer, & Weitzman, 1980), nor do the subjects become depressed.

Taken together, the REM sleep timing abnormalities of depressives are consistent with the hypothesis that the endogenous clock which regulates the timing of REM sleep (and temperature) runs "faster" than normal in endogenous depressive states. This hypothesis has not been critically tested in endogenously depressed patients, nor is it the only possible explanation for their REM sleep abnormalities. However, it fits with a fairly large body of chronobiological data on phase differences between depressives and normal individuals. When differences are found, they usually are that depressives display a phase advance of the rhythm compared to normals (Wehr & Goodwin, 1981; see below). In addition, virtually all of the effective biological treatments for depression (tricyclics, lithium, MAOIs, and even electroconvulsive therapy) have at least one biological effect in common: They suppress REM sleep (Chen, 1979). Furthermore, at least one drug from each of the above classes of antidepressants has been shown to slow circadian rhythms of some biological system (Wirz-Justice, 1983; see later). In summary, the REM sleep abnormalities found in endogenous depression not only provide a biological marker of the endogenously depressed state, but also represent one of the major sources of evidence suggesting that biological rhythm changes are a fundamental part of the pathophysiology of depressive illness.

Rhythms in Mood Switching

An interesting rhythmic phenomenon associated with sleep is the change from depression to mania. Several groups have found that the switch in mood toward mania occurs during the night (Dirlich et al., 1981; Doerr, von Zerssen, Fischler, & Schulz, 1979; Hanna, Jenner, & Souster, 1986; Sitaram, Gillin, & Bunney, 1978; Trapp, Eckert, Vastergaard, Sothern, & Halberg, 1979). These groups report less temporal consistency, however, in the switch from mania to depression.

Wehr and Goodwin (1983) found that some bipolar patients switched to mania after prolonged wakefulness (up to 48-hour sleep–wake cycles). The finding that the depression of these patients improved after self-selected sleep deprivation fits with the body of literature on therapeutic effects of imposed sleep deprivation (see below).

Recently, Hanna et al. (1986) demonstrated that the switch in mood in a 48-hour rapid cycler occurred at a precise time of night independent of sleep.

Diurnal Mood Variation

A well-known clinical aspect of depression is diurnal mood variation (Doerr et al., 1979; Sampson & Jenner, 1975; Wehr & Goodwin, 1981). Patients feel most depressed upon awakening and improve as the day continues, only to feel worse again the following morning. Rafaelson and Mellerup (1978) reviewed the literature on diurnal mood variations and found that not all studies could demonstrate diurnal mood changes in their patients by rating or questionnaire. Thus, more studies may be required to validate this well-accepted clinical phenomenon. Normal subjects do have diurnal rhythms in activation measures such as subjective alertness, with peak alertness occurring around noon (Monk, Leng, Folkard, & Weitzman, 1983).

Changes in the Core Temperature Rhythm

Circadian temperature rhythms have been examined in patients with affective disorders. Tupin (1973) reported that a subgroup of manic–depressives had a lower range of body temperature variation, that is, a lower amplitude of the rhythm. Dirlich et al. (1981) also observed that the amplitude of the body temperature rhythm was lower on depressed days than on "good days" in his single bipolar patient studied in temporal isolation. Pflug, Erikson, and Johnsson (1976) found that mean temperature was higher when a bipolar patient was depressed than during other phases of her affective illness. Higher mean temperature is not inconsistent with decreased amplitude, but suggests that the baseline is raised. Temporal isolation studies in our laboratory on depressed and age-matched normal women support both findings. Our depressed subjects show an increase in mean temperature and a decrease in temperature amplitude (Pollak, Moline, & Wagner, in preparation). Avery, Wildschiodtz and Rafaelsen (1982a, 1982b) attributed the decreased temperature amplitude to elevated nocturnal temperatures. Smallwood, Avery, Pascualy, and Prinz (1983) also reported an increase in nocturnal temperature in depressives, but did not find a change in amplitude compared to normal subjects. Thus, while it is clear that the temperature rhythm is modified in depression (toward increased means), the question of lowered amplitude may depend on other factors. Age is particularly important, since normal individuals over age 50 clearly show a reduction in circadian temperature amplitude (Weitzman et al., 1982). The phase relationships of the temperature rhythm to time of day and to other rhythms may also be altered by affective illness, as will be described in the next section.

Phase Shift Theory of Depression

The circadian physiology of individuals involves specific phase relationships between various rhythms. A change in phase relationships as the result of illness, for example, means that some rhythms have their usual timing with respect to solar day, while others have new timing. The internal relationship of one rhythm to another also becomes different. In general, the differences in phase between normal and depressed states are in the advance direction; that is, markers of rhythms such as peak secretion occur earlier. Wehr and Goodwin (1981) analyzed data from a large number of biochemical and physiological studies of circadian rhythms in depressives. They found almost uniformly that the acrophases were advanced in depression (Figure 9.1). Some specific endocrine and temperature studies will be mentioned here. The phase advance of REM sleep in depression has been discussed above.

The nocturnal secretion of cortisol becomes advanced in depressed patients (Fullerton et al., 1968a; Halbreich, Asnis, Shindledecker, Zumoff, & Nathan, 1985; Jarrett, Coble, & Kupfer, 1983). Halbreich et al. (1985) suggested that only the first secretory episode of cortisol during the night was advanced. Jarrett and colleagues (1983) concluded from their study that the hypothalamic–pituitary–adrenal axis has increased activity during sleep in depression, since sleep did not inhibit cortisol secretion as long as in normals. This phase advance in cortisol secretion persisted in patients after clinical remission. Other characteristics of cortisol secretion during remission do return to normal, however (see Adrenocorticotropic Hormone and Cortisol).

In a recent study using DST to test the phase advance of cortisol, no differences were found in the response to dexamethasone administered at 7 P.M. or 11 P.M. (Pepper, Davis, Davis, & Krieger, 1983). Although the authors state that their negative result sheds doubt on the phase-advance theory for cortisol, the study did not have controls, nor was sampling frequent enough to characterize the circadian rhythms before and after DST.

Some very interesting recent data on GH secretion in depression suggests that this hormone may have a phase-advanced sleep-related component (Mendlewicz et al., 1985). As described previously, GH is secreted in 4–6 episodes per day, and the largest daily episode is normally linked to the first 2 hours of sleep. In 7 of 8 unipolar depressed men, Mendlewicz et al. (1985) found a presleep surge in GH. Only 1 of 8 control subjects showed a similar GH secretion pattern. We have also observed such early GH surges in unipolar depressed women, in narcoleptic patients without medication (Moline, Wagner, & Pollak, unpublished data) and in normal women (Moline, Wagner et al., 1986).

Melatonin is a third hormone whose circadian rhythm is apparently phase advanced in affective disorders. Lewy (1983) reported that melatonin secretion begins earlier in manics than in depressives. In both manic and depressed patients, the dark-related onset of melatonin secretion starts before that

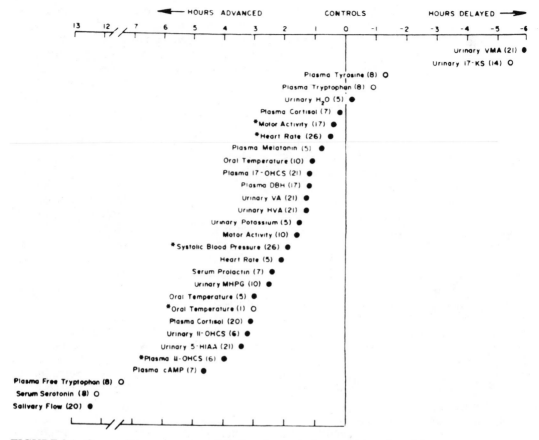

FIGURE 9.1. Composite graph representing the advanced phase positions found for various biological rhythms in patients with affective disorders. Reprinted by permission from Wehr, T. A., & Goodwin, F. K. (1981). Biological rhythms and psychiatry. In S. Arieti & H. K. H. Brodie (Eds.), *American Handbook of Psychiatry VII* (pp. 46–74). New York: Basic Books.

of normals. Wetterberg *et al.* (1984) have also measured a phase advance in peak melatonin in those patients with both depression and abnormal DST compared to patients with depression and normal DST. Nair and Hariharasubramanian (1984), however, have observed a phase delay in the onset of melatonin secretion. These differences indicate that there may be subgroups of depressives who have either phase-advanced or phase-delayed melatonin secretion.

Neurotransmitter metabolite rhythms have been examined in bipolar affective disorders. For example, urinary MHPG, a reflection of CNS norepinephrine metabolism, has a rhythm that is phase advanced by several hours in depression (Wehr, Muscettola, & Goodwin, 1980). Other neurotransmitter pre-

cursors or metabolites such as HVA and tryptophan may also be phase advanced (Wehr & Goodwin, 1981).

There is presently a question concerning whether the core temperature rhythm is phase advanced in depression (Wehr, Sack, Duncan, Mendelson, Rosenthal, Gillin, & Goodwin, 1985). From temperature data collected every 3 hours, Pflug *et al.* (1976) measured an earlier phase of peak temperature in a depressed bipolar patient. In manic–depressive patients, phase advances have been reported by Wehr, Wirz-Justice, and Goodwin (1983), but not by Tupin (1973), who instead found phase delays. Avery *et al.* (1982b) correlated REM latency with time from sleep onset to temperature minima and found that increasing REM latency (as occurs in many antidepressant treatments) decreased noctural temperature. The decrease in temperature values suggests that the temperature rhythm was phase delayed,[2] but could also mean that the evoked effect of sleep on temperature is greater in non-REM sleep than in REM sleep. In another study by the same group, however, no significant phase changes were found in patients when depressed or recovered (Avery *et al.*, 1982a). Two other studies have not found phase changes in depressed subjects without medication (Smallwood *et al.*, 1983) or with clomipramine treatment (Beersma, van den Hoofdakker, & van Berkestijn, 1983). These differences among studies may be due in part to methodological difficulties in estimating temperature phases, since the amplitude of the temperature rhythm decreases in depression. If the decrease in amplitude is large, the usual statistical techniques for calculating phase become less reliable.

In addition to the data supporting the view that many physiological rhythms assume stable advanced phases in depression is the observation that some rhythms may be desynchronized in patients with bipolar disorders. In studies of rapidly cycling manic–depressives, Kripke's group demonstrated that 5 of 7 patients had body temperature, activity, and urinary component rhythms that were "fast," that is, shorter than 24 hours, even though they were living in normal 24-hour environments (Atkinson, Kripke, & Wolf, 1975; Kripke, Mullaney, Atkinson, & Wolf, 1978). Pflug *et al.* (1976) also detected a fast component in the temperature rhythm of a manic–depressive patient. These data suggest that some bipolar patients have circadian rhythms that are internally desynchronized in the presence of normal 24-hour time cues. From a study of normal volunteers free-running in temporal isolation,

[2]Sleeping decreases temperature (an evoked effect). This evoked effect is independent of the variations in temperature due to the endogenous rhythm. Normally, the decrease in temperature due to sleep occurs at the same time that the endogenous component is also decreasing. The in-phase addition of these two components leads to low minima. When the temperature rhythm is advanced, the endogenous and evoked components are not in phase. When the components are added together in this case, the decrease in temperature is not as great. Thus, a delay of the endogenous temperature rhythm would restore the low minima.

Lund (1974) reported that those subjects who became internally desynchronized had a significantly higher degree of neuroticism and a greater tendency to complain of physical ailments. A subject who suicided following a phase-shift study was also found to have internally desynchronized rhythms during the baseline period of the study (Rockwell, Winget, Rosenblatt, Higgins, & Hetherington, 1978). It is not clear, however, if desynchrony is just a symptom or whether it causes or predisposes a susceptible person to the onset of illness.

TREATMENT OF AFFECTIVE DISORDERS BY CHRONOBIOLOGICAL TECHNIQUES

Taken together, the phase advances observed in endocrine and other rhythms support the hypothesis that depression changes circadian parameters. There are several ways to test this view, each of which involves resetting the advanced circadian rhythms toward more normal phase relationships with respect to the sleep–wake cycle and solar day. These include using light stimuli according to either a phase-response curve or a critical photosensitive interval, sleep deprivation, and pharmacological agents that delay phases. The first two techniques will be discussed below; the third is discussed in Circadian Rhythms and Psychotropic Drugs.

Light Therapy

Light has been used by several groups to treat depression. The rationale for the use of light depends on two theories and on the type of depression. The first theory is that the circadian system of humans, like other animals, is selectively responsive to pulses of light during the circadian day (Lewy *et al.*, 1983). Light stimuli given to an animal at dusk cause phase delays in rhythms such as the activity–rest cycle (Sridaran & McCormack, 1977). Light pulses near dawn cause advances in rhythms During most of the subjective day when light is normally present, pulses have no phase-shifting effect in animals. Rosenthal, Sack, James *et al.* (1984) reasoned that if depressed people were exposed to bright light (2500 lux at 3 meters) at an appropriate phase, some of their rhythms should phase delay and reestablish more normal phase relationships. This group used bright evening light and successfully elicited an antidepressant effect in patients with SAD (Rosenthal, Sack, James et al., 1984; James, Wehr, Sack, Parry, & Rosenthal, 1985). The effect took 2–4 days to appear, and relapses occurred along the same time course if treatment was discontinued. Another group (Sack, Lewy, Miller, & Singer, 1986) has also treated patients with major depression (not SAD) with evening light, and showed that indeed, a circadian rhythm was delayed (REM onset).

Patients with SAD have also been treated successfully with both dawn and dusk light stimulation (Lewy, Kern, Rosenthal, & Wehr, 1982; Lewy et al., 1983; Rosenthal, Sack, Carpenter, Parry, Mendelsohn, & Wehr, 1985; Rosenthal, Sack, Gillin et al., 1984; Rosenthal, Sack, James et al., 1984; Wirz-Justice, Bucheli, Graw, Kielholz, Fisch, & Woggon, 1986). Since these patients have recurring depressions as winter approaches which remit as photoperiods lengthen, artificially increasing the photoperiod should have an antidepressant effect. The effectiveness of the light treatment has depended on continued exposure to evening (and morning) light in these studies as well.

The second theory is based on the concept of a critical photosensitive interval during which light must be present to stimulate the circadian system or depression may occur in susceptible individuals (Kripke, 1984). This theory is derived mainly from studies of animal reproduction.[3] The photosensitive interval is postulated to occur in the early morning in normal people. In depression, the interval phase advances into the latter part of sleep during which light would not be present. Thus, light stimuli at the end of the night would stimulate the photosensitive interval of the circadian system and should relieve the depression. This theory may explain the effectiveness of the antidepressant actions of early or REM awakenings, sleep deprivation in the second half of the night, or phase advances of the rest–activity cycle, since each of these manipulations result in exposing the

depressed person to light during the presumed photosensitive interval.

Kripke, Risch, and Janowsky (1983a, 1983b) have used light stimuli at the end of the night to test the critical interval theory. They woke depressed patients 2 hours before their usual waketime and exposed them for 1 hour to either bright (1,000–2,000 lux) or dim red light. Only the bright light led to a small, but significant antidepressant effect, suggesting that the effect was specific to the light and not secondary to sleep or REM deprivation (see below).

The critical interval hypothesis and the phase-response curve are not compatible, however, in predicting when light should have antidepressant effects (Rosenthal, Sack, Jacobson, Parry, James, Tamarkin, Arendt, & Wehr, 1985). The light stimuli given at times according to the critical interval theory are in the morning, precisely that time of day when rhythms would phase advance according to the phase-response curve. Indeed, morning light pulses further decreased already short REM latencies in winter-depressive patients (Lewy, Sack, & Singer, 1984). Whether the shorter REM latencies were accompanied by an exacerbation of depressive symptoms was not reported, however. Lewy and colleagues postulated, however, that patients with SAD have phase-delayed rhythms, which, like the critical interval would also explain effective morning pulses. Most recently, Wehr and colleagues tested the photoperiodic theories and suggest that effective phototherapy may not depend on the timing of light exposure in SAD (Wehr, Jacobson, Sack, Arendt, Tamarkin, & Rosenthal, 1986). Thus, the chronobiological theories behind the antidepressant effects of light stimulation are incompatible, yet light therapy leads to clinical improvement. Clearly, more research is required to determine the role of light in treating depression, especially to assess whether light is effective in general for major depression or is limited to SAD.

Sleep Deprivation

Schulte, writing in the German literature, is credited with the first anecdotal observations that sleep deprivation ameliorates depression (Pflug, 1976; van den Burg & van den Hoofdakker, 1975). Numerous subsequent studies, reviewed by Gerner, Post, Gillin, and Bunney

[3]This animal research has shown that light must be present at particular phases of the day for the gonads to remain functional in seasonal reproducers such as the golden hamster (Elliott, 1976).

(1979), showed that a single night of total sleep deprivation resulted in 1 or 2 days of moderate to marked relief of symptoms (depressive mood, suicidality, and psychomotor inhibition) in 33–69% of patients. Patients with endogenous depression were found to be much more likely to respond than those diagnosed with neurotic depression in these studies. Svendsen (1976) sleep deprived 77 depressed patients, dividing them into three groups depending on whether they underwent a single night, once weekly, or twice weekly deprivation. All patients in the last two groups reportedly had endogenous depressions. Of 24 patients, 12 in the twice weekly deprivation group experienced a complete remission of their depressive episode. A similar result occurred in only 10 of the 57 patients who were less deprived of sleep. An unfortunate confounding factor in this study was that 94% of the patients were receiving concomitant antidepressant drugs. Nevertheless, the duration of drug therapy was unrelated to the outcome, suggesting that sleep deprivation might at least be synergistic with antidepressant medication in some patients. A much less robust effect of repeated sleep deprivation was found by Kvist and Kirkegaard (1980) in a group of 28 endogenously depressed patients, all of whom were off antidepressants for the duration of the study and who were followed for 6 months. Only 8 patients experienced a clinical remission of their depressions, and 5 of these relapsed within an average of 4 weeks.

Tolle and co-workers performed the original single night sleep deprivation experiments (Pflug & Tolle, 1971) and went on to try partial sleep deprivation as well. Interestingly, they found that waking the patients after the first half of a night's sleep produced a transitory improvement in depressive symptoms similar to that seen after total sleep deprivation (Schilgen & Tolle, 1980). However, keeping depressed patients up later than usual and then allowing them to sleep only half their usual amount had less effect (Goetze & Tolle, 1981). These studies are also confounded somewhat by the presence of antidepressant drugs taken for variable periods until the sleep deprivation night.

Sleep deprivation does not require concomitant exposure to bright light to produce successful antidepressant effects (Wehr,

Rosenthal, Sack, & Gillin, 1985). However, bright light may add to the effectiveness of sleep deprivation.

Selective sleep deprivation experiments have also been attempted. The observations that (1) reserpine, a drug well known to produce clinical depression, is almost unique in its ability to increase REM sleep, and (2) the efficacious antidepressants produce a large and sustained reduction in REM sleep, led to studies in which drug-free depressed patients were awakened whenever they entered REM sleep for 3 weeks (Vogel et al., 1975). Age-matched, equivalently depressed, and drug-free controls were initially deprived of an equal amount of non-REM sleep for 3 weeks, and some were then crossed over to the REM deprivation protocol. Patients were also divided into endogenous versus reactive subgroups prior to the deprivation procedure. Half (17/34) of the endogenous subgroup that underwent REM deprivation (either initially or secondarily) improved sufficiently to be discharged from the hospital with no other treatment. Of these 17, 13 remained well and off drug therapy for 6 months to 2 years following the REM deprivation. Of the reactive subgroup, 13 of 18 patients improved sufficiently to be discharged, but the improvement was independent of the type of deprivation. Follow-up evaluations showed that most had relapsed to some extent within 1.5 years after discharge. Eleven patients who had not responded to REM deprivation were treated later with imipramine, but 10 of them did not respond to drug therapy either. Finally, a later analysis of the recovery sleep data on these patients showed a positive correlation between the amount of REM on recovery nights (REM rebound) and the degree of improvement of depression (Vogel, McAbee, Barker, & Thurmond, 1977). This is similar to the findings of Gillin, Wyatt, Fram, and Snyder (1978). In the latter study, those patients treated with amitriptyline who showed a REM rebound upon withdrawal of the drug subsequently recovered. Similarly treated patients without REM rebound after withdrawal remained depressed. Furthermore, Vogel et al. (1980) found that the percentage increase of REM sleep in the last half of recovery sleep after REM deprivation was positively correlated with the change in Hamilton and global depression rating scale scores. Thus, the extent to which the REM sleep pattern normalized after REM deprivation was associated with the amount of improvement in depression.

All of the above results are reasonably consistent with the phase-advance hypothesis of endogenous depression. As outlined previously, the REM sleep abnormalities observed in endogenous depression can be viewed as one manifestation of an abnormal relationship between two endogenous oscillators. In depression, the more stable oscillator, which governs the timing of temperature, cortisol, and REM sleep rhythms, may have a shorter period than its more variable counterpart governing the timing of sleep, leading to rhythms that are phase advanced with respect to sleep. A logical extension of this model would predict that any maneuver that shifts the rhythms into more normal phase relationships should also ameliorate depression. Total sleep deprivation may permit the more stable rhythms to briefly lengthen in period by removing the evoked effects of sleep. Partial sleep deprivation in the second half of the night phase advances that day's wakefulness. Both maneuvers may prevent the postulated interaction of sleep with a sleep-sensitive circadian rhythm of depressive mood (Wehr & Wirz-Justice, 1981). Sleep deprivation in the first half of night may delay sleep even further out of phase with the stable rhythm of temperature. The relative lack of effect of this maneuver compared to the former two was mentioned above. Finally, REM deprivation could be viewed as "pulling" the stable rhythms into more normal phase positions, as evidenced by the partial normalization of REM sleep patterns on recovery nights.

While the empirical evidence reviewed in this section supports the phase-advance hypothesis, it is important to emphasize that direct and well-controlled tests of these ideas have been carried out only rarely. For example, a phase advance of the sleep period by 6 hours was reported to have resulted in a complete clinical remission of depression in a single bipolar patient (Wehr, Wirz-Justice, Goodwin, Duncan, & Gillin, 1979). However, this procedure had no effect in another patient (Uhde et al., 1981) and has subsequently been shown to have variable and temporary effects (Wehr & Goodwin, 1983).

CIRCADIAN RHYTHMS AND PSYCHOTROPIC DRUGS

Chronobiological factors are important in the effectiveness and toxicity of many therapeutic agents (Moore-Ede, Czeisler, & Richardson, 1983). For example, there are well-demonstrated rhythms in drug absorption, metabolism and excretion, and in tissue susceptibility (Reinberg, 1983). Some drugs that are used to treat psychiatric patients have been found to have chronobiological effects in animals (Baldessarini et al., 1981; Wehr et al., 1983).

Several classes of psychotropic drugs have been tested. These include tricyclic antidepressants (imipramine; Wirz-Justice et al., 1980), MAO inhibitors (clorgyline; Wirz-Justice et al., 1980), and lithium (Kripke et al., 1978; Rafaelson & Mellerup, 1978). All three types of drugs have been shown to lengthen the period of some circadian rhythms. Chronic administration of clorgyline clearly lengthened the activity rhythms of hamsters, while imipramine was less effective in this regard (Wirz-Justice et al., 1980). In addition, clorgyline and imipramine (1) changed the amplitude and 24-hour mean and (2) delayed the phase of brain adrenergic receptor rhythms (Wirz-Justice et al., 1980). Lithium has been reported by Kripke et al. (1978) and Welsh et al. (1986) to slow periods of circadian rhythms in depressed subjects.

That antidepressant drugs can alter circadian parameters lends credence to the phase-advance theory of depression described above. Lengthening the period of a rhythm would delay its phase during entrainment and reestablish more normal phase relationships between that rhythm and the sleep–wake cycle in depressed patients.

A seasonal effect on treatment using amitriptyline, a tricyclic antidepressant, has been reported by Swade and Coppen (1980). They found that depressed patients responded better to amitriptyline therapy in early fall than in early winter and spring. This finding is interesting in light of the reported seasonal increase in spring of hospital admissions for depression. Thus, not only is there a seasonal tendency for depression to occur, but the course of treatment may also be dependent on time of year.

PERTURBATIONS OF THE CIRCADIAN SYSTEM AND PSYCHOLOGICAL FACTORS

Two common circumstances in which everyday life disturbs the circadian system are shift work and crossing time zones rapidly. These conditions leave a person out of phase with the environment, and may also leave him or her unable to use traditional sources of time information that entrain circadian rhythms to 24-hour days. It is generally accepted that shift work and jet lag can result in psychological problems such as mood disturbances and performance deficits (Kripke, 1983). Monk and Folkard (1983) reviewed the literature on circadian rhythms and shift work and concluded that while rhythms are clearly disrupted under shift systems, the direct evidence for this disruption causing detrimental effects on subjective health is not strong. In addition, it may be that those individuals who suffer psychologically from shift work simply find more conventional jobs.

Nevertheless, a jet lag study conducted by Desir et al. (1981) found that anxiety and depression indices rose in normal subjects only after flying eastward. Eastward shifts, in general, require a longer period of adjustment than westward shifts because rhythms must advance to synchronize within the new time zone after eastward flights. Since the period of the endogenous physiological clock is longer than 24 hours, not only must the clock advance daily to keep on a 24-hour day, but it also would have to advance further to adjust to the new time zone. Westward flights, which involve delays in time, are in the natural direction of the circadian clock and therefore require less time for adjustment (Klein, Wegmann, & Hunt, 1972).

Jauhar and Weller (1982) examined psychiatric admissions directly from London's Heathrow Airport and found a significant relationship between direction of flight and affective disorder diagnosis. More patients were admitted for hypomania after flying eastward, and more were admitted for depression after westward journeys. The Jauhar and Weller (1982) study is consistent with the phase-advance theory of depression, as discussed in other sections of this chapter. According to the theory, delaying sleep relative to other, more slowly adjusting rhythms such as temperature and cortisol would create the phase disturbances measured in depression and could predispose a susceptible person to a depressive episode. This situation would be created in a westward flight.

CONCLUSIONS

This chapter has attempted to illustrate many of the chronobiological aspects of psychoneuroendocrinology and affective disorders. It is clear that a sense of time is important not only for obtaining blood samples for routine diagnostic purposes, but also for understanding multiple facets of affective disorders such as sleep disturbances and reduced hormone amplitudes. Further research will be required to understand fully the circadian rhythms of hormones, temperature, and sleep in diverse psychiatric conditions.

Acknowledgments

The authors are indebted to Drs. Timothy H. Monk and Jeffrey E. Fookson for technical advice, to David Gilbertson, Suellen Brown, and Barbara Mair for manuscript preparation, and to Ellie Hoey and Kenneth Tucker for data analysis.

Dr. Moline is the recipient of a Charles H. Revson Foundation fellowship in biomedical research.

References

Akiskal, H. S., Rosenthal, T. L., Haykal, R. F., Lemmi, H., Rosenthal, R. H., & Scott-Strauss, A. (1980). Characterological depressions. *Archives of General Psychiatry, 37*, 777–783.

Albers, H. E., Lydic, R., Gander, P. H., & Moore-Ede, M. C. (1984). Role of the suprachiasmatic nuclei in the circadian timing of squirrel monkeys. I. The generation of rhythmicity. *Brain Research, 300*, 275–284.

Altman, N., Sachar, E. J., Gruen, P. H., Halpern, F. S., & Eto, S. (1975). Reduced plasma LH concentration in postmenopausal depressed women. *Psychosomatic Medicine, 37*, 274–276.

Ansseau, M., Kupfer, D. J., & Reynolds, C. F., III (1985). Internight variability of REM latency in major depression, Implications for the use of REM latency as a biological correlate. *Biological Psychiatry, 20*, 489–505.

Arendt, J., Wirz-Justice, A., & Bradtke, J. (1977). Annual rhythm of serum melatonin in man. *Neuroscience Letters, 7*, 327–330.

Aschoff, J., Hoffman, K., Pohl, H., & Wever, R. (1975). Reentrainment of circadian rhythms after phase-shifts of the zeitgeber. *Chronobiologia, 2*, 23–78.

Aserinsky, E., & Kleitman, N. (1953). Regularly occurring periods of eye motility and concomitant phenomena during sleep. *Science, 118*, 273.

Atkinson, M., Kripke, D. F., & Wolf, S. R. (1975). Autorhythmometry in manic–depressives. *Chronobiologia, 2*, 325–335.

Avery, D., Wildschiodtz, G., & Rafaelsen, O. J. (1982a). Nocturnal temperature in affective disorder. *Journal of Affective Disorders, 4*, 61–71.

Avery, D., Wildschiodtz, G., & Rafaelsen, O. J. (1982b). REM latency and temperature in affective disorder before and after treatment. *Biological Psychiatry, 17*, 463–470.

Azuzikawa, M., Pekary, A. E., Hershman, J. M., & Parker, D. C. (1976). Plasma thyrothropin relationships in man. *Journal of Clinical Endocrinology and Metabolism, 43*, 533–542.

Baker, H. W., Santin, R. J., Burger, H. G., de Kretser, D. M., Hudson, B., Pepperell, R. J., & Bardin, C. W. (1975). Rhythms in the secretion of gonadotropins and gonadal steroids. *Journal of Steroid Biochemistry, 6*, 793–801.

Baldessarini, R. J., Campbell, A., Madsen, J., Herschel, M., Finkelstein, S., Smith, J. M., Majocha, R., & Arana, G. (1981). Chronopsychopharmacology. *Psychopharmacology Bulletin, 17*, 112–113.

Beck, U., & Marquetand, D. (1976). Effects of sleep deprivation in sleep-linked prolactin and growth hormone secretion. *Archiv Fuer Psychiatrie und Nervenkrankheiten, 223*, 35–44.

Beck-Friis, J., von Rosen, D., Kjellman, B.F., Ljunggren, J.-G., & Wetterberg, L. (1984). Melatonin in relation to body measures, sex, age, season, and the use of drugs in patients with major affective disorders and healthy subjects. *Psychoneuroendocrinology, 9*, 261–277.

Beersma, D. G. M., van den Hoofdakker, R. H., & van Berkestijn, H. W. B. M. (1983). Circadian rhythms in affective disorders. Body temperature and sleep physiology in endogenous depressives. *Advances in Biological Psychiatry, 11*, 114–127.

Besser, G. M., McNeilly, A. S., Anderson, D. C., Marshall, J. C., Harsoulis, P., Hall, R., Ormston, B. J., Alexander, L., & Collins, W. P. (1972). Hormonal responses to synthetic luteinizing hormone and follicle-stimulating hormone-releasing hormone in man. *British Medical Journal, 3*, 267–271.

Boyar, R. M., Finkelstein, J., & Roffwarg, H. (1973). Twenty-four hour luteinizing hormone and follicle-stimulating hormone secretory patterns on gonadal dysgenesis. *Journal of Clinical Endocrinology and Metabolism, 37*, 521–525.

Boyar, R. M., Katz, J., & Finkelstein, J. W. (1974). Anorexia nervosa, immaturity of the 24-hr. luteinizing hormone secretory pattern. *New England Journal of Medicine, 291*, 861–865.

Boyar, R., Finkelstein, J., & Roffwarg, H. P. (1972). Synchronization of augmented luteinizing hormone with sleep during puberty. *New England Journal of Medicine, 287*, 582–586.

Boyar, R., Perlow, M., Hellman, L., Kapen, S., Weitzman, E. D., & Hellman, L. (1972). Twenty-four-hour pattern of luteinizing hormone in normal men with sleep stage recording. *Journal of Clinical Endocrinology and Metabolism, 35*, 73–81.

Brown, G. M. (1975). Psychiatric and neurologic aspects of endocrine disease. *Hospital Practice, 10*, 71–79.

Carlson, H. E., Gillin, J. C., Gordon, P., & Snyder, F.

(1972). Absence of sleep-related growth hormone peaks in aged normal subjects and in acromegaly. *Journal of Clinical Endocrinology and Metabolism, 34*, 1102–1105.

Carmel, P. W., Araki, S., & Ferin, M. (1976). Prolonged stalk portal blood collection in rhesus monkeys. Pulsatile release of gonadotropin-releasing hormone. *Endocrinology, 99*, 243–248.

Carmen, J. S., Post, R. M., Buswell, R., & Goodwin, F. K. (1976). Negative effects of melatonin on depression. *American Journal of Psychiatry, 133*, 1181–1186.

Carpenter, W. T., & Gruen, P. H. (1982). Cortisol's effects on human mental functioning. *Journal of Clinical Psychopharmacology, 2*, 91–101.

Carroll, B. J., Curtis, G. C., & Mendels, J. (1976a). Neuroendocrine regulation in depression. II. Discrimination of depressed and nondepressed patients. *Archives of General Psychiatry, 33*, 1051–1058.

Carroll, B. J., Curtis, G. C., & Mendels, J. (1976b). Cerebrospinal fluid and plasma free cortisol concentrations in depression. *Psychological Medicine, 6*, 235–244.

Carskadon, M. A., & Dement, W. C. (1975). Sleep studies on a 90-minute day. *Electroencephalography and Clinical Neurophysiology, 39*, 145–155.

Carskadon, M. A., & Dement, W. C. (1980). Distribution of REM sleep on a 90-minute sleep–wake schedule. *Sleep, 2*, 309.

Chen, C.-N. (1979). Sleep, depression, and antidepressants. *British Journal of Psychiatry, 135* (review), 385–402.

Chihara, K., Kato, Y., Maeda, S., Ohgo, C., & Imura, H. (1976). Suppressive effect of L-DOPA on human prolactin release during sleep. *Acta Endocrinologica (Copenhagen), 81*, 19–27.

Coble, P. A., Kupfer, D. J., & Shaw, D. H. (1981). Distribution of REM latency in depression. *Biological Psychiatry, 16*, 453–466.

Coble, P. A., Kupfer, D. J., Spiker, D. G., Neil, J. F., & McPartland, R. J. (1979). EEG sleep in primary depression. *Journal of Affective Disorders, 1*, 131–138.

Czeisler, C. A., Zimmerman, J. C., Ronda, J. M., Moore-Ede, M. C., & Weitzman, E. D. (1980). Timing of REM sleep is coupled to the circadian rhythm of body temperature in man. *Sleep, 2*, 329–346.

Deguchi, T. (1978). Ontogenesis of circadian rhythm of melatonin synthesis in pineal gland of rat. *Journal of Neural Transmission, Supplement, 13*, 115–128.

Dement, W. C. (1976). Daytime sleepiness and sleep "attacks." In C. Guilleminault, W. C. Dement, & P. Passouant (Eds.), *Narcolepsy* (pp. 17–42). New York: Spectrum Publications.

Desir, D., van Cauter, E., Fang, V. S., Martino, E., Jadot, C., Spire, J. P., Pierre, N., Refetoff, S., Copinschi, G., & Golstein, J. (1981). Effects of "jet lag" on hormonal patterns. I. Procedures, variations in total plasma proteins, and disruption of adrenocorticotropin–cortisol periodicity. *Journal of Clinical Endocrinology and Metabolism, 52*, 628–641.

Desir, D., van Cauter, E., L'Hermite, M., Refetoff, S., Jadot, C., Caufriez, A., Copinschi, G., & Robyn, C. (1982). Effects of "jet lag" on hormonal patterns. II. Demonstration of an intrinsic circadian rhythmicity in plasma prolactin. *Journal of Clinical Endocrinology and Metabolism, 55*, 849–857.

Dirlich, G., Kammerloher, A., Schultz, H., Lund, R., Doerr, P., & von Zerssen, B. (1981). Temporal coordination of rest–activity cycle, body temperature, urinary free cortisol, and mood in a patient with 48-hour unipolar–depressive cycles in clinical and time cue-free environments. *Biological Psychiatry*, *16*, 163–179.

Doerr, P., von Zerssen, D., Fischler, M., & Schultz, H. (1979). Relationship between mood changes and adrenal cortisol activity in a patient with 48-hour unipolar–depressive cycles. *Journal of Affective Disorders*, *1*, 93–104.

Eastwood, M. R., & Stiasny, S. (1978). Psychiatric disorder, hospital admission, and seasons. *Archives of General Psychiatry*, *35*, 769–771.

Elliott, J. A. (1976). Circadian rhythms and photoperiodic time measurement in mammals. *Federation Proceedings, Federation of American Societies for Experimental Biology*, *35*, 2339–2346.

Feinberg, I., Braun, M., Koresko, R. L. & Gottleib, F. (1969). Stage 4 sleep in schizophrenia. *Archives of General Psychiatry*, *21*, 262–266.

Feinberg, I., Koresko, R. L., & Gottleib, F. (1965). Further observations on electrophysiological sleep patterns in schizophrenia. *Comparative Psychiatry*, *6*, 21–24.

Feinberg, I., Koresko, R. L., Gottlieb F., & Wender P. H. (1964). Sleep electroencephalographic and eye-movement patterns in schizophrenic patients. *Comparative Psychiatry*, *5*, 44–53.

Frangos, E., Athanassenas, G., Tsitourides, S., Psilolignos, P., Robos, A., Katsanou, N., & Bulgaris, C. (1980). Seasonality of the episodes of recurrent affective psychosis. *Journal of Affective Disorders*, *2*, 239–247.

Fullerton, D. T., Wenzel, F. J., Lorenz, F. N., & Fahs, H. (1968a). Circadian rhythm of adrenal cortical activity in depression. I. A comparison of depressed patients with normal subjects. *Archives of General Psychiatry*, *19*, 674–681.

Fullerton, D. T., Wenzel, F. J., Lorenz, F. N., & Fahs, H. (1968b). Circadian rhythm of adrenal cortical activity in depression. II. A comparison of types in depression. *Archives of General Psychiatry*, *19*, 682–688.

Gallagher, T. F., Yoshida, K., Roffwarg, H. P., Fukushima, D. K., Weitzman, E. D., & Hellman, L. (1973). ACTH and cortisol secretory patterns in man. *Journal of Clinical Endocrinology and Metabolism*, *36*, 1058–1073.

Gerner, R. H., Post, R. M., Gillin, J. C., & Bunney, W. (1979). Biological and behavioral effects of one night's sleep deprivation in depressed patients and normals. *Journal of Psychiatric Research*, *15*, 21–40.

Gillin, J. C., Duncan, W., Pettigrew, K. D., Frankel, B. L., & Snyder, F. (1979). Successful separation of depressed, normal, and insomniac subjects by EEG sleep data. *Archives of General Psychiatry*, *36*, 85–90.

Gillin, J. C., Wyatt, R. J., Fram, D., & Snyder, F. (1978). The relationship between changes in REM sleep and clinical improvement in depressed patients treated with amitriptyline. *Psychopharmacology*, *59*, 267–272.

Glass, A. R., Zavadil, A. P., Halberg, G., Cornelissen, G., & Schaaf, M. (1984). Circadian rhythm of serum cortisol in Cushing's disease. *Journal of Clinical Endocrinology and Metabolism*, *59*, 161–165.

Goetze, U., & Tolle, R. (1981). Antidepressive Wirkung des partiellen Schlafenturges wahrend de 1 Hafete der Nacht. *Psychiatrica Clinica*, *14*, 129–149.

Golstein, J., van Cauter, E., Linkowski, P., Vanhaelst, L., & Mendlewicz, J. (1980). Thyrotropin nyctohemeral pattern in primary depression: Differences between unipolar and bipolar women. *Life Sciences*, *27*, 1695–1703.

Gruen, P. H. (1978). Endocrine changes in psychiatric diseases. *Medical Clinics of North America*, *62*, 285–296.

Guilleminault, C., van den Hoed, J., & Mitler, M. (1978). Clinical overview of the sleep apnea syndromes. In C. Guilleminault & W. C. Dement (Eds.), *Sleep apnea syndromes* (pp. 1–12). New York: Alan R. Liss.

Halberg, F., Frank, G., Horner, R., Mathews, J., Aaker, H., Gravem, H., & Melby, J. (1961). The adrenal cycle in men on different schedules of motor and mental activity. *Experientia*, *17*, 282–284.

Halbreich, U., Asnis, G. M., Shindledecker, R., Zumoff, B., & Nathan, S. (1985). Cortisol secretion in endogenous depression. II. Time related functions. *Archives of General Psychiatry*, *42*, 909–914.

Halbreich, U., Grunhaus, L., & Menashe, B.-D. (1979). Twenty-four-hour rhythm of prolactin in depressive patients. *Archives of General Psychiatry*, *36*, 1183–1186.

Halbreich, U., Sachar, E. J., Asnis, G. M., Nathan, R. S., & Halpern, F. (1981). Studies of cortisol diurnal rhythm and cortisol response to *d*-amphetamine in depressive patients. *Psychopharmacology Bulletin*, *17*, 114–116.

Hanna, S. M., Jenner, F. A., & Souster, P. L. (1986). Electro-oculogram changes at the switch in a manic-depressive patient. *British Journal of Psychiatry*, *149*, 229–232.

Hume, K. I. (1980). Sleep adaptation after phase shifts of the sleep–wakefulness rhythm in man. *Sleep*, *2*, 417–435.

Insel, T. R., Gillin, J. C., Moore, A., Mendelson, W. B., Loewenstein, R. J., & Murphy, D. L. (1982). The sleep of patients with obsessive–compulsive disorder. *Archives of General Psychiatry*, *39*, 1372–1377.

Jamerson, D. C., Lynch, H. U., Post, R. M., Wurtman, R. J., & Bunney, W. F. (1977). Urinary melatonin rhythms during sleep deprivation in depressed patients and normals. *Life Sciences*, *20*, 1501–1509.

James, S. P., Wehr, T. A., Sack, D. A., Parry, B. L., Rogers, S., & Rosenthal, N. E. (1986). The dexamethaxone suppression test in seasonal affective disorder. *Comprehensive Psychiatry*, *27*, 224–226.

James, S. P., Wehr, T. A., Sack, D. A., Parry, B. L., & Rosenthal, N. E. (1985). Treatment of seasonal affective disorder with light in the evening. *British Journal of Psychiatry*, *147*, 424–428.

Jarrett, D. B., Coble, P. A., & Kupfer, D. J. (1983). Reduced cortisol latency in depressive illness. *Archives of General Psychiatry*, *40*, 506–511.

Jauhar, P., & Weller, M. P. I. (1982). Psychiatric morbidity and time zone changes: A study of patients from Heathrow Airport. *British Journal of Psychiatry, 140,* 231–235.

Jefferson, J. W. (1986). An early "study" of seasonal depression. *American Journal of Psychiatry, 143,* 261–262.

Jenner, F. A., Goodwin, J. C., Sheridan, M., Tauber, I. J., & Lobban, M. C. (1968). The effect of an altered time regime on biological rhythms in a 48-hour periodic psychosis. *British Journal of Psychiatry, 114,* 215–224.

Kapen, S., Boyar, R., Hellman, L., & Weitzman, E. D. (1970). Variations of plasma gonadotropin levels in normal subjects during the sleep–wake cycle. *Psychophysiology, 7,* 337.

Kapen, S., Boyar, R., Hellman, L., & Weitzman, E. D. (1976). The relationship of luteinizing hormone secretion to sleep in women during the early follicular phase: Effects of sleep reversal and a prolonged three-hour sleep–wake schedule. *Journal of Clinical Endocrinology and Metabolism, 42,* 1031–1039.

Kapen, S., Boyar, R., Perlow, M., Hellman, L., & Weitzman, E. D. (1973). Luteinizing hormone: Changes in secretory pattern during sleep in adult women. *Life Sciences, 13,* 693–701.

Kawamura, H., & Ibuka, N. (1978). Search for circadian rhythm pacemakers in the light of lesion experiments. *Chronobiologia, 5,* 69–88.

Kijne, B., Aggernaes, H., Fog-Moller, F., Anderson, H. H., Nissen, J., Kirkegaard, C., & Bjorum, N. (1982). Circadian variation of serum thyrotropin in endogenous depression. *Psychiatry Research, 6,* 277–282.

Klein, K. E., & Wegmann, H. M. (1974). The resynchronization of human circadian rhythms after transmeridian flight as a result of flight direction and mode of activity. In L. E. Sheving, F. Halberg, & J. E. Pauly (Eds.), *Chronobiology* (pp. 564–570). Tokyo: Igaku-Shoin.

Klein, K. E., Wegmann, H. M., & Hunt, B. I. (1972). Desynchronization of body temperature and performance circadian rhythm as a result of outgoing and homegoing transmeridian flights. *Aerospace Medicine, 43,* 119–132.

Krieger, D. T., Kreuzer, J., & Rizzo, F. (1969). Constant light: Effect on circadian pattern and phase reversal of steroid and electrolyte levels in man. *Journal of Clinical Endocrinology and Metabolism, 29,* 1634–1638.

Kripke, D. F. (1983). Phase-advance theories for affective illnesses. In T. A. Wehr & F. K. Goodwin (Eds.), *Circadian rhythms in psychiatry* (pp. 41–69). Pacific Grove, CA: Boxwood Press.

Kripke, D. F. (1984). Critical interval hypotheses for depression. *Chronobiology International, 1,* 73–80.

Kripke, D. F., Mullaney, D. J., Atkinson, M., & Wolf, S. (1978). Circadian rhythm disorders in manic-depressives. *Biological Psychiatry, 13,* 335–351.

Kripke, D. F., Risch, S. C., & Janowsky, D. (1983a). Bright white light alleviates depression. *Psychiatry Research, 10,* 105–112.

Kripke, D. F., Risch, S. C., & Janowsky, D. S. (1983b). Lighting up depression. *Psychopharmacology Bulletin, 19,* 526–530.

Kronauer, R. E., Czeisler, C. A., Pilato, S. F., Moore-Ede, M. C., & Weitzman, E. D. (1982). Mathematical model of the human circadian system with two interacting oscillators. *American Journal of Physiology, 242,* R3–R17.

Kulin, H. E., Moore, R. G., & Santner, S. J. (1976). Circadian rhythms in gonadotropin secretion in prepubertal and pubertal children. *Journal of Clinical Endocrinology and Metabolism, 42,* 770–773.

Kupfer, D. J. (1976). REM latency: A psychobiologic marker for primary depressive disease. *Biological Psychiatry, 11,* 159–174.

Kupfer, D. J. (1983). Application of the sleep EEG in affective disorders. In J. M. David & J. W. Mass (Eds.), *The affective disorders.* Washington, DC: American Psychiatric Press.

Kupfer, D. J., Foster, F. G., Coble, P., McPartland, R. J., & Ulrich, R. F. (1978). Application of EEG sleep for the differential diagnosis of affective disorders. *American Journal of Psychiatry, 135,* 69–74.

Kupfer, D. J., Shaw, D. H., Ulrich, R., Coble, P. A., & Spiker, D. G. (1982). Application of automated REM analysis in depression. *Archives of General Psychiatry, 39,* 569–573.

Kupfer, D. J., Spiker, D. G., Coble, P. A., Neil, J. F., Ulrich, R., & Shaw, D. H. (1981). Sleep and treatment prediction in endogenous depression. *American Journal of Psychiatry, 134,* 429–434.

Kupfer, D. J., Spiker, D. G., Rossi, A., Coble, P. A., Ulrich, R., & Shaw, D. (1983). Recent diagnostic and treatment advances in REM sleep and depression. In P. J. Clayton & J. E. Barrett (Eds.), *Treatment of depression: Old controversies and new approaches* (pp. 31–51). New York: Raven Press.

Kvist, J., & Kirkegaard, C. (1980). Effect of repeated sleep deprivation on clinical symptoms and the TRH test in endogenous depression. *Acta Psychiatrica Scandinavia, 62,* 494–502.

Lee, P. A., Plotnick, L. P., Steele, R. E., Thompson, R. G., & Blizzard, R. M. (1976). Integrated concentrations of luteinizing hormone and puberty. *Journal of Clinical Endocrinology and Metabolism, 43,* 168–172.

Lewy, A. J. (1983). Production and the human circadian system. *Progress in Neuro-Psychopharmacology and Biological Psychiatry, 7,* 551–556.

Lewy, A. J., Kern, H. A., Rosenthal, N. E., & Wehr, T. A. (1982). Bright artificial light treatment of a manic–depressive patient with a seasonal mood cycle. *American Journal of Psychiatry, 139,* 1496–1498.

Lewy, A. J., Nurnberger, J. I., Wehr, T. A., Pack, D., Becker, L. E., Powell, R., & Newsome, D. A. (1985). Supersensitivity to light, possible trait marker for manic–depressive illness. *American Journal of Psychiatry, 142,* 725–727.

Lewy, A. J., Sack, R. A., Fredrickson, R. H., Reaves, M., Denney, D., & Zielske, D. R. (1983). The use of bright light in the treatment of chronobiologic sleep and mood disorders: The phase-response curve. *Psychopharmacology Bulletin, 19,* 523–525.

Lewy, A. J., Sack, R. A., & Singer, L. L. (1984). Assessment and treatment of chronobiologic disorders using plasma melatonin levels and bright light exposure: The clock-gate model and the phase-response curve. *Psychopharmacology Bulletin, 20,* 561–565.

Lewy, A. J., Sack, R. L., & Singer, C. M. (1985). Immediate and delayed effects of bright light on human melatonin production, shifting "dawn" and "dusk" shifts the dim light melatonin onset (DLMO). *Annals of the New York Academy of Sciences, 453,* 253–259.

Lewy, A. J., Wehr, T. A., Goodwin, F. K., Newsome, D. A., & Markey, S. P. (1980). Light suppresses melatonin secretion in humans. *Science, 210,* 1267–1269.

Lewy, A. J., Wehr, T. A., Goodwin, F. K., Newsome, D. A., & Rosenthal, N. E. (1981). Manic–depressive patients may be supersensitive to light. *Lancet, 1,* 383–384.

Lewy, A. J., Wehr, T. A., Rosenthal, N. E., Nurnberger, J. I., Siever, L. J., Uhde, T. W., Newsome, D. A., Becker, L. E., Markey, S. P., Kopin, I. J., & Goodwin, F. K. (1982). Melatonin secretion as a neurobiological "marker" and effects of light in humans. *Psychopharmacology Bulletin, 18,* 127–129.

Linkowski, P., Van Cauter, E., Hoffman, G., Hubain, P., L'Hermite-Baleriaux, M., L'Hermite, M., & Mendlewicz, J. (1983). Circadian prolactin secretion and sleep in depression and mania. *Endocrine Society Abstracts,* 188.

Loewenstein, R. J., Weingartner, H., Gillin, J. C., Kaye, W., Eberts, M., & Mendelson, W. B. (1982). Disturbances of sleep and cognitive functioning in patients with dementia. *Neurobiology of Aging, 3,* 331–337.

Lucke, C., Hehrmann, R., & von Mayersbach, K. (1977). Studies on circadian variations of plasma TSH, thyroxine, and triiodothyronine in man. *Acta Endocrinologica (Copenhagen), 81,* 81.

Lund, R. (1974). Personality factors and desynchronization of circadian rhythms. *Psychosomatic Medicine, 36,* 224–228.

Menaker, M., Takahashi, V. S., & Eskin, A. (1978). The physiology of circadian pacemakers. *Annual Review of Physiology, 40,* 501–526.

Mendlewicz, J. (1982). Circadian variation of serum TSH in unipolar and bipolar depression. *Psychiatry Research, 7,* 388–389.

Mendlewicz, J., Kerkofs, M., Hoffman, G., & Linkowski, P. (1984). Dexamethasone suppression test and REM sleep in patients with major depressive disorder. *British Journal of Psychiatry, 145,* 383–388.

Mendlewicz, J., Linkowski, P., Branchey, L., Weinberg, U., Weitzman, E. D., & Branchey, M. (1979). Abnormal 24-hour pattern of melatonin secretion in depression. *Lancet, 2,* 1362.

Mendlewicz, J., Linkowski, P., Kerkhofs, M., Desmedt, D., Goldstein, G., Copinschi, G., & van Cauter, E. (1985). Diurnal hypersecretion of growth hormone in depression. *Journal of Clinical Endocrinology and Metabolism, 60,* 515–512.

Mendlewicz, J., van Cauter, E., Linkowski, P., L'Hermite, M., & Robyn, C. (1980). Current concepts. I. The 24-hour profile of prolactin in depression. *Life Sciences, 27,* 2015–2024.

Meyers, D. H., & Davies, P. (1978). The seasonal incidence of mania and its relationship to climatic variables. *Psychological Medicine, 8,* 433–440.

Milstein, V., Small, J. G., Shelbourne, D., & Small, I. F. (1976). Manic–depressive illness: Onset, diurnal temperature and season of birth. *Diseases of the Nervous System, 37,* 373–375.

Mims, R. B., & Bethune, J. E. (1974). Acromegaly with normal fasting growth hormone concentrations, but abnormal growth hormone regulation. *Annals of Internal Medicine, 81,* 781–784.

Moline, M. L., Monk, T. H., Wagner, D. R., Pollak, C. P., Kream, J., Fookson, J. E., Weitzman, E. D., & Czeisler, C. A. (1986). Human growth hormone is decreased during sleep in temporal isolation (free-running). *Chronobiologia, 13,* 13–19.

Moline, M. L., Pollak, C. P., & Wagner, D. R. Growth hormone secretion is elevated in young and middle-aged depressed women. (In preparation.)

Moline, M. L., Wagner, D. R., Pollak, C. P., & Kream, J. (1986). Sex differences in entrained growth hormone patterns in young, middle-aged and older subjects studied in temporal isolation. *Sleep Research, 15,* 48.

Monk, T. H., & Folkard, S. (1983). Circadian rhythms and shift work. In G. R. J. Hockey (Ed.), *Stress and fatigue in human performance* (pp. 97–121). Chichester: Wiley.

Monk, T. H., Leng, V. C., Folkard, S., & Weitzman, E. D. (1983). Circadian rhythms in subjective alertness and core body temperature. *Chronobiologia, 10,* 49–55.

Moore, R. Y. (1979). The anatomy of central neural mechanisms regulating endocrine rhythms. In D. T. Krieger (Ed.), *Endocrine rhythms* (pp. 63–87). New York: Raven Press.

Moore-Ede, M. C., Czeisler, C. A., & Richardson, G. S. (1983). Circadian timekeeping in health and disease. Part 2. Clinical implications of circadian rhythmicity. *New England Journal of Medicine, 309,* 530–536.

Nair, N. P. V., & Hariharasubramanian, N. (1984). Circadian rhythms and psychiatry. *British Journal of Psychiatry, 145,* 557–558.

Neal, J. F., Merikangas, J. R., Foster, F. G., Merikangas, K. R., Spiker, D. G., & Kupfer, D. J. (1980). Waking and all-night sleep EEGs in anorexia nervosa. *Clinical Electroencephalography, 11,* 9–15.

Newton, J., & Collins, W. P. (1972). Effect of synthetic luteinizing hormone-releasing hormone in women with menstrual disorders. *British Medical Journal, 3,* 271–273.

Okudaira, N., Kripke, D. F., & Webster, J. B. (1983). Naturalistic studies of human light exposure. *American Journal of Physiology, 245,* R613–R615.

Okuyama, H., Endo, M., Ohara, Y., Takase, S., & Itahara, K. (1977). Circadian rhythm of plasma cortisol in cases of prolonged coma. *Tohoku Journal of Experimental Medicine, 123,* 33–47.

Orem, J. M. (1984). Sleep. In R. M. Rosenberg (Ed.), *The clinical neurosciences* (pp. 589–607). Edinburgh & London: Churchill-Livingstone.

Orth, D. N., Island, D. P., & Liddle, G. W. (1969). Light synchronization of the circadian rhythm in plasma cortisol concentration in man. *Journal of Clinical Endocrinology and Metabolism, 29,* 479–486.

Oswald, I. (1970). Effects on sleep of amphetamine and its derivatives. In E. Costa & S. Garattini (Eds.), *Amphetamines and related compounds* (pp. 865–871). New York: Raven Press.

Parker, D. C., Pekary, A., & Hershman, J. U. (1976). Effect of normal and revised sleep–wake cycles upon nyctohemeral rhythmicity of plasma thyrotropin: Evidence suggesting an inhibiting influence of sleep.

Journal of Clinical Endocrinology and Metabolism, *43,* 318–329.

Parker, D. C., Rossman, L. G., Kripke, D. F., Gibson, W., & Wilson, K. (1979). Rhythmicities in human growth hormone concentrations in plasma. In D. T. Krieger (Ed.), *Endocrine rhythms* (pp. 143–173). New York: Raven Press.

Parker, D. C., Rossman, L. G., & VanderLaan, E. F. (1973). Sleep-related, nyctohemeral, and briefly episodic variation in human plasma prolactin concentrations. *Journal of Clinical Endocrinology and Metabolism, 36,* 1119–1124.

Parker, D. C., Rossman, L. G., & VanderLaan, E. F. (1974). Relation of sleep-entrained human prolactin release to REM–non-REM cycles. *Journal of Clinical Endocrinology and Metabolism, 38,* 646–651.

Parker, G., & Walter, S. (1982). Seasonal variation in depressive disorders and suicidal deaths in New South Wales. *British Journal of Psychiatry, 140,* 626–632.

Patel, Y. C., Alford, F. P., & Burger, H. G. (1972). The 24-hour plasma thyrotropin profile. *Clinical Science, 43,* 71–77.

Penny, R., Olambiwonnu, N. O., & Frasier, S. D. (1977). Episodic fluctuations of serum gonadotrophins in pre- and postpubertal boys and girls. *Journal of Clinical Endocrinology and Metabolism, 45,* 307–311.

Pepper, G. M., Davis, K. L., Davis, B. M., & Krieger, D. T. (1983). DST in depression is unaffected by altering the clock time of its administration. *Psychiatry Research, 8,* 105–109.

Pflug, B. (1976). Effects of sleep deprivation on depressed patients. *Acta Psychiatrica Scandinavica, 53,* 148–158.

Pflug, B., Erikson, R., & Johnsson, A. (1976). Depression and daily temperature: A long-term study. *Acta Psychiatrica Scandinavica, 54,* 254–266.

Pflug, B., & Tolle, R. (1971). Disturbance of the 24-hour rhythm in endogenous depression and the treatment of endogenous depression by sleep deprivation. *International Pharmacopsychiatry, 6,* 187–196.

Poland, R. E., Rubin, R. T., Clark, B. R., & Gouin, P. R. (1972). Circadian patterns of 17-OHCS and VMA excretion during sleep deprivation. *Diseases of the Nervous System, 33,* 456–458.

Pollak, C. P., Moline, M. L., & Wagner, D. R. Temperature rhythms in depressed young and middle-aged women. (In preparation.)

Prinz, P. N., Vitaliano, P. P., Vitiello, M. V., Bokan, J., Raskind, M., Peskind, E., & Gerber, C. (1982). Sleep, EEG and mental function changes in senile dementia of the Alzheimer's type. *Neurobiology of Aging, 3,* 361–370.

Rafaelson, O. J., & Mellerup, D. (1978). Circadian rhythms in depressive disorders. In S. Garattini (Ed.), *Depressive disorders* (pp. 409–417). Stuttgart: Schattauer.

Reame, N., Sauder, S. E., Kelch, R. P., & Marshall, J. C. (1984). Pulsatile gonadotropin secretion during the human menstrual cycle: Evidence for altered frequency of gonadotropin-releasing hormone secretion. *Journal of Clinical Endocrinology and Metabolism, 59,* 328–337.

Rebar, R. W., & Yen, S. S. C. (1979). Endocrine

rhythms in gonadotropins and ovarian steroids with reference to reproductive processes. In D. T. Krieger (Ed.), *Endocrine rhythms* (pp. 259–298). New York: Raven Press.

Rechtschaffen, A., & Kales, A. (1968). *A manual of standardized terminology, techniques, and scoring system for sleep stages of human subjects* (NIH Publication No. 204, pp. 1–57). Los Angeles, CA: Brain Information Service/Brain Research Institute.

Reinberg, A. (1983). Clinical chronopharmacology. In A. Reinberg & M. H. Smolensky (Eds.), *Biological rhythms and medicine* (pp. 211–263). New York: Springer-Verlag.

Rihmer, Z. (1980). Season of birth and season of hospital admission in bipolar depressed female patients. *Psychiatry Research, 3,* 247–251.

Rockwell, D. A., Winget, C. M., Rosenblatt, L. S., Higgins, E. A., & Hetherington, N. W. (1978). Biological aspects of suicide: Circadian disorganization. *Journal of Mental Disease, 166,* 851–858.

Rosenthal, N. E., Carpenter, C. J., James, S. P., Parry, B. L., Rogers, S. L. B., & Wehr, T. A. (1986). Seasonal affective disorder in children and adolescents. *American Journal of Psychiatry, 143,* 356–358.

Rosenthal, N. E., Lewy, A. J., Wehr, T. A., Kern, H. E., & Goodwin, F. K. (1983). Seasonal cycling in a bipolar patient. *Psychiatry Research, 8,* 25–31.

Rosenthal, N. E., Sack, D. A., Carpenter, C. J., Parry, B. L., Mendelson, W. B., & Wehr, T. A. (1985). Antidepressant effects of light in seasonal affective disorder. *American Journal of Psychiatry, 142,* 163–170.

Rosenthal, N. E., Sack, D. A., Gillin, J. C., Lewy, A. J., Goodwin, F. K., Davenport, Y., Mueller, P. S., Newsome, D. A., & Wehr, T. A. (1984). Seasonal affective disorders: A description of the syndrome and preliminary findings with light therapy. *Archives of General Psychiatry, 41,* 72–80.

Rosenthal, N. E., Sack, D. A., Jacobson, F. M., Parry, B. L., James, S. P., Tamarkin, L., Arendt, J., & Wehr, T. A. (1985). Consensus and controversy in seasonal affective disorder and phototherapy. Presented at the IVth World Congress of Biological Psychiatry.

Rosenthal, N. E., Sack, D. A., James, S. P., Parry, B. L., Mendelson, W. B., Tamarkin, L., & Wehr, T. A. (1984, November). *Seasonal affective disorder and phototherapy.* Presented at the New York Academy of Sciences.

Ross, J. L., Barnes, K. M., Brody, S., Merrian, G. R., Loriaux, D. L., & Cutler, G. B. (1984). A comparison of two methods for detecting hormone peaks: The effect of sampling interval on gonadotropin peak frequency. *Journal of Clinical Endocrinology and Metabolism, 59,* 1159–1163.

Rush, A. J., Erman, M. K., Giles, D. E., Schlesser, M. A., Carpenter, G., Vasavada, N., & Roffwarg, H. P. (1986). Polysomnographic findings in recently drug-free and clinically remitted depressed patients. *Archives of General Psychiatry, 43,* 878–884.

Rush, A. J., Giles, D. E., Roffwarg, H. P., & Parker, R. C. (1982). Sleep EEG and dexamethasone suppression test findings in outpatients with unipolar major depressive disorders. *Biological Psychiatry, 17,* 327–341.

Sachar, E. J. (1975). Twenty-four-hour cortisol secretory patterns in depressed and manic patients. *Progress in Brain Research*, *42*, 81–91.

Sachar, E. J., Hellman, L., Fukushima, D. K., & Gallagher, T. F. (1970). Cortisol production in depressive illness: A clinical and biochemical clarification. *Archives of General Psychiatry*, *23*, 289–298.

Sachar, E. J., Hellman, L., Roffwarg, H. P., Frieda, S., Fukushima, D. K., & Gallagher, T. F. (1973). Disrupted 24-hour patterns of cortisol secretion in psychotic depressives. *Archives of General Psychiatry*, *28*, 19–24.

Sack, R. L., Lewy, A. J., Miller, S., & Singer, C. M. (1986). Effects of morning versus evening bright light exposure on REM latency. *Biological Psychiatry*, *21*, 410–413.

Sampson, G. A., & Jenner, F. A. (1975). Editorial: Circadian rhythms and mental illness. *Psychological Medicine*, *5*, 4–8.

Sassin, J. F., Frantz, A. G., Kapen, S., & Weitzman, E. D. (1973). The nocturnal rise in human prolactin is dependent on sleep. *Journal of Clinical Endocrinology and Metabolism*, *37*, 436–440.

Sassin, J. F., Frantz, A. G., Weitzman, E. D., & Kapen, S. (1972). Human prolactin: 24-hour pattern with increased release during sleep. *Science*, *177*, 1205–1207.

Sassin, J. F., Hellman, L., & Weitzman, E. D. (1974). Twenty-four-hour growth hormone and cortisol secretion in acromegaly. *Transactions of the American Neurological Association*, *99*, 244–245.

Sassin, J. F., Parker, D. C., Mace, J. W., Gotlin, R. N., Johnson, L. C., & Rossman, L. G. (1969). Human growth hormone release: Relation to slow wave sleep at sleep–waking cycles. *Science*, *165*, 513–515.

Shilgen, B., & Tolle, R. (1980). Partial sleep deprivation as therapy for depression. *Archives of General Psychiatry*, *37*, 267–271.

Sitaram, N., Gillin, J. C., & Bunney, W. E., Jr. (1978). Circadian variation in the time of "switch" of a patient with 48-hour manic–depressive cycles. *Biological Psychiatry*, *13*, 567–574.

Smallwood, R. G., Avery, D. H., Pascualy, R. A., & Prinz, P. N. (1983). Circadian temperature rhythms in primary depression. *Sleep Research*, *12*, 215.

Spitzer, R. L., Endicott, J., & Robins, E. (1977). *Research diagnostic criteria (RDC) for a selected group of functional psychoses* (3rd ed.). New York: New York State Psychiatric Institute.

Sridaran, R., & McCormack, C. E. (1977). Predicting the time of ovulation in rats by monitoring running activity. *Federation Proceedings, Federation of American Societies for Experimental Biology*, *36*, 313.

Stern, M., Fram, D. H., Wyatt, R., Grinspoon, L., & Tursky, B. (1969). All-night sleep studies of acute schizophrenics. *Archives of General Psychiatry*, *20*, 470–477.

Svendsen, K. (1976). Sleep deprivation therapy in depression. *Acta Psychiatrica Scandinavica*, *64*, 184–192.

Svendsen, K., & Christensen, P. G. (1981). Duration of REM sleep latency as predictor of effect of antidepressant therapy. *Acta Psychiatrica Scandinavica*, *64*, 238–243.

Swade, C., & Coppen, A. (1980). Seasonal variations in biochemical factors related to depressive illness. *Journal of Affective Disorders*, *2*, 249–255.

Symonds, R. L., & Williams, P. (1976). Seasonal variation in the incidence of mania. *British Journal of Psychiatry*, *129*, 45–48.

Tamarkin, L., Reppert, S. M., & Klein, D. C. (1979). Regulation of pineal melatonin in the Syrian hamster. *Endocrinology*, *104*, 385–389.

Thase, M. E., Kupfer, D. J., & Spiker, D. G. (1984). Electroencephalographic sleep in secondary depression: A revisit. *Biological Psychiatry*, *19*, 805–814.

Touitou, Y., Lagoguey, M., Bogdan, A., Reinberg, A., & Beck, H. (1983). Seasonal rhythms of plasma gonadotropins: Their persistence in elderly men and women. *Journal of Endocrinology*, *96*, 15–21.

Trapp, G., Eckert, E. D., Vestergaard, P., Sothern, R. B., & Halberg, F. (1979). Psychophysiologic circadian rhythmometry on manic–depressive twins. *Chronobiologia*, *6*, 387–396.

Tupin, J. P. (1973). Diurnal temperature and manic–depression. *Lancet*, *2*, 843.

Uhde, T. W., Post, R. M., Ballenger, J. C., Cutler, N. R., Jimerson, D. C., Weitzman, E. D., & Bunney, W. E., Jr. (1981). Circadian rhythm and sleep deprivation in depression. In W. P. Koella (Ed.), *Sleep 1980* (pp. 23–26). Basel: Karger.

van den Burg, W., & van den Hoofdakker, R. (1975). Total sleep deprivation on endogenous depression. *Archives of General Psychiatry*, *32*, 1121–1125.

Vanhaelst, L., van Cauter, E., Degaule, J. P., & Golstein, J. (1972). Circadian variations of serum thyrotropin levels in man. *Journal of Clinical Endocrinology and Metabolism*, *35*, 479–482.

Vaugh, G. H., Allen, J. P., Tullis, W., Siler-Khodr, T. M., de la Pena, A., & Sackman, J. W. (1978). Overnight plasma profiles of melatonin and certain adenohypophyseal hormones in men. *Journal of Clinical Endocrinology and Metabolism*, *47*, 566–571.

Vekemans, M., Delvoye, P., L'Hermite, M., & Robyn, C. (1977). Serum prolactin levels during the menstrual cycle. *Journal of Clinical Endocrinology and Metabolism*, *44*, 989–993.

Vigneri, R., Pezzino, V., Squatrito, S., Callandra, A., & Maricchiolo, M. (1974). Sleep-associated growth hormone (GH) release in schizophrenics. *Neuroendocrinology*, *14*, 356–361.

Vogel, G. W., McAbee, R., Barker, K., & Thurmond, A. (1977). Endogenous depression improvement and REM pressure. *Archives of General Psychiatry*, *34*, 96–97.

Vogel, G. W., Thurmond, A., Gibbons, P., Sloan, K., Boyd, M., & Walker, M. (1975). REM sleep reduction effects on depression syndromes. *Archives of General Psychiatry*, *32*, 765–777.

Vogel, G. W., Vogel, F., McAbee, R. S., & Thurmond, A. J. (1980). Improvement of depression by REM sleep deprivation. *Archives of General Psychiatry*, *37*, 247–253.

Vollman, R. F. (1974). Some conceptual and methodological problems in longitudinal studies on human reproduction. In M. Ferin, F. Halberg, R. M. Richart & R. L. Van de Wiele (Eds.), *Biorhythms and human reproduction* (pp. 161–201). New York: Wiley.

Wagner, D. R. (1984). Sleep. *Generations, 9*, 31–37.

Walter, S. D. (1977). Seasonality of mania: A reappraisal. *British Journal of Psychiatry, 131*, 345–350.

Watson, S. J., & Madden, J. (1977). Melatonin and other pineal substances: Psychiatric and neurological implications. In E. Usdin, D. A. Hamber, & J. D. Barchas (Eds.), *Neuroregulators and psychiatric disorders* (pp. 193–200). London & New York: Oxford University Press.

Weeke, A., & Weeke, J. (1980). The 24-hour pattern of serum TSH in patients with endogenous depression. *Acta Psychiatrica Scandinavica, 62*, 69–74.

Weeke, J. (1973). Circadian variation of serum thyrotropin levels in normal subjects. *Scandinavian Journal of Clinical and Laboratory Investigation, 31*, 337–342.

Wehr, T. A., & Goodwin, F. K. (1981). Biological rhythms and psychiatry. In S. Arieti & H. K. H. Brodie (Eds.), *American handbook of psychiatry VII* (pp. 46–74). New York: Basic Books.

Wehr, T. A., & Goodwin, F. K. (1983). Biological rhythms in manic–depressive illness. In T. A. Wehr & F. K. Goodwin (Eds.), *Circadian rhythms in psychiatry* (pp. 129–184). Pacific Grove, CA: Boxwood Press.

Wehr, T. A., Jacobsen, F. M., Sack, D. A., Arendt, J., Tamarkin, L., & Rosenthal, N. E. (1986). Phototherapy of seasonal affective disorder. Time of day and suppression of melatonin are not critical for antidepressant effects. *Archives of General Psychiatry, 43*, 870–875.

Wehr, T. A., Muscettola, G., & Goodwin, F. K. (1980). Urinary 3-methoxy-4-hydroxyphenylglycol circadian rhythm. *Archives of General Psychiatry, 37*, 257–263.

Wehr, T. A., Rosenthal, N. E., Sack, D. A., & Gillin, J. C. (1985). Antidepressant effects of sleep deprivation in bright and dim light. *Acta Psychiatrica Scandinavica, 72*, 161–165.

Wehr, T. A., Sack, D. A., Duncan, W. C., Mendelson, W. B., Rosenthal, N. E., Gillin, J. C., & Goodwin, F. K. (1985). Sleep and circadian rhythms in affective patients isolated from external time cues. *Psychiatry Research, 15*, 327–339.

Wehr, T. A., & Wirz-Justice, A. (1981). Internal coincidence model for sleep deprivation and depression. In W. P. Koella (Ed.), *Sleep 1980* (pp. 26–33). Basel: Karger.

Wehr, T. A., Wirz-Justice, A., & Goodwin, F. K. (1983). Circadian rhythm disturbances in affective illness and their modification by antidepressant drugs. In J. M. David & J. W. Maas (Eds.), *The affective disorders*. Washington, DC: American Psychiatric Press.

Wehr, T. A., Wirz-Justice, A., Goodwin, F. K., Duncan, W., & Gillin, J. C. (1979). Phase advance of the circadian sleep–wake cycle as an antidepressant. *Science, 206*, 710–713.

Weinberg, U., D'Eletto, R. D., Weitzman, E. D., Erlich, S., & Hollander, C. S. (1979). Circulating melatonin in man: Episodic secretion throughout the light–dark cycle. *Journal of Clinical Endocrinology and Metabolism, 48*, 114–118.

Weitzman, E. D., Czeisler, C. A., Zimmerman, J. C., & Ronda, J. M. (1980). Timing of REM and stages III and IV sleep during temporal isolation in man. *Sleep, 2*, 391–407.

Weitzman, E. D., de Graaf, A. S., Sassin, J. F., Hansen, T., Godtlibsen, O. B., Perlow, M., & Hellman, L. (1975). Seasonal patterns of sleep and sleep stages and secretion of cortisol and growth hormone during 24-hour periods in northern Norway. *Acta Endocrinologica (Copenhagen), 78*, 65–76.

Weitzman, E. D., Fukushima, D. K., Perlow, M., Burack, B., Sassin, J. F., & Hellman, L. (1971). Persistence of the 24-hour pattern of cortisol secretion and growth hormone release in blind subjects. *Transactions of the American Neurological Association, 97*, 197–199.

Weitzman, E. D., Kahn, E., & Pollak, C. P. (1980). Quantitative analysis of sleep and sleep apnea before and after tracheostomy in patients with the hypersomnia–sleep apnea syndrome. *Sleep, 3*, 407–423.

Weitzman, E. D., & Kripke, D. F. (1981). Experimental 12-hour shift of the sleep–wake cycle in man: Effects on sleep and physiologic rhythms. In L. C. Johnson, D. L. Tepas, W. P. Colquhoun, & M. J. Colligan (Eds.), *The twenty-four-hour workday: Proceedings of a symposium on variations in work–sleep schedules* (pp. 125–149). Washington, DC: U.S. Department of Health and Human Services.

Weitzman, E. D., Kripke, D., Goldmacher, D., McGregor, P., & Nogeire, C. (1970). Acute reversal of the sleep–waking cycle in man: Effect on sleep stage patterns. *Archives of Neurology, 22*, 485–489.

Weitzman, E. D., Moline, M. L., Czeisler, C. A., & Zimmerman, J. C. (1982). Chronobiology of aging: Temperature, sleep–wake rhythms, and entrainment. *Neurobiology of Aging, 3*, 299–309.

Weitzman, E. D., Nogeire, C., Perlow, M., Fukushima, D., Sassin, J., McGregor, P., Gallagher, T. F., & Hellman, L. (1974). Effects of a prolonged 3-hour sleep–wake cycle on sleep stages, plasma cortisol, growth hormone, and body temperature in man. *Journal of Clinical Endocrinology and Metabolism, 38*, 1018–1030.

Weitzman, E. D., Zimmerman, J. C., Czeisler, C. A., & Ronda, J. (1983). Cortisol secretion is inhibited during sleep in normal man. *Journal of Clinical Endocrinology and Metabolism, 56*, 352–358.

Welsh, D. K., Nino-Murcia, G., Gander, P. H., Keenan, S., & Dement, W. C. (1986). Regular 48-hour cycling of sleep duration and mood in a 35-year-old woman, use of lithium in time isolation. *Biological Psychiatry, 21*, 527–537.

Wetterberg, L. (1978). Physiological and clinical studies. *Journal of Neural Transmission, Supplement, 13*, 289–310.

Wetterberg, L. (1983). The relationship between the pineal gland and the pituitary–adrenal axis in health, endocrine, and psychiatric conditions. *Psychoneuroendocrinology, 8*, 75–80.

Wetterberg, L., Beck-Friis, J., Aperia, B., & Peterson, U. (1979). Melatonin/cortisol ratio in depression. *Lancet, 2*, 1361.

Wetterberg, L., Beck-Friis, J., Kjellman, B. F., & Ljunggren, J. G. (1984). Circadian rhythms in melatonin and cortisol secretion in depression. *Advances in Biochemical Psychopharmacology, 39*, 197–205.

Williams, R. L., & Karacan, I. (1976). *Pharmacology of sleep*. New York: Wiley.

Williams, R. L., & Karacan, I. (1976). *Pharmacology of sleep*. New York: Wiley.

Wirz-Justice, A. (1983). Antidepressant drugs: Effects on the circadian system. In T. A. Wehr & F. K. Goodwin (Eds.), *Circadian rhythms in psychiatry* (pp. 235–264). Pacific Grove, CA: Boxwood Press.

Wirz-Justice, A., Bucheli, C., Graw, P., Kielholz. P., Fisch, H.-U., & Woggon, B. (1986). Light treatment of seasonal affective disorder in Switzerland. *Acta Psychiatrica Scandinavica, 74*, 193–204.

Wirz-Justice, A., Wehr, T. A., Goodwin, F. K., Kafka, M. S., Naber, D., Marangos, P. J., & Campbell, I. C. (1980). Antidepressant drugs slow circadian rhythms in behavior and brain neurotransmitter receptors. *Psychopharmacology Bulletin, 16*, 45–47.

Wolff, G., & Money, J. (1973). Relationship between sleep and growth in patients with reversible somatotropin deficiency (psychosocial dwarfism). *Psychological Medicine, 3*, 18–27.

Yen, S. S. C., Llerena, L. A., & Pearson, O. H. (1970). Disappearance rates of endogenous follicle-stimulating hormone in serum following surgical hypophysectomy in man. *Journal of Clinical Endocrinology and Metabolism, 30*, 325–329.

Yen, S. S. C., Vandenberg, G., & Tsai, C. C. (1974). Ultradian fluctuations of gonadotropins. In M. Ferin (Ed.), *Biorhythms and human reproduction* (pp. 203–218). New York: Wiley.

Zarcone, V. (1978). Alcoholism and sleep. *Advances in Biosciences, 21*, 29–38.

Zimmerman, J. C., Czeisler, C. A., Laxminarayan, S., Knauer, R. S., & Weitzman, E. D. (1980). REM density is dissociated from REM sleep timing during free-running sleep episodes. *Sleep, 2*, 409–415.

Zung, W. W. K., & Green, R. L. (1974). Seasonal variation of suicide and depression. *Archives of General Psychiatry, 30*, 89–91.

10 AGGRESSIVE AND ANTISOCIAL BEHAVIOR

MICHAEL H. SHEARD

Yale University Medical School
The Connecticut Mental Health Center

INTRODUCTION

Antisocial behavior is the outcome of many variables, biological, psychological, social, and situational. It is seen over a whole spectrum of psychiatric conditions and occurs in the normal population as well. This chapter will narrow the focus on those conditions where antisocial behavior of an aggressive type is a chronic, continuous, or frequent feature or where it is part of a pathological syndrome which can be operationally defined.

The most well known of this group of disorders is the antisocial personality disorder specified according to DSM-III (American Psychiatric Association, 1980) as having the characteristics listed in Table 10.1.

Childhood conduct disorders are enumerated according to unsocialized or socialized aggressive types with and without attention deficit disorder. Hare (1983) has reported that there is substantial agreement between DSM-III criteria and special personality rating scales for antisocial personality that he has developed (Hare, 1980) utilizing criteria derived from the classic description of Cleckley (1976). The difference between the two sets of criteria resides chiefly in Hare's use of judgments about internal qualities such as egocentricity, lack of remorse or shame, inability to love, and unreliability rather than wholly on external behavioral items as used in DSM-III. He points out that the strict use of DSM-III criteria may entail missing some

cases when early history is not readily obtainable or when the subject has not yet reached an age when behavior has occurred. Using these scales, Hare found about 30–40% of a criminal population in both a maximum secure prison and a medium secure facility were diagnosed as having an anitsocial personality disorder.

Clinical experience shows that the antisocial personality disorder is not a unitary condition, however, and neuroendocrine studies have to take this into account. There are subgroups which emphasize some characteristics more than others. For example, there is a subgroup with a history of attention deficit disorder in childhood and a later history of adult antisocial behavior (Satterfield, 1978). There is another with episodes of explosive violent behavior. Electrophysiological studies have revealed evidence for a group of antisocial disorders with slow electrodermal recovery from aversive stimuli indicative of poor avoidance learning (Hare & Cox, 1978; Syndulko, 1978). Another group maintains high levels of cardiac responsivity to aversive stimuli suggestive of somatic anxiety (Hare & Blevings, 1975; Lindner, Goldman, Dinitz, & Allen, 1970). Finally, a significant percentage of these subjects have an abnormal encephalogram either before or after activation techniques (Hill & Watterson, 1942; Monroe, 1970; Silverman, 1944). Research studies should therefore make an attempt to

TABLE 10.1. Characteristics of the Antisocial Personality Disorder as Specified According to DSM-III

A. Current age of at least 18

B. Onset before age 15 as indicated by a history of three or more of the following before that age:
   1. Truancy
   2. Expulsion or suspension from school for misbehavior
   3. Delinquency
   4. Running away from home overnight at least twice
   5. Persistent lying
   6. Repeated sexual intercourse in a casual relationship
   7. Repeated drunkenness or substance abuse
   8. Thefts
   9. Vandalism
   10. School grades markedly below expectations in relation to estimated or known IQ
   11. Chronic violation of rules at home and/or school (other than truancy)

C. At least four of the following manifestations of the disorder since age 18:
   1. Inability to sustain consistent work behavior as indicated by any of the following:
      a. Too frequent job changes (e.g., three or more jobs in 5 years not accounted for by nature of job or economic or seasonal fluctuation)
      b. Significant unemployment (e.g., 6 months or more in 5 years when expected to work)
      c. Serious absenteeism from work (e.g., 3 days or more of absence or lateness per month)
      d. Walking off jobs without other jobs in sight
   2. Lacking ability to function as a responsible parent as evidenced by one or more of the following:
      a. Child's malnutrition
      b. Child's illness resulting from lack of minimal hygiene standards
      c. Failure to obtain medical care for a seriously ill child
      d. Child's dependence on neighbors or nonresident relatives for food or shelter
      e. Failure to arrange for a caretaker for a child under 6 when parent is away from home
      f. Repeated squandering on personal items of money required for household necessities
   3. Failure to accept social norms with regard to lawful behavior as indicated by any of the following: repeated thefts, illegal occupation (pimping, prostitution, fencing, selling drugs), multiple arrests or felony conviction
   4. Inability to maintain enduring attachment to a sexual partner as indicated by two or more divorces and/or separations (legally married or not), desertion of a spouse, promiscuity (10 or more partners in a year)
   5. Irritability and aggressiveness as indicated by repeated physical fights or assaults, including spouse or child abuse
   6. Failure to honor financial obligations, as indicated by repeated defaulting on debts, failure to provide child support, failure to support other dependents on a regular basis
   7. Failure to plan ahead, or impulsivity
   8. Disregard for the truth—repeated lying
   9. Recklessness and disregard for others

D. Pattern of continuous antisocial behavior in which the rights of other are violated with no intervening period of at least 5 years without antisocial behavior between age 15 and present time (except when bedridden or confused)

E. Antisocial behavior is not due to either severe mental retardation, schizophrenia, or manic episodes

---

define homogeneous populations as much as possible.

Aggressive behavior is not a unitary concept either. Rather, aggression is a term which covers a wide range of behaviors serving different motivations and aimed at different goals. In animals, where controlled observations are more easily set up, as many as seven different types of aggressive behavior can be differentiated by means of the eliciting environmental situation and stimuli (Moyer, 1968). These different types of aggressive behavior can be reduced to two main categories. The first, called predatory or instrumental, is driven by needs, wishes, and desires for some reward. There is little or no affect involved unless an obstruction is placed in the way of obtaining the reward. There are marked individual differences in the nature and intensity of the aggression which can be called into the service of the instigating need or wish. The second category is called defensive or reactive. It is elicited by pain or threats of various kinds. The pain may be physical or emotional. Investigations into the neural substrates of aggressive behavior have revealed two main systems in mammalian brain, one for predatory or instrumental aggression and one for defensive aggression (Flynn, 1976). It is now well established by neuroendocrine investigations that sex hormones are taken up by select brain regions and affect neural behavioral and endocrine activity. It is of interest then to point out that an overlap exists between hormone-sensitive brain regions and regions from which attack can be elicited and either facilitated or suppressed in cats.

This chapter will discuss the genetic and chromosomal background for endocrinological findings in aggressive behavior followed by a review of endocrine influences on aggression in the prenatal, pubertal, and adult stages of human development. Where appropriate, reference will be made to animal studies. Basic information on antisocial behavior can be obtained from the comprehensive texts of Hare (1970), Reid (1978), and Hare and Schalling (1978).

GENETICS

Antisocial behavior of an aggressive type is more common in males, which throws suspicion on the Y chromosome. The evidence from twin and adoptive studies is suggestive of an important genetic contribution to antisocial behavior, although this evidence is by no means conclusive. There have been a number of concordance studies of criminals showing an increased rate in monozygotic twins. Eysenck and Eysenck (1978) summarized the data from several of these studies and estimated a concordance of 55% in monozygotic and 13% in dizygotic twins for criminal antisocial behavior. Christiansen (1968) has reported concordance rates for monozygotic twins as 33%. Shields (1975) in his review of psychiatric genetics was of the opinion that twin studies supported the genetic influence in criminality, but he provided no more convincing evidence than the concordance rates. Cloninger and Guze (1973) have stated that the monozygotic heritability is 0.70 and the dizygotic heritability is 0.28. They studied the psychiatric patterns in families of female criminals. An isolated case study has been described which supports genetic influence in a family of triplets. A pair of identical twins showed evidence of antisocial personality disorder, while the third member, dizygotic to the other two, did not. All these studies have difficulties such as the problem of zygosity and differential treatment. Adoption studies are better than concordance ones, but still suffer from some inescapable deficiencies, such as the difference in relative information from biological and adoptive parents. Also, very early, even intrauterine experiences could be important for later behavior. Nevertheless, the adoption model offers the best method so far.

The Kety, Rosenthal, Wender, and Schulsinger (1968) study is of this type. They found an increased prevalence of psychopathy (antisocial personality disorder) among the biological relatives of schizophrenics. Hutchings and Mednick (1975), studying criminality in adoptive and biological parents of male criminal adoptees, found that 50% of biological fathers of adopted criminals were criminal compared to 28% of fathers of noncriminal controls. However, results were in the same direction for adoptive fathers, though the magnitude was lower, indicating that both nature and nurture were playing an important role, though perhaps nature was exerting the greater influence. Additional positive studies have been performed by Crowe (1974) and Schulsinger (1972). In these studies, attempts were made to differentiate between "criminal" and "sociopathic" behavior. On the other hand, a negative study by Bohman (1971) found less antisocial behavior associated with children of criminal fathers than with controls.

CHROMOSOMAL STUDIES

There is now a body of data which addresses the problem of the linkage between sex chromosomes and aggressive antisocial behavior.

It is clear that males commit significantly more violent crimes than women, although recent evidence suggests that the incidence of violent crimes committed by women is increasing. This differential suggests a significance of the Y chromosome for aggressive behavior and the possibility, therefore, that the XYY chromosomal abnormality would show exaggerated aggressive behavior. Early reports from Scotland showing an increased prevalence of XYY genotype in subjects committing violence antisocial behavior gave impetus to this notion (Casey *et al.*, 1966). However, subsequent studies using better methods and better controls failed to reveal an association with either XXY or XYY to violent behavior (Kessler, 1975). A later study did find an increased conviction rate for XYY compared with other tall men; however, crimes were usually petty and non-aggressive (Hunter, 1977). An association between XYY, tallness, and mental subnormality has been demonstrated (Jacobs, Brunton, Melville, Britain, & McClemont, 1969), and it is possible that mental subnormality is the important variable accounting for increased conviction rates (Witkin, Mednick, & Schulsinger, 1976). Studies in this area require careful methodology and good design. Problems to be aware of are mosaicism, changes in karyotype over time, and even differences between tissue samples, within the same person.

In a careful review of over 260 references, Baker (1972) came to the conclusion that there was insufficient evidence to link 47 XXY or 47 XYY with aggressive behavior of crimes. While it appears generally correct to say that 47 XYY males do not show an unusually high degree of aggressive behavior, it is of interest to mention a report by Money *et al.* (1975). These authors described the characteristics of 13 of 28 cases of XYY karyotype on their records who displayed antisocial impulsive behavior. These subjects did not have subnormal IQs (mean 100.6, range 82–125) and 11 of the 13 had a history of assault against persons. However, it is not clear that these subjects necessarily had high androgen levels.

Most of these human studies have used criminality as an index rather than antisocial behavior per se. These two indices require more careful separation in genetic and behav-ior endocrine studies. Meanwhile, it is clear that there is a powerful interaction between genetic and environmental influences. The question remains as to how precisely genetic influences control the interaction with environment during development to either enhance or inhibit tendencies to antisocial behavior. Cloninger, Reich, and Guze (1975) used a Multifactorial Model of Disease Transmission to study genetic and environmental contributions to antisocial personality, hysteria, alcoholism, and criminality. They found a good fit of this model to family and twin data which suggested that genetic and environmental factors, though both very important, act independently rather than interdependently. Genetic influences may act in part through organic factors such as low cortical arousal thresholds of delayed autonomic recovery times as well as through altered endocrine regulation.

Fetal Androgenization

A consistent finding has been of more aggressiveness in males than females across many different cultures (Maccoby & Jacklin, 1974). Social training by itself cannot account for this difference because larger differences are found between 3- to 6-year-olds than 7- to 10-year-olds (D'Andrade, 1966). It is well accepted now that sexual differentiation is androgen dependent, and animal experimentation has shown that the brain can be critically affected at an early stage by exposure to androgens. Therefore, it has been a natural supposition that characteristic male sexual and aggressive behaviors are likewise facilitated by androgens. This has been shown to be true for rodents and nonhuman primates. For example, Conner, Levine, Wertheim, and Cummer (1969) found that testosterone increased aggression in male rats and males castrated at 21 days. On the other hand, neonatally castrated rats did not show increased aggression when given testosterone as adults; that is, they behaved like females. When neonatal female rats were treated with androgens, they showed increased aggression when treated with testosterone as adults (Powell, Francis, & Schneiderman, 1971). Studies with rhesus monkeys (Goy, 1968) have supported these findings in rodents. Prenatally androgenized female monkeys display more masculine-type behavior than normal females. Eaton, Goy, and Phoenix (1973) reported that when testosterone was administered to ovariectomized prenatally androgenized females in adulthood, they showed increased overt aggression, threat, sexual exploration, and display similar to males.

The evidence in humans is much less clear; however there are three clinical conditions which do lend some support to the notion that androgens are related to the process of masculinization and abnormal aggressive behavior. In two of the syndromes, the female fetus is exposed to androgenic substances either by progestin administered to the mother to prevent miscarriage or by abnormal androgen production by the adrenal gland with adrenogenital syndrome. The latter condition is the result of a recessive gene which causes excess adrenal androgen production instead of cortisol.

Reports on the behavior of progestin-masculinized girls (Ehrhardt & Money, 1967) and girls with adrenogenital syndrome (Money & Ehrhardt, 1972; Ehrhardt & Baker, 1974) compared with unrelated matched controls or unaffected siblings showed more tomboyish behavior, with a preference for male pursuits, and the subjects were more likely to initiate fights. In later life, however, they did not appear more dominant or aggressive (Money & Schwartz, 1976). Moreover, 9 boys with adrenogenital syndrome were not more aggressive than unaffected brothers (Ehrhardt & Mayer-Bahlburg, 1979). Reinisch (1977) has also reported on a group of children exposed to synthetic progestins compared to their unaffected siblings. They were found to be more individualistic and self-assured as measured by the Cattell Personality Questionnaire.

On the other hand, in the condition of androgen insensitivity, despite normal circulating androgens in a genetic male, the appearance and behavior is typically female (Masica, Money, Ehrhardt, & Lewis, 1969; Money & Ehrhardt, 1972). This condition has a genetic transmission and is associated with a defective androgen-binding molecule in receptor cells. The importance of this condition theoretically is that it reveals the importance of receptors in the determination of behavior in response to androgens. The assumption that the behavioral changes in

these conditions are simply hormonal has been critically challenged (Quadragno, Briscoe, & Quadragno, 1979). It is clear that many other factors could be playing a role, such as attitude and child-rearing practices of parents. Also, measurements of aggression were usually based solely on observations by parents. In the adrenogenital syndrome, it is not clear what effect cortisol therapy may itself have on behavior. Finally, the main androgen produced in the adrenogenital syndrome is androstenedione (Rivarola, Saez, & Migeon, 1967), while animal studies usually utilize testosterone.

Androgens have then two main functions. The first is to help determine the development of an androgen-sensitive neural substrate for aggressive behavior. The second is to provide a stimulus for this neural substrate once it si developed. This type of typical male behavior can be produced experimentally in female animals by administering androgens at a critical period of development and later in life by giving androgen injections.

ENDOCRINE CHANGES AT PUBERTY

A rapid rise in gonadal steriods occurs at the time of puberty which coincides in males with an increase in aggressive and competitive behavior. This is seen in both humans and apes (Hamburg, 1971). In young males, testosterone rises as much as fourfold within a year or so, with the time of greatest rise between 10 and 18 years. Adult levels are frequently reached within a 2-year period (Knorr, Bidlingmaier, Butenandt, Fendel, & Ehrt-Wehle, 1974). Other major endocrine changes also occur at this time, such as increased levels of growth hormone, luteinizing hormone (LH), prolactin, and thyroid-stimulating hormone (TSH) in females (Faiman & Winter, 1974). Thus, it would appear that young males would be a good population in whom to study the interrelationship of testosterone and aggressive behavior. Interesting evidence which tends to corroborate this was provided in a study by Kreuz and Rose (1972), to be discussed later. Here it suffices to note that they reported that levels of testosterone found in adults correlated positively with a history of violent behavior in the teen years.

Olweus, Mattson, Schalling, and Löw (1980) reported the results of a study correlating plasma testosterone in adolescent males with rating scales measuring aggression, impulsiveness, lack of frustration, tolerance, extroversion, and anxiety. Olweus (1975, 1977) has shown previously that aggressive behavior in preadolescent and adolescent subjects can be measured in a reliable and valid way. This has been a problem in adult studies utilizing rating scales. The plan of the study consisted of first completing the set of personality inventories and rating scales. Then 1 month later, a morning blood sample was taken for testosterone followed by a situation questionnaire designed to appraise anxiety. A physical examination was also performed. One month later a second morning blood sample was taken for testosterone.

The inventories measured physical and verbal aggression, aggressive attitudes and impulses, aggression inhibitory responses, lack of frustration tolerance, and antisocial behavior. Also measured were impulsiveness, anxiety, extroversion, and self-confidence. Peer ratings were used as a measure of validity. Fifty-eight boys, 15 to 17 years old, with a mean of 16, completed the study. The mean testosterone value was 544 ± 141.3 μg/100 ml with a range of 197–901 μg/100 ml. The test–retest reliability was 0.77. The correlation of pubertal stage and testosterone level was 0.44. Testosterone did not correlate with body build, but did correlate significantly with physical and verbal aggression scores and with lack of frustration tolerance. An analysis of individual items revealed the interesting finding that it was predominantly aggression in response to threat or unfair treatment which correlated most clearly with testosterone. As the authors point out, this may help to explain the poor correlations usually obtained with the Buss–Durkee Hostility Inventory (BDHI), which is relatively heterogenous in content, with none of the subscales clearly designed to measure provocation or threat. It should be emphasized that in this study, no correlation was found between self-reports of antisocial behavior and testosterone; however, this was a normal group of adolescents and the antisocial behavior was not of a physically aggressive type. In another study with male delinquents, the authors report a similar high correlation between aggression scores on items involving provocation and plasma testosterone.

ANDROGEN CORRELATES OF AGGRESSIVE BEHAVIOR IN ADULT MALES

Several attempts have been made to correlate testosterone levels with aggressive behavior in adults. In animals, particularly primates, the mating season is a time of increased aggression, with wounding and death (Kaufman, 1967; Vandenbergh & Vessey, 1968; Wilson & Boelkins, 1970). Persky, Smith, and Basu (1971) studied the relationship between testosterone concentrations and hostility as measured by the self-rated BDHI. They found a significant positive correlation between hostility and testosterone in a group of men aged 17–28 (mean age 22), but not in a group aged 31–66 (mean age 45), nor in a group of psychiatric patients with a mean age of 39. Meyer-Bahlburg, Boon, Sharma, and Edwards (1974) failed to replicate this result in a study comparing the plasma and urinary testosterone as well as production rate in a group of male college students (called high aggressive on the basis of scores on the BDHI) with a low-aggressive group.

Doering et al. (1974) studied a group of normal young men longitudinally and found no significant correlation between plasma testosterone and hostility either between or within subjects over time. Interestingly, in this last study there was a significant positive correlation between measures of depression and mean plasma testosterone. Perhaps in the normal individual, depression may be an index of aggression, "aggression turned inward," to use a psychodynamic interpretation. The problem with these studies is that it is unlikely that a normal population will vary sufficiently in aggressive behavior measurable by questionnaire to enable a correlation between testosterone and aggressive behavior to be found.

Indeed, several studies have shown that self-rated questionnaires such as the BDHI and the Hostility and Direction of Hostility Questionnaire correlate very poorly or not at all with overt aggressive behavior.

In another study of normals, Monti, Brown, and Corriveau (1977) found a poor correlation between BDHI scores of hostility and testosterone values. This was also true of a group of alcoholics studied by Persky *et al.* (1977). However, alcohol itself is known to depress plasma testosterone levels.

A relationship between plasma testosterone and behavioral ratings of aggressive behavior and agitation in 12 male patients aged 18–31 on an inpatient psychiatric ward has been reported by Kendenburg, Kendenburg, and Kling (1973). They found no difference between mean testosterone level between patient and control groups. However, within-subject correlations in the patient group between agitation or aggression and testosterone were highly significant. Agitation was negatively correlated and aggression positively correlated with testosterone levels.

In criminal populations there is a higher level of overt aggressive behavior, and studies have revealed some interesting findings. Kreuz and Rose (1972) selected a group of "fighters" and a group of "nonfighters" from male prisoners aged 19–32. Despite this difference in overt aggression, they found no difference in plasma levels of testosterone or in psychological tests between the two groups. However, they did find a positive correlation between testosterone levels and a past history of violent antisocial behavior in adolescence. Also they reported that those subjects with the highest testosterone had been convicted at a younger age than those with the lowest level. This finding, together with the Persky and Olweus studies, suggests that an important association between testosterone and aggression can occur during adolescence.

Studies by Rose, Holaday, and Bernstein (1972) in rhesus monkeys have shown the importance of social rank and the outcome of social conflict in the determination of testosterone levels. The dominant males increase and subordinates decrease their testosterone levels following resolution of conflicts. Mazur (1976) has also emphasized the importance of the relationship between testosterone and status in primate groups.

These variables were included in a study by Ehrenkranz, Bliss, and Sheard (1974) in male prisoners. Thirty-six subjects between the ages of 18 and 45 were selected from the general inmate population of a maximum security institution ($n = 860$). There were 12 subjects in each of three groups: a violent aggressive group, a socially dominant group, and a nonaggressive group. The aggressive group was characterized by evidence of overt physical aggression which was chronic and violent in character. These subjects were in prison for violent crimes and continued to display assaultiveness in prison. The socially dominant group was in prison for a variety of nonviolent crimes such as fraud, check passing, and drug-related felonies. They were on top in prison hierarchies and held key jobs. The nonaggressive group was in effect a control group and fell into neither of the first two groups. They were in prison for nonviolent crimes and were not socially dominant. Peer ratings validated the three groups in terms of leadership, dominance, and aggressiveness, in addition to the judgments of prison personnel. Subjects were not on medication and had no major physical or mental illness. There was no significant difference in height, weight, or age between the three groups. Plasma testosterone measured on three successive mornings between 8 and 8:15 A.M. had a high level of constancy and, moreover, the mean level was found to be approximately the same as that found in the study by Kreuz and Rose (1972) (8.15 μg vs. 8.45 μg/ml). These levels are higher than means usually reported for normal populations (around 6 μg/ml). The testosterone level for the aggressive group (10.10 μg/ml) was significantly higher than the level for the nonaggressive group (5.99 μg/ml). The testosterone level for the socially dominant group (9.36 μg/ml) was also significantly higher than that for the nonaggressive group. While the testosterone level was higher in the aggressive group than in the socially dominant group, the difference was not significant. The aggressive group scored significanlty higher on the BDHI than the other two groups on total score as well as the subscales of physical aggression, passive aggression, verbal aggression, and paranoia. However, there were no significant individual correlations between testosterone and socres on 57 psychological variables. The authors, however, did not rank individual aggressiveness in the aggressive group. An interesting finding was a significant negative correlation between levels of testosterone and scores on the Lykken test which can be interpreted as measuring anxiety around risk taking. In other words, the individuals with the highest plasma testosterone concentrations ranked themselves as taking the most risks and thus presumably had the least anxiety. The results of this study suggest that both excess aggressive behavior and dominant behavior can be associated with high testosterone in adult human males.

An interesting individual case illustrating a correlation between testosterone and aggressive behavior has been described by Matthews (1979). This subject was involved in a double-blind study of two antilibidinal drugs, benperidol and cyproterone acetate, in a prison population. The drugs were given in a double-blind crossover study. The individual in question, besides having a sexual problem, was pathologically aggressive. He had to mix as little as possible with other inmates and be housed in the prison hospital to avoid getting into heated fights. On cyproterone acetate he demonstrated a marked reduction in both sexual drive and pathological aggressiveness so that he could for the first time mix comfortably with other inmates. After the cyproterone acetate was stopped, he reverted to his former behavior and was then given benperidol. This time his sexual drive was reduced as before, but his pathological aggressiveness remained unabated. This subject's plasma testosterone was the highest of any member of the study and was reduced by cyproterone acetate, but not by benperidol. In the same report, however, 11 prisoners with violent crimes were found to have testosterone levels which did not differ significantly from 11 matched controls who were in prison for nonviolent crimes. Thus, while there are some suggestive findings that link testosterone with aggressive behavior, the evidence thus far is by no means conclusive, and many other variables are clearly involved.

The study by Olweus suggests a strong relationship between physical and verbal aggression and testosterone in response to provocation or threat in adolescence. It is interesting, therefore, that in another study by Scaramella and Brown (1978) testosterone levels in hockey players were found to correlate with aggressiveness in response to threat as judged by coaches. The evidence from both of these studies is consistent with the findings in rhesus monkeys (Rose, Bernstein, & Gordon, 1975) which showed the very large changes in testosterone that could occur as a result of conflict. Both social rank and outcome of the conflict appear important in determining levels of testosterone. This was investigated in humans in a study by Mazur and Lamb (1980) who measured testosterone in the winners and losers of a tennis game with a monetary prize. In two matches where the outcome was a decisive victory, the four losers showed drops in testosterone, while three out of four winners showed a rise in testosterone. In a third match with a very slim and thus rather indefinite victory, both winners and losers showed a fall in testosterone.

A study by Rada, Laws, and Kellner (1976) investigated plasma testosterone levels in sexual offenders. The offenders comprised 52 rapists and 12 child molesters. The mean age of the rapists was 26.1, with a range of 19–42, and of the child molesters 33.5, with a range of 22–48. The rapists were classified into four groups depending on the degree of violent behavior engaged in during the rape. Testosterone was measured from one venous blood sample obtained between 8:30 and 10 A.M. The range for normals was 225 μg/100 ml to 1412 μg/100 ml (mean 625 μg/100 ml), for rapists it was 181 μg/100 ml to 1236 μg/100 ml (mean 610 μg/100 ml), and for the child molesters it was 200 μg/100 ml to 911 μg/100 ml (mean 502 μg/100 ml). These results indicated that the range of testosterone for the total group of rapists and child molesters was not significantly different from normals. However, the authors did report that there was a significantly higher testosterone level in the most violent group of rapists from the other three groups and from normals. This group ($n = 5$) had a mean testosterone of 853 μg/100 ml.

EFFECTS OF CASTRATION

One would expect theoretically that if testosterone was linked to aggressive behavior, castration would lessen aggression. The effects of castration on aggressive behavior have not been well studied in either nonhuman primate or humans, though used as a technique for varied purposes in humans over centuries.

It has been used especially in Europe for sexual offenders. Bremmer (1959) followed up 244 cases and found a beneficial effect in reducing sexual offenses, but he specifically states that there was no effect on aggressive behavior or on other forms of antisocial behavior unrelated to sex offenses. This finding agrees with those of Vandenbergh and Vessey (1968) in rhesus monkeys. They studied 10 castrates, 4 as infants and 6 between 3 and 7 years of age. The monkeys were observed at 5 years of age and did not differ significantly in aggressive behavior from peers, though they did fall in dominance.

ENDOCRINE CORRELATIONS IN FEMALES

There exists in the literature and in medical lore suggestions and opinions that link dysphoria along with aggressive and antisocial behavior to various phases of the menstrual cycle (e.g., Beaumont, Richards, & Gelder, 1975; Dalton, 1964; Hamburg, Moos, & Yalum, 1968; J. F. O'Connor, Shelley, & Stern, 1974). A linkage with suicide has also been noted (Mandell & Mandell, 1967). Attempts have been made to correlate behavioral changes to changes in mood during the menstrual cycle. There is a well-described increase in negative affects, irritability, anxiety, depression, plus physical symptoms such as lethargy, painful breasts, and body swelling occurring in the few days prior to the onset of menstruation and for the first day or two of blood flow. This is known as the premenstrual syndrome, and many attempts have been made to correlate this with hormonal changes (see Haskett, Chapter 22). A role for estradiol was postulated by Frank (1931) and for a low progesterone level in the luteal phase by Dalton (1977). The evidence for an increase in violent aggressive outbursts is only fair. Morton, Additon, Addison, Hunt, and Sullivan (1953) gained information from 42 inmates of a women's prison farm guilty of violent crimes. They found that 62% committed their crimes during the premenstrual week and 17% during menstruation. However, this result depended entirely on the inmates' past memories and hence may not be reliable. Dalton found that older girl prefects aged 16–18 punished younger girls more often during the first 4 days of their periods and less often during the premenstrual 4 days. Hands, Herbert, and Tennent (1974) used frequency of confinement on a secure hospital ward, which treated violence in women patients, as an index of aggressive disturbance. They found that there were significantly more confinements in the premenstrual week than at other times. Ellis and Austin (1971) studied the relationship between aggressive acts as recorded by prison officials for 45 prison inmates over three menstrual cycles. One-third of 124 aggressive acts were physical attacks and the remainder verbal abuse. The aggressive acts were concentrated in the premenstrual and menstrual days and also were correlated with self-reports of increased irritability at these phases of the cycle. Rossi and Rossi (1980) studied 82 college women over a 40-day period and found negative moods correlated in time with the week preceding menstruation and the first day or two of the menses. They also pointed out that some women who were taking birth control pills did not report any mood changes. Since these women presumably did not experience normal shifts in estrogen and progesterone, perhaps mood shifts during the menstrual cycle are caused by hormone changes.

There have been several reports of lower progesterone concentrations during the luteal phase in patients with premenstrual syndrome (Bäckström & Carstensen, 1974; Bäckström, Wide, Sodegard, & Carstensen, 1976; Munday, Brush, & Taylor, 1981), but others have failed to confirm this finding (Andersch, Abrahamsson, Wendestam, Olhman, & Kahn, 1979; O'Brien, Selby, & Symonds, 1980; Taylor, 1979).

The results of a recent careful study by Bäckström et al. (1983) showed that the negative mood changes in women with premenstrual syndrome were linked to the luteal phase of the cycle, reaching a maximum in the last 5 days. The negative mood usually disappears within a day or two of the estradiol and progesterone reaching early follicular levels. Maximal positive moods were found when the preovulatory estradiol reached its peak. However, no actual differences in hormone levels were found between women with high and low degrees of cyclical mood change and, in particular, the earlier finding of a relative progesterone deficiency was not confirmed. Severe premenstrual syndrome can occur with a normal luteal phase. Thus, the underlying mechanism for premenstrual syndrome remains unknown at present, but the fact that the cyclic changes persist following hysterectomy (Bäckström, Boyle, & Baird, 1981) indicates that the explanation cannot be a psychological or physical reaction to menstruation itself. Since levels of plasma estrogens do not appear significantly related to the negative mood changes, is it possible that the latter could be related to plasma androgen levels? Persky *et al.* (1982) has reported that while androgen levels in women were related significantly to sexual response, they did not relate significantly to estimates of anxiety, depression, or hostility. The androgens measured were dehydroepiandrosterone, androstenedione, testosterone, and dihydrotestosterone and, of course, reflect predominantly adrenal function. Bancroft, Sanders, Davidson, and Warner (1983) also confirmed that plasma testosterone was not related to sexuality involving a partner, but was positively related to masturbation frequency.

Another hormone which may possibly be involved in premenstrual syndrome is aldosterone. Janowsku, Gorney, and Mandell (1967) suggest that irritability may be a result of the cyclic increase in aldosterone, since changes in weight, behavior, and aldosterone correlate well. They postulated that a resulting increase in sodium and water retention might then lead to neuronal irritability with associated psychic symptoms.

GONADOTROPIC HORMONES

Thus far, this chapter has concerned itself predominantly with gonadal hormones and aggressive behavior. The effects of gonadotropic hormones have been studied much less frequently. However, that there may well be important influences is suggested strongly by some animal experiments. For example, Inselman-Temkin and Flynn (1973) demonstrated that gonadectomy and follicle-stimulating hormone (FSH) decreased attack latencies in female cats and increased latencies in males. An increase in latency implies an inhibition of aggression and a decreased

latency a facilitation of aggression. On the other hand, LH, estradiol, and testosterone had the opposite effects, namely, increasing attack latencies in female cats and decreasing attack latencies in male cats. These altered latencies are presumably mediated via altered thresholds of the neural substrates for aggressive behavior resulting from the hormonal action.

Evidence from human studies is much scantier. However, in this connection, the work of Mendelson and his associates is of interest. Mendelson, Mello, and Ellingboe (1977) reported that alcohol suppresses gonadal hormones with a resulting increase in LH as a consequence of diminished gonadal steroid feedback control. Since alcoholism is associated with an increased aggressivity and increased risk taking, the data suggested that the increased LH could be a factor in the increased aggressivity. To obtain more evidence for this notion, Mendelson, Dietz, and Ellingboe (1982) investigated the relationship between postmortem plasma LH levels and antemortem violence. They found that violent antemortem behavior, such as committing suicide by gunshot or hanging or being killed during violent attack or physical struggle, was associated with significantly higher LH levels than with nonviolent antemortem behavior. These findings suggested that postmortem LH levels in males may be a biological indicator of violent behavior preceding death.

In contrast to these findings is a report by Sheard, Marini, and Giddings (1977), who measured LH and testosterone weekly during the course of a trial of lithium versus placebo on impulsive–aggressive behavior in 16- to 24-year-old male prisoners. Several studies have shown that lithium can inhibit pathological aggressiveness without adversely affecting other behaviors such as motor coordination or muscle strength. The mechanism of this action of lithium is poorly understood, but lithium is known to affect several endocrine systems. For example, it can interfere with the synthesis and release of iodinated thyroid hormones (T3 and T4) and produce goiter and clinical hypothyroidism. That this thyroid effect could be an explanation for an antiaggressive effect of lithium was considered unlikely in the above-mentioned study in spite of the fact that some animal studies have begun to appear suggesting a possible role for thyrotropin-releasing hormone (TRH), the hypothalamic releasing factor, in specific types of aggression. Malick (1976), for example, showed that TRH is a potent antagonist of isolation-induced aggression in mice. There was a rapid diminution of potency with time after dose, and tricodothyronine did not antagonize the fighting, suggesting the TRH was acting independently of the pituitary–thyroid axis. On the other hand, Marini and Sheard (1978) failed to demonstrate any effect of TRH on shock-elicited fighting in rats, indicating a specificity of the effect reported by Malick. Moreover, lithium can inhibit the aggression in both the isolation and shock-induced animal models.

By analogy with its action on the thyroid, it was considered possible that lithium could affect the gonads wtih an inhibition of the synthesis and release of testosterone, which might be reflected in a decrease of serum testosterone and an increase in LH. The authors reported that treatment with lithium for 3 months significantly reduced incidents of serious threatening or assaultive behavior and that this was accompanied by a significant increase in serum LH without any significant change in serum testosterone. It is likely that a temporary decline in serum testosterone was missed because of the weekly sampling, since a study of the effect of lithium on testosterone in rats (Prasad & Sheard, 1980) did show a temporary decline followed by a rise again to baseline, probably due to the compensatory rise in LH. The rise in serum LH in these young male subjects was then correlated with a decrease in aggressive behavior rather than an increase.

PEPTIDE HORMONES

Peptides can affect aggressive behavior, but so far there has been little work in this area. Brain and Evans (1977) have reported that ACTH-related peptides enhance fighting in male mice. It is known that adrenocortical activity is particularly responsive to stress and also to how the stress is perceived and dealt with as well as the origin of the stress. The variables of stress and conflict are particularly important in endocrine studies.

Guillemin et al. (1977) studied the influence of γ-endorphin and found agitation sometimes leading to aggressive behavior. Lastly, Nowell and Wouters (1975) have reported that injections of melanocyte-stimulating hormone can release an aggression-promoting pheromone in male mice, and Carroll and Steiner (1978) have implicated prolactin in premenstrual dysphoria.

HORMONE TREATMENT OF ANTISOCIAL BEHAVIOR

Hormone treatment for sexual offenses has largely replaced castration in Europe. Estrogenic treatment has been replaced by either cyproterone acetate or medroxyprogesterone because of the undesirable effects associated with estrogenic therapy such as gynecomastia, thrombophlebitis, weight gain, and osteoporosis. The rationale of all these therapies is a reduction of testosterone which results in a reduction of sexual drive regardless of stimulus target. Cyproterone acetate is a competitive inhibitor of endogenous and exogenous androgens at all androgen target organs. It also acts as a competitive inhibition in the hypothalamus–gonadal feedback system. It has also been postulated that there is a direct psychotropic effect on brain (Hermann & Beach, 1976). Mothes, Lehnert, Samimi, and Ufer (1972) reported on the results of treatment of 547 patients in three diagnostic categories. They claimed 85% of exhibitionist, 70% of homo- and heterosexual pedophilia, and 65–70% of heterosexual hypersexuality were successfully treated. However, the criteria of success and follow-up times were available. Petri (1975) reported on 20 patients treated with cyproterone acetate. He had a 3-year follow-up for 15 of these patients and found a success rate of 67% using a re-arrest criterion. He estimated a rate of 30% if more global psychosocial criteria were used. Berner, Brownstone, and Sluga (1983) published data on the treatment of 21 patients with rather severe sexual deviation. They were given 100 mg cyproterone acetate orally for from 1 to 2 years. The subjects were followed up for an average of 5 years and showed a re-arrest rate of 28% for sexual offenses. It may be noted here that the common assumption that sexual offenders tend to become more aggressive over time has not been proved. Rather, the pattern of behavior tends to remain the same (Gebhard, Gagnon, Pomeroy, & Christenson, 1965).

Laschet (1973) reported on 7 male patients who had committed sexual assault and murder who were successfully treated with cyproterone acetate. Laschet and Laschet (1975) provided data on 300 male patients with deviant sexuality. They found that sexual behavior was adequately inhibited in 80% of cases using 100 mg cyproterone daily by mouth. The remaining 20% required 200 mg orally per day. The effect occurs after about 1 week and reaches a maximum in 3 weeks. Cyproterone acetate can be given by intramuscular administration and a dose of 300–600 mg at intervals of 7–14 days appears equivalent to 100–200 mg given orally. It is important to note that the effects are reversible, though it may take up to 5 months until spermatogenesis is completely restored. Gynecomastia was reported to occur in about 20% of cases, and there is a temporary negative nitrogen balance. Laschet and Laschet are careful to point out that it is only the intensity of the sexual drive which is reduced and not the direction of the drive itself. They also emphasize that cyproterone is not a suitable agent for the treatment of aggressive pathology unless the aggression is sex related.

Cyproterone is not currently available for use in the United States and medroxyprogesterone has been used instead. Medroxyprogesterone is chemically close to progesterone itself and lowers testosterone levels by inhibiting LH. As a result, there is diminished activity of Leydig cells in addition, probably, to some block of testosterone receptors. Lloyd (1964) indicated that adolescent boys treated with medroxyprogesterone showed a reduction of hypersexual and aggressive activity. A series of reports by Money and associates have tended to confirm the usefulness of medroxyprogesterone, particularly when combined with counseling and other psychosocial interventions (Money, 1970; Money, Wiedeking, Walker, & Gain, 1976; Money et al., 1975). A wide variety of sexually deviant subjects were successfully treated, usually with the medroxyprogesterone given intramuscularly once a week. Berlin and Meinecke (1981) followed 20 paraphiliac men on medroxyprogesterone and reported that only 3 relapsed while taking the hormone. On the other hand, 10 of 11 subjects who stopped taking the medication relapsed. Money and Bennett (1981) also followed 20 subjects with deviant sexuality from 1 to 13 years on medroxyprogesterone. They report a modest long-term prognosis which was statistically significant, but some individual subjects showed a long-term remission. Additional positive results have been reported by Gagne (1981), who treated 48 men, and by Cordoba and Chapel (1983), who provide a detailed single case study involving the treatment with medroxyprogesterone of a 25-year old male with hypersexuality and heterosexual pedophilia. Of interest in this latter case was the indication from the subject's wife that there was a noticeable decrease in the subject's irritability as well as verbal and physical aggressiveness.

There does remain some controversy as to whether antiandrogen therapy can in fact reduce pathological aggressiveness unrelated to sexual behavior. An earlier report (Blumer & Migeon, 1975) has suggested that medroxyprogesterone acetate was helpful in reducing aggressive behavior in temporal lobe epilepsy. A recent paper has provided data on a controlled study of medroxyprogesterone versus injections of sterile water as an adjunctive treatment in 3 aggressive schizophrenic patients (M. O'Connor & Baker, 1983). Out of the 3 subjects, 2 improved in that episodes of violence were less frequent and psychiatric ratings of arousal, irritability, restlessness, and aggression decreased.

SUMMARY

There are many suggestive studies which involve a role for endocrines in the motivation and control of aggressive behavior. Sex and gonadotropic and possibly releasing hormones appear to have a direct action on excitation thresholds of the neural substrates for aggressive behavior. Many variables need to be taken into account when assessing the interrelationship between endocrines and aggressive behavior, among them the integrated balance of neuroendocrine functions with their circadian and pulsatile rhythms; the influence of stress, conflict, dominance, and status on endocrine function; the specificity of aggressive behavior patterns; learned behavior patterns becoming relatively independent of specific endocrine changes; the influence of genetic and environmental variables while behavior patterns are being learned; and social and psychological variables assuming a greater importance along with evolutionary development, with endocrine variables becoming less important.

References

American Psychiatric Association. (1980). *Diagnostic and statistical manual of mental disorders* (3rd ed.). Washington, DC: Author.

Andersch, B., Abrahamsson, L., Wendestam, C., Ohamn, R., & Kahn, L. (1979). Hormone profile in PMT: Effects of bromocriptine and diuretics. *Clinical Endocrinology (Oxford)*, *11*, 657–664.

Bäckström, T., & Carstensen, H. (1974). Estrogen and progesterone in plasma in relation to premenstrual tension. *Journal of Steroid Biochemistry*, *5*, 257–260.

Bäckström, C. T., Boyle, H., & Baird, D. T. (1981). Persistence of symptoms of premenstrual tension in hysterectomized women. *British Journal of Obstetrics and Gynecology*, *88*, 530–536.

Bäckström, T., Sanders, D., Leask, R., Davidson, D., Warner, P., & Bancroft, J. (1983). II. Hormone levels and their relationship to the premenstrual syndrome. *Psychosomatic Medicine*, *45*(6), 503–507.

Bäckström, T., Wide, L., Sodegard, R., & Carstensen, H. (1976). FSH, LH, TeBG capacity, estrogen, and progesterone in women with premenstrual tension during the luteal phase. *Journal of Steroid Biochemistry*, *7*, 473–476

Baker, D. (1972). Chromosome errors and antisocial behavior. *CRC Critical Reviews in Clinical Laboratory Sciences*, *3*, 41–101.

Bancroft, J., Sanders, D., Davidson, D., & Warner, P. (1983). Mood, sexuality, hormones, and the menstrual cycle. III. Sexuality and the role of androgens. *Psychosomatic Medicine*, *45*, 509–516.

Beaumont, R. J. V., Richards, D. H., & Gelder, M. G. (1975). A study of minor psychiatric and physical symptoms during the menstrual cycle. *British Journal of Psychiatry*, *125*, 431–434.

Berlin, F. S., & Meinecke, C. F. (1981). Treatment of sex offenders with antiandrogenic medication: Conceptualization, review of treatment modalities, and preliminary findings. *American Journal of Psychiatry*, *138*, 601–607.

Berner, W., Brownstone, G., & Sluga, W. (1983). The cyproteron acetate treatment of sexual offenders. *Neuroscience and Biobehavioral Reviews*, *7*, 441–443.

Blumer, D., & Migeon, C. (1975). Hormone and hormonal agents in the treatment of aggression. *Journal of Nervous and Mental Diseases*, *160*, 127–137.

Bohman, M. A. (1971). Comparative study of adopted children, foster children, and children in their biological environment born after undesired pregnancies. *Acta Paediatrica Scandinavica, Supplement*, *34*, 1–112.

Brain, D. F., & Evans, A. E. (1977). Acute influences of some ACTH-related peptides on fighting and adrenocortical activity in male laboratory mice. *Pharmacology, Biochemistry and Behavior*, *7*, 425–433.

Bremmer, J. (1959). *Asexualisation, a follow-up study of 244 cases.* New York: Macmillan.

Carroll, B. J., & Steiner, M. (1978). The psychobiology of premenstrual dysphoria: The role of prolactin. *Psychoneuroendocrinology*, *3*, 171–180.

Casey, M. D., Blank, C. E., Street, D. R. K., Segall, L. J., McDougall, J. H., McCraft, P. J., & Skinner, J. C. (1966). XYY chromosomes and antisocial behavior. *Lancet*, *2*, 659–660.

Christiansen, K. (1968). Threshold of tolerance in various population groups illustrated by results from a Danish criminological twin study. In A. V. S. deReuck (Ed.), *The mentally abnormal offender* (pp. 107–116). Boston: Little, Brown.

Cleckley, H. (1976). *The mask of sanity: An attempt to clarify some issues about the so-called psychopathic personality* (5th ed.). St. Louis, MO: C. V. Mosby.

Cloniger, C. R., & Guze, S. B. (1973). Psychiatric illnesses in the families of female criminals: A study of 288 first-degree relatives. *British Journal of Psychiatry*, *122*, 697–703.

Cloninger, C. R., Reich, T., & Guze, S. B. (1975). The multifactorial model of disease transmission: II. Sex differences in the familial transmission of sociopathy. *British Journal of Psychiatry*, *127*, 11–22.

Conner, R. L., Levine, S., Wertheim, G. A., & Cummer, J. F. (1969). Hormonal determinants of aggressive behavior. *Annals of the New York Academy of Sciences*, *159*, 760–776.

Cordoba, O. A., & Chapel, J. L. (1983). Medroxyprogesterone acetate anitandrogen treatment of hypersexuality in a pedophiliac sex offender. *American Journal of Psychiatry*, *140*, 1036–1039.

Crowe, R. R. (1974). An adoption study of antisocial personality. *Archives of General Psychology*, *31*, 785–791.

Dalton, K. (1964). *The premenstrual syndrome.* Springfield, IL: Charles C. Thomas.

Dalton, K. (1977). *Premenstrual syndrome and progesterone therapy.* London: Heinemann.

D'Andrade, R. (1966). Sex differences and cultural institutions. In E. Maccoby (Ed.), *The development of sex differences.* Stanford, CA: Stanford University Press.

Doering, C. H., McAdoo, B. C., Kraemer, H. C., Brodie, B. K. H., Dessert, N. J., & Hamburg, D. A. (1974). Plasma testosterone levels and psychologic measures in men over a two-month time span. In R. C. Friedman, R. M. Richart, & R. L. Van de Wiele (Eds.), *Sex differences in behavior* (pp. 413–431). New York: Wiley.

Eaton, G. G., Goy, R. W., & Phoenix, C. H. (1973). Effects of testosterone treatment in adulthood on sexual behavior of female pseudo hermaphrodite rhesus monkeys. *Nature (London), New Biology*, *242*, 119–120.

Ehrenkranz, J., Bliss, E., & Sheard, M. H. (1974). Plasma testosterone: Correlation with aggressive behavior and social dominance in man. *Psychosomatic Medicine*, *36*, 469–475.

Ehrhardt, A. A., & Baker, S. (1974). Fetal androgens, human central nervous system differentiation, and behavior sex differences. In R. Friedman, R. Richart, & C. R. Van de Wiele (Eds.), *Sex differences in behavior*. New York: Wiley.

Ehrhardt, A. A., & Meyer-Bahlburg, H. F. L. (1979). Prenatal sex hormones and the developing brain: Effects on psychosocial differentiation and cognitive function. *Annual Review of Medicine, 30,* 417–430.

Ehrhardt, A. A., & Money, J. (1967). Progestin-induced hermaphroditism and psychosexual identity in a study of ten girls. *Journal of Sex, Research, 3,* 83.

Ellis, D., & Austin, P. (1971). Menstruation and aggressive behavior in a correctional center for woman. *Journal of Criminal Law and Police Science, 62,* 388–395.

Eysenck, H, J., & Eysenck, S. B. G. (1978). Psychopathy, personality and genetics. In R. D. Hare & D. Schalling (Eds.), *Psychopathic behavior approaches to research*. London: Wiley.

Faiman, C., & Winter, J. S. D. (1974). Gonadotropins and sex hormone patterns in puberty: Clinical data. In M. M. Grumbach, G. D. Grave, & F. E. Mayer (Eds.), *Control of the onset of puberty* (pp. 32–55). New York: Wiley.

Flynn, J. P. (1976). Neural basis of threat and attack. In R. G. Grennel & S. Gabay (Eds.), *Biological foundations of psychiatry* (Vol. 1, pp. 273–295). New York: Raven Press.

Frank, R. T. (1931). The hormonal causes of PMT. *Archives of Neurology and Psychiatry, 26,* 1053–1057.

Gagne, P. (1981). Treatment of sex offenders with medroxyprogesterone acetate. *American Journal of Psychiatry, 138,* 644–646.

Gebhard, P., Gagnon, J., Pomeroy, W., Christenson, C. (1965). *Sex offenders*. New York: Harper & Row.

Goy, R. W. (1968). Organising effects of androgen on the behavior of rhesus monkeys. In R. D. Michael (Ed.), *Endocrinology and human behavior* (pp. 12–31). London: Oxford University Press.

Guillemin, R., Bloom, F., Rossier, F., Minicks, S., Hendriksen, S., Burgus, R., & Nicholas, L. (1977). Current physiological studies with endorphins. In I. McIntyre & M. Szelke (Eds.), *Molecular endocrinology* (pp. 251–267). Amsterdam: Elsevier.

Hamburg, D. A. (1971). Psychobiological studies of aggressive behavior. *Nature (London), 230,* 19–23.

Hamburg, D. A., Moos, R. H., & Yalum, I. D. (1968). Studies of distress in the menstrual cycle and the postpartum period. In R. P. Michael (Ed.), *Endocrinology and human behavior*. London: Oxford University Press.

Hands, J., Herbert, V., & Tennent, C. (1974). Menstruation and behavior in a special hospital. *Medicine, Science and the Law, 14,* 32–35.

Hare, R. D. (1970). *Psychopathy: Theory and research*. New York: Wiley.

Hare, R. D. (1980). A research scale of the assessment of psychopathy in criminal populations. *Personality and Individual Differences, 1,* 111–119.

Hare, R. D. (1983). Diagnosis of antisocial personality disorder in two prison populations. *American Journal of Psychiatry, 140,* 887–889

Hare, R. D., & Blevings, G. (1975). Conditional orienting and defensive responses. *Psychophysiology, 12,* 289–297.

Hare, R. D., & Cox, D. N. (1978). Psychophysiological research on psychopathy. In W. H. Reid (Ed.), *The psychopath: A comprehensive study of antisocial disorders and behaviors*. New York: Brunner/Mazel.

Hare, R. D., & Schalling, D. (1978). *Psychopathic behavior: Approaches to research*. Chichester, England: Wiley.

Herman, W. M., & Bleach, R. C. (1976). Psychotropic effects of androgens: A review of clinical observations and new human experimental findings. *Pharmacology and Psychiatry, 9,* 205–219.

Hill, J. D., & Watterson, D. (1942). EEG studies of psychopathic personalities. *Journal of Neurosurgery and Psychiatry, 5,* 47–65.

Hunter, H. (1977). XYY males. *British Journal of Psychiatry, 131,* 468–477.

Hutchings, B., & Mednick, S. A. (1975). Registered criminality in adoptive and biological parents of registered male criminal adoptees. *Proceedings of the American Psychopathological Association, 24,* 112–118.

Inselman-Temkin, B. R., & Flynn, J. P. (1973). Sex-dependent effects of gonadal and gonadotropic hormones on centrally elicited attack in cats. *Brain Research, 60,* 393–410.

Jacobs, P. A., Brunton, M., Melville, M. M., Britain, R. P., & McClemont, W. F. (1965). Aggressive behavior, mental subnormality and the XYY male. *Nature (London), 208,* 1351–1362.

Janowsky, E. S., Gorney, R., & Mandell, A. J. (1967). The menstrual cycle: Psychiatric and ovarian-adrenocortical hormone correlates: Case study and literature review. *Archives of General Psychiatry, 17,* 459–464.

Kaufman, J. H. (1967). Social relations of adult males in a free-ranging band of rhesus monkeys. In S. Altman (Ed.), *Social communication among primates*. Chicago, IL: University of Chicago Press.

Kendenburg, D., Kenbenburg, N., & Kling, H. (1973). *An ethological study in a patient group*. Presented at the annual meeting of the American Psychiatric Association, Honolulu, Hawaii.

Kessler, S. (1975). Extra chromosomes and criminality. In R. R. Fieve, D. Rosenthal, & H. Brill (Eds.), *Genetic research in psychiatry* (pp. 66–73). Baltimore: Johns Hopkins University Press.

Kety, S., Rosenthal, D., Wender, P., & Schulsinger, F. (1968). The types and prevalence of mental illness in biological and adoptive families of adopted schizophrenics. In D. Rosenthal & S. Kety (Eds.), *The transmission of schizophrenia*. Oxford: Pergamon Press.

Knorr, D., Bidlingmaier, F., Butenandt, O., Fendel, H., & Ehrt-Wehle, R. (1974). Plasma testosterone in male puberty: I. Physiology of plasma testosterone. *Acta Endocrinologica (Copenhagen), 75,* 181–194.

Kreuz, L. E., & Rose, R. M. (1972). Assessment of aggressive behavior and plasma testosterone in a young criminal population. *Psychosomatic Medicine, 34,* 321–332.

Laschet, U. (1973). Antiandrogen in the treatment of sex offenders: Mode of action and therapeutic outcome.

In J. Zulbin & J. Money (Eds.), *Contemporary sexual behavior* (pp. 311–318). Baltimore: Johns Hopkins University Press.

Laschet, U., & Laschet, L. (1975). Antiadrogens in the treatment of sexual deviations of men. *Journal of Steroid Biochemistry, 6,* 821–826.

Lindner, L., Goldman, H., Dinitz, S., & Allen, H. (1970). Antisocial personality type with cardiac lability. *Archives of General Psychiatry, 23,* 260–267.

Lloyd, C. W. (1964). Treatment and prevention of certain sexual behavioral problems. In C. W. Lloyd (Ed.), *Human reproduction and sexual behavior* (pp. 498–523). Philadelphia: Lea & Febiger.

Maccoby, E., & Jacklin, C. (1974). *The psychology of sex differences.* Stanford, CA: Stanford University Press.

Malick, J. (1976). Antagonism of isolation-induced aggression in mice by thyrotropin-releasing hormone (TRH). *Pharmacology, Biochemistry and Behavior, 5,* 665–669.

Mandell, A., & Mandell, M. (1967). Suicide and the menstrual cycle, *JAMA, Journal of the American Medical Association, 200,* 792–793.

Marini, J. L., & Sheard, M. H. (1978). Thyrotropin-releasing hormone (TRH): Lack of effect on shock-eicited fighting (SEF) in rats. *Communications in Psychopharmacology, 2,* 139–144.

Masica, D. N., Money, J., Ehrhardt, A. A., & Lewis, U. G. (1969). IQ fetal sex hormones and cognitive patterns: Studies in testicular feminizing syndrome of androgen insensitivity. *Johns Hopkins Medical Journal, 124,* 34–43.

Matthews, R. (1979). Testosterone levels in aggressive offenders. In M. Sandler (Ed.), *Psychopharmacology of aggression* (pp. 123–130). New York: Raven Press.

Mazur, A. (1976). Effects of testosterone on status in primate groups. *Folia Primatologica, 26,* 214–226.

Mazur, A., & Lamb, T. (1980). Testosterone, status and mood in human males. *Hormones and Behavior, 14(3),* 236–246.

Mendelson, J. H., Dietz, P. E., & Ellingboe, J. (1982). Postmortem plasma luteinizing hormone levels and antemortem violence. *Pharmacology, Biochemistry and Behavior, 17,* 171–173.

Mendelson, J. H., Mello, N. K., & Ellingboe, J. (1977). Effects of alcohol on pituitary gonadal hormones in normal males. *Journal of Pharmacology and Experimental Therapeutic, 202,* 676–682.

Meyer-Bahlburg, H. F. L., Boon, D., Sharma, M., & Edwards, J. A. (1974). Aggressiveness and testosterone measures in man. *Psychosomatic Medicine, 36,* 269–274.

Money, J. (1970). Use of an androgen-depleting hormone in the treatment of male sex offenders. *Journal of Sexual Research, 6,* 165–172.

Money, J., & Bennett, R. G. (1981). Postadolescent paraphiliac sex offenders: Antiandrogenic and counseling therapy follow-up. *International Journal of Mental Health, 10,* 122–133.

Money, J., & Ehrhardt, A. (1972). Gender dimorphic behavior and fetal sex hormones. *Records of Progress in Hormone Research, 28,* 735–754.

Money, J., & Schwartz, M. (1976). Fetal androgens in the early treated adrenogenital syndrome of 46 XY hermaphroditism; influence on assertive and aggressive types of behavior. *Aggressive Behavior, 2,* 19–30.

Money, J., Wiedeking, C. Walker, P. A., & Gain, D. (1976). Combined antiandrogenic and counseling program for treatment of 46 XY and 47 XYY sex offenders. In E. J. Sachar (Ed.), *Hormones, behavior and psychopatholgy* (pp. 105–120). New York: Raven Press.

Money, J., Wiedeking, C., Walker, P., Migeon, C., Meyer, W., & Borgaonkar, D. (1975). 47 XYY and 46 XY males with antisocial and/or sex-offending behavior: Antiandrogen therapy plus counseling. *Psychoneuroendocrinology, 1,* 165–173.

Monroe, R. R. (1970). *Episodic behavioral disorders.* Cambridge, MA: Harvard University Press.

Monti, P., Brown, W., & Corriveau, D. (1977). Testosterone and components of aggressive and sexual behavior in man. *American Journal of Psychiatry, 134,* 692–694.

Morton, J., Additon, H., Addison, R., Hunt, C., & Sullivan, J. (1953). A clinical study of premenstrual tension. *American Journal of Obstetrics and Gynecology, 65,* 1182–1191.

Mothes, C., Lenhert, J., Samimi, F., & Ufer, J. (1972). Klinische prüfung von cyproterone acetate bei sexual deviationen (Gesamtauswertung). In *Schering Symposium über sexual deviationen* (pp. 65–87). Braunschweig: Vieweg-Pergamon Press

Moyer, K. E. (1968). Kinds of aggression and their physiological basis. *Communications in Behavioral Biology, 2,* 65–87.

Munday, M. R., Brush, M. G., & Taylor, R. W. (1981). Correlations between progesterone, estradiol, and aldosterone levels in the premenstrual syndrome. *Clinical Endocrinology (Oxford), 14,* 1–9.

Nowell, N. W., & Wouters, A. (1975). Release of aggression-promoting pheromone by male mice treated with melanocyte-stimulating hormone. *Journal of Endocrinology, 65,* 36–37.

O'Brien, P. M. S., Selby, C., & Symonds, E. M. (1980). Progesterone, fluid, and electrolytes in premenstrual syndrome. *British Medical Journal, 1,* 1161–1163.

O'Connor, J. F., Shelley, E. M., & Stern, I. D. (1974). Behavioral rhythms related to the menstrual cycle. In M. Ferin, F. Halberg, R. M. Richard, & R. L. Van de Wiele (Eds.), *Biorhythms and human reproduction* (pp. 309–324). New York: Wiley.

O'Connor, M., & Baker, H. W. G. (1983). Depomedroxyprogesterone acetate as an adjunctive treatment in three aggressive schizophrenic patients. *Acta Psychiatrica Scandinavica, 67,* 399–403.

Olweus, D. (1975). *Development of a multifaceted aggression inventory for boys* (Reports from the Institute of Psychology, No. 6). University of Bergen.

Olweus, D. (1977). Aggression and peer acceptance in adolescent boys: Two short-term longitudinal studies of ratings. *Child Development, 48,* 1301–1313.

Olweus, D., Mattson, Ä., Schalling, D., & Löw, H. (1980). Testosterone, aggression, physical, and personality dimensions in normal adolescent males. *Psychosomatic Medicine, 42,* 253–269.

Persky, H., Dreisbach, L., Miller, W. R., O'Brien, C. P., Khan, M. A., Lief, H. I., Charney, N., & Strauss, D. (1982). The relation of plasma androgen levels to sexual behaviors and attitudes of women. *Psychosomatic Medicine, 44(4),* 305–319.

Persky, H., O'Brien, C. P., Fine, E., Howard, W. J., Khan, M. A., & Beck, R. W. (1977). The effects of alcohol and smoking on testosterone function and aggression in chronic alcoholics. *American Journal of Psychiatry, 134,* 621–625.

Persky, H., Smith, K. D., & Basu, G. K. (1971). Relation of psychologic measures of aggression and hostility to testosterone production in man. *Psychosomatic Medicine, 33,* 265–277.

Petri, H. (1975). Analytische kurztherapie bei sexuellen deviationen (mit bemerkungen zur antiandrogen therapie). In V. Sigusch (Ed.), *Therapie sexueller störungen* (pp. 180–214). Stuttgart: Thieme.

Powell, D. A., Francis, J., & Schneiderman, N. (1971). The effect of castration, neonatal injections of testosterone and previous experience with fighting on shock-elicited aggression. *Communications in Behavioral Biology, 5,* 371–377.

Prasad, V., & Sheard, M. H. (1080). The acute and chronic effect of lithium on serum testosterone in rats. *Communications in Psychopharmacology, 4,* 147–152.

Quadragno, D., Briscoe, R., & Quadragno, J. (1977). Effect of perinatal gonadal hormones on selected non-sexual behavior patterns: A critical assessment of the nonhuman and human literature. *Psychological Bulletin, 84,* 62–80.

Rada, R. T., Laws, D. R., & Kellner, R. (1976). Plasma testosterone levels in the rapist. *Psychosomatic Medicine, 38,* 257–268.

Reid, W. H. (1978). Genetic correlates of antisocial syndromes. In W. H. Reid (Ed.), *The psychopath: A comprehensive study of antisocial disorders and behaviors.* New York: Brunner/Mazel.

Reinisch, J. M. (1977). Prenatal exposure of human fetuses to synthetic progestin and estrogen affects personality. *Nature (London), 266,* 561–562.

Rivarola, M. D., Saez. J. M., & Migeon, C. J. (1967). Studies of androgens in patients with cogenital adrenal hyperplasia. *Journal of Clinical Endocrinology and Metabolism, 27,* 624–630.

Rose, R. M., Bernstein, I. S., & Gordon, T. P. (1975). Consequences of social conflict on plasma testosterone levels in rhesus monkeys. *Psychosomatic Medicine, 37,* 50–61.

Rose, R. M., Haladay, J. W., & Bernstein, J. S. (1971). Plasma testosterone, dominance rank, and aggressive behavior in rhesus monkeys, *Nature, 231,* 366.

Rossi, A., & Rossi, P. (1980) Body time and social time: Mood patterns by menstrual cycle phase and day of week. In J. Parsons (Ed.), *The psychobiology of sex differences and sex roles.* New York: McGraw-Hill.

Satterfield, J. H. (1978). The hyperactive child syndrome: A precursor of adult psychopathy? In R. D. Hare & D. Schalling (Eds.), *Psychopathic behavior approaches to research* (pp. 329–346). London: Wiley.

Scaramella, T. J., & Brown, W. A. (1978). Serum testosterone and aggressiveness in hockey players. *Psychosomatic Medicine, 40,* 262–265.

Schulsinger, F. (1972). Psychopathy: Heredity and environment. *International Journal of Mental Health, 1,* 190–206.

Sheard, M. H., Marini, J. L., & Giddings, S. (1977). The effect of lithium on testosterone and luteinizing hormone. *Journal of Nervous Disease, 38,* 765–769.

Shields, J. (1975). Some recent developments in psychiatric genetics. *Arch fuer Psychiatrie und Nervenkrankheiten, 220,* 347–360.

Silverman, D. (1944). The EEG of criminals. *Archives of Neurology (Chicago), 52,* 36–42.

Syndulko, K. (1978). Electrocortical investigations of sociopathy. In R. D. Hare & D. Schalling (Eds.), *Psychopathic behavior: Approaches to research* (pp. 145–155). London: Wiley.

Taylor, J. W. (1979). Plasma progesterone, estradiol 17β and premenstrual symptoms. *Acta psychiatric Scandinavica, 60,* 76–86.

Vandenbergh, J. G., & Vessey, S. (1968). Seasonal breeding of free-ranging rhesus monkeys and related ecological factors. *Journal of Reproduction and Fertility, 15,* 71–75.

Wilson, A. P., & Boelkins, R. (1970). Evidence for seasonal variations in aggressive behavior by M. mulatta. *Animal Behaviour, 18,* 719–724.

Witkin, A. A., Mednick, S. A., & Schulsinger, F. (1976). Criminality in XYY and XXY men. *Science, 193,* 547–555.

PART IV

THE EFFECT OF PSYCHIATRIC TREATMENT ON NEUROENDOCRINE PARAMETERS

11 NEUROENDOCRINE ASPECTS OF CONVULSIVE THERAPY: REVIEW OF RECENT DEVELOPMENTS

MAX FINK

School of Medicine, State University of New York at Stony Brook

Evidence of hypothalamic–pituitary dysregulation is such a frequent finding among patients with major depressive disorder that manifestations in abnormal test functions are now considered part of their pathophysiology. Failures in the regulation of cortisol, ACTH, thyrotropin stimulating hormone (TSH), growth hormone (GH), and prolactin (PRL) are well documented. At times, the dysregulation is so severe as to mimic the effects of glandular tumors, and depressive disorders must be considered in the differential diagnosis in patients with severe hormonal imbalances. Vegetative signs of anorexia, decreased weight, insomnia, decreased energy, and impaired libido are regular features found in depressed patients, reflecting hypothalamic–pituitary–adrenal, hypothalamic–pituitary–thyroid, and hypothalamic–pituitary–gonadal dysfunctions. The severity of the depressive illness is often matched by the severity of the hormonal dysregulation, and improvement in behavior is frequently associated with a normalization of neuroendocrine tests. There is much argument as to the significance and applications of any single measure of neuroendocrine function, but these problems reflect the primitive nature of our present diagnostic tools rather than questions about the intimate relationships between neuroendocrine substances and disorders in mood.

Electroconvulsive therapy (ECT) is an effective modifier of mood disorders, particularly for patients who are severely ill and who exhibit prominent vegetative symptoms. ECT is also a treatment of great mystery, its usage far outstripping our knowledge of its mode of action. It is little wonder then that the association of disordered mood, clinical efficacy of ECT, and neuroendocrine dysregulation has spawned diverse theories of the ECT process. In 1980, aware that hypothalamic dysfunction was a characteristic of major depressive disorders, Jan-Otto Ottosson and I suggested that induced seizures stimulated hypothalamic functions to redress hormonal imbalances, both by directly stimulating contrencephalic structures and by increasing the levels of activity of neurotransmitters (such as norepinephrine and acetylcholine) which affected hypothalamic cellular activity (Fink & Ottosson, 1980). Also, recognizing the direct behavioral effects reported after the administration of some natural peptides, we suggested that the operating action of ECT in elevating mood and altering cognition resulted from an increase in hypothalamic activity and the release of behaviorally active ("mood-elevating") peptides, to which we have given the name "antidepressin."

Neuroendocrine relationships in psychiatric patients have been subjected to much study, particularly as to the development of new tests, their utility in diagnostic classification, and more recently, as outcome measures and indices of physiological effect. In 1980 and 1982, I reviewed the reports of neuroendocrine tests as they relate to the ECT process (Fink, 1980, 1982). Many new studies have been published since then, so that it seems useful to review the observations reported since the winter of 1981.[1]

CORTISOL REGULATION

Much of our present interest is focused on variations in plasma cortisol levels and their response to oral dexamethasone (dexamethasone suppression test, DST) in patients with mental disorders. Many studies have sought to determine whether changes in cortisol regulation may be trait or state related; trait markers are useful to classify illnesses; state markers define the course of therapy or illness.

It is an interesting facet of the ECT process that clinical efficacy is inversely related to the severity of the disorder and that the more prominent the vegetative symptoms, the better the therapeutic results, seemingly independent of diagnostic classification; that is, severely depressed patients who are later classified as suffering from unipolar depression, bipolar depression, or schizoaffective disorders, with or without melancholia and with or without psychosis, generally do well with ECT. Indeed, of the depressive disorders the subgroup that is generally unresponsive is that which is classified as dysthymic disorder, or in the earlier classifications, as neurotic or secondary depression. These observations were recently reemphasized in the prospective rendom assignment Leicestershire study of ECT and sham ECT. In their report, Brandon *et al.* (1984) presented clinical results for three groups of patients—all depressives, depressives with delusions, and neurotic depressives, finding distinct differences in efficacy for the first two groups between patients treated with ECT and sham ECT, but not for the third.

In studies of the DST, it is unclear whether a test abnormality is a marker of a defined mental illness, perhaps providing a better classification of patients than the usual behavioral Chinese menu typology of DSM-III.

It is also unclear whether an abnormality of the DST in patients with severe mood disorder is a reliable sign of good prognosis with antidepressant treatment, including outcome after ECT. Abnormalities in cortisol regulation often accompany other signs of vegetative and mood disturbance. Thus, DST abnormality is a consistent feature of patients with good prognoses. And, in patients selected for ECT, good outcome is usually assured by the presence of severe mood disturbance, so that most studies fail to define a relationship between outcome and test abnormality precisely because the distribution of outcomes is skewed—most courses of ECT are successful.

A good example is reported by Extein, Kirstein, Pottash, and Gold (1983). In a retrospective study, these authors examined the response to tricyclic antidepressants or ECT of depressed patients who had both DST and TSH response tests before treatment. They found 13 patients with abnormalities in both tests, 9 with one test abnormality and 5 with neither. Physicians made the choice of treatment without knowledge of the test results and selected ECT for the patients with abnormalities in both tests more frequently than for patients with only one or no test abnormality. Of the 10 patients treated with ECT, 9 had a good clinical response. This very high therapeutic success rate made it difficult to find an association between test results and outcome.

Changes in cortisol measures with clinical course is another facet that has come under extensive study, and numerous authors have summarized the findings (Carroll, 1984; Baldessarini & Arana, 1985; Arana, Baldessarini, & Ornstein, 1985; Fink, 1986; Braddock, 1986). Carroll writes: "Gradual conversion of DST responses to normal occurs as patients improve with treatment. When the test results convert to normal before significant clinical change is evident, this is usually a good prognostic sign that the patient will eventually respond" (p. 183). He summarizes seven studies of DST conversion in relation to clinical response. All cases had abnormal DSTs on admission. Of 102 patients, 35 still had abnormal DST tests on discharge, and of these, 83% had a poor outcome even though treatment was continued in most cases. In two studies, suicides were

---

[1]This review will focus on studies in man. Important contributions from animal studies may be found in recent reviews by Grahame-Smith (1984), Cowen (1986), the volume edited by Lerer, Weiner, and Belmaker (1984); and that edited by Malitz and Sackeim (1986).

recorded among the patients with persistently abnormal DSTs. In contrast, 90% of the patients whose DSTs normalized had a good short-term response to treatment and were free of relapse for up to six months.

Baldessarini and Arana (1985) reach a similar conclusion. They summarize the data of 18 reports in patients with severe depression. Of 141 depressed patients who were DST nonsuppressors at initial assessment, 102 had a favorable response to antidepressant treatment. When DSTs were done at the end of treatment, 26 of 33 who had a positive DST had a poor clinical outcome on follow-up, while 11 of 44 with a negative DST had a poor outcome. They write: "... failure of an abnormal DST to normalize with follow-up and treatment is associated with a higher risk of poor clinical outcome and short-term prognosis. Thus, in 77 patients with major depressive disorder, the risk of poor outcome if the DST remained positive was nearly 79%, while the risk was only 25% if the DST converted to real normal cortisol suppression" (p. 28).

Electroconvulsive therapy has been a feature in only a few of these studies, since most patients have been treated with tricyclic antidepressants. The early reports of Albala et al. (1981), Greden et al. (1980), and Papakostas et al. (1981) suggested that the normalization of the DST was a predictor of good outcome with ECT. Other studies support these observations.

Coryell (1982) examined the DST in 42 depressed patients treated with ECT. Patients with an initial abnormal test response had better outcomes according to global ratings at the end of treatment than did patients with normal DSTs. But the outcome was not poor in either group, with only 3 patients with normal DSTs being rated as unimproved at discharge. In a 6-month follow-up of these patients, Coryell and Zimmerman (1983) failed to find any differences among the suppressors and nonsuppressors. Indeed, they reported that the 9 patients whose DSTs had converted at discharge from abnormal to normal were less likely to have a sustained remission than the 6 patients whose DSTs remained abnormal.

Yerevanian et al. (1983) reported DST and clinical results in 14 patients with RDC diagnoses of major depressive disorders with nonsuppressing DSTs on admission. Four patients received ECT; of these, the DST normalized in two and they were doing very well on follow-up; two failed to normalize— one was readmitted within 2 weeks and one was persistently anhedonic and unable to work. The findings among the drug-treated patients were similar with all nonnormalizers doing poorly on follow-up, and three committing suicide.

In a study of 18 severely depressed psychiatric inpatients with a positive DST on admission, Nemeroff and Evans (1984) treated 6 with ECT. In each the DST normalized, and each was rated as asymptomatic at follow-up. Of the 12 patients treated with medications alone, 5 were nonsuppressors at the end of treatment, and all required either further inpatient care or were symptomatic within 2 weeks to 4 months. Of the suppressors, 2 were readmitted within 2 months, and 5 were rated as asymptomatic in follow-up to 13 months.

Ames, Burrows, Davies, Maguire, and Norman (1984) studied 90 patients with primary depressive illness and reported that among 13 patients treated with ECT, they found the same degree of improvement using the Hamilton scale for the 6 nonsuppressors and the 7 suppressors at the time of first testing. These authors do not provide data as to outcome, but in their discussion they write: "It is our present practice to continue ECT in non-suppressors until normal suppression occurs. Further studies are needed to see whether this will help prevent the relapses that are common after ECT treatment" (pp. 312–313). Similar conclusions are expressed in reports by Holsboer, Liebl, and Hofschuster (1982), Rothchild and Schatzberg (1982), Ward, Strauss, and Ries (1982), Greden et al. (1983), Katona and Aldridge (1984), and Kutcher (1984).

Thus, in 1984 there was a consensus that an abnormal DST in patients with severe depression signified a good prognosis for antidepressant therapy, and that normalization of an abnormal DST could be considered an endpoint to a course of therapy. But the reports of Coryell (1982) and Coryell and Zimmerman (1982, 1983) were inconsistent. In his most recent report, Coryell (1986) obtained serial DSTs in 30 patients receiving ECT, and concluded that "serial DSTs do not appear to add information useful in predicting ECT response from week to week. Nor does the literature so far support the use of discharge DSTs in predicting relapse after ECT though the test clearly appears useful in this way for patients treated with antidepressants" (p. 65). Lipman *et al.* (1986a, b) also failed to find a relationship between the predischarge DST and either short-term improvement or 6-month follow-up status in depressed patients treated with ECT.

In a prospective study of the DST in patients referred for ECT, we studied 43 severely depressed patients; both at discharge and at 6-month follow-up, we also were unable to define a relationship with maintenance of improvement, rehospitalization, or suicide (Fink, Greenberg, & Gujavarty, in press). These studies by Coryell, Lipman and his co-workers, and our own do not encourage a clinical application for the DST in the management of patients during a course of ECT.

PROLACTIN AND ECT

Plasma PRL levels are another neuroendocrine measure of interest. The sharp increase in plasma PRL after a grand mal seizure, with peak activity about 30 minutes after the seizure and a rapid fall to baseline levels within 1 to 2 hours, is well documented (Arato, Erdos, Kurcz, Vermes, & Fekete, 1980; Carchedi *et al.*, 1978; Meco *et al.*, 1978; O'Dea, Gould, Hallberg, & Wieland, 1978; Öhman, Walinder, Balldin, & Wallin, 1976). The increase is found despite basal high levels which occur with the administration of chlorpromazine (Klimes, Vigas, Jurcovicova, & Wiedermann, 1978) or neuroleptic medication (Balldin, 1982), and the increase is not influenced by benzodiazepines (Arato & Bagdy, 1982; Balldin, 1982). The increase in plasma PRL with grand mal seizures is so characteristic that Trimble (1978) suggested that a plasma PRL increase be used to differentiate an epileptic fit from hysteria. Similar increases occur after complex partial seizures (Pritchard, Wannamaker, Sagel, Nair, & DeVillier, 1983).

The significance of PRL release for the ECT process remains unlcear. Does an increase in plasma PRL reflect a nonspecific release of humoral substances secondary to the physical stress of a seizure? Or does the PRL release reflect a specific aspect of the seizure, with significance for the convulsive therapy process? When increases in PRL with seizures were first described, many sought for the persistence of plasma PRL levels during the course of ECT, perhaps an increase which paralleled the clinical course. But no relationship between basal levels and clinical course was found. The amount of PRL released after the fifth or sixth seizure seemed to be the same as after the first, with the same time course, and with the levels returning to baseline within 1–2 hours after the seizure.

In the Northwick Park ECT and sham ECT study, PRL, cortisol, GH, and TSH serum levels were measured before and 15 minutes after the first and last treatments in 62 patients receiving either eight real or eight sham treatments. Prolactin levels increased in the patients with real seizures, with the degree of effect attenuated by about 30% by the end of the treatment course. Cortisol also increased with attenuation in the series, and no changes were noted for GH or TSH (Deakin, Ferrier, Crow, Johnstone, & Lawler, 1983).

Skrabenek, Balfe, Webb, Maguire, and Powell (1981) reported differences in time course of release for GH, FSH, PRL, and LH, but not for TSH and substance P. They concluded that the release of these substances was best interpreted as a nonspecific stress response. But Whalley *et al.* (1982) found differences in release rates for three neuroendocrine substances (PRL, nicotine-stimulated neurophysin, and estrogen-stimulated neurophysin) and concluded that hormone release was a specific effect of seizures. Differential effects on neuroendocrine release were also reported by O'Dea, Llerena, Hallberg, and Weiland (1979), Coppen, Rao, Bishop, Abou-Saleh, and Wood (1980a), Christie, Whalley, Brown, and Dick (1982), Pritchard *et al.* (1983), and Linnoila, Litovitz, Scheinin, Chang, and Cutler (1984). In the Pritchard *et al.* study, changes in PRL but little change in serum gonadotropins, TSH, GH, or cortisol were recorded after complex partial seizures. Linnoila *et al.* (1984) also found large increases in plasma PRL levels, but only relatively minor immediate effects on the major biogenic monoamine metabolites (MHPG, 5-HIAA, HVA) and GH in the plasma.

In the early reports of PRL levels during the course of ECT, it was generally reported that the amount of PRL liberated after each seizure, from the first to the last, was the same. However, recent quantitative studies suggest that the amount of PRL released may bear a relationship to the seizure-inducing stimulus or to seizure thresholds. Balldin (1982) found elevations in serum PRL at 15 minutes after ECT seizures in 35 of 37 patients. The increase in serum PRL was related to the duration of the seizure, but not to the duration of the stimulus. As noted earlier, the amount of PRL released after the eighth seizure was much less than after the first seizure in the Northwick Park trials (Deakin *et al.*, 1983). These authors also noted that the cortisol release after the first seizure was much greater than after the eighth seizure.

Much detailed attention to the PRL response to ECT has been given by Abrams and Swartz. In their most recent reports (Abrams & Swartz, 1985a, b), they find a fall in the amount of PRL released from the first to the last seizure. There also is an inverse relationship between the mean PRL release for the first four treatments and outcome ratings, with the larger PRL response associated with a slower treatment response. Postictal serum PRL levels are reported to be greater for seizures through bilateral electrode placements than after unilateral electrode placement. They conclude that the difference in PRL release reflects a difference in hypothalamic-stimulating effect, and that this difference may explain the reported therapeutic advantage of bilateral over unilateral ECT in the treatment of patients with melancholia (Swartz & Abrams, 1984). These findings were confirmed by Papakostas, Stefanis, Markianos, and Papadimitriou (1986). The same relationship of intensity of prolactin release and type of ECT-inducing current was reported for sinusoidal and brief pulse currents by Robin, Binnie, and Copas (1985). The PRL peak was maximal about 11 minutes after a seizure, with peaks greater in treatments using bilateral electrode placements than unilateral (Abrams & Swartz, 1985b). No relationship between PRL release and stimulus energy or seizure length was reported. Swartz (1985) proposed a mathematical model of the release of PRL and estimated that its half-life of elimination from the blood was 17.3 minutes, close to published metabolic measurements. Naloxone failed to block ECT-induced prolactin release (Papakostas, Stefanis, Markianos, and Papadimitriou, 1986).

Quantitative studies also find that ACTH and cortisol are released into the blood after induced seizures with different peaks— 5 minutes for ACTH and approximately 30 minutes for cortisol (Aperia, Thoren, Zettergren, & Wetterberg, 1984). The amount of cortisol and ACTH released after the first seizure is greater than after the last (Aperia *et al.*, 1984; Swartz & Chen, 1985). These latter authors also inferred a relationship to outcome for the fall in the amount of cortisol released during the treatment course, since this decrease was found in 10 of 11 patients who responded to ECT, while the one nonresponder showed the reverse, an increase in the amount of cortisol released after the last treatment than after the first.

Studies of PRL provide interesting associations between the hormonal effects of ECT and changes in behavior. The release of PRL is probably a specific response to seizures and not the result of a nonspecific stress response. The amount released is related to factors in seizure production, such as the strength of the stimulus and electrode location, and to changes in brain function which occur during the course of the therapy. PRL increase thus accompanies the rise in seizure threshold, development of persistent EEG changes, and mood changes which characterize clinical improvement.

TSH RESPONSE TO THYROTROPIN-RELEASING HORMONE (TRH)

The TSH response to an intravenous bolus of TRH is another test of hypothalamic–pituitary function. Following synthesis of TRH, demonstrations that it had mood-elevating effects alerted the profession to the psychoactive properties of these natural substances. Much of the early work is presented in the volume edited by Prange (1974). It soon became apparent that among severely depressed patients the amount of TSH (Δ_{max} TSH) stimulated by a bolus of TRH was less than that stimulated in normal controls. These data are reviewed by Loosen in Chapter 15 of this volume.

Following this lead, we and others examined the test among different psychiatric populations. We did not find as many abnormalities among our unipolar depressed patients as we did for the DST, nor did we find that the test was altered by a course of ECT (Papakostas, Fink, Lee, Irwin, & Johnson, 1981). Extein, Pottsh, and Gold (1981) examined the TSH response to TRH in unipolar depressed patients and controls, finding the Δ_{max} TSH lower among patients than among controls, and noted that the difference was not related to baseline thyroid functions, age, or sex. Later, they examined the TSH response to TRH in 14 patients with unipolar depression before and after treatment with ECT or antidepressant drugs and reported that the number with a Δ_{max} TSH greater than 7 μIU/ml increased from 0 to 9 of 14 after treatment. They concluded that the blunted TSH response was a state marker for active unipolar depression (Extein, Pottash, Gold, & Silver, 1982). In similar studies, Coppen, Rao, Bishop, Abou-Saleh, and Wood (1980b) failed to find abnormalities in the TSH response to TRH among various subtypes of depressive illness, nor did they find a change in the test response after ECT.

Krog-Meyer et al. (1984) recently reported the results of a prospective study of 39 patients with unipolar endogenous depression who recovered after ECT. TRH tests were done before and after a course of treatment. All patients received maintenance amitriptyline for 3 weeks and then were randomized to two groups based on the change in the Δ_{max} TSH response to TRH with treatment, one group with an increase after ECT greater than 2.0 mIU/ml, and the second group with a lesser increase in Δ_{max} TSH. The first group and half the second group received placebo for the next 6 months; the other half of the poor TSH responders received amitriptyline. After 6 months, the TSH response tests were repeated, and all patients received no further medication for 6 months. Persistent remission

was predicted for patients in Group 1 and relapse for those in Group 2. After 6 months, 3 of 15 patients in Group 1 and 9 of 13 in Group 2 who received placebo relapsed, while only 2 of 11 patients in Group 2 who recieved amitriptyline relapsed. The authors conclude that failure of the TSH response to TRH to normalize is a poor prognostic sign in depressed patients treated with ECT and, further, that maintenance with amitriptyline may prevent relapse.

The plasma PRL response to TRH, which is thought to be mediated by central 5-HT mechanisms, was studied in a variety of depressed patients without defining a difference among the groups or from control subjects. After ECT, the PRL response increased, which suggested an increased sensitivity of 5-HT receptors (Coppen et al., 1980b). Kirkegaard, Eskildsen, and Bjørum (1981) examined the PRL and GH responses to TRH and found that these measures also were obtunded in patients with depression. They noted that failure of the responses to normalize was a poor prognostic sign in the course of treatment.

In a direct comparison of the TRH test and the DST, Kirkegaard and Carroll (1980) made measurements in blood, cerebrospinal fluid (CSF), and urine in 20 depressed patients before and after a course of ECT. They failed to find correlations between serum TSH or Δ_{max} TSH, on the one hand, and serum and CSF cortisol or urinary excretion of cortisol, on the other hand. They did report a correlation between serum cortisol and plasma ACTH.

NEUROHORMONE RESPONSES AS INDICES OF RECEPTOR ACTION

As another index of the impact of seizures on central monoamine pathways, numerous authors, mainly in Great Britain, examined hormonal responses to receptor agonists and antagonists (Cowen, 1986). Studies of GH, plasma MHPG, and blood pressure response to clonidine reflect agonist actions on α_2-adrenoreceptors; increases in plasma ACTH, cortisol, and GH to amphetamine reflect agonist actions of α_1-adrenoreceptors; and the increase in GH and lowered PRL to subcutaneously injected apomorphine reflect dopamine agonist actions. In one study of the GH response to clonidine in patients during the course of ECT, no changes in response were measured (Slade & Checkley, 1980). Following a course of ECT in depressed patients, the cortisol response to methylamphetamine increased without a change in the GH response, suggesting an enhancement of α_1-adrenoreceptor-mediated responses with ECT.

In tests of the effects of apomorphine on GH, Costain, Cowen, Gelder, and Grahame-Smith (1982) reported a greater GH response after a course of ECT. The change was not attributable to concurrent antidepressant medication or to the process of recovery itself, so the authors concluded that these data were evidence of an enhanced dopamine-mediated response to ECT. In a study by Balldin, Granerus, Lindstedt, Modigh, and Walinder (1982), the GH response was not altered, but the suppression of PRL was enhanced, also suggesting an increase in dopamine-mediated responses. Studies by Christie et al. (1982) examined the GH, PRL, and cortisol responses to apomorphine in 12 severely depressed patients, 11 of whom exhibited delusions. They were examined before and after a successful course of ECT without finding any change in the apomorphine-mediated responses. (There was a decrease in basal plasma cortisol levels after the course of ECT, with the recovery from the depressive illness.)

Studies of postsynaptic catecholamine functions led Modigh, Balldin, Eden, Granerus, and Walinder (1981) to suggest that seizures may have long-term effects on dopaminergic systems. A review of the clinical reports found many in which ECT had salutary effects on Parkinson symptoms. In a direct test of this relationship, Balldin, Granerus, Lindstedt, Modigh, and Walinder (1981, 1982) reported that ECT did improve Parkinson symptoms in patients with the "on–off" phenomenon, independent of the effects on mood.

These sophisticated measures are interesting indices to brain functions, but in view of the present inconsistency of the measures, it is premature to derive any conclusions regarding the ECT process.

ENDORPHINS

Both plasma and CSF levels of β-endorphin immunoreactivity increase with ECT when samples are examined from 5 to 15 minutes after a seizure. The response after the later seizures is of the same degree as after the first, and the baseline values do not rise with the course of treatment (Emrich et al., 1979; Inturrisi, Alexopoulos, Lipman, Foley, & Rossier, 1982; Misiaszek, Cork, Hameroff, Finley, & Weiss, 1984). These findings are consistent with the earlier reports of the increase in plasma ACTH with induced seizures and with the animal studies of Belenky, Tortella, Hitzemann, and Holaday (1984). Whether these responses are specific to seizures or whether they are a general manifestation of systemic "stress" was examined by measurements in surgical patients before and after anesthesia (Cork, Hameroff, & Weiss, in press). These authors report similar increases in β-endorphin immunoreactivity as a result of anesthesia and surgery, suggesting that the endorphin response may not be specific to the ECT process.

DIABETES AND ECT

The influence of ECT on diabetes mellitus has recently come under scrutiny after reports that patients with diabetes may have decreased requirements for insulin following induced seizures (Fakhri, Fadhli, & Rawi, 1980). These authors reported that of 14 patients with diabetes mellitus, 8 had a remission of their diabetic symptoms after one or two induced seizures. In those who benefited, the diabetes was of recent origin and not insulin dependent. Case reports by Thomas, Goldney, and Phillips (1983) and Normand and Jenike (1984) also noted a fall in blood sugar with ECT and a reduced requirement for insulin, while Yudofsky and Rosenthal (1980) report a patient in whom insulin requirements increased. Finestone and Weiner (1984) report observations in 3 adult-onset diabetic patients who were treated with ECT for depression. In 1, fasting blood sugars fell, and in 2, the blood sugars rose, 1 of whom required an increase in his insulin dosage to maintain his fasting blood sugar values.

Jenike (1982), reflecting on the report by Fakhri et al. (1980), suggested that the hyperglycemia exhibited by some of the depressed patients was secondary to elevated cortisol and ACTH levels and that the effect of ECT in reducing plasma cortisol and ACTH also reduced the apparent hyperglycemia. Klimes,

Jurcovicova, Benetinova, Vigas, and Wiedermann (1980) reported an increase in plasma glucagon levels 30 minutes after induced seizures with small increases in blood glucose, effects which would result in a relative hyperglycemia.

DISCUSSION

What can we make of these observations? Interest in neuroendocrine mechanisms in patients with mental illnesses is high, and the variety of observations in the past few years is overwhelming. Much progress has been made in our understanding of two measures, cortisol and PRL, since these change dramatically during the ECT process.

The studies of cortisol may bear on clinical issues, particularly on the severity of symptomatology and on improvement in depressive illness. In our own practice, we were encouraged to repeat DST measures in our patients at biweekly intervals during a course of ECT, and failure of he DST to normalize by the end of our course of treatment caused us to reassess our decisions to end treatment; but we no longer follow this practice.

PRL measures provide a different window into brain functions. The levels seem unrelated to issues of mood or severity of depressive symptoms, but bear important relationships to the seizure itself. Plasma PRL levels at 15–45 minutes after a seizure reflect the intensity of the seizure. They are clearly related to the seizure and do not reflect a nonspecific stress effect. At the minimum, PRL levels provide another index of a cerebral seizure. Further study may help us resolve the questions of therapeutic efficacy and equivalence among seizures induced by different currents or through different electrode placements. As with the studies of cortisol, we are left with many questions. Is PRL release a specific effect of seizures and their duration or is the release a nonspecific stress effect? Do the levels or do changes in the levels bear a relationship to the clinical outcome or to the brain changes induced by the course of treatment? What is the relationship of PRL release to the release of other pituitary and hypothalamic peptides, and do measures of other peptides bear a relationship to clinical issues in the ECT process?

Observations with other neuroendocrine measures, such as the TSH response to TRH, the GH response to adrenergic receptor agonists, and β-endorphin immunoreactivity, are still too incomplete to illuminate the ECT process. These tests are difficult to administer, but their study is likely to provide additional insights into the ECT process and into the pathophysiology of depression, much as studies of cortisol and PRL have been helpful.

The interest in the effects of seizures on diabetes provides yet another window into centrencephalic physiology. At the minimum, the recent reports should reassure physicians that ECT is not a therapy for diabetes and that psychotic diabetic patients are at no additional or particular risk when they are subjected to treatment.

Have these studies influenced our theoretic view of the ECT process? The studies of cortisol and PRL provide interesting details into the neuroendocrine abnormalities in depression and the changes accompanying individual seizures and a course of therapy. The effects of seizures on receptor activity, particularly findings which implicate dopaminergic and serotoninergic receptors, refine and amplify the theory. While additional studies of the behavioral effects of peptides have been undertaken, these have been disappointing. Studies of the behavioral effects of vasopressin, ACTH fragments ($ACTH_{4-10}$, $ACTH_{4-9}$ analogue), des-Tyr-γ-endorphin, and β-endorphin have not defined populations of patients responsive to these peptides. It is probable that these peptides are not the active moiety in the mood-elevating reaction, and rather than become disheartened, the failure to find an active antidepressant substance among these early identified peptides should encourage us to increased efforts.

Acknowledgments

This work was aided, in part, by grants from the International Association for Psychiatric Research, Inc., St. James, New York 11780.

References

Abrams, R., & Swartz, C. M. (1985a). Electroconvulsive therapy and prolactin release: Relation to treatment response in melancholia. *Convulsive Therapy, 1,* 38–42.

Abrams, R., & Swartz, C. (1985b). Electroconvulsive therapy and prolactin release: Effects of stimulus parameters. *Convulsive Therapy*, *1*, 115–120.

Ames, D., Burrows, G., Davies, B., Maguire, K., & Norman, T. (1984). A study of the dexamethasone suppression test in hospitalized depressed patients. *British Journal of Psychiatry*, *144*, 311–313.

Aperia, B., Thoren, M., Zettergren, M., & Wetterberg, L. (1984). Plasma pattern of adrenocorticotropin and cortisol during electroconvulsive therapy in patients with major depressive illness. *Acta Psychiatrica Scandinavica*, *70*, 361–369.

Arana, G. W., Baldessarini, R. J., and Ornsteen, M. (1985). The dexamethasone suppression test for diagnosis and prognosis in psychiatry. Commentary and review. *Archives of General Psychiatry*, *42*, 1193–1204.

Arato, M., & Bagdy, G. (1982). Neuroendocrine study of the mechanism of action of electroconvulsive therapy. *Neuropsychobiology*, *8*, 162–168.

Arato, M., Erdos, A., Kurcz, M., Vermes, I., & Fekete, M. (1980). Studies on the prolactin response induced by electroconvulsive therapy in schizophrenics. *Acta Psychiatrica Scandinavica*, *61*, 239–244.

Baldessarini, R., & Arana, G. W. (1985). Does the dexamethasone suppression test have clinical utility in psychiatry? *Journal of Clinical Psychiatry*, *42*, 25–29.

Balldin, J. (1982). Factors influencing prolactin release induced by electroconvulsive therapy. *Acta Psychiatrica Scandinavica*, *65*, 365–369.

Balldin, J., Granerus, A. K., Lindstedt, G., Modigh, K., & Walinder, J. (1981). Predictors for improvement after electroconvulsive therapy in Parkinsonian patients with on–off symptoms. *Journal of Neural Transmission*, *52*, 199–211.

Balldin, J., Granerus, A. K., Lindstedt, G., Modigh, K., & Walinder, J. (1982). Neuroendocrine evidence for increased responsiveness of dopamine receptors in humans following electroconvulsive therapy. *Psychopharmacology*, *76*, 371–376.

Belenky, G. L., Tortella, F. C., Hitzemann, R. J., & Holaday, J. W. (1984). The role of endorphin systems in the effects of ECS. In B. Lerer, R. D. Weiner, & R. H. Belmaker (Eds.), *ECT: Basic mechanisms* (pp. 89–97). London: John Libbey.

Brandon, S., Cowley, P., McDonald, C., Neville, P., Palmer, R., & Wellstood-Eason, S. (1984). Electroconvulsive therapy: Results in depressive illness from the Leicestershire trial. *British Medical Journal*, *288*, 22–25.

Carchedi, F., Falaschi, P., Casacchia, M., Rocco, A., Meco, G., Cerbo, R., Saini, M., & Frajese, G. (1978). Changes in blood prolactin during electroconvulsive therapy? *Boletino—Societa Italiana Biologia Sperimentale*, *54*, 709–711.

Carroll, B. J. (1984). Dexamethasone suppression test in depression. *Advances in Biochemical Psychopharmacology*, *39*, 179–188.

Christie, J. E., Whalley, L. J., Brown, N. S., & Dick, H. (1982). Effect of ECT on the neuroendocrine response to apomorphine in severely depressed patients. *British Journal of Psychiatry*, *140*, 268–273.

Coppen, A., Rao, V. A., Bishop, M., Abou-Saleh, M. T., & Wood, K. (1980a). Neuroendocrine studies in affective disorders. I. Plasma prolactin response to thyrotropin-releasing hormone in affective disorders: Effect of ECT. *Journal of Affective Disorders*, *2*, 311–315.

Coppen, A., Rao, V. A., Bishop, M., Abou-Saleh, M. t., & Wood, K. (1980b). Neuroendocrine studies in affective disorders. II. Plasma thyroid-stimulating hormone response to thyrotropin-releasing hormone in affective disorders: Effect of ECT. *Journal of Affective Disorders*, *2*, 317–320.

Cork, R. C., Hameroff, S. R., & Weiss, J. L. (1985). Effects of halothane and fentanyl anesthesia on plasma β-endorphin immunoreactivity during cardiac surgery. *Anesthesia and Analgesia* (*Cleveland*), *64*, 677–680.

Coryell, W. (1982). Hypothalamic–pituitary–adrenal axis abnormality and ECT response. *Psychiatry Research*, *6*, 283–291.

Coryell, W. (1986). Are serial dexamethasone suppression tests useful in electroconvulsive therapy? *Journal of Affective Disorders*, *10*, 59–66.

Coryell, W., & Zimmerman, M. (1983). The dexamethasone suppression test and ECT outcome: A 6-month follow-up. *Biological Psychiatry*, *18*, 21–27.

Coryell, W., & Zimmerman, M. (1984). Outcome following ECT for primary unipolar depression: A test of newly proposed response predictors. *American Journal of Psychiatry*, *141*, 862–867.

Costain, D. W., Cowen, P. J., Gelder, M. G., & Grahame-Smith, D. G. (1982). Electroconvulsive therapy and the brain: Evidence for increased dopamine-mediated responses. *Lancet*, *1*, 400–404.

Cowen, P. J. (1986). Neuroendocrine responses as a probe into the mechanisms of action of electroconvulsive therapy. *Annals of the New York Academy of Sciences*, *642*, 163–171.

Deakin, J. F., Ferrier, I. N., Crow, T. J., Johnstone, E. C., & Lawler, P. (1983). Effects of ECT on pituitary hormone release: Relationship to seizure, clinical variables and outcome. *British Journal of Psychiatry*, *143*, 618–624.

Emrich, H. M., Höllt, V., Kissling, W., Fischler, M., Laspe, H., von Heinemann, H., Zerssen, D., & Herz, A. (1979). β-Endorphin-like immunoreactivity in cerebrospinal fluid and plasma of patients with schizophrenia and other neuropsychiatric disorders. *Pharmakopsychiatrie*, *12*, 269–276.

Extein, I., Kirstein, L. S., Pottash, A. L. C., & Gold, M. S. (1983). The dexamethasone suppression and thyrotropin-releasing hormone tests and response to treatment in unipolar depression. *International Journal of Psychiatry in Medicine*, *12*, 267–274.

Extein, I., Pottash, A. L. C., & Gold, M. (1981). The thyrotropin-releasing hormone test in the diagnosis of unipolar depression. *Psychiatry Research*, *5*, 311–316.

Extein, I., Pottash, A. L. C., Gold, M. S., & Silver, J. M. (1982). Thyroid-stimulating hormone response to thyrotropin-releasing hormone in unipolar depression before and after clinical improvement. *Psychiatry Research*, *6*, 161–169.

Fakhri, O., Fadhli, A. A., & Rawi, R. M. (1980). Effects of electroconvulsive therapy on diabetes mellitus. *Lancet*, *1*, 775–777.

Finestone, D. H., & Weiner, R. D. (1984). Effects of ECT on diabetes mellitus. *Acta Psychiatrica Scandinavica, 70,* 321–326.

Fink, M. (1980). Neuroendocrinology and ECT: A review of recent developments. *Comprehensive Psychiatry, 21,* 450–459.

Fink, M. (1982). Neuroendocrine aspects of convulsive therapy. In R. Abrams & W. Essman (Eds.), *Electroconvulsive therapy: Biological foundations and clinical applications* (pp. 187–198). New York: Spectrum Publications.

Fink, M. (1986). Neuroendocrine predictors of electroconvulsive therapy outcome: Dexamethasone suppression test and prolactin. *Annals of the New York Academy of Sciences, 462,* 30–36.

Fink, M., Greenberg, L., & Gujavarty, K. (in press). Serial dexamethasone suppression tests and clinical outcome in ECT. *Convulsive Therapy, 3.*

Fink, M., & Ottosson, J.-O. (1980). A theory of convulsive therapy in endogenous depression: Significance of hypothalamic functions. *Psychiatry Research, 2,* 49–61.

Grahame-Smith, D. G. (1984). The neuropharmacological effects of electroconvulsive shock and their relationship to the therapeutic effect of electroconvulsive therapy in depression. *Advances in Biochemical Psychopharmacology, 39,* 327–343.

Greden, J. F., Gardner, R., King, D., Grunhaus, B., Carroll, B. J., & Kronfol, Z. (1983). Dexamethasone suppression tests in antidepressant treatment of melancholia. *Archives of General Psychiatry, 40,* 493–500.

Holsboer, F., Liebl, R., & Hofschuster, E. (1982). Repeated dexamethasone suppression test during depressive illness: Normalisation of test result compared to clinical improvement. *Journal of Affective Disorders, 4,* 93–101.

Inturrisi, C. E., Alexopoulos, G., Lipman, R., Foley, K., & Rossier, J. (1982). β-Endorphin immunoreactivity in the plasma of psychiatric patients receiving electroconvulsive treatment. *Annals of the New York Academy of Sciences, 398,* 413–423.

Jenike, M. A. (1982). ECT and diabetes mellitus. *American Journal of Psychiatry, 139,* 136.

Katona, C. L., & Aldridge, C. R. (1984). Prediction of ECT response. *Neuropharmacology, 23,* 281–283.

Kirkegaard, C., & Carroll, B. (1980). Dissociation of TSH and adrenocortical disturbances in endogenous depression. *Psychiatry Research, 3,* 253–264.

Kirkegaard, C., Eskildsen, P. C., & Bjørum, N. (1981). Parallel changes of the responses of thyrotropin, growth hormone and prolactin to thyrotropin-releasing hormone in endogenous depression. *Psychoneuroendocrinology, 6,* 253–259.

Klimes, I., Jurcovicova, J., Benetinova, J., Vigas, M., & Wiedermann, V. (1980). Effect of glucose on the glucagon response after electroconvulsive therapy in man. *Hormone and Metabolic Research, 12,* 231–233.

Klimes, I., Vigas, M., Jurcovicova, J., & Wiedermann, V. (1978). Serum prolactin after electroconvulsive therapy in man. *Endokrinologie, 72,* 371–373.

Krog-Meyer, I., Kirkegaard, C., Kijne, B., Lumholtz, B., Smith, E., Lykke-Olesen, L., & Bjørum, N. (1984). Prediction of relapse with the TRH test and prophylactic amitriptyline in 39 patients with endogenous depression. *American Journal of Psychiatry, 141,* 945–948.

Kutcher, S. P. (1984). Clinical utility of dexamethasone suppression testing in the elderly depressive: Case report. *Canadian Journal of Psychiatry, 29,* 505–507.

Lerer, B., Weiner, R. D., & Belmaker, R. H. (Eds.). (1984). *ECT: Basic mechanisms.* London: John Libbey.

Linnoila, M., Litovitz, G., Scheinin, M., Chang, M.-D., Cutler, N. R. (1984). Effects of electroconvulsive treatment on monoamine metabolites, growth hormone, and prolactin in plasma. *Biological Psychiatry, 19,* 79–84.

Lipman, R. S., Backup, C., Bobrin, Y., Delaplane, J. M., Doeff, J., Gittleman, S., Joseph, R., & Kanefield, M. (1986). Dexamethasone suppression test as a predictor of response to electroconvulsive therapy. I: Inpatient treatment. *Convulsive Therapy, 2,* 151–160.

Lipman, R. S., Uffner, W., Schwalb, N., Ravetz, R., Lief, B., Levy, S., & Levenberg, D. (1986). Dexamethasone suppression test as a predictor of response to electroconvulsive therapy. II: Six-month follow-up. *Convulsive Therapy, 2,* 161–168.

Malitz, S., & Sackeim, H. A. (Eds.). (1986). *Electroconvulsive Therapy: Clinical and Basic Issues.* New York: New York Academy of Sciences.

Meco, G., Casacchia, M., Carchedi, F., Falaschi, P., Rocco, A., & Frajese, G. (1978). Prolactin response in repeated electroconvulsive therapy in acute schizophrenia. *Lancet, 1,* 999.

Misiaszek, J., Cork, R. C., Hameroff, S., Finley, J., & Weiss, J. L. (1984). The effect of electroconvulsive therapy on plasma β-endorphin. *Biological Psychiatry, 19,* 451–457.

Modigh, K., Balldin, J., Eden, S., Granerus, A. K., & Walinder, J. (1981). Electroconvulsive therapy and receptor sensitivity. *Acta Psychiatrica Scandinavica, 290,* 91–99.

Nemeroff, C. B., & Evans, D. L. (1984). Correlation between the dexamethasone suppression test in depressed patients and clinical response. *American Journal of Psychiatry, 141,* 247–249.

Normand, P. S., & Jenike, M. A. (1984). Lowered insulin requirements after ECT. *Psychosomatics, 25,* 418–419.

O'Dea, J. P., Gould, D., Hallberg, M., & Wieland, R. G. (1978). Prolactin changes during electroconvulsive therapy. *American Journal of Psychiatry, 135,* 609–611.

O'Dea, J. P. K., Llerena, L. A., Hallberg, M., & Wieland, R. G. (1979). Specificity of pituitary responses to electroconvulsive therapy. *Journal of the Irish Medical Association, 72,* 490–492.

Öhman, R., Walinder, J., Balldin, J., & Wallin, L. (1976). Prolactin response to electroconvulsive therapy. *Lancet, 2,* 936–937.

Papakostas, Y., Fink, M., Lee, J., Irwin, P., & Johnson, L. (1981). Neuroendocrine measures in psychiatric patients: Course and outcome with ECT. *Psychiatry Research, 4,* 55–64.

Papakostas, Y. G., Stefanis, C. C., Markianos, M., & Papadimitriou, G. N. (1985). Naloxone fails to block ECT-induced prolactin increase. *Biological Psychiatry, 20,* 1326–1327.

Papakostas, Y. G., Stefanis, C., Markianos, M., & Papadimitriou, G. N. (1986). Electrode placement and prolactin response to electroconvulsive therapy. *Convulsive Therapy, 2,* 99–107.

Prange, A. J. (Ed.). (1974). *The thyroid axis, drugs, and behavior.* New York: Raven Press.

Pritchard, P. B., III, Wannamaker, B. B., Sagel, J., Nair, R., & DeVillier, C. (1983). Endocrine function following complex partial seizures. *Annals of Neurology, 14,* 14–27.

Robin, A., Binnie, C. D., & Copan, J. B. (1985). Electrophysiological and hormonal response to three types of electroconvulsive therapy. *British Journal of Psychiatry, 147,* 707–712.

Rothschild, A. J., & Schatzberg, A. F. (1982). Fluctuating postdexamethasone cortisol levels in a patient with melancholia. *American Journal of Psychiatry, 139,* 129–130.

Skrabanek, P., Balfe, A., Webb, M., Maguire, J., & Powell, D. (1981). Electroconvulsive therapy (ECT) increases plasma growth hormone, prolactin, luteinizing hormone and follicle-stimulating hormone, but not thyrotropin or substance P. *Psychoneuroendocrinology, 6,* 261–267.

Slade, A. P., & Checkley, S. A. (1980). A neuroendocrine study of the mechanism of action of ECT. *British Journal of Psychiatry, 137,* 217–221.

Swartz, C. (1985). The time course of post-ECT prolactin levels. *Convulsive Therapy, 1,* 252–257.

Swartz, C., & Abrams, R. (1984). Prolactin levels after bilateral and unilateral ECT. *British Journal of Psychiatry, 144,* 643–645.

Swartz, C., & Chen, J.-J. (1985). Electroconvulsive therapy-induced cortisol release: Changes with depressive state. *Convulsive Therapy, 1,* 15–21.

Thomas, A., Goldney, R., & Phillips, P. (1983). Depression, electroconvulsive therapy, and diabetes mellitus. *Australian and New Zealand Journal of Psychiatry, 17,* 289–291.

Trimble, M. R. (1978). Serum prolactin in epilepsy and hysteria. *British Medical Journal, 2,* 1682.

Ward, N. G., Strauss, M. M., & Ries, R. (1982). The dexamethasone suppression test as a diagnostic aid in late onset paranoia. *Journal of Nervous and Mental Disease, 170,* 248–250.

Whalley, L. J., Rosie, R., Dick, H., Levy, G., Watts, A. G., Sheward, W. J., Christie, J. E., & Fink, G. (1982). Immediate increases in plasma prolactin and neurophysin, but not other hormones after electroconvulsive therapy. *Lancet, 2,* 1064–1068.

Yudofsky, S. C., & Rosenthal, N. E. (1980). ECT in a depressed patient with adult onset diabetes mellitus. *American Journal of Psychiatry, 137,* 100–101.

12 ANTIPSYCHOTICS, TRICYCLIC ANTIDEPRESSANTS, AND LITHIUM

HERBERT Y. MELTZER
GARY A. GUDELSKY
JAMES KOENIG

Case Western Reserve University School of Medicine

The effects of psychotropic drugs on the neuroendocrine axis have been of interest to psychiatry for both clinical and theoretical reasons. Psychotropic drugs may adversely affect the hypothalamus, pituitary, or the peripheral glands and impair various endocrine-dependent behaviors, for example, sex hormone and thyroid hormone-dependent behaviors. They may affect hormone secretion which is of interest for diagnostic testing, for example, basal plasma cortisol levels, the dexamethasone suppression test, the thyrotropin-releasing hormone test, or the endocrine challenge tests which are, at least for the present, solely of research interest in investigating, for example, the cortisol response to 5-hydroxytryptophan (5-HTP). Hormone responses to these agents may help to clarify their mechanism of action, for example, the prolactin (PRL) response to neuroleptics and the effect of lithium on the 5-HTP-induced increase in cortisol. Endocrine responses such as the PRL response to conventional neuroleptics may also be of value in monitoring drug absorption and metabolism and to predict clinical response. Hormone responses are also of value in clarifying which neurotransmitters are affected by acute and chronic administration of psychotropic drugs and hence may be relevant to their mechanism of action. The pattern of hormone responses may help to identify significant differences in drugs of the same class,

for example, the differences between conventional and atypical antipsychotic drugs. This chapter will consider the neuroendocrine effect of neuroleptics, antidepressants, and lithium, mainly with regard to any adverse effects on the peripheral glands and the mechanism of action of the psychotropic drugs.

EFFECT OF NEUROLEPTIC DRUGS

Effect on PRL Secretion

Mechanism

All major groups of neuroleptic drugs have the capacity to block dopamine (DA) receptors, including those in the pituitary gland. DA secreted into the pituitary portal circulation by the tuberoinfundibular DA (TIDA) neurons tonically inhibits PRL secretion (Gudelsky, 1981; MacLeod, 1976) via an action on DA_2 receptors, that is, those DA receptors which inhibit DA-stimulated adenylate cyclase activity (Creese, Schneider, & Snyder, 1977). Neuroleptic drugs stimulate PRL secretion by virtue of their ability to block pituitary DA receptors. Domperidone, a butyrophenone-type DA receptor antagonist with limited ability to penetrate the blood–brain barrier, stimulates PRL secretion in man, but it may not be as effective in this regard as agents which penetrate the

266

blood–brain barrier, suggesting a suprapituitary locus of action may also be relevant to the PRL-stimulating effect of these drugs (Browers, Assies, Wierslinga, Huizing, & Tytgat, 1980).

The potency of neuroleptic drugs to block striatal DA receptors is correlated with their ability to stimulate PRL secretion in man (Langer, Sachar, Gruen, & Halpern, 1977) and rodents (Meltzer, Paul, & Fang, 1977). Langer *et al.* (1977) reported a correlation of .96 between the relative PRL-releasing potencies and clinical antipsychotic potency of seven neuroleptic drugs: chlorpromazine (CPZ), fluphenazine, haloperidol, perphenazine, prochlorperazine, thiothixene, and trifluoperazine. In that study, one or more of the seven drugs, but not all seven, was administered to each of 12 subjects. This reduced the effect of individual differences in PRL responsiveness, but the analysis was flawed by an incomplete set of repeated measures in each subject. Thus, the magnitude of the correlation may be less than reported. However, the basic relationship between clinical potency and PRL response to conventional neuroleptic drugs is probably valid for acute doses of the conventional neuroleptics given acutely.

The pituitary DA_2 receptors on the lactotrophes are very similar to the DA_2 receptors in the striatum and mesolimbic system which mediate the extrapyramidal and antipsychotic effects of these agents, respectively (Meltzer, Simonovic, & So, 1983). The similarity of mechanisms between the antipsychotic and PRL-stimulating effects of conventional neuroleptics suggests that monitoring the PRL response to such neuroleptics may be of value in using neuroleptics clinically and in identifying new neuroleptics (Meltzer, Busch, So, Holcomb, & Fang, 1980; Meltzer & Fang, 1976). Specifically, it has been suggested that the PRL response to neuroleptics might (1) predict the dosage level for conventional neuroleptics and help to identify atypical neuroleptics because of their lesser effect on PRL secretion, (2) predict clinical response following a small, single dose, (3) correlate with plasma levels of neuroleptics and substitute for their direct determination, and (4) correlate with clinical response following subacute or chronic administration, thus providing an objective measure of the action of neuroleptic drugs (Meltzer, Busch, So, Holcomb, & Fang, 1980; Meltzer, Kane, Kolakowska, 1983).

Acute Effects of Neuroleptics on PRL Secretion

Despite the general correlation between DA receptor blockade and ability to stimulate PRL secretion, some neuroleptic drugs appear to be more potent than others in stimulating PRL secretion. The typical benzamide antipsychotic drugs such as sulpiride, tiapride, and metochlopramide produce maximal PRL secretion at doses which are far less than the doses required for an antipsychotic effect. This could be due to low penetration of these drugs into the limbic cortex and other areas relevant to their antipsychotic action. However, it may also be due to blockade of a subgroup of DA receptors which is most critical for inhibiting PRL secretion or via some other mechanism such as stimulating the release of a PRL-releasing factor (Meltzer, Simonovic, & So, 1983). Conversely, melperone, a butyrophenone, and clozapine, a dibenzodiazepine, are less potent in stimulating PRL secretion in man than would be expected on the basis of their antipsychotic potency (Bjerkenstadt, Emeroth, Harnyrd, & Sedvall, 1977; Meltzer, Goode, Schyve, Young, & Fang, 1979). This may be due, at least in the case of clozapine, to its ability to stimulate DA turnover, which counteracts the effect of DA receptor blockade. These two drugs also produce fewer extrapyramidal side effects and may be less likely to produce tardive dyskinesias. They are the best examples of atypical neuroleptics and may be readily identified by their anomalous effects on PRL secretion.

Schizophrenics have normal serum PRL levels when adequately free of neuroleptic drugs (Gruen *et al.*, 1978; Meltzer & Fang, 1976). It is customary to obtain serum or plasma for PRL determinations in the early morning hours in fasting subjects. Obtaining samples by direct venipuncture may sometimes produce a stress-induced elevation. Obtaining multiple samples over a 30-minute period through an indwelling venous catheter which has been in place for 30 minutes will give a better indication of basal PRL secretion. Radioimmunoassays for PRL differ considerably in sensitivity. Absolute values may differ despite use of standards obtained from the National Institutes of Health. It is therefore advisable to obtain PRL determinations from laboratories with considerable experience and which maintain high quality control. Because PRL elevations due to neuroleptics may be relatively small in males given low doses of neuroleptics, it is desirable to obtain pretreatment PRL levels if it is anticipated that the PRL response to neuroleptics will be monitored. In some instances, the PRL elevations due to neuroleptics will still be within the upper limit of normal (Laughren, Brown, & Williams, 1979). Measurement of the effect of neuroleptic drug treatment on serum PRL levels may be done no sooner than an hour after awakening to avoid the effects of the PRL surge during the last part of sleep.

Intramuscular (im) administration of CPZ in doses as low as 12.5 mg can increase serum PRL levels in normal volunteers (Meltzer & Busch, 1983). The PRL response to 25 or 50 mg im CPZ is not significantly different (Meltzer, Busch, Creese, Snyder, & Fang, 1981), indicating that the former dose produces maximal blockade of pituitary DA receptors. The PRL response during the first 2–3 hours correlates highly with the complete PRL response curve, which generally lasts for 6 hours (Busch, Fang, & Meltzer, 1979). There is marked intraindividual variability in the PRL response following intramuscular or oral neuroleptics among patients (Gruen et al., 1978; Meltzer, Busch et al., 1981) and controls (Langer et al., 1979; Rubin & Hays, 1979). The PRL response to haloperidol has been reported to be greater in the evening than the morning (Nathan, Sachar, Langer, Tabrizi, & Halpern, 1979). The PRL response to sulpiride was found to be reproducible when the interval between studies was at least 10 days (Pontiroli et al., 1979). With shorter intervals, the PRL response to the second dose of sulpiride was enhanced, possibly due to an enhanced storage of PRL after the initial administration of sulpiride.

The acute PRL response to neuroleptics is not significantly different in females and males (Meltzer, Busch et al., 1981; Schwinn et al., 1975). Haloperidol in doses of 0.25 and 0.5 mg im stimulates PRL secretion in normal volunteers in a dose-related manner

(Hays & Rubin, 1979; Rubin, O'Connor, Gorwin, & Tower, 1976). This is obviously lower than the dosage needed to produce an antipsychotic effect or extrapyramidal effects in most patients. This may be due to fewer DA receptors in the pituitary, the fact that the pituitary is outside of the blood–brain barrier, less presynaptic dopaminergic activity in the TIDA neurons (and hence less resistant to dopaminergic blockade), and greater nonspecific binding of neuroleptics to nonspecific sites in the striatal and mesolimbic regions. Differences in serum haloperidol concentrations accounted for 88% of the variability in the magnitude of the PRL response to the 0.5 mg im haloperidol dose in normal volunteers (Rubin & Hays, 1979). However, Nikotopoulou, Thorner, Grammer, and Lader (1977) found that the plasma PRL response to an oral dose of thioridazine did not correlate with plasma thioridazine or mesoridazine levels in 6 normal men and that drowsiness and electroencephalographic (EEG) changes correlated highly with the increase in PRL, but not with drug plasma concentrations. The PRL response to 0.5 mg im haloperidol was not significantly different in 6 male schizophrenics with tardive dyskinesia and 13 normal males (Asnis, Sachar, Langer, Halpern, & Fink, 1979), consistent with evidence from hormonal effects of DA agonist administration that tardive dyskinesia is not associated with postsynapitc DA hypersensitivity in the TIDA–pituitary axis (Tamminga, Smith, Pandey, Frohman, Davis, 1977).

When the PRL response to 12.5 and 25.0 mg CPZ was compared in unmedicated schizophrenics and controls (Meltzer & Busch, 1983), female but not male schizophrenics were found to have smaller increases in serum PRL than the controls, possibly indicating increased activity of the TIDA neurons or supersensitivity of pituitary DA receptors. Since the PRL response to apomorphine, a DA agonist, does not differ between schizophrenics and controls (Meltzer, Kolakowska et al., 1984), this suggests the difference between the female schizophrenics and normal controls could be due to increased presynaptic dopaminergic activity. Gruen et al. (1978) also found no difference in the PRL response to 25 mg CPZ between male schizophrenics and controls.

Effect of Chronic Neuroleptic Treatment on PRL Secretion

The ability of neuroleptic drugs to produce persistent antipsychotic effects presumably rests upon their ability to produce effective blockade of limbic system DA receptors (Meltzer & Stahl, 1976). The persistence of antipsychotic activity is presumptive evidence for continued effective DA receptor blockade. Elevation of serum PRL levels during chronic neuroleptic treatment is evidence for DA receptor blockade at the pituitary level. Following the initiation of oral neuroleptic treatment with even modest doses such as 100 mg CPZ at 9 A.M. and 9 P.M., serum PRL levels are elevated over baseline levels 12 hours after the last dose. The magnitude of the increase is usually dose related in both males and females until a dose of 400 mg CPZ at 9 A.M. and 9 P.M. is reached. Thereafter, no further increase in serum PRL occurs, indicating that all the DA receptors in the pituitary are blocked (Meltzer, Kane, & Kolakowska, 1983). However, acute oral or intramuscular doses of neuroleptics in the morning hours will increase serum PRL levels further in some subjects (Kolakowska, Braddock, Wiles, Franklin, & Gelder, 1981). Sampling at the time of peak plasma levels gives a better indication of the neuroleptic effect on pituitary DA receptors. This suggests that there could be a fairly rapid clearance of drug and PRL following the evening doses, even when the neuroleptic dose is far greater than the dose at which morning PRL levels plateau. It is well established that PRL elevations will trigger an increase in DA turnover in the TIDA neurons (Hokfelt & Fuxe, 1972), although it is disputed as to whether this occurs in a few hours (Selmanoff, 1985) or not before 12–26 hours (Gudelsky, Simpkins, Mueller, Meites, & Moore, 1976). An increase in DA turnover may also help to overcome the effects of the higher neuroleptic doses in the evening.

The magnitude of the PRL response to chronic neuroleptic administration is greater in females than males (Meltzer, Busch et al., 1981). With the exception of atypical neuroleptics such as clozapine and melperone, the PRL response to equivalent doses of the various neuroleptics is not significantly different. McCreadie et al. (1984) examined the effect of oral haloperidol, fluphenazine, flupenthixol, and the long-acting parenteral forms of the latter two drugs on plasma PRL levels and plasma levels of the different drugs at 8 A.M. and at the time of the peak plasma levels. They noted significant differences in the plasma PRL and plasma drug levels as a function of time, drug, and subject, and suggested this might have implications for drug assignment. However, it is possible that the doses of drugs chosen were not equivalent.

Parenteral neuroleptics such as fluphenazine decanoate produce long-lasting, dose-related increases in plasma PRL. After an initial injection of 12.5–50 mg im fluphenazine decanoate, plasma PRL levels begin to increase during the first 2 hours and reach a maximum and remain relatively stable over a 2- to 14-day period (Meltzer & Busch, 1983). They usually return to preinjection baseline levels after 2–4 weeks (Chalmers & Bennie, 1978; Meltzer, Goode, & Fang, 1978). The duration of the action of perphenazine enanthate on PRL secretion was only 2 days in males and 9 days in females (Lindholm, Gullberg, Ohman, & Sedvall, 1978). Haloperidol decanoate produced only a small increase in serum PRL levels in male schizophrenics at 7 days, but a more marked increase in female schizophrenics (Meco et al., 1985). Penfluridol, a long-acting oral neuroleptic, produces a PRL elevation for at least a week (Chouinard, Annable, & Collu, 1982). The duration of the PRL elevation in such cases may provide one measure of the need for repeated administration. After discontinuation of chronic treatment with parenteral neuroleptics, PRL elevations sometimes appear to persist for months (Wistedt, Wiles, & Kolakowska, 1981).

Withdrawal of oral neuroleptic drug administration leads to a return of serum PRL levels to baseline levels within 24–48 hours (Meltzer & Fang, 1976). This is not accompanied by loss of antipsychotic activity in most cases. This implies that the antipsychotic action of the neuroleptics is not necessarily dependent upon constant DA receptor blockade. The fact that the onset of the PRL response following initiation of neuroleptic treatment is much more rapid than the onset of the antipsychotic response is also evidence that there is no simple relationship between DA receptor blockade and antipsychotic action (Meltzer & Fang, 1976).

Correlation with Plasma Levels and Clinical Response

There has been extensive investigation as to whether serum PRL levels correlate with plasma levels of neuroleptics and provide a measure of clinical response. One would expect a good correlation with neuroleptic levels only if active metabolites are also measured, as is done with the radioreceptor assay, if the neuroleptic dose is below that which produces maximal PRL elevations and if there is appropriate provision for the sex effect on PRL levels. We have reviewed this in detail elsewhere (Meltzer, Kane, & Kolakowska, 1983).

There is considerable interest in using plasma PRL response as a measure of plasma neuroleptic levels. A good correlation would be expected until the neuroleptic achieves full blockade of pituitary DA receptors (Meltzer, Kane, & Kolakowska, 1983; Wiles, Kolakowska, McNeilly, Mandlebrote, & Gelden, 1976). For groups of patients, most studies have found a significant correlation between PRL levels and neuroleptic levels during chronic treatment (Bjørndal et al., 1980; Meltzer, Busch, Creese, Snyder, & Fang, 1981; Meltzer, Kane, & Kolakowska, 1983; Ravichandran et al., 1984).

There is mixed evidence concerning the relationship between plasma neuroleptic levels and clinical response in schizophrenic patients (Meltzer, Busch, Creese, Snyder, & Fang, 1981; Meltzer, Kane, & Kolakowska, 1983). A number of studies show no relationship (Bjørndal et al., 1980; Kolakowska, Gelder, & Orr, 1980; R. C. Smith et al., 1984). There are many factors which contribute to this, for example, using a wide range of neuroleptic dosages, failure to measure active metabolites and differences in DA turnover, postsynaptic DA receptor sensitivity, compensatory non-DA-dependent effects, the importance of DA to the psychotic process for specific patients, as well as the type of dependent measures. However, a group of positive studies used a variety of drugs: flupenthixol (Cotes, Crow, Johnstone, Bartlett, & Bourne, 1978), CPZ (Bowers, Heninger, & Meltzer, 1979; Meltzer & Fang, 1976; Meltzer et al., 1978), thioridazine (Ohman & Axelsson, 1978), and pimozide (Siris, van Kammen, & De Fraites, 1978), but PRL levels account for only a small proportion of the variance in clinical response. It is doubtful that measurement of serum PRL response has any specific predictive value for clinical response in clinical practice. However, it may be of help in evaluating possible problems in absorption and metabolism by determining if enough of a plasma level has been achieved to block pituitary DA receptors. This depends upon the absence of tolerance to the neuroleptic-induced PRL response.

Development of Tolerance

There is a variable pattern of tolerance to the DA receptor blocking properties of neuroleptic drugs. Thus, most patients develop tolerance to the clinical effects of neuroleptics on the extrapyramidal system, and some show tolerance to the increase in cerebrospinal fluid (CSF) homovanillic acid (HVA), the major metabolite of DA. Tolerance needs to be differentiated from pharmacokinetic factors such as decreased absorption or increased metabolism. There is conflicting evidence concerning the development of tolerance to the PRL response following chronic neuroleptic treatment. As will be discussed, some studies find that serum PRL levels return to baseline frequently, while others find persistent elevations. Factors such as dosage of drug prescribed, agent, route of administration, sex, duration of treatment, interval between administration and sampling, compliance, and sensitivity of the PRL assay must be considered to evaluate this literature.

Two rodent studies indicate a diminished PRL response to chronic neuroleptic administration: (1) Müller et al. (1980) found a progressive attenuation of the prolactin response in rats during 4 weeks of treatment with haloperidol or domperidone, 1 mg/kg daily. Somewhat similar data were reported at 24 hours after the sixth injection of haloperidol, clozapine, or penfluridol (Annunziato, Quattrone, Schettini, & Di Renzo, 1980).

Numerous studies show that the PRL response to a fixed dose of a variety of neuroleptics remains constant during the first 2–4 weeks of treatment (Meltzer, 1985; Meltzer & Fang, 1976), but one study reported tolerance developing over a 4-week period and again at 12–14 weeks (W. A. Brown & Laughren, 1981). The PRL assay in this study was not very sensitive and only a small number of subjects were included.

There is some evidence that some degree of tolerance develops to the PRL-stimulating effect of neuroleptic drugs in patients receiving these agents for more than a few years (see Meltzer, 1985, for review). For example, Naber, Steinbock, and Greil (1980) reported that serum PRL levels were within normal limits in many male and female schizophrenics treated with neuroleptics for 5–25 years. The PRL response to thyrotropin was within normal limits in these patients (Naber, Finkbeiner, Zander, & Ackenheil, 1980), indicating no impairment in PRL synthesis or release. However, the fact that serum PRL levels in these patients declined significantly after withdrawal of neuroleptic drugs, despite the finding that they were within the normal range prior to cessation of drug treatment, indicates that these agents were still partially blocking DA receptors (Naber et al., 1985). However, many studies report above normal serum PRL levels in the majority of chronic schizophrenic patients receiving neuroleptic treatment over many years. The reason for the discrepancy between studies may be, in part, dosage (Chouinard, Annable, Jones, & Collu, 1981; Tripodiankis, Markianos, & Garelis, 1983). The most relevant measure of tolerance may be plasma PRL/neuroleptic level ratios; low ratios may suggest tolerance and the possible need for increased dosage if inadequate clinical response is present.

Effect of Neuroleptics on the Hypothalamic–Pituitary–Gonadal Axis

There have been numerous reports of abnormalities in the function of the hypothalamic–gonadal axis in schizophrenics prior to the neuroleptic era or in patients who have not received neuroleptics for long periods of time (Brambilla & Penati, 1978). This includes amenorrhea, menstrual irregularity, testicular atrophy, decreased sperm count and motility, decreased libido and potency, and hormonal abnormalities such as low levels of FSH, LH, estrogens, and testosterone. Nevertheless, there is evidence that the fertility rate of married, nonhospitalized schizophrenics is not different from that of the general population (Shader, 1970b).

While there are conflicts between various reports, there is sufficient evidence to conclude that all gonadal abnormalities in neuroleptic-treated patients are not necessarily due to neuroleptics; that is, they may be related to schizophrenia per se, weight loss, sleep disturbance, stress, and so on. Only studies of pre- and posttreatment effects or of withdrawal of neuroleptics can produce data that can be reliably attributed to neuroleptic treatment. The effects of neuroleptics on multiple neurotransmitters, especially the cholinergic system, must be considered along with their antidopaminergic effects to understand how they influence sexual function.

Neuroleptic drugs can produce abnormalities in sexual maturation, ovarian function, testicular atropy, decreased sperm motility, decreased sexual activity, and infertility in laboratory rodents and nonhuman primates (DeWied, 1967; Shader, 1970a). In humans, chronic neuroleptic administration may produce galactorrhea and increase the incidence of amenorrhea, menstrual irregularity, impotence, ejaculatory dysfunction, and diminished libido. Virtually all neuroleptics have been associated with these effects on sexual behavior. Hyperprolactinemia may be the cause of the full range of these effects, especially galactorrhea (Arato, Erdos, & Polgar, 1979; D. A. Carter et al., 1982; J. N. Carter, Tyson, Tolis, Van Ulich, & Friesen, 1978; Ghadirian, Chouinard, & Annable, 1982). However, thioridazine is particularly associated with impotence and ejaculatory disturbances. The incident of such abnormalities in males has been reported to be about 50% in thioridazine-treated patients compared to 10–20% with other neuroleptics (Ghadirian et al., 1982), but no good, controlled survey data really exist. Menstrual disturbances may be as high as 90% (Ghadirian et al., 1982). The incidence of galactorrhea varies from 10% to 30% in most reports. There is no strict correlation between serum PRL levels and galactorrhea, indicating host factors are important. Gynecomastia in males is not related to enhanced PRL secretion; it may be more related to an abnormality in the ratio of estrogens to androgens (Forbes, 1978). There is no evidence to suggest neuroleptic drugs increase the risk of mammary carcinoma in humans (Schyve, Smithline, & Meltzer, 1978). These effects are reversible upon cessa tion of treatment, but since relapse within 2 years is all but inevitable in chronic schizophrenia, it may be more prudent to try substituting another neuroleptic for thioridazine or lowering the dosage to the minimum at which sexual function returns. Addition of bromocriptine, a potent DA agonist, at low dosages may be useful, since there is evidence that hyperprolactinemia may be the cause of the sexual dysfunction. On occasion, psychiatric patients will have PRL-secreting adenomas which can cause sexual dysfunction and require pharmacological or surgical intervention (Schwartz, Bauman, & Masters, 1982). The menstrual disturbances due to neuroleptics may also be related to hyperprolactinemia or a direct effect on the hypothalamic mechanisms controlling gonadotropin release (Thorner, 1977). Meco et al. (1985) found some evidence that hyperprolactemia was associated with sexual dysfunction in males receiving haloperidol decanoate. If the sexual dysfunction is not of great concern to the patient or his significant others, no change in medication may be indicated.

There have been numerous studies of the effect of hypothalamic hormones on pituitary and gonadal hormone secretion, as well as basal secretion, of these hormones in neuroleptic-treated patients. Beaumont et al. (1974) reported that 8 amenorrheic neuroleptic-treated females had absent midcycle LH peaks and variable basal LH levels, but normal estrogen and progesterone values. Premenopausal women with normal menses had no abnormalities of LH. Metoclopramide and sulpiride, two benzamide drugs, produced amenorrhea or oligomenorrhea in a high percentage of women given these agents for gastrointestinal disorders. The LH response to gonadotropin-releasing hormone (GnRH) was increased in these women, but basal LH and FSH levels were normal. The effects of these drugs on menstruation disappeared over several months after their cessation (Aono et al., 1978). Johnstone, Crow, and Cotes (1979), Naber, Steinbock, and Greil (1980) and Brown, Grof, and Grof (1981) also found no effect of chronic neuroleptic treatment on plasma LH levels. The LH response to GnRH in chronic neuroleptic-treated patients may be normal (D. A. Carter et al., 1982; Naber, Steinbock, &

Greil, 1980), enhanced (D. A. Carter et al., 1982; Tolis & Frank, 1979) or impaired (D. A. Carter et al., 1982). Exaggerated LH responses to LH-releasing hormone may be related to hyperprolactinemia (D. A. Carter et al., 1982). Ferrier, Cotes, Crow, and Johnstone (1982) reported a normal LH and diminished FSH response to GnRH in 18 male schizophrenics who had not received neuroleptic medication for at least a year, suggesting that the diminished or enhanced LH responses cited above may be neuroleptic related.

Plasma testosterone levels appear to be decreased by neuroleptic drugs in some patients (Beaumont et al., 1974; Brambilla, Guerrini, Guastalla, Rovere, & Riggi, 1975). There is some evidence that thioridazine may produce the largest decrease in serum testosterone levels (G. M. Brown et al., 1981; Laughren et al., 1979) or LH levels (G. M. Brown et al., 1981). However, many studies report basically normal androgen levels in most neuroleptic-treated male schizophrenics (Brooksbank et al., 1970; Johnstone et al., 1979; Martin-Du Pan, Baumann, Magrini, & Felber, 1979; Siris et al., 1980).

In summary, chronic neuroleptic administration has modest effects on hypothalamic–pituitary–gonadal function which may contribute to sexual dysfunction in schizophrenics. Many of these effects may be related to hyperprolactinemia. They may respond to reduced dosage or bromocriptine. The possibility that the sexual dysfunction is not related to the drug treatment must be considered.

EFFECT OF ANTIDEPRESSANTS ON NEUROENDOCRINE FUNCTION

Antidepressant drugs (other than lithium or neuroleptics that also have antidepressant action along with their primary effects upon mania and psychosis) have minimal effects upon the function of endocrine organs. Antidepressant drug treatment has very rarely been reported to produce gynecomastia in the male, breast enlargement and galactorrhea in the female, increased or decreased libido, impotence, abnormal glucose tolerance tests, or minor effects upon thyroid function tests. There is no evidence that antidepressant treatment produces abnormalities of the dexamethasone suppression test or the TRH stimulation test. Rather, administration of antidepressant agents is usually associated with normalization of DST nonsuppression and TRH blunting (see Chapters 2 and 3, this volume). The effects of antidepressant drugs on neuroendocrine function in man are mainly reflected in changes in the basal plasma concentrations of PRL, GH, and cortisol. In addition to the acute effects of antidepressant agents on hormone secretion, long-term treatment with antidepressants appears to alter the responsiveness of hypothalamic neurotransmitter mechanisms involved in the regulation of the release of pituitary hormones. Whereas the neuroendocrine effects of neuroleptics appear to be mediated primarily through hypothalamic dopaminergic mechanisms, antidepressant-induced changes in hormone secretion may involve serotonergic and/or adrenergic mechanisms. In view of the current concepts regarding 5-HT and norepinephrine (NE) in the etiology of depression, the neuroendocrine effects of antidepressants conceivably are important to an understanding of the mechanism of antidepressant action.

Acute Antidepressant Treatment and PRL Secretion

Imipramine and Desipramine

The acute administration of tricyclic antidepressants has been shown in several studies to result in an elevation of plasma PRL concentrations in healthy subjects and depressed patients. For example, desipramine (DMI) and chlorimipramine (CI) produce dose-related increases in plasma PRL concentrations after intravenous administration to normal volunteers (Laakman, Chuang, Gugath, Ortner, Schmauss, & Whittman, 1983, Laakman, Gugath, Kuss, & Zygan, 1984; Laakman, Schoen, Blaschke, & Wittman, 1985). CI was found to be 5–10 times more potent than DMI in this regard (Laakmann et al., 1983). Elevations in plasma PRL were found within 30 minutes after the infusion of 5 mg of CI or 50 mg of DMI. Recently, Calil et al. (1984) also reported that depressed patients given DMI (100 mg) per os (by mouth) exhibited an acute elevation of plasma PRL concentrations.

In contrast to the findings of Laakman et al. and Calil et al. are numerous reports that acute tricyclic antidepressant treatment fails to appreciably alter PRL secretion (Hughes, 1973; Jones, Luscombe, & Groom, 1977; Meltzer et al., 1977; Widerlov, Wide, & Sjøstrom, 1978). However, differences in drugs, drug dosages, routes of administration, and sampling procedures may account for some of these negative data. Laakmann has noted that the per os administration of CI caused no change in PRL secretion (Laakmann, Schumacher, & Beakert, 1977), whereas the intravenous administration of this antidepressant evoked a significant stimulation of PRL secretion (Laakmann et al., 1983). In many of the studies, PRL concentrations were determined in blood samples obtained from venipuncture as opposed to an indwelling catheter. Significant stress-related elevations of plasma PRL concentrations in control groups conceivably could have masked an antidepressant-induced elevation of plasma hormone levels.

The ability of DMI and CI to stimulate PRL secretion in man may be attributable to the inhibitory effects of these agents on 5-HT reuptake and the subsequent facilitation of serotonergic neurotransmission. Serotonergic stimulation of PRL secretion has been established in the rat (cf. Gudelsky, Simonovic, & Meltzer, 1984; Van de Kar & Bethea, 1982), but the data in man are less certain. MacIndoe and Turkington (1973) reported that L-tryptophan infused intravenously over a 20-minute period produced a 10- to 20-fold increase in serum PRL levels, with maximum concentrations 20–40 min after the beginning of the infusion. Charney, Heninger, Sternberg, Redmond, Leckman, Maas, and Roth (1982) also reported a significant but smaller increase in serum PRL levels in normal volunteers in response to an infusion of L-tryptophan. Oral L-tryptophan does not reliably increase serum PRL levels in man (Meltzer, Wiita, et al., 1982). Similarly, oral 5-hydroxytryptophan (5-HTP) also does not increase serum PRL levels in man (Meltzer, Wiita et al., 1982; Meltzer, Umberkoman-Wiita et al., 1984). However, direct-acting 5-HT agonists such as N,N-dimethyltryptamine (Meltzer, Wiita et al., 1982) and MK-212 (H. Y. Meltzer, Lowy, & Koenig, unpublished data) do increase serum PRL levels in man. The finding that the selective 5-HT uptake inhibitor CI is more potent than the selective NE uptake inhibitor DMI in elevating plasma PRL concentrations is consistent with the view that inhibition of 5-HT uptake is involved in the PRL-stimulating effect of these agents. In further support for 5-HT mediation of the PRL-releasing effects of CI and DMI is the fact that the administration of methysergide, a 5-HT antagonist, results in a significant attenuation of CI- and DMI-induced elevations of PRL concentrations (Laakmann et al., 1983; Laakmann, Gugath et al., 1984). However, methysergide does have some dopaminergic effects which could account for its PRL-lowering effects. Inhibition of the effects of these agents by more selective 5-HT antagonists such as ketanserin will be useful to establish this point.

Nevertheless, the contention that serotonergic mechanisms alone mediate the PRL-releasing effect of DMI recently has been questioned (Calil et al., 1984). These investigators reported that plasma PRL concentrations were increased after oral DMI, but not after the administration of the selective 5-HT uptake inhibitor zimelidine. The lack of effect of acute oral zimelidine administration of PRL secretion also had been observed in earlier studies (Potter et al., 1981; Syvalahti, Nagy, & Van Praag, 1979). Aside from pharmacokinetic factors, it would appear that interactions among several aminergic systems account for the PRL-releasing effect of DMI.

Other Antidepressants

The effects on serum PRL concentrations of numerous antidepressants other than DMI and CI have been reported. Halbreich, Assael, and Ben-David (1978) studied serum PRL concentrations in depressed patients in response to a 3-hour infusion of dibenzepine, a tricyclic antidepressant with strong noradrenergic and serotonergic properties. Dibenzepine produced a very marked but variable increase in serum PRL concentrations which persisted for up to 4 hours. The PRL-releasing effect of dibenzepine could be due to its serotonergic properties, but a neuroleptic component to its action was not ruled out.

A low dose of trazodone (10 mg per os),

one of the more recently introduced antidepressants, has been reported to produce a significant reduction of serum PRL concentrations in normal volunteers. This effect of trazodone was attributed by Rolandi, Magnani, Milesi, and Barreca (1981) to its antiserotonergic activity. However, an antiserotonergic action of trazodone to lower PRL levels presupposes a tonic serotonergic stimulation of PRL secretion in man, and there is little evidence in support of this supposition at the present time. However, we have demonstrated that trazodone, like other 5-HT antagonists, can block the increase in serum PRL produced by 5-HTP or the 5-HT agonist, quipazine, in rats (Meltzer, Simonovic et al., 1981). Trazodone is unique in that it is metabolized to a 5-HT agonist, m-chlorophenylpiperazine (m-CPP) (Melzacha et al., 1979). It would be expected if concentrations of m-CPP were sufficiently high that plasma PRL and cortisol concentrations could be elevated. There are no known reports to this effect, however. In contrast to the effects of trazodone in normal volunteers, a nonsignificant decrease in plasma PRL concentrations was reported after the intravenous administration of 200 mg trazodone to a group of depressed patients (Roccatagliata, DeCecco, Rossato, & Albano, 1979). A systematic investigation of the differences in the responses of controls and patients to trazodone in relation to plasma levels of m-CPP appears to be warranted.

Amoxapine, the demethylated derivative of the neuroleptic loxapine, is a clinically effective antidepressant (Hekimian, Friedhoff, & Deever, 1978; Rickels et al., 1981) which produces elevated plasma levels of PRL after both acute (Robertson, Berry, & Meltzer, 1982) and chronic (Anton, Sexauer, & Randall, 1983; Cooper et al., 1981; Gelenberg, Cooper, Duller, & Maloof, 1979; Robertson et al., 1982) treatment. Anton et al. (1983) have speculated that the 7-hydroxy metabolite of amoxapine, which exhibits neuroleptic properties (Coupet, Rauh, Szues-Myers, & Yunger, 1979), acts through the blockade of pituitary dopamine receptors to enhance the secretion of PRL. Supportive of this contention is the observation that 7-hydroxyamoxapine increases serum PRL concentrations in the rat (H. Y. Meltzer, unpublished observation).

Antidepressant agents which possess indirect DA agonist properties have been shown to produce an acute suppression of plasma PRL concentrations. Hence, the inhibitory effect of nomifensine (Masala, Alagra, Devilla, Delitala, & Rovasio, 1980; Müller, Genazzani, & Murru, 1978) and bupropion (Stern, Rogers, Fang, & Meltzer, 1979) on plasma concentrations of PRL may be attributed to an enhanced release of DA from tuberoinfundibular neurons and, hence, a greater DA-mediated inhibition of PRL secretion.

Chronic Antidepressant Treatment and PRL Secretion

Although PRL responses in normal volunteers or depressed patients to acute antidepressant treatment are variable and are dependent upon the agent and the route of administration, there are numerous reports that chronic treatment of depressed patients with antidepressant drugs results in an elevation of plasma PRL concentrations. It should be noted, however, that the magnitude of the reported increase is relatively small, especially when compared to the elevation of plasma concentrations of PRL induced by neuroleptic agents. Indeed, although plasma PRL concentrations after chronic antidepressant therapy are often elevated when compared to predrug baseline levels, concentrations often are still within the normal range.

Francis et al. (1976) reported that plasma PRL concentrations increased progressively during the course of oral CI treatment (150 mg daily). However, these investigators noted that in patients crossed over after 3 weeks of CI treatment to amitriptyline, plasma PRL concentrations returned to normal predrug values during the course of amitriptyline treatment. An increase in plasma PRL concentrations during the course of CI therapy also has been reported by other investigators (Cole, Groom, Links, O'Flanagan, & Seldrup, 1976; Jones et al., 1977; Laakmann et al., 1983). Of interest are the observations of Jones et al. (1977) and Laakmann et al. (1983) that there is no correlation between plasma PRL responses and clinical responses to treatment.

Chronic treatment of depressed patients with antidepressants other than CI also has been shown to elevate plasma PRL concentrations. Lisansky et al. (1984) have reported that there was a significant elevation in plasma PRL concentrations in patients whose depressive symptoms had improved during a 1-month period of amitriptyline treatment. Treatment of patients with DMI for 3–4 weeks also has been shown to produce elevated plasma concentration of PRL (Calil et al., 1984). However, treatment with the selective 5-HT uptake inhibitor zimelidine did not produce a similar effect (Calis et al., 1984).

In accord with these reports, Asnis, Nathan, Halbreich, Halpern, and Sachar (1980) have observed that PRL concentrations were significantly greater in recovered depressed patients when compared to values obtained during their illness. Increases in plasma PRL concentrations were noted in patients treated with DMI, imipramine, doxepine, or mianserin. It should be noted that increases in plasma concentrations of PRL also were observed in unmedicated patients who had recovered.

Thus, elevated plasma levels of PRL resulting from chronic antidepressant therapies may be related to a normalization of neurotransmitter mechanisms governing PRL secretion and may not be reflective of a direct effect per se of antidepressant drugs. In view of the stimulatory influence of 5-HT mechanisms on PRL secretion, it is tempting to speculate that antidepressant therapies enhance serotonergic mechanisms within the neuroendocrine axis. Asnis et al. (1980) raised an alternative interpretation of these data, namely, that a modest reduction of plasma PRL levels is associated with depressive illness. A reduction in serotonergic function could account for the diminished secretion of PRL in depression, consistent with current theories of reduced serotonergic tone as an underlying mechanism of depression.

Plasma PRL levels in depressed patients also have been shown to increase in response to treatment with monoamine oxidase inhibitors (MAOI). Chronic treatment with clorgyline (Slater, Shiling, Lipper, & Murphy, 1977), pargyline (Slater et al., 1977), deprenyl (Mendlewicz & Youdim, 1977), or phenelzine (Meltzer, Fang et al., 1982) has been reported to significantly elevate PRL levels in depressed patients. The elevation of PRL levels by chronic MAOI treatment contrasts with the acute suppressive effects of these agents on PRL secretion in the rat (Chen, Simpkins, Mueller, & Meites, & Moore, 1981; Gudelsky & Meltzer, 1984) and man (Meltzer, Fang, Tricon, & Robertson, 1982), which presumably is due to the enhancement of the dopaminergic suppression of PRL secretion (Gudelsky & Meltzer, 1984). One explanation for the effects of clorgyline, pargyline, deprenyl, and phenelzine treatment is that serotonergic mechanisms are facilitated to a greater extent than dopaminergic mechanisms after prolonged inhibition of monoamine oxidase. Cimoxatone, a reversible, selective inhibitor of type A monoamine oxidase (MAO) at low concentrations, was reported to produce a slight but significant reduction in circulating PRL levels in 6 normal vounteers in a placebo-controlled study (Strolin Benedetti et al., 1984). The decrease in PRL produced by cimoxatone was mainly evident in the lack of an increase in plasma PRL concentrations noted between 2 and 8 P.M. on the placebo day rather than a decline below baseline. The effect of cimoxatone was attributed to its ability to enhance dopaminergic activity by inhibition of both type A and type B MAO. It has been reported that chronic administration of cimoxatone to a group of depressed patients of either sex did not affect morning PRL levels (Strolin Benedetti et al., 1984).

Evidence for a stimulatory influence of 5-HT on PRL secretion in man includes the fact that the intravenous administration of the 5-HT precursor tryptophan to normal volunteers results in increased plasma PRL concentrations (Charney, Heninger, Reinhard, Sternberg, & Hafstad, 1982). Heninger, Charney, and Sternberg (1984) have reported recently that the PRL response to intravenous tryptophan is blunted in depressed patients compared to age- and sex-matched controls. Additionally, the PRL-releasing effect of morphine, whose mechanism of action involves serotonergic (Koenig, Mayfield, McCann, & Krulich, 1979) as well as dopaminergic (Gudelsky & Porter, 1979) mechanisms, also is diminished in depressed patients compared to controls. Charney, Heninger, and Sternberg (1984) have extended their study of the blunted PRL reponse to tryptophan administration in depressed patients and found that chronic treatment of depressed patients with DMI or amitriptyline significantly enhanced the tryptophan-induced elevation of plasma PRL concentrations. We have not replicated these results, however (H. Y. Meltzer, unpublished data). Although there are many possible pre- and postsynaptic mechanisms through which DMI and amitriptyline could facilitate serotonergic function, neuroendocrine data from rat studies are suggestive of an enhanced sensitivity of 5-HT receptors following chronic antidepressant treatment (Meltzer, Simonovic, Sturgeon, & Fang, 1981).

Antidepressants and GH Secretion

Laakman, Gugath et al. (1984), Laakman et al. (1977), and Laakman, Treusch, Schmauss, Schmitt, and Treusch (1982) have reported that serum GH concentrations are increased following the administration of DMI to normal volunteers, but that CI produced little effect. The GH-releasing effect of DMI has been confirmed by other investigators (Calil et al., 1984; Sawa, Odo, & Nakazawa, 1982) and has heen attributed to its ability to enhance noradrenergic outflow (Laakman et al., 1985). In contrast to the GH responses to DMI in normal volunteers, there are several reports that endogenously depressed patients exhibit no significant elevation in GH levels following DMI administration (Calil et al., 1984; Matussek & Laakman, 1981; Sawa et al., 1982). Moreover, Sawa et al. (1982) reported in a study involving a small number of depressed patients that the GH response to DMI increased upon clinical improvement. Consistent with this finding is the report of Calil et al. (1984), in which a significant GH response to DMI was observed in patients who had recurring major affective disorders, but who were not depressed at the time of DMI administration. Zimelidine had no effect on GH concentrations in plasma after acute dosage of normal volunteers (Syvalahti, Eneroth, & Ross, 1979).

The lack of GH response to DMI in depressed patients is supportive of the involvement of dysregulated noradrenergic mechanisms in the etiology of depression.

Thus, some depressed patients are thought to have hypersensitive presynatpic α_2-adrenergic reports and, consequently, reduced noradrenergic neuronal activity (Charney et al., 1981; Cohen et al., 1980; C. B. Smith, Garcia-Sevilla, & Hollingsworth, 1981). A desensitization of the α_2-adrenergic receptor by chronic antidepressant treatment (Charney et al., 1981) would then account for the normalization of the GH response to DMI patients after clinical recovery (Sawa et al., 1982).

Serum GH concentrations are increased by clonidine, and this response has been reported to be blunted in depressed patients (Charney, Heninger, Sternberg et al., 1982; Checkley, Slade, & Shur, 1981; Matussek et al., 1980; Siever, Uhde, Silberman et al., 1982). Treatment of depressives with DMI for 1 week has been shown to enhance the clonidine-induced stimulation of GH secretion (Corn, Hale, Thompson, Bridges, & Checkley, 1984; Glass, Checkley, Shur, & Dawley, 1982). This effect of DMI was attributed to its ability to acutely inhibit norepinephrine reuptake. However, following chronic (3 weeks) treatment of patients with DMI, the GH response to clonidine was found to be decreased compared to the response observed prior to treatment (Corn et al., 1984; Glass et al., 1982). This finding was interpreted as being indicative of an adaptive change of postsynaptic α-adrenergic receptors in response to the acute effects of DMI. Consistent with these data are the findings that the blunted GH response to clonidine in depressed patients is unaltered at 3–6 weeks of treatment with amitriptyline or clorgyline (Charney, Heninger, & Sternberg, 1982; Siever, Uhde, Insel, Roy, & Murphy, 1982).

Antidepressants and Cortisol Secretion

Laakman, Gugath et al. (1984), Laakman, et al. (1985), and Laakman, Wittman, Gugath, Mueller, Treusch, Wahlster and Stella (1984) have reported that DMI (15–50 mg iv) and CI (25 mg iv) significantly increase serum cortisol concentrations in normal volunteers. DMI also was observed to elevate plasma concentrations of ACTH (Laakman, Wittman et al., 1984). The cortisol responses to CI and DMI were attributed to the selective blockade of 5-HT and norepinephrine re-

uptake, respectively. Acute administration of zimelidine, a specific 5-HT reuptake blocker, partially prevented the expected decline in serum cortisol levels during the morning hours (Syvalahti et al., 1979). Although a stimulatory role for 5-HT in the secretion of cortisol is generally accepted, noradrenergic mechanisms are generally thought to be inhibitory to cortisol secretion. A pharmacological analysis of the DMI-induced increase in cortisol levels has not as yet been performed.

Serum cortisol levels have been shown to increase following the oral administration of 5-HTP (Meltzer, Umberkoman-Wiita et al., 1984). Furthermore, the cortisol response to 5-HTP in depressed patients was reported to be greater than that in normal volunteers (Meltzer, Umberkoman-Wiita et al., 1984). Chronic treatment of depressives with any one of several antidepressants (e.g., nortriptyline, imipramine, amoxapine, amitriptyline, maprotiline, or trazodone) was found to diminish the cortisol response to 5-HTP (Meltzer, Lowy, Robertson, Goodnick, & Perline, 1984).

The suppression of the cortisol response to 5-HTP by antidepressants was attributed to a normalization of serotonergic function followed by a down-regulation of 5-HT$_2$ receptors. These results contrast with the finding of Charney et al. (1984) of an enhancement of the PRL response to L-tryptophan after DMI or amitriptyline administration. Thus, it would appear that even within the neuroendocrine axis, chronic antidepressant treatment can facilitate some 5-HT-dependent process and, at the same time, suppress others. However, it has yet to be firmly established that either the 5-HTP-induced increase in cortisol or the L-tryptophan-induced increase in PRL is due to serotonergic mechanisms. Various effects of antidepressants on the uptake of the precursor, processing of the precursor into 5-HT, or on pre- and postsynaptic 5-HT mechanisms could account for the differences noted above.

Conclusions

Antidepressant agents do not usually produce serious endocrinological side effects. Whatever influence they have on neuroendocrine function is of an indirect consequence of their pharmacological actions. Basal hormone levels are not affected greatly by antidepressants per se, but plasma PRL concentrations may be most sensitive. The effects of antidepressants on hormone secretion are most apparent in neuroendocrine challenge studies in which the ability of antidepressants to alter noradrenergic, dopaminergic, or serotonergic receptor mechanisms may become evident.

EFFECT OF LITHIUM ON NEUROENDOCRINE FUNCTION

The effect of lithium carbonate on the neuroendocrine axis is of interest for two reasons. First, neuroendocrine studies have helped to reveal some of the biological effects of lithium which may be relevant to its efficacy in mania and depression. Second, chronic lithium administration may adversely affect some glands, especially the thyroid (Emerson, Dyson, & Utiger, 1973). Lithium treatment has also been reported to be associated with impaired glucose tolerance (Muller-Oerlinghausen, Passoth, Poser, & Schlecht, 1978) and the onset of diabetes mellitus (Johnston, 1977), impaired gastrin secretion (Lauritsen, Heltberg, Hornum, & Rehfeld, 1978), decreased testosterone levels (Sanchez, Murthy, Mehta, Shreeve, & Singh, 1976), and hypercalcemia and hyperparathyroidism (Christensson, 1976; Davis, Pfefferbaum, Krutzik, & Davis, 1982).

In order to understand the interaction of lithium with the endocrine system, a brief review of its effects on monoamine systems which regulate the neuroendocrine axis is in order. Lithium has been found to produce significant changes in brain DA metabolism in animals, but the results are conflicting. Most studies report an inhibitory effect of lithium; reductions in DA synthesis (Friedman & Gershon, 1973; Poitou & Bohoun, 1975), in the influx of the DA precursor tyrosine into brain slices (Laakso & Oja, 1979), and in brain tyrosine and DA levels (Engel & Berggren, 1980). However, chronic lithium administration has been reported to increase the synthesis and release of DA in the nigrostriatal region (Hesketh, Nicolaou, Arbuthnott, & Wright, 1978; Maggi & Enna, 1980) and the hypothalamus (Corrodi, Fuxe, & Schou, 1969). A sustained increase in the release of DA would be expected to decrease the number of DA receptors. Therefore, it was hypothesized that lithium would prevent the development of supersensitive DA receptors induced by chronic haloperidol treatment or 6-hydroxydopamine lesions. Pert, Rosenblatt, Civit, Pert, and Bunney (1978) reported no significant increase in DA receptor binding as well as no change in the sensitivity to the stereotypy induced by apomorphine. Consistent results were reported by Allikmets, Stanley, and Gershon (1979). These results were attributed to the ability of lithium to stabilize dopaminergic receptors. However, other authors have not confirmed either the binding data (Bloom et al., 1983; Staunton, Magistretti, Shoemaker, Deyo, & Bloom, 1982) or the behavioral effects (Reches, Wagner, Jackson, & Fahn, 1982) of simultaneous lithium plus neuroleptic administration.

The effect of lithium on serotonergic function has been well established. Chronic administration of lithium enhances the function of central serotonergic neurons and decreases the number of brain serotonin receptors (Maggi & Enna, 1980; Treiser & Kellar, 1979; Treiser et al., 1981). The increased function of serotonergic neurons was demonstrated by increased concentration CSF 5-hydroxyindoleacetic acid (5-HIAA), the major metabolite of 5-HT, in patients receiving lithium (Bowers & Heninger, 1977; Fyro, Petterson, & Sedvall, 1975), by increased activity of brain 5-HT neurons (Corrodi et al., 1969), and from the increased ability of the 5-HT neurons to take up tryptophan (Knapp & Mandell, 1973). The ability of lithium to enhance serotonergic function has been demonstrated in behavioral studies (Sangdee & Franz, 1980).

Lithium also has been reported to increase the number of α_2 receptor binding sites in whole brain (Rosenblatt, Pert, Tallman, Pert, & Bunney, 1979) and the forebrain in some (Kafka et al., 1982), but not all (Treiser & Kellar, 1979), studies. β-Adrenergic receptor number has been reported to decrease (Rosenblatt et al., 1979; Treiser & Kellar, 1979), increase (Kafka et al., 1982), or remain unchanged (Maggi & Enna, 1980) following chronic lithium treatment. GABA receptors in the striatum and hypothalamus appear to decrease following lithium treatment (Maggi & Enna, 1980). These neurochemical effects most likely contribute to the neuroendocrine effects to be described.

Adrenocorticotropin/Cortisol

The activity of the pituitary–adrenal axis is controlled by the secretion of corticotropin-releasing factor (CRF) from the hypothalamus and by the feedback of glucocorticoids on the activity of the CRF neurons in the hypothalamus as well as directly on the pituitary (for a review, see Streeten et al., 1984). There are several reports of lithium treatment resulting in elevated morning levels of glucocorticoids (Jacobs, 1978; Koenig, Meltzer, & Gudelsky, 1984; McEachron et al., 1982). This enhanced· secretion of glucocorticoids may be due to increased secretion of CRF and/or increased secretion of ACTH or altered circadian rhythms which control glucocorticoid secretion. There are no data to support the direct stimulatory effect of lithium on CRF secretion; however, there are data that support the latter possibilities. Thus, the in vitro incubation of either mouse pituitary tumor cells or normal rat pituitary cells with concentrations of lithium chloride which are therapeutically effective increase the release of ACTH from the cells (Zatz & Reisine, 1985). This appears to be the result of increased phosphatidylinositol metabolism and is not altered by exposure of the cells to other ACTH secretagogues such as CRF or phorbol esters (Zatz & Reisine, 1985). Lithium administration to rats for 3 weeks produces a significant delay in the circadian cycle of corticosterone (McEachron et al., 1983). Plasma levels of corticosterone were minimal at 2 A.M. in lithium-treated rats, while levels were at their nadir in control animals at 10 A.M. (McEachron et al., 1983).

In normal human subjects, plasma cortisol levels are elevated in the early morning and lower in the evening. Many patients with major depressive illnesses have persistently elevated levels of cortisol and a flattening of the circadian cortisol rhythm (Sachar Gruen, Altman, Halpern, & Frantz, 1976). The elevation of plasma adrenal corticosteroid levels in depressed patients may be due to increased release of CRF. Nemeroff and co-workers

(1985) have demonstrated that depressed patients typically have elevated CSF concentrations of CRF in the morning hours. However, it is not known whether increased CSF concentrations of CRF accurately reflect an increased secretion of CRF from hypothalamic neurons which regulate ACTH secretion from the anterior pituitary gland.

Lithium administration to either normal controls or patients has been reported to produce elevations in 9 A.M. cortisol levels (Brown, Laughren, & Mueller, 1979; Noyes, Ringdahl, & Andresen, 1971; Platman & Fieve, 1968). This effect may be sustained throughout the course of treatment and may be due to several factors, including altered cortisol-binding globulin and changes in the clearance of cortisol. However, we have been unable to observe an elevation in plasma cortisol in bipolar patients during lithium administration (Meltzer, Lowy et al., 1984). Some studies have reported that chronic lithium treatment may lower cortisol secretion in depressed patients (Muehlbauer & Mueller-Oerlinghausen, 1985; Smigan & Perris, 1984). Halmi, Noyes, and Millard (1972) have reported that normal male volunteers receiving lithium carbonate for 2 weeks had smaller circadian cortisol rhythms than normal males during a placebo period. However, if dexamethasone was used to suppress endogenous cortisol secretion followed later by an ACTH challenge, cortisol responses to ACTH (0.25 mg) were identical during both placebo and lithium treatment. These authors concluded that lithium does not affect the sensitivity of the adrenal to stimulation by ACTH.

As mentioned previously, lithium enhances the synaptic efficacy of 5-HT (Sangdee & Franz, 1980). In a recent study, Meltzer, Lowy et al. (1984) have reported that the administration of 5-HTP, a 5-HT precursor, to depressed patients elevated plasma concentrations of cortisol. Following the 5-HTP challenge, these patients were treated with lithium until the symptoms of depression improved. This period of treatment was approximately 24 days, after which the 5-HTP challenge was repeated. The cortisol reponse to 5-HTP following lithium administration was significantly greater than before lithium administration.

Other investigators demonstrated that the administration of fenfluramine to both manic–depressive patients without medication and normal controls did not alter the plasma levels of cortisol between 10 and 12 A.M. (Muehlbauer & Mueller-Oerlinghausen, 1985). These results taken together suggest that lithium has enhanced the ability of serotonin neurons to synthesize and release 5-HT, improving the efficiency of 5-HT neurotransmission.

The above-mentioned studies suggest that lithium may cause alterations in circulating levels of glucocorticoids in normal humans and rodents. However, these changes are not reflected in the manic–depressive patient. Some of these patients already are cortisol hypersecretors and lithium appears to normalize this hypersecretion (Muehlbauer & Mueller-Oerlinghausen, 1985; Smigan & Perris, 1984), perhaps by slowing circadian rhythms (McEachron et al., 1982). Additionally, lithium treatment may alter 5-HT neuron function involved in regulating glucocorticoid and/or ACTH secretion probably within the CNS.

In addition to the changes in cortisol and ACTH secretion, patients with affective illnesses have elevated plasma levels of β-endorphin (Risch, 1982). Stimulation of β-endorphin secretion from the anterior pituitary by CRF appears to be the primary regulatory factor of β-endorphin/β-lipotropin secretion. Additionally, β-endorphin in the intermediate lobe of the pituitary is under the inhibitory influence of the tuberohypophysial DA neurons. The source of the β-endorphin in the plasma of the depressed patients has yet to be investigated.

There have been very few studies investigating the effects of lithium on the endogenous opioid peptides. Our laboratory has provided the first demonstration that lithium administration to rodents increased plasma levels of β-endorphin. Furthermore, upon challenge with a 5-HT agonist, plasma concentrations of β-endorphin are increased, and lithium administration potentiates the 5-HT agonist-induced increased in the plasma levels of β-endorphin in the rat (Koenig et al., 1984). Also, in rodents, lithium treatment using lithium chloride injections increases the concentration of methionine- and leucine-enkephalin in the striatum. There were no changes in enkephalin concentrations in the septum, amygdala, medulla, hypothalamus,

or cortex (Gillin, Hong, Yang, & Costa, 1978). In contrast to CNS changes, lithium administration decreases methionine- and leucine-enkephalin levels in the pituitary gland (Yoshikawa & Hong, 1983). While the interpretation of these changes is difficult, they do suggest that lithium can alter the metabolism and the secretion of the endorphins and enkephalins.

Prolactin

As previously mentioned, the secretion of PRL from the pituitary gland is under the inhibitory control of DA, which is secreted by the tuberoinfundibular DA neurons of the hypothalamus. Serotonin has a stimulatory role with respect to PRL secretion. Serotonin appears to act both by inhibition of the release of DA (Pilotte & Porter, 1981) and stimulation of the secretion of a PRL-releasing factor (Clemens, Roush, & Fuller, 1978), but this remains unclear. In the experimental animal, lithium has been found to decrease basal plasma concentrations of PRL in a number of studies (Banerji, Parkening, Collins, & Rassoli, 1983; Koenig et al., 1984; Smythe, Brandstater, & Lazarus, 1979). However, there are contradictory findings (McIntyre, Kuhn, Demitriou, Fucek, & Stanley, 1983; Tanimoto, Maeda, & Chihara, 1981). Administration of a single dose of lithium chloride potentiated haloperidol-induced PRL secretion in rats (Tanimoto, Maeda, & Chihara, 1981). However, chronic lithium administration does not potentiate haloperidol-induced PRL secretion (Koenig et al., 1984; McIntyre et al., 1983) or other DA antagonist effects (Smythe et al., 1979). However, DA receptor subsensitivity may develop during lithium treatment as reflected by the augmentation of the effect of haloperidol or blunting of the ability of apomorphine to suppress PRL secretion in reserpinized animals (Meltzer, Simonovic et al., 1981; Tanimoto, Maeda, & Chihara, 1981). This subsensitivity may be due to increased tuberoinfundibular DA neuron activity (Corrodi et al., 1969; Koyama et al., 1985). In addition, acute treatment with lithium has been reported to be without effect on the increase of PRL secretion produced by 5-HTP of β-endorphin (Tanimoto et al., 1981). The administration of lithium to animals for longer periods does potentiate the PRL response to direct-acting 5-HT agonists or reserpine (Koenig et al., 1984; Meltzer, Simonovic et al., 1981). These findings in rats indicate that lithium enhances the responsiveness of 5-HT receptors which are involved in stimulating PRL secretion. This enhancement of 5-HT neurotransmission could produce a greater inhibition in the release of DA from the tuberoinfundibular DA neurons than usual (Pilotte & Porter, 1981) or a greater stimulation of the secretion of PRL-releasing factor from the median eminence (Clemens et al., 1978). In either case, a greater stimulation of PRL secretion following the administration of a 5-HT agonist would result.

The administration of lithium to normal or alcoholic individuals does not result in significant changes in plasma concentrations of PRL (G. M. Brown et al., 1981; Czernik & Kleesiek, 1979; Lal, Nair, & Guyda, 1978; Tanimoto, Maeda, Yamaguchi et al., 1981). These subjects were usually tested after receiving lithium for 12 days to 4 weeks, at which time the serum levels of lithium were within the therapeutic range. Similarly, manic–depressive patients given lithium also have normal serum concentration of PRL (Czernik & Kleesiek, 1979; Epstein, Sagel, Zabow, Pimstone, & Vinik, 1975; Goodnick & Meltzer, 1983; Nielson, Amidsen, Darleng, & Pedersen, 1977; Tanimoto, Maeda et al., 1981). However, in these studies, patients had been receiving lithium for longer periods of time (weeks to years). In a longitudinal study, lithium therapy for up to 90 days produced no changes in serum concentrations of PRL (Nielsen et al., 1977). In contrast to the study of Nielsen et al. (1977), W. A. Brown et al. (1979) reported a decrease in PRL secretion in depressed patients following lithium therapy. However, in this study, the secretion of PRL was determined over a 24-hour period, whereas the previous studies involved single samples.

Lal et al. (1978) reported that lithium treatment did not affect the ability of haloperidol to elevate serum PRL concentrations in alcoholics and several other nondepressed patients. This finding is very similar to the findings in experimental animals (Koenig et al., 1984; McIntyre et al., 1983). Goodnick and Meltzer (1983) reported that bipolar patients receiving lithium for 2–10 weeks were less sensitive to the PRL-lowering effects of apomorphine, indicating that lithium had decreased the sensitivity of the pituitary DA receptors to stimulation. This finding also agrees very well with the data derived from rodent studies (Meltzer, Simonovic et al., 1981).

Thyrotropin-releasing hormone (TRH) increases plasma concentrations of both PRL and TSH and can be used to determine the responsiveness of both the pituitary thyrotrope and lactotroph. TRH-induced PRL secretion is not altered by lithium treatment in normal controls (G. M. Brown et al., 1981; Czernik & Kleesiek, 1979; Epstein et al., 1975). Tanimoto, Maeda et al. (1981) reported that following the administration of lithium for 3–4 weeks, TRH-induced PRL secretion was unchanged in normal female subjects, but was enhanced in female manic patients. Therefore, there may be a differential effect of lithium on the lactotroph in bipolar patients and normal controls.

Finally, Slater, de la Vega, Skyler, and Murphy (1976) reported an enhancement of the PRL response to fenfluramine, an indirect 5-HT agonist, in depressed patients receiving lithium. However, these results could not be confirmed by Meuhlbauer (1984).

The effect of lithium treatment on the PRL response to insulin-induced hypoglycemia in normal volunteers and schizophrenics was reported by Grof, Grof, and Brown (1985). There was no difference in the PRL response before and after lithium treatment in the normal volunteers or in bipolars who relapsed on lithium, whereas the PRL response was markedly blunted in those who responded well to lithium.

Therefore, it appears that lithium alters the basal activity of the tuberoinfundibular DA neurons involved in regulating PRL secretion. In general, lithium enhances the activity of these neurons and decreases the sensitivity of the DA receptors on the pituitary lactotrophs. In manic patients, however, resting PRL concentrations are already low, making a further decrease in PRL concentrations difficult. However, the dynamic regulation of PRL secretion appears abnormal in manic–depressive illness. Manic–depressive patients, particularly females, have exaggerated PRL response to TRH. Lithium therapy further exaggerates these responses, suggesting that in some manic–depressive patients, the pituitary gland receptors for prolactin-releasing substances differ from those in normal (non-depressed) individuals. In addition, lithium increases the PRL-releasing ability of serotonergic stimuli in man and rodents, suggesting that one of lithium's most powerful actions is to increase the responsiveness of the brain's serotonergic neurons.

Thyrotropin

The secretion of TSH from the anterior pituitary is under the stimulatory control of hypothalamic TRH and under the negative feedback influence of the thyroid hormones T3 and T4. The secretion of TRH from the hypothalamus is controlled by CNS monoaminergic neurons. Norepinephrine is considered the major stimulatory input to TRH release and, subsequently, on TSH secretion. Currently, the role of serotonergic mechanisms in regulating TRH secretion is controversial. Data suggesting a stimulatory and inhibitory role have been provided (Krulich, 1982). In addition to the CNS monoamines and TRH, the secretion of TSH can be inhibited by somatostatin. In many situations, parallel changes occur in GH and TSH secretion indicative of some common regulatory mechanisms.

The administration of lithium to normal subjects for a minimum of 3 weeks did not cause any significant change in baseline levels of TSH, T3, or T4 uptake (Lauridsen, Kirkegaard, & Nerup, 1974; Tanimoto, Maeda et al., 1981). There did not appear to be a difference between sexes in these studies. However, when challenged with TRH, lithium enhanced the TSH response (Lauridsen et al., 1974; Tanimoto et al., 1981). Interestingly, the T3 response to TRH was decreased following lithium treatment. These results suggest that in normal controls, lithium has little effect on the thyroid axis, and while there may be an enhanced TSH response to TRH, the thyroid gland is less responsive to TSH stimulation.

The effect of lithium on the hypothalamic–pituitary–thyroid axis in patients with affective disorders appears at first glance to be qualitatively different from that of normal controls. These differences could be due to the following reasons and should be kept in mind. First, plasma levels of lithium in nor-

mal controls are less than the levels observed in patients receiving lithium therapeutically (Tanimoto, Maeda et al., 1981). Second, normal controls receive lithium for shorter time periods (3–4 weeks) than do patients (2 months–14 years). These differences in treatment regimes could account for the inability to observe thyroid function changes in normal controls.

Depressed patients usually do not have grossly abnormal thyroid function (Smigan, Wahlin, Jacobsson, & von Knorring, 1984; Tanimoto, Maeda et al., 1981). However, when studied after extended periods of lithium treatment (up to 14 years), abnormalities in thyroid function may manifest themselves. The majority of reports indicate that the plasma concentrations of T3 and T4 may be normal (Cowdry, Wehr, Zis, & Goodwin, 1983; Epstein et al., 1975; Lazarus, John, Bennie, Chalmers, & Crockett, 1981; Smigan et al., 1984; Takahashi, Kondo, Yoshimura, & Ochi, 1975; Tanimoto, Maeda et al., 1981) or perhaps slightly less than normal (Emerson et al., 1973; Transbol, Christiansen, & Baastrup, 1978). Additionally, FT4I, and FT3, and rT3 have been shown to be either decreased or within normal limits (Lazarus et al., 1981; Takahashi et al., 1975; Transbol et al., 1978).

In contrast to the mixed findings of investigations of the effect of lithium on T3 and T4, more consistent findings of TSH hypersecretion have been reported (Cowdry et al., 1983; Emerson et al., 1973; Epstein et al., 1975; Lazarus et al., 1981; Smigan et al., 1984); however, Tanimoto and co-workers were unable to observe increased TSH secretion. Emerson et al. (1973) have found the hypersecretion of TSH begins to appear during the first 3 months of lithium therapy. Additionally, as the duration of lithium therapy increases, there is a higher incidence of elevated TSH concentrations. In one study, the incidence of elevated levels of TSH occurs almost exclusively in females; there is even greater incidence of TSH hypersecretion in females above age 40 compared with other patients (Transbol et al., 1978). The general incidence of TSH hypersecretion varies from study to study, but is generally 20% of the lithium-treated subjects (Emerson et al., 1973; Lazarus et al., 1981; Transbol et al., 1978).

In patients with the rapid cycling form of

bipolar illness, there is a much higher incidence of TSH hypersecretion. Of the rapid cyclers studied retrospectively over 4 years, 83% were females and almost 90% had been treated with lithium for more than 1 year. Hypersecretion of TSH following lithium therapy was observed in 92% of this patient population, whereas 32% of the non-rapid cyclers showed the same effect. Following lithium therapy, 12 of 24 patients developed clinical hypothyroidism as compared with none of the non-rapid cycling patients. Returning the rapid cycling patients to a euthyroid state did not stop the rapid cycling illness (Cowdry et al., 1983).

About 25% of medicated depressed patients have decreased TSH responses following TRH challenge (for review, see Loosen & Prange, 1982). The administration of lithium to patients with depressive disorders not only normalizes, but potentiates the TSH response to TRH administration (Epstein et al., 1975; Lazarus et al., 1981; Takahashi et al., 1975; Tanimoto, Maeda et al., 1981; Yamaguchi, Tanimoto, & Kuromaru, 1980). During chronic lithium administration, TRH administration has been reported to produce an abnormal GH response in 4 out of 6 manic patients, but in none of 5 normal controls (Yamaguchi et al., 1980). Lithium levels were lower in the controls; however, the abnormal GH response could be a result of slight hypothyroidism (Hamada et al., 1976).

The presence of thyroid autoantibodies has been reported in lithium-treated patients (Lazarus et al., 1981). However, Emerson et al. (1973) report that lithium does not cause the production of antithyroid antibodies in patients who are negative at the outset of treatment. Further clarification of the presence of autoantibodies and its implications in lithium-induced changes in thyroid function are required.

These studies suggest that the function of the hypothalamic–pituitary–thyroid axis is particularly sensitive to the effects of lithium, and should be monitored carefully as the duration of lithium treatment is prolonged. Unfortunately, the effects of lithium therapy are not indicated by determination of T3 and T4 levels. The secretion of TSH in response to TRH is more revealing.

Arginine Vasopressin

Arginine vasopressin (AVP) or antidiuretic hormone respresents a unique neuroendocrine system. The cell bodies which synthesize AVP reside within the hypothalamus and transport their secretory products through the median eminence to the posterior lobe of the pituitary gland. The activity of the neurons producing AVP and, hence, the secretion of AVP is dependent on input from the osmoreceptors in the organum vasculosum of the lamina terminalis, subfornical, and subcommissural organs. These osmoreceptors monitor the tonicity of the CSF which reflects the hydration state of the body. For example, in circumstances which cause hyperosmolar states, AVP secretion is increased so that more water will be reabsorbed by the kidney in an effort to dilute the increased concentration of salts. Furthermore, the secretion of AVP from the posterior pituitary is influenced by many CNS neurotransmitters and neuropeptides (for review, see Sklar & Schrier, 1983).

The difficulty with determining the effects of lithium on AVP secretion is complicated by the fact that lithium is a monovalent cation, like sodium, which in many cases can substitute for sodium. Consequently, lithium could act at multiple sites within the body to alter AVP levels. However, one of the common side effects of lithium ingestion in many patients is polydipsia and polyuria. These side effects would suggest that either the secretion of AVP is decreased, resulting in water loss and increased thirst, or that the effects of AVP on the kidney are blocked, resulting in the same symptomatology. In many instances, the plasma levels of AVP in patients receiving lithium prophylactically are elevated (Hansen et al., 1982; Miller et al., 1979; Morgan, Penny, Hullin, Thomas, & Srinivasan, 1982) or unchanged (Baylis & Heath, 1978; Gold et al., 1983). In addition, urine levels of AVP have been reported to be increased by lithium therapy (Morgan et al., 1982; Penny, Hullin, Srinivasan, & Morgan, 1982). However, lithium therapy did not change urine output, plasma sodium concentrations, or plasma osmolality (Gold et al., 1983). In spite of the somewhat discordant results with regard to basal levels of AVP in plasma, uniform results have been obtained when the balance of body water is changed.

Challenging normal subjects with water deprivation dramatically increases plasma levels of AVP (Morgan et al., 1982), and the same occurs in drug-free manic–depressives (Miller et al., 1979). However, the prophylactic use of lithium of 3 weeks to 7 years results in a much greater AVP response to water deprivation than would be expected (Baylis & Heath, 1978; Hansen et al., 1982; Miller et al., 1979; Morgan et al., 1982). Similar findings of AVP hypersecretion have been reported by Gold et al. (1983) when infusions of hypertonic saline were used to perturb water homeostasis. The greater secretion of AVP would be expected to result in the excretion of a hyperosmolar urine; however, lithium-treated patients were unable to increase urinary osmolality (Baylis & Heath, 1978; Miller et al., 1979).

These studies suggest that lithium decreases the sensitivity of the kidney to AVP, probably by inhibiting the activity of adenyl cyclase (Kanba, Pfenning, & Richelson, 1984). Consistent with this hypothesis is the finding that the administration of exogenous AVP does not alter urinary osmolality (Miller et al., 1979). These findings suggest that lithium results in nephrogenic diabetes insipidus. The role of the CNS or pituitary in the development of lithium-induced AVP release has been overshadowed by a possible direct effect of lithium on the kidney; however, Clifton, Baricos, Eggert, and Wallin (1984) reported that lithium can increase AVP secretion from isolated neurohypophysial tissue. Consequently, a central component for the effect of lithium on AVP secretion cannot be completely ruled out.

In addition to its effects on AVP, lithium can affect two other hormones which influence electrolyte balance, but these effects appear to be transient. Thus, lithium administration increases aldosterone and renin concentrations during the first week of administration, but levels return to basal state thereafter (Aronoff, Evans, & Durrell, 1971; Shopsin, Sathananthari, & Gershon, 1973).

the neuroendocrine axis. Perhaps the most detrimental of the changes are the development of hypothyroidism and possible changes in AVP secretion and function. The development of hypothyroidism, while not life-threatening, could exacerbate or induce depression. Disturbances of AVP secretion and function could result in imbalances in serum electrolyte concentrations. Therefore, long-term lithium prophylaxis in manic–depressive patients should be accompanied by careful monitoring of selected aspects of endocrine function.

CONCLUSIONS

The effect of neuroleptics on the neuroendocrine axis is much more profound than those of the antidepressants and lithium. Neuroleptic drugs may influence sexual function directly or indirectly. They almost always elevate serum PRL levels, but tolerance may develop in some patients. The PRL response may be of clinical use in determining if at least moderate plasma levels of DA receptor blocking agents are present following neuroleptic administration; this could include how frequently a given dose of a long-acting parenteral neuroleptic should be given. PRL responses may identify atypical neuroleptics in man. PRL responses do not appear to be robust predictors or markers of clinical response. The effects of antidepressants on neuroendocrine function in man are mainly reflected in changes in the basal plasma concentrations of PRL, GH, and cortisol. They also have acute effects on PRL, GH, and cortisol secretion and may, with chronic administration, alter the responsiveness of hypothalamic neurotransmitter mechanisms involved in the regulation of the release of pituitary hormones. Neuroendocrine effects of lithium have been useful in understanding its mechanism of action. Its potential toxic effects on the thyroid, glucose tolerance, and electrolyte balance are also of clinical importance.

Summary

In summary, lithium administration to normal subjects and patients with manic–depressive disorders can produce multiple effects on

Acknowledgment

This work was supported, in part, by USPHS MH 41684 and a grant from the Cleveland Foundation. HYM is recipient of USPHS Research Scientist Award MH 47808.

References

Allikmets, L. H., Stanley, M., & Gershon, S. (1979). The effect of lithium on chronic haloperidol-enhanced apomorphine aggression in rats. *Life Sciences, 25,* 165–170.

Annunziato, L., Quattrone, A., Schettini, G., & Di Renzo, G. (1980). Supersensitivity of pituitary dopamine receptors involved in the inhibition of prolactin secretion. *Advances in Biochemical Psychopharmacology, 24,* 379–385.

Anton, R. F., Sexauer, J. D., & Randall, C. L. (1983). Amoxapine elevates serum prolactin in depressed men. *Journal of Affective Disorders, 5,* 305–310.

Aono, T., Miyaki, A., Shoji, T., Kinusaga, T., Onishi, T., & Kurachi, K. (1976). Impaired LH release following exogenous estrogen in patients with amenorrhea–galactorrhea syndrome. *Journal of Clincial Endocrinology and Metabolism, 42,* 696–702.

Arato, M., Erdos, A., & Polgar, M. (1979). Endocrinological changes in patients with sexual dysfunction under long-term neuroleptic treatment. *Pharmakopsychiatrie, 12,* 426–431.

Aronoff, M. S., Evans, R. G., & Durrell, J. (1971). Effects of lithium salts on electrolyte metabolism. *Journal of Psychiatric Research, 8,* 139–159.

Asnis, G. M., Nathan, R., Halbreich, U., Halpern, F., & Sachar, E. (1980). Prolactin changes in major depressive disorders. *American Journal of Psychiatry, 137,* 1117–1118.

Asnis, G. M., Sachar, E. J., Langer, G., Halpern, F. S., & Fink, M. (1979). Normal prolactin responses in tardive dyskinesia. *Psychopharmacology, 66,* 247–250.

Banerji, T. K., Parkening, T. A., Collins, T. J., & Rassoli, A. (1983). Lithium-induced changes in the plasma and pituitary levels of luteinizing hormone, follicile-stimulating hormone, and prolactin in rats. *Life Sciences, 33,* 1621–1627.

Baylis, P. H., & Heath, D. A. (1978). Water disturbances in patients treated with oral lithium carbonate. *Annals of Internal Medicine, 88,* 607–609.

Beaumont, P. J. V., Corker, C. S., Friesen, H. G., Kolakowska, T., Mandelbrote, B. M., Marshall, J., Murray, M. A. F., & Wiles, D. H. (1974). The effects of phenothiazines on endocrine function: II. Effects in men and postmenopausal women. *British Journal of Psychiatry, 124,* 420–430.

Bjerkenstadt, L., Eneroth, P., Härnryd, C., & Sedvall, G. (1977). Effects of melperone and thiothixene on prolactin levels in cerebrospinal fluid and plasma of psychotic women. *Archiv für Psychiatrie und Nervenkrankheiten, 224,* 281–293.

Bjørndal, N., Bjerre, M., Gerlach, J., Kristjansen, P., Magelund, G., Oestrich, I. H., & Waehrens, J. (1980). High-dosage haloperidol therapy in chronic schizophrenic patients: A double-blind study of clinical response, side effects, serum haloperidol, and serum prolactin. *Psychopharmacology, 67,* 17–23.

Bloom, F. E., Baetge, G., Deyo, S., Ettenberg, A., Koda, L., Magistretti, P. J., Shoemaker, W. J., & Staunton, D. A. (1983). Chemical and physiologicial aspects of the actions of lithium and antidepressant drugs. *Neuropharmacology, 22,* 359–365.

Bowers, M. B., & Heninger, G. R. (1977). Lithium: Clinical effects and cerebrospinal fluid acid monoamine metabolites. *Communications in Psychopharmacology, 1,* 135–145.

Bowers, M. B., Heninger, G. R., & Meltzer, H. Y. (1979). Cerebrospinal fluid (CSF) homovanillic acid (HVA), cyclic adenosine monophosphate (cAMP), prolactin, and serum prolactin in acute psychotic patients at two points during early chlorpromazine (CPZ) treatment. In E. Usdin, I. J., Kopin, & J. Banchas (Eds.), *Catecholamines: Basic and clinical frontiers* (Vol. 2, pp. 1893–1985). New York: Pergamon Press.

Brambilla, F., & Penate, G. (1978). Schizophrenia: Endocrinological review. In F. Brambilla, P. K. Bridges, E. Endroczi, & G. Heuser (Eds.), *Perspectives in endocrine psychobiology* (pp. 309–422). New York: Wiley.

Brambilla, F., Guerrini, A., Guastalla, A., Rovere, C., & Riggi, F. (1975). Neuroendocrine effects of haloperidol therapy in chronic schizophrenia. *Psychopharmocologia, 44,* 17–22.

Brooksbank, B. W. L., MacSweeney, D. A., Johnson, A. L., Cunningham, A. E., Wilson, D. A., & Coppen, A. (1970). Androgen secretion and physique in schizophrenia. *British Journal of Psychiatry, 117,* 417–420.

Browers, J. R., Assies, J., Wierslinga, W. M., Huizing, G., & Tytgat, G. N. (1980). Plasma prolactin levels after acute and subchronic oral administration of domperidone and of metoclopramide. *Clinical Endocrinology (New York), 72,* 435–440.

Brown, G. M., Grof, E., & Grof, P. (1981) Neuroendocrinology of depression: A discussion. *Psychopharmacology Bulletin, 17,* 10–12.

Brown, W. A., & Laughren, T. (1981). Low serum prolactin and early relapse following neuroleptic withdrawal. *American Journal of Psychiatry, 138,* 237–239.

Brown, W. A., Laughren, T. P., & Mueller, B. (1979). Endocrine effects of lithium in manic–depressive patients. In J. Obiols, C. Ballus, E. Gonzalez Mondus, & J. Pujol (Eds.), *Biological psychiatry today* (pp. 759–763). New York: Elsevier/North-Holland Biomedical Press.

Busch, D. A., Fang, V. S., & Meltzer, H. Y. (1979) Serum prolactin levels following intramuscular chlorpromazine: Two- and three-hour response as predictors of six-hour response. *Psychiatry Research, 1,* 153–159.

Calil, H., Lesiur, P., Gold, P., Brown, G. M., Zavadil, A. P., & Potter, W. (1984). Hormonal responses to zimelidine and desipramine in depressed patients. *Psychiatry Research, 13,* 231–242.

Carter, D. A., McGarrick, G. M., Norton, K. R. W., Paykel, E. S., Prysor-Jones, R. A., & Whitehead, S. A. (1982). The effect of chronic neuroleptic treatment on gonadotropin release. *Psychoneuroendocrinology, 7,* 201–207.

Carter, J. N., Tyson, J. E., Tolis, G., Van Ulich, S., & Friesen, H. G. (1978). Prolactin-secreting tumors and hypogonadism in 22 men. *New England Journal of Medicine, 299,* 847.

Chalmers, R. J., & Bennie, E. H. (1978). The effect of fluphenazine on basal prolactin concentrations. *Psychological Medicine, 8,* 483–486.

Charney, D. S., Heninger, G. R., Reinhard, J. F., Sternberg, D. E., & Hafstad, K. M. (1982). The effect of intravenous L-tryptophan on prolactin and growth hormone and mood in healthy subjects. *Psychopharmacology, 77*, 217–222.

Charney, D. S., Heninger, G. R., Sternberg, D. S., Redmond, D. E., Leckman, J. F., Maas, J. W., & Rorh, E. H. (1981). Presynaptic adrenergic receptor sensitivity in depression: The effect of chronic desipramine treatment. *Archives of General Psychiatry, 38*, 1334–1340.

Charney, D. S., Heninger, G. R., & Sternberg, D. E. (1982). Failure of chronic antidepressant treatment to alter growth hormone responses to clonidine. *Psychiatry Research, 7*, 135–138.

Charney, D. S., Heninger, G. R., Sternberg, D. E., Hafstad, K., Giddings, S., & Landis, H. (1982). Adrenergic receptor sensitivity in depression: Effects of clonidine in depressed patients and healthy subjects. *Archives of General Psychiatry, 39*, 290–294.

Charney, D. S., Heninger, G. R., & Sternberg, D. E. (1984). Serotonin function and mechanism of action of antidepressant treatment: Effects of amitryptyline and desipramine. *Archives of General Psychiatry, 41*, 359–365.

Checkley, S. A., Slade, A. P., & Shur, E. (1981). Growth hormone and other responses to clonidine in patients with endogenous depression. *British Journal of Psychiatry, 136*, 51–55.

Chen, H. T., Simpkins, J. W., Mueller, G. P., & Meites, J. (1977). Effects of pargyline on hypothalamic biogenic amines and serum prolactin, LH, and TSH in male rats. *Life Sciences, 21*, 533–541.

Chouinard, G., Annable, L., & Collu, R. (1982). Plasma prolactin levels: A psychiatric tool. In R. Collu (Ed.), *Brain peptides and hormones* (pp. 333–341). New York: Raven Press.

Chouinard, G., Annable, L., Jones, B. D., & Collu, R. (1981). Lack of tolerance to long-term neuroleptic treatment in dopamine tuberoinfundibular system. *Acta Psychiatrica Scandinavica, 64*, 353–362.

Christensson, T. A. (1976). Lithium, hypercalcaemia and hyperparathyroidism. *Lancet, 2*, 44.

Clemens, J. A., Roush, M. E., & Fuller, R. W. (1978). Evidence that serotonin neurons stimulate secretion of prolactin-releasing factor. *Life Sciences, 22*, 2209–2214.

Clifton, G., Baricos, R., Eggert, W., & Wallin, J. D. (1984). Effects of lithium on vasopressin secretion from isolated rate neurohypophysis. *Society for Neuroscience Abstracts*, p. 90.

Cohen, R. M., Campbell, I. C., Cohen, M. R., Torda, T., Pickar, D., Siever, L. J., & Murphy, D. L. (1980). Presynaptic noradrenergic regulation during depression and antidepressant drug treatment. *Psychiatry Research, 3*, 93–106.

Cole, E. N., Groom, G. S., Link, J., O'Flanagan, P. M., & Seldrup, J. (1976). Plasma prolactin concentrations in patients on chlomipramine. *Postgraduate Medical Journal, 52*, 93–150.

Cooper, D. S., Gelenberg, A., Wojcik, J., Saxe, V., Ridgway, E., & Maloof, F. (1981). The effect of amoxapine and imipramine on serum prolactin levels. *Archives of Internal Medicine, 14*, 1023–1025.

Corn, T. H., Hale, A. S., Thompson, C., Bridges, P. K.,

& Checkley, S. A. (1984). A comparison of the growth hormone responses to clonidine and apomorphine in the same patients with endogenous depression. *British Journal of Psychiatry, 144*, 636–639.

Corrodi, H., Fuxe, K., & Schou, M. (1969). The effect of prolonged lithium administration on cerebral monoamine neurons in the rat. *Life Sciences, 8*, 643–651.

Cotes, P. M., Crow, T. J., Johnstone, E. C., Bartlett, W., & Bourne, R. C. (1978). Neuroendocrine changes in acute schizophrenia as a function of clinical state and neuroleptic medication. *Psychological Medicine, 8*, 657–665.

Coupet, J., Rauh, C. E., Szues-Myers, V. A., & Yunger, L. M. (1979). 2-Chloro-11-(1-piperazinyl) dibenz b-, f,1,4-oxazepine (amoxapine), an antidepressant with antipsychotic properties—A possible role for 7-hydroxyamoxapine. *Biochemical Pharmacology, 28*, 2514–2515.

Cowdry, R. W., Wehr, T. A., Zis, A. P., & Goodwin, F. K. (1983). Thyroid abnormalities associated with rapid-cycling bipolar illness. *Archives of General Psychiatry, 40*, 414–420.

Creese, I., Schneider, R., & Snyder, S. H. (1977). [^{3}H]Spiroperidol labels dopamine receptors in pituitary and brain. *European Journal of Pharmacology, 46*, 377–381.

Czernik, A., & Kleesiek, K. (1979). Neuroendokrinologische veranderungen unter langzeitbehandlung mit lithiumsalzen. *Pharmakopsychiatrie, 12*, 305–312.

Davis, B. M., Pfefferbaum, A., Krutzik, S., & Davis, K. L. (1982). Lithium's effect on parathyroid hormone. *American Journal of Psychiatry, 138*, 489–492.

Demarest, K. T., & Moore, K. E. (1981). Type A monoamine oxidase catalyzes the intraneuronal deamination of dopamine within nigrostriatal, mesolimbic, tuberoinfundibular, and tuberohypophyseal neurons in the rat. *Journal of Neural Transmission, 62*, 175–187.

DeWied, D. (1967). Chlorpromazine and endocrine function. *Pharmacological Review, 19*, 251–288.

Emerson, C. H., Dyson, W. L., & Utiger, R. D. (1973). Serum thyrotropin and thyroxine concentrations in patients receiving lithium carbonate. *Journal of Clinical Endocrinology and Metabolism, 36*, 338–346.

Engel, J., & Berggren, U. (1980). Effects of lithium on behavior and central monoamines. *Acta Psychiatria Scandinavica* [Suppl.] *61* (Suppl. 280), 133–143.

Epstein, S., Sagel, J., Zabow, T., Pimstone, B., & Vinik, A. (1975). The effect of prolonged lithium carbonate administration on the thyrotropin and prolactin response to thyrotropin-releasing hormone. *South African Medical Journal, 49*, 1977–1979.

Ferrier, I. N., Cotes, P. M., Crow, T. J., & Johnstone, E. C. (1982). Gonadotropin secretion abnormalities in chronic schizophrenia. *Psychological Medicine, 12*, 263–273.

Forbes, A. P. (1978). Editorial: Chemotherapy, testicular damage, and gynecomastia: An endocrine "black hole." *New England Journal of Medicine, 299*, 42–43.

Francis, A. F., Williams, R., Cole, E. N., Williams, P., Link, J., & Hughes, D. (1976). The effect of clomipramine on prolactin levels—pilot studies. *Postgraduate Medical Journal, 52*, 87–91.

Friedman, E., & Gershon, S. (1973). Effect of lithium on brain dopamine. *Nature (London)*, *243*, 520.

Fyro, B., Petterson, V., & Sedvall, G. (1975). The effect of lithium treatment on manic symptoms and levels of monoamine metabolites in cerebrospinal fluid of manic–depressive patients. *Psychopharmacologica*, *44*, 99–103.

Gelenberg, A. J., Cooper, D. S., Duller, J. C., & Maloof, F. (1979). Galactorrhea and hyperprolactinemia associated with amoxapine therapy—report of a case. *JAMA, Journal of the American Medical Association*, *242*, 1900–1901.

Ghadirian, A. M., Chouinard, G., & Annable, L. (1982). Sexual dysfunction and plasma prolactin levels in neuroleptic-treated schizophrenic outpatients. *Journal of Nervous and Mental Disease*, *170*, 463–467.

Gillin, J. C., Hong, J.-S., Yang, H.-Y. T., & Costa, E. (1978). Met^5-enkephalin content in brain regions of rats treated with lithium. *Proceedings of the National Academy Sciences of the U.S.A.*, *75*, 2992–2993.

Glass, I. B., Checkley, S. A., Shur, E., & Dawley, S. (1982). The effect of desipramine upon central adrenergic function in depressed patients. *British Journal of Psychiatry*, *141*, 372–376.

Gold, P. W., Robertson, G. L., Post, R. M., Kaye, W., Ballenger, J., Rubinow, D., & Goodwin, R. K. (1983). The effect of lithium on the osmoregulation of arginine vasopressin secretion. *Journal of Clinical Endocrinology and Metabolism*, *56*, 295–299.

Goodnick, P. J., & Meltzer, H. Y. (1983). Effect of subchronic lithium treatment on apomorphine-induced change in prolactin and growth hormone secretion. *Journal of Clinical Psychopharmacology*, *3*, 239–243.

Grof, E., Grof, P., & Brown, G. M. (1985). Effects of long-term lithium treatment on prolactin regulation. In D. Kemali & G. Raeagni (Eds.), *Chronic treatments in neuropsychiatry* (pp. 81–87). New York: Raven Press.

Gruen, P. H., Sachar, E. J., Langer, G., Altman, N., Leifer, M., Frantz, A., & Halpern, F. S. (1978). Prolactin response to neuroleptics in normal and schizophrenic subjects. *Archives of General Psychiatry*, *35*, 108–116.

Gudelsky, G. A. (1981). Tuberoinfundibular dopamine neurons and the regulation of prolactin secretion. *Psychoneuroendocrinology*, *6*, 3–16.

Gudelsky, G. A., & Meltzer, H. Y. (1984). Function of tuberoinfundibular dopamine neurons in pargyline- and reserpine-treated rats. *Neuroendocrinology*, *38*, 51–55.

Gudelsky, G. A., & Porter, J. C. (1979). Morphine and opioid peptide-induced inhibition of the release of dopamine from tuberionfundibular neurons. *Life Sciences*, *25*, 1697–1702.

Gudelsky, G. A., Simonovic, M., & Meltzer, H. Y. (1984). Dopaminergic and serotonergic control of neuroendocrine function. *Monographs in Neural Sciences*, *10*, 85–102.

Gudelsky, G. A., Simpkins, J., Mueller, G. P., Meites, J., & Moore, K. E. (1976). Selective actions of prolactin on catecholamine turnover in the hypothalamus and on serum LH and FSH. *Neuroendocrinology*, *22*, 206–215.

Halbreich, U., Assael, M., & Ben-David, M. (1978). Prolactin secretion during and after noveril infusions to depressive patients. *Psychopharmacology*, *56*, 167–171.

Halmi, K. A., Noyes, R., & Millard, S. A. (1972). Effect of lithium on plasma cortisol and adrenal response to adrencorticotropin in man. *Clinical Pharmacology and Therapeutics*, *13*, 699–703.

Hamada, N., Uoi, K., Nishizaw, Y., Okamoto, T., Hasegawa, K., Morii, H., & Wada, M. (1976). Increase of serum GH concentration following TRH injection in patients with primary hypothyroidism. *Endocrinologie Japonica*, *23*, 5–10.

Hansen, H. E., Redersen, E. B., Orskov, H., Vestergaard, P., Amidsen, A., & Schou, M. (1982). Plasma arginine vasopressin, renal-concentrating ability, and lithium excretion in a group of patients on long-term lithium treatment. *Nephron*, *32*, 125–130.

Hays, S. E., & Rubin, R. T. (1979). Variability of prolactin response to intravenous and intramuscular haloperidol in normal adult men. *Psychopharmacology*, *61*, 17–24.

Hekimian, L. J., Friedhoff, A. J., & Deever, E. (1978). A comparison of the onset of action and therapeutic efficacy of amoxapine and amitriptyline. *Journal of Clinical Psychiatry*, *39*, 633–637.

Heninger, G. R., Charney, D. S., & Sternberg, D. E. (1984). Serotonergic function in depression: Prolactin response to intravenous tryptophan in depressed patients and healthy subjects. *Archives of General Psychiatry*, *41*, 398–402.

Hesketh, J. E., Nicolaou, N. M., Arbuthnott, G. W., & Wright, A. K. (1978). The effect of chronic lithium administration on dopamine metabolism in rat striatum. *Psychopharmacology*, *56*, 163–166.

Hokfelt, T., & Fuxe, K. (1972). Effects of prolactin and ergot alkaloids of the tuberoinfundibular dopamine (DA) neurons. *Neuroendocrinology*, *9*, 100.

Hughes, D. (1973). Clomipramine (anafranil) and prolactin secretion. *Journal of Internal Medical Research*, *1*, 317–320.

Jacobs, J. J. (1978). Effect of lithium chloride on adrenocortical function in the rat. *Proceedings of the Society for Experimental Biology and Medicine*, *157*, 163–167.

Johnston, B. B. (1977). Diabetes mellitus in patients on lithium. *Lancet*, *2*, 935–936.

Johnstone, E. C., Crow, T. J., & Cotes, P. M. (1979). Hormone levels in acute schizophrenia with and without neuroleptic medication. In J. Ohiols, C. Ballus, G. Gonzalez Moncius, & J. Payol (Eds.), *Biological psychiatry today* (pp. 476–481). New York: Elsevier/North-Holland Biomedical Press.

Jones, R. B., Luscombe, D. K., & Groom, G. V. (1977). Plasma prolactin concentrations in normal subjects and depressive patients following oral clomipramine. *Postgraduate Medical Journal*, *53*, 166–171.

Kafka, M. S., Wirz-Justice, A., Naber, D., Marangos, P. J., O'Donohue, T. L., & Wehr, T. A. (1982). The effect of lithium on circadian neurotransmitter receptor rhythms. *Neuropsychobiology*, *8*, 41–50.

Kanba, S., Pfenning, M., & Richelson, D. (1984). Lithium inhibits neuropeptide function. *American College of Neuropsychopharmacology Abstract*, p. 119.

Knapp, S., & Mandell, A. J. (1973). Short- and long-term lithium administration: Effect on the brain's serotonergic biosynthetic systems. *Science*, *180*, 645–647.

Koenig, J. I., Mayfield, M., McCann, S. M., & Krulich, L. (1979). Stimulation of prolactin secretion of morphine, role of the central serotonergic system. *Life Sciences*, *25*, 853–864.

Koenig, J. I., Meltzer, H. Y., & Gudelsky, G. A. (1984). Alterations of hormonal responses following lithium treatment in the rat. *Proceedings of the Eighth International Congress of Endocrinology*, p. 1037.

Kolakowska, T., Braddock. L., Wiles, D., Franklin, M., & Gelder, M. (1981). Neuroendocrine tests during treatment with neuroleptic drugs. *British Journal of Psychiatry*, *139*, 400–404.

Kolakowska, T., Gelder, M. G., & Orr, M. W. (1980). Drug-related and illness-related factors in the outcome of chlorpromazine treatment: Testing a model. *Psychological Medicine*, *10*, 335–343.

Koyama, T., Koenig, J. I., Meltzer, H. Y., & Gudelsky, G. A. (1985). Lithium enhances the activity of tuberoinfundibular and tuberohypophyseal dopaminergic neurons. *Society for Neuroscience*, *11*, 658.

Krulich, L. (1982). Neurotransmitter control of thyrotropin secretion. *Neuroendocrinology*, *35*, 139–147.

Laakman, G., Chuang, I., Gugath, M., Ortner, M., Schmauss, M., & Wittmann, M. (1983). Prolactin and antidepressants. In G. Tolis (Ed.), *Prolactin and prolactinomas* (pp. 151–161). New York: Raven Press.

Laakman, G., Gugath, M., Kuss, H.-J., & Zygan, K. (1984). Comparison of growth hormone and prolactin stimulation induced by chlorimipramine and desimipramine in man in connection with chlorimipramine metabolism. *Psychopharmacology*, *82*, 62–67.

Laakman, G., Schoen, H. W., Blaschke, D., & Wittman, M. (1985). Dose-dependent growth hormone, prolactin and cortisol stimulation after i.v. administration of desimipramine in human subjects. *Psychoneuroendocrinology*, *10*, 83–93.

Laakman, G., Schumacher, G., & Beakert, O. (1977). Stimulation of growth hormone secretion by desimpramine and chlorimipramine in man. *Journal of Clinical Endocrinology and Metabolsim*, *44*, 1010–1013.

Laakman, G., Treusch, J., Schmauss, M., Schmitt, E., & Treusch, U. (1982). Comparison of growth hormone stimulation induced by desimipramine, diazepam, and metachlazepam in man. *Psychoneuroendocrinology*, *7*, 141–146.

Laakman, G., Wittman, M., Gugath, M., Mueller, O. A., Treusch, J., Wahlster, U., & Stella, G. K. (1984). Effects of psychotropic drugs (desimipramine, chlorimipramine, sulpiride, diazepam) on the human HPA axis. *Psychopharmacology*, *84*, 66–70.

Laakso, M. L., & Oja, S. S. (1979). Transport of tryptophan and tyrosine in rat brain slices in the presence of lithium. *Neurochemical Research*, *4*, 411–423.

Lal, S., Nair, N. P. V., & Guyda, H. (1978). Effect of lithium on hypothalamic pituitary dopaminergic function. *Acta Psychiatrica Scandinavica*, *57*, 91–96.

Langer, G., Sachar, E. J., Gruen, P. H., & Halpern, F. S. (1977). Human prolactin response to neuroleptic drugs correlate with antischizophrenic potency. *Nature* (*London*), *266*, 639–640.

Langer, G., Sachar, E. J., Nathan, R. S., Tabrizi, M. A.,

Perel, J. M., & Halpern, F. S. (1979). Dopaminergic factors in human prolactin regulation: A pituitary model for the study of the neuroendocrine system in man. *Psychopharmacology*, *65*, 161–164.

Laughren, T. P., Brown, W. A., & Williams, B. W. (1979). Serum prolactin and clinical state during neuroleptic treatment and withdrawal. *American Journal of Psychiatry*, *136*, 108–110.

Lauridsen, U. B., Kirkegaard, C., & Nerup, J. (1974). Lithium and the pituitary thyroid axis in normal subjects. *Journal of Clinical Endocrinology and Metabolism*, *39*, 383–385.

Lauritsen, K. B., Heltberg, J., Hornum, I., & Rehfeld, J. F. (1978). Lithium inhibits basal and food-stimulated gastrin secretion. *Gastroenterology*, *75*, 59–60.

Lazarus, J. H., John, R., Bennie, E. H., Chalmers, R. J., & Crockett, G. (1981). Lithium therapy and thyroid function: A long-term study. *Psychological Medicine*, *11*, 85–92.

Lindholm, H., Gullberg, B., Ohman, A., & Sedvall, G. (1978). Effects of perphenazine enanthate injections on prolactin levels in plasma from schizophrenic women and men. *Psychopharmacology*, *57*, 1–4.

Lisansky, J., Fava, G. A., Buckman, M. T., Kellner, R. Fava, M., Zielezny, M., & Peake, G. T. (1984). Prolactin, amitriptyline and recovery from depression. *Psychopharmacology*, *84*, 331–335.

Loosen, P. T., & Prange, A. J., Jr. (1982). Serum thyrotropin response to thryotropin-releasing hormone in psychiatric patients: A review. *American Journal of Psychology*, *139*, 406–416.

MacIndoe, J. H., & Turkington, R. W. (1973). Stimulation of human prolactin secretion by intravenous infusion of L-tryptophan. *Journal of Clinical Investigation*, *52*, 1972–1978.

MacLeod, R. M. (1976). Regulation of prolactin secretion. In L. Martini & W. F. Ganong (Eds.), *Frontiers in neuroendocrinology* (vol. 4, pp. 169–194). New York: Raven Press.

Maggi, A., & Enna, S. J. (1980). Regional alterations in rat brain neurotransmitter systems following chronic lithium treatment. *Journal of Neurochemistry*, *34*, 888–892.

Martin-Du Pan, R., Baumann, P., Magrini, G., & Felber, J.-P. (1979). Neuroendocrine effects of chronic neuroleptic therapy in male psychiatric patients. *Psychoneuroendocrinology*, *3*, 245–252.

Masala, A., Alagra, S., Devilla, L., Delitala, G., & Rovasio, P. P. (1980). Inhibition of prolactin secretion by nomifensine in man. *Clinical Endocrinology* (*Oxford*), *12*, 237–241.

Matussek, N., Ackenheil, M., Hippius, J., Mueller, F., Schroder, H.-T., Schultes, H., & Wasilewski, B. (1980). Effect of clonidine on growth hormone release in psychiatric patients and controls. *Psychiatry Research*, *2*, 25–36.

Matussek, N., & Laakman, G. (1981). Growth hormone response in patients with depression. *Acta Psychiatrica Scandinavica*, *63* (Suppl. 290), 122.

McCreadie, R. G., Mackie, M., Wiles, D. H., Jorgensen, A., Hausen, V., & Menzies, C. (1984). Within-individual variation in steady-state plasma levels of different neuroleptics and prolactin. *British Journal of Psychiatry*, *144*, 625–629.

McEachron, D. L., Kripke, D. F., Hawkins, R., Hans, E., Pavilnac, D., & Deftos, L. (1982). Lithium delays biochemical circadian rhythms in rats. *Neuropsychobiology, 8*, 12–29.

McIntyre, I. M., Kuhn, C., Demitriou, S., Fucek, F. R., & Stanley, M. (1983). Modulating role of lithium on dopamine turnover, prolactin release, and behavior supersensitivity following haloperidol and reserpine. *Psychopharmacology, 81*, 150–154.

Meco, G., Falaschi, P., Cassachia, M., Rocco, A., Petrini, P., Rosa, M., & Agnoli, A. (1985). Neuroendocrine effects of haloperidol decanoate in patients with chronic schizophrenia. In D. Kemali & G. Raeagni (Eds.), *Chronic treatments in neuropsychiatry* (pp. 89–93). New York: Raven Press.

Meltzer, H. Y. (1985). Long-term effects of neuroleptic drugs on the neuroendocrine system. In D. Kemali & G. Racagni (Eds.), *Chronic treatments in neuropsychiatry* (pp. 59–68). New York: Raven Press.

Meltzer, H. Y., & Busch, D. (1983). Serum prolactin response to two doses of intramuscular chlorpromazine and oral chlorpromazine and psychopathology in schizophrenics: Implications for the dopamine hypothesis. *Psychiatry Research, 9*, 285–299.

Meltzer, H. Y., Busch, D. A., Creese, I. R., Snyder, S. H., & Fang, V. S. (1981). Effect of intramuscular chlorpromazine on serum prolactin levels in schizophrenic patients and normal controls. *Psychiatry Research, 5*, 95–105.

Meltzer, H. Y., Busch, D., So, R., Holcomb, H., & Fang, V. S. (1980). Neuroleptic-induced elevations in serum prolactin levels: Etiology and significance. In C. Baxter & T. Melnechuk (Eds.), *Perspectives in schizophrenia research* (pp. 149–176). New York: Raven Press.

Meltzer, H. Y., & Fang, V. S. (1976). The effect of neuroleptics on serum prolactin levels in schizophrenic patients. *Archives of General Psychiatry, 33*, 279–286.

Meltzer, H. Y., Fang, V. S., Tricou, B. J., & Robertson, A. (1982). Effect of antidepressants on neuroendocrine axis in humans. In E. Costa & G. Racagni (Eds.), *Typical and atypical antidepressants* (pp. 303–316). New York: Raven Press.

Meltzer, H. Y., Goode, D. J., & Fang, V. S. (1978). The effect of psychotropic drugs on endocrine function. I. Neuroleptics, precursors and agonists. In M. A. Lipton, A. DiMascio, & Killam (Eds.), *Psychopharmacology: A generation of progress* (pp. 509–529). New York: Raven Press.

Meltzer, H. Y., Goode, D. J., Schyve, P. M., Young, M., & Fang, V. S. (1979). Effect of clozapine on human serum prolactin levels. *American Journal of Psychiatry, 136*, 1550–1555.

Meltzer, H. Y., Kane, J. M., & Kolakowska, T. (1983). Plasma levels of neuroleptics, prolactin levels, and clinical response. In J. T. Coyle & S. J. Enna (Eds.), *Neuroleptics: Neurochemical, behavioral and clinical perspective* (pp. 255–279). New York: Raven Press.

Meltzer, H. Y., Kolakowska, T., Fang, V. S., Fogg, L., Robertson, A., Lewine, R., Strahilevitz, M., & Busch, D. (1984). Growth hormone and prolactin response to apomorphine in schizophrenia and the major affective disorders: Relation to duration of illness and depressive symptomatology. *Archives of General Psychiatry, 41*, 512–519.

Meltzer, H. Y., Lowy, M., Robertson, A., Goodnick, P., & Perline, R. (1984). Effect of 5-hydroxytryptophan on serum cortisol levels in major affective disorders. III. Effect of antidepressants and lithium carbonate. *Archives of General Psychiatry, 41*, 391–397.

Meltzer, H. Y., Paul, S. M., & Fang, V. S. (1977). Effect of flupenthixol and butaclamol isomers on prolactin secretion in rats. *Psychopharmacology, 51*, 181–188.

Meltzer, H. Y., Simonovic, M., & So, R. (1983). Effects of a series of substituted benzamides on rat prolactin secretion and [³H]spiperone binding to bovine anterior pituitary membranes. *Life Sciences, 32*, 2877–2886.

Meltzer, H. Y., Simonovic, M., Sturgeon, D., & Fang, V. S. (1981). Effect of antidepressants, lithium, and electroconvulsive treatment on rat serum prolactin levels. *Acta Psychiatrica Scandinavica, 63*, (Suppl. 290), 100–121.

Meltzer, H. Y., & Stahl, S. (1976). The dopamine hypothesis: A review. *Schizophrenia Bulletin, 2*, 19–76.

Meltzer, H. Y., Umberkoman-Wiita, B., Robertson, A., Tricou, B., Lowy, M., & Perline, R. (1984). Effect of 5-hydroxytryptophan on serum cortisol levels in major affective disorders. I. Enhanced response in depression and mania. *Archives of General Psychiatry, 41*, 366–374.

Meltzer, H. Y., Wiita, B., Tricou, B. J., Simonovic, B., & Fang, V. S. (1982). Effect of serotonin precursors and serotonin agonists on plasma hormone levels. *Advances in Biological Psychiatry, 34*, 117–140.

Melzacka, M., Boksa, J., & Maj, J. (1979). 1-(m-Chlorophenyl)-piperazine: A metabolite of trazodone isolated from rat urine. *Journal of Pharmacy and Pharmacology, 3*, 855–856.

Mendelewicz, H., & Youdim, M. B. H. (1977). Monoamine oxidase inhibitors and prolactin secretion. *Lancet, 2*, 507.

Miller, D. D., Dubovsky, S. L., McDonald, K. M., Katz, F. H., Robertson, G. L., & Schrier, R. W. (1979). Central, renal and adrenal effects of lithium in man. *American Journal of Medicine, 66*, 797–803.

Morgan, D. B., Penney, M. D., Hullin, R. P., Thomas, T. H., & Srinivasan, D. P. (1982). The responses to water deprivation in lithium-treated patients with and without polyuria. *Clinical Science, 63*, 539–554.

Muehlbauer, H. D. (1984). The influence of fenfluramine stimulation on prolactin plasma levels in lithium long-term treated manic–depressive patients and healthy subjects. *Pharmacopsychiatrie, 17*, 191–193.

Muehlbauer, H. D., & Mueller-Oerlinghausen, B. (1985). Fenfluramine stimulation of serum cortisol in patients with major affective disorders and healthy controls: Further evidence for a central serotonergic action of lithium in man. *Journal of Neural Transmission, 61*, 81–94.

Mueller-Oerlinghausen, B., Passoth, P. M., Poser, W., & Schlecht, W. (1978). Influence of long-term treatment with major tranquilizers or lithium salts on carbohydrate metabolism. *Arzneimittel-Forschung, 28* (9), 1522–1524.

Müller, E. E., Fregnan, G. B., Chieli, T., Cocchi, T., Frigerio, C., & Locatelli, V. (1980). Effects of neuroleptics on neuroendocrine mechanisms for gonadotropin secretion. *Advances in Biochemical Psychopharmacology, 24*, 387–397.

Müller, E. E., Genazzani, A. R., & Murru, S. (1978). Nomifensine: Diagnostic test in hyperprolactinemic states. *Journal of Clinical Endocrinology and Metabolism, 47,* 1352–1357.

Naber, D., Albus, M., Burke, H., Muller-Spahn, F., Munch, U., Reinertshofer, T., Wissmann, J., & Ackenheil, M. (1985). Neuroleptic withdrawal in chronic schizophrenia: CT and endocrine variables relating to psychopathology. *Psychiatry Research, 16,* 207–219.

Naber, D., Finkbeiner, B., Zander, K.-J., & Ackenheil, M. (1980). Effect of long-term neuroleptic treatment on prolactin and norepinephrine levels in serum of chronic schizophrenics: Relation to psychopathology and extrapyramidal symptoms. *Neuropsychobiology, 6,* 181–189.

Naber, D., Steinbock, H., & Greil, W. (1980). Effects of short- and long-term neuroleptic treatment on thyroid function. *Progress in Neuropsychopharmacology, 4,* 199–206.

Nathan, S. R., Sachar, E. J., Langer, G., Tabrizi, M. A., & Halpern, F. S. (1979). Diurnal variation in the response of plasma prolactin, cortisol, and growth hormone to insulin hypoglycemia in normal men. *Journal of Clinical Endocrinology and Metabolism, 49,* 231–235.

Nemeroff, C. B., Widerov, E., Bissette, G., Walleus, H., Karlsson, I., Eklund, K., Loosen, P. T., & Vale, W. (1985). Elevated concentrations of CSF corticotropin-releasing factor-like immunoreactivity in depressed patients. *Science, 226,* 1342–1344.

Nielsen, J. L., Amidsen, A., Darleng, S., & Pedersen, E. B. (1977). Plasma prolactin during lithium treatment. *Neuropsychobiology, 3,* 30–34.

Nikitopoulou, G., Thorner, M., Crammer, J., & Lader, M. (1977). Prolactin and psychophysiological measures after single doses of thioridazine. *Clinical Pharmacology and Therapeutics, 21,* 422–429.

Noyes, R., Ringdahl, I. C., & Andresen, N. J. C. (1971). Effect of lithium citrate on adrenocortical activity in manic–depressive illness. *Comparative Psychology, 12,* 337–347.

Ohman, R., & Axelsson, R. (1978). Relationship between prolactin response and antipsychotic effect of thioridazine in psychiatric patients. *European Journal of Clinical Pharmacology, 14,* 111–116.

Penny, M. D., Hullin, R. P., Srinivasan, D. P., & Morgan, D. B. (1982). The relationship between plasma lithium and the renal responsiveness to arginine vasopressin in man. *Clinical Science, 61,* 793–795.

Pert, A., Rosenblatt, J. E., Civit, C., Pert, C. B., & Bunney, W. E. (1978). Long-term treatment with lithium prevents the development of dopamine receptor supersensitivity. *Science, 201,* 171–173.

Pilotte, N. S., & Porter, J. C. (1981). Dopamine in hypophysial portal plasma and prolactin in systemic plasma of rats treated with 5-hydroxytryptamine. *Endocrinology (Baltimore), 108,* 2137–2141.

Platman, S. R., & Fieve, R. R. (1968). Lithium carbonate and plasma cortisol response in affective disorders. *Archives of General Psychiatry, 18,* 591–594.

Poitou, P., & Bohuon, C. (1975). Catecholamine metabolism in the rat brain after short and long term lithium administration. *Journal of Neurochemistry, 25,* 535–537.

Pontiroli, A. E., Gala, R. R., Pellicciotta, G., De Pasqua, A. D., Girardi, A. M., & Pozza, G. (1979). Studies on the reproducibility of human prolactin response to sulpiride, benserazide, insulin hypoglycemia, and arginine infusion. *Acta Endocrinologica (Copenhagen), 91,* 410–420.

Potter, W. Z., Calil, H. M., Extein, I., Gold, P. W., Wehr, T. A., & Goodwin, F. K. (1981). Specific norepinephrine and serotonin uptake inhibitors in man: A crossover study with pharmacokinetic, biochemical, neuroendocrine, and behavioral parameters. *Acta Psychiatrica Scandinavica, 63,* 152–162.

Ravichandran, G. K., Lu, R.-B., Shvartsbind, A., Misra, C. H., Ho, B. T., Kahn, M., & Smith, R. C. (1984). Prolactin response to single and multiple doses fo haloperidol in schizophrenic patients. *Psychiatry Research, 11,* 61–70.

Reches, A., Wagner, H. R., Jackson, V., & Fahn, S. (1982). Chronic lithium administration has no effect on haloperidol-induced supersensitivity of pre- and postsynaptic dopamine receptors in rat brain. *Brain Research, 246,* 172–177.

Rickels, K., Case, W. G., Werblosky, J., Csanalosi, I., Schless, A., & Weise, C. C. (1981). Amoxapine and imipramine in the treatment of depressed outpatients: A controlled study. *American Journal of Psychiatry, 138,* 20–24.

Risch, S. C. (1982). β-Endorphin hypersecretion in depression: Possible cholinergic mechanisms. *Biological Psychiatry, 17,* 1071–1079.

Robertson, A. G., Berry, R., & Meltzer, H. Y. (1982). Prolactin-stimulating effect of amoxapine and loxapine in psychiatric patients. *Psychopharmacology, 78,* 287–292.

Roccatagliata, G., DeCecco, L., Rossato, P., & Albano, C. (1979). Trazodone intravenously administered and plasma prolactin levels. *International Pharmacopsychiatry, 14,* 260–263.

Rolandi, E., Magnani, G., Milesi, G. M., & Barreca, T. (1981). Effect of a psychoactive drug, trazodone, on prolactin secretion in man. *Neuropsychobiology, 7,* 17–19.

Rosenblatt, J. E., Pert, C. B., Tallman, J. F., Pert, A., & Bunney, W. E. (1979). The effect of imipramine and lithium on α- and β-receptor binding in rat brain. *Brain Research, 160,* 186–191.

Rubin, R. T., & Hays, S. E. (1979). Variability of prolactin response to intravenous and intramuscular haloperidol in normal adult men. *Psychopharmacology, 61,* 17–24.

Rubin, R. T., Poland, R. E., O'Connor, D., Gorwin, P. R., & Tower, B. B. (1976). Selective neuroendocrine effects of low-dose haloperidol in normal adult men. *Psychopharmacology, 47,* 135–140.

Sachar, E. J., Gruen, P. H., Altman, N., Halpern, F. S., & Frantz, A. G. (1976). Use of neuroendocrine techniques in psychopharmacological research. In E. J. Sachar (Ed.), *Hormones, behavior and psychopathology* (pp. 161–176). New York: Raven Press.

Sancez, R. S., Murthy, G, G., Mehta, J., Shreeve, W. W., & Singh, F. R. (1976). Pituitary–testicular axis in patients on lithium therapy. *Fertility and Sterility, 27,* 667–669.

Sangdee, C., & Franz, D. C. (1980). Lithium enhancement of central 5-HT transmission induced by 5-HT precursors. *Biological Psychiatry, 15*, 59–75.

Sawa, Y., Odo, S., & Nakazawa, T. (1982). Growth hormone secretion by tricyclic and nontricyclic antidepressants in healthy volunteers and depressives. *Advances in the Biosciences, 40*, 309–315.

Schwartz, M. F., Bauman, J. E., & Masters, W. H. (1982). Hyperprolactinemia and sexual disorders in men. *Biological Psychiatry, 17*, 861–876.

Schwinn, G., Muhlen, A., Kobberling, J., Halves, E., Wenzel, K. W., & Meinhold, H. (1975). Plasma prolactin levels after TRH and chlorpromazine in normal subjects and patients with impaired pituitary function. *Acta Endocrinologica (Copenhagen), 79*, 663–676.

Schyve, P. M., Smithline, F., & Meltzer, H. Y. (1978). Neuroleptic-induced prolactin level elevations and breast cancer. *Archives of General Psychiatry, 35*, 1291–1301.

Selmanoff, M. (1985). Rapid effects of hyperprolactinemia on basal prolactin secretion and dopamine turnover in the medial and lateral median eminence. *Endocrinology (Baltimore), 116*, 1943–1952.

Shader, R. I. (1970a). Male sexual function. In R. I. Shader & A. DiMascio (Eds.), *Psychotropic drug side effects* (pp. 63–71). Baltimore: Williams & Wilkins.

Shader, R. I. (1970b). Pregnancy and pyschotropic drugs. R. I. Shader & A. DiMascio (Eds.), *Psychotropic drug side effects* (pp. 206–213). Baltimore: Williams & Wilkins.

Shopsin, B., Sathananthari, G. L., & Gershon, S. (1973). Plasma renin response to lithium in psychiatric patients. *Clinical Pharmacology and Therapeutics, 14*, 561–564.

Siever, L. J., Uhde, T. W., Insel, T. R., Roy, B. F., & Murphy, D. L. (1982). Growth hormone response to clonidine unchanged by chronic clorgyline treatment. *Psychiatry Research, 7*, 139–144.

Siever, L. J., Uhde, T. W., Silberman, E. K., Jimerson, D. C., Aloi, J. A., Post, R. M., & Murphy, D. L. (1982). The growth hormone response to clonidine as a probe of noradrenergic receptor responsiveness in affective disorder patients and controls. *Psychiatry Research, 6*, 171–176.

Siris, S. G., Siris, E. S., van Kammen, D. P., Doeherty, J. B., Alexander, P. E., & Bunney, W. E., Jr. (1980). Effect of dopamine blockade on gonadotropins and testosterone in men. *American Journal of Psychiatry, 137*, 211–215.

Siris, S. G., van Kammen, D. P., & De Fraites, E. G. (1978). Serum prolactin and antipsychotic responses to pimozide in schizophrenia. *Psychopharmacology Bulletin, 14*, 11–14.

Sklar, A. H., & Schrier, R. W. (1983). Central nervous system mediators of vasopressin release. *Physiological Reviews, 63*, 1243–1280.

Slater, S., de la Vega, C. E., Skyler, J., & Murphy, D. L. (1976). Plasma prolactin stimulation by fenfluramine and amphetamine. *Psychopharmacology Bulletin, 12*, 26–27.

Slater, S., Shiling, D. J., Lipper, S., & Murphy, D. L. (1977). Elevation of plasma prolactin by monoamine oxidase inhibitors. *Lancet, 2*, 275–276.

Smigan, L., & Perris, C. (1984). Cortisol changes in long--term lithium therapy. *Neuropsychobiology, 11*, 219–223.

Smigan, L., Wahlin, A., Jacobsson, L., & von Knorring, L. (1984). Lithium therapy and thyroid function tests. A prospective study. *Neuropsychobiology, 11*, 39–43.

Smith, C. B., Garcia-Sevilla, J. A., & Hollingsworth, P. J. (1981). α_2-Adrenoreceptors in rat brain are decreased after long-term tricyclic antidepressant drug treatment. *Brain Research, 210*, 413–418.

Smith, R. C., Baumgartner, R., Misra, C. H., Mauldin, M., Shvartsburd, A., Ho, B. T., & DeJohn, C. (1984). Haloperidol: Plasma levels and prolactin response as predictors of clinical improvement in schizophrenia: Chemical vs. radioreceptor plasma level assays. *Archives of General Psychiatry, 41*, 1044–1049.

Smythe, C. A., Brandstater, J. F., & Lazarus, L. (1979). Acute effects of lithium on central dopamine and serotonin activity reflected by inhibition of prolactin and growth hormone secretion in the rat. *Australian Journal of Biological Science, 32*, 329–334.

Staunton, D. A., Magistretti, P. J., Shoemaker, W. J., Deyo, S. N., & Bloom, F. E. (1982). Effects of chronic lithium treatment on dopamine receptors in the rat corpus striatum. II. No effect on denervation of neuroleptic-induced supersensitivity. *Brain Research, 232*, 401–412.

Stern, W. C., Rogers, J., Fang, V., & Meltzer, H. (1979). Influence of bupropion HCl (Wellbatrin), a novel antidepressant, on plasma levels of prolactin and growth hormone in man and rat. *Life Sciences, 25*, 1717–1724.

Streeten, D. H. D., Anderson, G. H., Dalakos, T. G., Seeley, T., Mallov, J. S., Eusebio, R., Sunderlin, F. S., Badawy, S. Z. A., & King, R. B. (1984). Normal and abnormal function of the hypothalamic–pituitary–adrenocortical system in man. *Endocrine Reviews, 5*, 371–394.

Strolin Benedetti, M., Eschalier, A., Lesage, A., Dordain, G, Rovei, V., Zarifian, E., & Dostert, P. (1984). Effect of a reversible and selective MAO-A inhibitor (cimoxatone) on diurnal variations in plasma prolactin level in man. *European Journal of Clinical Pharmacology, 26*, 71–77.

Syvalahti, E., Eneroth, P. R., & Ross, S. B. (1979). Acute effects of zimelidine and alaproclate, two inhibitors of serotonin uptake on neuroendocrine function. *Psychiatry Research, 1*, 110–120.

Takahashi, S., Kondo, H., Yoshimura, M., & Ochi, Y. (1975). Thyroid function levels and thyrotropin responses to TRH administration in manic patients receiving lithium carbonate. *Folia Psychiatrica et Neurologica Japonica, 29*, 231–237.

Tamminga, C. A., Smith, R. C., Pandey, G., Frohman, L. A., & Davis, J. M. (1977). A neuroendocrine study of supersensitivity in tardive dyskinesia. *Archives of General Psychiatry, 36*, 1199–1203.

Tanimoto, K., Maeda, K., & Chihara, K. (1981). Inhibition by lithium of dopamine receptors in rat prolactin release. *Brain Research, 223*, 335–342.

Tanimoto, K., Maeda, K., Yamaguchi, N., Chihara, K., & Fujita, T. (1981). Effect of lithium on prolactin responses to thyrotropin-releasing hormone in patients with manic state. *Psychopharmacology, 72*, 129–133.

Thorner, M. D. (1977). Prolactin: Clinical physiology and hyperprolactinemia. In L. Martini & G. M. Besser (Eds.), *Clinical neuroendocrinology* (pp. 319–366). New York: Academic Press.

Tolis, G., & Frank, S. (1979). Physiology and pathology of prolactin secretion. In G. Tolis, F. Labrie, J. B. Martin, & F. Naftolin (Eds.), *Clinical neuroleondocrinology: A pathophysiological approach* (pp. 291–317). New York: Raven Press.

Transbol, I., Christiansen, C., & Baastrup, P. C. (1978). Endocrine effects of lithium. I. Hypothyroidism, its prevalence in long-term treated patients. *Acta Endocrinologica (Copenhagen)*, *87*, 759–767.

Treiser, S. L., & Kellar, K. J. (1979). Lithium effects on adrenergic receptor supersensitivity in rat brain. *European Journal of Pharmacology*, *58*, 85–86.

Treiser, S. L., & Kellar, K. J. (1980). Lithium: effects on serotonin receptors in rat brain. *European Journal of Pharmacology*, *64*, 183–185.

Treiser, S. L., Cascio, C. S., O'Donohue, T. L, Thoa, N. B., Jacobowitz, D. M., & Kellar, K. J. (1981). Lithium increases serotonin release and decreases serotonin receptors in the hippocampus. *Science*, *213*, 1529–1531.

Tripodiankis, J., Markianos, M., & Garelis, E. (1983). Neurochemical studies on tardive dyskinesia. I. Urinary homovanillic acid and plasma prolactin. *Biological Psychiatry*, *18*, 337–345.

Van de Kar, L. D., & Bethea, C. L. (1982). Pharmacological evidence that serotonergic stimulation of prolactin secretion is mediated via the dorsal raphe nucleus. *Neuroendocrinology*, *35*, 225–230.

Widerlov, E., Wide, L., & Sjöstrom, R. (1978). Effects of tricyclic antidepressants on human plasma levels of TSH, GH, and prolactin. *Acta Psychiatrica Scandinavica*, *58*, 449–456.

Wiles, D. H., Kolakowska, T., McNeilly, A. S., Mandelbrote, B. M., & Gelder, P. U. (1976). Clinical significance of plasma chlorpromazine levels. I. Plasma levels of the drug, some of its metabolities, and prolactin during acute treatment. *Psychological Medicine*, *6*, 407–415.

Wistedt, B., Wiles, D., & Kolakowska, T. (1981). Slow decline of plasma drug and prolactin levels after discontinuation of chronic treatment with depot neuroleptics. *Lancet*, *1*, 1163.

Yamaguchi, N., Tanimoto, K., & Kuromaru, S. (1980). Growth hormone (GH) release following thyrotropin-releasing hormone (TRH) injection in manic patients receiving lithium carbonate. *Psychoneuroendocrinology*, *5*, 253–259.

Yoshikawa, K., & Hong, J.-S. (1983). The enkephalin system in the rat anterior pituitary: Regulation by gonadal steroid hormones and psychotropic drugs. *Endocrinology (Baltimore)*, *113*, 1218–1227.

Zatz, M., & Reisine, T. D. (1985). Lithium induces corticotropi in secretion and desensitization in cultured anterior pituitary cells. *Proceedings of the National Academy of Sciences of the U.S.A.*, *82*, 1286–1290.

13 MONOAMINE PRECURSORS

C. Z. LEMUS

H. M. van PRAAG

Albert Einstein College of Medicine/Montefiore Medical Center

PHYSIOLOGY OF MONOAMINERGIC SYSTEMS

With the increased interest in the biological aspects of psychiatric disorders in the past two decades, there has been an attempt to integrate knowledge from other areas of medicine into our understanding of these illnesses. For many years it has been well known that many endocrine disturbances are accompanied by psychiatric manifestations. The awareness that drugs such as neuroleptics, which affect monoamines (MA), also influence the secretion of certain hormones, and the fact that dysregulation of hormonal secretion exists in certain psychiatric disorders prompted researchers to investigate the interaction between MA and hormones and their possible pathogenetic significance.

The principal MA in the brain are serotonin (5-hydroxytryptamine, 5-HT), noradrenaline (NA), and dopamine (DA). 5-HT derives from the amino acid tryptophan, while the other two are synthesized from tyrosine. The synthesis of a certain MA will depend on, among other things, the brain level of its precursor and the activity of its rate-limiting enzyme.

Only about 1–2% of the 5-HT in the whole body is found in the brain. The synthesis of 5-HT begins with the uptake of tryptophan from plasma into the central nervous system (CNS). This is an active uptake process, and there is competition for this uptake mechanism from other amino acids, namely, tyrosine, phenylalanine, leucine, isoleucine, and valine. Therefore, the amount of tryptophan available in the brain for conversion into 5-HT depends not only on the plasma level of tryptophan, but also on the ratio of tryptophan to the plasma level of the other five competing amino acids (Wurtman, 1982). After gaining entry into the cell, tryptophan is hydroxylated at the 5 position to form 5-hydroxytryptophan (5-HTP). This reaction is catalyzed by the rate-limiting enzyme tryptophan hydoxylase. Subsequently, 5-HTP is decarboxylated by the enzyme aromatic amino acid decarboxylase to yield 5-HT (Figure 13.1).

The biosynthesis of NA and DA originate from a common substance, tyrosine. The hydroxylation of tyrosine by the enzyme tyrosine hydroxylase yields dopa which, in turn, is decarboxylated by the enzyme aromatic amino acid decarboxylase to produce DA. The enzyme dopamine-β-oxidase acts on DA to produce NA. Tyrosine hydroxylase is the rate-limiting step in the synthesis of these MA (Figure 13.2).

The MA function as neurotransmitters and the cell bodies of MAergic neurons are localized within discrete groups of nerve cells (for review, see Cooper, Bloom, & Roth, 1978). The 5-HT-containing neurons are localized near the raphe regions of the pons and upper brain stem. They consist of nine groups of cells of which the more caudal groups send

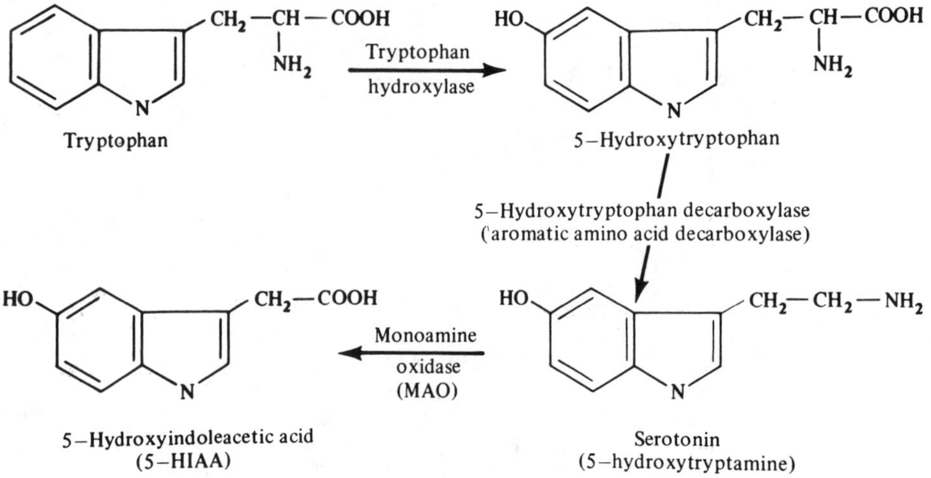

FIGURE 13.1. Metabolic pathway for the synthesis of serotonin. Tryptophan hydroxylase is the rate-limiting enzyme (Snyder, 1980).

projections to the medulla and spinal cord, while the more rostral groups innervate the telencephalon and diencephalon.

The NAergic cell bodies are mostly localized in the locus coeruleus, with some neurons found throughout the lateral ventral tegmental fields. There are five major NAergic tracts which stem from the locus coeruleus: (1) a central tegmental tract; (2) a ventral tegmental–medial forebrain bundle tract; (3) a central gray dorsal longitudinal fasciculus tract; (4) a tract which ascends in the superior cerebellar peduncle and innervates the cerebellar cortex; and (5) a tract

which descends into the mesencephalon and spinal cord. The first three tracts innervate thalamic and hypothalamic nuclei.

The DAergic system can be divided into three distinct parts:

1. The nigrostriatal system, whose cell bodies are localized in the compact zone of the substantia nigra while the fibers ascend to the caudate nucleus and the putamen. This system is involved in the extrapyramidal regulation of motor activity.
2. The mesolimbic and mesocortical system, with cell bodies in the ventral tegmental

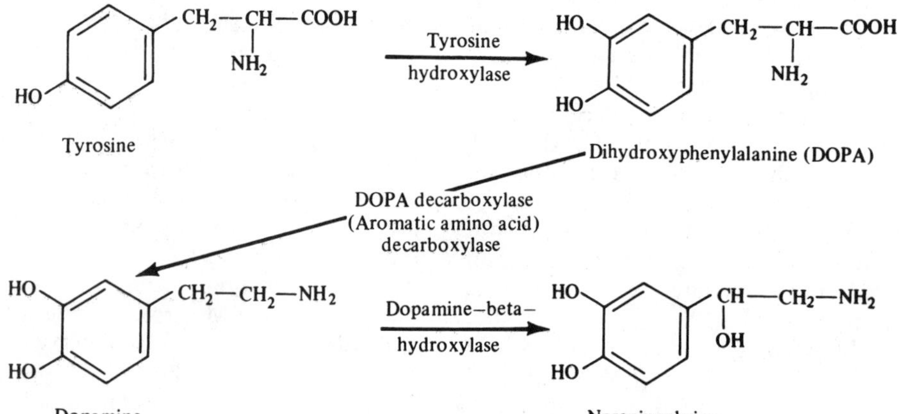

FIGURE 13.2. Metabolic pathway for the synthesis of the catecholamines dopamine and norepinephrine. Tyrosine hydroxylase is the rate-limiting enzyme (Snyder, 1980).

area and the fibers extending to certain nuclei of the limbic system (e.g., the nucleus accumbens and the olfactory bulb) and to the cerebral cortex. This system may be part of the cerebral system involved in mood and impulse regulation.

3. The tuberoinfundibular system, with cell bodies in the arcuate and paraventricular nuclei and fibers extending to the medial eminence. This system regulates the release of certain anterior pituitary hormones via the inhibiting and releasing factors in the hypothalamus.

The ascending MAergic pathways which originate in the midbrain and limbic system have been implicated in the regulation of mood. These same pathways seem to control the activity of hypothalamic nuclei which in turn control the secretion of anterior pituitary hormones. The neuroendocrine strategy affords a powerful means of looking indirectly at the activity of MAergic systems by measuring hormone levels in the peripheral circulation. This strategy has been used in two ways: (1) measuring hormone levels per se, and (2) measuring hormone levels after the manipulation of MA, either by increasing or decreasing their concentration or activity. The infusion of MA precursors has been used as a means to functionally up-regulate MAergic innervation, though another theory claims that increased MA availability leads to down-regulation of postsynaptic receptors and ultimately to diminished neuronal activity.

We will review studies that have used the latter strategy, administering MA precursors and subsequently measuring hormone levels in normal controls and psychiatric subjects. When analyzing the results of these studies, the concomitant administration of a peripheral decarboxylase inhibitor (PDI) such as carbidopa is an important factor to be considered. The administration of a PDI decreases the decarboxylation in peripheral tissues of the three aromatic amino acids (phenylalanine, 5-HTP, and histidine) and of dopa (Cooper et al., 1978), which in turn increases their bioavailability in the CNS (Mars, 1973).

EFFECT OF MONOAMINE PRECURSOR ADMINISTRATION ON CENTRAL MONOAMINE AVAILABILITY

The MA precursors tryptophan and tyrosine are available to the organism as food constituents present in a normal diet. Their effect on neurotransmitter synthesis is dependent on two conditions: (1) Brain levels of the precursor are subject to change, and (2) the rate-limiting enzyme in the synthesis of the neurotransmitter must not be saturated with substrate. Thus, an increase in the amount of available precursor would affect the rate of synthesis of the neurotransmitter. These two conditions are met in the case of the MA precursors.

In the 5-HTergic system, tryptophan hydroxylase is not normally saturated with tryptophan in vivo. Tryptophan administration has been found to increase brain tryptophan and 5-HT levels as well as the concentration of its major metabolite, 5-hydroxyindoleacetic acid (5-HIAA) (Fernström & Wurtman, 1971). Since tryptophan hydroxylase is specifically localized in 5-HTergic neurons, the increase in brain 5-HT following tryptophan administration is found only in 5-HT nerve cells. This is not the case after administration of 5-HTP because the enzyme aromatic amino acid decarboxylase is not restricted to 5-HTergic neurons. Hence, 5-HTP may be transformed to 5-HT in catecholaminergic neurons where it could act as a false transmitter, decreasing the effectivity of catecholaminergic transmission (Fuxe, Butcher, & Engel, 1971). An increase in brain 5-HT levels is not sufficient to determine whether increased tryptophan availability has a central effect. It is also necessary to prove an increase in 5-HTergic neurotransmission. To this effect tryptophan administration has been proved to stimulate behavioral responses that are dependent on 5-HTergic neurons such as reduced sleep latency (Griffiths, Lester, & Coulter, 1972; Hartmann, Cravens, & List, 1974) and inhibition of aggressive behavior in mice (Thurmond, Kramarcy, Lasley, & Brown, 1980).

The rate-limiting enzyme in the synthesis of catecholamines (CA) is tyrosine hydroxylase. It is relatively specific for its amino acid substrate tyrosine. *In vivo*, tyrosine hydroxylase is 70–80% saturated with tyrosine, and thus it would seem that adding tyrosine would only increase synthesis of CA by 15–20%. This is the case when the nerve cells are in a resting state. On the other hand, administration of tyrosine when the neurons are activated, such as after haloperidol blockage of postsynaptic receptors (Scally, Ulus, & Wurtman, 1977), leads to marked increases in turnover and release of DA and NA (Wurtman, Larin, Mostafapour, & Fernström, 1974). Hence, the ability of tyrosine to accelerate CA synthesis depends quantitatively on the firing rate of CAergic neurons (Wurtman, Hefti, & Melamed, 1981). Through observations of phenomena known to be CA dependent, it has been confirmed that increased tyrosine availability influences CAergic neurotransmission. Administration of tyrosine to hypertensive rats produces a marked fall in blood pressure (Sved, Fernström, & Wurtman, 1979b), thought to be mediated through NA. Tyrosine injection has also been found to decrease serum prolactin levels in rats with activated tuberoinfundibular DA neurons (Sved, Fernström, & Wurtman, 1979a).

In summary, increasing the availability of tryptophan and tyrosine is an adequate means, not only of increasing synthesis of neurotransmitters at the central level, but also of augmenting 5-HTergic and CAergic neurotransmission.

MONOAMINES AND PITUITARY HORMONE SECRETION

The MA act as neurotransmitters at the hypothalamic level and control the release or inhibition of hormones that control hormone release from the anterior pituitary. By using pharmacological agents which interfere with MA synthesis or metabolism and concurrently measuring hormone levels, some conclusions can be made as to the effect of a MA on a particular hormone. The pharmacological agents used have included enzyme inhibitors, neurotransmitter depletors, and releasers, receptor blockers and uptake inhibitors (for review, see Frohman, 1980, and Müller, Nistico, & Scapagnini, 1977) (Figure 13.3).

An enzyme blocker inhibits the synthesis of a MA by interfering at the metabolic pathway level. For example, α-methylparatyrosine inhibits tyrosine hydroxylase, affecting the synthesis of CA. Compounds that inhibit DA β-hydroxylase, such as disulfiram and fusaric acid, block the conversion of DA to NA. The neurotransmitter depletors, such as reserpine, interfere with the storage of MA. Uptake inhibitors, such as imipramine and desipramine, block the uptake of MA by nerve terminals, thereby increasing their concentration at the receptor sites. MA releasers, such as amphetamine and methylamphetamine, stimulate the release of CA and also block their reuptake by nerve terminals. The receptor blockers function by blocking both pre- and postsynaptic receptors. They include α-adrenergic blockers (e.g., phentolamine), β-adrenergic blockers (e.g., propranolol), DAergic blockers (e.g., haloperidol), and 5-HTergic blockers (e.g., cyproheptadine).

We will briefly mention the effect of these pharmacological agents on hormonal secretion, keeping in mind that their actions are not as specific as we would like to believe. Hence, simple extrapolation from their hormonal effects to one particular MA is not warranted (Table 13.1).

Corticotropin (ACTH)

All three MA seem to play a role in the release of ACTH. While L-dopa has no effect on ACTH secretion in humans, amphetamine increases plasma ACTH levels. This response is prevented if one gives an α blocker. β blockers enhance the ACTH release that occurs subsequent to insulin hypoglycemia. 5-HT antagonists decrease the ACTH response to insulin hypoglycemia (Plonk, Bivens, & Feldman, 1974).

Growth Hormone (GH)

Administration of CA alone has no effect on GH secretion in humans. Given in combination with a β blocker, they produce an increase in GH levels, which is inhibited if one adds an α blocker (Blackard & Heidingsfelder, 1968). Therefore, CA act in conjunction with both α- and β-adrenergic receptors in the control of GH secretion. L-Dopa also

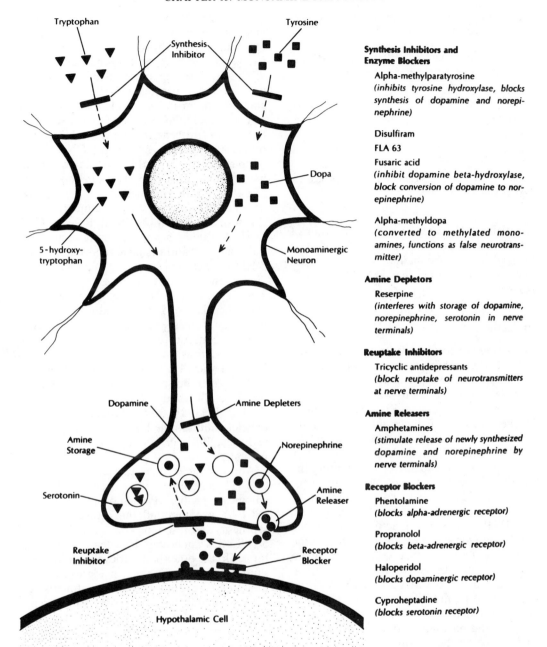

Tryptophan

Tyrosine

Synthesis Inhibitor

Dopa

5-hydroxy-tryptophan

Monoaminergic Neuron

Dopamine

Amine Depleters

Amine Storage

Norepinephrine

Serotonin

Amine Releaser

Reuptake Inhibitor

Receptor Blocker

Hypothalamic Cell

Synthesis Inhibitors and Enzyme Blockers

Alpha-methylparatyrosine
(inhibits tyrosine hydroxylase, blocks synthesis of dopamine and norepinephrine)

Disulfiram
FLA 63
Fusaric acid
(inhibit dopamine beta-hydroxylase, block conversion of dopamine to norepinephrine)

Alpha-methyldopa
(converted to methylated monoamines, functions as false neurotransmitter)

Amine Depletors

Reserpine
(interferes with storage of dopamine, norepinephrine, serotonin in nerve terminals)

Reuptake Inhibitors

Tricyclic antidepressants
(block reuptake of neurotransmitters at nerve terminals)

Amine Releasers

Amphetamines
(stimulate release of newly synthesized dopamine and norepinephrine by nerve terminals)

Receptor Blockers

Phentolamine
(blocks alpha-adrenergic receptor)

Propranolol
(blocks beta-adrenergic receptor)

Haloperidol
(blocks dopaminergic receptor)

Cyproheptadine
(blocks serotonin receptor)

FIGURE 13.3. Mechanisms by which pharmacological agents interfere with the synthesis or metabolism of monoamines (Frohman, 1980).

TABLE 13.1. Effects of Monoamines on Pituitary Hormone Secretion

	GH	PRL	ACTH
Norepinephrine			
α-adrenergic	↑	—	↑
β-adrenergic	↓	—	↓
Dopamine	↑	↓	(↓)
Serotonin	↓	↑	↑

Note. ↑, stimulates; ↓, suppresses; −, no change; ( ), possible effect.

stimulates GH secretion. Administration of 5-HTP increases GH release: this effect is blocked by cyproheptadine, a 5-HT antagonist. Thus, it appears that DA, NA, and 5-HT stimulate the release of GH.

Prolactin

Prolactin secretion is believed to be under the control of an inhibiting factor (PIF). DA is known to suppress prolactin secretion, and there is still debate as to whether DA itself may be the postulated PIF. DA receptor blockers such as haloperidol cause an increase in prolactin secretion. L-Dopa decreases prolactin secretion by increasing DA levels and is also capable of overcoming the receptor blockade caused by certain neuroleptics. 5-HT seems to have a stimulatory effect on prolactin secretion. Administration of 5-HTP stimulates prolactin release, while 5-HT antagonists such as cyproheptadine block this response. NA seems to have no effect on prolactin secretion.

In conclusion, the MA are involved in the secretion of pituitary hormones by acting at the hypothalamic level on the so-called inhibiting and releasing hormones, although a direct effect at the hypophyseal level cannot be excluded.

SEROTONIN PRECURSOR STUDIES

The role of brain 5-HT in the pathogenesis of certain types of depression has been a subject of interest for the past 20 years. There is evidence to support the hypothesis that brain 5-HT is reduced in patients with depression. A thorough review of this subject is

beyond the scope of this chapter. We will mention certain studies that have attempted to validate this hypothesis. The research strategies used have been postmortem studies of central 5-HT metabolism in suicide victims, studies of peripheral 5-HT metabolism, and measurement of 5-HT metabolites in cerebrospinal fluid (CSF). After the administration of probenecid (which inhibits the transport of 5-HIAA from the CNS to the peripheral circulation), most investigators have found decreased 5-HIAA in about 40% of patients with vital depression (Post, Ballenger, & Goodwin, 1980; Walinder, Skott, Carlson, Nagy, & Roos, 1976). Baseline CSF 5-HIAA studies have been more controversial, but some authors have reported lowered 5-HIAA levels in a subgroup of patients with vital (endogenous) depression (Asberg, Traskman, & Thoren, 1976; Traskman, Asberg, Bertilsson, & Sjöstrand, 1981). Postmortem studies have found decreased 5-HIAA concentrations in the raphe nuclei of suicide victims (Lloyd, Farley, Deck, & Hornykiewicz, 1974), while studies of peripheral MA metaboism have reported decreased platelet 5-HT uptake (Meltzer, Arora, Baber, & Tricou, 1981) and reduced density of platelet imipramine-binding sites (Langer & Briley, 1981) in populations of depressed patients.

Another tactic used to examine the role of 5-HT in depression has been the pharmacological probe. Parachlorophenylalanine (PCPA), a compound that decreases 5-HT synthesis, and reserpine which lowers central 5-HT levels can both induce depressive symptoms. On the other hand, tricyclic antidepressants and monoamine oxidase (MAO) inhibitors are both effective treatments for depression and share the property of increasing the amount of 5-HT available at central postsynaptic receptors. Similarly, the 5-HT precursors L-tryptophan and 5-HTP have been found to have antidepressant effect when administered alone (van Praag, 1981, 1982) or in combination with other antidepressants (Glassman & Platman, 1969; Walinder et al., 1976). Selective 5-HT reuptake inhibitors such as zimelidine also have an antidepressant effect. There is still much debate as to the significance of these findings in the pathogenesis of depressive illness. Many have not been consistently replicated and some persist after abatement of the depression. Further research in this area is still very relevant.

The effect of 5-HT precursors on neuroendocrine parameters would seem to be yet another way of investigating the role of 5-HT in depression. To this end, there have been numerous studies attempting to determine the hormonal response to the administration of 5-HT precursors, both in normal subjects and in patients with affective disorders. The hormones that have been studied the most have been ACTH, cortisol, prolactin, and GH.

Hypothalamic–Pituitary–Adrenal (HPA) Axis

Several studies have looked at the effect of 5-HT precursors on the HPA axis in normal volunteers. Administration of L-tryptophan (10 g orally) to 11 healthy volunteers by Woolf and Lee (1977) produced a gradual but significant decrease in serum cortisol by 45 minutes, with return to baseline by 90 minutes. Pretreatment with tryptophan 15 minutes before the intravenous (iv) administration of insulin significantly blunted the peak ACTH and cortisol response to hypoglycemia.

Modlinger, Schonmuller, and Arora (1980) studied 11 normal volunteers who received tryptophan (10 g orally) and reported significant rises in cortisol and ACTH, with peak levels occurring at 90 minutes for both hormones.

Hyyppa, Jolma, Lura, Langvik, and Kytomaki (1979) gave two different oral doses of L-tryptophan (2 g or 100 mg/kg) at 8:30 A.M. or 11:30 A.M. to 5 healthy subjects. The studies were carried out in a randomized manner at intervals of several days. A decline of plasma cortisol was seen with the 2 g dose at 8:30 A.M. but neither dose of L-tryptophan was capable of reducing cortisol secretion at 11:30 A.M. Eight male volunteers studied by Imura, Nakai, and Yoshimi (1973) were given 150 mg of 5-HTP orally without a PDI after an overnight fast. Plasma ACTH and cortisol rose significantly.

The results of 5-HT precursor loading on cortisol secretion in depressed patients are equally confusing. Westenberg, van Praag, de Jong, and Thyssen (1982) administered both precursors on separate days to 14 depressed patients and 12 healthy volunteers. On one test day, subjects recieved 5 g of L-tryptophan orally. Five days later, the subjects received 200 mg 5-HTP orally after being premedicated for 3 days with carbidopa to increase the concentration of 5-HTP reaching the brain. There was no significant change in the release of cortisol either in the depressed patients or in the controls.

Meltzer (1984) disputed these findings. He reported that the administration of 200 mg orally of D,L-5-HTP without carbidopa to 30 unmedicated depressed patients produced a significant increase in serum cortisol levels. Peak minus baseline cortisol levels following D,L-5-HTP was 6.3 ± 0.99 μg/dl compared to 2.0 ± 0.6 μg/dl following placebo ($p < .001$). Significant correlations were also found between the increase in serum cortisol following 5-HTP and (1) severity of depression and (2) history of suicide attempts (Meltzer, Perline, Tricou, Lowry, & Robertson, 1984).

The effect of treatment with lithium carbonate and antidepressants on tlhe cortisol response to 5-HTP has also been studied by Meltzer, Lowy, Robertson, Goodnick, and Perline (1984b). Treatment (3–5 weeks) with lithium carbonate or MAO inhibitors augmented the mean 5-HTP-induced increase in serum cortisol. On the other hand, tricyclic antidepressants diminished the serum cortisol response. These results are explained by the effect of these medications on 5-HT receptor sensitivity; lithium carbonate is believed to enhance 5-HT receptor sensitivity while tricyclic antidepressants diminish it. The contradictory results reported here could be due to a variety of factors, to be discussed later, including the different doses of precursors used and the absence or presence of carbidopa pretreatment. Further investigation with a more uniform methodology is needed before conclusions can be made (Table 13.2).

Prolactin

Prolactin is another hormone which has been extensively studied in relation to the 5-HTergic system. Charney, Heninger, Reinhard, Sternberg, and Hafstead (1982) gave 7 g of L-tryptophan IV over a 20-minute period to 10 volunteers. This induced a marked increase in serum prolactin in all the subjects.

TABLE 13.2. Survey of Serotonin Precursor Studies and the Hypothalamic–Pituitary–Adrenal (HPA) Axis

Author	Subjects	L-TP (g oral)	5-HTP (mg oral)	ACTH	Cortisol
Imura, Nakai, and Yoshimi (1973)	8 Normals	—	150	↑	↑
Woolf and Lee (1977)	11 Normals	10	—	→	→
Hyyppa, Jolma, Lura, Langvik, and Kytomakin (1979)	5 Normals	2	—		→
Modlinger, Schonmuller, and Arora (1980)	11 Normals	10	—	↑	↑
Westenberg, van Praag, de Jong, and Thyssen (1982)	12 Normals, 14 depressives	5	200 with PDI		No change
Meltzer et al. (1982)	30 Depressives	—	200		↑

TABLE 13.3. Representative Sample of Serotonin Precursor Studies and Prolactin

Author	Subjects	L-TP	5-HTP	Prolactin
Beck-Peccoz, Ferrari, Rondena, Sarrachi, and Faglia (1976)	10 Normals	—	200 mg oral	No change
Woolf and Lee (1977)	11 Normals	10 g oral	—	↑ (not significant)
Wiebe, Handmerger, and Hammon (1977)	8 Normals	90 mg/kg oral	—	No change
Lancranjan, Wirz-Justice, Puhringer, and Del Pozo (1977)	11 Normals	200 mg iv with PDI	—	↑
Hyyppa, Jolma, Lura, Langvik, and Kytomaki (1979)	5 Normals	2 g oral	—	No change
Fraser, Tucker, Grubb, Wigand, and Blackard (1979)	20 Normals	5 g oral	—	↑ (not significant)
Glass, Smallridge, Schaaf, and Dimond (1980)	8 Normals	5 g oral	—	No change
Charney, Heninger, Reinhard, Sternberg, and Hafstead (1982)	10 Normals	7 g iv	—	↑
Westenberg, van Praag, de Jong, and Thyssen (1982)	12 Normals, 14 depressives	5 g oral	200 mg oral with PDI	No change
Meltzer et al. (1982)	30 Depressives	—	200 mg oral	No change
Heninger, Charney, and Sternberg (1984)	25 Depressives	7 g iv	—	→

The percentage increase from baseline ranged widely (79–1100%), with the mean peak occurring at 60 minutes. There was no significant difference between male and female subjects, and no correlation between age and prolactin increase was found.

After administration of 10 g of oral L-tryptophan to 11 men, Woolf and Lee (1977) found a small but statistically significant rise in serum prolactin. On the other hand, several studies have failed to obtain prolactin release after administration of L-tryptophan. Fraser, Tucker, Grubb, Wigand, and Blackard (1979) gave 5 g of L-tryptophan orally to 20 normal volunteers and reported great individual variability in prolactin response, but no significant increase. Glass, Smallridge, Schaaf, and Dimond (1980), Hyyppa et al. (1979), and Wiebe, Handmerger, and Hammon (1977) obtained similar results with different doses of oral L-tryptophan.

The effect of 5-HTP on prolactin secretion is equally inconsistent. While Beck-Peccoz, Ferrari, Rondena, Parrachi, and Faglia (1976) failed to stimulate prolactin release after acute and chronic oral administration of 5-HTP without carbidopa, Lancranjan, Wirz-Justice, Puhringer, and Del Pozo (1977) reported a significant increase in prolactin plasma levels after giving L-5-HTP with a PDI.

In depressed subjects, oral administration of 5-HT precursors by Westenberg et al. (1982) and Meltzer, Tricou, Robertson, and Lowy (1983) produced no significant change in serum prolactin concentrations. Yet another study reports different findings, this time administering tryptophan by IV route (Heninger, Charney, & Sternberg, 1984). Twenty-five depressed patients who were drug free for 21 days were given 7 g of tryptophan IV over a 20-minute period, and the findings were compared with those of 19 age- and sex-matched controls. Both the female and male patients had a significantly blunted maximal prolactin response to IV tryptophan when compared to controls. This was true for all time points sampled and did not correlate with the severity of depression as scored by the Hamilton Depression Scale (Table 13.3).

The prolactin response to IV tryptophan has also been used as a means of studying the mechanism of action of different antidepressants. Charney, Heninger, and Sternberg (1984) reported that the prolactin rise induced by tryptophan was increased following 28–35 days of treatment with either desipramine or amitriptyline when compared with a preceding placebo period. In contrast, 2 weeks after abrupt cessation of amitriptyline treatment, the prolactin response to tryptophan was further enhanced, whereas this did not occur with cessation of desipramine therapy. This finding has implications for understanding the way in which these antidepressants interact with 5-HT receptors, suggesting that amitriptyline may produce 5-HT postsynaptic receptor blockade, whereas desipramine may lack this 5-HT receptor antagonist property.

The mechanism by which 5-HT precursors influence prolactin release has also been subject to investigation. While Lamberts and MacLeod (1978) believe that 5-HT stimulates prolactin secretion by influencing the DAergic system (which inhibits prolactin secretion), Takahara et al. (1981) state that 5-HT enhances prolactin release, not by inhibiting DAergic activity, but by stimulating a prolactin-releasing factor at the hypothalamic level. Both authors agree that 5-HT does not stimulate prolactin secretion when added to pituitary glands in vitro. Thus, 5-HT apparently does not act directly at the hypophyseal level.

Growth Hormone

As with other pituitary hormones, mixed results have been obtained when studying the effect of tryptophan on GH secretion in normal volunteers. Most groups report significant increases in GH concentration following L-tryptophan (Charney et al., 1982; Hyyppa, et al., 1979; Woolf & Lee, 1977) or 5-HTP administration (Imura et al., 1973; Lancranjan et al., 1977), with increases present at 60 minutes after oral ingestion of the precursor and lasting 120–180 minutes. No sex differences have been found. Others report modest rises in GH which are not statistically significant, with females showing higher values than males (Fraser et al., 1979), while some failed to produce any effect on basal or apomorphine-induced GH secretion (Lal, Young, Cervantes, & Guyda, 1980).

In depressive illness most studies concur

TABLE 13.4. Survey of Serotonin Precursor Studies and Growth Hormone

Author	Subjects	L-TP	5-HTP (mg oral)	Growth hormone
Imura, Nakai, and Yoshimih (1973)	8 Normals	—	150	↑
Woolf and Lee (1977)	11 Normals	10 mg oral	—	↑
Lancranjan, Wirz-Justice, Puhringer, and Del Pozo (1977)	11 Normals	200 mg iv with PDI	—	↑
Hyyppa, Jolma, Lura, Langrik, and Kytomaki (1979)	5 Normals	2 g oral	—	↑
Fraser, Tucker, Grubb, Wigand, and Blackard (1979)	20 Normals	5 g oral	—	↑ (not significant)
Lal, Young, Cervantes, and Guyda (1980)	7 Normals	3 g oral	—	No change
Charney, Heninger, Reinhard, Sternberg, and Hafstead (1982)	10 Normals	7 g iv	—	↑
Westenberg, van Praag, de Jong, and Thyssen (1982)	12 Normals, 14 depressives	5 g oral	200 with PDI	No change
Meltzer et al. (1982)	30 Depressives	—	200	No change
Ansseau, Doumont, Thiry, Greenen, and Legros (1983)	8 Depressives, 4 manics, 4 schizophrenics, and 4 normal controls	—	200	No change

that there is no effect of 5-HTP or L-tryptophan on GH secretion. Westenberg *et al.* (1982) reported that the mean peak GH concentrations between patients and controls were not significantly different after either oral tryptophan loading or 5-HTP plus carbidopa. Meltzer *et al.* (1983) found no effect of oral 5-HTP, this time without carbidopa, on serum GH levels. Ansseau, Doumont, Thiry, Greenen, and Legros (1983) also failed to elicit GH response after oral administration of 200 mg 5-HTP without carbidopa to a mixed sample of depressives, schizophrenics, manics, and normal controls (Table 13.4).

CATECHOLAMINE PRECURSOR STUDIES

Alterations in the DAergic system were initially linked to the pathogenesis of schizophrenic psychoses (Carlsson, 1978; Mattysse, 1973; Synder, Banerjee, Yamamura, & Greenberg, 1974; van Praag, 1967) based upon the following indirect considerations: (1) DA agonists, such as amphetamine, can provoke psychotic symptoms that mimic paranoid schizophrenia, and (2) the neuroleptics, although different in chemical structure, share the characteristics of producing DAergic blockade. This property has been correlated with their antipsychotic effect.

Subsequently, more direct methods of assessing CA function in schizophrenic subjects have been employed, namely, measurement of levels of CA and their metabolites in the CSF *in vivo* and postmortem studies of brain specimens obtained from schizophrenic patients.

CA research in schizophrenia has emphasized DA metabolism, though some studies have attempted to study NA metabolites. Homovanillic acid (HVA) in CSF, a direct metabolite of DA, originates mostly from the brain, whereas NA metabolites in CSF largely originate from the spinal cord.

The predicted elevation in CSF HVA levels in schizophrenia has not been found. To the contrary, investigators have reported no significant difference in the concentration of HVA in schizophrenics as compared to normal controls (Post, Fink, Carpenter, & Goodwin, 1975), while others have found decreased concentration of the metabolite in schizophrenics (Bowers, 1974; van Praag, 1977b). This finding would be consistent with hypersensitive postsynaptic DA receptors and would not support an increased turnover of DA.

Studies of DA receptors in postmortem brain tissue from schizophrenics using ligand binding techniques have yielded quite consistent results (Lee & Seeman, 1980; Mackay *et al.*, 1982), the most striking being an increase in the postsynaptic DA-2 receptors. It is difficult to determine whether the increase in DA receptor density occurs secondary to neuroleptic treatment or is an intrinsic feature of schizophrenia.

Another method of assessing the sensitivity of the DAergic system in schizophrenics is by administration of DA precursors—tyrosine and L-dopa—to pharmacologically produce neuroendocrine challenges to the DAergic system.

Because DA and NA share a common biosynthetic pathway, studies with L-dopa and tyrosine can also serve as probes to the NAergic system. Consequently, the results obtained after giving tyrosine or L-dopa will always be mixtures of DAergic and NAergic effects which are hard to differentiate.

The literature on precursor studies with tyrosine and L-dopa is even less extensive than that for 5-HT precursors, possibly due to the fact that neuroendocrine probes with drugs that act as agonists or receptor blockers have been a more popular approach when studying the DAergic and NAergic systems. Another factor is that until recently the enzyme tyrosine hydroxylase, which converts tyrosine to dopa, was considered to be saturated with substrate. Therefore, additional tyrosine administration would not lead to increased CA production and would not affect hormone levels. This has been disputed by Gibson and Wurtman (1978; for review, see Sved, 1983). It is now accepted that tyrosine hydroxylase is mostly, but not fully, saturated with tyrosine *in vivo* and that in the presence of increased tyrosine availability CA synthesis may increase by 20–30% of the normal rate, in particular in activated cells. We are not aware of any tyrosine/hormone studies. We will review studies that have looked at hormonal levels after L-dopa administration.

Growth Hormone

Boyd, Lebovitz, and Pfeiffer (1970) were the first to report the effect of L-dopa on GH secretion. A single oral dose of 0.5 g of L-dopa without a PDI given to 5 patients with Parkinson's disease caused a significant rise in plasma GH which persisted for 120 minutes after the administration of the drug. Eddy, Jones, Chakmahjian, and Silverthorne (1971) gave single oral dose increments of L-dopa (250, 500, and 1000 mg) on 3 consecutive days to 7 healthy males and obtained a GH release with peak levels within 60–180 minutes after ingestion and return to baseline levels by 240 minutes. Generally, the duration and magnitude of the GH response was dose related.

Mars and Genuth (1973) tested the effect of a PDI on the GH response to L-dopa. Ten healthy volunteers underwent two L-dopa tests 3 days apart. On each day they received 250 mg L-dopa orally, but were premedicated with a PDI on one occasion. Following L-dopa alone, the mean peak increment in GH was 9.2 mg/ml. Pretreatment with a PDI resulted in augmented plasma L-dopa levels at all sampling times and a mean peak increment in GH of 15.6 mg/ml.

Mims, Scott, Modelu, and Bethune (1975) also reported an increase of GH secretion after the oral administration of 1 g of L-dopa without a PDI to 12 male control subjects.

In another study, Rotrosen, Angrist, Gershon, Sachar, and Halpern (1976) gave 500 mg L-dopa orally without PDI to 22 schizophrenics and 9 controls. Elevations of plasma GH were seen in most subjects, with schizophrenics showing an earlier response and an earlier decline in plasma levels. Mean plasma GH peak values were not significantly different between schizophrenics and controls. On the other hand, Tamminga, Smith, Pandey, Frohman, and Davis (1977) reported significantly decreased GH response to oral L-dopa in 11 drug-free schizophrenic patients compared to 11 controls.

Sachar, Frantz, Altman, and Sassin (1973) have studied the effect of L-dopa on GH secretion in patients with affective disorders. Initial reports indicated a diminished GH response to L-dopa in unipolar depressed patients when compared to normal controls. However, another study conducted with unipolar depressed postmenopausal women and age-matched unipolar and bipolar depressed men found no significant difference in the GH response to L-dopa in the depressed groups when compared to their respective normal controls. Comparison within the normal control group showed that postmenopausal women had significantly lower GH responses than the age-matched men. This finding was not related to plasma dopa concentrations, but might be due to decreased estrogen availability, as estrogens have been known to potentiate GH responses to insulin (Sachar et al., 1975).

In conclusion, most studies concur that L-dopa and other DA agonists produce a GH release in normal controls. The GH response

TABLE 13.5. Survey of Studies on Growth Hormone Response to L-Dopa Administration

Author	Subjects	L-Dopa (oral)	Growth hormone
Eddy, Jones, Chakmahjian, and Silverthorne (1971)	7 Normals	250, 500, 1000 mg	↑
Mars and Genuth (1973)	10 Normals	250 mg with PDI	↑
Mims, Scott, Modelu, and Bethune (1975)	12 Normals	1 g	↑
Boyd, Lebovitz, and Pfeiffer (1970)	5 Parkinson's disease	0.5 g	↑
Tamminga, Smith, Pandey, Frohman, and Davis (1977)	11 Schizophrenics	500 mg	↓
Rotrosen et al. (1978)	22 Schizophrenics, 9 controls	500 mg	↑
Sachar et al. (1975)	19 Depressives	500 mg	↓

to L-dopa in psychiatric subjects (depressives and schizophrenics) is more variable, with investigators reporting both increases and decreases in GH levels (Table 13.5).

Prolactin

In 1971, Kleinberg, Noel, and Frantz reported that the well-known increase in prolactin levels that follows neuroleptic administration was inhibited with L-dopa pretreatment. Subsequently, several investigators looked at the effect of L-dopa on prolactin levels in drug-free schizophrenic subjects. Tamminga *et al.* (1977) measured prolactin levels in 11 unmedicated schizophrenic patients. Baseline values were similar to those of controls and were within normal limits. After oral ingestion of 500 mg L-dopa, both schizophrenic and control groups suppressed prolactin levels, but the schizophrenics had a blunted response compared to the control group.

Examination of prolactin response to L-dopa in chronic unmedicated schizophrenics by Rotrosen *et al.* (1978) showed a significant suppression of prolactin in all subjects which was slightly greater than in the control group.

The relatively few experimental studies done with DA precursors and prolactin confirm the results obtained with DA agonists, namely, there is a significant suppression of prolactin levels. This suppression is similar in normals, schizophrenics, and depressives (Table 13.6).

SUMMARY AND CONCLUSIONS

The wide range of results from the studies reviewed points out the very complicated in-terrelations between MA precursors, MA, and hormone secretion. The neuroendocrine response to 5-HT precursors is very variable in relation to cortisol, ACTH, and prolactin, both in normal controls and in depressives, with different studies reporting an increase, a decrease, or no change in the plasma levels of these hormones after administration of L-tryptophan or 5-HTP. The GH response to 5-HT precursors is more consistent, with most investigators in agreement that L-tryptophan and 5-HTP produce a GH release in normal subjects and no effect in depressed patients.

The findings of L-dopa administration are less uniform, with findings of GH release and prolactin suppression in normal controls and variable results in psychiatric subjects.

The evidence presented in these studies cannot be evaluated as a homogeneous data base because of the different methodologies used. There is great variability in the dose of precursor, the route of administration, the presence or absence of a PDI, and the ovarian activity of the female subjects. We will look briefly at each of these factors separately.

Dose of Precursor

Overloading the system by administration of large amounts of a particular precursor can have several effects. We will discuss the effect of each precursor on MAergic systems separately (van Praag & Lemus, 1986).

Tryptophan

Administration of large amounts of tryptophan may affect the ratio of tryptophan to

TABLE 13.6. Prolactin Response to L-Dopa Administration in Psychiatric Subjects: Representative Sample

Author	Subjects	L-Dopa (mg oral)	Prolactin
Tamminga, Smith, Pandey, Frohman, and Davis (1977)	11 Schizophrenics	500	↓
Rotrosen *et al.* (1978)	22 Schizophrenics, 9 controls	500	↓
Sachar, Frantz, Altman, and Sassin (1973)	19 Depressives	500	↓

the plasma level of the other five large neutral amino acids (leucine, isoleucine, valine, phenylalanine, and tyrosine) which share the same uptake process (Wurtman, 1982). Therefore, surplus L-tryptophan would interfere with tyrosine transport into the CNS and diminish CA synthesis. Another system affected by tryptophan administration is the so-called kynurenine shunt. Less than 3% of dietary L-tryptophan is converted to 5-HT. Most of it is metabolized by the liver enzyme tryptophan pyrrolase to nicotinic acid via intermediate formation of kynurenine. Some tryptophan is used for protein synthesis and a small fraction is converted to tryptamine. In conclusion, although oral administration of L-tryptophan leads to increased 5-HT availability in the CNS, the effect is probably not selective. Both CAergic and non-MAergic systems are affected as well.

5-Hydroxytryptophan

A substantial proportion of orally administered 5-HTP is converted to 5-HT in 5-HTergic neurons. The relevant enzyme, 5-HTP decarboxylase, however, is found not only in 5-HTergic neurons, but also in CAergic nerve cells (Yuwiler, Geller, & Eiduson, 1959). Consequently, 5-HTP is transformed to 5-HT in CAergic neurons as well. This extraneous 5-HT acts as a false transmitter, decreasing the effectivity of CAergic transmission (Fuxe et al., 1971). In turn there is an increased synthesis of both DA and NA (Everet, 1979) which can be viewed as compensatory. Thus, L-5-HTP administration affects not only the 5-HTergic system, but also has a dual effect on CAergic systems: formation of false transmitter and increased CA production.

L-Dopa

Administration of L-dopa increases DA levels and DA synthesis in DAergic neurons and supposedly DAergic activity as well. Although L-dopa increases NA metabolism (Gershon, Goodwin, & Gold, 1970) its effect on neuronal activity in NAergic neurons is not clear. Since L-dopa and L-5-HTP are decarboxylated by the same enxyme, aromatic amino acid decarboxylase, the L-dopa that enters 5-HTergic neurons is transformed

to DA which could function as a false transmitter (Cooper et al., 1978).

There are no indications of a compensatory increase in 5-HT synthesis, possibly due to the fact that 5-HTP and L-dopa compete for the same uptake mechanism into the CNS, causing less 5-HTP to enter the CNS.

Tyrosine

Tyrosine hydroxylase, the enzyme that converts tyrosine to dopa, is restricted to CAergic neurons (Nagatsu, Levitt, & Underfriend, 1964). As mentioned previously, recent studies indicate that this enzyme is not fully saturated and that administration of L-tyrosine, though not increasing CA levels, indeed leads to increases in turnover and release of DA and NA (Gibson & Wurtman, 1977; Wurtman et al., 1974). Large amounts of tyrosine may interfere with 5-HT synthesis by competing with tryptophan for the same uptake mechanism into the CNS.

In summary, the assumption that a given precursor will only affect a particular MAergic system is false. This lack of selectivity creates problems when trying to attribute a hormonal response to a particular neurotransmitter.

Route of Administration

Adequate absorption of an orally administered precursor should be determined before a conclusion can be reached as to its effect on the CNS. Plasma amino acid measurements are essential.

Peripheral Decarboxylase Inhibitor

The addition of a PDI can increase the plasma level of 5-HTP and dopa by interfering with the process of decarboxylation in peripheral tissues and thereby increasing the amount of available precursor. Although two studies might be administering the same dose of precursor, the challenge to the system will be different and much greater if one of them included a PDI in the design. Another element to be considered is the fact that a PDI per se is capable of eliciting prolactin secretion, possibly by acting at the pituitary level (Glass et al., 1980). The influence of PDIs on other hormones has not yet been studied.

Ovarian Activity

Decreased estrogen availability might influence GH response to L-dopa, as estrogens are known to potentiate GH responses to insulin. Different points in the menstrual cycle should be considered as a variable when measuring hormonal responses, particularly in relation to prolactin.

The relatively small number of studies done using MA precursors as neuroendocrine probes and the often conflicting results obtained point out the need for further investigation in this area. In future studies, attention should be paid to monitor plasma tryptophan/large neutral amino acid ratios, titrate the dose of MA precursor given to avoid supramaximal stimulation, and measure MA metabolites in CSF in an attempt to ascertain which neuronal system is being stimulated.

References

Ansseau, M., Doumount, A., Thiry, D., Greenen, V., & Legros, J. J. (1983). Interest of 5-hydroxytryptophan (5-HTP) as a neuroendocrine marker in depressive illness. *Acta Psychiatrica Belgica*, *83*, 50–56.

Asberg, M., Traskman, L., & Thoren, P. (1976). "Serotonin depression": A biochemical subgroup within the affective disorders? *Science*, *191*, 478–480.

Beck-Peccoz, P., Ferrari, C., Rondena, M., Parrachi, A., & Faglia, G. (1976). Failure of oral 5-hydroxytryptophan administration to affect prolactin secretion in man. *Hormone Research*, *7*, 303–307.

Blackard, W. G., & Heidingsfelder, S. A. (1968). Adrenergic receptor control mechanism for growth hormone secretion. *Journal of Clinical Investigation*, *47*, 1407–1414.

Bowers, M. B. (1974). Central dopamine turnover in schizophrenic syndromes. *Archives of General Psychiatry*, *31*, 50–54.

Boyd, A. E., Lebovitz, H. E., & Pfeiffer, J. B. (1970). Stimulation of human growth hormone secretion by L-dopa. *New England Journal of Medicine*, *283*, 1425–1429.

Carlsson, A. (1978). Antipsychotic drugs, neurotransmitters and schizophrenia. *American Journal of Psychiatry*, *135*, 164–173.

Charney, D. S., Heninger, G. R., Reinhard, J. F., Sternberg, D. E., & Hafstead, K. M. (1982). The effect of IV L-tryptophan on prolactin, growth hormone, and mood in healthy subjects. *Psychopharmacology*, *78*, 38–43.

Charney, D. S., Heninger, G. R., & Sternberg, D. E. (1984). Serotonin function and mechanism of action of antidepressant treatment. *Archives of General Psychiatry*, *41*, 359–365.

Cooper, J. R., Bloom, F. E., & Roth, R. H. (1978). *The biochemical basis of neuropharmacology*. London & New York: Oxford University Press.

Eddy, S. L., Jones, A. L., Chakmahjian, Z. H., & Silverthorne, M. C. (1971). Effect of levodopa (L-dopa) on human hypophyseal trophic hormone relaese. *Journal of Clinical Endocrinology and Metabolism*, *33*, 709–712.

Everet, G. M. (1979). Effects of 5-hydroxytryptophan on brain levels of monoamines and the dopamine metabolite DOPAC. In E. Usdin, I. J. Kopin & J. Barchas (Eds.), *Catecholamines: Basic and clinical frontiers*. New York: Pergamon Press.

Fernström, J. D., & Wurtman, R. J. (1971). Brain serotonin content: Physiological dependence on plasma tryptophan levels. *Science*, *173*, 149–152.

Fraser, W. M., Tucker, H. S., Grubb, S. R., Wigand, J. P., & Blackard, W. G. (1979). Effect of L-tryptophan on growth hormone and prolactin release in normal volunteers and patients with secretory pituitary tumors. *Hormones and Metabolic Research*, *11*, 149–155.

Frohman, L. A. (1980). Neurotransmitters as regulators of endocrine function. In D. T. Krieger & J. C. Hughes (Eds.), *Neuroendocrinology* (pp. 44–57). Sunderland, MA: Sinauer Assoc.

Fuxe, K., Butcher, L. L., & Engel, J. (1971). DL-5-Hydroxytryptophan-induced changes in central monoamine neurons after peripheral decarboxylase inhibition. *Journal of Pharmacology*, *23*, 420–424.

Gershon, E. S., Goodwin, F. K., & Gold, P. (1970). Effects of L-tyrosine and L-dopa on norepinephrine (NE) turnover in rat brain *in vivo*. *Pharmacologist*, *12*, 268.

Gibson, C. J., & Wurtman, R. J. (1977). Physiological control of brain catechol synthesis by brain tyrosine concentration. *Biochemical Pharmacology*, *26*, 1137–1142.

Gibson, C. J., & Wurtman, R. J. (1978). Physiological control of brain norepinephrine synthesis by brain tyrosine concentration. *Life Sciences*, *22*, 1399–1406.

Glass, A. R., Smallridge, R. C., Schaaf, M., & Dimond, R. C. (1980). Absent prolactin response to L-tryptophan in normal and acromegalic subjects. *Psychoneuroendocrinology*, *5*, 261–265.

Glassman, A., & Platman, S. R. (1969). Potentiation of a monoamine oxidase inhibitor by tryptophan. *Journal of Psychiatric Research*, *7*, 83–88.

Griffiths, W. J., Lester, B. K., & Coulter, J. D. (1972). Tryptophan and sleep in young adults. *Psychophysiology*, *9*, 345–356.

Hartmann, E., Cravens, J., & List, S. (1974). Hypnotic effects of L-tryptophan. *Archives of General Psychiatry*, *31*, 394–397.

Heninger, G. R., Charney, D. S., & Sternberg, D. E. (1984). Serotonergic function in depression. *Archives of General Psychiatry*, *41*, 398–402.

Hyyppa, M. T., Jolma, T., Lura, J., Langvik, V. A., & Kytomaki, O. (1979). L-Tryptophan treatment and the episodic secretion of pituitary hormones and cortisol. *Psychoneuroendocrinology*, *4*, 29–35.

Imura, H., Nakai, Y., & Yoshimi, T. (1973). Effect of 5-hydroxytryptophan (5-HTP) on growth hormone and ACTH release in man. *Journal of Clinical Endocrinology and Metabolism*, *36*, 204–206.

Kleinberg, D. L., Noel, G. L., & Frantz, A. G. (1971). Chlorpromazine stimulation and L-dopa suppression of plasma prolactin in man. *Journal of Clinical Endocrinology and Metabolism*, *33*, 873–876.

Lal, S., Young, S. N., Cervantes, P., & Guyda, H. (1980). Effect of L-tryptophan on apomorphine-induced growth hormone secretion in normal subjects. *Pharmakopsychiatrie Neuro-Psychopharmakologie*, *13*, 331–335.

Lamberts, S. W. J., & MacLeod, R. M. (1978). The interaction of the serotonergic and dopaminergic systems on prolactin secretion in the rat. *Endocrinology (Baltimore)*, *103*, 287–295.

Lancranjan, I., Wirz-Justice, A., Puhringer, W., & Del Pozo, E. (1977). Effect of L-5-hydroxytryptophan infusion on growth hormone and prolactin secretion in man. *Journal of Clinical Endocrinology and Metabolism*, *45*, 588–593.

Langer, S. Z., & Briley, M. (1981). High-affinity [^{3}H]-imipramine binding; a new biological tool for studies in depression. *Trends in NeuroSciences*, *4*, 28.

Lee, T., & Seeman, P. (1980). Elevation of brain neuroleptic/dopamine receptors in schizophrenia. *American Journal of Psychiatry*, *137*, 191–197.

Lloyd, K. J., Farley, I. J., Deck, J. H. N., & Hornykiewicz, O. (1974). Serotonin and 5-hydroxyindoleacetic acid in discrete areas of the brain stem of suicide victims and control patients. *Advances in Biochemical Psychopharmacology*, *11*, 387–397.

Mackay, A. V. P., Iversen, L. L., Rossor, M., Spokes, E., Bird, E., Arregui, A., Creese, I., & Snyder, S. H. (1982). Increased brain dopamine and dopamine receptors in schizophrenia. *Archives of General Psychiatry*, *39*, 991–997.

Mars, H. (1973). Modification of levodopa effect by peripheral decarboxylase inhibition. *Archives of Neurology (Chicago)*, *28*, 91–95.

Mars, H., & Genuth, S. M. (1973). Potentiation of levodopa stimulation of human growth hormone by systemic decarboxylase inhibition. *Clinical Pharmacology and Therapeutics*, *14*, 390–394.

Mattysse, S. (1973). Antipsychotic drug actions: A clue to the neuropathology of schizophrenia? *Federation Proceedings, Federation of American Societies for Experimental Biology*, *32*, 200–205.

Meltzer, H. Y. (1984). Serotonergic function in the affective disorders: The effect of antidepressants and lithium on the 5-hydroxytrytophan-induced increase in serum cortisol. *Annals of the New York Academy of Sciences*, *430*, 115–137.

Meltzer, H. Y., Arora, R. C., Baber, R., & Tricou, B. J. (1981). Serotonin uptake in blood platelets of psychiatric patients. *Archives of General Psychiatry*, *38*, 1322–1326.

Meltzer, H. Y., Lowy, M., Robertson, A., Goodnick, P., & Perline, R. (1984). Effect of 5-hydroxytryptophan on serum cortisol levels in major affective disorders. III. Effect of antidepressants and lithium carbonate. *Archives of General Psychiatry*, *41*, 391–397.

Meltzer, H. Y., Perline, R., Tricou, B. J., Lowy, M., & Robertson, A. (1984). Effect of 5-hydroxytryptophan on serum cortisol levels in major affective disorders. II. Relation to suicide, psychosis and depressive symptoms. *Archives of General Psychiatry*, *41*, 379–387.

Meltzer, H. Y., Tricou, B. J., Robertson, A., & Lowy, M. (1983). Hormone response to 5-hydroxytryptophan. *Psychiatry Research*, *10*, 151–152.

Mims, R. B., Scott, C. L., Modelu, O., & Bethune, J. E.

(1975). Inhibition of L-dopa-induced growth hormone stimulation by pyridoxine and chlorpromazine. *Journal of Clinical Endocrinology and Metabolism*, *40*, 256–259.

Modlinger, R. S., Schonmuller, J. M., & Arora, S. O. (1980). Adrenocorticotropin release by tryptophan in man. *Journal of Clinical Endocrinology and Metabolism*, *50*, 360–363.

Müller, E. E., Nistico, G., & Scapagnini, U. (1977). *Neurotransmitters and anterior pituitary function*. New York: Academic Press.

Nagatsu, T., Levitt, M., & Underfriend, S. (1964). Tyrosine hydroxylase: The initial step in norepinephrine biosynthesis. *Journal of Biological Chemistry*, *239*, 2910–2917.

Plonk, J. W., Bivens, C, H., & Feldman, J. M. (1974). Inhibition of hypoglycemia-induced cortisol secretion by the serotonin antagonist cyproheptidine. *Journal of Clinical Endocrinology and Metabolism*, *38*, 836–840.

Post, R. M., Ballenger, J. C., & Goodwin, F. K. (1980). Cerebrospinal fluid studies of neurotransmitter function in manic and depressive illness. In J. H. Wood (Ed.), *Neurobiology of CSF*. New York: Plenum Press.

Post, R. M., Fink, E., Carpenter, W. T., & Goodwin, F. K. (1975). Cerebrospinal fluid amine metabolites in acute schizophrenia. *Archives of General Psychiatry*, *32*, 1063–1069.

Rotrosen, J., Angrist, B. M., Clark, C., Gershon, S., Halpern, F., & Sachar, E. J. (1978). Suppression of prolactin by dopamine agonists in schizophrenics and controls. *American Journal of Psychiatry*, *135*, 949–951.

Rotrosen, J., Angrist, B. M., Gershon, S., Sachar, E. J., & Halpern, F. S. (1976). Dopamine receptor alteration in schizophrenia: Neuroendocrine evidence. *Psychopharmacology*, *51*, 1–7.

Sachar, E. J., Altman, N., Gruen, P. H., Glassman, A., Halpern, F. S., & Sassin, J. (1975). Human growth hormone response to levodopa. *Archives of General Psychiatry*, *32*, 502–503.

Sachar, E. J., Frantz, A. J., Altman, N., & Sassin, J. (1973). Growth hormone and prolactin in unipolar and bipolar depressed patients: Responses to hypoglycemia and L-dopa. *American Journal of Psychiatry*, *130*, 1362–1366.

Scally, M. D., Ulus, I. H., & Wurtman, R. J. (1977). Brain tyrosine levels control striatal dopamine synthesis in haloperidol-treated rats. *Journal of Neural Transmission*, *41*, 1–6.

Snyder, S. H. (1980). *Biological aspects of mental disorder*. London & New York: Oxford University Press.

Snyder, S. H., Banerjee, S. P., Yamamura, H. I., & Greenberg, D. (1974). Drugs, neurotransmitters, and schizophrenia. *Science*, *184*, 1243–1253.

Sved, A. F. (1983). Precursor control of the function of monoaminergic neurons. *Nutrition and the Brain*, *6*, 223–275.

Sved, A. F., Fernström, J. D., & Wurtman, R. J. (1979a). Tyrosine administration decreases serum prolactin levels in chronically reserpinized rats. *Life Sciences*, *25*, 1293–1300.

Sved, A. F., Férnström, J. D., & Wurtman, R. J. (1979b). Tyrosine administration reduces blood pressure and enhances brain norepinephrine release in spontaneously hypertensive rats. *Proceedings of the National Academy of Sciences of the U.S.A., 76,* 3511–3514.

Takahara, J., Yamauchi, J., Numi, M., Kageyama, J., Aoki, Y., Fujino, K., Hashimoto, K., & Ofuji, T. (1981). Mechanism of prolactin release by 5-hydroxytryptophan. *Life Sciences, 29,* 1463–1466.

Tamminga, C. A., Smith, R. C., Pandey, G., Frohman, L. A., & Davis, J. M. (1977). A neuroendocrine study of supersensitivity in tardive dyskinesia. *Archives of General Psychiatry, 34,* 1199–1203.

Thurmond, J. B., Kramarcy, N. R., Lasley, S. M., & Brown, J. W. (1980). Dietary amino acid precursors: Effect on central monoamines, aggression, and locomotor activity in the mouse. *Pharmacology, Biochemistry and Behavior, 12,* 525–532.

Traskman, L., Asberg, M., Bertilsson, L., & Sjöstrand, L. (1981). Monoamine metabolites in CSF and suicidal behavior. *Archives of General Psychiatry, 38,* 631–636.

van Praag, H. M. (1967). The possible significance of cerebral dopamine for neurology and psychiatry. *Psychiatria, Neurologia, Neurochirurgia, 70,* 361–379.

van Praag, H. M. (1977). The significance of dopamine for the mode of action of neuroleptics and the pathogenesis of schizophrenia. *British Journal of Psychiatry, 130,* 463–474.

van Praag, H. M. (1981). Management of depression with serotonin precursors. *Biological Psychiatry, 16,* 290–310.

van Praag, H. M. (1982). Serotonin precursors in the treatment of depression. In B. T. Ho, J. C. Schoolar, & E. Usdin (Eds.), *Serotonin in biological psychiatry* (pp. 259–286). New York: Raven Press.

van Praag, H. M., & Lemus, C. (1986). Monoamine precursors in the treatment of psychiatric disorders. In R. J. Wurtman & J. J. Wurtman (Eds.), *Nutrition and the brain* (Vol. 7). New York: Raven Press.

Walinder, J., Skott, A., Carlson, A., Nagy, A., & Roos, B. E. (1976). Potentiation of the antidepressant action of clomipramine by tryptophan. *Archives of General Psychiatry, 33,* 1384–1389.

Westenberg, H. G. M., van Praag, H. M., de Jong, J. T. V. M., & Thyssen, J. H. H. (1982). Postsynaptic serotonergic activity in depressive patients: Evaluation of the neuroendocrine strategy. *Psychiatry Research, 7,* 361–371.

Wiebe, R. H., Handmerger, S., & Hammon, D. B. (1977). Failure of L-tryptophan to stimulate prolactin secretion in man. *Journal of Clinical Endocrinology and Metabolism, 45,* 1310–1312.

Woolf, P. D., & Lee, L. (1977). Effect of the serotonin precursor, tryptophan, on pituitary hormone secretion. *Journal of Clinical Endocrinology and Metabolism, 45,* 123–133.

Wurtman, R. J. (1982). Nutrients that modify brain function. *Scientific American, 42,* 50–59.

Wurtman, R. J., Hefti, F., & Melamed, E. (1981). Precursor control of neurotransmitter synthesis. *Pharmacological Reviews, 32,* 315–335.

Wurtman, R. J., Larin, F., Mostafapour, S., & Fernström, J. D. (1974). Brain catechol synthesis: Control by brain tyrosine concentration. *Science, 185,* 183–184.

Yuwiler, A., Geller, E., & Eiduson, S. (1959). Studies on 5-hydroxytryptophan decarboxylase. I. *In vitro* inhibition and substrate interaction. *Archives of Biochemistry and Biophysics, 80,* 162–173.

PART V

THE USE OF NEUROENDOCRINE MARKERS IN PSYCHIATRY

14 THE DEXAMETHASONE SUPPRESSION TEST: A REVIEW

DWIGHT L. EVANS

ROBERT N. GOLDEN

University of North Carolina School of Medicine

INTRODUCTION

Since the publication of the 1981 work by Carroll and associates on the use of the dexamethasone suppression test (DST) as a specific laboratory test for the diagnosis of melancholia, considerable interest and controversy have arisen regarding the clinical utility of the DST as an adjunct in the diagnosis of depression. The DST was developed and used first in endocrinology as a test for Cushing's syndrome (Liddle, 1960; Nugent, Nichols, & Tyler, 1965; Pavlotos, Smilo, & Forsham, 1965). The use of the DST as a measure of hypothalamic–pituitary–adrenal (HPA) axis activity was soon adopted by psychiatric researchers (Carroll & Davies, 1970; Carroll, Martin, & Davies, 1968; Stokes, 1966, 1972) who were looking for a more specific physiological measure of the HPA axis in order to extend the observations of Sachar (1967a, 1967b) and earlier investigators (Gibbons & McHugh, 1963; McClure, 1966) who found evidence of HPA hyperactivity in depression as measured by plasma cortisol.

Sufficient evidence accumulated to suggest hyperactivity of the HPA axis in patients with major depression (Carroll & Mendels, 1976; Stokes, Pick, Stoll, & Nunn, 1975). Carroll, Feinberg et al. (1981) standardized the DST procedure for use in patients with depression and reported a 67% sensitivity, 96% specificity, and 94% diagnostic confidence for the diagnosis of melancholia in hospitalized psychiatric patients. A multitude of concordant and discordant reports have followed this 1981 study, and it is generally accepted that the DST has research utility (Hirshfield, Koslow, & Kupfer, 1983). The clinical utility of the DST has been questioned (Hirshfield, Koslow, & Kupfer, 1983), and further research and clinical experience has been recommended (Freedman & Glass, 1983) in order to determine the clinical utility of the DST in the assessment and treatment of major depressive disorders.

DST PROCEDURES

Dexamethasone is a synthetic glucocorticoid which, when administered at night to normal subjects, produces suppression of serum cortisol for at least 24 hours. The overnight DST was standardized by Carroll, Feinberg et al. (1981). Recommendations for the dose of dexamethasone, time of administration, and times of blood sampling for serum cortisol determination were made to yield maximal sensitivity, specificity, and diagnostic confidence for the use of the DST in the diagnosis of melancholia. This standardized test consists of a 1 mg oral dose of dexamethasone at 11 P.M., followed by serum cortisol determinations at 4 P.M. and 11 P.M. the following day. An abnormal test result (nonsuppression of serum cortisol following dexamethasone) is defined as a serum cortisol concentration of greater than 5 μg/dl at either 4 P.M. or 11 P.M. This cutoff criterion may vary based on the serum cortisol assay and laboratory methods, as will be reviewed below.

FACTORS THAT MAY RENDER DST RESULTS INVALID

Medical Exclusion Criteria

Valid interpretation of the DST requires that patients be, in general, physically healthy and physiologically stable. Medical and metabolic factors known to render the results of the DST invalid have been reviewed (Arana, Baldessarini, & Ornsteen, 1985; Carroll, 1983b; Carroll, Feinberg et al., 1981).

A number of factors may produce false positive DST results, such as the following:

Major medical illnesses such as acute congestive heart failure, uncontrolled hypertension or diabetes mellitus [and possibly controlled insulin-dependent diabetes mellitus (Cameron, Kronfol, Greden, & Carroll, 1984; Hudson et al., 1984)], advanced renal or hepatic disease, Cushing's disease or syndrome, toxic or infectious processes, and advanced cancer [but probably not cancer itself (Evans et al., 1986)] will produce false positive DST results.

Drugs with a capacity to induce hepatic microsomal enzymes and therefore increase the rate of dexamethasone metabolism may produce abnormal results. Thus, anticonvulsants (such as phenytoin and carbamazepine) and sedative hypnotics (such as barbiturates, meprobamate, glutethimide, methaqualone, and methyprylon) may produce false-positive DST findings. Alcohol abuse and possibly narcotic drugs and reserpine may also produce false-positive DSTs. The effects of anticonvulsants and barbiturates may continue for 3 weeks after discontinuation of these medications (Carroll, Feinberg et al., 1981).

Acute drug withdrawal may produce false-positive results as seen in alcohol withdrawal. Recent reports suggest that withdrawal from antidepressants, antipsychotics, and benzodiazepines also may be associated with abnormal findings.

Physiological instability brought on by fever, dehydration, and severe nausea and vomiting may produce false positives. Dehydration may be a particular problem in the recently admitted psychotic patient (Carroll, 1983b), and the DST should be performed after these patients are physiologically stable.

Severe weight loss from malnutrition (Smith, Bledsoe, & Chhetri, 1975), anorexia nervosa (Bethge, Nagel, Solbach, Wiegelmann, & Zimmermann, 1970), or rigid dieting [with normal body weight (Berger, Pirke, Doerr, Krieg, & von Zerssen, 1983; Edelstein, Roy-Byrne, Fawzy, & Dornfeld, 1983)] may produce false positives. Although weight loss is a sign of depression, weight loss did not account for the DST results in studies of depressed patients (Feinberg & Carroll, 1984; Holsboer, Steiger, & Maier, 1983).

Pregnancy and high-dose estrogens may produce false positives, but oral contraceptives do not appear to affect the DST.

Alterations in daily rhythms as seen in people working rotating shifts or in airline travelers may be associated with false-positive DSTs (Carroll, 1983b). A greater than 3-hour phase advance has been associated with DST nonsuppression (Krieger, Allen, Rozzo, & Krieger, 1971), while a phase advance of 3 hours does not appear to affect the DST results (Carroll, Martin, & Davies, 1968; Pepper, Davis, Davis, & Krieger, 1983).

A number of factors that may produce false-negative DST results have been reviewed (Carroll, 1983b) and include hypopituitarism, Addison's disease, synthetic steroid therapy, indomethacin (Mathe, 1983) and perhaps other nonsteroidal antiinflammatory medications, and high-dose cyproheptadine.

Psychiatric drugs including antidepressants (such as lithium, TCAs, MAOIs), neuroleptics, and benzodiazepines do not produce false positives (Carroll, Feinberg et al., 1981). The effects of electroconvulsive therapy (ECT) on the DST has not been fully determined, but the DST can probably be obtained after 4 days following the last ECT treatment (Carroll, Feinberg et al., 1981). High-dose benzodiazepines (greater than 25 mg/day diazepam) have been suggested to produce false-negative DST results (Carroll, Feinberg et al., 1981; Langer, Schonbeck, Konig, Lesch, & Schussler, 1979), as have tricyclic antidepressants and L-tryptophan (Nuller & Ostroumova, 1980), but Carroll (1983b) notes that there is no convincing evidence that TCAs, benzodiazepines, or L-tryptophan produce false negatives.

TECHNICAL FACTORS

A major factor that may account for the considerable variation in the available DST reports is the laboratory method of serum cortisol determination (Arana, Baldessarini, & Ornsteen, 1985; Carroll, 1983b; Meltzer & Fang, 1983). Most laboratories use either the competitive protein binding assay [which was used in the standardization of the DST (Carroll, Feinberg *et al.*, 1981)] or radioimmunoassay (RIA) methods to measure serum cortisol, and most hospitals and commercial laboratories are well prepared to measure with sufficient accuracy and precision the elevated serum cortisol levels found in Cushing's disease and Cushing's syndrome. However, use of the DST for the diagnosis of depression requires that the relatively low levels of post-dexamethasone serum cortisol be measured with accuracy and precision. Therefore, the assay should be modified for a sensitivity of $1-2\ \mu g/dl$ and for accuracy in the 3- to $7\text{-}\mu g/dl$ range. Moreover, considerable variation exists in the available commercial RIA kits (Ritchie, Carroll, Olton, Shively, & Feinberg, 1985), yielding different cutoff values. Thus, the $5\ \mu g/dl$ cutoff criterion for nonsuppression cannot be simply adopted by each laboratory. Each laboratory should adopt its own cutoff criterion for nonsuppression based on studies of normal and psychiatric controls (Carroll, 1983b; Meltzer & Fang, 1983). In addition, the clinician should know the quality control methods of the laboratory and whether the laboratory participates in testing such as that carried out by the College of American Pathologists or Wellcome Reagents; results in the middle range for standards in the $5\text{-}\mu g/dl$ range should be achieved (Meltzer & Fang, 1983). Furthermore, the clinician should assure that regular reliability testing is performed by the laboratory.

STATISTICAL FACTORS

Certain fundamental principles of statistics must be understood in order to interpret meaningfully the use of the DST in different clinical settings (inpatient vs. outpatient) and in different centers. Factors such as prevalence of depression in the study population (Baldessarini, Finklestein, & Arana, 1983; Carroll, 1983b; Carroll, Feinberg *et al.*, 1981)

and diagnostic concordance between centers (Carroll, 1983b; Carroll, Feinberg *et al.*, 1981) can affect the performance of the DST. A working knowledge of sensitivity, specificity, and predictive value (diagnostic confidence) will help the clinician to evaluate the clinical usefulness of the DST (and other laboratory tests).

The sensitivity of a test refers to the frequency of positive test results (true positive rate) in a population of patients who, according to the "gold standard" that the test is compared to, have the condition that the test is meant to identify (see Table 14.1). Thus, a DST sensitivity of 50% for the diagnosis of depression means that the DST is abnormal (positive) in 50% of the patients who have depression based on the gold standard (usually RDC or DSM-III criteria); conversely it also implies that the test will be normal incorrectly (false negative) in the remaining 50% of depressed patients.

The specificity of a test refers to the frequency of negative test results (true negative rate) in a population of patients who do not have the condition that the test is meant to identify. Thus, specificity of 90% for the diagnosis of depression means that the DST is normal (true negative) in 90% of the patients studied who do not have depression (based on the gold standard) and incorrectly abnormal (false positive) in 10% of the patients studied who do not have depression.

Both sensitivity and specificity are defined based on the test's performance compared to an existing gold standard. A "perfect" test, that is, one with 100% sensitivity and specificity, is only perfect in regard to its ability to correctly identify abnormal and normal as defined by the gold standard. Thus, if the gold standard for comparison for the DST is a clinician's diagnosis based on DSM-III criteria and if the DST were to have 99% sensitivity and 99% specificity, then the DST would be extremely accurate in predicting the results of a clinician's DSM-III diagnosis.

Sensitivity and specificity, in theory at least, are constant features of a test itself and are not affected by the population to which the test is applied. The predictive value (diagnostic confidence), on the other hand, depends on the prevalence of the disease in the population studied. For the clinician who receives a test result and wonders how

TABLE 14.1. "Gold Standard" in Test Results

Test results (+ or −)	Disease present (+)	Disease absent (−)	Evaluation
+	A	B	Sensitivity = A/A + C
−	C	D	Specificity = D/D + B
			Positive predictive value = A/A + B
			Negative predictive value = D/C + D
Disease prevalence = 50% (100 subjects studied)			
+	25	5	Sensitivity = 25/50 = 50%
−	25	45	Specificity = 45/50 = 90%
			Positive predictive value = 25/30 = 83%
	50	50	Negative predictive value = 45/70 = 64%
Disease prevalence = 10% (100 subjects studied)			
+	5	9	Sensitivity = 5/10 = 50%
−	5	81	Specificity = 81/90 = 90%
			Positive predictive value = 5/14 = 35%
	10	90	Negative predictive value = 81/86 = 94%

confident he or she can be that the result is correct, positive and negative predictive values are, in a way, more relevant than sensitivity and specificity, although the latter two characteristics of the test, along with disease prevalence, affect the predictive value. Positive predictive value refers to the percentage of positive test results that are true positives; negative predictive value refers to the percentage of negative test results that are true negatives. In other words, positive predictive value answers the question of what the odds are that a particular positive test result is correct. A few examples illustrate how disease prevalence influences positive and negative predictive values (see Table 14.1).

Assume that the DST has a sensitivity of 50% and a specificity of 90%. If the prevalence of depression in the population to which the test is applied is 50% (as in the 1981 Carroll, Feinberg *et al.* validation study), then the positive predictive value will be 83%. This means that there is an 83% chance that a patient with an abnormal test result has a true positive (i.e., correct) test result and only a 17% chance that the test

result is a false positive. On the other hand, the negative predictive value is only 64%; that is, the odds are 64 out of 100 that a negative or normal test result truly reflects the absence of depression.

The predictive values change as disease prevalence changes. With a prevalence of 10% (closer to the actual estimated prevalence of depression in an urban community), the positive predictive value of the DST would be only 35% even though the specificity and sensitivity remain the same. Thus, there is a 65% chance that an abnormal DST result might be a false positive if obtained from a population with a disease prevalence of 10%. On the other hand, the negative predictive value in such a population would rise to 94%. Thus, with decreasing prevalence of disease, the positive predictive value of a diagnostic test diminishes and the negative predictive value increases. On the other hand, the DST will have a relatively greater positive predictive value when applied to a population with a larger prevalence of depression (i.e., an acute inpatient service) than when applied to a population where prevalence is relatively low (i.e., as a screening test in a primary care clinic).

Another factor that can affect the performance of the DST is diagnostic concordance between clinicians. Considerable variation in diagnosis can exist in both clinical practice and well-controlled research studies (Helzer et al., 1977; Spitzer, Endicott, & Robins, 1978). Since clinical diagnosis is the gold standard (the independent variable) used to define the sensitivity and specificity of the DST, variance in diagnostic opinions can seemingly affect the sensitivity and specificity of the test. The apparent test performance will be much less powerful than the actual test performance, even with 75% interrater reliability; the sensitivity, specificity, and diagnostic confidence for a positive test result will be each significantly reduced (Carroll, 1983b). Thus, diagnostic variability may account for some of the reported variability in sensitivity and specificity of the DST for the diagnosis of depression.

ADDITIONAL FACTORS

Age

Does the age of the subject affect his or her response to a dexamethasone challenge? There are two types of data pertinent to this question: (1) studies of the DST in subpopulations of patients at each end of the age spectrum (i.e., in geriatric subjects and in children), and (2) studies analyzing the relationship between postdexamethasone cortisol levels and patient ages that cover a broad range. Alexopoulos and colleagues (1984) reported on the DST in geriatric depression. They studied 73 depressed patients with a median age of 72 years. Dividing their subjects into two groups at the median, they found a nonsuppression rate of 86% in the older subgroup and of 58% in the subgroup of patients less than 72 years old. At the other end of the spectrum, at least three groups have studied prepubertal children. Weller, Weller, Fristad, Preskorn, and Teare (1985) found DST nonsuppression in 82% of 50 depressed prepubertal children, with nonsuppression rates of only 28% and 11% in nondepressed age-matched psychiatric inpatients and nonhospitalized healthy control children, respectively (Weller et al., 1985).

Geller, Rogol, and Knitter (1983) found DST positive results in only 2 of 14 depressed children, but used a dexamethasone dose of 20 μg/kg. Ascarnov, Carison, and Lesser (1985) gave 0.5 mg dexamethasone challenge to 7 children with major depression, 6 with dythymia, and 17 without affective illness. Based on their results, they estimated that the DST has a sensitivity of 86% and specificity of only 53% in detecting major depression in prepubertal children. Zis (1986), however, pointed out that when the cutoff criterion for nonsuppression is changed to 7.1 μg/dl, then the data of Petty et al. (1985) demonstrate a sensitivity of 57% and, a specificity of 88%.

Looking at subjects over a broad range of age, does one find that DST results correlate with age? The answer appears to depend on what type of subjects are studied. Brown and Qualls (1981) found that depressed patients with abnormal DST results were older than depressed patients with normal suppression. Davies et al. (1984) also reported more frequent DST nonsuppression in depressed men 55 years or older compared to depressed men younger than 55. Whiteford's group recently reported that the mean 8:00 A.M. postdexamethasone cortisol concentration in depressed inpatients younger than 50 years old was only half of that found in depressed inpatients older than 50 (Whiteford et al., 1986). On the other hand, in a carefully controlled study which examined hourly cortisol levels 24 hours before and after dexamethasone administration in healthy volunteers, the pre- and postdexamethasone cortisol profiles were no different in young healthy subjects (mean age 28 years) and older healthy volunteers (mean age 70 years) (Tiongco, Harihan, Haskett, & Greden, 1986). Tourigny-Rivard, Raskind, and Rivard (1981) also found no correlation between age and postdexamethasone cortisol levels in normal subjects. Fogel and Satel (1985) reported a significant correlation between age and post-DST cortisol levels in depressed patients, but not in nondepressed patient controls. Nelson, Khan, Orr, and Tamragouri (1984) studied 227 patients and found a significant interaction between age and nonsuppression rates in depressed men, but not in nondepressed men, depressed women, or nondepressed women. Finally, Greden, Tiongco, Haskett, Grunhaus, and Kotun (1986), studying depressed patients, psychiatric controls, and normal subjects over a broad range of age, found that increased age increased significantly and progressively with post-DST cortisol concentrations in depressed patients, but not in the other two groups. The mechanism(s) through which age might affect the DST in depressed patients, but not other psychiatric patients or healthy subjects, awaits further elucidation.

Plasma Dexamethasone

One potential confounding variable in pharmacological challenge paradigms such as the DST is interindividual differences in pharmacokinetics. For the DST, variance in the plasma dexamethasone concentration following oral administration of a standard (1 mg) dose may contribute to differences in cortisol response. To date, we have found eight studies which have assayed plasma dexamethasone concentrations in more than 350 psychiatric patients. In all of these studies, a significant inverse correlation was found between plasma dexamethasone levels and post-DST plasma cortisol values (Arana, Workman, & Baldessarini, 1984; Berger, irke, Doerr, Krieg, & von Zerssen, 1984; Carr, Morris, & Gilliland, 1986; Carroll, Schroeder et al., 1980; Holsboer, Haack, Gerken, & Vesci, 1984; Johnson, Hunt, Kerr, & Caterson, 1984; Lowy, Reder, Antel, & Meltzer, 1986; Stokes, Stoll, Lasley, & Sikes, 1986). Taken together, these studies suggest that individual or illness-related differences in absorption and/or metabolism of dexamethasone may influence the outcome of the DST. Could the phenomenon of nonsuppression in major depression be simply a reflection of reduced bioavailability of dexamethasone in patients with that disorder? Two sets of data suggest that the answer is no. Lowy et al. (1986) found no difference in serum dexamethasone levels in normal controls compared to hospitalized psychiatric patients, although in their preliminary report of this work they do not specify how many of the latter group were, in fact, diagnosed with major depression (Lowy et al., 1986). In a more complete study of this question, Carr et al. (1986) found no significant difference in serum dexamethasone concentrations between subjects with major depression and those with other psychiatric disorders. In fact, many of their depressed patients had fairly high serum dexamethasone concentrations. Using analysis of covariance, they found that diagnostic group differences in post-DST cortisol levels were maintained even after controlling for serum dexamethasone concentrations. These authors suggest that small but perhaps clinically significant increases in the specificity and positive predictive value of the DST may be obtained if serum dexamethasone concentrations are taken into account in determining DST response categorization. Given the relative complexity and expense of measuring serum dexamethasone concentrations, we feel it is unlikely that this will become common practice in most clinical settings.

Stress

Researchers have speculated that the degree of nonsuppression of cortisol by dexamethasone is a variable that reflects the quantity of stress or distress experienced by the patient rather than relating to a specific diagnosis (Mellsop, Hutton, & Delahunt, 1985). Kalin's work with primates supports this hypothesis: Acute behavioral stress can partially override the cortisol suppressive effects of dexamethasone in monkeys (Kalin & Shelton, 1984). Several investigators have tested this hypothesis in "naturalistic" studies of different types of stress. Das and Berrios (1984) gave DSTs to 21 bereaved first-degree relatives; two had positive DSTs during the period of acute bereavement, but normal DSTs 3 months later. Ceulemans, Westenberg, and van Pragg (1985) found that 19 of 40 patients who were about to undergo surgery were DST positive, whereas none of their 20 control subjects had abnormal DSTs. Coccaro, Prudie, Rothpearl, and Nurnberg (1984) found retrospectively that depressed patients who received DSTs within the first 2 days of psychiatric admission were more likely to demonstrate abnormal suppression than depressed patients tested on the third through sixth day of admission, suggesting that the acute stress of psychiatric hospitalization may increase the likelihood of dexamethasone nonsuppression. In a particularly interesting investigation, Baumgartner, Graf, and Kurten (1985) studied 16 psychiatrists in an academic department who underwent the "acute stress" of presenting a 40- to 60-minute paper at a departmental clinical conference. DSTs were performed, with cortisol sampling at the completion of each presentation (the sampling times ranged from 3:20 P.M. to 6:00 P.M.). The DST was then repeated in each subject 1 week later at an identical sampling time. Seven of the psychiatrists had abnormal DSTs on the day of their presentation, yet none failed to suppress on their control day. Thus, several investigations looking at various types of stress support the hypothesis that stress per se might affect DST results. However, in the majority of studies, subjects were not systematically evaluated to definitively rule out the presence of depressive illness. Also, the majority of DST studies, including Carroll's validation paper (Carroll, Feinberg et al., 1981), found substantially lower rates of DST nonsuppression in nondepressed but severely ill patients (e.g., schizophrenics) who could be expected to be under considerable stress. In addition, we studied 3 patients who had experienced markedly traumatic life events and who met criteria for posttraumatic stress disorder. Each of the patients had a normal DST (Evans, Burnett, & Nemeroff, 1983; Evans & Nemeroff (in press a). While it is plausible that a stress-responsive system such as the HPA axis could be altered through chronic stress, the exact relationship between stress per se and DST results awaits further elucidation.

CLINICAL FINDINGS (SENSITIVITY AND SPECIFICITY)

Since the initial report (Carroll, Feinberg et al., 1981) of high sensitivity (67%) and high specificity (96%), numerous studies have found both concordant (Aggernaes et al., 1983; Agren & Wide, 1982; Arana et al., 1985; Carroll, 1982; Holden, 1983; Kasper & Beckmann, 1983; Mendlewicz, Charles, & Frankson, 1982; Schatzberg et al., 1983; Schlesser, Winokur, & Sherman, 1980) and discordant (Amsterdam, Caroff, & Conn, 1982; Arana et al., 1985; Ceulemans et al., 1985; Dewan, Pandurangi, Boucher, Levy, & Major, 1982; Hallström et al., 1983; Raskind,

Pesking, Rivard, Veith, & Barnes, 1982; Spar & Gerner, 1982; Stokes et al., 1984) results. It should be noted that in the 1981 report by Carroll, Feinberg and associates, the diagnosis of depression was based not only on the presenting signs and symptoms of depression, but also on family history as well as past psychiatric history and treatment (Carroll, Feinberg et al., 1980; Carroll, Feinberg et al., 1981). These clinical diagnosis may yield more homogeneous groups of nondepressed and depressed patients than would the simple application of DSM-III criteria without the application of this clinical gestalt; this could account for the high sensitivity and specificity of the DST in the initial study and also for some of the discrepancy in the DST results in subsequent studies.

A selected review of the available studies addressing the sensitivity and specificity of the DST for the diagnosis of depression should provide answers concerning the potential clinical utility of the DST in the assessment and treatment of depression. An important consideration when comparing DST results obtained in psychiatric inpatients compared to psychiatric outpatients is the fact that most DSTs done in the inpatient setting include postdexamethasone serum cortisol determinations at 4 P.M. and 11 P.M. while most outpatient evaluations include only the 4 P.M. serum cortisol determination. The 4 P.M. serum cortisol will detect approximately 80% of the abnormal DST results (Carroll, Feinberg et al., 1981). In other words, approximately 20% of the abnormal DST results will be missed if only the 4 P.M. sample is obtained. This fact obviously affects the performance of the DST and the sensitivity findings of the DST for the diagnosis of depression in the outpatient setting where the sensitivity will be necessarily lower if only the 4 P.M. sample is obtained. Also, there may be considerably less chance of noncompliance in inpatient studies and hence less chance for false-positive tests based on missed dexamethasone administration.

Sensitivity

The sensitivity of the DST for the diagnosis of depression has varied somewhat in the available studies. A review of early studies

(Carroll, 1983a) pooled data on approximately 1,000 patients and found a combined sensitivity of 45%. A more recent review of approximately 5,000 patients found a combined sensitivity of 44% (Arana *et al.*, 1985). These combined data include both inpatient and outpatient DST results and, as indicated above, the sensitivity will be higher in the inpatient studies using two (4 P.M. and 11 P.M.) blood samplings than in the outpatient protocols using only one (4 P.M.) blood sampling, for example, 67% for inpatients and 49% for outpatients (Carroll, Feinberg *et al.*, 1981). In the earlier review (Carroll, 1983a), the sensitivity ranged from 24% to 100%, but the dose of dexamethasone varied from 0.5 mg to 2 mg and the cutoff criterion for an abnormal test varied; in addition, blood sampling ranged from 1 to 3 samples per DST. The more recent review included only the 1 mg DST, and the sensitivity generally ranged from approximately 40% to 60% (mean 44%) across the various studies. However, inpatient and outpatient studies were included and the schedule of blood sampling varied across the studies. In a recent study (Evans & Nemeroff, in press a), we found an abnormal DST in 63% of hospitalized patients meeting criteria for major depression ($n = 104$). In summary, the DST appears moderately sensitive for the diagnosis of depression, with between approximately 40% to 60% of depressed patients showing abnormal DST results.

As noted in the recent DST review of over 5,000 patients (Arana *et al.*, 1985), the rate of DST abnormality increases across the range of normal controls, acute grief, dysthymic disorders, major depression without melancholia, major depression with melancholia, major depression with psychosis, mixed mania, and severely suicidal depressives. This may suggest that DST abnormality represents an increasing degree of severity of depression and/or a more biologically distinct subtype of depression. Consistent with this relationship is the finding of not only an increasing rate of DST nonsuppression, but a higher absolute postdexamethasone serum cortisol concentration across the range of patients from those with depressive symptoms to those with major depression without melancholia, major depression with melancholia, and major depression with psychosis

(Evans, Burnett, & Nemeroff, 1983; Evans & Nemeroff, 1983b; Evans & Nemeroff, in press a).

Specificity

One of the controversies surrounding the clinical use of the DST is whether the DST is specific for the diagnosis of depression; that is, is there a high false-positive rate for abnormal DSTs in psychiatric disorders other than depression? Here, a critical reading of the available studies is necessary to understand and address this controversy. Two recent reviews (Arana *et al.*, 1985; Carroll, 1985) have summarized specificity data for the DST and an inspection of these two reviews and available studies is instructive.

Considerable data now exist which confirm that the DST is highly specific for depression when compared to normal controls; DST results in over 1,000 normal controls yield a specificity of 92.8% (Arana *et al.*, 1985). The specificity data from three studies of patients with panic and phobic disorders is similar to that found in normal controls and suggest that the DST is highly specific for major depression when compared to panic and phobic disorder (Curtis, Cameron, & Nesse, 1982; Lieberman *et al.*, 1983; Sheehan *et al.*, 1983). Curtis and associates (1982) studied 17 patients with active panic attacks (agoraphobia with panic attacks or panic disorder) and found an abnormal DST in 3 patients. However, 2 of the patients with an abnormal DST were in acute alcohol withdrawal and had normal DSTs following detoxification from alcohol; the third patient met criteria for major depression. Lieberman and associates (1983) found normal suppression of serum cortisol in 10 out of 10 patients with panic disorder who were administered the DST. In a similar study, Sheehan and associates (1983) studied 51 patients with agoraphobia with panic attacks and found abnormal DST results in 6 patients. When the RIA results were compared to the competitive protein binding method, it was found that 7.125 μg/ml by RIA corresponded to 5.0 μg/dl by competitive protein binding; 4 of 51 patients had abnormal DSTs using this corrected cutoff criterion. The findings of these three outpatient studies taken together suggest that the DST has a very high specificity for major depression when compared to panic and phobic disorders. In fact, if the 2 patients with alcohol withdrawal and the 1 patient with major depression are excluded (Curtis et al., 1982) and the appropriate cutoff criterion is used in the Sheehan et al. (1983) study, only 4 of 78 patients with panic attacks had a positive DST (95% specificity).

If the DST is to have clinical utility, it is important for the test to distinguish between affective disorder and schizophrenia. Arana et al. (1985) pooled data on 275 schizophrenic patients, reported a combined specificity of 87%, and suggested that with this specificity the DST may be clinically useful in separating schizophrenia from depression, mania, or acute psychosis. It should be noted that the often quoted early study by Dewan and associates (1982), who found only 70% specificity, used a relatively imprecise fluorometric assay that might be expected to give false-positive DST results (and seemingly lower specificity) with the 5 $\mu g/dl$ cutoff criterion. Carroll (1985) notes a 94% DST specificity for schizophrenia in his recent review. A recent study by Herz, Fava, Molnar, and Edwards (1985) found 73% abnormal DSTs in newly hospitalized schizophrenic patients ($n = 15$). The DST was performed on the first day of admission, and it is unclear whether these abnormal DST findings represent the acute effect of hospitalization (Clower, 1985; Herz, Molnar, & Fava, 1985) or physiological instability (Carroll & Haskett, 1985; Haskett, Zis, Albala & Carroll, 1983). However, it appears that for clinical use, the DST should not be performed during the first 3 days of acute hospitalization (Carroll, Feinberg et al., 1981; Haskett et al., 1983).

In addition to having apparent potential clinical utility in distinguishing major depression from schizophrenia, the DST appears to strongly distinguish affective psychosis (psychotic depression and mixed bipolar disorder) from schizophrenia (Arana et al., 1985). Any capacity of the DST to aid in the detection of affective psychosis and in the separation of affective psychosis from schizophrenia suggests an important potential clinical utility in the diagnostic assessment and selection of proper treatment for patients presenting with psychosis.

The DST findings are more variable in patients diagnosed as having atypical psychosis, schizophreniform disorder, and schizoaffective disorder. Arana et al. (1985) reviewed DST findings on nearly 100 patients with one of these diagnoses and found a combined specificity of 65%, suggesting a high false positive rate (35%). Since these diagnoses, particularly schizoaffective and atypical psychosis, are not well defined and are used generally for patients who present with atypical symptoms and who are often difficult to diagnose using current descriptive criteria, it is, of course, possible that some of these patients are suffering from an affective disorder. To the extent that this proves to be the case, the abnormal DSTs would be true positives and therefore could be useful in identifying affective disorder in this population of patients. This possibility is consistent with Targum's (1983) follow-up findings on schizophreniform disorder, but further study is necessary.

The concept that the DST is a biological marker not only for major depression, but for affective disorder in general is an important concept and is consistent with the DST findings in mania. Although early reports (Schlesser et al., 1980) suggested that the DST was negative in mania, much evidence has accumulated to suggest that the DST is positive at a high rate in patients in the mixed manic state and the dysphoric manic state, but at a lower rate in patients in the euphoric manic state (Evans & Nemeroff, in press a; Evans & Nemeroff, 1983a, 1984a & b; Feinberg & Opler, 1984; Krishnan, Maltbie, & Davidson, 1983). This high rate of DST abnormality seems consistent with the fact that mania and depression are each phases of the same affective disorder and can even coexist in the mixed (and perhaps the dysphoric) manic state. Therefore, rather than viewing these DST results in mania as evidence for poor specificity of the DST (Graham et al., 1982), it seems more consistent to view the DST as a potential marker for major affective disorder, which includes both depression and mania.

An early report (Insel, Kalin, Guttmacher, Cohen, & Murphy, 1982) on the use of the DST in obsessive–compulsive disorder has often been interpreted to suggest that the DST is positive in obsessive–compulsive disorder and therefore is nonspecific for major depression. Although the DST was positive

(8 A.M., 4 P.M., 11 P.M.) in 6 of 16 patients with obsessive–compulsive disorder, 4 of the 6 patients also were major depressed. Thus, the abnormal DST findings covaried with depression rather than obsessive–compulsive disorder, which is consistent with a more recent study in which the DST was 100% specific with no positive DST results (4 P.M.) in 18 obsessive–compulsive patients (Lieberman et al., 1985).

The psychiatric presentation of elderly patients is often one of depression, dementia, or depression superimposed upon dementia. Because major depression and dementia often share certain common signs and symptoms, the clinical differentiation between the two conditions can be very difficult. The cognitive impairment seen in depressed patients has led to the concept of depressive pseudodementia. Several early reports suggested that the DST might be useful in distinguishing depressive pseudodementia from dementia (McAllister, Ferrell, Price, & Neville, 1982; Rudorfer & Clayton, 1981, 1982). However, the DST findings in patients with dementia are variable. Carnes, Smith, Kalin, and Bauwens (1983) found normal DST results in all of the 14 demented patients they studied, and Castro, Lemaire, Toscano-Aguilar, and Herchuelz (1983) found normal DST findings in 13 of 15 patients with dementia. However, Spar and Gerner (1982) and Raskind et al. (1982) found abnormal DSTs in 9 of 17 (53%) and 7 of 15 (47%) demented patients, respectively. Several of the patients in the Spar and Gerner (1982) study were severely demented, and the patients in the Raskind et al. (1982) study were so severely demented that meaningful speech was grossly impaired. Therefore, it appears that the DST will be falsely positive in patients with advanced dementia. Thus, Grunhaus, Dilsaver, Greden, and Carroll (1983) suggested that the severity and state of dementia may be better correlated with DST nonsuppression than dementia per se. Further study will be necessary to determine if the DST has any utility in identifying major depression in patients with early and/or mild to moderate dementia.

A relationship between alcoholism and depression has been suggested based on both epidemiological data (Weissman et al., 1977) and family history investigation (G. Winokur, Behar, Van Valkenburg, & Lowry, 1978). It is clinically important, but often difficult to diagnose major depression in patients with alcoholism. Although acute withdrawal from alcohol was included in the medical exclusion criteria for the DST (Carroll, Feinberg et al., 1981), numerous studies have examined the use of the DST in the acute withdrawal phase and after withdrawal from alcohol in alcoholic patients with and without major depression. A review of the available studies suggests that the DST is positive in a high percentage of alcoholic patients in acute withdrawal, a finding consistent with the medical exclusion criteria. Swartz and Dunner (1982) studied 43 alcoholic patients without major depression and found that 33% showed an abnormal DST result during the first week of abstinence (median 5 days following admission). Nelson et al. (1984) studied 28 alcoholic patients after 5 days of abstinence and found a nonsuppression rate of 39%. Targum, Capodanno, Unger, and Advani (1984) studied 83 alcoholic patients without major depression and found a 19% rate of nonsuppression during the first week of abstinence.

If the DST is performed after approximately 3 weeks of abstinence, the false-positive DST results decrease considerably and the DST appears to be specific for the diagnosis of depression. Khan et al. (1984) administered the DST to 66 nondepressed alcoholic patients an average of 21 days after the last alcohol use and found only 6% positive DSTs. Kroll, Palmer, and Greden (1983) studied 38 alcoholic patients during the fourth week of abstinence (21–28 days) and found a nonsuppression rate of 18%; when the coexistence of depression and alcoholism was considered, it appeared that approximately 10% of the alcoholics without apparent depression had false-positive DST results. Targum, Wheadon, Chastek, McCabe, & Advani (1982) studied 28 alcoholic patients (14 with and 14 without major depression) between the 6th and 28th day (median 14.6 days) of abstinence and found nonsuppression in 64% of the depressed alcoholics and in none of the nondepressed alcoholics. Ravi et al. (1984) reported a 63% nonsuppression rate for alcoholic patients tested after 5 days of abstinence and an 11% nonsuppression rate when the patients were tested again after 25 days of abstinence; none of the patients met clinical criteria for major depression. Dackis *et al.* (1984) studied 32 alcoholic patients without major depression and found a 20% nonsuppression rate among the 15 patients in acute withdrawal during the first week of abstinence and normal DST findings in all 32 alcoholic patients tested during the fourth week of abstinence. In summary, the DST is positive in a high percentage of patients in acute alcohol withdrawal, but can be performed after approximately 3 weeks of abstinence, with a low false-positive rate. Thus, the DST may prove useful in identifying major depression in recently withdrawn (approximately three weeks) alcoholic patients.

Although developmental vicissitudes can complicate the assessment of depression in the adolescent patient, several studies (Puig-Antich, 1982; Robbins, Allessi, Yanchyshyn, & Colfer, 1982; Stroeber & Carlson, 1982) suggest that depression can be diagnosed using the same descriptive criteria as used in the adult patient. Considerable variability exists among the studies using the DST in adolescent patients. The reported sensitivity of the DST for the diagnosis of major depression has ranged from a high of 64% (Hsu *et al.*, 1983) and 53% (Extein, Rosenberg, Pottash, & Gold, 1982) to a low of 36% (Ha, Kaplan, & Foley, 1984) and 25% (Robins *et al.*, 1983). In addition, some investigators have found high specificity [92% (Extein *et al.*, 1982) and 100% (Robbins *et al.*, 1983)], while others have found a lower specificity (Hsu *et al.*, 1983; Targum & Capodanno, 1983). Hsu and associates (1983) found a high DST-positive rate in adolescents with a mood disturbance other than major depression (31%) and in adolescents with nonaffective diagnoses (33%). However, Hsu and associates (1983) included adolescents with conditions that are associated with DST nonsuppression such as alcoholism and substance abuse as well as eating disorders. Targum and Capodanno (1983) found an 83% specificity and suggested that some adolescents may present with affective symptoms that differ from adult patients and that the DST may be positive in these adolescents who do not meet criteria for an affective disorder at the time of initial presentation, but who later go on to manifest an overt major affective disorder. This suggestion is con-

sistent with our clinical findings and DST results in 4 adolescents who showed nonsuppression on the DST and who did not meet criteria for a major affective disorder at the time of admission to our hospital, but who later manifested a major affective disorder (*n* = 3) or a probable affective disorder (*n* = 1) (Evans, Nemeroff, Haggerty, & Pedersen, in press b). Further clinical use of the DST is necessary to determine if there is a subset of adolescents who show atypical affective symptoms and DST nonsuppression.

The relationship between stroke and depression has been under investigation in recent years, and more than 30% of stroke patients have been reported to have significant depression, particularly during the first year (and perhaps 2 years) after stroke (Lipsey, Robinson, Pearlson, Ras, & Price, 1985; Robinson & Price, 1982; Robinson, Starr, Kubos, & Price, 1983; Robinson, Starr, & Price, 1984). Robinson and associates (1984) found that 25% of acute stroke patients have major depression, and Lipsey and associates (1985) reported that depression following stroke can be successfully treated with nortriptyline. Therefore, the clinical recognition of depression in the post-stroke patient is important and, if recognized, may lead to effective treatment of the depression. The DST has been used in post-stroke patients to identify depression, and the initial reports are encouraging (Finklestein *et al.*, 1982; Lipsey *et al.*, 1985; Reding *et al.*, 1985; Ross & Rush, 1981). Finklestein and associates (1985) studied 25 stroke patients and 13 nonstroke patients and found that the rates of depression, vegetative disturbance, and abnormal DSTs were higher in the stroke patients than in the controls: depression, 48% versus 0%; vegetative disturbance, 52% versus 8%; abnormal DST, 52% versus 8%. Follow-up DSTs in 2 patients were consistent with the clinical state. Reding and associates (1985) studied 78 patients on average 7 weeks following stroke and found that 38 patients (49%) had an abnormal DST. Only 8 A.M. and 4 P.M. cortisols were obtained following dexamethasone; the 8 A.M. cortisol was 47% sensitive and 87% specific for depression, and the 4 P.M. cortisol was 55% sensitive and 83% specific for depression. Lipsey and associates (1985) studied 48 patients who met criteria for major depression and who had a stroke less than 1 year prior to the DST and found a significant relationship between post-stroke major depression and abnormal DST results; 67% of the major depressed patients had a positive DST compared to 30% of the nondepressed patients. These findings taken together suggest that the DST may identify major depression in approximately 50% (Finklestein et al., 1982; Reding et al., 1985) or more (Lipsey et al., 1985) of poststroke patients and may be useful as a monitor of antidepressant treatment response (Finklestein et al., 1982). However, the extent and location of the lesion in stroke patients may need to be considered in the interpretation of DST results in these patients (Evans & Nemeroff, 1985; Feibel, Kelly, Lee, & Woolf, 1983; Lipsey et al., 1985). Further study is necessary to determine if the DST is sufficiently specific for major depression in the poststroke patient (Lipsey et al., 1985) in order for the DST to have general clinical utility in this population of patients.

In considering the application of the DST to patients with borderline personality disorder, two points should be kept in mind: (1) The diagnosis of major depression and borderline personality disorder are not mutually exclusive, and reports of DST nonsuppression in borderline patients do not necessarily call into question the specificity of the test unless the studies have controlled for the presence of concurrent affective illness. (2) Some psychiatrists have argued that borderline personality disorder may, in fact, be a "form fruste" of affective illness and, hence, might be expected to share some of the neuroendocrine characteristics of depression. In fact, at least one neuroendocrine correlate of affective disease, a blunted TSH response to TRH challenge, has been described in borderline patients (Garbutt, Loosen, Tipermas, & Prange, 1983).

Several investigators have studied the DST in carefully diagnosed borderline patients. Beeber, Kline, Pies, and Manring (1984) reported on 13 borderline patients who also met Research Diagnostic Criteria (RDC) for unipolar major depression without psychosis; 8 of these patients had positive DST results. Soloff, George, and Nathan (1982) studied 19 borderline patients and observed nonsuppression in 3, all of whom were depressed as

well. Baxter, Edell, Gerner, Fairbanks, and Swirtsman (1984) found that 19 of 26 borderlines had positive DST results, but again, 18 of the nonsuppressors had affective illness as well. Finally, Carroll, Greden et al. (1981) studied 21 patients with borderline personality disorder as a principal diagnosis; 10 also met RDC for endogenous depression. The DST was positive in 13 (62%) of these patients; 8 patients had both endogenous depression and a positive DST. When the patients "identified" as having endogenous depression by the RDC and by an abnormal DST were compared, the degree of congruence was moderate; the two "measures" were in agreement in 67% of the cases. Further studies comparing the DST in borderline patients without depression to controls should help clarify the correlation between HPA dysregulation and borderline syndrome per se.

The DST has been studied in patients with eating disorders. Two important issues are related to these studies: (1) Weight loss itself as discussed above may affect the cortisol response to dexamethasone even when it occurs outside of the context of psychiatric illness [e.g., in obese but otherwise healthy subjects undergoing weight reduction through dieting (Berger et al., 1983; Edelstein et al., 1983)]. Many patients with eating disorders may be either malnourished, underweight, or have rapid fluctuations in weight, and DST results may be affected by these factors. (2) Both bulimia and anorexia nervosa have been linked to depressive illness based on family studies, phenomenology, and response to antidepressant medication (Pope & Hudson, 1982; Pyle, Mitchell, & Eckerd, 1982; A. Winokur, March, & Mendels, 1980). If, in fact, eating disorders and major depression represent different presentations of the same genotypic biological disorder, then DST nonsuppression in patients with eating disorders would not necessarily reflect poor specificity of the DST.

A number of investigators have studied the DST in patients with anorexia nervosa. Walsh et al. (1978) found that 3 out of 3 anorectic patients exhibited DST nonsuppression. Bethge and colleagues (1970), using a 3 mg dexamethasone dose and 9 A.M. cortisol sampling time, found that 4 of 8 anorectics who were 51–55% underweight were

DST positive; only 1 of 6 patients who were 20–31% underweight failed to suppress. In a more extensive study, Gerner and Gwirtsman (1981) found that 21 of 22 anorectics were DST positive. The average weight for this group was only 66.5% (+1.7%) of ideal weight. There was no difference in post-DST cortisol levels in the subgroup of anorectics diagnosed as also having major or minor depression compared to the other anorectic subjects in their study.

The DST has also been studied in patients with bulimia. Hudson *et al.* (1983) reported DST nonsuppression in 23 of 47 (47%) bulimics; Gwirtsman, Roy-Byrne, Yager, and Gerner (1983) found abnormal DSTs in 67% of 18 bulimics; Mitchell, Pyle, Hatsukami, and Boutaroff (1984) reported that 50% of their 28 bulimics had positive DSTs. Mitchell *et al.* (1984) found that postdexamethasone cortisol levels did not correlate with weight; however, most of their subjects were normal weight, with few low-weight patients. Interestingly, while Gwirtsman *et al.* (1983) found no differences between their DST-positive and DST-negative bulimics in regard to presence of depression or family histories, Mitchell *et al.* (1984) reported that their DST-positive bulimics were more likely to have first-degree relatives with affective disorders than their DST-negative patients. Thus, it appears that patients with eating disorders have a higher than expected frequency of DST nonsuppression. For bulimia, at least, this does not appear to be entirely attributable to weight loss. However, further research is necessary to determine the extent to which genetic vulnerability to depression may account for the DST nonsuppression seen in this population.

Chronic pain syndromes, like several of the psychiatric disorders discussed above, have been considered by some to be a variant form of depressive illness (Blumer & Heilbronn, 1981). Based on this construct, Blumer, Zorick, Heilbronn, and Roth (1982) applied the DST to 20 chronic pain patients and found a nonsuppression rate of 50%. However, they did not systematically apply standardized diagnostic criteria to tease out those pain subjects who met RDC or DSM-III criteria for depression. France, Krishan, Houpt, and Maltbie (1984) studied 42 patients with chronic low back pain related to definite organic pathology; 9 of the 22 patients who also met DSM-III criteria for major depression had positive DST results, while none of the 20 pain patients without concomitant depression were DST positive. In a more recent report from this group, these findings have been extended to a larger group of 80 pain patients where 40% of depressed pain patients had DST nonsuppression and none of the nondepressed pain patients were DST positive (France & Krishnan, 1985). These studies suggest that chronic pain syndromes without accompanying major depression are associated with DST suppression. Therefore, the DST may be moderately sensitive in identifying the chronic pain patient with concomitant major depression.

ANTIDEPRESSANT TREATMENT RESPONSE

Early reports suggested that the DST might be useful in predicting the response to antidepressant treatment in general (Brown & Shuey, 1980) and to specific antidepressant medications (Amsterdam *et al.*, 1983; Beckman, Holzmuller, & Fleckenstein, 1984; Brown, Haier, & Qualls, 1980; Greden *et al.*, 1981; Nelson, Orr, Stevenson, & Shane, 1982). Arana and associates (1985) recently pooled data on over 300 patients from eight separate studies and reported only an 11.1% difference in the treatment response rate between DST-positive and DST-negative patients (DST positive, 75.5%; DST negative, 64.4%). We found no significant difference in the antidepressant response rate between DST nonsuppressors and suppressors, though there was a trend for a greater response rate among nonsuppressors: nonsuppressors, 13 of 15 (87%); suppressors, 13 of 19 (68%). Furthermore, 6 of the 8 (75%) patients who did not respond to treatment showed dexamethasone suppression (Simon, Nemeroff, & Evans, 1986). The available studies of treatment response and DST status have not controlled for placebo response or for "nonsomatic" antidepressant treatment such as psychotherapy. Arana *et al.* (1985) note that a recent report (Shrivastava, Schwimmer, Browne, & Arito, 1985) found a high response rate to placebo in DST-negative patients, and these authors (Arana *et al.*,

1985) suggest that the treatment response rate to antidepressant medications could be even higher in the DST-positive patients. The implication is that DST-positive patients, as a group, might require somatic antidepressant treatment, while DST-negative patients, as a group, might respond without drug treatment. In fact, Carroll (1985) suggests that in general a technically valid, positive DST in a depressed patient warrants somatic antidepressant treatment. This possibility clearly requires further controlled study, but gains some support from clinical observations (Carroll, 1985) and research study (Rush, 1984). In a study comparing the response to cognitive therapy, Rush (1984) reported that DST-positive [and shortened rapid eye movement (REM) latency on electroencephalograms] endogenously depressed patients ($n = 5$) failed to respond to cognitive therapy (4 of 5 could not even complete treatment), whereas DST-negative (and normal REM latency) nonendogenously depressed patients responded to cognitive therapy ($n = 8$ of 9 responded).

There is no evidence available to suggest that an abnormal DST will predict a response to a particular antidepressant medication. An early study by Brown and Shuey (1980) suggested that DST nonsuppressors responded preferentially to antidepressants with relatively predominant norepinephrine reuptake blockade (imipramine or desipramine), and that DST suppressors responded preferentially to relatively predominant serotonin reuptake blockade (amitriptyline and chlomipramine). Subsequent studies found no difference in treatment response for imipramine versus amitriptyline in DST nonsuppressors (Greden et al., 1981; Nelson et al., 1982) or between amitriptyline and imipramine in DST suppressors. Furthermore, Amsterdam et al. (1983) found a poorer response to desipramine in DST nonsuppressors compared to DST suppressors. In a recent preliminary study comparing the antidepressant treatment response rate of maprotiline (a relatively predominant norepinephrine reuptake blocker) and trazodone (a relatively predominant serotonin reuptake blocker), we found no difference in the response rate for the two treatment groups; 13 of 17 (76%) patients responded in each of the treatment groups. In addition, there was no

significant treatment effect on the response rate for the DST-positive patients versus the DST-negative patients; 86% of the DST-positive patients responded to maprotiline and 88% of the DST-positive patients responded to trazodone. Furthermore, 70% of the DST-negative patients responded to maprotiline and 67% of the suppressors responded to trazodone (Simon et al., 1986). Thus, any preferential response to specific antidepressants that may exist between DST suppressors and nonsuppressors awaits additional study.

In summary, further study will be necessary to confirm if DST-positive depressed patients require somatic antidepressant treatment and if DST status might even be helpful in selecting the specific type of antidepressant treatment (somatic and/or psychotherapeutic). However, at the present time any such conclusions would be premature. Although there is some evidence that a positive DST in a depressed patient may suggest a need for somatic treatment (Carroll, 1985; Rush, 1984), the choice of antidepressant treatment should be based on clinical grounds and should include, when clinically indicated, the use of neuroleptics, lithium, and ECT in addition to antidepressant drugs. Furthermore, there is no convincing evidence that DST-negative patients with major depression should receive any less (or different) antidepressant treatment than DST-positive, major depressed patients.

TREATMENT OUTCOME

A number of early studies reported that the DST normalizes in depressed patients after treatment and clinical recovery (Albala, Greden, Tarika, & Carroll, 1981; Brown & Shuey, 1980; Carroll, 1982; Greden et al., 1980), and several studies suggested that the DST may predict the risk of relapse after treatment (Goldberg, 1980a, 1980b; Greden et al., 1980).

Two recent reviews have summarized the available studies on DST normalization, clinical response, and treatment outcome. Carroll (1985) pooled data on 102 patients who had an abnormal DST on admission and again upon repeat testing around the time of discharge and noted that 34% of the patients studied had an abnormal repeat DST. Of these patients, 83% had a poor clinical outcome. Arana and associates (1985) pooled data from 13 studies and found that 77% of the patients who remained DST positive or again became DST positive had a poor outcome (including relapse) or a fatal outcome compared to a poor outcome in only 19% of the patients who showed normalization of the DST.

Thus, the DST could be a marker to monitor recovery from major depression. In one of the more recent studies (Nemeroff & Evans, 1984), we found that continued DST nonsuppression (patients failed to normalize the abnormal DST from initial testing on admission to repeat testing at discharge) was associated with poorer clinical response and increased risk of relapse compared to patients whose DST normalized. Further controlled study will be necessary to assess this clinical use of the DST, but the findings to date suggest that this may be one of the most clinically useful of the potential uses of the DST in clinical psychiatry.

The association between a positive DST result and suicide has been suggested by several investigators (Carroll, Greden, & Feinberg, 1981; Coryell & Schlesser, 1981; Targum, Rosen, & Capodanno, 1983). A positive DST was present in 10 of the 11 major depressed patients who went on to suicide [Carroll, Greden, & Feinberg (1981) ($n = 1$ of 1)]. Furthermore, an additional 11 depressed patients underwent serious suicide attempts, and all were DST positive (Carroll, Greden, & Feinberg, 1981). Carroll, Greden, & Feinberg (1981) reported also 3 DST-negative patients (schizophrenia, organic brain disease, anxiety neurosis) who went on to complete suicide. In addition, Targum and associates (1983) found abnormal DSTs in 14 of 17 (82%) suicidal patients (suicide attempts requiring hospitalization) compared to 9 of 32 (20%) nonsuicidal patients. Of the 17 suicidal patients, 5 reattempted suicide within 6 months after discharge and all 5 were DST positive; 3 of the 5 failed to normalize their abnormal DST. A relationship between DST abnormality and suicide in the adolescent patient has also been suggested (Robbins & Alessi, 1985). Thus, a positive DST in a depressed patient might alert the clinician to a higher risk of suicide. However, as emphasized previously (Carroll, 1985), a negative DST in other populations who are at high risk for suicide (such as schizophrenics and alcoholics) or in depressed patients who appear at risk for suicide should not lessen the concern or care necessary to prevent a suicide attempt in these patients.

CLINICAL GUIDELINES AND POTENTIAL USES OF THE DST IN CLINICAL PSYCHIATRY

The following guidelines and potential clinical uses of the DST are derived from the findings of the individual studies reported above and incorporate points made in recent reviews of the DST (Arana et al., 1985; Carroll 1983b, 1985).

1. The DST should be used in patient populations in which there is a high prevalence and a high clinical suspicion of affective disorder and should not be used as a screening test for affective disorder in unselected populations.
2. The DST may be used to confirm a diagnosis of major affective disorder or may be used as an adjunct in the clinical assessment of patients where the diagnosis is less clear-cut. The DST may help identify major affective disorder in adult patients who do not meet full criteria for major affective disorder at the time of the initial presentation, but who later show overt evidence of affective disorder. The DST may have a similar utility in those adolescent patients who present with atypical signs and symptoms of affective disorder and who later meet descriptive criteria for affective disorder. Early treatment intervention could result if this potential use of the DST is confirmed by further research study and clinical experience.
3. Valid interpretation of the DST requires that patients are, in general, medically healthy, physiologically stable, and are not taking medications known to render the results of the DST invalid. The affects of anticonvulsants and barbiturates may continue for 3 weeks after discontinuation, and DSTs performed before this time may be falsely positive.
4. Every effort should be made to ensure patient compliance in taking the dexamethasone.

5. The laboratory method used to measure serum cortisol should be sensitive and precise in the low range (3–7 μg/dl) of serum cortisol concentrations, and, if possible, the cutoff criterion for nonsuppression should be standardized by the local laboratory using normal controls and psychiatric controls.

6. To maximize avoiding an invalid, abnormal DST result, the DST should not be performed during the first 3 days of admission to the hospital. This is especially important in the acutely psychotic patient who may be physiologically unstable from poor food and fluid intake. If the acutely psychotic patient is in good food and fluid balance before the DST is performed, the DST may be useful in distinguishing the psychotic affective disorder patient from the schizophrenic patient.

7. To maximize the sensitivity of the DST, both 4 P.M. and 11 P.M. postdexamethasone blood samples should be obtained whenever possible. Approximatley 20% of the true positive test results will be missed in the major depressed patients if only the 4 P.M. sample is obtained.

8. The DST should not be performed during acute alcohol withdrawal, but can be administered after approximately 3 weeks of abstinence. The DST may be useful in helping to confirm a diagnosis of major depression in alcoholic patients who are beyond the acute phase of alcohol withdrawal.

9. While a valid, positive DST can confirm the diagnosis of major depression, a negative DST is not inconsistent with a diagnosis of major depression or with the need for antidepressant treatment of the major depression. The DST, like any laboratory test, is but one piece of information that should be used by the clinician in patient assessment. However, the DST may separate major affective disorder patients into more homogeneous groups, and further research may determine treatment guidelines based, in part, on DST status.

10. The DST may be useful in assessing the response to treatment. Persistently abnormal DST results based on repeated testings may be associated with poor outcome as well as increased risk of relapse of depression and therefore may support the need for continued antidepressant treatment. Normalization of the DST prior to clinical recovery may support the continuation of the current antidepressant treatment. However, no evidence exists to suggest that normalization of the DST would permit discontinuation of the current antidepressant treatment. Longitudinal assessment of clinical course and results of repeated DSTs will be necessary to address this issue more fully.

11. Repeated use of the DST in the longitudinal clinical care of affective disorder patients may be useful in predicting or assessing relapse of the affective disorder. If the clinician has established (based on past clinical course and DST results) that the patient has an abnormal DST when psychiatrically ill and a normal DST when clinically well, a change from a normal DST to an abnormal DST might suggest an impending relapse and may help in decisions regarding treatment. It is not an uncommon clinical situation for patients to develop mild to moderate signs and symptoms of affective disorder which may or may not be the early signs of relapse. An abnormal DST in this clinical context might be helpful in guiding treatment decisions, but further research is necessary to confirm the utility of the DST in this regard.

12. An abnormal DST in a depressed patient might increase clinical concern regarding the risk of suicide. However, a normal DST in other populations at risk for suicide (alcoholics and schizophrenics) and in depressed patients should not be used to lessen the concern over suicide when clinical assessment supports a high suicide risk.

13. The DST does not appear to be useful in distinguishing major depression from dementia, although further work is necessary to determine if the DST can identify depression in patients with early, mild dementia.

14. The DST may be helpful in identifying the presence of major depression in patients after stroke, and if this finding is

borne out by further study, this use of the DST could lead to the necessary antidepressant treatment of stroke patients with depression.

CONCLUSIONS

The 1 mg overnight DST is a simple laboratory test first used for Cushing's syndrome and recently used in psychiatry as a putative marker of major depression. The DST has been researched extensively and has received unprecedented use in clinical psychiatry. It has sparked both considerable interest in the use of laboratory tests in psychiatry and controversy regarding the clinical utility of the DST for the diagnosis and treatment of major affective disorders.

The DST is moderately sensitive for the diagnosis of major affective disorder, and approximately 50% of major affective disorder patients will have an abnormal test result. The rate of DST abnormality increases across the range of diagnoses from normal controls, acute grief, dysthymic disorder, major depression without melancholia, major depression with melancholia, to major depression with psychosis and mixed mania.

The specificity of the DST for the diagnosis of major depression appears to be sufficiently high to distinguish (with moderate sensitivity) patients with major depression from normal controls as well as from patients with obsessive–compulsive disorder, panic disorders, schizophrenia, alcoholism (after 3 weeks of abstinence), and possibily strokes and pain disorders. The DST may prove particularly helpful in distinguishing patients with psychotic affective disorders from patients with schizophrenia or nonaffective psychoses. However, the DST should not be administered to acutely psychotic patients until they are physiologically stable; therefore, the DST is not useful in identifying affective psychoses in these patients because of the high false-positive rate. In addition, the DST does not appear to be useful in identifying depression in patients with eating disorders, borderline disorders, or dementia.

The DST may be a useful marker of treatment response in those depressed patients with an abnormal DST. Failure to normalize the abnormal DST may be associated with poorer clinical outcome and increased risk of relapse. In addition, the DST may prove to be a marker of relapse of depression in patients who develop an abnormal DST after having normalized it upon recovery previously. This could alert the clinician to adjust the antidepressant dose or to reinitiate antidepressant treatment. There is evidence also that an abnormal DST in a depressed patient might be associated with a higher risk of suicide; a normal DST should not lessen the concern regarding suicide in depressed or nondepressed patients.

As is the case with all laboratory tests, the clinician should use the test as an adjunct in the clinical assessment of the patient. It should be emphasized that the DST is not to be used as a screening test for major affective disorder, and the test will be most useful in patient populations with a high prevalence of affective illness and those who are selected on the basis of a high likelihood of having an affective disorder.

The research application of the DST is established and will evolve further as the test receives additional use in the clinical setting. The potential limitations and uses of the DST in the clinical setting have already received considerable attention. If the clinician gives consideration to all of the factors necessary for a technically valid DST, each clinician can gain experience with the DST and can help determine potential clinical uses. Available studies suggest that at the present time the DST may have its main clinical use in diagnosing selected patients with suspected depression (particularly patients with affective psychosis), and, in addition, as a marker of recovery and as a monitor of continued treatment response and relapse. Only further controlled study and clinical use will determine the ultimate utility of the DST for the assessment and treatment of major affective disorder in clinical psychiatry.

Separate from its clinical utility, the DST has considerable value as a research tool in probing the pathophysiology of affective illness. By identifying a particular subtype of depressed patient, it provides a more homogenous group of subjects in which to test hypotheses about the biological bases of depression and its treatment. It has already drawn a considerable amount of attention and interest to the field of biological research and has helped to nurture the development of other "challenge strategies" in psychiatric research.

References

Aggernaes, H., Kirkegaard, C., Krog-Meyer, I., Kijne, B., Larsen, J. K., Lund Laursen, A., Lykke-Olesen, L., Mikkelsen, P. L., Rasmussen, S., & Bjorum, N. (1983). Dexamethasone suppression test and TRH test in endogenous depression. *Acta Pscyhiatrica Scandinavica, 67*, 258–264.

Agren, H., & Wide, L. (1982). Patterns of depression reflected in pituitary–thyroid and pituitary–adrenal endocrine changes. *Psychoneuroendocrinology, 7*, 309–327.

Albala, A. A., Greden, J. F., Tarika, J., Carroll, B. J. (1981). Changes in serial dexamethasone suppression tests among unipolar depressives receiving electroconvulsive treatment. *Biological Psychiatry, 16*, 551–560.

Alexopoulos, G. S., Young, R. L., Koesis, J. H., Brockner, N., Butler, T. A., & Stokes, P. E. (1984). Dexamethasone suppression test in geriatric depression. *Biological Psychiatry, 19*, 1567–1571.

Amsterdam, J. D., Winokur, A., Caroff, S. N., & Conn, J. (1982). The dexamethasone suppression test in outpatients with primary affective disorder and healthy control subjects. *American Journal of Psychiatry, 139*(3), 287–291.

Amsterdam, J. D., Winokur, A., Lucki, I., Caroff, S., Snyder, P., & Rickels, K. (1983). A neuroendocrine test battery in bipolar patients and healthy subjects. *Archives of General Psychiatry, 40*, 515–521.

Arana, G. W., Baldessarini, R. J., & Ornsteen, M. (1985). The dexamethasone suppression test for diagnosis and prognosis in psychiatry. *Archives of General Psychiatry, 42*, 1193–1204.

Arana, G. W., Workman, R. J., & Baldessarini, R. J. (1984). Association between low plasma levels of dexamethasone and elevated levels of cortisol in psychiatric patients given dexamethasone. *American Journal of Psychiatry, 141*, 1619–1620.

Baldessarini, R. J., Finklestein, S., & Arana, G. W. (1983). The predictive power of diagnostic tests and the effect of prevalence of illness. *Archives of General Psychiatry, 40*, 596–573.

Baumgartner, A., Graf, K. J., & Kurten, I. (1985). The dexamethasone suppression test in depression, in schizophrenia, and during experimental stress. *Biological Psychiatry, 20*, 675–679.

Baxter, L., Edell, W., Gerner, R., Fairbanks, L., & Swirtsman, H. (1984). Dexamethasone suppression test and axis I diagnoses in inpatients with DSM-III borderline personality disorder. *Journal of Clinical Psychiatry, 45*, 150–153.

Beckman, H., Holzmuller, B., & Fleckenstein, P. (1984). Clinical investigations into antidepressive mechanisms. II. Dexamethasone suppression test predicts response to nomifensine or amitriptyline. *Acta Psychiatrica Scandinavica, 70*, 341–353.

Beeber, A. R., Kline, M. D., Pies, R. W., & Manring, J. M., Jr. (1984). Dexamethasone suppression test in hosptialized depressed patients with borderline personality disorder. *Journal of Nervous and Mental Disease, 172*, 301–303.

Berger, M., Pirke, K. M., Doerr, P., Krieg, C., & von Zerssen, D. (1983). Influence of weight loss on the dexamethasone suppression test. *Archives of General Psychiatry, 40*, 585–586.

Berger, M., Pirke, K. M., Doerr, P., Krieg, C., & von Zerssen, D. (1984). The limited utility of the dexamethasone suppression test for the diagnostic process in psychiatry. *British Journal of Psychiatry, 145*, 372–382.

Bethge, H., Nagel, A. M., Solbach, H. G., Wiegelmann, W., & Zimmermann, H. (1970). Disturbance of cortisol regulation of adrenocortical function in anorexia nervosa, parallels to endogenous depression and Cushing's syndrome. *Materia Medica Nordmark, 22*, 204–214.

Blumer, D., & Heilbronn, M. (1981). The pain-prone disorder: A clinical and psychological profile. *Psychosomatics, 22*, 395–402.

Blumer, D., Zorick, F., Heilbronn, M., & Roth, T. (1982). Biological markers for depression in chronic pain. *Journal of Nervous and Mental Disease, 170*, 425–428.

Brown, W. A., Haier, R. J., & Qualls, C. B. (1980). Dexamethasone suppression test identifies subtypes of depression which respond to different antidepressants. *Lancet, 1*, 928–929.

Brown, W. A., & Qualls, C. B. (1981). Pituitary–adrenal distribution in depression: Marker of a subtype with characteristic clinical features and response to treatment? *Psychiatry Research, 4*, 115–128.

Brown, W. A., & Shuey, I. (1980). Response to dexamethasone and subtype of depression. *Archives of General Psychiatry, 37*, 747–751.

Cameron, O. G., Kronfol, Z., Greden, J. F., & Carroll, B. J. (1984). Hypothalamic–pituitary–adrenocortical activity in patients with diabetes mellitus. *Archives of General Psychiatry, 41*, 1090–1095.

Carnes, M., Smith, J. C., Kalin, N. H., & Bauwens, S. F. (1983). The dexamethasone suppression test in demented outpatients with and without depression. *Psychiatry Research, 9*, 337–334.

Carr, V., Morris, H., & Gilliland, J. (1986). The effect of serum dexamethasone concentrations in the dexamethasone suppression test. *Biological Psychiatry, 21*, 735–743.

Carroll, B. J. (1982). The dexamethasone suppression test for melancholia. *British Journal of Psychiatry, 140*, 292–304.

Carroll, B. J. (1983a). Biological markers and treatment response. *Journal of Clinical Psychiatry, 44*, 30–40.

Carroll, B. J. (1983b). Dexamethasone suppression test. In R. C. W. Hall & T. P. Beresford (Eds.), *Handbook of psychiatric diagnostic procedures*. New York: Spectrum Publications.

Carroll, B. J. (1985). Dexamethasone suppression test: A review of contemporary confusion. *Journal of Clinical Psychiatry, 46*, 13–24.

Carroll, B. J., & Davies, B. M. (1970). Clinical associations of 11-hydroxycorticosteroid suppression and nonsuppression in severe depressive illness. *British Medical Journal, 1*, 789–791.

Carroll, B. J., Feinberg, M., Greden, J. F., Haskett, R. E., James, N. M., Steiner, M., & Tarika, J. (1980). Diagnosis of endogenous depression: Comparison of clinical, research and neuroendocrine criteria. *Journal of Affective Disorders, 2*, 177–194.

Carroll, B. J., Feinberg, M., Greden, J. F., Tarika, J., Albala, A. A., Haskett, R. F., James, N. M., Kronfol, Z., Lohr, N., Steiner, M., de Vigne, J. P., & Young, E. (1981). A specific laboratory test for the diagnosis of melancholia. *Archives of General Psychiatry, 38*, 15–22.

Carroll, B. J., Greden, J. F., & Feinberg, M. (1981). Suicide, neuroendocrine dysfunction and CSF 5-HIAA concentrations in depression. In B. Angrist (Ed.), *Recent advances in neuropsychopharmacology.* Oxford: Pergamon Press.

Carroll, B. J., Greden, J. F., Feinberg, M., Lohr, N., James, N., Steiner, M., Haskett, R. F., Albala, A. A., de Vigne, J. P., & Tarika, J. (1981). Neuroendocrine evaluation of depression in borderline patients. *Psychiatric Clinics of North America, 4*, 89–99.

Carroll, B. J., & Haskett, R. F. (1985). The DST in newly hospitalized patients. *American Journal of Psychiatry, 143*, 999–1000.

Carroll, B. J., Martin, F. I. R., & Davies, B. M. (1968). Resistance to suppression by dexamethasone of plasma 11-OHCS levels in severe depressive illness. *British Medical Journal, 3*, 285–287.

Carroll, B. J., & Mendels, J. (1976). Neuroendocrine regulation in affective disorders. In E. J. Sachar (Ed.), *Hormones, behavior and psychopathology.* New York: Raven Press.

Carroll, B. J., Schroeder, K., Makhopadhyay, S., Greden, J. F., Feinberg, M., Ritchie, J., & Tarika, J. (1980). Plasma dexamethasone concentrations and cortisol suppression response in patients with endogenous depression. *Journal of Clinical Endocrinology and Metabolism, 51*, 433–437.

Castro, P., Lemaire, M., Toscano-Aguilar, M., & Herchuelz, A. (1983). Depression, dementia, and the dexamethasone suppression test. *American Journal of Psychiatry, 140*, 386.

Ceulemans, D. L., Westenberg, H. G., & van Pragg, H. M. (1985). The effects of stress on the dexamethasone suppression test. *Psychiatry Research, 14*, 189–195.

Clower, C. G. (1985). The DST in newly hospitalized patients. *American Journal of Psychiatry, 142*, 999.

Coccaro, E. F., Prudie, J., Rothpearl, A., & Nurnberg, H. G. (1984). Effect of hospital admission on DST results. *American Journal of Psychiatry, 141*, 982–985.

Coryell, W., & Schlesser, M. A. (1981). Suicide and the dexamethasone suppression test in unipolar depression. *American Journal of Psychiatry, 138*, 1120–1121.

Curtis, G. C., Cameron, O. G., & Nesse, R. M. (1982). The dexamethasone suppression test in panic disorder and agoraphobia. *American Journal of Psychiatry, 139*, 1043–1046.

Dackis, C. A., Bailey, J., Pottash, A. L. C., Stuckey, R. F., Extein, I. L., & Gold, M. S. (1984). Specificity of the DST and the TRH test for major depression in alcoholics. *American Journal of Psychiatry, 141*, 680–683.

Das, M., & Berrios, G. E. (1984). Dexamethasone suppression test in acute grief reaction. *Acta Psychiatrica Scandinavica, 70*, 278–281.

Davis, K. L., Davis, B. M., Mathe, A. A., Morris, R. C.,

Rothpearl, A. B., Levy, M. I., Gorman, L. K., Berger, P. (1984). Age and the dexamethasone suppression test in depression. *American Journal of Psychiatry, 141*, 872–874.

Dewan, M. J., Pandurangi, A. K., Boucher, M. L., Levy, B. F., & Major, L. F. (1982). Abnormal dexamethasone suppression test results in chronic schizophrenic patients. *American Journal of Pscyhiatry, 139*, 1501–1503.

Edelstein, C. K., Roy-Byrne, P., Fawzy, F. I., & Dornfeld, L. (1983). Effects of weight loss on the dexamethasone suppression test. *American Journal of Psychiatry, 140*, 338–341.

Evans, D. L., Burnett, G. B., & Nemeroff, C. B. (1983). The dexamethasone suppression test in the clinical setting. *American Journal of Psychiatry, 140*, 586–589.

Evans, D. L., McCartney, C. F., Nemeroff, C. B., Raft, D., Quade, D., Golden, R. N., Haggerty, J. J., Holmes, V., Simon, J. S., Droba, M., Mason, G. A., & Fowler, W. C. (1986). Depression in women treated for gynecological cancer: Clinical and neuroendocrine assessment. *American Journal of Psychiatry, 143*, 447–452.

Evans, D. L., & Nemeroff, C. B. (1983a). The dexamethasone suppression test in mixed bipolar disorder. *American Journal of Psychiatry, 140*, 615–617.

Evans, D. L., & Nemeroff, C. B. (1983a). Use of the dexamethasone suppression test using DSM-III criteria on an inpatient psychiatric unit. *Biological Psychiatry, 18*, 505–511.

Evans, D. L., & Nemeroff, C. B. (1984a). The dexamethasone suppression test in organic affective syndrome. *American Journal of Psychiatry, 141*, 1465–1467.

Evans, D. L., & Nemeroff, C. B. (1984b). The dexamethasone suppression test in the mixed manic state: Reply. *American Journal of Psychiatry, 141*, 146–147.

Evans, D. L., & Nemeroff, C. B. (1985). The DST and organic affective disorder: Reply. *American Journal of Psychiatry, 142*, 992.

Evans, D. L., & Nemeroff, C. B. (in press a). The clinical use of the dexamethasone suppression test in DSM-III affective disorders: Correlation with the severe depressive subtypes of melancholia and psychosis. *Journal of Psychiatry Research.*

Evans, D. L., Nemeroff, C. B., Haggerty, J. J., & Pederson, C. A. (in press b). Use of the dexamethasone suppression test with DSM-III criteria in psychiatrically hospitalized adolescents. *Psychoneuroendocrinology.*

Extein, I., Rosenberg, G., Pottach, A. L. C., & Gold, M. S. (1982). The dexamethasone suppression test in depressed adolescents. *American Journal of Psychiatry, 139*, 1617–1619.

Feibel, J., Kelly, M., Lee, L., & Woolf, P. (1983). Loss of adrenocortical suppression after acute brain injury: Role of increased intracranial pressure and brain stem function. *Journal of Clinical Endocrinology and Metabolism, 57*, 1245–1250.

Feinberg, M., & Carroll, B. J. (1984). Biological markers for endogenous depression: Effect of age, severity of illness, weight loss and polarity. *Archives of General Psychiatry, 41*, 1080–1085.

Feinberg, S. S., & Opler, L. A. (1984). Bipolar disorder, mixed, and the DST. *American Journal of Psychiatry*, *141*, 145–146.

Finklestein, S., Benowitz, L. I., Baldessarini, R. J., Arana, G. W., Levine, D., Woo, E., Bear, D., Moya, K., & Stoll, A. L. (1982). Mood, vegetative disturbance, and the dexamethasone suppression test after stroke. *Annals of Neurology*, *12*, 463–468.

Fogel, B. S., & Satel, S. L. (1985). Age, medical illness and the DST in depressed general hospital inpatients. *Journal of Clinical Psychiatry*, *46*, 95–97.

France, R. D., & Krishnan, K. R. (1985). The dexamethasone suppression test as a biological marker of depression in chronic pain. *Pain*, *21*, 49–55.

France, R. D., Krishan, K. R., Houpt, J. L., & Maltbie, A. A. (1984). Differentiation of depression from chronic pain with the dexamethasone suppression test and DSM-III. *American Journal of Psychiatry*, *141*, 1577–1579.

Freedman, D. X., & Glass, R. M. (1983). Editorial note: Testing endocrine tests in clinical psychiatry. *Archives of General Psychiatry*, *40*, 587–588.

Garbutt, J. C., Loosen, P. T., Tipermas, A., & Prange, A. J., Jr. (1983). The TRH test in patients with borderline personality disorder. *Psychiatry Research*, *9*, 107–113.

Geller, B., Rogol, A. D., & Knitter, E. F. (1983). Preliminary data on the dexamethasone suppression test in children. *American Journal of Psychiatry*, *140*, 620–622.

Gerner, R., & Gwirtsman, H. (1981). Abnormalities of dexamethasone suppression test and urinary MHPG in anorexia nervosa. *American Journal of Psychiatry*, *138*, 650–655.

Gibbons, J. L., & McHugh, P. R. (1963). Plasma cortisol in depressive illness. *Journal of Psychiatric Research*, *1*, 162–171.

Goldberg, I. K. (1980a). Dexamethasone suppression test as indicator of safe withdrawal of antidepressant therapy. *Lancet*, *1*, 376.

Goldberg, I. K. (1980b). Dexamethasone suppression tests in depression and response to treatment. *Lancet*, *2*, 92.

Graham, P. M., Booth, J., Boranga, G., Galhenage, S., Myres, C. M., Teoh, C. L., & Cox, L. S. (1982). The dexamethasone suppression test in mania. *Journal of Affective Disorders*, *4*, 201–211.

Greden, J. F., Albala, A. A., Haskett, R. F., James, N. M., Goodman, L., Steiner, M., & Carroll, B. J. (1980). Normalization of dexamethasone suppression test: A laboratory index of recovery from endogenous depression. *Biological Psychiatry*, *15*, 449–458.

Greden, J. F., Kronfol, Z., Gardner, R., Feinberg, M., Mukhopadhyay, S., Albala, A., & Carroll, B. (1981). Dexamethasone suppression test and selection of antidepressant medications. *Journal of Affective Disorders*, *3*, 389–396.

Greden, J. F., Tiongco, D., Haskett, R. F., Grunhaus, L., & Kotun, J. (1986). *Interactions between depression and aging in HPA dysregulation*. Presented at the 41st annual meeting of the Society of Biological Psychiatry, Washington, DC, No. 155.

Grunhaus, L., Dilsaver, S., Greden, J. F., Carroll, B. J.

(1983). Depressive pseudodementia: A suggested diagnostic profile. *Biological Psychiatry*, *18*, 215–225.

Gwirtsman, H., Roy-Byrne, P., Yager, J., & Gerner, R. (1983). Neuroendocrine abnormalities in bulimia. *American Journal of Psychiatry*, *140*, 559–563.

Ha, H., Kaplan, S., & Foley, C. (1984). The dexamethasone suppression test in adolescent psychiatric patients. *American Journal of Psychiatry*, *141*, 421–423.

Hallström, T., Samuelsson, S., Balldin, J., Walinder, J., Bengtsson. C., Nystrom, E., Andersch, B., Lindstedt, G., & Lundberg, P. (1983). Abnormal dexamethasone suppression test in normal females. *British Journal of Psychiatry*, *142*, 489–497.

Haskett, R. F., Zis, A. P., Albala, A. A., & Carroll, B. J. (1983). *DST performance during first 48 hours of admission*. Presented at the 38th annual meeting of the Society of Biological Psychiatry, Los Angeles, CA. P. 134.

Helzer, J. E., Clayton, P. J., Pambakian, R., Reich, T., Woodruff, R., & Reveley, M. (1977). Reliability of psychiatric diagnosis. II. The test–retest reliability of diagnostic classification. *Archives of General Psychiatry*, *34*, 136–141.

Herz, M. I., Fava, G. A., Molnar, G., & Edwards, L. (1985). The dexamethasone suppression test in newly hospitalized schizophrenic patients. *American Journal of Psychiatry*, *142*, 127–129.

Herz, M. I., Molnar, G., & Fava, G. (1985). The DST in newly hospitalized patients. *American Journal of Psychiatry*, *142*, 1000.

Hirschfeld, R. M., Koslow, S. H., & Kupfer, D. J. (1983). The clinical utility of the dexamethasone suppression test in psychiatry, *JAMA, Journal of the American Medical Association*, *250*, 2172–2174.

Holden, N. L. (1983). Depression and the Newcastle scales: Their relationship to the dexamethasone suppression test. *British Journal of Psychiatry*, *142*, 505–512.

Holsboer, F., Haack, D., Gerken, A., & Vecsci, P. (1984). Plasma dexamethasone concentrations and differential suppression response of cortisol and corticosterone in depressives and controls. *Biological Psychiatry*, *19*, 281–291.

Holsboer, F., Steiger, A., & Maier, W. (1983). Four cases of reversion to abnormal dexamethasone suppression test response as indicator of clinical relapse: A preliminary report. *Biological Psychiatry*, *18*, 911–916.

Hsu, L. K. G., Molcan, K., Cashman, M. A., Lee, S., Lohr, J., & Hindmarsh, D. (1983). The dexamethasone suppression test in adolescent depression. *Journal of the American Academy of Child Psychiatry*, *22*, 470–473.

Hudson, J. I., Hudson, M. S., Rothschild, A. J., Vignati, L., Schatzberg, A. F., & Melby, J. C. (1984). Abnormal results of the dexamethasone suppression tests in nondepressed patients with diabetes mellitus. *Archives of General Psychiatry*, *41*, 1086–1095.

Hudson, J. I., Pope, H. G., Jr., Jones, J. M., Laffer, P. S., Hudson, M. S., & Melby, J. C. (1983). Hypothalamic–pituitary–adrenal axis hyperactivity in bulimia. *Psychiatry Research*, *8*, 111–117.

Insel, T. R., Kalin, N. H., Guttmacher, L. B., Cohen, R. M., & Murphy, D. L. (1982). The dexamethasone suppression test in patients with primary obsessive-compulsive disorder. *Psychiatry Research, 6,* 153–160.

Johnson, G. F., Hunt, G., Kerr., & Caterson, I. (1984). Dexamethasone suppression test (DST) and plasma dexamethasone levels in depressed patients. *Psychiatry Research, 13,* 305–313.

Kalin, N. H., & Shelton, S. E. (1984). Acute behavioral stress affects the dexamethasone suppression test in rhesus monkeys. *Biological Psychiatry, 19,* 113–117.

Kasper, S., & Beckmann, H. (1983). Dexamethasone suppression test in a pluri diagnostic approach: Its relationship to psychopathological and clinical variables. *Acta Psychiatrica Scandinavica, 68,* 31–37.

Khan, A., Ciraulo, D. A., Nelson, W. H., Becker, J. T., Nies, A., & Jaffe, J. H. (1984). Dexamethasone suppression test in recently detoxified alcoholics: Clinical implications. *Journal of Clinical Psychopharmacology, 4,* 94–97.

Krieger, D. T., Allen, W., Rizzo, F., & Krieger, H. P., (1971). Characterization of the normal temporal pattern of plasma corticosteroid concentrations. *Journal of Clinical Endocrinology and Metabolism, 32,* 266–284.

Krishnan, R. R., Maltbie, A. A., & Davidson, J. R. T. (1983). Abnormal cortisol suppression in bipolar patients with simultaneous manic and depressive symptoms. *American Journal of Psychiatry, 140,* 203–205.

Kroll, P., Palmer, C., & Greden, J. F. (1983). The dexamethasone suppression test in patients with alcoholism. *Biological Psychiatry, 18,* 441–450.

Langer, G., Schonbeck, G., Koinig, G., Lesch, O., & Schussler, M. (1979). Hyperactivity of hypothalamic-pituitary–adrenal axis in endogenous depression. *Lancet, 2,* 524.

Liddle, G. W. (1960). Tests of pituitary–adrenal suppressibility in the diagnosis of Cushing's syndrome. *Journal of Clinical Endocrinology and Metabolism, 20,* 1539–1560.

Leiberman, J. A., Brenner, R., Lesser, M., Coccaro, E., Borenstein, M., & Kane, J. M. (1983). Dexamethasone suppression tests in patients with panic disorder. *American Journal of Psychiatry, 140,* 917–919.

Lieberman, J. A., Kane, J. M., Sarantoakos, S., Cole, K., Howard, A., Borenstein, M., Novacenko, H., & Puig-Antich, J. (1985). Dexamethasone suppression tests in patients with obsessive-compulsive disorder. *American Journal of Psychiatry, 142,* 747–751.

Lipsey, J. R., Robinson, R. G., Pearlson, G. D., Rao, K., & Price, T. R. (1985). The dexamethasone suppression test and mood following stroke. *American Journal of Psychiatry, 141,* 318–323.

Lowy, M. T., Reder, A. T., Antel, J. P., & Meltzer, H. Y. (1986). *Serum dexamethasone levels and the DST.* Presented at the 139th annual meeting of the American Psychiatric Association, Washington, DC. No. 177.

Mathe, A. A. (1983). False normal dexamethasone suppression test and indomethacin. *Lancet, 2,* 714.

McAllister, T. W., Ferrell, R. B., Price, T. R. P., Neville, M. B. (1982). The dexamethasone suppression test in two patients with severe depressive pseudodementia. *American Journal of Psychiatry, 139,* 479–481.

McClure, D. J. (1966). The diurnal variation of plasma cortisol levels in depression. *Journal of Psychosomatic Research, 10,* 189–195.

Mellsop, G. W., Hutton, J. D., & Delahunt, J. W. (1985). Dexamethasone suppression test as a simple measure of stress? *British Medical Journal, 290,* 1804–1806.

Meltzer, H. Y., & Fang, V. S. (1983). Cortisol determination and the dexamethasone suppression test. *Archives of General Psychiatry, 40,* 501–505.

Mendlewicz, J., Charles, G., & Frankson, J. M. (1982). The dexamethasone suppression test in affective disorder: Relationship to clinical and genetic subgroups. *British Journal of Psychiatry, 141,* 464–470.

Mitchell, J. E., Pyle, R. S., Hatsukami, D., & Boutaroff, L. I. (1984). The dexamethasone suppression test in patients with bulimia. *Journal of Clinical Psychiatry, 45,* 508–511.

Nelson, W. H., Khan, A., Orr, W. W., & Tamragouri, R. N. (1984). The dexamethasone suppression test: Interaction of diagnosis, sex, and age in psychiatric inpatients. *Biological Psychiatry, 19,* 1293–1304.

Nelson, W. H., Orr, W. W., Stevenson, J. M., & Shane, S. R. (1985). Hypothalamic–pituitary–adrenal axis activity and tricyclic response in major depression. *Archives of General Psychiatry, 39,* 1033–1036.

Nemeroff, C. B., & Evans, D. L. (1984). Correlation between the dexamethasone suppression test in depressed patients and clinical response. *American Journal of Psychiatry, 141,* 247–249.

Nugent, C. A., Nichols, T., & Tyler, F. H. (1965). Diagnosis of Cushing's syndrome. Single dose dexamethasone suppression tests. *Archives of Internal Medicine, 116,* 172–176.

Nuller, J. L., & Ostroumova, M. N. (1980). Resistance to inhibiting effects of dexamethasone in patients with endogenous depression. *Acta Psychiatrica Scandinavica, 61,* 169–177.

Pavlotos, F. C., Smilo, R. P., & Forsham, P. H. (1965). A rapid screening test for Cushing's syndrome. *JAMA, Journal of the American Medical Association, 193,* 720–723.

Pepper, G. M., Davis, B. M., & Krieger, D. T. (1983). DST in depression is unaffected by altering the clock time of its administration. *Psychiatry Research, 8,* 105–109.

Petty, L. K., Ascarnov, J. R., Carison, G. A., & Lesser, L. (1985). The dexamethasone suppression test in depressed, dysthymic, and nondepressed children. *American Journal of Psychiatry, 142,* 631–633.

Pope, H. G., Jr., & Hudson, J. I. (1982). Treatment of bulimia with antidepressants. *Psychopharmacology, 78,* 176–179.

Puig-Antich, J. (1982). The use of RDC criteria for depressive disorders in children and adolescents. *Journal of the American Acadmey of Child Psychiatry, 21,* 291–293.

Pyle, R. L., Mitchell, J. E., & Eckerd, E. D. (1981). Bulimia: A report of 34 cases. *Journal of Clinical Psychiatry, 42,* 60–64.

Raskind, M., Peskind, E., Rivard, M. E., Veith, R., & Barnes, R. (1982). Dexamethasone suppression test and cortisol circadian rhythm in primary degenerative dementia. *American Journal of Psychiatry, 139,* 1468–1471.

Ravi, S. D., Dorus, W., Park, Y. N., Collins, M. C., Reid, R. W., & Borge, C. F. (1984). The dexamethasone suppression test and depressive symptoms in early and late withdrawal from alcohol. *American Journal of Psychiatry*, 141, 1445–1448.

Reding, M., Orto, L., Willensky, P., Fortuna, I., Day, N., Steiner, S. F., Gehr, L., & McDowell, F. (1985). The dexamethasone suppression test: An indicator of depression in stroke but not a predictor of rehabilitation outcome. *Archives of Neurology (Chicago)*, 42, 209–212.

Ritchie, J. C., Carroll, B. J., Olton, P. R., Shively, V., & Feinberg, M. (1985). Plasma cortisol determination for the dexamethasone suppression test: Comparison of competitive protein binding and commercial radioimmunoassay methods. *Archives of General Psychiatry*, 42, 493–497.

Robbins, D. R., & Alessi, N. E. (1985). Suicide and the dexamethasone suppression test in adolescence. *Biological Psychiatry*, 20, 94–119.

Robbins, D. R., Alessi, N. E., Yanchyshyn, G. W., & Colfer, M. V. (1982). Preliminary report on the dexamethasone suppression test in adolescents. *American Journal of Psychiatry*, 139, 942–943.

Robbins, D. R., Alessi, N. E., Yanchyshyn, G. W., & Colfer, M. V. (1983). The dexamethasone suppression test in psychiatrically hospitalized adolescents. *Journal of the American Academy of Child Psychiatry*, 22, 467–469.

Robinson, R. G., & Price, T. R. (1982). Poststroke depressive disorders: A follow-up study of 103 outpatients. *Stroke*, 13, 635–641.

Robinson, R. G., Starr, L. B., Kubos, K. L., & Price, T. R. (1983). A two-year longitudinal study of poststroke mood disorders: Findings during the initial evaluation. *Stroke*, 14, 746–741.

Robinson, R. G., Starr, L. B., & Price, T. R. (1984). A two-year longitudinal study of mood disorders following stroke: Prevalence and duration at 6 months follow-up. *British Journal of Psychiatry*, 144, 256–262.

Ross, E. D., & Rush, A. J. (1981). Diagnosis and neuroanatomical correlates of depression in brain-damaged patients: Implications for a neurology of depression. *Archives of General Psychiatry*, 38, 1344–1354.

Rudorfer, M. V., & Clayton, P. J. (1981). Depression, dementia and dexamethasone suppression. *American Journal of Psychiatry*, 138, 701.

Rudorfer, M. V., & Clayton, P. J. (1982). Pseudodementia: Use of the DST in diagnosis and treatment monitoring. *Psychosomatics*, 23, 429–431.

Rush, J. A. (1984). A phase II study of cognitive therapy of depression. In J. B. W. Williams & R. L. Spitzer (Eds.), *Psychotherapy research: Where are we and where should we go?* New York: Guilford Press.

Sachar, E. J. (1967a). Corticosteriods in depressive illness. I. A reevaluation of control issues and the literature. *Archives of General Psychiatry*, 17, 544–553.

Sachar, E. J. (1967b). Corticosteroids in depressive illness. II. A longitudinal psychoendocrine study. *Archives of General Psychiatry*, 17, 554–557.

Schatzberg, A. F., Rothchild, A. J., Stahl, J. B., Bond, T. C., Rosenbaum, A. H., Lofgren, S. B., MacLaughlin, R. A., Sullivan, M. A., & Cole, J. O. (1983). The dexamethasone suppression test: Identification of subtypes of depression. *American Journal of Psychiatry*, 140, 88–91.

Schlesser, M. A., Winokur, G., & Sherman, B. M. (1980). Hypothalamic–pituitary–adrenal axis activity in depressive illness: Its relationship to classification. *Archives of General Psychiatry*, 37, 737–743.

Sheehan, D. V., Claycomb, J. B., Surman, O. S., Baer, L., Coleman, J., & Gelles, L. (1983). Panics attacks and the dexamethasone suppression test. *American Journal of Psychiatry*, 140, 1063–1064.

Shrivastava, R. V., Schwimmer, R., Browne, W. A., & Arito, M. (1985, May). *DST predicts poor placebo response in depression.* Presented at the annual meeting of the American Psychiatric Association, Dallas, TX. No. 94.

Simon, J. S., Nemeroff, C. B., & Evans, D. L. (1986). *The dexamethasone suppression test and antidepressant response in major depression.* Presented at the Forty-first annual meeting of the Society of Biological Psychiatry. No. 191.

Smith, S. R., Bledsoe, T., & Chhetri, M. K. (1975). Cortisol metabolism and the pituitary–adrenal axis in adults with protein calorie malnutrition. *Journal of Clinical Endocrinology and Metabolism*, 40, 43–52.

Soloff, P. H., George, A., & Nathan, R. S. (1982). The dexamethasone suppression test in patients with borderline personality disorders. *American Journal of Psychiatry*, 193, 1621–1623.

Spar, J. E., & Gerner, R. (1982). Does the dexamethasone suppression test distinguish dementia from depression? *American Journal of Psychiatry*, 139, 238–240.

Spitzer, R. L., Endicott, J., & Robins, E. (1978). Research diagnostic criteria. Rationale and reliability. *Archives of General Psychiatry*, 35, 773–782.

Stokes, P. E. (1966). Pituitary suppression in psychiatric patients. The Endocrine Society (USA), 48th meeting abstracts. *Endocrinology (Baltimore)*, 78, (Suppl.).

Stokes, P. E. (1972). Studies on the control of adrenocortical function in depression. In T. A. Williams, M. M. Katz, & J. A. Shield (Eds.), *Recent advances in the psychobiology of the depressive illnesses*. Washington, DC: U. S. Government Printing Office.

Stokes, P. E., Pick, G. R., Stoll, P. M., & Numm, W. D. (1975). Pituitary–adrenal function in depressed patients: Resistance to dexamethasone suppression. *Journal of Psychiatry Research*, 12, 271–281.

Stokes, P. E., Stoll, P. M., Koslow, S. H., Maas, J. W., Davis, J. M., Swann, A. C., & Robins, E. (1984). Pretreatment DST and hypothalamic–pituitary–adrenocortical function in depressed patients and comparison groups. *Archives of General Psychiatry*, 41, 257–267.

Stokes, P. E., Stoll, P. M., Lasley, B. J., & Sikes, M. A. (1986). *Plasma dexamethasone level and cortisol response.* Presented at the 139th annual meeting of the American Psychiatric Association, Washington, DC. No. 176.

Stroeber, M., & Carlson, G. (1982). Bipolar illness in adolescents with major depression. *Archives of General Psychiatry*, 39, 1309–555.

Swartz, C. M., & Dunner, F. J. (1982). Dexamethasone suppression testing of alcoholics. *American Journal of Psychiatry*, 39, 1309–1312.

Targum, S. D. (1984). Persistent neuroendocrine dysregulation in major depressive disorder: A marker for early relapse. *Biological Psychiatry 19*, 305–318.

Targum, S. D. (1983). Neuroendocrine dysfunction in schizophreniform disorder: Correlation with six-month clinical outcome. *American Journal of Psychiatry, 140*, 309–313.

Targum, S. D., Byrnes, S. M., & Sullivan, A. C. (1982). Subtypes of unipolar depression distinguished by the dexamethasone suppression test. *Journal of Affective Disorders, 4*, 21–27.

Targum, S. D., & Capodanno, A. E. (1983). The dexamethasone suppression test in adolescent psychiatric inpatients. *American Journal of Psychiatry, 140*, 589–591.

Targum, S. D., Capodanno, A. E., Unger, S., & Advani, M. (1984). Abnormal dexamethasone tests in withdrawing alcoholic patients. *Biological Psychiatry, 19*, 401–405.

Targum, S. D., Rosen, L., & Capodanno, A. E. (1983). The dexamethasone suppression test in suicidal patients with unipolar depression. *American Journal of Psychiatry, 140*, 877–879.

Targum, S. D., Wheadon, D. E., Chastek, C. T., McCabe, W. J., & Advani, M. T. (1982). Dysregulation of hypothalamic–pituitary–adrenal axis function in depressed alcoholic patients. *Journal of Affective Disorders, 4*, 347–353.

Tiongco, D. D., Hariharan, M., Haskett, R. F., & Greden, J. F. (1986). *Age effects on HPA regulation and dexamethasone plasma levels in normal subjects.* Presented at the 41st annual meeting of the Society of Biological Psychiatry, Washington, DC. No. 195.

Tourigny-Rivard, M. F., Raskind, M., & Rivard, D. (1981). The dexamethasone suppression test in an elderly population. *Biological Psychiatry, 16*, 1177–1184.

Walsh, B. T., Katz, J. L., Levin, J., Kream, J., Fukushima, D. K., Hellman, L. D., Weiner, H., & Zumoff, B. (1978). Adrenal activity in anorexia nervosa. *Psychosomatic Medicine, 40*, 499–506.

Weissman, M. M., Pottenger, M., Kleber, H., Ruben, H., Williams, D., & Thompson, D. W. (1977). Symptom patterns in primary and secondary depression. *Archives of General Psychiatry, 34*, 854–862.

Weller, E. B., Weller, R. A., Fristad, M. A., Preskorn, S. H., & Teare, M. (1985). The dexamethasone suppression test in prepubertal depressed children. *Journal of Clinical Psychiatry, 46*, 511–513.

Whiteford, H. A., Peabody, C. A., Thiemann, M. S., Kraemer, H. C., Csernansky, J. G., & Berger, P. A. (1986). *The effect of age on the dexamethasone suppression test in major depressive disorder.* Presented at the 41st annual meeting of the Society of Biological Psychiatry, Washington, DC. No. 199.

Winokur, A., March, V., & Mendels, J. (1980). Primary affective disorder in relatives of patients with anorexia nervosa. *American Journal of Psychiatry, 137*, 695–698.

Winokur, G., Behar, D., Van Valkenburg, C., & Lowry, M. (1978). Is a familial definition of depression both feasible and valid? *Journal of Nervous and Mental Disease, 166*, 764–767.

Zis, A. (1986). The dexamethasone suppression test in depressed children. *American Journal of Psychiatry, 143*, 128–129.

15 THE TRH STIMULATION TEST IN PSYCHIATRIC DISORDERS: A REVIEW

PETER T. LOOSEN

Veterans Administration Medical Center, Nashville

INTRODUCTION

Psychoendocrinology occupied center stage in biological psychiatry during the first decades of this century (Bleuler, 1954; Laignel-Lavastine, 1919). At that time, investigators were well aware of clinical associations between endocrine and psychiatric disorders, but there existed no framework within which they could be understood. This framework, that is, the crucial understanding of brain–endocrine interactions was soon to be provided. Yalow and her colleague Berson (Yalow, 1978) developed radioimmunoassay methods allowing measurement of hormones in body fluids with high specificity and sensitivity. Scharrer and Scharrer (1939) demonstrated that certain cells of the hypothalamus possess secretory properties, thus introducing the concept of neurosecretion. Harris (1955) recognized the importance of the portal venous system which connects the hypothalamus and the pituitary gland. He proposed that the hypothalamus secretes neurohormones into this system and thus regulates the anterior pituitary gland. This hypothesis has been confirmed and several "hypothalamic hypophysiotropic hormones" have been isolated and chemically characterized by, among others, Guillemin (1978), Schally (1978), and Vale, Spiess, Rivier, and Rivier (1981). One of these is thyrotropin-releasing hormone (TRH). Its relevance as a psychoendocrine research tool is the subject of the present review.

THE TRH TEST

TRH is a tripeptide (Boler, Enzmann, Folkers, Bowers, & Schally, 1969; Burgus, Dunn, Desiderio, & Guillemin, 1969) that is found primarily in the central nervous system (CNS) (Jackson & Reichlin, 1974; Morely, Garvin, Pekary, & Hershman, 1977; Winokur & Utiger, 1974). Under physiological conditions, TRH release is controlled by a variety of stimuli of hypothalamic origin (Figure 15.1). Endocrinologically, TRH stimulates release of thyrotropin (TSH) and prolactin from the anterior pituitary gland (Burger & Patel, 1977; Sawin & Hershman, 1976). TSH release, in turn, stimulates the thyroid gland to secrete thyroid hormones. Thus, TRH can be considered the highest member in the hierarchy of the so-called hypothalamic–pituitary–thyroid axis (Figure 15.1).

The TRH test, that is, measurement of serum TSH following TRH administration, has become a standard procedure. It is inexpensive, safe, rapidly accomplished, depends upon a radioimmunoassay now generally available, and does not require a high level of patient cooperation. These features commend its use no less in psychiatry than in endocrinology. In regard to the TRH test in psychoendocrinology, it is important to note that in psychiatric patients with a diminished or blunted TSH response to TRH, no endocrine explanation has yet been identified. It is also worth noting that administration of

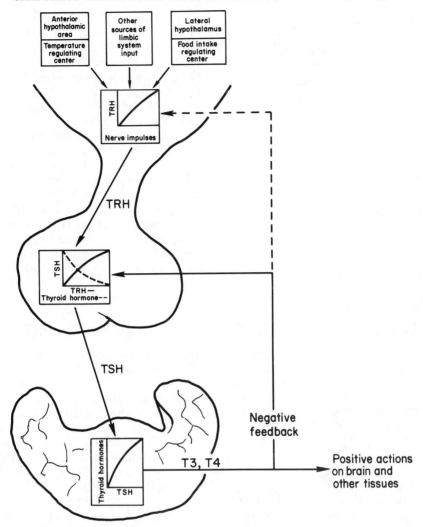

FIGURE 15.1. The hypothalamic–pituitary–thyroid axis. Note that TSH secretion from thyrotroph cells in the anterior pituitary is regulated by an interplay of both stimulatory (TRH) and inhibitory (thyroid hormones) effects.

TRH sometimes induces a partial and temporary behavioral effect toward increased well-being in both psychiatric patients and normal subjects. This behavioral change is most prominent 6 hours after injection (Figure 15.2); it is observed in only a few subjects, and no predictor of this change has yet been determined. In general, behavioral changes after TRH administration are much more controversial than endocrine response, namely, the TSH response. We have dis-

cussed this matter in detail elsewhere (Loosen & Prange, 1980).

Technique

The technique used by psychiatric investigators follows guidelines developed in endocrinology (Anderson *et al.*, 1971; Ingbar & Woeber, 1981; Sawin & Hershman, 1976). Variables to be controlled are nutritional state of the subject (e.g., recent weight loss,

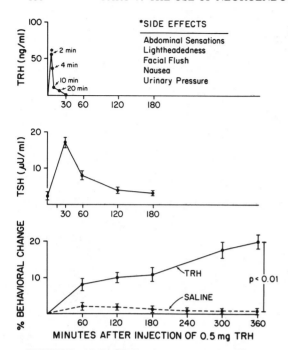

FIGURE 15.2. TRH plasma levels, TSH responses, and behavioral changes after administration of 0.5 mg TRH in normal controls. TRH levels were measured in 11 normal subjects, and TSH and behavioral data were collected in 20 normal subjects. All data have been described elsewhere in detail (Loosen, Wilson, & Prange, 1980; Loosen, Youngblood, & Dew, 1983).

percentage of deviation from ideal weight), menstrual history (e.g., day of menstrual cycle during the time of testing), dose of TRH, rate and route of administration, and time of blood sampling. We inject TRH at about 9 A.M. in a standarized dose (0.5 mg) after an overnight fast, with the subject in a recumbent position throughout the ensuing experiment. An intravenous catheter may be inserted to assure easy access for blood sampling. Intravenous administration of TRH is preferred to oral administration to avoid the potentially confounding variable of differential absorption. The TSH response to TRH is linear between doses of 0.1–0.4 mg, above which a plateau is reached; the dose suggested (0.5 mg) is therefore slightly supramaximal. This has the advantage of avoiding false-positive TSH blunting. As regards time of sampling, there is overwhelming evidence that the peak TSH response occurs about 30

minutes after TRH injection (Loosen & Prange, 1982). In normal subjects, $\Delta 30$ TSH (i.e., TSH at 30 minutes minus baseline) yields nearly as much information as a detailed assessment of the entire TSH response for 3 hours (Loosen, Mason, & Prange, 1982; Wilkin, Baldet, & Papachristou, 1979). However, use of $\Delta 30$ TSH as the main variable in psychiatric patients results in 5–7% false-positive TSH blunting (Schlesser, Rush, Fairchild, Crowley, & Orsulak, 1983). If accuracy in identifying "TSH blunters" is of high priority, one may therefore choose to subtract peak TSH values occurring 15, 30, or 45 minutes after TRH administration from baseline TSH values (Δ_{max} TSH). This approach does not produce false positives, and it requires only four blood samples for TSH assay: TSH 0, TSH 15, TSH 30, and TSH 45 (Schlesser et al., 1983).

Side Effects and Patients at Risk

The test provokes only mild and short-lasting subjective reactions. TRH "side effects" such as nausea, urinary urgency, facial flush, lightheadedness, and abdominal sensations occur immediately after TRH injection (Loosen & Prange, 1980) and coincide nicely with the ascending curve of TRH plasma levels (Loosen, Youngblood, & Dew, 1983). They persist for about 2 minutes (Figure 15.2). The half-life time of exogenous TRH in human plasma is approximately 5–6 minutes (Loosen, Youngblood, & Dew, 1983). There are three medical conditions in which the administration of TRH may be dangerous. The first two concern high blood pressure and heart disease. TRH may induce a short-lasting increase in blood pressure during the first 2 minutes following injection (Borowski, Garofano, Rose, & Levy, 1984; Zaloga et al., 1984). This may complicate an underlying heart disease and may explain the severe headaches and transient amaurosis reported to have ensued shortly after TRH injection in hypertensive patients (Drury, Belchetz, McDonald, Thomas, & Besser, 1982). The third condition concerns the history of head injury and/or seizure disorder. Patients with such a history, even when treated with anticonvulsant medications and being seizure-free for an extended period of time, may experience a seizure following TRH administration

(Dolva, Riddervold, & Thorsen, 1983; Maeda & Tanimoto, 1981). However, this side effect appears to occur only in a small percentage of patients. Dolva *et al.* (1983) reported convulsions in 3 of 1,500 patients tested with TRH. Nonetheless, it seems advisable that special precautions (e.g., very slow injection and/or lowering the dose of TRH) be taken when the TRH test is administered to patients with hypertension, cardiac disease, or a history of seizure disorder.

Confounding Variables

The TRH test is usually not affected by neuroleptics (Naber, Steinbock, & Greil, 1980) or tricyclic antidepressants (Kirkegaard *et al.*, 1977; Widerlov, Wide, & Sjöstrom, 1978), but certain other factors are likely to invalidate results. Among these factors are increasing age (Snyder & Utiger, 1972), being male (Haigler, Pittman, Hershman, & Baugh, 1971; Wenzel, Meinhold, & Herpach, 1974), acute starvation (Burger, Weissel, & Berger, 1980; Carlson, Drenick, Chopra, & Hershman, 1977; Croxson, Hall, Kletzky, Jaramillo, & Nicoloff, 1977; Portnay *et al.*, 1974; Spencer, Lum, Wilber, Kaptein, & Nicoloff, 1983), chronic renal failure (Czernichow, Dauzet, Brayer, & Rappoport, 1976), Klinefelter syndrome (Smals *et al.*, 1977), repetitive administration of TRH (Frey & Haug, 1977; Rabello, Snyder, & Utiger, 1974; Snyder & Utiger, 1973; Spencer, Greenstadt, Wheeler, Kletzky, & Nicoloff, 1980; Staub *et al.*, 1978), and administration of somatostatin (Vale *et al.*, 1973), calcitonin (Isaac, Merceron, Caillens, Raymond, & Ardaillou, 1980), neurotensin (Nemeroff, Bissette, & Manberg, 1980), dopamine (Besses, Burrow, & Spaulding, 1975; Burrow, May, Spaulding, & Donabedian, 1977; Kaptein, Kletzky, Spencer, & Nicoloff, 1980; Kaptein, Spencer, & Kamiel, 1980; Leebaw, Lee, & Woolf, 1978; Thorner *et al.*, 1978), and thyroid hormones or glucocorticoids (Burger & Patel, 1977). Moreover, several drugs are known to cause abnormal TRH test results (Joffe, Gold, Uhde, & Post, 1984; Ramey *et al.*, 1976; Wenzel, 1981) (Table 15.1). These factors need to be considered whether one performs the TRH test for psychoendocrine purposes or for diagnosis of endocrine disease.

TABLE 15.1. Substances Causing Abnormal TRH Test Results

False-positive results	False-negative results
Dopamine	Metoclopramide
Lisuride	Sulpiridine
L-Dopa	Chlorpromazine
Cyproheptadine	Biperidine
Methysergide	Haloperidol
Somatostatin	Cimetidine
Growth hormone	Estrogen (males)
Salicylates	Iodine
Morphine	Iodine-contrast dyes
Heroin	Amiodarone
Fenclofenac	Lithium
Glucocorticoids	Spironolactone
Thyroid hormones	Theophylline
Etiroxate HCL	
Calcitonin	
Carbamazepine	

Definition of TSH Blunting

The TRH test has been widely used in psychiatric patients. It is now clear from more that 55 studies involving more than 1,200 patients that the TRH-induced response is blunted in about 25% of depressed patients (Loosen & Prange, 1982). What is less clear, however, is how to express this fault most usefully. It is possibly more helpful to classify patients as blunted or nonblunted than to compare group means. Comparison of group means does not appear to firmly establish that an abnormality exists, to what it is correlated, and how it persists over time. The work of Amsterdam, Winokur, and Mendels (1979), Winokur, Amsterdam, Caroff, Snyder, and Brunswick (1982), and Wolkin *et al.* (1984) illustrates this. These investigators reported that some depressed patients, but none of the normal controls, had a blunted TSH response to TRH. The mean TSH response, however, did not differ significantly from that of controls.

How, then, can patients with an abnormal TSH response be classified? One could employ a traditional standard and require that to be abnormal, a patient's TSH value be more than two standard deviations from the mean of a sufficiently large number of appropriate controls. This statistical definition may in fact be preferred in the future. As working definition of a blunted TSH response, we have required that a patient's maximum increase in serum TSH above baseline (Δ_{max} TSH) after TRH administration be less than that found in *any* of our age- and sex-matched normal subjects. This conservative definition probably excludes from any blunted group some patients whose responses are in fact abnormally low. Conversely, any blunted group so defined is probably uncontaminated by false positives, and this is an obvious advantage if the group is to be studied additionally. We have studied 73 normal men and women from 20 to 70 years of age; their mean age was 39.6 ± 1.4 ($\bar{x} \pm SEM$) years. Subjects with a personal or family history of mental illness were excluded. Since the lowest Δ_{max} TSH found in the normal population was $5.6\,\mu U/ml$, we arbitrarily defined a blunted response as a Δ_{max} TSH less than $5.0\,\mu U/ml$. Using this definition, we found TSH blunting in 13 of 50 (26%) pa-

tients, both men and women, with primary depression whose diagnoses were based on DSM-III and Research Diagnostic Criteria (RDC) (Figure 15.3)

Quite obviously, the definition of blunting, that is, the specification of the cutoff point, will largely influence its frequency. For example, M. S. Gold *et al.* (1981) recently reported TSH blunting in 75% of depressed patients. They defined the fault as a Δ_{max}TSH less than $7.0\,\mu U/ml$. In contrast, Schlesser *et al.* (1983) found TSH blunting in 39% of patients with primary depression. They defined blunting as a Δ_{max} TSH less than $5.0\,\mu U/ml$.

Test–Retest Reliability

Evaluation of the test–retest reliability of a blunted TSH response is complicated by the fact that depression, by nature, is a cycling disorder. To study test–retest reliability, one must assure, therefore, that depressed

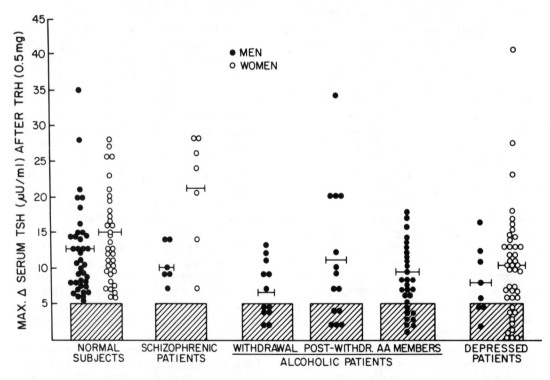

FIGURE 15.3. TSH response to TRH, 0.5 mg iv, in 73 normal subjects, and 13 schizophrenic, 55 alcoholic, and 50 depressed patients. Depressed patients were studied during an acute episode of depression; alcoholic patients were studied during acute withdrawal, after such withdrawal, and during prolonged sobriety. Maximum increases in serum TSH above baseline (Δ_{max} TSH) after TRH of less than $5.0\,\mu U/ml$ reflect TSH blunting. They are shown in the shaded area. All data have been presented in detail elsewhere (Loosen & Prange, 1982; Loosen *et al.*, 1979; Loosen, Wilson, Dew, & Tipermas, 1983).

patients who have shown TSH blunting initially are retested during a state of comparable disease severity. This may be within the same episode or during a comparable, later episode. To complicate matters, retesting within the same episode will require delay of treatment. This is often difficult and when it is done, the disorder is subject to spontaneous changes. (Data of other investigators who have retested depressed patients in remission pertain rather to state–trait considerations, and this will be reviewed below.) However, preliminary data from our own laboratory indicate that the test–retest reliability of a blunted TSH response is acceptable in both depressed and alcoholic patients. In depression, we retested 6 of 10 patients with TSH blunting, and all showed blunted responses on second testing (Loosen, Kistler, & Prange, 1983). In alcoholic patients who had shown abstinence from alcohol for more that 2 years and who were free of any psychiatric symptoms at the time of testing, we retested 5 patients with TSH blunting, and 4 showed blunted responses on second testing (Loosen, Wilson, Dew, & Tipermas, 1983).

Specificity

In biological marker research, one is confronted with three major definitions of a given test: (1) sensitivity, that is, the incidence of true-positive results obtained when a test is applied to patients known to have the disease; (2) specificity, that is, the incidence of true-negative results obtained when a test is applied to subjects known to be free of the disease; and (3) predictive value, that is, the percentage of positive results that are true positives when the test is applied to a population containing both healthy and diseased subjects (Galen & Gambino, 1975). In clinical practice, sensitivity and specificity are usually inversely related, that is, the higher the sensitivity, the lower the specificity. With these definitions in mind, what can be said about the specificity of TSH blunting within psychiatric disorders? It is clearly not specific for depression as it has also been observed in some patients with mania, alcoholism, borderline personality disorder, chronic pain, and, infrequently, schizophrenia. These findings are discussed in detail below. However,

the infrequent occurrence of TSH blunting in schizophrenic patients and the observation that the TSH response to *in vivo* flooding therapy is normal in patients with phobic disorders (Nesse, Curtis, & Brown, 1982) render it doubtful that the fault is just a correlate of mental distress.

THE TRH TEST IN DEPRESSION

Frequency

Prange, Wilson, Lara, Alltop, and Breese (1972) first reported TRH test results in 10 women with primary unipolar depression. Two patients showed virtually absent TSH responses, although they were euthyroid at the time of testing. As noted above, more than 55 studies involving more than 1,200 patients reported findings consistent with this original observation. Five studies involving 36 patients have been negative (Loosen & Prange, 1982). In summary, these data clearly indicate that the TSH response to TRH is not normal in some depressed patients. If one assesses the data reported to date in regard to frequency of TSH blunting in depression—as opposed to examining mean TSH values—then an approximate 25% frequency in *primary* depression is found (Loosen & Prange, 1982).

State–Trait Considerations

Is TSH blunting in depression limited to the acute state of the disorder (state marker), or can it also be observed during remission (trait marker)? In studies which have addressed this question TSH was administered both during the acute state and after clinical remission. In eight studies the TSH response, being reduced in depression, normalized or "improved" upon recovery (Agren, 1981; Asnis, Nathan, Halbreich, Halpern, & Sachar, 1980; Brambilla, Smeraldi, Bellodi, Sacchetti, & Mueller, 1980; Grégoire, Brauman, de Buck, & Corrilain, 1977; Hatotani, 1977; Kjellman, 1983; Linkowski, Brauman, & Mendlewicz, 1981; Tsutsui, Yamazaki, Namba, & Tsushima, 1979). Unfortunately, all studies listed above compared *mean* TSH responses as they occurred in depression and remission; they thus did not allow to assess whether a blunted TSH response in depression persisted into remission. However, seven reports identifying individual responses demonstrated that, in some depressed patients, a blunted TSH response did not normalize during remission (Coppen, Montgomery, Peet, & Bailey, 1974; Kirkegaard & Carroll, 1980; Kirkegaard, Norlem, Lauridsen, Bjorum, & Christiansen, 1975; Loosen, Prange, Wilson, Lara, & Pettus, 1977; Maeda et al., 1975; Papakostas, Fink, Lee, Irwin, & Johnson, 1981; Targum, 1983). One of these reports is particularly revealing. Targum (1983) reported that only 8 of 19 patients (42%) with primary depression normalized their TSH response at the time of symptomatic recovery, suggesting that TSH blunting in depression may normalize in fewer than half of patients during remission. Two recent reports on TSH blunting in remitted depressed patients are consistent with this view. Kathol, Sherman, Winokur, Lewis, and Schlesser (1983) studied 28 outpatients who had recovered from depression for an average of 1 year. Four patients (14%) showed TSH blunting. P. T. Loosen and J. C. Garbutt (unpublished data) studied 22 depressed outpatients in remission and found TSH blunting in 3 (14%) patients. If, as shown above, the approximate frequency of TSH blunting in acutely depressed patients is 25%, then a frequency of 14% in remitted patients suggests that less than half of patients "escaped" blunting when shifting into remission. Thus, at least in some depressed patients, TSH blunting does indeed persist into remission (this, of course, does not necessarily imply persistence over a prolonged period of time). In a similar way, TSH blunting has been observed in alcoholic patients both during acute withdrawal and 1 week later when all withdrawal symptoms had shown complete remission (to be discussed below).

Prediction of Outcome

If, in depressed patients, the TRH test is assessed in regard to its possible usefulness as a predictor of treatment outcome, two questions come to mind: (1) Does Δ_{max} TSH allow to assess whether a "good" response has occurred to standard antidepressant treatment? (2) Does it predict early (or late) relapse in patients who have shown remission during such treatment?

Several independent investigators (Kirkegaard, 1981; Krog-Meyer et al., 1984; Langer et al., 1980; Targum, 1983) have examined whether the TRH test is useful in assessing a good clinical response to treatment with tricyclics or electroconvulsive therapy (ECT) and in predicting early relapse after tricyclic- or ECT-induced remission. TRH tests were performed both in depression and during remission, and the difference in Δ_{max} TSH between first and second testing ($\Delta\Delta_{max}$ TSH) was used as the endocrine variable. Langer et al. (1980) and Kirkegaard (1981) concluded that a positive trend in $\Delta\Delta_{max}$ TSH (i.e., a Δ_{max} TSH that is bigger on second testing than on first) was correlated with a good response to treatment. However, Targum (1983) reported that normalization of TSH blunting, defined as a $\Delta\Delta_{max}$ TSH > 2.0 μU/ml, "was not significantly correlated with the timing of symptomatic improvement." Kirkegaard (1981), Targum (1983), and Krog-Meyer et al. (1984) also concluded that a persistently low TSH response (i.e., a $\Delta\Delta_{max}$ TSH < 2.0 μU/ml) predicts early relapse, usually within 6 months. These data, however, could not be replicated by Langer et al. (1980) who found that Δ_{max} TSH levels on second testing increased in most patients in order to decrease again just before relapse into depression. The findings of Krog-Meyer et al. (1984) are of interest in an additional way. They reported that the danger of relapse, as predicted by a $\Delta\Delta_{max}$ TSH value < 2.0 μU/ml, can be prevented if patients are placed on amitriptyline maintenance.

In discussing these outcome data, a word of caution seems necessary. First, different doses of TSH were used by Langer's, Kirkegaard's, and Targum's group. Second, the patients of Langer et al. (1980) were studied during continued antidepressant treatment, whereas the patients of Kirkegaard (1981) were tested when without medication. Third, differences in maximum TSH between two tests as small as the ones reported above are difficult to interpret because they are close to the expected range of both intraindividual variation (Sawin & Hershman, 1976) and intra- as well as interassay variation (Loosen, Kistler, & Prange, 1983; Loosen, Wilson,

Dew, & Tipermas, 1983; Schlesser *et al.*, 1983). Nevertheless, Kirkegaard (1981), in discussing these issues in detail, demonstrated that by optimizing both test conditions and TSH assay, only approximately 15% of patients are misclassified due to intraindividual and methodological variations.

Sources of Variance

Presumably all the factors listed above that influence the TSH response in normal subjects or in nonpsychiatric patients can influence the response in psychiatric patients as well. The need for age- and sex-matched control groups is obvious, and most investigators have controlled for these factors. Other factors tend to be uncommon (e.g., chronic renal failure, Klinefelter syndrome) or are usually excluded (e.g., hyperthyroidism). An exception is nutritional state, and one must control for this in light of the profound appetite disturbances which often accompany depression. Acute fasting is known to induce TSH blunting (Burger *et al.*, 1980; Carlson *et al.*, 1977; Croxson *et al.*, 1977; Portnay *et al.*, 1974; Spencer *et al.*, 1983). Interestingly, however, the magnitude of the TSH response is normal in anorexia nervosa, though peak responses are usually delayed (to be discussed below).

In depression, possible associations between TSH blunting and several clinical factors have been appraised (Table 15.2).

Age, Severity of Illness, and Previous Drug Intake

There seems to be no association between TSH blunting and age (Brambilla *et al.*, 1980, M. S. Gold *et al.*, 1980; Loosen *et al.*, 1977; Takahashi, Kondo, Yoshimura, & Ochi, 1974), severity of depression (Burger & Patel, 1977; Coppen *et al.*, 1974; M. S. Gold *et al.*, 1980; Hollister, Davis, & Berger, 1976; Kirkegaard & Carroll, 1980; Loosen *et al.*, 1977; Maeda *et al.*, 1975; Papakostas *et al.*, 1981; Takahashi *et al.*, 1974), and previous drug intake (Brambilla *et al.*, 1980; Burger & Patel, 1977; Kirkegaard, Bjorum, Cohn, & Lauridsen, 1978; Loosen *et al.*, 1977). The latter, of course, excludes long-term lithium

TABLE 15.2. Factors Associated with a Reduced TSH Response in Depression

Clinical factors	
Age	No
Body surface	No
Antidepressant drugs	No
Severity of illness	No
Subtypes of depression:	
Primary vs. secondary	Unknown
Unipolar vs. bipolar	No
Duration of illness	Yes
State–trait occurrence	Yes
History of violent suicide attempts	Yes
Endocrine factors	
Serum thyroid hormone elevation	No
Serum cortisol elevation and	
DST abnormalities	No
Dopamine	No
Somatostatin	Unknown
TRH pharmacokinetics	Unknown
Basal TSH and 24-hour	
TSH rhythm	Unknown
Neurotensin	Unknown

administration. Lithium's thyroid-suppressant effects result in increased TSH responses after TRH (Lauridsen, Kirkegaard, & Nerup, 1974; Lazarus, John, Bernie, Chalmers, & Cruchett, 1981; Tanimoto, Maeda, Yamaguchi, Chihara, & Fujita, 1981).

Subtypes and Duration of Depression

The TRH test does not presently seem to aid in the distinction between primary and secondary depression (although the majority of TSH blunting is observed in major depression) or between unipolar and bipolar subgroups (Loosen & Prange, 1982). There is, however, evidence of a possible association between TSH blunting and duration of illness. Takahashi *et al.* (1974) have shown that patients with chronic depression show TSH blunting at a higher frequency than do nonprotracted depressives of the same age.

Suicidal Behavior

Agren (1981) and Kjellman (1983) reported a significant negative association between Δ_{max} TSH and history of suicidal behavior.

Linkowski, Van Wettere, Kerkhofs, Brauman, and Mendlewicz (1983), studying 51 depressed women, extended these findings. They found Δ_{max} TSH values to be equally distributed in patients with and without history of suicidal behavior, but there was a striking association between *violent* suicidal behavior and a virtually absent TSH response (Δ_{max} TSH $< 1.0 \, \mu U/ml$). Of 51 patients, 12 had an absent TSH response to TRH; 7 of these 12 patients had a history of violent suicidal behavior (as compared to 4 of 39 patients in whom Δ_{max} TSH was larger than $1.0 \, \mu U/ml$). These investigators also reported a higher frequency of suicide in patients with absent Δ_{max} TSH values during a 5-year follow-up period.

Body Surface

Since TRH is normally injected in a standard dose (0.5 mg) and not in a dose related to body weight, it seems possible that patients with large body surface (and increased distribution space) have less TRH delivered to thyrotroph cell receptors (resulting in TSH blunting). In fact, Kjellman (1983) found Δ_{max} TSH in normal subjects, but not in depressed patients, to be negatively associated with height and weight. Agren and Wide (1982) reported a negative correlation between height and Δ_{max} TSH in depressed patients. However, using Δ_{max} TSH as an independent variable, we did not find body weight, height, or body surface to be significantly different in patients with TSH blunting if compared to age-, sex-, and diagnosis-matched patients with normal TSH responses and to normal subjects (Loosen, Kistler, & Prange, 1983).

Our group has studied additional endocrine factors as to their relevance to TSH blunting in primary depression (Table 15.2). These are serum thyroid hormone and cortisol levels, somatostatin in cerebrospinal fluid (CSF), dopamine, TRH pharmacokinetics, and basal TSH.

Serum Thyroid Hormones

The majority of studies have unequivocally shown that depressed patients with TSH blunting are not hyperthyroid (Loosen & Prange, 1982). Some patients with TSH blunting may even show low serum thyroid hormone levels (Hatotani et al., 1977; Takahashi et al., 1974), probably indicating a disturbance in feedback inhibition. The concept of a disturbed feedback inhibition is further supported by our preliminary findings that (1) pretreatment with a single dose of thyroid hormones blunts the TRH-induced TSH response in normal subjects, but not in depressed patients (Loosen, Wilson, & Prange, 1980), and (2) that patients with TSH blunting, but not normal subjects or patients with normal TSH responses, show a significant positive association between serum T4 levels at baseline (i.e., before TRH administration) and the TRH-induced TSH response (Loosen, Kistler, & Prange, 1983).

Serum Cortisol

Interest in serum cortisol elevation as a possible cause for TSH blunting derives from two major observations: First, cortisol is known to reduce the TSH response both in patients with endocrine disorders and in normal subjects (Nicoloff, Fisher, & Appleman, 1969; Otsuki, Dakoda, & Baba, 1973; Re, Kourides, Ridgeway, Weintraub, & Maloof, 1976; Wilber & Utiger, 1969). Second, activation of the pituitary–adrenocortical axis is a hallmark of primary depression (Carroll 1982, Carroll & Mendels, 1976; Sachar, 1975). However, several investigators did not find any association between the TSH response and serum cortisol levels in depression (Extein, Pottash, & Gold, 1981; M. S. Gold et al., 1980; Kirkegaard & Carroll, 1980; Langer et al., 1980; Papakostas et al., 1981; Sachar, Halbreich, Asnis, Nathan, & Halpern, 1980).

Somatostatin (SRIF)

SRIF is known to inhibit TSH release in both animals (Arimura & Schally, 1976) and man (Azukizawa, Pekary, Hershman, & Parker, 1976; Hall et al., 1973; Lucke, Hoeffken, & von zur Muehlen, 1975; Siler, Yen, Vale, & Guillemin, 1974; Weeke, Hansen, & Lundboek, 1974). It is thus theoretically possible that TSH blunting in depressed patients is due to increased SRIF activity. We studied SRIF-like immunoreactivity (SRF-LI) in CSF of 10 normal subjects and 23 patients with major depression. All subjects also received a TRH test. Six depressed patients showed a blunted TSH response, defined as a Δ_{max} TSH less than 5 μU/ml. There was a significant negative correlation between SRF-LI and basal TSH, but not between SRF-LI and TRH-induced TSH response in depressed patients (Bisette *et al.*, 1984). These data support an earlier report by Agren and Lundqvist (1984) who demonstrated a significant curvilinear correlation between CSF-SRIF and serum TSH levels in 85 patients with major depression. However, it remains to be determined whether TSH blunting is a function of increased SRIF activity.

Dopamine

Dopamine and prodopaminergic drugs are known to attenuate the TRH-induced TSH response (Besses *et al.*, 1975; Burrow *et al.*, 1977; Kaptein, Kletzky *et al.*, 1980; Leebaw *et al.*, 1978; Spaulding, Burrow, Donabedian, & van Woert, 1972; Thorner *et al.*, 1978), suggesting that TSH blunting in depression may be due to increased dopaminergic inhibition of thyrotroph cells. In fact, Birkhaeuser *et al.* (1980) reported that metoclopramide (a dopamine receptor blocker), 10 mg orally, normalized TSH blunting in depressed patients, but not in patients with "preclinical" hyperthyroidism. However, we have not been able to replicate this finding. We studied 21 depressed patients twice with the TRH test: initially and after 1 week of haloperidol, 2 mg twice daily orally. Although haloperidol significantly increased serum prolactin levels, it had no effect on basal or TRH-induced TSH levels. Furthermore, 4 of 5 patients with TSH blunting initially had a blunted TSH response when retested after haloperidol (Loosen, Garbutt, & Tipermas, 1986). These data do not support the notion that TSH blunting in depression is due to increased inhibitory input by dopamine. This is further supported by the observation that prolactin responses are usually normal in patients with TSH blunting (Loosen, Kistler, & Prange, 1983).

TRH Pharmacokinetics

We have recently measured serum TRH levels in 11 normal subjects and 2 patients with TSH blunting after administration of 0.5 mg TRH. In normal subjects, maximum (peak) TRH concentrations occurred consistently 2 minutes after injection; they ranged from 8.1 to 75.1 ng/ml, (Figure 15.2). In contrast, the 2 patients with TSH blunting had peak TRH levels that were well beyond the normal range (104 and 140 ng/ml, respectively), though their TRH disappearance rates, both *in vivo* and *in vitro*, were similar to those of normal subjects (Loosen, Youngblood, & Dew, 1983). These findings, of course, suggest that the thyrotroph cells in patients with TSH blunting are less responsive to TRH stimulation rather than that less TRH is available to stimulate these cells. Possible explanations for this lack of thyrotroph cell responsivity are discussed in detail below.

Basal TSH and 24-Hour TSH Secretion

Our group has assessed possible associations between baseline TSH levels and TSH blunting. Initially, we found mean baseline TSH levels to be significantly reduced in patients with TSH blunting, but not in patients with normal TSH responses (Loosen, Kistler, & Prange, 1983). In a later report using a different patient population, we found mean baseline TSH levels to be significantly reduced both in patients with and without TSH blunting as compared to normal controls. However, no significant difference emerged when patients with TSH blunting were compared to patients with normal TSH responses (Loosen, Wilson, Dew, & Tipermas, 1983). We concluded that the "data are inconclusive with regard to the question of whether low baseline TSH levels are related to TSH blunting rather than to being mentally ill" (p. 703). Kjellman (1983) recently reported that depressed patients had lower baseline, Δ_{max}, and mean 24-hour TSH levels than did normal subjects. Patients also showed a significant positive correlation between Δ_{max} TSH and 24-hour TSH levels. When patients were retested during clinical remission, Δ_{max} TSH and 24-hour TSH increased significantly. Similar data were reported by Rubin *et al.* (1980) who studied 24-hour TSH secretion and the TRH-induced TSH response in 1 depressed patient. During depression, the TSH response to TRH was blunted and the

24-hour TSH secretion reduced. Both variables normalized upon remission.

THE TRH TEST AND OTHER PUTATIVE BIOLOGICAL MARKERS

The purpose of this section is to discuss possible associations between TSH blunting and other biological markers, particularly those that are relevant for depression. They are as follows: the dexamethasone suppression test (DST), sleep markers such as shortened rapid eye movement (REM) latency, monoamine metabolite levels in different body fluids, and the as yet not well-understood syndrome of "multiple pituitary faults." Most of these markers have been studied as dependent variables (diagnosis being the independent variable), and only recently has attention been directed to how they may interact with the TRH test. Information gained from such comparisons may aid in a better understanding of the pathophysiology of TSH blunting and, perhaps, allow a more refined use of the TRH test as a clinical marker.

The DST

One important rationale for administering both the DST and the TRH test in the population is, as noted above, to evaluate whether TSH blunting is due to increased pituitary–adrenocortical axis activity. Ten investigators (Asnis et al., 1980; Banki, Vojnik, Arato, Papp, & Kovacz, 1985; Davis et al., 1981; Extein et al., 1981; Fleming, Extein, Sternbach, Pottash, & Gold, 1983; Langer et al., 1980; Papakostas et al., 1981; Rush et al., 1983; Targum, Sullivan, & Byrnes, 1982; Winokur et al., 1982) have administered both tests to patients with major depression. Their results indicate that cortisol nonsuppression after dexamethasone and TSH blunting do not show any clear association. In fact, DST abnormalities and TSH blunting seem to be independent phenomena, suggesting that neither abnormality is an (endocrine) epiphenomenon of the other. Three studies (Banki et al., 1985; Extein et al., 1981; Targum et al., 1982) are of interest in an additional way. They showed that a higher sensitivity can be achieved in identifying depressed patients if the two tests are used together. For example,

in the study of Extein et al. (1981), 30% of patients were abnormal on both tests, 34% showed TSH blunting, and 20% failed to suppress on the DST. Only 16% were normal on both tests. Targum et al. (1982) found 33% of depressed patients (and 89% of nondepressed patients) to be normal on both tests. Banki et al. (1985) administered both tests to 63 psychiatric inpatients and 15 normal controls. Patients had the diagnosis of major depression, schizophrenia, alcohol dependence, and adjustment disorder with depressed mood. Four measures [TSH, prolactin (PRL), growth hormone (GH), and cortisol] were subjected to a discriminant function analysis in order to assess the best possible separation of patients. Only one significant function emerged, and only three measures (postdexamethasone cortisol, TSH, and PRL response to TRH) proved to be important to successfully discriminate depressed patients from normal controls in 97% of cases. However, it still remains to be determined whether the predictive value of a combined TRH test and DST is greater than the predictive value of either test alone.

REM Latency

The sleep EEG has become a powerful tool in diagnosing depressed patients, particularly those with primary depression. Based on such variables as shortened REM latency and REM density, it appears to discriminate primary from secondary depressive disorder. Kupfer (1976) reported that REM latency and density allowed identification of primary depression with greater than 80% accuracy. Gillin, Duncan, Pettigrew, Rankel, and Snyder (1979) showed that a shortened REM latency was characteristic of 64% of inpatients with primary depression. Feinberg, Gillin, Carroll, Greden, and Zis (1982) reported similar findings. It can therefore be assumed that about 60–80% of patients with primary depression show characterstic sleep EEG abnormalities.

Rush and his associates (1983) administered the DST, the TRH test, and EEG sleep recordings to 22 patients with primary depression. Thirteen patients (59%) were identified by either a reduced REM latency or by a blunted TSH response, whereas all three tests detected 15 (68%) patients.

Monamine Metabolites

Five investigators have studied possible associations between parameters of monoamine metabolism and the TRH-induced TSH response in depressed patients. Of course, these studies were guided by two observations: (1) Monoamine metabolite dysfunctions have been widely described in depression, leading to both the catecholamine (Schildkraut, 1965) and the indoleamine (Coppen, Prange, Whybrow, & Noguera, 1972) hypothesis of depression; and (2) monoamines, serving as neurotransmitters, are intimately involved in neuroendocrine regulation, including the regulation of the hypothalamic–pituitary–thyroid axis (Loosen & Prange, 1982).

Three investigators assessed possible associations between urinary 3-methoxy-4-hydroxyphenyglycol (MHPG, a norepinephrine metabolite) and TRH-induced TSH response and obtained conflicting results. Davis et al. (1981), studying 42 men with primary depression, found a significant association between TSH blunting and high urinary MHPG excretion. Sternbach et al. (1983), studying 51 patients with unipolar depression, found a significant positive correlation between urinary MHPG levels and TSH response in men, but not in women. Brambilla et al. (1980), studying 29 depressed patients during depression and 15 patients during remission, reported no relationship between urinary MHPG and TSH response.

Two groups assessed possible relationships between TSH response and measures of serotonergic activity. P. W. Gold, Goodwin, Wehr, and Rebar (1977), studying 23 patients with primary depression, found a significant negative correlation between TSH response and 5-hydroxyindoleacetic acid (5-HIAA, a serotonin metabolite) levels in CSF. Robertson, Tricou, Fang, and Meltzer (1982), studying 58 euthyroid depressed patients, reported a significantly reduced uptake of labeled serotonin in blood platelets of patients with TSH blunting as compared to normal controls.

Multiple Pituitary Faults

In endocrine disorders, abnormalities involving the pituitary gland are rarely limited to a one-cell system. If applied to depression, this notion suggests that depressed patients may—aside from reduced TSH secretion by the thyrotroph cells—show additional faults in other adenohypophysial cells. In fact, recent evidence supports this view. Brambilla et al. (1978) studied 14 depressed patients and found that 10 patients showed a paradoxical GH response to TRH, whereas 8 responded (paradoxically) to TRH with increased follicle-stimulating hormone (FSH) and luteinizing hormone (LH) secretions. These latter faults were observed in addition to TSH blunting in some patients. In a later report, the same investigators (Brambilla et al., 1980) studied 29 depressed patients with TRH; 9 patients showed TSH blunting, 15 had an exaggerated prolactin response, 16 showed a paradoxical GH response, 11 had a paradoxical LH response, and 8 had a paradoxical FSH response. In some patients, prolactin, GH, and LH responses persisted into remission. Winokur et al. (1983) administered the TRH test to 32 healthy subjects and 45 patients with major depression; 7 patients showed TSH blunting, 8 had blunted prolactin responses, 4 showed a paradoxical GH response, and 10 an exaggerated FSH response to TRH. Twelve depressed patients (27%), but no controls, had two or more abnormal hormonal responses.

Whereas the studies cited above emphasize the presence of abnormal prolactin, GH, FSH, and LH responses to TRH in depressed patients, there is also evidence of increased variability in hormonal responses to a variety of other endocrine stimuli. Winokur et al. (1982) administered TRH, LHRH, and the insulin tolerance test to 26 patients with primary depression and to 24 normal controls. Normal ranges were established by use of log-transformed control values. Seven control subjects (29%) and 25 depressed patients (96%) had at least one abnormal response, and 15 depressed patients (58%) had two or more abnormal responses. Using a similar design, Amsterdam et al. (1983) reported that 9 control subjects (41%) and 17 bipolar patients (72%) had at least one abnormal response. Twelve bipolar patients (55%), but no control, had two or more abnormal responses.

Taken together, these studies indicate that in major depression there is increased variability in hormonal responses involving several neuroendocrine axes. No consistent pattern of abnormality has yet emerged. However, the association of two or more abnormalities seems particularly characteristic for depression, as it is never seen in normal controls.

THE TRH TEST IN OTHER PSYCHIATRIC DISORDERS

Evaluation of TRH-induced TSH responses in psychiatric disorders other than depression is important from three points of view. First, for any given biological marker, one must evaluate specificity, that is, the incidence of true-negative results obtained when a test is applied to subjects known to be free of the disease (Galen & Gambino, 1975). Second, comparison of TRH test results gained from different psychiatric populations may provide information as to possible biological similarities between these populations. This seems particularly relevant in conditions that share certain symptoms (e.g., affective disturbances) with depression. Third, such comparison will allow to assess to what degree TRH test abnormalities are related to mental distress per se rather than to any given psychiatric diagnostic classification.

Mania

Seven studies have investigated the TRH-induced TSH response in manic patients. Takahashi et al. (1974) found it somewhat reduced in 8 patients. McLarty, O'Boyle, Spencer, and Ratcliffe (1975) studied 21 manic patients taking lithium and found exaggerated TSH responses, but these results probably indicate lithium-induced hypothyroidism. Consistent with this interpretation, Tanimoto et al. (1981) found normal TSH responses in 6 manic patients before lithium treatment; after lithium treatment their TSH responses were exaggerated. Kirkegaard et al. (1978) found the TSH response in 14 manic patients somewhat diminished. M. S. Gold et al., (1980) studied 2 patients as they shifted from depression to mania. Both patients showed a change from normal to blunted responses when becoming manic. In a recent report from the same group, Extein, Pottash, Gold, and Cowdry (1982) found 18

of 30 manic patients showing a blunted TSH response, as defined by a Δ_{max} TSH less than 7.0 μU/ml. Wolkin et al. (1984) reported that 3 of 8 manic patients showed a blunted TSH response, as defined by a Δ_{max} TSH below 5.9 μU/ml (lowest quartile of distribution). However, 6 of these patients were on psychotropic medications when tested.

Alcoholism

Loosen, Prange, and Wilson (1979) studied 33 male depressed alcoholics. None had a diagnosis, personal history, or family history of primary depression. In all cases, alcoholism had preceded diagnosable depression. Twelve men received TRH during acute alcohol withdrawal, and 14 men were retested with TRH in the postwithdrawal state 1 week after the first injection. At that time all symptoms of withdrawal (e.g., tremor, sweating, agitation) had shown complete remission. Of 12 patients, 6 (50%) showed blunted TSH responses after TRH during acute withdrawal, and 5 of 14 (36%) after withdrawal (Figure 15.3). Moreover, findings in the acute state suggested thyroid activation and increased central dopaminergic activity, as evidenced by elevated baseline levels of total T4 and FT4 index, as well as elevated GH and reduced prolactin levels at baseline (Table 15.3). These abnormalities returned to normal levels in the remission state (Table 15.3). However, persistence of TSH blunting in some patients suggested that the fault may not have been solely state dependent. It became necessary, therefore, to study a group of abstinent alcoholics. To achieve this goal, we welcomed the collaboration of a local Alcoholics Anonymous (AA) group. Twenty-nine male AA members were studied (Loosen, Wilson, Dew, & Tipermas, 1983). All had been diagnosed as alcoholic during previous hospitalizations, and all had a proven record of sobriety for at least 2 years. Although some patients had a personal history of depression, all were free of depressive symptoms when receiving TRH.

In addition to a "euthyroid sick syndrome," evidenced by low levels of T3, high levels of reverse T3, and normal levels of T4 (Table 15.3), 9 of 29 patients (31%) showed TSH blunting, defined as Δ_{max} TSH < 5.0 μU/ml. TSH blunting was not

TABLE 15.3. Summary of Endocrine Findings in Alcoholic Patients[a]

	Acute withdrawal	Postwithdrawal	Abstinence
FT4	↑	NC	NC
Total T4	↑	NC	NC
T3	NC	NC	↓
rT3	NS	NS	↑
T3/T4 ratio	NS	NS	↓
T3U	NC	NC	↓
TBG	NS	NS	↑
TSH B	NC	NC	↓
TSH P	↓	↓	↓
PRL B	↓	NC	NC
PRL P	NC	NC	NC
GH B	↑	NC	NC
Cortisol B	NC	NC	NC
Testosterone B	NC	NC	NC

[a]Patients were studied during acute alcohol withdrawal ($n = 12$), after such withdrawal ($n = 14$), and during sobriety for more than 2 years ($n = 29$). These data have been described in detail elsewhere (Loosen et al., 1979; Loosen, Wilson, Dew, Tipermas, 1983). N.C. = No change; N.S. = Not studied.

associated with duration of abstinence and family or personal history of depression. Serum concentrations of prolactin, cortisol, and testosterone were similar in TSH blunters and nonblunters. Patients as a whole showed significantly reduced levels of TSH at baseline; however, these levels were significantly reduced in those with and those without TSH blunting, and the difference between the two groups was not statistically significant. Because patients showed evidence for a euthyroid sick syndrome, we evaluated possible associations between thyroid hormones and TSH blunting. In general, thyroid hormone disturbances did not follow the blunting–nonblunting dichotomy. Neither values of the free T4 index nor concentrations of total T4, T3, and reverse T3 were correlated with TSH blunting. Furthermore, changes in reverse T3 were not associated with changes in the TSH response; that is, TSH blunting was not due to increased levels of reverse T3.

If one compares the two studies cited above, marked differences and some similarities emerge in regard to the results of the TRH test. First, in contrast to patients in acute withdrawal, patients in remission and abstinent alcoholics did not show any sign of thyroid activation, nor was there evidence for a central hyperdopaminergic state. This suggests that both findings are possibly more closely related to the acute withdrawal state. Second, among the abstinent alcoholics, the euthyroid sick syndrome was most prominent; this was not seen in acutely withdrawn or remitted patients. Third, the incidence of TSH blunting was highest in the acute state (50%); thereafter it was similar in both remitted (36%) and abstinent (31%) patients. Because TSH blunting was observed in both some acutely ill and some abstinent alcoholics, it may represent a trait marker, at least in some patients. However, that TSH blunting in alcoholism is not always a trait marker is suggested by the increased frequency of blunting in acutely ill patients (which, of course, points to a possible role of acute withdrawal on TSH blunting).

The occurrence of TSH blunting in depression and alcoholism deserves special mention. Clinical and epidemiological studies (Goodwin & Erickson, 1979) have revealed that there are features shared by patients with these conditions: (1) Patients often show elements of both disorders and frequently it is impossible to determine which, if either, is primary and which is secondary; (2) both conditions exhibit high rates of suicide; (3) lithium, the drug of choice for the prevention of recurrent depression, may have similar beneficial effects in chronic alcoholic patients; and (4) genetic relationships between alcoholism and depression have also been noted. Whether TSH blunting represents a biological link that parallels the other similarities between alcoholism and depression mentioned above remains to be determined.

Anorexia Nervosa

Several studies have assessed hypothalamic–pituitary–thyroid axis function in patients with anorexia nervosa. Resting levels of TSH appear to be normal in this condition (Beumont, George, Pimstone, & Vinik, 1976; Brown, Garfinkel, Jeuniewic, Moldofsky, & Stancer, 1977; Lundberg, Walinder, Werner, & Wilde, 1972; Moshang & Utiger, 1977). TRH-induced TSH responses have also been reported to be normal in magnitude, although they are usually delayed (Aro, Lamberg, & Pelkonen, 1975; Croxson & Ibbertson, 1977; Jeuniewic, Garfinkel, & Moldofsky, 1978; Lundberg et al., 1972; Miyai, Toshihide, Azukizawa, Ishibashi, & Kumahara, 1975; Vigersky, Loriaux, Andersen, Mecklenburg, & Vaitukaitis, 1976; Wakeling et al., 1979), and weight gain is sometimes followed by an increase of Δ_{max} TSH levels (Leslie, Isaacs, Gomez, Ragatt, & Bayliss, 1978; Wakeling et al., 1979). Delayed TSH responses seem to be related to starvation rather than being causally associated with the disease. They have also been reported to occur in secondary amenorrhea associated with simple weight loss (Vigersky et al., 1976). Pathophysiologically they may indicate hypothalamic dysfunction or altered plasma TSH clearance (Brown et al., 1977).

Borderline Personality Disorder

The syndrome described as borderline personality disorder is etiologically and nosologically complex, and undoubtedly, heterogeneous, hence, the effort to operationally define its diagnostic classification (Gunderson, Kolb, & Austin, 1981; Perry & Klerman, 1980; Spitzer, Endicott, & Gibbon, 1979).

Several lines of evidence suggest the potential usefulness of the TRH test in patients with borderline personality disorder. First, depression is often observed in borderline patients (Stone, 1980). Second, there is a greater incidence of depression in relatives of borderline patients than in relatives of schizophrenic patients (Loranger, Oldham, & Tulis, 1982; McGlashan, 1983). Third, there is evidence that biological markers thought to be specific for depression are also at fault in borderline patients. For example, Carroll et al. (1981) reported DST abnormalities in 13 of 21 borderline patients; only 8 of them had received RDC diagnoses of major depression. Reus (1982) also reported DST abnormalities in some borderline patients who did not fulfill criteria for major depression. Furthermore, Akiskal (1981) and McNamara et al. (1984) reported that some patients with borderline personality disorder (although not depressed) had significantly reduced REM latency measures.

We administered the TRH test to 15 patients with the primary diagnosis of borderline personality disorder. Twelve patients carried the additional diagnosis of depression, substance abuse, or both. Prolactin levels were normal in these patients. A blunted TSH response to TRH was found in 7 patients, 2 of whom were neither depressed during testing nor did they have the additional diagnosis of depression and/or substance abuse. TSH blunting was not associated with such factors as thyroid status, serum cortisol, weight, height, or body surface (Garbutt, Loosen, Tipermas, & Prange, 1983).

Taken together, these data derived from three biological tests suggest that the borderline personality disorder may be more closely linked to the affective disorders than to the schizophrenia syndrome.

Schizophrenia

Nine studies have assessed pituitary–thyroid axis function in patients suffering from schizophrenia or other syndromes characterized by psychotic features. Two early studies found baseline TSH levels to be significantly elevated in schizophrenic patients (Dewhurst, El Kabir, Exley, Harris, & Mandelbrote, 1968; Dewhurst, 1969). In the former study, elevations of baseline TSH levels were significantly associated with clinical ratings of paranoid ideations.

Seven studies have assessed the TRH-induced TSH response in schizophrenic patients; they also provide data on the TSH response in depression for comparison. As one will see below, such comparison is fruitful in assessing frequency of TSH blunting in schizophrenic patients. Loosen *et al.* (1977) injected TRH, 0.4 or 0.5 mg, in schizophrenic and depressed women. Of 23 depressed, 6 (26%), but none of the 9 schizophrenic women, showed TSH blunting, defined as a Δ_{max} TSH < 5.0 μU/ml. M. S. Gold *et al.* (1981) injected TRH, 0.5 mg, in depressed and schizophrenic patients. Of 41 unipolar depressed patients, 31 (76%), but none of the 14 schizophrenic patients, showed TSH blunting, defined as Δ_{max} TSH < 7.0 μU/ml. However, in a later report from the same group, Extein *et al.* (1982) demonstrated TSH blunting (defined as a Δ_{max} TSH < 7.0 μU ml) in 8 of 30 schizophrenic patients (27%) and in 18 of 30 manic patients (60%). Banki *et al.* (1985) administered TRH, 0.2 mg, to 63 women with one of the following four diagnoses: depression, alcoholism, schizophrenia, and adjustment disorder. Of 19 depressed women, 12 (63%), 7 of 10 alcoholic women (70%), 6 of 20 schizophrenic women (30%), and 5 of 14 women with adjustment disorder (36%) showed TSH blunting, defined as a Δ_{max} TSH < 5.0 μU/ml. Although each patient group differed significantly from individual controls in regard to frequency of TSH blunting, the TRH test still subdivided patients into two subgroups: Depressed and alcoholic patients had significantly lower mean Δ_{max} TSH levels than patients with schizophrenia or adjustment disorders. Wolkin *et al.* (1984) injected TRH, 0.5 mg, in 8 normal volunteers and 14 depressed, 8 manic, and 17 schizophrenic patients. One schizophrenic (6%) and 3 depressed patients (21%) showed TSH blunting, as defined by a Δ_{max} TSH less than 5.0 μU/ml. However, if the lowest quartile was used for defining the fault (i.e. Δ_{max} TSH less than 5.9 μU/ml), 5 schizophrenic (29%) and 4 depressed patients (29%) showed blunting, suggesting a similar frequency of TSH blunting in the two conditions. The authors concluded that TRH test abnormalities "exist in both schizophrenia and affective disorders, with the latter illness having the more severe endocrine disturbances." Ferrier, Johnstone, Crow, and Rimon-Rodriguez (1983) injected TRH, 0.2 mg, in 18 chronic schizophrenic and 9

control subjects and found the TSH response to be normal in patients. However, here it is worth mentioning that 6 of the 9 control subjects had a history of some psychiatric disorder. Five subjects suffered from "long-standing neurotic symptoms . . . mainly of a depressive nature," and one had the diagnosis of manic–depressive psychosis. However, no subject showed symptoms of depression at the time of testing. Koenig, Aschauer, Langer, Resch, and Schoenbeck (1984) injected TRH, 0.4 mg, in patients with a depressive or paranoid hallucinatory syndrome. Of 74 depressed patients, 41 (55%) and 21 of 54 patients with paranoid hallucinatory syndrome (40%) showed TSH blunting, defined as a Δ_{max} TSH < 5.0 μU/ml. However, there was no nosological reference as to whether patients with paranoid hallucinatory syndrome also fulfilled criteria for schizophrenia.

Taken together, these data indicate that TSH blunting may indeed occur in some schizophrenic patients. However, in most studies involving both schizophrenic and depressed patients, the frequency of TSH blunting appars to be lower in schizophrenic than in depressed patients.

Chronic Pain

Krishnan and France (1984) administered the TRH test to 24 patients with chronic low back pain. Pain complaints corresponded well with organic findings such as radiculopathy, positive electromyographs, and/or positive radiographic findings. Diagnostically, 14 patients also fulfilled DSM-III criteria for major depression, while the remaining 10 patients did not satisfy such criteria. Of patients without depression, 20% and 29% of patients with depression showed TSH blunting, defined as a Δ_{max} TSH < 5.0 μU/ml. The authors concluded "that the blunted TSH response might be a measure of some common abnormality" (of the two conditions). Unfortunately, however, there was no control for drug status at the time of testing. It is thus possible that TSH blunting in some chronic pain patients was due to short- or long-term effects of analgetics (e.g., morphine, fenclofenac, aspirin) and/or glucocorticoids (Wenzel, 1981). Regimens containing both analgetics and glucocorticoids are commonly used in that condition.

SIGNIFICANCE OF TSH BLUNTING

A blunted TSH response to TRH has been observed in some depressed, manic, alcoholic, borderline, and schizophrenic patients. The fault is thus not specific for depression, or, for that matter, for any of the psychiatric nosological classifications studied to date. Nevertheless, TSH blunting may have both heuristic and practical clinical value (though at present both are more potential than actual), and it seems justified to consider in a preliminary way its value in regard to pathophysiology and clinical utility. Here, it is important to recall that the observation of TSH blunting in depression may be valuable in one way, while a blunted response in the other psychiatric conditions may be valuable in quite another way.

Pathophysiological Significance

A prominent difficulty in studying brain function in man, apart from its complexity, is the fact that, for obvious reasons, the human brain cannot be studied directly. Thus, "windows" (Carroll, 1978) have, by necessity, been utilized; and here the neuroendocrine system—more precisely TSH secreted by the anterior pituitary gland—provides an important mode of access. In brief, the thyrotroph cells in the anterior pituitary are regulated not only by feedback messages from the periphery (e.g., thyroid hormones, cortisol, possibly dopamine), but also via the portal venous system by hormones secreted by neurons in the hypothalamus. These hormones are TRH, somatostatin, and possibly neurotensin; they are regulated, at least in part, by neurons from other brain regions which depend for transmission upon the secretion of substances of traditional interest to the psychiatrist—acetylcholine, norepinephrine, dopamine, serotinin, and the like. Thus, if the relevant physiological connections were known, one could infer from measurement of TSH about activity of transmitters in the brain. However, as we have pointed out elsewhere (Loosen & Prange, 1982), "it is difficult to

draw conclusions about amine transmitters from pituitary hormone measurements. At every level of the system there are complex interactions of multiple factors of opposing signs."

In addition to the neuroendocrine window strategy, one can assemble sufficient evidence to posit two preliminary endocrine hypotheses for TSH blunting. The first hypothesis suggests that TSH blunting in depressed patients may be due to chronic hypersecretion of (endogenous) TRH. In this condition, the thyrotroph cells in the anterior pituitary are thought to become hyporesponsive to TRH, possibly because of downregulation of thyrotroph TRH receptors. After TRH challenge, these patients would then show TSH blunting. This hypothesis rests partly on studies in which TRH was given chronically to normal subjects (Ahuja, Baumgarten, & Oeff, 1980; Bremner, Abreu, Stockigt, Kretser, & Burger, 1977; Frey & Haug, 1977; Mongioi et al., 1983; Rabello et al., 1974; Retiene, Schulz, & Mueller, 1973; Snyder & Utiger, 1973; Staub et al., 1978). Spencer et al. (1980) also reported that normal subjects showed an inhibition of the normal TSH rise during evening hours and a loss of the diurnal TSH rhythm after chronic TRH administration. Golstein, Van Cauter, Linkowski, Vanhaelst, & Mendlewicz (1980) and Kjellman (1983) reported that the latter finding occurs (without TRH treatment) in depressed patients. However, A. Weeke and Weeke (1980) found no difference in the 24-hour TSH rhythm between patients with primary depression and normal subjects, and Kijne et al. (1982) found no difference in the 24-hour TSH rhythm when patients were studied during depression and again after remission. Here it is worth noting that depressed patients with TSH blunting often show low TSH levels at baseline and normal prolactin levels. After chronic low-dose TRH stimulation, however, one would expect both levels to be somewhat increased (Bremner et al., 1977; Mongioi et al., 1983; Spencer et al., 1980).

The second hypothesis regards the status of the thyrotroph cells which may be primarily disordered or receiving increased inhibitory input in patients with TSH blunting. This notion is supported by the following findings: (1) Levels of T4 and T3 were sometimes low in patients with TSH blunting, suggesting a disturbance in feedback inhibition (Loosen & Prange, 1982); (2) baseline levels of TSH were low in some depressed and alcoholic patients, though there was no significant difference between those with and those without TSH blunting (Loosen, Kistler, & Prange, 1983; Loosen, Wilson, Dew, & Tipermas, 1983); (3) patients with TSH blunting had, by definition, a low TSH response to TRH, but the TSH increase above baseline was highly significant (Loosen, Kistler, & Prange, 1983); and (4) 2 patients with TSH blunting showed, after TRH administration, higher peak TRH serum levels than did normal subjects (Loosen, Youngblood, & Dew, 1983). Taken together, these findings suggest that thyrotroph cells in patients with TSH blunting may receive increased inhibitory input (the notion that these cells may be primarily disordered is presently not testable). What substances, then, could account for such inhibition of thyrotroph cells? As discussed above, thyroid hormones, cortisol, and dopamine—all known to exert inhibitory effects on TSH secretion—are unlikely to cause TSH blunting in the psychiatric conditions studied to date. However, here it is worth noting that it still remains to be determined whether small alterations in the *free* concentration of thyroid hormones are responsible for TSH blunting. Excessive somatostatin activity could cause TSH blunting in some depressed patients (Agren & Lundgvist, 1984; Bissette et al., 1984); it would also account for another prominent neuroendocrine finding in that condition, that is, diminished GH response to insulin-induced hypoglycemia (Gruen, Sachar, Altman, & Sassin, 1975). However, recent studies reporting *low* somatostatin levels in CSF of depressed patients do not support this view (Gerner & Yamada, 1982; Post et al., 1983). Furthermore, neurotensin is known to reduce the TRH-induced TSH response in rats (Nemeroff et al., 1980). However, interactions between neurotensin and TSH have not yet been studied in normal human subjects, let alone patients in whom TSH blunting does occur. It is also possible that thyrotroph cells receive increased inhibitory input by other as yet unidentified or untested substances.

Clinical Utility

Since the first description of a blunted TSH response in depressed patients (Prange et al., 1972), the employment of neuroendocrine strategies and the search for biological markers for one or another mental illness have become ever more important research strategies. This effort, however, has produced some confusion. First, neuroendocrine measures, as we have shown, rest upon complex physiological processes. Second, the notion of biological markers, as has been suggested elsewhere (Prange & Loosen, 1981), is based on concepts that are poorly defined as to their application to psychiatric research. Third, psychiatric nosology, to which a biological finding is to be assigned, is often confusing and, by nature, only vaguely defined. As we (Loosen & Prange, 1982; Prange & Loosen, 1981) and others (Carroll, 1982) have pointed out, biological findings should be called "markers" only after they have fulfilled stringent criteria such as acceptable sensitivity, specificity, and predictive value. To date, the TRH test only approximates these criteria as a marker for depression.

In order to critically analyze factors such as specificity and sensitivity of TSH blunting in depressive disorders, one must consider the nature of problems inherent in psychiatric nosology. Depression tends to grade into normalcy rather than separate from it. Thus, there is a need to reach consensus about clinical definitions of more severe depression in order to circumvent the potential problem of falsely low sensitivity of TSH blunting associated with broad definitions of depression. This has been recognized, and most of the studies reviewed here have administered TRH to patients with primary depression. However, even in this condition a consensus does not exist. For example, the diagnosis of "endogenous" depression can vary from 24% to 72% of a given population of depressed patients (Davidson, Turnbull, Strickland, & Belyea, 1984).

Aside from specificity and sensitivity, biological markers are defined as state or trait markers. This definition is particularly useful in psychiatric disorders with a predominantly cycling course (e.g., depression, alcoholism). A state marker is an aspect of an (acute) illness, and as such it is not present before or after illness. Its utility lies in aiding in diagnosis. In contrast, a trait marker will be present before, during, and after an illness. It helps, therefore, in assessing the likelihood of an illness. With this consideration in mind, what can be said about TSH blunting in both depression and alcoholism? It is sometimes a state marker and sometimes a trait marker. The fact that as a state marker it can occur in depression and acute states of alcoholism without persisting into remission suggests that it may play a role in the pathophysiology of these conditions, though the interpretation of mechanism is uncertain and, possibly, heterogeneous in nature. The fact that as a trait marker TSH blunting can occur in depressed patients in remission and in abstinent alcoholics suggests that it may be helpful in identifying subjects with high vulnerability for these conditions. An efficient way to assess the utility of TSH blunting as a trait marker is to study its occurrence in first-degree relatives of an affected (i.e., depressed or alcoholic) proband. Brambilla et al. (1980) have made a promising start in this direction. They found that 2 of 6 phenotypically normal relatives of a depressed proband showed blunting. Furthermore, Robertson et al. (1982), studying 10 nonpatient controls with the TRH test, found that 6 had a personal history of previous minor depression, alcohol abuse, or a family history of treated depressive disorder. Of these 6 controls, 5 had blunted TSH response, whereas no blunting was observed in the remaining 13 controls. Unfortunately, however, these authors did not distinguish between personal and family history of depression and alcohol abuse.

In addition to its possible use as a state or trait marker, TSH blunting has shown promising clinical utility in several ways. The phenomenon may aid in assessing the response to standard antidepressant treatment, predicting outcome to such treatment, assessing the risk for violent suicide attempts, and describing relationships between different psychiatric diagnoses.

COMMENT

An important conclusion from this work is that the TRH test has excellent research and empirical clinical value. For more that two

centuries investigators and clinicians have suspected relationships between the thyroid axis and behavior, especially affective state, but investigations of these relationships have suffered from the criticism that no disorder in thyroid axis function could be identified. This criticism can now be removed. Moreover, if one assumes that depression must be understood as a process (and the clinical course of the disease strongly supports this view), then the study of process requires longitudinal observation. Here it is worth recalling that the majority of studies cited in this review are based on the administration of TRH during the acute illness and that only a few studies retested patients during symptomatic recovery. Clearly, what is needed are longitudinal studies using repeated TRH administrations both during depression and after remission over an extended period of time. Such studies are likely to remove our present uncertainties in regard to test–retest reliability of TSH blunting, its state or trait nature, its usefulness for monitoring treatment response and predicting outcome, and its possible association with duration of the disease and suicidal behavior. They are also likely to show whether the TSH response has a seasonal variation and whether it is affected by long-term antidepressant treatment.

References

Agren, H. (1981). Biological markers in major depressive disorders: A clinical and multivariate study. *Acta Universitatis Upsalliensis, Abstracts of Uppsala Dissertations from the Faculty of Medicine, 405.*

Agren, H., & Lundqvist, G. (1984). Low levels of somatostatin in human CSF mark depressive episodes. *Psychoneuroendocrinology, 9,* 233–248.

Agren, H., & Wide, L. (1982). Patterns of depression reflected in pituitary–thyroid and pituitary–adrenal endocrine changes. *Psychoneuroendocrinology, 7,* 309–327.

Ahuja, S., Baumgarten, S., & Oeff, K. (1980). Repetitive intravenous TRH stimulations at short intervals in euthyroid and hypothyroid subjects. *Acta Endocrinologica (Copenhagen), 93,* 20–24.

Akiskal, H. S. (1981). Subaffective disorders: Dysthymic, cyclothymic and bipolar II disorders in the "borderline" realm. *Psychiatric Clinics of North America, 4,* 25–46.

Amsterdam, J. D., Winokur, A., Lucki, I., Caroff, S. Y., Snyder, P., & Rickels, K. (1983). A neuroendocrine test battery in bipolar patients and healthy subjects. *Archives of General Psychiatry, 40,* 515–521.

Amsterdam, J. D., Winokur, A., & Mendels, J. (1979). *Multiple hormonal response to TRH in depressed patients.* Abstracts of the Tenth International Congress of the International Society of Psychoneuroendocrinology, Park City, UT.

Anderson, M. S., Bowers, C. J., Kastin, A. J., Schalch, D. S., Schally, A. V., Snyder, P. J., Utiger, R. D., Wilber, J. F., & Wise, A. J. (1971). Synthetic TRH, a potent stimulator of thyrotropin secretion in man. *New England Journal of Medicine, 285,* 1279–1283.

Arimura, A., & Schally, A. V. (1976). Increase in basal and TRH-stimulated TSH by passive immunization with antiserum to SRIF in rats. *Endocrinology (Baltimore), 98,* 1069–1072.

Aro, A., Lamberg, B. A., & Pelkonen, R. (1975). Dysfunction of the hypothalamic–pituitary axis in anorexia nervosa. *New England Journal of Medicine, 292,* 594–595.

Asnis, G. M., Nathan, R. S., Halbreich, U., Halpern, F. S., & Sacher, E. J. (1980). TRH test in depression. *Lancet, 1,* 424–425.

Azukizawa, M., Pekary, E., Hershman, J. R., & Parker, D. C. (1976). Plasma TSH, thyroxine, and T3 relationships in man. *Journal of Clinical Endocrinology and Metabolism, 43,* 533–542.

Banki, C. M., Vojnik, M., Arato, M., Papp, Z., & Kovacz, A. (1985). Dexamethasone suppression and multiple hormonal responses to TRH in some psychiatric disorders. *Archives of Psychiatry and Neurological Sciences, 235,* 32–37.

Besses, G. S., Burrow, G. N., & Spaulding, S. W. (1975). Dopamine infusion acutely inhibits the TSH and prolactin response to TRH. *Journal of Clinical Endocrinology and Metabolism, 41,* 985–988.

Beumont, P. J. V., George, G. C. W., Pimstone, B. L., & Vinik, A. I. (1976). Body weight and the pituitary response to hypothalamic-releasing hormones in patients with anorexia nervosa. *Journal of Clinical Endocrinology and Metabolism, 43,* 487–496.

Birkhaeuser, M. H., Staubb, J. C., Grani, R., Girard, J., Noelpp, B., & Good, E. (1980). *Dopaminergic control of TSH response to TRH in depressive patients* (p. 61). Abstracts of the Eleventh International Congress of the International Society of Psychoneuroendocrinology, Florence, Italy.

Bissette, G., Walleus, H., Widerlov, E., Karlsson, I., Eklundt, K., Loosen, P. T., & Nemeroff, C. B. (1984). *Reduction of CSF concentration of SRIF-LI in dementia, major depression, and schizophrenia.* Abstracts of the annual meeting of the Society for Neuroscience, Anaheim, CA.

Bleuler, M. (1954). *Endokrinologische Psychiatrie.* Stuttgart: Thieme.

Boler, J., Enzmann, F., Folkers, K., Bowers, C. Y., & Schally, A. V. (1969). The identity of chemical and hormone properties of the thyrotropin-releasing hormone and pyroglutamyl-histadyl-prolineamide. *Biochemical and Biophysical Research Communications, 37,* 505–510.

Borowski, G. D., Garofano, C. D., Rose, L. I. & Levy, R. A. (1984). Blood pressure response to TRH in euthyroid subjects. *Journal of Clinical Endocrinology and Metabolism, 58,* 197–200.

Brambilla, F., Smeraldi, E., Bellodi, L., Sacchetti, E., & Mueller, E. E. (1980). Neuroendocrine correlates and monoaminergic hypothesis in primary affective disorders (PAD). In F. Brambilla, G. Racagni, & D. de Wied (Eds.), *Progress in psychoneuroendocrinology* (pp. 235–245). Amsterdam: Elsevier/North-Holland Biomedical Press.

Brambilla, F., Smeraldi, E., Sacchetti, E., Flammetta, N., Lochi, D., & Mueller, E. (1978). Deranged anterior pituitary responsiveness to hypothalamic hormones in depressed patients. *Archives of General Psychiatry, 35,* 1231–1238.

Bremner, W. J., Abreu, R., Stockigt, J. R., Kretser, D. M., & Burger, H. G. (1977). Pituitary thyroid responses to 4-hour constant infusions of TRH in man. *Journal of Clinical Endocrinology and Metabolism, 45,* 981–987.

Brown, G. M., Garfinkel, P. E., Jeuniewic, N., Modlofsky, H., & Stancer, H. C. (1977). Endocrine profiles in anorexia nervosa. In R. Vigersky (Ed.), *Anorexia nervosa* (pp. 123–135). New York: Raven Press.

Burger, A. G., & Patel, Y. C. (1977). TSH and TRH: Their physiological regulation and the clinical application of TRH. In L. Martini & G. M. Besser (Eds.), *Clinical neuroendocrinology* (pp. 31–69). New York: Academic Press.

Burger, A. G., Weissel, M., & Berger, M. (1980). Starvation induces a partial failure of triiodothyronine to inhibit the thyrotropin response to thyrotropin-releasing hormone. *Journal of Clinical Endocrinology and Metabolism, 51,* 1064–1067.

Burgus, R., Dunn, T. F., Desiderio, D., & Guillemin, R. (1969). Structure moleculaire du facteur hypothalamique hypophysitrope TRF d'origine ovine: Mise en évidence spectrometrie de mass de la séquence, PCA-His-Pro-NH2. *l'Academie des Sciences, Hebdomadaires des Seances de Compte Rendus, 269,* 1870–1873.

Burrow, G. M., May, P. B., Spaulding, S. W., & Donabedian, R. K. (1977). TRH and dopamine interaction affecting pituitary hormone secretions. *Journal of Clinical Endocrinology and Metabolism, 45,* 76–72.

Carlson, H. E., Drenick, E. J., Chopra, I. J., & Hershman, J. M. (1977). Alterations in basal and TRH-stimulated serum levels of TSH, prolactin, and thyroid hormones in starved obese men. *Journal of Clinical Endocrinology and Metabolism, 45,* 707–713.

Carroll, B. J. (1978). Neuroendocrine functions in psychiatric disorders. In M. A. Lipton, A. de Mascio, & K. F. Killam (Eds.), *Psychopharmacology: A generation of progress* (pp. 487–497). New York: Raven Press.

Carroll, B. J. (1982). The dexamethasone suppression test for melancholia. *British Journal of Psychiatry, 140,* 292–304.

Carroll, B. J., Greden, J. F., Feinberg, M., Lohr, N., James, N. M., Steiner, M., Haskett, R. F., Albala, A. A., de Vigne, J. P., & Jarika, J. (1981). Neuroendocrine evaluation of depression in borderline patients. *Psychiatric Clinics of North America, 4,* 89–99.

Carroll, B. J., & Mendels, J. (1976). Neuroendocrine regulation in affective disorders. In E. J. Sachar (Ed.), *Hormones, behavior and psychopathology* (pp. 193–224). New York: Raven Press.

Coppen, A., Montgomery, S., Peet, M., & Bailey, J. (1974). Thyrotropin-releasing hormone in the treatment of depression. *Lancet, 2,* 433–434.

Coppen, A., Prange, A. J., Jr., Whybrow, P. C., & Noguera, R. (1972). Abnormalities of indoleamines in affective disorders. *Archives of General Psychiatry*, *26*, 474–478.

Croxson, M. S., Hall, T. D., Kletzky, O. A., Jaramillo, J. E., & Nicoloff, J. T. (1977). Decreased serum thyrotropin induced by fasting. *Journal of Clinical Endocrinology and Metabolism*, *45*, 560–568.

Croxson, M. S., & Ibbertson, H. K. (1977). Low serum triiodothyronine (T3) and hypothyroidism in anorexia nervosa. *Journal of Clinical Endocrinology and Metabolism*, *44*, 167–174.

Czernichow, P., Dauzet, M. C., Brayer, M., & Rappoport, R. (1976). Abnormal TSH, PRL and GH response to TSH-releasing factor in chronic renal failure. *Journal of Clinical Endocrinology and Metabolism*, *43*, 630–637.

Davidson, J., Turnbull, C., Strickland, R., & Belyea, M. (1984). Comparative diagnostic criteria for melancholia and endogenous depression. *Archives of General Psychiatry*, *41*, 506–511.

Davis, K. L., Hollister, L. E., Mathe, A. A., Davis, B. M., Rathpearl, M. A., Faull, K. F., Hsieh, J. Y., Barchas, J. D., & Berger, P. A. (1981). Neuroendocrine and neurochemical measurement in depression. *American Journal of Psychiatry*, *138*, 1555–1562.

Dewhurst, K. E., El Kabir, D. T., Exley, D., Harris, G. W., & Mandelbrote, B. M. (1968). Blood levels of TSH, protein-bound iodine, and cortisol in schizophrenia and affective states. *Lancet 2*, 1160–1162.

Dewhurst, K. E., El Kabir, D. T., Harris, G. W., & Mandelbrote, B. M. (1969). Observations on the blood concentration of thyrotropic hormone (TSH) in schizophrenia and affective states. *British Journal of Psychiatry*, *115*, 1003–1011.

Dolva, L. O., Riddervold, F., & Thorsen, R. K. (1983). Side effects of TRH. *British Medical Journal*, *281*, 532.

Drury, P. L., Belchetz, P. E., McDonald, W. I., Thomas, D. G. T., & Besser, G. M. (1982). Transient amaurosis and headaches after TRH. *Lancet*, *1*, 218–219.

Extein, I., Pottash, A. L. C., & Gold, M. S. (1981). Relationship of TRH test and dexamethasone suppression test abnormalities in unipolar depression. *Psychiatry Research*, *4*, 49–53.

Extein I., Pottash, A. L. C., Gold, M. S., & Cowdry, R. W. (1982). Using the protirelin test to distinguish mania from schizophrenia. *Archives of General Psychiatry*, *39*, 77–81.

Feinberg, M., Gillin. J. C., Carroll, B. J., Greden, J. F., & Zis, A. P. (1982). EEG studies of sleep in the diagnosis of depression. *Biological Psychiatry*, *17*, 305–316.

Ferrier, I. N., Johnstone, E. L., Crow, T. J., & Rincon-Rodriguez, J. (1983). Anterior pituitary hormone secretions in chronic schizophrenia. Responses to administration of hypothalamic-releasing hormones. *Archives of General Psychiatry*, *40*, 755–761.

Fleming, J. E., Extein, I., Sternbach, H. A., Pottash, A. L. C., & Gold, M. S. (1983). The thyrotropin-releasing hormone and dexamethasone suppression tests in the familial classification of depression. *Psychiatry Research*, *9*, 53–58.

Frey, H. M. M., & Haug, E. (1977). Effect of prolonged oral administration of TRH on plasma levels of thyrotropin and prolactin in normal individuals and in patients with primary hypothyroidism. *Acta Endocrinologica (Copenhagen)*, *85*, 744–752.

Galen, R. S., & Gambino, S. R. (1975). *Beyond normality*. New York: Wiley.

Garbutt, J. C., Loosen, P. T., Tipermas, A., & Prange, A. J. Jr. (1983). The TRH test in borderline personality disorder. *Psychiatry Research*, *9*, 107–113.

Gerner, R. H., & Yamada, T. (1982). Altered neuropeptide concentration in cerebrospinal fluid of psychiatric patients. *Brain Research*, *238*, 298–302.

Gilling, J. C., Duncan, W., Pettigrew, K. D., Rankel, B. L., & Snyder, F. (1979). Successful separation of depressed, normal and insomniac subjects by EEG sleep data. *Archives of General Psychiatry*, *36*, 85–90.

Gold, M. S., Pottash, A. L. C., Ryan, N., Sweeney, D. R., Davies, R. K., & Martin, D. M. (1980). TRH-induced TSH response in unipolar and secondary depression: Possible utility in clinical assessment and differential diagnosis. *Psychoneuroendocrinology*, *5*, 147–155.

Gold, M. S., Pottash, A. L. C., Extein, I., Martin, D. M., Howard, E., Mueller, E. A., & Sweeney, D. R. (1981). The TRH test in the diagnosis of major and minor depression. *Psychoneuroendocrinology*, *6*, 159–169.

Gold, P. W., Goodwin, F. K., Wehr, T., & Rebar, R. (1977). Pituitary thyrotropin response to thyrotropin-releasing hormone in affective illness: Relationship to spinal fluid amine metabolites. *American Journal of Psychiatry*, *134*, 1028–1031.

Golstein, J., Van Cauter, E., Linkowski, P., Vanhaelst, L., & Mendlewicz, J. (1980). Thyrotropin nyctohemeral pattern in primary depression: Differences between unipolar and bipolar women. *Life Sciences*, *27*, 1695–1703.

Goodwin, D. W., & Erickson, C. K. (Eds.). (1979). *Alcoholism and affective disorders*. New York: Spectrum Publications.

Grégoire, F., Brauman, J., de Bruck, R., & Corrilain, J. (1977). Hormone release in depressed patients before and after recovery. *Psychoneuroendocrinology*, *2*, 303–312.

Gruen, P. H., Sachar, E. J., Altman, N., & Sassin, J. (1975). Growth hormone response to hypoglycemia in postmenopausal women. *Archives of General Psychiatry*, *32*, 31–33.

Guillemin, R. (1978). Peptides in the brain: The new endocrinology of the neuron. *Science*, *202*, 90–402.

Gunderson J. G., Kolb J. E., & Austin, V. (1981). The diagnostic interview for borderline patients. *American Journal of Psychiatry*, *138*, 896–903.

Haigler, E. D., Jr., Pittman, J. A., Jr., Hershman, J. M., & Baugh, C. M. (1971). Direct evaluation of pituitary thyrotropin reserve utilizing synthetic thyrotropin-releasing hormone. *Journal of Clinical Endocrinology and Metabolism*, *33*, 573–581.

Hall, R., Besser, G. M., Schally, A. V., Coy, D. H., Evered, D., Goldie, D. J., Kastin, A. J., McNeilly, A. S., Mortimer, C. H., Phenekos, C., Turnbridge, W. M. G., & Weightmann, D. (1973). Actions of SRIF in healthy men and in acromegaly. *Lancet*, *2*, 581–584.

Harris, G. W. (1955). *The pituitary gland*. London: Edward Arnold.

Hatotani, N., Normura, J., Yamaguchi, T., & Kitayama, J. (1977). Clinical and experimental studies of the pathogenesis of depression. *Psychoneuroendocrinology, 2*, 115–130.

Hollister, L. E., Davis, K. L., & Berger, P. A. (1976). Pituitary response to TRH in depression. *Archives of General Psychiatry, 33*, 1393–1396.

Ingbar, S. H., & Woeber, K. A. (1981). The thyroid gland. In R. H. William (Ed.), *Textbook of endocrinology* (pp. 117–248). Philadelphia: Saunders.

Isaac, R., Merceron, R., Caillens, G., Raymond, J. P., & Ardaillou, R. (1980). Effects of calcitonin on basal and TRH-stimulated prolactin secretion in man. *Journal of Clinical Endocrinology and Metabolism, 50*, 1011–1015.

Jackson, I. M. D., & Reichlin, S. (1974). Thyrotropin-releasing hormone (TRH): Distribution in hypothalamic and extrahypothalamic brain tissues of mammalian and submammalian chordates. *Endocrinology (Baltimore), 96*, 854–862.

Jeuniewic, N., Brown, G. M., Garfinkel, P. E., & Moldofsky, H. (1978). Hypothalamic function as related to body weight and body fat in anorexia nervosa. *Psychosomatic Medicine, 40*, 187–198.

Joffe, R. T., Gold, P. W., Uhde, T. W., & Post, R. M. (1984). The effects of carbamazepine on the TSH. *Psychiatry Research, 12*, 161–166.

Kaptein, E. M., Kletzky, O. A., Spencer, C. A., & Nicoloff, J. T. (1980). Effects of prolonged dopamine infusion on anterior pituitary function in normal males. *Journal of Clinical Endocrinology and Metabolism, 51*, 488–491.

Kaptein, E. M., Spencer, C. A., & Kamiel, M. B. (1980). Prolonged dopamine administration and thyroid economy in normal and critically ill subjects. *Journal of Clinical Endocrinology and Metabolism, 51*, 387–393.

Kathol, R. G., Sherman, B. M., Winokur, G., Lewis, D., & Schlesser, M. (1983). Dexamethasone suppression, protirelin stimulation, and insulin infusion in subtypes of recovered depressive patients. *Psychiatry Research, 9*, 99–106.

Kijne, B., Aggernaes, H., Fog-Moller, F., Harrestrup-Andersen, J., Nissen, J., Kirkegaard, C., & Bjorum, N. (1982). Circadian variation of serum thyrotropin in endogenous depression. *Psychiatry Research, 6*, 277–282.

Kirkegaard, C. (1981). The thyrotropin response to thyrotropin-releasing hormone in endogenous depression. *Psychoneuroendocrinology, 6*, 189–212.

Kirkegaard, C., Bjorum, N., Cohn, D., Faber, J., Lauridsen, U. B., & Nerup, J. (1977). Studies on the influence of biogenic amines and psychoactive drugs on the prognostic value of the TRH stimulation test in endogenous depression. *Psychoneuroendocrinology, 2*, 131–136.

Kirkegaard, C., Bjorum, N., Cohn, D., & Lauridsen, V. B. (1978). TRH stimulation test in manic–depressive disease. *Archives of General Psychiatry, 35*, 1017–1023.

Kirkegaard, C., & Carroll, B. J. (1980). Dissociation of TSH and adrenocortical disturbances in endogenous depression. *Psychiatry Research, 3*, 253–364.

Kirkegaard, C., Norlem, N., Lauridsen, U. B., Bjorum, N., & Christiansen, C. (1975). Protirelin stimulation test and thyroid function during treatment of depression. *Archives of General Psychiatry, 32*, 1115–1118.

Kjellman, B. F. (1983). *The function of the hypothalamic–pituitary–thyroid axis in affective disorders*. Karolinska Institute, Department of Psychiatry and Medicine, St. Goran's Hospital, Stockholm, and University of Linkoping, Department of Psychiatry, Stockholm, Sweden

Koenig, G., Aschauer, H., Langer, G., Resch, F., & Schoenbeck, G. (1984). *TSH response to TRH in patients of various psychiatric diagnoses and in normal controls* (p. 19). Abstracts of Fifteenth International Congress of the International Society of Psychoneuroendocrinology, Vienna, Austria.

Krishnan, K. R., & France, R. D. (1984). *TRH stimulation test in chronic pain*. Abstracts of the annual meeting of the American Psychiatric Association, Los Angeles, CA.

Krog-Meyers, J., Kirkegaard, C., Kijne, B., Lumholtz, B., Smith, E., Lykke-Olson, L., & Bjorum, N. (1984). Prediction of relapse with TRH test and prophylactic amitriptyline in 39 patients with endogenous depression. *American Journal of Psychiatry, 141*, 945–948.

Kupfer, D. J. (1976). REM latency: A psychological marker for primary depressive disease. *Biological Psychiatry, 11*, 159–174.

Laignel-Lavastine, M. (1919). *The internal secretion and the nervous system*. New York: Nervous & Mental Disease Publishing Co.

Langer, G., Schonbeck, G., Kornig, G., Reiter, H., Schussler, M., Aschauer, H., & Lesch, O. (1980). Evidence for neuroendocrine involvement in the therapeutic effects of antidepressant drugs. In F. Brambilla, G. Racagni, & D. de Wied (Eds.), *Progress in psychoneuroendocrinology* (pp. 197–208). Amsterdam: Elsevier/North-Holland Biomedical Press.

Lauridsen, U. B., Kirkegaard, C., & Nerup, J. (1974). Lithium and pituitary–thyroid axis in normal subjects. *Journal of Clinical Endocrinology and Metabolism, 39*, 383–385.

Lazarus, J. H., John, R., Bennie, E. H., Chalmers, J., & Crochett, G. (1981). Lithium therapy and thyroid function: A long-term study. *Psychological Medicine, 11*, 85–92.

Leebaw, W. E., Lee, L. A., & Woolf, P. D. (1978). Dopamine affects basal and augmented pituitary hormone secretion. *Journal of Clinical Endocrinology and Metabolsim, 47*, 480–487.

Leslie, R. D. G., Isaacs, A. J., Gomez, J., Ragatt, P. F., & Bayliss, R. (1978). Hypothalamic–pituitary–thyroid function in anorexia nervosa: Influence of weight gain. *British Medical Journal, 2*, 526–528.

Linkowski, P., Brauman, H., & Mendlewicz, J. (1981). Thyrotropin response to TRH in unipolar and bipolar affective illness. *Journal of Affective Disorders, 3*, 9–16.

Linkowski, P., Van Wettere, J. P., Kerkhofs, M., Brauman, H., & Mendlewicz, J. (1983). Thyrotropin response to thyreostimulin in affectively ill women. Relationships to suicidal behavior. *British Journal of Psychiatry, 143*, 401–405.

Loosen P. T., Garbutt J. C., & Tipermas, A. (1986). The TRH test during dopamine receptor blockade in depressed patients. *Psychoneuroendocrinology, 11,* 327–336.

Loosen, P. T., Kistler, K., & Prange, A. J., Jr. (1983). The use of the TRH-induced TSH response as an independent variable. *American Journal of Psychiatry, 140,* 700–703.

Loosen, P. T., Mason, G. A., & Prange, A. J., Jr. (1982). The TRH test in normal subjects: Methodological considerations. *Psychoneuroendocrinology, 7,* 147–153.

Loosen, P. T., & Prange, A. J., Jr. (1980). TRH: A useful tool for psychoneuroendocrine investigation. *Psychoneuroendocrinology, 5,* 63–80.

Loosen, P. T., & Prange, A. J., Jr. (1982). The serum thyrotropin (TSH) response to thyrotropin-releasing hormone (TRH) in depression: A review. *American Journal of Psychiatry, 139,* 405–416.

Loosen, P. T., Prange, A. J., Jr., & Wilson, I. C. (1979). TRH (Protirelin) in depressed alcoholic men: Behavioral changes and endocrine responses. *Archives of General Psychiatry, 36,* 540–547.

Loosen, P.T., Prange, A. J., Jr., Wilson, I. C., Lara, P. P., & Pettus, C. (1977). Thyroid-stimulating hormone response after thyrotropin-releasing hormone in depressed, schizophrenic and normal women. *Psychoneuroendocrinology, 2,* 137–148.

Loosen, P. T., Wilson, I. C., Dew, B. W., & Tipermas, A. (1983). TRH in abstinent alcoholic men. *American Journal of Psychiatry, 130,* 1145–1149.

Loosen, P. T., Wilson, I. C., & Prange, A. J., Jr., (1980). Endocrine and behavioral changes in depression after TRH: Alteration by pretreatment with thyroid hormones. *Journal of Affective Disorders, 2,* 267–278.

Loosen, P. T., Youngblood, W. W., & Dew, B. (1983). Plasma levels of exogenous TRH in normal subjects and two patients with TSH blunting. *Psychopharmacology Bulletin, 19,* 325–327.

Loranger, A. Q., Oldham, J. M., & Tulis, E. H. (1982). Familial transmission of DSM-III borderline personality disorder. *Archives of General Psychiatry, 39,* 795–799.

Lucke, C., Hoeffken, B., & von zur Muehlen, A. (1975). The effect of somatostatin on TSH levels in patients with primary hypothyroidism. *Journal of Clinical Endocrinology and Metabolism, 416,* 1082–1084.

Lundberg, P. O., Walinder, J., Werner, I., & Wide, L. (1972). Effects of thyrotropin-releasing hormone on plasma levels of TSH, FSH, LH and GH in anorexia nervosa. *European Journal of Clinical Investigation, 2,* 150–153.

Maeda, K., Kato, Y., Ohgo, S., Chihara, K., Yoshimoto, Y., Yamaguchi, N., Kuromaru, S., & Imura, H. (1975). Growth hormone and prolactin release after injection of thyrotropin-releasing hormone in patients with depression. *Journal of Clinical Endocrinology and Metabolism, 40,* 501–505.

Maeda, K., & Tanimoto, K. (1981). Epileptic seizures induced by TRH. *Lancet, 1,* 1058–1059.

McGlashan, T. H. (1983). The borderline syndrome. II. Is it a variant of schizophrenia or affective disorder? *Archives of General Psychiatry, 40,* 1319–1324.

McLarty, D. G., O'Boyle, J. H., Spencer, C. A., & Ratcliffe, J. G. (1975). Effects of lithium in hypothalamic–pituitary thyroid function in patients with affective disorders. *British Medical Journal, 3,* 623–626.

MacNamara, E., Reynolds, C. F., Soloff, P. H., Mathias, R., Rossi, A., Spiker, D., Coble, P. A., & Kupfer, D. J. (1984). EEG sleep evaluation of depression in borderline patients. *American Journal of Psychiatry, 141,* 182–186.

Miyai, K., Toshihide, Y., Azukizawa, M., Ishibashi, K., & Kumahara, Y. (1975). Serum thyroid hormones and thyrotropin in anorexia nervosa. *Journal of Clinical Endocrinology and Metabolism, 40,* 344–348.

Mongioi, A., Aliffi, A., Vicari, E., Coniglione, F., Scapagnini, V., & d'Agata, R. (1983). Down-regulation of prolactin secretion in men during continuous TRH infusion: Evidence for induction of pituitary desensitization by continuous TRH administration. *Journal of Clinical Endocrinology and Metabolism, 56,* 904–907.

Morley, J. E., Garvin, T. J., Pekary, A. E., & Hershman, J. M. (1977). Thyrotropin-releasing hormone in the gastrointestinal tract. *Biochemical and Biophysical Research Communications, 79,* 314–318.

Moshang, T., Jr., & Utiger, R. D. (1977). Low triiodothyronine euthyroidism in anorexia nervosa. In R. Vigersky (Ed.), *Anorexia nervosa* (pp. 263–270). New York: Raven Press.

Naber, D., Steinbock, H., & Greil, W. (1980). Effects of short- and long-term neuroleptic treatment of thyroid function. *Progress in Neuropsychopharmacology, 49,* 199–206.

Nemeroff, C. B., Bissette, G., & Manberg, P. J. (1980). Neurotensin-induced hypothermia: Evidence for an interaction with dopaminergic systems and the hypothalamic–pituitary–thyroid axis. *Brain Research, 195,* 68–86.

Nesse, R. M., Curtis, G. C., & Brown, G. M. (1982). Phobic anxiety does not affect plasma levels of TSH in man. *Psychoneuroendocrinology, 7,* 69–74.

Nicoloff, J. T., Fisher, D. A., & Appleman, M. D. (1979). The role of glucocorticoids in the regulation of thyroid function in man. *Journal of Clinical Investigation, 49,* 1922–1929.

Otsuki, M., Dakoda, M., & Baba, S. (1973). Influence of glucocorticoids on TRH-induced TSH response in man. *Journal of Clinical Endocrinology and Metabolism, 36,* 95–102.

Papakostas, V., Fink, M., Lee, J., Irwin, P., & Johnson, L. (1981). Neuroendocrine measures in psychiatric patients: Course and outcome to treatment. *Psychiatry Research, 4,* 55–65.

Perry, J. C., & Klerman, G. L. (1980). Clinical features of the borderline personality disorder. *American Journal of Psychiatry, 137,* 165–173.

Portnay, G. K., O'Brian, J. T., Bush, J., Vagenakis, A. G., Azizi, F., Arky, R. A., Ingbar, S. J., & Braverman, L. E. (1974). The effect of starvation on the concentration and binding of thyroxine and triiodothyronine in serum and on the response of TRH. *Journal of Clinical Endocrinology and Metabolism, 39,* 191–194.

Post, R. M., Rubinow, D. R., Gold, P. W., Ballenger, J. C., Goodwin, F. K., Pickard, D., Naber, D., Uhde, T. W., Reichlin, S., Bollinger, J., & Bunney, W. E., Jr. (1981). Somatostatin and opiate peptides in CSF of affectively ill patients: Effects of carbamazepine. In C. Perris, G. Struwe, & B. Jansson (Eds.), *Biological Psychiatry* (pp. 345–345). Amsterdam: Elsevier/ North-Holland Biomedical Press.

Prange, A. J., Jr., & Loosen, P. T. (1981). Somatic findings in affective disorders: Their status as risk factors. In D. A. Regier, & G. Allen (Eds.), *Risk factor research in the major mental disorders* (pp. 69–79). Washington, DC: U.S. Government Printing Office.

Prange, A. J., Jr., Wilson, I. C., Lara, P. O., Alltop, L. B., & Breese, G. R. (1972). Effect of thyrotropin-releasing hormone in depression. *Lancet*, *2*, 999–1002.

Rabello, M. B., Snyder, P. J., & Utiger, R. D. (1974). Effects of the pituitary–thyroid axis and prolactin secretion of single and repetitive oral doses of thyrotropin-releasing hormone (TRH). *Journal of Clinical Endocrinology and Metabolism*, *39*, 571–578.

Ramey, T. N., Burrow, G. N., Spaulding, S. W., Donabedian, R. K., Speroff, L., & Frantz, A. G. (1976). The effect of aspirin and indomethacin on the TRH response in man. *Journal of Clinical Endocrinology and Metabolism*, *43*, 107–114.

Re, R. B., Kourides, I. A., Ridgeway, E. C., Weintraub, B. D., & Maloof, F. (1976). The effect of glucocorticoid administration on human pituitary secretion of thyrotropin and prolactin. *Journal of Clinical Endocrinology and Metabolism*, *43*, 338–346.

Retiene, K., Schulz, F., & Mueller, A. (1973). Moglichkeiten der Anwendung von Thyreotropin-releasing hormone. *Medizinische Klinik* (*Munich*), *68*, 1146–1150.

Reus, I. V. (1982). Pituitary–adrenal disinhibition as the independent variable in the assessment of behavioral symptoms. *Biological Psychiatry*, *17*, 317–326.

Robertson, A. G., Tricou, B. J., Fang, V. S., & Meltzer, H. Y. (1982). Biological markers for depressive illness. *Psychopharmacology Bulletin*, *18*, 120–122.

Rubin, R. T., Poland, R. E., Blodgett, A. L. N., Winston, R. A., Forster, B., & Carroll, B. J. (1980). Cortisol dynamics and dexamethasone pharmacokinetics in primary endogenous depression: Preliminary findings. In F. Brambilla, C. Racagni, & D. de Wied (Eds.), *Progress in psychoneuroendocrinology* (pp. 223–234). Amsterdam: Elsevier/North-Holland Biomedical Press.

Rubinow, D. R., Gold, P. W., Post, R. M., Balenger, J. C., Cowdry, R., Bollinger, J., & Reichlin, S. (1983). CSF somatostatin in affective illness. *Archives of General Psychiatry*, *40*, 409–412.

Rush, A. J., Schlesser, M. A., Roffwarg, H. P., Giles, D. E., Orsulak, P. J., & Fairchild, C. (1983). Relationships among the TRH, REM latency and dexamethasone suppression tests: Preliminary findings. *Journal of Clinical Psychiatry*, *44*, 23–29.

Sachar, E. J. (1975). Psychiatric disturbances associated with endocrine disorders. In D. X. Freedman & J. E. Dyrud (Eds.), *American handbook of psychiatry* (Vol. 4, pp. 299–313). New York: Basic Books.

Sachar, E. J., Halbreich, U., Asnis, G., Nathan, R. S., & Halpern, M. A. (1980). Neuroendocrine disturbance in depression. In F. Brambilla, G. Racagni, & D. de Wied (Eds.), *Progress in psychoneuroendocrinology* (pp. 263–272). Amsterdam: Elsevier/ North-Holland.

Sawin, C. T., & Hershman, J. M. (1976). Clinical use of thyrotropin-releasing hormone. *Pharmacology & Therapeutics, Part C*, *1*, 351–366.

Schally, A. V. (1978). Aspects of hypothalamic regulation of the pituitary gland. *Science*, *202*, 18–28.

Scharrer, E., & Scharrer, B. (1939). Secretory cells within the hypothalamus. *Research Publications— Association for Research in Nervous and Mental Disease*, *20*, 170–194.

Schildkraut, J. J. (1965). The catecholamine hypothesis of affective disorders: A review of supporting evidence. *American Journal of Psychiatry*, *122*, 509–522.

Schlesser, M. A., Rush, A. J., Fairchild, C., Crowley, G., & Orsulak, P. (1983). The thyrotropin-releasing hormone stimulation test: A methodological study. *Psychiatry Research*, *9*, 59–67.

Siler, T. M., Yen, S. S. C., Vale, W., & Guillemin, R. (1974). Inhibition by somatostatin on the release of TSH induced in man by TRH. *Journal of Clinical Endocrinology and Metabolism*, *38*, 742–745.

Smals, A. G. H., Kloppenberg, P. W. C., Lequin, R. L., Beex, L., Ross, A., & Benraad, T. J. (1977). The pituitary–thyroid axis in Klinefelter's syndrome. *Acta Endocrinologica (Copenhagen)*, *84*, 72–90.

Snyder, P. J., & Utiger, R. D. (1972). Response to thyrotropin-releasing hormone (TRH) in normal man. *Journal of Clinical Endocrinology*, *34*, 380–385.

Snyder, P. J., & Utiger, R. D. (1973). Repetitive administration of thyrotropin-releasing hormone results in small elevations of serum thyroid hormones and in marked inhibition of thyrotropin response. *Journal of Clinical Investigation*, *52*, 2305–2312.

Spaulding, G. W., Burrow, G. N., Donabedian, R., & van Woert, M. (1972). L-Dopa suppression of thyrotropin-releasing hormone response in man. *Journal of Clinical Endocrinology and Metabolism*, *35*, 182–185.

Spencer, C. A., Greenstadt, M. A., Wheeler, W. S., Kletzky, O. A., & Nicoloff, J. T. (1980). The influence of long-term low-dose thyrotropin-releasing hormone infusions on serum thyrotropin and prolactin concentrations in man. *Journal of Clinical Endocrinology and Metabolism*, *51*, 771–775.

Spencer, C. A., Lum, S. M. C., Wilber, J. F., Kaptein, E. M., & Nicoloff, J. T. (1983). Dynamics of serum TSH and thyroid hormone changes in fasting. *Journal of Clinical Endocrinology and Metabolism*, *56*, 883–888.

Spitzer, R. L., Endicott, J., & Gibbon, M. (1979). Crossing the border into borderline personality and borderline schizophrenia: The development of criteria. *Archives of General Psychiatry*, *36*, 17–24.

Staub, J. T., Girard, J., Mueller-Brand, J., Noelpp, B., Werner-Zodrow, I., Baur, V., Heitz, P., & Gemsenjaeger, E. (1978). Blunting of TSH response after repeated oral administration of TRH in normal and hypothyroid subjects. *Journal of Clinical Endocrinology and Metabolism*, *46*, 260–266.

Sternbach, H. A., Kirstein, L., Pottash, A. L. C., Gold, M. S., Extein, I., & Sweeney, D. R. (1983). The TRH test and urinary MHPG in unipolar depression. *Journal of Affective Disorders*, *5*, 233–237.

Stone, M. (1980). *The borderline syndrome: Constitution, personality and adaptation*. New York: McGraw-Hill.

Takahashi, S., Kondo, H., Yoshimura, M., & Ochi, Y. (1974). Thyrotropin responses to TRH in depressive illness: Relation to clinical subtypes and prolonged duration of depressive episodes. *Folia Psychiatrica et Neurologica Japonica, 28,* 355–365.

Tanimoto, K., Maeda, K., Yamaguchi, N., Chihara, K., & Fujita, T. (1981). Effect of lithium on prolactin response to TRH in patients with manic state. *Psychopharmacology, 72,* 129–133.

Targum, S. D. (1983). The application of serial neuroendocrine challenge studies in the management of depressive disorder. *Biological Psychiatry, 18,* 3–19.

Targum, S. D., Sullivan, A. C., & Byrnes, S. M. (1982). Neuroendocrine interrelationships in major depressive disorder. *American Journal of Psychiatry, 139,* 282–286.

Thorner, M. O., Ryan, S. M., Wass, J. A. H., Jones, A., Bouloux, P., Williams, S., & Besser, G. M. (1978). Effect of the dopamine agonist, lergotrile mesylate, on circulating anterior pituitary hormones in man. *Journal of Clinical Endocrinology and Metabolism, 47,* 372–378.

Tsutsui, S., Yamazaki, Y., Namba, Y., & Tsushima, M. (1979). Combined therapy of T3 antidepressants in depression. *Journal of International Medical Research, 7,* 138–146.

Vale, W., Brazeau, P., Rivier, C., Rivier, J., Grant, G., Burgus, R., & Guillemin, R. (1973). Inhibitory hypophysiotropic activity of hypothalamic somatostatin. *Federation Proceedings, Federation of American Societies for Experimental Biology, 32,* 211.

Vale, W., Spiess, J., Rivier, C., & Rivier, J. (1981). Characterization of a 41-residue ovine hypothalamic peptide that stimulates secretion of corticotropin and β-endorphin. *Science, 213,* 1394–1397.

Vigersky, R. A., Loriaux, D. L., Andersen, A. R. E., Mecklenburg, R. S., & Vaitukaitis, J. L. (1976). Delayed pituitary hormone response to LRF and TRF in patients with anorexia nervosa and with secondary amenorrhea associated with simple weight loss. *Journal of Clinical Endocrinology and Metabolism, 43,* 893–900.

Wakeling, A., DeSourza, V. A., Gore, M. B. R., Sabur, M., Kingstone, D., & Boss, A. M. B. (1979). Amenorrhea, body weight and serum hormone concentrations, with particular reference to prolactin and thyroid hormones in anorexia nervosa. *Psychological Medicine, 9,* 265–272.

Weeke, A., & Weeke, J. (1980). The 24-hour pattern of serum TSH in patients with endogenous depression. *Acta Psychiatrica Scandinavica, 62,* 69–74.

Weeke, J., Hansen, A. P., & Lundboek, K. (1974). The inhibition by somatostatin of the TSH response to TRH in normal subjects. *Scandinavian Journal of Laboratory Investigation, 33,* 101–103.

Weeke, J., Hansen, A. P., & Lundboek, K. (1975). Inhibition by somatostatin of the basal levels of serum TSH in normal men. *Journal of Clinical Endocrinology and Metabolism, 41,* 168–171.

Wenzel, K. W. (1981). Pharmacological interference with *in vitro* test of thyroid function. *Metabolism, Clinical and Experimental, 30,* 717–732.

Wenzel, K. W., Meinhold, H., & Herpach, M. (1974). TRH-stimulations-test mit alters-und geschlechtsabhangigem TSH-Anstieg bei Normalpersonen. *Klinische Wochenschrift, 52,* 722–727.

Widerlov, E., Wide, L., & Sjöstrom, R. (1978). Effects of tricyclic antidepressants on human plasma levels of TSH, GH, and prolactin. *Acta Psychiatrica Scandinavica, 58,* 449–456.

Wilber, J. F., & Utiger, R. D. (1969). The effect of glucocorticoids on the thyrotropin secretion. *Journal of Clinical Investigation, 48,* 2096–2103.

Wilkin, T. J., Baldet, L., & Papachristou, C. (1979). The TRH test: Which is the best index of the TSH release? *Annee Endocrinologique, 40,* 495–500.

Winokur, A., Amsterdam, J., Caroff, S., Snyder, P. J., & Brunswick, D. (1982). Variability of hormonal responses to a series of neuroendocrine challenges in depressed patients. *American Journal of Psychiatry, 139,* 39–44.

Winokur, A., Amsterdam, J. D., Oler, J., Mendels, J., Snyder, P. J., Caroff, S. N., & Brunswick, D. J. (1983). Multiple hormonal response to protirelin (TRH) in depressed patients. *Archives of General Psychiatry, 40,* 525–531.

Winokur, A., & Utiger, R. D. (1974). TRH: Regional distribution in the rat brain. *Science, 185,* 265–267.

Wolkin, A., Peselow, E. D., Smith, M., Lautin, A., Kahn, I., & Rotrosen, G. (1984). TRH test abnormalities in psychiatric disorders. *Journal of Affective Disorders, 6,* 273–281.

Yalow, R. (1978). Radioimmunoassay: A probe for the fine structure of biologic systems. *Science, 200,* 1236–1245.

Zaloga, G. P., Chernow, B., Zajtchuk, R., Chin, R., Rainey, T. G., & Lake, C. R. (1984). Diagnostic dosages of TRH elevate blood pressure by noncatecholamine mechanisms. *Archives of Internal Medicine, 144,* 1149–1152.

16 PROVOCATIVE CHALLENGES OF GROWTH HORMONE AND PROLACTIN SECRETION IN SCHIZOPHRENIC AND AFFECTIVE DISORDERS

S. CRAIG RISCH
LEWIS L. JUDD

University of California, San Diego

INTRODUCTION

This chapter overviews studies of the anterior pituitary hormones, growth hormone and prolactin in psychiatric disorders. Both stress paradigms and psychopharmacological perturbation interventions have been used to delineate the pathophysiology of psychiatric illnesses and to provide laboratory studies as aids in diagnosis and as tools to predicting efficacy of psychopharmacological treatments.

The conceptual basis of these studies is that these hormones provide a "window to the brain," since (1) many psychiatric disease statuses are accompanied by various hormonal dysregulations, and (2) many of the limbic–hypothalamic neurotransmitter systems involved in anterior pituitary hormone regulation have been hypothesized to be dysfunctional and underlie the pathogenesis of specific psychiatric illnesses. Classical examples include the dopamine hypothesis of schizophrenia and the catecholamine hypothesis of affective disorders.

There is an extensive literature implicating aberrant ("up-regulated") mesolimbic and mesocortical dopamine neurotransmission in the pathophysiology of hallucinations and delusions in schizophrenia and other psychoses. Studies of prolactin, in large part regulated by tuberoinfundibular and incerto-hypothalamic dopamine [prolactin inhibiting factor (PIF)], have been carried out in the hope that these systems, like the mesolimbic and mesocortical systems, may also be dysregulated and may provide some insight into the nature of this putative dysregulation. Likewise, many studies have implicated abnormal limbic catecholamine (i.e., dopamine, norepinephrine, and serotonin) neurotransmission in depression and mania. These same central nervous system (CNS) neurotransmitters regulate anterior pituitary growth hormone and prolactin secretion. Provocative challenges of growth hormone and prolactin secretion in affective disorder patients have revealed significant, possibly disease-specific abnormalities.

Unfortunately, with some notable exceptions, provocative challenges of prolactin and growth hormone in patients with specific psychiatric disorders have been inconsistent and of limited clinical utility.

These conflicting results presumably reflect such issues as diagnostic heterogeneity and lack of sufficient age, sex, diet, activity, menstrual cycle, menopausal status, medication status, and duration of illness controls.

However, the literature suggests that future studies using more specific hypotheses and more refined methodologies may provide significant insights into the pathogenesis of specific psychiatric disease states as well as provide laboratory markers for diagnosis and data to help choose and monitor psychopharmacological treatments.

GROWTH HORMONE PHYSIOLOGY

Basal growth hormone secretion tends to have spontaneous bursts during the day, averaging 6–7 bursts per 24 hours, and decreasing in frequency with age (van Praag, 1982). Growth hormone is markedly augmented by circulating estrogen, and plasma growth hormone concentrations may vary markedly with menstrual cycle and menopausal status. Secretion is stimulated by stress, exercise, hypoglycemia, certain hormones (insulin), and a variety of medications, such as amphetamine, L-dopa, apomorphine, and clonidine. Growth hormone secretion is stimulated by dopamine, norepinephrine, and serotonin. Growth hormone secretion increases during slow wave sleep, usually early after onset of sleep in the first non-REM phase (Brown, Seggie, Chambers, & Ettigi, 1978).

PROLACTIN PHYSIOLOGY

Basal plasma prolactin levels are higher among women (mean 8 ng/ml) than mean 5 ng/ml). Concentrations rise during sleep to approximately 20–25 ng/ml (Horrobin, Mtabaji, Karmali, Manku, & Nassa, 1976). Prolactin is released in a pulsatile manner with no apparent fixed periodicity. Exercise, stress, and many different medications may affect prolactin levels. Dopamine (putative PIF) tonically inhibits anterior pituitary prolactin secretion, while serotonin is believed stimulatory, particularly during sleep. Opiates and opioid peptides also stimulate prolactin secretion presumably via inhibition of tuberoinfundibular dopamine turnover. It is also believed that prolactin feeds back to regulate itself ("short-loop feedback") (Thorner, 1977).

PROVOCATIVE CHALLENGES OF GROWTH HORMONE IN SCHIZOPHRENIA

Basal plasma growth hormone concentrations in patients with schizophrenia do not differ from normals (Loosen & Prange, 1980; Prange, Loosen, Wilson, Meltzer, & Fang, 1979).

A number of investigators have utilized dopamine agonists (i.e., L-dopa and apomorphine) to pharmacologically challenge anterior pituitary growth secretion in both schizophrenics and controls. Since the pathogenesis of schizophrenia is believed to involve increased mesolimbic and mesocortical dopamine activity, it has been hypothesized that patients with schizophrenia might have an augmented response to dopaminergic agonists. In fact, many investigators have reported a significantly augmented prolactin response to apomorphine in acute schizophrenics with positive symptoms of psychosis as compared with chronic schizophrenics or controls (Casper, Davis, Pandey, Garver, & Dekirmenjian, 1977; Cleghorn, Brown, Brown, Kaplan, & Mitton, 1983; Ettigi, Nair, Lal, Cervantes, & Guyda, 1976; Ferrier, Johnstone, & Crow, 1984; Pandey et al., 1977; Rotrosen et al., 1979; Tamminga, Smith, Pandey, Frohman, & Davis, 1977).

In general, growth hormone responses to apomorphine in chronic schizophrenia with negative symptoms of psychosis tend to be blunted (Ferrier et al., 1984; Pandey et al., 1977; Rotrosen et al., 1979). An exaggerated growth hormone response to apomorphine in acute schizophrenic patients may predict a favorable response to treatment (Hollister, Davis, & Berger, 1980), while an exaggerated response in chronic schizophrenics may predict relapse (Cleghorn, Brown, Brown, Kaplan, Dermer, et al., 1983). Tamminga et al. (1977) report that while schizophrenics in general may demonstrate a blunted growth hormone response to apomorphine, there is no significant difference in growth hormone response to apomorphine in schizophrenics with or without tardive dyskinesia. Meltzer et al. (1984) studied growth hormone responses to apomorphine in a large group of unmedicated, hospitalized, psychotic patients and found no differences in growth hormone among various diagnostic groups. However, the apomorphine-induced growth hormone response correlated significantly with psychosis ratings and negative symptom scale scores. Growth hormone response was inversely related to duration of illness, but the correlation was independent of age effect only in patients with major depression. A blunted growth hormone response to intravenously administered methylphenidate in schizophrenia has also been reported (Janowsky *et al.*, 1978). This effect appeared independent of medication status.

In summary, although there is some variability, apomorphine-induced growth hormone responses in schizophrenics may be (1) elevated in acute schizophrenia with positive symptoms, or in chronic schizophrenics about to relapse, and that an exaggerated response may predict a favorable response to treatment; and (2) blunted in chronic schizophrenia with negative symptoms. However, a blunted growth hormone response to apomorphine is not specific to schizophrenia and therefore is of little diagnostic value. However, the test may be useful in predicting and monitoring pharmacotherapy.

PROVOCATIVE CHALLENGES OF PROLACTIN IN SCHIZOPHRENIA

Basal plasma prolactin concentrations do not differ statistically from normals in patients with schizophrenia (Brambilla *et al.*, 1976; Gruen, 1978b; Meltzer, Sachar, & Frantz, 1974; Rotrosen *et al.*, 1978).

As reviewed by Rubin and Hayes (1980) and Gruen (1978b), there is an extensive literature studying pituitary prolactin secretion in response to acute and chronic neuroleptization. It was hoped that putative dysregulation of mesolimbic and mesocortical dopamine neurotransmission in schizophrenia might be reflected in the tuberoinfundibular and incertohypothalamic dopaminergic systems regulating anterior pituitary prolactin secretion. Specifically, it was hoped that patients with schizophrenia might have different prolactin response to neuroleptic challenges than controls, that prolactin responses in individuals would predict therapeutic efficacy, and that monitoring prolactin levels in neuroleptic pharmacotherapy might be useful in predicting relapse. Unfortunately, the literature in

this regard has been almost uniformly unrewarding (Gruen, Sachar, Altman *et al.*, 1978; Gruen, Sachar, Langer *et al.*, 1978; Langer, Sachar, & Gruen, 1978; Meltzer & Busch, 1983; Meltzer, Busch, & Fang, 1983, Meltzer, Busch, Robertson, Tricou, & Fang, 1981; Sachar, Gruen, & Altman, 1977; Silverstone & Cookson, 1983). There are several likely explanations for these largely negative results. First, there is no a priori reason to believe that disturbances in mesolimbic and/or mesocortical dopaminergic neurotransmission would be generalized to or reflected in tuberoinfundibular and incertohypothalamic dopaminergic neurotransmission and anterior pituitary prolactin secretion. In addition, doses of neuroleptics necessary for antipsychotic efficacy far exceed doses which maximally stimulate prolactin secretion. Furthermore, in some cases, tolerance, especially in men, may develop in the prolactin response to chronic neuroleptization. As noted, the above prolactin response may differ in men and women, and as prolactin is extremely estrogen sensitive, may differ with phases of the menstrual cycle. As discussed by Rubin and Hayes (1980) in terms of monitoring pharmacotherapy, prolactin may not be useful for predicting relapse, as plasma levels may stay elevated for weeks after discontinuation of neuroleptic medication. For predicting efficacy, not only are there marked interindividual differences in magnitude of prolactin response to neuroleptics, but also in time course of response. This means that single time point determinations could be misleading, while extended blood sampling protocols might be impractical in acutely psychotic patients.

Thus, while prolactin responses to putative neuroleptics (assuming they enter the brain) have been useful as one component of screening for possible neuroleptic agents in preclinical animal models, provocative challenges with neuroleptics in schizophrenia have added little to our understanding of the pathogenesis of the disorder, nor have they proved of any clinical utility.

Apomorphine, a direct dopamine receptor agonist, suppresses pituitary prolactin secretion. However, as reviewed by Meltzer *et al.* (1984), studies of apomorphine challenges· of prolactin secretion in schizophrenia have been inconsistent and remain controversial.

PROVOCATIVE CHALLENGES OF GROWTH HORMONE IN AFFECTIVE DISORDERS

As noted, interpretation of basal growth hormone plasma concentrations is confounded by stress, activity, diet, obesity, sex, menopausal status, stage of menstrual cycle, medication status, and many other factors. However, in general, when these factors have been controlled, basal plasma concentrations of growth hormone have been reported to not be significantly different between depressed patients and normal controls (Gruen, 1978a).

One of the most extensively studied provocative challenges of growth hormone in affective disorders has been insulin-induced hypoglycemia. After controlling for the above variables, the minimally clinical adequate response is usually defined as a change in plasma growth hormone response greater than 5 ng/ml after at least a 50% drop in blood glucose level (Gruen, 1978a; Sachar, 1976). Although early studies were marked by lack of the above-described adequate controls, the consensus of the literature suggests that an inadequate or "blunted" growth hormone response to insulin-induced hypoglycemia is a substantive neuroendocrine "marker" in endogenous depression (Casper et al., 1977; Grof, Brown, & Grof, 1982b; Gruen, Sachar, Altman, & Sassin, 1975; Kathol, Sherman, Winokur, Lewis, & Schlesser, 1983; Mueller, Heninger, & McDonald, 1969; Sachar, Finkelstein, & Hellman, 1971; Sachar, Frantz, Altman, & Sassin, 1973; Winokur, Amsterdam, Caroff, Snyder, & Brunswick, 1982). This abnormality appears more common in unipolar depressed patients than in bipolar depressed patients (Kathol et al., 1983; Sachar et al., 1973). This growth hormone resistance to insulin challenge also occurs in prepubertal children with major depression, perhaps with a greater frequency than in adults (Puig-Antich, Novacenko, Davies, Chambers et al., 1984; Puig-Antich et al., 1981; Puig-Antich & Weston, 1983). These depressed children also secrete significantly more growth hormone during sleep, and there is little overlap between this abnormality and insulin resistance (Puig-Antich & Weston, 1983). Both these abnormalities tend to persist for long periods after clinical recovery (Puig-Antich, Goetz et al., 1984; Puig-Antich, Novacenko, Davies, Tabrizi et al., 1984).

In contrast, challenge studies to growth hormone secretion with dopamine agonists apomorphine and L-dopa have been unrewarding in differentiating depressed patients from controls (Casper et al, 1977; Gruen, 1978a; Insel & Siever, 1981; Linkowski, Brauman, & Mendlewicz, 1983; Maany, Mendels, Frazer, & Brunswick, 1979; Meltzer et al., 1984; Mendlewicz, Linkowski, & Van Cauter, 1979; Sachar et al., 1975).

Amphetamine challenges of growth hormone secretion differ in mechanism from L-dopa and apomorphine in that they involve both noradrenergic neurotransmission. However, despite an early report by Langer, Heinze, Reim, and Mattussek (1976) of significantly lower growth hormone secretion in response to amphetamine challenges in endogenously depressed patients and significantly higher responses in reactively depressed patients as compared with controls, subsequent studies have failed to replicate these findings (Checkley, 1979, 1980; Halbreich et al., 1982).

Unlike these unrewarding results in differentiating depressed patients from controls with growth hormone responses to apomorphine, L-dopa, and amphetamine (reviewed above), a reduced growth hormone response to clonidine (an α-receptor agonist) has emerged as one of the most powerful and substantive markers for neuroendocrine dysfunction in depression (Charney, Heninger, Sternberg, Hafstad et al., 1982; Checkley, Slade, & Shur, 1981; Matussek et al., 1980; Siever, Insel, & Uhde, 1981). Furthermore, of both theoretical interest and clinical utility, treatment of patients with tricyclic antidepressants or monoamine oxidase inhibitors does not appear to alter the growth hormone response to clonidine (Charney, Heninger, & Sternberg, 1982; Siever, Uhde, Insel, Roy, & Murphy, 1982). Also of interest is a similar blunting or reduced growth hormone response to clonidine in patients with obsessive–compulsive illness, which together with an increased frequency of abnormal dexamethasone suppression test (DST) and shortened rapid eye movement (REM) sleep latency, suggest that they may share similar biological abnormalities with depressed patients (Siever et al., 1983).

Desmethylimipramine (DMI) stimulates growth hormone secretion. A reduced growth hormone response to DMI has also been observed in depressed patients as compared with controls (Glass, Checkley, Shur, & Dawling, 1982; Laakman & Benkert, 1980; Laakman, Benkert, Neurlinger, Werder, & Erhardt, 1978). These observations, like those with clonidine, support the notion that this abnormality may be selectively nora-drenergically, rather than dopaminergically, mediated.

From the above review, it appears that depressed patients manifest reduced growth hormone responses to clonidine, DMI, and, to a lesser extent, insulin. These observations suggest that noradrenergic systems, at least in part, may mediate the pathogenesis of this neuroendocrine abnormality and that further studies appear warranted.

PROVOCATIVE CHALLENGES OF PROLACTIN IN AFFECTIVE DISORDERS

The literature with respect to basal plasma prolactin levels in affective disorders has been conflicting. This may reflect differences in failing to control for sex (women tend to have higher plasma prolactin than men), phase of the menstrual cycle, time of day for sampling, and possibly unipolar–bipolar dichotomies. Asnis, Nathan, Halbreich, Halpern, and Sachar (1980), Judd, Risch et al. (1982), Linkowski, Brauman, and Mendlewicz (1980), and Mendlewicz, Van Cauter, Lindowski, L'Hermite, and Robyn (1980) have all reported lower basal prolactin levels in depressed patients. However, in the study of Mendlewicz et al. (1980), while prolactin levels were lower in bipolar patients, they were elevated in unipolar patients. In the study of Linkowski et al. (1980), basal prolactin levels were significantly lower in pre- and postmenopausal bipolar patients and in postmenopausal unipolar patients, but not in premenopausal unipolar patients. In the study by Asnis et al. (1980), basal prolactin levels in depressed patients increased significantly with recovery. Halbreich, Grunhaus, and Ben-David (1979) reported an altered 24-hour rhythm of prolactin secretion in depression, with a statistically significant eleva-

tion in prolactin levels in the evening. Thus, basal plasma concentrations may differ in depressed patients and controls, and these differences when present may confound interpretations of provocative challenge tests.

As with growth hormone, insulin stimulates prolactin secretion. Several investigators (Grof et al., 1982b; Grof, Brown, & Grof, 1983; Winokur et al., 1982) have reported a significantly reduced or blunted prolactin responsivity to insulin challenge in depressed patients, particularly those with primary or endogenous depression. This abnormality persists during the depressive state, but normalizes on recovery. An increased or augmented prolactin response to insulin challenge in bipolar patients has preliminarily been reported to predict relapse into mania (Grof, Brown, & Grof, 1982a). In contrast, prepubertal children with major depressive disorder have been reported not to differ significantly from controls in prolactin response to insulin challenge despite confirmed abnormalities in growth hormone response (Puig-Antich, Novacenko, Goetz et al., 1984).

These observations suggest abnormalities of prolactin responsivity to insulin challenges in major depressive disorder and that concurrent monitoring of both growth hormone and prolactin in the insulin tolerance test is warranted.

Dopaminergic agonists, L-dopa, apomorphine, and carbidopa generally suppress prolactin in normals. However, as reviewed by Insel and Siever (1981), studies of dopaminergic agonist challenges of prolactin secretion in affective disorder patients have reported conflicting findings with normal, blunted, and augmented responses in affective disorder patients as compared with controls, and no consistent findings have emerged (Garfinkel, Brown, Warsh, & Stancer, 1979; Gold & Goodwin, 1977; Linkowski et al., 1983; Meltzer et al., 1984; Mendlewicz et al., 1979).

Heninger, Charney, and Sternberg (1984) have recently reported a marked blunting of prolactin response to intravenous tryptophan in depressed patients as compared with age- and sex-matched controls. These findings implicate serotonergic mechanisms in dysfunctional growth hormone secretion in depression and warrant further studies.

Finally, Judd, Parker et al. (1982) and Judd, Risch et al. (1982) have reported significantly attenuated prolactin response to methadone challenge in depressed patients as compared with controls. These depressed patients also had significantly lower basal (premethadone) plasma prolactin concentrations. These findings may suggest dysfunctions opioid receptor physiology in prolactin abnormalities in depression.

Thus, abnormalities in insulin tolerance and possibly serotonergic and endogenous opioid peptide receptor physiology have been preliminary implicated in the possible dysregulation of prolactin secretion in depression.

CONCLUSIONS

From the above review, it appears manifest that abnormalities in growth hormone and prolactin secretion occur in both schizophrenia and affective disorders and may be elicited and studied by a variety of provocative challenge tests. Although careful attention must be placed on controlling adequately for a large number of interacting variables, it appears that such studies may prove valuable in understanding the pathogenesis of these disorders and in developing standardized laboratory tests to aid in diagnosis and monitoring of treatment.

References

Asnis, G. M., Nathan, R. S., Halbreich, U., Halpern, F. S., & Sachar, E. J. (1980). Prolactin changes in major depressive disorders. *American Journal of Psychiatry*, 137(9), 117–118.

Brambilla, F., Fuastalla, A., Guerrini, A., Rovere, C., Legnani, G., Sarno, M., & Riggi, F. (1976). Prolactin secretion in chronic schizophrenia. *Acta Psychiatria Scandanavia*, 54(4), 131–153.

Brown, G. M., Seggie, J. A., Chambers, J. W., & Ettigi, P. G. (1978). Psychoendocrinology and growth hormone: A review. *Psychoneuroendocrinology*, 3(2), 131–153.

Casper, R. C., Davis, J. M., Pandey, G. N., Garver, D. L., & Dekirmenjian, H. (1977). Neuroendocrine and amine studies in affective illness. *Psychoneuroendocrinology*, 2(2), 105–113.

Charney, D. S., Heninger, G. R., & Sternberg, D. E. (1982). Failure of chronic antidepressants, desmethylimipramine and amitriptyline, on the growth hormone response to clonidine. *Psychiatry Research*, 7, 135–138.

Charney, D. S., Heninger, G. R., Sternberg, D. E., Hafstad, K. M., Giddings, S., & Landis, D. H. (1982). Adrenergic receptor sensitivity in depression. Effects of clonidine in depressed patients and healthy subjects. *Archives of General Psychiatry*, 39(3), 290–294.

Checkley, S. A. (1979). Corticosteroid and growth hormone responses to methylamphetamine in depressive illness. *Psychological Medicine*, 9, 107–115.

Checkley, S. A. (1980). A neuroendocrine study of adrenoceptor function in endogenous depression. *Acta Psychiatria Scandanavia, Supplementum*, 280, 211–217.

Checkley, S. A., Slade, A. P., & Shur, E. (1981). Growth hormone and other responses to clonidine in patients with endogenous depression. *British Journal of Psychiatry*, 138, 51–55.

Cleghorn, J. M., Brown, G. M., Brown, P. J., Kaplan, R. D., Dermer, S. W., MacCrimmon, D. J., & Mitton, J. (1983). Growth hormone responses to apomorphine HCl in schizophrenic patients on drug holidays and at relapse. *British Journal of Psychiatry*, 142, 482–488.

Cleghorn, J. M., Brown, G. M., Brown, P. J., Kaplan, R. D., & Mitton, J. (1983). Growth hormone responses to graded doses of apomorphine HCl in schizophrenia. *Biological Psychiatry*, 18(8), 875–885.

Ettigi, P., Nair, N. P., Lal, S., Cervantes, P., & Guyda, H. (1976). Effects of apomorphine on growth hormone and prolactin secretion in schizophrenic patients with or without oral dyskinesia, withdrawn from chronic neuroleptic therapy. *Journal of Neurology, Neurosurgery and Psychiatry*, 39, 870–876.

Ferrier, I. N., Johnstone, E. C., & Crow, T. J. (1984). Hormonal effects of apomorphine in schizophrenia. *British Journal of Psychiatry*, 144, 349–357.

Garfinkel, P. E., Brown, G. M., Warsh, J. J., & Stancer, H. C. (1979). Neuroendocrine responses to carbidopa in primary affective disorders. *Psychoneuroendocrinology*, 4(1), 13–20.

Glass, I. B., Checkley, S. A., Shur, E., & Dawling, S. (1982). The effect of desipramine upon central adrenergic function in depressed patients. *British Journal of Psychiatry*, 141, 372–376.

Gold, P. W., & Goodwin, F. K. (1977). Neuroendocrine response to levodopa in affective illness. *Lancet*, 1, 1007.

Grof, E., Brown, G. M., & Grof, P. (1982a). Neuroendocrine responses as an indicator of recurrence liability in primary affective illness. *British Journal of Psychiatry*, 140, 320–322.

Grof, E., Brown, G. M., & Grof, P. (1982b). Prolactin response to hypoglycemia in acute depression. *Progress in Neuro-Psychopharmacology & Biological Psychiatry*, 6(4–6), 487–490.

Grof, E., Brown, G. M., & Grof, P. (1983). Neuroendocrine strategies in affective disorders. *Progress in Neuro-Psychopharmacology. Biological Psychiatry*, 7(4–6), 557–562.

Gruen, P. H. (1978a). Endocrine changes in psychiatric diseases. *Medical Clinics of North America*, 62(2), 285–296.

Gruen, P. H. (1978b). The prolactin response in clinical psychiatry. *Medical Clinics of North America*, 62(1), 409–424.

Gruen, P. H., Sachar, E. J., Altman, N., Langer, G., Tabrizi, M. A., & Halpern, F. S. (1978). Relation of plasma prolactin to clinical response in schizophrenic patients. *Archives of General Psychiatry*, 35(10), 1222–1227.

Gruen, P. H., Sachar, E., Altman, N., & Sassin, S. (1975). Growth hormone responses to hypoglycemia in postmenopausal depressed women. *Archives of General Psychiatry, 32*, 31–33.

Gruen, P. H., Sachar, E. J., Langer, G., Altman, N., Leifer, M., Frantz, A., & Halpern, F. S. (1978). Prolactin responses to neuroleptics in normal and schizophrenic subjects. *Archives of General Psychiatry, 35*(1), 108–116.

Halbreich, U., Grunhaus, L., & Ben-David, M. (1979). Twenty-four-hour rhythm of prolactin depressive patients. *Archives of General Psychiatry, 36*(11), 1183–1186.

Halbreich, U., Sachar, E. J., Asnis, G. M., Quitkin, F., Nathan, R. S., Halpern, F. S., & Klein, D. F. (1982). Growth hormone response to dextroamphetamine in depressed patients and normal subjects. *Archives of General Psychiatry, 39*(2), 189–192.

Heninger, G. R., Charney, D. S., & Sternberg, D. E. (1984). Serotonergic function in depression. Prolactin response to intravenous tryptophan in depressed patients and healthy subjects. *Archives of General Psychiatry, 41*(4), 398–402.

Hollister, L., Davis, K., & Berger, P. (1980). Apomorphine in schizophrenia. *Communications in Psychopharmacology, 4*(4), 277–281.

Horrobin, D. F., Mtabaji, J. P., Karmali, R. A., Manku, M. S., & Nassar, B. A. (1976). Prolactin and mental illness. *Postgraduate Medical Journal, 52*(3 suppl.), 79–86.

Insel, T. R., & Siever, L. J. (1981). The dopamine system challenge in affective disorders: A review of behavioral and neuroendocrine responses. *Journal of Clinical Psychopharmacology, 1*(4), 207–213.

Janowsky, D. S., Leichner, P., Parker, D., Judd, L., Huey, L., & Clopton, P. (1978). The effect of methylphenidate on serum growth hormone: Influence of antipsychotic drugs and diagnosis. *Archives of General Psychiatry, 35*, 1384–1389.

Judd, L. L., Parker, D. C., Janowsky, D. S., Segal, D. S., Risch, S. C., & Huey, L. Y. (1982). The effect of methadone on the behavioral and neuroendocrine responses of manic patients. *Psychiatry Research, 7*(2), 163–170.

Judd, L. L., Risch, S. C., Parker, D. C., Janowsky, D. S., Segal, D. S., & Huey, L. Y. (1982). Blunted prolactin response. A neuroendocrine abnormality manifested by depressed patients. *Archives of General Psychiatry, 39*(12), 1413–1416.

Kathol R. G., Sherman, B. M., Winokur, G., Lewis, D., & Schlesser, M. (1983). Dexamethasone suppression, protirelin stimulation, and insulin infusion in subtypes of recovered depressive patients. *Psychiatry Research, 9*(2), 99–106.

Kathol, R. G., Winokur, G., Sherman, B. M., Lewis, D., & Schlesser, M. (1984). Provocative endocrine testing in recovered depressives. *Psychoneuroendocrinology, 9*(1), 57–67.

Laakman von G., & Benlert, O. (1980). Neuroendokrinologie und Psychopharmaka. *Arzneimittel-Forschung, 28*, 1277–1280.

Laakmann von G., Benkert, O., Neurlinger, E., Werder, K. V., & Erhardt, F. (1978). Beeinflussung der Hypophysen-Vorderlappen-hormon-Sekretion nach akuter und chroniscker Gabe von Desipramin. *Arzneimittel-Forschung, 28*, 1292–1294.

Langer, G., Heinz, G., Reim, B., & Matussek, N. (1976). Reduced growth hormone responses to amphetamine in "endogenous" depressive patients: Studies in normal, "reactive" and "endogenous" depressive, schizophrenic, and chronic alcoholic subjects. *Archives of General Psychiatry, 33*(12), 1471–1475.

Langer, G., Sachar, E. J., & Gruen, P. H. (1978). Prolactin response to neuroleptic drugs in normal and schizophrenic subjects. *Psychopharmacology Bulletin, 14*(1), 8–9.

Linkowski, P., Brauman, H., & Mendlewicz, J. (1980). Prolactin secretion in women with unipolar and bipolar depression. *Psychiatry Research, 3*(3), 265–271.

Linkowski, P., Brauman, H., & Mendlewicz, J. (1983). Prolactin and growth hormone response to levodopa in affective illness. *Neuropsychobiology, 9*(2–3), 108–112.

Loosen, P. T., & Prange, A. J., Jr. (1980). Thyrotropin-releasing hormone (TRH): A useful tool for psychoneuroendocrine investigation. *Psychoneuroendocrinology, 5*(1), 63–80.

Maany, I., Mendels, J., Frazer, A., & Brunswick, D. (1979). A study of growth hormone release in depression. *Neuropsychobiology, 5*(5), 282–289.

Matussek, N., Ackenheil, M., Hippius, H., Müller, F., Schroder, H. T., Schultes, H., & Wasilewski, B. (1980). Effect of clonidine on growth hormone release in psychiatric patients and controls. *Psychiatry Research, 2*(1), 25–36.

Meltzer, H. Y., & Busch, B. (1983). Serum prolactin response to chlorpromazine and psychopathology in schizophrenics: Implications for the dopamine hypothesis. *Psychiatry Research, 9*(4), 285–299.

Meltzer, H. Y., Busch, D. A., & Fang, V. S. (1983). Serum neuroleptic and prolactin levels in schizophrenic patients and clinical response. *Psychiatry Research, 9*, 271–283.

Meltzer, H. Y., Busch, O. A., Robertson, A., Tricou, B. J., & Fang, V. S. (1981). Prolactin secretion: An update. *Psychopharmacology Bulletin, 17*(3), 168–172.

Meltzer, H. Y., Kolakowska, T., Fang, V. S., Fogg, L., Robertson, A., Lewine, R., Strahilevitz, M., & Busch, D. (1984). Growth hormone and prolactin response to apomorphine in schizophrenia and the major affective disorders. Relation to duration of illness and depressive symptoms. *Archives of General Psychiatry, 41*(5), 512–519.

Meltzer, H. Y., Sachar, E. J., & Frantz, A. G. (1974). Serum prolactin levels in unmedicated schizophrenic patients. *Archives of General Psychiatry, 31*, 564–569.

Mendlewicz, J., Linkowski, P., & Van Cauter, E. (1979). Some neuroendocrine parameters in bipolar and unipolar depression. *Journal of Affective Disorders, 1*(1), 25–32.

Mendlewicz, J., Van Cauter, E., Linkowski, P., L'Hermite, M., & Robyn, C. (1980). Current concepts: I. The 24-hour profile of prolactin in depression. *Life Sciences, 27*(22), 2015–2024.

Mueller, P. S., Heninger, G. R., & McDonald, R. K. (1969). Insulin tolerance test in depression. *Archives of General Psychiatry, 21*, 578–594.

Pandey, G. M., Garver, D. L., Tamminga, C., Erickson, S., Ali, S. I., & Davis, J. M. (1977). Postsynaptic supersensitivity in schizophrenia. *American Journal of Psychiatry, 134*(5), 518–522.

Prange, A. J., Jr., Loosen, P. T., Wilson, I. C., Meltzer, H. Y., & Fang, V. S. (1979). Behavioral and endocrine responses of schizophrenic patients to TRH (protirelin). *Archives of General Psychiatry, 36*(10), 1986–1093.

Puig-Antich, J., Goetz, R., Davies, M., Tabrizi, M. A., Novacenko, H., Hanlon, C., Sachar, E. J., & Weitzman, E. D. (1984). Growth hormone secretion in prepubertal children with major depression. IV. Sleep-related plasma concentrations in a drug-free, fully recovered clinical state. *Archives of General Psychiatry, 41*(5), 479–483.

Puig-Antich, J., Novacenko, H., Davies, M., Chambers, W. J., Tabrizi, M. A., Krawiec, V., Ambrosini, P. J., & Sachar, E. J. (1984). Growth hormone secretion in prepubertal children with major depression. I. Final report on response to insulin-induced hypoglycemia during a depressive episode. *Archives of General Psychiatry, 41*(5), 445–460.

Puig-Antich, J., Novacenko, H., Davies, M., Tabrizi, M. A., Ambrosini, P., Goetz, R., Bianca, J., Goetz, D., & Sachar, E. J. (1984). Growth hormone secretion in prepubertal children with major depression. III. Response to insulin-induced hypoglycemia after recovery from a depressive episode and in a drug-free state. *Archives of General Psychiatry, 41*(5), 471–475.

Puig-Antich, J., Novacenko, H., Goetz, R., Corser, J., Davies, M., & Ryan, N. (1984). Cortisol and prolactin responses to insulin-induced hypoglycemia in prepubertal major depressives during episode and after recovery. *Journal of the American Academy of Child Psychiatry, 23*(1), 49–57.

Puig-Antich, J., Tabrizi, M. A., Davies, M., Goetz, R., Chambers, W. J., Halpern, F., & Sachar, E. J. (1981). Prepubertal endogenous major depressives hyposecrete growth hormone in response to insulin-induced hypoglycemia. *Biological Psychiatry, 16*(9), 801–818.

Puig-Antich, J., & Weston, B. (1983). The diagnosis and treatment of major depressive disorder in childhood. *Annual Review of Medicine, 34*, 231–245.

Rotrosen, J., Angrist, B., Clark, C., Gershon, S, Halpern, F. S., & Sachar, E. J. (1978). Suppression of prolactin by dopamine agonists in schizophrenics and controls. *American Journal of Psychiatry, 135*(8), 949–951.

Rotrosen, J., Angrist, B., Gershon, S., Poquin, J., Branchey, L., Oleshansky, M., Halpern, F., & Sachar, E. J. (1979). Neuroendocrine effects of apomorphine: Characterization of response patterns and application to schizophrenia research. *British Journal of Psychiatry, 135*, 444–456.

Rubin, R. T., & Hayes, S. E. (1980). The prolactin secretory response to neuroleptic drugs: Mechanisms, applications and limitations. *Psychoneuroendocrinology, 5*(2), 121–137.

Sachar, E. J. (1976). Neuroendocrine dysfunction in depressive illness. *Annual Review of Medicine, 27*, 389–396.

Sachar, E. J., Altman, N., Gruen, P., Glassman, A., Halpern, F. S., & Sassin, J. (1975). Human growth hormone response to levodopa. Relation to menopause, depression and plasma dopamine concentration. *Archives of General Psychiatry, 32*, 502–503.

Sachar, E. J., Finkelstein, J., & Hellman, L. (1971). Growth hormone responses in depressive illness. *Archives of General Psychiatry, 25*2, 263–269.

Sachar, E. J., Frantz, A. G., Altman, N., & Sassin, J. (1973). Growth hormone and prolactin in unipolar and bipolar patients: Responses to hypoglycemia and L-dopa. *American Journal of Psychiatry, 130*, 1362–1367.

Sachar, E. J., Gruen, P. H., & Altman, N. (1977). The use of the prolactin response in clinical psychopharmacology (proceedings). *Psychopharmacology Bulletin, 13*(1), 60–61.

Siever, L. J., Insel, T. R., Jimerson, D. C., Lake, C. R., Uhde, T. W., Aloi, J., & Murphy, D. L. (1983). Growth hormone response to clonidine in obsessive-compulsive patients. *British Journal of Psychiatry, 142*, 184–187.

Siever, L. J., Insel, T. R., & Uhde, T. W. (1981). Noradrenergic challenges in the affective disorders. *Journal of Clinical Psychopharmacology, 1*(4), 193–206.

Siever, L. J., Uhde, T. W., Insel, T. R., Roy, B. F., & Murphy, D. L. (1982). Growth hormone response to clonidine unchanged and chronic clorgyline treatment. *Psychiatry Research, 7*(2), 139–144.

Silverstone, T., & Cookson, J. (1983). Examining the dopamine hypotheses of schizophrenia and of mania using the prolactin response to antipsychotic drugs. *Neuropharmacology, 22*(4), 539–541.

Tamminga, C. A., Smith, R. C., Pandey, G., Frohman, L. A., & Davis, J. M. (1977). A neuroendocrine study of supersensitivity in tardive dyskinesia. *Archives of General Psychiatry, 34*(10), 1199–1203.

Thorner, M. O. (1977). Prolactin: Clinical physiology and the significance and management of hyperprolactemia. In L. Martini & G. M. Besser (Eds.), *Clinical neuroendocrinology* (pp. 320–355). New York: Academic Press.

van Praag, H. M. (1982). The significance of biological factors in the diagnosis of depressions. II. Hormonal variables. *Comparative Psychiatry, 23*(3), 216–226.

Winokur, A., Amsterdam, J., Caroff, S., Snyder, P. J., & Brunswick, D. (1982). Variability of hormonal responses to a series of neuroendocrine challenges in depressed patients. *American Journal of Psychiatry, 139*(1), 39–44.

17 CORTISOL SECRETION IN PSYCHIATRIC DISORDERS

GREGORY M. ASNIS
CARMEN Z. LEMUS

Albert Einstein College of Medicine/Montefiore Medical Center

INTRODUCTION

Increased hypothalamic–pituitary–adrenal (HPA) activity, as evidenced by increase in plasma, cerebrospinal fluid (CSF) and urinary cortisol, and nonsuppression to dexamethasone, is the most consistently reported biological abnormality of major depressive disorder (MDD) (Butler & Besser, 1968; Carroll, Curtis, & Mendels, 1976a; Doig, Mummery, Wills, & Elbes, 1966; Gibbons & McHugh, 1962; Sachar, Hellman, Roffwarg, Halpern, Fukushima, & Gallagher, 1973; Stokes et al., 1984; Traskman, Tybring, Asberg, Bertilsson, Lantto, & Schalling, 1980).

Although MDD is the psychiatric disorder that is most associated with increased HPA activity, the literature describes cases of schizophrenia, stress states, etc. as also demonstrating increased HPA activity (Franzen, 1971; Katz, Weiner, Gallagher, & Hellman, 1970; Sachar, Mason, Kolmer, & Artiss, 1963). Sachar, Halbreich, Asnis, Nathan, & Halpern (1980) have commented that it is not surprising that MDD has disturbed HPA functions due to the frequent presence of symptoms suggesting hypothalamic involvement (e.g., disturbance of mood, appetite, sleep, libido, and autonomic function). Needless to say, since many of these hypothalamic signs may also occur in patients with other psychiatric states, (non-MDDs) disturbance of HPA activity may not be specific for MDD.

The literature on HPA axis function in psychiatric patients has almost exclusively focused on MDD, neglecting normal as well as pathological controls. Although increased HPA activity involves increased secretion of diverse peptides and hormones (CRF, ACTH), this chapter will focus exclusively on a review of cortisol secretion per se. In addition, it will present an overview of cortisol secretion in psychiatric disorders (depression and schizophrenia in comparison to normal controls), by reviewing three levels of cortisol assessment (see Table 17.1).

BASAL CORTISOL

The most replicated neuroendocrine abnormality of depressive illness has been disturbance in cortisol secretion. The latter has been studied by various techniques, including 24-hour urinary cortisol production rates determined by isotope dilutional methods, 24-hour urine-free cortisol collections, and sampling plasma cortisol every 20–30 minutes over 24 hours, as well as CSF cortisol assessments (Butler & Besser, 1968; Carroll et al., 1976a; Doig et al., 1966; Gibbons & McHugh, 1962; Sachar et al., 1973; Stokes et al., 1984; Traskman et al., 1980).

The major finding of these above studies is that of cortisol hypersecretion. As can be seen in Figure 17.1, depressives have an excess of cortisol in the afternoon, evening and early morning hours, have nocturnal hypersecretion (normal subjects have minimal

TABLE 17.1. Strategies for Assessing Cortisol Secretion

---

1. Assessment of basal cortisol.
   a. Mean 1–4 P.M. Afternoon Cortisol Test.
2. Assessment of cortisol suppression.
   a. Dexamethasone Suppression Test (DST).
3. Assessments of cortisol stimulation.
   a. Insulin Tolerance Test (ITT).
   b. Dextroamphetamine Cortisol Test.
   c. Desipramine Cortisol Test.

---

cortisol levels during this time, $<5\mu g/dl$), and have relative flattening of the circadian cortisol curve. In addition, depressives have increased number of cortisol secretory episodes (Sachar *et al.*, 1980b). Further work by our group has demonstrated the complexities of these findings. Depressives may have an altered ultradian rhythm, a flattened cortisol curve, as well as cortisol hypersecretion, but each one of these abnormalities may be independent of each other (Halbreich, Asnis, Shindledecker, Zumoff, & Nathan, 1985b).

The phenomenon of cortisol hypersecretion appears to be predominantly a state-related finding, apparently normalizing after clinical recorery (Sachar, 1975). The clinical correlates for cortisol hypersecretion within depressive illness have been sought and remain illusory. Despite early reports suggest-

ing an association with anxiety, severity of illness, and psychosis, these findings have not been replicated.

Our group has found that age is an important factor associated with cortisol hypersecretion in endogenous depression. This was originally found in the most detailed assessment of plasma cortisol—24-hour cannula study with blood sampling every 30 minutes—as well as in single plasma cortisol assessments (Asnis, Sachar, Halbreich, Nathan, Novacenko, & Ostrow, 1981). Subsequent to our reports, other investigators have replicated this finding (Halbreich, Asnis, Zumoff, Nathan, & Shindledecker, 1984; Stokes *et al.*, 1984). Interestingly, this relationship appears to break down after clinical recovery, suggesting an interaction of illness and age. Increasing age is associated with a norepinephrine decrease in the hypothalamus. Apparently this is not enough to result in a cortisol change in normal aging in man. Perhaps a further decrease of norepinephrine secondary to depression results in this age-dependent relationship in the endogenously depressed state.

The specificity of cortisol hypersecretion for endogenous depressive illness has not been adequately studied. We thus chose to reevaluate cortisol hypersecretion in a large group of depressives, schizophrenics and normal controls; the mean 1–4 P.M. plasma corti-

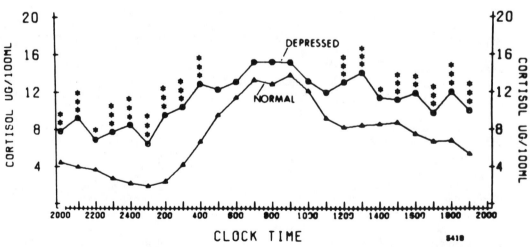

FIGURE 17.1. Mean hourly cortisol concentration in a group of 7 depressives and 54 normal controls. *$p < .05$; **$p < .01$; ***$p < .001$.

sol was chosen as a comprehensive measure of cortisol secretion, since it is highly correlated with the mean 24-hour cortisol level (every 30 min for 24 hours) in depressives, normal controls, and medical patients with various physical illnesses (Halbreich, Zumoff, Kream, & Fukushima, 1982; Halbreich, Asnis, Shindledecker, Zumoff, & Nathan, 1985a).

The 1–4 P.M. plasma cortisol test thus is a short procedure (involving a small butterfly needle inserted in a forearm vein with sampling every 30 minutes) and is economical in both cost and time, in contrast to a 24-hour cannula study. Since Asnis et al. (1981) demonstrated that endogenous depressives over the age of 50 had significantly higher plasma cortisol than those less than 50 years old, and most of the patient groups had three or fewer patients over 50 years old, we will only present data on patients 18–50 years old.

As can be seen from Table 17.2, we studied a large group of patients ($n = 135$) (depressed inpatients and outpatients, schizophrenic inpatients) and normal controls ($n = 32$).

As subjects were evaluated with at least a semistructured interview (depressed inpatients and normal controls were given SADS interview) and given an RDC diagnosis when applicable; normal controls received Research Diagnostic Criteria (RDC) diagnosis of "never mentally ill." All depressives were rated using the Hamilton Depression Scale within 48 hours of the neuroendocrine procedure—the mean 1–4 P.M. plasma cortisol assessment.

As can be seen in Table 17.2, the MDD–endogenous (ED) inpatients had the highest 1–4 P.M. plasma cortisol and was the only patient group that differed from the normal controls (8.20 ± 3.20 μg/dl versus 6.54 ± 2.11 μg/dl, $t = 2.81$, $p < .01$). Furthermore the MDD–ED inpatients differed significantly from MDD–ED and MDD–nonED outpatients, but were not significantly different from the schizophrenic inpatients.

Cortisol hypersecretion was arbitrarily defined as a value greater than 2 SDs above the mean 1–4 P.M. plasma cortisol level of the normal controls, > 10.8 μg/dl. The frequency of cortisol hypersecretion across diagnostic groups is presented in Table 17.3. MDD–ED inpatients had a significantly greater prevalence (22%) than any of the other diagnostic groups except for schizophrenic inpatients.

Interestingly, none of the depressed outpatinets were cortisol hypersecretors.

Since endogenously depressed inpatients were the only group that was different from the normal controls, a series of univariate analysis was performed evaluating the mean 1–4 P.M. plasma cortisol in relation to RDC subtypes (unipolar, agitated, retarded, simple, psychotic) and the lifetime diagnoses of bipolar disorder and intermittent depressive disorder. No RDC subtype differed significantly. In contrast, the presence of both lifetime diagnoses examined had significantly higher cortisol levels (bipolar, $n = 14$ versus unipolar disorder, $n = 27$, 10.0 SD 2.8 μg/dl versus 7.3 SD 3.0 μg/dl; $F = 7.7$, $p < .01$; intermittent depressive disorder, $n = 13$ versus nonintermittent depressive disorder, $n = 28$, 9.0 SD 3.2 μg/dl versus 6.5 SD 2.6 μg/dl; $F = 5.7$, $p < .03$). A multiple regression analysis was performed with the following independent variables: age, Hamilton score, and the RDC diagnoses of bipolar and intermittent depressive disorder. Only the bipolar group remained significant: $F = 4.1$, $p = .05$.

Bipolar ED inpatients had a significantly higher cortisol than all other groups, including the schizophrenic inpatients. As can be seen from Table 17.3, bipolar ED inpatients had a significantly higher prevalence rate of cortisol hypersecretion than unipolar ED inpatients, schizophrenics, normal controls, as well as the depressed outpatients. MDD–ED inpatients with a unipolar subtype did not differ from normals or other pathological controls.

Cortisol hypersecretion occurred predominantly in severe endogenously depressed inpatients. The prevalence of cortisol hypersecretion was 22%, a modest figure in comparison to that which has been reported in the past, 40–50% (Sachar et al., 1973; Stokes et al., 1984). This low figure is probably a function of young age groups studied (18–50 years) since cortisol hypersecretion increases dramatically in endogenous depressives above age 50 (Asnis et al., 1981).

MDD–ED inpatients differed from normal controls and most other depressed outpatient groups, but did not differ from the other inpatient group—schizophrenics. Thus it is possible that increased cortisol may relate to severe illnesses requiring hospitalization.

TABLE 17.2. Mean 1–4 P.M. Plasma Cortisol in Psychiatric Patients and Normal Controls

	Intermittent or minor depression outpatients	MDD–nonED outpatients	MDD–ED outpatients	MDD–ED inpatients	Schizophrenic inpatients	Normal controls
Number of patients	14	23	13	41	19	32
Age (years)	35.1, SD 8.9	35.1, SD 7.0	37.9, SD 9.0	34.1, SD 9.1	30.6, SD 9.1	29.7, SD 8.5
HDS	13.0, SD 3.0	15.0, SD 5.0	21.0, SD 8.0	25.0, SD 5.0	—	—
Mean 1–4 P.M. plasma cortisol (μg/dl)	6.8, SD 1.9	6.1, SD 1.6	6.2, SD 2.0	8.2, SD 3.2	7.3, SD 3.0	6.5, SD 2.1[a]
Age versus cortisol	−.07	−.21	.43	.09	−.12	−.13
HDS versus cortisol	−.16	−.11	−.07	−.15	—	—

Significant cortisol contrasts

MDD–ED inpatients versus MDD–ED outpatients $t = 2.54$, $p < .02$
MDD–ED inpatients versus normals $t = 2.81$, $p < .01$
MDD–ED inpatients versus MDD–nonED outpatients $t = 3.24$, $p < .01$

[a]Diagnosis: $F = 3.03$, $df = 5,135$, $p < .02$.

TABLE 17.3. Prevalence of Cortisol Hypersecretion in Psychiatric Patients and Normal Controls

Diagnosis	Number of patients	Prevalence
Intermittent or minor depressive disorder outpatients	14	0%
MDD non-ED outpatients	23	0%
MDD–ED outpatients	13	0%
MDD–ED inpatients[a]	41	22.0%
Schizophrenic inpatients	19	10.5%
Normal controls	32	0%

[a]Bipolar ED inpatients $n = 14$ Prevalence 43.8%.
[a]Unipolar ED inpatients $n = 27$ Prevalence 11.1%.

Furthermore, the stress of hospitalization may contribute to high cortisol; although all patients were in the hospital for a minimum of 1 week prior to testing, this may not have been an adequate time for adaptation.

A retrospective evaluation of MDD–ED inpatients did reveal that bipolar depression was the RDC diagnosis with the highest prevalence rate of cortisol hypersecretion, significantly higher than all other patient groups (43% for bipolars, 11% for unipolars, 15% for schizophrenics). Interestingly MDD–ED inpatients with a unipolar subtype did not differ from normal controls or schizophrenics. A more intensive evaluation of bipolar disorder in inpatients and outpatients is in order.

DEXAMETHASONE SUPPRESSION TEST

The dexamethasone suppression test (DST) is a test that has been used in evaluating limbic–hypothalamic–pituitary activity. Dexamethasone is a synthetic steroid many times more potent than corticosteroid. Ingestion of dexamethasone in normal subjects turns off the endogenous secretion of ACTH and cortisol by negative feedback inhibition for at least 24 hours (Krieger, Allen, Rizzo, & Krieger, 1971; McHardy-Young, Harris, Lessoff, & Lyne, 1967). Although the DST was first widely used by endocrinologists to diagnose Cushing's syndrome, various investigators have found that many depressives have nonsuppression of cortisol to dexamethasone; this has ranged from prevalence

rates of 30–70% depending on the dose of dexamethasone (Arana, Baldessarini, & Ornstein, 1985).

The 2 mg DST was originally utilized in psychiatry in the 1970s (Carroll, Curtis, & Mendels, 1976b). It was found to be sensitive (40%) and highly specific (95%). In 1981 a major turning point took place in DST research. Carroll et al. (1981) reported that reducing the dose of dexamethasone from 2 mg to 1 mg dramatically increased the sensitivity without sacrificing the specificity; subsequently most studies have switched to the 1 mg DST.

Since this test appeared to offer a simple laboratory aid in diagnosing and investigating major depressive disorder, there was an explosion of studies that emanated since 1981. What started to arise in the literature was that 1 mg DST might not be as highly specific for depression as originally believed. Various reports have found that nonsuppression to dexamethasone was not infrequently seen in patients with bulimia, dementia, dysthymia, schizophrenia, etc. Arana et al. (1985) have reviewed this issue in depth.

We report here a 1 mg DST study that we conducted in a group of endogenous depressives, schizophrenics and normal controls. We studied 57 hospitalized patients (ages 16–68) and 30 normal controls. All depressives and normals were given the Schedule for Affective Disorders and Schizophrenia (SADS) (Endicott & Spitzer, 1978) and all schizophrenics were evaluated with a semistructured clinical interview. The patients and normal controls were diagnosed according to Research Diagnostic Criteria

(RDC) of Spitzer, Endicott, and Robins (1978) as follows: depressives had a major depressive disorder (MDD), endogenous subtype ($n = 40$, mean age 41, SD 13 years); schizophrenics had chronic ($n = 13$) and subchronic ($n = 4$) schizophrenia (mean age 27, SD 6 years); normal controls ($n = 30$, mean age 30, SD 9 years) met RDC criteria of never mentally ill. All depressives had a minimum Hamilton depression score of ≥ 18.

Since the depressives were significantly older than the other 2 groups, we examined the effect of age on postdexamethasone cortisol levels in each group; all Pearson correlation coefficients were nonsignificant ($r = -.18$ for normals, $r = -.04$ for depressives, and $r = -.31$ for schizophrenics). The depressives had a significantly higher prevalence of nonsuppression to 1 mg DST than normals or schizophrenics (see Table 17.4). This study confirms most prior reports finding that nonsuppression to 1 mg dexamethasone occurs significantly more frequently in major depressive disorder than in schizophrenics and normal controls. Furthermore, the DST is highly specific (92.4%) for depressives when normal subjects are controls, but specificity markedly decreases when schizophrenics are controls (Asnis, Eisenberg, Lemus, & Halbreich, 1986), thus sacrificing the usefulness of the DST for diagnosing MDD.

As can be seen in Table 17.5, reports of DST nonsuppression in schizophrenia vary from 0 to 35%, with a mean rate of 23% for studies performing 4 P.M. and 11 P.M. postdexamethasone cortisol samplings (Asnis *et al.*, 1986; Berger, Pirke, Doerr, & Krieg,

1984; Castro, Lemaire, Toscano-Aguilhar, & Herchulez, 1983; Coppen, Abow-Saleh, Milln, Metcalfe, Harwood, & Bailey, 1983; Dewan, Pandurangi, Boucher, Levy, & Major, 1982; Gold, Pottash, Extein, & Sweeney, 1981; Greden, Kronfol, Gardner, Feinberg, & Carroll, 1981; Hwang, Zander, & Garvey, 1984; Nelson, Khan, & Orr, 1984; Rihmer & Arato, 1984; Sawyer & Jeffries, 1984; Schlesser, Winokur, & Sherman, 1980; Stokes *et al.*, 1984; Targum, 1983).

What might be responsible for the high prevalence rate of DST nonsuppression in schizophrenia? Several studies have found that schizoaffectives have prevalence rates of nonsuppression to dexamethasone similar to or higher than MDDs. Thus the presence of depressive symptomatology appears to be a major determinant. Although the studies reviewed in Table 17.5 exclude schizoaffective disorder, it is possible that depressive symptoms per se might influence the DST in schizophrenia. Table 17.5 suggests that this is not a likely possibility since many of the studies excluded patients who had depressive symptoms and still found high rates of nonsuppression.

The DST is influenced by stress. It has been clearly demonstrated that DSTs performed within 1–2 days of hospitalization have higher rates of nonsuppression than after 1 week of hospitalization in the same patients. Although this has been predominantly reported in MDD (Carroll *et al.*, 1981; Coccaro, Prudic, Rothpearl, & Nurnberg, 1984), Berger *et al.* (1984) demonstrated this phenomenon in schizophrenics: 33% were nonsuppressors on day 1 or 2 of hospitaliza-

TABLE 17.4. DST in Depressives, Schizophrenics, and Normal Controls

	Number of subjects	Nonsuppressors	Suppressors
Depressives	40	21 (52.5%)	19 (47.5%)
Schizophrenics	17	4 (23.5%)	13 (76.5%)
Normal controls	30	2 (6.7%)	28 (93.3%)

For all diagnostic groups $\chi^2 = 17.38$, $p < .0002$.

Depressives versus normal controls, $\chi^2 = 14.30$ with Yates correction, $p < .001$.

Depressives versus schizophrenics, $\chi^2 = 4.60$ with Yates correction, $p < .05$.

Schizophrenics versus normal controls, $\chi^2 = 4.60$ with Yates correction, $p = $ NS.

TABLE 17.5. The 1 mg DST in Schizophrenia: A Review

Study (Year)	Sampling times 8 A.M.	4 P.M.	11 P.M.	Schizophrenics N	Nonsuppressors (%)	Depressed R/O	Nonsuppressors (%) MDDs	Controls
Berger et al. (1984)		*	*	21	33	+	44	11
Castro et al. (1983)		*		23	30	+		
Coppen et al. (1983)		*		41	20	+	81	12
Dewan et al. (1982)[a]		*		20	30	+		
Gold et al. (1981)	*	*	*	20	0	−	48	
Greden et al. (1980)		*	*	24	8	+	54	
Hwang et al. (1984)	*	*	*	13	15	−	33	
Nelson et al. (1984)		*	*	14	29	−	62	
Rihmer et al. (1984)	*	*		20	5	−	66	4
Sawyer et al. (1984)		*	*	20	35	−		
Schlesser et al. (1980)	*			48	0	+	52	
Stokes et al. (1984)	*			12	17	−	34	10
Targum (1980)		*	*	14	7	+	43	8
Asnis et al. (1986)		*	*	17	24	+	52	7

[a]Fluorometric assay.

TOTALS: All times $n = 307$,   16% nonsuppressors.
4–11 P.M. $n = 194$,   23% nonsuppressors.
8 A.M. $n = 60$,   3% nonsuppressors.

tion but only 19% remained nonsuppressors 7–10 days later. Most of the studies assessed in Table 17.5 did not specify precisely how soon after hospitalization the DST was performed (but generally within 7–10 days of hospitalization); thus, this may be one of the factors contributing to the wide variance of DST nonsuppression rates in schizophrenia. We do not think that this is a major factor, particularly since our own study presented here found a high prevalence of nonsuppression in schizophrenics who had been hospitalized a minimum of 1 week prior to testing.

The dose of dexamethasone itself may be contributing to DST nonsuppression in schizophrenia. Studies demonstrating high prevalence rates of nonsuppression in schizophrenia almost uniformly have used the 1 mg DST. Unfortunately, there are only three studies in the literature examining the 2 mg DST in schizophrenia with a total sample size of 25 schizophrenics (Brown, Johnston, & Mayfield, 1979; Hotsboer, 1983; Shulman & Dieold, 1977). Of these, Shulman and Dieold used a fluorometric assay which is rather nonspecific. In the other two studies, using reliable assays (competitive protein binding) only 1 of 17 schizophrenics was found to be nonsuppressor, for a prevalence rate of 6%. This rate for schizophrenia is similar to that reported for normal controls (Zimmerman & Coryell, 1985). Furthermore, in our study presented here, 4 of the 17 schizophrenic nonsuppressors to 1 mg dexamethasone were retested 1 week later with 2 mg of dexamethasone; all became suppressors to the 2 mg DST. Thus, the 1 mg DST in schizophrenia has a sizable prevalence rate of nonsuppression causing a significant number of false positive DSTs. The 2 mg DST appears to significantly reduce this rate. A reevaluation of the 2 mg DST is in order.

ASSESSMENTS OF CORTISOL STIMULATION

The Insulin Tolerance Test

The insulin tolerance test (ITT) is one of the classic provocative challenges of the HPA axis in endocrinology: insulin induces hypoglycemia with a subsequent hormonal re-

sponse. One must achieve a decrease of blood glucose of at least 50% to ensure a reliable release of hormones—human growth hormone, cortisol, and prolactin (Howanitz & Howanitz, 1984). The literature has consistently found that depressives have a blunted growth hormone response to insulin (Gregoire, Brauman, DeBock, & Corvilain, 1977; Mueller, Heninger, & McDonald, 1969; Sachar, Finkelstein, & Hellman, 1970). Whether the cortisol response in depressives or other diagnostic categories is different from normal controls is unclear.

In order to study the cortisol response to ITT in depressives, we have matched by age and sex, a small group of endogenously depressed inpatients with a group of chronic schizophrenic inpatients and normal control outpatients who had at least a 50% decrease in blood glucose during an ITT.

The subjects fasted from midnight and came to the laboratory early the next morning. At 9 A.M. a butterfly needle was inserted in a forearm vein and kept patent with heparinized saline. Samples for cortisol were taken every 15 minutes for 30 minutes after which time 0.1 IU/kg mixed with 5 cc normal saline was administered over 60 seconds; subsequently, samples were taken every 15 minutes for 90 minutes for cortisol; glucose was assessed via a glucose analyzer every 5 minutes for 45 minutes and then every 15 minutes for the rest of the study. As can be seen in Table 17.6, there was no difference in the cortisol response to ITT (peak cortisol, $F = 0.88$, or Δ cortisol, $F = 1.07$) among the groups studied—depressives and schizophrenics did not differ from normal controls.

Our findings with the ITT suggest that the cortisol response to ITT does not differentiate patients (depressives and schizophrenics) from normal controls.

The ITT clearly is an extremely potent releaser of cortisol. The magnitude of the response is many times greater than the cortisol response to pyrogen, arginine vasopressin, tyrosine vasopressin, ovine CRH (Clayton, Librik, Gardner, & Guillemin, 1963; DeBold et al., 1984), intravenous dextroamphetamine and IM desipramine (Asnis, unpublished data).

Why might the ITT be a stimulating test that finds no differences among patients and normal controls? The ITT stimulus may be

TABLE 17.6. The Cortisol Response to ITT in 13 Depressives, Schizophrenics, and Normal Controls

	Depressives	Schizophrenics	Normals
Age	33.6, *SD* 8.9	33.8, *SD* 9.6	31.8, *SD* 8.7
Basal cortisol (μg/dl)	10.6, *SD* 2.1	11.4, *SD* 5.6	11.6, *SD* 4.0
Peak cortisol response (μg/dl)	22.4, *SD* 5.0	24.2, *SD* 6.8	21.4, *SD* 2.9
Δ cortisol (peak–basal)	11.8, *SD* 5.1	12.8, *SD* 5.9	9.9, *SD* 3.7

suprathreshold, causing a maximal cortisol release despite whatever neurotransmitter or receptor differences that might exist among diagnostic groups.

The mechanisms of action determining the cortisol response to ITT appear not to be highly selective. Although serotonin appears to be the predominant neurotransmitter associated with cortisol release to ITT (Cavagnini, Raggi, Micossi, DiLandro, & Invitti, 1976; Prescott, Kendal-Taylor, Weightman, Watson, & Ratcliffe, 1984), others have found a significant cholinergic influence (Copolov, Jethwa, Stern, Clements, & Funder, 1983). Further confounding the issue of specificity is in fact that the peripheral release of catecholamines resulting from the stress of hypoglycemia may influence the release of cortisol at the level of the adrenal gland (Plotsky, 1985).

Thus, the ITT may be a supramaximal stimulus, as well as a nonspecific probe effecting multiple neurotransmitters, which limits its usefulness as a selective probe for cortisol secretion.

The need for a more specific provocative test that is nonstressful as well as a submaximal stimulus to cortisol secretion is highly desirable.

The Dextroamphetamine Cortisol Test

As reviewed in the prior section on ITT, the use of more selective neurotransmitter probes to evaluate cortisol secretion in man is clearly indicated. In particular, a noradrenergic probe seemed warranted since NE is one of the neurotransmitters implicated in depressive illness (Bunney & Davis, 1965) as well as the regulation of cortisol secretion (Jones, Hillhouse, & Burden, 1976).

A few researchers have pursued this line of investigation. Amphetamines, which release

and prevent the reuptake of NE from presynaptic neurons, have been utilized as a noradrenergic probe by several investigators. Besser, Butler, Landon, and Rees (1969) and Rees, Butler, Gosling, and Besser (1970) found that IV methylamphetamine stimulated the release of cortisol in normal subjects. Furthermore, this was blocked by an α-adrenergic blocker, thymoxamine; these data were provocative in that it suggested that NE might be stimulatory to cortisol via α-noradrenergic receptors. Checkley *et al.* (1979) evaluated the cortisol response to intravenous methylamphetamine 0.2 mg/kg in endogenous depressives and several groups of pathological controls (Checkley, 1979). The endogenous depressives differed from the pathological controls with a significantly diminished cortisol response which normalized after clinical recovery. These findings were consistent with a NE deficit and/or an α-noradrenergic receptor insensitivity in endogenous depression.

Our group has utilized intravenous dextroamphetamine as a noradrenergic probe. We first explored the response of 0.1 mg/kg iv administered in the morning in a small group of normal males ($n = 5$) and a group of endogenous depressives ($n = 11$). The normals had a brisk release of cortisol by 30 minutes in contrast to the depressives who failed to release cortisol (Sachar, Asnis, Nathan, Halbreich, Tabrize, & Halpern, 1980a).

In an expanded project of dextroamphetamine 0.1 mg/kg iv, including the original sample that was studied by Sachar *et al.* (1980a), we evaluated 11 endogenous depressives (9 women and 2 men, 51.9, *SD* 11.0 years old), 8 chronic schizophrenic men (27.5, *SD* 5.5 years old), and 14 normal controls (8 women and 6 men, 36.5, *SD* 13.8 years old). Patients were hospitalized and drug free for a minimum of 10 days. All subjects were studied after an overnight fast. A butterfly needle was inserted in a forearm vein at 9 A.M. Thirty minutes later, a baseline sample was obtained for cortisol and immediately thereafter, dextroamphetamine 0.1 mg/kg iv was infused over 1 minute. Subsequently, blood samples were obtained every 15 minutes for 90 minutes.

As can be seen in Figure 17.2, the mean post-amphetamine cortisol response (mean 15–90 min cortisol level minus baseline cortisol level at time 0) was significantly different between all three groups studied; $F = 5.70$, $p < .025$. Schizophrenics and the normals had a significantly greater cortisol response ($t = 2.89$, $p < .05$ and $t = 2.77$, $p < .05$, respectively) than the normal controls. Furthermore, the schizophrenics had a trend for even a greater response than the normal controls.

These data further support the notion that endogenous depressives have a NE deficit and/or noradrenergic insensitivity. They also suggest that schizophrenics have a heightened cortisol release to dextroamphetamine; the latter is indicative of hyperfunction of NE in schizophrenia, which has recently been reported (Bird, Spokes, & Iverson, 1979; Carlsson, 1979).

Further work by our group with dextroamphetamine had changed from 0.1 mg/kg to an increased dose of 0.15 mg/kg since the latter dose was found to cause a more consistent release of cortisol within normal subjects

(Halbreich, Sachar, Asnis, Nathan, & Halpern, 1981; Sachar et al., 1980a). In addition, the release of cortisol was found to be greater in the evening compared to the morning, with a greater discrimination between depressives and normal controls (Sachar, Halbreich, Asnis, Nathan, Halpern, & Ostrow, 1981). Preliminary work by Sachar et al. using dextroamphetamine, 0.15 mg/kg, in the evening found that 78% of endogenous depressives failed to release cortisol (an adequate release was defined as 1.5 μg/dl rise above baseline level at 30 minutes) in comparison to 13% of the normal controls (Sachar et al., 1981). Recently, Stewart et al. (1984) has evaluated a heterogeneous group of depressed outpatients with 0.15 mg/kg iv dextroamphetamine and found that an inadequate release of cortisol occurred significantly more often in depressed patients with MDD in contrast to depressed patients with non-MDD (intermittent and minor depressive disorder) and normal controls. Interestingly, within the patients with MDD, there was no difference between endogenous and nonendogenous subtypes. Still to be clarified is the cortisol response to 0.15 mg/kg of dextroamphetamine in schizophrenics.

The Desipramine Cortisol Test

Exploring the effect of intramuscular desipramine (im DMI), another noradrenergic agonist, in normals and depressives, was particularly inviting since DMI, in contrast to amphetamines, is highly selective for NE and has a minimal effect on behavior and mood factors which could affect cortisol (Randrup & Braestrup, 1977).

Early work with intraperitoneal DMI in animals suggested an ACTH release (Fuxe et al., 1978). Recently, Laakmann et al. (1985) reported a release of cortisol to im and iv desipramine in normal controls.

A pilot study was conducted (Asnis, Lemus, & Halbreich, 1986) evaluating the cortisol response to 75 mg im DMI over 2 hours in a group of 13 endogenous depressives (8 males and 5 females), 23 to 64 years old (mean age 38.7, SD 9.4 years) and 20 normal controls (10 females and 10 males) 18 to 52 years old (mean age 33.0, SD 11.6 years). Depressives did not differ from normals in regard to age ($t = 1.50$, two-tailed t test) or sex ($\chi^2 = 0.42$). All subjects were assessed by a rater with the

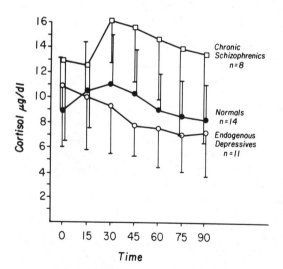

FIGURE 17.2. Cortisol response to d-amphetamine 0.1 mg/kg in schizophrenics versus depressives and normals.

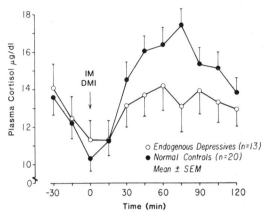

FIGURE 17.3. The cortisol response to 75 mg im DMI.

SADS (Endicott & Spitzer, 1978); depressives were given an RDC diagnosis of MDD, endogenous subtype and normals were given an RDC diagnosis of never mentally ill. Depressives were hospitalized and free of psychotropic medication for at least 10 days prior to the study. All patients were moderately depressed with a Hamilton score of ≥ 18 (mean 25.5, SD 7.6) on the day of the DMI test.

Figure 17.3 demonstrates the cortisol response in depressives and normal controls. A repeated measures analysis of variance was performed on the group and time effects and their interaction. The group effect was not significantly larger than the between subject effect ($F = 1.06$, df 1/31, $p = .31$); there was a significant time and a Group × Time interaction ($F = 13.65$, df 10/307, $p = .001$ and $F = 2.68$, df 10/307, $p = .003$, respectively). The means of individual cells were compared at equivalent time points between groups as planned comparisons. It was found that these means were not significantly different at time points prior to 45 minutes or subsequent to 75 minutes. Significant differences did occur between 45 and 75 minutes ($p = .01$ at 45 minutes, $p = .02$ at 60 minutes, $p = .0001$ at 75 minutes).

The cortisol change scores (post-DMI cortisol minus baseline cortisol) of endogenous depressives and normal controls at the significant times (45–75 minutes) were evaluated for cutoff values that would best discriminate endogenous depressives from normal controls. A cutoff of 1.5 µg/dl increase above baseline at 45 minutes most significantly discriminated between normals and

depressives. This criterion was the same as the one found best in discriminating endogenous depressives from normal controls utilizing the dextroamphetamine cortisol test (Sachar *et al.*, 1981). The Δ45 minute cortisol is seen in Figure 17.4 where a cutoff of 1.5 µg/dl identified 7 of 13 depressives and 1 of 20 normals (Fisher exact test = .003).

It was decided on the basis of the repeated measures effect to convert the post-DMI cortisol levels to change scores from baseline (time 0) in order to examine the effect of potential covariates: (1) basal cortisol just prior to im DMI; (2) age; and (3) sex. As can be seen in Table 17.7, basal plasma cortisol just prior to im DMI and sex were significant covariates in contrast to age. But only basal cortisol accounted for a sizable portion of the variance (30.9%). Nonetheless, the group difference (depressives versus normal controls) still remained highly significant after covarying out any of these factors.

Although an actual placebo study was not conducted to rule out the possibility that the DMI cortisol response might be a placebo response (or due to cortisol diurnal rhythmicity, stress of venipuncture, etc.) a non-DMI procedure day with assessments of cortisol was available for comparison to several time points of the DMI day, for many subjects. This non-DMI day procedure (from which the 1–4 P.M. plasma cortisol test was taken) was an assessment of basal plasma cortisol involving an insertion of

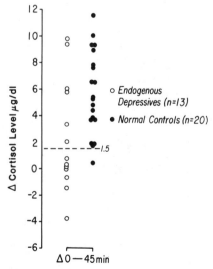

FIGURE 17.4. The Δ45 minute cortisol response to 75 mg im DMI.

TABLE 17.7. Mean Post-DMI Cortisol Response (Baseline Corrected) of Endogenous Depressives versus Normal Controls and the Effect of Covariates

	Mean $\pm$ SD basal cortisol (μg/dl)	Mean $\pm$ SD post-DMI cortisol (μg/dl)	Basal plasma cortisol[a]	Sex[a]	Age[a]
Controls $n = 20$	10.31 ± 3.04	4.68 ± 1.34	4.49	4.61	4.84
Depressives $n = 13$	11.31 ± 3.77	1.86 ± 1.55	2.14	1.91	1.80
F for covariates			4.58^{b}	5.58	0.37
F for group before/ after controlling for covariate	0.70	33.09^{c}	26.72^{c}	33.70^{c}	39.91^{c}

[a]Mean post-DMI response adjusted for the particular covariate.
[b]$p < .02$.
[c]$p < .001$.

a cannual in a forearm vein from 9 to 10 A.M., with sampling of cortisol every 30 minutes for a minimum of 7 hours (time for DMI was always at 9:30 A.M., 30 minutes after the cannula insertion. Cortisol levels on the non-DMI day were used only after a 30-minute adaptation to a postcannula insertion).

Cortisol values from the DMI day were compared to the non-DMI day using correlated t tests at each time point for both normals and depressives (Figures 17.5 and 17.6).

As can be seen, both normals and depressives had higher cortisol levels on the DMI day versus the non-DMI day (from 30 to 120 minutes, which represents post-DMI administration times).

Thus, the cortisol response to DMI appears not to be due to placebo response, diurnal rhythmicity, stress of venipuncture, etc. To definitively rule out a placebo effect, we are currently conducting a double blind im DMI versus im placebo (saline) study.

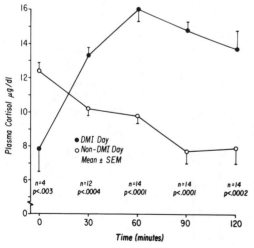

FIGURE 17.5. Plasma cortisol in a DMI day versus a non-DMI day in normal controls.

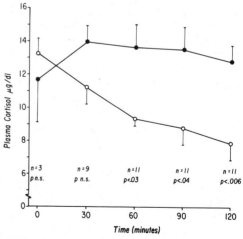

FIGURE 17.6. Plasma cortisol in a DMI day versus a non-DMI day in endogenous depressives.

CONCLUSIONS

The multiple strategies used in this chapter to assess cortisol secretion in psychiatric disorders basically find that disturbances of cortisol secretion occur predominantly in MDD. Although not conclusive, most evidence suggests that these disturbances normalize after clinical recovery and are thus state-related phenomena.

The usefulness of these cortisol assessments as laboratory tests for diagnosing major depressive illness is fraught with difficulties. Thus far, many of these assessments, although earlier thought to be highly specific for MDD, have been found to be less specific than originally believed.

The DST was one of the first of these measures of cortisol secretion to be used as a laboratory test for depression. As reviewed, the 1 mg DST appears to be rather nonspecific for depressive illness. Whether this nonspecificity is due to decrease in dose of dexamethasone from 2 mg to 1 mg awaits clarification. Cortisol hypersecretion, which was also originally believed to be highly specific for MDD, falls short of an ideal laboratory test for MDD. This chapter also reviews stimulatory probes of cortisol secretion, nonselective (ITT), as well as those more selective (intravenous dextroamphetamine and intramuscular desipramine). Once again, these tests find a high prevalence of abnormalities in MDD, but whether they prove to be highly specific needs to be ascertained.

Since basal cortisol is influenced by so many diverse factors and is controlled by multiple neurotransmitters, our work has shifted its emphasis onto more specific probes of cortisol secretion—intravenous dextroamphetamine and intramuscular desipramine—which might reflect specific receptor functions. In regard to the DMI cortisol response, this assessment appears to be independent of age, in contrast to basal cortisol and the DST. Furthermore, although it is negatively correlated with basal cortisol, the differences found between depressives and normals remain highly significant after controlling for this factor.

Although our focus is on the more specific noradrenergic probes, many of the more general probes, that is, basal cortisol and DST,

still need further investigation. It is logical to think these methods of cortisol assessment should be interrelated, however, it is also possible that these measurements evaluate different aspects of the neuroendocrine system and therefore may not be associated. For example, basal cortisol may be normal representing a compensated state, whereas the receptor sensitivity to cortisol regulation may be altered. The latter may be demonstrated by an abnormal cortisol response to a suppressive (steroid) or stimulant probe.

Whether any of these assessments of cortisol secretion prove to be laboratory aids in diagnosing depression is perhaps much less important than whether they identify biochemical and/or clinical correlates of homogeneous groups of patients. For example, if the cortisol response to DMI is reflective of a predominantly α-noradrenergic receptor stimulation as suggested by Laakmann et al. (1986), then our finding of a reduced cortisol response to DMI in depressives may suggest a biochemically homogeneous group of patients with an α-noradrenergic subsensitivity and/or a NE deficit. This finding may be relevant to clinical issues, such as treatment response to NE reuptake inhibitors.

References

Arana, G. W., Baldessarini, R. J., & Ornstein, M. (1985). The dexamethasone suppression test for diagnosis and prognosis in psychiatry. *Archives of General Psychiatry, 42,* 1193–1204.

Asnis, G. M., Lemus, C. Z., & Halbreich, U. (1986). The desipramine cortisol test—A selective noradrenergic challenge. *Psychopharmacology Bulletin, 22,* 571–578.

Asnis, G. M., Eisenberg, J., Lemus, C. Z., & Halbreich, U. (1986). Dexamethasone suppression test in schizophrenia—study and review. *Neuropsychobiology, 15,* 571–578.

Asnis, G. M., Sachar, E, J., Halbreich, U., Nathan, R. S., Novacenko, H., & Ostrow, L. C. (1981). Cortisol secretion in relation to age in major depression. *Psychosomatic Medicine, 43,* 235–242.

Berger, M., Pirke, K. M., Doerr, P., & Krieg, J. C. (1984). The limited utility of the DST for the diagnostic process in psychiatry. *British Journal of Psychiatry, 145,* 372–382.

Besser, G. M., Butler, P. W. P., Landon, J., & Rees, L. (1969). Influence of amphetamines on plasma corticosteroid and growth hormone levels in man. *British Medical Journal, 4,* 528–530.

Bird, E. D., Spokes, E. G., & Iversen, L. L. (1979). Brain norepinephrine and dopamine in schizophrenia. *Science, 204,* 93–94.

Brown, W. A., Johnston, R., & Mayfield, D. (1979). The 24-hour DST in a clinical setting: Relationship to diagnosis, symptoms and response to treatment. *American Journal of Psychiatry, 136,* 543–547.

Bunney, W. E., & Davis, J. M. (1965). Norepinephrine in depressive reactions: A review. *Archives of General Psychiatry, 13,* 483–494.

Butler, P. W. P., & Besser, G. M. (1968). Pituitary–adrenal function in severe depressive illness. *Lancet, 1,* 1234–1236.

Carlsson, A. (1979). Introduction. In E. Usdin and I. J. Kopin (Eds.), *Catecholamines: Basic and clinical frontiers* (pp. 1845–1847). New York: Pergamon Press.

Carroll, B. J., Curtis, G. C., & Mendels, J. (1976a). Cerebrospinal fluid and plasma free cortisol concentrations in depression. *Psychological Medicine, 6,* 235–244.

Carroll, B. J., Curtis, G. C., & Mendels, J. (1976b). Neuroendocrine regulation in depression: II. Discrimination of depressed from nondepressed patients. *Archives of General Psychiatry, 33,* 1051–1058.

Carroll, B. J., Feinberg, M., Greden, J. F., Tarika, J., Albala, A. A., Hasket, R. F., James, N., Kronfol, Z., Lohr, R., Steiner, M., Vigne, J. P., & Young, E. (1981). A specific laboratory test for the diagnosis of melancholia—standardization, validation and clinical utility. *Archives of General Psychiatry, 38,* 15–22.

Castro, P., Lemaire, M., Toscano-Aguilhar, M., & Herchuelz, A. (1983). Abnormal DST results in patients with chronic schizophrenia. *American Journal of Psychiatry, 140,* 1261.

Cavagnini, F., Raggi, U., Micossi, P., DiLandro, A., & Invitti, C. (1976). Effect of an antiserotonergic drug, metergoline, on the ACTH and cortisol response to insulin hypoglycemia and lysine–vasopressin in man. *Journal of Clinical Endocrinology and Metabolism, 43,* 306–312.

Checkley, S. A. (1979). Corticosteroid and growth hormone responses to methylamphetamine in depressive illness. *Psychological Medicine, 9,* 107–116.

Clayton, G., Librik, L., Gardner, R., & Guillemin, R. (1963). Studies on the circadian rhythm of pituitary adrenocorticotropic release in man. *Journal of Clinical Endocrinology and Metabolism, 23,* 975–980.

Coccaro, E. F., Prudic, J., Rothpearl, A., & Nurnberg, H. G. (1984). Effect of hospital admission on DST results. *American Journal of Psychiatry, 141,* 982–985.

Copolov, D., Jethwa, J., Stern, A., Clements, J., & Funder, J. (1983). Insulin hypoglycemia and cholinergic blockade: Response of plasma immunoreactive beta-endorphin. *Clinical Endocrinology, 19,* 575–580.

Coppen, A., Abow-Saleh, M., Milln, P., Metcalfe, M., Harwood, J., & Bailey, J. (1983). DST in depression and other psychiatric illness. *British Journal of Psychiatry, 142,* 498–504.

DeBold, C., Sheldon, W., DeCherney, G., Jackson, R., Alexander, A., Vale, W., Rivier, J., & Orth, D. (1984). Arginine vasopressin potentiates adrenocorticotropin release induced by ovine corticotropin releasing factor. *Journal of Clinical Investigation, 73,* 533–538.

Dewan, M. J., Pandurangi, A. K., Boucher, M. L., Levy, B. F., & Major, L. F. (1982). Abnormal dexamethasone suppression test results in chronic schizophrenic patients. *American Journal of Psychiatry, 139,* 1501–1503.

Doig, R. J., Mummery, R. V., Wills, M. R., & Elbes, A. (1966). Plasma cortisol levels in depression. *British Journal of Psychiatry, 112,* 1263–1267.

Endicott, J., & Spitzer, R. L. (1978). A diagnostic interview: The schedule for affective disorders and schizophrenia. *Archives of General Psychiatry, 35,* 837–844.

Franzen, G. (1971). Serum cortisol in chronic schizophrenia. *Acta Psychiatrica Scandinavica, 47,* 150–162.

Fuxe, K., Ogren, S. O., Everitt, B. J., Agnati, L. F., Eneroth, P., Gustafsson, J. A., Jonsson, G., Skett, P., & Holm, A. C. (1978). The effect of antidepressant drugs of the imipramine type on various monoamine systems and their relation to changes in behavior and neuroendocrine function. In S. Garattine (Ed.), *Depressive disorders* (pp. 67–94). Stuttgart, New York: F. K. Schattauer.

Gibbons, J. L., & McHugh, P. R. (1962). Plasma cortisol in depressive illness. *Journal of Psychiatric Research, 1,* 162–171.

Gold, M. S., Pottash, A. L. C., Extein, I., & Sweeney, D. R. (1981). Diagnosis of depression in the 1980s. *JAMA, Journal of the American Medical Association, 245,* 1562–1564.

Greden, J. F., Kronfol, Z., Gardner, R., Feinberg, M., Carroll, B. J. (1981). Neuroendocrine evaluation of schizoaffectives with the DST. In C. Perris, G. Struwe, & B. Jansson (Eds.), *Proceedings of the World Congress on Biological Psychiatry* (pp. 461–468). Amsterdam: Elsevier.

Gregoire, F., Brauman, H., DeBock, R., & Corvilain, J. (1977). Hormone release in depressed patients before and after recovery. *Psychoneuroendocrinology, 2,* 303–312.

Halbreich, U., Sachar, E. J., Asnis, G. M., Nathan, R. S., & Halpern, F. S. (1981). Diurnal cortisol responses to dextroamphetamine in normal subjects. *Psychoneuroendocrinology, 6,* 223–229.

Halbreich, U., Zumoff, B., Kream, J., & Fukushima, D. K. (1982). The mean 1300–1600 h plasma cortisol concentration as a diagnostic test for hypercortisolism. *Journal of Clinical Endocrinology and Metabolism, 54*(6), 1262–1264.

Halbreich, U., Asnis, G. M., Zumoff, B., Nathan, R. S., & Shindledecker, R. (1984). Effect of age and sex on cortisol secretion in depressives and normals. *Psychiatry Research, 13,* 221–229.

Halbreich, U., Asnis, G. M., Shindledecker, R., Zumoff, B., & Nathan, R. S. (1985a). Cortisol secretion in endogenous depression. I. Basal plasma levels. *Archives of General Psychiatry, 42,* 904–908.

Halbreich, U., Asnis, G. M., Shindledecker, R., Zumoff, B., & Nathan, R. S. (1985b). Cortisol secretion in endogenous depression. II. Time-related functions. *Archives of General Psychiatry, 42,* 909–914.

Holsboer, F. (1983). The DST in depressed patients: Clinical and biochemical aspects. *Journal of Steroid Biochemistry, 19,* 251–257.

Howanitz, J. H., & Howanitz, P. J. (1984). Evaluation of endocrine function. In J. B. Henry (Ed.), *Clinical diagnosis and management by laboratory methods* (pp. 299–345). Philadelphia: Sanders.

Hwang, S., Zander, J., & Garvey, M. (1984). DST: Use of two different dexamethasone doses. *Journal of Clinical Psychiatry, 45,* 390–392.

Jones, M. T., Hillhouse, E., & Burden, J. (1976). Secretion of corticotropin-releasing hormone *in vivo.* In L. Martini & W. F. Ganong (Eds.), *Frontiers in Neuroendocrinology,* Vol. 4. New York: Raven Press.

Katz, J. L., Weiner, H., Gallagher, T. F., & Hellman, L. (1970). Stress, distress and ego defenses. *Archives of General Psychiatry, 23,* 131–142.

Krieger, D. T., Allen, W., Rizzo, F., & Krieger, H. P. (1971). Characterization of the normal temporal pattern of plasma cortisol levels. *Journal of Clinical Endocrinology, 32,* 266–287.

Laakmann, G., Schoen, H. W., Blaschke, D., & Wittman, M. (1985). Dose-dependent growth hormone, prolactin and cortisol stimulation after i.v. administration of desimipramine in human subjects. *Psychoneuroendocrinology, 10* (1), 83–93.

Laakmann, G., Wittman, M., Schoen, H. W., Zygan, K., Weiss, A., Meissner, R., Mueller, O. A., & Stalla, G. K. (1986). Effect of receptor blockers (methysergide propranolol, phentolamine yokimisine and pragosin) on desimipramine-induced pituitary hormone stimulation on human-II. Hypothalamo–pituitary–adrenocortical axis. *Psychoneuroendocrinology, 11,* 475–489.

McHardy-Young, S., Harris, P. W. R., Lessoff, M. H., & Lyne, C. (1967). Single dose dexamethasone suppression test for Cushing's syndrome. *British Medical Journal, 1,* 740–744.

Mueller, P. S., Heninger, G. R., & McDonald, R. K. (1969). Insulin tolerance test in depression. *Archives of General Psychiatry, 21,* 587–594.

Nelson, W. H., Khan, A., Orr, W. W., & Tamragouri, R. N. (1984). The DST: Interaction of diagnosis, sex, and age in psychiatric inpatients. *Biological Psychiatry, 19,* 1293–1304.

Plotsky, P. (1985). Hypophysiotropic regulation of adenohypophysial adrenocorticotropin secretion. *Federation Proceedings, Federation of American Societies for Experimental Biology, 44,* 207–213.

Prescott, R., Kendall-Taylor, P., Weightman, D., Watson, J., & Ratcliffe, W. (1984). The effect of ketanserin, a specific serotonin antagonist, on the prolactin, growth hormone, ACTH, and cortisol responses to hypoglycemia in normal subjects. *Clinical Endocrinology, 20,* 137–142.

Randrup, A., & Braestrup, P. (1977). Uptake inhibition of biogenic amines by newer antidepressant drugs: Relevance to the dopamine hypothesis. *Psychopharmacology, 53,* 309–314.

Rees, L., Butler, P. W. P., Gosling, C., & Besser, G. M. (1970). Adrenergic blockade and the corticosteroid and growth hormone responses to methylamphetamine. *Nature, 228,* 565–566.

Rihmer, Z., & Arato, M. (1984). The DST as a clinical aid and research tool in patients with affective disorders. *Psychopharmacology Bulletin, 20,* 174–177.

Sachar, E. J., Mason, J. W., Kolmer, H., & Artiss, K. (1963). Psychoendocrine aspects of acute schizophrenic reactions. *Psychosomatic Medicine, 25,* 510–537.

Sachar, E. J., Finkelstein, J., & Hellman, L. (1970). Growth hormone responses in depressive illness: I. Response to insulin tolerance test. *Archives of General Psychiatry, 25,* 263–269.

Sachar, E. J., Hellman, L., Roffwarg, H. P., Halpern, F. S., Fukushima, D, K., & Gallagher, T. F. (1973). Disrupted 24-hour patterns of cortisol secretion in psychotic depression. *Archives of General Psychiatry, 28,* 19–24.

Sachar, E. J. (1975). Neuroendocrine abnormalities in depressives illness. In E. J. Sachar (Ed.), *Topics in psychoendocrinology.* New York: Grune & Stratton.

Sachar, E. J., Asnis, G. M., Nathan, R. S., Halbreich, U., & Tabrize, M. A., Halpern, R. S. (1980a). Dextroamphetamine and cortisol in depression. *Archives of General Psychiatry, 37,* 755–757.

Sachar, E. J., Halbreich, U., Asnis, G. M., Nathan, S., & Halpern, F. S. (1980b). Neurotransmitter regulation of cortisol secretion in depression: Studies of the response to dextroamphetamine. In E. E. Muller (Ed.), *Neuroactive drugs in endocrinology* (pp. 293–307). Amsterdam: Elsevier/North-Holland Biomedical Press.

Sachar, E. J., Halbreich, U., Asnis, G. M., Nathan, R. S., Halpern, F. S., & Ostrow, L. (1981). Paradoxical cortisol responses to dextroamphetamine in endogenous depression. *Archives of General Psychiatry, 38,* 1113–1117.

Sawyer, J., & Jeffries, J. J. (1984). The DST in schizophrenia. *Journal of Clinical Psychiatry, 45,* 399–402.

Schlesser, M. A., Winokur, G., & Sherman, B. M. (1980). HPA axis activity in depressive illness. *Archives of General Psychiatry, 37,* 737–743.

Shulman, R., & Dieold, P. (1977). A two dose DST in patients with psychiatric illness. *Canadian Psychiatric Association Journal, 22,* 417–421.

Spitzer, R. L., Endicott, J., & Robins, E. (1978). Research diagnostic criteria: Rationale and reliability. *Archives of General Psychiatry, 35,* 773–782.

Stewart, J. W., Quitkin, F., McGrath, P. J., Liebowitz, M. R., Harrison, W., Robbin, J. G., Novancenko, H., Puig-Antich, J., & Asnis, G. M. (1984). Cortisol response to dextroamphetamine stimulation in depressed outpatients. *Psychiatry Research, 12*(3), 195–206.

Stokes, P. E., Stoll, P. M., Koslow, S. H., Maas, J. W., Davis, J. M., Swann, A. C., & Robins, S. E. (1984). Pretreatment DST and hypothalamic–pituitary–adrenocortical function in depressed patients and comparison groups: A multicenter study. *Archives of General Psychiatry, 41,* 257–266.

Targum, S. D. (1983). The application of serial neuroendocrine challenge studies in the management of depressive disorder. *Biological Psychiatry, 18,* 3–19.

Traskman, L., Tybring, G., Asberg, M., Bertilsson, L., Lantto, B., & Schalling, D. (1980). Cortisol in the CSF of depressed and suicidal patients. *Archives of General Psychiatry, 37,* 761–767.

Zimmerman, M., & Coryell, W. (1985). Limited utility of the 1-mg dexamethasone suppression test as a measure of hypercortisolism. *Archives of General Psychiatry, 42,* 200–201.

18 HYPOTHALAMIC–PITUITARY–ADRENAL AXIS PEPTIDES IN AFFECTIVE DISEASE: FOCUS ON THE ACTH/β-ENDORPHIN SYSTEM

STANLEY J. WATSON
HUDA AKIL
ELIZABETH YOUNG
University of Michigan Medical Center

INTRODUCTION

The focus of this chapter involves several different, but related topics dealing with the integration of basic neurobiology and endocrinology, with clinical science studies of affective disease. We begin with a summary of the anatomy, biochemistry, and physiology of the ACTH/β-endorphin/β-lipotropin (ACTH/β-E/β-LPH) system in anterior pituitary. A strong emphasis is placed on this system because of its pivotal role in relaying and integrating the responses of the nervous system to stress. Furthermore, it is clear that as a field, our understanding of the hypothalamic–pituitary–adrenal (HPA) axis's response to depression is actively moving "up" from the adrenal to the pituitary and its peptides, ACTH and β-endorphin (β-E). In the second section of the chapter, we discuss biochemical-regulatory studies of the ACTH/β-E/β-LPH-producing cell in the anterior lobe of pituitary (known as a "corticotroph"), focusing on the conditions of high demand in rat pituitary. These studies were conducted to obtain some understanding of the regulatory ("coping") strategies used by the corticotroph as it handles increased demand. We are certainly not proposing that stress (be it acute or chronic) is an animal model of depression. Rather, we are attempting to use these animal studies to understand possible mechanisms of control available along the axis—some of which may become evident in the pituitary of depressed humans. In effect, we hope to learn how the depressed pituitary responds and perhaps what its inputs must have been to adopt that regulatory strategy. The third section presents an overview of clinical science studies of affective disease, with an emphasis on pituitary peptides and their dysregulation in depression (the parallel studies on corticoid dysregulation are presented by Evans and Golden, Chapter 14, this volume). In this section, we will attempt to reach some tentative conclusions about the state of knowledge of corticotroph functioning in depression. Finally, there will be a brief future-oriented section in which the probable next generation of studies will be discussed. They will cover the range from better versions of current peptide measurement protocols through challenge with corticotropin-releasing factor (CRF) and arginine vasopressin (AVP) agonists and eventually antagonists, and finally postmortem measurement of levels of mRNA coding for the several enzymes, receptors, and hormones of the HPA axis of depressed individuals.

ACTH, β-ENDORPHIN, AND β-LIPOTROPIN: BIOGENESIS, RELEASE, AND FEEDBACK REGULATION

In order to be able to extend the HPA studies more directly into pituitary and brain, it is necessary to measure ACTH and/or its cosynthesized peptides (β-E and β-lipotropin) and to understand their regulation and release in the anterior pituitary. It is now well known that ACTH derives from a larger precursor molecule which also gives rise to a number of other peptides, including β-lipotropin (β-LPH) and its carboxy terminal opioid β-E, including three copies of the $ACTH_{4-10}$ active core, as part of melanocyte-stimulating hormone structures (Figure 18.1). This precursor has thus been termed proopiomelanocortin, or POMC (Mains, Eipper, & Ling, 1977; Nakanishi et al., 1979; Roberts, Budarf, Baster, & Herbert, 1979; Roberts & Herbert, 1977). The orderly events leading to the maturation of the precursor into individual peptide products are fairly well understood (Eipper & Mains, 1980, 1981; Mains et al., 1977). These are known to be different in pituitary and brain and differ between the anterior and neurointermediate lobes of the pituitary of many species (Akil, Shiomi, & Matthews, 1985; Akil, Veda, & Lin, 1981; Chrétien & Seidah, 1981; Eipper & Mains, 1980, 1981; Herbert, 1981; Krieger, Liotta, Brownstein, & Zimmerman, 1980;

Mains & Eipper, 1981). Since humans have no intermediate lobe, we need only describe anterior lobe POMC processing and release. The corticotrophs of the anterior lobe store $ACTH_{1-39}$, β-LPH, a smaller amount of β-E (the β-LPH:β-E ratio is approximately 2:1), and the entire 16,000 MW (16K) peptide at the N terminus (Chrétien & Seidah, 1981). Processing into smaller peptides such as α-MSH, α- or γ-endorphin, or posttranslational events such as N-acetylation of β-E or amidation of α-MSH appear to be the hallmark of the intermediate lobe and occur only to a very small extent in the anterior lobe (Akil et al., 1981; Mains & Eipper, 1981; Zakarian & Smyth, 1982). Thus, in the plasma of human subjects, we see β-LPH and $β-E_{1-31}$ (with a preponderance of β-LPH in normals) (Cahill, Matthews, & Akil, 1983) and $ACTH_{1-39}$. However, in humans, we have no evidence of products such as N-acetyl-β-E, which we detect in rat and monkey plasma and which are devoid of opioid activity (Akil et al., 1981). No studies in plasma have characterized the peptides derived from the 16K N-terminal piece of POMC.

Since β-LPH/β-E and ACTH are costored in the same secretory granules, they are thought to be coreleased (Guillemin et al., 1977), although the differential release of β-E versus β-LPH in vivo has not been well studied. Nevertheless, measurement of either total ACTH-like immunoreactivity or total β-like immunoreactivity (which includes both β-LPH and β-E) (see Figure 18.1). would reflect the activity of the corticotrophs. It should be noted in passing that the peripheral functions of β-LPH and β-E have not been elucidated (see Akil & Watson, 1983, for review), although γ-MSH, which derives from the 16K N-terminal peptide, has been shown to potentiate ACTH-induced steroidogenesis (Pedersen, Brownie, & Ling, 1980).

The release of the POMC products (ACTH, β-LPH, β-E, N-terminals peptide) is thought to be triggered by a variety of hypothalamic factors, including AVP (Vale & Fleischer, 1968) and the more recently sequenced CRF (Vale, Speiss, Rivier, & Rivier, 1981). The use of pituitary cultures along with in vivo studies has shown direct effects of CRF on the corticotrophs, liberating both β-E/β-LPH and ACTH (Rivier & Vale, 1983;

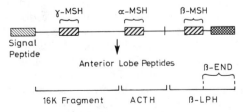

FIGURE 18.1. The proopiomelanocortin (POMC) precursor in the anterior lobe of pituitary can give rise to ACTH, β-endorphin, β-lipotropin, and other peptides from the 16K fragment.

Turkelson *et al.*, 1981; Vale *et al.*, 1981). AVP-induced release and CRF-induced release have been shown to be synergistic (Turkelson *et al.*, 1982), and there findings have been replicated by us (Young & Akil, 1985). As we shall discuss later, the release of POMC products by these hypothalamic peptides is affected not only by the concentration of the releasing factors, but by the propensity of ACTH and β-E to be released.

STEROID FEEDBACK TO THE PITUITARY

The HPA axis (Figure 18.2) regulates many of its functions through inhibitory feedback of cortisol on both the pituitary and hypothalamus. As early as 1948, Sayers and Sayers demonstrated that pretreatment with corticosteroids prevented the depletion of adrenal ascorbate induced by stress or ACTH administration. Their work suggested that corticosteroids could inhibit ACTH secretion if administered immediately prior to a stress as well as if administered a number of hours earlier. The critical nature of this glucocorticoid feedback from the adrenal to the pituitary is most clearly demonstrated by the impact of adrenalectomy on ACTH secretion; this is, adrenelectomy leads to elevated basal levels of plasma ACTH levels as well as hyperresponsiveness of ACTH release following stress. Administration of glucocorticoids after adrenalectomy lowers basal plasma ACTH levels as well as regulating the ACTH response to stress (Dallman & Jones, 1973; Dallman, Jones, Vernikos-Danellis, & Ganong, 1972; Dallman & Yates, 1969; Jones, Brush, & Neame, 1972). These studies suggest the corticosteroids act at both the hypothalamic and pituitary levels to control CRF release, as well as ACTH release in response to CRF.

Steroid feedback seems to operate through two relatively independent types of mechanisms, a rate-sensitive fast feedback system and a delayed (or proportional) feedback system. These appear to operate through separate steroid receptors, since steroid metabolites 11-deoxycorticosterone and 11-deoxycortisol antagonize fast feedback, but are active in delayed feedback studies (Jones, Tiptaft, Brush, Fergusson, & Neame, 1974). The purposes of these two systems appear to

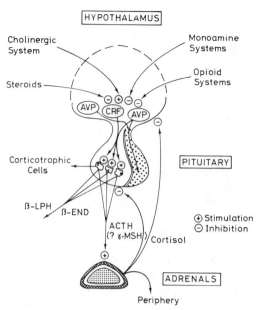

FIGURE 18.2. The hypothalamic–pituitary–adrenal (HPA) axis involves several peptide hormones in the hypothalamus (corticotropin-releasing factor, AVPD, oxytocin) and their regulation by other brain sites and substances (acetylcholine, monoamines, endorphins, steroids, etc.). These hypothalamic peptides (chiefly CRF and AVP) cause the release of ACTH and β-endorphin from anterior pituitary and thereby the release of corticosteroids from adrenal. Adrenal corticoids feed back on the pituitary and hypothalamus to negatively control CRF, AVP, ACTH, and so on.

be different, with the fast feedback system maintaining a fine control over basal secretion of ACTH and operating in the times of acute demand, while delayed feedback maintains the overall set point of the system (Jones, Gillham, Greenstein, Beckford, & Holmes, 1982). The time parameters of these feedback systems suggest that fast feedback directly influences releasability of ACTH and other POMC peptides in times of stress, while delayed feedback is involved in the regulation of transcription of the POMC gene and subsequent synthesis of the precursor and processing to its end products. Roberts and co-workers (1979), using AtT-20 mouse pituitary tumor cells, and Birnberg, Lissitizky, Hinman, and Herbert (1983), using pituitaries from adrenalectomized rats, demonstrated that 6–8 hours after dexamethasone administration the corticotroph decreased the specific POMC mRNA content. The studies strongly support the contention that steroids directly affect POMC gene regulation. Similarly, this decrease in POMC biosynthesis is reflected in a subsequent decrease in overall POMC peptide content of the pituitary a number of hours after dexamethasone administration. Thus, the time frame of delayed feedback (approximately 10 hours) fits with the regulation of gene transcription and mRNA translation seen by Roberts *et al.* (1979). This delayed feedback sets limits on the content of the gland and the overall products available for release (releasable pools). During acute stress, the biosynthesis and processing of POMC to ACTH and β-E may increase, but only within the bounds of POMC mRNA available for translation. In sum, long-term (or delayed) feedback is necessary to regulate biosynthesis of ACTH and β-E, and fast feedback is necessary to modulate release from the releasable pools. Studies by Dallman *et al.* (1972) have confirmed that both the delayed feedback system and the fast feedback system must be in operation to produce *normal* ACTH release after stress in adrenalectomized rats.

There appears to be substantial evidence supporting the existence of a similar fast feedback mechanism in man. Daly, Reader, Alaghband-Zadeh, and Halsmann (1979) infused cortisol in normals at 3 mg/hour and observed a fall in plasma ACTH during the period the cortisol level was rising, a plateau in ACTH levels after 2 hours, and a drop in ACTH levels when the rate of infusion was increased to 6 mg/hour. These data parallel the work on fast feedback in rat, including saturability at high cortisol levels. Delayed feedback also appears to operate in humans, since patients with adrenocortical atrophy (Addison's disease) show elevated plasma ACTH levels, similar to those seen in adrenalectomized animals, and a reduction in plasma ACTH levels with corticosteroid replacement therapy (Bethune, Nelson, & Thorn, 1957).

HPA AXIS REGULATION IN CHRONIC STRESS

Although a number of investigators have looked at the effects of acute stress on the HPA axis, the work on repeated (or chronic) stress is less clear. Using a bioassay system for ACTH, Dallman and Jones (1973) report an increased release of ACTH to a subsequent stress within an 8-hour period after the first stress. De Souza and Van Loon (1982) suggest a decreased release of corticoids to a subsequent stress. Since similar plasma ACTH rises were seen in control and previously stressed groups, De Souza and Van Loon (1983) hypothesized that other peptides, for example, enkephalins, may be responsible for this inhibition. In CRF infusion studies, C. Rivier and Vale (1983) have demonstrated a decreased release of ACTH to a second CRF infusion *in vivo*. Although glucocorticoids may play a regulatory role in this decreased responsiveness, they do not appear to be the sole mechanism, since analogous changes are seen in adrenalectomized rats. All these studies agree that more than one regulatory mechanism at multiple levels of the HPA axis appear to be involved in the observed changes. The involvement of several levels of HPA axis feedback make the interpretation of these data difficult, suggesting that *in vivo* studies alone may not be able to sort out the issues of pituitary regulation of release. Additionally, none of the above studies has addressed a repeated stress paradigm.

We have elected to use repeated daily sessions of footshock as a chronic stress stimulus. This form of stress has been well studied and appears to stimulate the release of the endogenous opioids from pituitary and adrenal (Akil, Madden, Patrick, & Barchas, 1976; Amir & Amit, 1979; Lewis, Cannon, & Liebeskind, 1980). Using a short-term *in vitro* anterior pituitary culture system from rats who have been stressed immediately prior to sacrifice, we were able to investigate the effects of previous stress on the response to CRF or other releasers in this "open-loop" controlled system. Additionally, we have explored sensitivity to negative steroid feedback on release of POMC peptides.

Three different stress paradigms were explored: (1) a one-time footshock stress immediately prior to decapitation (acute stress); (2) the same footshock parameter (for one-half hour), but applied daily for 14 days, with a 24-hour recovery period prior to decapitation (chronic stress/rest); and (3) chronic footshock as in (2), with the last shock stress session immediately prior to decapitation (chronic stress/acute stress) (Young & Akil, 1985). These three groups are always contrasted with an untreated, unhandled control group. Thus, the differences between the acute stress group and the chronic stress/acute stress group relate to the previous stress history of the animal. Likewise, the differences between the naive unhandled control rats and the chronic stress/rest groups are similarly related to their history of stress (or lack of same). It should be noted that the control and chronic stress/rest groups have similar plasma corticoid, ACTH, and β-E levels at the time of decapitation. Additionally, the acute stress and chronic stress/acute stress groups show similar plasma corticoid, ACTH, and β-E rises in plasma levels at the time of decapitation immediately after the stress session. Thus, several differences within these two sets of groups cannot be attributed to acute release of pituitary or adrenal hormones.

ACUTE STRESS

When reponse to the secretagogues CRF or AVP is examined after acute stress (using rapid primary cultures of anterior pituitary), it becomes clear that acute stress causes a decrease reponse to these releasers. In the case of AVP-stimulated release of β-E or ACTH, a blunted response to AVP is seen across several doses, from 0.1 nM to 10 nM. In contrast, a clearly blunted response to CRF is seen only at the threshold dose of 0.01 nM. This agrees with the work of Rivier and Vale (1983) that previous administration of CRF produces a decreased responsiveness of a subsequent dose of CRF within the next 6–8 hours. Thus, a previous stressor inhibits the subsequent response of POMC peptides to CRF or AVP. Since animals in the acute stress group show elevated plasma steroids at the time of decapitation, perhaps this decreased response to CRF or AVP is a reflection of steroid negative feedback on the pituitary. Indeed, a similar decrease in response to AVP and CRF is produced by administration of steroids prior to decapitation. Consequently, it appears that previous stress impairs the response to a subsequent stress.

Pulse-chase experiments (reflecting new protein synthesis) show that immediately af-

ter acute stress, the biosynthetic rate of POMC is elevated such that the rate of incorporation into the precursor is 50% higher, and that $t_{1/2}$ of conversion from POMC to β-LPH and β-E is accelerated twofold. Thus, release appears to elicit a compensatory increase in rate of biosynthesis. This acceleration probably accounts for the minor changes in AL content in spite of the substantial release in plasma (Akil et al., 1985).

CHRONIC STRESS

If a stressful stimulus is repeated over a number of days (chronic stress), adaptation appears to occur. Animals who have been chronically stressed and who are allowed 24 hours to recover show normal plasma hormone responses to the secretagogues AVP and CRF. Yet, in fact, there is a recent suggestion that these animals are actually supersensitive to CRF. This supersensitivity is most clearly seen in the chronic stress/acute stress group. The chronic stress/acute stress group no longer manifests a blunted response to CRF. In fact, they show a more robust response to 0.01 nM CRF. Thus, the same treatment (acute stress prior to sacrifice) that causes a blunted response to CRF in normal rats causes an increased response to CRF in rats with a history of chronic stress. This difference is most pronounced with a threshold dose of CRF. These data suggest that negative steroid feedback on the pituitary has been attenuated in these animals. In both groups of chronically stressed rats, we see an increase in pituitary content of POMC-derived peptides, which could partially explain the increased release of ACTH and β-E to CRF stimulation. However, these elevated peptide levels cannot explain the further increased release seen after acute stress in chronically stressed rats. It seems as though in a chronically stressed rat, acute stress now has a facilitating influence on pituitary release to CRF. In addition, recent data suggest a loss of the normal inhibitory influence of glucocorticoids.

Pulse-chase experiments show that compensatory changes are different in the AL of chronically stressed rats. At least the $t_{1/2}$ of POMC is even longer than controls, possibly because the content of β-E is already so high. When the animals are studied immediately poststress (chronic/acute), the biosynthetic rate is not particularly accelerated. A slight decrease in $t_{1/2}$ is evidenced by the chronic/acute group when compared to the chronic/rest group, but the change is minimal when contrasted to the effect of acute stress in previously naive rats. Thus, it appears as though, with repeated activation, the AL exhibits a different strategy for coping with demand. Rather than exhibiting a secondary rise in biosynthesis following release, it stores a great deal more material in the releasable pool such that the recurrent demand causes relatively less perturbation in the system. This observation is supported by POMC mRNA quantitation studies showing a 28% increase in AL after chronic stress. Thus, it is likely that the increased storage of peptide in the releasable pool is derived from this higher translational capacity.

Although these chronically stressed rats may appear normal in resting conditions, the increase in pituitary peptide content and rate of biosynthesis, the increase in POMC mRNA, the increase in releasability of ACTH and β-E, and the decrease in sensitivity to glucocorticoid feedback on release argue that these animals have very different pituitaries and very different regulatory strategies than control animals. Yet, when we examine the plasma levels of ACTH, β-E, or corticosterone in the acute stress and chronic stress/acute stress groups, we see no difference between them in the levels of these hormones after stress. Other levels of HPA axis (perhaps fast feedback) appear to be able to compensate for this increased releasability of ACTH and β-E. That these differences in releasability only become evident with challenges to the pituitary strongly supports the strategy of investigating HPA axis abnormalities in human diseases with dynamic challenges to the regulatory mechanisms. This chronic stress animal model in many ways resembles humans with Cushing's disease secondary to a pituitary adenoma, with an increase content of POMC-derived peptides and a decreased sensitivity to glucocortiocoid negative feedback. This parallel suggests that the regulatory strategies revealed in this chronic stress rat model are basic to a number of conditions and may shed further light on the HPA axis dysfunction of endogenous depression (ED).

RELEASE OF β-E WITH STRESS

But what is the role of β-E in this system? Is authentic β-E present in or released from these primary anterior lobe cultures? Are there changes in processing of β-E from β-LPH in stress? We are beginning to explore these questions (Young, Lewis, & Akil, 1986). Examining both pituitary cultures after CRF stimulation and plasma after acute footshock stress, we have concluded there is a release of β-E from the anterior lobe in rats. Although the intermediate lobe may contribute to the pool of circulating β-E-like peptides in rat, the tremendous rise in β-E size material with stress, paralleling the rise seen in ACTH released from the anterior lobe, suggests that the anterior lobe releases β-E, not just β-LPH. In fact, plasma sieving experiments show a 2:1 ratio of β-E to β-LPH. This occurs despite the occurrence of approximately 2.5-fold more β-LPH than β-E in the anterior lobe. This ratio is confirmed by studies with anterior lobe cultures from both normal and acutely stressed rats by looking at the culture medium for unstimulated and stimulated release. Although the ratio of β-E to β-LPH in unstimulated release in the medium of control animal pituitary cultures is 1:1, CRF stimulation results in a greater release of β-E, so the ratio of β-E to β-LPH is 2:1. Again, this argues strongly that β-E (vs. β-LPH) is the primary end product of anterior lobe POMC processing. Similarly, the preferential release of β-E by CRF suggests that this opiate-active peptide plays a substantial role in stress and HPA axis regulation and feedback during stress.

What are the effects of chronic stress on this pituitary system? Looking at the plasma from chronically stressed rats immediately after a stress session, we continue to see an increase in β-E with stress. However, other work in our laboratory has shown that the intermediate lobe is also induced with chronic stress and now releases both true β-E as well as amino and carboxyl terminally altered β-E (Akil et al., 1985). Thus, the plasma data in chronic stress are rather difficult to interpret. Looking at anterior lobe pituitary cultures from chronically stressed rats, either immediately after stress of 24 hours after the last stress, we see proportionately more release of β-LPH than in control or acute stress anterior lobe pituitary cultures. In the case of chronically stressed/acute stress rat pituitary cultures, we see a predominance of β-LPH over β-E released after CRF stimulation. This shift in the peptide released, from β-E to predominantly β-LPH, with chronic stress further supports that these animals utilize different regulatory strategies than control animals. To summarize, our chronic stress model has shown that a response to chronic stress occurs in the anterior lobe. The primary changes are (1) an increase in pituitary content of POMC-related peptides and POMC mRNA, (2) increased sensitivity to releasers such as CRF, (3) a decreased sensitivity to negative steroid feedback on CRF-induced release from pituitary cultures, and (4) a shift in the ratio of β-E to β-LPH released by CRF stimulation in favor of β-LPH. To assess whether the regulatory strategies demonstrated in our chronic stress paradigm are of value in understanding clinical disorders requires similar investigations in human disorders.

POMC PEPTIDE REGULATION IN AFFECTIVE DISEASE

A number of investigators have shown adrenal steroid dysregulation in ED (Brown, Johnston, & Mayfield, 1979; Carptenter & Bunney, 1971; Carroll, 1972; Carroll, Curtis, & Mendels, 1976; Carroll & Mendels, 1976; Carroll et al., 1981; Rubin & Mandell, 1966; Sachar, 1967; Sachar, Hellman, Fukushima, & Gallagher, 1970; Sachar et al., 1973). It is presumed that this regulatory abnormality occurs secondary to alterations in central neurotransmitters which result in excessive release of CRF or alterations in the steroid feedback inhibition of CRF release. It should be recognized that a number of regulatory levels intervene between the presumed defect (brain neurotransmitters) and measured abnormality (adrenal corticosteroid release). Thus, it is important to examine pituitary regulation to determine if the defect in feedback regulation occurs at the pituitary as well as adrenal level. A number of recent studies have directly approached this issue. Most investigators have examined either ACTH or β-E plasma levels before and after the administration of dexamethasone, a potent syn-

thetic steroid, in order to examine the effects of a challenge to the system. In general, most of these clinical studies have divided the patients into endogenous and nonendogenous depressives, as well as subdivided the endogenous depressives into subgroups of cortisol suppressors and nonsuppressors (after dexamethasone administration). While the division into endogenous and nonendogenous depressives may be reasonable on a theoretical basis, the subdivision of endogenous depressives into cortisol suppressors and nonsuppressors is not necessarily sound, since these patients are not distinguishable clinically from each other.

Fang, Tricou, Robertson, and Meltzer (1981) compared ACTH plasma levels before and after dexamethasone administration (using the DST paradigm) in endogenous and nonendogenous depressives. They report no significant differences between cortisol suppressors and nonsuppressors in plasma ACTH levels after dexamethasone administration. Although there was a tendency for cortisol nonsuppressors to have higher postdexamethasone ACTH values than suppressors, because of the large between-subjects variation in postdexamethasone ACTH levels in cortisol nonsuppressors, this difference was not significant. The authors conclude that the cortisol "escape" is less related to elevated ACTH and may result from abnormal adrenal regulation. In contrast, Reus, Joseph, and Dallman (1982) noted higher postdexamethasone plasma ACTH levels in endogenously depressed patients who were cortisol nonsuppressors. They also found significantly higher 8 A.M. predexamethasone plasma ACTH values in these same patients. These data are supported by Kalin, Weiler, and Shelton (1982) who also found evidence of pituitary dysregulation in endogenous depression, noting higher plasma ACTH levels in cortisol nonsuppressors both before and after dexamethasone administration.

The poor correlation between ACTH and cortisol levels in the plasma of endogenous depressives seen by Fang et al. (1981) was also noted by Sherman, Pohl, Schlecter, and Winokur (1982). This lack of concordance suggests a genetic component to this disturbance, since it seems to be present in relatives of endogenously depressed patients as well as in affected patients. Although such dissociation of ACTH and cortisol regulation may indicate adrenal dysfunction, other explanations are also possible. It seems clear that each level of the HPA axis (Figure 18.2) may attempt to compensate for abnormalities at other levels. Thus, while each HPA level may reflect input from higher levels, it also may use its own regulatory mechanisms to modulate its response to this input. Viewed from this perspective, one might expect that average plasma ACTH or β-E levels would demonstrate more variability among endogenous depressives than among normal controls; that is, endogenous depressives may not be a homogenous group, but rather represent some individuals with high plasma ACTH and high cortisol levels, while other individuals may show high cortisol levels which inhibit pituitary ACTH release, resulting in normal plasma ACTH levels. Consequently, one might hypothesize that the pituitaries of different patients may use different adaptive strategies to compensate for the HPA axis abnormality, resulting in wide variations in resting ACTH or β-E levels in the endogenous depressives. This hypothesis is consistent with the data of Fang *et al.* (1981) showing wide variations in ACTH levels (and regulation) after dexamethasone administration as well as our own data on β-E levels before and after dexamethasone in endogenous depressives (Matthews, Akil, Greden, & Watson, 1982; Matthews *et al.*, 1986). Because of this probable complexity, a number of different challenges to the HPA axis may prove useful in delineating the various regulatory strategies that are used to compensate for the underlying abnormalities seen in depression.

The approach in our studies has been to examine plasma β-E/β-LPH levels at 4 P.M. both before and after dexamethasone administration in endogenous depressives, other psychiatric disorders, and normal controls (Matthews *et al.*, 1986). Blood samples are drawn through indwelling intravenous catheters inserted $1\frac{1}{2}$ hours prior to sampling to minimize possible "stress" effects of the blood-drawing procedure. Four samples are drawn between a 3:30 and 4:30 P.M. time period to control for possible secretory episodes. This 4 P.M. time period is a quiescent period for the HPA axis, and we have in fact found very few secretory bursts. We have

defined suppression as a decrease in mean β-E levels after dexamethasone administration, such that the average pre- and postvalues plus or minus the standard error of the mean do not overlap; that is, the two values are defined as not different if their standard errors overlap. Using this criterion for "abnormality," we can show suppression of plasma β-E after dexamethasone administration in the vast majority of normal subjects and in psychiatric controls. In contrast, quite a large number of endogenous depressives fail to suppress β-E levels after dexamethasone. In two independent samples from different hosptials and different investigators, between 50% and 69% of endogenous depressives failed to suppress β-E levels after dexamethasone administration. The sample with the highest nonsuppression rate included substantially more delusional depressives, suggesting that severity of illness may be related to disordered pituitary regulation.

Are the same patients who are abnormal on postdexamethasone plasma β-E levels also abnormal on cortisol measures? Surprisingly, this is not necessarily the case. In our samples (over 30 endogenous depressives), more patients fail to suppress plasma β-E levels after dexamethasone than fail to suppress cortisol levels. This dissociation of POMC peptides and cortisol supports the hypothesis that each level of the HPA axis may try to compensate for abnormalities at other levels. Using failure to suppress to dexamethasone on either cortisol or β-E measures as a criterion, we can now identify 72% of the endogenously depressed patients, while only 8% of the normal controls show abnormal suppression on these measures. However, the point of our investigations is not to construct a β-E laboratory test for depression, but to understand pituitary regulation in depression. From a regulation standpont, it is of interest that a number of the most severely depressed patients not only failed to suppress β-E levels after administration, but also clearly increased their postdexamethasone plasma β-E levels. In general, these data support the hypothesis that the defect in HPA axis is present above the adrenal level.

To assist in developing a model for the HPA axis regulatory abnormality in ED, it is useful to compare ED to Cushing's disease, the prototypical HPA axis disorder. In ED, abnormal long-term steroid feedback on both β-E/ACTH and cortisol levels has been shown, similar to the findings in Cushing's disease. In contrast with Cushing's disease, only a few investigators report significant differences in basal plasma levels of β-E or ACTH between endogenous depressives and nonendogenous or normal controls (Kalin et al., 1981; Reus et al., 1982). It is unclear if this finding is simply a result of more variability in pituitary regulation in ED or if it is indicative of differences in pathogenesis or severity between ED and Cushing's disease. In addition to abnormalities in long-term steroid feedback, failure to suppress plasma ACTH levels with cortisol infusion (fast feedback) has been demonstrated in Cushing's disease (Fehm et al., 1977). Similar studies have been undertaken in ED. Work by Carr et al. (1984) has demonstrated a paradoxical increase in plasma ACTH levels after infusion of cortisol in 2 of 10 endogenous depressives. Because of their small number of controls, it is unclear whether the other endogenous depressives who did not show this paradoxical response demonstrated abnormalities in the rate of ACTH suppression to cortisol infusion, as seen in Cushing's patients (Fehm et al., 1977; Reader, Robertson, Alaghband-Zadeh, & Daly, 1980). In collaboration with Drs. Reus and Dallman, we have conducted similar preliminary studies which demonstrate an increase in β-E levels after the infusion of cortisol in endogenous depressives, similar to the paradoxical response of ACTH to cortisol infusion seen in Cushing's disease. In the case of the report by Carr et al. (1984), the 2 patients with abnormal cortisol-induced fast feedback inhibition of ACTH release demonstrated normal cortisol suppression in the standard dexamethasone suppression test, suggesting a dissociation of delayed and fast feedback systems in some patients. This suggests that both delayed and fast feedback may be altered in ED and that abnormal HPA axis regulation may be present in more endogenously depressed patients than demonstrated by previous studies on delayed feedback alone.

The response to infusion of CRF in endogenously depressed patients may provide the most exciting new clues to understanding HPA axis abnormalities present in this illness(es). A report by Gold et al. (1984) demonstrated a substantially decreased response to CRF in four depressed subjects, in marked contrast to the increased response to CRF seen in Cushing's disease. Although the number of subjects in the Gold et al. study is small, the data suggest that the response of endogenous depressives to CRF shows a different pathophysiology than Cushing's disease (Catania et al., 1984; Gold et al., 1984; Lystras et al., 1984; Mueller, Dorr, Hagen, Stalla, & Werder, 1982; Mueller, Stalla, & von Werden, 1983; Orth et al., 1982, 1983; Pieters et al., 1983). Holsboer, Gerhen et al. (1984) reported no difference in plasma ACTH between endogenous depressives and nonendogenous depressive to oCRF infusion, despite the fact that endogenous depressives show elevated resting plasma steroids. More recently, Holsboer, Bardeleben et al. (1984) reported a blunted ACTH response but a normal cortisol response to hCRF. Again the sample size is small, but the response is different from the response seen in Cushing's patients. These studies need to be interpreted with caution, since (1) the numbers of subjects are small, and (2) in the reports by Holsboer, Berdeleben et al. (1984) and Holsboer, Gerhen et al. (1984) there are clear differences between baseline cortisol levels of the endogenous depressives and control subjects; this may also be true of the report by Gold et al. (1984). Work by Hermus, Pieters, Smals, Benraad, and Kloppenborg (1984) showed, in normal subjects, that individual basal cortisol levels are highly negatively correlated to ACTH and cortisol levels after CRF infusion. That is, that baseline cortisol inhibits ACTH release after cortisol. This negative control by steroids of CRF-induced release does not appear to be present in Cushing's disease patients. Although endogenous depressives may show some of the same features as Cushing's disease, the disturbance is not as severe and may be due to different HPA axis disturbances. For example, endogenous depressives may still show glucocorticoid modulation of the response to CRF, and normal control and depressives may need to be matched for basal cortisol levels before the response to CRF infusion can be interpreted. Finally, it should be noted that most of these studies have employed high doses of CRF that test the maximal output of the system, but do not address the possibility of a shift in threshold dose or an increased sensitivity to lower doses of CRF.

In Cushing's disease, the pathophysiology of the increased response to CRF is fairly clear: There is an increase in total stores of ACTH/β-E accompanied by a decrease in sensitivity to negative steroid feedback. In depression, the situation is unfortunately unclear. Even if depression is accompanied by an increase in CRF release, as long postulated, it is unclear to what degree CRF receptor down-regulation occurs and how that would influence the HPA axis. Work by Vale and colleagues (Rivier & Vale, 1983; Vale et al., 1983) and our own work (Young & Akil, 1985) suggest that down-regulation of the CRF receptor in vivo or even after chronic, continuous exposure to CRF in vitro is relatively small in magnitude (Vale et al., 1983; Young & Akil, 1985). Since CRF appears to act as a promoter of both biosynthesis and release, down-regulation of CRF receptors might be outweighed by an increase of ACTH in the releasable pools (Vale et al., 1983). Thus, a decreased response to CRF infusion as demonstrated by Gold et al. (1984) would not be the expected result. It may be that the final answer will await another level of studies further up the HPA axis, that is, studies evaluating the neurotransmitter regulation of CRF neurons themselves. Studies by Risch (1982) have attempted to address this issue by measuring the β-E response to infusion of physostigmine, a cholinesterase inhibitor, which appears to promote acetylcholine-induced release of CRF from the hypothalamus. These investigators found an increased release of β-E into the plasma after physostigmine administration in endogenous depressives (in contrast to controls), suggesting either an increased release of CRF or an increased pituitary sensitivity to CRF. If we return to our previous hypothesis that different levels of the HPA axis may use their own regulatory mechanisms to compensate for dysfunction at another level of the HPA axis, one might speculate that a number of different regulatory strategies with differing sensitivities to releasers and feedback may be used by the system, presenting a picture that is far from homogeneous.

FUTURE DIRECTIONS

The study of the dysregulation of the HPA axis in affective disease is at a very early stage. As a field, we have just begun to generate the technical and a theoretical base for the detailed study of the brain and endocrine biology of mental disease. The pituitary peptide studies summarized above clearly need to be replicated, expanded, and improved. Among the necessary factors to be considered is the standardization of plasma peptide measures (ACTH and β-E), the coordinate measure of both substances in the same patients, and consideration of intrinsic biological variables such as sex, age, and menstrual status.

Releasing factor challenge studies need to be broadened from CRF to include AVP and their interaction. These studies (and their logical counterparts using CRF and AVP antagonists) should be a rich source of information about corticotroph function and, by implication, the input of the CRF and AVP systems from the hypothalamus.

Finally, in a few years, it should be possible to study the brain chemistry of depression more directly (albeit postmortem) via the quantitation of specific mRNAs. It has become clear that the mRNA coding for a particular peptide (CRF, AVP, POMC), receptor (corticosteroid, ACTH, cholinergic muscarinic), enzyme (dopamine β-hydroxylase, tyrosine hydroxylase, choline acetylase), or peptide-processing enzyme reflect both general cellular regulation and use of those materials in the 24–48 hours prior to death. As such, knowledge of the specific levels of these mRNAs reflects the synthesis rates in the particular cells of origin. For example, if one could quantitate CRF mRNA in the paraventricular nucleus of hypothalamus of accidental death victims ("normals") and endogenously depressed subjects, it would be possible to infer CRF cellular activity (and probable CRF release rate). Such a study (or its analogue in pituitary with POMC mRNA, or the choline acetylase mRNA in the nucleus basalis acetylcholine system) would be very valuable in determining how these various neuronal systems are regulated in ED. While such studies would be very useful, they still would not imply causation, merely major brain regulatory events. The genetics of the disease(s) itself, that is, its cause(s), will involve a variety of types of new information, including very careful, patient population characterization followed by more detailed molecular genetics of the central nervous system itself.

Acknowledgments

This work was supported by NIMH Grant MH36168 (SW), NIDA Grant DA02265 (HA), and NIMH RSDA Grant MH00427 (EY).

References

Akil, H., Madden, J., Patrick, R. L., & Barchas, J. D. (1976). Stress-induced increase in endogenous opiate peptides; concurrent analgesia and its partial reversal by naloxone. In H. W. Kosterlitz (Ed.), *Opiates and endogenous opioid peptides* (pp. 63–79). Amsterdam: Elsevier.

Akil, H., Shiomi, H., & Matthews, J. (1985). Induction of the intermediate pituitary by stress: Synthesis and release of a nonopioid form of β-endorphin. *Science, 227,* 424–426.

Akil, H., Ueda, Y., & Lin, H.-S. (1981). A sensitive coupled HPLC/RIA technique for separation of endorphins: Multiple forms of β-endorphin in rat pituitary intermediate versus anterior lobe. *Neuropeptides (Edinburgh), 1,* 429–446.

Akil, H., & Watson, S. J. (1983). β-Endorphin and biosynthetically related peptides in the CNS. In L. Iversen, S. Iversen, & S. Snyder (Eds.), *Handbook of psychopharmacology* (Vol. 16, pp. 209–253). New York: Plenum Press.

Amir, S., & Amit, Z. (1979). The pituitary gland mediates acute and chronic pain responsiveness in stressed and nonstressed rats. *Life Science, 24,* 439–448.

Bethune, J. E., Nelson, D. H., & Thorn, G. W. (1957). Plasma adrenocorticotrophic hormone in Addison's disease and its modification by the administration of adrenal steroid. *Journal of Clinical Investigation, 36,* 1701–1707.

Birnberg, N. C., Lissitizky, J.-C., Hinman, M., & Herbert, E. (1983). Glucocorticoids regulate proopiomelanocortin gene expression *in vivo* at the levels of transcription and secretion. *Proceedings of the National Academy of Sciences of the U.S.A., 80,* 6982–6986.

Brown, W. A., Johnston, R., & Mayfield, D. (1979). The 24-hour dexamethasone suppression test in a clinical setting: Relationship to diagnosis, symptoms, and response to treatment. *American Journal of Psychiatry, 136,* 543–547.

Cahill, C. A., Matthews, J. D., & Akil, H. (1983). Human plasma β-endorphin-like peptides: A rapid, high recovery extraction technique and validation of radioimmunoassay. *Journal of Clinical Endocrinology and Metabolism, 56,* 992–997.

Carpenter, W. T., & Bunney, W. E. (1971). Adrenal cortisol activity in depressive illness. *American Journal of Psychiatry, 128,* 1–40.

Carr, D. B., Wool, C., Lydiard, B., Fisher, J., Gelenberg, A., & Klerman, G. (1984). Rate-sensitive inhibition of ACTH release in depression. *American Journal of Psychiatry, 141,* 590–592.

Carroll, B. J. (1972). The hypothalamic–pituitary–adrenal axis: Functions, control mechanisms and methods of study. In B. Davies, B. J. Carroll, & R. M. Mowbray (Eds.), *Depressive illness: Some research studies* (pp. 23–201). Springfield, IL: Charles C. Thomas.

Carroll, B. J., Curtis, G. C., & Mendels, J. (1976). Neuroendocrine regulation in depression. II. Discrimination of depressed from nondepressed patients. *Archives of General Psychiatry, 33,* 1051–1058.

Carroll, B. J., & Mendels, J. (1976). Neuroendocrine regulation in affective disorders. In E. Sachar (Ed.), *Hormones, behavior and psychopathology* (pp. 193–224). New York: Raven Press.

Carroll, B. J., Feinberg, M., Greden, J. F., Tarika, J., Albala, A., Haskett, R., James, N., Kronfol, Z., Lohr, N., Steiner, M., de Vigne, J. P., & Young, E. A. (1981). A specific laboratory test for the diagnosis of melancholia. *Archives of General Psychiatry, 38,* 15–22.

Catania, A., Cantalassa, L., Orsatti, A., Mosca, G., Minonzio, F., Motta, P., Reschini, E., & Zanussi, C. (1984). Plasma ACTH response to the corticotropin releasing factor in patients with Cushing's disease. Comparison with the lysine vasopressin test. *Metabolism: Clinical and Experimental, 33*(5), 478–481.

Chrétien, M., & Seidah, N. (1981). Chemistry and biosynthesis of proopiomelanocortin: ACTH, MSHs, endorphins and their related peptides. *Molecular and Cellular Endocrinology, 21,* 101–127.

Dallman, M. F., & Jones, M. T. (1973). Corticosteroid feedback control of ACTH secretion: Effect of stress-induced corticosterone secretion on a subsequent stress response in the rat. *Endocrinology (Baltimore), 92,* 1367–1375.

Dallman, M. F., Jones, M. T., Vernikos-Danellis, J., & Ganong, W. F. (1972). Corticosteroid feedback control of ACTH secretion: Rapid effects of bilateral adrenalectomy on plasma ACTH in the rat. *Endocrinology (Baltimore), 91,* 961–968.

Dallman, M. F., & Yates, F. E. (1969). Dynamic asymmetries in the corticosteroid feedback path and distribution-metabolism-binding elements of the adrenal–cortical system. *Annals of the New York Academy of Sciences, 156,* 696–721.

Daly, J. R., Reader, S. C. J., Alaghband-Zadeh, J., & Halsmann, P. (1979). Observations on feedback regulation of corticotropin (ACTH) secretion in man. In M. T. Jones, B. Gillham, M. F. Dallman, & S. Chattopadhyay (Eds.), *Interaction within the brain–pituitary–adrenocortical system* (pp. 181–188). London: Academic Press.

De Souza, E., & Van Loon, G. (1982). Stress-induced inhibition of the plasma corticosterone response to a subsequent stress in rats: A nonadrenocorticotropin-mediated mechanism. *Endocrinology (Baltimore), 110,* 23–33.

Eipper, B., & Mains, R. (1980). Structure and function of proadrenocorticotropin/endorphin and related peptides. *Endocrine Reviews, 1,* 247–262.

Eipper, B. A., & Mains, R. E. (1981). Further analysis of posttranslational processing of β-endorphin in rat intermediate pituitary. *Journal of Biological Chemistry*, *256*, 5689–5695.

Fang, V. S., Tricou, B. J., Robertson, A., & Meltzer, H. Y. (1981). Plasma ACTH and cortisol levels in depressed patients: Relation to dexamethasone suppression test. *Life Sciences*, *29*, 931–938.

Fehm, H. L., Voigt, K. H., Lang, R., Beinert, K. E., Kummer, G. W., & Pfeiffer, E. F. (1977). Paradoxical ACTH response to glucocorticoids in Cushing's disease. *New England Journal of Medicine*, *297*, 904–907.

Gold, P. W., Chrousos, G., Kellner, C., Post, R., Roy, A., Augerinos, P., Schulte, H., Oldfield, E., & Loriaux, D. (1984). Psychiatric implications of basic and clinical studies with corticotropin releasing factor. *American Journal of Psychiatry*, *141*, 619–627.

Guillemin, R., Vargo, T., Rossier, J., Minick, S., Ling, N., Rivier, C., Vale, W., & Bloom, F. (1977). β-Endorphin and adrenocorticotropin are secreted concomitantly by the pituitary gland. *Science*, *197*, 1367–1369.

Herbert, E. (1981). Discovery of proopiomelanocortin—a cellular polyprotein. *Trends in Biochemistry*, *6*, 184–188.

Hermus, A., Pieters, G., Smals, A., Benraad, T., & Kloppenborg, P. (1984). Plasma adrenocorticotropin, cortisol and aldosterone responses to corticotropin releasing factor: Modulatory effects of basal cortisol levels. *Journal of Clinical Endocrinology and Metabolism*, *58*, 187–191.

Holsboer, F., Bardeleben, U., Gerken, A., Stalla, G. K., & Mueller, O. A. (1984). Blunted corticotropin and normal cortisol response to human corticotropin releasing factor in depression. *New England Journal of Medicine*, *311*, 1127.

Holsboer, F., Gerhen, A., Steiger, A., Benkert, O., Mueller, O., & Stalla, G. (1984). Corticotropin-releasing factor induced pituitary adrenal response in depression. *Lancet*, *1*, 55.

Jones, M. T., Brush, F. R., & Neame, R. L. B. (1972). Characteristics of fast feedback control of corticotropin release by corticosteroids. *Journal of Endocrinology*, *55*, 489–497.

Jones, M. T., Gillham, B., Greenstein, B. D., Beckford, A., & Holmes, M. C. (1982). Feedback action of adrenal steroids. In D. Canten & D. Pfaff (Eds.), *Current topics in neuroendocrinology: Adrenal action on brain*. Berlin: Springer-Verlag.

Jones, M. T., Tiptaft, E. M., Brush, F. R., Fergusson, D. A. N., & Neame, R. L. B. (1974). Evidence for dual corticosteroid receptor mechanisms in the feedback control of ACTH secretion. *Journal of Endocrinology*, *60*, 223–233.

Kalin, N. H., Weiler, S. J., & Shelton, S. E. (1982). Plasma ACTH and cortisol concentrations before and after dexamethasone. *Psychiatry Research*, *7*, 87–92.

Krieger, D. T., Liotta, A. S., Brownstein, M. J., & Zimmerman, E. A. (1980). ACTH, β-lipotropin and related peptides in brain, pituitary and blood. *Recent Progress in Hormone Research*, *36*, 277–345.

Lewis, J. W., Cannon, J. T., & Liebeskind, J. C. (1980). Opioid and nonopioid mechanisms of stress analgesia. *Science*, *208*, 623–625.

Lystras, H., Grossman, A., Perry, L., Tomlin, S., Wass, J. A., Coy, D. H., Schally, A. V., Rees, L. H., & Besser, G. M. (1984). Corticotropin releasing factor: Responses in normal subjects and patients with disorders of the hypothalamus and pituitary. *Clinical Endocrinology (Oxford)*, *20*(1), 71–80.

Mains, R. E., & Eipper, B. A. (1981). Differences in the posttranslational processing of β-endorphin in rat anterior and intermediate pituitary. *Journal of Biological Chemistry*, *265*, 5683–5688.

Mains, R. E., Eipper, B. A., & Ling, N. (1977). Common precursor to corticotropins and endorphins. *Proceedings of the National Academy of Science of the U.S.A.*, *74*, 3014–3018.

Matthews, J., Akil, H., Greden, J., Charney, D., Weinberg, V., Rosenbaum, A., & Watson, S. (1986). β-Endorphin/β-lipotropin-like immunoreactivity in endogenous depression: Effect of dexamethasone. *Archives of General Psychiatry*, *43*, 374–381.

Matthews, J., Akil, H., Greden, J., & Watson, S. J. (1982). Plasma measures of β-endorphin-like immunoreactivity in depressives and other psychiatric disorders. *Life Sciences*, *31*, 1867–1870.

Mueller, O., Dorr, H. G., Hagen, B., Stalla, G. K., & von Werder, K. (1982). Corticotropin releasing factor (CRF) stimulation test in normal controls and patients with disturbances of the hypothalamic-pituitary-adrenal axis. *Klinische Wochenschrift*, *60*, 1485–1891.

Mueller, O., Stalla, G., & von Werder, K. (1983). Corticotropin releasing factor: A new tool for the differential diagnosis of Cushing's syndrome. *Journal of Clinical Endocrinology and Metabolism*, *57*, 227–229.

Nakanishi, S., Inoue, A., Kita, T., Nakamura, M., Chang, A. C. Y., Cohen, S. N., & Numa, S. (1979). Nucleotide sequence of cloned cDNA for bovine corticotropin-β-lipotropin precursor. *Nature (London)*, *274*, 423–427.

Orth, D. N., DeBold, C. R., DeCherney, G. S., Jackson, R. V., Alexander, A. N., Rivier, J., Rivier, C., Spiess, J., & Vale, W. (1982). Pituitary microadenomas causing Cushing's disease respond to corticotropin-releasing factor. *Journal of Clinical Endocrinology and Metabolism*, *55*, 1017–1019.

Orth, D. N., Jackson, R. V., DeCherney, G. S., DeBold, R. C., Alexander, A. N., Island, D. P., Rivier, J., Rivier, C., Spiess, J., & Vale, W. (1983). Effect of synthetic ovine corticotropin-releasing factor: Dose-response of plasma adrenocorticotropin and cortisol. *Journal of Clinical Investigation*, *71*, 587–595.

Pedersen, R. C., Brownie, A., & Ling, N. (1980). Proadrenocorticotropin/endophin-derived peptides: Coordinate action on adrenal steriodogenesis. *Science*, *208*, 1044–1045.

Pieters, G., Hermus, A., Smals, A., Bartelink, A., Benraad, T., & Kloppenlorg, P. (1983). Responsiveness of the hypophyseal–adrenocorticol axis to corticotropin releasing factor in pituitary-dependent Cushing's disease. *Journal of Clinical Endocrinology and Metabolism*, *57*, 513–516.

Reader, S. C. J., Robertson, W. R., Alaghband-Zadeh, J., & Daly, J. R. (1980). Negative effects on adrenocorticotropin secretion by cortisol in Cushing's syndrome. *Journal of Endocrinology*, *87*, 60–61.

Reus, V. I., Joseph, M. S., & Dallman, M. F. (1982). ACTH levels after the dexamethasone suppression test in depression. *New England Journal of Medicine, 306,* 238–239.

Risch, S. C. (1982). β-Endorphin hypersecretion in depression: Possible cholinergic mechanisms. *Biological Psychiatry, 17,* 1071–1079.

Rivier, C., & Vale, W. (1983). Influence of the frequency of ovine corticotropin releasing factor administration on adrenocorticotropin and corticosterone secretion in rat. *Endocrinology (Baltimore), 113,* 1422–1426.

Roberts, J. L., Budarf, M. L., Baster, J. D., & Herbert, E. (1979). Selective reduction of proadrenocorticotropin/endorphin proteins and messenger ribonucleic acid activity in mouse pituitary tumor cells by glucocorticoids. *Biochemistry, 18,* 4907–4915.

Roberts, J. L., & Herbert, E. (1977). Characterization of a common precursor of corticotropin and β-lipotropin: Cell-free synthesis of the precursor identification of corticotropin peptides in the molecule. *Proceedings of the National Academy of Sciences of the U.S.A., 74,* 5300–5304.

Rubin, R., & Mandell, A. (1966). Adrenocorticoid activity in pathological emotional states: A review. *American Journal of Psychiatry, 123,* 384–400.

Sachar, E. J. (1967). Corticosteroids in depressive illness. *Archives of General Psychiatry, 17,* 544–553.

Sachar, E. J., Hellman, L., Fukushima, D. K., & Gallagher, T. F. (1970). Cortisol production in depressive illness. *Achives of General Psychiatry, 23,* 289–298.

Sachar, E. J., Hellman, L., Roffwarg, H. P., Halpern, F. S., Fukushima, D. K., & Gallagher, T. F. (1973). Disrupted 24-hour patterns of cortisol secretion in psychotic depression. *Archives of General Psychiatry, 28,* 19–24.

Sayers, G., & Sayers, M. A. (1948). Regulation of pituitary adrenocorticotroph activity during the response of the rat to acute stress. *Endocrinology (Baltimore), 40,* 265–273.

Sherman, B., Pfohl, B., Schlecter, J., & Winokur, G. (1982). Dissociation of plasma cortisol and ACTH responses to dexamethasone (dex) in healthy subjects and depressed patients. *Clinical Research, 30,* 722A.

Turkelson, C. M., Arimura, A., Culler, M. D., Fishback, J. B., Groot, K., Kanda, M., Luciano, M., Thomas, C. R., Chang, D., & Shimizu, M. (1981). *In vivo* and *in vitro* release of ACTH by synthetic CRF. *Peptides (New York), 2,* 425–429.

Turkelson, C. M., Thomas, C. R., Amimura, A., Chang, D., Chang, J. K., & Shimizu, M. (1982). *In vitro* potentiation of the activity of synthetic ovine corticotropin-releasing factor by arginine vasopressin. *Peptides (New York), 1,* 111–113.

Vale, W., & Fleischer, N. (1968). Inhibition of vasopressin-induced ACTH release from the pituitary by glucocorticoids *in vitro. Endocrinology (Baltimore), 83,* 1232–1236.

Vale, W., Speiss, J., Rivier, J., & Rivier, C. (1981). Characterization of 41-residue ovine hypothalamic peptide that stimulates secretions of corticotropin and β-endorphin. *Science, 213,* 1394–1397.

Vale, W., Vaughan, J., Smith, M., Yamamoto, G., Rivier, J., & Rivier, C. (1983). Effects of synthetic ovine corticotropin-releasing factor, glucocorticoids, catecholamines, neurohypophyseal peptides and other substances on cultured corticotropic cells. *Endocrinology (Baltimore), 113,* 1121–1130.

Young, E. A., & Akil, H. (1985). Corticotropin releasing factor stimulation of adrenocorticotropin/β-endorphin release: Effects of acute and chronic stress. *Endocrinology (Baltimore), 117,* 23.

Young, E. A., Lewis, J. W., & Akil, H. (1986). The preferential release of β-endorphin from the anterior pituitary lobe by corticotropin releasing factor (CRF). *Peptides, 7,* 603–607.

Zakarian, S., & Smyth, D. (1982). β-Endorphin is processed differentially in specific regions of rat pituitary and brain. *Nature (London), 296,* 250–252.

PART VI

THE EFFECTS OF HORMONES ON BEHAVIOR

19 BEHAVIORAL EFFECTS OF NONOPIOID PEPTIDES IN HUMANS

MARK A. SMITH
CHARLES B. NEMEROFF

Duke University Medical Center

Interest in the possibility that peptides might influence animal behavior occurred long before the development of sensitive radioimmunoassays and receptor binding techniques which would later demonstrate that peptides and their receptors exist throughout the central nervous system (CNS). Beginning with the pioneering work of de Wied concerning the CNS effects of ACTH analogues devoid of adrenocortical activity and vasopressin analogues devoid of antidiuretic activity, a number of animal behaviors were found to be influenced directly by neuropeptides quite independent of their peripheral actions. Subsequently, more neuropeptides were discovered and soon were found to influence brain–behavior functions, including thirst, appetite, sexual behavior, learning and memory, sleep, motor activity, nociception, and thermoregulation. These behavioral effects induced by peripherally administered peptides were viewed with skepticism because of the blood–brain barrier's relative impermeability to peptides. Nevertheless, during the past 10 years additional evidence has accumulated implicating peptides in the modulation of brain function of animals. This naturally led to the investigation of neuropeptide effects in humans, which is the subject of this chapter.

In the present treatise, we will review clinical investigations concerning the role of nonopioid peptides in several normal brain functions as well as in psychiatric disorders. We will focus on the following peptides: angiotensin II (AII), cholecystokinin (CCK), insulin, adrenocorticotropin (ACTH), vasopressin, gonadotropin-releasing hormone (GnRH), delta sleep-inducing peptide (DSIP), thyrotropin-releasing hormone (TRH), calcitonin, and melanocyte-stimulating hormone-release inhibiting factor (MIF). The rationale for studying the peptides that was derived from previous preclinical research studies will be briefly described and then the relevant clinical studies will be reviewed. The general strategy for studying the effect of peptides on behavior is to (1) observe behavioral effects in response to peripheral administration of peptide agonists, (2) block the physiological effects of endogenous peptides by administering their antagonists, and (3) measure endogenous levels of the peptide in tissues and body fluids by radioimmunoassay. This strategy will provide a framework for presenting evidence on the behavioral effects of peptides and their mechanism of action. However, measurement of neuropeptides in cerebrospinal fluid (CSF) will be mentioned only briefly, since this topic has been reviewed recently in detail (Iversen, Iversen, & Snyder 1983; Nemeroff & Bissette, 1986). Finally, the last part of the chapter will discuss possible mechanisms mediating the behavioral effects of peptides.

ANGIOTENSIN II

Thirst, the desire to drink liquids, can be seen as a behavioral mechanism to control fluid volume, blood pressure, and electrolyte balance. Angiotensin II (AII) plays a physiological role in fluid and electrolyte balance and therefore is in a key position to control thirst as well.

AII is an octapeptide synthesized in the circulation by successive cleavage of precursors through the action of two enzymes, renin and angiotensin converting enzyme. All the components of the renin–angiotensin system are also found in brain. However, many and possibly all of the central effects of AII may be mediated via circumventricular organs which lack the tight junctions between capillary endothelial cells that comprise the blood–brain barrier. Thus, the problem of how a polar molecule such as angiotensin could be produced in the periphery and yet influence brain function is readily explained by the existence of angiotensin receptors in circumventricular organs. The mechanism of action of other centrally acting peptides is less obvious, as will be discussed later. AII has several effects on fluid and electrolyte balance (for review, see Reid, 1984). It increases blood pressure, and the CNS site of action of this effect seems to be the area postrema in the medulla oblongata, though direct effects on arteriolar smooth muscle may also play an important role. AII also releases aldosterone from the adrenal cortex which, in turn, acts at the distal tubule to enhance sodium reabsorption. Also of significance to this discussion is the fact that AII increases vasopressin secretion, and in the rat, hypophysectomy reduces the pressor effect of AII by 50% (Severs, Summy-Long, Taylor, & Connor, 1970).

In animals, AII has two well-defined behavioral effects; it stimulates drinking and increases sodium appetite. A variety of experiments have shed light on the dipsogenic action of this peptide (Phillips, 1984). Fitzsimons was the first to demonstrate that water intake is elevated in a number of situations in which the activity of the renin–angiotensin system is increased. These situations include hypovolemia, water deprivation, renal artery constriction, and vena caval ligation (Fitzsimons, 1969). Second, in the rat and dog, drinking can be stimulated by low doses of AII that are within the physiological range (Trippodo, McCaa, & Buyton, 1976). Finally, nephrectomy or administration of sub-

stances that reduce the net functional activity of the renin–angiotensin system such as saralasin and captopril reduce water intake (Barney, Threatte, & Fregly, 1983). The sites of the dipsogenic action of AII appear to be the subfornical organ and the organum vasculosum of the lamina terminalis (OVLT). Destruction of either organ abolishes drinking responses elicited by centrally or peripherally administered AII (Fitzsimons, 1980). Plasma sodium is increased not only through the indirect effects of aldosterone, but also by AII itself. Slow intracranial infusions of AII into rats cause an increase in sodium intake in rats (Fitzsimons, 1978).

Human Studies

Several recent case reports measuring renin activity in various clinical situations are concordant with the hypothesis that AII may play a role in thirst regulation in humans. A 16-month-old infant with a renin-secreting Wilms' tumor was noted to drink one-half gallon of water per day (Sheth, Tank, Blaedel, & Good, 1978). Plasma renin was elevated 50-fold. The polydipsia was alleviated after surgical removal of the tumor. Two other children with polydipsia have been identified who had renal artery stenosis and elevated renin activity (Chevalier, 1984). Treatment of the stenosis decreased their water intake. Propranolol, a β-adrenergic receptor antagonist which decreases renin activity, also decreased thirst. An adult with sudden onset of drinking more than 4 liters of water per day was found to have a renal artery thrombosis and high renin activity (Denamur, Kaloustian, Veyssier, & Plouin, 1984).

No reports have measured AII or renin activity in patients with psychogenic polydipsia. However, some psychiatric patients who develop hyponatremia have elevated plasma vasopressin concentrations. The etiology and pathogenesis of these disturbances in fluid and electrolyte balance remain obscure.

Because of angiotensin's pressor effects, evaluation of the effects of large doses of AII in humans on water intake has not been conducted. Such experiments will be required before we can conclude that AII plays a physiological role in human thirst, as it is believed to do in other mammals.

CHOLECYSTOKININ

Satiety

Perhaps the most compelling evidence for a behavioral effect of a peptide exists for CCK, a hormone in the proximal small intestine which causes contraction of the gallbladder. Satiety has often been associated with a feeling of fullness. Thus, nerve signals from a distended stomach were assumed to convey a satiety signal and terminate eating. Teleologically, it is not surprising that gut hormones such as CCK might play a role in feeding behavior. It has long been known that animals eat more when they sham feed compared to when they eat naturally, and when food enters the digestive tract, this stimulus may elicit the release of humoral substances. However, the notion of a humoral mechanism of satiety was entertained seriously when Gibbs, Young, and Smith (1973) administered a 10% pure extract of CCK and found a dose-dependent inhibition of food intake in the rat. The satiety effect of CCK-33 or CCK-8 persists for 30 minutes after each intraperitoneal (i.p.) injection. It had no effect on water intake and did not produce its effect by making food aversive, as determined in the bait shyness paradigm, but controversy over the issue of whether CCK induces satiety by an effect secondary to malaise has still not been resolved (Deutsch & Hardy, 1977). The behavioral action of CCK depends on the presence of a sulfate group on the tyrosine in the seventh position from the carboxy-terminal end (for review, see Smith, 1984).

A physiological role for CCK in satiety must now be considered more plausible because the mechanism of action of CCK appears to be mediated by gastric vagal afferent fibers on the peripheral side of the blood–brain barrier. Gastric vagotomy abolishes the satiating effect of CCK-8 in rats (Smith, Jerome, Gushin, Eterno, & Simansky, 1981). Moreover, the abdominal vagus possesses specific CCK-8 receptors, as demonstrated with autoradiography, accessible to blood-borne CCK (Zarbin, Wamsley, Innis, & Kuhar, 1981). The vagal afferents project to the nucleus tractus solitarius.

Human Studies

The first study examining the satiety effects of CCK in humans employed a 20% pure CCK preparation which was given intravenously to 10 normal subjects (Sturdevant & Goetz, 1976). Although rapid intravenous infusion of the CCK given over a 30-second period prior to eating significantly decreased food intake, a slower 20-minute infusion produced the opposite effect—a 22% increase in food intake. No significant side effects occurred in this double-blind study. A second study using the synthetic C-terminal octapeptide of CCK failed to demonstrate a satiety effect (Greenway & Bray, 1977). However, the doses used were small (usually 20 μg/kg), and the subjects had a time limit of 20 minutes in which to ingest the food.

Subsequent clinical studies seemed to confirm the hypothesis that CCK was a satiety signal in humans as well as animals. Kissileff, Pi-Sunyer, Thornton, and Smith (1981) gave CCK-8 as a 10 to 15-minute intravenous infusion which closely resembled the fairly rapid physiological rise in plasma CCK levels during a meal (Lilja et al., 1984). This double-blind study found a significant decrease in food intake of the normal subjects. Specifically, CCK caused the nonobese male subjects to stop eating sooner without any associated subjective changes in fullness, taste, or feelings of hunger. CCK's ability to shorten the duration of the meal without changing the rate of eating is consistent with a satiety rather than aversive effect. Although this study used liquid food, CCK also seems to decrease intake of solid food (Stacher, Steinringer, Schnierer, Schneider, & Winklehner, 1982). When larger doses of CCK were given intravenously, the nonobese subjects reported feelings of fullness and satiety. Objective tests of sensorimotor performance and heart rate indicated decreased activation in response to CCK. Moreover, θ activity on electroencephalography (EEG) also increased with CCK infusions consistent with postprandial satiety and deactivation.

Another study using obese men showed similar satiety effects of CCK as seen in normal weight controls (Pi-Sunyer, Kissileff, Thornton, & Smith, 1982). Thus, obese humans, like obese rats, are apparently not resistant to the satiety effect of CCK. Whether obese or bulimic humans release smaller quantities of CCK in response to a meal compared to normals remains to be determined. Sensitive and specific radioimmunoassays for plasma CCK now exist which should make such physiological experiments feasible (Izzo, Brugge, & Praissman, 1984). However, studies already completed suggest that CCK may be of therapeutic value in eating disorders and obesity.

Schizophrenia

Based on compelling evidence of colocalization of CCK and dopamine in the mesolimbic system (Hokfelt *et al.*, 1980) and evidence that CCK concentrations in brains of schizophrenics are lower than normal (Wang, White, & Voigt, 1984), the effects of treatment with CCK or a related homologous decapeptide, ceruletide, on the symptoms of schizophrenia have been studied. Moroji, Watanabe, Aoki, and Itoh (1982) treated 20 chronic schizophrenic patients maintained on antipsychotic drugs with a single injection of ceruletide (0.3 or 0.5 μg/kg iv), and the Brief Reactive Rating Scales (BPRS) was used to rate symptoms in an open study. After the low dose, 5 of the 12 patients showed improvement in mood and 1 patient reported a reduction in auditory hallucinations. After the high dose of the peptide, improved mood was noted in 16 patients and reduction in auditory hallucinations was observed in 3 patients. These improvements were reported to persist for 3 weeks after injection. Another group has studied the effects of CCK-33 (0.3 μg/kg iv) in chronic schizophrenia (Bloom, Nair, & Schwartz, 1983; Nair, Bloom, & Nestoros, 1982). Six chronic paranoid schizophrenic patients maintained on neuroleptic drugs were studied in their first trial. In this open, uncontrolled study, CCK produced a significant reduction in the BPRS score, which was maintained for 6 weeks. In a second study, a single dose of CCK-8 (0.04 μg/kg iv) was administered to 8 chronic schizophrenic patients maintanied on neuroleptic drugs. A rapid improvement in psychopathology was observed and their BPRS and Present State Examination scores were significantly reduced. In contrast, no changes in the nurses observation scale were observed. Peak improvement was observed 6 days post-CCK injection.

Stimulated by these preliminary findings, three research groups have evaluated the effects of ceruletide in schizophrenia using a double-blind, placebo-controlled protocol. The results have been quite disappointing. Hommer *et al.* (1984) treated 8 neuroleptic-treated schizophrenic patients with ceruletide (increasing intramuscular doses beginning at 0.3 μg/kg twice per day to reach a final dose of 0.6 μg/kg). The peptide produced no amelioration in schizophrenic symptoms as assessed by several rating scales, including the BPRS. Albus, Ackenheil, Munch, and Naber (1984) have conducted both an open study (6 patients) and a double-blind study (20 patients) with ceruletide. No antipsychotic effects of the peptide were observed. Lotstra, Verbanck, Mendlewicz, and Vanderhaeghen, (1984) found no effect of caerulein (30–300 pmole/kg for 9 days) in 9 schizophrenics. Finally, Mattes, Hum, Rochford, and Orlosky (1985), in a double-blind study of 17 chronic neuroleptic-treated schizophrenic patients, administered ceruletide (0.6 μg/kg im) or placebo (1 week apart). The evaluation included ratings of 29 variables related to prognosis in schizophrenia as well as BPRS and SCL-90 scales. No beneficial effects of the peptide were observed.

There is clearly good evidence that CCK acts as a satiety agent. This is supported by the fact that it transmits its signal via gastric vagal afferent fibers, thus avoiding the need to invoke "physiological prestidigitation" in order to explain how a peptide might cross the blood–brain barrier in sufficient quantities to influence behavior. No clear evidence has accrued to suggest that abnormalities in peptide secretion are responsible for the eating disturbances seen in anorexia, bulimia, obesity, depression, and so on. However, there is sufficient circumstantial evidence to warrant further investigation. Regardless of the etiology of these eating disorders, CCK may be of real therapeutic value in treating disorders such as obesity and bulimia.

CALCITONIN

Appetite

Calcitonin is a 32 amino acid peptide produced in the C cells of the thyroid which elicits hypocalcemic and hypophosphatemic effects. Calcitonin receptors exist in the human hypothalamus, limbic system, and possibly the circumventricular organs (Sagar, Henke, & Fischer, 1984). An inhibitory effect of peripherally administered calcitonin on eating in rats was demonstrated by Freed, Perlow, and Wyatt (1979). This action of calcitonin is long-lasting (24 hours) when compared to that of CCK (minutes). In a retrospective study of 9 psychiatric patients who received a single subcutaneous injection of salmon calcitonin, the weights were reduced slightly (2%), but significantly at 12–36 hours after receiving the calcitonin compared to 1 week before or after (Perlow, Freed, Carman, & Wyatt, 1980). This group also examined plasma calcitonin concentrations in anorexic patients, but found no difference from controls (Freed, Bing, Anderson, & Wyatt, 1984), and no significant differences were noted in those who binged on food. It is therefore unclear at this time whether calcitonin has an effect on human appetite or satiety. Calcitonin gene-related peptide, which has been found in the CNS, may have anorexic effects that are more potent than calcitonin (Morley, Krahn, Gosnell, Billington, & Levine, 1984).

Affect

Disorders of calcium metabolism can sometimes produce changes in affect. For instance, depression and lethargy are often seen in patients with hypercalcemia due to hyperparathyroidism. Conversely, hypocalcemic states can produce irritability, paranoia, and mania-like syndrome. Calcitonin reduces serum calcium and phosphorus concentrations while increasing CSF calcium concentrations. Thus, it was of interest to evaluate its effects on mood. Carman, Wyatt, Smith Post, and Ballenger (1984) have recently reviewed this subject. In two trials, calcitonin was administered to 8 unmedicated manics and 22 manic patients on lithium and/or neuroleptics. Calcitonin significantly attenuated the irritability, euphoria, and hyperactivity in 26 of the 30 patients. Depression was increased in most of the patients. Reduced CSF calcitonin in patients with mania has also been reported by this group. Another group found that calcitonin caused improvements in agitation, anxiety, and mood in 9 depressed subjects in an open study (Mussini, Agricola, Moia, Fiore, & Rivolta, 1984).

Whether the reduction of hyperactivity is a direct effect of calcitonin or secondary to serum calcium changes and subsequent alterations in CNS excitability remains to be determined. It will also be of interest to determine if calcitonin gene regulatory peptide possesses behavioral effects.

Analgesia

Recently there have been several open trials concerning the effects of calcitonin in various pain states. For example, Gennari et al. (1985) studied the effects of salmon and human calcitonin in cancer patients with painful osteolytic metastases. Salmon calcitonin was more effective in reducing bone pain than human calcitonin and placebo. Moreover, there was a significant increase in plasma β-endorphin-like immunoreactivity in the patients treated with salmon calcitonin.

INSULIN

Insulin was probably the first peptide observed to influence human behavior. Early in the century physicians had noticed the hunger and improved nutrition in diabetic patients treated with insulin. Pitfield (1923) was perhaps the first to treat malnourished patients with insulin. This does not appear to be a direct effect of insulin per se but rather is mediated by a decrease in blood glucose levels which in turn is "sensed" by specific cells in the ventromedial area of the hypothalamus, that is, the glucostat (Mayer, 1955). The hunger induced by insulin is a behavioral response to the abnormal hypoglycemic state.

More recent studies have suggested that insulin may also act directly to decrease eating. Insulin receptors have been found in circumventricular organs, and several reports suggest that insulin administered intravenously raises CSF insulin levels. However, recently Reiser, Lenz, Bernstein, and Dorn (1985) concluded from a clinical study involving measurement of insulin in CSF and blood of humans that insulin-like immunoreactivity in CSF is independent of plasma insulin levels. When insulin is infused at a slow rate into the periphery such that hypoglycemia is prevented, however, food intake decreases and there is a decrease in body weight. Intracerebroventricular injection of insulin into baboons decreases food intake in a dose-dependent manner (Woods, Lotter, McKay, & Porte, 1979). Obese humans have been reported to have increased CSF insulin concentrations when compared to normals, suggesting that CNS insulin may serve to signal an excess in adipose tissue (Owen, Reichard, Boden, & Shuman, 1974). Thus, an excess of insulin may serve as a satiety signal if it is not obviated by the appetite-stimulating effects of hypoglycemia.

GONADOTROPIN-RELEASING HORMONE

Sexual Behavior

It is well known that sexual receptivity in female mammals such as the rat is closely linked to changes in estrogen and progesterone secretion during the ovarian (e.g., estrus or menstrual) cycle. The secretion of these gonadal steroids as well as testosterone secretion in the male are controlled by the pituitary gonadotropic hormones, luteinizing hormone (LH) and follicle-stimulating hormone (FSH), which are in turn regulated by the hypothalamic peptide gonadotropin-releasing hormone (GnRH). GnRH-induced release of LH occurs just prior to the onset of the sexual receptive period in the female rat. Furthermore, the fact that GnRH is present in areas such as the medial preoptic-anterior hypothalamus which are known to influence sexual behavior suggested that GnRH might mediate the central regulation of sexual libido. Subcutaneous injections of GnRH which potentiated sexual behavior in estrogen-primed ovariectomized and/or hypophysectomized female rats provided the first evidence for a behavioral effect of GnRH (Moss & McCann, 1973; Pfaff, 1973). Intraventricular injection of a potent GnRH antagonist profoundly reduced normal sexual receptivity in female rats, suggesting that GnRH has a physiological role in regulating sexual behavior in the rat (Dudley, Vale, Rivier, & Moss, 1982). The ability of GnRH to stimulate male and female sexual behavior independently of steroid hormones now seems fairly well established in animals.

The effects of GnRH on human sexual behavior are suggestive but inconclusive. Early clinical studies examined the endocrine and behavioral effects of GnRH in men, some of whom probably had hypogonadism. GnRH induced an increase in libido and frequency of erections and ejaculations concurrently with an increase in plasma LH and testosterone levels in a patient who had undergone delayed puberty and who initially had low LH and testosterone levels (Van Loon & Brown, 1975). In 4 patients with oligospermia, GnRH produced an increase in libido and sexual potency after 1 month of treatment despite no change in plasma testosterone concentrations (Schwartzstein et al., 1975). GnRH may have had a potent placebo effect in these studies. However, in a double-blind study involving 20 sexually impotent men who had no apparent endocrine abnormalities and had previously been unable to sustain normal erections, GnRH given as nasal spray for 14 weeks produced a statistically significant increase in sexual performance after 6 weeks (Benkert, Jordan, Dahlen, Schneider, & Gammel, 1975). Another double-blind study with subcutaneous injections of GnRH also produced an increase in the spontaneity of erections without any apparent change in mood (Davies et al., 1976). Likewise, McAdoo et al. (1978) found no change in mood or behavior, but did report an increase in speed of performance on certian motor tasks and increased alertness in normal males within 3 hours after intravenous administration of GnRH. These changes coincided with an increase in plasma testorterone levels. However, Evans and Distiller (1979) found that GnRH facilitated the ability of erotic stimuli to produce an erection in normal males within 40 minutes of injection before significant changes in plasma testosterone has occurred. Although these results are of interest, more studies are required before the clinical efficacy of GnRH may be ascertained. The effects of GnRH antagonists on normal libido would be of interest as well.

Affective Disorders

The only report we are aware of concerning treatment with GnRH in affective disorders is a brief note by German and Stampfer (1979). In this uncontrolled study of 20 patients with major depression (unipolar or bipolar) and 8 patients with "stress-associated" depression (no criteria for either diagnosis), each patient received a single intramuscular injection of GnRH (500 μg). All 27 patients reported improved sleep the following night and the 8 patients characterized as stress-associated depressions continued to have improved sleep for several months. No indication of concurrent medication status was provided, no controls were included, and no statistical comparison was performed.

DELTA SLEEP-INDUCING PEPTIDE

The search for sleep-inducing substances has a long history, beginning with reports that CSF or serum from sleep-deprived dogs induced sleep when introduced into the fourth ventricle of normal dogs. The fact that heating to 65°C destroyed the sleep-inducing properties of the fluid suggested that the active substance might be a peptide or protein. Monnier went on to find that a substance isolated from cerebral venous blood of rabbits whose medial thalamic nuclei had been electrically stimulated produced slow wave sleep when injected into normal animals (Monnier & Hosli, 1964). The substance was identified as a nonapeptide and termed delta sleep-inducing peptide (DSIP) (Schoenenberger & Monnier, 1977). DSIP appears to modulate sleep when injected peripherally into animals and humans.

A group in Switzerland has postulated that DSIP may function to reset sleep–wake cycles rather than serve as an immediate hypnotic agent. In 6 of 7 patients with insomnia, 2 weeks of DSIP injections produced 7 months of relief from insomnia as well as an increase in daily performance (Kaeser, 1984). In a double-blind study, three injections of DSIP produced a statistically significant increase in REM sleep, a decrease in arousal from sleep, and a decrease in the proportion of Stage I sleep as well as an increase in daytime performance in insomniacs (Schneider-Helmert, 1984). Once again, these effects seemed to last for weeks after the injection period and were thought to represent a change in the circadian sleep–wake cycle. Recently, Schneider-Helmert (1985) has comprehensively reviewed the clinical trials with DSIP. The peptide appears to be a safe and effective agent that improves sleep quality and quantity after intravenous injection.

Reduced levels of DSIP were recently found in the CSF of patients with depression (Lindstrom, Ekman, Walleus, & Widerlov, 1985). Interestingly, there was a trend, though not significant, in which DSIP levels were inversely correlated to the magnitude of the sleep disturbance in these patients.

ACTH

The concept that hormones secreted by the pituitary might influence adaptive behavior stemmed from the observation that hypophysectomized rats had deficits in the acquisition and retention of learned behaviors (Applezweig & Baudry, 1955). The pioneering studies of de Wied (1965) showed that treatment with ACTH and MSH normalized the defective learning of hypophysectomized rats and supported the idea that these hormones might play a physiological role in memory and attention.

Adrenocorticotropic hormone (ACTH) and related peptides such as MSH, which shares 13 amino acids with ACTH, delayed extinction of avoidance behavior in rats. The animals were trained to initiate a response in order to avoid receiving an aversive stimulus such as a painful electric shock. After learning to avoid the shock, the shock was turned off and the animals tested to determine how long they continued to respond in the absence of negative reinforcement (extinction trial). Animals given α-MSH during the extinction period continued to respond during extinction longer than controls (Bohus & de Wied, 1966). The ACTH neuropeptides were also found to facilitate acquisition of shuttle box avoidance behavior and alleviate the amnesia produced by CO_2 inhalation of electroconvulsive shock in rats (Sandman & Kastin, 1981).

Although these early studies suggested that ACTH-related peptides might enhance short-term memory processes, later studies indicated that these substances might influence attention or motivational processes rather than memory per se. Rats trained with a two-choice visual discrimination task to avoid shock by running to the white door did not learn faster when treated with MSH. However, when the task was reversed such that the black door was the correct response, rats treated with MSH required approximately 50% fewer trials to solve this reversal learning problem, suggesting that the animals might be more attentive to a change in the test (Sandman and & Kastin, 1981). A separate study by Martinez, Vasquez, Jensen, Soumiren-Mourat, and McGaugh (1979) indicated that $ACTH_{4-9}$ enhanced acquisition of passive avoidance behavior only when administered prior to training. When given immediately after training or 1 hour prior to retention testing, it was ineffective.

Thus, most studies indicate that ACTH/MSH increases selective attention, allowing the animal to focus on the task at hand. There is no good evidence that these peptides have any effect on consolidation or retrieval of memory. Either peripheral or central (parafasicular thalamic area) administration causes a delay in extinction. The behavioral effects of the ACTH analogues are generally short-lived, lasting from 1 to 24 hours. The effects of the ACTH peptides are not dependent on their endocrine actions, since they are effective in hypophysectomized or adrenalectomized animals. In addition, analogues such as $ACTH_{4-10}$, which are devoid of endocrine action, are capable of enhancing attention and motivation.

Human Studies

Most clinical studies are in agreement with animal studies in which ACTH-related peptides were found to influence attention. Endroczi, Lissak, Fekete, and de Wied (1970) were the first to demonstrate that ACTH had a behavioral effect in humans. Administration of this peptide to normal volunteers caused an attenuation of habituation to a repeated sound stimulus. Miller, Kastin, Sandman, Fink, and Van Veen (1974) gave an intravenous injection of $ACTH_{4-10}$ (30 mg) to 20 male medical students prior to a test session in which the volunteers had to discriminate between two warning signals before they made the appropriate response. The peptide treatment did not influence the reaction time, but it did alter the EEG in the interval between a response and the next warning signal, with a significant increase in α frequency consistent with increased vigilance. The subjects also showed decreased

anxiety and improved visual retention in the Benton Visual Retention Test, but did not improve their performance of a verbal task.

A series of studies by Sandman and his colleagues indicated that ACTH improves attention. In the first study, subjects were given $ACTH_{4-10}$ (15 mg iv) over 4 hours in a double-blind design (Sandman, George, Nolan, van Riezen, & Kastin, 1975). Subjects had to make a visual discrimination between two stimuli differing in form and color. Initially they had to select a certain color. During the testing period another color was made "correct" by the investigator (intradimensional shift), while in a later part of the experiment a form was made relevant instead of a color (extradimensional shift). The treated subjects showed a significantly more rapid ability to compensate for a change in color (intradimensional shift) and a slower ability to adapt to a change in form as the relevant stimulus (extradimensional shift) compared to control subjects. The authors concluded that $ACTH_{4-10}$ increased selective attention to the exclusion of other environmental cues. It took 4 hours for the effects of the ACTH to be apparent. ACTH did not influence complex learning and a verbal memory task. Further physiological evidence of ACTH's influence on attentional processes was suggested by its ability to augment heart rate deceleration during the presentation of novel stimuli (Sandman *et al.*, 1977). Finally, Ward, Sandman, George, and Shulman (1979) examined the effects of $ACTH_{4-10}$ (30 mg/subcutaneously) in 12 male and 12 female volunteers on their ability to remember if the items presented during a trial were part of an earlier presented set ranging between 1 and 4 items. The subjects pressed one key if the item was a member of the memory set and a second key if it was not. Data were plotted as a linear relation between reaction time and set size. Treatment with $ACTH_{4-10}$ reduced the reaction time by a fixed amount independently of the size of the memory set (1–4 items). Had memory been affected, reaction time would have been enhanced only for sets three and four. Thus, it was concluded that $ACTH_{4-10}$ facilitated attention to environmental stimuli rather than memory per se.

Gaillard and Sanders (1975) showed that ACTH analogues improved performance possibly by reducing mental fatigue. Normal volunteers treated with placebo showed only a slight improvement in their performance of a repeated serial task during a 30-minute continuous test period. Their learning by repetition was offset by increased errors and decreased reaction time toward the end of the trial. However, subjects treated with ACTH (30 mg/s.c.) showed fewer errors and faster reaction times later in the repeated visual discrimination trials. This suggests that ACTH improved their ability to concentrate so that performance did not decline toward the end of the test period. A second study using a very potent $ACTH_{4-9}$ analogue (5 mg by mouth) supported the idea that ACTH prevented the deterioration of reaction time and helped the subject to concentrate during continuous performance (Gaillard & Varey, 1979).

It is possible that the effects of ACTH differ, depending on sex and personality of the subjects. Veith, Sandman, George, and Stevens (1978) evaluated the effect of ACTH in women during their menstrual phase (plasma ACTH low) or during midcycle (plasma ACTH high). Verbal memory was slightly but not significantly better in women at midcycle compared to menstruation when given placebo. ACTH significantly improved verbal memory in women during menstruation (when endogenous ACTH was low), but impaired a visual reversal discrimination task in these women. These results are in contrast to previous studies using males in which ACTH had no effect on verbal memory, but enhanced visual discrimination and attention. Men were not included in Veith's study, so no direct comparison can be made, although Gaillard and Varey (1979) and Ward et al. (1979) examined both women and men and could detect no sex differences. Breier, Kain and Kanzett (1979) examined the effects of ACTH on introverted and extroverted males. ACTH improved mental performance only in extroverted subjects.

There is little or no evidence of an effect of ACTH on memory. $ACTH_{4-10}$ (30 mg/s.c.) did not alter consolidation or retrieval of memory when administered 30 minutes after unilateral electroconvulsive therapy (ECT) (d'Elia & Frederiksen, 1980). Failure of ACTH to influence an active conditioned avoidance response in humans has also been noted (Miller, Fischer, Groves, Rudrauff, & Kastin, 1977). Normal subjects were given $ACTH_{4-10}$ or diluent and then were taught to avoid an electric shock by pressing a key during a safe interval between a warning signal and the shock. ACTH did not influence either acquisition or extinction. This is in contrast to results obtained in lower animals, but of course such a task is much more difficult for animals.

Effects on Mentally Impaired Patients

Normal elderly subjects improved slightly or not at all when given ACTH analogues. Dornbush and Volavka (1976) found a slight increase in reaction time, but no change in mental capacity. Miller, Groves, Bopp, and Kastin (1980) reported improvement in visual retention and the effect was greater in men than in women. Those with a mild "organic dementia" showed an increase in "mood and vigor" and a trend toward decreased reaction time (Branconnier, Cole, & Gardos, 1979). No change in the Bender–Gestalt test or Wechsler Memory Scale was noticed. Moreover, in contrast to Miller et al. (1974), a decrease in the α rhythm on EEG was seen in these mildly demented patients (mostly in females).

Although decreases in ACTH levels in CSF have been observed in patients with Alzheimer's disease (Facchinetti et al., 1984), no improvement in mental performance was seen in 38 female Alzheimer patients given Org2766, the potent $ACTH_{4-9}$ analogue (40 mg p.o./day) (Martin et al., 1983). However, these patients were very severely demented.

Mentally retarded subjects have been reported to respond to ACTH fragments. Sandman, George, Waike, and Nolan (1976) repeated their visual dimensional shift protocol in a double-blind fashion in mentally retarded subjects. Treatment with ACTH once again improved performance on the intradimensional shift (color). However, ACTH also improved their ability to recognize that form was the correct parameter (extradimensional shift). In another study, $ACTH_{4-9}$ appeared to improve the work performance of mentally retarded subjects during a 2-week period (Sandman, Walker, & Lawton, 1980). Additionally, the drug also increased communication and sociability in these subjects.

In contrast to the successes with mentally retarded subjects, hyperactive and "learning disabled" children showed no improvement (Rappoport, Quinn, Copeland, & Burg, 1976).

Conclusions

ACTH might play a role in attention and memory, but further clinical studies will be necessary in order to clarify the subject. In humans and animals, ACTH seems to influence attention. Most of the studies in humans have used visual discrimination tasks in order to test the effects of ACTH. It might be helpful to supplement these data with more studies exploring the influence of ACTH-related peptides on the human EEG as a quantitative index of attention. The P300 wave is thought to be related to attentional processes. Does ACTH specifically alter the P300 wave or other evoked potentials? Combining evoked potential and brain electrical activity mapping (BEAM) may shed light on the role of ACTH in attention and motivation.

VASOPRESSIN

In addition to its well-known ability to increase the permeability of the renal collecting ducts to alter water reuptake and its direct action on the smooth muscle of the arterioles to increase blood pressure, arginine vasopressin (AVP) appears to mediate some behavioral processes as well. In particular, vasopressin has been implicated in memory. This was initially suggested by the observation that removal of the posterior pituitary from the rat interfered with the maintenance of escape behavior (de Wied, 1965). Pitressin, a crude extract of posterior pituitary tissue, was able to restore the normal rate of extinction. De Wied hypothesized that vasopressin delayed the extinction of a previously learned behavior by enhancing the memory trace. However, during the extinction phase, an animal is continuing to display the learned avoidance behavior despite the absence of negative reinforcement, the shock. Thus, an alternative hypothesis might be that retention of a learned behavior during extinction reflects a decreased ability to adapt to new environmental contingencies. However, vasopressin has minimal effects on the rate of acquisition of aversively motivated behaviors. Therefore, unlike ACTH, vasopressin seems to influence memory rather than attentional or motivational processes.

In addition to vasopressin's ability to reverse abnormal extinction behavior in posterior lobectomized rats, further evidence for a role of vasopressin in memory came from the following observations (de Wied, 1984). First, vasopressin increases resistance to extinction of avoidance behavior for days to weeks after a single injection. Second, the effects are apparently not due to its endocrine or pressor activities because analogues such as desglycinamide lysine vasopressin, which are devoid of such classical effects, are still capable of delaying extinction in passive avoidance tests. Third, Brattleboro rats with hereditary diabetes insipidus which are unable to synthesize vasopressin, display deficits in the consolidation of memory, which are reversed by peripheral vasopressin administration. Fourth, injection of an vasopressin antagonist into normal rats facilitated extinction—just the opposite of the peptide's effect (Le Moal et al., 1981). Vasopressin affects both consolidation and retrieval of the memory trace. When vasopressin is injected 1 hour after the initial learning trial, it enhanced retention of the memory upon retesting 24 hours later (consolidation). Moreover, vasopressin also improves retention when injected 1 hour prior to retrial (retrieval).

Human Studies

Investigation in humans tends to support a role for vasopressin in modulating memory, but the results differ in several important respects from the animal studies. Legros et al. (1978) were the first to examine the effect of vasopressin on memory and learning in normal humans after they had previously noted a decrease in neurophysin plasma levels in men older than age 50. In a double-blind study employing 23 normal males (aged 50–65) who received 16 IU AVP intranasally for 3 days, they found a significant improvement in attention, concentration, and motor rapidity as well as in immediate and delayed free recall memory. In another study examining the effects of the long-acting vasopressin analogue 1-desamino-8-D-arginine vasopressin (DDAVP), serial learning and word recall were improved in 6 young normal subjects after 2 weeks of treatment with the peptide (Weingartner, Gold, Ballinger, Smallberg, Summers, Rubinow, Post, & Goodwin, 1981). Beckwith, Petros, Kanaan-Beckwith, Cook, and Hang (1982) found that DDAVP increased selective attention in normal humans. In a single case study, vasopressin influenced only attention and arousal and had no effect on memory (Fehm-Wolfsdorf, Born, Voigt, & Fehm, 1984). However, in a recent double-blind crossover study, 48 healthy young and old males were given DDAVP daily for 1 week and then were tested for short-term memory by the Sternberg paradigm and for long-term memory by responding to a given word with words of that category beginning with a specified letter (Nebes, Reynolds, & Horn, 1984). DDAVP improved both short- and long-term episodic memory, but did not affect semantic memory or simple response time. In addition, the memory facilitation by DDAVP was similar regardless of age. They concluded that vasopressin enhanced actual memory retrieval rather than increasing general arousal. Therefore, studies in normal humans tend to support a role for vasopressin in memory consolidation and retrieval although unlike results from animal studies, vasopressin may influence human attention and motivation as well.

Effects on Memory-Impaired Individuals

In older individuals with Alzheimer's disease, DDAVP given 1 hour prior to testing significantly enhanced semantic memory (Weingartner, Kaye, Gold, Smallberg, Peterson, Gillin, & Ebert, 1981). Another study found improvement in verbal associative memory and visual recognition memory in 9 patients with progressive senile dementia treated for 1 week with lysine–vasopressin (Ferris & Reisberg, 1981). Of 4 depressed patients treated with DDAVP for 2 weeks 3 also showed increased recall of words independently of a change in mood (Weingartner, Gold, Ballenger, Smallberg, Summers, Rubinow, Post, & Goodwin, 1981). These effects on cognition persisted for 4 weeks after termination of drug treatment. In this same study, 2 depressed patients were given a list of words and asked to recall them 5 hours after ECT. DDAVP markedly improved their recall

compared to saline control. Likewise, Partap, Jos, and Dye (1983) found that AVP reversed the retrograde amnesia produced by ECT in 57 schizophrenics. In both these studies, vasopressin or DDAVP was administered for at least 1 week during the ECT treatments. Lehrer, Zabow, Egnal, and Belmaker (1983) failed to find an effect of vasopressin on ECT-induced amnesia, but DDAVP was administered only twice 2–3 hours after the ECT and 30 minutes prior to memory testing.

Oliveros *et al.* (1978) first reported therapeutic effects of lysine–vasopressin in patients with retrograde amnesia. Several studies were then conducted on alcohol-induced memory disturbances such as those seen in Korsakoff's syndrome in which access to long-term memory seems to be impaired. Le Bouef, Lodge, and Eames (1978) found a marked improvement associated with vasopressin treatment on performance in the Wechsler memory scale. However, Blake, Dodd, and Grimley-Evans (1978) were unable to demonstrate such an effect. Moreover, Laczi, Van Ree, Balogh *et al.* (1983) treated 14 patients with Korsakoff's syndrome for 7 days with intranasal desglycinamide–arginine vasopressin (DGAVP) and found no effect on attention or short- or long-term memory. Finally, Hennekens-Schinkel, Wintzen, and Lanser (1985) conducted a double-blind crossover study of the effects of DGAVP in 16 patients with memory disorders, including Alzheimer's disease, Korsakoff's syndrome, and head injury. No beneficial effects of the peptide were noted.

Vasopressin's effects on memory have been examined in several other syndromes, with mixed results. DDAVP helped 3 children with Lesch–Nyhan disease to learn an active avoidance task, though the positive results may have been due to normal repetitive learning because DDAVP was only administered on the last trial (Anderson, David, Bonnet, & Dancis, 1979). In a controlled double-blind crossover study, a small but statistically insignificant effect of DDAVP on various learning tasks was seen in children with an attention-deficit disorder (Eisenberg, Chazan-Gologorsky, Hattab, & Belmaker, 1984). Likewise, word list memory was not improved by DDAVP in Down's syndrome (Eisenberg, Hamberger-Bar, & Belmaker, 1984).

An important question is whether patients with central diabetes insipidus have impaired learning and memory as seen in Brattleboro rats. One study suggests that they do (Laczi et al., 1982), while another study by the same group found no difference in baseline performance between patients and controls (Laczi, Van Ree, Wagner et al., 1983). However, the control group in the later study was composed of hospitalized patients of different ages with a variety of diseases. Despite the uncertainty concerning baseline deficits in memory, DDAVP or DGAVP (with virtually no pressor effect) improved both short-term and long-term memory in diabetes insipidus patients as well as controls. DGAVP increased attention only in control subjects. However, both these studies tested the vasopressin analogues after an initial placebo treatment so that improvement with vasopressin may have been due, at least in part, to learning during the first placebo trial. Additional studies with diabetes insipidus patients using a double-blind crossover design are needed to resolve the important issue of vasopressin effects on memory deficits in these subjects.

Conclusions

Vasopressin is suggested to influence primarily memory and possibly attention either through its own action or secondarily via release of ACTH. It is relatively long acting in contrast to the short-term effects of ACTH. This situation is also complicated by the recent observation that oxytocin may impair memory (Fehm-Wolfsdorf et al., 1984b). Before the role of vasopressin in human memory can be more firmly established, a number of investigations need to be conducted. First, do patients with central diabetes insipidus possess memory deficits? Will vasopressin reverse these deficits? Additional studies with diabetes insipidus patients using a double-blind crossover design are needed to resolve the improtant issue of vasopressin's effects or possible memory deficits in these subjects. Second, is vasopressin's effect central or secondary to some peripheral effect such as changes in blood pressure?

Packard and Ettenberg (1985) found that vasopressin, but not DGAVP (which is devoid of pressor and endocrine activity), influ-enced extinction of a spatial learning task in rats. Further clinical studies with DGAVP are needed. Le Moal et al. (1981) used a vasopressin antagonist in rats to block the pressor effect of vasopressin. This antagonist blocked not only the vascular response, but also the behavioral effects of exogenous vasopressin. No behavioral studies in humans have been carried out using the vasopressin antagonist.

A physiological role for vasopressin in memory would be strengthened if a vasopressin antagonist could be shown to interfere with normal memory function. Clearly it is important to evaluate vasopressin's effects in a variety of test situations and to minimize its effects on the autonomic nervous system before one can ascertain whether peripheral administration of vasopressin truly influences human memory.

Affective Disorders

Gold and his colleagues (1984) have scrutinized the vasopressinergic system in affective disorders (see earlier) and have also studied the effects of a behaviorally active vasopressin analogue that is devoid of pressor activity, DDAVP, on cognitive function in depressed patients. The peptide was administered intranasally (40–160 μg/day for 2–7 weeks) to 4 depressed patients; controls received 60 μg DDAVP per day for 2–3 weeks. A statistically significant increase in learning and memory scores was observed in both the depressed patients and the control subjects after DDAVP treatment. In 2 of the 4 depressed patients, DDAVP produced an apparent antidepressant effect. Three other depressed patients exhibited improved cognitive function without any significant effect on their depressed mood.

Schizophrenia

Lysine-8-vasopressin was administered as a nasal spray to 19 schizophrenics in a double-blind crossover placebo-controlled study (Korsgaard, Casey, Damgaard-Pedersen, Jorgensen, & Gerlach, 1981). Some of the negative symptoms such as lack of energy were significantly improved using the BPRS scale, but 6 patients became agitated or aggressive during the vasopressin treatment.

THYROTROPIN-RELEASING HORMONE

Affective Disorders

The effects of TRH have been intensively studied in patients with affective disorders, and these findings have been comprehensively reviewed by Prange and his co-workers (Loosen & Prange, 1984; Prange & Loosen, 1984b). In 1972, Prange and Wilson reported that TRH (500 μg iv) produced a prompt, partial, but significant, antidepressant effect in 10 unipolar depressed women. The study used a placebo-controlled, double-blind crossover design, and the behavioral responses were assessed with the Hamilton Rating Scale for depression. Similar results were obtained by Kastin, Ehrensing, Schalch, and Anderson (1972). A large number of clinical trials with TRH have subsequently been conducted—the results have been quite disappointing. It is now clear that TRH is not a clincially efficacious antidepressant agent. However, one finding which has been confirmed many times is that approximately 25% of depressed patients exhibit a blunted or absent TSH response after intravenous TRH administration. This finding is described in detail in Chapter 15 of this volume.

Schizophrenia

The effects of TRH have been most widely studied in affective disorders, but a few studies with schizophrenic patients have been conducted as well. This literature has been reviewed most recently by Loosen and Prange (1984) in a comprehensive treatise. In general, the results are disappointing with the exception of one research group. In a single blind study, TRH was administered orally (4 mg/day) to 62 chronic (neuroleptic-treated) schizophrenic patients. A beneficial effect was reported in 75% of the patients within 2 weeks. A double-blind study of 143 chronic schizophrenic patients, by the same Japanese group, confirmed the initial finding. Motivation and social contact was repeatedly most improved. The studies in which TRH was administered intravenously to schizophrenic patients have been disappointing. Moreover, several investigators have reported that TRH worsens the symptoms of paranoid schizophrenic patients.

MELANOCYTE INHIBITORY FACTOR

The antidepressant effects of MIF-1 were first described by Ehrensing and Kastin (1974, 1978). In their first double-blind study, depressed women (involutional melancholia or manic–depressive illness, depressed type) received oral MIF-1 (60 or 150 mg) for 6 days. The lower dose was more effective than the higher one; 4 of 5 patients improved in the low-dose group. In their second study, this same group examined the effects of daily MIF-1 (75 or 750 mg, orally) in 8 depressed patients using a randomized double-blind design. Again the lower dose produced greater improvement than the higher one, or placebo, as assessed by four different depression rating scales. Recently, Levy, DeNigris, and Davis (1982) compared the effects of orally administered MIF-1 (60 mg/day) with imipramine (75 mg/day), a clinically efficacious trycyclic antidepressant, in patients fulfilling RDC criteria for major depressive disorder. Of the 6 patients receiving MIF-1, 3 did very poorly and were dropped from the study. These authors concluded that this tripeptide was devoid of antidepressant properties and was certainly not superior to imipramine. In contrast, van der Welde (1983) reported a rapid and robust antidepressant effect of MIF-1. In this study, 20 psychiatric inpatients (15 males, 5 females) who fulfilled RDC criteria for major depressive disorder were assigned in a double-blind study to either daily MIF-1 (60 mg orally) or imipramine (150 mg in a divided dose). The Hamilton and Zung Rating Scales as well as a global assessment scale were utilized, and the data were statistically evaluated by analysis of variance for repeated measures. The study was designed so that patients not improving after 1 week would be dropped—2 MIF-treated patients and 4 imipramine-treated patients were removed from the trial. Both MIF-1 and imipramine exerted a significant antidepressant effect, but the MIF-1 effect was more rapid; on day 8 of the study, the MIF-treated group had significantly lower Hamilton Rating Scale scores than the imipramine-treated group. These findings are concordant with those of Ehrensing and Kastin and indicate that MIF-1 may indeed possess antidepressant properties. Further work is clearly warranted in larger patient populations with this peptide.

CONCLUSIONS

We have reviewed the human trials of exogenous peptides with respect to their effects on normal and abnormal behavior. We have not discussed the now voluminous literature on the adenohypophyseal hormone responses to hypothalamic releasing factors in psychiatric patients. These findings have been comprehensively reviewed by Gold and Chrousos (1985) for CRF, and Prange and Loosen (1984b) and Loosen (Chapter 15, this volume) for TRH. Compared with animal studies, there is less convincing evidence that exogenous peptides influence human behavior. There are three main problems with the clinical studies:

1. Access to the CNS. Peripherally injected peptides apparently do not cross the blood–brain barrier to any appreciable extent (Meisenberg & Simmons, 1983). Even if the effects of the peripherally injected peptides were mediated by the extremely small fraction which entered the CSF via the choroid plexus or circumventricular organs or by some other mechanism, it would be impractical to administer large quantities of these peptides parentally, thus precluding their use clinically. With the exception of a few case reports in which peptides have been administered intrathecally, there are no studies of the direct central effects of these peptides. The microinjection of peptides into various brain regions of animals greatly strengthens the argument that they may influence animal behavior. Because similar experiments are impossible to conduct in humans, it is unlikely that we will gain much additional knowledge about the central effects of peptides until hydrophobic lipophilic analogues can be synthesized which cross the blood–brain barrier in appreciable quantities. However, it is also important to recognize that extraordinarily small quantities of neuropeptides are required to act at CNS receptors. Thus, even if only 1% of administered peptide reaches the CNS, it may produce appreciable neurochemical behavioral effects.

It is clear that some peptides truly influence behavior by acting at a receptor site on the peripheral side of the blood–brain barrier. CCK at vagal afferent nerves and angiotensin at the subfornical organ and OVLT are two such examples. Not coincidentally, the best evidence for a behavioral effect of a peptide in humans exists for CCK.

Until it is proved that other peptides have a peripheral site of action via vagal afferents, act to change local blood flow in the brain, or are carried to the hypothalamus by retrograde transport in the hypothalamic–hypophysial portal system, their putative centrally mediated behavioral effects will remain unconvincing.

2. Peripheral endocrine effects. Trying to determine whether the peptides have a direct behavioral effect is rendered even more difficult by the myriad of processes they influence in the periphery. Clearly vasopressin and ACTH have some sort of effect on attention and possibly memory, but are these effects secondary to general arousal, changes in blood pressure, and so on? The use of analogues devoid of classical endocrine effects helps to clarify these problems, but controversy still exists.

3. Lack of studies with peptide antagonists. Few potent and specific neuropeptide antagonists exist. However, with the exception of naloxone, the few that do exist have not been exploited to any degree in evaluating the role of neuropeptides in behavior. It is difficult to prove a physiological role for a substance based on experiments in which the substance is administered exogenously. Blocking the endogenous substance via the administration of an antagonist or antiserum is more instructive. Clinical studies using peptide antagonists are warranted.

Thus, with the possible exception of CCK, there is no conclusive evidence that neuropeptides influence human behavior. Until analogues are created which can readily gain access to the CNS or an ingenious sytem to deliver the peptides into the CNS is developed, there is little hope that peptides can be routinely used in a clinical setting. However, as the physiological role of each of the more than 40 neuorpeptides thus far identified in the brain becomes more evident, the development of a successful, novel treatment strategy designed to alter neuropeptide systems becomes more likely.

Acknowledgments

We are grateful to Mary Lassiter for preparation of this manuscript. The authors' research is supported by NIMH MH-39415, MH-40524, MH-40159, MH-42088, and NIA AG-05128. Charles B. Nemeroff is the recipient of a Nanaline H. Duke Fellowship from Duke University Medical Center.

References

Albus, M., Ackenheil, M., Munch, U., & Naber, D. (1984). Ceruletide: A new drug for the treatment of schizophrenic patients? *Archives of General Psychiatry, 41,* 528.

Anderson, L. T., David, R., Bonnet, K., & Dancis, J. (1979). Passive avoidance learning in Lesch-Nyhan disease: Effect of 1-desamino-8-arginine vasopressin. *Life Sciences, 24,* 905–910.

Applezweig, M. H., & Baudry, F. D. (1955). The pituitary-adrenocortical system in avoidance learning. *Psychological Reports, 1,* 417–420.

Barney, C. C., Threatte, R. M., & Fregly, M. J. (1983). Water deprivation-induced drinking in rats: Role of angiotensin II. *American Journal of Physiology, 244,* R244–R248.

Beckwith, B. E., Petros, T., Kanaan-Beckwith, S., Cook, D. I., & Hang, R. J. (1982). Vasopressin analogue (DDAVP) facilitates concept learning in human males. *Peptides (New York), 3,* 627–630.

Benkert, O., Jordan, R., Dahlen, H. G., Schneider, H. P. G., & Gammel, G. (1975). Sexual impotence: A double-blind study of LHRH nasal spray versus placebo. *Neuropsychobiology, 1,* 203–210.

Blake, D. R., Dodd, M. J., & Grimley Evans, J. (1978). Vasopressin in amnesia. *Lancet, 1,* 608.

Bloom, D. M., Nair, N. P. V., & Schwartz, G. (1983). CCK-8 in the treatment of chronic schizophrenia. *Psychopharmacology Bulletin, 19,* 361–363.

Bohus, B., & de Wied, D. (1966). Inhibitory and facilitatory effect of two related peptides on extinction of avoidance behavior. *Science, 153,* 318–320.

Branconnier, R. J., Cole, J. O., & Gardos, G. (1979). $ACTH_{4-10}$ in the amelioration of neuropsychological symptomatology associated with senile organic brain syndrome. *Psychopharmacology, 61,* 161–165.

Breier, C., Kain, H., & Konzett, H. (1979). Personality-dependent effects of the $ACTH_{4-10}$ fragment on test performances and on concomitant autonomic reactions. *Psychopharmacology, 65,* 239–245.

Carman, J. S., Wyatt, E. S., Smith, W., Post, R. M., & Ballenger, J. C. (1984). Calcium and calcitonin in bipolar affective disorder. *Frontiers of Clinical Neuroscience, 1,* 340–355.

Chevalier, R. L. (1984). Polydipsia and enuresis in childhood renin-dependent hypertension. *Journal of Pediatrics, 104,* 591–592.

Davies, T. F., Mountjoy, C. Q., Gornes-Pan, A., Wat-son, M. J., Hanker, J. P., Besser, G. M., & Hall, R. (1976). A double-blind crossover trial of gonadotropin-releasing hormone (LHRH) in sexually impotent men. *Clinical Endocrinology (Oxford), 5,* 601–607.

D'Elia, G., & Frederiksen, S.-O. (1980). $ACTH_{4-10}$ and memory in ECT-treated and untreated patients. *Acta Psychiatrica Scandinavica, 62,* 418–428.

Denamur, E., Kaloustian, E., Veyssier, P., & Plouin, P. F. (1984). Polyuria–polydipsia syndrome showing a renal infarction. *Clinical Nephrology, 22,* 107–108.

Deutsch, J. A., & Hardy, W. T. (1977). Cholecystokinin produces bait shyness in rats. *Nature (London), 266,* 196.

de Wied, D. (1965). The influence of the posterior and intermediate lobe of the pituitary and pituitary peptides in the maintenance of a conditioned avoidance behavior in rats. *International Journal of Neuropharmacology, 4,* 157–167.

de Wied, D. (1984). The importance of vasopressin in memory. *Trends in Neurosciences, 7,* 62–63.

Dornbush, R. L., & Volavka, J. (1976). $ACTH_{4-10}$: A study of toxicological and behavioral effects in an aging sample. *Neuropsychobiology, 2,* 350–360.

Dudley, C. A., Vale, W., Rivier, J., & Moss, R. L. (1982). The effect of LHRH antagonist analogues and an antibody to LHRH on mating behavior in female rats. *Peptides (New York), 2,* 393–396.

Ehrensing, R. H., & Kastin, A. J. (1974). Melanocyte-stimulating hormone release inhibiting hormone as an antidepressant: A pilot study. *Archives of General Psychiatry, 35,* 63–65.

Ehrensing, R. H., & Kastin, A. J. (1978). Dose-related biphasic effects of prolyl-lewcyl-glycinamide (MIF) in depression. *American Journal of Psychiatry, 135,* 562–566.

Eisenberg, J., Chazan-Gologorsky, S., Hattab, J., & Belmaker, R. H. (1984). A controlled trial of vasopressin treatment of childhood learning disorder. *Biological Psychiatry, 19,* 1137–1141.

Eisenberg, J., Hamberger-Bar, R., & Belmaker, R. H. (1984). The effect of vasopressin treatment on learning in Down's syndrome. *Journal of Neural Transmission, 60,* 143–147.

Endroczi, E., Lissak, K., Fekete, T., & de Wied, D. (1970). Effects of ACTH on EEG habituation in human subjects. *Progress in Brain Research, 32,* 254–262.

Evans, I. M., & Distiller, L. A. (1979). Effects of luteinizing hormone-releasing hormone on sexual arousal in normal men. *Archives of Sexual Behavior, 8,* 385–395.

Facchinetti, F., Nappi, G., Petraglia, F., Martignoni, E., Sinforano, E., & Gerazzani, A. R. (1984). Central ACTH deficit in degenerative and vascular dementia. *Life Sciences, 35,* 1691–1697.

Fehm-Wolfsdorf, G., Born, J., Voigt, K.-H., & Fehm, H.-L. (1984a). Behavioral effects of vasopressin. *Neuropsychobiology, 11,* 49–53.

Fehm-Wolfsdorf, G., Born, J., Voigt, K.-H., & Fehm, H.-L. (1984b). Human memory and neurohypophyseal hormones: Opposite effects of vasopressin and oxytocin. *Psychoneuroendocrinology, 9,* 285–292.

Ferris, S. H., & Reisberg, B. (1981). Clinical studies of neuropeptide treatment in impaired elderly. *Biological Psychiatry, 16,* 986–989.

Fitzsimons, J. T. (1969). The role of a renal thirst factor in drinking induced by extracellular stimuli. *Journal of Physiology (London)*, 201, 349–368.

Fitzsimons, J. T. (1978). Angiotensin, thirst and sodium appetite: Retrospect and prospect. *Federation Proceedings, Federation of American Societies for Experimental Biology*, 37, 2669–2675.

Fitzsimons, J. T. (1980). Angiotensin stimulation of the central nervous system. *Reviews of Physiology, Biochemistry and Pharmacology*, 87, 117–167.

Freed, W. J., Bing, L. A., Anderson, A. E., & Wyatt, R. J. (1984). Calcitonin as an anorectic agent. In N. S. Shah & A. G. Donald (Eds.), *Psychoneuroendocrine dysfunction* (pp. 83–109). New York: Plenum Press.

Freed, W. J., Perlow, M. J., & Wyatt, R. D. (1979). Calcitonin: Inhibitory effect on eating in rats. *Science*, 206, 850–852.

Gaillard, A. W. K., & Sanders, A. F. (1975). Some effects of $ACTH_{4-10}$ on performance during a serial reaction task. *Psychopharmacology*, 42, 201–208.

Gaillard, A. W. K., & Varey, C. A. (1979). Some effects of an $ACTH_{4-9}$ analogue (ORG 2766) on human performance. *Physiology and Behavior*, 23, 79–84.

Gash, D. M., & Thomas, G. J. (1983). What is the importance of vasopressin in memory processes? *Trends in Neurosciences*, 6, 197–198.

Gennari, C., Chierichetti, S. M., Piolini, M., Vibelli, C., Agnusdei, D., Civitelli, R., & Gonnelli, S. (1985). Analgesic activity of salmon and human calcitonin against cancer pain: A double-blind, placebo-controlled clinical study. *Current Therapeutic Research*, 38, 298–308.

German, G. A., & Stampfer, H. G. (1979). Hypothalamic releasing factor for reactive depression. *Lancet*, 2, 789.

Gibbs, J., Young, R. C., & Smith, G. P. (1973). Cholecystokinin decreases food intake in rats. *Journal of Comparative and Physiological Psychology*, 84, 488–495.

Gold, P. W., Ballenger, J. C., Robertson, G. L., Weingartner, H., Rubinow, D. R., Hoban, M. C., Goodwin, F. K., & Post, R. M. (1984). Vasopressin in affective illness: Direct measurement, clinical trials and response to hypertonic saline. In R. M. Post & J. C. Ballenger (Eds.), *Neurobiology of mood disorders* (pp. 323–339). Baltimore: William & Wilkins.

Gold, P. W., & Chrousos, G. P. (1985). Clinical studies with corticotropin-releasing factor: Implications for the diagnosis and pathophysiology of depression, Cushing's disease and adrenal insufficiency. *Psychoneuroendocrinology*, 10, 401–419.

Greenway, F. L., & Bray, G. A. (1977). Cholecystokinin and satiety. *Life Sciences*, 21, 769–772.

Hokfelt, T, Rehfeld, J. F., Skirboll, L., Ivemark, B., Goldstein, M., & Markey, K. (1980). Evidence of coexistence of dopamine and CCK in mesolimbic neurons. *Nature (London)*, 285, 476–478.

Hommer, D. W., Pickar, D., Roy, A., Ninan, P., Boronow, J., & Paul, S. M. (1984). The effects of ceruletide in schizophrenia. *Archives of General Psychiatry*, 41, 617–619.

Iversen, L. L., Iversen, S. D., & Snyder, S. H. (Eds.). (1983). Neuropeptides. *Handbook of psychopharmacology* (Vol. 16, pp. 1–577). New York: Plenum Press.

Izzo, R. I., Brugge, W. R., & Praissman, M. (1984). Immunoreactive cholecystokinin in human and rat plasma: Correlation of pancreatic secretion in response to CCK. *Regulatory Peptides*, 9, 21–34.

Jennekens-Schinkel, A., Wintzen, A. R., & Lanser, J. B. K. (1985). A clinical trial with desglycinamide arginine vasopressin for the treatment of memory disorders in ? an. *Progress in Neuro-Psychopharmacology and Biological Psychiatry*, 9, 273–284.

Kaeser, H. E. (1984). A clinical trial with DSIP. *European Neurology*, 23, 386–388.

Kastin, A. J., Ehrensing, R. H., Schalch, D. S., & Anderson, M. S. (1972). Improvement in mental depression with decreased thyrotropin response after administration of thyrotropin-releasing hormone. *Lancet*, 2, 740.

Kissileff, H. R., Pi-Sunyer, F. Z., Thornton, J., & Smith, G. P. (1981). C-terminal octapeptide of cholecystokinin decreases food intake in man. *American Journal of Clinical Nutrition*, 34, 154–160.

Korsgaard, S., Casey, D. E., Damgaard-Pedersen, N. E., Jorgensen, A., & Gerlach, J. (1981). Vasopressin in anergic schizophrenia. *Psychopharmacology*, 74, 379–382.

Laczi, F., Valkusz, Z., Laszlo, F. A., Wagner, A., Jardanhazy, T., Szasz, A., Szilard, J., & Telegdy, G. (1982). Effects of lysine-vasopressin and 1-deamino-8-D-arginine-vasopressin on memory in healthy individuals and diabetes insipidus patients. *Psychoneuroendocrinology*, 7, 185–193.

Laczi, F., Van Ree, J. M., Balogh, L., Szasz, A., Jardanhazy, T., Wagner, A., Garpar, L., Valkusz, Z., Dobranovics, I., Szilard, J., Laszlo, F. A., & de Wied, D. (1983). Lack of effect of desglycinamide-argine-vasopressin (DGAVP) on memory in patients with Korsakoff's syndrome. *Acta Endocrinologica (Copenhagen)*, 104, 177–182.

Laczi, F., Van Ree, J. M., Wagner, A., Valdusz, Z. S., Jardanhazy, T., Kovacs, G. L., Telegdy, G., Szilard, J., Laszlo, R. A., & de Wied, D. (1983). Effects of desglycinamide-arginine-vasopressin (DGAVP) on memory processes in diabetes insipidus patients and nondiabetic controls. *Acta Endocrinologica (Copenhagen)*, 102, 205–212.

Le Boeuf, A., Lodge, J., & Eames, P. G. (1978). Vasopressin and memory in Korsakoff syndrome. *Lancet*, 2, 1370.

Legros, J. J., Gilot, P., Soron, X., Claessens, J., Adam, A., Moeglen, J. M., Audibert, A., & Berchier, P. (1978). Influence of vasopressin on learning and memory. *Lancet*, 1, 41–42.

Le Moal, M., Koob, G. F., Koda, L. Y., Bloome, F. E., Manning, M., Sawyer, W. H., & Rivier, J. (1981). Vasopressin receptor antagonist prevents behavioural effects of vasopressin. *Nature (London)*, 291, 491–493.

Lerer, B., Zabow, T., Egnal, N., & Belmaker, R. H. (1983). Effect of vasopressin on memory following electroconvulsive therapy. *Biological Psychiatry*, 18, 831–834.

Levy, M. L., DeNigris, Y., & Davis, K. L. (1982). Rapid antidepressant activity of melanocyte inhibiting factor: A clinical trial. *Biological Psychiatry*, 17, 259–263.

Lilja, P., Wiener, I., Inone, K., Fried, G., Greeley, G., & Thompson, J. (1984). Release of cholecystokinin in response to food and intraduodenal fat in pigs, dogs and man. *Surgery, Gynecology and Obstetrics, 159,* 557–561.

Lindstrom, L. H., Ekman, R., Walleus, H., & Widerlov, E. (1985). Delta sleep-inducing peptide in cerebrospinal fluid from schizophrenics, depressives and healthy volunteers. *Progress in Neuro-Psychopharmacology and Biological Psychiatry, 9,* 83–90.

Loosen, P. T., & Prange, A. J., Jr. (1984). Hormones of the thyroid axis and behavior. In C. B. Nemeroff & A. J. Dunn (Eds.), *Peptides, hormones and behavior* (pp. 533–577). New York: Spectrum Publications.

Lotstra, F., Verbanck, P., Mendlewicz, J., & Vanderhaeghen, J. J. (1984). No evidence of antipsychotic effect of caerulein in schizophrenic patients free of neuroleptics: A double-blind crossover study. *Biological Psychiatry, 19,* 877–882.

Martin, J. C., Ballinger, B. R., Cockran, L. L., McPherson, F. M., Pigache, R. M., & Tregaskis, D. (1983). Effect of a synthetic peptide, ORG2766, on inpatients with severe senile dementia. *Acta Psychiatrica Scandinavica, 67,* 205–207.

Martinez, J. L., Vasquez, B. J., Jensen, R. A., Soumiren-Mourat, B., & McGaugh, J. L. (1979). $ACTH_{4-9}$ analogue (ORG2766) facilitates acquisition of inhibitory avoidance response in rats. *Pharmacology, Biochemistry and Behavior, 10,* 145–147.

Mattes, J. A., Hum, W., Rochford, J. M., & Orlosky, M. (1985). Ceruletide for schizophrenia: A double-blind study. *Biological Psychiatry, 20,* 533–538.

Mayer, J. (1955). Regulation of energy intake and the body weight: The glucostatic theory and the lipostatic hypothesis. *Annals of the New York Academy of Sciences, 63,* 15–43.

McAdoo, B. C., Doering, C. H., Kraemer, H. C., Dessert, N., Brodie, H. K. H., & Hamburg, D. A. (1978). A study of the effects of gonadotrophin releasing hormone on human mood and behavior. *Psychosomatic Medicine, 40,* 199–209.

Meisenberg, G., & Simmons, W. H. (1983). Peptides and the blood barrier. *Life Sciences, 32,* 2611–2623.

Miller, L. H., Fischer, S. C., Groves, G. A., Rudrauff, M. E., & Kastin, A. J. (1977). $MSH/ACTH_{4-10}$ influences on the CAR in human subjects: A negative finding. *Pharmacology, Biochemistry and Behavior, 7,* 417–419.

Miller, L. H., Groves, G. A., Bopp, M. J., & Kastin, A. J. (1980). A neuroheptopeptide influence on cognitive functioning in the elderly. *Peptides (New York), 1,* 55–57.

Miller, L. H., Kastin, A. J., Sandman, C. A., Fink, M., & Van Veen, W. J. (1974). Polypeptide influences on attention, memory and anxiety in man. *Pharmacology, Biochemistry and Behavior, 2,* 663–668.

Monnier, M., & Hosli, L. (1964). Dialysis of sleep and waking factors in blood of the rabbit. *Science, 146,* 796–798.

Morley, J. E., Krahn, D. D., Gosnell, B. A., Billington, C. J., & Levine, A. S. (1984). Interrelationships between calcitonin and other modulators of feeding behavior. *Psychopharmacology Bulletin, 20,* 463–465.

Moorji, T., Watanabe, N., Aoki, N., & Itoh, S. (1982).

Antipsychotic effects of ceruletide (cerulein) in chronic schizophrenia. *Archives of General Psychiatry, 39,* 485–486.

Moss, R. L., & McCann, S. M. (1973). Induction of mating behavior in rats by luteinizing hormone-releasing factor. *Science, 182,* 177–179.

Mussini, M., Agricola, R., Moia, G. C., Fiore, P., & Rivolta, A. (1984). A preliminary study on the use of calcitonin in clinical psychopathology. *Journal of International Medical Research, 12,* 23–29.

Nair, N. P., Bloom, D. M., & Nestoros, J. N. (1982). Cholecystokinin appears to have antipsychotic properties. *Progress in Neuro-Psychopharmacology and Biological Psychiatry, 6,* 509–512.

Nebes, R. D., Reynolds, C. F., & Horn, L. C. (1984). The effect of vasopressin on memory in the healthy elderly. *Psychiatry Research, 11,* 49–59.

Nemeroff, C. B., & Bissette, G. (1986). Neuropeptides in psychiatry. In P. A. Berger & H. K. H. Brodie (Eds.), *The American handbook of psychiatry* (Vol. 8). New York: Basic Books.

Oliveros, J. C., Jandali, M. K., Timsit-Berthier, M., Romy, R., Benghezal, A., Audibert, A., & Moeglen, J. M. (1978). Vasopressin amnesia. *Lancet, 1,* 42.

Owen, O. E., Reichard, G. A., Boden, G., & Shuman, C. R. (1974). Comparative measurements of glucose, β-hydroxybutyrate, acetoacetate, and insulin in blood and cerebrospinal fluid during starvation. *Metabolism, Clinical and Experimental, 23,* 7–14.

Packard, M. G., & Ettenberg, A. (1985). Effects of peripherally injected vasopressin and desglycinamide vasopressin on the extinction of a spatial learning task in rats. *Regulatory Peptides, 11,* 51–63.

Partap, M., Jos, C. J., & Dye, C. J. (1983). Vasopressin-8-lysine in prevention of ECT-induced amnesia. *American Journal of Psychiatry, 140,* 946–947.

Perlow, M. J., Freed, W. J., Carman, J. S., & Wyatt, R. J. (1980). Calcitonin reduces feeding in man, monkey and rat. *Pharmacology, Biochemistry and Behavior, 12,* 609–612.

Pfaff, D. W. (1973). Luteinizing hormone-releasing factor potentiates lordosis, behavior in hypophysectomized ovarectomized female rats, *Science, 182,* 1148–1149.

Phillips, M. I. (1984). Angiotensin and drinking: A model for the study of peptide action in the brain. In C. B. Nemeroff & A. J. Dunn (Eds.), *Peptides, hormones and behavior* (pp. 423–462). New York: Spectrum Publications.

Pi-Sunyer, F. X., Kissileff, H. R., Thornton, J., Smith, G. P. (1982). C-terminal octapeptide of cholecystokinin decreases food intake in obese men. *Physiology and Behavior, 29,* 627–630.

Pitfield, R. L. (1923). On the use of insulin in infantile inanition. *New York Medical Journal, 118,* 217–218.

Prange, A. J., Jr., & Loosen, P. T. (1984a). Aspects of thyroid axis function in depression. In N. S. Shah & A. G. Donald (Eds.), *Psychoneuroendocrine dysfunction* (pp. 431–442). New York: Plenum Press.

Prange, A. J., Jr., & Loosen, P. T. (1984b). Peptides in depression. In E. Usdin *et al.* (Eds.), *Frontiers in biochemical and pharmacological research in depression* (pp. 127–145). New York: Raven Press.

Prange, A. J., Jr., & Wilson, I. C. (1972). Thyrotropin-releasing hormone (TRH) for the immediate relief of depression: A preliminary report. *Psychopharmacologia, 26*, 82.

Rappoport, J. L., Quinn, P. O., Copeland, A. P., & Burg, C. (1976). ACTH$_{4-10}$: Cognitive and behavioral effects in hyperactive, learning-disabled children. *Neuropsychobiology, 2*, 291–296.

Reid, I. (1984). Actions of angiotensin II on the brain: Mechanisms and physiologic role. *American Journal of Physiology, 246*, F533–F543.

Reiser, M., Lenz, E., Bernstein, H.-G., & Dorn, A. (1985). Insulin-like immunoreactivity in human cerebrospinal fluid is independent of insulin blood levels. *Human Neurobiology, 4*, 53–55.

Sagar, S. M., Henke, H., & Fischer, J. A. (1984). Calcitonin and calcitonin gene-related peptide in the human brain. *Psychopharmacology Bulletin, 20* 447–450.

Sandman, C. A., George, J., Nolan, J., van Riezen, H., & Kastin, A. (1975). Enhancement of attention in man with ACTH/MSH$_{4-10}$. *Physiology and Behavior, 15*, 427–431.

Sandman, C. A., George, J., Walke, B. B., & Nolan, J. (1976). Neuroheptapeptide MSH/ACTH$_{4-10}$ enhances attention in the mentally retarded. *Pharmacology, Biochemistry and Behavior, 5*(Suppl. 1), 23–28.

Sandman, C. A., & Kastin, A. J. (1981). The influence of fragments of the LPH chains on learning, memory and attention in animals and man. *Pharmacology & Therapeutics, 13*, 39–60.

Sandman, C. A., George, J., McCanne, T. R., Nolan, J. D., Kaswan, J., & Kastin, A. J. (1977). MSH/ACTH$_{4-10}$ influences behavioral and psychological measures of attention. *Journal of Clinical Endocrinology and Metabolism, 44*, 884–891.

Sandman, C. A., Walker, B. B., & Lawton, C. A. (1980). An analog of MSH/ACTH$_{4-9}$ enhances interpersonal and environmental awareness in mentally retarded adults. *Peptides (New York), 1*, 109–114.

Schneider-Helmert, D. (1984). DSIP in insomnia. *European Neurology, 23*, 358–363.

Schneider-Helmert, D. (1985). Clinical evaluation of DSIP. In A. Wauquier, J. M. Gaillard, J. M. Monti, & M. Radulovacki (Eds.), *Sleep* (pp. 279–289). New York: Raven Press.

Schoenenberger, G. A., & Monnier, M. (1977). Characterization of a delta electroencephalogram (sleep)-inducing peptide. *Proceedings of the National Academy of Sciences of the U.S.A., 74*, 1282–1286.

Schwartzstein, L, Aparicio, N. J., Turner, D., Calamera, J. C., Mancini, R., & Schally, A. V. (1975). Use of synthetic luteinizing hormone-releasing hormone in treatment of oligospermic men: A preliminary report. *Fertility and Sterility, 26*, 331–336.

Severs, W. B., Summy-Long, J., Taylor, J. S., & Connor, J. D. (1970). A central effect of angiotensin: Release of pituitary pressor material. *Journal of Pharmacology and Experimental Therapeutics, 174*, 27–34.

Sheth, K. J., Tank, T. T., Blaedel, M. E., & Good, T. A. (1978). Polydipsia, polyuria, and hypertension associated with renin-secreting Wilms' tumor. *Journal of Pediatrics, 92*, 921–924.

Smith, G. P. (1984). Gut hormones and feeding behavior. Intuitions and experiments. In C. B. Nemeroff & A. J. Dunn (Eds.), *Peptides, hormones and behavior* (pp. 463–495). New York: Spectrum Publications.

Smith, G. P., Jerome, C., Cushin, B. J., Eterno, R., & Simansky, K. F. (1981). Abdominal vagotomy blocks the satiety effect of cholecystokinin in the rat. *Science, 213*, 1036–1037.

Stacher, G, Steinringer, H., Schnierer, G., Schneider, C., & Winklehner, S. (1982). Cholecystokinin octapeptide decreases intake of solid food in man. *Peptides (New York), 3*, 133–136.

Sturdevant, R. A. L., & Goetz, H. (1976). Choelcystokinin both stimulates and inhibits human food intake. *Nature (London), 261*, 714–715.

Trippodo, N. C., McCaa, R. E., & Buyton, A. C. (1976). Effect of prolonged angiotensin II infusion on thirst. *American Journal of Physiology, 230*, 1063–1066.

Van der Welde, C. D. (1983). Rapid clinical effectiveness of MIF-1 in the treatment of major depressive illness. *Peptides (New York), 4*, 297–300.

Van Loon, G. R., & Brown, G. M. (1975). Secondary drug failure occurring during chronic treatment with LHRH: Appearance of an antibody. *Journal of Clinical Endocrinology and Metabolism, 41*, 640–643.

Veith, J. L., Sandman, C. A., George, J. M., & Stevens, V. C. (1978). Effects of MSH/ACTH$_{4-10}$ on memory attention and endogenous hormone levels in women. *Physiology and Behavior, 20*, 43–50.

Wang, R. Y., White, F. J., & Voigt, M. M. (1984). Cholecystokinin, dopamine and schizophrenia. *Trends in Pharmacological Sciences, 5*, 436–438.

Ward, M. M., Sandman, C. A., George, J. M., & Shulman, H. (1979). MSH/ACTH$_{4-10}$ in men and women: Effects upon performance of an attention and memory task. *Physiology and Behavior, 22*, 669–673.

Weingartner, H., Gold, P. W., Ballenger, J. G., Smallberg, S., Summers, K., Rubinow, D. R. Post, R. M., & Goodwin, F. K. (1981). Effects of vasopressin on human memory functions. *Science, 211*, 601–603.

Weingartner, H., Kaye, W., Gold, P., Smallberg, S., Peterson, R., Gillin J. C., & Ebert, M. (1981). Vasopressin treatment of cognitive dysfunction in progressive dementia. *Life Sciences, 29*, 2721–2726.

Woods, S. C., Lotter, E. C., McKay, L. D., & Porte, D. (1979). Chronic intracerebroventricular infusion of insulin reduces food intake and body weight of baboons. *Nature (London), 283*, 503–505.

Zarbin, M. A., Wamsley, J. H., Innis, R. B., & Kuhar, M. J. (1981). Cholecystokinin receptors: Presence and axonal flow in the rat vagus nerve. *Life Sciences, 29*, 697–705.

20 THE EFFECTS OF OPIOIDS ON BEHAVIOR: POSSIBLE ROLE IN PSYCHOTOGENESIS

CLAUDIA SCHMAUSS

HINDERK M. EMRICH

Max Planck Institute for Psychiatry, Munich

INTRODUCTION

The discovery of endogenous opioids and their specific receptors in the central nervous system (CNS) has been followed by intensive research attempting to understand their role in pain, behavior, and endocrine functions.

Both pharmacological and binding studies have provided evidence of multiple opioid receptor subtypes (Lord, Waterfield, Hughes, & Kosterlitz, 1977; Martin, Eades, Thompson, Huppler, & Gilbert, 1976), which differentially associate with various opiate-mediated effects (for review, see Martin, 1984). Although the pharmacological profile of the effects of opiates on the processing of nociceptive information and some aspects of neuroendocrine regulation is reasonably well described, little is known about the nature of opiate-induced effects on mood, emotions, learning, memory, and so on in man.

Regarding opioid effects on behavior, perhaps the oldest view is that opioids alter consciousness by decreasing sensory input (i.e., attenuating nociceptive transmission), thus increasing probability of sleep, production of stupor, immobility, atactic walking, catalepsy, etc. Opioids slow α activity and increase δ activity in electroencephalography (EEG), preceded by a period of arousal and EEG desynchronization. On the other hand, opioids exert both convulsive and anticonvulsive effects, probably through different receptor mechanisms (for review, see Martin, 1984).

The role of endorphins in mediation of behavioral reinforcement has been extensively demonstrated with self-administration (exogenous opioids) and self-stimulation (endogenous opioids) behavior (naloxone reversible) (see Belluzzi & Stein, 1982). Further research suggested a role of endogenous peptides in memory formation (Koob & Bloom, 1983). Belluzzi and Stein (1982) reported that morphine and enkephalins in high doses consistently facilitate memory formation, whereas lower doses have been reported to exert response retention deficits related to amnesia evoked by the low-dose opioid.

Additionally, opioids have been suggested to be involved in the regulation of pleasure, reward, and emotions (Belluzzi & Stein, 1977). Among the subjective effects opiates exerted in man are those described for opiate agonist–antagonists by Martin (1984): (1) feeling of well-being; (2) sedation, tiredness, sleepiness; and (3) dysphoria (racing thoughts, irritability, inability to concentrate, delusion, hallucinations). Within the subjective effects in man there is a complete concordance between the ability of opioid agonist–antagonists to produce euphoria and increased scores in the LSD scale.

Since opioids, in general, do not exert unique effects on behavior, different mechanisms of action are thought to be responsible for different behavioral effects. It is suggested that opioids act either as a neurotransmitter or as a neuromodulator by presynaptically regulating the release, or postsynaptically regulating the receptor number or affinity of other neurotransmitters.

OPIATE–DOPAMINE INTERACTION

Of particular importance in certain mental diseases is the interaction of opiates with dopaminergic neurotransmission. The limbic dopaminergic system, for example, is thought to be related to the major psychopathology of schizophrenia, the nigrostriatal dopaminergic system is thought to be related to the extrapyramidal symptoms and some of the motor functions in schizophrenia and, finally, the incertohypothalamic and tuberoinfundibular dopaminergic system regulates pituitary prolactin release. An increase in prolactin levels often correlates well with clinical improvement of schizophrenia.

There are six lines of evidences for an opioid modulation of dopaminergic neurotransmission:

1. Anatomical and biochemical data. Anatomical and biochemical data reveal an interaction beween opioid receptors and dopaminergic neurotransmission on dopaminergic nerve terminals, cell bodies, and afferent nerve endings (Johnson, Sarand, & Stumf, 1980; Llorens-Cortes, Pollard, & Schwartz, 1979; Murrin, Coyle, & Kuhar, 1980). Additionally, endogenous enkephalin levels correlate well with the endogenous dopamine content in various brain areas (Yang, Hong, & Costa, 1977), and there is evidence suggesting a functional relationship between these two systems and compensatory changes in enkephalin levels following destruction of the nigrostriatal dopaminergic system (Thal, Sharpless, Hirschhorn, Horavitz, & Makman, 1983) or chronic impairment of dopaminergic neurotransmission. At the receptor level chronic morphine enhances the affinity of $[^3H]$spiroperidol binding (Bhargava, 1983) and opiates induce a naloxone reversible noncompetitive inhibition of dopamine-stimulated adenylate cyclase (Neff, Parenti, Gentleman, & Olianas, 1981) (see Table 20.1).

2. Electrophysiological effects of opiates on A10 dopaminergic neurons. Systemically or iontophoretically applied morphine or phencyclidine alters the spontaneous activity of ventral tegmental (VTA) dopaminergic neurons (Freeman & Bunney, 1984; Gysling & Wang, 1983) (see Table 20.2).

3. Opiate effect on dopaminergic turnover in the striatum. Opiates alter striatal dopamine release, reuptake, and metabolism (for review, see Schmauss & Emrich, 1985) (Table 20.2). In a reverse manner, dopamine neurons projecting from the arcuate nucleus of the hypothalamus to the intermediate lobe of the pituitary interact with receptors on the pars intermedia cells and tonically inhibit the release of β-endorphin. Additionally, chronic and acute D_2-postsynaptic dopamine receptor blockade with haloperidol increases the biosynthesis of β-endorphin in the pituitary (Table 20.1).

4. Opioid's effect on contralateral rotation and stereotypy. Functionally, opiates affect stereotypy induced by dopamine agonists and contralateral rotation elicited by dopamine agonists in animals with unilateral lesions of the nigrostriatal pathway (for review, see Schmauss & Emrich, 1985) (Table 20.2).

5. Phencyclidine's effect on dopaminergic mechanisms. Phencyclidine (PCP), a putative σ-opioid receptor agonist (Brady, Balster, & May, 1982; Vaupel, 1983; Zukin & Zukin, 1981) increases the activity of striatal dopamine system by increasing the release (Vickroy & Johnson, 1982) and $[^3H]$dopamine uptake inhibition (Vickroy & Johnson, 1980), inhibits pituitary prolactin release (Lozorsky et al., 1983), and has a biphasic effect on A9 and A10 dopamine neuronal firing (Freeman & Bunney, 1984). Some of the effects evoked by PCP are blocked by haloperidol, but PCP renders resistance to naloxone (Vaupel, 1983). Severe psychosis, elicited by PCP, most closely resembles the clinical features of schizophrenia (Cohen, Rosenbaum, Luby, Gottlieb, & Yelen, 1962). Preclinical and clinical data reveal that even the PCP-induced psychosis can be effectively treated with neuroleptics (Luisada & Brown, 1976).

TABLE 20.1. Effect of Dopamine Agonists and Chronic Haloperidol on Endogenous Opioid Content and Release

	Hypothalamic β-endorphin content	Striatal Met[5]-enkephalin content	Striatal ME-IR[a] release
Dopamine agonists	Decrease (Locatelli, Petraglia, Penalva, & Panerai, 1983)	—	Increase (Pasinetti, Govoni, Giovine, Spano, & Trabucchi, 1984)
Acute and chronic haloperidol	Increase (Höllt, Haarmann, Seizinger, & Herz, 1982)	Increase (Hong et al., 1979)	—

[a]Met-enkephalin immunoreactivity.

419

TABLE 20.2. Effect of Opioids on Dopamine Functions[a]

Function	Morphine	Enkephalin thiorphan	Naloxone	Endorphins α	Endorphins γ	Endorphins β	PCP
Excitability of dopamine neurons	↑ Spontaneous firing in VTA, SNC	—	—	—	—	—	Biphasic effect on A9, A10 neurons (excitation, followed by inhibition)
Pituitary prolactin release	Increase	Increase	No effect	—	—	—	Decrease
Dopamine turnover Hypothalamic	↓ DOPAC ↑ HMV ↓ α-MT	↓ DOPAC ↑ HMV ↓ α-MT	= DOPAC = HMV = α-MT	↓ HMV			
Striatonigral	↓ DOPAC	↓ DOPAC			↓ DA ↓ DOPAC ↓ HMV	= DA = DOPAC = HMV	↑[³H]DA ↑ DOPAC ↑ HMV
Dopamine reuptake Hypothalamus Striatum						↑ V_{max} ↑ V_{max}	↑ V_{max} ↑ V_{max}
Lateral rotation Ipsilateral	Antagonism of amphetamine's effect		Antagonism of amphetamine's effect				Stimulation of rotation
Contralateral	Antagonism of apomorphine's effect Stimulation of rotation (naloxone reversible)		Enhancement of apomorphine's effect				
Behavioral stereotypy	Enhancement		Inhibition of apomorphine's effect; potentiation with amphetamines				Enhancement

[a]Reprinted by permission of the publisher from "Dopamine and the effects of opioids" by C. Schmauss and H. M. Emrich. *Biological Psychiatry 20*:1211–1231. Copyright 1985 by Elsevier Science Publishing Co., Inc.

6. Opioid's effect on pituitary prolactin release. The tuberoinfundibular dopamine neurons originate in the mediobasal hypothalamus and terminate in the median eminence and posterior pituitary. The terminals of these neurons are in close proximity to capillaries of the hypothalamic–pituitary vascular system, nerve terminals and axons of peptidergic neurons, and ependymal cells in the median eminence. Dopamine released from the tuberoinfundibular dopaminergic system located in the medial-palisade zone can be transported via the hypothalamic–pituitary portal vascular system to the anterior pituitary to activate receptors on the lactotrophs and thereby reduces prolactin secretion. The release of prolactin is depolarization induced, calcium and sodium dependent, and can be inhibited by dopamine agonists, suggesting an autoinhibition of a presynaptic receptor (autoreceptor) (Eriksson, Modigh, Carlsson, & Wikström, 1983; Gudelsky, Passaro, & Meltzer, 1983; Sakar et al., 1983). Prolactin itself regulates its own secretion while increasing the synthesis and release of dopamine from the tuberoinfundibular neurons. Additionally, there is some evidence that a part of the haloperidol-induced increase of striatal dopamine is mediated by prolactin (Van Loon, Shum, George, & Shin, 1983).

In general, increased release of prolactin in both animals and man has been reported during many kinds of stress. Restraint stress and heat stress have been shown to be potent stimulators of prolactin release, and this effect has been shown to be naloxone reversible, indicating that endogenous opioids may play a significant role in elevating prolactin during stress (Van Vugt, Bruni, & Meites, 1978). It has been suggested that endogenous opioids stimulate prolactin release either by inhibiting dopamine neurons or by a direct opioid-mediated stimulatory effect. The latter appears to be unlikely, since naloxone alone does not affect prolactin release, nor does naloxone pretreatment affect opioid-stimulated prolactin release (Cheung, 1984). A suppression of dopamine-mediated inhibition of prolactin release is supported by the results of Reymond, Kaur, and Porter

(1983), who demonstrated that intracerebroventricularly applied morphine significantly decreased median eminence DOPAC and portal blood dopamine in rats. It is therefore most likely that morphine, endorphins, and enkephalins inhibit the release and synthesis of hypothalamic dopamine and thus enhance pituitary prolactin release.

Hypothalamic β-endorphin with cell bodies located on the arcuate nucleus and basal tuberal region is presumably the source of endogenous β-endorphin involved in the regulation of pituitary prolactin release through a modulatory effect on hypothalamic dopaminergic activity. But continuous application of β-endorphin leads to a loss of the suppressive effect of β-endorphin on dopamine, suggesting the development of receptor subsensitivity which follows initial exposure to opiate agonists (Cheung, 1984). It might be that endogenously released β-endorphin initially stimulates basal prolactin release, but subsequently develops subsensitivity to endogenous opioids.

The endorphin excess or deficiency hypothesis of schizophrenia and depression could therefore be proved, for example, by estimating the opioid-stimulated prolactin response. Judd et al. (1982) originally postulated a blunted prolactin response to methadone in patients suffering from endogenous depression, but subsequent investigations revealed rather conflicting results. In unmedicated patients suffering from schizophrenia, Meltzer, Busch, and Fang (1981) reported slightly increased to normal prolactin levels. We therefore tested the effect of the partial opiate agonist buprenorphine on prolactin levels in healthy volunteers, patients suffering from schizophrenia, and patients with major depressive disorders. Buprenorphine, administered sublingually at various doses, produced a dose-dependent effect on the rise of plasma prolactin levels (Figures 20.1–20.3). The rise in plasma prolactin levels appeared slowly, with a peak effect 4 hours after application of the drug (Figure 20.1).

Naloxone (5–10 mg intravenously) did not significantly change the plasma prolactin levels. Only the highest dose of naloxone used in this study (10 mg) slightly, but insignificantly reduced plasma prolactin levels 1 hour postdrug application (Figures 20.2 and 20.3). Interestingly, no rebound increase of plasma

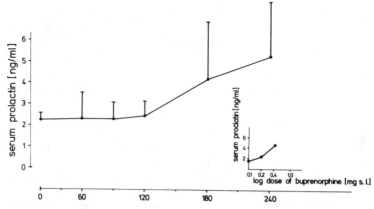

FIGURE 20.1. The effect of buprenorphine (0.2 mg sublingual) on serum prolactin levels. Ordinate: Serum prolactin levels (ng/ml); abscissa: Time in minutes. Each point represents the mean ± SEM of determinations made in five probands. Inset diagram: Dose–response curve for the effect of buprenorphine on serum prolactin levels. Abscissa: Dose of buprenorphine (log scale) (mg); ordinate: serum prolactin levels (ng/ml). Reprinted by permission of the publisher from "Dopamine and the effects of opioids" by C. Schmauss and H. M. Emrich. *Biological Psychiatry 20*:1211–1231. Copyright 1985 by Elsevier Science Publishing Co., Inc.

prolactin levels after a single high dose of naloxone stimulation could be observed. In unmedicated patients suffering from paranoid-hallucinatory psychosis ($n = 7$; DSM-III diagnostic criteria) and patients suffering from major depression ($n = 7$; Research Diagnostic Criteria, RDC), the response to 0.2 mg buprenorphine on plasma prolactin levels revealed no difference to the control group and no indication for an opiate receptor sub- or supersensitivity in both diseases

(Figure 20.4). The baseline prolactin levels varied slightly, but did not differ from the baseline of the control group.

Although our data do not prove any sub- or supersensitivity of opioid receptors in the incertotuberoinfundibular region in patients with schizophrenia and major depressive disorders, determinations of prolactin levels appear to be of great value in relation to the clinical outcome of both psychiatric diseases. Swigar, Jatlow, Goicoechea, Opsahl, and

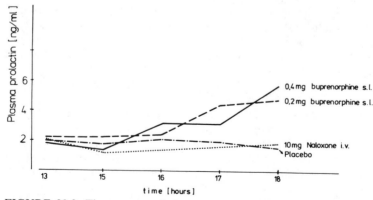

FIGURE 20.2. Time course of changes in plasma prolactin levels after buprenorphine (0.2 and 0.4 mg), placebo, and naloxone (10 mg) applications as estimated in one proband. Ordinate: Serum prolactin levels (ng/ml); abscissa: daytime hours.

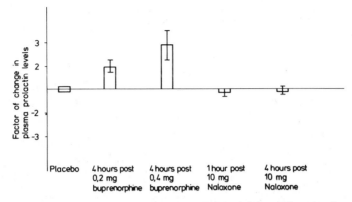

FIGURE 20.3. Effect of buprenorphine (0.2 and 0.4 mg sl) and naloxone (10 mg iv) on plasma prolactin levels in humans. Ordinate: Factor of change in plasma prolactin levels (poststimulation prolactin levels/baseline prolactin levels). Each column represents the mean ± SEM of determinations made in 10 probands.

Bowers (1984) demonstrated a close correlation of rise in plasma prolactin levels and clinical improvement in psychotic women treated with a constant dose of haloperidol. Thus, the antipsychotic effect of neuroleptics, mediated through central dopaminergic mechanisms, might be reflected by drug interference with dopaminergic prolactin-regulating neurons in the hypothalamus and the prolactin response could be used as a good correlate for an antipsychotic effect in schizophrenia (Larsson, Öhman, Wallin, Wallinder, & Carlsson, 1984). The same is true for antidepressant-like drugs, since clinical recovery from depression goes parallel with an increase of plasma prolactin (Lisansky et al., 1984).

DO OPIOIDS HAVE ANTIPSYCHOTIC EFFECTS?

Considering the evidence presented thus far, it seems not unlikely that effects evoked by opiate agonists or antagonists on schizophrenic symptomatology are, at least to some extent, mediated via dopaminergic mechanisms. There is no convincing evidence thus far for such a hypothesis. It is possible, however, that opiates with different opiate receptor selectivity differentially affect dopaminergic neurotransmission, and it is generally thought that schizophrenia is due to a functional overactivity of the dopamine neuronal system. But, it was also suggested that the endogenous opioid system might be overactive in schizophrenia (Terenius, Wahlström, Lindström, & Widerlöv, 1976). Extensive studies using naloxone in patients suffering from schizophrenia revealed only minimal effects, and the observed antipsychotic effect appeared 2–7 hours after the naloxone application, that is, the latency of the onset of the antipsychotic effect exceeds the plasma $t_{1/2}$ more than four times (Figure

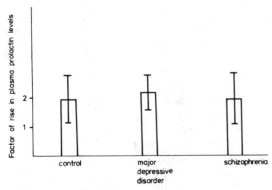

FIGURE 20.4. Increase of plasma prolactin levels after 0.2 mg buprenorphine stimulation in the control group ($n = 10$), in patients with major depressive disorders ($n = 7$), and in patients with acute schizophrenia ($n = 7$). Ordinate: Factor of rise in plasma prolactin levels (poststimulation prolactin levels/baseline prolactin levels).

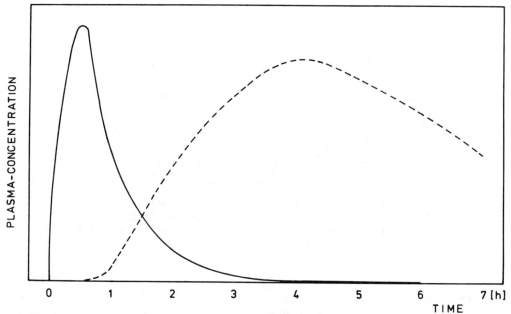

FIGURE 20.5. Schematic representation of the kinetic of intravenously administered naloxone (solid line) and the counterbalance release of β-endorphin (dotted line).

20.5) (Emrich, 1984; Emrich *et al.*, 1977). The most likely explanation for the late-onset antipsychotic effect evoked by naloxone is that a single dose of the antagonist elicits a rebound release of endogenous opioids which actually might be responsible for the observed antipsychotic effect. Such a dose-dependent effect of naloxone on pituitary β-endorphin secretion had been recently demonstrated in rats (Levin, Sharp, & Carlsson, 1984). Therefore, in line with these findings, opiate agonists administered to schizophrenics should exert an antipsychotic effect. Several attempts have been undertaken to prove the effect of β-endorphin on schizophrenic target symptoms, but the results of clinical studies are scarce (for review, see Schmauss & Emrich, 1985).

In a double-blind placebo-controlled study, we tested the effects of buprenorphine (0.2–0.4 mg) on schizophrenic target symptoms in newly admitted, unmedicated schizophrenic inpatients (*n* = 10; DSM-III diagnostic criteria). Psychopathological changes were scored using the IMPS scale and a behavioral observation scale (VBS) with eight graduations of intensity of target

symptoms adapted to the prominent psychotic delusion or hallucinations.

Our results can be summarized as follows:

1. Of 10 patients, 2 almost classically responded to buprenorphine with a time-dependent decrease of psychotic target symptoms and showed constant psychopathological features during the placebo period. Figure 20.6 demonstrates the results obtained with 1 of the 2 patients. Both patients were younger than 20 years of age, had their first schizophrenic episode, and had never been exposed to neuroleptics until entering the study.

2. Six further patients responded as shown for one patient of this group in Figure 20.7. An antipsychotic effect of buprenorphine could be obtained, but was inconsistent over the time period of testing. Patients in this group were older than 20 years of age, had more than one schizophrenic episode in their life, had been exposed to neuroleptics sometime in their life, and had already established some residual symptoms of their disease.

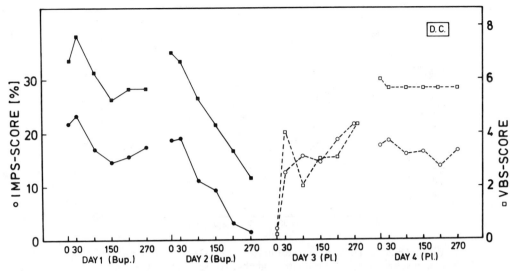

FIGURE 20.6. Effect of 0.2 mg buprenorphine on psychotic target symptoms. The drug was administered on Days 1 and 2 (solid lines); placebo was administered on Days 3 and 4 (dotted line). Left ordinate represents the IMPS rating score (%); right ordinate represents the score obtained from the behavioral observation scale (VBS), with a graduation of severity of psychotic target symptoms from 1 to 8. (●), IMPS during verum testing: (○), IMPS during placebo testing; (■), VBS during verum testing for one major psychotic symptom; (□), VBS for placebo testing of the major psychotic symptom.

3. Two further patients either did not respond to buprenorphine or showed an impairment of the psychopathological symptoms. Figure 20.8 demonstrates the result for one patient of this group. Both patients suffered from a chronic course of their disease, with negative symptoms in-between the exacerbation periods. During this study, these patients additionally had been on low doses of neuroleptics.

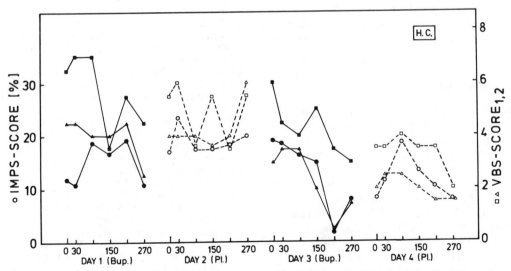

FIGURE 20.7. The drug was administered on Days 1 and 3; placebo was administered on Days 2 and 4. Ordinates and abscissa: See Figure 20.6. Two major psychotic symptoms have been scored in the VBS. (■), VBS_1, and (▲), VBS_2 during the verum test period; (□), VBS_1, and (△), VBS_2 during the placebo period.

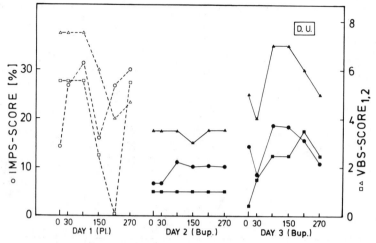

FIGURE 20.8. The drug was administered on Days 2 and 3; placebo was administered on Day 1. Ordinates and abscissa: see Figure 20.6. Two major psychotic symptoms have been scored in the VBS. (■) VBS_1 and (▲) VBS_2 during the verum days and (□) VBS_1 and (△) VBS_2 during the placebo period.

These data indicate that the effect of buprenorphine on psychotic symptoms is dependent on the course of the disease, especially with the number of schizophrenic episodes, and, thus, previous exposure to neuroleptics and the degree of residual symptoms. Such considerations might be of importance in evaluating clinical results of treatment, since it is likely that patients demonstrate varying degrees of changes of limbic dopaminergic neurotransmission.

CONCLUSIONS

In summary, there is no general concept regarding the effect of opioids on behavior and certain mental diseases. Opiates exert different effects in different systems and test assays. These differences might reflect selective activations of subpopulations of opioid receptors, pre- versus postsynaptic effects on opioid receptors, or different modulatory effects on "classical neurotransmission." Thus, the effects of some opioids on schizophrenic target symptoms might reflect opioid-induced modulation of limbic dopamine neurotransmission, which, finally, could be responsible for the antipsychotic effect induced by opioids.

References

Belluzzi, J. D., & Stein, L. (1977). Enkephalin may mediate euphoria and drive reduction reward. *Nature (London)*, *266*, 556–558.

Belluzzi, J. D., & Stein, L. (1982). Brain endorphins: Possible role in long-term memory. *Annals of the New York Academy of Sciences*, *398*, 221–229.

Bhargava, H. N. (1983). Binding of [³H]spiroperidol to striatal membranes of rats treated chronically with morphine. *Neuropharmacology*, *22*, 1357–1361.

Brady, K. T., Balster, R. L., & May, E. L. (1982). Stereoisomers of *N*-allylnormetazocine: Phencyclidine-like behavioral effects in squirrel monkeys and rats. *Science*, *215*, 178–180.

Cheung, C. Y. (1984). Does β-endorphin modulate basal dopamine-inhibited prolactin release by an action at the anterior pituitary? *Neuroendocrinology*, *39*, 489–495.

Cohen, B. C., Rosenbaum, G., Luby, E. D., Gottlieb, J. S., & Yelen, D. (1982). Comparison of phencyclidine hydrochloride (sernyl) with other drugs. *Archives of General Psychiatry*, *6*, 395–401.

Emrich, H. M. (1984). Endorphins in psychiatry. *Psychiatric Development*, *2*, 97–114.

Emrich, H. M., Cording, C., Pirée, S., Kölling, A., von Zerssen, D., & Herz, A. (1977). Indication of an antipsychotic action of the opiate antagonist naloxone. *Pharmacopsychiatry*, *10*, 265–270.

Eriksson, E., Modigh, K., Carlsson A., & Wikström, H. (1983). Dopamine receptors involved in prolactin secretion pharmacologically characterized by means of 3-PPP enantiomers. *European Journal of Pharmacology*, *96*, 29–36.

Freeman, A. S., & Bunney, B. S. (1984). The effects of phencyclidine and *N*-allylnormetazocine on midbrain dopamine neuronal activity. *European Journal of Pharmacology*, *104*, 287–293.

Gudelsky, G. A., Passaro, E., & Meltzer H. Y. (1983). Effect of two dopamine agonists, TL99 and 3-PPP, on prolactin secretion in the rat. *European Journal of Pharmacology*, *90*, 423–425.

Gysling, K., & Wang, R. Y. (1983). Morphine-induced activation of A10 dopamine neurons in the rat. *Brain Research*, *277*, 119–127.

Höllt, V., Haarmann, B. R., Seizinger, B., & Herz, A. (1982). Chronic haloperidol treatment increases the level of *in vitro* translatable messenger ribonucleic coding for the β-endorphin/adrenocorticotropin precursor proopiomelanocortin in the pars intermedia of the rat pituitary. *Endocrinology (Baltimore)*, *110*, 1885–1891.

Hong, J. S., Yang, H. Y., Gillin, J. C., Guilio, A. M., Fratta, W., & Costa, E. (1979). Chronic treatment with haloperidol accelerates the biosynthesis of enkephalin in the rat brain. *Brain Research*, *160*, 192–195.

Johnson, R. P., Sarand, M., & Stumf, W. E. (1980). A topographic localization of enkephalin on the dopamine neurons of the rat substantia nigra and ventral tegmental area demonstrated by combined histofluorescence immunohistochemistry. *Brain Research*, *196*, 566–571.

Judd, L. L., Risch, S. C., Parker, D. C., Janowsky, D. S., Segal, D. S., & Huey, L. Y. (1982). Blunted prolactin response. *Archives of General Psychiatry*, *39*, 1413–1416.

Koob, G., & Bloom, F. E. (1983). Memory, learning, and adaptive behaviors. In D. T. Krieger, M. J. Brownstein, & J. B. Martin (Eds.), *Brain peptides*, (pp. 369–389. New York: Wiley (Interscience).

Larsson, M., Öhman, R., Wallin, L., Wallinder, J., & Carlsson, A. (1984). Antipsychotic treatment with α-methyltyrosine in combination with thioridazine: Prolactin response and interaction with dopaminergic precursor pools. *Journal of Neural Transmission*, *60*, 115–132.

Levin, E. R., Sharp, B., & Carlsson, H. E. (1984). Studies of naloxone-induced secretion of β-endorphin immunoreactivity in dogs. *Life Sciences*, *35*, 1535–1545.

Llorens-Cortes, C., Pollard, H., & Schwartz, J. C. (1979). Localization of opiate receptors in the substantia nigra evidenced by lesion studies. *Neuroscience Letters*, *12*, 165–170.

Lisansky, J., Fava, G. A., Buckman, M. T., Kellner, R., Fava, M., Zielezny, M., & Peake, G. T. (1984). Prolactin, amitryptiline, and recovery from depression. *Psychopharmacology*, *84*, 331–335.

Locatelli, V., Petraglia, F., Penalva, A., & Panerai, A. E. (1983). Effect of dopaminergic drugs on hypothalamic and pituitary immunoreactive β-endorphin concentration in the rat. *Life Sciences*, *33*, 1711–1717.

Lord, J. A., Waterfield, A. A., Hughes, J., & Kosterlitz, H. W. (1977). Endogenous opioid peptides: Multiple agonists and receptors. *Nature (London)*, *267*, 495–499.

Lozovsky, D., Saller, C. F., Bayorh, M. A., Chiueh, C. C., Rice, K. C., Burke, T. R. Jr., & Kopin, I. J. (1983). Effect of phencyclidine on rat prolactin, dopamine receptor and locomotor activity. *Life Sciences*, *32*, 2725–2731.

Luisada, P. V., & Brown, B. I. (1976). Clinical management of the phencyclidine psychosis. *Clinical Toxicology*, *9*, 539–545.

Martin, W. R. (1984). Pharmacology of opioids. *Pharmacological Reviews*, *35*(4), 283–323.

Martin, W. R., Eades, C. G., Thompson, J. A., Huppler, R. E., & Gilbert, P. E. (1976). The effect of morphine- and nalorphine-like drugs in the nondependent and morphine-dependent chronic spinal dog. *Journal of Pharmacology and Experimental Therapeutics*, *197*, 517–532.

Meltzer, H. Y., Busch, D., & Fang, V. S. (1981). Hormones, dopamine receptors, and schizophrenia. *Psychoneuroendocrinology*, *6*, 17–36.

Murrin, L. C., Coyle, J. T., & Kuhar, M. J. (1980). Striatal opiate receptors: Pre- and postsynaptic localization. *Life Sciences*, *27*, 1175–1183.

Neff, N. H., Parenti, M., Gentleman, S., & Olianas, M. C. (1981). Modulation of dopamine receptors by opiates. In G. L. Gessa & G. U. Corsini (Eds.), *Apomorphine and other dopaminomimetics* (pp. 193–200). New York: Raven Press.

Pasinetti, G., Govoni, S., Giovine, S., Spano, P. F., & Trabucchi, M. (1984). Dopamine enhances Met-enkephalin efflux from rat striatal slices. *Brain Research*, *293*, 364–367.

Reymond, M. J., Kaur, C., & Porter, J. C. (1983). An inhibitory role for morphine on the release of dopamine into hypophysial portal blood and on the synthesis of dopamine in tuberoinfundibular neurons. *Brain Research*, *262*, 253–258.

Sakar, D. K., Gottschall, P. E., Meites, J., Horn, A., Dow, R. D., Fink, G., & Cuello, A. C. (1983). Uptake and release of [³H]dopamine by median eminence. Evidence for presynaptic dopaminergic receptors and for dopaminergic feedback inhibition. *Neuroscience*, *10*, 821–830.

Schmauss, C., & Emrich, H. M. (1985). Dopamine and the action of opiates: a reevaluation of the dopamine hypothesis of schizophrenia. With special consideration of the role of endogenous opioids in the pathogenesis of schizophrenia. *Biological Psychiatry*, *20*, 1211–1231.

Swigar, M. E., Jatlow, P. I., Goicoechea, N., Opsahl, C., & Bowers, M. B. (1984). Ratio of serum prolactin to haloperidol and early clinical outcome in acute psychosis. *American Journal of Psychiatry*, *141*, 1281–1283.

Terenius, L., Wahlström, A., Lindström, L., & Widerlöv, E. (1976). Increased CSF levels of endorphins in chronic psychosis. *Neuroscience Letters*, *3*, 157–162.

Thal, L. J., Sharpless, N. S., Hirschhorn, I. D., Horowitz, S. G., & Makman, M. H. (1983). Striatal Met-enkephalin concentration increases following nigrostriatal denervation. *Biochemical Pharmacology*, *32*, 3297–3301.

Van Loon, G. R., Shum, A., George, S. R., & Shin, S. H. (1983). Prolactin increases the activity of tuberoinfundibular and nigroneostriatal dopamine neurons: Prolactin antiserum inhibits the haloperidol-induced increases in dopamine synthesis rates in median eminence and striatum of rats. *Brain Research Bulletin*, *10*, 539–545.

Van Vugt, D. A., Bruni, J. F., & Meites, J. (1978). Naloxone inhibition of stress-induced increase in prolactin secretion. *Life Sciences, 22*, 85–90.

Vaupel, D. B. (1983). Naltrexone fails to antagonize the sigma effects of PCP and SKF 10,047 in the dog. *European Journal of Pharmacology, 92*, 269–274.

Vickroy, T. W., & Johnson, K. M. (1980). *In vivo* administration of phencyclidine inhibits [³H]dopamine accumulation by rat brain striatal slices. *Substance and Alcohol Actions/Misuse, 1*, 351–354.

Vickroy, T. W., & Johnson, K. M. (1982). Similar dopamine-releasing effects of phencyclidine and non-amphetamine stimulants in striatal slices. *Journal of Pharmacology and Experimental Therapeutics, 223*, 669–674.

Yang, H. Y., Hong, J. S., & Costa, E. (1977). Regional distribution of Leu- and Met-enkephalin in rat brain. *Neuropharmacology, 16*, 303–307.

Zukin, R. S., & Zukin, S. R. (1981). Multiple opiate receptors: Emerging concepts. *Life Sciences, 29*, 2681–2690.

PART VII

THE HUMAN LIFE CYCLE

21 BEHAVIORAL INFLUENCES OF PRENATAL HORMONES

JUNE MACHOVER REINISCH
STEPHANIE A. SANDERS
Indiana University

Hormones present during embryonic and fetal development are thought to influence later behavior by either imposing organization on the neural system (Goy, 1968; Goy & McEwen, 1980; Harris, 1964; Phoenix, Goy, Gerall, & Young, 1959; Young, Goy, & Phoenix, 1964) or sensitizing the organism to later hormonal stimulation (Beach, 1945, 1971). Evidence indicates that the prenatal hormone environment affects gender role, especially many of those behaviors that are characteristically thought to distinguish between the sexes. Whether the early hormonal milieu plays a primary role in the formation of gender identity and/or sexual orientation has yet to be determined. In this context, it is important to keep in mind the power of postnatal sociopyschological environmental influences, which act as powerful determinants of behavior in all mammals, particularly humans for whom an exceedingly long preadult period of development exists.

A second important era of hormonal impact occurs at puberty when, after several years of relative endocrine quiescence, the pituitary–gonadal axis is reactivated in the male and activated for the first time in the female. At this time, the gonadal steroids stimulate the development of the secondary sexual characteristics and activate sexually dimorphic patterns which may have been established during the earlier period of differentiation. The impact of the onset of adult hormonal levels at puberty, and the obvious physical changes that ensue, affect simultaneously both the individual's response to the environment and the environment's response to the individual. The interaction among prenatal hormonal influences, pubertal changes, and the socioenvironmental response to the organism contributes significantly to the coalescence of adult gender identity, gender role, and sexual orientation.

The purpose of this chapter is to present some theoretical issues relevant to an understanding of the influence gonadal hormones during gestation may have on human behavioral development. To this end, we will first present a brief overview of the process of sexual differentiation and the evidence supporting the notion that the prenatal hormonal milieu may predispose on organism to develop sexually dimorphic traits, abilities, and/or behaviors (for more extensive reviews of this literature, see Ellis, 1982; Hines, 1982; Reinisch, 1974, 1983; Reinisch & Sanders, 1984; Sanders & Reinisch, 1985). This is followed by a discussion of the current models which view masculinity and femininity as multidimensional and thus, not by necessity, inversely related. Finally, we will explore the process by which interactions between the biological organism and the sociological environment serve to magnify sexual dimorphisms of behavior.

It is a commonly held misconception that gender identity (whether the individual considers himself or herself to be male or female), sex role conformity (the degree to which one's behavior conforms to cultural stereotypes of how males and females should behave), and sexual orientation (sexual/romantic attraction to the opposite sex, same sex, or both sexes) are highly correlated. This chapter comments on the relative independence and/or interrelationship of behavioral dimensions related to these aspects of sexual differentiation.

NORMAL SEXUAL DIFFERENTIATION

Since prenatal genital differentiation provides the model for understanding sexual development in general, a brief discussion of the process is relevant as an introduction to our comments regarding the influence of hormones on human behavioral development.

During the major portion of embryonic development, the human female and male are virtually identical in terms of morphology, including the internal and external genital primordia. The initial difference between the sexes is chromosomal/genetic. Male cells include one X and one Y sex chromosome in addition to the 22 pairs of autosomes shared by both sexes, while female cells are characterized by a pair of X chromosomes.

A mammal's genotype does not directly determine the development of the male or female phenotype, although it probably does influence the ease with which the hormonal agents that do direct male and female differentiation operate. The genotype does, however, dictate the differentiation of the gonads. In the male, the gonads begin to differentiate into testes at approximately 6 weeks postconception followed closely by the commencement of testosterone production (Sitteri & Wilson, 1974). The presence of testosterone and its metabolites (in particular, dihydrotestosterone) masculinizes the internal and then the external genitalia. In the female, estradiol synthesis begins at the same time as the fetal testes commence testosterone production; however, the ovary remains undifferentiated well into the fetal stage. Plasma levels of estradiol are similar in male and female fetuses. Thus, estrogens appear not to play an indispensable role in the development of the female phenotype. (It is possible that histological differentiation of the ovary may be mediated by local action of estradiol in an analogous manner to the putative role of testosterone in testicular maturation.) It is the relative absence of hormones from the fetal gonads that permits the expression of the female phenotype (for review, see George, Griffin, Leshin, & Wilson, 1981).

In summary, masculine differentiation occurs because the fetal testis, which is actively producing androgen and a substance inhibiting the development of the female anlagen, imposes masculinity against the basic feminine trend of the body, whereas feminine differentiation proceeds in the absence of hormonal influence. This model can be applied to all sexually dimorphic differentiation, be it morphological, physiological, neurological, or behavioral. The strong presence of a masculinizing factor is essential fr male development, and the relative absence of hormonal influence is essential for female development.

SEX DIFFERENCES IN THE CENTRAL NERVOUS SYSTEM

The central nervous system in a number of species appears to be sexually dimorphic as well (De Vries, De Bruin, Uylings, & Corner, 1984; Gorski, 1987; Goy & McEwen, 1980; MacLusky & Naftolin, 1981). The list of morphological and physiological brain differences identified between males and females and predicated on early hormonal differences has been steadily increasing during the past decade and a half (Gorski, 1987; Reinisch, 1983). Sex differences have been found in various nuclei of the hypothalamus, the cerebellum, hippocampus, amygdala, and cerebral cortex. Differences are expressed in biochemical and physiological parameters such as oxidative metabolism, protein content, serotonin levels, RNA metabolism, and cholinesterase activity. Male and female brains also differ with regard to morphology, including such dimensions as neural connections, volume of cell nuclei, dendritic field patterns, and size of brain nuclei. Most of this reseach has been conducted with rodents; however, there is reason to believe that similar sex differences determined by a comparable prenatal hormonal milieu exist in human brains.

Recently, morphological sex differences in

the human brain have been reported. A sexually dimorphic cell group in the preoptic area of the hypothalamus has been described in humans (Swaab & Fliers, 1985), which is analogous to the sexually dimorphic nucleus (SDN) found in rats (Gorski, Gordon, Shryne, & Southam, 1978). The volume of this SDN in men was found to be 2.5 times as large as that in women and contained 2.2 times as many cells. This laboratory has also observed a sex difference in the shape of the suprachiasmatic nucleus of the human hypothalamus which is not associated with differences in overall volume, cell density, or total cell number (D. F. Swaab, E. Fliers, & T. Partiman, unpublished observation, reported in Swaab & Hofman, 1984). A few years ago, deLacoste-Utamsing and Holloway (1982) reported that human females had a larger posterior fifth of the corpus callosum, although there was no difference in total callosal area, and females had lower brain weights than did males. Witelson (1985) failed to confirm these findings and suggest "the possibility of a complex sex factor which, in interaction with hand preference, may be related to the size of some segment of the posterior half of the callosum" (p. 666). Of course, at the present time the relationship between these structural differences and any behavioral differences is speculative.

Most studies of differential brain functioning in male and female mammals focus on interhemispheric laterality (see McGlone, 1980, for review). Work on the intrahemispheric localization of various language functions using electrical stimulation techniques (Ojemann, 1983) and more frequent reporting of sexual arousal or orgasm related to temporal lobe epileptic seizures by women than by men (Remillard et al., 1983) indicate additional sexually dimorphic organizational differences in the human brain.

In the upcoming years, it is likely that there will be an increasing number of reports of both anatomical and functional sex differences in the human brain. On the assumption that the brain provides the biological foundation for behavior, it appears logical to further assume that these sex differences in the structure and function of neural tissue probably are related to at least some of the identified behavioral sex differences.

Another avenue through which sexually dimorphic brain differentiation may affect behavior is through the regulation of the pituitary–gonadal axis. Hypothalamic releasing factors are responsible for the regulation of gonadotropin release from the anterior pituitary. Males and females differ with respect to the pattern of gonadotropin release. Males exhibit a tonic or acyclic pattern, while the female pattern is cyclic. Like the external genital primordia, the hypothalamus is initially undifferentiated early in development, and the presence of androgen during some "critical" or "sensitive" period appears to determine the male pattern of tonic gonadotropin release (e.g., Barraclough, 1961, 1966; Barraclough & Gorski, 1961; Gorski, 1973; Gorski & Barraclough, 1963; Gorski & Wagner, 1965). In the absence of androgen, the female pattern of cyclic follicle stimulating hormone and luteinizing hormone release develops, mediating growth of the follicle, ovulation, and corpora lutea formation which together characterize menstrual and estrous cycles. Further, behavioral patterns which are linked to hormonal regulation are probably affected via this same mechanism. These principles of sexual development are especially relevant for infrahuman mammals in which there appears to be less cortical control over behavior.

PRENATAL HORMONES AND BEHAVIOR

Sex-typical behavior, like morphology and physiology, is influenced by the presence or absence of androgen during early development. Although virtually all behaviors seen in the male are apparent in the female, and vice versa, there are some behaviors which are exhibited at higher frequencies in one sex or the other. In nonhuman mammals, many of these behaviors are directly associated with reproduction. However (and most interesting for this discussion), a wide range of behaviors not directly related to mating which are sexually dimorphic are affected by prenatal hormonal stimulation. There are several sources of evidence supporting the notion that the prenatal hormone environment affects human behavioral development: (1) experiments with laboratory animals; (2) descriptions of patients with clinical endocrine syndromes; and (3) evaluations of human offspring whose mothers were treated during pregnancy with exogenous hormones. Several comprehensive reviews of this literature have been published during the past two decades (see Ellis, 1982; Hines, 1982; Reinisch, 1974, 1983; Reinisch & Sanders, 1984; Sanders & Reinisch, 1985).

Laboratory Animal Experiments

The only true experiments in behavioral endocrinology are conducted with laboratory animals, since studies evaluating human subjects cannot include the most fundamental component of experimental design—random assignment of subjects to treatment and control groups prior to the administration of hormones (Reinisch & Gandelman, 1978). Various species have been observed in an attempt to ascertain the role of prenatal exposure to gonadal hormones as determinants of subsequent behavior. The subjects of these experiments have primarily been rodents, although several very significant studies have been conducted with infrahuman primates.

Experiments to evaluate the influence of hormones during early life on the adult mating behavior of many mammals from rats to monkeys involve either (1) the addition of androgens during pre- or perinatal development of the female in an attempt to interfere with female differentiation and enhance masculine behavior patterns, or (2) androgen deprivation of the male by castration or chemical interference during early development in an attempt to feminize morphology and behavior. These studies have demonstrated that exposure to steroid hormones during an early critical period for sex behavior differentiation affects the expression of sexually dimorphic behavior patterns. Regardless of genetic sex, if a developing organism is exposed to gonadal steroids, particularly testosterone (the most potent androgen), both genital morphology and adult mating behavior will be masculinized. The relative absence of sex hormones, particularly testosterone, will assure feminine development of both genitalia and mating behavior. For example, in rodents, male behavior patterns include the masculine mating posture of mounting, intromission, ejaculation, and ultrasonic vocalizations. Behavioral patterns seen most frequently in female ro-

dents include the feminine mating posture of lordosis, darting, hopping, and ear wiggling (Beach, 1971). Morphological and behavioral masculinization of female mice which developed contiguous to male fetuses *in utero* has also been reported (Gandelman, vom Saal, & Reinisch, 1977; Hauser & Gandleman, 1983; vom Saal & Bronson, 1978, 1980). Thus, testosterone from littermates can have virilizing developmental consequences.

Perhaps most relevant in its implications for human behavioral development are those studies which demonstrate the effects of critical period hormonal intervention on sexually dimorphic behaviors that are *not* directly related to reproduction. Hormonal influences on behaviors of this kind have been identified in many mammalian species, including rodents and monkeys, and derive from observations of activity level, grooming, aggression, avoidance, exploration, urination posture, parenting, sleep patterns, play, and threat (see reviews by Ellis, 1982; Goy, 1981; Goy & McEwen, 1980; Hines, 1982; Reinisch, 1974, 1983; Reinisch & Sanders, 1984; Sanders & Reinisch, 1985). Studies of such non-mating-linked behaviors of animals are particularly relevant to the understanding of human development. Sex differences in these behaviors appear to be more analogous to the behavioral differences found between human males and females than are sex differences in animal mating behaviors, which are most closely tied to hormonal state and reproduction than is the case for humans.

Studies of Clinical Endocrine Syndromes

It should now be apparent that, in at least infrahuman mammals, early exposure to gonadal steroids profoundly influences the substrata mediating male and female behavior. Many effects similar to those produced experimentally in laboratory animals have been identified in human patients with chromosomal/genetic anomalies, resulting in abnormally high or low effective hormone levels during fetal development.

Adrenogenital syndrome is an example of a human clinical disorder analogous to the laboratory animal experiments in which androgen is administered to the developing organism. Human females born with this syndrome exhibit virilized external genitalia resulting from pathologically high levels of adrenal androgen produced during gestation by their own adrenal glands in response to an enzymatic deficiency. A series of studies of these children throughout development suggests that excess prenatal androgen affected not only genital morphology, but also had a lasting influence on psychosexual, personality, and cognitive development (Lewis, Money, & Epstein, 1968; Money & Ehrhardt, 1972; Money & Schwartz, 1976, 1977; Reinisch, Gandleman, & Speigel, 1979). As would be expected from the animal experiments, these females' behavior was masculinized on many dimensions, including activity level, interests, maternalism, and toy preferences, and was characterized by themselves and their parents as "tomboyish." In general, such reports suggest an effect on gender role behavior rather than on gender identity.

Recently, a study (Slijper, 1984) compared boys and girls with this syndrome to diabetic, healthy, and same-sex sibling controls using an instrument that assesses gender role behavior and parental interviews. It concluded that "the effect on gender role behaviour is not necessarily explained by hormonal action alone; being sick plays a role" (Slijper, 1984, p. 419). Further, it speculated that the shift toward more masculine behavior in adrenogenital females might be an indirect effect of uncertainty of gender identity generated by parental doubts. Clearly, more research into the psychosocial factors related to this syndrome is needed to elucidate the relationship of both hormonal and environmental components of congenital adrenal hyperplasia as these relate to behavioral outcomes.

Patients suffering from androgen insensitivity syndrome provide an example of human subjects with an early hormonal history similar to laboratory animal males deprived of androgen stimulation during the critical period for sexual differentiation. Androgen insensitivity, as the name implies, manifests itself as an inability of the cells to utilize the androgen produced by the testes of these patients despite XY chromosomes. The result is the birth and development of chromosomal males with normal testes producing normal titers of androgen whose external appearance is female. They are reared unconditionally as females and are most likely to come to the attention of the medical community during adolescence when menarche fails to occur. Studies of these individuals reveal that their behavior, attitudes, interests, and appearance are indistinguishable from those of unequivocally reared genetically, hormonally, and morphologically normal females (Money & Ehrhardt, 1972; Money & Ogunro, 1974; Reinisch et al., 1979).

Studies of these types of patients support the notion that humans are affected by the early hormone environment in a manner similar to that of other mammals.

Prenatal Exposure to Exogenous Sex Hormones

The offspring of mothers administered steroid hormones for various problems of pregnancy provide certain advantages as subjects for the evaluation of the behavioral effects of prenatal exposure to hormones as compared to patients with genetically based endocrine abnormalities such as those already described. Primary among these advantages is the absence of the confounding genetic factor that caused the hormonal abnormality and that may continue to exert its influence throughout development and/or be connected to other genetic determinants of behavior. Individuals exposed to hormones prenatally via medical treatments of their mothers are not subject to the continued influence of the hormones beyond the termination of drug administration. Therefore, these subjects can be evaluated for prenatal exposure alone since their development subsequent to the gestational exposure is undisturbed. Although this exposure more closely parallels that of experimental laboratory animals, the model is limited in that women are rarely treated with testosterone during pregnancy.

Hormones that are administered for pregnancy maintenance include synthetic progestins which do, however, have androgenic potential to varying extents. The synthetic progestins have been shown to exert influence on the development of human behavior (Hines, 1982; Reinisch, 1977, 1981, 1983; Reinisch & Sanders, 1984; Sanders & Reinisch, 1985). The alteration in behaviors which are manifested as a result of prenatal exposure to these hormones can, in general, be characterized as masculinizing. The few investigations in which the behavioral effects of these compounds have been evaluated indicate an influence of prenatal exposure on a broad spectrum of behaviors, including activity level, interests, toy preferences, clothing preferences, maternalism, mental abilities, masculinity/femininity, self-esteem personality/temperament, aggression/assertion, and the likelihood of marriage (Beral & Colwell, 1981; Ehrhardt, Meyer-Bahlburg, Feldman, & Ince, 1984; Ellis, 1982; Hines, 1982; Kester, 1984; Kester, Green, Finch, & Williams, 1980; *Lancet*, 1981; Reinisch, 1977, 1981, 1983; Reinisch et al., 1979; Reinisch & Karow, 1977; Reinisch & Sanders, 1982; Sanders & Reinisch, 1985; Zussman, Zussman, & Dalton, 1975).

The nature of the behavioral outcome appears to be dependent upon both the species of the animal and its sex as well as on the type of hormonal intervention (chemical nature of the compound, timing of exposure, dosage, and duration of treatment). For example, personality development appeared to be differentially affected, depending on the nature of prenatal hormone exposure (Reinisch, 1977; Reinisch & Karow, 1977). When subjects exposed to combinations of estrogen and progestin were examined, offspring exposed primarily to progestin were found to be more "independent," "self-assured," and "self-sufficient" than unexposed sibling controls, whereas those exposed to higher proportions of estrogen were more "group dependent" and "group oriented."

Differential effects due to various treatment regimes were also reported by Kester *et al.* (1980). Males exposed prenatally to diethylstilbesterol (DES) recalled the most stereotypically masculine boyhoods, whereas progesterone-exposed males recalled the least. Males exposed to a combination of both DES and progesterone reported high sex drive, while low sex drive was reported by males exposed to synthetic progestins. Those exposed only to natural progesterone *in utero* were most likely to report erectile failure. A recent study (Hines & Shipley, 1984) compared women exposed prenatally to DES to their unexposed sisters on sexually dimorphic cognitive abilities and cerebral lateralization. No differences were found with respect to

visuospatial and verbal ability. However, the performance of DES-exposed women appeared to be masculinized on a dichotic listening task in that they demonstrated an enhanced right ear advantage and a strong negative correlation between right and left ear scores.

The apparent paradox of masculinization due to estrogen exposure has been explained via the "aromatization hypothesis." Within brain cells, testosterone can be converted to estradiol by means of an aromatizing enzyme. It is believed that estrogen acts at the cellular level to masculinize many aspects of neural and behavioral development in some, but not all, species (e.g., Baum, Carrick, Erskine, Gallagher, & Shim, 1983; Goy, 1981; Goy & McEwen, 1980; Naftolin, 1979; Plapinger & McEwen, 1978). During normal development, endogenous estradiol from the fetoplacental unit appears to be rendered relatively inert by binding with α-fetoprotein in rodents and estrogen binding protein in humans. DES (which is a nonsteroidal synthetic estrogen) does not bind to these proteins and can reach the brain in a biologically active form capable of exerting a masculinzing effect. However, there is some doubt as to the applicability of the aromatization hypothesis to human sexual differentiation. Dihydrotestosterone, a nonaromatizable androgen, is capable of organizing masculine sexual behavior in monkeys and guinea pigs, but not in rats, mice, or hamsters, which are masculinized by aromatizable androgens and/or estrogens (Goy & McEwen, 1980). Whether this mechanism or another unrelated pharmacological action is responsible for the behavioral effects of prenatal exposure to DES in humans remains unclear. Finally, controversy exists with regard to the behavioral effects of DES in humans. Some laboratories have reported feminizing effects of prenatal exposure to DES (Reinisch, 1977; Reinisch & Karow, 1977; Yalom, Green, & Fisk, 1973). This may reflect the relative independence of masculinization and feminization or differences in dosage, timing, and duration of DES treatment among groups studied.

Our recent study of aggression/assertion in synthetic progestin (19-nor-17α-ethynyl-testosterone, 19-NET) -exposed offspring provides both an exemplar and a further extension of the boundaries of our understanding of early hormonal influence (Reinisch, 1981). Human offspring whose mothers were administered synthetic progestins with virilizing potential during pregnancy were tested with a pencil-and-paper instrument designed to assess the potential for aggressive behavior by eliciting verbal indications of subjects' responses to a variety of common conflict situations. Scores were obtained for physical aggression, verbal aggression, nonaggressive coping, and withdrawal. In general, males at all ages choose more physically aggressive responses than do females on this measure (Reinisch & Sanders, 1986). As would be expected from the research outlined above, when female subjects exposed prenatally to progestins were compared to their unexposed sisters, their physical aggression scores were significantly higher. However, progestin-exposed males also exhibited higher physical aggression scores than their unexposed brothers, suggesting that additional stimulation with potentially virilizing hormones may induce increased masculine response in human males as well as females (Reinisch & Sanders, 1984).

Whether higher physical aggression scores reflect an increased probability of aggressive action in real-life situations has not yet been definitively determined. However, in a recent pilot study of young adults (18 males and 20 females) who were exposed prenatally to medically prescribed barbiturates and their cohort-matched, unexposed controls (in preparation from our laboratory), physical aggression scores from this measure were positively correlated with self-reported frequency of violent acts during adolescence. The observed influence of hormones during gestation on later aggression, particularly in human males, suggests that individual differences in the frequency of aggressive behavior may be related in part to natural variations in hormone levels prior to birth.

It is relevant to note briefly here that substances other than hormones may have the capacity to affect the development of gender-related behavior patterns in humans and laboratory animals. An example of such a widely prescribed and abused drug is phenobarbital (a barbiturate), which, by means of its influence on liver metabolic activities, affects the metabolism of testosterone and thereby the course of normal prenatal masculinization (Reinisch & Sanders, 1982). Based upon the evaluation of laboratory animals exposed during early development to barbiturates, these substances appear to demasculinize or femininize males. As already noted, in a preliminary evaluation of a small number of subjects on a narrow set of dimensions, barbiturates appear to be either masculinizing or developmentally disruptive.

In summary, exogenous hormones administered prenatally appear to influence the behavioral development of humans in a manner parallel to that of laboratory animals. Next, data are presented which suggest that naturally occurring variation in endogenous prenatal hormone levels may contribute to observed sex differences in behavior as well as variation in the degree of masculinization or feminization within each sex.

Perinatal Endogenous Hormones

The majority of research examining the influence of early hormone exposure on human behavioral development has utilized samples of patients with various clinical endocrine disorders or subjects exposed *in utero* to exogenous hormones that were administered to their mothers for medical reasons (see above). A few studies have been conducted relating levels of gonadal steroids (including testosterone, estrogen, and progesterone) present in umbilical cord blood sampled at birth with subsequent behavioral development. One advantage to these studies is that they provide insight into the effects of "normal" levels of endogenous hormones, albeit at a unique moment in development. Although the critical or sensitive period for hormonal influence on genital differentiation occurs much earlier during gestation (Abramovich, 1974; George et al., 1981), the critical period(s) for other sexually dimorphic dimensions of morphology, physiology, and behavior might extend through gestation and early infancy. For example, there is a postnatal rise in testosterone between Days 10 and 61 of life in human male infants (Forest, Lecoq, Salle, & Bertrand, 1981; Forest, Sizonenko, Cathiard, & Bertrand, 1974), which may be relevant to· sexual differentiation.

Differences in hormonal concentrations at delivery in the umbilical cord blood of males and females have been noted in both humans (Forest et al., 1974; Maccoby, Doering, Jacklin, & Kraemer, 1979) and rhesus monkeys (Resko, 1974a, 1974b). Circulating testosterone levels are higher in males than in females at birth, whereas estrogen concentrations are comparable between sexes. Data regarding sex differences in levels of progesterone present at birth are contradictory (Forest & Cathiard, 1978; Hagemenas & Kittinger, 1972; Laatikainen & Peltonen, 1974; Maccoby et al., 1979; McDonald, Yoshinaga, & Greep, 1973; Resko, 1975). Any sex difference in progesterone at birth is probably not robust and would be unlikely to contribute significantly to the development of sex differences in behavior (Maccoby et al., 1979). Birth order effects on hormone concentrations in cord blood have been noted for estrogens (Maccoby et al., 1979; Shutt, Smith, & Shearman, 1974; Smith, Shutt, & Shearman, 1975) and progesterone (Maccoby et al., 1979), with higher levels found in firstborns.

Jacklin, Maccoby, and Doering (1983) reported on a longitudinal study in which timidity was assessed in 6- to 18-month-old children (84 boys and 78 girls) by presentation of a novel toy. The child's responses were then related to his or her concentrations of sex hormones (androstenedione, testosterone, estrone, estradiol, and progesterone) which were present in umbilical cord blood at birth. For boys, significant negative correlations were reported between timidity and cord concentrations of testosterone and progesterone, whereas estradiol was positively related to timidity. For girls, however, no significant correlations were found between hormones and timidity. A follow-up study (Jacklin, Maccoby, Doering, & King, 1984) examined muscular strength during the first 3 years of life in relation to sex of the infant and umbilical cord blood hormone profiles (5 hormones listed above). Small but significant sex differences in strength were found. Cord progesterone levels were positively correlated with strength for boys, but negatively correlated with strength for girls.

In their most recent report on this longitudinal project, Marcus, Maccoby, Jacklin, and Doering (1985) evaluated the predominant mood state of 104 children during the first 2 years of life as it related to the hormonal profiles of their cord blood at birth. Boys were reported to be in a happy/excited mood more often than girls, and girls were reported to be in a quiet/calm mood more often than boys. For boys, androstenedione (at trend levels), estrogen, and progesterone were positively correlated with boys' happy/excited mood and negatively correlated with their time spent in a quiet/calm mood. Hormone–mood relationships for girls were almost always in the opposite direction from boys and did not attain significance. Since the concentrations of the five hormones measured covary, a component score representing the common variance of all the hormones together was generated. This "all hormone" component was positively correlated with boys' happy/excited mood scores and negatively correlated with their quiet/calm moods. The sex difference in the direction of the hormone effect was found to be significant. A separate "androgens" component showed no correlation to predominant mood for either sex.

These data provide support for the hypothesis that differences in endogenous levels of hormones during early postnatal development may influence personality and temperament in later life. The fact that all of these studies report sex differences in the relationships among hormones and timidity, strength, mood, and activity level (C. N. Jacklin, E. E. Maccoby, & C. H. Doering, unpublished data reported in Marcus et al., 1985) suggests that "if hormones do have an organizational effect on the organism, the nature of the effect is different for the two sexes" (Marcus et al., 1985, p. 338). This conclusion is consistent with some of the data reported above which suggest that each genetic sex may provide a distinct substrate for some types of hormonal action.

PRENATAL HORMONES AND SEXUAL ORIENTATION

During the past decade, psychoendocrine theories of sexual orientation have come to focus on the role of hormones during fetal development. Studies of adult endocrine status have, in general, failed to consistently differentiate between homosexuals and heterosexuals (Gladue, Green, & Hellman, 1984; Gooren, in preparation; Gooren, Rao, van Kessel, & Harmsen-Louman, 1984; Gooren, van Kessel, & Harmsen-Louman, 1983; Sanders, Bain, & Langevin, 1984a, 1984b; Sanders, Langevin, & Bain, 1983; for review, see Meyer-Bahlburg, 1984). Based upon animal models, Dörner (1976) has postulated that prenatal androgen insufficiency in males and prenatal androgen excess in females leads to homosexuality by means of the development of "pseudohermaphroditism" of the central nervous system.

There are a number of problems in extrapolating from animal models of sex behavior to human sexual orientation (Beach, 1979):

1. Is increased lordosis (female sexual behavior) in a male animal or mounting (male sexual behavior) in a female animal equivalent to homosexuality in humans? Isn't a male mounting another male "homosexual" as well? Some animal studies have focused on preferences for proximity to males versus females rather than copulatory patterns in an attempt to use animal models to draw inferences about the derivation of human sexual orientation. Further research is necessary to establish the validity of all such comparisons to human sexual orientation.
2. The hormonal manipulations required to produce inversions of sexual behavior often lead to alterations of the genitalia as well. However, human homosexuals have normal primary and secondary sexual characteristics.
3. Even data derived from laboratory experiments with animals are not in full agreement with the prenatal hormone imbalance theory of the etiology of homosexuality in that the type of sexual behavior displayed, especially among prenatally treated females, is dependent on whether exogenous hormones are administered in adulthood, the nature of the hormone (estrogen vs. testosterone), and the social context (e.g., sex, age, and status of companions) such that the same animal may lordose in the presence of a male and mount in the presence of a female (see Goldfoot & Neff, 1987; Meyer-Bahlburg, 1984; Phoenix & Chambers, 1982; Phoenix, Jensen, & Chambers, 1983; Whalen, 1974; Whalen & Edwards, 1967).

To date, the number of human subjects studied with respect to sexual orientation with known abnormal prenatal hormone histories due to endocrine disorders or medical treatment of their mothers is too small to draw any definite conclusions about the influence of hormones during prenatal development on human sexual orientation. A few studies provide preliminary evidence that the prenatal hormonal milieu may make some contribution to the development of sexual orientation. When compared to women with androgen insensitivity or Müllerian duct aplasia (absence of internal female organs), women with early-treated adrenogenital syndrome (see above) were found to have increased bisexual imagery and/or experience, although the majority were primarily heterosexual (Money & Schwartz, 1977; Money, Schwartz, & Lewis, 1984, Schwartz & Money, 1983). A recent study of women exposed prenatally to DES (Ehrhardt *et al.*, 1985) reported higher bisexual or homosexual tendencies in DES-exposed women as compared to women with abnormal Pap smear findings and unexposed sisters. Although the effect is larger when nonsiblings are compared and one-tailed tests are used, the findings are still suggestive that prenatal exposure to this nonsteroidal estrogen may contribute to a decrease in heterosexual exclusivity. (As discussed, estrogens appear to have masculinizing potential, at least in the developing rat.) However, studies of offspring of progestogen-treated pregnancies failed to demonstrate significant increases in homosexuality (Kester *et al.*, 1980; Money & Matthews, 1982; Zussman *et al.*, 1975).

Replications and studies of subjects exposed to other maternal treatment regimes are necessary to clarify the extent to which the prenatal hormone environment may affect sexual orientation. Whether the putative prenatal hormonal influence on sexual orientation is direct or indirect [i.e., exerting its effect via alteration of personality and temperament variables which may be related to gender role conformity (Reinisch, 1977)] remains unclear.

PUBERTAL HORMONES
AND BEHAVIOR

The complex interplay of the effects of androgen exposure during the prenatal critical period, hormonal activation of puberty, and social, psychological, and cultural factors is interestingly portrayed in the case histories of individuals evidencing the syndrome of 5α-reductase deficiency (for review and in depth discussion, see Rubin, Reinisch, & Haskett, 1981). In brief, individuals with 5α-reductase deficiency have testes that produce normal amounts of testosterone during prenatal life, but they are partially or completely missing the enzyme which converts testosterone into dihydrotestosterone. During prenatal development, it is dihydrotestosterone that is responsible for virilization of the external genital primordia. Therefore, the internal genitalia which are dependent upon testosterone for their differentiation develop normally, and presumably the brain is exposed to normal amounts of androgen. However, due to the enzymatic deficiency, these genetic males are born with ambiguous external genitalia which are more female-like than male-like. At puberty when their testes resume production of testosterone, these individuals experience significant somatic masculinization and their clitoris-like phalluses are considerably enlarged, since testosterone alone is responsible for genital enlargement at puberty.

Considerable controversy has been generated regarding interpretation of the rather unusual behavioral developmental history of a group of these individuals discovered in the Dominican Republic. It appeared upon superficial examination of the data that these individuals, assigned and reared as females, change both their gender identity (the primary identification as male or female) and their gender role (behavioral differences related to sex which are culturally influenced) in response to the hormonal stimulation and the resulting morphological virilization that accompany male puberty (Imperato-McGinley, Guerrero, Gautier, & Peterson, 1974; Imperato-McGinley, Peterson, & Gautier, 1981; Imperato-McGinley, Peterson, Gautier, & Sturla, 1979; Imperato-McGinley et al., 1980). These researchers concluded that the most significant factor in the development of

male gender identity is the presence of testosterone prenatally, perinatally, and especially pubertally. This view is in contrast to the more widely held belief that sex of rearing is the primary determinant of gender identity (Money, 1977; Money & Ehrhardt, 1972). This seemingly unusual capacity to assume successfully an adult male gender identity/role following a more or less consistent rearing as female can only be understood by thorough examination of the influences exerted on the members of the Dominican kindred by a combination of hormonal, social, cultural, and psychological factors. As would be predicted from the evidence obtained in laboratory animal studies, other human clinical syndromes, and subjects exposed exogenously to additional hormones, it is most likely the interaction of a complex series of factors (biological and socioenvironmental) that results in the adult gender identity/role of these individuals.

These factors include the following in rough order of their temporal influence:

1. Testosterone exposure at normal male levels *in utero* has a concomitant influence on masculine brain development. This stimulation would be expected, as in girls with adrenogenital syndrome or those whole mothers were treated with potentially virilizing synthetic progestins, to produce tomboyish behavior in unambivalently assigned and reared girls and to facilitate the adoption of masculine behavior patterns for either sex.

2. At birth, these individuals possess genitalia that are not distinctly male or normally female. Even if they are labeled as female, possession of abnormally appearing genitalia would be expected to alter the response of parents and other members of the family and community as well as stimulate self-doubt contributing to a foundation for gender confusion. The likelihood is that in most cases, the sex of rearing is somewhat equivocal, since the two villages where these individuals have been born and raised during the past 80 years have a special name for the affected children which translates as "penis at 12 (years old)."

3. This very traditional and conservative society applies narrow sex role definitions,

places great emphasis on gender differences in behavior, and confers higher status and more freedom to males. Individuals who do not fit easily into the prescribed roles (such as tomboyish girls) are likely to experience ambivalence about their assigned gender and may welcome the alternate choice that is offered by pubertal masculinization. Appraisal of the case histories of patients with 5α-reductase deficiency from more industrialized, less traditional societies reveals that individuals evidencing this syndrome do not, in general, change either gender identity or role in response to their paradoxical pubertal experience.

4. At puberty, in response to testicular hormonal stimulation, individuals with 5α-reductase deficiency are morphologically masculinized. The response of the individual and the sociocultural environment to this pubertal hormonal alteration of morphology, resulting in the differentiation of masculine secondary sexual characteristics combined with the effects of the stimulation by testosterone of a central nervous system masculinely organized or sensitized during prenatal development, lead the majority of 5α-reductase-deficient individuals to choose to assume a male gender identity/role. This transformation typically occurs after several years of conflict. All those who accomplish this transition successfully appear also to develop sexual relationships with adult females despite their infertility. Infertility is due primarily to perineal hypospadias common to all affected males as well as abnormalities of spermatogenesis in many of these individuals (Imperato-McGinley *et al.*, 1981; Wilson, Griffin, Leshin, & McDonald, 1983).

Although individuals with 5α-reductase deficiency constitute an unusual case, this complex of influences contributing in sequence to the development and differentiation of adult gender identity/role and sexual orientation is similar for all humans. These data also serve as evidence of the likely influence that prenatal, perinatal, and pubertal hormones have on development of these outcomes.

MODELS OF MASCULINITY AND FEMININITY

The studies reported above provide examples of the complex sequence of events and matrix of possible influences and outcomes with respect to the role of prenatal hormones in behavioral development. They also reveal the inadequacy of the notion that masculinity and femininity reside on a single dimension, so that the more masculine an organism's behavior, the necessarily less feminine it must be. Such a unidimensional or polar model (Figure 21.1A) does not incorporate findings that demonstrate the reduction of male-like behavior with no concomitant increase in the frequency or strength of feminine behavior, or the circumstances that result in an organism capable of exhibiting high levels of both masculine and feminine behavior, depending upon environmental and/or internal stimuli. In fact, it has been demonstrated that depending upon the experimental manipulation of timing, dosage, duration, and/or type of gonadal steroid hormone administered, subsequent behavior can be masculinized, demasculinized, feminized, and/or defeminized regardless of genetic sex.

Based upon these data, two alternative two-dimensional models of sexual differentiation and expression have been proposed. The orthogonal or independent model (Figure 21.1B: Bem, 1974; Berzins, Welling, & Wetter, 1978; Constantinople, 1973; Heilbrun, 1976; Spence, Helmreich, & Stapp, 1974; Whalen, 1974) and the oblique or correlated model (Figure 21.1C: Reinisch, 1976) suggest that masculinity and femininity are relatively independent behavioral dimensions. These models imply that reduction of masculinity results in demasculinization with no necessary increase in feminine behavior (femininization). Conversely, a decrease in feminine behavior is labeled as defeminization and is not necessarily expected to be accompanied by an increase in masculine behavior (masculinization). The difference between the orthogonal and oblique models resides in the degree of independence which is understood to exist between masculinity and femininity. While the orthogonal model proposes complete independence, the oblique model suggests, based upon experimental data from laboratory animal research as well

A. BIPOLAR

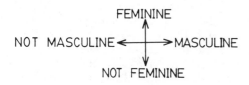

B. ORTHOGONAL

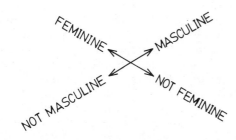

C. OBLIQUE

FIGURE 21.1. Models of masculinity and femininity.

as studies of humans, that some degree of correlation exists between the dimensions of masculinization/demasculinization and feminization/defeminization.

These principles have been incorporated into measures for the evaluation of human gender role by such researchers as Bem in the Bem Sex Role Inventory (Bem, 1974, 1977) and Spence, Helmreich, and Stapp in the Personal Attributes Questionnaire (Spence & Helmreich, 1978; Spence et al., 1974) by the inclusion of four possible classifications for males and females—Masculine (high masculine score, low feminine score), Feminine (high feminine score, low masculine score), Androgynous (high scores on both dimensions), and Undifferentiated (low scores on both dimensions).

It should be noted that the various behavioral and physiological systems appear to develop independently of one another. Thus, one system may be stereotypically masculine while another is not, for example, pseudo-hermaphrodites whose phenotypes are not consistent with their genotypes, transsexuals in which biological and psychological sex are discrepant, or the male homosexual who is a stereotypically masculine football player. Evidence from sex role measures (e.g., Bem Sex Role Inventory, Personal Attributes Questionnaire) clearly demonstrates that large proportions of both the male and female populations fall in each of the four sex role categories—Androgynous, Feminine, Masculine, and Undifferentiated (Spence & Helmreich, 1978).

Further, systems differ with respect to the applicability of the one- versus two-dimensional models. For example, a unipolar model applies well to the development of the external genitalia in which masculinization is the opposite of feminization. There are also certain personality dimensions such as submissive-dominant for which one extreme is stereotypically masculine, while the opposite is feminine (at least in American culture). The two-dimensional model applies to the internal sexual apparatus developed independently by the Wolffian and Müllerian systems; the development of one does not preclude the development of the other. A normal female would be demasculinized with respect to the Wolffian system and feminized with respect to the Müllerian system. On sex role inventories, personality traits such as emotionality and competitiveness load only on the femininity and masculinity scales, respectively.

INTERACTION BETWEEN BIOLOGICAL AND SOCIOENVIRONMENTAL FACTORS

Based on data such as those reviewed above, it seems clear that the early prenatal hormone environment does influence physical and behavioral development in similar ways across a number of mammalian species, including humans. Certain sex differences in behavioral patterns, perception, cognitive abilities, personality, and temperament are mediated by the degree to which the fetus is exposed to endogenous or exogenous hormones. However, this influence is not absolute or deterministic. Rather, it is probably best to conceptualize the effect of the early hormone environment, particularly in relation to human development, as "influencing" the development of personality or temperament, or "predisposing" the individual's cognitive abilities or behavioral potential in a certain direction; that is, the early hormonal milieu bestows a bias on the neural system which then facilitates the acquisition and maintenance of behaviors more characteristic of one sex than the other. Generally speaking, the presence of androgenic substances during prenatal development will shift this predisposition toward that which is considered typical of the average male. This masculinization can occur regardless of genetic sex. The relative absence of masculinizing agents during this sensitive period will encourage the expression of traits and behavioral patterns in a direction characteristic of the average female.

It must be remembered that the environment has a profound impact on behavior not only via reinforcement and punishment, but also via the principles described in social learning theory. The more cognitively oriented the species, the more difficult it is to predict behavior based simply upon biological information. In a society which holds strongly divergent sex stereotypes, it is expected that the biologically influenced sexual dimorphisms of behavior would be magnified by socioenvironmental factors.

In humans, behavior is also judged and regulated by the individual's self-concept. Self-concept is determined and modulated by a complex of factors, including cognitive, temperamental, and physical factors which may predispose the individual to exhibit certain behaviors and not others.

Bem's Gender Schema Theory (1985, 1987) suggests that gender role conformity results in part from the assimilation of the self-concept to gender role stereotypes. As children learn their society's "gender schema," they learn which attributes are associated with their sex and model their behavior after that pattern. Further, the child learns to evaluate his or her own adequacy according to these gender stereotypes. "The gender schema becomes a prescriptive standard or guide and self-esteem becomes its hostage" (Bem, 1987).

The degree to which a person's gender identity or sexual orientation is correlated with gender role conformity is also highly variable. For some men, for example, being a "macho" is an essential part of their feeling that they are male. For some women, being a mother is an intrinsic part of their concept of womanhood. Thus, gender role conformity depends not only on behavioral predispositions which may be influenced by the early hormone environment, but also on the degree to which the individual has internalized society's values regarding conformity to sex role stereotypes and the degree to which he or she believes such conformity forms the foundation of his or her maleness or femaleness. Such stereotypes are culturally specific and reflect the values of a given society at a particular time in history.

Multiplier Effect

From the moment of birth through adulthood, interactions between the organism and the environment yield behavioral sex differences in two ways (Reinisch et al., 1979). First, males and females perceive certain stimuli differently (Gandelman, 1983). Perceptual, cognitive, and temperament differences probably lead to differences in interpretation of and response to the environment. Second, most societies treat males and females differently based upon the sex assigned at birth and sex of rearing.

The more divergent the sex stereotypes are within a culture, the more one would expect to see biologically determined sexual dimorphisms in behavior magnified by postnatal socioenvironmental influences. However, it is important to note that in strongly gender-stereotyped cultures, traits or roles may be differentially attributed to the sexes in the absence of or even contrary to a biologically based rationale. For example, based upon physiological sex differences (e.g., height and weight, oxygen and food consumption, sensory thresholds), women are more suited to be astronauts than are men. On the other hand, even if there were no societal "rules" regarding what is appropriate behavior for males and females, one would still presumably find some quantitative differences in the frequency of behaviors displayed when groups of males and females were compared, although the discrepancies would be much smaller.

The interaction between the organism and the environment in the development of sexual

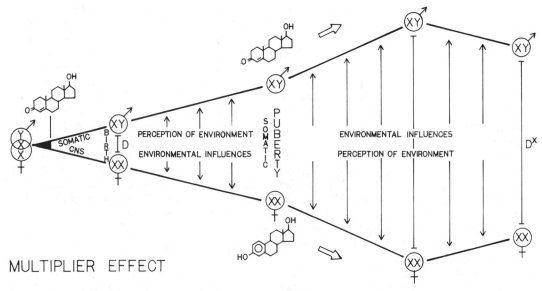

MULTIPLIER EFFECT

FIGURE 21.2. Role of the interaction between biological factors and the environment in the development of sex differences.

dimorphisms in human behavior can be conceptualized as a "multiplier effect" (derived from Wilson, 1975) (Figure 21.2). At conception, only chromosomal/genetic differences exist. During normal development, this leads to the production of androgens in male fetuses, resulting in divergent prenatal hormonal environments for males and females. The prenatal hormonal milieu produces somatic and central nervous system morphological dimorphisms between the sexes which lead to psychological differences. Thus, there are small but significant sex differences in appearance, behavior, and responsiveness at birth to which the social environment immediately responds (Reinisch, Rosenblum, Rubin, & Schulsinger, under review). With the announcement of the child's sex, cultural influences begin to magnify the initially small sex differences. Each successive interaction alters the organism slightly. The modified organism then perceives and responds to the environment slightly differently and, in turn, is perceived and responded to in a slightly different fashion. Through this dynamic transaction among biological, psychological, and social factors—between the organism and its environment—sex differences in behavior emerge. At puberty, when the physical differences between the sexes are dramatically

increased, so are the perceptual discrepancies and societal expectations of how the individual should behave. All these factors serve to maximize overall sex differences during the early adult/reproductive years. There is some evidence that androgyny increases and thus, sex differences decrease with age (Maracek, 1979) following the reproductive years.

It is important to mention that the variability of abilities and behavioral frequencies among individuals within a sex is great and that small mean differences between males and females for specific traits are accompanied by highly overlapping distributions. For example, generally speaking, men perform better on certain spatial tasks, while women exhibit better performances on certain verbal tasks. However, many females achieve higher scores on spatial tasks than does the average male. In fact, the average sex difference is one-half standard deviation (Jere Levy, personal communication).

SUMMARY

Substantial evidence suggests that hormones present during critical periods of gestation appear to influence behavioral development, specifically gender role, by alteration of the central nervous system. At present, data supporting the hypothesis that prenatal hormones affect sexual orientation are much less convincing. Even considering data from individuals with 5α-reductase deficiency, gender identity appears to be more closely correlated with the sex of rearing than with prenatal hormonal history. Thus, the prenatal hormone environment appears to exert its strongest influence on behavioral predispositions or gender role. Any suggested influence on sexual orientation and/or gender identity must remain tentative until further evidence accrues and, in any case, may be secondary to effects of gender role behaviors. In societies with divergent gender stereotypes, sex differences in behavior are magnified as a result of successive interactions between the organism and its environment.

Acknowledgments

This work was supported in part by the National Institute of Child Health and Human Development grant HD 17655 and the Indiana University general fund (to JMR). We gratefully acknowledge the support of M. Lowengrub and K. Gros Louis and The Kinsey Institute staff, the library assistance of G. Pershing, N. Alfonso, and M. Davis, and editorial comments by C. Kaufman.

References

Abramovich, D. R. (1974). Human sexual differentiation—*in utero* influences. *British Journal of Obstetrics and Gynaecology, 81*, 448–453.

Barraclough, C. A. (1961). Production of anovulatory, sterile rats by single injections of testosterone proprionate. *Endocrinology (Baltimore), 67*, 62–67.

Barraclough, C. A. (1966). Modification in the CNS regulation of reproduction after exposure of prepubertal rats to steroid hormones. *Recent Progress in Hormone Research, 22*, 503–539.

Barraclough, C. A., & Gorski, R. A. (1961). Evidence that the hypothalamus is responsible for androgen-induced sterility in the female rat. *Endocrinology (Baltimore), 68*, 68–79.

Baum, M. J., Carrick, J. A., Erskine, M. S., Gallagher, C. A., & Shim, J. H. (1983). Normal differentiation of masculine sexual behavior in male ferrets despite neonatal inhibition of brain aromatase or 5α-reductase activity. *Neuroendocrinology, 36*, 277–284.

Beach, F. A. (1945). Bisexual mating behavior in the male rat: Effects of castration and hormone administration. *Physiological Zoology, 18*, 390–402.

Beach, F. A. (1971). Hormonal factors controlling the differentiation, development, and display of copulatory behavior in the ramstergig and related species. In E. Tobach, L. R. Aronson, & E. Shaw (Eds.), *Biopsychology of development* (pp. 249–296). New York: Academic Press.

Beach, F. A. (1979). Animal models for human sexuality. *Ciba Foundation Symposium 62* (new series), 113–143.

Bem, S. L. (1974). The measurement of psychological androgyny. *Journal of Consulting and Clinical Psychology, 42*, 155–162.

Bem, S. L. (1977). On the utility of alternative procedures for assessing psychological androgyny. *Journal of Consulting and Clinical Psychology, 45*, 196–205.

Bem, S. L. (1985). Gender schema theory. In T. B. Sonderegger (Ed.), *Nebraska symposium on motivation 1984: Psychology and gender* (Vol. 32). Lincoln: University of Nebraska Press.

Bem, S. L. (1987). Masculinity and femininity exist only in the mind of the perceiver. In J. M. Reinisch, L. A. Rosenblum, & S. A. Sanders, *Masculinity/femininity: Basic perspectives.* New York: Oxford University Press.

Beral, V., & Colwell, I. (1981). Randomized trial of high doses of stilbesterol and ethisterone therapy in pregnancy: Long-term follow-up of the children. *Journal of Epidemiology and Community Health, 39*, 155–160.

Berzins, J. I., Welling, M. A., & Wetter, R. E. (1978). A new measure of psychological androgyny based on the Personality Research Form. *Journal of Consulting and Clinical Psychology, 46*, 126–138.

Constantinople, A. (1973). Masculinity–femininity: An exception to a famous dectum? *Psychological Bulletin, 80*, 389–407.

de Lacoste-Utamsing, C., & Holloway, R. L. (1982). Sexual dimorphism in the human corpus callosum. *Science, 216*, 1431–1432.

De Vries, G. J., De Bruin, J. P. C., Uylings, H. B. M., & Corner, M. A. (Eds.) (1984). *Progress in brain research: Vol. 61. Sex differences in the brain.* Amsterdam: Elsevier.

Dörner, G. (1976). *Hormones and brain differentiation.* Amsterdam: Elsevier.

Ehrhardt, A. A., Meyer-Bahlburg, H. F. L., Feldman, J. F., & Ince, S. E. (1984). Sex-dimorphic behavior in childhood subsequent to prenatal exposure to exogenous progetogens and estrogens. *Archives of Sexual Behavior, 13*(5), 457–477.

Ehrhardt, A. A., Meyer-Bahlburg, H. F. L., Rosen, L. R., Feldman, J. F., Veridiano, N. P., Zimmerman, I., & McEwen, B. S. (1985). Sexual orientation after prenatal exposure to exogenous estogen. *Archives of Sexual Behavior, 14*(1), 57–75.

Ellis, L. (1982). Developmental androgen fluctuations and the five dimensions of mammalian sex (with emphasis upon the behavioral dimension and the human species). *Ethology and Sociobiology, 3*, 171–197.

Forest, M. C., & Cathiard, A. M. (1978). Ontogenic study of plasma 17α-hydroxyprogesterone in the human. I. Postnatal period: Evidence for transient ovarian activity in infancy. *Pediatric Research, 12*, 5–11.

Forest, M. G., Lecoq, A., Salle, B., & Bertrand, J. (1981). Does phenobarbital treatment affect testicular and adrenal functions and steroid binding in plasma in infancy? *Journal of Clinical Endocrinology and Metabolism, 52*, 103–110.

Forest, M. G., Sizonenko, P. C., Cathiard, A. M., & Bertrand, J. (1974). Hypophysogonadal function in humans during the first year of life. *Journal of Clinical Investigation, 53*, 819–828.

Gandleman, R. (1983). Gonadal hormones and sensory function. *Neuroscience and Biobehavioral Reviews, 7*, 1–17.

Gandleman, R., vom Saal, F. S., & Reinisch, J. M. (1977). Contiguity of male foetuses affects morphology and behaviour of female mice. *Nature (London), 266*, 722–724.

George, F. W., Griffin, J. E., Leshin, M., & Wilson, J. D. (1981). Endocrine control of sexual differentiation in the human. In M. J. Novy, & J. A. Resko (Eds.), *Fetal endocrinology* (pp. 341–357). New York: Academic Press.

Gladue, B. A., Green, R., & Hellman, R. E. (1984). Neuroendocrine response to estrogen and sexual orientation. *Science, 225*, 1496–1499.

Goldfoot, D. A., & Neff, D. A. (1987). Assessment of behavioral sex differences in social contexts: Perspectives from primatology. In J. M. Reinisch, L. A. Rosenblum, & S. A. Sanders (Eds.), *Masculinity/ femininity: Basic perspectives.* New York: Oxford University Press.

Gooren, L. (in preparation) Biomedical theories of sexual orientation: A critical examination. In D. P. McWhirter, S. A. Sanders, & J. M. Reinisch (Eds.), *Homosexuality/Heterosexuality.* New York: Oxford University Press.

Gooren, L. J. G., Rao, B. R., van Kessel, H., & Harmsen-Louman, W. (1984). Estrogen positive feedback on LH secretion in transsexuality. *Psychoneuroendocrinology, 9*(3), 249–259.

Gooren, L. J. G., van Kessel, H., & Harmsen-Louman, W. (1983). Gonadotrophin response to estrogen administration in transsexuality [Abstract]. *Neuroendocrinology Letters, 5*, 130.

Gorski, R. A. (1973). Perinatal effects of sex steroids on brain development and function. *Progress in Brain Research, 39*, 149–163.

Gorski, R. A. (1987). Sex differences in the rodent brain: Their nature and origin. In J. M. Reinisch, L. A. Rosenblum, & S. A. Sanders (Eds.), *Masculinity/ femininity: Basic perspectives.* New York: Oxford University Press.

Gorski, R. A., & Barraclough, C. A. (1963). Effects of low dosages of androgen on the differentiation of hypothalamic regulatory control of ovulation in the rat. *Endocrinology (Baltimore), 73*, 210–216.

Gorski, R. A., Gordon, J. H., Shryne, J. E., & Southam, A. M. (1978). Evidence for a morphological sex difference within the medial preoptic area of the rat brain. *Brain Research, 148*, 333–346.

Gorski, R. A., & Wagner, J. W. (1965). Gonadal activity and sexual differentiation of the hypothalamus. *Endocrinology (Baltimore), 76*, 226–239.

Goy, R. W. (1968). Organizing effects of androgens on the behavior of rhesus monkeys. In R. P. Michael (Ed.), *Endocrinology and human behavior* (pp. 12–310). London: Oxford University Press.

Goy, R. W. (1981). The differentiation of male social traits in female rhesus monkeys by prenatal treatment with androgens: Variations in types of androgens, duration, and timing of treatments. In M. J. Novy & J. A. Resko (Eds.), *Fetal endocrinology* (pp. 319–340). New York: Academic Press.

Goy, R. W., & McEwen, B. S. (1980). *Sexual differentiation of the brain.* Cambridge, MA: MIT Press.

Hagemenas, F. C., & Kittinger, G. W. (1972). The influence of fetal sex of plasma progesterone levels. *Endocrinology (Baltimore), 91*, 253–256.

Harris, G. W. (1964). Sex hormones, brain development and brain function. *Endocrinology (Baltimore), 75*, 627–648.

Hauser, H., & Gandleman, R. (1983). Contiguity to males *in utero* affects avoidance responding in adult female mice. *Science, 220*, 437–438.

Heilbrun, A. B. (1976). Measurement of masculine and feminine sex role identities as independent dimensions. *Journal of Consuting and Clinical Psychology, 44*, 183–190.

Hines, M. (1982). Prenatal gonadal hormones and sex differences in human behavior. *Psychological Bulletin, 92*(1), 56–80.

Hines, M., & Shipley, C. (1984). Prenatal exposure to diethylstilbesterol (DES). and the development of sexually dimorphic cognitive abilities and cerebral lateralization. *Developmental Psychology, 20*(1), 81–94.

Imperato-McGinley, J., Guerrero, L., Gautier, T., & Peterson, R. E. (1974). Steroid 5α-reductase deficiency in man: An inherited form of male pseudohermaphroditism. *Science, 186*, 1213–1215.

Imperato-McGinley, J., Peterson, R. E., & Gautier, T. (1981). Male pseudohermaphroditism secondary to 5α-reductase deficiency: A review. In M. J. Novy & J. A. Resko (Eds.), *Fetal endocrinology* (pp. 359–382). New York: Academic Press.

Imperato-McGinley, J., Peterson, R. E., Gautier, T., & Sturla, E. (1979). Androgens and the evolution of male gender identity among male pseudohermaphrodites with 5α-reductase deficiency. *New England Journal of Medicine, 300*, 1233–1237.

Imperato-McGinley, J., Peterson, R. E., Leshin, M., Griffin, J. E., Cooper, G., Draghi, S., Berenyi, M., & Wilson, J. D. (1980). Steroid 5α-reductase deficiency in a 65-year-old male pseudohermaphrodite: The natural history, ultrastructure of the testes and evidence for inherited enzyme heterogeneity. *Journal of Clinical Endocrinology and Metabolism, 50*, 15–22.

Jacklin, C. N., Maccoby, E. E., & Doering, C. H. (1983). Neonatal sex-steroid hormones and timidity in 6- to 18-month-old boys and girls. *Developmental Psychobiology, 16*(3), 163–168.

Jacklin, C. N., Maccoby, E. E., Doering, C. H., & King, D. R. (1983). Neonatal sex-steroid hormones and muscular strength of boys and girls in the first three years of life. *Developmental Psychology, 17*(3), 301–310.

Kester, P. A. (1984). Effects of prenatally administered 17α-hydroxyprogesterone caproate on adolescent males. *Archives of Sexual Behavior, 13*(5), 441–455.

Kester, P. A., Green, R., Finch, S. J., & Williams, K. (1980). Prenatal "female hormone" administration and psychosexual development in human males. *Psychoneuroendocrinology, 5*, 269–285.

Laatikainen, T., & Peltonen, J. (1974). *Levels of estriol, estriol sulfate, progesterone, and neutral steroid mono- and disulfates in umbilical cord arterial and venous plasma* (Vol. 32). Paris: INSERM.

The Lancet (1981). Prenatal determination of adult sexual behavior. November *21*, 1149–1150.

Lewis, V. G., Money, J., & Epstein, R. (1968). Concordance of verbal and nonverbal ability in the adrenogenital syndrome. *Johns Hopkins Medical Journal, 122*, 192–195.

Maccoby, E. E., Doering, C. H., Jacklin, C. N., & Kraemer, H. (1979). Concentrations of sex hormones in umbilical cord blood: Their relation to sex and birth order of infants. *Child Development, 50*, 632–642.

MacLusky, N. J., & Naftolin, F. (1981). Sexual differentiation of the central nervous system. *Science, 211*, 1294–1302.

Maracek, J. (1979). Social change, positive mental health, and psychological androgyny. *Psychology of Women Quarterly, 3*, 241–247.

Marcus, J., Maccoby, E. E., Jacklin, C. N., & Doering, C. H. (1985). Individual differences in mood in early childhood: Their relation to gender and neonatal sex steroids. *Developmental Psychobiology, 18*, 327–340.

McDonald, G. J., Yoshinaga, K., & Greep, B. O. (1973). Progesterone values in *Macaca mulatta* near term. *American Journal of Physical Anthropology, 38*, 201–206.

McGlone, J. (1980). Sex differences in human brain asymmetry: A critical survey. *Behavioral and Brain Sciences, 3*, 215–263.

Meyer-Bahlburg, H. F. L. (1984). Psychoendocrine research on sexual orientation. Current status and future options. *Progress in Brain Research, 61*, 375–398.

Money, J. (1977). Determinants of human gender identity/role. In J. Money & H. Musaph (Eds.), *Handbook of sexology* (pp. 57–80.). New York: Elsevier.

Money, J., & Ehrhardt, A. A. (1972). *Man and woman, boy and girl.* Baltimore: Johns Hopkins University Press.

Money, J., & Matthews, D. (1982). Prenatal exposure to virilizing progestins: An adult follow-up study of twelve women. *Archives of Sexual Behavior, 11*(1), 73–83.

Money, J., & Orgunro, C. (1974). Behavioral sexology: Ten cases of genetic male intersexuality with impaired prenatal and pubertal androgenization. *Archives of Sexual Behavior, 3*, 181–205.

Money, J., & Schwartz, M. F. (1976). Fetal androgens in the early treated adrenogenital syndrome of 46,XX hermaphroditism: Influence on assertive and aggressive types of behavior. *Aggressive Behavior, 2*, 19–30.

Money, J., & Schwartz, M. (1977). Dating, romantic and nonromantic friendships, and sexuality in 17 early-treated adrenogenital females, aged 16–25. In P. A. Lee, L. P. Plotnick, A. A. Kowarski, & C. J. Migeon (Eds.), *Cogenital adrenal hyperplasia* (pp. 419–431). Baltimore: University Park Press.

Money, J., Schwartz, M., & Lewis, V. G. (1984). Adult erotosexual status and fetal hormonal masculinization and demasculinization: 46,XX congenital virilizing adrenal hyperplasia (CVAH) and, 46,XY androgen insensitivity syndrome (AIS) compared. *Psychoneuroendocrinology, 9*(4), 405–414.

Naftolin, F. (1979). Endocrinology of the developing fetus. *Contemporary Obstetrics/Gynecology, 13*, 155–160.

Ojemann, G. A. (1983). The intrahemispheric organization of human language, derived with electrical stimulation techniques. *Trends in NeuroSciences, 16*, 184–189.

Phoenix, C. H., & Chambers, K. C. (1982). Sexual behavior in adult gonadectomized female pseudohermaphrodite, female, and male rhesus monkeys (*Macaca mulatta*) treated with estradiol benzoate and testosterone proprionate. *Journal of Comparative and Physiological Psychology, 96*, 823–833.

Phoenix, C. H., Goy, R. W., Gerall, A. A., & Young, W. C. (1959). Organizing action of prenatally administered testosterone proprionate on the tissues mediating mating behavior in the female guinea pig. *Endocrinology (Baltimore), 65*, 369–372.

Phoenix, C. H., Jensen, J. N., & Chambers, K. C. (1983). Female sexual behavior displayed by androgenized female rhesus macaques. *Hormones and Behavior, 17*, 146–151.

Plapinger, L., & McEwen, B. S. (1978). Gonadal steroid–brain interactions in sexual differentiation. In J. B. Hutchinson (Ed.), *Biological determinants of sexual behaviour* (pp. 153–214). New York: Wiley.

Reinisch, J. M. (1974). Fetal hormones, the brain, and human sex differences: A heuristic integrative review of the recent literature. *Archives of Sexual Behavior, 3*, 51–90.

Reinisch, J. M. (1976). Effects of prenatal hormone exposure on physical and psychological development in humans and animals: With a note on the state of the field. In E. J. Sacher (Ed.), *Hormones, behavior and psychopathology* (pp. 69–94). New York: Raven Press.

Reinisch, J. M. (1977). Prenatal exposure of human foetuses to synthetic progestin and oestrogen affects personality. *Nature (London), 266*, 561–562.

Reinisch, J. M. (1981). Prenatal exposure to synthetic progestins increases potential for aggression in humans. *Science, 211*, 1171–1173.

Reinisch, J. M. (1983). Influence of early exposure to steroid hormones on behavioral development. In W. Everaerd, C. B. Hindley, A. Bot, & J. J. van der Werff ten Bosch (Eds.), *Development in adolescence: Psychological, social and biological aspects* (pp. 63–113). Boston: Martinus Nijhoff Publishers.

Reinisch, J. M., & Gandelman, R. (1978). Human research in behavioral endocrinology: Methodological and theoretical consideration. In G. Dorner & M. Kawakami (Eds.), *Hormones and brain development* (pp. 77–86). Amsterdam: Elsevier/North-Holland Biomedical Press.

Reinisch, J. M., Gandelman, R., & Spiegel, F. S. (1979). Prenatal influences on cognitive abilities: Data from experimental animals and human genetic and endocrine syndromes. In M. A. Wittig & A. C. Petersen (Eds.), *Sex-related differences in cognitive functioning* (pp. 215–239). New York: Academic Press.

Reinisch, J. M., & Karow, W. G. (1977). Prenatal exposure to synthetic progestins and estrogens: Effects on human development. *Archives of Sexual Behavior, 6*, 257–288.

Reinisch, J. M., Rosenblum, L. A., Rubin, D. B., & Schulsinger, M. F. (under review). Sex differences in behavioral milestones during the first year of life.

Reinisch, J. M., & Sanders, S. A. (1982). Early barbiturate exposure: The brain, sexually dimorphic behavior, and learning. *Neuroscience and Biobehavioral Reviews, 6*, 311–319.

Reinisch, J. M., & Sanders, S. A. (1984). Prenatal gonadal steroidal influences on gender-related behavior. *Progress in Brain Research, 61*, 407–416.

Reinisch, J. M., & Sanders, S. A. (1986). A test of sex differences in aggressive response to hypothetical conflict situations. *Journal of Personality and Social Psychology, 50*, 1045–1049.

Remillard, G. M., Andermann, F., Testa, G. F., Gloor, P., Aubé, M., Martin, J. B., Feindel, W., Guberman, A., & Simpson, C. (1983). Sexual ictal manifestations predominate in women with temporal lobe epilepsy: A finding suggesting sexual dimorphism in the human brain. *Neurology, 33*, 323–330.

Resko, J. A. (1974a). The relationship between fetal hormones and the differentiation of the central nervous system in primates. In W. Montagna & W. A. Sadler (Eds.), *Reproductive behavior* (pp. 211). New York: Plenum Press.

Resko, J. A. (1974b). *Sex steroids, in the circulation of the fetal and neonatal rhesus monkey: A comparison of male and female fetuses* (vol. 32). Paris: INSERM.

Resko, J. A. (1975). Fetal hormones and their effects on the differentiation of the central nervous system of primates. *Federation Proceedings, Federation of American Societies for Experimental Biology, 34*, 1650–1655.

Rubin, R. T., Reinisch, J. M., & Haskett, R. (1981). Postnatal gonadal steroid effects on human sexually dimorphic behavior: A paradigm of hormone-environmental interaction. *Science, 211*, 1318–1324.

Sanders, R. M., Bain, J., & Langevin, R. (1984a). Adrenal hormones and established sexuality in the adult human male. Unpublished manuscript.

Sanders, R. M., Bain, J., & Langevin, R. (1984b). Peripheral sex hormones, homosexuality, and gender identity. In R. Langevin (Ed.), *Erotic preference, gender identity, and aggression in men* (pp. 227–247). Hillsdale, NJ: Erlbaum.

Sanders, R. M., Langevin, R., & Bain, J. (1983). Hormones and human sexuality [Abstract]. *Neuroendocrinology Letters, 5*, 129.

Sanders, S. A., & Reinisch, J. M. (1985). Behavioral effects on humans of progesterone-related compounds during development and in the adult. *Current Topics in Neuroendocrinology, 5*, 175–205.

Schwartz, M. F., & Money, J. (1983). Dating, romance and sexuality in young adult adrenogenital females. *Neuroendocrinology Letters, 5*, 132.

Shutt, D. A., Smith, I. D., & Shearman, R. J. (1974). Fetal plasma steroids in relation to parturition. III. The effect of parity and method of delivery upon umbilical oestrone and oestradiol levels. *Journal of Obstetrics and Gynaecology of the British Commonwealth, 81*, 986–970.

Sitteri, P., & Wilson, J. D. (1974). Testosterone formation and metabolism during male sexual differentiation in the human embryo. *Journal of Clinical Endocrinology and Metabolism, 38*, 113–125.

Slijper, F. M. E. (1984). Androgens and gender role behaviour in girls with congenital adrenal hyperplasia (CAH). *Progress in Brain Research, 61*, 417–422.

Smith, I. D., Shutt, D. A., & Shearman, R. P. (1975). Foetal plasma steroid concentration related to gestational age and method of delivery. *Journal of Steroid Biochemistry, 6*, 657–662.

Spence, J. T., & Helmreich, R. L. (1978). *Masculinity and femininity: Their psychological dimensions, correlates and antecedents.* Austin: University of Texas Press.

Spence, J. T., Helmreich, R. L., & Stapp, J. (1974). The PAQ: A measure of sex-role stereotypes and M-F. *JSAS Catalogue of Selected Documents in Psychology, 4*, 127.

Swabb, D. F., & Fliers, E. (1985). A sexually dimorphic nucleus in the human brain. *Science, 228*, 1112–1115.

Swabb, D. F., & Hoffman, M. A. (1984). Sexual differentiation of the human brain: A historical perspective. *Progress in Brain Research, 61*, 361–374.

vom Saal, F. S., & Bronson, F. H. (1978). *In utero* proximity of female mouse fetuses to males: Effect on reproductive performance during later life. *Biology of Reproduction, 19*, 842–853.

vom Saal, F. S., & Bronson, F. H. (1980). Sexual characteristics of adult female mice are correlated with their blood testosterone levels during prenatal development. *Science, 208*, 597–599.

Whalen, R. E. (1974). Sexual differentiation: Models, methods and mechanisms. In R. C. Friedman, R. M. Richart, & R. L. Vande Wiele (Eds.), *Sex differences in behavior* (pp. 467–481). New York: Wiley.

Whalen, R. E., & Edwards, D. A. (1967). Hormonal determinants of the development of masculine and feminine behavior in male and female rats. *Anatomical Record, 157*, 173–180.

Wilson, E. O. (1975). *Sociobiology: The new synthesis* (pp. 11–13). Cambridge, MA: Belknap Press, Harvard University.

Wilson, J. D., Griffin, J. E., Leshin, M., & McDonald, P. C. (1983). The androgen resistance syndromes: 5α-reductase deficiency, testicular feminization, and related disorders. In J. B. Stannbury, J. B. Wyngaarden, D. S. Fredricks, J. L. Goldstein, & M. S. Brown (Eds.), *The metabolic basis of inherited disease* (pp. 1001–1026). New York: McGraw-Hill.

Witelson, S. F. (1985). The brain connection: The corpus callosum is larger in left-handers. *Science, 299*, 665–668.

Yalom, I. D., Green, R., & Fisk, N. (1973). Prenatal exposure to female hormones: Effect on psychosexual development in boys. *Archives of General Psychiatry, 28*, 554–561.

Young, W. C., Goy, R. W., & Phoenix, C. H. (1964). Hormones and sexual behavior. *Science, 142*, 212–218.

Zussman, J. U., Zussman, P. P., & Dalton, K. (1975). *Postpubertal effects of prenatal administration of progesterone.* Presented at the Society for Research in Child Development, Denver, CO.

22 PREMENSTRUAL SYNDROME

ROGER F. HASKETT

University of Michigan Medical Center

INTRODUCTION

In many women, regular changes in emotions and behavior appear to be linked to specific phases of the menstrual cycle (Moos *et al.*, 1969). This association has been described for centuries (De Wees, 1843), but the phenomena are now receiving widespread attention, especially the premenstrual syndrome (PMS): a group of negative affects and other emotional and behavioral changes that occur in some women for 5–10 days before the onset of menses. Following this increased awareness of PMS, specialized clinics have appeared in many locations and physicians are encouraged to recognize PMS as an entity and provide treatment (Dalton, 1977). Unfortunately, this growing enthusiasm for intervention has not been accompanied by a corresponding increase in our understanding of the disorder. The pathogenesis and specific treatment of PMS, even its precise definition, remain subjects of much disagreement. Although some individuals have questioned the validity of PMS as a discrete diagnostic category (Parlee, 1973; Ruble, 1977), the subject has received sufficient attention in the popular and scientific literature to ensure that some women will continue to seek help for disturbances that they perceive to be related to their menstrual cycles. Clinicians must, therefore, be familiar with appropriate methods for evaluating PMS and, while recognizing that questions of etiology, natural history, and treatment are far from settled,

should attempt to differentiate between some of the disturbances that are often included within this broad descriptive category.

DEFINITION AND DIAGNOSIS

The defining characteristics of PMS should be considered on two dimensions: the time course of the disturbance and the typical clinical features. The timing of PMS has been emphasized since Frank's original report (1931) and is of fundamental importance. The symptoms usually appear 5–10 days before menstruation, with rapid relief after the onset of menses. In a few women, however, the duration of PMS is extended by the occurrence of symptoms at the presumed time of ovulation, or midcycle, and continues throughout the entire luteal phase. Notwithstanding some variation in its duration, an essential characteristic of PMS is the complete remission of clinical features during the majority of the follicular phase. This follicular remission of symptoms distinguished PMS, a disturbance that is specific to the premenstruum, from a premenstrual worsening of ongoing physical or psychiatric disorder. Failure to attend to this "normality criterion" is a common source of variability in the use of this diagnostic label.

Remission of the disorder with the appearance of menstruation is particularly useful, since it delineates PMS from dysmenorrhea, the physically painful disturbance that accompanies menstrual flow. Primary dysmenorrhea occurs in young postmenarchal women and is not associated with demonstrable pelvic pathology. Symptoms appear within hours of the onset of menses and consist of cramping pelvic and lower abdominal pain, often associated with nausea, vomiting, headache, and fatigue. This disorder usually becomes less severe with increasing age and often disappears after pregnancy. There is evidence that the etiology of primary dysmenorrhea involves the prostaglandin system. Elevated levels of prostaglandins have been documented in the menstrual blood of women with this disorder, and nonsteroidal antiinflammatory agents that inhibit prostaglandin synthesis and/or activity have been reported to provide relief from the symptoms (Chan, Dawood, & Fuchs, 1979; Lundstrom, Green, & Svanborg, 1979; Schwartz, Zor, Lindner, & Naor, 1975). Secondary dysmenorrhea describes the painful menses associated with pelvic pathology such as endometriosis or chronic pelvic inflammatory disease. Although women with dysmenorrhea may suffer from associated negative affects or behavioral disturbance, it is uncommon for these women to experience emotional changes during menses in the absence of physical symptoms. Diagnosis is sometimes more difficult in women with PMS whose symptoms do not abruptly remit with the onset of menses. This variant of PMS in which the negative effects persist through several days of menstrual flow can usually be distinguished from dysmenorrhea by the onset of symptoms during the midlate luteal phase. Clinically, this diagnostic distinction is important, since there is no evidence that PMS and dysmenorrhea are etiologically related and there is minimal support for the use of antiinflammatory agents in the treatment of PMS (Wood & Jakubowicz, 1980).

Description of the typical clinical features of PMS should include consideration of a "severity criterion" as well as a list of common symptoms and signs. There is some indication that although the prevalence of severe PMS may be low, mild premenstrual symptoms are common in women of reproductive age. In a recent epidemiological survey of 1,083 women (Andersch, 1980), 70% reported mild or moderate premenstrual changes, and 92% reported at least one pre

menstrual change. Only 2–3%, however, reported severe or distressing premenstrual symptoms, and few (10%) believed treatment necessary. Similar findings were obtained from a study of an English family practice (Clare, 1983). Nearly all women (98%) reported some premenstrual change in at least one item, but the global severity of disturbance was usually low. The distribution of individual scores was skewed, with most reporting minimal changes (modal score of 10, range 0–102). The relationship between these common, mild, and isolated premenstrual symptoms and the less frequent, severe form of PMS is unclear. These findings suggest, however, that failure to consider the global severity of the premenstrual disturbance will result in the application of the PMS label to most women, a practice that raises many legitimate clinical and social questions.

The list of clinical features that comprise the phenomenology of PMS has tended to expand since Frank (1931) described a series of women with "premenstrual tension syndrome." This disorder included a combination of emotional and physical disturbances, but the most prominent was a feeling of "indescribable tension." Other clinicians have subsequently added to the clinical features of PMS so that some descriptions include disturbances from almost every system in the body, with no distinction between core symptoms and variable accompaniments (Dalton, 1977; May, 1976; Moos, 1968; Rees, 1953). It is likely that many of the features included in these accounts of the phenomenology of PMS represent a premenstrual exacerbation of long-standing problems rather than part of a specific time-limited premenstrual syndrome. One response to the great interindividual variability in the phenomenology of PMS has been to divide the syndrome into a number of subtypes (Abraham, 1980; Halbreich, Endicott, Schacht, & Nee, 1982; Steiner & Carroll, 1977). Separation of the physical features of PMS (tissue swelling and weight gain) from the emotional and behavioral disturbances has some empirical support. Diuretics have been reported to preferentially ameliorate the tissue swelling symptoms of PMS (Andersch, Hahn, Wendestam, Ohman, & Abrahamsson, 1978) and to be generally effective in the treatment of PMS when the symptoms are associated with substantial weight gain (Werch & Kane, 1976). Subdivision of PMS according to the particular psychological changes is of less established clinical utility. Although this approach has heuristic value, overlap between proposed subtypes is common (Halbreich & Endicott, 1982), and the validity of these distinctions remains to be demonstrated.

One approach to characterizing the typical clinical features of PMS utilizes both normality and severity criteria. This involves the study of only those women who suffer from severe premenstrual disturbance, but who have no evidence of psychopathology or physical illness at other times in their menstrual cycle. One study of 42 women who met these criteria obtained concurrent symptom ratings with the Menstrual Distress Questionnaire (MDQ) (Moos, 1968) during the follicular and premenstrual phases of their cycles and identified those items that changed most in severity in the greatest number of women (Haskett, Steiner, Osmun, & Carroll, 1980). The five most highly ranked items of emotional change were irritability, depression, tension, mood swings, and restlessness. The study included subjects with psychological and/or physical premenstrual symptoms, provided that the overall disturbance was severe and time-limited. The two most commonly reported physical changes were "swelling of abdomen, breasts, or ankles" and "painful or tender breasts." In addition, several other frequently reported items reflected the impaired functioning that was experienced by this particular group of women. These included decreased efficiency, increased accidents, difficulty in concentration, distractibility, lowered motor coordination, and lowered school or work performance. The relationship between the emotional/behavioral and physical changes was inconsistent. Some women reported both types of disturbance, but a substantial proportion of subjects experienced severe psychological symptoms of PMS without concurrent physical discomfort.

It should be emphasized that these premenstrual changes were identified in a group of women whose overall disturbance was much more severe than had been reported in earlier studies of presumptively normal women. The mean total score on the MDQ for the women with severe PMS changed from 74 in the follicular phase to 135 premenstrually compared with corresponding values of 58–67 and 74–86, respectively, in other studies (Gruba & Rohrbaugh, 1975; Moos, 1968; Rouse, 1978). There is no evidence to suggest that the changes associated with severe PMS are commonly expressed in the general female population.

The findings from this study also demonstrated a crucial aspect of PMS research. The symptom profile of PMS appears to be greatly influenced by the characteristics of the study population. As defined previously, women with only PMS should have minimal or no symptoms during the follicular phase. Although all study subjects reported this "normality" criterion during follicular phase interviews, it was possible to retrospectively distinguish between a subgroup of women whose self-report of symptoms on the MDQ confirmed the complete remission of PMS at menses and a subgroup of women whose MDQ scores remained elevated at the follicular phase visit. Examination of the individual symptoms of premenstrual change revealed a different profile in the two subgroups. The women with minimal symptoms during the follicular phase described a premenstrual syndrome in which the symptoms of irritability, tension, and emotional lability were most prominent. By comparison, the subgroup with persistently higher levels of disturbance during the follicular phase more commonly reported physical discomfort and incapacity with associated depression.

Several reviews have addressed important methodological concerns that are of practical importance to the clinician (Abplanalp, Haskett, & Rose, 1980; Dennerstein & Burrows, 1979; Rubinow & Roy-Byrne, 1984). There is general agreement that the accurate assessment of symptom fluctuation during the menstrual cycle requires longitudinal collection of concurrent ratings. Although frequently used in past studies, it has been suggested that retrospective accounts of premenstrual disturbance often reflect beliefs about the menstrual cycle instead of the subjective experience of changes (Abplanalp, Donnelly, & Rose, 1980; Ruble, 1977; Ruble & Brooks-Gunn, 1979) and are affected by the mood present when the rating is completed (Sampson & Prescott, 1981). There is often low agreement between retrospectively collected accounts of premenstrual symptomatology and subsequent concurrent ratings (May, 1976; Sampson & Jenner, 1977), although the disparity may be less during the assessment of women with severe PMS (Endicott & Halbreich, 1982; Haskett et al., 1980). In addition, it appears that concurrent self-ratings more readily detect a low level of disturbance than is reported at interviews.

Selection of the appropriate frequency for concurrent rating can be more difficult. Since the duration of PMS may vary, the best description of the premenstrual disturbance and the follicular phase remission will be obtained by daily ratings. Many scales have been constructed and no single instrument has demonstrated clear superiority. Pragmatic concerns, such as compliance, may influence the decision. A clinician may choose to identify the time-limited course of the disturbance and its global severity rather than obtain an extensive description of the clinical features of PMS. It could be argued that considering the lack of specificity of individual PMS symptoms, the time course and severity characteristics contribute most to the diagnostic process. One suggested method involves the daily rating of two to three symptoms by visual analogue scale (Rubinow, Roy-Byrne, Hoban, Gold, & Post, 1984).

Another system uses a 36-item questionnaire (PMRS) and operationally defined diagnostic criteria (Steiner, Haskett, & Carroll, 1980). These instruments were tested to determine whether their administration on only two occasions in the follicular and premenstrual phases could identify women with severe, but time-limited, premenstrual disturbance (Haskett & Abplanalp, 1983). This study also included women suffering from severe PMS, with physical and/or emotional symptoms, but no other disorder. It is notable that in both studies, less than 1 in 5 of the volunteers qualified for these global selection criteria. This also supports the indication that the severe form of PMTS has a low prevalence in the general population. The women in this study were grouped according to whether they met the diagnostic criteria for PMS at interview and reported the presence of few items (≤ 5) on the PMRS at a follicular phase visit and a high score (≥ 14)

on the PMRS during the premenstrual phase. Concurrent daily symptom reports confirmed that women selected by these criteria were suffering from a substantial psychological disturbance that was confined to the premenstruum. This subgroup reported significantly increased negative mood scores in the premenstruum, but a very low level of symptomatology during the other phases of the menstrual cycle. Daily symptom ratings of five somatic discomfort items did not, however, support a particular association between somatic discomfort and the psychological form of PMS, although both types of disturbance could coexist. There was no significant difference in the somatic symptom profiles over the menstrual cycle between the subgroup of women who met these diagnostic criteria for PMS and the women who did not.

In summary, debate continues about the most appropriate defining criteria and classification system for PMS. We should, however, attempt to decrease some of the confusion by restricting the diagnosis of PMS to those premenstrual disturbances that are time-limited and associated with an almost complete remission of symptoms during the follicular phase. This will differentiate specific premenstrual disorders from the common premenstrual exacerbations of a wide range of clinical disturbances. The latter could continue to be named premenstrual change or menstrual distress. This does not imply that PMS cannot coexist with other disturbances, but until a more precise method is available for identifying PMS, mixed syndromes should be considered separately and potential confounds clearly acknowledged. From a clinical perspective, it is also unhelpful to include disturbance of all ranges of severity under the diagnosis of PMS. There is evidence that symptoms of similar form but much milder severity can occur in many women and are not associated with any significant dysfunction or disability. The diagnosis of PMS should be restricted to those syndromes that are of sufficient severity that they produce a noticeable disturbance in functioning or lead to a request for relief of symptoms.

The nosology of premenstrual disorders should also reflect the lack of a demonstrated association between psychological and somatic symptoms in the premenstruum. PMS has been used to refer to either or both types of disturbance, and a name that specifically identifies the constellation of emotional and behavioral symptoms is needed. Possibilities include the original term, Premenstrual Tension Syndrome, or, in the more modern style, Premenstrual Dysphoric Disorder.

ETIOLOGY AND PATHOPHYSIOLOGY

The previously described problems with syndrome definition and heterogeneity of study populations have clearly contributed to the lack of progress in understanding the etiology or pathophysiology of PMS. Numerous hypotheses have been considered in the past 50 years, and several excellent reviews have examined the evidence that has been collected in attempts to explain the origins of this disorder (Rausch & Janowsky, 1982; Reid & Yen, 1981; Rubinow & Roy-Byrne, 1984; Steiner & Carroll, 1977). The most recent of these have concluded that no single etiological hypothesis can be substantiated, although some remain optimistic that a link will be found between hormone-related changes in neurotransmitter levels and the fluctuations in emotions and behavior that may occur during the menstrual cycle of some women.

Although most clinicians acknowledge that psychological and environmental factors appear able to influence the severity and specific manifestations of PMS, the search for an etiology for PMS has concentrated on biological factors. In particular, the relationship between PMS symptoms and the menstrual cycle has directed much attention to the possible pathogenetic effect of hormone imbalance. Many hypotheses have been based upon a temporal correlation between a purportedly abnormal hormone level and the appearance of emotional and behavioral changes in the premenstruum. This approach has been used to support theories of estrogen excess, progesterone deficiency or withdrawal, altered estrogen–progesterone ratio, and hyperprolactinemia. Apart from the obvious weaknesses of moving from a positive correlation to a causal theory, interpretation of many studies is severely limited by inconsistent and imprecise syndrome definition, lack of appropriate control populations, esti-

mation of endocrine function from single blood samples and variable definitions of menstrual cycle phase. In addition, etiological theories that depend upon a specific alteration in a hormone level usually fail to account for the lack of symptomatology during other times that the particular abnormality is present (Steiner, Haskett, Carroll, Hays, & Rubin, 1984). The association of a particular endocrine abnormality with the clinical features of PMS could be just as reasonably considered to be a consequence of altered central neurotransmitter activity rather than the cause of the syndrome. Neuroendocrine regulation of the normal menstrual cycle involves a complex interaction between fluctuations in central neurotransmitter systems and the secretion of various hormones, especially those from the anterior pituitary and ovary. Although neurotransmitter dysfunction has been implicated in some forms of psychopathology and there is evidence that alterations in neurotransmitters or gonadal hormones can affect behavior (Rubin, Reinisch, & Haskett, 1981), hypotheses that consider these relationships in humans are not easily testable.

TREATMENT

For many of the same reasons, the search for an effective treatment for PMS has been as inconclusive or contradictory as the studies of this condition's etiology. Several interventions have gained enthusiastic support, including the use of progesterone or pyridoxine, but their specific efficacy has not been demonstrated in appropriately designed studies. Minimal evidence supports the use of lithium or other psychotropic medications in the treatment of pure PMS, although the management of PMS in women with primary psychiatric disorders will be considered in the next section. Interruption of pituitary–ovarian cycling with danazol (Day, 1979; Dennerstein, Judd, & Davies, 1983) or a gonadotropin-releasing hormone (GnRH) agonist (Muse, Cetel, Futterman, & Yen, 1984) does appear capable of alleviating premenstrual symptoms, but the potential hazards of these agents has not been sufficiently evaluated for them to be generally recommended for the treatment of PMS. Perhaps the most consistent findings are that PMS appears to respond favorably to most interventions in uncontrolled studies and there is a prominent placebo effect in almost all controlled studies (Smith, 1975). Characterization of the natural history of this placebo response is limited by the absence of longitudinal systematic follow-up.

The failure to unequivocally demonstrate efficacy, however, should not be taken as proof that all interventions are ineffective. Methodological weaknesses in many studies, such as heterogeneous study populations and low symptom severity, increase the possibility that a positive finding might have been missed. Clinicians treating PMS today should acknowledge the uncertainties about the "specific benefit" component of the risk–benefit ratio, and the choice of any pharmacological treatment should be greatly influenced by the possibility of serious risks or side effects. Many women with PMS report an improvement in symptoms when provided with support and explanations. They are often relieved to learn that these recurring changes in emotions and behavior are a function of their reproductive physiology rather than a manifestation of severe personality instability.

RELATIONSHIP BETWEEN PREMENSTRUAL SYNDROME AND PSYCHIATRIC DISORDER

The relationship between PMS and psychiatric disorder has intrigued many clinicians, but has not proved to be easily answered. The design of most studies has aimed in one of two directions: to determine the prevalence of PMS in women with psychiatric disorder and compare it with the normal population or, conversely, to search for evidence of increased psychopathology in women with PMS. Early studies utilized global concepts of psychopathology, such as neurosis, but more recently attention has focused on a possible relationship between PMS and affective disorder. In particular, some investigators have suggested that PMS may be a manifestation or model for affective disorder or may predict the past or future occurrence of typical psychiatric syndromes.

Review of the literature reveals several attempts to determine whether the presence of psychopathology increases the risk that a woman will suffer from PMS or influences its presentation. In a study of psychiatric outpatients more that 30 years ago, Rees (1953) reported that PMS occurred much more commonly in patients with neurosis than in normal controls. Rees found a positive correlation between the intensity of PMS and the severity of their neurosis. This study, however, contained an important confound. Neurosis and emotional stability were not syndromal diagnoses, but were ratings on a continuum that were derived from clinical interviews and questionnaires containing a number of symptoms commonly included in the description of PMS. This problem has continued to interfere with the interpretation of subsequent studies and, particularly when retrospective self-report is the source of data, it is difficult to be sure that raters are clearly distinguishing between specific premenstrual symptoms and disturbances that persist at other times. Despite these concerns, Rees (1953) did note that severe PMS could occur in normal women with no evidence of neurosis or personality instability. Subsequently, Coppen (1965) examined the prevalence of paramenstrual symptoms in three groups of psychiatric patients and compared this with controls. He found that symptoms of menstrual disorder which included menstrual pain as well as PMS has an increased prevalence in women with neurotic diagnoses, but a normal prevalence in women with affective disorders and a reduced prevalence in women with schizophrenic diagnoses. The timing of specific paramenstrual symptoms did not differ between patients and controls; both groups reported irritability, depression, and swelling in the premenstruum. Patients and controls reported a significant association between PMS symptoms and neuroticism scores. There was no relationship between dysmenorrhea and neuroticism in the normal controls, but neurotic patients had an increased prevalence of dysmenorrhea. These findings suggest that PMS, like dysmenorrhea, occurs in some women regardless of the presence of psychopathology. When these menstrual disorders occur in women with psychiatric problems, however, there appears to be a relationship between the severity of both types of disorder.

An indication of an increased frequency of PMS in patients with an affective disorder came from a report by Kashiwagi, McClure, and Wetzel (1976). They found that 43% of a group of neurology patients with functional headache met criteria for a premenstrual affective syndrome. It was also noted that a large proportion of these patients qualified for a diagnosis of affective disorder and that women with a history of affective disorder had a higher prevalence of premenstrual affective symptoms (65%) than women with other diagnoses (14%) or normal controls (21%). Comparable findings were reported using a system for subtyping PMS (Endicott, Halbreich, Schacht, & Nee, 1981). A similar proportion of women (62%) who met Research Diagnostic Criteria (RDC) (Spitzer, Endicott, & Robins, 1978) for a past diagnosis of Major Depressive Disorder (MDD) also met their criteria for a "major" depressive premenstrual syndrome compared with only 13% of patients with a nonaffective diagnosis and 7% of controls. Two other categories of PMS—water retention and impaired social functioning—also occurred with significantly different frequencies between patients with a past diagnosis of MDD and normal controls. Interestingly, current affective disorder was not significantly associated with a higher prevalence of premenstrual disturbance compared to normal controls. This latter finding agreed with a earlier study of 63 patients with affective disorder who were attending a lithium clinic (Diamond, Rubinstein, Dunner, & Fieve, 1976). When these women were compared with 25 controls, there was no significant difference between the groups in the prevalence and severity of premenstrual symptoms. This applied for both somatic and affective symptoms. There was, however, an increased frequency of hospitalization for exacerbation of affective disorder during the premenstrual and menstrual phases. The authors concluded that women with a diagnosis of affective disorder who were not in episode experience menstruation similarly to controls, whereas the appearance of premenstrual and menstrual changes during an affective episode produces an exacerbation of symptoms, sometimes leading to hospitalization.

Major differences in subject characteristics interfere with comparisons of studies that have evaluated women with PMS for evidence of psychiatric disorder. College students reporting premenstrual symptoms were more likely to have a past history and family history of depression, to seek psychiatric help, and to develop an affective episode during the subsequent year (Schuckit, Daly, Herrmann, & Hineman, 1975; Wetzel, Reich, McClure, & Wald, 1975). Although these students met criteria for a premenstrual affective syndrome, only 3–8% reported severe symptoms. This is in contrast to a study of women with severe PMS whose clinical features and adrenocortical function were compared with that found in patients with MDD (Haskett, Steiner, & Carroll, 1984). Although absence of past psychiatric disorder was a selection criterion for this study, the cross-sectional phenomenology of the premenstrual disturbance qualified for the psychiatric diagnosis of MDD. It did not, however, resemble an endogenous depression, and adrenocortical functioning was normal.

In women with a current psychiatric diagnosis, increased symptomatology during the premenstruum should be considered initially as a premenstrual exacerbation rather than demonstrating the coexistence of a separate diagnosis of PMS. There are many reports that psychiatric disorders worsen more often during the premenstrual phase than would be expected by chance. Dalton (1959) found an increased rate of admission during the premenstrual and menstrual phases, with no significant difference between subjects with diagnoses of depression and schizophrenia. Of admissions, 45% occurred during 29% of the menstrual cycle (8/28). Similar results have been reported from surveys of psychiatric admission in Denmark (Kramp, 1968) and the United States (Janowsky, Gorney, Castelnuovo-Tedesco, & Stone, 1969). More recently, it has been reported that the increased rate of admission to hospital during the paramenstrual period can be related to the patient's diagnosis (Abramowitz, Baker, & Fleischer, 1982). Whereas 69% of patients with a diagnosis of depression were admitted during the 8 days of the premenstrual and menstrual phases, only 37% of patients with a diagnosis of schizophrenia were admitted at this time. The concentration of admissions around the onset of menses was even more pronounced for the 2-day interval consisting of the last premenstrual day and the day of onset of menstrual flow. Of all admissions for depression, 41% occurred at this time (7% of the menstrual cycle), as did 12% of admissions for schizophrenia. The authors suggested that this difference in admission rate between diagnoses did not support claims that the paramenstrual admission peak was merely a function of sociocultural expectations. Although these results are persuasive, the method of fixing cycle phase in these patients is cause for some concern. In most cases, it was done at the admission interview or by noting the time of menses during hospitalization. There are numerous reports of altered menstrual cycle rhythms associated with various psychological or environment stresses, and the possibility that admission to hospital could have produced the onset of menses deserves consideration. This would artefactually raise the frequency of women in the premenstrual phase at the time of admission. There have been similar reports linking suicide to the premenstrual phase, but Wetzel and McClure (1972) reviewed the methodological problems that raise significant questions about this particular observation.

One report utilizing a more precise method for determining menstrual cycle phase provided some interesting, if unexplained, findings (MacKinnon, MacKinnon, & Thomson, 1959). One hundred and two women, aged from 18 to 46, who had died suddenly or with an uncertain diagnosis were subjected to a postmortem examination at which their phase of menstrual cycle was fixed by endometrial histology. Subjects were grouped according to cause of death: suicide, accident, or disease. Of the women, irrespective of diagnosis, 87% died during the 14-day luteal phase as compared with 11% and 2% in the follicular and menstrual phases, respectively. There was no significant difference between diagnostic groups in the proportion of deaths occurring during the luteal phase. Road trauma and skull fractures accounted for the deaths of more than half of the accident group and, together with 5 deaths from carbon monoxide poisoning, comprised 80% of women dying from accidents. Cardiovascular deaths were a common occurrence in the group whose death was due to disease.

An uncommon but dramatic association between psychopathology and the premenstruum is seen in women with the disorder called Periodic Psychosis, included under Atypical Psychosis in DSM-III. Women with this diagnosis are essentially normal between menses, but during the premenstrual phase they suffer from recurrent and severe psychotic episodes that remit rapidly after the onset of menses. These women are distinguishable from patients with chronic psychotic illnesses who may experience premenstrual exacerbations of symptoms and from women with typical PMS who are never psychotic. Periodic psychosis appears around menarche (Altschule & Brem, 1963; Endo, Daiguji, Asano, Yamashita, & Takahashi, 1978), which is earlier than the usual time of presentation for PMS, which is during a woman's fourth decade. The pathogenesis of these disorders is not yet known, but several possibilities deserve consideration. The descriptions of some patients in the literature are compatible with a rapid-cycling bipolar affective disorder (Horwitz & Harris, 1936; Lingjaerde & Bredland, 1954; Williams & Weekes, 1952). Another not necessarily incompatible proposal is that some premenstrual psychotic disorders may be the result of temporal lobe epilepsy (Price, 1980). Some patients with epilepsy suffer from an increased frequency of seizures in the premenstruum which is possibly related to ovarian hormone-induced changes in seizure threshold (Backstrom, 1976; Backstrom, Zetterlund, Blom, & Romano, 1984; Laidlaw, 1956). Out of 7 women with periodic psychoses (Endo, Daiguji, Asano, Yamashita, & Takahashi, 1978), 5 were found to have electroencephalogram (EEG) abnormalities, and 2 suffered from at least one grand mal seizure. Price (1980) reported the successful treatment of one woman with carbamazepine, but others have stabilized this condition with agents that interfere with normal hypothalamic–pituitary–gonadal cycling (Berlin, Bergey, & Money, 1982; Felthous, Robinson, & Conroy, 1980).

Two observations appear justified by the literature on the relationship between PMS and psychiatric disorder: (1) Severe PMS can occur in women with no evidence of other psychopathology. (2) Some women with a diagnosis of past or current psychiatric disorder may report the features of PMS in addition to their other diagnosis. In these latter circumstances, the lack of specificity of PMS symptoms may make it very difficult to determine whether the woman is suffering from two disorders or that her psychiatric diagnosis is more noticeable during the premenstruum. Clinicians that are confronted with the presence of significant psychopathology during the premenstrual phase should attempt to answer the following question: Does the woman suffer only from PMS, a time-limited premenstrual disturbance, or are these premenstrual changes occurring in someone with clear evidence of a psychiatric disorder at other times? This decision can only be made by evaluating the woman during several phases of the menstrual cycle, using a combination of repeated interviews and a diary or self-rating instruments. Concurrent psychiatric disorders should be treated with appropriate biological and/or psychological interventions and, if successful, this will often result in an acceptable reduction of premenstrual symptoms. Women with premenstrual disturbances should not be diagnosed as suffering from a personality disorder unless there is clear evidence of a lifelong pattern of emotional difficulty that is present at times other than the premenstruum. The longitudinal relationship between PMS affective disorder remains unclear and requires further investigation with appropriately selected subject groups.

CONCLUSION

Women presenting for assistance with emotional and behavioral disturbance during the premenstruum may be suffering from PMS. Severe PMS does not appear to be a common condition, but it should be recognized and distinguished from minor emotional changes that may occur during the premenstruum and from premenstrual exacerbations of psychiatric illness.

Clinicians need to be aware of the serious deficiencies and inconsistencies that exist in the PMS literature. Many of the claims for effective treatments cannot be supported by adequate data and, although a few may prove to be appropriate, some skepticism is still justified. Many women report that support and education are associated with a significant improvement in their symptoms.

Improvements in the methodology used in research into PMS are of direct relevance to the clinical evaluation of these conditions. Assessment of clinical features must be concurrent, since retrospective accounts are often misleading. The evaluation must include at least one entire menstrual cycle and may need to extend over several cycles. Although PMS and other psychiatric disorders may coexist, the distinction is of practical significance, since primary psychiatric disorder should be treated first with standard interventions.

References

Abplanalp, J. M., Donnelly, A. F., & Rose, R. M. (1980). Psychoendocrinology of the menstrual cycle: I. Enjoyment of daily activities and moods. *Psychosomatic Medicine, 41,* 587–604.

Abplanalp, J. M., Haskett, R. F., & Rose, R. M. (1980). The premenstrual syndrome. *Psychiatric Clinics of North America, 3,* 327–347.

Abraham, G. E. (1980). The premenstrual syndromes. In L. K. McNall (Ed.), *Contemporary obstetric and gynecologic nursing* (Vol. 3). St Louis, MO: C. V. Mosby.

Abramowitz, E. S., Baker, A. H., & Fleischer, S. F. (1982). Onset of depressive psychiatric crises and the menstrual cycle. *American Journal of Psychiatry, 139,* 475–478.

Altschule, M. D., & Brem, J. (1963). Periodic psychosis of puberty. *American Journal of Psychiatry, 119,* 1176–1178.

Andersch, B. (1980). *Epidemiological, hormonal and water balance studies on premenstrual tension.* Thesis, University of Göteburg.

Andersch, B., Hagn, L., Wendestam, C., Ohman, R., & Abrahamsson, L. (1978). Treatment of premenstrual tension syndrome with bromocriptine. *Acta Endocrinologica (Copenhagen), 88,* (Suppl. 216), 165–174.

Backstrom, T. (1976). Epileptic seizures in women related to plasma estrogen and progesterone during the menstrual cycle. *Acta Neurologica Scandinavica, 54,* 321–347.

Backstrom, T., Zetterlund, B., Blom, S., and Romano, M. (1984). Effects of intravenous progesterone infusions on the epileptic discharge frequency in women with partial epilepsy. *Acta Neurologica Scandinavica, 69,* 240–248.

Berlin, F. S., Bergey, G. K., & Money, J. (1982). Periodic psychosis of puberty: A case report. *American Journal of Psychiatry, 139,* 119–120.

Chan, W. Y., Dawood, M. Y., & Fuchs, F. (1979). Relief of dysmenorrhea with the prostaglandin synthetase inhibitor ibuprofen: Effect on prostaglandin levels in menstrual fluid. *American Journal of Obstetrics and Gynecology, 135,* 102–108.

Clare, A. W. (1983). Psychiatric and social aspects of premenstrual complaint. *Psychological medicine* (Monograph Supplement No. 4). Cambridge, England: Cambridge University Press.

Coppen, A. (1965). The prevalence of menstrual disorder in psychiatric patients. *British Journal of Psychiatry, 111,* 155–167.

Dalton, K. (1959). Menstruation and acute psychiatric illnesses. *British Medical Journal, 1,* 148–149.

Dalton, K. (1977). *The premenstrual syndrome and progesterone therapy.* London: Heinemann.

Day, J. (1979). Danazol and the premenstrual syndrome. *Postgraduate Medical Journal, 55,* (Suppl. 5), 87–89.

Dennerstein, L., & Burrows, G. D. (1979). Affect and the menstrual cycle. *Journal of Affective Disorders, 1,* 77–92.

Dennerstein, L., Judd, F., & Davies, B. (1983). Psychosis and the menstrual cycle. *Medical Journal of Australia, 1,* 524–526.

De Wees, W. P. (1843). *A treatise on the diseases of females.* Philadelphia: Lee & Blanchard.

Diamond, S. B., Rubenstein, A. A., Dunner, D. L., Fieve, R. R. (1976). Menstrual problems in women with primary affective illness. *Comprehensive Psychiatry, 17,* 541–548.

Endicott, J., & Halbreich, U. (1982). Retrospective report of premenstrual depressive changes: Factors affecting confirmation of daily ratings. *Psychopharmacology Bulletin, 18,* 109–112.

Endicott, J., Halbreich, U., Schacht, S., & Nee, J. (1981). Premenstrual changes and affective disorders. *Psychosomatic Medicine, 43,* 519–529.

Endo, M., Daiguji, M., Asano, Y., Yamashita, I., & Takahashi, S. (1978). Periodic psychosis recurring in association with menstrual cycle. *Journal of Clinical Psychiatry, 39,* 456–461.

Felthous, A. R., Robinson, D. B., & Conroy, R. W. (1980). Prevention of menstrual psychosis by an oral contraceptive. *American Journal of Psychiatry, 137,* 245–246.

Frank, R. T. (1931). The hormonal causes of premenstrual tension. *Archives of Neurology and Psychiatry, 26,* 1053–1057.

Gruba, G. H., & Rohrbaugh, M. (1975). MMPI correlates of menstrual distress. *Psychosomatic Medicine, 37,* 265–273.

Halbreich, U., & Endicott, J. (1982). Classification of premenstrual syndromes. In R. C. Friedman (Ed.), *Behavior and the menstrual cycle.* New York: Dekker.

Halbreich, U., Endicott, J., Schacht, S., & Nee, J. (1982). The diversity of premenstrual changes as reflected in the Premenstrual Assessment Form. *Acta Psychiatrica Scandinavica, 65,* 46–65.

Haskett, R. F., & Abplanalp, J. M. (1983). Premenstrual tension syndrome: Diagnostic criteria and selection of research subjects. *Psychiatry Research, 9,* 125–138.

Haskett, R. F., Steiner, M., & Carroll, B. J. (1984). A psychoendocrine study of premenstrual tension syndrome. *Journal of Affective Disorders, 6,* 191–199.

Haskett, R. F., Steiner, M., Osmun J. N., and Carroll, B. J. (1980). Severe premenstrual tension: Delineation of the syndrome. *Biological Psychiatry, 15,* 121–139.

Horwitz, W. A., & Harris, M. M. (1936). Study of a case of cyclic psychic disturbances associated with menstruation. *American Journal of Psychiatry, 92,* 1403–1412.

Janowsky, D. S., Gorney, R., Castelnuovo-Tedesco, P., & Stone, C. B. (1969). Premenstrual–menstrual increases in psychiatric hospital admission rates.

American Journal of Obstetrics and Gynecology, 103, 189–191.

Kashiwagi, T., McClure, J. N., & Wetzel, R. D. (1976). Premenstrual affective syndrome and psychiatric disorder. *Diseases of the Nervous System, 37,* 116–119.

Kramp, J. L. (1968). Studies on the premenstrual syndrome in relation to psychiatry. *Acta Psychiatrica Scandinavica, Supplementum, 203,* 261–267.

Laidlaw, J. (1956). Catamenial epilepsy. *Lancet, 2,* 1235–1237.

Lingjaerde, P., & Bredland, R. (1954). Hyperestrogenic cyclic psychosis. *Acta Psychiatrica et Neurologica Scandinavica, 29,* 355–360.

Lundstrom, V., Green, K., & Svanborg, K. (1979). Endogenous prostaglandins in dysmenorrhea and the effect of prostaglandin synthetase inhibitors (PGSI) on uterine contractility. *Acta Obstetrica et Gynecologica Scandinavica, 86,* (Suppl.), 51–56.

MacKInnon, I. L., MacKinnon, P. C. B., & Thomson, A. D. (1959). Lethal hazards of the luteal phase of the menstrual cycle. *British Medical Journal, 1,* 1015–1017

May, R. R. (1976). Mood shifts and the menstrual cycle. *Journal of Psychosomatic Research, 20,* 125–130.

Moos, R. H. (1968). The development of a Menstrual Distress Questionnaire. *Psychosomatic Medicine, 30,* 853–867.

Moos, R. H., Kopell, B. S., Melges, F. T., Yalom, I, D., Lunde, D. T., Clayton, R. B., & Hamburg, D. A. (1969). Fluctuations in symptoms and moods during the menstrual cycle. *Journal of Psychosomatic Research, 13,* 37–44.

Muse, K. H., Cetel, N. S., Futterman, L. A., & Yen, S. S. C. (1984). The premenstrual syndrome: Effects of "medical ovariectomy." *New England Journal of Medicine, 311,* 1345–1349.

Parlee, M. B. (1973). The premenstrual syndrome. *Psychological Bulletin, 80,* 454–465.

Price, T. R. P. (1980). Temporal lobe epilepsy as a premenstrual behavioral syndrome. *Biological Psychiatry, 14,* 957–963.

Rausch, J. L., & Janowsky, D. S. (1982). Premenstrual tension: Etiology. In R. C. Friedman (Ed.), *Behavior and the menstrual cycle.* New York: Dekker.

Rees, L. (1953). Psychosomatic aspects of the premenstrual tension syndrome. *British Journal of Psychiatry, 99,* 62–73.

Reid, R. L., & Yen, S. S. C. (1981). Premenstrual syndrome. *American Journal of Obstetrics and Gynecology, 139,* 85–104.

Rouse, P. (1978). Premenstrual tension: A study using the Moos Menstrual Questionnaire. *Journal of Psychosomatic Research, 22,* 215–222.

Rubin, R. T., Reinisch, J. M., & Haskett, R. F. (1981). Postnatal gonadal steroid effects on human sexually dimorphic behavior: A paradigm of hormone–environmental interaction. *Science, 211,* 1318–1324.

Rubinow, D. R., & Roy-Byrne, P. (1984). Premenstrual syndromes: Overview from a methodologic perspective. *American Journal of Psychiatry, 141,* 163–172.

Rubinow, D. R., Roy-Byrne, P., Hoban, M. C., Gold, P. W., & Post, R. M. (1984). Prospective assessment of menstrually related mood disorders. *American Journal of Psychiatry, 141,* 684–686.

Ruble, D. N. (1977). Premenstrual symptoms: A reinterpretation. *Science, 197,* 291–292.

Ruble, D. N., & Brooks-Gunn, J. (1979). Menstrual symptoms: A social cognition analysis. *Journal of Behavioral Medicine, 2,* 171–193.

Sampson, G. A., & Jenner, P. A. (1977). Studies of daily recordings from the Moos Distress Questionnaire. *British Journal of Psychiatry, 130,* 265–271.

Sampson, G. A., & Prescott, P. (1981). The assessment of the symptoms of premenstrual syndrome and their response to therapy. *British Journal of Psychiatry, 138,* 399–405.

Schuckit, M. A., Daly, V., Herrmann, G., & Hineman, S. (1975). Premenstrual symptoms and depression in a university population. *Diseases of the Nervous System, 35,* 516–517.

Schwartz, A., Zor, U., Lindner, H. R., & Naor, S. (1975). Primary dysmenorrhea: Alleviation by an inhibitor of prostaglandin synthesis and action. *Obstetrics and Gynecology (New York), 44,* 709–712.

Smith, S. L. (1975). Mood and the menstrual cycle. In E. J. Sachar (Ed.), *Topics in psychoendocrinology.* New York: Grune & Stratton.

Spitzer, R. L., Endicott, J. & Robins, E. (1978). *Research Diagnostic Criteria (RDC) for a selected group of function disorders* (3rd ed.). New York: New York State Psychiatric Institute.

Steiner, M., & Carroll, B. J. (1977). The psychobiology of premenstrual dysphoria: Review of theories and treatments. *Psychoneuroendocrinology, 2,* 321–335.

Steiner, M., Haskett, R. F., & Carroll, B. J. (1980). Premenstrual tension syndrome. The development of research diagnostic criteria and new rating scales. *Acta Psychiatrica Scandinavica, 62,* 177–190.

Steiner, M., Haskett, R. F., Carroll, B. J., Hays, S. E., & Rubin, R. T. (1984). Plasma prolactin and severe premenstrual tension. *Psychoneuroendocrinology, 9,* 29–35.

Werch, A., & Kane, R. E. (1976). Treatment of premenstrual tension with metolazone: A double–blind evaluation of a new diuretic. *Current Therapy Research, 19,* 565–572.

Wetzel, R. D., & McClure, J. N. (1972). Suicide and the menstrual cycle: A review. *Comprehensive Psychiatry, 13,* 369–374.

Wetzel, R. D., Reich, T., McClure, J. N., Jr., & Wald, J. A. (1975). Premenstrual affective syndrome and affective disorder. *British Journal of Psychiatry, 127,* 219–221.

Williams, E. Y., & Weekes, L. R. (1952). Premenstrual tension associated with psychotic episodes. *Journal of Nervous and Mental Disorders, 116,* 321–329.

Wood, C., & Jakubowicz, D. (1980). The treatment of premenstrual symptoms with mefenamic acid. *British Journal of Obstetrics and Gynecology, 87,* 627–630.

23 HORMONES AND STRESS

SUSANNA GOLDSTEIN

Cornell University Medical Center

URIEL HALBREICH

State University of New York at Buffalo

INTRODUCTION

Modern studies of stress and disease were started early in this century by Cannon (1929). He studied bodily changes associated with pain, hunger, fear, and rage and showed an activation of the sympathetic adreno-medullary system in response to emotional stimuli as well as to well-known physiological stimuli such as blood loss. Later, Selye (1936) focused on the pituitary–adrenocortical system and suggested the concept of "general adaptation syndrome" (GAS)—a nonspecific physiological response to stimuli or stressors which includes activation of the sympathetic nervous system, the adrenal medulla, and the adrenal cortex. Selye's theory of stress and diseases of adaptation had enormous influence on medical thinking and research throughout the world (Selye, 1946). Subsequently, those who became disenchanted with this type of research embraced the argument that the correlational data generated cannot support the generalization that the endocrine mechanisms of GAS were important in disease. Also, the field became thoroughly confusing because of the lack of a clear definition of stress and continuing semantic disputes. Some researchers referred to stress as the provocative agent, event, or stimulus, while others called the response "stress." These and other definitions were often used interchangeably in the same report. Stress research was also hindered by the difficulty of sorting out cognitive and physiological stimuli: Mason (1975), in a series of studies, had demonstrated that the conventional laboratory situation, which is designed for the study of physical stressors such as immobility, exercise, and cold, stress response is not elicited when stressors are presented in a way that eliminates their psychological sequelae, while emotional disturbance, when present, serves as a potent stimulus of pituitary–adrenocortical secretion.

The difficulty in formulating an objective, reliable, and valid measurement of emotional events seems to have discouraged present-day stress research after the explosion of human and primate studies in this field in the 1960s and 1970s. The past 5 years have seen more advances in neurobiology on the molecular, cellular, or simple animal model level, with only very cautious attempts to generalize the results. In addition, most of the recent research has been focused on changes in the central nervous system, while the earlier studies of endocrine responses to stress were mainly focused on changes in hormonal levels in the peripheral blood.

This chapter will attempt to integrate the findings of earlier studies, extensively reviewed elsewhere (Rose, 1984), and those of more recent studies.

SPECIFIC HORMONAL RESPONSES TO STRESS

The Pituitary–Adrenal Axis

The adrenocortical hormones and ACTH were focused on most in stress research since

Selye's work. There are more studies that measure cortisol response to stress than for any other hormone and these have been extensively reviewed (Rose, 1980, 1984). Levels of cortisol were reported to be elevated in association with a wide array of situations having various levels of physical and emotional involvement: after crying, in normal human infants; in infants with a stormy postnatal course (Cathro, Forsyth, & Cameron, 1969); following surgery (Kahlet & Binder, 1973) and in anticipation of surgery (Czeisler, Moore, & Regestein, 1976); in anticipation of examination (Mason, 1968a); at admission to hospital (Mason, 1968a); during prolonged, exhausting exercise such as marathon running (Newmark, Timathongkam, Martin, Cooper, & Rose, 1976); in anticipation of exhausting exercise (Mason *et al.*, 1973); and when moving (relocating) (Kral, Grad, & Berenson, 1968).

The most brisk cortisol response occurs at first exposure to the stressful stimulus. Repeated exposure leads to adaptation, with extinguishing of the adrenocortical arousal (Mason, 1968a; Pollard, Bassett, & Cairncross, 1976; Ursin, Baade, & Levine, 1978). Adaptation of the hormonal response or the lack of response is interpreted by some researchers as reflecting the effectiveness of the defenses or coping style of the individual in protecting him- or herself from feelings of being stressed (Poe, Rose, & Mason, 1970; Rose, Poe, & Mason, 1968; Wolff, Friedman, Hofer, & Mason, 1964; Wolff, Hofer, & Mason, 1964), regardless of the psychological adaptive value of the defense employed. The impact of any potentially stressful event seems to be dependent on the perception of the individual who is exposed to it, and this perception is crucial in determining his or her adrenocortical responses (Bourne, Rose, & Mason, 1967, 1968). These observations have been made in humans as well as animals.

Social variables have also been shown to be relevant in determining response to stress: When a dominant, aggressive individual is subjected to a task that involves avoidance of punishment, this may be perceived as a highly stressful ("novel") stimulus, with concomitant brisk cortisol increase, while for the subordinate, submissive individual, this kind of situation is "usual" and therefore nonstressful (Mason, Brady, & Tolliver, 1968).

Despite the findings that endocrine adaptation to stress occurs relatively rapidly, chronically stressed animals have more rapid endocrine responses to other novel stimuli than do unexposed controls (Sakellaris & Vernikos-Danellis, 1975).

The Pituitary–Adrenal Axis in Psychiatric Disorders

Some patients with schizophrenia and affective disorders have increased levels of cortisol secretion (Halbreich, Asnis, Shindledecker, Zumoff, & Nathan, 1985; Sachar *et al.*, 1973). In schizophrenia, elevated cortisol has been interpreted as an indicator of the amount of stress experienced, whereas changes in depression, which include decreased suppressibility of plasma cortisol by dexamethasone, are assumed to reflect a central pathogenetic abormality, that is, altered levels of neurotransmitters in the brain.

A puzzling, but consistent lack of increase of plasma cortisol levels had been demonstrated in panic attacks, whether spontaneous, situational, or lactate induced. Researchers attempted to explain the lack of cortisol response in these seemingly highly stressful situations by habituation; that is, the panic attack does not have the quality of novelty that may be required to induce increase of cortisol.

Central Nervous System Effects of Glucocorticoids

Chronic hypersecretion of glucocorticoids, stimulated by chronic stress, was shown to reduce (down-regulate) the number of glucocorticoid receptors in specific areas of the brain in patients (Sapolsky, Krey, & McEwen, 1984).

A recent study in rats has shown that the activity of the pituitary–adrenal axis may physiologically modulate the permeability of the blood–brain barrier to macromolecules from the blood into the brain interstitium (Long & Holaday., 1985). Increased availability of circulating cortisol, stimulated by stress, may indirectly decrease the central actions of diffusion-limited humoral substances and drugs.

β-Endorphin and Pro-opiomelanocortin-Derived Peptides

Following the observation that the hypothalamic–pituitary–adrenal (HPA) system is activated in response to stress, animal and human studies suggested that there is also an increase in plasma β-endorphin in these conditions and that there is a linkage between the stress-induced responses of the endogenous opioid system and the HPA axis. This linkage is consistent with the common origin of plasma β-endorphin and ACTH (Guillemin et al., 1977).

The increase of β-endorphin levels may contribute to increased tolerance to pain following stress (stress-induced analgesia), as observed in animals (Akil, Mayer, & Liebeskind, 1976) and humans (Willner, Dehen, & Cambier, 1981). This observation is supported also by the negative correlation found between surgical stress-induced β-endorphin levels and postoperative morphine requirements (Cohen, Pickar, Dubois, & Bunney, 1982). Interestingly, a significant negative relationship between preoperative hormone levels and postoperative opiate usage was found. This suggests that physical trauma during surgery may not be a major determinant of the variability of patient need for postoperative morphine. Rather, the patient's physiological arousal prior to surgery, which may be dependent upon innate responsiveness of an arousal system and/or responses to physiological stress, may be the major determinant of postoperative pain and may also predict the degree of physiological response to surgical stress (Cohen et al., 1982).

So far, it is unclear if circulating β-endorphin levels are directly involved in behavioral responses to stress. However, β-endorphin may be a marker of central nervous system arousal. This marker role may not be unique to plasma β-endorphin, as the release of other pituitary peptides was shown to be increased by stress (Guillemin et al., 1977). α-Melanocyte-stimulating hormone (α-MSH) along with β-endorphin are secreted mainly by the intermediate lobe of the pituitary, and β-lipotropin (β-LPH) along with ACTH are released by the anterior lobe (Eipper & Mains, 1980). The intermediate lobe peptide secretion is stimulated by epinephrine which is known to increase in response to stress (Smelik, 1984)

via a β-adrenergic mechanism that is blocked by propranolol (Berkenbosh, Tilders, & Vermes, 1983). In addition, it is inhibited by the dopaminergic innervation (Smelik, Berkenbosch, Vermes, & Tilders, 1983). Thus, the intermediate lobe, linked and modulated by the catecholamine system, seems to be centrally involved in the response to emotional stress. In addition, repeated stress induces the biosynthesis and release of β-endorphin-like opioid-inactive substance from the intermediate lobe of rats (Akil, Shiomi, & Matthews, 1985). It is possible that this and similar substances, while devoid of opioid activity, have other biological effects in chronic stress response.

A particularly interesting area of research is related to the influence of endorphins on stress-related feeding. Various stressors, such as tail pinch, induce feeding in rats. This effect was shown to be significantly reduced by administration of low doses of the narcotic antagonist, naloxone. In contrast, hyperphagia induced by insulin was not decreased by naloxone. These results are concordant with the hypothesis that endorphins may be involved in mediating stress-induced eating. Thus, narcotic antagonists may be considered as putative anorexogenic agents (Lowy, Maickel, & Yim, 1980; Morley & Levine, 1980).

Vasopressin

This area of research is fraught with conflicting results. Stress has been known to be associated with antidiuresis but, nevertheless, vasopressin is not released by all stress stimuli. Rather, it appears that levels of circulating vasopressin decrease after a variety of stress stimuli (Knepel, Nutto, & Hertting, 1982). There is some evidence that β-endorphin is responsible for inhibition of vasopressin release (Knepel et al., 1982). However, it seems that a portion of vasopressin neurons does respond to stress in a fashion similar to CRF neurons; there is evidence for co-localization of CRF and vasopressin in hypothalamic paraventricular nucleus neurons. This would account for the observations that vasopressin strongly potentiates the effect of CRF on anterior pituitary ACTH secretion (Gillies, Linton, & Lowry, 1982).

Growth Hormone

Studies of the response of growth hormone (GH) to stress have mainly focused on GH's relationship to associated psychological parameters. Thus, several studies have demonstrated that some individuals exhibit an increase of plasma GH levels after exposure to stress. The responders have been identified by clinical evaluations and by psychological testing as anxious or "neurotic" and as exhibiting an additional factor. For example, in a study of cardiac catheterization as an acute stress, patients who were anxious and not "engaged" with the physician doing the procedure had an elevation of GH during the procedure (Green, Corron, Schalch, & Schreiner, 1970). Another study compared responses to watching a stressful movie and found that GH responders had high scores on the "psychological defensiveness" scale of the Minnesota Multiphasic Personality Inventory (MMPI) (Kurakawa et al., 1977). A recent study explored GH in older people during a stressful interview and found that anxiety in conjunction with defensiveness, interpreted as "nonengagement," that is, the subject avoids the emotional state the interviewer attempts to elicit, predicted "GH responders" (Kosten, Jacobs, Mason, Wohby, & Atkins, 1984). GH increase was demonstrated in a variety of other situations as well: surgery (Newsom & Rose, 1971), venipuncture (Rose & Hurst, 1975), tests and examinations (Miyabo, Asato, & Mizushima, 1977), and in particular, the anticipation of stressful events (Kosten et al., 1984; Salter, Fluck, & Stimmler, 1972). While GH response rarely occurs in the absence of cortisol response (Abplanalp, Livingston, 1977), there are situations in which GH response does not parallel adrenal response (G. M. Brown, Seggie, Chambers, Prakash, & Ettigi, 1978). The dissociation may be related to stimulus intensity. It was hypothesized that a more intense stimulus is needed to provoke release of GH than cortisol (Abplanalp et al., 1977; Rose & Hurst, 1975) or that the GH responses are specific to certain coping styles such as independence (W. A. Brown & Heninger, 1976) or the level of defensiveness of the subject.

The normal episodic secretion of GH complicates the interpretation of GH response to stress.

Prolactin

Prolactin (PRL) rises during surgery (Noel, Suh, Stone, & Frantz, 1972) and procedures such as gastroscopy, proctoscopy, and pelvic examinations (Koninckx, 1978), as well as for parachute jumping and motion sickness (Eversmann, Gottsman, Uhlich, von Wender, & Scriba, 1978). The PRL response may be dissociated form the cortisol and GH response and, like GH, the PRL response has a higher threshold of stimulus intensity than cortisol. This issue is complicated and multifaceted because PRL is also episodically secreted in response to other nonstressful stimuli (e.g., nipple stimulation).

A number of authors have described a possible "protective" effect of hyperprolactinemia against stressful stimuli. This effect was demonstrated by marked resistance to stress-induced changes in body temperature and diminished stress response of the hypothalamic–pituitary–adrenal (HPA) axis in hyperprolactinergic rats (Drago & Scapagnini, 1984). On the other hand, the HPA system can influence the PRL response to stress. Low plasma levels of plasma cortisol and high plasma concentrations of ACTH potentiate the PRL response to stress (Drago & Scapagnini, 1984), while long-term ACTH treatment inhibits PRL release induced by stress (Fekete, Stark, Kanyicska, Herman, & Palkovitz, 1980).

It is hypothesized that various hyperprolactinemic states may have "psychosomatic" determinants: Several studies reported that most women with these disorders, but not matched controls, were reared under chronic stress conditions related to an absent, violent, or alcoholic father (Sobrinho et al., 1984). This observation was supported by another study which reported that neurotic women, but not normal controls, respond to psychological stress with increased PRL (Miyabo et al., 1977).

Gonadal Hormones

The effect of stress on the human male reproductive system was first documented in prisoners sentenced to death who were waiting for execution. They showed arrested spermatogenesis (McGrady, 1984). Other studies reported a decrease of testosterone (T) levels in the plasma of men undergoing basic army training and combat stress (Rose, 1969), surgical stress (Charters, Odell, & Thompson, 1969), and psychological stress (Kreuz, Rose, & Jennings, 1972). Decrease in T did not appear to be related to a fall in follicle-stimulating hormone (FSH) or luteinizing hormone (LH) (Carstensen et al., 1973), or to an increase in ACTH. In fact, elevated cortisol plasma levels seem to be responsible for T suppression in men (Schiason, Durand, & Monszowicz, 1978) and primates (Sapolsky, 1985). The implications of these findings may be that in situations of elevated cortisol levels, such as depression, circulating T levels may be decreased. However, the behavioral significance of decreased levels of T is unclear.

Stress has been shown to delay the onset of puberty in male rhesus monkeys (Rose, 1980). Prenatal stress in pregnant rats leads to more feminine behavior in the male offspring (Ward, 1972), mediated by a fall in T detected in the male fetuses of stressed mothers (Ward & Weisz, 1980). These observations were not repeated in humans, but they raise intriguing questions about the influence of maternal stress during critical periods of fetal development on psychosocial behavior of the offspring.

While the T level decreases in males under stress, it has been hypothesized that psychological stress may play a role in the initiation of inappropriate gonadotropin secretion, chronic anovulation, and androgen excess in females, resulting in polycystic ovary syndrome (PCO) (Lobo, Granger, Paul, Goebelsmann, & Mishell, 1983).

Stress is implicated in the pathogenesis of certain conditions of cessation of the regular menstrual cycle in young women undergoing psychologically stressful experiences, such as separation. It has been proposed that these conditions, called stress amenorrhea, hypothalamic amenorrhea, or psychogenic amenorrhea, are initiated and maintained by inappropriate gonadotropin secretion reflecting neuroendocrine changes caused by psychological stress. Similar mechanisms may interfere with ovulation and produce reproductive failure (psychogenic infertility). Psychotherapy or appropriate efforts to deal with the emotional stress (improved coping) were claimed to be beneficial in the treatment of amenorrhea and infertility in some women (Reichlin, Ablanalp, Labrum, Schwartz, & Sommer, 1979).

Another circumstance in which stress is implicated as causing disruption of the menstrual cycle is athletic amenorrhea (Baker, 1981). This condition was described in female marathon runners as well as ballet dancers and was attributed to many factors, including body composition (leanness), hyperprolactinemia, hyperandrogenism, and stress. Here stress refers to the mechanical intensity of athletic training and the psychological strain of competition (Rebar & Cumming, 1981). However, it was shown that the increase in PRL occurring during exercise (Shangold, Gatz, & Tysen, 1981) fails to occur in amenorrheic athletes (Loucks & Horvath, 1984), and therefore menstrual cycle disruption in these women cannot be sustained by hyperprolactinemia. Also, psychological tests applied to eumenorrheic and amenorrheic athletes failed to show differences between the two groups (Loucks & Horvath, 1984). The researchers interpreted these results as proof against the involvement of stress in reproductive dysfunction in athletes. However, this issue is still open to debate and research, especially when increasing numbers of women are engaging in athletic training.

Catecholamines

Levels of the peripheral catecholamines (epinephrine and norepinephrine) increased rapidly when the organism is confronted with a variety of stressful stimuli (Carruthers, 1977). Stimuli that appear threatening, distressing, or novel increase both circulating catecholamines and corticoids. However, cortisol response decreases rapidly with adaptation, while catecholamines remain elevated, possibly reflecting the need for vigilance and increased effort. Most stimuli that are effective in raising catecholamine levels stimulate both epinephrine and norepinephrine. However, a large increase in epinephrine is associated with attention and vigilance, as in flying, motor car driving, piece-wage work, exposure to crowded public transportation, mental stress (Akerstedt et al., 1983), and public speaking (Dimsdale & Moss, 1980). Norepinephrine excretion, on the other hand, appears to respond more to physical stress and activity (Howley, 1976). Lundberg (1980) constructed an intriguing model of the relationship between catecholamine and cortisol secretion in response to stressful conditions:

> Effort without distress is accompanied by sympathetic–adrenal activation whereas the pituitary–adrenal system may be suppressed, provided the individual is in control of the situation. Effort with distress is accompanied by sympathetic–adrenal as well as pituitary–adrenal activation. Distress without effort, i.e., feeling helpless, passive, seems to be associated mainly with increased cortisol excretion. (p. 460)

This model is useful in explaining and predicting the pattern of endocrine response in many situations, but a notable exception is panic attacks during which the individual endures great distress, accompanied by feelings of helplessness, without significant response of either the HPA system or catecholamines.

Catecholamine Changes in the Central Nervous System

Following acute cold swim tests in rats, hypothalamic epinephrine concentrations were markedly lowered and remained decreased for 24 hours, while norepinephrine concentrations decreased, but returned to baseline within 14 hours. With repeated stress, norepinephrine and epinephrine turnover was decreased and their absolute concentrations were increased in the hypothalamus and hippocampus, while there was little effect on serotonin and dopamine. The decreased turnover of norepinephrine and epinephrine under chronic stress is implicated in the behavioral and endocrine changes observed in these animals (Roth, Mefford, & Barchas, 1982).

Stress, Catecholamines, and Illness

A study that explored the complex relationship between stress and physical and emotional disorders measured plasma catecholamine levels in response to stress in combination with behavioral observations and physiological parameters in spontaneously hypertensive and normotensive rats. This study concluded that the spontaneously hypertensive rats have a more marked response of the central nervous system to stress, reflected in behavioral activation and peripheral secretion of catecholamines. However blood pressure response to catecholamines was more striking in the hypertensive rats, and this appeared to be the result of reduced β_2-adrenoreceptor-mediated vasodilation. With repeated stress, the number of β-receptors may be even further diminished and the net vasoconstrictor effect of catecholamines enhanced (Kopin, McCarty, Torda, & Yamaguchi, 1980). This combination of central nervous system hyperreactivity to stress and susceptibility of a particular peripheral effector system to the development of pathological changes may explain, at least in part, the complexity of "psychosomatic" disorders.

Another study of human subjects assessed sympathetic nervous system activity in those exposed to graded orthostatic and isometric stress during monthly hospital visits. After the first session, the experimental subjects practiced a technique that elicited a relaxation response. The concentrations of plasma norepinephrine during subsequent graded stresses were significantly higher, with no changes in the control group. The groups did not differ in their heart rate and blood pressure response. These observations were interpreted as reflecting reduced norepinephrine endorgan responsivity elicited by regular practice of the relaxation response (more norepinephrine is required to produce compensatory increases in heart rate and blood pressure) (Hoffman et al., 1982). Other examples of observed elevated catecholamines without high blood pressure occur in patients with ulcers (Brandsborg, Brandsborg, Lovgreen, & Christensen, 1978) and depressed patients (Wyatt, Portnoy, Kupfer, Snyder, & Engelman, 1971). These patients do not become hypertensive, presumably because compensatory mechanisms for maintaining a normal blood pressure appear to be functioning adequately, but abnormalities in other effector systems may be responsible for the development of abnormal functional states in other systems, which with prolonged or repeated exposure may result in illness.

THE STRESS THEORY OF AGING

The stress theory of aging combines the cellular hypothesis of "wear and tear" and auto-intoxication (production of substances, e.g., hydrogen peroxide, which are toxic to the cell) with neuroendocrinological theories of aging involving the HPA axis. According to the stress theory, exposure to repeated stressful stimuli over the years eventually exhausts the ability of the organism to maintain its homeostasis. The breakdown of homeostasis is expressed by the process of aging and death.

This theory is based on Selye's (1946) "general adaptation syndrome," which implies that individuals are born with a limited amount of "adaptive energy" which is progressively used up by each exposure to stress. Exposure to stimuli (stresses) induces a sequence of events leading first to the activation of defense mechanisms necessary for survival (the so-called alarm reaction), following by a period of enhanced adaptive capacity (the stage of resistance), and terminating in a loss of the capacity to adapt (the stage of exhaustion). The HPA axis synchronizes the neural input from stress stimuli with hormonal secretion and the sensitivity of the target tissues to hormonal actions. The life cycle of the individual mirrors the sequence of neuroendocrine response to stress: At infancy, adaptive capacity is not completely developed; in adulthood, resistance reaches an optimum (maximum adaptive capacity); thereafter, gradual exhaustion sets in, with declining available adaptive reserves, leading to death (Timiras, 1983).

Neuroendocrine Dissociations in Stress

Although stress-induced activation of pituitary hormones seems to follow a common pattern, several neuroendocrine dissociations in stress have been described in animals and man. For example, in experimental anxiety states induced by exposing phobic patients to their feared objects, GH responses are common, whereas no rise occurs in plasma cortisol levels, despite a marked behavioral arousal. In the same patients, a cortisol response (without a GH response) occurs when the subjects first enter the testing laboratory knowing that they will not be exposed to the feared object. In an attempt to explain this, it was hypothesized that the cortisol system in these subjects is responsive to novelty or distant apprehension, but not to the induced phobic anxiety (Curtis, Nesse, Buxton, Wright, & Lippman, 1976). Another example of dissociated endocrine response to stress is seen with electroconvulsive therapy (ECT). The most striking hormonal response to ECT is a rise in plasma PRL levels (Öhman, Wallinder, Balldin, Wallin, & Abrahansson, 1976). However, a variable cortisol level usually occurs, but no change in GH secretion can be demonstrated following ECT (Elithorn, Bridges, Hodges, & Jones, 1968).

SUMMARY

Stress should not be defined by hormonal responses. Just because a stress hormone rises does not make the stimulus stressful (e.g., highly pleasurable or erotic stimuli), and a condition may be highly stressful without a concomitant rise in stress hormones (e.g., panic attacks).

There are specific patterns of endocrine responses which may be associated with specific classes of stimuli, and it is not possible to define a "generalized" stress hormone. The pattern of endocrine response to stress may be modulated also by coping style as well as earlier experience and perception of the stimulus by the subject.

The functional consequences of endocrine changes that are associated with stressful events are unclear. Endocrine response to stress may be a reflection of the way the brain operates in adaptation. Accordingly, hormonal changes that occur following stressful stimuli can help us to infer some aspects of central nervous system functioning. Alternatively, Selye's tradition equates stress and disease, and hormonal responses to stress reflect maladaptation or pathophysiology of some diseases. Most of the data available today are based on human studies which, at best, can demonstrate correlations. In order to establish a caustative role of stress in disease, there is a need for animal models and long-term studies that include repeated experiences and allowances for individual differences in response. Among the many intriguing questions for future research is that generated by the ultimate result of repeated exposure to the same stressor. Does such a result reflect habituation, immunization, or breakdown?

References

Abplanalp, J. M., Livingston, L., Rose, R. M., & Sandwisch, D. (1977). Cortisol and growth hormone responses to psychological stress during the menstrual cycle. *Psychosomatic Medicine, 39*, 158–177.

Akerstedt, T., Gillberg, M., Hjemdahl P., Sigurdson K., Gustavson, I., Daleskeg, M., & Pollare, T. (1983). Comparison of urinary and plasma catecholamine responses to mental stress. *Acta Psychiatrica Scandinavica, 117*, 19–26.

Akil, H., Mayer, D. J., & Liebesking, J. (1976). Antagonism of stimulation-produced analgesia by naloxone, a narcotic antagonist. *Science, 191*, 961–962.

Akil, H., Shiomi, H., & Matthews, J. (1985). Induction of the intermediate pituitary by stress: Synthesis and release of a nonopioid form of β-endorphin. *Science, 227*, 424–426.

Baker, E. R. (1981). Menstrual dysfunction and hormonal status in athletic women: A review. *Fertility and Sterility, 36*, 691.

Berkenbosh, F., Tilders, F. J. H., & Vermes, I. (1983). β-Adrenoreceptor activation mediates stress-induced secretion of β-endorphin-related peptides from the intermediate lobe, but not anterior pituitary. *Nature (London), 305*, 237–239.

Bourne, P. G., Rose, R. M., & Mason, J. W. (1967). Urinary 17-OHCS levels: Data on seven helicopter ambulance medics in combat. *Archives of General Psychiatry, 17*, 104–110.

Bourne, P. G., Rose, R. M., & Mason, J. W. (1968). 17-OHCS levels in combat—special forces "A" team under threat of attack. *Archives of General Psychiatry, 19*, 135–140.

Brandsborg, O., Brandsborg, M. N. A., Lovgreen, N. A., & Christensen, N. J. (1978). Increased plasma noradrenaline and serum gastrin in patients with duodenal ulcer. *European Journal of Clinical Investigation, 8*, 11–14.

Brown, G. M., Seggie, J. A., Chambers, J. W., Prakash, G., & Ettigi, P. G. (1978). Psychoendocrinology and growth hormone: A review. *Psychoneuroendocrinology, 3*, 131–153.

Brown, W. A., & Heninger, G. (1976). Stress-induced growth hormone release: Psychologic and physiologic correlates. *Psychological Medicine, 38*, 145–147.

Cannon, W. B. (1929). *Bodily changes in pain, hunger, fear and rage: An account of recent research into the function of emotional excitement* (2nd ed.). New York: Appleton.

Carruther, M. E. (1977). The chemical anatomy of stress. In P. Kielholz (Ed.), (pp. 53–58). Berne: Huber.

Carstensen, H., Amer, B., Amer, L. *et al.* (1973). The postoperative decrease of plasma testosterone in man after major surgery in relation to plasma FSH and LH. *Journal of Steroid Biochemistry, 4*, 45–55.

Cathro, D. M., Forsyth, C. C., & Cameron, J. (1969). Adrenocorticol response to stress in newborn infants. *Archives of Disease in Childhood, 44*, 88–95.

Charters, A. C., Odell, W. D., & Thompson, J. C. (1969). Anterior pituitary function during surgical stress and convalescence. Radioimmunoassay measurement of blood TSH, LH, FSH and growth hormone. *Journal of Clinical Endocrinology and Metabolism, 29*, 63–71.

Cohen, M. R., Pickar, B., Dubois, M., & Bunney, W. E. (1982). Stress-induced plasma β-endorphin immunoreactivity may predict postoperative morphine usage. *Psychiatry Research, 6*, 7–12.

Curtis, G., Nesse, R., Buxton, M., Wright, J., Lippman, D. (1976). Neuroendocrine response to stress in phobic patients. *Comprehensive Psychiatry, 17*, 153–160.

Czeisler, C. A., Moore, E., & Regestein, Q. R. (1976). Episodic 24-hour cortisol secretory patterns in patients awaiting elective cardiac surgery. *Journal of Clinical Endocrinology and Metabolism, 42*, 273–283.

Dimsdale, J. E., & Moss, J. (1980). Plasma catecholamines in stress and exercise. *JAMA, Journal of American Medical Association, 243*, 340–342.

Drago, F., & Scapagnini, V. (1984). Prolactin–ACTH interactions in the neuroendocrine responses to stress. In E. Usdin, R. Kvetnansky, & J. Axelrod (Eds.), *Stress: The role of catecholamines and other neurotransmitters* (pp. 311–324). New York: Gordon & Breach.

Eipper, B. A., & Mains, R. E. (1980). Structure and biosynthesis of proadrenocorticotropin endorphin and related peptides. *Endocrine Reviews, 1*, 1–27.

Elithorn, A., Bridges, P. K., Hodges, J. R., & Jones, M. T. (1968). Cortisol and growth hormone responses to electroconvulsive therapy. *British Journal of Psychiatry, 114*, 575–580.

Eversmann, T., Gottsman, M., Uhlich, E., von Wender, K., & Scriba, P. C. (1978). Increased secretion of growth hormone, prolactin, antidiuretic hormone and cortisol induced by the stress of motion sickness. *Aviation, Space and Environmental Medicine, 53*–57.

Fekete, M. I. K., Stark, E. B., Kanyicska, J. P., Herman, M. J., & Palkovitz, M. (1980). Inhibition of stress-induced hormonal changes by chronic ACTH treatment: Possible relationships with changes of monaminergic transmission in the central nervous system. In E. Usdin, R. Kventnansky, & J. Kopin (Eds.), *Catecholamines and stress.* New York: Elsevier/North-Holland.

Gillies, G. E., Linton, E. A., & Lowry, P. J. (1982). Corticotropin-releasing activity of the new CRF is potentiated several times by vasopressin. *Nature (London), 295*, 355–357.

Greene, W. A., Corron, G., Schalch, D. S., & Schreiner, B. F. (1970). Psychologic correlates of growth hormone and adrenal responses of patients undergoing cardiac catheterization. *Psychosomatic Medicine, 32*, 599–614.

Guillemin, R., Vargo, T., Rossier, Y., Minick, S., Ling, N., Rivier, C., Vale, W., & Bloom, F. (1977). β-Endorphin and adrenocorticotropin are secreted concomitantly by the pituitary gland. *Science, 197*, 1367–1369.

Halbreich, U., Asnis, G. M., Shindledecker, K., Zumoff, B., & Nathan, R. S. (1985). Cortisol secretion in endogenous depression. I. Basal plasma levels. *Archives of General Psychiatry, 42*, 904–908.

Hoffman, J. W., Benson, H., Arns, P. A., Stainbrook, G. L., Landsberg, L., Young, J. B., & Gill, A (1982). Reduced sympathetic nervous system responsivity associated with relaxation response. *Science, 215*, 190–192.

Howley, E. T. (1976). The effect of different intensities of exercise on the secretion of epinephrine and norepinephrine. *Medicine and Science in Sports, 8*, 219–222.

Kahlet, H., & Binder, C. (1973). Alterations in distribution volume and biological half-life of cortisol during major surgery. *Journal of Clinical Endocrinology and Metabolism, 36*, 330–333.

Knepel, W., Nutto, D., & Hertting, G. (1982). Evidence for inhibition by β-endorphin of vasopressin release during foot shock-induced stress in the rat. *Neuroendocrinology, 34*, 353–356.

Koninckx, P. (1978). Stress hyperprolactinemia in clinical practice. *Lancet, 1* (8058), 273.

Kopin, I. J., McCarty, R., Torda, T., & Yamaguchi, I. (1980). Catecholamines in plasma and responses to stress. In E. Usdin, R. Kvetnansky, & J. Kopin (Eds.), *Catecholamines and stress: Recent advances* (pp. 197–204). Amsterdam: Elsevier/North-Holland.

Kosten, T. R., Jacobs, S., Mason, J., Wohby, V., & Atkins, S. (1984). Psychological correlates of growth hormone responses to stress. *Psychosomatic Medicine, 46*, 49–58.

Kral, V. A., Grad, B., & Berenson, J. (1968). Stress reactions resulting from the relocation of an aged population. *Canadian Journal of Psychiatry, 13*, 201–209.

Kreuz, L. E., Rose, R. M., & Jennings, R. (1972). Suppression of plasma testosterone levels and psychological stress. *Archives of General Psychiatry 26*, 479–482.

Kurakawa, N., Suematsu, H., Tamai, H., Esaki, M., Aoki. H., & Ikemi, Y. (1977). Effect of emotional stress on human growth hormone secretion. *Journal of Psychosomatic Research, 21*, 231–235.

Lobo, R. A., Granger, L. R., Paul, W. L., Goebelsmann, U., & Mishell, D. R. (1983). Psychological stress and increases in urinary norepinephrine metabolites, platelet serotonin and adrenal androgens in women with polycystic ovary syndrome. *American Journal of Obstetrics and Gynecology, 145*, 496–502.

Long, J. B., & Holaday, J. W. (1985). Blood–brain barrier: Endogenous modulation by adrenal-corticol function. *Science, 227*, 1580–1582.

Loucks, A. B., & Horvath, S. M. (1984). Exercise-induced stress responses of amenorrheic and eumenorrheic runners. *Journal of Clinical Endocrinology and Metabolism, 59*, 1109–1120.

Lowy, M. T., Maickel, R. P., & Yim, G. K. W. (1980). Naloxone-induced reduction of stress-related feeding. *Life Sciences, 24*, 2113–2118.

Lundberg, U. (1980). Catecholamine and cortisol excretion under psychologically different laboratory conditions. In E. Usdin, R. Kvetnansky, & J. Kopin (Eds.), *Catecholamines and stress: Recent advances* (pp. 455–460). Amsterdam: Elsevier/North-Holland.

Mason, J. W. (1968a). A review of psychoendocrine research on the pituitary–adrenal cortisol system. *Psychosomatic Medicine, 30*, 576–607.

Mason, J. W. (1968b). A review of psychoendocrine research on the sympathetic–adrenal medullary system. *Psychosomatic Medicine, 30*, 631–653.

Mason, J. W. (1975). A historical view of the stress field: Part One. *Journal of Human Stress, 1*, 6–12.

Mason, J. W., Brady, J., & Tolliver, G. A. (1968). Plasma and urinary 17-hydroxycorticosteroid responses to 72-hour avoidance sessions in the monkey. *Psychosomatic Medicine, 36*, 608–630.

Mason, J. W., Hartley, H., Kotchen, T. A., Mougey, E. H., Ricketts, P. T., Lee Roy, G., & Jones, C. (1973). Plasma cortisol and norepinephrine responses in anticipation of muscular exercise. *Psychosomatic Medicine, 35*, 406–414.

McGrady, A. V. (1984). Effects of psychological stress on male reproduction: A review. *Archives of Andrology, 13*, 1–7.

Miyabo, S., Asato, T., & Mizushima, N. (1977). Prolactin and growth hormone responses to psychological stress in normal and neurotic subjects. *Journal of Clinical Endocrinology and Metabolism, 44*, 947–951.

Morley, T. E., & Levine, A. S. (1980). Stress-induced eating is mediated through endogenous opiates. *Science, 209*, 1259–1260.

Newmark, S. R., Timathongkam, T., Martin, R. P., Cooper, K. H., & Rose, L. I. (1976). Adrenocortisol response to marathon running. *Journal of Clinical Endocrinology and Metabolism, 42*, 393–394.

Newsom, H. H., & Rose, J. C. (1971). The response of human adrenocorticotropic hormone and growth hormone to surgical stress. *Journal of Clinical Endocrinology and Metabolism, 33*, 481–487.

Noel, G. L., Suh, H. K., Stone, J. G., & Frantz, A. G. (1972). Human prolactin and growth hormone release during surgery and other conditions of stress. *Journal of Clinical Endocrinology and Metabolism, 35*, 840–851.

Öhman, R., Walinder, J., Balldin, J., Wallin, L., & Abrahannson, E. (1976). Prolactin response to electroconvulsive therapy. *Lancet 2* (7992), 736–737.

Poe, R. O., Rose, R. M., & Mason, J. W. (1970). Multiple determinants of 17-hydroxycorticosteroid excretion in recruits during basic training. *Psychosomatic Medicine, 32*, 369–378.

Pollard, I., Bassett, J. R., & Cairncross, K. D. (1976). Plasma glucocorticoid elevation and ultrastructural changes in the adenohypophysis of the male rat following prolonged exposure to stress. *Neuroendocrinology, 21*, 312–330.

Rebar, R. W., & Cumming, D. C. (1981). Reproductive function in women athletes. *JAMA, Journal of the American Medical Association, 246*, 1590.

Reichlin, S., Ablanalp, J. M., Labrum, A. H., Schwartz, N., & Sommer, B., & Taymor, M. (1979). The role of stress in female reproductive dysfunction. *Journal of Human Stress, 5*(2), 38–45.

Rose, R. M. (1969). Androgen responses to stress. I. Psychoendocrine relationships and assessment of androgen activity. *Psychosomatic Medicine, 31*, 405–417.

Rose, R. M. (1980). Endocrine responses to stressful psychological events. *Psychiatric Clinics of North America, 3*, 251–276.

Rose, R. M. (1984). Overview of endocrinology of stress. In G. M. Brown & S. H. Koslow (Eds.), *Neuroendocrinology and psychiatric disorders* (pp. 95–122). New York: Raven Press.

Rose, R. M., Bourne, P. G., Pie, R. O., Mougey, E. H., Collins, D. R., & Mason, J. W. (1969). Androgen responses to stress. II. Excretion of testosterone, epitestosterone, androsterone and etoicholanolone during basic combat training and under threat of attack. *Psychosomatic Medicine, 31,* 418–436.

Rose, R. M., & Hurst, M. W. (1975). Plasma cortisol and growth hormone responses to intravenous catheterization. *Journal of Human Stress, 1,* 22–36.

Rose, R. M., Poe, R. O., & Mason, J. W. (1968). Psychological state and body size as determinants of 17-OHCS excretion. *Archives of Internal Medicine, 121,* 406–413.

Roth, K. A., Mefford, I. M., & Barchas, J. D. (1982). Epinephrine, norepinephrine, dopamine and serotonin: Differential effects of acute and chronic stress on regional brain amines. *Brain Research, 239,* 417–424.

Sachar, E. J., Hellman, L., Roffwarg, H. P., Halpern, F. S., Fukushima, D. K., & Gallagher, T. F. (1973). Disrupted 24-hour patterns of cortisol secretion in psychotic depression. *Archives of General Psychiatry, 28,* 19–24.

Sakellaris, P. C., & Vernikos-Danellis, J. (1975). Increased rate of response of the pituitary–adrenal system in rats adapted to chronic stress. *Endocrinology (Baltimore), 97,* 597–602.

Salter, C., Fluck, D. C., & Stimmler, L. (1972). Effect of open heart surgery on growth hormone levels in man. *Lancet, 21.*

Sapolsky, R. M. (1985). Stress-induced suppression of testicular function in the wild baboon. *Endocrinology (Baltimore), 116,* 2273.

Sapolsky, R. M., Krey, L. C., & McEwen, B. S. (1984). Stress down-regulates corticosterone receptors in a site-specific manner in the brain. *Endocrinology (Baltimore), 114,* 287–292.

Schiason, G., Durand, F., & Monszowicz, I. (1978). Effects of glucocorticoids on plasma testosterone in men. *Acta Endocrinologica (Copenhagen), 89,* 126–131.

Selye, H. (1936). A syndrome produced by diverse noxious agents. *Nature (London), 138,* 32.

Selye, H. (1946). General adaptation syndrome and diseases of adaptation. *Journal of Clinical Endocrinology and Metabolism, 6,* 117.

Shangold, M. M., Gatz, M. L., & Thysen, B. (1981). Acute effects of exercise on plasma concentrations of prolactin and testosterone in recreational women runners. *Fertility and Sterility, 35,* 699.

Smelik, P. G. (1984). Factors determining the pattern of stress responses. In E. Usdin, R. Kvetnansky, & J. Axelrod (Eds.), *Stress: The role of catecholamines and other neurotransmitters* (pp. 17–25). New York: Gordon & Breach.

Smelik, P. G., Berkonbosch, F., Vermes, I., & Tilders, F. J. H. (1983). The role of catecholamines in the control of the secretion of proopiocortin-derived peptides from the anterior and intermediate lobes and its implications in the response to stress. In K. Bhatnager (Ed.), *The anterior pituitary gland* (pp. 113–126). New York: Raven Press.

Sobrinho, L. G., Nunes, C. P., Calhaz-Jorge, C., Afonso, A. M., Pereira, M. C., & Santos, M. A. (1984). Hyperprolactinemia in women with paternal deprivation during childhood. *Obstetrics and Gynecology (New York), 64,* 465–468.

Timiras, P. S. (1983). Neuroendocrinology of aging. Retrospective, current and prospective views. In T. Meites (Ed.), *Neuroendocrinology of aging* (pp. 5–30). New York: Plenum Press.

Ursin, H., Baade, E., & Levine, S. (1978). *Psychobiology of stress.* New York: Academic Press.

Ward, I. L., & Weisz, J. (1980). Maternal stress alters plasma testosterone in fetal males. *Science, 207,* 328–329.

Willner, J. C., Dehen, H., & Cambier, J. (1981). Stress-induced analgesia in humans: Endogenous opioids and naloxone-reversible depression of pain reflexes. *Science, 212,* 689–691.

Wolff, C. T., Friedman, S. B., Hofer, M. A., & Mason, J. W. (1964). Relationship between psychological defenses and mean urinary 17-hydroxycorticosteroid excretion rates. I. A predictive study of parents of fatally ill children. *Psychosomatic Medicine, 26,* 576–591.

Wolff, C. T., Hofer, M. A., & Mason, J. W. (1964). Relationship between psychological defenses and mean urinary 17-hydroxycorticosteroid excretion rates. II. Methodological and theoretical considerations. *Psychosomatic Medicine, 26,* 592–609.

Wyatt, R. J., Portnoy, B. D., Kupfer, J., Snyder, F., & Engelman, K. (1971). Resting plasma catecholamine concentrations in patients with depression and anxiety. *Archives of General Psychiatry, 24,* 65–71.

24 AGING AND HORMONES

URIEL HALBREICH

State University of New York at Buffalo

SUSANNA GOLDSTEIN

Cornell University Medical Center

INTRODUCTION

In 1889, Brown-Sequard suggested that "the feebleness of old men is in part due to the diminution of the function of the testicles" and injected testicular fluid into old men ". . . with the conviction that I would obtain with it stable augmentation of the power of the nervous centers and especially the spinal cord" (cited by Timiras, 1983). This statement set forth the axiom that aging is due to endocrine changes. Indeed, since these early landmark observations and clinical trials, the studies and theories of the neuroendocrinology of aging have become more sophisticated. However, basically theories of cause and effect in this relationship fall into two areas: (1) Changes in various aspects of endocrine systems cause, or at least contribute to the aging process; and (2) the aging process of regulatory central nervous system (CNS), mechanisms causes age-related changes in various hormonal axes. A third and probably more promising theory is a combination of the previous two, that is that during the aging process there are continuous and supposedly desynchronized changes in the CNS and hormonal systems and their multiple and intricate interrelationships. At present, the strengths and weaknesses of any of the theories are a matter of debate, and the cause and effect sequence is a matter of speculation.

Therefore, in this chapter we will only present examples of age-related changes in some hormonal axes that have been relatively widely studied. We will attempt to emphasize the point that age variable should be well controlled in every study of hormonal changes in psychiatric patients and controls. This chapter is not intended to provide a comprehensive review of all hormonal systems, nor does it intend to illuminate all aspects of this multifactorial field. We will not enter into the intriguing theories of endocrine causes of aging; rather, we will present only one side of the coin—facts about age-related changes in peripherally measured hormones. The other side of the coin and the integration of the two is beyond the scope of this chapter.

AGING AND HUMAN GROWTH HORMONE

The basal secretion of the pituitary growth hormone (GH) is closely related to sleep—mostly to Stages III and IV (slow wave sleep). The age-related decrease in GH peaks during sleep was already reported in the early 1970s (Carlson, Gillin, Gordon, & Snyder, 1972; Finkelstein, 1972), and this has been considered to be an indication of the decline of integrity of GH release with age (D. C. Parker, Sassin, Mace, Gotlin, & Rossman, 1969). This is not a direct, simple relationship because even though slow wave sleep has been reported to decrease with age (Webb, 1971), these stages correlated significantly with GH levels in a total group of young and old men, but not in each of them separately (Prinz, Weitzman, Cunningham, & Karacan, 1983). Even though total GH secretion during sleep as well as total 24-hour secretion of GH declines with age and approaches zero in some older subjects (Finkelstein, Roffwarg, Boyer, Kream, & Hellman, 1972; Rudman, Kutner, Rogers *et al.*, 1981), the main difference between young and old men is during the first 3 hours of the night, while the hormonal levels during the rest of the night and during the day do not differ (Prinz *et al.*, 1983). The reason for the limitation of the age effect of GH to the first 3 hours of sleep and not to the other 21 hours of the day or night is unclear. Nonetheless, the phenomenon itself is quite well established because two other groups (Dudle, Ensinck, Palmer, & Williams, 1973; Shibasaki, 1984) did not find any change with age in basal morning levels of GH. Our own data (Figure 24.1) confirm the negative correlation between age and night GH levels which were apparent mostly during the beginning of the night when young subjects had higher secretory peaks of GH which were almost absent in older subjects.

The relationship between GH and age is not limited to elderly people. It is best demonstrated in the finding that mean secretion rate of GH is higher in adolescents than in prepubertal children, young adults, or older adults (Finkelstein *et al.*, 1982).

GH response to most stimuli is decreased with age. It has been shown that GH response to L-dopa (Sachar, 1975) and to dextroamphetamine (Halbreich, Asnis, Halpern, Tabrizi, & Sachar, 1980; Halbreich *et al.*, 1982) is decreased in older subjects. This finding as well as the decrease of basal GH during sleep (Plotnik, Thompson, Beitins, & Blizzard, 1974) was suggested as being attributable to decreased levels of estrogen in postmenopausal women (Frantz & Rubkin, 1965; Plotnik *et al.*, 1974; Sachar, 1975). The situation is somewhat less clear in regard to insulin-induced hypoglycemia (ITT). While reduced GH response with age was reported by some groups (Laron, Doron, & Amikam, 1969; Merimee & Feinberg, 1971), no change or no significant change was reported by others (Cartlidge, Black, Hall, & Hall, 1970; Kalk, Vinik, Pimstone, & Jackson, 1973; Laron *et al.*, 1979; Sachar, Finkelstein, & Hellman, 1971).

As opposed to insulin, which in young normal subjects causes an increase in GH levels, glucose usually causes inhibition in GH

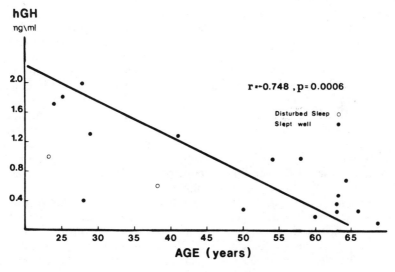

FIGURE 24.1.

release in normal subjects— "glucose pulse" (Glick & Goldsmith, 1968). Paradoxical rise with age in GH levels after glucose loading was reported by Dilman (1971), but this was not confirmed by Dudle et al. (1973). This finding supports the suggestion that the pituitary reserve of GH is preserved with age. This notion is also supported by the preservation of basal levels of GH during most of the day and the inconclusive and probably nonuniversal blunted response to GH to various stimuli.

There is a suggestion that while the pituitary reserve of GH is not influenced by age, its responsiveness declines. This is based on the report (Shibasaki et al., 1984) that after age 40 there is a very steep decline in GH response to growth hormone releasing factor (GHRF). It is worthwhile to note that the decline with age was not gradual—mean levels of GH were stable for age groups 20–39, then they abruptly dropped, and from ages 40 to 79 they were stabilized again, but in very low levels.

The importance of GHRF is that is exerts its effects on the pituitary (Guillemin et al., 1982), while pharmacological agents act mostly through central neurotransmitters and hypothalamic pathways. Hence, we may assume that in cases where there was a decrease of GH response to a stimulus with age, it was at least partially due to decreased responsivity to GHRF. Again, because the pituitary content of GH probably does not vary with age (Gershberg, 1957), this may be attributed to increased secretion of somatostatin in older men or to a decreased sensitivity of the somatotroph to GHRF.

As is the case with other hormonal systems, the different responses to stimuli with age may be due to factors that have nothing to do with the system in focus. They may be a result of the longer half-life of a pharmacological agent or may be related to changes in other pharmacokinetic variables (Ebert, Vankammen, & Murphy, 1971).

Other parameters that may influence GH release in the aged (and may also be important in the control or release of other hormones) are (1) adipose tissue—in the aged there is a relative increase in adipose content and a decrease in lean body mass (Dudle et al., 1973; Myhre, & Kessler, 1966, cited in Dudle et al., 1973). Blunted GH responses may be secondary to that accumulation of fat (Ball, El-Khodary, & Canary, 1972; Crockford & Salmon, 1970; Sims et al., 1968, cited in Dudle et al., 1973); (2) higher concentrations of fasting blood sugar in older people might inhibit GH release (Glick & Goldsmith, 1968, cited in Dudle et al., 1973); (3) there is a progressive decrease in weight of the pituitary gland with age (Shanklin, 1953, cited in Dudle et al., 1973). Nonetheless, the pituitary reserve for GH as well as ACTH (Blichert-Toft & Hummer, 1976), thyroid-stimulating hormone (TSH) (Mayberry, Gharib, Bilstad, & Sizemore, 1971), and gonadotropins (Carlson et al., 1972) may be maintained intact in the elderly (Dudle et al., 1973).

In summary, the importance of the age variable in GH responsiveness to GHRF, especially at age 40 and older, cannot be underscored because blunted GH response to various stimuli (notably amphetamine, clonidine, and desmethylimipramine) has been suggested as a biological marker or a test for endogenous depression, as an indication of an abnormal α_2-receptor activity. If it does have any significance for this purpose, it may be limited to patients who are 40 years old or younger.

AGING OF THE HYPOTHALAMIC–PITUITARY–ADRENAL (HPA) SYSTEM

The HPA system has been the center of studies in behavioral endocrinology for over two decades (Carroll Martin, & Davis, 1968; Gibbons & McHugh, 1962; Sachar et al., 1973). This is attributed to the fact that a psychiatric community, anxious to find biological correlates of mood disorders, enthusiastically embraced the reports of abnormalities of this system in depression. This abnormality was reported in two main findings: cortisol hypersecretion and a relative nonsuppressibility of cortisol in response to the administration of dexamethasone (the Dexamethasone Suppression Test—DST). Between 30% and 75% of endogenously depressed patients were reported to demonstrate an abnormality of the HPA system (Carroll et al., 1981; Schlesser, Winokur, & Sherman, 1981; Stokes et al., 1984).

Recently, a more cautious examination of the meaning and application of the DST and other parameters of HPA abnormality is replacing the conclusions drawn during the initial period of research. As part of that process, variables that may influence the HPA axis, including diet, weight loss, situational stress, and others, are carefully being studied. Not surprisingly, we have recently witnessed an increased number of reports in which the effect of age on cortisol secretion and DST was examined. In this section, we will first review the evidence for the influence of age on the spontaneous secretion of cortisol in normals and depressed patients and then the data pointing to a decreased suppressibility of cortisol in response to dexamethasone, an abnormal DST, in the elderly. The scarce data on a potential influence of age on diurnal and ultradian rhythm of cortisol secretion will be discussed briefly.

The literature is consistent that in normal men, there is no significant change with age in levels of cortisol. However, earlier reports were based mostly on single blood drawings (Drafta, Schindler, Stroe, & Neacsu, 1982; Kaalud-Jensen & Blichert-Toft, 1971; Kley, Nieschlag, Wiegelmen, Solbach, & Kruskemper, 1975). There is one report of diminished levels of cortisol in geriatric subjects (Grad, Rosenberg, Liberman, Trachtenberg, & Kral, 1971). We have recently reported (Halbreich, Asnis, Shindledecker, Zumoff, & Nathan, 1984; Halbreich, Asnis, Zumoff, Nathan, & Shindledecker, 1985a) a lack of correlation between mean 24-hour plasma cortisol (PC) levels and age in a group of 40 normal men. The same finding is confirmed with the Afternoon Cortisol Test (ACT) (Halbreich et al., 1984). The HPA system may age differently in normal men and women. While the mean 24-hour PC does not change with age in men, it does increase in women. Postmenopausal women had mean 24-hour PC levels higher than younger women. A significant positive correlation between mean 24-hour PC and age was found in younger women ($r = .57$, $p = .0067$), but not in postmenopausal women, even though the direction of correlation was the same. A similar tendency is found with the ACT levels (Figure 24.2); a drop of cortisol levels of normal women immediately after menopause is demonstrated with the ACT results, even though the numbers are not large enough to firmly solidify this issue.

Mean 24-hour PC levels of endogenously depressed men and women ($n = 32$) were found to positively correlate with age (Halbreich et al., 1984). This finding confirmed previous suggestions based on 2 to 3 single predexamethasone cortisol samples (Asnis et al., 1981; Stokes et al., 1984) and was confirmed by data based on 1–4 P.M. cortisol levels (Asnis et al., 1983). The association between age and cortisol levels in depressives is probably state dependent because it has been shown to disappear after recovery from an episode of endogenous depression (ED) (Asnis et al., 1981). In summary, spontaneous levels of cortisol increase with age in depressed men and women, but not in

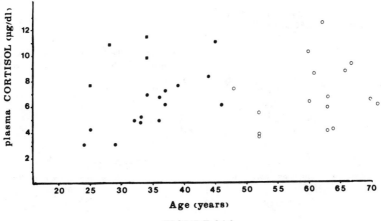

FIGURE 24.2.

normal men or postmenopausal women. It appears that there is an increase of cortisol levels with age in younger normal women. The reason for this sex and age difference in normal subjects is unclear at present, though one may speculate that gonadal hormones may play a role in that phenomenon.

The effect of age on the DST was and still is being studied extensively. It has been reported that plasma levels of cortisol after dexamethasone administration are higher in elderly than in young depressed patients or normal controls (Asnis *et al.*, 1981; Davis *et al.*, 1984; Dilman, Lapin, & Oxenkrug, 1979; Oxenkrug, Pomara *et al.*, 1983; Stokes *et al.*, 1984). A positive linear correlation between postdexamethasone cortisol levels (or their log transformation—because they are not normally distributed) and age has been reported in depressed patients (Davis *et al.*, 1984; Nelson, 1982; Nelson, Khan, Orr, & Tamragouri, 1984; Nelson, Orr, Shane, & Stevenson, 1984) as well as normal controls (Oxenkrug, Pomara *et al.*, 1983). A significant contribution of age to the variance of the postdexamethasone cortisol levels in normal subjects (Feinberg & Carroll, 1984; Oxenkrug, Branconnier *et al.*, 1983) has also been reported. A nonsignificant tendency toward abnormality of DST in older normals was reported by Brown and Shuey (1980), Tourigny-Rivard, Raskind, and Rivard (1981), and Amsterdam, Winokur, Caroff, and Conn (1982), but Mandlewicz *et al.* (1982) did not find any relationship. A linear

relationship between age and postdexamethasone cortisol levels was not found in a large group of depressed patients and normal controls (Carroll *et al.*, 1981), but a reanalysis of the data by the same group (Feinberg & Carroll, 1984) suggested that their DST results might have a cubic relationship with age.

The circadian rhythm of cortisol secretion has been reported not to be influenced by age (Dean & Felton, 1979); Krieger, 1972; Serio, Piolanti, Romano, DeMagistris, & Guisti, 1970). These studies, however, included small groups of subjects and/or were performed with infrequent blood sampling. Recently, we have found (Halbreich, Asnis, Shindledecker, Zumoff, & Nathan, 1985b) an inverse correlation between the timing of peak values of plasma cortisol (acrophase) and age in a group of 72 normal subjects and a nonsignificant tendency in the same direction in 32 EDs (Figure 24.3). This finding indicates that cortisol levels peak earlier (phase advance) with older age. This issue still needs further clarification.

The effect of age on cortisol response to external stimuli has been less well studied probably because most of the studies on this issue were done with young normal men as a control group. It appears that cortisol response to stimulation by stress, ACTH, or insulin-induced hypoglycemia (Insulin Tolerance Test—ITT) is the same in young and elderly normal subjects. The cortisol response of postmenopausal women to dextroam-

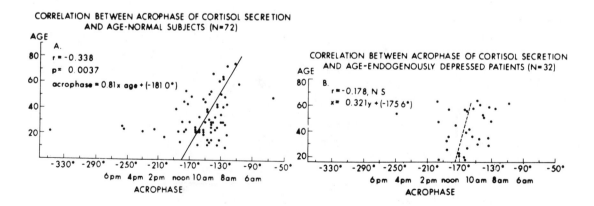

FIGURE 24.3.

phetamine is nonsignificantly lower than that of young normal men (Halbreich *et al.*, 1981), but this slight difference may be attributed to sex difference and not necessarily to age. This area of the age effect on the responsiveness of the HPA system to external environmental or pharmacological stimulation is still unclear.

In summary, age affects baseline levels of cortisol in depressed patients. Postdexamethasone cortisol levels of depressed and normal subjects are affected as well. There may be a sexual dimorphism in the age–cortisol interrelationship, but this is still unclear. It is obvious that the age variable should be controlled for in any study of the HPA system. There have been at least two attempts (Halbreich *et al.*, 1984; Oxenkrug, Branconnier *et al.*, 1983) at formulating equations for the expected endogenous and post-DST levels of cortisol for a given age in order to provide an aid in controlling for the age effect. The validity and usefulness of such equations still remain to be seen.

AGING AND THE HYPOTHALAMIC–PITUITARY–THYROID (HPT) SYSTEM

The prevalence of hypothyroidism increases with age and is higher in the elderly as compared to younger populations (Bahemuka & Hodkinson, 1975; Jeffreys, Hoffenberg, Farran, Fraser, & Hodkinson, 1972; Lloyd & Goldberg, 1961; Sawin, Chopra, Azizi, Mannix, & Bachrach, 1979; Sawin, Herman, Molitch, London, & Kramer, 1983). Often hypothyroidism in the elderly is not presented clinically and there are very few apparent symptoms, if any (Bahemuka & Hodkinson, 1975; Evered *et al.*, 1973a, b). In most cases, such an abnormality is discovered only after screening for HPT malfunction (Sawin *et al.*, 1979; 1983; Tunbridge *et al.*, 1977).

Until quite recently, age-related changes in the HPT system were mostly studied in the thyroid gland itself and its hormonal products. The pituitary gland and its responsiveness to stimulation with hypothalamic thyrotropin-releasing hormone (TRH) as well as the TSH (thyrotropin, thyroid-stimulating hormone) responses to feedback mechanisms from the thyroid hormones is the focus of some more recent investigations. As is apparent from the following details, dynamic studies of the entire functioning of the HPT system are still scarce.

Several studies show no age-related changes in serum T4 levels (Braverman, Dawber, & Ingbar, 1966; Gregerman, Gaffnez, & Shock, 1962; Hesch, Catz, Pape, Schmidt, & Muhlen, 1976; Nicod, Burger, Staeheli, & Vallotton, 1976; Nishikawa *et al.*, 1981; Oddie, Meade, & Fisher, 1966; Rubenstein *et al.*, 1973; Sawin *et al.*, 1979; Westgren *et al.*, 1976). Another (Lipson *et al.*, 1979) study reported that serum T4 levels were lower in women over 60 years of age, but not in older men, and another group reported decreased T4 levels in older subjects of both sexes (Herrmann, Rusche, Kroll, Hilger, & Kruskemper, 1974). Still another study reports increased T4 in elderly women (Britton *et al.*, 1975). T4 turnover is prolonged as a function of age (Gregerman *et al.*, 1962; Inada, Koshiyama, Torizuka, Akagi, & Miyake, 1964; Oddie *et al.*, 1966), a factor which may influence plasma levels.

Serum T3 concentrations showed a significant decline with age (Fisher *et al.*, 1977; Hansen, Skovsted, & Siersbaek-Nielsen, 1975; Hesch *et al.*, 1976; Hermann *et al.*, 1974; Nishikawa *et al.*, 1981; Rubenstein *et al.*, 1973; Westgren *et al.*, 1976). This was also found for the FT3 index (Caplan Wickus, Glasser, Davis, & Wahner, 1981). Other reports find a T3 decrease in either older men (Snyder and Utiger, 1972a) or older women (Britton *et al.*, 1975) or in both, but later in women than in men (Sawin *et al.*, 1979).

An intriguing study (Olsen, Lariberg, & Weeke, 1978) did not find a change in serum T3 with aging per se in the absence of disease. The low T3 in the elderly was attributed to varying degrees of chronic disease. This finding raises the issue of "normalcy" and adequate normative levels for older people because the definition of aging per se may include a higher degree of disease or dysfunction.

Most authors explain the decrease of blood T3 levels in old age by a shift of peripheral T4 monodeiodination from T3 to rT3 (Burrow *et al.*, 1977; Faber *et al.*, 1976). rT3 itself is a potent inhibitor of T4-T3 conversion, which furhter decreases peripheral T3 generation (Hufner & Grussendorf, 1978). In addition, T3 production by the thyroid gland per se may be decreased in old age (Szabolcs *et al.*, 1981).

Serum rT3 concentrations were found to be significantly elevated in subjects over 70 years of age; however, they were widely scattered (Nicod *et al.*, 1976; Nishikawa *et al.*, 1981). Another study showed decreased rT3 in serum after age 50 in females, while males had stable rT3 values (Lipson *et al.*, 1979). Hence, this issue is still debatable.

Serum, 3,5-T2, 3,3′-T2, and 3′,5′-T2 levels (monodeiodination products of T3 and rT3 metabolism) showed an inverse correlation with age (Burger & Sokoloff, 1977; Faber, Carsten, Lumholtz, Nielsen, & Friis, 1979; Nishikawa *et al.*, 1981). Since serum T4 concentrations are fairly constant throughout life, the decrease in serum T2s with age suggests that the sequential monodeiodination of T4 through T3 or rT3 might be slowed down in the elderly. The observation that both 3,3′-T2 and 3′,5′-T2 (metabolites of rT3) are decreased while rT3 is elevated suggests decreased 5- and 3-deiodinating activities with age, which is consistent with the observed prolonged turnover of T4 in the elderly. This issue is still unsettled because in a recent study, no decline in T2s was found (Caplan *et al.*, 1981), a fact that casts some doubt on the above hypothesis.

The hypothalamic content of TRH does not change with age (C. R. Parker & Porter, 1984), while an increase in serum levels of the pituitary TSH is fairly common in the elderly, especially in women. This frequently occurs when levels of the thyroid hormones T4 and T3 are within normal limits (Odell, Wilber, & Utiger, 1967; Sawin *et al.*, 1979). No age-related difference was demonstrated in the response of T4 and T3 to TSH (Szabolcs *et al.*, 1981), indicating that the response of the thyroid gland to TSH is not diminished in old age. The TSH response to repeated TRH stimulation becomes blunted earlier in the elderly, which may mean that the pituitary TSH content is more readily exhaustible by TRH in old age, resulting in decreased levels of TSH (Szabolcs *et al.*, 1981). This may be due to the stronger suppressive effect of T3 on the pituitary in old age (Szabolcs *et al.*, 1981). In any case, that phenomenon raises a more generalized aspect. It may show that even though the pituitary reserve is intact in the elderly, the responsiveness of the gland or its sensitivity to stimuli or feedback mechanisms is altered. An emphasis on this aspect shifts the focus of studies from that of determinations of basal hormonal levels to studies involving active and dynamic interventions in the system.

In conclusion, it seems that the most sensitive single index of aging of the thyroid regulator system is elevated plasma levels of thyrotropin (TSH). This may be compensating for low levels of triiodothyronine (T3), while levels of thyroxine (T4) are usually within normal limits for younger people. The feedback mechanism between the thyroid and the pituitary glands is probably more sensitive in the elderly because older people need less oral thyroxine to bring the elevated TSH levels to what is considered levels of a euthyroid state. This issue is unclear at present because the reason for the lower oral dose of T4 may be a slower metabolism (Gregerman *et al.*, 1962; Oddie *et al.*, 1966; Richey & Bender, 1977) or an altered binding of the thyroid hormones (Braverman *et al.*, 1966). Also, some of the contradictions in the cited reports may result from sex differences—T4 metabolism may be decreased with age in older men, but not in older women (Gregerman *et al.*, 1962; Wenzel & Horn, 1975).

CHANGES IN REPRODUCTIVE HORMONES IN MALES THROUGH AGING

Several studies reported that circulating levels of total and free testosterone (T) decrease progressively with advancing age (Drafta *et al.*, 1982; Muta, Kato, Akamine, & Ibayashi, 1981; Stearns *et al.*, 1974; Takahashi *et al.*, 1983; Zumoff *et al.*, 1982). As reported in a group of recent studies, the average difference in levels of serum T between young and old males was −14% (Neaves, Johnson, Porter, Parker, & Petty, 1984). Others failed to confirm this finding in aging men who were in optimal health (Harman & Tsitouras, 1980; Neaves *et al.*, 1984; Sparrow, Bosse, & Rowe, 1980). A recent study of 220 subjects (Davidson *et al.*, 1983) found mainly a decreased circulating level of free T accompanied by large increases in luteinizing hormone (LH) and follicle-stimulating hormone (FSH) and no age-related change in estradiol or prolactin (PRL). The changes in hormonal levels may particularly account for the age-related decline observed in sexual activity and capacity, as well as quality of experience reported by the aging male subjects in that study. T levels of aged men, though decreased, were mostly within the normal range, which is suggestive of an age-related, altered threshold of the elements that respond to androgen. This more dynamic assumption may also account for the maintenance of sexual function in many aging men. Similar conclusions were reached in studies on rats (Gray, Smith, Dorsa, & Davidson, 1981) and in another study in human males (Tsitouras, Martin, & Harman, 1982).

While the issue of whether serum T levels decrease, increase, or remain unchanged is still unsettled, many investigators agree that the testes of aged men are deficient in their ability to secrete T or it precursors in response to stimulation by gonadotropins (Harman & Tsitouras, 1980; Harman, Tsitouras, Costa, & Blackman, 1982; Mastragiacomo, Feghali, Foresta, & Ruzza, 1982) due to their decreased population of Leydig cells. In some aging men, the loss of Leydig cells is modest enough to be compensated for by the higher stimulation of the surviving cells with elevated plasma LH. These men will have normal plasma levels of T; in others the loss of Leydig cells is so great that the testes can no longer respond adequately (Mastragiacomo et al., 1982).

The secretory reserve for T, demonstrated by response to stimulation with human chorionic gonadotropin (hCG), appears to be somewhat diminished with age (Harman & Tsitouras, 1980; Longcope, 1973). This is compatible with the hypothesis that the Leydig cells of older men are functioning closer to their maximum capacity in order to compensate for a reduction in their number. Stimulation with hCG unmasks the deficit in Leydig cells, which could be qualitative as well as quantitative.

The inconsistency of studies concerning T levels and aging might be due to different sampling time: Studies involving morning samples have often shown an age-related decline, while those using afternoon samples failed to show such a decrease. This may be explained by a marked attenuation or an absence of the circadian rhythm of serum T in elderly men. In one report, the early morning rise in T levels characteristic of young men was not present in older men (Bremner, Vitiello, & Prinz, 1983). However, another study (Murono, Nankin, Lin, & Osterman, 1982) reported that older men maintained diurnal rhythms of T and other androgens, similar to the pattern in young men.

Several studies report an increase of estrogen (free estrone and estradiol) levels with advancing age in normal males (Baker, Burger, deKretser, & Hudson, 1977; Drafta et al., 1982; Myking, Thorsen, & Stoa, 1980). However, another major estrogenic component in plasma—estrone sulfate—showed a moderate decrease with age (Myking et al., 1980), which may point to a decreased binding capacity in the aged. Because plasma estrogens originate in nearly equal amounts from direct testicular secretion and from peripheral conversion of T and androstenedione (Longcope, Kato, & Horton, 1969), the increase in levels of estrogen in the presence of decreased T levels and the correlation between estrogen and T (Drafta et al., 1982) may suggest an increased peripheral conversion in old age. The increased levels of estrogen in aging men may further be responsible for inhibition of production of testicular androgen and a further decrease in its levels.

As is the case with other systems, this hormone–age relationship is still open to speculation because other studies (e.g., Zumoff et al., 1982) found no association between age and estrone and estradiol.

In the human male, serum levels of FSH and LH increase with age. As reported in several recent studies, the average change in serum LH in older men as compared to younger men was +110%, and in serum FSH it was +155% (Davidson et al., 1983; Harman & Tsitouras, 1980; Harman et al., 1982; Muta et al., 1981; Neaves et al., 1984; Sparrow et al., 1980; Takahashi et al., 1983; Zumoff et al., 1982). However, another study (Zumoff et al., 1982) reported no age-related change in levels of LH. Elevated LH and FSH, along with decreased T and excessive pituitary responsiveness to synthetic luteinizing hormone-releasing hormone (LHRH) in the elderly male (Wasada, 1978), may suggest a primary testicular insufficiency at senescence [decline in Leydig cell function (Takahashi et al., 1983)], with secondary compensatory increases in gonadotropin secretion. Alternatively, aging may induce an elevation of set point to sex steroids in the hypothalamic–pituitary axis. This hypothesis is supported by the finding that the hypothalamic–pituitary axis of the aged is more strongly resistant (in other words, is less sensitive) to the effects of sex steroids (Muta et al., 1981). Another explanation which may have some factual support (Neaves et al., 1984; Warner, Santen, & Dufau, in press) is that in older age the pituitary produces LH with reduced biological potency relative to its ability to immunoassay. The first hypothesis is more consistent with age-related changes in other systems.

The pituitary responsiveness to synthetic LHRH in elderly males is still unclear. In one study an increased responsiveness has been demonstrated (Wasada, 1978), while another (Harman et al., 1982) showed a small, but significant tendency for LH and FSH responses to LHRH to be both diminished and delayed in healthy aging men. Another study (Winters & Troen, 1982) showed only significantly delayed peak LH responses to LHRH, with a slower decrease after the peak. These changes may represent primary pituitary or hypothalamic deficiency in aging men. These data may also suggest an alteration in the control of the releasable LH pool and a prolonged secretion of the hormone after LHRH stimulation, indicating an altered hypothalamic–pituitary function associated with aging.

In summary, in most men the function of the reproductive system is maintained through older age. This is achieved by an intricate compensatory mechanism and by changes in the responsivity of the various steps in the hypothalamic–pituitary–gonadal (HPG) system in men.

REPRODUCTIVE HORMONES ALONG THE LIFE CYCLE IN FEMALES

Serum levels of estradiol decline gradually over many years before and after the cessation of menstruation (Furuhashi, Suzukii,

Abe, Yamaya, & Yakahashi, 1977). There is, however, no evidence of marked morphological changes in the ovaries for some time after the menopause (Procope, 1969). A statistically significant decline of serum levels of progesterone with age precedes that of serum levels of estradiol (Furuhashi et al., 1977).

Blood levels of LH and FSH become progressively elevated during the premenopausal period (Reyes, Winter, & Faiman, 1977), reaching their peaks 1–3 years after menopause, and remain high for at least the ensuing 10 years (Furuhashi et al., 1977). A gradual decrease in plasma levels of LH is observed in some women several decades after menopause (Chakravarti, Collins, Newton, Ovan, & Studd, 1977). This is consistent with a report by Wide, Nillius, Gemzell, and Ross (1973) of highest levels of FSH and LH levels in women aged 51–60 years and significantly lower levels after 60 years of age, suggesting that senescence of pituitary function occurs as a part of the systemic aging process.

An age-related dynamic alteration of the function of the HPG system in women is demonstrated by the report that a positive correlation between serum levels of estradiol and the serum levels of LH/FSH was found in the 20–29 age group, while no correlation was found in women between 30 and 49 years of age, and postmenopausal women showed a negative correlation (Furuhashi et al., 1977).

FSH in extracts of pituitaries of young women was reported to have a low in vivo biological activity in relation to in vitro biological or immunological activity when compared to the FSH of elderly women or men (Wide & Hobson, 1982). This difference may be due to a more rapid metabolic clearance of FSH in mice used in the in vivo biological assay (Wide & Wide, 1984), but it is still an intriguing possibility. It seems that estrogens may influence the production of forms of FSH, with more rapid rates of disappearance, and that this may be of physiological importance for the pulsatile stimulation of the ovaries and for ovarian pituitary feedback control of FSH secretion. Age-related changes in the biological activity of hormones that immunologically are similar to those at a younger age can probably be demonstrated in other systems. This may be an important factor in the age–hormone relationship.

The amount of LHRH in the hypothalamus of women varies as a function of age and reproductive status. In women of reproductive age (16–49), the mean hypothalamic content of LHRH is two times greater than that of postmenopausal women (50–78 years of age) (C. R. Parker & Porter, 1984); this decrease is not the result of aging per se, but rather a consequence of diminished ovarian function, since younger women who had bilateral ovariectomy had the same low hypothalamic LHRH as older women (C. R. Parker & Porter, 1984). Moreover, the decrease in hypothalamic content of LHRH occurs after rather than before menopausal ovulatory failure. The impact of altered function of LHRH neurons on the activity of other neuronal structures could be of importance in some changes in brain function that occur with aging.

In view of the reduced frequency of LH pulses observed by middle age in rodents of both sexes and the similar patterns of cycle variance with aging in mice and women, it has been proposed by Finch, Felicio, Mobbs, and Nelson (1984) that the lengthening of menstrual cycles during the years close to menopause could result from a slowed frequency of pulses of LHRH. At present, no data are available on the mechanism by which aging may influence the frequency of gonadotropin pulses in women. There are only very limited observations of morphological changes in aging human hypothalamus, demonstrating altered fluorescent emission patterns and neuronal hypertrophy in some areas of the hypothalamus (Sheehan & Kavacs, 1982). Neuronal mechanisms have at least one clearly demonstrated role in menopause. The hot flashes that usually appear after estrogen levels become very low during menopause are assumed to result from hypothalamic events in which β-adrenergic receptors are implicated (Judd, 1983). It is intriguing that the hot flashes spontaneously disappear in many women after 1–5 years (Yen, 1977). Because hot flashes are an event influenced by the CNS, their spontaneous extinction strongly implies a change in the hypothalamus, for example, slowed down norepinephrine turnover (Yen, 1977). Another possibility is that the sustained neuronal hyperactivity implied by sustained high levels of LH secretion eventually causes the attrition of some neurons associated with the control of tonic or episodic LHRH secretion.

Although aging in the female is characterized by a progressive decrease of estrogen secretion by the ovary (Furuhashi et al., 1977), the aging ovary is still capable of producing both androstenedione and T (Vermeulen, 1976). Studies of hormonal levels in ovarian vein blood of postmenopausal women suggest that aged ovaries secrete more T but less androstenedione than young ovaries (Judd, 1976). Levels of androstenedione in the blood decline gradually from the 20s to the 50s (Purifoy, Koopmans, & Tatum, 1980) and after the menopause levels are similar to those of prepubertal females (L. N. Parker, Sack, Fisher, & Odell, 1978). It has been suggested that this decline may be due to reduced adrenal secretion. The existence of an "adrenopause" similar to "adrenarche" was suggested (Crilly, Marshall, & Nordin, 1979).

Levels of free T in the plasma of older females were found to be widely variable (Purifoy et al., 1980), similar to the great variability in levels in aged males. Individual variation in sex anabolic hormone production may contribute to variation in the mental and physical well-being of the elderly female, as these hormones have been shown to have a positive effect on mood, energy level, libido, memory, and so on in aged females (Caldwell, 1954). The association of sociocultural factors with a variation in hormone level should also be considered. Purifoy and his colleagues (1980) found a positive correlation of androgen levels with occupational status in their subjects; females over age 50 with extradomestic careers had significantly higher mean androstenedione and T values than those who were housewives. The increase in the relative proportion of T compared to other sex steroids in the aging female may have morphological, physiological, and behavioral effects: A slight increase in facial hair is a well-known morphological effect of aging in females, while increased aggression has been noted in elderly female mammalian species (Hrdy & Hrdy, 1976), and an increase in assertiveness and political activity was reported among older females in some societies (Murphy & Murphy, 1974).

PROLACTIN LEVELS AND AGING

Age-related changes in plasma PRL level are controversial. In several studies, it was claimed that in women there is a decrease in plasma levels of PRL with age (Djursing, Hagen, Moller, & Christiansen, 1981; Vekemans, 1975), but other studies show no differences in plasma PRL between young (premenopausal) and old (postmenopausal) women (Notelovitz, Ware, Buhi, & Dougherty, 1982). In mean, a trend towards increasing levels with aging was observed, indicating a sex dichotomy (Vekemans & Robyn, 1975). Another indication of such a dichotomy is the report of no circannual rhythm in plasma PRL either in young or in elderly men (Djursing et al., 1981; Touitou, Carayon, Reinberg, Bogdan, & Beck, 1983), while a circannual rhythm of PRL was demonstrated in young (Tarquini et al., 1979) and elderly women (Touitou et al., 1983). This issue, however, is in need of additional clarification because in two other studies (Davidson et al., 1983; Neaves et al., 1984), there was no age-related change in serum levels of PRL in normal males.

Surgical menopause (oophorectomy) appears to be associated with elevated (albeit within normal range) levels of PRL in young and older women compared to levels of PRL in premenopausal and naturally menopausal women. These data may indicate that increasing age per se, independent of hormonal milieu, has no effect on PRL (Notelovitz et al., 1982).

Human pituitary PRL cells do not regress with old age, and there is no apparent difference in the incidence, distribution, granulation, or immunoreactivity of PRL cells between aging males and females (Kovacs, Ryan, Horvath, Penz, & Ezrin, 1977). This finding is another indication that, in general, the integrity and reserve of the pituitary gland is maintained with aging. We are unaware of detailed studies of the age effect on the responsivity and sensitivity of the system.

As is the case with other systems, the diurnal rhythm of PRL may alter with age (Hans et al., 1979, 1980). Our own (yet unpublished) data show a significant contribution of age to the variance of acrophase (timing of highest levels of PRL: $F = 6.49$, $p = .0142$, $df = 1/46$). Aged subjects tend to have an earlier acrophase—phase advance. No sex difference was found in that phenomenon.

COMMENTS

As a rule, the activity of most hormonal systems alters with age, even though there are some exceptions to this generalization. The age-related change may be viewed on two levels. In most cases, there is a decreased activity on various (mostly peripheral) glands. However, when hormonal systems are evaluated in terms of their entirety, a change in the intricate feedback network and homeostasis of the systems can be demonstrated. This results in an increase with age of some hormones and changes in sensitivity and responsiveness of some binding-mediated mechanisms.

The decreased peripheral activity may be due to alterations in several mechanisms: (1) activity of regulatory neurotransmitters, including synthesis rate, discharge to the synaptic cleft, sensitivity of the post- and presynaptic receptors, and activity of enzymes that participate in synthesis and metabolism of neurotransmitters; (2) the number of cells participating in any hormonal chain usually decreases with age as well as number of receptor sites; (3) binding and responsiveness of receptors usually decrease with age, although, due to decrease in stimulus, there may be a compensatory hypersensitivity; (4) mechanisms inside the postsynaptic cell which mediate the response to the hormone (e.g., ATP–cyclic AMP system) are subject to aging effects as well. Two of these mechanisms will be demonstrated in detail below.

Aging and Changes in Neurotransmitter Activity

Decrease with aging of activity of major neurotransmitter systems has been postulated. Probably it is not accurate to assume that there is a universal decline in number of cells and activity of all neurotransmitters in the brain. Rather, there is a selective change which is different in various areas of the CNS as well as in different neurotransmitters systems (Enna, Samorajski, & Beer, 1981; Timiras, 1983). Probably there is a selective decrease with age in number of catecholaminergic (CA) neurons in several areas of the brain (Gottfries, 1982; Toffano *et al.*, 1980), while there is no decrease in number and level of activity of various serotonergic systems (Timiras, 1982). The selective alterations in various neurotransmitters and in various areas of the CNS led to a theory (Enna *et al.*, 1981) that in aging there is a desynchronization of balance between neurotransmitters, which contributes to dysregulation of homeostasis of hormonal systems (as well as other regulatory mechanisms).

The decline with age of CA activity is at least partially due to a decrease in activity of the enzyme tyrosine hydroxylase (TH) in several areas of the CNS (E. G. McGeer & McGeer, 1976; P. L. McGeer & McGeer, 1978) (TH is a major step in the synthesis of CA). The selectivity of age-related decline in enzyme activity is demonstrated by these investigators' finding that in the same areas there was almost no decline in levels of choline acetyltransferase (CAT) and glutamic acid decarboxylase (GAD). A significant selective decrease in the number of cells with age has been demonstrated for dopaminergic neurons (P. L. McGeer, McGeer, & Suzuki, 1977) and noradrenergic cells (Brody, 1976). An increase in the metabolism of CA with age is also indicated by reports of an increased activity of monoamine oxidase (MAO) (Robinson, 1975).

Changes in Neurotransmitters and Hormonal Receptors with Aging

As a rule (Makman *et al.*, 1980; Timiras, 1983), "neuronal cells' responsiveness to chemical (transmitter or hormonal) stimulation decreases with age." This is in addition to a decreased number of binding sites (Roth, 1979).

There is a possibility that with age there is a decrease in flexibility of some regulatory systems. The compensatory or adaptive ability of postsynaptic receptors to respond to the decreased availability of neurotransmitters is decreased. It has been shown (Greenberg & Weiss, 1979) that while young animals respond to depletion of CA by reserpine with increased postsynaptic sensitivity of β-adrenergic receptors, this compensatory response is blunted in aged animals. Decreased regional receptor responsiveness has been demonstrated also in the DA system (Govanni, Memo, Saiani, Spano, & Trabucchi, 1980; Thal, Horowitz, Dvorkin, & Makman, 1980), but it is unclear (Abrass, 1983) if this is due to a real alteration in the receptor's sensitivity or a decreased number of cells or receptor sites.

The age-related alteration of receptor responsivity is not limited to regulatory neurotransmitters. Actually, this is better documented in several hormonal systems in the hypothalamus (Dilman, 1976). Decreased sensitivity of the hypothalamus to negative-feedback influences from the periphery has been proposed for corticosteroids (Reigle, 1973). This phenomenon may contribute to the high prevalence of nonsuppression of cortisol in response to dexamethasone in the aged as well as to the increase of basal levels of cortisol with age. Similarly, there is a decreased responsivity with age of the hypothalamus and pituitary to the negative-feedback mechanism exerted by gonadal steroids (Shaar, Euker, Reigle, & Meites, 1975). The decreased sensitivity may lead to high levels of gonadotropin-releasing hormones and gonadotropins in postmenopausal women.

It should be noted that it is more accurate to refer to age-related changes as changes in homeostasis and not as significant increases or decreases in the activity of systems. Some components of a given system decline with age, while the activity of others may increase. Furthermore, some of the components that would be expected to change as part of a compensatory adaptive mechanism do not change in advanced age due to impairment of one or more homeostatic mechanisms. In some cases, such "nonadapting" mechanisms lead to added vulnerability of the entire system due to its inability to react with the necessary flexibility to internal as well as external changes. Thus, this can lead to a state of imbalance from which the aged CNS and the entire body will have difficulty in returning to normal functioning.

Acknowledgments

The reported studies and the preparation of this chapter were supported in part by NIMH Grant RO1-37111 and The Ritter's Foundation. We greatly appreciate the assistance of Juliet Lesser, Ph.D., and Kathleen Bacon, Ph.D.

References

Abrass, I. B. (1983). *Hormone receptors in aging* (Section 1, pp. 1–4). New York: Roche Publications.

Amsterdam, J. D., Winokur, A., Caroff, S. N., & Conn, J. (1982). The dexamethasone suppression test in outpatients with primary affective disorder and healthy control subjects. *American Journal of Psychiatry, 139,* 287–291.

Asnis, G. M., Halbreich, U., Quitkin, F., Endicott, J., Puig-Antich, J., & Sachar, E. J. (1983). Mean 1–4 P.M. plasma cortisol levels may distinguish various depressive subtypes [summary]. *Proceedings of the Annual Meeting of the American College of Neuropsychopharmacology,* p. 119.

Asnis, G. M., Sachar, E. J., Halbreich, U., Nathan, R. S., Novacenko, H., & Ostrow, L. C. (1981). Cortisol secretion in relation to age in major depression. *Psychosomatic Medicine, 43,* 235–242.

Bahemuka, M., & Hodkinson, H. M. (1975). Screening for hypothyroidism in elderly inpatients. *British Medical Journal, 2,* 601–603.

Baker, H. W. G., Burger, H. G., deKretser, D. M., & Hudson, B. (1977). Endocrinology of aging: Pituitary testicular axis. In V. H. T. James (Ed.), *Proceedings of the Fifth International Congress of Endocrinology* (Vol., 2, pp. 479–483). Amsterdam: Excerpta Medica Foundation.

Ball, M. F., El-Khodary, A. Z., & Canary, J. J. (1972). Growth hormone response in the thinned obese. *Journal of Clinical Endocrinology and Metabolism, 34,* 498–511.

Blichert-Toft, M., & Hummer, L. (1976). Immunoreactive corticotrophin reserve in old age in man during and after surgical stress. *Journal of Gerontology, 31,* 539–545.

Braverman, L. E., Dawber, N. A., & Ingbar, S. H. (1966). Observations concerning the binding of thyroid hormones in sera of normal subjects in varying age. *Journal of Clinical Investigation, 45,* 1273–1279.

Bremmer, W. J., Vitiello, M. V., & Prinz, P. N. (1983). Loss of circadian rhythmicity in blood testosterone levels with aging in normal men. *Journal of Clinical Endocrinology and Metabolism, 56,* 1278–1281.

Britton, K. E., Ellis, S. M., Miralles, J. M., Quinn, V., Cayley, A. C. D., Brown, B. L., & Ekins, R. P. (1975). Is "T4 toxicosis" a normal biochemical finding in elderly women? *Lancet, 2,* 141–142.

Brody, H. (1976). An examination of cerebral cortex and brainstem aging. In R. D. Terry & S. Gershon (Eds.), *Aging* (Vol. 3, pp. 177–181). New York: Raven Press.

Brown, W. A., & Shuey, I. (1980). Response to dexamethasone and subtype of depression. *Archives of General Psychiatry, 37,* 747–751.

Burger, A., & Sokoloff, C. (1977). Serum 3,3′-L-diiodothyronine, a direct radioimmunoassay in human serum: Method and clinical results. *Journal of Clinical Endocrinology and Metabolism, 45,* 384–391.

Burrow, A. K., Cooper, E., Shakespear, R. A., Aickin, C. M., Fraser, S., Hesch, R. D., & Burke, C. W. (1977). *Clinical Endocrinology (Oxford), 7,* 289–300.

Caldwell, B. M. (1954). An evaluation of psychologic effects of sex hormone administration in aged women. *Journal of Gerontology, 9,* 168–174.

Caplan, R. H., Wickus, G., Glasser, J. E., Davis, K., & Wahner, H. W. (1981). Serum concentrations of the iodothyronines in elderly subjects: Decreased triiodothyronine T2 and free T3 index. *Journal of the American Geriatric Society, 29,* 19–24.

Carlson, H. E., Gillin, J. C., Gordon, P., & Snyder, F. (1972). Absence of sleep-related growth hormone peaks in aged normal subjects and in acromegaly. *Journal of Clinical Endocrinology and Metabolism, 34,* 1102–1105.

Carroll, B. J., Feinberg, M., Greden, J. F., Tarika, J., Albala, A. A., Haskett, R. F., Kronfol, Z., Lohr, N., Stener, J. M., DeVigne, J. P., & Young, E. (1981). A specific laboratory test for the diagnosis of melancholia. *Archives of General Psychiatry, 38,* 15–22.

Carroll, B. J., Martin, F. I. R., & Davis, B. (1968). Resistance to suppression of dexamethasone of 11-OCHS levels in severe depressive illness. *British Medical Journal, 3,* 285–287.

Cartlidge, N. E. F., Black, M. M., Hall, M. R. P., & Hall, R. (1970). Pituitary function in the elderly. *Gerontologia Clinica, 12,* 65–70.

Chakravarti, S., Collins, W. P., Newton, J. R., Ovan, D. H., & Studd, J. W. W. (1977). Endocrine changes and symptomatology after oophorectomy in premenopausal women. *British Journal of Obstetrics and Gynaecology, 84,* 769–775.

Crilly, R. G., Marshall, D. H., & Nordin, B. E. (1979). Effect of age on plasma androstenedione concentration in oophorectomized women. *Clinical Endocrinology (Oxford), 10,* 199–201.

Crockford, P. M., & Salmon, P. A. (1970). Hormones and obesity: Changes in insulin and growth hormone secretion following surgically induced weight loss. *Canadian Medical Association Journal, 103,* 147–150.

Davidson, J. M., Chen, J. J., Crapo, L., Gray, G. D., Greenleaf, W. J., & Catania, J. A. (1983). Hormonal changes and sexual function in aging man. *Journal of Clinical Endocrinology and Metabolism, 57,* 71–77.

Davis, K. L., Davis, B. M., Mathé, A. A., Mohs, R. C., Rothpearl, A. B., Levy, M. I., Gorman, L. K., & Berger, P. (1984). Age and the dexamethasone suppression test in depression. *American Journal of Psychiatry, 141,* 872–874.

Dean, S., & Felton, S. P. (1979). Circadian rhythm in the elderly: A study using a cortisol-specific radioimmunoassay. *Age and Ageing, 8,* 243–245.

Dilman, V. M. (1971). Age-associated elevation of hypothalamic threshold to feedback control and its role in development, aging, and disease. *Lancet, 1,* 1211–1219.

Dilman, V. M. (1976). The hypothalamic control of aging and age-associated pathology. The elevation mechanism of aging. In A. V. Everitt & J. A. Burgess (Eds.), *Hypothalamus, pituitary, and aging* (pp. 634–667). Springfield, IL: Charles C. Thomas.

Dilman, V. M., Lapin, J. P., & Oxenkrug, G. F. (1979). Serotonin and aging. In W. B. Essman (Ed.), *Serotonin in health and disease* (pp. 111–212). New York: Spectrum Publications.

Djursing, H., Hagen, C., Moller, J., & Christiansen, C. (1981). Short- and long-term fluctuations in plasma prolactin concentration in normal subjects. *Acta Endocrinologica (Copenhagen), 97,* 1–6.

Drafta, D., Schindler, A. E., Stroe, E., & Neacsu, E. (1982). Age-related changes of plasma steroids in normal adult males. *Steroid Biochemistry, 17,* 687–692.

Dudle, R. J., Ensinck, J. W., Palmer, H. E., & Williams, R. H. (1973). Effect of age in growth hormone secretion in man. *Journal of Clinical Endocrinology and Metabolism, 37,* 11–16.

Ebert, M. H., Vankammen, D. P., & Murphy, D. L. (1971). Plasma levels of amphetamine and behavioral response. In L. A. Gottshalk & S. Merlis (Eds.), *Psychokinetics of psychoactive drugs: Blood levels and clinical response* (pp. 157–169). New York: Spectrum Publications.

Enna, S. J., Samorajski, T., & Beer, B. (Eds.). (1981). *Aging: Vol. 17. Brain neurotransmitters and receptors in aging and age-related disorders.* New York: Raven Press.

Evered, D. C., Ormston, B. J., Smith, P. A., Hall, R., & Bird, T. (1973a). Grades of hypothyroidism. *British Medical Journal, 1,* 657–662.

Evered, D. C., Young, E. T., Ormston, B. J., Menzies, R., Smith, R. A., & Hall, R. (1973b). Treatment of hypothyroidism: A reappraisal of thyroxine therapy. *British Medical Journal, 3,* 131–134.

Faber, J., Carsten, C., Lumholtz, I. B., Nielsen, K. S., & Friis, T. (1979). Measurement of serum 3′,5′-diiodothyronine and 3,3′-diiodothyronine concentrations in normal subjects and in patients with thyroid and nonthyroid disease: Studies of 3′,5′-diiodothyronine metabolism. *Journal of Clinical Endocrinology and Metabolism, 48,* 611–617.

Faber, J., Friis, T., Kirkegaard, C., Luridsen, U. B., Nerup, J., Rogowski, P., & Siersback-Nielsen, K. (1976). Thyroid hormone response to varying doses of TSH. *Acta Endocrinologica (Copenhagen), 83,* 737–744.

Feinberg, M., & Carroll, B. J. (1984). Biological "markers" for endogenous depression. *Archives of General Psychiatry, 41,* 1080–1085.

Finch, C. E., Felicio, L. S., Mobbs, C. V., & Nelson, J. F. (1984). Ovarian and steroidal influences on neuroendocrine aging processes in female rodents. *Endocrine Reviews, 5,* 467–497.

Finkelstein, J. W., Roffwarg, H. P., Boyer, R. M., Kream, J., & Hellman, L. (1972). Age-related changes in the 24-hour spontaneous secretion of growth hormone. *Journal of Clinical Endocrinology and Metabolism, 35,* 665–670.

Fisher, D. A., Sack, J., Oddie, T. H., Pekavy, A. E., Hershman, J. M., Lam, R. W., & Parolow, M. E. (1977). Serum T4, TBG, T3 uptake, reverse T3, and TSH concentrations in children 1 to 15 years of age. *Journal of Clinical Endocrinology and Metabolism, 45,* 191–198.

Frantz, A. G., & Rubkin, M. T. (1965). Effect of estrogen and sex difference on secretion of human growth hormone. *Journal of Clinical Endocrinology and Metabolism, 25,* 1470–1480.

Furuhashi, N., Suzuki, M., Abe, T., Yamaya, Y., & Takahashi, K. (1977). Changes of hypophysioovarian endocrinological function by aging in women. *Tohoku Journal of Experimental Medicine, 121,* 231–238.

Gershberg, H. (1957). Growth hormone content and metabolic actions of human pituitary gland. *Endocrinology (Baltimore), 61,* 160–165.

Gibbons, J. L., & McHugh, P. R. (1962). Plasma cortisol in depressive illness. *Journal of Psychiatry Research, 1,* 162–171.

Glick, S, M., & Goldsmith, S. (1968). The physiology of growth hormone secretion. In A. Pecile & E. Müller (Eds.), *Growth hormone* (pp. 84–88). Amsterdam: Excerpta Medica Foundation.

Gottfries, C. G. (1982). Brain, monoamines, and aging. In R. D. Terry, C. L. Bolis, & G. Toffano (Eds.), *Aging* (Vol. 18, pp. 161–168). New York: Raven Press.

Govanni, S., Memo, M., Saiani, L., Spano, P. F., & Trabucchi, M. (1980). Impairment of brain neurotransmitter receptors in aged rats. *Mechanism of Ageing and Development, 12,* 39–46.

Grad, B., Rosenberg, G. M., Liberman, H., Trachtenberg, J., & Kral, V. A. (1971). Diurnal variation of serum cortisol level of geriatric subjects. *Journal of Gerontology, 26,* 351–357.

Gray, G. D., Smith, E. R., Dorsa, D. M., & Davidson, J. M. (1981). Sexual behavior and testosterone in middle-aged male rats. *Endocrinology (Baltimore), 109,* 1597–1604.

Greenberg, L. H., & Weiss, B. (1979). Ability of aged rats to alter β-adrenergic receptors of brain in response to repeated administration of reserpine and desmethylimipramine. *Journal of Pharmacology and Experimental Therapy, 211,* 309–316.

Gregerman, R. I., Gaffnez, G. W., & Shock, N. W. (1962). Thyroxine turnover in euthyroid man with special references to changes with age. *Journal of Clinical Investigation, 41,* 2065–2074.

Guillemin, R., Brazeau, P., Bohlen, P., Esch, F., Ling, N., & Wehrenberg, W. B. (1982). Growth hormone-releasing factor from a human pancreatic tumor that caused acromegaly. *Science, 218,* 585–587.

Halbreich, U., Asnis, G. M., Halpern, F. S., Tabrizi, M. A., & Sachar, E. (1980). Diurnal growth hormone response to dextroamphetamine in normal young men and postmenopausal women. *Psychoneuroendocrinology, 5,* 339–344.

Halbreich, U., Sachar, E. J., Asnis, G. M., Nathan, R. S., & Halpern, F. S. (1981). Diurnal cortisol responses to dextroamphetamine in normal subjects. *Psychoneuroendocrinology, 6,* 223–229.

Halbreich, U., Asnis, G. M., Shindledecker, R., Zumoff, B., & Nathan R. S. (1985a). Cortisol secretion in depression. I. Basal levels. *Archives of General Psychiatry, 41,* 904–908.

Halbreich, U., Asnis, G. M., Shindledecker, R., Zumoff, B., & Nathan, R. S. (1985b). Cortisol secretion in depression. II. Time-related functions. *Archives of General Psychiatry, 42,* 909–914.

Halbreich, U., Asnis, G. M., Zumoff, B, Nathan, R. S., & Shindledecker, R. S. (1984). Effect of age and sex on cortisol secretion in depressives and normals. *Psychiatry Research, 13,* 221–229.

Halbreich, U., Sahcar, E. J., Asnis, G. M., Quitkin, F, Nathan, R. S., Halpern, F., & Klein, D. F. (1982). Growth hormone response to dextroamphetamine in depressed patients and normal subjects. *Archives of General Psychiatry, 39,* 189–192.

Hansen, J. M., Skovsted, L., & Siersbaek-Nielsen, K. (1975). Age-dependent changes in iodine metabolism and thyroid function. *Acta Endocrinologica (Copenhagen), 79,* 60–65.

Harman, S. M., & Tsitouras, P. D. (1980). Reproductive hormones in aging men. I. Measurement of sex steroids, basal luteinizing hormone and Leydig cell response to human chorionic gonadotropin. *Journal of Clinical Endocrinology and Metabolism, 51*, 35–40.

Harman, S. M., Tsitouras, P. D., Costa, P. T., & Blackman, M. R. (1982). Reproductive hormones in aging men: Basal pituitary gonadotropin responses to LHRH. *Journal of Clinical Endocrinology and Metabolism, 54*, 547–551.

Haus, E., Halberg, F., Nelson, W., Lakatua, D. J., Kawasaki, R., Vero, M., Vezono, K., & Omae, T. (1979). Age effects upon circadian amplitude in a concomitant study of 12 hormones in plasma of women. *Chronobiologia (Milan), 6*, 266–272.

Haus, E., Lakatua, D. J., Halberg, F., Halberg, E., Cornelissen, G., Sackett, L. L., Berg, H. C., Kawasaki, T., Veno, M., Vezono, K., Matsuoka, M., & Omae, T. (1980). Chronobiological studies of plasma prolactin in women in Kyushu, Japan and Minnesota, U.S.A. *Journal of Clinical Endocrinology and Metabolism, 51*, 632–640.

Herrmann, J., Rusche, H. J., Kroll, J. J., Hilger, P., & Kruskemper, H. L. (1974). Free triiodothyronine (T3) and thyroxine (T4) serum levels in old age. *Hormone and Metabolic Research, 6*, 239–240.

Hesch, R. D., Catz, J., Pape, J., Schmidt, E., & Muhlen, A. (1976). Total and free T3 and TBG concentrations in elderly human persons. *European Journal of Clinical Investigation, 6*, 139–145.

Hrdy, S. B., & Hrdy, D. B. (1976). Hierarchical relations among female hanuman langurs (primates: colobinae, presbytisentellus). *Science, 193*, 913–915.

Hufner, M., & Grussendorf, M. (1978). Correlation of reverse-T3 and 3,3′-T2 (T2′) plasma concentration under physiological and experimental conditions in man. *Acta Endocrinologica (Copenhagen), 89*, 679–686.

Inada, M., Koshiyama, K., Torizuka, K., Akagi, H., & Miyake, T. (1984). Clinical studies on the metabolism of (131 J) labeled L-thyroxine. *Journal of Clinical Endocrinology and Metabolism, 24*, 775–784.

Jeffreys, P. M., Hoffenberg, R., Farran, H. E. A., Fraser, P. M., & Hodkinson, H. M. (1972). Thyroid function tests in the elderly. *Lancet, 1*, 924–927.

Judd, H. L. (1976). Hormonal dynamics associated with the menopause. *Clinical Obstetrics and Gynecology, 19*, 775–788.

Judd, H. L. (1983). Pathophysiology of menopausal hot flushes. In J. Meites (Ed.), *Neuroendocrinology of aging* (p. 173). New York: Plenum Press.

Kaalud-Jensen, H., & Blichert-Toft, M. (1971). Serum corticotrophin, plasma cortisol and urinary excretion of 17-ketogenic steroids in the elderly (age group: 66–94 years). *Acta Endocrinologica (Copenhagen), 66*, 25–34.

Kalk, W. J., Vinik, A. I., Pimstone, B. L., & Jackson, W. P. U. (1973). Growth hormone response to insulin hypoglycemia in the elderly. *Journal of Gerontology, 28*, 431–433.

Kley, H. K., Nieschlag, E., Wiegelman, W., Solbach, H. G., & Kruskemper, H. L. (1975). Steroid hormones and their binding in plasma of male patients with fatty liver, chronic hepatitis and liver cirrhosis. *Acta Endocrinologica (Copenhagen), 79*, 275–285.

Kovacs, K., Ryan, N., Horvath, E., Penz, G., & Ezrin, C. (1977). Prolactin cells of the human pituitary gland in old age. *Journal of Gerontology, 32*, 534–540.

Krieger, D. (1972). Characterization of normal temporal pattern of cortisol levels. *Journal of Clinical Endocrinology and Metabolism, 34*, 380–384.

Laron, Z., Doron, M., & Amikam, B. (1969). Plasma growth hormone in men and women over 70 years of age. In D. Brunner & E. Jokl (Eds.), *Medicine and sport*. White Plains, NY: Phiebig.

Lipson, A., Nicoloff, E. L., Hsu, T. H., Kasecamp, W. R., Drew, H. M., Shakir, R., & Wagner, H. N., Jr. (1979). A study of age-dependent changes in thyroid function tests in adults. *Journal of Nuclear Medicine, 20*, 1124–1130.

Lloyd, W. H., & Goldberg I. J. L. (1961). Incidence of hypothyroidism in the elderly. *British Medical Journal, 2*, 1256–1259.

Longcope, C. (1973). The effect of human chorionic gonadotropin on plasma steroid levels in young and old men. *Steroids, 21*, 583–592.

Longcope, C., Kato, T., & Horton, R. (1969). Conversion of blood androgens to estrogens in normal adult men and women. *Journal of Clinical Investigations, 48*, 2191–2201.

Makman, M. H., Gardner, E. L., Thal, L. J., Hirschhorn, I. D., Seeger, T. F., & Bhargava, G. (1980). Central monoamine receptor systems: Influence of aging, lesion and drug treatment. In R. C. Adelman, J. Roberts, G. T. Baker, III, S. I. Baskin, & V. J. Cristofalo (Eds.), *Neural regulatory mechanisms during aging* (pp. 91–127). New York: Alan R. Liss.

Mastragiacomo, I., Feghali, G., Foresta, C., & Ruzza, G. (1982). Andropause: Incidence in pathogenesis. *Archives of Andrology, 9*, 293–298.

Mayberry, W. E., Gharib, H., Bilstad, J. M., & Sizemore, G. W. (1971). Radioimmunoassay for human thyrotrophin. *Annals of Internal Medicine, 74*, 471–480.

McGeer, E. G., & McGeer, P. L. (1976). Neurotransmitter metabolism in the aging brain. In R. D. Terry & S. Gershon (Eds.), *Aging* (Vol. 3, pp. 389–403). New York: Raven Press.

McGeer, P. L., & McGeer, E. G. (1978). Aging and neurotransmitter systems. In C. E. Finch, D. E. Potter, & A. D. Kenny (Eds.), *Aging and neuroendocrine relationships*. New York: Plenum Press.

McGeer, P. L., McGeer, E. G., & Suzuki, J. S. (1977). Aging and extrapyramidal function. *Archives of Neurology (Chicago), 34*, 33–35.

Mendlewitz, J., Charles, G., & Franckson, J. M. (1982). The dexamethasone suppression test in affective disorders: Relationship to clinical and genetic subgroups. *British Journal of Psychiatry, 141*, 464–470.

Merimee, T. J., & Feinberg, S. F. (1971). Studies of the sex-based variation of human growth hormone secretion. *Journal of Clinical Endocrinology and Metabolism, 33*, 896–902.

Murono, E. P., Nankin, H. R., Lin, T., & Osterman, J. (1982). The aging Leydig cell. V. Diurnal rhythms in aged men. *Acta Endocrinologica (Copenhagen), 99*, 619–623.

Murphy, Y., & Murphy, R. F. (1974). *Women of the forest*. New York: Columbia University Press.

Muta, K., Kato, K., Akamine, Y., & Ibayashi, H. (1981). Age-related changes in the feedback regulation of gonadotrophin secretion by sex steroids in men. *Acta Endocrinologica (Copenhagen)*, *96*, 154–162.

Myhre, L. G., & Kessler, W. V. (1966). Body density and potassium 40 measurements of body composition as related to age. *Journal of Applied Physiology*, *21*, 1251–1256.

Myking. O., Thorsen, T., & Stoa, K. F. (1980). Conjugated and unconjugated plasma oestrogens—oesterone, oestradiol, and oestriol—in normal human males. *Journal of Steroid Biochemistry*, *13*, 1215–1220.

Neaves, W. B., Johnson, L., Porter, J. C., Parker, C. R., Jr., & Petty, C. S. (1984). Leydig cell numbers, daily sperm production, and serum gonadotropin levels in aging men. *Journal of Clinical Endocrinology and Metabolism*, *59*, 756–763.

Nelson, W. H. (1982). Effect of age on DST results [Letter]. *American Journal of Psychiatry*, *139*, 1376.

Nelson, W. H., Khan, A., Orr, W. W., & Tamragouri, R. N. (1984). The dexamethasone suppression test: Interaction of diagnosis, sex, and age in psychiatric inpatients. *Biological Psychiatry*, *19*, 1293–1304.

Nelson, W. H., Orr, W. W., Shane, S. R., & Stevenson, J. M. (1984). Hypothalamic–pituitary–adrenal axis activity and age in major depression. *Journal of Clinical Psychiatry*, *45*, 120–124.

Nicod, P., Burger, A., Staeheli, V., & Vallotton, M. B. (1976). A radioimmunoassay for 3,3′,5′-triiodo-L-thyronine in unextracted serum—method and clinical results. *Journal of Clinical Endocrinology and Metabolism*, *42*, 823–829.

Nishikawa, M., Inada, M., Naito, K., Ishii, H., Tanaka, K., Mashio, Y., & Imura, H. (1981). Age-related changes of serum 3,3′-diiodothyronine, 3′,5′-diiodothyronine, and 3,5-diiodothyronine concentrations in man. *Journal of Clinical Endocrinology and Metabolism*, *52*, 517–522.

Notelovitz, M., Ware, D. M., Buhi, C. W., & Dougherty, M. C. (1982). Prolactin: Effects of age, menopausal status, and exogenous hormones. *American Journal of Obstetrics and Gynecology*, *143*, 225–227.

Oddie, T. H., Meade, J. H., Jr., & Fisher, D. A. (1966). An analysis of published data on thyroxine turnover in human subjects. *Journal of Clinical Endocrinology and Metabolism*, *26*, 425–436.

Odell, W. D., Wilber, J. F., & Utiger, R. D. (1967). Studies of thyrotropin physiology by means of radioimmunoassay. *Recent Progress in Hormone Research*, *23*, 47–85.

Olsen, T., Lariberg, P., & Weeke, J. (1978). Low serum triiodothyronine and high serum reverse triiodothyronine in old age: An effect of disease, not age. *Journal of Clinical Endocrinology and Metabolism*, *47*, 1111–1115.

Oxenkrug, G. F., Branconnier, R. J., McIntyre, I., Pomara, N., Stanley, M., Herto-Traux, N. E., & Gershon, S. (1983). *Factors influencing serum cortisol response to dexamethasone in normal volunteers.* Presentation at the annual meeting of the American College of Neuropsychopharmacology, San Juan, PR.

Oxenkrug, G. F., Pomara, N., McIntyre, I., Branconnier, R. J., Stanley, M., & Gershon, S. (1983). Aging and cortisol resistance to suppression by dexamethasone: A positive correlation. *Psychiatry Research*, *10*, 125–130.

Parker, C. R., Jr., & Porter, C. J. (1984). Luteinizing hormone-releasing hormone in the hypothalamus of women: Effects of age and reproductive status. *Journal of Clinical Endocrinology and Metabolism*, *58*, 488–491.

Parker, D. C., Sassin, J. F., Mace, J. W., Gotlin, R. W., & Rossman, L. G. (1969). Human growth hormone release during sleep: Electroencephalographic correlation. *Journal of Clinical Endocrinology and Metabolism*, *29*, 871–874.

Parker, L. N., Sack, J., Fisher, D. A., & Odell, W. D. (1978). Adrenarche: Prolactin, gonadotropins, adrenal androgens, and cortisol. *Journal of Clinical Endocrinology and Metabolism*, *46*, 396–401.

Plotnik, L. P., Thompson, R. G., Beitins, I., & Blizzard, R. M. (1974). Integrated concentration of growth hormone correlated with stage of puberty and estrogen levels in girls. *Journal of Clinical Endocrinology and Metabolism*, *38*, 436–439.

Prinz, P. N., Weitzman, E. D., Cunningham, G. R., & Karacan, I. (1983). Plasma growth hormone during sleep in young and aged men. *Journal of Gerontology*, *38*, 519–524.

Procope, B. J. (1969). Studies on the urinary excretion, biological effects, and origin of estrogens in postmenopausal women. *Acta Endocrinologica (Copenhagen)*, *Supplementum*, *135*, 9–83.

Purifoy, F. E., Koopmans, L. H., & Tatum, R. W. (1980). Steroid hormones and aging: Free testosterone, testosterone, and androstenedione in normal females aged 20–87 years. *Human Biology*, *52*, 181–191.

Reigle, G. D. (1973). Chronic stress effects on adrenocortical responsiveness in young aged rats. *Neuroendocrinology*, *11*, 1–10.

Reyes, F. I., Winter, J. S. D., & Faiman, C. (1977). Pituitary–ovarian relationships preceding the menopause: I. A cross-sectional study of serum follicle-stimulating hormone, luteinizing hormone, prolactin, estradiol, and progesterone levels. *American Journal of Obstetrics and Gynecology*, *129*, 557–564.

Richey, D. P., & Bender, A. D. (1977). Pharmokinetic consequences of aging. *Annual Review of Pharmacology and Toxicology*, *17*, 49–65.

Robinson, D. S. (1975). Changes in monoamine oxidase and monoamines with human development and aging. *Federation Proceedings, Federation of American Societies for Experimental Biology*, *34*, 103–107.

Roth, G. S. (1979). Hormone receptor changes during adulthood and senescence: Significance for aging research. *Federation Proceedings, Federation of American Societies for Experimental Biology*, *38*, 1910–1914.

Rubenstein, H. A., Bulter, V. P., Jr., & Werner, S. C. (1973). Progressive decrease in serum triiodothyronine concentration with human aging: Radioimmunoassay following extraction of serum. *Journal of Clinical Endocrinology and Metabolism*, *37*, 247–253.

Rudman, D., Kutner, M. H., Rogers, C. M., Lubin, M. F., Flemming, G. A., & Bain, R. P. (1981). Impaired growth hormone secretion in the adult "population." *Journal of Clinical Investigation*, *67*, 1361–1369.

Sachar, E. J. (1975). Evidence for neuroendocrine abnormalities in the major mental illnesses. In D. X. Freedman (Ed.), *Biology of the major psychoses* (pp. 347–358). New York: Raven Press.

Sachar, E. J., Altman, N., Gruen, P. H., Glassman, A., Halpern, F., & Sassin, J. (1975). Human growth hormone response to levodopa: Relation to menopause, depression, and plasma dopa concentration. *Archives of General Psychiatry, 32,* 502–503.

Sachar, E. J., Finkelstein, J., & Hellman, L. (1971). Growth hormone response in depressive illness. *Archives of General Psychiatry, 25,* 263–269.

Sachar, E. J., Hellman, I., Roffwarg, H. P., Halpern, F. S., Fukushima, D. F., & Gallagher, R. F. (1973). Disrupted 24-hour patterns of cortisol secretion in psychotic depression. *Archives of General Psychiatry, 28,* 19–24.

Sawin, C. T., Chopra, D., Azizi, F., Mannix, J. E., & Bachrach, P. (1979). The aging thyroid, *JAMA, Journal of the American Medical Association, 242,* 247–250.

Sawin, C. T., Herman, T., Molitch, M. E., London, M. H., & Kramer, S. M. (1983). Aging and thyroid: Decreased requirement for thyroid hormone in older hypothyroid patients. *American Journal of Medicine, 75,* 206–209.

Schlesser, M. A., Winokur, G., & Sherman, B. M. (1980). Hypothalamic–pituitary–adrenal axis activity in depressive illness: Its relationship to classification. *Archives of General Psychiatry, 37,* 737–743.

Serio, M., Piolanti, P., Romano, S., DeMagistris, L., & Guisti, G. (1970). The circadian rhythm of plasma cortisol of subjects over 70 years of age. *Journal of Gerontology, 25,* 95–97.

Shaar, C. J., Euker, J. S., Reigle, G. D., & Meites, J. (1975). Effects of castration and gonadal steroids on serum LH and prolactin in old and young rats. *Journal of Endocrinology, 66,* 45–51.

Shanklin, W. M. (1953). Age changes in the histology of the human pituitary. *Acta Anatomica, 19,* 290–304.

Sheehan, H. L., & Kovacs, K. (1982). Neurophyophysis and hypothalamus. In J. M. B. Bloodworth (Ed.), *Endocrine pathology* (pp. 45–99). Baltimore: Williams & Wilkins.

Shibasaki, T., Shizume, K., Nakahara, M., Masuda, A., Jibiki, K., Demura, H., Wakabayashi, I., & Ling, N. (1984). Age-related changes in plasma growth hormone response to growth hormone-releasing factor in man. *Journal of Clinical Endocrinology and Metabolism, 58,* 212–214.

Sims, E. A., Goldman, R. F., Gluck, C. M., Horton, E. S., Kelleher, P. C., & Rowe, D. W. (1968). Experimental obesity in man. *Transactions of the Association of American Physicians, 81,* 153–170.

Snyder, P. J., & Utiger, R. D. (1972a). Response to thyrotropin releasing hormone (TRH) in normal man. *Journal of Clinical Endocrinology and Metabolism, 34,* 380–384.

Snyder, P. J., & Utiger, R. D. (1972b). Thyrotropin response to thyrotropin releasing hormone in normal females. *Journal of Clinical Endocrinology and Metabolism, 34,* 1096–1098.

Sparrow, D., Bosse, R., & Rowe, J. W. (1980). The influence of age, alcohol consumption, and body build on gonadal function in men. *Journal of Clinical Endocrinology and Metabolism, 51,* 508–512.

Stearns, E. L., MacDonnel, J. A., Kaufman, B. J., Paduci, R., Lucman, T. S., Winter, J. S. D., & Faiman, C. (1974). Declining testicular function with age. *American Journal of Medicine, 57,* 761–766.

Stokes, P. E., Stoll, P. M., Koslow, S. H., Mass, J. W., Davis, J. M., Swann, A. C., & Robins, E. (1984). Pretreatment DST and hypothalamic–pituitary–adrenocortical function in depressed patients and comparison groups. *Archives of General Psychiatry, 41,* 257–263.

Szabolcs, I., Szilagyi, G., Goth, M., Kovacs, Z. S., Weber, M., & Halasz, T. (1981). Plasma triiodothyronine response to thyrotropin releasing hormone, thyrotropin, and propranolol in old age. *Experimental Gerontology, 16,* 309–316.

Takahashi, J., Higashi, Y., LaNasa, J. A., Yoshida, K. I., Winters, S. J., Oshima, H., & Troen, P. (1983). Studies of the human testis. XVIII. Simultaneous measurement of nine intratesticular steroids: Evidence for reduced mitochondrial function in testis of elderly men. *Journal of Clinical Endocrinology and Metabolism, 56,* 1178–1187.

Tarquini, B., Gheri, R., Romano, S., Costa, A., Cagnoni, M., Lee, J. K., & Halberg, F. (1979). Circadian mesor hyperprolactinemia in fibrocystic mastopathy. *American Journal of Medicine, 66,* 229–237.

Thal, L. J., Horowitz, S. G., Dvorkin, B., & Makman, M. H. (1980). Evidence for loss of brain [³H]spiroperidol and [³H]ADTN binding sites in rabbit brain with aging. *Brain Research, 192,* 185–194.

Timiras, P. S. (1982). Neuroendocrine theories of aging: Homeostasis and stress. In A. Vernadakis & P. S. Timiras (Eds.), *Hormones in development and aging* (pp. 551–586). New York: SP Medical and Scientific Books.

Timiras, P. S. (1983). Neuroendocrinology of aging. In J. Meites (Ed.), *Neuroendocrinology of aging* (pp. 5–30). New York: Plenum Press.

Toffano, G., Calderini, G., Battistella, A., Scapagnini, U., Gaiti, A., Ponzio, F., Algeri, S., & Crews, F. (1982). Biochemical changes related to neurotransmission in the aging brain. In R. D. Terry, C. L. Bolis, & G. Toffano (Eds.), *Aging: Vol. 18. Neural aging and its implications in human neurological pathology* (pp. 119–128). New York: Raven Press.

Touitou, Y., Carayon, A., Reinberg, A., Bogdan, A., & Beck, H. (1983). Differences in the seasonal rhythmicity of plasma prolactin in elderly human subjects: Detection in women but not in men. *Journal of Endocrinology, 96,* 65–71.

Tourigny-Rivard, M. F., Raskind, M., & Rivard, D. (1981). The dexamethasone suppression test in an elderly population. *Biological Psychiatry, 16,* 1177–1184.

Tsitouras, P. D., Martin, C. E., & Harman, S. M. (1982). Relationship of serum testosterone to sexual activity in healthy elderly men. *Journal of Gerontology, 37,* 288–293.

Tunbridge, W. M. G., Evered, D. C., Hall, R., Appleton, D., Brewis, F., Clark, J., Evans, J. G., Young, E., Bird, T., & Smith, P. A. (1977). The spectrum of thyroid disease in a community: The Wickham survey. *Clinical Endocrinology (Oxford), 7,* 481–493.

Vekemans, M., & Robyn, C. (1975). Influence of age on serum prolactin levels in women and men. *British Medical Journal, 4,* 738–739.

Vermeulen, A. (1976). The hormonal activity of the postmenopausal ovary. *Journal of Clinical Endocrinology and Metabolism, 42,* 247–253.

Warner, B. A., Santen, R. J., Dufau, M. (in press). Leiding cell dysfunction with aging: Role of a qualitative abnormality in LH. *Annals of the New York Academy of Science.*

Wasada, T. (1978). The changes in serum levels of FSH, LH, LHa and β-subunit and prolactin and in pituitary responsiveness to synthetic LHRH and TRH in normal subjects with aging. *Fukuoka Igaku Zasshi, 69,* 506–518.

Webb, W. B. (1971). Sleep, biological rhythms and aging. In W. B. Coloquhoun (Ed.), *Biological rhythms and human performance* (p. 155). New York: Academic Press.

Wenzel, K. W., & Horn, W. R. (1975). Triiodothyronine (T3) and thyroxine (T4) kinetics in aged men. *International Congress Series—Excerpta Medica, 361,* 89–90.

Westgren, U., Burger, A., Ingenmansson, S., Melander, A., Tibblin, S, & Wohlin, E. (1976). Blood levels of 3,5,3″-triiodothyronine and thyroxine: Differences between children, adults, and elderly subjects. *Acta Medica Scandinavica, 200,* 493–495.

Wide, L., & Hobson, B. M. (1982). Qualitative difference in follicle-stimulating hormone activity in the pituitaries of young women compared to that of men and elderly women. *Journal of Clinical Endocrinology and Metabolism, 56,* 371–375.

Wide, L., Nillius, S. T., Gemzell, C., & Ross, P. (1973). Serum levels and urinary excretion of FSH and LH in healthy men and women. *Acta Endocrinologica (Copenhagen), Supplementum, 174,* 41–58.

Wide, L., & Wide, M. (1984). Higher plasma disappearance rate in the mouse for pituitary follicle stimulating hormone of young women compared to that of men and elderly women. *Journal of Clinical Endocrinology and Metabolism, 58,* 426–429.

Winters, S. J., & Troen, P. (1982). Episodic luteinizing hormone (LH) secretion and the response of LH and follicle stimulating hormone to LH-releasing hormone in aged men: Evidence for coexistent primary testicular insufficiency and an impairment in gonadotropin secretion. *Journal of Clinical Endocrinology and Metabolism, 55,* 560–565.

Yen, S. S. C. (1977). The biology of menopause. *Journal of Reproductive Medicine, 18,* 287–296.

Zumoff, B., Strain, G. W., Kream, J., O'Connor, J., Rosenfeld, R. S., Levin, J., & Fukushima, D. K. (1982). Age variation of the 24-hour mean plasma concentrations of androgens, and gonadotropins in normal adult men. *Journal of Clinical Endocrinology and Metabolism, 54,* 534–538.

INDEX